SECOND EDITION

HUMAN SEXUALITY TODAY

BRUCE M. KING

PRENTICE HALL, UPPER SADDLE RIVER, NEW JERSEY 07458

Library of Congress Cataloging-in-Publication Data

King, Bruce M.
   Human sexuality today / Bruce M. King. — 2nd ed.
   p.   cm.
   Includes bibliographical references and index.
   ISBN 0-13-014994-2
   1. Sex instruction for youth—United States. 2. Sex. 3. Sex
(Biology) 4. Sex (Philosophy) 5. Hygiene, Sexual—United States.
I. Title.
HQ35.2.K56   1996
306.7—dc20
          95-42690
          CIP

Editorial/production supervision: Mary Rottino
Acquisitions editor: Heidi Freund
Interior and cover design: Carole Anson
Manufacturing buyer: Tricia Kenny
Cover art: Celia Johnson
Marketing manager: Michael Alread
Editorial assistant: Jeff Arkin

©1996, 1991 by Prentice-Hall, Inc.
Simon & Schuster/A Viacom Company
Upper Saddle River, New Jersey 07458

Printed in the United States of America
10 9 8 7 6 5 4 3 2 1

ISBN 0-13-014994-2

Prentice-Hall International (UK) Limited, *London*
Prentice-Hall of Australia Pty. Limited, *Sydney*
Prentice-Hall Canada Inc., *Toronto*
Prentice-Hall Hispanoamericana, S.A., *Mexico*
Prentice-Hall of India Private Limited, *New Delhi*
Prentice-Hall of Japan, Inc., *Tokyo*
Simon & Schuster Asia Pte. Ltd., *Singapore*
Editora Prentice-Hall do Brasil, Ltda., *Rio de Janeiro*

TO GAIL

WITHOUT WHOM THIS BOOK WOULD NEVER HAVE BEEN POSSIBLE

AND

TO LESLIE, JOHN, KATIE, AND COREY

MAY I ALWAYS BE A POSITIVE INFLUENCE IN THEIR LIVES.

BRIEF CONTENTS

CONTENTS

PREFACE

When I set about to write this book, my major goal was to have students come away feeling good about themselves while learning about their sexuality. The AIDS crisis has forced many people to realize the need for human sexuality education. However, I believe that factual information can be presented in a warm, nonthreatening way. Sexual responsibility can be taught without making sex something negative. It is essential that students be given facts so they can make responsible decisions. But it is equally important that they complete their course in human sexuality with positive feelings about sex and their own sexuality. I have tried to achieve a balance between facts and understanding to meet this end.

My students' response to the several textbooks I had used was that the books were "too dry," "too sterile," and "too long." Feedback from students was an essential part of the writing process as I strove to create a book that was factual and thorough, yet readable and warm. The numerous case histories (contributed by students who wanted to share their experiences with others) are not used as substitutes for scientific studies, but to supplement them and make the material more humanistic. My writing style is purposely conversational in many places, but scientific results have not been sacrificed. For example, the section on HIV/AIDS is as thorough and updated as can be found in any human sexuality textbook.

The final test for any textbook is whether or not students will read it, learn from it, and enjoy it. Two classroom testing versions of this book were used with over 6,000 students before the first edition was published. As a result of feedback from students and reviewers, the book has continually evolved in an attempt to create an ever better product.

FEATURES NEW TO THE SECOND EDITION

The cost of textbooks to students has become an increasing concern to many faculty. In addition to the cost of the primary textbook, already prohibitive for some, there is the additional cost of the student study guide. It has been the goal of Prentice Hall and myself to publish a high-quality textbook at the lowest possible expense to the students. To meet this goal, the second edition has become *a totally self-contained textbook*, with the study guide included within the textbook itself at no additional cost to the student. The study guide has more questions than the one that accompanied the first edition, and includes an interactive review, true-false questions, matching, and fill-in-the-blanks questions. In paperback form, the entire textbook, with study guide, costs substantially less than almost all other human sexuality textbooks (without study guide).

In addition to the study guide, the personal experience workbook that was available as a supplement to the first edition is now included within the text at the end of each chapter (entitled "Personal Reflections"). A Resource Guide has been added to the appendix. Several new pedagogical features have also been added:

- Each chapter begins with a clear, concise list of chapter objectives;
- A list of key terms, with page numbers, concludes each chapter (definitions can be found in the running glossary and end-of-book glossary);
- For students who wish to pursue a subject matter further, the book now contains over twice the citations as the first edition;
- Special boxes are now limited to two important themes—sexuality and health, and cross-cultural comparisons.

In addition to greatly expanding the amount of material on cross-cultural studies, a new chapter on communication concludes the text (part of this was previously included as an appendix). The chapter on homosexuality has been expanded and reorganized into a chapter entitled "Sexual Orientation" and relocated so that it follows the chapter on gender identity and gender roles and precedes the chapter on life-span sexual development. Other than these two changes, the organization of the chapters remains the same.

The chapters on birth control and sexually transmitted diseases appear early in the book, before the chapters on sexual behavior and relationships, in order to emphasize the importance of sexual responsibility.

ACKNOWLEDGMENTS

I offer my greatest gratitude to Dr. Cameron Camp, who helped write the classroom testing versions and the first edition of the book. His friendship and support will always be appreciated. Thanks also to Anne Downey for her input on the first edition. Others who helped in the early development of the book include Vic Hughes, Cheryl Stout, Desiree Comeaux, Chantelle Boudreaux, and Kathryn King. I thank Corbie Johnson, who typed the present edition.

Thanks to everyone at Prentice Hall who worked on this book. Special thanks to Pete Janzow for having faith in me, Heidi Freund for her direction, Mary Rottino for her hard work in production, and Carole Anson for her creative design expertise.

My sincere appreciation and thanks to the following colleagues for their valuable input and constructive feedback in reviewing the first edition of this book: Susan Graham-Kresge, University of Southern Mississippi; Kendra Jeffcoat, Palomar College; Deborah R. McDonald, New Mexico State University; Ken Murdoff, Lane Community College; Janet A Simons, University of Iowa; and Janice D. Yoder, University of Wisconsin-Milwaukee.

Finally, I cannot thank enough the thousands of students who provided me with chapter reviews and/or case histories. This book was written with students in mind. I hope it helps them to lead healthier, happier, and more fulfilling lives.

ABOUT THE AUTHOR

BRUCE KING RECEIVED HIS PH.D. IN BIOPSYCHOLOGY FROM THE UNIVERSITY OF CHICAGO IN 1978. HE HAS TAUGHT HUMAN SEXUALITY TO OVER 25,000 STUDENTS AT THE UNIVERSITY OF NEW ORLEANS SINCE 1981. HE HAS CONDUCTED HUMAN SEXUALITY WORKSHOPS FOR PHYSICIANS, PUBLIC SCHOOL TEACHERS, STAFF MEMBERS WORKING WITH THE MENTALLY RETARDED, AND PARENTAL GROUPS. IN ADDITION TO CONDUCTING RESEARCH IN THE FIELD OF HUMAN SEXUALITY, DR. KING HAS CO-AUTHORED A TEXTBOOK ON STATISTICS AND HAS PUBLISHED OVER 50 PAPERS ON THE BIOLOGICAL BASIS OF FEEDING BEHAVIOR AND OBESITY. HE IS AN HONORARY MEMBER OF THE GOLDEN KEY NATIONAL HONOR SOCIETY FOR EXCELLENCE IN TEACHING.

CHAPTER ONE

Human Sexuality Today

WHY A COURSE IN HUMAN SEXUALITY?

WHEN YOU HAVE FINISHED STUDYING THIS CHAPTER, YOU SHOULD BE ABLE TO:

1. EXPLAIN THE NEED FOR, AND BENEFIT OF, SEXUALITY EDUCATION;

2. EXPLAIN HOW, EVEN THOUGH WE MAY HAVE EXTENSIVE SEXUAL EXPERIENCE, IT IS POSSIBLE FOR US TO KNOW VERY LITTLE ABOUT HUMAN SEXUALITY;

3. DESCRIBE CULTURAL PERSPECTIVES OTHER THAN OUR OWN WITH REGARD TO SEXUAL BEHAVIORS AND ATTITUDES;

4. DESCRIBE WHAT MAKES SOMETHING SEXUALLY ATTRACTIVE AND HOW THAT CAN CHANGE OVER TIME OR BE DIFFERENT IN OTHER CULTURES;

5. EXPLAIN THE HISTORICAL INFLUENCE OF JUDAISM AND CHRISTIANITY ON CONTEMPORARY ATTITUDES ABOUT SEXUALITY;

6. SUMMARIZE THE VICTORIAN ERA'S SEXUAL VIEWS AND ITS INFLUENCE ON OUR SEXUAL VALUES AND BEHAVIORS TODAY;

7. EXPLAIN THE CONTRIBUTIONS OF SIGMUND FREUD, HAVELOCK ELLIS, ALFRED KINSEY, AND MASTERS AND JOHNSON TO THE FIELD OF SEXUALITY; AND

8. UNDERSTAND ISSUES OF SURVEY CONSTRUCTION AND THE METHODS USED TO SELECT SAMPLES.

IN THE FALL OF 1981, THE PSYCHOL-
OGY DEPARTMENT AT THE UNIVER-
SITY OF NEW ORLEANS OFFERED A
new course in human sexuality. In its first semester, the
course had an enrollment of 110 students in one section. Within a year, the course had grown to 950 students per semester, with another 300 to 400 people
turned away for lack of room. A weekend section has
subsequently brought the total current enrollment up
to nearly 1,100 students per semester. Nearly half of
the colleges and universities around the country now
offer a course in human sexuality (Polyson, Lash, &
Evans, 1986), and many of them have had similar experiences.

Why are so many students taking a course in human sexuality? **Sexuality** is
certainly an important part of
our lives. We need only to look
at the world population of
more than five billion to see
that sexual motivation is quite
strong. Although it is necessary
for procreation, it is doubtful
that many people think of this
on more than just an occasional basis when having
sexual intercourse. Sex can be a source of great
physical and emotional pleasure, enhancing our sense
of health and well-being. It can relieve tensions and
anxieties. It can boost self-esteem and make us feel
more masculine or feminine. It is also the vehicle
through which couples can express their affection for
one another.

So why the need for a course in human sexuality?
Surely, someone in your life took the time and responsibility to educate you about this important topic. Surveys in my course have consistently revealed that fewer
than one third (and often fewer than 10 percent) of the
over 1,000 students per semester have ever had a serious
and meaningful discussion with their parents about sex
(see King, Parisi, & O'Dwyer, 1993). These survey
results are consistent with national findings (T.D.
Fisher, 1987; Janus & Janus, 1993). For those few who
did, in many cases it was just a single discussion—one
"birds and bees" talk that was supposed to prepare them
for life. The students generally received little information from their parents, other than a description
of intercourse and the fact that it could result in pregnancy. Here are a few comments that I have received
from students regarding their prior sex education.
These were selected not because they were unusual, but
because they were typical of the many comments received (on the end of semester course evaluations).

> **Sexuality**
> All of the sexual attitudes, feelings, and behaviors associated with being human. The term does not refer specifically to a person's capacity for erotic response or to sexual acts, but to a dimension of one's personality.

"My father thinks this class is a waste because he feels people instinctively know
how to deal with their sexuality. Maybe I'm just

a freak of nature, but I've never had any instincts explaining any of this to me."

"My boyfriend doesn't like me taking the
course. He says, 'You don't need a
classroom to teach you about sex. I'll teach
you everything you need to know.'"

"Until now my parents never spoke to me
about sex. I'm from a very strict family.
They made me feel as though it was a sinful
subject to talk about."

"I remember my mother finding a book my
sister was reading and screaming at her, so
everyone in the house could hear, about what
an awful, dirty book it was. It wasn't pornography. It was a book on sex education. She just
wanted to learn something correctly."

"When I was young the word sex was
never brought up. My mother had one
short talk with me, and that was to explain
what a period is."

"The only time my parents discussed sex
with me was after they found some condoms in my dresser drawers."

(from the author's files)

Students also provided the following comments
regarding the usefulness of a human sexuality course.
Apparently, it's never too late to learn.

"I'm glad I registered in the class. I sure
thought I knew it all and found I knew
very little. I've been married six years and knew
little about my own body, much less about my
husband's."

"I am 32 years old. I am a paramedic with
eight years of street experience. I have
personally delivered nine babies and assisted
with countless other births. I have personally
been sexually active for 15 years. I thought I
knew it all. This course has taught me a lot."

"When selecting this course, the thought
came to me that it would be a very
easy class because I knew everything about
sex because mother told me. After all, there
are 18 of us in the family. Boy, was I wrong. I've
learned more in one semester than mother
could teach me in 20 years."

" Just knowing about sex is just not enough. If I was taught about sex at home or in school in 1954, I may not have had 11 children before I was 28."

" I was very surprised at the amount of material I learned. I thought it was going to be just about sex. There is a lot more to sex than just sex."

(from the author's files)

Where, then, did most of us learn about sex? You may find it hard to believe, but it has been estimated that the average child sees over 2,000 references to sex every year on television alone (Brown, Childers, & Waszak, 1990; Greenberg et al., 1987). Most of these show the pleasurable aspects of sexual relations, but there is seldom any mention of responsibility for one's sexual behavior. Soap operas, for example, routinely show couples initiating sexual activities (Strouse & Fabes, 1985), but there is seldom any mention of birth control. Many R-rated movies have sexually explicit scenes with full frontal nudity. Many stores have erotic magazines on open display. Advertisements (such as those for Calvin Klein) use sex to sell products. Sex is everywhere, and children are exposed to it all day long.

In the face of all this, parents continue to be silent with their children on the subject of sex. However, this too is a source of sex education. Making something mysterious only makes many adolescent children want to know more about it. With their parents remaining silent, most young people turn to their friends and the media for their sexual information (Papini et al., 1988; Rogers & Strover, 1980; Thornburg, 1981). Much of this information is incorrect, and as a result a majority of Americans are amazingly ignorant about sexual behaviors and sexual health (Reinisch, 1990). Many believe, for example, that people over 60 do not have sex, that masturbation is physically harmful, or that anal intercourse causes AIDS. What this all adds up to is that many people do not fully understand or appreciate

the consequences of engaging in sexual relations. Over half of American teenagers have had sexual intercourse before their seventeenth birthday (Centers for Disease Control and Prevention, 1992; Laumann et al., 1994; Seidman & Rieder, 1994), yet only a fifth of sexually active teenagers in the United States use contraception on a regular basis. Each year in the United States one in ten teenage girls gets pregnant (Jones et al., 1986) and one in seven sexually active teens contracts a sexually transmitted disease (U.S. House of Representatives Select Committee, 1987). Most young people do not know the symptoms of sexually transmitted diseases and do not know where to turn if they think they have one.

So, once again, why the need for a course in human sexuality? Probably because you desire to have factual information about a subject that plays, or will play, an important role in your life. Human sexuality courses are designed to do just that. If parents are not going to assume the responsibility, the next best alternative is the schools. Surveys consistently show that the vast majority of Americans support the teaching of sex education in schools. A 1985 Harris poll, for example, found that 85 percent of Americans favor the teaching of sex education in high school, and a more recent survey conducted by Samuel and Cynthia Janus found that 90 percent approved (Janus & Janus, 1993). A 1985 Gallup poll found that 85 percent of those surveyed believed that sex education

(Cartoon by Mike Luckovich reproduced with permission of The New Orleans Times-Picayune/The States Item)

(Cartoon by Mike Luckovich reproduced with permission of *The New Orleans Times - Picayune/The States Item*)

should not be limited to reproductive biology and venereal disease, but should include a discussion of birth control as well. Sex education curricula are available for elementary and secondary schools (SIECUS, 1991), yet only half of U.S. high schools and only a third of junior high schools offer courses in sex education (Kenny, Guardad, & Brown, 1989). Many of the sex education courses that are offered omit topics like safer sex practices and birth control (Forrest & Silvermann, 1989).

Canada, England, and many northern European countries have extensive sex education programs, and the teenage pregnancy rates are much lower in these countries than in the United States (Dryfoos, 1985; Westoff, 1988). Courses that include advice to teenagers about resisting peer pressure have proven to be especially successful in reducing the number of teenage pregnancies (Howard & McCabe, 1990). However, the purpose of human sexuality courses is much more than just learning about reproduction and sexually transmitted diseases. People want to feel comfortable with their own sexuality and to feel good about themselves. Knowledge about their bodies and understanding their feelings and emotions help people achieve this. No part of our bodies should be shrouded in mystery. Understanding our partners' bodies will help in verbal and nonverbal communication and prevent unnecessary problems. Appreciating that all people are sexual beings can give us a greater understanding of our children, parents, grandparents, and friends. Studies show that sex education courses in schools typically result in substantial gains in knowledge and a more tolerant attitude of others (DiClimente et al., 1989; Kilmann et al., 1981; Kirby, 1984). The tolerance that develops with sex education is particularly important. Understanding that people are different from ourselves without condemning them is an important part of getting along with others. ■

A SEXUAL KNOWLEDGE QUIZ

Many of you may already be sexually experienced, and as a result, may think that you do not need a course in human sexuality. There is more to sexuality, however, than engaging in sexual intercourse. See how well you do on the following 50-question quiz. Do not be afraid to admit that you do not know the correct answer (don't guess)—no one except yourself is going to see the results. The answers are at the end of the quiz.

	True	False	Don't Know
1. Erections in human males result, in part, from a bone that protrudes into the penis.	_____	_____	_____
2. Sperm can only be produced in an environment several degrees lower than normal body temperature.	_____	_____	_____
3. The hymen is a reliable indicator of whether or not a female is a virgin.	_____	_____	_____
4. The inner two thirds of the vagina is highly sensitive to touch.	_____	_____	_____
5. Nipple erection is a common sign of sexual arousal in men.	_____	_____	_____
6. Most men and women are capable of multiple orgasms.	_____	_____	_____
7. Breast size in women is related to the number of mammary glands.	_____	_____	_____
8. Before puberty, boys can reach orgasm, but they do not ejaculate.	_____	_____	_____
9. During sexual intercourse, orgasm in women results from direct stimulation of the clitoris by the penis.	_____	_____	_____
10. Menstrual discharge consists of shredded uterine tissue, blood, and cervical mucus.	_____	_____	_____
11. It is medically unsafe to have sex during menstruation.	_____	_____	_____
12. Ovulation generally occurs just before menstruation.	_____	_____	_____

	True	False	Don't Know

13. After a vasectomy, a man can reach orgasm but does not ejaculate.

14. AIDS is the diagnosis for people who have human immuno-deficiency virus (HIV).

15. A female can get pregnant as soon as she starts having menstrual periods.

16. The combination birth control pill works primarily by preventing implantation of a fertilized egg.

17. Taking the oral contraceptive pill results in fewer serious health problems than do pregnancy and childbirth.

18. Women show their highest levels of sexual desire at the time of ovulation.

19. There are over 12 million new cases of sexually transmitted diseases in the United States each year.

20. The major cause of AIDS is homosexuality.

21. Gonorrhea is the most common type of sexually transmitted disease in the United States.

22. Most women do not show symptoms in the early stages of gonorrhea or chlamydia.

23. Gonorrhea, syphilis, and herpes can be successfully treated with antibiotics.

24. In vitro fertilization involves a process where part of fetal development occurs in a test tube.

25. It is usually safe to have sexual intercourse during the seventh and eighth months of pregnancy.

26. "Prepared childbirth" (e.g., Lamaze) refers to delivering a baby without the use of drugs.

27. Most healthy people in their sixties or older continue to engage in sexual behavior.

28. People are capable of erection or vaginal lubrication as early as infancy.

29. Excessive masturbation can cause serious medical problems.

30. The majority of married couples engage in oral-genital sex.

31. Women who masturbated to orgasm during adolescence generally have less difficulty reaching orgasm during intercourse than women who never masturbated.

32. Couples who have sex very frequently when young generally engage in sex less often than others when old (due to burn-out).

33. Adult male homosexuals have lower than normal levels of male hormones.

34. Douching is an effective method of birth control.

35. Recent evidence indicates that environmental factors are most important in determining one's sexual orientation.

	True	False	Don't Know
36. Prostitutes are generally hypersexual and have pathological sexual needs.	_____	_____	_____
37. Most convicted rapists committed their crimes because of an uncontrollable sex drive.	_____	_____	_____
38. There is a demonstrated link between the availability of pornography and sex crimes.	_____	_____	_____
39. It is against the law in many states for a married couple to engage in sexual behaviors other than penile-vaginal intercourse.	_____	_____	_____
40. Most cases of child molestation involve an acquaintance or relative of the child.	_____	_____	_____
41. A pregnant female can transmit syphilis to the unborn baby.	_____	_____	_____
42. Exhibitionists and voyeurs often attempt to rape their victims.	_____	_____	_____
43. Nocturnal emissions ("wet dreams") are often an indication of a sexual problem.	_____	_____	_____
44. Alcohol is a central nervous system excitant that enhances sexual performance.	_____	_____	_____
45. Humans can crossbreed with animals using artificial insemination techniques.	_____	_____	_____
46. Women's sexual desire decreases sharply after menopause.	_____	_____	_____
47. Vaginal infections can be prevented by regular use of feminine hygiene products.	_____	_____	_____
48. A woman's ability to have vaginal orgasms is related to penis size.	_____	_____	_____
49. Oral herpes can be transmitted to another person by oral-genital sexual relations.	_____	_____	_____
50. Unless testosterone is present during embryological development, nature has programmed everyone to be born a girl.	_____	_____	_____

ANSWERS—CHAPTER 1

1. false
2. true
3. false
4. false
5. true
6. false
7. false
8. true
9. false
10. true
11. false
12. false
13. false
14. false (only in the final stages)
15. true
16. false
17. true
18. false (no good evidence for this)
19. true
20. false (homosexuality does not cause AIDS)
21. false
22. true
23. false
24. false
25. true
26. false
27. true
28. true
29. false
30. true
31. true
32. false
33. false
34. false
35. false
36. false
37. false
38. false
39. true
40. true
41. true
42. false
43. false
44. false
45. false
46. false
47. false
48. false
49. true
50. true

These questions were not intended to be tricky or difficult. They are representative of the type of material that is covered in this book. How did you do? Fewer than one fourth of the students in my classes are able to answer 40 or more correctly at the beginning of the semester. Fewer than half get 35 or more correct. Did you really know all the ones that you got right, or did you just make a correct guess on some of them? If you were not certain of the answers to some of the questions, then that is sufficient reason to read this book. ■

CROSS-CULTURAL COMPARISONS

It should come as no surprise that people are different. Some people like short hair, while others like it long. Some like blue eyes, while others prefer brown. Some people like to dress up. Some like to dress down. People's sexual attitudes and behaviors differ as well. Some people, for example, have sexual intercourse only in the **missionary position** (i.e., the female lying on her back with the male on top— so called because Christian missionaries instructed people that other positions were unnatural). Others prefer a variety of positions. Some people are most aroused by looking at breasts or a hairy chest. Other people become highly aroused by looking at legs and buttocks.

Missionary position

A face-to-face position of sexual intercourse in which the female lies on her back and the male lies on top with his legs between hers. It was called this because Christian missionaries instructed people that other positions were unnatural.

We learn to accept that other people in our own culture are different from ourselves and do not regard them (or most of them) as abnormal because their behavior falls within the "normal" range of responses. What is normal, however, is defined by the community in which we live. As different as we are, we share much in common. An outsider, such as a person from a different country, is often regarded as very strange by many people. Unfortunately, Americans have a reputation around the world of being egocentric, that is, of viewing our own behaviors and customs as correct or the way things ought to be (a perception leading to the image of the "ugly American"). We must not lose sight of the fact, however, that if we traveled to another country we would probably be regarded as strange. One country's customs and beliefs should not be regarded as correct or normal and another's incorrect or abnormal (in this book, I will make an exception in the case in which a culture sanctions sexual abuse). Instead, the world can be viewed as one large community, with the behavior and beliefs of all its people falling into the normal range of responses.

The topics covered in some chapters of this book are the same for all peoples of the world (e.g., anatomy, physiology, hormones). When the book covers behaviors and attitudes, it will be primarily from the perspective of people in the United States. Behaviors of people in other cultures will be presented in special boxes, beginning with Box 1-A in this chapter. However, before going on, here is a brief introduction to sexual attitudes and behaviors in a few other cultures around the world. Some of them may seem funny, but remember, *we seem just as strange to them* as they seem strange to us.

SEXUAL ATTRACTIVENESS

Cultures differ with regard to which parts of the body they find to be erotic. The sight of a navel is considered highly arousing in Samoa. This generally is not true in the United States, but did you know the TV censors would not allow Barbara Eden to have her navel exposed on the television show "I Dream of Jeannie" in the 1970s? A knee is considered to be erotic in New Guinea and the Celebes Islands. When anthropologist Martha Ward visited New Guinea in the early 1970s, she deboarded the plane wearing a miniskirt, blouse, and brassiere, customary clothing for American women at that time. She caused quite a ruckus. She wrote the following letter to one of her colleagues in the United States:

Dear Len,
I have had to change my manner of dressing. Thank goodness for the Sears Catalog. The minidresses and short skirts you all are wearing in the States cause quite a stir here. It seems that breasts are regarded as normal female equipment and useful only for feeding babies. Clothing for many women consists of a large towel or three yard length of brightly colored cloth. This is worn around the waist inside the house or in the yard. . . . (In public) if you have on a bra, you don't need a blouse. Bras are considered proper dress for women. Those black Maidenforms with the heavy stitched cups are particularly valued. When Americans are not around, it is sufficient to cover oneself only from the waist down. . . .

Breasts are not really erogenous, but legs are. Particularly that sexy area on the inside of the knee! No more miniskirts for me. Fitting in and observing local customs means that I have lengthened my skirts to below the knee. . . .

The American men watch women with nothing on above the waist. The Pohnpeian men comment on American women with short skirts. I am now dressed to please the standards of two cultures. . . .

(From *Nest in the Wind: Adventures in Anthropology on a Tropical Island* by Martha C. Ward, 1989, Waveland Press, Inc.)

Many groups of people find body weight to be an important determinant of sexual attractiveness. There is a great deal of pressure in our culture, for example, for men and women to remain thin. It is no coincidence that fashion models are very thin and that movie stars who are considered to be "sexy" have thin waistlines. In many other countries, however, these people would not be considered attractive. For example, women whom most American men would consider obese are found highly attractive in some other cultures. Adolescent girls are sometimes kept in huts and fed high-calorie diets in order to become more attractive (Gregersen, 1982).

What is considered to be sexually attractive can also change over time. Plump women, for example, were also considered to be most attractive in Western cultures a few centuries ago. If you don't believe this, just look at some famous paintings of nude women that were done two or three hundred years ago (see Figure 1-1).

American men find female breasts to be very sexually arousing (just recall the large number of magazines for men that show bare-breasted women). There are many areas of the world, however, where naked female breasts have no erotic significance at all (see Figure 1-2). They are important only to hungry babies. On the other hand, Polynesian men are as fascinated with the size, shape, and consistency of female genitals (particularly the mons veneris) as American men are with breasts (Marshall, 1971). In some African cultures, a woman's labia minora are considered to be the most erotic part of her body.

Although walking around naked in public would be considered highly deviant by most people in the United States, there are some cultures in New Guinea and Australia where people go about completely naked. They do, however, have firm rules about staring at other persons' genitals. The Zulus of South Africa also have public rituals that call for people to be naked. They believe that a flabby body results from immoral behavior, and thus if someone refuses to undress for these rituals, it is taken as a sign of trying to hide his or her immorality (Gregersen, 1982). These attitudes about the human body are in marked contrast to those that

FIGURE 1-1   RUBENS' "THE THREE GRACES," PAINTED IN 1630, IS A GOOD EXAMPLE OF HOW CULTURAL IDEALS CHANGE OVER TIME. THINNESS IS CONSIDERED TO BE PHYSICALLY ATTRACTIVE TODAY, BUT A THIN WOMAN IN RUBENS' TIME WOULD HAVE BEEN CONSIDERED UNATTRACTIVE.

FIGURE 1-2   THIS NEW GUINEA GIRL IS DRESSED UP TO GO COURTING AND FIND A HUSBAND. AS IN
MANY OTHER AREAS OF THE WORLD, BARE BREASTS HAVE NO EROTIC SIGNIFICANCE. IN
SOME AREAS OF NEW GUINEA, MALES WEAR ONLY A PENIS SHEATH—A PIECE OF
BAMBOO THAT FITS OVER THE PENIS AND ATTACHES AROUND THE WAIST BY A STRING.
SOME NEW GUINEA TRIBES WEAR NOTHING AT ALL.

prevail in Islamic societies, where women must cover their entire body and most of their face when they leave the privacy of their homes (Lindholm & Lindholm, 1980).

In some cultures people carve holes in their lips, while in others they stretch their lips or necks, or wear needles through their noses. It is obvious from the lack of universal standards that attitudes about the human body, and what is considered to be sexually attractive, are learned responses.

SEXUAL BEHAVIORS AND ATTITUDES

Kissing is a highly erotic and romanticized part of sexual relations in Western cultures. You will probably be surprised to learn, therefore, that this practice is not shared by all people. "When the Thonga first saw Europeans kissing they laughed, expressing this sentiment: 'Look at them—they eat each other's saliva and dirt' " (Ford & Beach, 1951). Chinese and Japanese peoples never kissed (at least until recently). In fact, foreplay before intercourse is entirely unheard of in some cultures.

When you were growing up, many of you probably heard the story of the Hudson Bay Eskimos. It was once the custom for an Eskimo husband to share his wife with any traveler who stayed in the igloo overnight. Western males' eagerness to take advantage of this custom eventually brought it to an end.

Anthropologists believe the most sexually permissive group of people in the world to be the Mangaians, who live on the Cook Islands in the South Pacific

(Marshall, 1971). Mangaian boys and girls play together until the age of three or four, but after that they separate into sex-age groups during the daytime for the remainder of their lives. When the boys approach adolescence, the arrival of manhood is recognized by superincision of the penis (cutting the skin of the penis lengthwise on top). As the wound heals, the boy is instructed in all aspects of sex, including how to bring a female to orgasm, which is considered important. Girls receive similar instructions from older women. The boy is then given to an experienced woman, who removes the superincision scab during intercourse and teaches the boy an array of sexual techniques. After that, the boys actively seek out girls at night, and have sex an average of 18 to 20 times a week. Mangaian adolescents are encouraged to have sex with many partners and engage in all types of sexual activities, including different positions of intercourse, oral-genital sex, anal sex, and axillary sex (e.g., placing the penis between the breasts or the armpit).

Many other societies in the South Pacific, including Samoa and Pohnpei, similarly encourage their teenage children to enjoy sexual relations (Ward, 1989). In some of these cultures the boys go into the huts where teenage girls live and have sex with them while the girls' parents are present. The parents ignore them and act as if the children are invisible. In all of these societies the physical pleasure of both sexes is emphasized (women have orgasm as often as men) and emotional attachments come later. They regard our custom of emphasizing love before sex to be very strange.

The most sexually repressive society in the world is believed to be the Inis Baeg, a fictitious name (coined by anthropologists to provide biographical immunity) for a group of people who live on an island off the coast of Ireland (Messenger, 1971). Any mention of sex is a taboo, so that children are never told about things like menstruation and pregnancy, which are greatly feared. Nudity is strictly forbidden, to the extent that although they depend on fishing to survive, most of the Inis Baeg never learn how to swim (which requires taking off some clothing) and usually drown if they are in a boating accident. Children wear smocks and their mothers do not entirely undress them during bathing, but instead wash one arm or leg at a time. Married adults never even see each other completely naked. Sexual relations are not regarded as something positive by either sex. Foreplay is unheard of, and intercourse, which is always done in the missionary position, is completed as quickly as possible because men consider it to be debilitating to their health (women almost never have orgasm).

If the Mangaians and Inis Baeg represent the two extremes, where do we fall on this continuum? In many ways our behavior is permissive and we live in the so-called sexual revolution, but our attitudes about sex are often less than positive (evidenced by the fact that parents and children rarely talk about it together, for example). The constant sexual themes on TV, in movies, in magazines, and on the radio give our children one type of message—sex is fun, sex is exciting, sex is great. At the same time, the same children get another type of message from their parents, school, and church—sex is not for you! Is it any wonder that many Americans have ambivalent attitudes about sex? Sex is something good on the one hand, yet bad on the other. We fall somewhere between the Mangaians and Inis Baeg. We are permissive, yet repressed. To see how we arrived at this point in the 1990s, we must examine the history of sexual attitudes in our own culture. ■

HISTORICAL PERSPECTIVES

JUDAISM

Life for the Biblical Jews was harsh. Living in nomadic tribes that roamed the desert areas of what is now referred to as the Middle East, it was considered a great advantage to have many children. The Jews were directed to do so in the first chapter of the first book of the Old Testament:

> And God blessed them, and God said to them, "Be fruitful and multiply, and fill the earth and subdue it . . ."

> (Genesis 1:28,
> Revised Standard Version)

Having many children assured the survival of the Jewish people. Thus, the primary purpose of sex for the Hebrews was considered to be procreation. This view had a major impact on Western thought about sexuality and is still influential today, even though there is no longer any fear of the world running out of people.

Male children were especially valued because of their dual roles as providers and defenders. In the strongly patriarchal Hebrew society, females were regarded as property (of fathers or husbands), and there were many rules to guarantee that material property be passed on to legitimate offspring. Thus, the Hebrews were very concerned with the social consequences of sex. Sex outside of marriage, for example, was severely condemned and punished. A Jewish woman caught committing adultery was stoned to death, but a man who committed adultery was considered only to have violated the other man's property rights. Rape, too, was considered to be a violation of property rights. The punishment for homosexuality and bestiality was death (Leviticus 18:22–29). Celibacy was looked upon as neglecting one's obligations and was regarded as sinful.

In contrast to those harsh views, the Old Testament presents a positive view of sex within a marriage (Gordis, 1978). A good example of this can be found in the Song of Solomon (Song of Songs):

> How graceful are your feet in sandals,
> O queenly maiden!
> Your rounded thighs are like jewels,
>   the work of a master hand.
> Your naval is a rounded bowl
>   that never lacks mixed wine.
> Your belly is a heap of wheat,
>   encircled with lilies.
> Your two breasts are like two fawns,
>   twins of a gazelle. . . .
> How fair and pleasant you are,
>   O loved one, delectable maiden!
> You are stately as a palm tree,
>   and your breasts are like its clusters.
> I say I will climb the palm tree
>   and lay hold of its branches.
> Oh, may your breasts be like clusters of the vine,
>   and the scent of your breath like apples,

and your kisses like the best wine
that goes down smoothly,
gliding over lips and teeth.

(Song of Solomon 7:1–9,
Revised Standard Version)

The genitals were not considered to be obscene, for God had created Adam and Eve in his own image. Sex between husband and wife was cause for rejoicing, a gift from God. A married couple could engage in any sexual activity with only one restriction—the husband had to ejaculate within his wife's vagina (not doing so was considered "spilling of seed" because it could not lead to having children). Although Jewish women had second-class status, a Jewish wife could take an active role in sexual relations. In fact, her sexual rights were guaranteed in the marriage contract. For example, husbands were not allowed to change jobs without the wife's consent if it meant a change in conjugal rights. The ancient Hebrews did not distinguish between physical and spiritual love.

THE GREEKS AND ROMANS

The ancient Greeks and Romans, like the Jews, placed a strong emphasis on marriage and the family. Although procreation was viewed as the primary purpose of marital sex, a couple had children for the state, not God. Unlike the Biblical Jews, Greek and Roman men were allowed considerable sexual freedom outside the marriage. In Greece, sexual relations between adult males and adolescent boys in a teacher-student relationship were not only tolerated, but encouraged as part of the boy's intellectual, emotional, and moral development. Greek women were viewed as second-class citizens, bearers of children with little or no legal status. Roman women were considered to be property of their husbands, but they enjoyed more prominence than Greek women.

The Greeks idealized the human body and physical beauty (as evident in their art), but in the late part of the Greek era there was a strong emphasis on spiritual development and a denial of physical pleasures. The basis for this change was **dualism**, the belief that body and soul are separate (and antagonistic). Dualism gave rise to an *ascetic philosophy*, which taught that from wisdom came virtue, and that these could only be achieved by avoiding strong passions. Plato, for example, believed that a person could achieve immortality by avoiding sexual desire and striving for intellectual and spiritual love (thus the term "platonic" for sexless love). As you will see next, dualism was a major influence on early Christian leaders.

Dualism
The belief that body and soul are separate and antagonistic.

CHRISTIANITY

Like the theology of the later-period Greeks, Christian theology separated physical love from spiritual love. The period of decline of the Roman empire, which coincided with the rise of Christianity, was marked by sexual excess and debauchery. The views of the early Christians regarding sex were in part the result of an attempt to keep order.

There is little written record about Jesus' views on sex. It is known that except for grounds of adultery, He forbade divorce. It is written in the Gospel of Matthew that He said, "Whosoever looketh on a woman to lust after her hath committed adultery with her already in his heart." Thus, it was not enough for a Christian to conform behaviorally, but there was to be purity of inner thoughts as well.

The teachings of the early Christian writers reflect their own personal struggles with sexual temptation. The most influential of the early writers was **St. Paul** (A.D. ?–67), who was a fanatical persecutor of Christians until he had a vision. St. Paul regarded the body as evil and struggled to control it:

For I know that nothing good dwells within me, that is, in my flesh. I can will what is right, but I cannot do it. For I do not do the good I want, but the evil I do not want is what I do. . . . For I delight in the law of God, in my inmost self, but I see in my members another law at war with the law of my mind and making me captive to the law of sin which dwells in my members.

(Romans 7:18, 7:22–23,
Revised Standard Version)

St. Paul blamed Eve for the expulsion from the Garden of Eden and viewed women as temptresses. He strongly believed, as did many others, that the second coming of Christ (signifying the end of the world) would occur in his lifetime and preached that a celibate lifestyle was the way to heaven. Marriage was only for the weak-willed:

It is well for a man not to touch a woman. . . . To the unmarried and the widows I say that it is well for them to remain single as I do. But if they cannot exercise self-control, they should marry. For it is better to marry than to be aflame with passion.

(Corinthians 7:1, 7:8–9,
Revised Standard Version)

Thus, Paul regarded marriage as a compromise (and a rather poor one at that) to deal with the problems of the flesh. His followers believed that women should be subordinate to men, and therefore, should assume the bottom position during sexual intercourse.

St. Jerome (about A.D. 340–420), who spent years fasting in the desert trying to get rid of visions of dancing girls, said a man who loved his wife too passionately was guilty of adultery. Pope John Paul II created some controversy within the Catholic Church when he appeared to echo the beliefs of St. Jerome:

Adultery in the heart is committed not only because a man looks in a certain way at a woman who is not his wife . . . but precisely because he is looking at a woman that way. Even if he were to look that way at his wife, he would be committing adultery.

(October 8, 1980)

Another major influence on Christian beliefs was **St. Augustine** (A.D. 354–430), whose life was full of conflict, beginning with a pagan father and a Christian mother. He had a mistress and a son at an early age, but he continued to have numerous sexual affairs into his early thirties, including some with male friends (Boswell, 1980). He is reported to have prayed, "Give me chastity and continence, but do not give it yet" (*The Confessions of St. Augustine*, Book VIII, chap. 7).

*"If sex is dirty and disgusting, why should
I save it for someone I love?"*

After reading the works of St. Paul, he converted to Christianity and thereafter led an ascetic life. It was he, more than anyone else, who solidified the Church's antisexual attitude. Augustine believed that all sexual intercourse was sinful, and thus all children were born from the sin of their parents. As a result of the downfall of Adam and Eve, he argued that sex was shameful and equated with guilt. Augustine denounced sex between a husband and wife for the purpose of pleasure, and thus opposed sexual relations during pregnancy or after menopause. He even considered marital sex for procreational purposes to be an unpleasant necessity:

They who marry . . . , if the means could be given them of having children without intercourse with their wives, would they not with joy unspeakable embrace so great a blessing? Would they not with great delight accept it?

(Goergen, 1975)

Augustine not only departed from the Hebrews in denying the pleasures of (marital) sex, but in the process also differed from them by showing complete disgust for the human body: "Between feces and urine we are born."

Augustine's beliefs were systematized by St. Thomas Aquinas (1225–1274) and became doctrine in 1563. Any sexual behavior that was done for pleasure and excluded the possibility of procreation was considered lust and a sin against nature. In descending order of infamy, this included bestiality, homosexuality, intercourse in "unnatural" positions, and masturbation. Although not all Christians today are of the same denomination, they all share the same early history, and thus, they all have been influenced by the beliefs of St. Paul and St. Augustine.

In the sixteenth century, Martin Luther (1483–1546) and John Calvin (1509–1564) organized revolts against the Catholic church. Some of their followers later came to be known as Puritans. The *Reformation* movement, as it was called, included an opposition to celibacy. Luther advocated, for example, that priests and nuns be allowed to marry to solve the problem of lust. Adultery, homosexuality, and masturbation were still viewed as sinful and severely punished (because of the perceived threat to the family unit), but the linkage of sex with love in marital relationships was emphasized. Thus, the Puritans had a positive view of sex within the marriage, and this attitude was brought over to New England in this country. The Puritans proved their worthiness of going to heaven not by denying the pleasurable aspects of marital sex, but by living frugal and industrious lives.

VICTORIANISM

The nineteenth century is often referred to as the **Victorian era**, after Queen Victoria (1817-1901), who ruled in England for most of the century. It was an era of public prudery and purity. All pleasurable aspects of sex were denied. Women, who just a few centuries before had been considered sexual temptresses, were now viewed as asexual (i.e., having no interest in sex) and as innocent as children. Men were the ones who were viewed as responsible for lust. According to Victorian moralists, a woman's place was in the home, and wives engaged in sex only to perform their "wifely duties." Women's dresses covered the neck, back, and ankles, and the prudery was carried to such an extreme that even

Victorian era

The period during the reign of Queen Victoria of England (1819-1901). With regard to sexuality, it was a time of great public prudery (the pleasurable aspects of sex were denied) and many incorrect medical beliefs.

piano legs were covered. At the dinner table, it was considered improper to ask for a "breast" of chicken.

The medical views of the nineteenth century generally supported the antisexuality views of that era. A prominent Swiss physician named Tissot had published a book in 1758 in which he claimed that masturbation could lead to blindness, consumption, other physical disorders, and insanity. This view had numerous supporters in the medical community, including Dr. Benjamin Rush (1745–1813), the father of American psychiatry. The eminent German Dr. Richard von Krafft-Ebing classified sexual disorders in his *Psychopathia Sexualis* (1886), in which the predominant theme was a link between sexuality and disease. A group of British doctors claimed to have evidence that touching a menstruating female could spoil hams (*British Medical Journal*, 1878). To the Victorians, including physicians of that era, loss of semen was thought to be as detrimental to a male's health as loss of blood (a belief that had originated from the Greek physician Hippocrates; Haller & Haller, 1977). As a result of these beliefs, parents often went to ridiculous lengths to prevent masturbation (see Hall, 1992) and nocturnal emissions ("wet dreams," or spermatorrhea as it was called then), including having their male children castrated or circumcised, or making them wear antimasturbation inventions to bed at night. Two such inventions are shown in Figure 1-3. The "spermatorrhea ring" was invented by a Dr. J. L. Milton in the 1800s, while the "surgical appliance" was patented by

A

B

FIGURE 1-3 TWO ANTISEX DEVICES INVENTED AND PATENTED DURING THE VICTORIAN ERA: (A) A SPERMATORRHEA RING TO PREVENT NOCTURNAL EMISSIONS; (B) A "SURGICAL APPLIANCE" MADE OF LEATHER STRAPS AND METAL POCKETS TO PREVENT MASTURBATION.

one J. E. Heyser in 1911. Patents were even issued for devices designed to prevent horses from masturbating.

The amount of misinformation that was distributed by the medical community during this time period is really quite appalling. Consider, for example, a book entitled, *Perfect Womanhood* by Mary Melendy, M.D., Ph.D., published in 1903. It was an advice book for women, and in addition to the usual warnings about masturbation and excess sex, contained the following advice about when it was safest to have intercourse (to avoid pregnancy):

It is a law of nature—to which there may be some exceptions—that conception must take place at about the time of the menstrual flow. . . .

It may be said with certainty, however, that from ten days after the cessation of the menstrual flow until three days preceding its return, there is little chance of conception, while the converse is equally true.

. . . This law is to the effect that if the conception takes place in the early part of the menstrual period a female child will be the result; if in the latter part, a male child will be born.

These beliefs were based on the fact that most non-human mammalian females have a bloody discharge at the time of ovulation (the optimal time of conception to occur). As you will learn in Chapter 3, this is not true for human females (ovulation occurs about two weeks before the menstrual discharge begins); yet some people still believe it.

The private lives of Victorians may not have been as repressed as the image of modesty and prudery they conveyed in public. A recently discovered questionnaire of 45 married women conducted by Dr. Celia Mosher in 1892 reveals that most of the women desired and enjoyed sex (Mosher, 1980). There was also a great deal of hypocrisy during this era. Prostitution and pornography flourished and extramarital affairs were common (Trudgill, 1976).

THE TWENTIETH CENTURY

It was not unusual for our great-great-grandfathers, whether they worked on the farm or in the city, to put in 12- to 16-hour days, often six days a week. Child labor was common, so that many children were also working these hours. In addition to puritanical Victorian ideals, the lack of leisure time limited the opportunities for sexual relations.

The industrial revolution slowly changed all this. Mechanization and more efficient means of production eventually led to shorter work weeks, freeing people to engage in leisure activities. The invention of the automobile allowed people to get away from the watchful eyes of their parents and neighbors. For the first time, Americans had two things necessary to engage in leisure sex: time and mobility. The growing women's rights movement eventually resulted in more equality for women, and they began to take an active role in sexual matters (they were not the passive, asexual creatures portrayed by Victorian moralists). With the invention of penicillin in 1940, people worried less about sexually transmitted diseases such as syphilis and gonorrhea. Unlike before, they could now be cured. In the 1960s, the birth control pill and the IUD became available, so that having sexual intercourse could be spontaneous and worry-free (from unwanted pregnancies). In addition to time and mobility, people now believed they were protected from unwanted side effects.

As a result, we entered the so-called **sexual revolution**, where more people than in the past were supposedly engaging in more sex, beginning at an earlier age, and with more partners. We have already discussed how movies, TV, and magazines portrayed sexual relations (including premarital and extramarital sex) as exciting and desirable. The newest generation of Americans was under pressure, not to abstain from premarital sex, but to engage in it.

> **Sexual revolution**
> A period in U.S. history, beginning in about 1960, of increased sexual permissiveness.

Although more people are now engaging in premarital sex, oral-genital sex, and trying different positions than was the case in past generations (to mention a few of the many examples that could be given), many people have just as many anxieties and feelings of discomfort about their own sexuality as before. The influences of the early Christian church and Victorian era obviously have not fully disappeared. As a result, many people have ambivalent feelings about sex. We are more permissive, yet still repressive. It is no wonder that so many people still have so many questions, doubts, and fears about sex. ■

SEX AS A SCIENCE

Until the last few centuries, religious theology was the primary influence in intellectual endeavors. The rise of science was slow and was met with much resistance.

Galileo (1564–1642), for example, was forced to publicly recant (or face excommunication) his support for Copernicus' theory that the earth moved around the

FIGURE 1-4   SIGMUND FREUD. THE FATHER OF PSYCHOANALYSIS, FREUD LIVED DURING THE VICTORIAN ERA, A PERIOD OFTEN DESCRIBED AS BEING INDISCRIMINATELY ANTISEXUAL, YET HE IS GIVEN THE MAJOR CREDIT FOR SHOWING THE IMPORTANCE OF SEXUALITY IN HUMAN BEHAVIOR AND MOTIVATIONS.

sun and not vice versa, as stated in Church doctrine. People's desire for facts and knowledge could not be stifled, however, and the following centuries saw great advances in the biological and physical sciences. Science slowly replaced religion as the authority on most subjects.

Unfortunately, sexual behavior as a subject for scientific investigation met with more resistance than most others. As we have already discussed, even the medical professionals of the nineteenth and early twentieth centuries were guilty of allowing their personal moral beliefs to interfere with their treatment of sexual subjects. It has not been until the last few decades that researchers interested in studying sexual behavior have been able to apply the two tools necessary for scientific inquiry: observation and measurement. Let us take a brief look at a few individuals who were most responsible for making sexual behavior a serious, objective field of study. Further details of their work will be discussed in later chapters.

SIGMUND FREUD (1856–1939)

Sigmund Freud, more than anyone else, is responsible for demonstrating the influence of sexuality in human life (Figure 1-4). It is all the more remarkable that he did so during the antisexual atmosphere of the Victorian era.

Freud believed that there were three subsystems of the personality. The *id*, Freud said, was present at

birth and was directed at immediate gratification. This was not always possible or socially acceptable, so the *ego* developed as a realistic servant of the id (it only postponed immediate gratification). Opposed to both of these was the *superego*, which was the internal representation of all the traditional ideals of society as taught by the parents. These three systems were in constant conflict, a great deal of which was unconscious. Adult behavior, according to Freud, was determined largely by the outcome of these conflicts at different stages of development. Sexual energy, or *libido* as Freud called it, was said to be channeled into particular areas of the body at different ages. First was the oral stage (in which the center of eroticism was the mouth), then the anal stage, followed by the phallic, latency, and genital stages. You will learn of these stages in greater detail in the chapter on development. Freud claimed that if the conflicts were not properly resolved, neuroses (psychological problems) could result during adulthood. He developed psychoanalysis as a means for evaluating and treating unconscious conflicts.

Although many people disagree with Freud's theory today (see, for example, *Time* magazine, November 29, 1993), he remains important for emphasizing sexual motivation and sexuality in infants and children. However, like other Victorian doctors, Freud had many incorrect beliefs about sex, including the idea that loss of semen was as detrimental to a male's health as loss of blood.

HAVELOCK ELLIS (1859–1939)

When he was a young man in the 1800s, Ellis had frequent nocturnal emissions (wet dreams), which at the time were called spermatorrhea because Victorian physicians believed it to be caused by the same thing that caused gonorrhea. The end result, Ellis was told, would be blindness, insanity, and eventual death. He wanted to commit suicide, but was too fearful, so instead kept a diary to document his death by this dreaded "disease." When his eyesight and reasoning did not deteriorate over the passing months, Ellis concluded that loss of semen did not really lead to death, and he became angry at the misconceptions held by the medical profession. In order to spare others the emotional trauma that he had suffered, Ellis devoted the remainder of his life to sexual research (although he reputedly remained a virgin himself). He argued that women were not asexual and that such behaviors as masturbation and homosexuality should be considered normal.

Ellis published six volumes entitled *Studies in the Psychology of Sex* between 1897 and 1910, and a seventh in 1928. His tolerant view of sexuality was in marked contrast to that of the Victorian moralists and was a major influence on researchers for several generations (Figure 1-5).

ALFRED C. KINSEY (1894–1956)

Nearly everyone, of course, has heard of Kinsey's surveys on sexual behavior (1948, 1953). When asked to teach a course on marriage at Indiana University in 1938, Kinsey was amazed to find how little objective data there were on sexual behavior. He started collecting his own data by giving questionnaires to his students,

FIGURE 1-5   HAVELOCK ELLIS. THIS ENGLISH RESEARCHER PUBLISHED SEVEN VOLUMES ABOUT THE PSYCHOLOGY OF SEX BETWEEN 1897 AND 1928. HIS VIEWS WERE REMARKABLY TOLERANT COMPARED TO MOST VICTORIAN PHYSICIANS AND SCIENTISTS.

but soon decided that personal interviews resulted in a greater amount of more detailed data. He was joined by Wardell Pomeroy and Clyde Martin. They conducted interviews with over 12,000 men and women (Figure 1-6).

Kinsey's work opened the doors to a whole new field of research, but it did not come without a price. His findings that most people masturbated, that many people engaged in oral-genital sex, that women could have multiple orgasms, and that many men had had a homosexual experience shocked many people. He was accused of being antifamily and amoral. One Columbia University professor stated that "there should be a law against doing research dealing exclusively with sex" (*New York Times*, April 1, 1948). His work is still the target of impassioned attacks today (e.g., Reisman & Eichel, 1990). Kinsey died an embittered man in 1956, but the Institute for Sex Research at Indiana University continues to be a major center for the study of human sexuality.

MASTERS AND JOHNSON

Kinsey paved the way for scientific behavioral studies of sexual behavior, but functional anatomy and physiological studies of sex were still limited to experiments with laboratory animals. Dr. Denslow Lewis, a prominent Chicago gynecologist, presented the first frank discussion of the physiology of sex to the annual meeting of the American Medical Association in 1899. He graphically described erection, vaginal lubrication, and even noted that women could have multiple orgasms (and thus enjoyed sex!). His paper was not well accepted. When Lewis finished with his

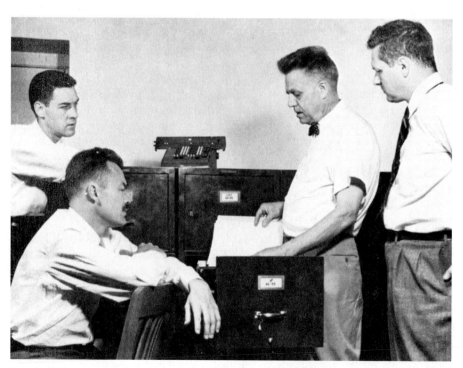

FIGURE 1-6   ALFRED C. KINSEY AND COLLEAGUES. THIS COLLEGE PROFESSOR'S SURVEYS OF MALE SEXUAL BEHAVIORS IN 1948 AND FEMALE SEXUAL BEHAVIORS IN 1953 MARKED THE BEGINNING OF THE MODERN ERA OF SEXUALITY RESEARCH. FROM LEFT TO RIGHT: CLYDE MARTIN, PAUL GEBHARD, KINSEY, WARDELL POMEROY.

presentation, Dr. Howard Kelly, the leading gynecologist of the day, responded, "I do hope we shall not have to go into details in discussing this subject. Its discussion is attended with more or less filth and we besmirch ourselves by discussing it in public." Papers read at meetings of the American Medical Association were routinely published in the *Journal of the American Medical Association*, but the journal refused to publish Lewis's.

Over half a century later, William Masters, a physician, and Virginia Johnson, a behavioral scientist, did not believe that experiments with rats could tell us a great deal about sexual behavior in people (Figure 1-7). Ford and Beach (1951) had published a book a few years earlier in which they included observations of each other having sexual intercourse with their wives, but it lacked objectivity. Therefore, in 1954, Masters and Johnson started to directly observe and record the physiological responses in humans engaged in sexual activity under laboratory conditions. Their results, which were based on over 10,000 episodes of sexual activity of 312 men and 382 women, were not published until 1966 (*Human Sexual Response*). Although some people were shocked at their observational approach ("scientific peeping Toms"), most people in the medical community appreciated the importance of their findings. As in all other areas of medical science, the understanding of anatomy and physiology led to methods for treating clinical problems and abnormalities. The behavioral approach to treating sexual dysfunctions (based on Masters and Johnson's work) has helped thou-

FIGURE 1-7 WILLIAM MASTERS AND VIRGINIA JOHNSON. THEIR LABORATORY STUDIES OF THE PHYSIOLOGICAL RESPOSNES THAT NORMALLY OCCUR DURING SEXUAL AROUSAL LED TO THE DEVELOPMENT OF MODERN DAY SEXUAL THERAPY TECHNIQUES.

sands of people to overcome problems and has contributed to improving their sexual relations and overall satisfaction with life. ∎

SCIENTIFIC METHODOLOGY: SURVEYS AND SAMPLES

Throughout this book you will see statistics about sexual behaviors (e.g., percentages of people, frequencies of behavior). In order to know such things, it was necessary for someone like Kinsey, for example, to ask people about their sexual attitudes and behaviors. This means taking a **survey**. It is not possible, of course, to interview everyone in the entire United States, so researchers must take a **sample** (a subset) from this population. There have been many such surveys, some of which you may have heard of: the Kinsey report, the Hunt report (done for *Playboy*), the Hite report, and surveys done by *Redbook, Cosmopolitan,* and other magazines. Sometimes the results of these surveys agree, but in other cases they disagree, sometimes considerably. Which ones should we trust to be true? Are any of them accurate?

Survey
A study of people's attitudes, opinions, or behaviors.

Sample
A subset of a population of subjects.

It might seem to make sense to some of you that the accuracy of a survey would depend on the size of the sample (i.e., the number of people surveyed). Although sample size is important, there are other factors which, if not considered, can negate any advantage obtained by using a large sample. The classic example that bigger is not necessarily better is a survey conducted in 1936 by a magazine called the *Literary Digest*. The magazine sent questionnaires to ten million people whose names were gathered from lists of telephone and automobile owners. They asked the people whether they were going to vote for Roosevelt or Landon in the upcoming presidential election. Over two million people responded, and the results indicated that the Republican Landon would beat the incumbent Democrat Roosevelt by a landslide. In fact, Roosevelt beat Landon by a landslide. As a result, the *Literary Digest* lost credibility, which was one of the reasons it went out of business shortly thereafter.

How could a survey that included such a large

number of people have been so wrong? The country was in the middle of the Great Depression, and most people were worrying about whether they could continue to buy food to feed their families. Only financially secure people could afford to own a car and have a telephone, and they tended to vote Republican. Most of the voters were registered as Democrats. In other words, despite the large sample size, this survey was grossly inaccurate because of a built-in bias. It surveyed only a small subgroup of the population and was not representative of the entire country. For a sample to be accurate, it must be taken randomly.

What is random sampling? Does it mean blindly picking out names in a phone book or stopping people on the street? No, for these types of samples might have the same type of built-in biases as the *Literary Digest* survey. A **random sample** is one in which observations are drawn so that each possible sample of that size has an equal chance of being selected (see Minium, King, & Bear, 1993, p. 234). A special type of random sample is a *stratified random sample*, the type used by the Gallup and Harris polls to predict the outcome of presidential elections today. Before they take their surveys, they break the entire country down by sex, race, education, income, geographical location, and many other factors. They know, for example, exactly what percentage of the population is white, Protestant, college educated, and living in the Northeast. Their sample survey includes this percentage of people with these characteristics. As a result, the Gallup and Harris surveys are rarely off by more than a few percentage points (and because both are done scientifically, they generally agree as well). Yet both polls survey only about 2,500 people out of an estimated 100 million voters.

Kinsey's two studies were quite large (5,300 males and 5,940 females), but his samples were not randomly drawn from the U.S. population. They overrepresented Midwestern, white, college-educated people, and also included a disproportionately large number of inmates from local prisons. Surveys conducted by magazines are also generally quite large, sometimes with over 100,000 respondents, but are they representative of the country as a whole? What kind of people read *Playboy* or *Hustler*? What kind of people read *Cosmopolitan* or *Ladies Home Journal*? One third of the respondents to a 1982 *Playboy* magazine questionnaire said that they had engaged in group sex. Do you really believe this to be true for the entire country?

There are more problems in taking a survey of people's sexual behavior than making sure it is repre-

> **Random sampling**
>
> A sampling procedure in which observations are drawn so that each possible sample of that size has an equal chance of being selected.

sentative of the population. Ask yourself the following questions:

1. How often do you masturbate?
2. How many sexual partners have you had in your lifetime?
3. Do you have sexual intercourse in different positions?
4. Do you engage in oral-genital sex?
5. Have you ever had a homosexual experience?
6. Have you ever had an extramarital affair?

Answering some of these questions may have made you or anyone else feel uncomfortable, for these are very personal questions. How would we know that the people we are surveying are telling the truth? Some people might try to make themselves look good by lying when answering questions about their personal life, so some questionnaires contain "truth items," that is, questions such as, "Have you ever told a lie?" It is assumed that everyone has told a lie in his or her life (maybe just a little one), so someone responding negatively to this item would be assumed to be not telling the truth. Incorrect answers, however, are not necessarily the result of intentional deceit, but can also be due to faulty recall. How well do you remember all the events of your childhood, for example? If couples are surveyed, what does the interviewer do if there are discrepancies in the answers given by the two people? How can the interviewer decide who is telling the truth (or is it a case that they both recall events differently)? With regard to sex surveys, two problems are particularly troublesome. Some people may exaggerate their sexual experiences, while others may try to hide certain aspects of their sexuality. Surveys often find, for example, that the number of female sexual partners reported by men is greater than the number of male partners reported by women (see Morris, 1993). Problems like these can sometimes be minimized if the survey is done by questionnaire rather than by interview, and the questions can be answered anonymously, that is, the respondent is assured that no one (including the person doing the survey) will ever know who he or she is.

Okay, so now you know enough to design a good sex survey. First you stratify the population of people in which you are interested, and then you randomly sample a specified number of people from each of the subgroups. The questionnaires will be filled out anonymously and contain a few items to check for truthfulness. After all this, however, there is another major problem that plagues sex survey research. What do we do when people refuse to participate? In Morton Hunt's survey (1975), which was an attempt to update Kinsey's (1948, 1953) data, only 20 percent of the people contacted agreed to participate. Shere Hite's often-cited surveys (1976, 1981, 1987) had only a 3–6 percent response rate. From a scientific point of view it is necessary that everyone randomly selected to be in the survey complete it, but it probably would not surprise you to learn that many people refuse to answer questions like those in the previous list. We cannot force people to do so. This is a problem of volunteer bias. Are there differences between people who agree to participate in the survey and those who do not? Should we assume that people who refuse to answer are more conservative in their views and behavior than those who do answer? Or, maybe these people are trying to hide something. Moreover, it is possible that the only difference in sexual behaviors between these two groups is that one regards it as something very private, not to be shared with others. The fact of the matter is that we will never know for sure, and the greater the number of people in a survey who refuse to participate, the more cautious we should be in making generalizations about the population.

What then can we conclude from most of the surveys that were done between 1948 and 1990? Although we may never know exactly how many people engage in a particular behavior, or the exact frequency with which people engage in various behaviors, there has often been enough agreement among the many different surveys to allow us to feel confident in making generalizations.

Today, there are calls from many sources to update what we know about sexual behavior of people in the United States. The Centers for Disease Control and Prevention argued the need for a new national survey (to combat AIDS) in the spring of 1988. In 1989, a panel of the National Academy of Science's National Research Council asked federal agencies to fund new surveys of sexual behavior in order to help with AIDS

prevention (*New York Times,* February 28, p. C1). In the same year, the U.S. Department of Health and Human Services was getting ready to test a new survey in order to acquire information about the increase in teenage pregnancies, sexually transmitted diseases, and sexual abuse of children. The Department initially approved $15 million for a large survey of 20,000 Americans that would be led by sociologist Edward Laumann. However, U.S. Senator Jesse Helms of South Carolina introduced an amendment in the Senate to eliminate funding for surveys of sexual behavior (saying that they were designed to "legitimize homosexual lifestyles") and the White House Office of Management and Budget eventually blocked the attempts at funding (*APA Monitor,* July 1989, p. 34; *University of Chicago Magazine,* October 1992, p. 14). Attempts to revive the surveys on a smaller scale were squashed by the government in 1991 (*APA Monitor,* November 1991, p. 1). The British government similarly blocked funding of sexual surveys in that country (Maddox, 1989).

Despite the new political obstacles, a few groups of researchers are proceeding with new sexual surveys, using more scientifically based sampling procedures than ever before. Samuel and Cynthia Janus published *The Janus Report on Sexual Behavior* in 1993, a cross-sectional national survey begun in 1988. Laumann and his colleagues eventually received $1.7 million from private foundations, and after scaling down their project, in 1992 they interviewed 3,432 randomly selected adults (Laumann et al., 1994). This is the most scientifically conducted sexual survey to date and we will refer to their results often. In time it is hoped that people (and governments) will come to recognize that surveys of sexual behavior are not an invasion of privacy, but research with potentially great social benefit. ∎

SEXUALITY EDUCATION TODAY

Kinsey's surveys (1948, 1953) were met with much public outrage, but surveys of people's behaviors and attitudes have since become commonplace, so that we now have a good idea of what can be considered normal sexual behaviors. Physiological studies with humans rather than animals have become accepted within the scientific community as well. As a result, we now have a large body of data on human sexual responses. The emerging field of sexual therapy has provided us with much information on sexual dysfunctions. Interestingly, it has been found that there is a link between a sexually restrictive upbringing and adult sexual problems.

For the first time in our history, we are in a position to teach factual information to our children about human sexuality. What was just in our recent past a

taboo subject for discussion even within the family is now offered in many schools. Only three states had mandated sexuality education in all school districts in 1986, but this number had increased to 23 by the end of 1989 (deMauro, 1990). Twenty-three other states had made recommendations for the teaching of sexuality education.

This book teaches all aspects of human sexuality. You will learn about anatomy, physiology, the effects of hormones, pregnancy and childbirth, sexual development, behavior, sexual abuse, contraception, sexually transmitted disease, and many other topics. The book does not advocate one lifestyle over another, and I hope that everyone who finishes the book will feel more comfortable with his or her own sexuality.

BOX 1-A

CROSS-CULTURAL PERSPECTIVES: SEX EDUCATION

Children learn of sex from a variety of sources, including parents, brothers and sisters, friends, the media, and school. Parents' attitudes about the sexuality of their children vary considerably across cultures. In many cultures, parents are very permissive, either promoting sexual relations among adolescents and sometimes preadolescent children (as in the Mangaian culture or the Muria Gond of India), or at least tolerating it (as with the !Kung of Africa) (Elwin, 1968; Marshall, 1971; Shostak, 1981). In other cultures, parents are very restrictive and never mention sex or normal bodily functions such as menstruation to their children, and severely restrict premarital sexual relations (as in the case of the Inis Baeg of Ireland or in most Islamic cultures) (Ammar, 1954; Messenger, 1971). In a survey of 141 societies, Broude and Greene (1976) found 25 percent to be highly permissive and another 25 percent highly restrictive.

Some anthropologists believe that attitudes about premarital sexual exploration become more restrictive the more complex the culture is (Murdock, 1964). Although Western cultures have become more tolerant in the post-Victorian era, it is still the case that American parents are the primary source of sexual information for only a minority of children (T.D. Fisher, 1987; King et al., 1993; Thornburg, 1981), and even those parents who do talk to their children about sex are unlikely to tell them that one purpose for sex is enjoyment (Goldman & Goldman, 1982).

In Europe, the United States, and other English-speaking countries, schools are increasingly becoming the primary source of information about sex (Penland, 1981). The country with probably the longest history of school sex education is Sweden, which made it compulsory for all children (starting at age 8) in 1956. Schools in Sweden and Denmark do not have special sex education classes, but instead integrate lessons throughout the curriculum. Pre-adolescent Swedish children's knowledge of sexual anatomy and behaviors (including the pleasurable aspects) is far superior to that of most North American children (Goldman & Goldman, 1982), yet the teenage pregnancy rate in Sweden is substantially lower (Westoff, 1988). In our own country, many states have now mandated sex education (de Mauro, 1990). Interestingly, completion of a comprehensive sexuality education program increases the likelihood that students will talk to their own children about sex in the future (King et al., 1993). In 1993, the World Health Organization called for more sex education in schools.

In many parts of the world, government or international agencies are playing a role in sex education. In June 1988, then U.S. Surgeon General Everett Koop's office mailed a brochure entitled ''Understanding AIDS'' to 107 million American households. The Chinese government published a booklet in 1980 entitled *Sexual Knowledge* that was designed to help the Chinese combat the less restrictive sexual morals of Western countries. (Chinese students are much more conservative in their attitudes about sex compared to most U.S. students; Chan, 1990.) In underdeveloped African and Asian countries, the World Health Organization and the International Planned Parenthood Federation have developed innovative programs to deal with sexual health education (Senanayake, 1992).

The primary source of sexual information may vary from culture to culture, but there is a definite trend in the direction of enlightenment. In Western cultures the sexual education of children has increasingly become an integrative responsibility shared by parents, schools, and the government. ■

KEY TERMS

ascetic philosophy 11	missionary position 7	sexuality 2
dualism 11	procreation 10	St. Augustine 12
Havelock Ellis 15	random sample 18	St. Paul 11
Sigmund Freud 15	Reformation 12	survey 17
Alfred Kinsey 16	sample 17	Victorian era 13
Masters and Johnson 16	sexual revolution 14	

PERSONAL REFLECTIONS

1. From whom (or from where) did you acquire most of your information about sex (e.g., parents, friends, teachers, the media)?

2. Did your parents discuss sexuality with you? If not, why do you suppose they did not? If yes, was it ongoing discussions or just one or two "birds and bees" talks? Do you think that one or two talks can adequately prepare most people for a lifetime of sexual relations and problems?

3. From whom do you hope your children will learn about sexuality? Do you plan to play a role in their sex education?

4. Do you believe that sexuality education should be taught in school? If so, beginning at what level? Why?

5. Christian views about sex were strongly influenced by St. Paul and St. Augustine, who believed that the only legitimate reason to engage in sex was for procreation (to have children). How do you feel about engaging in sex for pleasure?

6. How do you feel about sex as a subject for scientific study? Explain.

SUGGESTED READINGS

Caron, S. L., & Bertran, R. M. (1988, April). What college students want to know about sex. *Medical Aspects of Human Sexuality.*

Davenport, W. (1977). Sex in cross-cultural perspective. In F. Beach (Ed.), *Human sexuality in four perspectives* (Baltimore: Johns Hopkins Press. A comparison of different sexual attitudes and behaviors around the world.

D'Emilio, J., & Freedman, E. (1988). *Intimate matters: A history of sexuality in America.* New York: Harper & Row. A very scholarly history.

Gordon, S. (1982, Fall/Winter). Sexuality education in the 1980's—no more retreats. *Journal of Sex Education and Therapy,* Vol. 8.

Hall, E. (1986, June). New directions for the Kinsey Institute. *Psychology Today.* A profile of June Reinisch, the director of the Kinsey Institute.

Marshall, D. S. (1971, February). Too much in Mangaia. *Psychology Today.*

Messenger, J. L. (1971, February). Sex and repression in an Irish folk community: The lack of the Irish. *Psychology Today.*

Murray, L. (1983, October). Daring pioneers of sex research. *Science Digest.*

Suggs, D. N., & Miracle, A. W. (1993). *Culture and human sexuality.* Pacific Grove: Brooks/Cole. Cross-cultural essays about human sexuality.

CHAPTER TWO

Human Sexuality Today

OUR SEXUAL AND REPRODUCTIVE ANATOMY

WHEN YOU HAVE FINISHED STUDYING THIS CHAPTER, YOU SHOULD BE ABLE TO:

1. EXPLAIN WHY LEARNING CORRECT ANATOMICAL TERMS IS IMPORTANT;

2. DESCRIBE EACH PART OF THE EXTERNAL FEMALE ANATOMY: MONS VENERIS, LABIA MAJORA, LABIA MINORA, CLITORIS, HYMEN, VAGINAL AND URETHRAL OPENINGS, AND EXPLAIN ITS FUNCTION(S);

3. BE ABLE TO DISCUSS ATTITUDES ABOUT AN INTACT HYMEN AND THEIR IMPLICATIONS FOR WOMEN OF DIFFERENT CULTURES;

4. UNDERSTAND WHY EARLY DETECTION OF BREAST CANCER CAN SAVE LIVES AND EXPLAIN HOW TO PERFORM A BREAST SELF-EXAMINATION;

5. EXPLAIN THE RISKS ASSOCIATED WITH BREAST AUGMENTATION OPERATIONS;

6. LIST AND DESCRIBE EACH OF THE FEMALE INTERNAL ANATOM-ICAL STRUCTURES: VAGINA, UTERUS, FALLOPIAN TUBES, AND OVARIES, AND EXPLAIN ITS FUNCTION(S);

7. EXPLAIN THE IMPORTANCE OF AN ANNUAL PELVIC EXAMINA-TION AND PAP SMEAR FOR FEMALE HEALTH;

8. DESCRIBE EACH OF THE STRUCTURES OF THE EXTERNAL AND INTERNAL MALE ANATOMY: PENIS, SCROTUM, TESTICLES, EPI-DIDYMIS, VAS DEFERENS, EJACULATORY DUCTS, URETHRA, PROSTATE GLAND, SEMINAL VESICLES, AND COWPER'S GLANDS, AND EXPLAIN ITS FUNCTION(S);

9. DISCUSS THE ADVANTAGES AND DISADVANTAGES OF ROUTINE CIRCUMCISION;

10. EXPLAIN HOW TO PERFORM A TESTICULAR SELF-EXAMINATION;

11. IDENTIFY THE EARLY SIGNS OF PROSTATE PROBLEMS; AND

12. DESCRIBE HOW OTHER PARTS OF THE BODY (LIPS, MOUTH, HAIR, BUTTOCKS, ETC.) MAY ALSO BE CONSIDERED PART OF OUR SEXUAL ANATOMY.

MANY OF THE FIRST WORDS THAT WE EVER LEARN ARE ANATOMICAL TERMS. PARENTS OFTEN SPEND hours teaching their young children to point to and say different parts of the body such as the mouth, eyes, ears, and nose. Unfortunately, when naming body parts, many parents simply skip from arms, chest, and "tummy" to legs, knees, and feet, completely omitting any mention of the genitals and anus. Other parents teach their children the correct anatomical word for all other parts of the body, but substitute such "cute" words as "weeney," "booty," "peanut," and "talleywacker" for the genitals. As for functions of this mysterious body area, many of us are simply taught during toilet training to make "pee-pees" and "poopoos." Although some parents became sexually experienced without ever knowing the correct anatomical terms, many others who know better nevertheless feel very uncomfortable with teaching their children to say the words "penis" or "vagina."

As we grow older we learn new words from our peers that describe our sexual anatomy or behavior, but quite often these are slang terms. Men are more likely than women to use slang terms when referring to their own **genitalia**,

Genitalia
The reproductive organs of the male or female.

but many students use no word at all to refer to their partner's or their own genitals (Fischer, 1989). Very few students use the word "intercourse" when referring to the act of copulation. The use of slang terminology and the discomfort that many people feel about using the correct words reflect the ambivalent feelings that many people have about sex. There is perhaps no better example of the distorted negative attitudes that some people have toward sex than the common use of the word "fuck" instead of intercourse. It is frequently used to express displeasure ("What the fuck is going on here?"), trouble ("I got fucked over at work"), or aggression ("Fuck you!"); yet at many other times we think of sexual intercourse as a pleasurable experience. The word "fuck," by the way, probably originated from the middle English word "fucken." At one time it was not considered improper to use, but it acquired its negative connotations in the mid-1600s.

Many of the slang terms used to describe our sexual anatomy also have negative connotations. A commonly used term for the external female genitalia, for example, is "pudendum," which is derived from a Latin word meaning "something to be ashamed of." Similarly, the slang term "prick" is often used in a derogatory manner.

Slang terms can also result in misinformation about one's sexual anatomy and behavior. In response to one of the items on a questionnaire given the first day of class in human sexual behavior, many students

indicated that they believed that an erection in human males occurs when a bone protrudes from the base of the penis. This belief should not be surprising, for after all, why else would an erection be called a "boner"? Slang terms such as "cherry," "nuts," and "pussy" can also be very misleading.

It is not the intent of the author to teach "dirty" words or slang terminology. In fact, a course in human sexuality often results in an increase in the use of proper terms (Fischer, 1989). We must acknowledge the fact, however, that many of us come to class with a sexual vocabulary that consists almost entirely of slang words. The question that many students have, of course, is, "What good will it do to learn the correct anatomical terms, which are almost always Latin or Greek?" The lack of such knowledge obviously does not hinder most people from becoming sexually experienced. Knowledge of sexual anatomy may help dispel any misleading information acquired through use of slang terms, but will it help make us better sexual partners? It may be very helpful, particularly if it results in our becoming less inhibited about our own body and that of our partner. Many people have never even examined themselves (possibly because many parents discouraged or punished such behavior during childhood) and are ashamed of their genitals rather than view them as a source of pleasure and a positive part of their anatomy. This is more often true of women than men (Barbach, 1980; Hite, 1976). Here are a few comments that I received from students when I was using a classroom testing version of this book:

"As for the illustrations in Chapter 2, I thought they were good and very well illustrated, but they were rather embarrassing to look at."

"Figure 2-2 made me feel uncomfortable. I felt as if everyone could see me."

"The diagrams and illustrations are quite to the point. Somehow I still find these photographs repulsive."

"The pictures in this chapter were quite graphic. I wish they were on another separate page so that we wouldn't have to look at them the entire time we read a particular page. Even just reading this by myself was a little embarrassing."

"I had difficulties looking at the pictures without embarrassment and shame. I should be able to look without any bad feelings."

(from the author's files)

No one should feel embarrassed or ashamed about any part of their own body, including their genitals. If you have never done so, I encourage you to examine yourself during this part of the course. By making us more aware of our own body and that of our partner (or future partner), a chapter on basic anatomy might result in our becoming more comfortable with exploring other aspects of our sexuality as well.

In the act of sexual intercourse, you share in mutual bodily stimulation with your partner. Intercourse means "communication" (*Webster's New World Dictionary*), but communication, whether verbal or tactile, is not possible without some basic knowledge. Should your sexual relations result in having children, it is hoped that someday you will teach them about their bodies without having to resort to slang and/or cute terminology that avoids the basic facts of life (see Chapter 10). ■

EXTERNAL FEMALE ANATOMY

You can see the location of the female reproductive system in Figure 2-1. A picture of the external female genitalia, collectively known as the **vulva** (Latin for "covering"), is shown in Figure 2-2. The vulva consists of the mons veneris, the labia majora, labia minora, clitoris, and vaginal and urethral openings. When examining herself (which requires use of a hand mirror) a woman should not consider herself to be abnormal if she does not look identical to the drawing in Figure 2-2. As in all other parts of the body, the female genitalia vary in appearance from person to person, differing in size, shape, and color (see Figure 2-3). Many women have ambivalent feelings about their genitalia (remember the

> **Vulva**
> A term for the external female genitalia, which includes the mons veneris, labia majora, labia minora, clitoris, vaginal opening, and urethral opening.

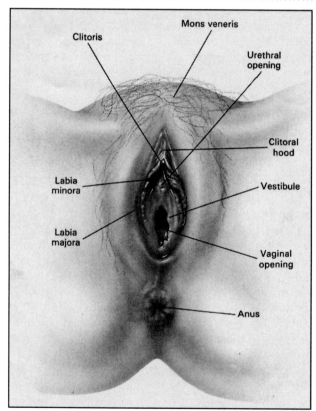

FIGURE 2-2   THE FEMALE GENITALIA (VULVA) WITH THE LABIA PARTED TO SHOW THE VAGINAL AND URETHRAL OPENINGS.

use of the term pudendum). The feelings that a woman has toward her genitalia, however, are often a reflection of the self-concept she has about her overall physical appearance.

THE MONS VENERIS

Translated from Latin, **mons veneris** means "mount of Venus" and refers to the soft layer of fatty tissue overlaying the area where the pubic bones come together. Venus, of course, was the Roman goddess of love and the mons area is considered

> **Mons veneris**
> The soft layer of fatty tissue that overlays the pubic bone in females. It becomes covered with pubic hair during puberty.

FIGURE 2-1   ANATOMICAL LOCATION OF THE FEMALE REPRODUCTIVE SYSTEM.

FIGURE 2-3   TWO VARIATIONS IN THE APPEARANCE OF FEMALE GENITALIA.

to be very erotic after puberty when it becomes covered with hair. Prior to the early 1970s, magazines such as *Playboy* and *Penthouse* considered pubic hair too explicitly erotic for publication and the hair was airbrushed out of photographs. Pubic hair varies considerably in color, texture, and waviness.

Our sensitivity to touch is dependent on the density of nerve endings in a particular area of skin. Areas such as the lips and fingertips have a high density of nerve endings and thus are very sensitive to touch, while areas such as the back have a much lower density of nerve endings and are much less sensitive to touch. Because of numerous nerve endings in the mons area, many women find gentle stimulation of the mons to be pleasurable.

Although the soft layer of fatty tissue cushions the pubic region during intercourse, one can only speculate as to what purpose nature intended pubic hair to serve. Some researchers believe that this pocket of hair on an otherwise mostly hairless body serves to be sexually attractive visually. However, there are small glands at the base of the pubic hairs, and it was probably nature's intention that pubic hair serves to trap secretions that occur during sexual arousal (chemical sex arousers?). Of course, pubic hair on females also traps vaginal secretions. Males of most mammalian species find vaginal odors to be erotically stimulating, and similar results have been found for humans under laboratory conditions (Hassett, 1978). Many people in Western cultures,

however, are conditioned to have negative feelings about such odors (see the section on the vagina). Shaving the pubic hair is a recent but increasingly popular practice among American women, although this practice may result in chafing, irritation of the skin, and possible infection from ingrown hairs.

THE LABIA

The labia consists of two outer (**labia majora** or major lips) and two inner (**labia minora** or minor lips) elongated folds of skin, which, in the sexually unstimulated state, cover (and thus protect) the vaginal and urethral openings. The outer surfaces of the labia majora become covered with hair at the time of puberty. The labia majora extend from the mons to the hairless bit of skin between the vaginal opening and anus called the **perineum**. Because the perineum often tears during childbirth, physicians commonly make an incision in it (called an *episiotomy*) prior to delivery (see Chapter 7). When sewing up this area, some old-fashioned doctors add an extra stitch to tighten the vaginal opening (called a husband's knot as its only purpose is

Labia majora

Two outer elongations extending from the mons to the perineum in females. Its outer surfaces become covered with pubic hair during puberty.

Labia minora

Two hairless elongations located between the labia majora in females. They meet at the top of the vulva to form the clitoral hood.

Perineum

Technically refers to the entire pelvic floor, but more commonly is used to mean the hairless bit of skin between the anus and either the vaginal opening (in females) or scrotum (in males).

to increase the male's pleasure when sexual intercourse is resumed). After childbirth it is not uncommon for the labia majora to remain apart to some extent in the unstimulated state.

The pinkish and hairless labia minora are located between, and sometimes protrude beyond, the labia majora. Among the bush people of Africa, particularly the Hottentots, elongation of the labia minora is considered to be highly erotic, and females are instructed to pull on them from early childhood. Some "Hottentot Aprons," as they are called, can hang as much as seven inches in length.

The labia minora, which meet at the top to form the **clitoral hood** (or prepuce), are very sensitive to touch. They have numerous blood vessels that become engorged with blood during sexual stimulation, causing them to swell and turn bright red or wine-colored.

Clitoral hood
The part of the labia minora that covers the clitoris in females.

Located at the base of the labia minora are the **Bartholin's glands**, which, during prolonged stimulation, contribute a few drops of an alkaline fluid to the inner surfaces via ducts. The small amount of fluid does not make a significant contribution to vaginal lubrication during sexual intercourse, but it does help to counteract the normal acidity of the outer vagina (sperm cannot live in an acidic environment). Infection or cysts of the Bartholin's glands sometimes occur, and a physician should be consulted if there is any local swelling or irritation.

Bartholin's glands
Glands located at the base of the labia minora in females that contribute a small amount of an alkaline fluid to their inner surfaces during sexual arousal.

The Clitoris

The **clitoris** (Greek, meaning "hill" or "slope") develops from the same embryonic tissue as the penis and has at least as many nerve endings as the much larger penis, making it extremely sensitive to touch. In fact, it is the only structure in either males or females with no known function other than to focus sexual sensations (Masters & Johnson, 1970). The only visible portion is the *glans*, which in a sexually unaroused woman looks like a small, shiny button located just below the hood of skin formed where the two labia minora meet. The visible part of the clitoris measures about one quarter to one inch in length, but contrary to what some people may believe, the sexual pleasure of females is not related to the size of the clitoris

Clitoris
A small, elongated, erectile structure in females that develops from the same embryonic tissue as the penis. It has no known reproductive function other than to focus sexual sensations.

(Money, 1970). Another popular myth is that greater sexual responsiveness in women is linked to the shorter the distance between the vaginal opening and clitoral glans (so that the penis can more easily stimulate the clitoris); but this, too, is not true. The penis, in fact, usually does not come into direct contact with the clitoris during sexual intercourse.

Most of the clitoris is not visible. The body or *shaft* of the clitoris is located beneath the clitoral hood. It divides to form two much larger structures called *crura* (Latin for "legs"), which fan out and attach to the pubic bone. Like the penis, the clitoris is made up of spongy tissue (two *corpora cavernosa*) that becomes engorged with blood during sexual arousal. This causes it to increase in size; but because of the way it is attached to the pubic bone, the clitoris does not actually become erect like the penis. Any form of sexual arousal may result in engorgement and enlargement of the clitoris. If sexual stimulation continues, the previously visible clitoris pulls back against the pubic bone and the glans disappears from view beneath the clitoral hood.

During sexual intercourse, the thrusting of the penis only indirectly stimulates the clitoris by causing the clitoral hood to rub back and forth over the glans. Surgical removal of the clitoral hood (*clitoral circumcision*) in order to directly expose the clitoris was once a common practice in order to enhance responsivity in wives who were thought to be "frigid." Problems with sexual desire or attaining orgasm, however, are only rarely the result of an anatomical problem.

Surgical removal of the clitoris was sometimes performed in the United States and Europe during Victorian times in order to eliminate masturbation and prevent female children from growing up "oversexed." Female circumcision is no longer performed in America, of course, but it is very common in Middle Eastern countries, parts of Africa, Malaysia, and Indonesia (see Box 4-A).

Thickened secretions called *smegma* can accumulate beneath the clitoral hood and result in discomfort during sexual intercourse by causing the glans to stick to the clitoral hood. The secretions can generally be removed, however, by bathing thoroughly.

The Vaginal Opening

The vaginal and urethral openings are visible only if the labia minora are parted. The area between the two labia minora is sometimes referred to as the **vestibular area** (Latin for "entrance hall") and the vaginal opening as the *introitus* (Latin for "entrance"). The vaginal opening, which is very sensitive to stimulation, is not a permanently open orifice ready for penetration

Vestibular area
A term sometimes used to refer to the area between the two labia minora.

Bulbocavernosus muscle

A ring of sphincter muscles that surround the vaginal opening in females or the root of the penis in males.

Vestibular bulbs

These surround the vaginal opening and fill with blood during sexual arousal, resulting in swelling of the tissues and a narrowing of the vaginal opening.

Hymen

The thin membrane that partially covers the vaginal opening in many sexually inexperienced women. Its presence or absence, however, is really a very poor indicator of prior sexual experience.

by the penis. It is surrounded by the **bulbocavernosus muscle**, a ring of sphincter muscles similar to the sphincter muscles surrounding the anus. Sexually experienced women can learn to voluntarily contract or relax these muscles during intercourse, and during childbirth the vaginal opening expands enough to accommodate delivery of a baby. In sexually inexperienced women, on the other hand, these muscles may involuntarily contract as a result of extreme nervousness, making penetration very difficult. The **vestibular bulbs**, which are located underneath the sphincter muscles on both sides of the vaginal openings, also help the vagina to grip the penis by swelling with blood during sexual arousal.

In sexually inexperienced females a thin membrane called the **hymen** (named after the Greek god of marriage) may partially cover the opening to the vagina. It is found only in human females (and perhaps female horses) and has no known physiological function. The hymen may have one (annular hymen), two (septate hymen), or several openings (cribriform hymen) that allow for passage of menstrual flow. In the rare instance that the hymen has no opening (imperforate hymen), a simple surgical incision can be made at the time of first menstruation. The vaginal opening of women who have given birth is sometimes referred to as the *parous introitus* ("passed through").

The presence of the hymen has been used by men throughout history as proof of virginity. In the time of the Biblical Hebrews a newlywed woman who did not bleed during first intercourse was sometimes stoned to death.

> But if the thing is true, that the tokens of virginity were not found in the young woman, then they shall bring out the young woman to the door of her father's house, and the men of her city shall stone her to death with stones, because she has wrought folly in Israel by playing the harlot in her father's house; so you shall purge the evil from the midst of you.
>
> (Deuteronomy 22:20–21, Revised Standard Version)

Even in many parts of the world today a newlywed wife can be divorced or exiled if her husband believes her to be unchaste (Ford & Beach, 1951). Many Muslims, Chinese, and Moroccans display a blood-stained sheet on the wedding night as proof of a new bride's chastity. It was once the custom in some cultures for a priest to devirginate a woman. In other cultures girls are ritually "deflowered" with stone phalluses or horns. Although these extreme customs are not found in Western cultures, many American men nevertheless expect their female partner to bleed during first intercourse.

> "A girlfriend of mine, a few years ago, told me that she was a virgin, so naturally I figured that after we had sex she would bleed. Then, when she didn't I felt upset and betrayed."

> "When my girlfriend and I first had intercourse it was just understood by listening to my peers that she was supposed to bleed and I should see some kind of skin hanging (hymen). This didn't happen and for years it bothered me because I thought she lied to me when she told me that I was her first. It wasn't until after taking this course that I realized how ignorant my friends and I were."

> "Being very athletic came natural for me and by the time I was 12, I had won four athletic trophies and many certificates. My mother took me to a doctor right after I made 14 and he told her that I was not a virgin because my hymen was not in place. I cried for 2 weeks. It was not true. My life was very traumatic for the next 6 months. Now at 40 years old, I am still angry."

(from the author's files)

In actuality, the hymen is really a very poor indicator of whether or not a female is sexually experienced, and there is often very little bleeding or discomfort during first sexual intercourse. In fact, pain during first intercourse often reflects a woman's attitudes about sex (Weis, 1985). Not all women are born with a hymen, and many others are born with an incomplete membrane. The hymen sometimes ruptures during vigorous physical activity or insertion of a tampon, and in some women the opening in the hymen only stretches rather than tears during first intercourse (and thus there would be no bleeding). Even most doctors would have a difficult time determining whether or not a female is sexually experienced. Nevertheless, it has become a common practice in Japan and some northern European countries for sexually experienced women to have a hymen reconstructed by a plastic surgeon prior to marriage (at great expense, it might be added). It speaks rather poorly of our attitudes about sex that many newlywed women are expected to bleed and experience great discomfort and pain in order to please their husbands. Untold millions of women throughout history have probably suffered much grief (or even death) for failing to display what many men wrongly believe to be an appropriate response to first intercourse.

The Urethral Opening

Urine passes from the bladder through a small tube called the **urethra** and out the urethral opening, which is located below the clitoris and above the vaginal opening. The male's urethra serves for the passage of sperm as well as urine, but the female's urinary system is not related to her reproductive system.

Urethra
The passageway from the bladder to the exterior of the body. In males, it also serves as a passageway for semen during ejaculation.

Cystitis is an inflammation of the bladder with symptoms of frequent and burning urination. It is often caused by the transmission of intestinal bacteria to the urethral opening. Women are more susceptible to this than men because of the closer distance of the anus to the urethral opening. Thus, after a bowel movement a woman should not wipe herself in the direction from the anus to the vulva (see Chapter 5).

The Breasts

Although breasts are not part of a woman's reproductive system, they are considered to be highly erotic by most men in Western societies and therefore we must consider them part of a woman's sexual anatomy. Recall from Chapter 1, however, that female breasts have no erotic significance in many cultures around the world. (Remember the native women in the movie *Mutiny on the Bounty* who were naked from the waist up? Their naked breasts were erotic only to the English sailors.)

Breasts
In females, located on the front of the chest, providing milk for infants.

Breasts develop at puberty as a result of increasing levels of the hormone estrogen, which is produced by the ovaries. Thus, the breasts are really a secondary sex characteristic, just as is pubic hair. Interestingly, it is common for one breast (usually the left) to be slightly larger than the other. Males also have a slight increase in estrogen levels after puberty, and many show a slight increase in breast size as a result (called *gynecomastia*). This may cause embarrassment for some young teenage boys, but the condition usually disappears within a few years.

Each adult female breast consists of 15–20 *mammary* (milk-producing) *glands* (see Figure 2-4). A separate duct connects each gland to the nipple, which is made up of smooth muscle fibers and also has lots of nerve fibers (making the nipples sensitive to touch). When a woman becomes sexually aroused, the smooth muscle fibers contract and the nipples become erect. The darkened area around the nipple is called the *areola*, and becomes even darker during pregnancy. The small bumps on the areola are glands that secrete oil to keep the nipples lubricated during breast-feeding.

Mammary glands
Milk-producing glands of the breast.

Hormone changes in the late stages of pregnancy cause the mammary glands to start producing milk, but

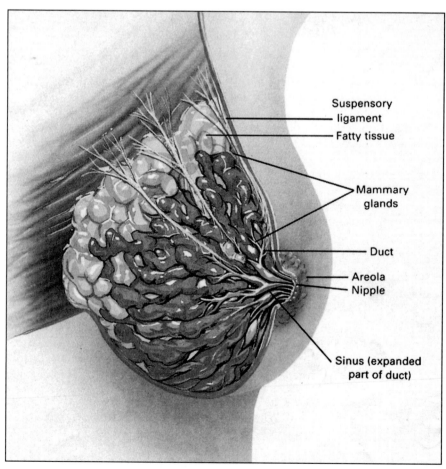

FIGURE 2-4   ANATOMY OF THE FEMALE BREAST.

Suspensory ligament
Fatty tissue
Mammary glands
Duct
Areola
Nipple
Sinus (expanded part of duct)

secretions from the breasts can also happen at other times (a condition known as *galactorrhea*) as a result of certain drugs, birth control pills, stress, and rough fabrics rubbing against the breasts. Some people (including males) have inverted nipples or an extra nipple, but this generally does not pose a health problem.

Breasts vary in size from woman to woman (see Figure 2-5). Breast size is not determined by the number of mammary glands, which is about the same for all women, but by the amount of fatty tissue packed between the glands. This is determined primarily by heredity. Although some men believe that large-breasted women have a greater sexual capacity than small-breasted women, there is really no relation between breast size and sensitivity to touch (Masters & Johnson, 1966). Large breasts do not have a greater number of nerve endings than small breasts. Nevertheless, because of the attention that many males give to breast size, some women attempt to enlarge their breasts.

Breast augmentation exercises and the lotions and mechanical devices advertised in women's magazines do not work (remember, breast size is determined by the amount of fatty tissue). Injections of liquid silicone were once popular to enhance breast size, but the complication rate eventually proved to be nearly 60 percent (e.g., infection, excessive hardness, deformities). Plastic surgeons then began to implant soft pouches filled with silicone to increase the size of breasts, and at least two million American women had their breasts enlarged in this manner. However, as with silicone injections, there were some complications. It was recognized early that in about 20 percent of women a fibrous capsule formed around the implant, making the breast hard, tight, and unnatural in appearance (Arrillaga et al., 1977), and despite advances the number of these types of complications has not changed (Norman Cole, president of the American Society of Plastic and Reconstructive Surgeons, in testimony before an FDA panel, November 12, 1991). Perhaps as many as 14 percent of im-

plants eventually ruptured (Food and Drug Administration), raising concerns because silicone had been found to cause cancer in animals. Other studies showed that leaking silicone could possibly cause autoimmune disease (antibodies attacking the body's own tissues, resulting in arthritis or lupus), but later studies downplayed the risks of cancer or connective-tissue disease (Bryant & Brashier, 1995; Gabriel et al., 1994; Sanchez-Guerrero et al., 1995).

Talk-show host Jenny Jones has had six operations because of the damage her implants did to her breasts. She was quoted in *People* magazine as saying, "I hate my body a thousand times more now than I ever did before. . . . I would sell everything I own to be able to have the body back that I gave up." Students in my class have relayed similar experiences:

" Recently I learned that one of my breast implants is leaking. My lymph nodes in my right breast are engorged with silicone. This will worry me for the rest of my life."

" My mom had a breast augmentation job done about 2 years ago and has had nothing but problems. She started growing too much scar tissue and lumps in her breasts, and now, after all the pain and money and aggravation she went through, she's having them removed this summer. I know she did it for my dad, but she can never tell me enough times how sorry she is she ever did it."

(from the author's files)

In 1992, the Food and Drug Administration (FDA) severely restricted silicone implants for purely cosmetic purposes, but left them available for women with mastectomies (breast removal), for whom they felt the emotional benefits outweighed the other risks.

FIGURE 2-5   SOME VARIATIONS IN THE APPEARANCE OF FEMALE BREASTS.

Manufacturers had to settle billions of dollars in liability cases, but are now making saline-filled implants and experimenting with soybean oil. However, these new implants will not eliminate the problem of encapsulation with hardening of the breasts.

Many naturally large-breasted women would like to be smaller:

" I currently wear a D-D cup. . . . My chest has become a large nuisance. It is hard for me to dance, jog, or any kind of activity that involves moving around a lot. Finding clothes is very hard. . . . I just recently talked to a friend of mine who had a breast reduction. I really want to have this operation. It would make me feel better about myself.''

(from the author's files)

Breast reduction involves removing some of the fatty tissue, and although it generally has fewer complications, it can cause scars or leave numbness in parts of a breast.

Cancer of the breasts is the second major cause of cancer death in women. Women are advised, therefore, to learn how to examine themselves in order to make an early, possibly life-saving, detection (see Box 2-A). ■

BOX 2-A

SEXUALITY AND HEALTH: BREAST CANCER AND EXAMINATION

Other than skin cancer, cancer of the breasts is the most common type of cancer (and the second leading cause of cancer death) in women, with over 180,000 new cases and 46,000 deaths per year (American Cancer Society). The odds of getting breast cancer have been increasing over the last few decades, and the latest statistics show that one in eight American women will develop breast cancer in her lifetime (Harris, 1994). It is less well known, but men can get breast cancer, too (about 2,500 this year).

The cause(s) of breast cancer is unknown, but there are some factors that put a woman at high risk. These include a family history of breast cancer, being older than 50 years, never giving birth or having the first child after age 30, starting menstruation before age 12, or undergoing menopause after age 55 (see Gail et al., 1989). The rate of breast cancer in North America and Northern Europe is much higher than in Asia or black Africa (Goodman, 1991), but much of these geographical variations are believed to be due to differences among cultures in the just-mentioned risk factors (Henderson & Bernstein, 1991). Some of the other factors that have been implicated as risks are obesity or a diet high in fats or lack of exercise (Bernstein et al., 1994; Kritchevsky, 1990; Kushi et al., 1992), alcohol consumption (Longnecker et al., 1992), smoking (Calle et al., 1994), and exposure to the pesticide DDT (Wolff et al., 1993). Estrogen (a hormone released by the ovaries) has long been thought to be a cause of breast cancer (see Toniolo et al., 1995), but results of studies looking at the effects of birth control pills (containing estrogen) or postmenopausal estrogen replacement therapy have been inconsistent (Cobleigh et al., 1994; Colditz et al., 1995; Sattin et al., 1986, Stanford et al., 1995, Steinberg et al., 1991). The present consensus is that if the pill or replacement therapy do increase the risk, it is only very slight and only with long-term (4–5 years or more) use (Malone, Daling, & Weiss, 1993; Stanford et al., 1995, Steinberg et al., 1991; Romieu, Berlin, & Colditz, 1990). How little is known about breast cancer is revealed by the fact that only about half of all cases are associated with any of the known risk factors.

About half of all cases of breast cancer have spread beyond the breast before they are discovered (Centers for Disease Control and Prevention). However, with early detection, there is a 90 percent survival rate (American Cancer Society) and with a little instruction, the female herself is most likely to make a life-saving early detection. Some women are reluctant or fearful to examine themselves or go to a doctor after discovering a lump. When then First Lady Betty Ford publicly announced in 1974 that she would have surgery for a self-discovered lump, she probably saved thousands of lives by making the subject less of a taboo. Nancy Reagan's breast surgery in 1987 reemphasized the importance of early detection.

Women should examine their breasts on a monthly basis. The best time is after menstruation ends when estrogen levels are low and the breasts are not tender or swollen. Women who are pregnant, postmenopause, or do not menstruate regularly should examine themselves at a regular time each month. First, examine yourself in front of a mirror. Do this with your hands at your sides, then with your hands on your hips, and finally with your hands raised above your head. Look for any bulging, flattening, dimpling, or redness. The symptoms are usually painless. In each position, examine one breast with the opposite hand. With fingers flat, press gently in small circular motions starting at the top and check the outermost part of the entire breast in clockwise fashion (see Figure 2-6). It is normal to have a ridge of firm tissue in the lower curve of each breast. After completion, move your fingers an inch closer to the nipple and make another complete check around the breast. At least three to four complete circles around the breast will be required. Be sure to examine under your arms as well because this is one of the most common areas for cancer to occur. In addition, examine the nipple by squeezing and note any discharge. Repeat the same procedure on the other breast. When done, examine yourself again during a bath or shower, as it is often easier to detect a lump, hard knot, or thickening when the skin is wet and slippery. Finally, report any suspected abnormality to your doctor immediately.

> "I am a 33-year-old nurse that has instructed many other women about self-examination, but unfortunately, did not practice what I preached. After one of your lectures I did examine my breasts and was horrified to find a small lump. . . ."

(from the author's files)

Unfortunately, by the time many women discover a lump, the cancer has already spread to other parts of their bodies. As a result, the American Cancer Society has been strongly recommending that women start having a **baseline mammogram** (breast X-ray) to find can-

FIGURE 2-6   BREAST SELF-EXAMINATION.

cers that are too small to be felt by hand. They suggest one baseline mammogram be taken between the ages of 35 and 40, another every one to two years between the ages of 40 to 49, and an annual breast X-ray after the age of 50. Eleven leading medical organizations endorsed this schedule in 1989. The amount of radiation used is quite small and the American Cancer Society believes that the long-term benefits far outweigh any potential risks. In fact, the number of cancers detected by mammograms has doubled since the mid-1980s (President's Cancer Panel, 1993). Unfortunately, many women were left confused when in 1993 the National Cancer Institute withdrew its endorsement of mammograms for women under age 50 (except in cases where there is a family history of breast cancer; They claimed that routine screening of women aged 40 to 49 had not proven effective (see Kerlikowske et al., 1995), but please note that all organizations urge mammograms for women aged 50 and older. If you are under age 50, talk to your doctor about what is best for you.

Eight out of ten lumps that are discovered are benign (noncancerous). They are known as *fibrocystic disease* (cysts) or fibroadenomas.

"When I was 15 years old, I discovered a breast lump accidentally while bathing. That was one of the scariest days of my life. My doctors told me I had fibrocystic disease. The day before my eighteenth birthday, I had surgery to remove another lump."

(from the author's files)

Therefore, do not panic if you find a lump in your breast, as the chances are good that it is not malignant. However, there is some evidence that having benign tumors increases the risk of future breast cancer among premenopausal women (London et al., 1992).

Biopsies are now being done by needle, which is faster, more exact, and less painful than the conventional surgical biopsy. If you should have a lump and it is diagnosed as cancerous, a number of surgical procedures might be performed: (1) radical mastectomy, in which the entire breast, underlying muscle, and lymph nodes are removed; (2) modified radical mastectomy, in which the breast and lymph nodes, but not the underlying muscles, are removed; (3) simple mastectomy, in which only the breast is removed; and (4) lumpectomy (or quadrectomy), in which only the lump and a small bit of surrounding tissue is removed, followed by radiation therapy. A committee of 15 experts assembled by the National Institutes of Health in 1990 concluded that with early detection, lumpectomy and radiation treatment can be as effective as radical mastectomy (also see Fisher et al., 1989, 1993). (It was later found that one of the investigators used fraudulent data, but reanalysis of the remaining data revealed the same beneficial effect for lumpectomy and other studies confirmed this; Lee-Feldstein et al., 1994.) In cases of cancer that has spread to the lymph nodes, the established procedure includes chemotherapy. In addition to these treatments, anti-estrogen drugs (e.g., tamoxifen) are often given to women who have, or have had, breast cancer.

Whatever the therapy, it is common for women with breast cancer to experience serious sexual problems and adjustments (Fallowfield & Hall, 1991; Kaplan, 1992a). The reaction of a woman's partner is important. A woman who has had a breast removed needs to be reassured by her partner that she is not going to be loved less than before. Would you expect your partner to love you less if you lost a toe, foot, leg, finger, hand, or arm? Of course not. So why should it be any different if your partner loses a breast? This may seem obvious to you, but your partner will probably want to hear you say it. Breast reconstruction through plastic surgery is often possible (over 50,000 breast cancer patients choose to do this every year), but counseling for both the female and her partner is equally important.

For more information and to help find the most appropriate tests and therapies, call the National Cancer Institute hotline: 1-800-4-CANCER. ∎

INTERNAL FEMALE ANATOMY

The vagina, uterus, Fallopian tubes, and ovaries are often referred to as the female's reproductive system (see Figure 2-7). The vagina serves as a depository for the male's sperm. Eggs are produced by the ovaries. During a woman's reproductive years, one or more eggs will mature on a monthly basis and be released from an ovary and picked up by one of the Fallopian tubes. It is in the Fallopian tube that an egg and a sperm unite to start a new living being. The fertilized egg then travels through the tube and implants itself within the uterus (see Chapter 7).

The Vagina

We have already discussed the vaginal opening as part of the genitalia or external anatomy, yet the **vagina** (Latin for "sheath") is really an internal structure located behind the bladder and in front of the rectum. It serves not only as a depository for sperm during sexual intercourse, but also as the birth canal and thus is capable of expanding to about four inches in diameter. However, contrary to what some men may believe, the vagina is not an open orifice always ready to accommodate the insertion of a penis. In the unstimulated state it is about three to five inches long and its walls are collapsed. It is not until a woman becomes sexually aroused that the walls of the inner two thirds of the vagina begin to expand to accommodate a penis. The vaginal opening actually narrows during sexual arousal (see Chapter 4).

The vaginal walls have three layers. The inner layer has a soft mucosal surface similar to the inside of the mouth. Prior to puberty, the walls of the vagina are thin and relatively inelastic. The rising levels of female hormones at puberty cause the vaginal walls to thicken and become more elastic and highly vascularized (i.e., having lots of blood vessels). Vaginal lubrication during sexual arousal results from the walls of the vagina becoming engorged with blood, with the resulting

> **Vagina**
>
> The sheathlike canal in the female that extends from the vulva to the cervix and that receives the penis during intercourse.

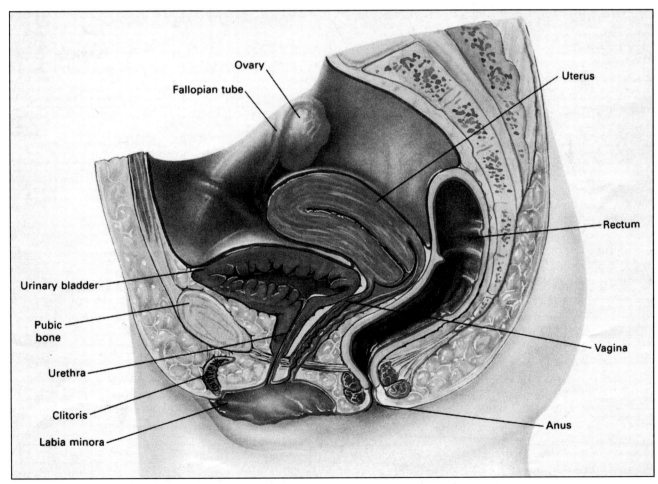

FIGURE 2-7(A)   THE INTERNAL FEMALE REPRODUCTIVE SYSTEM FROM A SIDE VIEW.

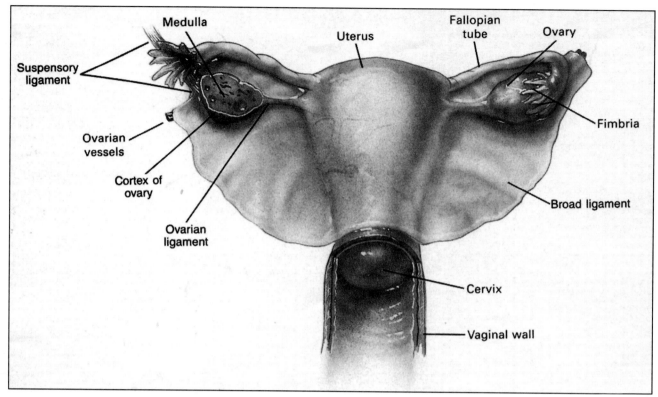

FIGURE 2-7(B)   THE INTERNAL FEMALE REPRODUCTIVE SYSTEM FROM A FRONTAL VIEW.

pressure causing fluid (super-filtered blood plasma) to be secreted from the mucosal lining. At menopause (the time in life when a female's reproductive capacity ends) the ovaries atrophy, and the consequent loss of hormones causes the walls of the vagina to again become thin and inelastic, similar to the condition before puberty. There is also a decrease in the blood supply to the vaginal walls after menopause, resulting in decreased vaginal lubrication, and thus many older women may require a lubricant during sexual intercourse.

The vagina is a self-cleansing organ. Many potentially harmful bacteria from the outside environment are destroyed by other bacteria that are found naturally within the vagina. In addition, the walls of the vagina continually secrete fluids that help to maintain an acidic environment. A healthy vagina has a musky odor. Vaginal odors act as a sexual stimulant to the males in most mammalian species. Vaginal secretions from female rhesus monkeys, for example, contain fatty acids called copulins, which attract the male monkeys. A similar substance has been found in human vaginal secretions, and one study reported that when married women rubbed perfumes containing the human copulin on their breasts before going to bed many of their husbands showed increased sexual activity (Morris & Udry, 1978).

In laboratory studies most men do not find musky vaginal odors to be offensive (Hassett, 1978). Humans,

however, are often raised to believe that vaginal odors are offensive. If a person hears enough dirty jokes and stories about vaginal odors before becoming sexually experienced, he or she will come to believe it even if it is not true. How, then, did these stories get started? Probably because most females will occasionally get a vaginal infection that can be accompanied by a foul odor (see Chapter 5 on vaginitis). These infections can be easily and quickly cured. In order to sell their products, however, advertisers of feminine hygiene sprays and douches generally imply that vaginal odors are always offensive and must be masked with a perfumy substance. The fact is that these products do not cure vaginal infections and generally make them worse by further changing the chemical environment of the vagina.

> "A year ago I started using a feminine hygiene deodorant spray. I had used this spray for an average of 5 months before I realized that my discharge was abnormal. . . . After talking with my doctor I found that I had a yeast infection. All of this could have been avoided if I had only stayed away from feminine deodorant sprays."

(from the author's files)

Recent studies have found that regular douching increases the risk of getting pelvic inflammatory disease (see Chapter 5), a serious infection of a woman's reproduction system (Forrest et al., 1989; Wolner-Hanssen et al., 1990). Women should avoid using douches unless told to do so by a physician.

Although the vaginal opening is very sensitive to touch, the walls of the inner two thirds of the vagina are relatively insensitive to touch as a result of having few nerve endings. It has been demonstrated that some women cannot even tell when their inner vaginal walls are being touched by a probe (Kinsey et al., 1953). Does this mean that the presence of a penis in the vagina does not contribute to a woman's subjective feelings of pleasure during sexual intercourse? Not necessarily. Although the vaginal walls are sparse in nerve endings, the vagina is surrounded by a large muscle, the **pubococcygeus (PC) muscle**, which is more richly innervated with nerves. It has been found that women who have little vaginal sensation during intercourse (some report that they cannot even feel the penis) have a weak pubococcygeus muscle (Kegel, 1952). As a result, some sex therapists have advocated daily exercises to strengthen this muscle in order to enhance pleasure during sexual intercourse (Barbach, 1976; Graber, 1982; Perry & Whipple, 1981). The exercises are called **Kegel exercises**. They are the same exercises that many physicians instruct women to do after having a baby in order to regain urinary control. The pubococcygeus muscle controls urine flow, but becomes stretched and weak during pregnancy, causing many women to suffer from urinary incontinence.

For those women interested, one learns to do Kegel exercises as follows: (1) learn to know what it feel like to contract the PC muscle by stopping yourself in the middle of urinating with your legs apart; (2) after you know what it feels like to contract the PC muscle, insert a finger into your vagina and bear down until you can feel the muscle squeeze your finger, and (3) once you can do this, start doing daily Kegels without a finger inserted. Physicians and therapists suggest practicing ten contractions of three seconds each three times a day. The best thing about Kegel exercises is that they can be done anytime and anywhere and no one else knows what you are doing.

There may be an exception to the statement that the vaginal walls are relatively insensitive to touch. Some women have a small sensitive spot on the front wall of the vagina at about the level of the top of the pubic bone. This has been named the **Grafen-berg spot (G spot)** after the German doctor who first reported it in 1950 (Perry & Whipple, 1981) and stimulation of it often leads to an orgasm that some women say feels different from an orgasm caused by clitoral stimulation (see Chapter 4). Originally it was claimed that all women had a G spot (Ladas, Whipple, & Perry, 1982), but more recent studies suggest that only 10 percent or fewer women have this area of heightened sensitivity (Alzate & Londono, 1984).

One in every 4,000 to 5,000 girls are born without a vagina (Harnish, 1988). When this occurs, physicians are usually able to surgically construct one.

> **Pubococcygeus muscle**
> The major muscle in the pelvic region. Voluntary control over this muscle (to aid in preventing urinary incontinence or to enhance physical sensations during intercourse) is gained through Kegel exercises.

> **Kegel excercises**
> Exercises that are designed to strengthen the pubococcygeus muscle that surrounds the bladder and vagina.

> **Grafenberg spot**
> A small, sensitive area on the front wall of the vagina found in about 10 percent of women.

The Uterus

It is within the **uterus**, or womb, that a fertilized egg will attach itself and become an embryo and then a fetus. Resembling a small, inverted pear, the uterus in women who have not had children measures only about three inches long and three inches across at its broadest portion, but it is capable of tremendous expansion. The *cervix*, the narrow end of the uterus, projects into the back of the vagina and can be easily felt (as a slippery bump) by inserting a finger into the back of the vagina. The broad part of the uterus is called the *fundus*. Ligaments hold the uterus in the pelvic cavity at about a 90 degree angle to the vagina, although in some women it may tilt slightly forward or backward.

The uterus has three layers: the innermost *endometrium* where the fertilized egg implants; a middle, strong layer of muscles called the *myometrium*, which contracts during labor; and an external cover called the *perimetrium*. The endometrium thickens and becomes rich in blood vessels after ovulation, but it is sloughed off and discharged from the female's body during menstruation if fertilization does not occur. Glands within the cervix secrete mucus throughout the female's menstrual cycle and the change in the consistency of this mucus is often used to tell when ovulation has occurred. The cervical opening, or *os* (Latin for "mouth"), is normally no wider than the diameter of a matchstick, but it dilates to 10 centimeters (about 4 inches) at childbirth to allow delivery of the baby.

Unfortunately, the cervix is the site of one of the most common types of cancer in women. It is extremely important, therefore, that all females, whether sexually inexperienced or sexually active, go to a physician for an annual examination and Pap smear (see Box 2-B).

> **Uterus**
> The womb. The hollow, muscular organ in females where the fertilized egg normally implants.

> **Endometrium**
> The inner, mucous membrane of the uterus where a fertilized egg implants. Its thickness varies with the phase of the menstrual cycle.

BOX 2-B

SEXUALITY AND HEALTH: CANCER OF THE FEMALE REPRODUCTIVE SYSTEM

CANCER OF THE CERVIX

There are approximately 60,000 new cases of cervical cancer in the United States every year, of which 13,500 are invasive (have spread beyond the surface of the cervix). The average age of women diagnosed with cervical cancer is 45, but it can happen at almost any age (E. Hill, 1987). Women at high risk include those who began having sexual intercourse at an early age or who have had numerous sexual partners (Clarke et al., 1985), and those whose partners have had numerous sexual partners (Slattery et al., 1989). Cancer of the cervix is rare among nuns and celibate women. It is not sex per se that is believed to be the cause of cervical cancer, but viruses that are spread during sexual activity, such as human papillomavirus and herpes virus (Slattery et al., 1989). Regular use of barrier methods of contraception (condoms, diaphragms) reduces the risk of getting cervical cancer (Slattery et al., 1989). Women who smoke also have a higher risk of cervical cancer (Daling et al., 1992; Gram, Austin, & Stalsberg, 1992), probably by weakening the body's defenses and making it easier for the cancer-causing viruses to have their effect (Burger et al., 1993).

A pelvic exam and **Pap smear** test (named after Dr. Papanicolaou, who developed the test) are a necessary part of female health care. The risk of developing cervical cancer is only about one fourth as great for women who get Pap smears regularly as it is for women who do not (Shy et al., 1989). Most cervical cancer-related deaths occur in women who do not get regular Pap tests. Many women are nevertheless reluctant to get a Pap smear because of embarrassment. The first step, therefore, is to find a doctor with whom you are comfortable and who shows concern for his or her patients (such as warming the instruments to body temperature before use). In the examination room, the woman lies flat on her back with her legs apart by having her feet in foot rests called stirrups. An instrument called a speculum, which is shaped like a duckbill, is inserted into the vagina and gently opened so that the vaginal walls and cervix may be inspected. A cotton swab or thin wooden stick is used to gently skim the surface of the cervix in order to collect cells, which are then examined under a microscope for abnormalities. During the exam, the doctor will also check the vaginal walls and vulva for possible infections. Some doctors may include a rectal exam at this time also. The entire process generally takes only a few minutes, and although some women may experience some discomfort, it is generally not painful.

> **Pap smear**
>
> Named for Dr. Papanicolaou, who developed it; a test for cancer of the cervix in females.

"Human sexuality class has made me more educated about my body and I became more aware. Before I entered this class I was very scared of going to the gynecologist for a visit (age 20). Recently I went for my first visit and found my fears were ridiculous. It was not bad at all and I even felt better to find out I was OK."

"At the beginning of the semester you mentioned UNO's Health Services and I decided to check them out. When the results of my Pap smear came in, I had tested positive. I had stage II dysplasia. I had cryotherapy. . . . If it had not been for this class I don't know how long I would have waited to get a Pap smear or what the results would have been."

(from the author's files)

Any detected abnormalities of cells are treated according to severity. An estimated one million women per year are found to have low-grade lesions (which includes mild dysplasia and cellular changes due to human papillomavirus). In the precancerous stage, the localized abnormal cells are often destroyed by extreme cold (cryotherapy) or intense heat (electrocoagulation). Because most precancerous abnormalities are slow to develop and have a low risk of becoming cancer, some physicians are calling for a watch-and-wait strategy at this stage (Bergström et al., 1993; Solomon, 1993). Precancerous abnormalities in cells often take as long as 8 years before they start to invade other tissues. If the cancer progresses, warning signs may include bleeding between menstrual periods, excessive bleeding during periods, and bleeding after menopause. However, sometimes there are no symptoms. If cancer of the cervix is found, a woman may have to have a hysterectomy (surgical removal of the uterus). This will end her reproductive capabilities, of course, but it does not interfere with sexual desire or make her less feminine in appearance (Schover, 1988).

> " I thought after my hysterectomy my vagina would dry up and I would lose my sexual desire. It has been five years and I still take hormones but I haven't dried up and I have reached my sexual peak. Within these five years I have felt better about my self sexually. . . . "

(from the author's files)

The American Cancer Society advises women that regular checkups should begin when they start having sexual intercourse, or at age 18 even if they are sexually inexperienced. Annual checkups are required at first because the Pap smear test has a rather high false negative rate (Solomon, 1993). After three initial negative tests, your doctor may tell you to come back less often.

Pelvic exams are also done to fit a diaphragm or IUD, to check for vaginal infections, and to examine the uterus during pregnancy. Many women assume that their doctor routinely checks for sexually transmitted disease when taking a Pap smear, but most do not unless specifically asked to do so. If you have had multiple sexual partners (and are thus at high risk to get a sexually transmitted disease), you should consider these additional tests at this time.

CANCER OF THE ENDOMETRIUM AND OVARIES

Cancer of the endometrium is also very common, with an estimated 33,000 new cases and 10,000 deaths per year in the United States (American Cancer Society). Typically, the first symptom is abnormal vaginal bleeding, so if you should experience this, go to a physician immediately. He or she will make a diagnosis by dilation and curretage (D & C). Should cancer be found, your doctor will probably recommend a hysterectomy, but radiation, drug, or hormonal therapies are also used sometimes.

Ovarian cancer is a rare disease (lifetime risk of less than 1.5%), but a deadly one. It causes the death of more American women each year (approximately 13,300) than either cervical or endometrial cancer (Cannistra, 1993). Most cases are found in women approaching or after menopause (50–59 years). It is more common in women who have never been pregnant, and less so in women who use oral contraceptives. Recently, a consortium of principal investigators of 12 studies reported that the use of fertility drugs was associated with an increased risk of ovarian cancer (Whittemore et al., 1992). However, the highest risk factor is a family history of ovarian cancer (Lynch & Lynch, 1992).

Cancer of the ovaries is usually painless in the early stages. Thus the tumors are often quite large by the time they are discovered, making effective treatment difficult. Today, there is a blood test for women at high risk (it tests for CA-125, a protein produced by cancerous ovarian cells). Treatment usually involves removal of the ovaries and radiation.

Many ovarian cysts are benign (noncancerous), but can become quite large. Recently, surgeons at Stanford University removed a cyst weighing 303 pounds (the woman herself weighed 210 pounds after the operation). Studies show that in the case of benign cysts, removal of the cyst alone results in fewer problems than does hysterectomy (surgical removal of the uterus). ■

The Fallopian Tubes

Extending 4 inches laterally from both sides of the uterus are the **Fallopian tubes**, or oviducts, as they are sometimes called. There is no direct physical connection between the Fallopian tubes and the ovaries, but the fingerlike projections at the end of the tubes (called *fimbria*) brush against the ovaries. After an egg is expelled from an ovary into the abdominal cavity at ovulation, it is picked up by one of the fimbria. If a sperm fertilizes the egg, it will usually do so within the tube. The fertilized egg then continues its three-to-four-day trip through the tube and normally implants itself in the endometrium of the uterus. Anatomical abnormalities and infections can block the tube and cause sterility (sperm cannot meet egg) or a tubal pregnancy (a fertilized egg implants itself within the tube). The latter poses a serious health threat because the tubes are not capable of expanding like the uterus. Tying off and cutting, or cauterizing the tubes (*tubal ligation* or *laparoscopy*) is a popular means of birth control for couples who

> **Fallopian tubes**
> The passageway that the egg follows on the way to the uterus.

already have all the children they want (see Chapter 6).

The Ovaries

The **ovaries** are the female gonads and develop from the same embryonic tissue as the male gonads, the testicles. They are suspended by ligaments on both sides of the uterus. The ovaries have two functions: to produce eggs (*ova*) and female hormones (*estrogen* and *progesterone*). A female has all the immature eggs that she will ever have at birth, as many as 300,000 to 400,000, each contained within a thin capsule to form what is called a **primary follicle**. At puberty, one or more of the follicles is stimulated to mature on about a monthly basis (the menstrual cycle). When mature, the follicle is called a *Graafian follicle*. This process ends at menopause, and thus only about 400 of the several hundred thousand ova will ever mature during a female's lifetime. In contrast, the male's testes produce millions of new sperm every day. ■

> **Ovary**
> The female gonad in which ova are produced.

> **Primary follicle**
> An immature ovum enclosed by a single layer of cells.

EXTERNAL MALE ANATOMY

Generally speaking, men have a better idea than women of what their genitals look like. Not only is the male genitalia more visible than the female structures, but boys are taught at a very young age to hold their penis while urinating and thus may be less inhibited than girls to touch and examine themselves. Although they differ in appearance, many of the male structures develop from the same embryonic tissue as female structures (the penis and clitoris, for example). The male reproductive system and genitalia are shown in Figures 2-8 and 2-9. Penises differ in appearance just like any other part of the body, and men should not consider themselves to be abnormal if they do not look identical to this drawing.

The Penis: Outer Appearance

The **penis** (Latin for "tail") has both a reproductive and a urinary function. It serves to deposit sperm in the female's vagina and to eliminate urine from the bladder. When unaroused, the penis is soft and hangs between the legs, but it hardens and becomes erect during sexual stimulation, thus enabling penetration of the vagina. The average size of the penis in the unstimulated (flaccid) condition is 3.75 inches

> **Penis**
> The male organ for sexual intercourse and the passageway for sperm and urine.

Figure 2-8   Anatomical location of the male reproductive system.

FIGURE 2-9   A CIRCUMCISED (LEFT) AND UNCIRCUMCISED (RIGHT) PENIS.

in length and 1.2 inches in diameter, and six inches in length and 1.5 inches in diameter when erect. In a rare condition called micropenis, the penis never develops to more than 1 inch in length (usually due to low levels of the male hormone testosterone; Aaronson, 1994). In Chapter 4, we will consider whether penis size is important for women's sexual satisfaction.

The skin of the penis is very loose to allow for expansion during erection. At birth the skin folds over the *glans*, the smooth rounded end of the penis, but many males have had their *foreskin* cut off in a surgical procedure known as **circumcision** (see Figure 2-9). If you should have a son, be sure to teach him that good hygiene includes cleaning under the foreskin (see Box 2-C). However, when bathing a newborn, do not pull back forcibly on the foreskin for the first several months because it is often partially adhered to the penis during this time (Paige, 1978b). In some boys it is still adhered at 3 years of age (see Williams, Chell, & Kapila, 1993).

Circumcision

In males, the removal of all or part of the foreskin of the penis. In females, the removal of the clitoral hood.

THE PENIS: INTERNAL STRUCTURE

The penis has three parts: the body or shaft, the glans, and the root. Only the first two parts are visible (see Figure 2-10). In cross-section, the *shaft* of the penis can be seen to consist of three parallel cylinders of spongy-like tissue, two *corpora cavernosa* (or "cavernous bodies") on top and a *corpus spongiosum* (or "spongy body") on the bottom. Each is contained in its own fibrous sheath. The corpora cavernosa do not extend the full length of the penis. Instead, the spongy body expands greatly in front to form the round smooth *glans*. The raised rim at the border of the shaft and glans is called the *corona* (and is the most sensitive to touch of any part of the penis). The *urethra*, which serves as a passageway for urine and sperm, runs through the corpus spongiosum, and thus the urethral opening (or meatus) is normally located at the tip of the glans. It occasionally is located to one side of the glans, but this poses no major medical problem.

The *root* of the penis consists of the expanded ends of the cavernous bodies, which fan out to form *crura* and attach to the pubic bone (note the similarity in structure to the clitoris), and the expanded end of the spongy body (called the *bulb*). The root is surrounded by two muscles (bulbocavernosus and ischiocavernosus) which aid in urination and ejaculation.

In human males, an erection does not result from a bone protruding into the penis as occurs in some mammalian species (e.g., dogs), nor does it result from voluntary contraction of a muscle. When a male becomes sexually aroused, the arteries going to the penis dilate, and the many cavities of the cavernous and spongy bodies fill with blood. Valves in the veins that drain the penis simultaneously close. Expansion of the sinuses and contraction of the muscles at the base of the penis may further aid this process by pressing against the veins and partially cutting off the drainage. In brief, an erection results from the spongy tissues of the penis becoming engorged (filled) with blood. Detumescence, or loss of erection, is not as well understood, but probably occurs as a result of the arteries beginning to constrict, thus removing pressure from the veins and allowing drainage.

Some men have an abnormal curvature of the penis due to injury to the uretha and/or cavernous bodies, developmental urethral abnormalities, or Peyronie's disease (Gregory & Purcell, 1989). If too extreme, this can cause pain during erection. Attempting to prolong erections by use of "cock rings" or rubber bands around the penis can severely damage the penile tissues, as can masturbating with vacuum cleaners (Benson, 1985). Men can also "fracture" their penis (rupture the cavernous bodies) during sexual intercourse, which may require surgery (Adduci & Ross, 1991).

THE SCROTUM

The sac located beneath the penis is called the **scrotum**. It holds the testicles outside of the body cavity. Sperm are produced in the testicles, but they can only be produced in an environment several degrees lower than the normal body temperature of 98.6 degrees Fahrenheit. Scrotal temperature is typically about 93 degrees Fahrenheit. The skin of the scrotum is sparsely covered with hair and has many sweat glands that aid in temperature regulation. The scrotum also has small muscle fibers that contract when it is cold to help draw the testicles closer to the body cavity for warmth. When it is hot, the muscle fibers relax and the testes are suspended farther away from the body cavity.

Scrotum

The pouch beneath the penis that contains the testicles.

In tropical areas of the world, it is not uncommon for men to suffer from elephantiasis of the scrotum (caused by a parasite), in which the scrotum can get as large as a basketball. ■

BOX 2-c

CROSS-CULTURAL PERSPECTIVES/SEXUALITY AND HEALTH: MALE CIRCUMCISION

Circumcision has been performed on males since at least 4,000 B.C. Egyptian mummies dating from this period give evidence of it, and the Greek geographers and historians Herodotus and Strabo later wrote about observing it in their travels (Larue, 1989; Manniche, 1987). The ancient Egyptians and Ethiopians performed circumcisions for cleanliness (Herodotus), and the practice was borrowed by the Hebrews at about the time of Abraham (the custom later fell into disuse, but was revived by Moses). Today, Jewish boys are circumcised on the eighth day of life to symbolize the covenant with God made by Abraham (Genesis 17:10). Muslim boys are also circumcised as part of a religious ceremony, but at 13 years of age.

In many cultures today the operation is done as a puberty rite, and sometimes involves more than the cutting away of the foreskin. It is done with crude instruments and without anesthesia. The Mangaians and other South Pacific islanders cut lengthwise along the top of the penis (superincision) all the way to the stomach (Marshall & Suggs, 1971). Primitive tribes in central Australia make a slit to the depth of the urethra along the entire length of the lower side of the penis (subincision) so that males urinate at the base of the penis, requiring that they sit like women (Gregersen, 1982). Still other cultures insert rods with brushes, bells, or pins attached to the end (Brown, 1990). Many anthropologists believe that these customs are performed as symbolic pledges of loyalty to the group (Paige & Paige, 1981).

In the United States and England, circumcision became popular during the nineteenth century because Victorian physicians believed that circumcised penises were less sensitive and that the operation would therefore prevent masturbation and hypersexuality. Remember from Chapter 1 that Freud and other physicians of that day believed that loss of semen was just as detrimental to a male's health as loss of blood (Haller & Haller, 1977), and that an array of maladies, including insanity, awaited the masturbator. Circumcision reached its height in popularity between World Wars I and II, but then fell out of favor in most English-speaking countries. Presently, only one quarter or fewer of male babies are being circumcised in countries such as England, Canada, New Zealand, and Australia, leaving the United States as the only country in which circumcision is still performed for nonreligious reasons on a majority of boys. About 60 percent of newborn baby boys are circumcised yearly in the United State (National Center for Health Statistics).

Circumcising boys' penises, of course, did not stop them from masturbating. In fact, Masters and Johnson do not believe that circumcision affects a male's sexual function whatsoever (Masters, Johnson, & Kolodny, 1992).

Today, the reason most commonly given by American physicians for circumcision is to ensure proper hygiene, but there is considerable debate about this even within the medical community. Glands located beneath the foreskin secrete an oily substance that gets mixed with dead cells to form a cheesy substance called **smegma**, which can cause the foreskin to adhere to the underlying glans of the penis. Without proper hygiene, the smegma serves as a possible breeding ground for bacteria. Several studies have found that many young boys have poor genital hygiene (see Schoen, 1990). Cancer of the penis is rare, but some early studies reported that it was more common in uncircumcised males (see Rotolo & Lynch, 1991). However, penile cancer was no more

Smegma
The cheesy secretion of sebaceous glands that can cause the clitoris to stick to the clitoral hood or the foreskin of the penis to stick to the glans.

common among uncircumcised men who regularly cleaned under their foreskin than among circumcised men. There were also some early reports of an increased risk of cervical cancer in women married to uncircumcised men, but later studies failed to find a cause–effect relationship (Brinton et al., 1989; Poland, 1990).

Occasionally, there are serious health risks associated with circumcision, including hemorrhage, infection, and amputation (Poland, 1990; Snyder, 1989; Thompson, 1990). In addition, circumcision is usually done on infant boys without the use of anesthesia, and although some physicians are advocating the use of local pain killers (Stang et al., 1988), for most infants it is a painful operation that causes them to cry for hours (Howard, Howard, & Weitzman, 1994; Tyler, 1988). Neonatal circumcision may affect pain responses for several months (Taddio et al., 1995).

> "When I had my son in the 70s I thought after his circumcision he was set in that area. After a coule of weeks I had to take him to the doctor's office because his penis had become red and inflamed. . . . ''

> "When I was 10 years old, I saw my baby brother get circumcised. I hated to see the pain that he was going through. I could not see why a baby should go through it at all. So I have decided to not let my baby boy go through that kind of pain. I just won't!''

> (from the author's files)

As a result of these concerns, both the American Academy of Pediatrics and the American College of Obstetricians and Gynecologists took a joint stand against the routine circumcision of newborns (*Guidelines for Perinatal Care*, 1983). However, since that time there have been concerns raised about increased risks of urinary tract infections in uncircumcised boys (Fergusson, Lawton, & Shannon, 1988; Herzog, 1989; Wiswell et al., 1987). Some studies have also raised the possibility that circumcision makes it less likely that a male would be infected with a sexually transmitted disease (including HIV, the virus that causes AIDS) if he were able to have unprotected intercourse with an infected partner (Bongaarts et al., 1989; Cook, Koutsky, & Holmes, 1994; Hira et al., 1990). Other studies have cast doubt on this (Chiasson et al., 1990; Donovan, Bassett, & Bodsworth, 1994). Nevertheless, largely because of the urinary tract infection studies, the American Academy of Pediatricians in 1989 decided to take a neutral stand on the matter, allowing parents and physicians to decide for themselves (see Schoen, 1990). There are still many physicians, however, who feel that the benefits do not outweigh the risks (see Poland, 1990). There is one circumstance in which there is little argument as to whether circumcision is justified medically—when the foreskin is too tight and cannot be pulled back over the glans (a condition known as *phimosis*). This causes pain during erection.

All of these medical arguments are no doubt very confusing to most parents. Many probably choose circumcision just so that their baby boys will look like dad.

> "I will have my son circumcised because I don't want him to feel different.''

> (from the author's files)

On the other hand, today some circumcised men are paying surgeons to reconstruct their foreskin (Greer et al., 1982). My advice to parents is that you educate yourself about both sides of the argument (I suggest Poland, 1990, and Schoen, 1990, in addition to this box) and then make a decision that feels right for you. ∎

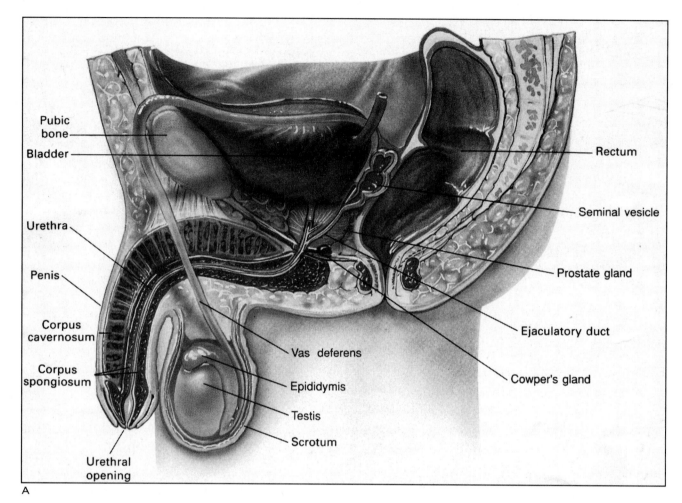

Pubic bone

Bladder

Urethra

Penis

Corpus cavernosum

Corpus spongiosum

Urethral opening

Rectum

Seminal vesicle

Prostate gland

Ejaculatory duct

Cowper's gland

Vas deferens

Epididymis

Testis

Scrotum

A

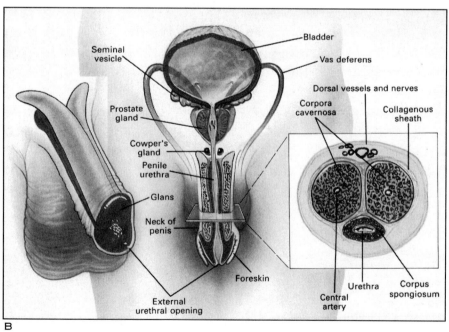

Seminal vesicle

Prostate gland

Cowper's gland

Penile urethra

Glans

Neck of penis

External urethral opening

Bladder

Vas deferens

Dorsal vessels and nerves

Corpora cavernosa

Collagenous sheath

Foreskin

Central artery

Urethra

Corpus spongiosum

B

FIGURE 2-10   THE INTERNAL MALE REPRODUCTIVE SYSTEM (A) FROM A SIDE VIEW AND CROSS-SECTION OF THE PENIS; (B) FROM A FRONTAL VIEW.

INTERNAL MALE ANATOMY

The male internal reproductive system consists of the testicles, a duct system to transport sperm out of the body, the prostate gland and seminal vesicles that produce the fluid in which the sperm are mixed, and the Cowper's gland (see Figure 2-10).

THE TESTES

The **testicles** (the male gonads) develop from the same embryonic tissue as the ovaries (the female gonads). Like the ovaries, the testes have two functions—to produce sperm and to produce male hormones. Millions of new sperm are produced each day in several hundred *seminiferous tubules*, which if laid end to end would measure over a quarter of a mile in length. In between the seminiferous tubules are cells called *interstitial cells of Leydig*, which produce male hormones. Male (or masculinizing) hormones are called *androgens*. The most important is *testosterone*, and you will find many references to this hormone in later chapters.

> **Testicles**
> The male gonads that produce sperm and male hormones.

Each testicle is suspended in the scrotum by the *spermatic cord* and is enclosed by a tight, fibrous sheath. The testes normally descend into the scrotum about 2 months before birth, but fail to descend in about 3–4 percent of male births, a condition known as *cryptorchidism* (McClure, 1988). This usually corrects itself, but if not it can result in sterility and an increased risk of hernia and cancer of the testicles (McClure, 1988; Rao, Wilkinson, & Benton, 1991).

In right-handed men it is normal for the left testicle to hang lower than the right one, and vice versa in left-handed men (don't ask why). Both testicles, however, should be about the same size. The testes are very sensitive to pressure and men differ as to whether they like to have them touched during sexual relations.

Men and parents of male children should be aware of several health problems associated with the testicles. The virus that is responsible for mumps, for example, causes the testes to swell painfully, and the pressure against the fibrous sheath can crush the seminiferous tubules, resulting in sterility if mumps occurs after puberty. In an uncommon condition called *testicular torsion*, the spermatic cord twists and cuts off the blood supply to the testicles, necessitating removal if not corrected in time. This is generally accompanied by severe pain, and males should go to a doctor immediately if much pain is experienced. The testes are also the site of a relatively rare but deadly form of cancer (see Box 2-D).

The word testes, by the way, is derived from a Latin word for witness (to testify). People shake hands when completing a deal or giving an oath today, but in Biblical times one held the testicles of the person to whom they gave the oath. The idea was that if one broke his oath, the children of the other person had the right to take revenge.

THE DUCT SYSTEM

After sperm are produced in the seminiferous tubules, they pass through a four-part duct system (epididymis, vas deferens, ejaculatory duct, and urethra) before being expelled from the penis during an ejaculation. The seminiferous tubules converge to form the **epididymis**, coiled tubes (about 20 feet long if uncoiled) that can be felt on the top and back of each testicle. Sperm mature as they travel through the epididymis (Cooper, 1990). From here the sperm pass into the paired 14- to 16-inch **vas deferens**, which transports them out of the scrotum and up and over the bladder toward the prostate gland. Many sperm are stored in the expanded end of the vas, called the *ampulla*, prior to ejaculation. Tying off and cutting the vas (*vasectomy*) is the sterilization procedure that is performed in men, similar to tubal ligation in women.

> **Epididymis**
> The elongated cordlike structure on the back of a testicle. It is the first part of the duct system that transports sperm out of a male's body.

> **Vas deferens**
> The second part of the duct system that transports sperm out of a male's body.

During orgasm, rhythmic muscular contractions force the sperm into the **ejaculatory ducts**, short (about 1 inch long) paired tubes that run through the prostate gland, where they are mixed with fluids from the prostate and seminal vesicles to form *semen*. The two ejaculatory ducts open into the **urethra**, which passes through the spongy body of the penis. Sphincter muscles surround the part of the urethra coming from the bladder. These involuntarily contract during an erection so that urine does not get mixed with semen.

> **Ejaculatory duct**
> One inch-long paired tubes that pass through the prostate gland. The third part of the duct system that transports sperm out of a male's body.

> **Urethra**
> The passageway from the bladder to the exterior of the body. In males, it also serves as a passageway for semen during ejaculation.

THE PROSTATE GLAND AND SEMINAL VESICLES

Although an average ejaculation contains about 200–300 million sperm, they make up very little of the total volume. Most of the volume is seminal fluid from the seminal vesicles (accounting for about 70 percent of the fluid) and the prostate gland (about 30 percent). Among other substances, the **seminal vesicles** (misnamed because anatomists once thought that was where sperm were stored prior to ejacu-

> **Seminal vesicles**
> Two structures in the male that contribute many substances to the seminal fluid.

BOX 2-D

SEXUALITY AND HEALTH:
TESTICULAR CANCER AND SELF-EXAMINATION

Cancer of the testicles is not very common, accounting for only 1 percent of all cancers in males (about 6,100 new cases per year), but it is the most common type of cancer in men aged 20 to 35 (National Cancer Institute, 1992). Men at highest risk are those whose testicles did not descend into the scrotum until the age of six, or whose mother had pelvic X-rays or took diethylstilbestrol (DES) during pregnancy. White males have a higher incidence of this type of cancer than do Black or Hispanic men. Cancer of the testicles is not related to masturbation, frequent sex, or sexually transmitted diseases.

The most common symptom is a small lump or a testicle that is slightly enlarged. In the first stages of testicular cancer, the tumors are painless; thus it is important that all men (particularly those in the high-risk gorups) examine themselves regularly. Once a month is advised.

Examine yourself after a warm bath or shower. This causes the testicles to descend and the skin of the scrotum to relax. Examine your testicles one at a time by placing both thumbs on top and the middle and index fingers on bottom (see Figure 2-11). Gently roll your testicle between the thumbs and fingers. When doing so, you will also feel your epididymis, which feels like a spongy rope on the top and back of each testicle.

FIGURE 2-11   PROSTATE SELF-EXAMINATION.

Not all abnormal lumps are cancerous, but if it should be, treatment usually involves surgical removal of the infected testicle and chemotherapy. The cancer rarely spreads to the other testicle, and the uninfected testicle can produce enough male hormones for normal sex drive and enough sperm to father a child. Synthetic implants can be inserted into the scrotum to give the male a normal appearance.

At one time cancer of the testicles was usually fatal, but today it is one of the most curable cancers if *it is detected early and treated right away*. A self-examination takes only about 3 minutes once a month. Isn't it worth your time? ■

lation) secrete fructose, prostaglandins, and bases. Fructose (a sugar) activates the sperm and makes them mobile, while prostaglandins cause contractions of the uterus, aiding movement through that structure. Bases neutralize the normal acidity of the vagina so that sperm will not be destroyed on their way to the more favorable alkaline environment of the uterus. The **prostate**

Prostate gland

A gland in males that surrounds the urethra and neck of the bladder and which contributes many substances to the seminal fluid.

gland secretes all of these substances and a substance (fibrinogenase) that causes semen to temporarily coagulate after ejaculation, thus helping to prevent spillage from the vagina. More recently, it has been found that the prostate also secretes a powerful antibiotic, possibly to protect the male and female reproductive systems from infection. The prostate is the site of the second most common type of cancer found in males and should be checked annually as men reach the age of 40 (see Box 2-E).

BOX 2-E

SEXUALITY AND HEALTH:
PROSTATE PROBLEMS AND EXAMINATION

Cancer of the prostate is the most common nonskin cancer among men in the United States, with approximately 200,000 new cases and 38,000 deaths each year (American Cancer Society; Coleman & Kaplan, 1993). An average of one in every eight men will be diagnosed with prostate cancer by age 85. The rates are considerably higher among black men than among white men. Although the cause of prostate cancer is still unclear, two suspected risk factors are high testosterone levels and dietary fat. The good news is that cancer of the prostate is usually a very slow-growing type of cancer. The 5-year survival rate for all patients is 78 percent. Many men show no symptoms in the early stages. As the cancer advances, symptoms may include difficulty in urination or a frequent need to urinate (especially at night), blood in the urine, and/or continuing pain in the lower back or pelvic region.

When then President Ronald Reagan underwent prostate surgery in 1987, he probably did a lot of men a favor by bringing their attention to this chestnut-sized gland that surrounds the urinary tract at the base of the bladder. Since that time, both the diagnosis and treatment of prostate cancer has undergone revolutionary changes. The traditional method to diagnose prostate cancer has been the rectal examination, in which a physician feels the prostate for any abnormalities. Although the test will continue to be widely used, nearly 70 percent of the cancers detected by the method are already in an advanced stage. In 1994, the Food and Drug Administration approved the first blood test for detecting prostate cancer. The test measures levels of prostate-specific antigen (PSA), a substance produced by prostate cells. PSA levels are higher in men with prostate cancer (Catalona et al., 1991). The American Cancer Society has recommended that all men have a yearly PSA test starting at age 50. Another diagnostic technique is called transrectal ultrasound, in which ultrasound provides a TV picture to guide the physician while making a needle biopsy, but some physicians believe the the PSA test and rectal exam are sufficient for most cases (Stamey, 1992).

Prostate cancer traditionally has been treated by either radical prostatectomy (surgical removal of the prostate, seminal vesicles, and other tissues), radiation, or castration. However, side effects of these treatments often include impotency and urinary incontinence (inability to control the bladder), and many men feel that the cures are worse than the disease (Litwin, 1993). Because localized prostate cancer is slow to develop and surgery or radiation have limited benefits (Adolfsson, Steineck, & Whitmore, 1993) and unwanted side effects, many experts are now advising that the best treatment is ''watchful waiting''— doing nothing (except regular monitoring) until there is a threat that the cancer will spread to surrounding tissue (Fleming et al., 1993; Lu-Yao et al., 1993).

Cancer is not the only problem a man can have with his prostate. Inflammatory infections (e.g., prostatitis), sometimes resulting from untreated sexually transmitted diseases, can occur. In addition, as men grow older it is common for the prostate to enlarge as a result of overgrowth of normal prostate tissue. This condition, called *benign prostatic hyperplasia*, affects up to 80 percent of men over the age of 60 (Roehrborn & McConnell, 1991). The overgrowth pinches off the urethra, causing an increase in frequency or a difficulty in urination. The traditional treatment has been transurethral prostatectomy, in which the prostate tissue is removed by an instrument inserted through the urethra. However, about 10–15 percent of operated men suffer complications, including impotence (although some cases may be psychologically caused). Today, there are an increasing number of physicians who believe that unless the urethra is completely blocked or there are other bothersome symptoms (such as urinary difficulties) the best approach is again watchful waiting (Denis et al., 1992; Wasson et al., 1995). Meanwhile, initial results are promising for treatment with a drug called Proscar (finasteride), which blocks the hormone that causes enlargement of the prostate gland (Gormley et al., 1992).

If you are male, to be safe you should start going in for a prostate exam at least once a year starting at age 40. ■

The Cowper's Glands

Cowper's glands

Two pea-shaped structures located beneath the prostate gland in males that secrete a few drops of an alkaline fluid prior to orgasm.

The **Cowper's**, or bulbourethral **glands**, are two pea-sized structures located beneath the prostate. They secrete a few drops of an alkaline fluid (a base) that may appear at the tip of the penis prior to orgasm. The fluid neutralizes the normal acidity of the urethra, and thus sperm are not destroyed when passing through the penis during ejaculation. Many couples use withdrawal as a contraceptive technique (i.e., the male withdraws his penis from his partner's vagina just prior to orgasm), but the Cowper's glands fluid often contains sperm, making this an unreliable method of birth control (see Chapter 6). ■

OUR SEXUAL BODIES

Does our sexual anatomy include only the genitals and breasts? Of course not. Most of us are attracted to and aroused by many other parts of our partner's body. For example, the lips and mouth, which have numerous nerve endings, are very sensitive to touch and are certainly erogenous areas. Kissing is an important part of sexual relations for most people, and it is no accident that women try to make themselves more attractive by wearing lipstick.

Although not sensitive to touch, hair is a very important part of our sexual anatomy, and people spend a great deal of money getting it cut and groomed in the latest attractive styles. Balding men often spend a great deal of money for expensive toupees, and many men love the touch and smell of women's soft and shiny hair. Many women find a man's hairy chest to be a sexual turn on. Eyes, too, can be an erogenous part of the body. Do women spend a great deal of time putting on eye makeup because it will improve their eyesight? Eye contact between two people can be an initial and ongoing form of sexual communication (the "windows of our souls").

The buttocks are considered highly erotic to a lot of people. They are really just a large bunch of muscles covered by fat and skin with relatively few nerve endings, yet people wear tight and skimpy bikini bottoms or swim trunks to the beach in order to look more attractive. Incidentally, the males of other primate species mount the female from behind during sex, and the buttocks of the females become swollen and red when she is sexually receptive, which acts as a sexual stimu-lant to the males. Male-from-behind is the preferred position of sexual intercourse for many humans as well, especially in other cultures.

In addition to specific parts of the body, one's overall physical appearance is an important part of sexual attractiveness. Unfortunately, in today's society, magazines, television, and movies overemphasize a person's visual appearance to the point that people can't help but compare themselves to those who are considered physically beautiful. Many Americans have become obsessed about their bodies and have become so image-conscious that they pay thousands of dollars for face lifts, breast or penis enlargements, hair transplants, and even padding for their buttocks and legs. But is sex only for the very beautiful? Of course not. Physical appearance might make us sexually appealing to others at first, but a good healthy sexual life involves having *sensuality*, which encompasses all of our senses and who we are as a total person. A person's voice, feel, taste, smell, and personality can all be sensual and contribute to his or her sexuality. For example, an overweight person who appreciates the importance of touching and taking his or her time may be a much better sexual partner than one who physically may be a perfect "10."

Think how boring the world would be if we all looked the same, even if all our bodies were perfect. We each have different ideas and standards as to what we find sexually arousing. Some people are attracted to outdoorsy types, while others are more aroused by a person's intellect. Some men are preoccupied with becoming bald, but many women find bald men to be sexy. We are all unique, and if we can appreciate that uniqueness and love ourselves, then we also have the capacity to truly care for others. Chances are, our partner has (or will have as he or she grows older) as many unique physical features as we do. In the long run, human tenderness and caring, being interesting and interested, and loving and being loved are more important than physical appearance. In the excitement of sexual relations with someone we truly enjoy and care for, a paunchy midline, bald spot, or a small penis or small breasts are not important. We all have the capacity to be sensual beings, and we all have bodies that are sexual.

KEY TERMS

androgens   43
areola   28
Bartholin's glands   26
baseline mammogram   31
breasts   28
bulb, of penis   39
bulbocavernosus muscle   27
cervix   35
circumcision   26, 40
clitoral hood   26
clitoris   26
corona   39
corpora cavernosa   26, 39
corpus spongiosum   39
Cowper's glands   46
crura   26, 39
cryptorchidism   43
cystitis   28
ejaculatory ducts   43
endometrium   35
epididymis   43
episiotomy   25
Fallopian tubes   38
fibrocystic disease   32
fimbria   38
follicle   38

foreskin   39
fundus   35
galactorrhea   29
genitalia   23
glans   26, 39
Grafenberg (G) spot   35
gynecomastia   28
hymen   27
hysterectomy   37
introitus   26
Kegel exercises   35
labia majora   25
labia minora   25
Leydig, cells of   43
lumpectomy   32
mammary glands   28
mastectomy   32
mons veneris   24
nipple   28
os   35
ova   38
ovaries   38
Pap smear   36
pelvic exam   36
penis   38
perineum   25

phimosis   41
prostate gland   44
pubic hair   25
pubococcygeus (PC) muscle   35
root, of penis   39
scrotum   39
semen   43
seminal vesicles   43
seminiferous tubules   43
sensuality   46
shaft   26, 39
smegma   26, 40
sperm   43
spermatic cord   43
testicular torsion   43
testicles   43
tubal ligation   38
urethra   28, 39, 43
uterus   35
vagina   33
vas deferens   43
vasectomy   43
vestibular area   26
vestibular bulbs   27
vulva   24

PERSONAL REFLECTIONS

1. Do you use sexual slang terms (a) to refer to your genitalia, or (b) when you are upset? Why? If you do, list below the terms you use, then write the correct word next to each. Say each correct term out loud a few times. Are you comfortable doing this, or uncomfortable? Could you use these terms in normal conversation with others without being embarrassed or uncomfortable (if you cannot, explain why—after all, do you use the slang terms)?

2. What are your feelings when you look at drawings such as Figures 2-2 and 2-9? If you experience any discomfort or anxiety, explain why?

3. The biblical Jews believed that humans were created in the image of God, and therefore were not ashamed of any part of their bodies, including their genitals. How do you feel about this? How do you feel about your own body? (Don't just respond "good" or "bad," but explain in some detail.)

4. As part of this chapter, I have suggested that you examine your own genitals. Were you able to do this without feelings of guilt or anxiety? If not, try to explain why you have negative feelings about looking at this part of your body.

5. (a) Women: Have you been to a physician for a pelvic examination? (b) Women aged 35 or older: Have you had a mammogram? (c) Men aged 40 or older: Have you been to a physician for a prostate examination? If you have not, explain why (lack of time is not an acceptable excuse).

6. Do you regularly examine your breasts or testicles for abnormal lumps? If the answer is no, why not? (Neither procedure takes long, so once again lack of time is not a valid excuse.)

7. If in the future you should have a male baby, do you plan to have him circumcised? Why or why not?

8. What body parts of others do you find to be most sexually arousing? Why? Do you think this is a learned response or is it biologically determined? If the latter, how do you account for the fact that people in other cultures may not be aroused by parts of the body that you find to be arousing (see Chapter 1)?

SUGGESTED READINGS

Boston Women's Health Book Collective (1992). *The new our bodies, ourselves* (4th ed.). New York: Simon & Schuster. For women, with an emphasis on health care.

Castleman, M. (1985, September). Prostate: The misunderstood gland. *Ms.*

Diagram Group. (1976). *Man's body: An owner's manual.* New York: Paddington Press, Bantam Books paperback. For men, with an emphasis on health care.

Hoffman, S. A. (1989, April). UTIs: Everything you need to know about urinary tract woes. *American Health.* Urinary tract infections are very common in women. This article discusses causes and preventive steps.

Love, S. *Dr. Susan Love's breast book.* Reading, MA: Addison-Wesley. All about breast care with many illustrations.

CHAPTER THREE

Human Sexuality Today

HORMONES, MENSTRUATION, AND BEHAVIOR

WHEN YOU HAVE FINISHED STUDYING THIS CHAPTER, YOU SHOULD BE ABLE TO:

1. IDENTIFY AND DESCRIBE THE HORMONES OF THE ENDOCRINE SYSTEM THAT ARE INVOLVED IN REPRODUCTION;

2. DESCRIBE THE FOUR PHASES OF THE MENSTRUAL CYCLE;

3. EXPLAIN THE DIFFERENCE BETWEEN MENSTRUAL AND ESTROUS CYCLES;

4. UNDERSTAND THE REASONING BEHIND THE NEGATIVE ATTITUDES FOR HAVING SEX DURING MENSTRUATION AND REALIZE THEIR LACK OF FACTUAL BASIS;

5. DEFINE AND EXPLAIN MENSTRUAL PROBLEMS SUCH AS AMENORRHEA, PREMENSTRUAL SYNDROME (PMS), DYSMENORRHEA, ENDOMETRIOSIS, AND TOXIC SHOCK SYNDROME (TSS);

6. UNDERSTAND THE DANGEROUS EFFECTS OF TAKING ANABOLIC STEROIDS; AND

7. UNDERSTAND THE RELATIONSHIP BETWEEN HORMONES AND SEXUAL DESIRE.

THE ENDOCRINE SYSTEM

WHAT ARE HORMONES? DO YOU KNOW WHAT THEY DO? ALTHOUGH MOST PEOPLE HAVE HEARD OF HORmones, very few are certain of their function. Many men believe that hormones only affect female behavior. This is incorrect. Hormones, in fact, play a crucial role in both sexes. They are important for growth (growth hormone), metabolism (thyroid hormone), water retention (antidiuretic hormone), reaction to stress (cortisol), and many other functions in males and females. They are also important for the development and maintenance of our reproductive system and influence our sexual behavior.

Hormones are chemical substances that are released into our bloodstream by ductless **glands** found throughout the body (see Figure 3-1). They are carried in the blood to other parts of the body where they exert their effect. Hormones released by one gland often cause another gland to release its hormones. This network of ductless glands is called the **endocrine system**.

The testicles and ovaries are part of the endocrine gland system. The testes manufacture and release **testosterone**, which is often referred to as the "male hormone," while the ovaries produce the "female hormones" **estrogen** and **progesterone**. However, testosterone is also produced in small amounts by the ovaries, and estrogen in small amounts by the testes. The adrenal glands (located near the kidney) also produce small amounts of these hormones, so that all three of them are found in both males and females.

What causes the testicles and ovaries to secrete their hormones? There is another gland located at the base of the brain called the **pituitary gland**. It releases eight different hormones into the bloodstream. Two of these have their effect on the ovaries and testicles and are thus called *gonadotropins* ("gonad-seeking"). In women, **follicle-stimulating hormone (FSH)** stimulates the maturation of a follicle (an immature egg) in one of the ovaries. This was its first known function and thus how it received its name. However, FSH is also released by the male's pituitary to stimulate the production of sperm in the testicles.

A second pituitary gonadotropin hormone goes by two names. In women it is called **luteinizing hormone (LH)** and triggers ovulation (release of an egg). In men the same hormone is known as **interstitial cell-stimulating hormone (ICSH)** and stimulates the testicles to produce male hormones.

The pituitary was once called the "master gland" of the body because many of its hormones (like FSH and LH)

Hormones
Chemical substances that are secreted by ductless glands into the bloodstream. They are carried in the blood to other parts of the body where they exert their effects on other glands or target organs.

Endocrine system
A network of ductless glands that secrete their chemical substances, called hormones, directly into the bloodstream, where they are carried to other parts of the body to exert their effect.

Testosterone
A hormone that is produced by the testicles (and in very small amounts by the ovaries and adrenal glands).

Estrogen
A hormone that is produced by the ovaries (and in very small amounts by the testes and adrenal glands).

Progesterone
A hormone that is produced in large amounts by the ovaries after ovulation. It prepares the endometrium of the uterus to nourish a fertilized egg.

Pituitary gland
A gland located at the base of the brain that secretes eight hormones, including follicle-stimulating hormone and luteinizing hormone.

Follicle-stimulating hormone (FSH)
A gonadotropin hormone released by the pituitary gland that stimulates the development of a follicle in the ovary and the production of sperm in the testicles.

Luteinizing hormone (LH)
A gonadotropin hormone that is released by the pituitary. A large increase in LH signals the onset of ovulation. Also see interstitial cell-stimulating hormone.

Interstitial cell-stimulating hormone (ICSH)
A hormone produced in the anterior pituitary gland that stimulates the testicles to produce male hormones. In females the same hormone triggers ovulation and is called luteinizing hormone.

FIGURE 3-1   LOCATION OF THE ENDOCRINE GLANDS.

influence the activities of other glands (like the ovaries and testicles). We now know, however, that the brain controls the release of pituitary hormones (maybe the brain should be called the master gland). The release of gonadotropin hormones from the pituitary, for example, is under control by additional hormones (called *releasing hormones*) that are manufactured in a part of the brain called the *hypothalamus* (Guillemin, 1980). The brain receives sensory input from the external environment and also from all the organs of the body, and responds to these stimuli not only by causing our muscles to work, but also by stimulating the release of hormones from the pituitary when they are needed.

Menstrual cycle
The monthly cycle of hormonal events in a female that leads to ovulation and menstruation.

Female gonadotropin and gonadal hormone levels show cyclic fluctuations, referred to as the **menstrual cycle**, throughout most of a woman's adult life. Male hormone levels, on the other hand, are relatively stable. What accounts for the difference? Are female pituitary glands different from male pituitary glands? Research with animals has shown that when male pituitary glands are transplanted into females, these glands also begin to secrete FSH and LH cyclically. Thus, the difference is in the hypothalamus of the brain, not the pituitaries. A woman's hypothalamus is, in fact, different in both its structure and connections than a man's hypothalamus, and it is this that accounts for why women show cycles in FSH and LH and men do not (Whalen, 1977).

In this chapter you will learn about the role of hormones in the female menstrual cycle, and whether or not hormones are important for sexual desire. I will save a discussion of the role of hormones in development for a later chapter. ■

THE MENSTRUAL CYCLE

A female, you recall, has about 400,000 immature ova at birth. Each egg is surrounded by other cells within a thin capsule of tissue to form what is called a **follicle**. A female does not produce any new eggs during her lifetime, but starting at puberty one (and occasionally more) of the eggs will start maturing on about a monthly basis. Each month the endometrium of the uterus thickens and becomes highly vascularized (having lots of blood vessels) in preparation for implantation of a fertilized egg. If the egg is not fertilized by a sperm, uterine tissues are discharged from the body accompanied by bleeding (**menstruation**), and a new ovum starts to mature. This process will end at menopause (when the ovaries shrivel up to the point that no eggs can mature, usually around the age of 50), and thus an average woman will have about 400 menstrual cycles in her lifetime.

Follicle
Found in the ovary, a sac containing an ovum and surrounding follicular cells.

Menstruation
The monthly discharge of endometrial tissue, blood, and other secretions from the uterus that occurs when an egg is not fertilized.

The average length of an adult human menstrual cycle is about 28 days. I will describe the hormonal events that occur in a 28-day cycle as consisting of four phases. In numbering the days, it is convenient to start with an easily recognizable event. Because all women know when they start menstruating, we will refer to the start of menstruation as day one. In actuality, however, menstruation is really the last of the four phases of the cycle, so we will begin with the events that occur after menstruation on day five (see Figure 3-2). Try not to be confused by the system used for numbering days. As you will soon learn, consistent 28-day cycles

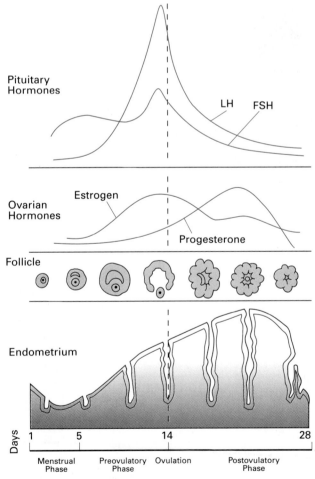

FIGURE 3-2   HORMONAL, OVARIAN, AND UTERINE CHANGES DURING A 28-DAY MENSTRUAL CYCLE.

are not very common, so the numbers of the days in parentheses will be different for shorter and longer cycles.

PREOVULATORY PHASE (DAYS 5 TO 13)

This phase is also referred to as the *follicular* or *proliferative phase*. The pituitary secretes relatively high levels of follicle-stimulating hormone (FSH) which, as the name implies, stimulates the development of a follicle in the ovary. The growing follicle, in turn, becomes a temporary endocrine gland and secretes increasingly higher levels of estrogen. Estrogen is carried in the bloodstream back to the brain and pituitary, where it inhibits further release of FSH. Estrogen also stimulates release of luteinizing hormone (LH) from the pituitary and promotes proliferation (growth) of the endometrium of the uterus. Near the end of this phase, estrogen levels reach their peak, which triggers a release of LH from the pituitary (called the *LH surge*).

OVULATION (DAY 14)

The LH surge (along with a sharp increase in FSH) signals the onset of ovulation within 12 to 24 hours. By this time, the mature follicle (called a Graafian follicle) has moved to the surface of the ovary (see Figure 3-3). At **ovulation**, the follicle ruptures and the ripe ovum is expelled into the abdominal cavity, where it will soon be picked up by a Fallopian tube. Only the ovum is expelled during ovulation. The cells that had surrounded it in the follicle remain in the ovary and now have a new name, the **corpus luteum**. In addition, the hormonal changes induce a change in the quantity and consistency of cervical mucus (from white and sticky to clear and slippery like an egg white) to provide a more hospitable environment for sperm.

Ovulation
The expulsion of an egg from one of the ovaries.

Corpus luteum
The follicular cells that remain in the ovary after the follicle expels the ovum during ovulation. They begin to secrete progesterone in large quantities in the postovulatory stage.

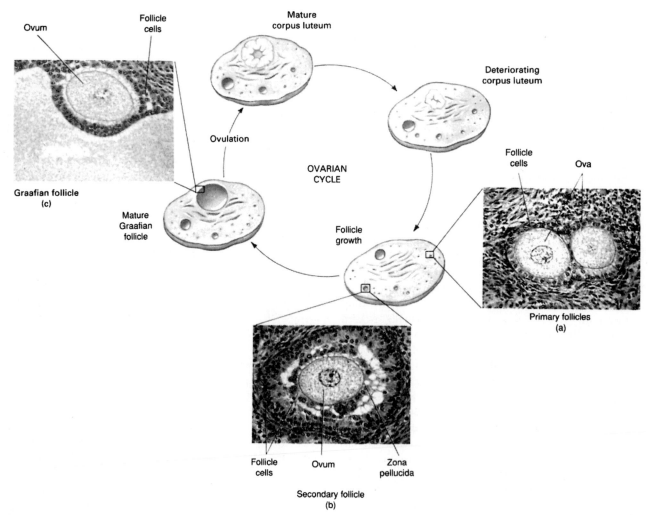

FIGURE 3-3   CHANGES THAT TAKE PLACE IN THE OVARY DURING A MENSTRUAL CYCLE.

Mittelschmerz
Abdominal pain at the time of ovulation.

Some women experience lower abdominal cramps for about a day during ovulation. This is sometimes referred to as **Mittelschmerz** (German for "middle pain"). It is more common among young females than older women.

Postovulatory Phase (Days 15 to 28)

This phase is also referred to as the **luteal** or **secretory phase**. The cells of the corpus luteum, which are already secreting estrogen, also begin to secrete large levels of progesterone after ovulation. Progesterone inhibits further release of LH from the pituitary, and further prepares the thickened endometrium in case the egg is fertilized. The endometrium develops small blood vessels, and its glands secrete nourishing substances. If the egg is fertilized by a sperm, it continues its trip through the Fallopian tube and implants itself in the endometrium. The developing placenta produces the hormone *human chorionic gonadotropin* (HCG), which ensures that the corpus luteum will continue to secrete estrogen and progesterone for months to come to maintain the endometrium.

But how often in a female's reproductive lifetime will one of her eggs be fertilized and result in pregnancy? Not too often. Most of the time fertilization does not occur, and in the absence of implantation, the corpus luteum degenerates, and there is a sharp decline in estrogen and progesterone near the end of this phase.

Menstruation (Days 1 to 4)

With the decline in levels of estrogen and progesterone, there is loss of the hormones that were responsible for the development and maintenance of the endometrium. The endometrium is sloughed off and discharged over a 3- to 7-day period. Menstruation consists of shredded endometrial tissue, cervical mucus, and blood (about 4–6 tablespoons over the entire menstrual period). The loss of estrogen (which was inhibiting the release of FSH, you recall) also results in the pituitary once again secreting FSH, and a new cycle begins. ∎

MENSTRUAL CYCLE LENGTH

In the previous section you learned that the average length of women's menstrual cycles is 28 days. However, most cycles do not last exactly 28 days. There is considerable variability from female to female and from cycle to cycle in the same female. One study of over 2,000 women found that 87 percent of them had cycles which varied by at least 7 days (Chiazze et al., 1968). The normal range is from 21 to 40 days (Vollman, 1977). Ovulation, however, is almost always 14 days (plus or minus a day or so) before the start of menstruation, so that it is the length of the preovulatory phase that usually varies (Willson & Carrington, 1991). Many things can affect the length of the menstrual cycle, including stress, nutrition, illness, drugs, and, as you will see next, other women's cycles. ∎

MENSTRUAL SYNCHRONY

The sexual behavior of animals is greatly influenced by their sense of smell. If you have ever owned a female cat or dog, you know about this. When your pet was "in heat," male animals from all over the neighborhood started showing up in your yard. They were attracted by natural body scents called **pheromones** produced by substances secreted by your pet. Many people use perfumes and colognes to enhance their sexual attractiveness, but is there any evidence that human sexuality is influenced by natural body odors?

Pheromones
Chemical substances secreted externally by animals that convey information to, and produce specific responses in, members of the same species.

The answer appears to be "yes." In a study of 135 college coeds, Martha McClintock (1971) found that roommates came to have similar menstrual cycles while living together over the course of a year. At the beginning of the year, their cycles were an average of 8.5 days apart, but were an average of 4.9 days apart by the end of the year. Mothers and daughters who live together also display menstrual synchrony (Weller & Weller, 1993). McClintock suggested that it was some undetermined natural body odor that synchronized women's cycles. Results of later studies support her hypothesis. Women who were regularly smeared under the nose with sweat collected from the underarms of other women began to have menstrual cycles that coincided with those of the sweat donors (Preti et al., 1986). In a similar experiment, it was found that women with abnormal menstrual cycles who were regularly smeared under the nose with underarm secretions collected from men began to show more normal cycles (Cutler et al., 1986), as is usually found for women who have sex regularly with men (Veith et al., 1983). ∎

MENSTRUAL VERSUS ESTROUS CYCLE

Does a woman's interest in sexual relations differ depending on the phase of her menstrual cycle? Well, apparently some people think so:

Dear Abby: You advised "Mismatched," the woman whose sexual appetite didn't match her husband's, to seek therapy. Bad advice, Abby. It's just another example of the guilt trip that has been laid on women ever since Freud and Kinsey came along with their crackpot theories about sex.

It is a biological truth that female mammals, which includes human beings, have a brief period of sexual desire when the ovum is ready for impregnation by the male.

This period is easily observed in wild mammals and is familiar to owners of female dogs and cats. We humans have chosen to ignore its existence, and try to make our females feel guilty because they desire sex far less frequently than males, whom nature created to be always ready for action.

A woman who loves her husband will willingly accommodate his need for sexual pleasure even if she does not desire it at the time. For this she will receive another kind of pleasure—the pleasure of pleasing her husband.

Happily Married

Dear Married: The female of the human species need not be in her fertile phase to desire sex. The biological "truth" you cited is a misconception. (No pun intended.)

(Taken from the "Dear Abby" column by Abigail Van Buren. Copyright 1984, Universal Press Syndicate. Reprinted with permission. All rights reserved.)

That is correct, Abby! There are some obvious differences between women and cats and dogs. Human females, for example, do not walk on all fours or bark or meow. So why is it so difficult for some people to believe that sexual desire in human females may be determined differently than in nonhuman species? Only females of the human species and a few other primate species (mostly apes) have menstrual cycles. The females of other species, including cats and dogs, have **estrous cycles**. Although owners of female cats and dogs may have noticed some periodic estrous discharge, these animals do not have a menstrual period. In some species the endometrium is reabsorbed rather than shed if fertilization does not occur. The slight discharge (called spotting) occurs during ovulation, and it is only at this time that the female is sexually receptive (in "heat" or estrus) to the male.

> **Estrous cycle**
> The cycle of hormonal events that occurs in most nonhuman mammals. The females are sexually receptive ("in heat" or estrus) to males only during ovulation.

A few studies have found a slight peak in human female sexual interest at about the time of ovulation (Diamond, Diamond, & Mast, 1972; Rossi & Rossi, 1980), but other studies have reported that sexual arousability is highest at other times of the cycle (Bancroft et al., 1983; Slob, Ernste, & Tenbosch, 1991). Recent studies have found that sexual interest is greatest during the preovulatory phase (Silber, 1994; Zillmann, Schweitzer, & Mundorf, 1994). While the evidence for a link between female sexual arousability and the menstrual cycle is inconsistent and contradictory (see Meuwissen & Over, 1992), the important point is that women, unlike the females of most other mammalian species, can become sexually aroused at any time of the cycle. There is a drop in sexual activity for many couples during menstruation (e.g., Silber, 1994), but this is probably the result of negative social and cultural learning rather than the result of hormones.

Why have a few species evolved to have menstrual cycles (in females)? What purpose does menstruation serve? Recently, it has been proposed that the adaptive significance of menstruation is to rid the body of bacteria carried into the uterus by sperm (Profet, 1993) or to eliminate abnormal embryos (Clarke, 1994), but there is little evidence yet to support either theory. ■

ATTITUDES ABOUT MENSTRUATION: HISTORICAL PERSPECTIVES

The Biblical Hebrews regarded a menstruating woman ("Niddah" in Hebrew) as unclean or "impure," and believed that she could transfer her condition of uncleanliness to a man during sexual intercourse:

When a woman has a discharge of blood which is her regular discharge from her body, she shall be in her impurity for seven days, and whoever touches her shall be unclean until the evening.

And everything upon which she lies during her impurity shall be unclean; everything also upon which she sits shall be unclean. And whoever touches her bed shall wash his clothes, and

BOX 3-A

CROSS-CULTURAL PERSPECTIVES: ATTITUDES ABOUT MENSTRUATION

In our own culture, we have a long history of negative attitudes about menstruation. The book of Leviticus in the Bible instructed that no one touch a woman while she was in her "impurity," and as recently as the Victorian era physicians advised that menstruating females be kept away from the kitchen or pantry so that they would not spoil hams (*British Medical Journal*, 1878). Menstrual blood was regarded as a pollutant, and menstruating women as impure or unclean. Social isolation was thought to be necessary in order to protect others, as if a menstruating woman had a contagious disease.

Today, **menstrual taboos** (as they are often called) persist in many cultures around the world, including such geographically diverse places as central Africa, Alaska, and the South Pacific. For example, the Havik Brahmins of southern India believe that if a woman touches her husband while she is menstruating, it will shorten his life (Ullrich, 1992), similar to the belief by Sambian (Melanesia) males that menstrual blood endangers their health (Herdt, 1993). The Lele of the Congo believe that if a menstruating woman enters the forest it will ruin hunting for the men (Douglas, 1966), while the Thonga of South Africa believe that sex with a menstruating woman will cause them to be weak in battle (Ford & Beach, 1951).

Menstrual taboos
Incorrect, negative attitudes about menstruating females.

FIGURE 3-4   MENSTRUAL HUTS IN NEW GUINEA WHERE MENSTRUATING FEMALES ARE ISOLATED FOR 7 DAYS.

In order to ensure that a menstruating woman have no contact with men, many cultures require that she remain in a small menstrual hut (usually on the outskirts of the community) for an entire week. Figure 3-4 shows an example of such a hut in New Guinea (Ward, 1989). This practice is carried to an extreme among the Kolish Indians of Alaska, who lock young girls in a small hut for as long as a year after their first menstruation (Delaney et al., 1988). Other cultures do not use special huts, but require that a woman sleep outside of the house while she is menstruating (Ullrich, 1992).

It is a common practice in these cultures to introduce menstrual taboos to young girls during initiation ceremonies held about the time of first menstruation (Schlegel & Barry, 1979, 1980). These ceremonies are rites of passage into adulthood, signifying that the girls are ready for sexual activity or marriage. Anthropologists believe that the taboos serve to emphasize the low status and inferiority of women in these cultures, where the social organization (including division of labor) is based on gender (Harper, 1964). Formal menstrual taboos are most frequently observed in small food-gathering or horticultural societies (Schlegel & Barry, 1979, 1980). The taboos decrease in importance with increased educational and professional opportunities, and increased marriage age, for women, resulting in a less dominant role for men. These changes occurred rather rapidly (over 20 years), for example, among the Havik Brahmin of India (Ullrich, 1992).

Larger societies generally do not have formal adolescent initiation ceremonies, and there are even some cultures in which the people do not have negative attitudes about menstruation. In Japan, for example, parents celebrate a daughter's first menstruation in a positive manner (Delaney, et al., 1988).

"Growing up, I was not told much about sex by my parents. As a result I felt uncomfortable about beginning menstruation. My best friend's mom, on the other hand, who was from Japan, told her about menstruation early and openly. When she began menstruation, she felt comfortable telling her mom and according to the custom of her native country, a celebration dinner was planned to celebrate her entrance into womanhood."

(from the author's files)

Which girl do you suppose felt better about herself as a blossoming woman during adolescence? ∎

bathe himself in water, and be unclean until the evening. . . . And if any man lies with her, and her impurity is on him, he shall be unclean seven days; and every bed on which he lies shall be unclean.

(Leviticus 15:19–21, 24,
Revised Standard Version)

and

If a man lies with a woman having her sickness, and uncovers her nakedness, he has made naked her fountain, and she has uncovered the fountain of her blood; both then shall be cut off from among their people.

(Leviticus 20:18,
Revised Standard Version)

Sexual intercourse was strictly forbidden for 7 days from the time a woman first noticed menstrual blood. If no blood was noticed on the eighth day, she immersed herself in a mikveh (ritual bath) and was again considered "pure." The menstrual taboo later was extended to all physical contact, and a Niddah was required to leave her home and stay in a special house called "a house for uncleanliness" (Nid. 7:4). Orthodox Jews still adhere to a literal interpretation of the passages in Leviticus. (See also Box 3-A.)

Attitudes about menstruation were even more negative during the time of the Roman Empire. Consider, for example, this passage from the Roman historian Pliney (A.D. 77) describing the possible effects of menstrual blood (Delaney, Lupton, & Toth, 1988):

Contact with it turns new wine sour, crops touched by it become barren, grafts die, seeds in gardens are dried up, the fruit of trees falls off . . . the edge of steel and the gleam of ivory are dulled, hives of bees die, even bronze and iron are at once seized by rust, and a horrible smell fills the air, to taste it drives dogs mad and infects their bites with an incurable poison.

As you will see in the next section, many people in the United States still have very negative attitudes about menstruation today. ∎

ATTITUDES ABOUT MENSTRUATION TODAY

Although our country no longer has formal menstrual taboos, there are still many people who believe menstrual myths—incorrect negative beliefs about menstruation. Here are a few of the many provided by students in my class:

"When I was about ten, I was told that if a woman was on her menstrual cycle, she shouldn't visit friends who had infant boys because the baby would get a strain."

"My mother told me to tie a piece of black thread around my baby's foot when I went out in public. She claimed that women menstruating would give the baby colic."

"When you had your period not to cook or go around the stove while cooking red gravy because it would curdle."

"All my mother said was, 'Never wash your hair when you are on your period. It will give you cramps.' Not being able to wash my hair for almost a week was pure torture. The grease was unbelievable."

(from the author's files)

Myths that women should avoid bathing, swimming, and exercise during menstruation are common (see Cumming, Cumming, & Kieren, 1991). Bathing, washing one's hair, and swimming are not the only things many women do without during menstruation. Results of a survey published in 1978 indicated that the vast majority of Americans aged 55 or older had never had sexual intercourse while the female was menstruating (Paige, 1978a). More recent studies also find that American men and women seldom initiate sex during menstruation (Harvey, 1987; Silber, 1994). This abstinence is a direct reflection of negative attitudes about menstruation. When people can be persuaded to try sexual intercourse during menstruation, they are often surprised by their reaction:

"My girlfriend sometimes wanted to have sex while she was menstruating. However, I was always reluctant. After taking this course I decided to give it a shot. Much to my surprise, I didn't mind it at all. In fact, she enjoys herself more than normal."

"The first time my girlfriend and I had sex during menstruation I told her that she was going to have to remove the condom afterwards without me looking. The thought of it disgusted me. But as we started, we found that we enjoyed it much more because we did not have to worry about getting her pregnant, it relaxed her afterwards, and because of the added fluids, she was much more lubricated. Now we look forward to sex during menstruation."

"I enjoy making love to my boyfriend while I'm having my periods. It might be messy, but it gives me pleasure, and most important it makes my period light the next day. Anyone who hasn't tried making love this way is crazy. If their only excuse is that it's messy, haven't they ever heard of a shower."

(from the author's files)

A 1981 survey by the manufacturers of Tampax found that one quarter of Americans believed that menstruation was not an acceptable topic in the home, and two thirds believed it was not an acceptable topic in social situations. Menstruation was not even mentioned on television until 1973 (an episode of "All in the Family"), and drew considerable criticism when it was.

In her book, *Outrageous Acts and Everyday Rebellions*, female activist Gloria Steinem (1983) asked what our attitudes about this subject would be if men were the ones who menstruated?

Clearly, menstruation would become an enviable, boastworthy, masculine event:

Men would brag about how long and how much.

Young boys would talk about it as the envied beginning of manhood. Gifts, religious ceremonies, family dinners, and stag parties would mark the day. . . .

Sanitary supplies would be federally funded and free. Of course, some men would still pay for the prestige of such commercial brands as Paul Newman Tampons, Muhammad Ali's Rope-a-Dope Pads, John Wayne Maxi-Pads, and Joe Namath Jock Shields—'For those Light Bachelor Days!'

There is nothing dirty or nasty about menstruation, and with a little education, it is not even mysterious, but rather a basic, important biological function. The discharge consists of nothing more than some shredded endometrial tissue, mucus, and a small amount of bleeding. From a contraceptive perspective, menstruation is the safest phase of the cycle in which to have otherwise unprotected intercourse (although conception is still remotely possible). Fortunately, young people are apparently becoming more enlightened. The same 1978 survey that found that a majority of older people had never had sex during menstruation also reported that only 28 percent of people under the age of 35 had avoided sex during this phase.

What are your attitudes about menstruation? Do you regard it as a normal physiological event, or is it something about which you or your sexual partner feel ashamed or embarrassed? Test your attitude by answering one of the following two questions. Women, would you feel comfortable asking your boyfriend or husband to buy you some tampons or sanitary napkins at the store? Some women are even embarrassed to buy them for themselves:

"Before taking this class I didn't realize what effect attitudes (about sexuality) in the U.S. had on me. When I went to the store to buy sanitary napkins I would try to hide them until I was getting ready to pay for them. I would not want a man to see me pay for them. I felt that they would think or say she's on her period."

(from the author's files)

Men, if your girlfriend or wife asked you to do so, would you feel comfortable buying her some tampons or sanitary napkins at the store?

If you would be uncomfortable, ask yourself why. No one feels uncomfortable about buying toilet paper at the store. The reason for this, of course, is that we all know that everyone has bowel movements. It is a normal physiological event. Well, nearly all women will menstruate on a monthly basis for 30 to 40 years of their lives. Menstruation is also a normal physiological occurrence.

"One class session you asked how many men would buy tampons for their girlfriend. I don't think that is a fair question, because I wouldn't ask my girlfriend to buy condoms for me."

(from the author's files)

"Oh, don't be such a wimp, Edwards. Surely you can pick me up a package of tampons on your lunch hour."

(Reproduced by Special Permission of *Playboy* magazine: Copyright © 1985 by Playboy.)

When a person buys condoms, it is with the intent of having sex. Tampons and sanitary napkins are not used for sexual relations. In fact, menstruation has nothing to do with whether or not a female is sexually experienced. Sexually inexperienced as well as sexually experienced women menstruate. No one should feel ashamed or embarrassed, or be made to feel so, about a normal bodily function. ∎

MENSTRUAL PROBLEMS

Many women experience problems that are associated in some manner with the menstrual cycle.

AMENORRHEA

Amenorrhea refers to the *absence of menstruation*. This is normal, of course, when a female is pregnant and is not unusual during breast-feeding or in the first few months after discontinuing use of birth control pills. It is also common for menstrual cycles to be irregular during the first few years after **menarche** (a girl's first menstrual period), but with the exception of these reasons, women should be having menstrual periods on about a monthly basis from the late teens until they approach menopause, at which time their cycles will again become irregular. However, up to 3 percent of women in their reproductive years have amenorrhea (Schachter & Shoham, 1994).

Amenorrhea
The absence of menstruation.

Menarche
The term for a female's first menstrual period.

A woman's health can affect her hormone levels. There is a relation between body fat levels and age of menarche. Girls with high body fat levels generally start menstruating at a younger age than girls with low levels of body fat. Amenorrhea is common among female athletes (Shangold, 1985), although intense exercise and stress may also contribute to this (Prior & Vigna, 1991). Women with the eating disorder anorexia nervosa are often considerably underweight and as a result rarely menstruate (Schweiger, 1991). Adult females who are not menstruating regularly should not assume, however, that it is due to diet or low body fat levels. A failure to menstruate (or menstruate regularly) may also be due to pituitary or ovarian problems, and thus amenorrhea can affect a woman's health. For example, the low levels of estrogen usually associated with amenorrhea often results in long-term problems such as osteoporosis and cardiovascular disease (Schachter & Shoham, 1994). Thus a premenopausal woman who is not menstruating regularly should consult a physician.

PREMENSTRUAL SYNDROME

In recent years, **premenstrual syndrome (PMS)** has received more attention than any other menstrual-related problem. PMS refers to a group of physical and/or emotional changes that many women experience in the last 3–14 days *before the start of their menstrual period*. Physical symptoms may include bloating, breast tenderness, abdominal swelling, swollen hands and feet, weight gain, constipation, and headaches. Emotional changes may include depression, anxiety, tension, irritability, and an inability to concentrate (Andersch et al., 1986). Women with PMS do not usually have all of these symptoms. Also, some women are more bothered with the physical symptoms than the emotional changes, while for others it is just the reverse. These inconsistencies have led some researchers to doubt whether or not there really is such a thing as PMS. What distinguishes PMS from other conditions with similar symptoms is the regularity with which the symptoms occur, and the rapid relief experienced once menstruation begins.

> **Premenstrual syndrome (PMS)**
> A group of physical and/or emotional changes that many women experience in the last 3–14 days before the start of their menstrual period.

> "I am a 29-year-old female who is suffering with PMS. It starts exactly 2 weeks before my menstrual period. I can tell when my PMS starts because I start to get very frustrated for no reason at all. Little things that I can normally handle seem impossible at this time. I start to regret that I have children and I desire a divorce from my husband. It seems like the walls are closing in on me and I suddenly get the urge to run away. I can't make any sense out of myself at this time and a lot of times I think of suicide. I know that I am going thru PMS but I have no control of my emotions and actions, and thinking. I hate myself at this time. As soon as a drop of blood is released from my body (menstruation) I feel like all my stress and anxieties are released with that blood. All of a sudden I feel like myself again."
>
> (from the author's files)

The American Psychiatric Association recently decided to classify some of the more severe symptoms of PMS as a mental illness (called premenstrual dysphoric disorder, or PMDD, in the 1994 edition of the *Diagnostic and Statistical Manual of Mental Disorders*). To be diagnosed with PMDD, a woman's symptoms must "markedly interfere" with social relations, work, or education, and include at least one of the following symptoms: markedly depressed mood, marked anxiety or tension, persistent and marked irritability or anger, or "marked affective liability" (e.g., sudden sadness).

Women with PMS generally have normal hormone levels (Rubinow et al., 1988). Thus, some researchers have concluded that PMS results not from a hormone excess or deficiency, but from an imbalance in the estrogen/progesterone ratio. PMS clinics once prescribed progesterone as a therapy, but studies have shown that this results in no significant improvement (Freeman et al., 1990). One study found that PMS symptoms were not relieved by artificially inducing menstruation and concluded that endocrine events do not directly cause the symptoms (Schmidt et al., 1991). Alternatively, the hormones may act in combination with certain brain chemicals (very possibly a neurotransmitter called serotonin) to produce the symptoms. Bloating may be due to adrenal hormones responsible for water retention. Although the cause(s) of PMS is uncertain, some of the symptoms can be relieved by medication and diet changes. Diuretics ("water pills"), for example, can be prescribed to eliminate the excess body fluid causing bloating and swelling, and cutting down on salt intake can also help this. Caffeine (found in coffee, tea, many soft drinks, and chocolate) should be avoided because its stimulating effect will worsen problems like nervousness, irritability, and anxiety (Rossignol et al., 1989). A carbohydrate-rich (but not chocolate), protein-poor diet may improve the negative emotional changes of PMS (Wurtman et al., 1989). Very recently, doctors have found that the anti-depressant drug Prozac (Fluoxetine) substantially reduces the tension and irritability in many women with severe premenstrual syndrome (Steiner et al., 1995). Prozac inhibits brain serotonin.

Although a hormonal basis for PMS is suspected, social and cultural factors can also play a role. For example, stress increases the severity of PMS symptoms (Mills, 1988). Several researchers have noted that PMS is greatest in women who have a very negative attitude about menstruation (often due to their husbands' behavior). With so many people still treating menstruation as a taboo, it is no wonder that some women are depressed during the few days before it begins. A negative attitude like this will only exaggerate any hormonally caused emotional problems (Brooks, Ruble, & Clarke, 1977).

Many women normally experience some mood fluctuations, but only a few have premenstrual problems that are severe enough to interfere with normal functioning (Keye, 1983). Nevertheless, Dr. Katharina Dalton has published numerous articles claiming that marital conflicts (including spouse and child abuse), job absenteeism, accidents, suicide attempts, and criminal acts are more common in the 2 or 3 days before the start of menstruation than at other times of the menstrual cycle (Dalton, 1959, 1960, 1964, 1980). PMS has even been successfully used as a defense in criminal cases in Europe, and similar attempts have been made in this country. It should be noted, however, that many do not believe Dalton's studies are valid (Fausto-Sterling, 1985; Koeske, 1983).

Feminists, who for years denied that menstruation makes any difference in behavior, worry that the new attention to PMS will reopen charges of biological inferiority and keep women out of positions of responsibility. Former Vice President Hubert Humphrey's personal physician, you may recall, publicly stated that women were unfit to hold high public office because of their "raging hormonal influences." Some feminists are also concerned that the use of PMS as a legal defense might eventually even be used against them in divorce and child custody cases.

Research in this area is relatively recent, and much of it has been poorly done, so it is difficult to make conclusions at this point. Generalizations for all women are certainly unfounded. Interestingly, a couple of studies have reported that males have cycles in testosterone levels and that depression was correlated with high testosterone (Doering et al., 1978). More research is obviously needed here as well.

DYSMENORRHEA

Many women experience *painful abdominal cramps during menstruation*, although perhaps not with every menstrual period. Painful menstrual cramps are called dysmenorrhea, and symptoms can also include backaches, headaches, a feeling of being bloated, and nausea. There are two types of dysmenorrhea—primary and secondary. It is called **primary dysmenorrhea** if the symptoms are not associated with any pelvic abnormalities, and **secondary dysmenorrhea** when pelvic disorders are found. Secondary dysmenorrhea is often caused by endometriosis (see next section), pelvic inflammatory disease (see Chapter 5), or ovarian cysts.

Dysmenorrhea
Painful menstruation.

Primary dysmenorrhea is not a psychological condition, as was once believed. It is the result of an overproduction of *prostaglandins*, substances that cause contractions of the uterus. The symptoms may be severe enough to cause many women to occasionally miss work or school.

"My periods used to ruin five days out of the month. I could barely get out of bed with extreme cramps to the point of nausea. Nothing helped, not even over the counter medicine. It just put me to sleep and didn't help with the pain. I have been on birth control pills for almost a year. It is the best thing that ever happened. I haven't experienced any pain."

"The cramps kept me doubled over for days at a time, feeling like I was going to die.

Only recently did I find out about drugs like Advil. . . ."

"Sex actually seems to relieve the severity of the cramps for a while. . . ."

(from the author's files)

All three of these personal experiences reflect common (and usually successful) ways of alleviating primary dysmenorrhea. Drugs like ibuprofen (trade names Motrin, Advil, and others) inhibit the production of prostaglandins. Many physicians prescribe birth control pills for women who suffer from dysmenorrhea (Nabrink et al., 1990). Finally, Masters and Johnson (1966) reported that orgasms relieve the symptoms, at least temporarily.

ENDOMETRIOSIS

The endometrium of the uterus grows and thickens during each menstrual cycle and is then shed and discharged during menstruation. **Endometriosis** refers to a condition that occurs in 15 percent of premenopausal women in which the *endometrial tissue also grows outside the uterus.* This may include the Fallopian tubes, ovaries, external surface of the uterus, vagina, pelvic cavity, and other places. The out-of-place tissues also grow and then break apart and bleed during the menstrual cycle, but the blood cannot drain normally (like the inner uterine lining). The abnormal bleeding becomes surrounded with inflammation and scar tissue forms, and in many cases causes adhesions (abnormal growth that binds organs together). Endometriosis is often found in women being investigated for infertility (Gruppo italiano, 1994).

Endometriosis
The growth of endometrial tissue outside of the uterus.

Many women with endometriosis suffer severe cramps and abdominal soreness, especially at menstruation, and often there is excessive menstrual bleeding. Some women experience deep pelvic pain during sexual intercourse as well.

"I have had problems with severe menstrual cramps since I was a junior in high school. The pain got worse and worse over the years. I would have to wear a tampon and 2 sanitary napkins just to catch the blood. It was awful. I remember missing many days of school because the pain was so severe I could not walk. I went to my OBGYN and he prescribed all types of medication for the pain, but nothing worked. Then it was discovered that I had endometriosis."

(from the author's files)

BOX 3-B

SEXUALITY AND HEALTH: ANABOLIC STEROIDS

In their pursuit to be the best, athletes are always looking for an edge over their competitors. Megavitamins, pain killers, stimulants—all have been used in the desire to win. Today, there is another substance that is widely used for this purpose by athletes, from high school football players to world-class Olympians: synthetic **anabolic steroids** (the more correct name is anabolic-androgenic steroids). These steroid hormones are derivatives of testosterone. They have masculinization (androgenic) effects and also promote growth by enhancing protein uptake of the muscle cell (the anabolic effect).

> **Anabolic steroids**
> Synthetic steroid hormones that combine the growth (anabolic) effects of adrenal steroids with the masculinizing effects of androgenic steroids.

When administered in proper dosages by a physician, anabolic steroids often have therapeutic value for recovery from illness or surgery, treatment of osteoporosis, healing of fractures, severe burns, stimulation of appetite, and muscular dystrophy. In an attempt to gain weight, build muscle mass and strength, many athletes started taking many times (often 100 times) the normal dose (see Strauss, 1991). More than 300,000 people a year use steroids in this country, including many nonathletes who do it for cosmetic (to look good) purposes (Buckley et al., 1988; Yesalis et al., 1993).

The use of anabolic steroids, however, can have serious harmful effects (see Strauss, 1991). These include high blood pressure and other serious cardiovascular disease, tumors of the liver and prostate gland, decrease in size of the testicles and impaired reproductive function in men, and gynecomastia in men (lumps in the breast tissue). Steroids can also stunt growth in boys who have not reached their full height. Taking anabolic steroids will *not* make a male's penis bigger, and steroids are likely to cause acne.

Women who take steroids also risk sterilization, masculinization of the fetus should pregnancy occur, and a much greater than normal chance of breast cancer. Anabolic steroids have a marked masculinizing effect in women as well (e.g., facial hair growth, male pattern baldness, deepening of the voice), which is not reversed by discontinuing use of the drugs.

Although anabolic steroids often boost energy and self-esteem (at least temporarily), other behavior changes may include anxiety, irritability, depression, impaired judgment, and paranoid delusions. One study found that one third of steroid abusers suffered mild to severe mental disorders as a result of using the synthetic hormones (Pope & Katz, 1988). Steroid use increases aggressiveness and antisocial behavior (Yesalis et al., 1993).

Here are some personal experiences by students taking my course:

> "My friends and I worked out in high school. It was a goal of mine to be bigger and stronger than the others. I decided to take anabolic steroids. Not sure how to do it, I had another inexperienced friend help me inject it into my buttocks. About two weeks later I noticed my testicles were getting smaller. In another week I started to get severe abdominal pains. . . . "

> "I am 19 years old and started using steroids last summer. I wanted to bench press 500 pounds. I gained about 40 pounds. These steroids tended to make me irritable and edgy. I occasionally got bad acne on my back and my testicles shrunk a good bit. . . . "

> "When I was playing football in college I had a roommate who also played football. This friend of mine felt that he needed that extra edge on all the other players, so he decided to start taking steroids. After taking them for a couple

of years he started to develop lumps in his chest. His attitude started to change in a more violent way. By this time the steroids had started to control his actions. He went through many ups and downs with his attitude. Finally a year before I left he was unable to function anymore on the field and in the classroom.''

(from the author's files)

Many high school athletes and some college athletes probably take anabolic steroids without knowing much about their side effects, but many world-class athletes who know better continue to do so. Fifteen athletes were stripped of 23 medals at an international meet in Caracas, Venezuela, in 1983, and another 12 American athletes withdrew rather than be tested. In the most publicized case, Canadian sprinter Ben Johnson was stripped of his 1988 Olympic gold medal in the 100-meter dash for taking steroids.

Many champions (probably most) have earned their medals without ever taking steroids. Why then do some persist in light of the dangers? In addition to physical training, most athletes get themselves ''psyched up'' when competing. Some athletes are easily ''psyched out,'' especially if they believe that the drug their competitor is taking gives them an edge. In two independent surveys, world-class athletes were asked if they could take a drug that would make them Olympic champion, but kill them within 1–5 years afterward, would they do it. A majority responded yes (Goldman, Bush, & Klatz, 1987; Mirkin, & Hoffman, 1978). This may be a sad commentary on our attitude about winning, but an anabolic steroid is not the miracle drug that will turn someone into a champion. It may, however, cause you serious harm.

For additional information, read *Anabolic Steroids: Losing at Winning*, published by the U.S. Food and Drug Administration. To receive a copy, write to Dept. 533T, Consumer Information Center, Pueblo, Colorado 81009. ■

However, many women with endometriosis show no symptoms, and thus there is some debate as to whether it should be regarded as a disease (see Moeu, 1995). For women who have symptoms, relief can often be achieved with hormone therapy that reduces estrogen levels (Barbieri & Gordon, 1991). In some cases surgical removal of the abnormal abdominal tissue is required, and the use of laparoscopy shows particular promise (Cook & Rock, 1991).

TOXIC SHOCK SYNDROME

'' I work at a local hospital. . . . One evening a patient came in with flu-like symptoms. The woman got progressively sicker as time went by and her color was actually turning purple in tint. The doctor looked her over from head to toe and then stated that he had found an old tampon in the back of her vagina. He diagnosed her with TSS. The patients's symptoms were getting worse so we went ahead with an emergency transfer by helicopter. After she left, the clerk answered the phone and told us it was the helicopter. Our patient had died. . . . ''

(from the author's files)

Toxic shock syndrome (TSS) is caused by toxins produced by a bacterium (*Staphylococcus aureus*). Symptoms include a sudden high fever, vomiting, diarrhea, fainting or dizziness, low blood pressure, and a red rash (that resembles a bad sunburn). It sometimes results in death. Although children and men can get TSS, over 85 percent of cases are related to menstruation (Bryner, 1989; Reingold, 1983).

There were over 300 cases of TSS in 1980 when the Centers for Disease Control released the first published report of the disease. Most of the cases were in women using extraabsorbent tampons, particularly the Rely brand. The number of cases of TSS fell dramatically after highly absorbent tampons were removed from the market (Petitti & Reingold, 1988) and there are now fewer than 20 cases a year.

Women who use tampons should change them three or four times a day, and switch to sanitary napkins at night before going to bed. If any of the previously described symptoms should develop during menstruation, be sure to see a doctor immediately. ■

> **Toxic shock syndrome**
>
> A syndrome (e.g., high fever, vomiting, diarrhea, dizziness) caused by toxins produced by the *Staphylococcus aureus* bacterium.

HORMONES AND SEXUAL DESIRE

Is the degree of our sexual desire related to our level of hormones? Do people with high sex drives have high levels of hormones and people with low sex drives low levels? Are some hormones more important for sexual desire than others?

Research on sex and hormones rely heavily upon two types of studies: those investigating the effects of administration of hormones, and those investigating the effects of loss of hormones (usually after surgical removal of the ovaries or testicles). We will restrict ourselves to human studies, because as you have already learned (menstrual versus estrous cycles), the differences between human sexual behavior and the sexual behavior of most nonhuman mammalian species is so great as to make generalizations from studies with laboratory animals very questionable.

As you will see in Chapter 10, the loss of estrogen and progesterone in women at menopause (or after surgical removal of the ovaries) does not reduce sexual desire or responsivity in most women (Kinsey et al., 1953; Masters & Johnson, 1966), and some show an increase in sexual behavior because they no longer worry about getting pregnant. In those postmenopausal women who do show a decrease in sexual desire, estrogen-replacement therapy alone generally has no effect (Myers et al., 1990).

There is stronger evidence for testosterone playing a role in sexual desire. In normal young men, 6 to 8 milligrams of testosterone are produced every day (95% by the testicles and 5% by the adrenal glands), but there is a gradual decline as a man grows older. Men who are sexually active often have high testosterone levels, but we do not know which came first (the old chicken and egg question; Udry et al., 1985). Men exposed to sexually explicit pictures show a short-term increase in testosterone levels (Rowland et al., 1987). Very low levels of testosterone have been associated with erectile problems and loss of desire, especially if the impaired hormone production existed before puberty (Bancroft, 1984; Davidson, 1984). The sexual behavior of adult males who experience impaired testosterone production may or may not be drastically altered. In the cases where impaired testosterone production does lead to loss of desire, hormone replacement therapy generally restores sexual desire. It was once believed that elevating testosterone levels beyond a minimal threshold had no further effect on sexual desire (Bancroft, 1980), but more recent studies have found that administration of testosterone enhances sexual desire and activity even in men with normal hormone levels (Moss, Panzak, & Tarter, 1993; O'Carroll & Bancroft, 1984).

In some parts of the world, men who are used as harem attendants are forced to have their testicles removed (castration or *orchiectomy*) so that they will not be interested in the women they are supposed to protect. In many cases it works, especially if they were not yet sexually experienced at the time of castration, but there are also stories of these eunuchs, as they are called, having the time of their lives (like a rooster guarding a henhouse). Similarly, males castrated for medical reasons sometimes lose interest in sex, but others lead a normal sex life. Some men have continued to lead a normal sex life for as long as 30 years after castration (Ford & Beach, 1951). One cannot rule out the possibility that a decrease in sexual interest after castration might be due in part to a negative psychological reaction to having mutilated genitals.

Castration has also been performed on sex offenders in European countries, and most of the subjects have shown a decrease in sexual desire and behavior. In Europe and in the United States, some judges now offer male sex offenders a choice between prison and chemical castration with an antiandrogen drug called Depo-Provera (medroxyprogesterone acetate). This drug (and others like it) severely reduces testosterone production, and often reduces interest in sex (Cooper & Cernovovsky, 1992; Money, 1987c). Some experts feel that antiandrogen drugs may be useful when combined with psychotherapy, but since castration does not always eliminate sexual desire, this is certainly an unproven "cure" (especially since the primary motivation for most rapes is nonsexual, as you will learn in Chapter 15).

It appears that testosterone is also the most important hormone for sexual desire in women. Small amounts of testosterone (0.5 milligram) are normally produced daily by a woman's ovaries and adrenal glands. Several studies have found that testosterone levels in women are directly related to measures of sexual behavior and desire (Alexander & Sherwin, 1993; Persky et al., 1982; Sherwin, 1988). A deficiency in testosterone produces a marked decrease in sexual desire and responsiveness in women (Kaplan & Owett, 1993). Although estrogen generally has no effect on sexual activity in postmenopausal women (see above), women administered testosterone after menopause or removal of the ovaries often show enhanced sexual desire (Bachmann, 1992; Sherwin et al., 1985). However, in at least one study the effect was found to be rather small (Myers et al., 1990).

In conclusion, a stronger case can be made for testosterone influencing sexual desire in both sexes than for estrogen and progesterone. Human sexual desire, however, appears to be less affected by changes in hormone levels than for that of nonhuman species, as many people continue to show normal sexual behavior after loss of all gonadal hormones. Once people have become sexually experienced, the brain plays an equal, if not greater, role in our level of desire.

KEY TERMS

adrenal glands   50
amenorrhea   58
anabolic steroids   61
corpus luteum   52
dysmenorrhea   60
endocrine system   50
endometriosis   60
estrogen   50
estrous cycle   54
follicle   38, 51
follicle-stimulating
   hormone   50
follicular phase   52
FSH   50
gonadotropins   50

HCG   53
hormones   50
human chorionic
   gonadotropin   53
ICSH   50
interstitial cell-stimulating
   hormone   50
LH   50
luteal phase   53
luteinizing hormone   50
menarche   58
menopause   51
menstrual cycle   51
menstrual taboo   55
menstruation   51

Mittelschmerz   53
orchiectomy   63
ovaries   38, 50
ovulation   52
pheromones   53
pituitary gland   50
PMS   59
premenstrual syndrome   59
progesterone   50
proliferation phase   52
prostaglandins   60
secretory phase   53
testicles   43, 50
testosterone   50
toxic shock syndrome   62

PERSONAL REFLECTIONS

1. How was menstruation first described to you: as something positive (e.g., "becoming a woman"), as just a fact of life, or as something negative? What effect do you think these early experiences havehad on your present attitudes about menstruation?

2. Are you able to talk about menstruation in your family? If not, why?

3. (a) Men: Could you go to the store and buy some sanitary napkins or tampons for your girlfriend or wife without embarrassment or anxiety? If not, why?
   (b) Women: Could you ask your boyfriend or husband to go to the store to buy you some sanitary napkins or tampons without embarrassment or anxiety? If not, why?

4 For those of you having sexual relations, do you have sexual intercourse with your partner during menstruation? If not, why?

5 Do you regard menstruation as a normal physiological process that is experienced by all women in good health (between puberty and menopause)? If you answer yes, but answered no to Question 2, 3, or 4, you are not being consistent–examine your feelings more carefully.

6 Do you or your partner suffer from premenstrual syndrome? If the answer is yes, is it possible that any negativity that you or your partner have about menstruation may contribute to it? What do you do about PMS?

SUGGESTED READINGS

Boston Women's Health Book Collective. (1992). *The new our bodies, ourselves* (4th ed.). New York: Simon & Schuster.

Delaney, J., Lupton, M. J., & Toth, E. (1988). *The curse: A cultural history of menstruation*. Urbana and Chicago: University of Illinois Press.

Gallagher, W. (1988, March). Sex and hormones. *Atlantic Monthly*.

Gastell, B. (1986, January/February). A gift from Mother Nature. *St. Raphael's Better Health*. Discusses myths about menstruation.

Goleman, D. (1988, 18 October). Chemistry of sexual desire yields its elusive secrets. *The New York Times*. Discusses the role of testosterone in men's and women's sexual desire.

Golub, S. (1992). *Periods: From menarche to menopause*. Newbury Park, CA: Sage Publications. Excellent and very thorough.

Harrison, M. (1985). *Self-help for Premenstrual Syndrome*. New York: Random House.

Hopson, J., and Rosenfeld, A. (1984, August). PMS: Puzzling monthly symptoms. *Psychology Today*.

Paige, K. E. (1973, April). Women learn to sing the menstrual blues. *Psychology Today*. Discusses the negative attitudes about menstruation in our culture.

Steinem, G. (1978, October). If men could menstruate. *Ms*. A humorous and political view of menstruation.

U.S. Food and Drug Administration. *Anabolic steroids: Losing at winning*.

CHAPTER FOUR

Human Sexuality Today

SIMILARITIES AND DIFFERENCES IN OUR SEXUAL RESPONSES

WHEN YOU HAVE FINISHED STUDYING THIS CHAPTER, YOU SHOULD BE ABLE TO:

1. LIST AND DESCRIBE THE PHASES OF THE SEXUAL RESPONSE CYCLE IN THE ORDER OF THEIR OCCURRENCE;

2. UNDERSTAND THE PROCESS OF VAGINAL LUBRICATION AND PENILE ERECTION;

3. DESCRIBE THE ORGASMIC PLATFORM AND THE "SEX-TENSION FLUSH";

4. DESCRIBE THE TWO STAGES OF MUSCULAR CONTRACTIONS INVOLVED IN MALE ORGASM AND DIFFERENTIATE BETWEEN THE VARIOUS KINDS OF FEMALE ORGASM;

5. DESCRIBE THE FEMALE MULTIPLE ORGASM AND THE MALE REFRACTORY PERIOD;

6. EXPLAIN AND DISCUSS SEVERAL CONTROVERSIES ABOUT ORGASM;

7. UNDERSTAND THE ROLE OF PENIS SIZE IN SEXUAL PLEASURING;

8. DISCUSS THE VALIDITY OF REPUTED APHRODISIACS; AND

9. EXPLAIN AND DISCUSS THE PRACTICE OF FEMALE GENITAL MUTILATION IN OTHER CULTURES.

THE PRIMARY TOOLS OF BEHAVIORAL SCIENTISTS ARE OBSERVATION AND MEASUREMENT. THE MECHANISMS involved in most human behaviors have been under investigation since the last century, but because of the negative attitudes that prevailed since the Victorian era, human sexual behavior was considered off-limits as a subject for scientific inquiry. The first major surveys of human sexual behavior were not published until the middle of this century (Kinsey et al., 1948, 1953). Then in 1966, William Masters and Virginia Johnson published their book entitled *Human Sexual Response*, based on direct laboratory observation of hundreds of men and women engaged in sexual activity on thousands of occasions (see Chapter 1). Human sexuality as a topic for research was thereafter no longer taboo. In this chapter, you will learn about the physiological responses that occur during sexual arousal. The emotional and psy-

chological aspects of sexuality will be discussed in later chapters.

Prior to Masters and Johnson, men and women were thought to be quite different in their sexual responses. Men, for example, were thought to heat up like light bulbs, while women, who many thought were incapable of orgasm, were believed to respond only after long periods of foreplay. Masters and Johnson focused on the physiological responses during sexual activity and emphasized the similarities, rather than the differences, between the two sexes. Some researchers now believe, however, that Masters and Johnson were too intent on showing that men's and women's sexual responses are similar (Tiefer, 1991). Research conducted in the last 30 years has shown that although men's and women's sexual responses are a lot more similar than once believed, there are some important differences between the sexes, as well as some individual differences among each gender. ∎

MODELS OF SEXUAL RESPONSE

Masters and Johnson describe the physiological responses that take place in men and women as occurring in four phases: (1) excitement, (2) plateau, (3) orgasm, and (4) resolution. They refer to this response pattern as the **sexual response cycle**. Although there is little argument concerning the specific responses, it must be emphasized that the phases are only a convenient model. Even Masters and Johnson admit that the phases are arbitrarily defined, and rather than indicating a noticeable shift, they often flow together. Hardly anyone, for example, would be aware of the precise moment they left the excitement phase and entered the plateau phase.

Other researchers and therapists have proposed models that divide the sexual responses into fewer or more phases than the model used by Masters and

Sexual response cycle

The physiological responses that occur during sexual arousal, which many therapists and researchers have arbitrarily divided into different stages.

Johnson. Many sex therapists have found, for example, that some people never become sexually excited (the first phase in Masters and Johnson's model) because of a lack of sexual desire or an aversion to sex (see Chapter 13). As a result, some therapists have suggested that desire be included as the first phase of the sexual response cycle (Kaplan, 1979; Zilbergeld & Ellison, 1980). Helen Kaplan, a well-known sex therapist, has proposed a model for the sexual responses that has only three phases: desire, excitement, and orgasm. From a subjective point of view, her model is appealing because most people would be able to distinguish the change in phases. However, because of the historical importance of Masters and Johnson's studies, this book will follow their four-phase model and simply add Kaplan's desire phase to the beginning. None of these models, however, should be viewed as being right or wrong. They are merely different ways of looking at the same experience. ∎

THE SEXUAL RESPONSE CYCLE

DESIRE

Desire, according to Helen Kaplan (1979),

Is experienced as specific sensations which move the individual to seek out, or become receptive to, sexual experiences. These sensations are produced by the physical activation of a specific neural system in the brain. When this system is active, a person is ''horny''; he may feel genital sensations or he may feel vaguely sexy,

interested in sex, open to sex, or even just restless.

The addition of a desire phase has been very popular with many sex therapists, particularly those who feel that the subjective aspects of sexual responsiveness (how one thinks and feels emotionally) are as important as the

Desire

". . . Is experienced as specific sensations which move the individual to seek out, or become receptive to, sexual experiences" (Kaplan, 1979). Kaplan and others have suggested that desire precedes excitement as the first stage of the sexual response cycle.

Full erection

Partially
stimulated
state

Unstimulated state

Partial elevation
of testes

EARLY EXCITEMENT

Uterus

Bladder

Clitoris
enlarges

Vaginal
lubrication
begins

Labia swell

EARLY EXCITEMENT

Cowper's gland
secretion

Color deepens

Prostate
enlarges

Scrotum thickens

Increase in
size of testes

Testes fully elevated

Cowper's
gland
secretes
a few
drops of
fluid

PLATEAU

Uterus elevates

Vagina
expands

Orgasmic platform

Labia changes color

PLATEAU

Penile
contractions

Seminal vesicles
contract

Urethral contractions

Contractions move
the seminal fluid
through the urethra

Prostate
gland
contracts

Rectal
sphincter
contracts

ORGASM

Contractions
in uterus

Rectal
sphincter
contracts

Rhythmic contractions
in orgasmic platform

ORGASM

FIGURE 4-1 SEXUAL RESPONSE COMPARISON BETWEEN MALE AND FEMALE.

physiological responses. A person can have the physiological response (e.g., erection) without feeling aroused, or can feel highly aroused but fail to have the physiological responses.

Once a person has sexual desire, stimulation of any of the five senses, or the imagination, can lead to sexual excitement. The physiological responses that occur during excitement and the remaining phases do not differ with different stimuli. The responses are the same regardless of whether the arousing stimuli are tactile, visual, auditory, olfactory, or taste, or whether the source of arousal is another person of the opposite sex or of the same sex, or oneself (fantasy and/or masturbation).

Vasocongestion

Refers to tissues becoming engorged (filled) with blood.

Myotonia

A build-up of energy in nerves and muscles, resulting in involuntary contractions.

We can describe most of the responses that occur in terms of two basic physiological processes: vasocongestion and myotonia. **Vasocongestion** refers to tissues becoming engorged (filled) with blood, while **myotonia** refers to a buildup of energy in nerves and muscles resulting in involuntary contractions.

Excitement

MALES. The first physical sign of arousal in males, of course, is *erection of the penis* resulting from the spongy-like tissues of the corpora cavernosa and corpus spongiosum becoming engorged with blood (see Figure 4-1). This vasocongestive response begins within 3 to 8 seconds after stimulation begins, but usually does not result in a full erection right away. Many men, however, worry if they do not have a "steel-hard" erection immediately upon stimulation. Remember, this is just the initial phase of the response cycle, and it is not unusual for men to be easily distracted at first by either mental or external stimuli, resulting in fluctuation of the firmness of erection.

Excitement

The first stage of the sexual response cycle as proposed by Masters and Johnson. The first signs are erection in the male and vaginal lubrication in the female.

Vasocongestion of the penis results from nerve impulses causing dilation of the arteries that carry blood to the penis. To better understand this, look at Figure 4-2. There are two centers in the spiral cord responsible for erection. The more important of the two is located in the lowest (sacral) part of the spinal cord. Nerve impulses caused by stimulation of the penis travel to this center, which then sends nerve impulses back to the arteries in a reflex action to initiate dilation of the arteries (and vasocongestion). Many men with their spinal cord cut above the sacral erection center can still get erections in this reflexive manner, although they cannot feel stimulation of the penis (Weiss, 1978). This is true for quadriplegics as well as

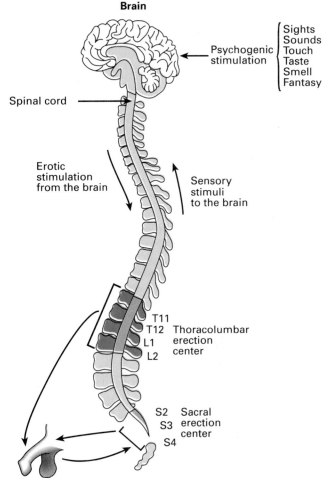

FIGURE 4-2   NEURAL MECHANISMS INVOLVED IN AN ERECTION.

paraplegics (Alexander, Sipski, & Findley, 1993). In men with intact spinal cords, nerve impulses from the brain (generated by such things as sights, sounds, and fantasies) are carried to the erection center and result in vasocongestion. A second erection center located higher in the spinal cord (thoracolumbar) also receives impulses originating in the brain and thus it too contributes to psychologically caused erections. Although vasocongestion of the penis sounds like a mechanically easy process, a number of things can interfere with it, including physical or emotional stress and/or fatigue (see Chapter 13).

Vasocongestion of the penis is not the only response that happens in men during the excitement phase. The scrotum thickens (muscle layer contracts) and the spermatic cord shortens, thus elevating the testicles toward the body. Late in the excitement phase the testicles also start to become engorged with blood and slightly enlarge (see Figure 4-1). In addition, nipple erection occurs in some men (but this is not related to a man's masculinity or femininity).

FEMALES. *Vaginal lubrication*, the first sign of sexual arousal in females, also begins within seconds after the start of stimulation. It happens as a result of the vaginal walls becoming engorged with blood and the consequent pressure causing the walls to secrete drops of fluid (superfiltered blood plasma) on the inner surfaces. Thus, the first physiological response in males and females is a vasocongestive response, and it begins within seconds of stimulation in both sexes. However, while it is difficult for a man not to notice that his penis is getting firm, many women may not be aware that their vagina is lubricating for several minutes. Even when vaginal lubrication is noticed, some women, particularly young women, may not attribute it to sexual arousal (Heiman, 1975) and may instead believe that it is a variation in their vaginal discharge or a sign of infection.

Many men mistake the presence of vaginal lubrication to mean that their female partner is ready to begin intercourse. Although lubrication makes vaginal penetration easier and prevents irritation during thrusting, remember that this is just the first physiological response experienced by a woman and does not mean that she is emotionally, or even physically, ready to begin sexual intercourse. There is also no relation between the amount of lubrication and the level of arousal. Lubrication may actually slow down during the following plateau phase, which is a much higher state of arousal.

In addition to vaginal lubrication, the labia majora, which normally cover and protect the vaginal opening, flatten and begin to move apart. The walls of the vagina, which are collapsed in the unstimulated state, begin to balloon out and the cervix and uterus pull up, thus getting the vagina ready to accommodate a penis (see Figure 4-1). The clitoris, which is made up of two corpora cavernosa, becomes engorged with blood, resulting in an increase in diameter of the shaft (and

length in 10 percent of women) and a slight increase in diameter of the glans. As a result, the clitoris is more prominent during the excitement phase than at any other time (see Figure 4-3).

The nipples also become erect during the excitement phase, but this is as a result of contraction of small muscle fibers, not vasocongestion. Vasocongestion of breast tissues is responsible, however, for a slight increase in breast size late in the excitement phase.

PLATEAU

The **plateau** phase is a period of high sexual arousal that potentially sets the stage for orgasm. In some people this phase may be quite short, and in others it might last a long time and be as satisfying as orgasm.

Plateau

The second stage of the sexual response cycle as proposed by Masters and Johnson. Physiologically, it represents a high state of arousal.

MALES. In men, the diameter of the penis further increases, especially near the corona. In addition, the testes become fully engorged with blood (increasing in size by 50 to 100 percent) and continue to elevate and rotate until their back surfaces touch the perineum, an indication that orgasm is near (see Figure 4-1). The Cowper's glands secrete a few drops of clear fluid that may appear at the tip of the penis. About 25 percent of men experience a sex flush on various areas of their skin (see below).

FEMALES. In women, many things occur during this period that make the plateau phase distinct from the excitement phase (see Figure 4-1). While the inner two thirds of the vagina continues to expand like an inflated balloon and the uterus continues to elevate (creating a "tenting effect" in the vaginal walls), something quite different happens in the tissues of the outer third of the vagina. These tissues become greatly engorged with

FIGURE 4-3 CHANGES IN THE CLITORIS AND LABIA DURING SEXUAL AROUSAL.

blood and swell, a reaction that Masters and Johnson call the *orgasmic platform*. The swelling of tissues results in a narrowing of the vaginal opening by 30 to 50 percent. Thus, the tissues of the outer third of the vagina grip the penis during this stage (negating the importance of penis size, according to Masters and Johnson).

Changes in blood flow cause a measles-like rash to appear on areas of the skin early in the plateau stage (or late in the excitement stage). This "*sex-tension flush,*" as it is called, occurs in 50 to 75 percent of women and generally appears on the breasts, upper abdomen, and buttocks, but it can appear on any part of the body.

There are three additional responses that occur in women during the plateau phase which are sometimes misinterpreted by men to mean that the female is no longer aroused, when in fact she is at a very heightened stage. First, the clitoris pulls back against the pubic bone and disappears beneath the clitoral hood (see Figure 4-3). Second, the breasts, and particularly the areola, become engorged with blood and swell, increasing in size by 20 to 25 percent in women who have not breast-fed a baby and to a lesser extent in those who have. This obscures the nipple erection that was so prominent in the excitement phase. Third, the secretion of fluids from the vaginal walls may slow down if the plateau phase is prolonged (the Bartholin's glands secrete a few drops of fluid during this stage, but not enough to contribute to lubrication). Some men may worry about the disappearance of some responses that were so prominent during the initial excitement phase, but once again, these are the normal physiological responses when women become highly aroused. The glans of the clitoris, for example, is extremely sensitive to touch at this stage, and indirect stimulation is generally sufficient to maintain arousal. In fact, some women find direct stimulation of the clitoris during this phase to be too intense and less pleasurable than indirect stimulation.

The labia minora also become greatly engorged with blood during the plateau phase, resulting in a doubling or tripling in thickness and a vivid color change (from pink to rosy red or wine color). The thickening of the labia minora helps to further push the labia majora apart and expose the vaginal opening. Masters and Johnson claim that the color change in the labia minora means that a woman is very close to orgasm.

The changes that occur in the plateau phase in males obviously are not as distinct as the changes that occur in females. Although the responses that occur in women prior to orgasm can justifiably be divided into two phases, there are those who disagree with such a division for men (e.g., Robinson, 1976). They claim that the plateau phase in males is really just an advanced stage of excitement, and that Masters and Johnson included a plateau phase for males only because they were determined to show the similarities between men and women.

Orgasm

THE ESSENCE OF ORGASM. With continued and effective stimulation, people experience intense physical sensations lasting a few seconds that are referred to collectively as orgasm (climax or "coming"). Masters and Johnson define orgasm as a sudden discharge of the body's accumulated sexual tension, while *Webster's Dictionary* defines it as "the climax or culmination of a sexual act." But do either of these definitions describe the real essence of orgasm? If a Martian were to land on earth and ask you what an orgasm is, how would you describe it? Hemingway wrote that during orgasm "the earth moved," but, except for a few people in California who might have been having sex when an earthquake struck, I doubt if this is an experience shared by many. When asked to describe an orgasm, people often respond with such descriptions as "throbbing," "a rush," "an avalanche," "earth-shattering," "waves of pleasure," and "an explosion." From these descriptions, our Martian might have trouble distinguishing between an orgasm and the Fourth of July ("bombs bursting in air"). Obviously, it is difficult to adequately describe orgasm in words, although we generally might be able to express the feeling that "it sure feels good!" I guess that you have to have had one to really know what it is.

Interestingly, men and women describe orgasm similarly. When physicians and psychologists were presented with descriptions of orgasm, they were unable to distinguish which had been written by men or women (Vance & Wagner, 1976; Wiest, 1977).

Using electrophysiological recording equipment, Masters and Johnson (1966) found that orgasm consisted of rhythmic muscular contractions in specific parts of the body that initially occurred every 0.8 seconds, but then diminished in intensity and regularity. Others have reported that the first contractions are only 0.6 seconds apart (Bohlen et al., 1980), but the really important thing is that for the first time definite physiological responses could be identified in specific tissues.

Is an orgasm really nothing more than rhythmic

Orgasm

The brief, but intense, sensations (focused largely in the genitals but really a whole body response) experienced during sexual arousal. At this time, rhythmic muscular contractions occur in certain tissues in both the male and female. The third stage of the sexual response cycle, as proposed by Masters and Johnson.

muscular contractions in a few genital tissues? Did Masters and Johnson record what an orgasm actually is, or merely what it looks like? Recent studies have been unable to find a relationship between a person's perception of orgasm and the muscular contractions. Contractions often begin before a person's perception of orgasm begins and end before the person reports orgasm to be over. Moreover, strong contractions are sometimes seen with "mild" orgasms, while weak contractions are sometimes associated with orgasms that are perceived as intensely pleasurable (Bohlen et al., 1980, 1982; Levin & Wagner, 1985). In short, researchers can measure the contractions, but they can't measure the pleasure. The perception of the orgasm can be measured only by the individual person. Subjectively, people report a feeling of pleasure focused initially in the genitals and then spreading throughout the entire body. This has led some experts to conclude that the essence of orgasm lies not in the genitals, but in the brain (see Gallagher, 1986). Evidence for this is provided by the recent finding that some women can experience orgasm in response to imagery alone, in the absence of any physical stimulation (Whipple, Ogden, & Komisaruk, 1992).

Additional proof lies in the fact that some paraplegics, and quadriplegics, people whose spinal cord has been transected, report having orgasms (Alexander et al., 1993; Gallagher, 1986; Kettle et al., 1991). They display the typical heart rate changes, muscle tensions, and sex flushes that nonspinal damaged people show. A male paraplegic might be capable of having erections during arousal, but would not be able to feel them, so the sexual response is clearly in the brain. Stimuli, such as emotions, visual and nongenital physical input, and fantasy obviously come to play a major role with disabled people (as well as most others).

In summary, it appears that orgasm is a perceptual experience (generated in the brain, thus not always requiring genital stimulation), and that its occurrence is subjective (Whipple et al., 1992).

MALES. In males, orgasm occurs in two stages. In the first stage, called *emission*, rhythmic muscular contractions in the vas deferens, prostate gland, and seminal vesicles force the sperm and prostate and seminal fluids into the ejaculatory ducts, thus forming *semen*. Sphincter muscles (circular bands of muscle fibers) contract and close off the part of the urethra that goes through the prostate and the semen causes it to swell to two to three times its normal size (called the urethral bulb). These initial contractions give men a feeling of ejaculatory inevitability (the famous "I'm coming")—the feeling that orgasm is about to happen and cannot be put off.

In the second stage, called *expulsion*, these contractions are joined by contractions in the urethra and muscles at the base of the penis to force the semen from the penis—**ejaculation**. During this stage, the sphincter muscles surrounding the part of the urethra coming from the bladder are tightly contracted so that urine is not mixed with semen. A few men have a medical problem known as *retrograde ejaculation* in which the sphincter muscle that allows passage of semen through the penile urethra closes (instead of opening) and the sphincter muscle surrounding the part of the urethra from the bladder opens (instead of closing), thus forcing semen into the bladder instead of out of the body.

> **Ejaculation**
> The expulsion of semen from the body.

Although ejaculation occurs at about the same time as orgasm in adult males, *they are really two different events*. Orgasm refers to the subjective pleasurable sensations while ejaculation refers to the release of semen from the body. The passage of semen through the penis has nothing to do with the sensation of orgasm or the intensity of orgasm. Think about it; if the passage of fluid through the uretha were the cause of the pleasurable sensations, at what other times during the day would males have a very intense orgasm (but do not)? Orgasm and ejaculation, in fact, do not always occur together. Before puberty, for example, boys can have orgasm, but do not ejaculate (the prostate and seminal vesicles do not enlarge until then). Ejaculation in the absence of orgasm has also been reported with some types of illness and medications.

FEMALES. Incredible as it may seem, until just a few decades ago many people (including many physicians and therapists) did not believe that women had orgasms. In fact, as late as 1976, a graduate school professor of mine was still telling students that women were not capable of orgasm. This mistaken belief was due in part to attitudes left over from the Victorian era. Women, at that time, were not supposed to enjoy sex and participated only to "do their wifely duties." Sex was something that men did to women when they could not control their own desires; thus the female's role was merely passive. This belief was also partly based on comparative studies. Symons (1979) found that nonhuman female primates living in the wild rarely, if ever, experience orgasm (even if they are physiologically capable, the males mate too quickly for it to occur). It was not until Masters and Johnson recorded electrophysiological responses from females that the debate was finally ended. Similar to men, women also had rhythmic muscular contractions in specific tissues that were initially 0.8 seconds apart. The structures included the tissues of the outer third of the vagina (the orgasmic platform), the uterus, and the anal sphincter muscles. Unlike males, female orgasms occur in a single stage without the sense of inevitability (the sense of "coming") that men have.

RESOLUTION

MALES. Resolution is defined as a return to the unaroused state. In men, this involves a loss of erec-

Resolution

The fourth and final stage of the sexual response cycle as proposed by Masters and Johnson. It refers to a return to the unaroused state.

tion, a decrease in testicle size and their movement away from the body cavity, and disappearance of the sex flush in those who have it. Loss of erection (detumescence) is due to the blood flow to the penis return-

ing to normal. Some of the excess blood is pumped out by the orgasmic contractions, and normal blood flow then returns as the arteries begin to constrict and the veins open. The testes had become swollen with blood during the plateau phase, and if orgasm is delayed or not achieved, males may experience testicular aching (what is sometimes known as "blue balls"). The discomfort is only temporary and is not dangerous (and the testicles and scrotum do not turn blue).

Many men, of course, are capable of reaching orgasm two or more times while having sex. If emotional and/or physical stimulation continues after an orgasm, a man's physiological responses may not fall all the way to preexcitement phase levels, but they will drop below plateau level for some period of time. Partial or full erection may be possible, but he will be unable to have another orgasm until his responses build up to plateau level again. (Remember, it is not possible to have an orgasm until one's responses have built up to the high-intensity level Masters and Johnson call plateau.) The period of time after an orgasm in which it is physiologically impossible for a male to achieve another or-

gasm is called the **refractory period** (see Figure 4-4). The length of the refractory period increases with age and differs from individual to individual and from occasion to occasion. If a man continues to have sexual stimulation after reaching orgasm, the refractory period will generally get longer with each orgasm.

Refractory period

In males, the period of time after an orgasm in which their physiological responses fall below the plateau level, thus making it impossible for them to have another orgasm (until the responses build back up to plateau).

Increased stimulation, of course, can shorten the duration of the refractory period. Successive introductions of new female partners, for example, can keep male laboratory animals performing for prolonged periods of time. This is known as the "Coolidge effect," named after the American president. President and Mrs. Coolidge were being conducted on separate tours of a farm. When she reached the henhouse, Mrs. Coolidge asked the farmer whether the continuous and vigorous sexual activity of the hens was really the work of just one rooster. After the farmer acknowledged, "Yes," Mrs. Coolidge responded, "You might point that out to Mr. Coolidge." Her statement was relayed to the President, who then asked the farmer whether the rooster had sex with a new hen each time. When the farmer responded, "Yes," Mr. Coolidge replied, "You might point that out to Mrs. Coolidge."

FEMALES. Similar to what happens in males, a female's physiological responses generally drop below the plateau level after orgasm and return to the unaroused state (see the first solid line in Figure 4-4). Some women, however, are capable of having true **multiple orgasms**—two, three, four, or numerous (limited only by the point of physical exhaustion) full orgasms in quick succession without dropping below the

Multiple orgasms

Having two or more successive orgasms without falling below the plateau level of physiological arousal.

plateau level (the dotted line in Figure 4-4). They must be capable, of course, of having the first orgasm, and additional orgasms are only possible with continued sexual desire and effective stimulation. As many as 10 percent of sexually experienced women have never had an orgasm (the wavy line in Figure 4-4). Only about 14 to 16 percent of women regularly have multiple orgasms (Athanasiou et al., 1970; Kinsey et al., 1953), but perhaps as many as 40 percent

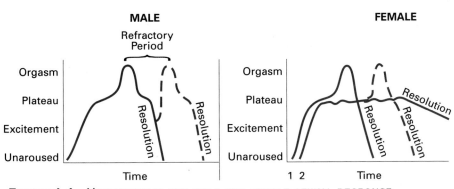

FIGURE 4-4 VARIATIONS IN THE MALE AND FEMALE SEXUAL RESPONSE CYCLE.

have experienced them occasionally (Darling, Davidson, & Jennings, 1991). Thus, the female sexual response cycle is quite variable. In fact, it is best not to think of "the" human sexual response cycle (a universal model that applies to everybody on all occasions), but rather to "a" human sexual response cycle that differs from person to person and from occasion to occasion (Tiefer, 1991).

Among those women who have experienced multiple orgasms, only a few do so in all of their sexual encounters. Many women report that multiple orgasms are most easily experienced during masturbation, when they are not distracted by the partner and when sexual fantasy is maximal.

> "
> . . . sometimes (I get) two or three orgasms right after each other. I can have multiple orgasms as much as eight times in a row, but this is only during masturbation."
>
> (from the author's files)

Many physicians and psychoanalysts (mostly men) refused to believe Kinsey when he first reported multiple orgasms in women in 1953. In a book entitled *Kinsey's Myth of Female Sexuality*, for example, it was stated that "one of the most fantastic tales the female volunteers told Kinsey (who believed it), was that of multiple orgasm . . ." (Bergler & Kroger, 1954). Fourteen percent of the women in Kinsey's famous survey reported having multiple orgasms, yet it was not until

Masters and Johnson (1966) physiologically recorded multiple orgasms that many people accepted it as truth. Unfortunately, the pendulum may now have swung too far, with some people misinterpreting Masters and Johnson's findings to mean that all women who have learned to have a single orgasms can (or should) have multiple orgasms.

Multiple orgasms, as well as simultaneous orgasms (with one's partner), have become the one and only goal in sex for some men and women. This can be self-defeating, as they feel like failures when it is not achieved. Many individuals are completely satisfied by a single orgasm, and they should not put additional pressure on themselves by treating sex like an Olympic event. When people watch the Olympics, it never occurs to them that they should be able to run a 4-minute mile or perform incredible feats on the parallel bars. Many of the same people, however, feel that they have to go for a gold medal every time they have sex. This sexual Olympics mentality can only detract from having a good, healthy, and sexually satisfying experience and can lead to sexual problems as well (see Chapter 13).

At some point, after a single or multiple orgasm(s), a woman's responses will start to fall below plateau level and return to normal. The blood drains from the breasts and the tissues of the outer third of the vagina, the sex flush disappears, the uterus comes down, and the vagina shortens in width and length. The clitoris returns to its normal position within seconds, but the glans may be extremely sensitive to touch for several minutes. Perspiration may appear on both the female and male, but is often unrelated to the degree of physical exertion.

CONTROVERSIES ABOUT ORGASMS

ARE ALL WOMEN CAPABLE OF ORGASM DURING SEXUAL INTERCOURSE?

> "Unfortunately, I have yet to learn how to have an orgasm with a partner during intercourse, but I have no problem reaching orgasm during oral sex. . . . "
>
> (from the author's files)

About 5 to 10 percent of American women have never had an orgasm under any circumstances (Spector & Carey, 1990). Shere Hite (1976) reported that only 30 percent of adult women experience orgasm regularly during intercourse without simultaneous stimulation of the clitoris. Others put the figure at 40 to 50 percent (Fisher, 1973; Kinsey et al., 1953; Wilcox & Hager, 1980). However, in a recent, well-conducted study, Laumann and colleagues (1994) found that 75 percent

of married women and 62 percent of single women usually or always had an orgasm during sexual intercourse. Even so, this still leaves a sizable minority of women who do not. Both psychosocial and biological factors appear to play a role in women's ability to reach orgasm (Raboch & Raboch, 1992). From years of experience in her own clinical practice, sex therapist Helen Kaplan (1974) concluded, "There are millions of women who are sexually responsive, and often multiply orgasmic, but who cannot have an orgasm during intercourse unless they receive simultaneous clitoral stimulation." Kaplan and others reached this conclusion after interviewing many women who reported that they desired and enjoyed sex, became highly aroused, but had never had an orgasm with a male partner (and some reported having had many partners) without simultaneous clitoral stimulation. On the other hand, Masters and Johnson (1966) and others (Barbach, 1980) claim to have successfully treated similar women and believe that all women in good health are capable of orgasm during intercourse without additional stimulation. We will return to this issue in Chapter 13.

HOW MANY TYPES OF FEMALE ORGASM ARE THERE?

Sigmund Freud, unlike many of his Victorian colleagues, not only believed that women had orgasms, but he started another controversy when he said that there were two types of female orgasms, one due to clitoral stimulation and one resulting from vaginal sensations. Moreover, he claimed that clitoral orgasms were infantile and a sign of immaturity (because they were caused by noncoital acts) while vaginal orgasms were "authentic" and "mature" and a sign of normal psychosexual development (the result of stimulation by the penis). "The elimination of clitoral sexuality," he wrote, "is a necessary precondition for the development of femininity." This belief was adopted by his followers and caused many women to feel badly or even seek analysis because they could not experience a vaginal orgasm. Freud's views, which were made without any physiological data, have since been refuted by modern sex researchers. It is not true that just because the vagina provides pleasure for the penis, that the reverse also must be the case.

Kinsey (1953), who doubted the authenticity of vaginal orgasms, had five gynecologists touch the vaginal walls of 879 women with a probe. Most women could not tell when their vagina was being stimulated, but were very much aware when their clitoris was touched. Physiologically speaking, the inner two thirds of the vagina has few nerve endings, but it is possible, of course, that the vagina is more sensitive to stimulation during sexual arousal, which Kinsey did not test.

Masters and Johnson (1966) later reported that all female orgasms were physiologically the same. No matter whether the source of stimulation was clitoral or vaginal, identical rhythmic muscular contractions were recorded in the same structures and the focus of subjective sensation was the clitoris. The clitoris is indirectly stimulated by the penis during vaginal penetration, you recall (by the clitoral hood), but the same contractions were recorded from women who reached orgasm from breast stimulation alone. According to Masters and Johnson's early physiological research, an orgasm is an orgasm, regardless of the source of stimulation. In other words, Masters and Johnson initially denied the existence of vaginal orgasms.

As you learned earlier, while scientists can measure contractions, they can't measure the pleasure. Several studies have found that women subjectively distinguish between orgasms caused by clitoral stimulation during masturbation and orgasms during intercourse (which were described as "fuller, but not stronger," "more internal," and "deeper" [e.g., Bentler & Peeler, 1979; Butler, 1976; Seaman, 1972]).

"I believe I've had clitoral orgasms, vaginal orgasms, and the blended type. All of these feel different. . . . For me the best type of orgasm is the blended type because I feel it all over and when it is over my body trembles as if I had just stopped running."

(from the author's files)

In fact, some women say that they have never had an orgasm from clitoral stimulation—that their orgasms always result from vaginal stimulation.

"I am a 30 yr. old woman who has been sexually active since my late teens. I've always been very responsive sexually, resulting in multiple, intense orgasms during intercourse. The significant point is, I have orgasms during intercourse, but never during oral sex or direct clitoral stimulation. My orgasms are strictly vaginal, they are never clitoral. I'd always felt fine about this until I had a relationship with a man who said there was something wrong with me because I did not reach orgasm during oral sex. He made me feel so bad that I literally lost all of my self-esteem and self-confidence. I truly believed I was abnormal. It took me a long time to get over these feelings of inadequacy. I know now that I am okay. I may not be the same as most other women, but there is nothing 'wrong' with me. I consider myself lucky . . . not different."

(from the author's files)

If the walls of the inner two thirds of the vagina are so sparse in nerve endings, what could be the anatomical basis for vaginal orgasms? Recall from Chapter 2 that the muscle which surrounds the vagina, the pubococcygeus (PC) muscle, is more richly innervated with nerve endings than the vaginal walls, and that women who report vaginal sensations during intercourse tend to have strong PC muscles (Kinsey et al., 1953). In 1982, Ladas, Whipple, and Perry suggested in their book, *The G Spot*, another possible basis for a vaginal orgasm. The **Grafenberg spot**, or **G spot**, was first described by the German gynecologist Ernst Grafenberg (1950) in the 1940s. It was described as being a very sensitive area about the size of a dime located on the front wall of the vagina about halfway between the back of the pubic bone and the front of the cervix (just under the bladder). It swells when stimulated and a woman's first reaction (lasting a few seconds) may be an urge to urinate.

Grafenberg spot
A small, sensitive area on the front wall of the vagina found in about 10 percent of women.

BOX 4-A

CROSS-CULTURAL PERSPECTIVES: MUTILATION OF FEMALES' GENITALS

Mutilation of females' genitals has been a common practice in many cultures since antiquity. The Greek geographer Agatharchides, for example, made note in the second century B.C. of the clitoral excision of Ethiopian women (Widstrand, 1964). In England and the United States, various forms of clitoral circumcision were used in the late nineteenth and early twentieth centuries as a medical treatment for ``frigidity,'' ``nymphomania,'' and masturbation.

Today, female genital mutilation is still performed in many parts of the world (see Figure 4-5). Some cultures practice *clitoridectomy*, removal of the clitoris, while others subject females to the more extreme *infibulation*, which involves cutting away the entire clitoris and labia minora and parts of the labia majora, and then sewing together (sometimes with thorns) the raw sides of the vulva except for a small opening for urine and menstrual flow (Giorgis, 1981). The procedure is usually done by an older village woman with an unsterilized knife and without anesthesia, requiring that the ``victim'' be tied or held down. It is usually done during early childhood, but in some cases, such as in Nigeria, it is performed just prior to marriage (Messenger, 1971). Many of the girls suffer hemorrhage or shock, and some die, and long-term effects include chronic uterine, vaginal, and pelvic infections, cysts, and abscesses (Abu-el-Futuh Shandall, 1967).

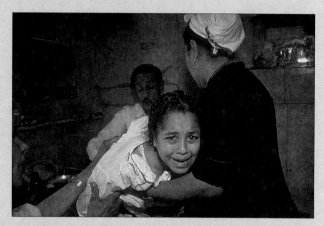

FIGURE 4-5   A GIRL IN CAIRO IS CIRCUMCISED (SIPA PRESS/CATHERINE LEROY)

Well over 80 million females presently living have been mutilated in this manner (Hosken, 1989). This includes nearly all women in Somalia, Ethiopia, Sudan, and Egypt, and about half the women in Kenya, with smaller numbers in other African countries (Lightfoot-Klein & Shaw, 1991). It is also common in several Middle Eastern countries and in parts of Indonesia, Malaysia, and the India-Pakistan subcontinent. Most of the cultures in which genital mutilation is practiced are Muslim, but it is also known to have been committed by Christians and some Ethiopian Jews.

Why are girls subjected to this mutilation? In the words of Ragiya Dualeh Abdalla, a Somali woman who denounced the practice in her 1982 book *Sisters of Affliction*:

> ``The various explanations and mystifications offered to justify the practice. . . . all emanate from men's motive to control women economically and sexually and as personal objects.''

There is no real comparison here to male circumcision, a practice that has little obvious effect on male sexuality. Genital mutilation substantially reduces sexual pleasure. Most genitally mutilated women do not enjoy sex, and for many sexual intercourse is painful (Abu-el-Futuh Shandall, 1967; Lightfoot-Klein, 1989). The men, for whom sexual pleasure is reserved exclusively, believe that the elimination of sexual desire in women ``frees them to fulfill their real destiny as mothers.''

A second, but related, reason is economic. The countries where genital mutilation is practiced are strongly patriarchal, and thus there is great concern in guaranteeing the inheritance of property from fathers to legitimate sons. Women are regarded as property and often sold in marriage. The sewing together of the vulva guarantees that a new wife is a virgin on the wedding night (the vulva is partially cut open by the male), and the elimination of sexual desire reduces infidelity, so that any offspring are almost assuredly the husband's. Infibulated women are fully cut open at childbirth, and then partially restitched afterwards.

In 1992, the World Health Organization unanimously approved tougher action to end the practice of female genital mutilation, as had the Organization of African Unity in 1990. The Egyptian government promised in 1994 that it would introduce a law to ban the practice. However, ancient customs are slow to change. Today, as populations emigrate, there is often a clash of cultural values. A Gambian woman living in France was sentenced to a year in prison in 1993 for hiring a woman to circumcise her two young girls. More and more, physicians in this country and in Europe are being asked to perform the mutilation (or the restitching after childbirth). This has posed an ethical dilemma for many physicians. However, in 1995, the American College of Obstetricians and Gynecologists officially opposed physicians in the United States performing these procedures. ∎

Ladas, Whipple, and Perry described three types of orgasm. In the *tenting type* described by Masters and Johnson (1966) and Helen Kaplan (1974), orgasm results from clitoral stimulation (which travels via the pudendal nerve) and is characterized by the buildup and discharge of myotonia in the orgasmic platform (which closes) and the pubococcygeus muscle. In the *A-frame type*, orgasm results from stimulation of the Grafenberg spot (which travels via the pelvic nerve) and is characterized by the uterus pushing down instead of elevating, no orgasmic platform, and the buildup and discharge of myotonia in the deeper vaginal muscles. G spot stimulation was often associated with the emission of fluid from the urethra at orgasm. A third type was described as *blended*. Remember, though, that some recent studies suggest that only 10 percent or less of women even have a distinct G spot (Alzate & Londono, 1984; Masters, Johnson, & Kolodny, 1992).

Ladas, Whipple, and Perry's classification is somewhat similar to the three types of female orgasm suggested earlier by Singer and Singer (1972). They distinguished between *vulval orgasms*, which are characterized by rhythmic contractions of the orgasmic platform (induced by direct clitoral stimulation or intercourse), and *uterine orgasms*, caused by repeated penis-cervix contact (deep stimulation) that displaces the uterus and stimulates the membrane lining of the abdominal wall. The latter type are characterized by gasping breathing and involuntary breath-holding, and, unlike the vulval type, are followed by a refractory period. A *blended type* was also noted. It has been found that orgasmic contraction of the pelvic muscles lasts less than a second, while a uterine contraction can last for as long as 30 seconds.

Is all this just a question of semantics, that is, peo-ple confusing the stimulus with the response? The most effective stimulus for erection in men is touching the glans of the penis (light pressure stimulates the pudendal nerve), but the orgasmic contractions come from the base of the penis and perineum (deep pressure stimulates the pelvic nerve). Yet no one argues whether there are glans or perineal orgasms in males. Instead, men are viewed as having a total-body orgasm, with different ranges of the same experience (some are mild and others intense). Although most women do not have a distinct G spot, for many the front wall of the vagina is a more sensitive area than other parts of the vagina (Darling, Davidson, & Conway-Welch, 1990) and may be "part and parcel of the female's clitoral/vaginal sensory arm of the orgasmic reflex" (Schultz et al., 1989).

So do women have different types of orgasms, or do they experience different ranges of one orgasm that has both clitoral and vaginal components? The circumstances and emotional climate can certainly affect the experience (e.g., masturbation versus having sex with a partner). As psychiatrist and sex therapist Helen Kaplan (who believes that there is just one type of orgasm) says: "You use the same muscles to eat a hamburger that you use to eat a dinner at Lutece, but the experiences are very different" (note: Lutece is a fancy, expensive restaurant; quoted by Gallagher, 1986). As for the opinion of the author of this text, a male, I prefer the view of William Masters, who said: "Physiologically, an orgasm is an orgasm, though there are degrees of intensity. But psychologically—don't ask me about women. I'm a man, and I know that I don't know" (Gallagher, 1986).

Even if it should be proven beyond doubt that there are two or more different types of female orgasm, there is one thing that all sex therapists agree on today—that one type should not be viewed as infantile, immature, or less important, and another type as mature, authentic, or more important. In short, a woman should not worry about what kind of orgasm she has. As Barbara Seaman (1972) writes, "The liberated orgasm is any orgasm a woman likes."

Do Women Ejaculate During Orgasm?

Adult males ejaculate during orgasm, but do women also ejaculate? Crude novelettes written for the purpose of arousing men often describe female orgasm as including "great gushes of fluid flowing down her thighs." References to female ejaculation have also appeared in better-known fictional novels (e.g., D. H. Lawrence's *Lady Chatterley's Lover*, 1930) and in marriage manuals (Van de Velde, 1930). Actually, the emission of a fluid by some women during orgasm was noted as early as 300 years ago by the Dutch embryologist Regnier de Graff, who described the fluid as coming from the small glands surrounding the urethral opening. This was confirmed in the modern scientific literature by Ernst Grafenberg (after whom the G spot was named) in 1950. The emission of fluid in some women was described as a dribble and in others as a gushing stream.

> "I have always achieved vaginal orgasms with fluid. The fluid is clear and white. It has no odor and is not unpleasant. I thought all women have this type of orgasm."

> "The first time I emitted a fluid, I thought I had urinated on myself and my boyfriend. I mean it was *all over*. My boyfriend kept looking at me real strange and I couldn't explain it. After the first time I kept making sure that I went to the bathroom before we had intercourse. When it happened after I knew I couldn't have that much fluid in my bladder. I got a little worried, but my boyfriend enjoyed watching me 'let loose' and got very excited."

(from the author's files)

Prior to the 1980s, women who emitted a fluid during orgasm were almost always told by physicians that they suffered from urinary incontinence, which is the inability to control urination during stress (which also happens to some women during a sneezing bout).

In 1981, however, three articles on female ejaculation appeared in *The Journal of Sex Research*, and this was followed in 1982 by a book about the Grafenberg spot and ejaculation (Ladas, Whipple, and Perry). They confirmed that the fluid was emitted not from the vagina, but from **Skene's glands** located in the urethra (Belzer, 1981; Perry and Whipple, 1981). These glands were thought to develop from the same embryological tissue as the male prostate (Heath, 1984; Sevely & Bennett, 1978), and the fluid, which was said to differ in color (clear to milky-white) and odor from urine, was found to contain prostatic acid phosphatase, an enzyme found in prostate secretions (Addiego et al., 1981). A few researchers have even begun to refer to the Skene's glands as the female prostate ("a small, functional organ that produces female prostatic secretion and possesses cells with neuroendocrine function, comparable to the male prostate"; Zaviacic & Whipple, 1993). Female ejaculation, it is claimed, is seen most often with stimulation of the Grafenberg spot and in women who have a strong pubococcygeus muscle (Perry & Whipple, 1981; Zaviacic et al., 1988). However, as yet there is no evidence of an anatomical link between the front wall of the vagina and the Skene's glands (Alzate & Hoch, 1986).

How many women emit a fluid (ejaculate) during orgasm? Perry and Whipple claimed in their initial article that "perhaps 10 percent of females" did so, but later claimed in their book that perhaps as many as 40 percent of females had experienced it, on occasion. More recent studies agree with this (Darling, Davidson, & Conway-Welch, 1990; Zaviacic et al., 1988). Masters and Johnson, on the other hand, found that only 14 of 300 women they surveyed had experienced emission of fluid at orgasm, but in those who did, the fluid was again found not to be urine (Masters, 1982). However, a later study (which included Beverly Whipple on the research team) of six female "ejaculators" found that the fluid emitted could not be distinguished from urine (Goldberg et al., 1983). It would appear, therefore, that while it can no longer be doubted that some women emit a fluid from the urethra during orgasm, there is some question as to the nature of the fluid. No doubt some women do suffer from stress-induced incontinence, but in others it may actually be a true ejaculation.

Can Men Have Multiple Orgasms?

Masters and Johnson originally took the position that only women could have true multiple orgasms—two or more orgasms within a short time without dropping below plateau. Whenever they recorded orgasm with ejaculation from men, it was always followed by a refractory period. Only when a man's level of arousal built back up to the plateau level could he have

Skene's glands

Glands located in the urethra of some women that are thought to develop from the same embryological tissue as the male prostate, and which may be the source of a fluid emitted by some women during orgasm.

another orgasm. However, two survey studies question whether there is a true gender difference in the ability to have multiple orgasms. The first study reported 13 men who said that they had multiple dry "mini-orgasms," by withholding ejaculation, before having a full wet orgasm (i.e., with ejaculation). The wet orgasm was always followed by a refractory period (Robbins & Jensen, 1978). In the second study, 21 men reported experiencing a variety of multiple orgasms (Dunn & Trost, 1989). Some had one or more "dry" orgasms before ejaculating, while others had an orgasm with ejaculation followed by one or more dry orgasms. As you have learned by now, scientists have always been the last ones to believe people's claims about experiencing different (from most others) types of orgasm. Until someone records rhythmic muscular contractions during multiple dry orgasms, that will probably be the case here as well. ■

PENIS SIZE: DOES IT MATTER?

In an article written for *Cosmopolitan* (1984), Michael Barson stated that, "for a man, the one emotion more disquieting than his own sense of not being big enough is the terror of finding himself in bed with a woman who shares his opinion." It should not be surprising that many men have anxieties about the size of their penis, for penis size has been a focus of attention throughout history. Priapus, the Greco-Roman god of procreation, was always displayed as having an enormous penis. Many writers have also described the penis in exaggerated terms. In the novel, *Justine*, by the Marquis de Sade, for example, the hero's penis was described as "of such length and exorbitant circumference that not only had I never clapped eyes upon anything comparable, but was absolutely convinced that nature had never fashioned another as prodigious; I could scarcely surround it with both hands, and its length matched that of my forearm." In D. H. Lawrence's *Lady Chatterley's Lover*, the gameskeeper's penis was even given its own name (John Henry). More recently, penis size has been emphasized in magazine centerfolds and erotic X-rated movies. Zilbergeld (1978), a noted sex therapist, has said that "it is not much of an exaggeration to say that penises in fantasyland come in only three sizes—large, gigantic, and so big you can barely get through the front door." All of this tends to leave the impression that penis size is related to virility, that is, the ability of a man to sexually please a woman, so that even men with a normal-sized penis may wish they were larger.

> " Penises come in a variety of shapes and sizes ... and about the only thing most penises have in common is that they are the wrong size or shape as far as their owners are concerned. In the many hours we have spent talking to men in and out of therapy, we have heard every conceivable complaint about penises. They are too small (the most common complaint), too large, too thin, too thick, stand up at too small (or great) an angle when erect, bend too much to the right, or left, or in the middle, or don't get hard enough when they are erect."
>
> (Zilbergeld, 1978)

> " I have an inferiority complex about my penis size. Even though my penis is larger than normal (about 7 inches). . . . No matter how many women tell me that my penis is large, I still have that complex."
>
> (from the author's files)

Breast size in women is relatively easy to assess, but for most heterosexual males the only opportunity to compare themselves to others is in the locker room, where they may get a false impression. The average size of a flaccid penis is about 3.5 to 3.75 inches in length and 1.0 to 1.2 inches in diameter. Researchers at the Kinsey Institute have found, however, that there is considerable more variation in penis size in the flaccid condition than in the erect state. Penises that appear small when flaccid display a proportionately greater increase in size upon erection than penises that appear large in the unaroused state (Jamison & Gebhard, 1988). Frequent intercourse does not cause a penis to get larger. Penis size is also not related to height, weight, or race (see Eldridge Cleaver's book *Soul on Ice* for a discussion of how the story that black men have larger penises got started).

This is not to say, however, that all penises are the same size when erect. The average size of an erect penis (measured along the bottom) is about 6 inches in length and 1.5 inches in diameter, with the vast majority of men measuring between 5 and 7 inches in length (Alfred C. Kinsey Institute). In Kinsey's research, the smallest erect penis measured was 1 inch long and the largest, 10 inches long (Pomeroy, 1972).

Today, some men are paying thousands of dollars each to have their penises made thicker by liposuction.

However, the American Society for Aesthetic Plastic Surgery has issued a statement warning that the safety of this procedure has not yet been established. Before any man considers having this operation, let us examine whether the size of a male's penis really is important in pleasing a woman during sexual intercourse.

In order to answer this, we must first reexamine some basic facts about female anatomy. A woman's vagina, you will recall, is neither a bottomless cavern nor an open hole always ready to accommodate a penis. In the unaroused state, the vagina measures 3 to 5 inches in length and its walls are collapsed. When a woman becomes sexually aroused, the walls of the inner two thirds of the vagina expand and its depth averages about 6 inches, which perhaps not coincidentally is the same length as the average penis (isn't nature wonderful?). In its capacity to physically stimulate the vagina, therefore, there is no real advantage to having a penis any longer than about 6 inches, for there is no place for it to go. And do not forget, the walls of the inner two thirds of the vagina are relatively sparse in nerve endings anyway. The tissues of the vaginal opening are highly sensitive to touch, but recall that the vaginal opening narrows when a women is highly sexually aroused, minimizing the importance of penis size. Most important, remember that the focus of physical sensations in most women is not the vagina, but the clitoris, which usually doesn't come into direct physical contact with the penis during intercourse. Thrusting of the penis only stimulates the clitoris indirectly by causing the clitoral hood to rub back and forth over the clitoral glans.

Do women consider the size of a penis important? In one study, it was found that the idea of a large penis was not even important for psychological arousal (Fisher, Branscombe, & Lemery, 1983). In another study, several hundred women were asked what was most important to them during sexual intercourse. Not one mentioned penis size (Zilbergeld, 1978). Some expressed a personal preference when questioned further

(e.g., circumcised or uncircumcised), but it was never a high priority. In surveys conducted in my class, only once has a woman expressed a preference for large penises.

> "I love men who have big dicks. They don't have to be hudge (sic) or anything, but I much prefer the larger size."
>
> (from the author's files)

For the large majority of women, penis size was not important. Here are some typical responses:

> "Penis size—of course it doesn't matter!"
>
> "And about penis size, we don't care!"
>
> "Also, penis size doesn't mean anything, especially to women."
>
> "It's not what you have that's so important, but how you use it."
>
> "It's not the size, but the performance that counts."
>
> "It is not the size of the ship that matters, but the motion of the ocean."
>
> (from the author's files)

In fact, *Forum* editor Philip Nobile found that most women preferred an average size penis. The women in these surveys were more concerned with their male partner taking his time and his total response to her during sexual intercourse. The quality of the entire sexual experience (not the length of the penis) was the important factor in sexual enjoyment and satisfaction. ∎

APHRODISIACS: DO THEY HELP?

People have searched for **aphrodisiacs**, substances that enhance sexual desire or prolong sexual performance (named after the Greek goddess of love, Aphrodite), for centuries. At one time or another, over 500 substances have been believed to be aphrodisiacs, including bull's testicles, powdered rhinoceros horns, elephant sperm, turtle eggs, ginseng roots, vitamin E, as well as common foods like bananas, potatoes, tomatoes, asparagus,

Aphrodisiacs
Substances that enhance sexual desire or performance.

garlic, and radishes (Stark, 1982). Many people like to believe that oysters are an aphrodisiac, but the fact is that none of these has any physiological effect on sexual responsivity. Any temporary improvement in sexual functioning is purely a psychological effect (believing that it will work can be arousing), but the effect will wear off shortly.

Spanish fly (*cantharides*), made from powdered beetles that are found in Spain, is perhaps the most famous reputed aphrodisiac. Taken orally, the active substance causes inflammation and irritation of the urinary and genital tracts, which some may interpret as lust. In males, Spanish fly can cause a painful, persistent erection (priapism), even when there is no desire for sex. This is a dangerous drug, a poison, which can result in abdominal and urinary tract ulcers, diarrhea, severe pain, and even death.

Alcohol is commonly believed to enhance sexual desire and responsivity. One of its initial effects is dilation of blood vessels in the skin, which gives us a feeling of warmth and well-being. A drink or two depresses certain areas of your brain, making you less inhibited about engaging in sex (and other behaviors that you might not ordinarily do; Crowe & George, 1989). The loss of inhibitions can even result in a person engaging in sexual behaviors that are at high risk for contracting HIV (the virus that causes AIDS) and other sexually transmitted diseases (Buffum, 1988). In addition, alcohol is often used as an excuse by people who have high levels of guilt about engaging in sex (Lang et al., 1980). Although alcohol may make a person less inhibited about engaging in sex, any more than a single drink can impair the nervous system responses needed to engage in sex. As stated by Shakespeare in *Macbeth*, "it provokes the desire, but it takes away from the performance." Alcohol, in fact, is an **anaphrodisiac**, a suppressant of sexual functioning. In even moderate amounts it can cause erectile problems in men (Farkas & Rosen, 1976; Rosen, 1991) and difficulty in reaching orgasm in both sexes (Malatesta, 1979, 1982; Rosen, 1991). Chronic alcoholics almost always have sexual problems (Rosen, 1991).

Anaphrodisiac
Substances that suppress sexual functioning.

Some illegal drugs also have reputations as sexual stimulants. Cocaine is a central nervous system stimulant, and thus may give the user a temporary burst of energy and feeling of self-confidence, but the drug's effects are often equally due to heightened expectations and the social situation in which it is used (i.e., like alcohol, drugs give people an excuse that they can use afterwards for having sex). The use of cocaine, however, can often result in erectile failures and difficulties reaching orgasm (Cocores, Dackis, & Gold, 1986). Heavy, chronic use of cocaine generally leads to nearly total sexual dysfunction—impotency and inability to reach orgasm—although abusers may still try to engage in sex compulsively (Washton, 1989). Some people have tried rubbing cocaine on the clitoris to increase female responsivity, but cocaine is in fact a topical anesthetic (i.e., it deadens nerve endings). A few men have suffered permanent nerve and tissue damage, requiring amputation, as a result of injecting cocaine directly into their penis (*New York Times*, 1988).

Amphetamines ("speed" or "uppers") in low doses can also give the user a burst of energy (sometimes used for marathon sexual encounters), but decrease sexual functioning in higher doses (Buffom et al., 1981) and can result in severe paranoia if used chronically. Amyl nitrate ("poppers" or "snappers"), which is used medically for treatment of coronary disease (it dilates blood vessels), is inhaled just prior to orgasm by some people in order to intensify the sensations (Cohen, 1979). This can be especially dangerous for people with heart or blood pressure problems. In order to intensify orgasm during masturbation, some people have attempted to cut off their oxygen supply (anoxia) by hanging, a practice which has resulted in several deaths.

Most marijuana users report that the drug improves sexual pleasure (Goode, 1972; Kolodny, Masters, & Johnson, 1979). It does not increase desire or arousal, or intensify orgasms, but it enhances relaxation, thus allowing increased awareness of touch. Men who use marijuana chronically, however, may experience erectile problems, lowered testosterone levels, and decreased sperm production (Kolodny, 1981; Kolodny et al., 1974).

Among young people, a drug known as "Ecstasy" (3, 4-methylenedioxymethaphetamine, or MDMA) has become popular as an aphrodisiac. Proponents claim that it enhances a user's sense of well-being and empathy without the visual distortions of other hallucinogens. MDMA was originally a "designer drug," designed to be very similar to banned drugs, but just different enough in structure to escape the law. However, it too is now outlawed. Research has shown that it causes permanent brain damage and some users have experienced psychotic episodes. What's more, designer drugs are manufactured in clandestine labs without stringent quality control, and sometimes just a small unintended alteration in the chemical structure has devastating effects. A botched batch of designer drugs in the early 1980s, for example, caused permanent Parkinson's disease in numerous young people in California.

Most recently, studies have focused on pharmacological agents that affect central nervous system neurotransmitters—the chemical substances that allow brain cells to "talk" to one another (Rosen & Ashton, 1993). Of these, *yohimbine hydrochloride*, a substance derived from the sap of an African tree, has received the most attention because of a report that it caused intense sexual arousal in male rats (Clark, Smith, & Davidson, 1984). Although initial studies suggested that it might also have a positive effect on sexual desire in humans, a recent review of the work found that over half of people tested showed no response (Rosen, 1991). There is some evidence, however, that yohimbine is of some help in men with psychologically caused impotence (see Segraves, 1991).

Another psychopharmacological agent that might affect sexual responses is oxytocin, a pituitary hormone that promotes ejection of milk. It was recently reported that a woman who was prescribed this hormone as a nasal spray experienced intense sexual desire afterwards (Anderson-Hunt & Dennerstein, 1994), but it is too early to make general conclusions from a single case study.

Despite the lack of scientific evidence for most chemicals tried as aphrodisiacs, some people will probably continue to search for a problem-free drug that enhances sexual performance. Their efforts would probably be better rewarded if they instead took the time to learn how to communicate and be intimate with their partners. We will discuss how to do this in later chapters. ■

AND AFTERWARDS?

You have just read Masters and Johnson's description of the sexual response cycle as ending with orgasm and the physiological responses returning to normal, but an individual does not have to stop paying attention to his or her partner as soon as he or she reaches orgasm (e.g., by rolling over and going to sleep or lighting up a cigarette). This is one of the things that distinguishes human beings from other species. It is a rare couple who can experience simultaneous orgasms on any more than an occasional basis, which means that most of the time, someone will get there first. If it is the male, this will often mean loss of erection. Stimulation of one's partner, however, is not totally dependent on the functioning of the genitals. Sexual intimacy is a whole-body response, involving lips, tongue, hands, and emotional responsivity. Even if your partner has reached orgasm, the time afterwards can be a period of mutual touching, hugging, and emotional intimacy. When Ann Landers asked her female readers in 1985 if they would forego "the act" if they could be held closely, 100,000 women responded and 72,000 of them said yes. Touching is necessary for a baby's emotional well-being, and we do not lose that need as we grow older. Sexual intimacy is more than genital thrusting and orgasm. It is having someone to touch and to touch you. It is a sense of closeness, a sense of partnership. This next section is a good example of that. ■

SEXUALITY AND THE HANDICAPPED

Is sexual pleasure reserved only for the young and beautiful? Judging by the number of jokes about sexual behavior of elderly, obese, and other people whom our society often labels as "unattractive," many people apparently think so. These negative attitudes are often extreme in the case of the handicapped. What about people who are blind, deaf, spinal cord-damaged, or suffer from other physical disabilities? What about the mentally retarded? Do these groups of people have sexual desires and feeling? If so, should they be allowed to express those desires?

In this chapter you have learned about the effects of one kind of physical disability on sexual functioning (i.e., the effects of spinal cord damage on the ability to achieve erection and/or orgasm). However, as difficult as a handicapped person's disabilities may make it to physically engage in sex, a greater barrier to most handicapped individuals having a sexual relationship is society's attitude about them. For example, I recently received the following note from a spinal-damaged student:

"Recently my boyfriend's mother wanted him to explain to me that she wants

grandchildren. I guess she assumed that because I'm in a wheelchair that I'm incapable of having children. Her ignorance amazed me. People who are in wheelchairs, whether they be paraplegics or quadriplegics, are no less sexually able. Sexuality is basically psychological, in terms of its influence upon a person's overall behavior. Thus, the fact that one is paralyzed from the neck down or from the hips down doesn't discount from one's sexual drive or fertility."

(from the author's files)

Many people treat physically and mentally handicapped adults as if they are asexual or childlike and think it ridiculous that these groups should even have any interest in sex (Asch & Rousso, 1985). Parents of handicapped children sometimes try to protect them by withholding sexual information, while friends and acquaintances of handicapped adults oftentimes try to protect them by never discussing the subject in their presence. Even the medical profession, which has perfected many ways to assure the reproductive capabilities of disabled persons, has only recently begun to realize the importance of patient and staff sexual education and counseling to deal with the emotional, self-esteem, and social issues that may impair sexual functioning (Alexander et al., 1993; Rieve, 1989).

The well-intended, but incorrect, assumptions of those who would protect the handicapped by denying their sexuality is that they believe the handicapped have more important things to worry about. In the case of spinal cord-damaged people, for example, who generally have no genital sensations, it is often assumed that they would (or should) not be interested in sex, but instead should be most concerned about physically rehabilitating the functional parts of their bodies.

Are sexual relations really so unimportant that they should be given such a low priority? To answer this, we must first ask why it is that people engage in sex. Is it possible for a person to enjoy sexual relations even if he or she cannot have sexual intercourse? Is sexual pleasure restricted to genital sensations (e.g., is a man's sexuality focused exclusively in his penis)? There are many reasons that people engage in sexual relations besides the physical pleasure of genital sensations. Sexual relations are important to many people for the shared intimacy. Recall that paralyzed individ-

uals often become highly sensitive to touch in their functional body parts, but equally important to the physical intimacy is the opportunity for emotional intimacy provided by the closeness of sexual relations. Hugging, holding, kissing, and shared affections are as important in sexual relations as intercourse for many people. Physical closeness can also be very psychologically exciting (see Figure 4-6). Here is part of a letter from the husband of a woman who had undergone three years of surgeries and rehabilitation for severe spinal cord damage suffered in an automobile accident:

"In July 'Susan' felt well enough to try once more. Sex was very good that day . . . we took it slow and easy. . . . We compensated with lots of holding and touching, something that often had been lacking in our pre-accident relationship. Incredibly, just holding each other in bed became very satisfying, and it actually seemed to bring us closer together emotionally."

(from the author's files)

FIGURE 4-6   WE ARE ALL SEXUAL BEINGS.

People with spinal cord damage often show a decrease in sexual desire and satisfaction after the injury, but the sexual desire of the partner can help overcome this. Spinal cord-injured individuals may show a decrease in sexual intercourse, but often compensate with other sexual activities (Alexander et al., 1993). There are, in fact, many ways to enjoy sexual relations besides intercourse.

Different handicaps present different problems in one's ability to have sexual relations, but none of the physical problems are as great an obstacle to healthy sexuality as society's attitude about handicapped people. Remember, regardless of what we look like or our physical or mental capabilities, we are all sexual beings. (See Chipouras et al., 1979, for a sexual bill of rights for disabled people. A list of resources on sex and disability may be found in *SIECUS Report,* 14 March, 1986.)

KEY TERMS

anaphrodisiac   81

aphrodisiac   80

clitoridectomy   76

desire   67

ejaculation   72

erection process   69

excitement   69

Grafenberg (G) spot   35, 75

infibulation   76

Helen Kaplan   67

Masters and Johnson   16, 67

multiple orgasm   73

myotonia   69

orgasm   71

orgasmic platform   71

plateau   70

refractory period   73

resolution   73

retrograde ejaculation   72

semen   43, 72

sex-tension flush   71

sexual response cycle   67

Skene's glands   78

vaginal lubrication process   70

vasocongestion   69

PERSONAL REFLECTIONS

1 Do you think it is important that we know the physiological responses that normally occur during sexual arousal? Is it important that physicians and therapists have this information? What do you think about studies, such as those by Masters and Johnson, that require observing and recording individuals engaged in sex? If your opinion is negative, how else could we learn about the normal physiological responses during sexual arousal?

2. List the physiological responses that you experience during sexual arousal (e.g., vaginal lubrication, nipple erection, Cowper's glands secretion, sex-tension flush, etc.). How do you feel about your responses? Are you comfortable with them or do some cause you anxiety? Why? What about your partner's responses?

3. Do you know what factors influence your continued arousal as you go through the excitement, plateau, and orgasm phases of the sexual response cycle? Do you know what will give you the most pleasure (what kinds of stimulation)? Do you know what pleases your partner most? Is it assumption or fact? Have you talked with your partner about how best to please each other? If not, why not?

4. Do you judge your sexual experiences by your ability to reach, or your frequency of, orgasm? Your partner's orgasm? Why? Many women do not experience orgasm during intercourse. How do you think they feel about it? How would you feel if it were you? Is it necessary to have an orgasm to enjoy sex?

5. Do you wish you had different sized/shaped breasts or a different penis? How would you like to be different? Why? How important is the size of a person's penis or breasts in sexually pleasing a partner compared to a person's mind (his or her attitude about sex)?

6. We do not mutilate women's genitals in this country to deny them their sexuality. Do we deny women's sexuality in other ways? How?

7. If you were to have an accident and become physically handicapped, do you think you would still want to hug, hold, kiss, and share affections (and have sex, if possible) with your partner? How do you presently react when you see a handicapped person engaging in these behaviors?

SUGGESTED READINGS

Gallagher, W. (1986, February). The etiology of orgasm. *Discover.*

Konner, M. (1988, March/April). Is orgasm essential? *The Sciences.*

Lightfoot-Klein, H. (1989). *Prisoners of ritual: An odyssey into female genital circumcision in Africa.* Binghamton, NY: Haworth Press.

Masters, W., & Johnson, V. (1966) *Human sexual response.* Boston: Little, Brown. The classic work.

Raphael, B. J. (1974, January). The myth of the male orgasm. *Psychology Today.* (Originally printed in the *Village Voice.*) A satire on male attitudes about female orgasm.

White, D. (1981, September). Pursuit of the ultimate aphrodisiac. *Psychology Today.* Reviews the scientific evidence.

CHAPTER FIVE

SEXUALLY TRANSMITTED AND SEXUALLY RELATED DISEASES

WHEN YOU HAVE FINISHED STUDYING THIS CHAPTER, YOU SHOULD BE ABLE TO:

1. EXPLAIN WHAT CAUSES SEXUALLY TRANSMITTED DISEASES, HOW THEY ARE SPREAD, AND WHO CAN GET THEM;

2. DESCRIBE THE SYMPTOMS FOR GONORRHEA, CHLAMYDIA, SYPHILIS, CHANCROID, HERPES, HEPATITIS, VENEREAL WARTS, AIDS, TRICHOMONIASIS, PUBIC LICE, AND SCABIES;

3. UNDERSTAND THAT FOR MANY STDs IT IS POSSIBLE TO BE INFECTED AND HAVE NO SYMPTOMS (FOR PARTICULAR STDs, NAME WHICH GENDER IS MORE LIKELY TO BE ASYMPTOMATIC, AND AT WHAT STAGE);

4. DESCRIBE THE METHOD OF DIAGNOSIS AND TREATMENT FOR EACH STD;

5. SUMMARIZE THE COMPLICATIONS THAT CAN OCCUR IF STDs ARE NOT TREATED EARLY;

6. DISCUSS THE POSSIBLE EFFECTS ON THE FETUS AND NEWBORN IF A PREGNANT WOMAN HAS VARIOUS STDs;

7. DESCRIBE THE THREE TYPES OF VAGINITIS AND DISCUSS VAGINAL HEALTH CARE; AND

8. DISCUSS SAFER SEX PRACTICES.

SEXUALLY TRANSMITTED DISEASES (STDs) ARE PRESENTLY AT EPIDEMIC PROPORTIONS. IN FACT, *for all Americans presently between the ages of 15 and 55, one in four will have at least one sexually transmitted disease sometime in their life* (Centers for Disease Control and Prevention). It is to everyone's advantage, therefore, that we educate ourselves about the causes, symptoms, modes of transmission, and treatments for these diseases. If left untreated, some of these diseases can cause sterility, blindness, and even death, not to mention ruined relationships. ∎

WHO GETS THEM AND WHAT ARE THEY?

Some people believe that sexually transmitted diseases are punishment for having sinful or immoral sex and that only promiscuous persons get STDs. They talk as if they believe that sexual behavior causes the diseases. These beliefs are not only incorrect, but they can be cruel, for tens of thousands of loyal and faithful men and women have caught these diseases from unfaithful partners; and a similar number of innocent newborn children have contracted them from infected mothers.

"I got gonorrhea from my boyfriend. I, myself, thought that I was engaged in a monogamous relationship. However, it was not monogamous for him. . . .''

''. . . I had never had sex with anyone else before I got married. Well, I was married 5 years and had never cheated. I came down with genital herpes. . . .''

"Over the past two years, I have had one steady boyfriend. I have never slept around and I thought he was faithful to me. I would have put my life on the line to prove this. During these two years I have contracted chlamydia three times, PID, and trichomonas. . . .''

"My first time having sex was at 16. My only fear was getting pregnant. My boy friend said he was infertile so I couldn't get pregnant. We had sex. Approximately one month later I found out I had gonorrhea. I had no idea I could be a victim of an STD.''

"I am a 48-year-old woman who contracted a sexually transmitted disease from my husband. As a result, I had to have a total hysterectomy. . . .''

(from the author's files)

These people were not promiscuous, yet they still became infected with a sexually transmitted disease. What causes STDs? It is not sexual behavior per se that causes STDs; the behavior is merely the mode of transmission for bacteria, viruses, or parasites that must be present for the diseases to be transmitted. *Sexually transmitted diseases are spread, for the most part, by sexual contact* (including vaginal and anal intercourse and oral-genital contact) *with someone who has the bacteria, viruses, or parasites that cause the diseases.*

Bacteria are very small single-celled organisms. They lack a nuclear membrane but have all the genetic material (RNA and DNA) and metabolic machinery to reproduce themselves. **Viruses** are just a protein shell around a nucleic acid core. They have RNA or DNA, but not both, and thus cannot reproduce themselves. They invade host cells that provide the material to manufacture new virus particles. The bacteria and viruses responsible for STDs have been reported to live outside the body

Bacteria

Small, single-celled organisms that lack a nuclear membrane, but have all the genetic material (RNA and DNA) to reproduce themselves.

Virus

A protein shell around a nucleic acid core. They have RNA or DNA, but not both, and thus cannot reproduce themselves. They invade host cells that provide the material to manufacture new virus particles.

TABLE 5-1
STDs IN THE UNITED STATES

TYPE OF SEXUALLY TRANSMITTED DISEASE	ESTIMATED NEW CASES PER YEAR IN THE U.S. (1995)
Chlamydia	4,000,000
Trichomoniasis	3,000,000+
Gonorrhea	800,000
Human Papillomavirus Infection	500,000–1,000,000
Genital Herpes	200,000–500,000
Syphilis	113,000
Hepatitis B (sexually transmitted)	50,000–100,000
AIDS	85,000
HIV infection	?

Source: Centers for Disease Control and Prevention and studies cited in text.

for only a short period of time. The common belief that you can catch these diseases from a toilet seat is greatly exaggerated, although it might be possible to expose yourself to the bacteria or virus by using a damp towel soon after someone with a disease uses it (and in this case, you are more likely to spread it to your eyes than to your genitals).

Some people believe (or at least would like to believe) that sexually transmitted diseases occur only in, or primarily in, the poor, uneducated, or minority groups. Sexually transmitted diseases, however, are nondiscriminating. The bacteria or viruses that cause these disease do not care if you are white, black, yellow, or brown, or if you are on welfare or a millionaire, bathe every day or only once a week, or if you are a grade school dropout or college-educated. In fact, at least one of these diseases (chlamydia) is at epidemic proportions among college students today. The point (here and in the previous case histories) is that anyone having sex is at some risk for contracting a sexually transmitted disease.

Some of these diseases were once called **venereal diseases**

Venereal diseases

Term originally used to refer to gonorrhea, syphilis, and three other diseases that are spread almost exclusively by sexual contact.

(after the Roman goddess of love, Venus), but these generally included diseases that are spread almost exclusively by sexual contact (gonorrhea, syphilis, and three other lesser known diseases). Today, the description **sexually transmitted diseases** is generally preferred and refers to these and other infectious diseases which can be, but are not always, transmitted by sexual contact.

There are still other diseases of the sexual organs that are caused by overgrowths of yeast or fungal organisms found naturally in the body, and these too can sometimes be passed on during sex. I will refer to these as **sexually related diseases**. A few other sexually transmitted diseases are not really diseases at all, but rather infestations of parasites (pubic lice and scabies) that are transmitted from person to person during sexual contact. ■

Sexually transmitted diseases

Term used to refer to diseases that can be, but are not necessarily always, transmitted by sexual contact. This term is generally preferred to the term "venereal diseases."

Sexually related diseases

A disease of the reproductive system or genitals that is not contracted through sexual activity. Often refers to overgrowths of bacteria, yeasts, viruses, or fungal organisms that are found naturally in sexual or reproductive organs.

WHERE DID THEY COME FROM?

Some people argue that humans first contracted sexually transmitted disease by having sex with animals, but no animal species is known to have gonorrhea or syphilis. It is more likely that previously harmless bacteria or viruses mutated (they are highly susceptible to change) into the strains causing disease. Although where and how STDs originated remains questionable, some of these sexually transmitted diseases have been around for at least a few thousand years, as many famous Greeks, Romans, and Egyptians (including Cleopatra) were described as having the symptoms. In fact, public kissing was banned for a period in Roman times because of an epidemic of a disease that was described as being identical to what we now know as herpes. An epidemic of syphilis also swept through Europe in the early 1500s, and it is still hotly debated whether Columbus and his sailors brought it back from the New World, or vice versa (e.g., Luger, 1993; Rosebury, 1971). In fact, Columbus died of advanced syphilis.

The fact is that it does not really matter where or how STDs originated; they are here to stay and we must deal with them. In our own country, there have been major outbreaks of STDs from time to time, most recently after World War I and again after the war in

Vietnam. The present epidemic situation can probably be attributed to several factors:

1. the discovery of penicillin and other antibiotics (about the time of WWII) made people less fearful about contracting an STD;
2. a large drop between the end of World War II and 1955 in the amount of federal funds available for STD prevention (due possibly because of an overconfidence in antibiotics);
3. the new sexual freedom that many people believed to be possible as a result of the birth control pill and other reliable means of birth control;
4. the shift from use of the condom as a means of birth control, which is also highly effective in preventing the spread of STDs, to use of the birth control pill; and
5. lack of education or just plain ignorance.

Surveys of teenagers indicate that many know very little about sexually transmitted diseases, although they believe themselves to be well informed (National Adolescent Student Health Survey, 1989).

Many people are unaware, for example, that they can have an STD but show no symptoms and still be contagious. As a result, they do not seek treatment as early as they should. I will discuss some precautionary measures to help avoid contracting sexually transmitted diseases, and what to do in case you should get one. First, let us examine the symptoms and treatment for some of the most widely known diseases. ■

GONORRHEA

Gonorrhea (from the Greek *gonos* for "seed" and *rhoia* for "flow," but also known as "the clap" or "the drip") is probably the oldest of the STDs. Its symptoms are described in Leviticus in the Old Testament, which dates back to about 1500 B.C., and were also described in detail by Greek physicians. The number of cases of gonorrhea declined in most industrialized countries in the 1980s, but the Centers for Disease Control and Prevention estimate that there are still 800,000 new cases a year in the United States. Here, the rate of infection is considerably higher among African-Americans than it is among Hispanics or whites (Coutinho, 1994).

> **Gonorrhea**
> A sexually transmitted disease caused by the *Neisseria gonorrhoeae* bacterium (often referred to as the gonococcus), which lives on mucous membranes.

SYMPTOMS AND COMPLICATIONS

Gonorrhea is caused by a bacterium (*Neisseria gonorrhoeae*, often referred to as the gonococcus) that is named after Albert Neisser, who discovered it in 1879. It lives on warm, moist mucous membranes (located in the urethra, vagina, rectum, mouth and throat, and eyes). A person gets gonorrhea by his or her mucous membranes coming into contact with another person's infected membranes. Because of the location of these membranes in the body, this normally occurs only during intimate contact. However, your chances of catching it from having vaginal intercourse once with an infected person are not 100 percent. A man's risk of infection during intercourse with an infected woman is about 30 to 50 percent, while a woman has about a 50 to 60 percent chance of catching it the first time she has intercourse with an infected man (Platt et al., 1983; Rein, 1977). The gonococcus can also infect the anus and rectum (during anal intercourse) and the throat (during

oral-genital sex, particularly fellatio), but less is known about the relative risk by these means of transmission. The gonococcus has been found to survive for a short time outside the body. Although there was a reported case of infants in a nursery being infected with gonorrhea from a contaminated fever thermometer, your chances of getting it from nonsexual contact, particularly a dry toilet seat, are extremely remote.

In males who become infected during intercourse, the gonococcus bacteria invade and cause inflammation of the urethra (*gonococcal urethritis*). This usually results in a thick pus-like, white or yellowish discharge from the urethra ("drip"), starting 2 to 10 days after infection (see Figure 5-1). There is generally an irritation or burning sensation at the urethral opening, and urination is often frequent and painful. Because the symptoms are painful and obvious, most men seek treatment immediately. However, *about 5 to 20 percent of men show no symptoms* (asymptomatic), while in others the early symptoms disappear. These asymptomatic males are still infected and can pass the gonococcus to new partners. If left untreated, it spreads up the male's

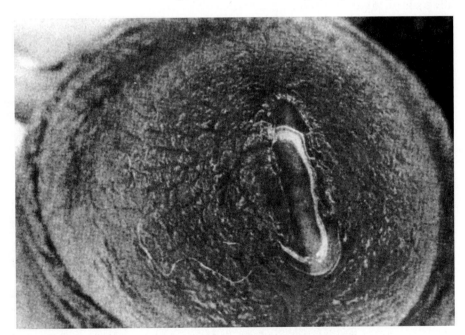

FIGURE 5-1   THE PUS-LIKE DISCHARGE FROM THE PENIS CAUSED BY GONORRHEA.

reproductive system and causes inflammation of the prostate, seminal vesicles, bladder, and epididymis. By this time the male usually experiences severe pain and fever. If still left untreated, the resulting scar tissue can cause sterility. In rare cases, it may get into the bloodstream and cause inflammation of the joints (*gonococcal arthritis*), heart, or brain covering, or it may be transmitted to the eyes by a contaminated hand. It rarely, however, results in death.

In females, the gonococcus initially invades the cervix, but unlike males, *most women show no symptoms during the early stages.* They are often unaware of their infection unless told by an infected male partner, and thus can unknowingly pass gonorrhea on to new partners. In the 20 to 40 percent of women who show symptoms, there may be an abnormal vaginal discharge and irritation of the vulva and urethra, causing burning during urination. Because so many women are asymptomatic, they often go untreated, and the gonococcus spreads through the uterus into the Fallopian tubes. In up to 40 percent of untreated women, the tubes become swollen and inflamed, a condition known as **pelvic inflammatory disease (PID)**, with symptoms of severe abdominal pain and fever (see later section). Hospitalization may be necessary at this stage. PID can cause scarring of the Fallopian tubes, blocking passage of the sperm and egg, a common cause of sterility and tubal pregnancies in women (see Chapter 7).

Pelvic inflammatory disease or PID

A bacterially caused inflammation of a female's reproductive tract, particularly the Fallopian tubes, that can result in sterility. The most common (though not the only) cause is untreated gonorrhea and/or chlamydia.

If a pregnant woman contracts gonorrhea, the fetus will not be affected because the gonococcus normally is not carried in the bloodstream. However, a baby's eyes can become infected at delivery as it passes through the infected cervix and vagina (a condition called *gonococcal opthalmia neonatorum*; see Figure 5-2). This can rapidly lead to blindness. In some developing countries, 3–15 percent of babies are at risk, but the rate for gonorrhea in pregnant women in the United States is less than 1 percent, and most states require that an antibiotic or silver nitrate drops be put into all babies' eyes at birth to prevent possible infections (Laga, Meheus, & Piot, 1989).

DIAGNOSIS AND TREATMENT

Most individuals with symptoms will seek treatment immediately. Remember, however, that many people (particularly females) have no early symptoms. Therefore, if you suspect that you have had sex with someone who has gonorrhea, see a doctor as soon as possible. Males who have a urethral discharge may be diagnosed quickly by an examination of the pus under a microscope. This is not 100 percent accurate, however, and the only sure way is to have a culture test. This is almost always done in women with suspected gonorrhea. A cotton swab is inserted into the area of suspected infection (about one-half inch up the urethra in males, into the cervix in females, or in the throat or rectum of either sex) and the cells are then grown in culture for a couple of days and tested.

FIGURE 5-2   EYE INFECTIONS CAUSED BY GONORRHEA (LEFT) AND HERPES (RIGHT).

There is no blood test for gonorrhea, because the gonococcus ordinarily does not invade the bloodstream.

There was little that could be done for people with gonorrhea prior to the discovery of antibiotics. The urethral inflammation caused by gonorrhea often caused blockage in men, and because the male's urethra also serves as the passageway for urine it was often necessary to clean it out with a "pipe cleaner." Fortunately, penicillin was discovered about the time of World War II and proved to be highly effective. Unfortunately, the bacterium developed resistance to penicillin over time. A dosage of 150,000 units was given to people for gonorrhea in the 1940s, but by the 1980s the standard dosage was nearly 5 million units, and there were some strains that could not be destroyed with any dose (*penicillinase Neisseria gonorrhoeae*). There were only about 8,000 reported cases of penicillin-resistant gonorrhea in 1985, but the number of cases had increased to 56,616 in 1989. Many physicians had switched to tetracycline in the early

1980s, but by the end of the decade the bacterium was becoming resistant to it as well (Plasma-mediated, 1990). To complicate matters, many people who are diagnosed with gonorrhea are also found to have another sexually transmitted disease called chlamydia, which is treated with tetracycline or an erythromycin. To combat these multiple problems, most physicians today treat gonorrhea with a drug called ceftriaxone (which is presently effective against all strains) followed by a week of tetracycline or an erythromycin (Handsfield, 1990; Moran & Zenilman, 1990; Schwarcz et al., 1990). In the future, it may be possible to combat the spread of gonorrhea by vaccinating people (Sparling et al., 1994).

Should you ever be diagnosed with gonorrhea, be sure to tell all your recent partners that they may have gonorrhea so that they, too, can be treated. Gonorrhea is not like chicken pox, where you become immune after having had the disease. You can catch gonorrhea again if you again have sex with someone infected with the gonococcus. ∎

CHLAMYDIA AND NONGONOCOCCAL URETHRITIS

Any inflammation of the urethra not caused by the gonococcus is called **nongonococcal** (or **nonspecific**) **urethritis** (**NGU**). This term is often reserved for men with an inflamed urethra, but the organisms that cause it cause infection in women (**cervicitis**) as well. There are several organisms that can cause infection (including *Ureaplasma urealyticum* and *Trichomonas vaginalis*), but the one that is most frequently responsible today is *Chlamydia trachomatis*. The infection caused by this sexually transmitted bacterium is called **chlamydia**.

> **Nongonococcal (nonspecific) urethritis or NGU**
> Refers to any inflammation of the urethra that is not caused by the *Neisseria gonorrhoeae* (gonococcus) bacterium.

> **Chlamydia**
> A sexually transmitted disease caused by the *Chlamydia trachomatis* bacterium, which lives on mucous membranes.

In most states physicians are not legally required to report patients that they treat for chlamydia, but it is certainly more common than gonorrhea, with an estimated 4 million new cases in the United States this year (Centers for Disease Control and Prevention). Chlamydia is especially prevalent in teenagers and young adults and is more common among whites than African-Americans (Zimmerman et al., 1990). In one study, 8 percent of college women who came into the college health service for a routine gynecological exam were found to have chlamydia (Swinker, 1986). Another study found that 5.7 percent of sexually active college women had chlamydia (Malotte et al., 1990).

Yet another study found that one third of college students coming into the health clinic for genital problems had chlamydia (Samuels, 1989).

Because many students have never heard of chlamydia, they think that it cannot be all that bad. In fact, although its initial symptoms are usually milder than those of gonorrhea, if left untreated it is more likely than gonorrhea to cause damage to the reproductive organs.

SYMPTOMS AND COMPLICATIONS

Like the gonococcus, Chlamydia trachomatis lives only on mucous membranes. Chlamydia is spread when infected membranes of one person come into contact with membranes of another person.

If a person with chlamydia shows early symptoms, he or she will start doing so within 1 to 3 weeks after infection. The early symptoms are milder than but similar to, and sometimes mistaken for, those of gonorrhea: irritation and burning of the urethra (but usually not painful) and a discharge (usually thin and clear rather than puslike). However, most women and a large proportion of men have no symptoms at all in the initial stage.

> "I found out that I had chlamydia when my girlfriend handed me a bottle of pills and told me to follow the instructions. I didn't even know what chlamydia was. . . . I had no idea I had an STD. . . ."

"When I was attending LSU, I went to see the doctor for a regular gynecological exam. The nurse suggested that I consider some other tests for STDs because some of them had few or no symptoms. At first I declined, thinking that I had not slept with many people and, also, that if I had anything I would surely know from symptoms. But I changed my mind and was tested. When I called for results, I was shocked to find out that I was positive for chlamydia."

(from the author's files)

If left untreated, the infection spreads through the reproductive system, which can cause infection of the prostate and epididymis in men, and possible sterility (Greendale et al., 1993), and **pelvic inflammatory disease** resulting in scarred Fallopian tubes with consequent sterility or increased risk of tubal pregnancy in women (Brunham et al., 1988; Sherman et al., 1990). At this stage the infection can be quite painful and require hospitalization. Research has shown that *a single attack of chlamydia is about three times more likely than gonorrhea to cause sterility in women.* Babies born to women who have chlamydia at the time of delivery can get eye infections (*chlamydia conjunctivitis*) and/or nose-throat infections, or even pneumonia (an estimated 182,000 cases per year; Schacter et al., 1986). There is an increased risk of stillbirths, premature deliveries, and death as well. In underdeveloped countries, the chlamydia bacteria often cause an eye infection called *trachoma*, which is spread to other people's eyes by flies. It is the leading cause of blindness in those areas. In tropical countries, chlamydia is also responsible for a serious sexually transmitted disease called

lymphogranuloma venereum (LGV) (there are fewer than 400 cases annually in the United States). If left untreated, LGV causes the inguinal lymph nodes to swell, followed by swelling of the penis, labia, or clitoris (some-times enormously so, resulting in elephantiasis of the external genitalia).

Lymphogranuloma venereum or LGV

A sexually transmitted disease that is common in tropical countries and which is caused by chlamydia. If left untreated, it causes swelling of the inguinal lymph nodes, penis, labia, or clitoris.

DIAGNOSIS AND TREATMENT

Until recently, the only way to diagnose chlamydia was with culture tests that were expensive and technically demanding, sometimes taking up to a week to complete. In the 1990s, several nonculture tests (that detect chlamydial antigens or nucleic acids) became available that could give results in a matter of minutes. However, studies have found that these tests are not as sensitive as the culture tests, and thus often "miss" people who really have chlamydia (Lin et al., 1992; Schachter et al., 1992). The Food and Drug Administration approved a urine test for males in 1993, and although they have not yet approved a urine test for females, recent studies indicate that a female urine test used in Europe is better than either the culture or antigen test (and thus should be approved shortly; Lee et al., 1995).

If chlamydia is confirmed, it is usually treated with tetracycline, doxycycline, or erythromycin, but because in some cases the infection persists, some doctors are using newer antibiotics such as azithromycin (Martin et al., 1992). Remember, many people have no symptoms in the early stages, so if you think you have had sex with someone who has chlamydia, seek treatment immediately. ■

PELVIC INFLAMMATORY DISEASE (PID) IN WOMEN: A LIKELY CONSEQUENCE OF UNTREATED CHLAMYDIA OR GONORRHEA

In both the sections on gonorrhea and chlamydia, I referred to pelvic inflammatory disease as a possible consequence in women if the diseases went untreated. PID is a general term for an infection that travels from the lower genital tract (vagina and cervix) to the Fallopian tubes (and sometimes the surrounding structures such as the ovaries and pelvic cavity; Berger, Weström, & Wolner-Hanssen, 1992). It results from infection with a variety of organisms, but 50 to 75 percent of cases are caused by *Chlamydia trachomatis* or *Neisseria gonorrhoeae* (Brunham et al., 1988; Rice & Schachter, 1991).

Over one million cases of PID occur each year in the United States (Cates, Rolfs, & Aral, 1990), requiring about 182,000 hospitalizations (Rolfs, Galaid, & Zaidi, 1992). One in seven women of reproductive age have had PID (Aral, Mosher, & Cates, 1991). The direct medical expenses totaled $2.73 billion in 1990 (Washington & Katz, 1991).

Symptoms may include tenderness or pain in the lower abdomen (sometimes to the extent that standing up straight is impossible), high fever, and chills. However, three times as many women experience a persistent low-grade infection with either no symptoms or intermittent abdominal cramps (Wolner-Hansen, Kiviat, & Holmes, 1989). In these "silent" infections (i.e., the women do not go to a physician for diagnosis) the long-term inflammation can result in pelvic adhesions and abscesses.

The inside diameter of a Fallopian tube is only about that of a human hair; thus, even a small amount of scar tissue can result in a life-threatening ectopic (tubal) pregnancy or permanent sterility (Cates et al., 1990). The chances of sterility increase from 11 percent of women after one case of PID to 54 percent of women with three episodes (Weström, 1980). Largely because of the increase in sexually transmitted diseases, the rates for ectopic pregnancies and infertility have increased dramatically in young women during the last two decades. Over 40 percent of ectopic pregnancies are directly related to STDs and pelvic inflammatory disease (Coste et al., 1994). STDs account for 125,000 new cases of infertility a year in the United States (*Reproductive Health Digest*, 1988).

Because PID is so closely associated with the acquisition of chlamydia and gonorrhea, it should not be surprising that the major risk factors for PID are related to sexual behavior: early age for first experience of intercourse and history of multiple partners (Aral et al., 1991; Lidegaard & Helm, 1990). Interestingly, there is also an increased risk from douching (probably by forcing the bacteria into the uterus) and smoking (by impaired tubal ciliary function or impaired immune response; Forrest et al., 1989; Wolner-Hanssen et al., 1990; Scholes, Daling, & Stergachis, 1992).

Is there anything that women can do to minimize the chances of getting PID? One option, of course, is to reduce one's number of sexual partners. But many of us may be sexually monogamous and still have several (monogamous) partners over time. Barrier methods of contraception, such as male or female condoms and the diaphragm, and spermicides (including the sponge), reduce the risk of PID by reducing the risk of sexually transmitted diseases (Lidegaard & Helm, 1990; Washington, Cates, & Wasserheit, 1991; see Box 6-A). The birth control pill increases the risk of lower genital tract chlamydial infections, but decreases the risk of PID, while IUDs increase the risk of PID (see Chapter 6). It is very important that women having sexual relations have regular pelvic examinations (and perhaps ask their doctor to test for gonorrhea and chlamydia if they have had new partners since their last exam). ■

SYPHILIS

The consequences of untreated gonorrhea or chlamydia can be serious, but untreated **syphilis** is far worse, being responsible for the deaths of over 100 million people worldwide in this century alone (Chiappa & Forish, 1976). As stated earlier, some people have speculated that Columbus brought it back from the New World (Catterall, 1974; but see Luger, 1993 for another explanation), while others have speculated that the disease evolved from the treponema organism, which causes the skin disease yaws in tropical areas. They believe that when humans migrated to cooler climates, the skin provided a less desirable environment, and the organism retreated to the genitals and anus, becoming a sexually transmitted disease. Whatever the origin, there is no written description of the disease's symptoms prior to the time of Columbus.

It was once thought that gonorrhea and syphilis were the same disease. In the 1700s, an English doctor named John Hunter tried to prove this by inoculating his own penis with the pus from a patient with gonorrhea. He thought he had proven his hypothesis when he developed the symptoms of both diseases (the patient had simply had both diseases). *Treponema pallidum* (commonly called the *spirochete*), the spiral-shaped bacterium that causes syphilis, was finally identified in 1905.

The United States has made great efforts to eradicate syphilis by tracking down the sexual contacts of infected persons (and most states require premarital and prenatal blood tests). With the discovery of antibiotics, the number of new cases dropped to around 7,000 in the late 1950s, but it started rising again in the 1960s. Another decline in the early 1980s gave health officials hope, but there was an explosive increase in the middle to late 1980s (Rolfs & Nakashima, 1990). The incidence of syphilis decreased among whites and Asian-Americans during this time, remained stable among Hispanics, but increased dramatically among African-Americans. By 1990, syphilis was nearly 50 times more common among African-Americans than whites. These ethnic differences are not direct risk factors for syphilis, but are instead related to more specific risks. Syphilis is particularly bad in the inner cities where there is widespread unemployment, poverty, poor education and health care, and a greater frequency of prostitution. The Centers for Diseases Control and Prevention estimate that there will be about 113,000 new cases of syphilis a year in the United States.

Syphilis

A sexually transmitted disease caused by the *Treponema pallidum* bacterium (spirochete), which can also pass directly through any cut or scrape into the bloodstream.

Symptoms and Complications

The vast majority of cases of syphilis are transmitted by sexual contact. However, unlike the bacteria that causes gonorrhea and chlamydia, which require contact of mucous membranes for transmission, the spirochete can also pass directly through any little cut or scrape of the skin into the bloodstream. This means that one could potentially get syphilis by merely touching the sores of another person, as has happened to some dentists and physicians. If a person has been infected by the spirochete, the first symptoms generally appear 2 to 4 weeks later. If many bacteria are transmitted, the incubation period can be as short as 10 days, but if only a few are transmitted, the sores can take as long as 90 days to appear. The symptoms generally occur in four stages.

The **primary stage** begins with the appearance of a very ugly ulcerlike (raised edges with a crater) sore called a **chancre** (see Figure 5-3) at the site where the spirochete entered the body (usually the penis, cervix, lips, tongue, or anus). The chancre is full of bacteria and highly infectious, but even though the chancre looks awful, it is usually painless and, thus, some people do not seek treatment. Because the painless chancre generally appears on the cervix in women, they usually are unaware that they are infected during the initial stage unless they get a pelvic exam. Even if a person is not treated, the sore will disappear in a few weeks. However, the spirochete continues to be carried throughout the person's bloodstream and thus individuals remain infected *and* infectious even after the chancre disappears.

Symptoms of the **secondary stage** of syphilis appear within a few weeks to a few months after the chancre heals. The main symptom is an **itchless, painless rash** that appears all over the body, including the palms of the hands and soles of the feet (see Figure 5-4). In the moist areas around the genitals, the rash appears as large sores called *condylomata lata*, which break and ooze a highly infectious fluid (full of

Chancre
The painless sore that is the main symptom of the primary stage of syphilis.

FIGURE 5-3A   A PRIMARY STAGE SYPHILIS CHANCRE ON THE PENIS.

FIGURE 5-3B   A PRIMARY STAGE SYPHILIS CHANCRE ON THE LABIA.

FIGURE 5-4   SECONDARY STAGE SYPHILIS RASH ON THE PALMS AND ABDOMEN.

bacteria). Other symptoms can include a sore throat, a persistent low fever, nausea, loss of appetite, aches and pains, and sometimes even hair loss. These symptoms are bothersome enough that many infected people will seek treatment, but many people mistake the symptoms for the measles, an allergic reaction, or some other disease (syphilis is sometimes called "the great imitator"). If treatment is not obtained, these symptoms, like the chancre of the primary stage, will also disappear after a few months and not return.

An infected person now enters the symptomless **latent stage**, and after about a year is no longer contagious any more because the spirochete is no longer found on the mucous membrane surfaces. This stage may last for years with no noticeable signs, but all the while the bacteria are attacking the internal organs of the body, particularly the heart and blood vessels, and brain and spinal cord.

About two thirds of the people with untreated syphilis will not experience any more problems with the disease, while one third will develop serious complications as a result of the accumulated organ damage. They are now in the **late** (or **tertiary**) **stage**. Large ulcers called *gummas* often appear on the skin and bones. Damage to the heart and blood vessels frequently results in death, while damage to the central nervous system can lead to paralysis, insanity, and/or deafness.

Particularly heartbreaking is the fact that *an unborn baby can catch syphilis from an infected mother*. This happens because the spirochete travels in the common blood supply between the mother and the fetus. If it is not diagnosed and treated, the fetus will be aborted, stillborn, or born with a rather advanced stage called **congenital syphilis**. Complications of congenital syphilis can include deformation of the bones and teeth, blindness, deafness, and other abnormalities that can result in an early death (see Figure 5-5). Blood tests for syphilis are done routinely during pregnancy tests, and if detected the disease can be treated. Congenital syphilis is most common in babies born to mothers who never went for a prenatal checkup (Ricci et al., 1989). There were 4,352 cases of congenital syphilis cases in 1991.

> ### Gumma
> A soft, gummy tumor that occurs in late (tertiary) syphilis.

DIAGNOSIS AND TREATMENT

The spirochete taken from a chancre or sore can be identified under a microscope, but blood tests are almost always done as well (some conditions, such as Lupus and some types of arthritis, and some flu vaccines, can cause a false positive test result). The saddest thing about any suffering and/or deaths that occur from syphilis is that the spirochetes are so easily eradicated with antibiotics. Penicillin is very effective, with the amount and duration of treatment depending on the stage of infection (although there is some controversy about the manner in which penicillin should be used; Zenker & Rolfs, 1990). There have been some indications in the last few years, however, that the bacteria that cause syphilis may be developing some resistance to penicillin, but this is not a major problem as yet. Although antibiotics can eradicate the bacteria at any stage, it cannot reverse any organ damage that may have already occurred if the disease is left untreated until the late stage. It is important, therefore, that people seek treatment as early as possible. ∎

FIGURE 5-5   A BABY BORN WITH CONGENITAL SYPHILIS.

LESS COMMON BACTERIAL STDs

There are other types of bacterially caused STDs that are common in tropical climates, but rare in the United States. I have already mentioned lymphogranuloma venereum (see the section on chlamydia), and two additional examples are chancroid and granuloma inguinale. **Chancroid** is caused by *Hemophilus ducreyi*

Chancroid

A sexually transmitted disease caused by the *Hemophilus ducreyi* bacterium, that is characterized by small, painful bumps.

FIGURE 5-6   TWO ADJACENT CHANCROID LESIONS ON THE PENIS.

and is characterized by small bumps on the genitals or other sites that rupture into soft craterlike sores (see Figure 5-6). The incubation period from the time of infection to the appearance of the first sores is only 1 to 8 days. Unlike the syphilis chancre, chancroid is painful. The lymph nodes in the groin area often become inflamed and swollen. There are only about 1,000 to 2,000 new cases per year in the United States, where it is spread mainly by sexual contact, but in moist tropical areas it can be spread by nonsexual physical contact as well. Chancroid is treated with erythromycin or ceftriaxone (Schmid, 1990).

Granuloma inguinale is rare in the United States, with fewer than 50 cases per year. The main symptom is a painless pimple which then ulcerates and spreads to surrounding areas, permanently destroying the tissue (causing death if not treated). It is treated with tetracycline.

Granuloma inguinale

A rare (in the United States) sexually transmitted disease that is characterized by ulceration of tissue.

Shigellosis is another uncommon sexually transmitted disease. It is contracted from exposure to feces infected with the *Shigella* bacteria (a result of behavior such as oral stimulation of the anus). Symptoms include acute diarrhea, fever, and pain. Thirty percent of the cases in the United States occur in male homosexuals. Shigellosis is treated with tetracycline or ampicillin. ∎

Shigellosis

A disease that can be contracted during sexual activity by exposure to feces containing the *Shigella* bacterium.

HERPES

Before all the attention given to AIDS, herpes was the media's favorite STD, appearing on the cover of *Time* and *Newsweek* and even the subject of a feature article in *Rolling Stone* magazine. Although it doesn't receive the attention it used to, herpes is still with us, infecting several hundred thousand Americans every year, including at least 200,000 to 500,000 cases of genital herpes (Centers for Disease Control and Prevention). Unlike gonorrhea, chlamydia, and syphilis, there is no cure for herpes. The men and women infected this year will be added to those who already have it, making the total number of genital herpes sufferers at least 30 million (Centers for Disease Control and Prevention). Some studies estimate that at least one in six Americans is infected with genital herpes (Aral & Holmes, 1991). All of these individuals can potentially infect new partners.

Herpes (from a Greek word meaning "to creep") has been with us for a long time. It is *spread by direct skin-to-skin contact* (from the infected site on one person to the site of contact on another person). A terrible epidemic in Roman times led the emperor Tiberius to ban public kissing. It was finally identified as a virus in the 1940s, with two different types (I and II) of the virus being identified in the mid-1960s. The type I virus is much more common than the type II (see Burke, 1993 for a review of many studies). Both types cause painful blisters, but at that time there was a 95 percent site-specificity: 95 percent of people with fever blisters or a cold sore around the mouth had *herpes simplex virus type I* (and thus this type was called "oral herpes"), and 95 percent of people with blisters around the genitals had *herpes simplex virus type II* (which thus came to be called "genital herpes"). Only 5 percent of individuals with blisters on the mouth had type II, and vice versa. Thus, it was commonly believed that HSV type I was acquired by kissing and HSV type II only by sexual intercourse.

By 1980, there was no longer a strong site-specificity, particularly in young people. In some clinics, 20 to 35 percent of those persons who had blisters on the genitals had the type I virus rather than type II, and 30 percent who had blisters on the mouth had type II herpes rather than type I (Corey et al., 1983; Peter et al., 1982). Some believe that this is due to the increased popularity of oral-genital sexual behavior in recent decades. Whether or not this is true, it is certain that *both the type I and type II viruses can be transferred from mouth to genitals, and vice versa. The two viruses are not different clinically, as both cause the same painful symptoms.* Nevertheless, many persist in their mistaken belief that oral herpes can only be caught by kissing and genital herpes only through intercourse. Perhaps this letter to Ann Landers will be more persuasive:

Dear Ann Landers: I got genital herpes from my boyfriend of two years from an innocent fever blister on his lip. I could not believe a woman could get a venereal disease from indulging in oral sex with someone who had a simple cold sore. My doctor cultured it and sure enough it came back Herpes Simplex Type I (the oral kind). But now I have genital herpes.

I developed a high fever after being exposed to the virus on his lip. That virus caused two fever blisters on my genitals. They reappear every two months and are quite painful.

My boyfriend dumped me when he learned I was infected. He remains ``pure'' and does not come down with a sexually transmitted disease, while I am alone and scared. There is no justice! Please, Ann Landers, inform the public at once. Tell them what can happen if a person has contact with those innocent-looking sores near the mouth.

Sign Me Dumb and Angry

Dear Angry: I have printed this information in my column more than once. Several readers wrote to say I was ill-informed, stupid, and just plain nuts. Thanks for your testimony.

(Reprinted with permission granted by Ann Landers and Creators Syndicate.)

A person with blisters on the mouth cannot only transfer the virus to another person's genitals, and vice versa, but a person with herpes can transfer it to other parts of his or her own body by touch, including the eyes, as well. This is referred to as *autoinoculation.* I will refer to herpes blisters on the mouth as **oral herpes** and blisters on the genitals as **genital herpes**, without worrying whether the blisters were caused by the type I or type II virus (see Figure 5-7). Although oral herpes can be contracted through oral-genital sex, experts believe most cases of oral herpes in adults to be reactivations of latent infections acquired during childhood (Centers for Disease Control and Prevention). The virus can be easily spread by even a quick, casual kiss and thus *it should not be assumed that a person suffering an attack of oral herpes was recently involved in sexual activity.* By the way, not all mouth ulcers are caused by the herpes virus; they can also be caused by bacteria, allergic reactions, or autoimmune (canker sores) responses. However, "fever blisters" and most cold sores are herpes.

There are actually seven human herpes viruses, but only types I and II are sexually spread. The herpes simplex virus types I and II are very closely related to the viruses that cause chicken pox in children and shingles in adults (Varicellazoster virus), infectious mononucleosis (Epstein-Barr virus), and cytomegalic ("large-cell") inclusion disease in infants (Cytomegalovirus).

> **Oral herpes**
>
> Herpes infection in or around the mouth. It can be caused by herpes simplex virus types I or II.

> **Genital herpes**
>
> Herpes infection in the genital region. It can be caused by herpes simplex virus types I or II.

A   B   C

FIGURE 5-7   HERPES BLISTERS ON THE MOUTH (A) AND PENIS (B). PHOTO (C) SHOWS ULCERATED HERPES LESIONS ON THE PENIS.

SYMPTOMS—PRIMARY ATTACK

Symptoms of the initial herpes attack normally appear about 2 to 20 days after contact with an infected person, with an average of 6 days. The symptoms occur in three stages. In stage one, or the **prodrome stage**, the person feels a tingling, burning, itching, or anestheticlike sensation on the skin surface where he or she came into contact with the virus. Sometimes the symptoms are more diffuse, and in the case of genital herpes, for example, the infected person may feel pain running down the buttocks and thighs. These initial signs indicate the beginning of *viral replication and shedding* (i.e., viruses traveling from the source, free to incorporate into other cells). Therefore, the individual should cease immediately all intimate contact involving the infected area.

Within a few hours the skin surface will break into a rash, which is followed a short time later by the appearance of fluid-filled *blisters* called *vesicles*. These can be excruciatingly painful (see Figure 5-7). After a while the vesicles break open and resemble pustules and then ulcerated running sores. Although herpes lesions generally resemble blisters, some people have sores that are more ulcerative in appearance (Corey, 1988). These symptoms mark the second or **vesicle stage**, which can last from 2 to 3 weeks. The first, or primary, herpes attack includes more than just painful blisters, however. The person often has flulike symptoms, suffering muscle aches and pains, headache, fever, and swollen lymph glands. Urination can be quite painful for those with genital herpes (catheterization is sometimes required), and even walking or sitting is sometimes extremely painful.

The sores eventually begin to develop scales and form *scabs*. This is the third or **crusting-over stage**. Concomitant bacterial infection of the sores sometimes occurs during this stage, but the lesions eventually heal without leaving a scar. Viruses are still being shed during the crusting-over stage; thus, intimate contact with the infected area should be avoided until all the sores are fully healed. The average duration of a primary attack is about 20 days in women and about 16–17 days in men (Corey et al., 1983).

The primary attack is so severe because the person has not yet built up antibodies to the virus. A person can have more than one primary attack, however. An individual could have a primary attack after exposure to the type I virus, for example, and later be exposed to the type II virus and have another primary attack (Al Samarai et al., 1989). Primary attacks to different strains of the same virus are also possible. A person with genital herpes, therefore, should not assume that it is safe to have intercourse with someone who also has herpes.

RECURRENT ATTACKS

During the primary herpes attack, some viruses migrate up sensory nerves from the infected site to the nerve's ganglion (the nerve cell center): the sacral nerve ganglion in the case of genital herpes and the trigeminal nerve ganglion in the case of oral herpes. The viruses become dormant (inactive) when they reach the ganglion. About one third of those who have suffered primary herpes symptoms never again have another attack, but the remaining cases are evenly divided between those who suffer occasional attacks and those who suffer regular recurrent attacks. A recurrent attack occurs as a result of the virus reactivating and traveling down the sensory nerve to or near the same area as the initial sores, where it again starts multiplying. Genital herpes infections are six times more likely to recur as oral infections (Lafferty et al., 1987), and people with genital herpes suffer an average of four recurrent attacks a year. Recurrent attacks are usually less severe than the primary attack (because the individual now produces antibodies) and generally last only from 5 to 10 days.

What causes recurrent attacks? *Stress* to the immune system, either of a physical or emotional nature, seems to be the major cause. A recurrent attack can be brought on by illness, fatigue, menstruation, too much sunlight, and/or anxiety.

ASYMPTOMATIC AND UNRECOGNIZED INFECTIONS

The herpes viruses are most easily spread when sores (blisters or ulcerations) are present. The sores are an obvious sign of viral shedding and infected persons can take measures to prevent the spread of the virus to other persons at this time. However, in many people the symptoms are mild, while still other individuals are asymptomatic shedders of the virus. In fact, as many as 50–80 percent of people infected with herpes simplex type II in the genital region are unaware of their infectious potential (Koutsky et al., 1992a; see Burke, 1993). Half or more of these individuals have clinically recognizable symptoms, but the symptoms are so mild that the individuals do not recognize them as herpes.

"The guy I had been dating for two years told me that he had 'jock itch' and showed me a sore at the base of his penis. I didn't know what jock itch even looked like, much less herpes, so I believed him. His sore went away. About a month later another sore came up, so he went to the doctor . . . told him he had herpes. Two days later I had a sore on my labia. . . . The doctor diagnosed the sore as herpes."

(from the author's files)

In other words, it is possible to spread herpes even when the symptoms are so mild that the person does not know he or she is infected, or in some people even when there are no symptoms at all.

SERIOUS COMPLICATIONS

We generally think of herpes blisters occurring only on the mouth and genitals (or anal area), but *the blisters may appear on any part of the body*. The virus can spread to the eyes (by touching blisters that appear elsewhere on the body and then rubbing the eyes, or by using saliva to insert contact lenses), resulting in **herpes Keratitis** or ocular herpes. It is *the leading cause of infectious blindness in the United States today* (see Figure 5-2). Symptoms escalate from feeling like you have something in your eye to marked irritation and pain, often accompanied by conjunctivitis (inflammation of the mucous membrane). Small lesions will often be visible on the eyeball and result in scarring as they heal (it is the scars that eventually cause blindness). So, if you have herpes, be sure to wash your hands if you touch the sores.

Occasionally, dormant oral or facial herpes migrates to the brain rather than to the face, resulting in **herpes encephalitis**, a rare but often fatal condition. Primary attacks of herpes sometimes include inflammation of the membranes covering the brain and spinal cord (**herpes meningitis**), but full recovery usually follows.

The herpes viruses also play a role in the development of atherosclerosis and artery-blocking blood clots, and promote cholesterol deposits (Hajjar, 1993; Key et al., 1990). The results include increased risk of atherosclerosis and heart attack.

Women with genital herpes run a four to eight times greater risk of getting cancer of the cervix than women who have never had herpes (Graham et al., 1982). The relationship between herpes and cancer is poorly understood (herpes is not necessarily the cause, but perhaps a cofactor in susceptibility). Women who have genital herpes should get a Pap smear test twice a year instead of once.

Herpes can result in serious complications during pregnancy. A primary attack during pregnancy is generally more severe than usual, and recurrent attacks tend to occur more frequently. The stress of delivery may also bring on a recurrent attack. The greatest risk is to the unborn or newborn baby, particularly for women who have a primary attack after the thirty-second week of gestation. The virus ordinarily does not get into the bloodstream, but there is a higher than normal rate of premature births, spontaneous abortions, and congenital malformations (e.g., brain damage, mental retardation), suggesting the possibility that the virus can cross the placenta (Stone et al., 1989).

The greatest risk to the baby is at birth as it passes through the infected cervix and vagina. **Neonatal herpes** is devastating. If a woman has an active case of genital herpes during delivery, there is at least a 50 percent chance that the baby will catch it. The first signs appear 4 to 21 days after birth. Fifty percent of infants who get herpes at birth die or suffer permanent and severe neurological problems (Binkin & Alexander, 1983). Eye infections, widespread skin eruptions, and damage to internal organs can occur as well. The disease is so virulent in newborns because they have no defenses to fight off the infection. Unfortunately, it is not possible to assess the risk of spreading infection to the baby by looking for symptoms in the mother prior to birth. Most babies who become infected are born to mothers who do not display genital blisters at the time of delivery (Stone et al., 1989). It is for these reasons that most doctors prefer to deliver babies by cesarean section to women with genital herpes. Because many people with the herpes virus have no symptoms, or symptoms they do not recognize to be herpes (see previous section), pregnant women are advised to get a blood test (Kulhanjian et al., 1992). An active case of oral herpes is not a risk factor at the time of delivery, but parents (or anyone else) with an active case of oral herpes should avoid kissing or fondling the baby.

DIAGNOSIS AND TREATMENT

First, the bad news. As yet, there is no cure for herpes. Nothing you can do or take will rid your body of the herpes virus. The virus lies dormant in the ganglion cells between active outbreaks, and the potential for another attack is always there. Herpes sufferers nevertheless remain persistent in their attempts to find a home cure. Treatments such as applying baking soda, bleach, ether, yogurt compresses, seaweed, and even peanut butter or snake venom to the blisters have all been tried. None of these has proven effective in scientific tests, but just the attempt to do something probably makes some people feel better. Some of these home remedies, however, have proven to make matters even worse in some cases (e.g., ether). Creams and ointments should also be avoided because they help to spread the virus to adjacent areas and prevent drying. Many people are attempting to control herpes via diet, such as eating foods high in L-lysine (e.g., fish, meat, milk, beans, cheese, eggs) and avoiding foods high in arginine (e.g., nuts, chocolate, whole wheat bread, raisins, oatmeal, brown rice). The Centers for Disease Control and Prevention indicate that there is no merit to these specific diet claims.

A culture test is available for a positive identification. Now the good news. Although there is no known cure for herpes, there is a drug presently available that relieves symptoms and speeds up the healing process during the primary attack. The drug is called *acyclovir* (marketed under the name Zovirax) and is marketed both as an ointment and as a tablet. For people who have frequent recurrent attacks, daily tablets may be taken safely for at least 5 years (Goldberg et al., 1993). Acyclovir is not a cure, however, and recurrent attacks will return once the drug is discontinued. The antiviral drugs used to treat ocular herpes and herpes encephalitis (vidarabine and idoxuridine) are ineffective when applied topically to oral-genital herpes, but can be administered intravenously for treatment of neonatal herpes.

There is real hope for a herpes vaccine in the near future (Burke, 1993). In the meantime, it is recommended that sufferers reduce stress, wash their hands regularly to prevent autoinoculation, and do not wear nylon or tight-fitting underwear. Furthermore, because the herpes virus can live outside the body for a while, such items as towels and toothbrushes should not be shared. Intimate contact with the infected area should certainly be avoided during an active attack; and because some people shed the virus when they have no symptoms, the use of condoms for those with genital herpes (or for individuals whose partner has herpes) is recommended between active attacks.

The Personal Side of Herpes

Most people with oral herpes continue to lead normal lives. A person with oral herpes can engage in sexual intercourse without worrying about infecting his or her partner, but kissing or oral-genital relations during an active attack should be avoided, of course.

Genital herpes is almost always contracted by intimate sexual contact. Recall, too, that people with genital herpes usually have frequent recurrent attacks. Besides the physical symptoms, individuals suffering with genital herpes almost always have some psychological difficulties adjusting to their infection. They often pass through several stages: shock, emotional numbing, isolation and loneliness, and sometimes severe depression and impotence. Initially, there is often a frantic search for a second or even third doctor's opinion (denial), a lot of "Why me?" responses, guilt, and anger. The anger is sometimes directed at the medical profession for its inability to cure herpes, but almost always at the partner responsible and/or the opposite sex in general. Some herpes sufferers have filed "kiss-and-don't-tell" lawsuits against the people who gave them herpes (in 1992, a Louisiana woman was awarded $125,000 from her ex-husband). *Time* magazine (August 2, 1982) reported testimonials from men and women who had deliberately infected dozens of partners for revenge (e.g., one Los Angeles woman stated that when she first got it, she wanted to pass it on to everyone for vengeance until everyone had it, and it became normal). Others invest a great deal of time and effort in experimental drugs, fad diets, and even faith healers.

After the initial shock, many genital herpes sufferers have feelings of ugliness, self-loathing, and guilt. The reactions of others may make them feel like "social lepers." As a result, some may have sexual problems and others may just swear off sex. A 1993 survey of readers of *the helper* (a magazine for people with herpes) found that in the previous 12 months 52 percent had suffered depression and fear of rejection, 36 percent had feelings of isolation, and 10 percent had self-destructive feelings (Catotti, Clarke, & Catoe, 1993).

> "In my early 20's I felt a painful sore on my vagina. I had no idea what it was. At the time I hadn't had many partners. Later I had another eruption. My doctor told me I had herpes. Needless to say, I was shocked. I went through a denial phase that followed many nights of wet pillow. It took me years to accept it. . . . "
>
> (from the author's files)

So, how should we deal with personal relationships if we have herpes? First of all, accept the fact that although there is no cure, you do not have the plague. *The use of condoms will minimize the chances of infecting a partner* (in case there is viral shedding without symptoms). You should try to minimize the stress in your life, and if you have frequent or long-lasting attacks, talk to your doctor about taking acyclovir. Lastly, tell a new partner in advance of having an intimate relationship with them. You should not just tell them that you have herpes, but should educate them—teach them about herpes in order to reduce unfounded fears or dispel false myths. Most people can tell when they are about to have a recurrent attack and should refrain from sex at this time. You might still be rejected occasionally, but chances are this type of person would run off during any other type of crisis as well. Many couples have enjoyed long-lasting relationships where one partner had herpes and had not infected the other.

In summary, the best thing that herpes sufferers can do is to educate themselves and engage in consciousness raising for themselves and their partner. Here is the address of an organization that can provide the herpes sufferer with current up-to-date information on herpes research, therapy, and care:

American Social Health Association
P.O. Box 13827
Research Triangle Park, NC 27709 ■

HEPATITIS

Hepatitis is an inflammation of the liver that can have many causes. **Hepatitis A (infectious hepatitis)** is caused by a small virus (HAV) and is spread by direct or indirect contact with contaminated feces. Thus, the disease can be spread sexually (by contact with the anus of an infected person during sex) and has a higher incidence in male homosexuals than in other groups. However, it is most often spread through nonsexual means, such as infected individuals handling food, or by consumption of shellfish taken from contaminated waters.

Hepatitis A, B, and C

Liver infections caused by a virus. Type A is spread by direct or indirect contact with contaminated feces. Type B is transmitted by infected blood or body fluids, with 25 to 50 percent of the cases contracted during sex. Type C is spread mainly by contaminated blood, but is possibly spread during sexual intercourse in some cases.

Hepatitis B (serum hepatitis) is caused by a different, larger virus (HBV) and is transmitted by infected blood or body fluids such as saliva, semen, and vaginal secretions (Zuckerman, 1982). It can cause a number of liver diseases, including cancer and cirrhosis. There are more than 300 million people worldwide who are infected with this virus (Ayoola, 1988). At least 25 percent, and perhaps as many as 50 percent, of the 200,000 annual cases in the United States are spread during sex (Brandt, 1982; Centers for Disease Control and Prevention). The disease is most common in homosexual males (particularly those who engage in anal sex) and drug users who share needles. One can also get the virus during a blood transfusion, and over two thirds of pregnant females infected with hepatitis B pass the infection to their babies. The antiviral drug interferon is effective in about one third of patients (Perrillo et al., 1990). About 90 percent of persons with hepatitis recover, but up to 10 percent remain infected and thus become carriers of the disease. The Centers for Disease Control and Prevention and the American Academy of Pediatricians have recommended that *all* children (babies as well as adolescents) be vaccinated against the hepatitis B virus, and others have advised that everyone be vaccinated (Hoofnagle, 1989).

Hepatitis C, which is caused by still another virus (HCV), was not identified as a specific virus until 1988. About 150,000 Americans are infected each year and about half of them remain chronically infected. As yet, there is no vaccine available. People with hepatitis C are 25 times more likely to develop cancer of the liver than noninfected individuals (Resnick & Koff, 1993). The hepatitis C virus is most commonly spread through intravenous drug use and transfusions. Although the virus can be spread during sex (Alter et al., 1989; Peano et al., 1992), most researchers believe that this is uncommon (Osmond et al., 1993; Weinstock et al., 1993a).

The incubation period (time period before symptoms appear) is 2 to 6 weeks for hepatitis A and 6 weeks to 6 months for hepatitis B. The symptoms can be mild (poor appetite, diarrhea) to severe (fever, vomiting, pain, fatigue, jaundiced or yellow tinge of skin and eyes, and dark urine). If you ever get hepatitis, avoid alcohol entirely because it can damage the infected liver. ■

GENITAL HUMAN PAPILLOMAVIRUS INFECTION

Many of you probably have never heard of genital human papillomavirus (HPV) infection. If it were not for all the attention the media has given to AIDS, however, you no doubt would be reading and hearing a great deal more about this very common and sometimes life-threatening sexually transmitted disease.

Human papillomaviruses (HPV)

Viruses that cause abnormal growths in epithelial cells. There are over 70 types. A few (types 6 and 11) cause genital warts, while others (types 16, 18, 31, 33, and 45) can lead to cancer of the cervix.

Human papillomaviruses only infect epithelial cells (the covering of internal and external surfaces of the body). At present, over 70 different types have been identified (de Villiers, 1989). We can divide them into three broad categories: (1) those that cause a rare skin condition (epidermodysplasia verruciformis) that appears as reddish plaques, (2) those that cause nongenital warts (including common, plantar, and flat warts), and (3) those that cause warts in the genital and anal area (although these can also cause problems in the mouth, pharynx, and larynx).

Genital warts (condyloma-acuminata)

Warts in the genital (and anal) region caused by human *papillomaviruses* (mainly types 6 and 11). The warts look like cauliflower-like growths.

There are about 25 different human papillomaviruses that can cause ano-genital warts (called *condyloma-acuminata*). However, the large majority of genital warts are caused by HPV types 6 and 11.

The genital human papillomaviruses are usually spread by sexual intercourse (or oral-genital sex in some cases) and are highly contagious. In fact, there will be 500,000 to 1 million new cases this year, which makes HPV infection *the most common sexually transmitted disease caused by viruses in the United States.* It has been estimated that one in three adults has HPV (Aral & Holmes, 1991). One study found that 20 percent of sexually active 14- to 18-year-old girls were infected with HPV (Schoolnik, 1988) and another study reported that more than 40 percent of college women had HPV infections (Bauer et al., 1991).

Most people with HPV infections do not develop warts, but instead have invisible flat patches of abnormal cells (called *subclinical HPV infection*) that cannot be detected except by a physician with special tests (Gordon, 1990). This means, of course, that a person can be infected, not be aware of it, and unknowingly transmit the virus to new sexual partners. For those people who develop warts, the first symptoms generally appear anywhere from 3 weeks to 8 months after contact with an infected person. Ano-genital warts (often called venereal warts) are soft, pink (or whitish), and resemble a growth of cauliflower (single or in clusters; see Figure 5-8). They can cause itching, irritation, or bleeding. In males, the warts generally appear on the penis, scrotum, and/or anus, but they can also grow within the urethra. In females, the warts can appear on the cervix and walls of the vagina as well as the vulva and anus, and thus the virus can be transmitted to a newborn baby during vaginal delivery. Women are much more likely than men to develop visible warts (and serious complications—see below) because the cervix has a zone of cells that are continually undergoing cell division (which makes it easier for the viruses to exploit). The skin of the penis, on the other hand, resists transformation by the virus.

"I contracted venereal warts from a married woman I frequently slept with. I then gave

FIGURE 5-8   VENEREAL WARTS ON THE PENIS CAUSED BY HUMAN PAPILLOMAVIRUS.

them to my girlfriend. I did not know I had the affliction until she was diagnosed during a semiannual exam with her gynecologist. The removal procedure for me as a male was rather simple as opposed to her treatment. Her first treatment involved cryogenically freezing her cervix. After that unsuccessful attempt they resorted to laser surgery. She is still not cured. If I could change things I would. We're not together anymore, but I still pray for her. I surely will never forget and I practice safe sex with just my new girlfriend."

"When I was 17 years old I went to the doctor for a Pap smear. He found pre-malignant warts on my cervix. When he informed me that they were sexually transmitted, I didn't want to believe him. I went to an all-girls Catholic high school and the guys I slept with were usually from a boys' Catholic high school. I would never think that I would get a STD. I always thought STDs happened to lower class people.

My doctor performed laser surgery to get rid of the warts. A year and a half later I had another outbreak, had surgery, and within seven weeks after the surgery they came back. These last two times they weren't just on the cervix, they spread all the way to the vulva. . . . I have abstained from sex since the beginning of the second outbreak."

(from the author's files)

Women with HPV infections have a greatly increased risk of developing cervical and/or vulvar cancer (Koutsky et al., 1992b). Approximately 90 percent of women with cervical cancer are found to have HPV infections (Lowy, Kirnbauer, & Schiller, 1994). However, only a few of the human papillomaviruses are found in cervical cancers: HPV 31, HPV 33, HPV 45, HPV 18 (in 10–20 percent of cases) and in particular, HPV 16 (in at least 40–60 percent of cases). HPV 16 has also been found in about 30 percent of breast tumors (Lonardo, Venuti, & Marcante, 1992). Note that these types of HPV are different from the two types that cause most genital warts (types 6 and 11). What this means, of course, is that *most women with HPV infections who are at risk of developing cervical cancer will have no visible symptoms.* Because of this, a regular pelvic exam and Pap smear are an essential part of female health care. Women who test positive for HPV should have Pap smears at least every 6 months.

We do not yet fully understand how some types of HPV lead to cancer. Most researchers believe that other risk factors are involved (i.e., it is a complex interaction of many risk factors; Reeves et al., 1994; Schneider,

1993). Some of the risk factors associated with (but not necessarily the direct cause of) cervical cancer are high number of sexual partners, early age at first intercourse, and immune system suppression.

Two thirds of the partners of infected women also have HPV infections (Krebs, 1989). While HPV has been associated with cancer of the penis, it is much less likely that the viruses will lead to cancer in men (as was also the case for visible warts, you recall).

Small external warts can be treated by applying a solution of podophyllin (sold in stores as Condylox), which causes them to dry up. Larger warts can be removed by cauterization or minor surgery. Internal warts are often removed by laser surgery. For HPV infections of the cervix, cryotherapy (freezing) is the preferred therapy. Injection with the antiviral drug interferon has shown some promise (Stellato, 1992). However, none of these methods gets rid of the viruses, and thus recurrences of the warts are common (see previous case histories; Kraus & Stone, 1990). It is not surprising, therefore, that people with HPV infections are also affected emotionally by the disease, and in the case of women, have anxieties about cancer (Persson, Dahlof, & Krantz, 1993). In the future, it is likely that a vaccine will be developed to prevent HPV infection (Galloway, 1994). ■

MOLLUSCUM CONTAGIOSUM

Molluscum contagiosum

A sexually transmitted virus with symptoms that look like small pimples filled with kernels of corn.

Molluscum contagiosum is a painless wartlike growth that is caused by a sexually transmitted (pox) virus. There is only one case of this in the United States for every 100 cases of gonorrhea (Hatcher et al., 1994). The growths are usually one to five mm in diameter and look like small pimples filled with a kernel of corn. They can be treated with podophyllin or freezing. ■

HIV INFECTION AND AIDS

"When a person has sex, they're not having it just with that partner. They're having it with everybody that partner has had it with for the past ten years."

Otis Bowen, former U.S. Secretary of Health and Human Services

In the early 1980s, doctors in California were puzzled when five men were diagnosed with *Pneumocystis carinii pneumonia*, a rare respiratory infection usually seen only in people with depressed immune systems. Several young men in Miami were simultaneously diagnosed as having *Kaposi's sarcoma*, a rare cancer of the capillary system that appears as purple blotches on the skin (see Figure 5-9). It, too, is a sign of a depressed immune system. More and more cases of depressed immune systems began to appear, but it was not until September 1982 that the new disease was given a name: **Acquired Immunodeficiency Syndrome (AIDS)**.

It was not until the spring of 1984 that the cause of AIDS was identified as a virus (actually a special kind of virus called a retrovirus). Dr. Robert Gallo of the U.S. National Cancer Institute called the virus *human T-cell lymphotropic virus-III* (HTLV-III) and said that it was one of the family of HTLV viruses. Dr. Luc Montagnier of the Pasteur Institute in Paris, France, simultaneously and independently identified the virus and named it *lymphadenopathy-associated virus* (LAV), after the swollen lymph nodes that are among the early AIDS symptoms. There is a controversy about which group discovered the virus

AIDS (acquired immuno-deficiency syndrome)

A fatal disease caused by a virus (HIV) that destroys the immune system. It is spread by intimate sexual activity (the exchange of bodily fluids) or contaminated blood.

FIGURE 5-9   KAPOSI'S SARCOMA LESIONS ON TWO PATIENTS WITH AIDS.

first, but after a decade in which several hundred thousand people died of AIDS, that hardly seems important anymore. The virus is now referred to by everyone as **human immunodeficiency virus** or **HIV**.

Actually, there are two related retroviruses that cause AIDS—HIV-1 and HIV-2. HIV-1 has accounted for almost all the cases in the United States, but HIV-2 (which was first observed in the United States in 1987) is not uncommon in Western African countries. In fact, in West Africa it is not uncommon for individuals to be infected with both HIV-1 and HIV-2 (George et al., 1992).

Human immuno-deficiency virus (HIV)

A virus that kills CD4 cells, eventually resulting in AIDS.

HIV and the Body's Immune System

The **immune system** is that part of your body that defends you against bacteria, viruses, fungi, and cancerous cells. White blood cells, or *lymphocytes*, are the main line of defense in this system. There are several types. One type, called **CD4 cells** (also called *helper T cells* and *T4 lymphocytes*) have the job of recognizing the disease-causing agents and then signaling another type of white blood cell (*B cells*) to produce antibodies. The antibodies bind to the recognized agents so that they can be identified by yet another type of white blood cell, the *killer T cells* (T is for the thymus gland, where the cells develop). The CD4 cells then signal the killer T cells to destroy the identified disease-causing agents. In addition to CD4 cells, there are also *suppressor T cells* that suppress the activity of the B cells and killer T cells. A person normally has twice as many CD4 (helper) cells as suppressor T cells.

Immune system

Refers to bodily mechanisms involved in the production of antibodies in response to bacteria, viruses, and cancerous cells.

Recall now that viruses must invade and live in normal body cells (called host cells) in order to replicate themselves. The human immunodeficiency virus attacks and enters the CD4 cells. When the CD4 cells are activated during an infection, HIV reproduces itself, and in the process damages or destroys the host CD4 cell. The replicated virus then invades other CD4 cells. Thus, HIV destroys the cells that ordinarily would work to fight it off. Declining numbers of CD4 cells begin occurring early in the course of HIV infection (Lang et al., 1989), and the victim eventually has fewer helper (CD4) T cells than suppressor T cells, leaving the body defenseless against viruses, bacteria, and other infection-causing agents.

CD4 white blood cells are not the only body cells invaded by HIV. The virus has also been found in cells of the brain, gastrointestinal tract, kidney, lungs, cerebrospinal fluid, and other blood and plasma cells.

However, it is the destruction of CD4 cells that leads to the disease we call AIDS.

Progression of HIV Infection

After invading the body, HIV reproduces unchecked during the first few weeks, reaching enormous levels in the bloodstream. The newly infected person may experience flulike symptoms during this time. The body's immune system then launches a huge counterattack that kills the virus by the billions, reducing it to very low levels (Daar et al., 1991). In time, however, the virus regains the upper hand by slowly killing off the CD4 cells.

A normal, healthy person has between 1000 and 1,200 CD4 cells per cubic millimeter of blood. Although CD4 cell counts generally decline with time, people with HIV show no visible symptoms in the first stage of the infection, called **asymptomatic HIV infection**. This stage often lasts for years.

Infected persons generally start to show symptoms of a weakened immune system when their CD4 cell count falls below 500 per cubic millimeter of blood. Symptoms may include loss of appetite, recurrent diarrhea, loss of body weight, low-grade fever (often accompanied by "night sweats"), swollen lymph nodes, and "colds," "flus," and yeast infections that linger on and on. At this point, the infection is called **symptomatic HIV infection** (formerly called *AIDS related complex* or *ARC*).

HIV infection is not called **AIDS** until it has become life-threatening. As the CD4 cell count approaches 200 per cubic millimeter of blood, infected persons' immune systems have become so weakened that they fall prey to what are referred to as **opportunistic infections**—diseases such as lymphomas, Kaposi's sarcoma, Pneumocystis carinii pneumonia, recurrent bacterial pneumonia, pulmonary tuberculosis, cryptococcal meningitis, wasting syndrome, and invasive cervical cancer (Hankins & Handley, 1992; and see Katlama & Dickinson, 1993). These are often accompanied by severe mental disorders and/or emaciation (Maj, 1990). Many AIDS patients are infected with a mycoplasma (a primitive microorganism that doesn't even have cell walls) known to kill people who are not even infected with HIV (Lo et al., 1989). Dr. Montagnier has speculated that the mycoplasma makes HIV more powerful (see Wright, 1990). In 1993, the Centers for Disease Control and Prevention expanded the definition of AIDS to include anyone whose CD4 cell count was below 200, whether or not they had yet fallen victim to an opportunistic disease. Some people whose CD4 cell counts have dropped

Opportunistic diseases

Term used to refer to a variety of diseases that occur in individuals with a very weakened immune system, as occurs in AIDS.

below 200 have gone 3 years or longer without developing AIDS-related illnesses (Hoover et al., 1995). In the end, however, AIDS patients die as a result of the opportunistic infections (not as a direct result of HIV).

A few researchers have doubted the belief that AIDS is caused by HIV depleting CD4 cells. One researcher, for example, proposed that it is not HIV infection per se that causes AIDS, but high-risk behaviors (such as drug use and promiscuous homosexual activity) associated with HIV infection (Duesberg, 1989, 1990). However, others have shown that high-risk behavior individuals who are not infected with HIV do not develop AIDS (Ascher et al., 1993; Schecter et al., 1993). In the summer of 1992, several individuals were discovered to have AIDS-like symptoms (including depleted CD4 cells) without HIV (e.g., Laurence et al., 1992), causing a scare that a new, unknown virus could also cause AIDS. It was later found that this condition is very rare, has numerous causes, and is not evidence against HIV as the cause of AIDS (Fauci, 1993).

Once an individual is infected with HIV, how long does it take to develop a full-blown case of AIDS? Fewer than 5 percent of persons will develop AIDS within the first 3 years after infection with HIV-1; about 15 percent within 5 years; 50 percent in 10 years; and *at least* two thirds within 14 years (Bacchetti & Moss, 1989; Buchbinder et al., 1994; Gauvreau et al., 1994; Lemp et al., 1990; Rutherford et al., 1990; Veuglelers et al., 1993). Many of the remainder will have already reached the symptomatic HIV infection stage. Not as much is known about HIV-2, but there is some evidence that persons infected with this virus may take longer to develop AIDS than those infected with HIV-1 (Whittle et al., 1994). People who experience acute primary HIV infection ("flulike" symptoms or worse upon initial exposure) are more likely to develop AIDS earlier than people who are asymptomatic upon initial infection (Lindback et al., 1994; Sinicco et al., 1993). People who already have a weakened immune system (as a result of illness, age, or abuse of drugs, for example) will also generally show a rapid progression to AIDS.

Nevertheless, some infected persons (as many as 5 to 10 percent) carry HIV with them for 10–15 years without signs of damage—little or no decrease in their CD4 cells (Buchbinder et al., 1994). How is this possible? There is no difference between these individuals and those who progress to AIDS in prior exposure to sexually transmitted diseases or recreational drugs. One likely explanation is that a viral regulatory gene product (a protein) "tells" infected cells when to start reproduction of the virus, and in some individuals this protein remains in check. Even so, psychosocial processes (e.g., amount of stress) may also play a role (Capitano

& Lerche, 1991). Obviously, we are far from completely understanding the HIV replication process.

How long can an HIV-infected person expect to live after being diagnosed with AIDS? The news is not good. Even with antiviral therapy (see later section), the average survival time is only about a year (Friedland et al., 1991; Lemp et al., 1992), or about 3 years in individuals whose CD4 cell counts drop below 200 but do not initially have clinical diseases (Keet et al., 1994). Men tend to survive slightly longer than women, and young people longer than older people (Melnick et al., 1994).

WHERE DID HUMAN IMMUNODEFICIENCY VIRUS COME FROM?

There is no question that HIV-1 and HIV-2 are new to the human species, but where did they come from? "Conspiracy" theories are popular. At one time, the Soviets blamed it on U.S. biological experiments gone awry. Filmmaker Spike Lee publicly said that "AIDS is a government-engineered disease" targeted at gays, African-Americans, and Hispanics (November 1992). Another person circulated a booklet claiming that "WHO, the World Health Organization, murdered Africa with the AIDS virus" (Douglass, 1988). He, as well as others, said that the virus was injected into people with various vaccines (e.g., smallpox, hepatitis B). *Rolling Stone* magazine claimed HIV was introduced to humans during testing of a polio vaccine in Africa in the late 1950s (the polio virus was grown in monkey kidney cells, and the article suggested that the cells were contaminated with a monkey virus).

Scientific studies of the origins of HIV have, indeed, implicated nonhuman primates, but do not support conspiracy theories (see Desrosiers, 1990; Gao et al., 1992; Myers, MacInnes, & Korber, 1992). There is a diverse pool of nonhuman primate (*simian*) *immunodeficiency viruses* (SIV). The viruses are found in rhesus monkeys, sooty mangabeys, African green monkeys, and chimpanzees. Some individuals have been found to be infected with strains of HIV-2 that are more closely related to SIV than to any previously known human virus (Gao et al., 1992; Hahn, 1990). HIV-2 can infect baboons and rhesus macaques (Castro et al., 1991). In other words, for HIV-2 there is considerable evidence that humans acquired it through cross-species transmission, that is, that it "may simply be simian immunodeficiency viruses residing in and adopting to a human host" (Myers et al., 1992). Researchers have yet to find an SIV with the same degree of similarity to HIV-1, but some strains with notable similarities have been discovered.

The cross-species transmission almost certainly first took place in Africa. Tests of old blood samples have established that HIV-1 was in central Africa in the

1960s, and Kaposi's sarcoma was showing up at a high rate in this area in the 1970s. Features of modern society, such as worldwide travel, promiscuous sexual activities, and sharing of syringes and hypodermic needles, probably greatly helped the spread of the virus.

How Is HIV Spread?

What is the evidence concerning the transmission of HIV? Some people worry about catching it from just breathing the same air as, or touching objects previously held by, AIDS victims. Some neighbors of AIDS victims worry about mosquitoes. Some people have even quit donating blood. Can you get AIDS merely by casual contact with an HIV-infected person?

If HIV could be contracted from casual contact, you would expect that family members of AIDS patients (all living together) would be at great risk. However, no family member of an AIDS patient has ever become infected by sharing household facilities and items and no child has ever become infected by just playing with or living with an AIDS-infected brother or sister (Friedland et al., 1990; Gershon, Ulahov, & Nelson, 1990). HIV has sometimes been found in body fluids such as tears and saliva, but not in high enough concentrations to pose a threat. A protein found in saliva helps block HIV from infecting human cells (McNeely & Wahl, 1995). In fact, the concentrations in saliva are so low that your chance of acquiring HIV by being bitten by an HIV-infected individual is extremely unlikely (Richman & Rickman, 1993).

In the final stages of AIDS, patients cannot hold food down, often have uncontrollable diarrhea, and generally sweat profusely. Yet except for a few people who inadvertently stuck themselves with a contaminated needle and a few others whose skin was exposed to a large amount of contaminated blood (which may have entered the body through a small cut), none of the doctors, nurses, and other medical personnel who have cared for the most seriously ill AIDS patients on a daily basis have ever developed an HIV infection.

Malaria and some other diseases are spread by mosquitoes, but it is certain that HIV is not spread in this manner (Castro et al., 1988). If it were, we would be seeing a much larger number of children and elderly people with AIDS.

There is no need for panic—*HIV is not spread by casual contact.* There are three main ways in which HIV is transmitted: (1) sexual contact with an infected person; (2) exposure to infected blood (i.e., mainly needle sharing among I.V. drug users); and (3) perinatal transmission (i.e., an infected mother can transmit the virus to a fetus through their shared blood). Thus, *HIV is transmitted almost exclusively by intimate sexual contact and contaminated blood.* Let us examine each of these means of transmission.

In a book published in 1990, the author claimed

that it was a myth that HIV could be spread by sex between heterosexuals (Fumento, 1990). Believe me; it is no myth. HIV has been found in the semen and vaginal fluids of HIV-infected individuals (see Alexander, 1990; Kiessling, 1992), although not in all infected persons. Remember, the concentrations of HIV are greatest at the very beginning of the infection, then decrease dramatically, and then increase again as the disease progresses toward the AIDS stage (Daar et al., 1991). This means that the risk of transmission of HIV is greatest in the first 60 days and in the symptomatic HIV and AIDS stages (De Vincenzi et al., 1994; Jacquez et al., 1994). Of course, HIV is also in blood, so any sexual activity in which bleeding occurs would greatly increase the risk (e.g., anal intercourse; vigorous vaginal intercourse; open sore on the penis, vagina, or cervix; menstruation; Padian, Shiboski, & Jewell, 1990; Seidlin et al., 1993). Sores on the genitals caused by other sexually transmitted diseases greatly increase the risk of HIV transmission (see Wasserheit, 1991).

Studies show that HIV is at least twice as easy to transmit from an infected male to a female partner than vice versa (European study Group, 1992; Nicolosi et al., 1994; Padian, Shiboski, & Jewell, 1991). In one case, the same man infected 11 women by sexual contact (Clumeck et al., 1989). But female-to-male transmission has been well documented (see also Seidlin et al., 1993).

Most experts believe that the risk of HIV transmission during oral-genital sex is very small, but it has been known to occur between heterosexual or male homosexual partners (Lifson et al., 1990; Rozenbaum et al., 1988; Spitzer & Weiner, 1989). Female-to-female transmission of HIV during oral-genital sex has not been observed (Petersen et al., 1992). Transmission during kissing is highly unlikely.

Let me summarize what we know about HIV transmission during sex. Stage of infection and bleeding are factors that increase the risk. In terms of behavior, HIV is spread most easily during anal intercourse (because of bleeding, even if it is slight; see Caceres & Griensven, 1994), followed by vaginal intercourse (especially when there are open sores) and occasionally during oral sex.

As previously mentioned, a second major way in which HIV is transmitted is by exposure to contaminated blood. Needle-sharing drug users are at especially high risk (Chitwood et al., 1990). But what about our chances of getting HIV should we ever need a blood transfusion? At one time this was a major concern. Several thousand people contracted HIV from blood transfusions before screening tests were begun in 1985. Today, because all blood is tested, your chances are only one in 61,171 of becoming infected by a transfusion (Busch et al., 1991). A few units of infected blood still get through because the test cannot tell if a person has just been infected (see section on testing). Unfortunately, many people in the United States have stopped donating blood out of fear of getting AIDS, and as a result, there is a severe shortage of blood in many parts of the country. At blood donation centers in the United States needles are sterilized and used only once. You will not get AIDS from donating blood!

The third major way that HIV is transmitted is perinatally—from infected woman to fetus. The Centers for Disease Control and Prevention estimate that in the United States, 6,000 to 7,000 women a year who become pregnant are infected with HIV, and that 1,500 to 2,000 of their babies become infected (a transmission rate of about 25 percent; CDC, 1994; see also Gwinn et al., 1991). Evidence suggests that most infections occur very late in pregnancy or during delivery (European Collaborative Study, 1994b). There is some evidence, for example, that the risk can be reduced if delivery is by cesarean section (European Collaborative Study, 1994a). Breastfeeding increases the risk of mother-to-child transmission (Datta et al., 1994; European Collaborative Study, 1992; Van de Perre et al., 1992). The rapidity with which children infected with HIV progress to AIDS is associated with the severity of the mother's infection (Blanche et al., 1994). Most infected children show symptoms of HIV infection by 6 months of age (European Collaborative Study, 1991). By 1 year of age, about a fourth have AIDS and many have died (Blanche et al., 1994). Although the disease progresses more slowly in the remainder, many will suffer serious problems (e.g., deafness, mental retardation) that affect their ability to communicate (several papers at the 1994 conference of the American Speech-Language-Hearing Association). With immature and weakened immune systems, all eventually fall prey to various opportunistic diseases.

Because of the attention it has received in the media, one other potential means of transmission needs to be discussed. Many Americans have become afraid of contracting HIV from an infected health care professional (e.g., physician, dentist). These fears developed when it was widely reported that seven patients of an HIV-infected Florida dentist (who died of AIDS) became infected with HIV (Ou et al., 1992). A 1994 segment of the television investigative news show "60 Minutes" later cast doubt on whether the patients had actually acquired HIV from the dentist, but the case nevertheless raised the important issue of patients' rights.

What are the facts about your risk of contracting HIV from a health care professional? Studies of thousands of patients of HIV-infected surgeons and dentists reveal that the risk is practically nonexistent (Dickinson et al., 1993; Mishu et al., 1990; Rogers et al., 1993). Nevertheless, because chemical disinfectants do not always kill the virus (Sattar & Springthorpe, 1991), surgeons and dentists are now required to steam clean their instruments and wear protective gloves. Expert review panels will decide on a case-by-case basis whether HIV-infected health professionals may continue performing surgical procedures (American College of Physicians, 1994; Lo & Steinbrook, 1992). Conclusion: There is no good reason to avoid getting regular health and dental checkups.

WHO HAS HIV/AIDS?

HIV infection is not confined to the United States; it is a true pandemic disease. The World Health Organization estimated that, worldwide, about 17 million people had been infected with HIV (including those who had already died of AIDS) by the start of 1995. They were estimating 40 million cases by the year 2000, and the U.S. Census Bureau's World Population Profile said 121 million could be infected by 2020. A report from the Harvard School of Public Health was considerably more pessimistic. By the early part of next century, life expectancy in the hardest hit countries will be 9–25 years less than before HIV (U.S. Census Bureau).

At the start of 1995, well over half of the world's cases were in subSaharan Africa, where HIV is believed to have originated. Countries such as Uganda, Zambia, and Rwanda have been devastated. In some places as many as one out of every four people are infected with HIV (see Way & Stanecki, 1993). AIDS is the leading cause of death among adults in many African cities and has overwhelmed the hospitals (e.g., DeCock et al., 1990).

HIV may have originated in Africa, but the World Health Organization says that "the most alarming trends of HIV infection are in south and southeast Asia where the epidemic is spreading in some areas as fast as it was a decade ago in subSaharan Africa." In places like Thailand it was once confined to users of intravenous drugs and prostitutes, but it has now spread into the general population in epidemic form (Berkley, 1993).

India is another country where HIV has reached epidemic proportions (Pfutzner et al., 1992). The World Health Organization estimates that already over one third of the prostitutes in Bombay are infected with HIV, and similar numbers are being found among patients in some of the city's STD clinics.

In South America, more than 2 million people are believed to have HIV. Spread of the infection may initially have been helped by unregulated blood banks, but once in the population it spread rapidly as a result of cultural attitudes that encourage male promiscuity. HIV spread rapidly into the heterosexual community. In Brazil, for example, there was only one woman with AIDS for every 124 men with AIDS in 1984, but by 1993 the ratio was down to four men to every AIDS-infected woman.

In Africa, HIV infection is a true heterosexual disease. Half, or more, of the millions of people presently infected with HIV are women (Berkley et al., 1990). As a result, thousands of children have been born with HIV. Heterosexual transmission is helped by high numbers of cases of other sexually transmitted diseases that cause genital ulcerations (e.g., syphilis, chancroid;

WHO Consensus Statement, 1989; also see Wasserheit, 1992). Worldwide, over 3 million women and children will probably die of AIDS in the 1990s (Chin, 1990).

What about the United States? In 1994, there were 78,126 reported cases of AIDS in the 50 states. However, it is generally accepted that many cases (perhaps as many as a third) of AIDS and AIDS-related deaths are never reported (U.S. General Accounting Office, 1989; Gertig, Marion, & Schechter, 1991; Hessol et al., 1992). At the start of 1995, there had been a cumulative total of 426,978 reported cases of AIDS in the United States. Over 60 percent of these had already died. The Centers for Disease Control and Prevention estimate that at least 1 million more Americans are presently infected with the human immunodeficiency virus. By the mid 1990s, AIDS had become *the leading cause of death among Americans aged 25 to 44*, ahead of accidents, cancer, and heart disease (Centers for Disease Control and Prevention, 1995).

Although HIV infection is a heterosexual disease worldwide, to date, AIDS has been largely confined to specific subgroups in the United States (see Figure 5-10). In 1994, 44 percent of the new cases of AIDS occurred among homosexual or bisexual men, and 27 percent occurred among heterosexual intravenous (injecting) drug users. Another 5 percent were gay intravenous drug users. Twelve percent acquired HIV by unknown means. Ten percent acquired HIV through heterosexual contact.

The large majority of new cases in 1994 still occurred among men (a reflection of the high prevalence among homosexual and bisexual men). However, the number of new AIDS cases who are women is increasing dramatically, from only 7

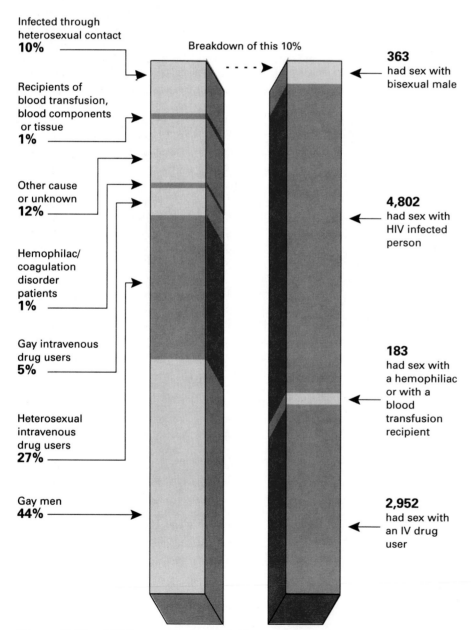

Who has AIDS

In 1994, there were 79,674 cases of AIDS reported among adults and adolescents nationwide. The cases break down like this:

Of the 10% infected through heterosexual contact: 8,300 people

Infected through heterosexual contact **10%**

Breakdown of this 10%

Recipients of blood transfusion, blood components or tissue **1%**

Other cause or unknown **12%**

Hemophilac/ coagulation disorder patients **1%**

Gay intravenous drug users **5%**

Heterosexual intravenous drug users **27%**

Gay men **44%**

363 had sex with bisexual male

4,802 had sex with HIV infected person

183 had sex with a hemophiliac or with a blood transfusion recipient

2,952 had sex with an IV drug user

FIGURE 5-10   AIDS CASES FOR 1994, UNITED STATES.

percent of all new cases in 1985 to 18 percent in 1994. A disproportionate number of AIDS cases occurred among African-Americans (nearly 40 percent) and Hispanics (about 19 percent), particularly those in low-income groups (Fife & Mode, 1992). Among women diagnosed with AIDS in 1994, three fourths were African-American or Hispanic. These latter statistics reflect the high prevalence among inner city intravenous drug users.

Why have so many cases in the United States shown up in the male homosexual community? Politician Patrick Buchanan was quoted as saying, "The poor homosexuals. They have declared war on nature, and now nature is exacting an awful retribution." However, you have already learned that a person's sexual behavior, or sexual orientation, per se does not cause HIV infection. To become infected, you must come into contact with the human immunodeficiency virus. The virus cannot tell whether you are homosexual or heterosexual. The reason it first spread so rapidly among the male homosexual community here is threefold: many gay men had numerous, often hundreds, of sexual partners; the common practice of unprotected anal intercourse; and a new disease with a long incubation period. Before anyone even knew that HIV/AIDS existed, the virus had already been spread to tens of thousands of male homosexuals.

Keep in mind that knowing who was diagnosed with AIDS in 1994 does not tell us who had HIV. Remember, *those people diagnosed with AIDS in the middle 1990s are those who first became infected with HIV 5–15 years ago.* Individuals who become infected with HIV in the middle 1990s probably will not reach the stage of infection we call AIDS until the years 2000 to 2010. So,where is HIV now? Is it spreading into the heterosexual, intravenous drug-free, community?

The answer is yes. Overall, the prevalence is still quite low, based on blood tests of military recruits, Job Corps applicants, and first-time blood donors (e.g., McNeil et al., 1991). However, the rate is considerably higher for heterosexuals who have had numerous sexual partners. Masters, Johnson, and Kolodny (1988) reported that among heterosexuals with six or more sexual partners a year, 7 percent of the women and 5 percent of the men tested positive for HIV. Similar results have been reported by others (Kelen et al., 1988).

The most likely pathways by which HIV will first spread into the heterosexual community are through bisexual men and intravenous drug users infecting their heterosexual partners (Chu et al., 1992; Doll et al., 1992; Lewis, Watters, & Case, 1990; vanden Hoek, van Haastrecht, & Coutinho, 1990). Another likely route of infection is through prostitutes, many of whom are intravenous drug users. A 1990 study of 1305 female prostitutes across the United States found that 6.7 percent tested positive for HIV (Khabbaz et al., 1990). In some cities the infection rate is as high as 25 percent for female prostitutes and 50 percent or higher for male homosexual prostitutes (Boles & Elifson, 1994; McKeganey, 1994). Many men who pay prostitutes for sex do not use condoms (Leonard, Freund, & Platt, 1989).

Ten percent of the new cases of AIDS in 1994 were people who became infected with HIV by heterosexual transmission, up from only 1.9 percent in 1985. The Centers for Disease Control and Prevention say this is a conservative estimate. Already, *over half of all new AIDS cases in U.S. women are due to heterosexual transmission.* AIDS is already the leading cause of death among African-American women aged 15 to 44 in New York state and New Jersey and is the fourth leading cause of death among all U.S. women aged 25 to 44 (CDC, 1995). By the end of 1995, more than 45,000 U.S. children will have been left motherless because of AIDS (Michaels & Levine, 1992). Researchers at the HIV Infection in Women Conference (1995) predicted that by the year 2000 HIV infection will surpass heart disease as the second leading cause of death.

Despite the tremendous amount of publicity about AIDS, including the fact that worldwide the large proportion of cases are acquired by heterosexual transmission, many heterosexuals in the United States still do not believe that they can get HIV. If you still are not convinced, there is no better evidence than what happened in Haiti, where, as one researcher stated, you can see "how rapidly and dramatically the AIDS virus can spread in a promiscuous heterosexual population." In 1983, 71 percent of the cases of AIDS occurred among male homosexuals and intravenous drug users, the same as presently found here. By the late 1980s, the large majority of new AIDS patients were heterosexuals (Pape & Warren, 1993). Only 15 percent of patients with AIDS in 1979–1982 were females, but by 1991–1992, nearly half the new AIDS patients were females. As a result, the number of children with AIDS has increased dramatically (6.6 percent of the total number of cases in 1989). In urban areas, 10 percent of the adult population is infected with HIV, and AIDS is the leading cause of death among sexually active adults. One of the reasons HIV spread so rapidly in Haiti is the common acceptance of multiple sexual partners (in one study it was not uncommon to have had more than 10 partners a year) and the common use of prostitution (Pape et al., 1990).

Perhaps there aren't as many people with as many multiple sexual partners in the United States as in Haiti, or as many men who solicit services of prostitutes, but that doesn't mean that HIV will not spread among heterosexuals here, only that it will spread more slowly. Dr. Ward Cates of the Centers for Disease Control and Prevention said, "Anyone who has the least ability to look into the future can already see the potential for this disease being much worse than anything mankind has seen before."

The Human Side of AIDS

The deaths of people like actor Rock Hudson and tennis star Arthur Ashe, and the news that basketball great Magic Johnson was infected with HIV, made the disease more personal for many people—it had affected "someone they knew." But with each passing year, there are more and more people who do not have to read a newspaper to get a first-hand experience with AIDS. AIDS is more than a disease; it is a personal tragedy, not only for the patient but for the family and loved ones as well. Some students in my course have asked me to share their experiences. Here are a few:

"My reaction to a low T-cell test was devastating. It was like a bomb exploding inside or a knife through the heart. My time is near and each day is a gift to cherish. . . . finding out I was HIV positive was not as shocking as finding out that what I have changed to improve the quality of my life makes little difference in my life expectancy. . . ."

"My father has AIDS. You really don't know the severity of a problem until you're faced with it. Watching my father die has been extremely painful and stressful. . . ."

"We are discussing STDs and AIDS in class and although these are issues that are in the media constantly, I still believe that most students don't think that AIDS can happen to them. I have seen AIDS happen firsthand. People need to know that this is a reality in all of our lives. I learned in one of the most painful ways I can imagine. Two years ago my older brother died of AIDS. I was only 19, he was 24. It had been said that everyone's lives would be touched by AIDS, and when I was younger I didn't believe it. Now I do. I was with my brother when he died, as was my whole family. We did not know he had AIDS until two weeks before he died. He had hidden it from us. He came home to die. It changed my life.

Believe me, AIDS is real. Don't wait for someone close to you to die before you take it seriously. Don't wait to test positive before you believe in AIDS. I think my brother thought he was invincible. I used to think I was, too, until the night he died."

(from the author's files)

Testing for HIV

Until recently, the standard tests for HIV did not test for the virus directly, but instead detected antibodies to the virus that are produced by an infected person's immune system. These tests are still widely used, but accurate testing requires multiple tests. Blood is first checked with the ELISA (enzyme-linked immunosorbent assay) test. However, the test can result in "false positives" (i.e., uninfected blood testing positive). A recent flu vaccination can sometimes produce a false positive, for example (Mac Kenzie, et al., 1992). To assure against false positives, the ELISA test is repeated if the results are positive. If there is a second positive indication, the blood is tested again with either the Western Blot or IFA (immunofluorescent assay) tests. These are more expensive and demanding tests that give information about particular antibodies. A negative test result means only that a person *probably* has not been infected with HIV. Remember, it often takes several months for an infected person's body to start producing antibodies to the virus, so it is possible for someone to be infected and not test positive. In fact, studies have found that in a few cases HIV can "hide" in blood cells, sometimes for years, without those cells expelling antibodies into the blood serum.

In December 1994, the Food and Drug Administration approved a new test that measures the presence of antibodies to HIV in saliva. The saliva is checked with the ELISA test and positive results are then confirmed with the Western Blot blood test. The saliva test is much less accurate than the blood test, but may be more appealing to some people than blood tests.

The HIV-antibody tests are very effective in detecting HIV infection in individuals who are already showing symptoms (and thus have high levels of HIV and antibodies to HIV). They are not as reliable in screening HIV-infected persons who are still healthy. Today, there is a new test that directly tests for HIV. The technique is called the polymerase chain reaction (PCR) and it can detect a single HIV-infected white blood cell among 100,000 healthy ones. Even this technique is being refined and improved (Piatuk et al., 1993).

At the start of 1995, there was considerable controversy over approval of a home HIV testing kit. Three companies were seeking Food and Drug Administration approval for drugstore sales of the kits. Purchasers of the kits would simply prick a finger and then send dried blood to a lab. They would learn by telephone whether or not they were infected with HIV (identification would be by a number on the kit, and thus would be anonymously done). Infected persons would talk to a counselor. Supporters, which include the Centers for Disease Control and Prevention, say that the kits will increase the number of people who are aware of their infection, and can then stop spreading the virus. Opponents worry that employers might (illegally) use the tests, or that some people might kill themselves if they learned by phone that they had HIV. Then there are questions about lab accuracy, and the problem of how the home tests will affect tracking of the epidemic (physicians currently report new cases to the CDC). This issue probably will have been decided by the FDA by the time you are reading this.

Treatment for HIV/AIDS

At the beginning of 1995, there were only four anti-retroviral drugs on the market to treat HIV infections, and 43 other drugs approved for treatment of AIDS-related illnesses. The antiretroviral drugs (technically called nucleoside analogs) slow the progression of HIV infection by blocking an essential enzyme (called reverse transcriptase) needed for the virus to replicate itself. The four drugs are zidovudine (AZT), didanosine (ddI), zalcitabine (ddC), and stavudine (d4T). However, these drugs do not rid an infected individual of HIV; *there is no cure for HIV infection.*

The first and most commonly used antiviral drug is AZT. The initial studies were very promising, indicating that the drug delayed the onset of AIDS and prolonged life (e.g., Fischl et al., 1989; Graham et al., 1992; Volberding et al., 1990). However, some subsequent studies have delivered more sobering news. For many HIV-infected patients, AZT's side effects (e.g., anemia) made them so ill that it offset any advantage of postponing onset of AIDS (Lenderking et al., 1994; Oddone et al., 1993). Moreover, the virus quickly becomes resistant to AZT, and because patients taking the drug have often continued to spread the virus, there are now AZT-resistant strains of the virus. Two large-scale studies found that while AZT delayed AIDS onset when given early (CD4 cell counts above 200), it did not prolong life (Hamilton et al., 1992; Nordic Medical Research Council, 1992). A more recent study found that early treatment with AZT in symptom-free patients did not even delay the onset of symptoms of HIV infection (Concorde Coordinating Committee, 1994). It is now the general consensus that AZT may boost survival in the first year (in those who can tolerate the side effects), but that its benefits fade very rapidly.

A recent study found that when HIV-infected women were treated with AZT and their babies were treated for 6 weeks after birth, it reduced the likelihood that the babies would be infected by two thirds (interim results of an international study, *Lancet*, 1994).

However, in 1995, the National Institutes of Health dropped AZT from a clinical trial among children after it proved to cause a high proportion of side effects.

As is the case with AZT, ddI, ddC, and d4T have serious side effects (e.g., all cause nerve problems in the hands and feet, and pancreatitis with ddI) and thus their use is limited. For those HIV-infected patients who can tolerate them, the drugs might possibly be used in combination (Chow et al., 1993). This approach of using a "cocktail" of different drugs was adopted from the field of cancer therapy and has brought new optimism to AIDS therapists.

Researchers continue to try other drugs. On-and-off infusions of interleukin-2, a natural protein that regulates the body's immune defenses, has been reported to increase CD4 cell counts in persons with symptomatic HIV infection (Kovacs et al., 1995). At the 10th International Conference on AIDS held in Yokohama, Japan, in 1994, scientists presented promising preliminary data for gene therapy. The procedure involves inserting protective new genes (a protein) into the CD4 cells. They hoped to start testing the gene therapy on infected babies sometime during 1995. At another national medical meeting in early 1995, scientists gave promising results for new drugs that block another key viral enzyme. The drugs, called protease inhibitors, were said to be much more effective than AZT (Kolata, 1995). But a recent study found that HIV can quickly become resistant to this class of drugs as well (Condra et al., 1995).

The final stages of AIDS are so debilitating that the person must be hospitalized or cared for entirely by others. In the absence of community-based treatment resources for AIDS patients, hospitals have had to assume the major burden for medical and psychosocial support services. The average hospital bill for an AIDS patient is about $70,000. The total lifetime cost of treating a person infected with HIV (from time of infection until death) is about $119,000 (Hellinger, 1993). This has already resulted in a drastic increase in billings to Medicaid and a budget crisis for many tax-supported big city hospitals. Many insurance companies are refusing to insure HIV-infected individuals, with many companies requiring blood tests for high-risk individuals. Because AIDS is an incurable disease, many health authorities believe that there will be more emphasis on easing a patient's final days in a hospice with volunteer workers rather than heroic measures to prolong lives.

Because it is presently incurable, the prevention of HIV infection depends on preventing transmission of, and avoiding exposure to, the virus. An ideal way to combat HIV would be to develop a vaccine. Scientists are identifying subunits of the virus that, when injected into the body, will stimulate the production of protective antibodies. Due to the rapid spread of HIV world-wide, health officials have lowered their expectations that a vaccine be 100 percent effective (see Haynes, 1993). In November 1994, the World Health Organization decided that the two most widely tested HIV vaccines were ready for large-scale human testing. Both vaccines are derived from a protein (gp 120), located on the surface of the virus, that attaches to human cells. When injected, the vaccines cause the body to make antibodies that target the gp 120 protein, thus interfering with the protein's ability to attach with the CD4 cell. However, Dr. Anthony Fauci of the U.S. National Institutes of Health said that the two vaccines will probably offer only a 30 percent chance of protection. In early 1995, a scientific advisory panel urged the Food and Drug Administration to allow final clinical trials of a vaccine developed by Dr. Jonas Salk, inventor of the first polio vaccine. About two dozen other vaccines are presently being tested with humans on a smaller scale.

The emotional impact of finding out that you have AIDS or are infected with HIV can be devastating. Severe depression is common in the early phases of HIV infection and again at the symptomatic stage, and the suicide rate is 17 to 66 times greater in individuals diagnosed with AIDS than in the general population (see Kalichman & Sikkema, 1994). On the other hand, many people have led productive lives for years after being diagnosed with AIDS (Kiecolt-Glaser & Glaser, 1988). There is increasing evidence that the immune system can be affected by a positive or negative attitude (Siegel, 1989). It is important, therefore, that HIV-infected individuals not give up hope and receive as much positive support as possible.

PUBLIC REACTIONS TO AIDS

"Despite the laws of the land, discrimination continues to play a brutal and important role in the lives of those infected with HIV. The extent and the cruelty of such discrimination have been brought forth in heartrending testimony to the National Commission at each of its many hearings. As a colleague and I wrote recently, 'the pain, suffering and despair of the disease alone are dreadful enough. The added stigma makes it virtually unbearable. You lose not only your life, but also your pride, your job, your insurance, your friends and your family. Posterity remembers you for dying of AIDS, not for having lived.'"

Dr. David Rogers (1992), vice chair of the National Commission on AIDS

The 1993 movie *Philadelphia*, starring Tom Hanks, focused attention on the pervasiveness of stigma related to AIDS and the discrimination often directed at HIV-infected individuals. A sizable minority of the public have feelings of anger, disgust, or fear toward persons with AIDS, and over a third of Americans feel that "people with AIDS should be legally separated from others to protect the public health" (Herek & Capitanio, 1993). In 1993, Congress did, in fact, pass a bill that banned immigration by HIV-infected foreigners.

The public's fear of AIDS has been fueled by well-publicized cases of individuals who knowingly put others at risk. In 1992, health officials in Michigan confined a woman after she was accused of having sex with six men without telling them she was infected with HIV. An HIV-infected man in Oakland, California was arrested after he set out to "ritually infect future sex partners out of spite." In Louisiana, an HIV-infected man was convicted after having sexual intercourse with his girlfriend without telling her of his infection.

But the negativity directed at people with AIDS is not limited to the few who would knowingly spread the disease. Some children who innocently contracted AIDS, such as Ryan White of Kokomo, Indiana (who became infected with HIV from a blood transfusion and later died of AIDS), have been temporarily barred from attending school. In Florida, the home of three hemophiliac children with AIDS was burned to the ground when they attempted to go to public school. Some victims have been fired from their jobs.

How should we as a society deal with the HIV epidemic? First of all, it is important to educate the public that the virus is not spread by any type of casual contact, and thus there is no medical basis to avoid nonsexual interactions with infected individuals. Most states now have laws that protect HIV-infected persons against discrimination in the workplace and housing. Ensuring the privacy and equal treatment of persons with HIV infection is essential to the success of testing, treatment, and outreach programs. Public health officials will not gain the confidence and cooperation of infected individuals if these persons are not legally protected from stigma and irrational prejudice.

It is the disease that is frightening, not the people who have it.

—Former President Ronald Reagan

Some medical journals have argued that there should be more routine testing of people's blood for HIV (for example, testing of all hospital patients, health care workers, pregnant women, and newborns; Angell,

1991). Others have called for more widespread testing (Kutchinsky, 1992). The intent is that most people would not knowingly spread the virus if they knew they were infected. Routine testing is already done for syphilis (e.g., when people apply for a marriage license, during prenatal exams). However, some people oppose mandatory testing because of possible civil rights violations (positive test results might be passed on to employers and insurance companies).

One likely way to reduce the spread of HIV is education, but there is even controversy about that. Former U.S. Surgeon General C. Everett Koop, a noted conservative, startled many people when he advocated the teaching of sex education, including facts about AIDS, beginning in elementary school. Former U.S. Secretary of Education William Bennett, on the other hand, opposed Koop and wanted to stress moral values and abstinence from sex until marriage. In June 1988, the Surgeon General's office mailed a brochure entitled "Understanding AIDS" to 107 million American households. The Surgeon General emphasized that if an individual is not in a monogamous relationship, the next best way to reduce the risk of HIV infection is always to use condoms. However, others oppose the promotion of condoms.

A big question, of course, is whether or not education about AIDS will convince people to change their lifestyles. The Surgeon General's office has been educating and warning people about the long-term dangers of smoking since 1964 (is there really anyone who hasn't heard that smoking can cause lung cancer?), yet many people continue to smoke.

The Effect of AIDS on Sexual Behavior

Have AIDS, and AIDS prevention programs, resulted in long-term changes in sexual behavior in the general population? In a review of 77 studies, Choi and Coates (1994) concluded that the answer was unequivocally yes. Studies in the 1980s showed a dramatic increase in safer sex behaviors among male homosexuals (e.g., Ekstrand, Coates, & McKusick, 1988). There was a marked increase in the use of condoms and a decrease in the number of sexual partners. The heterosexual community was slower to respond, but here, too, some improvement has been found (e.g., DeBuono et al., 1990; Samuel et al., 1991; Sonenstein, Pleck, & Ku, 1989). In 1995, the Centers for Disease Control and Prevention reported that among sexually active teens, 53 percent reported using condoms the last time they had sex. Condom use was highest among men who believed that condoms are effective in preventing HIV infection (e.g., Hingson et al., 1990; Siegel et al., 1991). Among heterosexuals, African-American men were much more likely than white men to have increased

their use of condoms and/or reduced their number of sexual partners (Catania et al., 1993; Melnick et al., 1993; Tanfer et al., 1993).

However, not everyone is practicing safer sex behaviors, and several studies have reported some very disturbing trends. For example, in the male homosexual community there has been some relapse from safer sex practices, particularly among young gay men (Handsfield & Schwebke, 1990; Stall et al., 1990). A 1993 study by the Department of Health in San Francisco concluded that "AIDS education campaigns have failed to make an impression on San Francisco's gay youths, who continue to contract HIV by engaging in dangerous sex practices" (Krieger, 1993).

Among heterosexuals, a very large national survey conducted in the early 1990s found that while use of condoms may have increased, only a small minority of sexually active adults used them all the time (Catania et al., 1992). Another study of adolescent and young adult males found that males decreased their use of condoms as they grew older. The authors concluded that "early progress in fostering safer behaviors among young men slowed and possibly stopped as the nation entered the 1990s" (Ku, Sonenstein, & Pleck, 1993). In addition, several studies found that among college students, the number who reported having had six or more sexual partners in their lifetime had not decreased during the 1980s, and may have actually increased (Bishop & Lipsitz, 1988; DeBuono et al., 1990; Reinisch et al., 1992). A recent study concluded that "roughly 85 percent of the adult population aged 18 to 50 were estimated to be at some risk for behavioral exposure to HIV virus with regard to reported sexual-behavior" and that "over time, those who could be considered at no risk have declined as a proportion of the population" (Campostrini & McQueen, 1993).

Most disturbing are findings that there are some people who apparently have no regard for their own health or the health of others. For example, many people who have had a sexually transmitted disease in the past still do not take precautions to prevent another infection in the future (O'Campo et al., 1992). In fact, a sizable minority of people who discover that they are infected with HIV continue to engage in unsafe sexual activity (Cleary et al., 1991). Many keep their infections secret from their partners (Marks, Richardson, & Maldonado, 1991). King and Anderson (1994) recently reported that some people might be willing to accept death by AIDS for an opportunity to engage in a few years of unlimited sexual partners.

Results like these indicate strongly that HIV will continue to spread for some time to come. What precautions are you taking to prevent becoming infected? Be sure to read the section on safer sex. ∎

PARASITIC INFESTATIONS

Viral and bacterial diseases are not the only things that can be transmitted from one person to another during sex. It is also possible to pick up parasites from an infested person. Condoms will do little good in preventing these types of infestations.

Pubic lice (*Pediculosis pubis,* also known as *Pthirus pubis,* or "crabs") are 1–2 millimeter long, grayish (or dusky red after a meal of blood), six-legged parasites that attach themselves to pubic hair and feed on human blood (see Figure 5-11). They cause intense itching.

> **Pubic lice**
> Also known as "crabs," an infestation of the parasite *Pediculosis pubis,* which attach themselves to pubic hair and feed on blood.

" I was a senior in high school and I was sleeping with a guy who I had been involved with for a year. For about two weeks I had been itching in the pubic area. The longer it went on, the more irritating it got. Finally, I examined my pubic hair and found little crab-looking things. I was shocked and disgusted...."

" ...I noticed an itching down in my pubic area. It got extensively annoying so I took a look to see what was happening down there. I almost started to scream when I noticed little flat insects crawling around that area...."

(from the author's files)

The lice do not live for more than a day off the human body, but any eggs that fall off can survive and hatch up to a week later. You could, therefore, pick them up from the sheets, towels, or clothing of an infested person. Normal bathing will not wash the lice off, but you can eliminate them by applying pyrethrin products (e.g., one percent permethrin cream rinse) or 1% lin-

dane (Kwell) lotion, cream, or shampoo to the infested area *and all other hairy body areas.* Repeat the treatment in seven to 10 days (Meinking & Taplin, 1990). Be sure also to clean all clothing, sheets, and towels that might be infested in very hot water (or have them dry cleaned) to avoid reinfestation.

Scabies is a contagious infestation of 0.3–0.4 millimeter long, pearly white, parasitic itch mites (*Sarcoptes scabiei;* see Figure 5-11). The mites burrow under the skin to lay their eggs, resulting at first in itchy, red, pimplelike bumps when the eggs hatch. Large patches of scaling skin result if the mites are not immediately destroyed. Secondary bacterial infection is common. The itch mite is acquired by close contact with infested persons (sexual contact is not necessary) and thus is most common in people living and sleeping in crowded conditions. However, the mite "is notorious for its lack of respect for person, age, sex or race, whether it be in the epidermis of an emperor or a slave, a centurion or a nursling, it makes itself perfectly at home with undiscriminating impudence and equal obnoxiousness" (Friedman, 1947). Scabies has traditionally been treated with 1 percent lindane, but

> **Scabies**
> A contagious infestation of parasitic mites (*Sarcoptes scabiei*) that burrow under the skin and lay their eggs.

A

B

FIGURE 5-11   (A) TWO *PTHIRUS PUBIS* (CRAB LICE). (B) GRAVID FEMALE *SARCOPTES SCABIEI* MITE. (DAVID TOPLIN & TERRY MEINKING: SCABIES, LICE, AND FUNGAL INFECTIONS. *PRIMARY CARE,* 16(3), 551–568. DEPT. OF DERMATOLOGY AND CUTANEOUS SURGERY, AND EPIDEMILOGY AND PUBLIC HEALTH, UNVERSITY OF MIAMI SCHOOL OF MEDICINE, MIAMI, FLORIDA.)

recent work has shown that permethrin 5 percent cream may be more effective (Taplin et al., 1991). Should you ever get scabies, be sure also to wash all your sheets, towels, and clothing to avoid re-infestation.

Pinworms (*Enterobius vermicularis*) live in the large intestine and are generally gotten through nonsexual contact with the eggs. The female pinworms leave the rectum at night and lay their eggs around the anus, which results in intense itching (see Weber, 1993). Pinworms are common in children, who pass them from one to another by hand-to-mouth contact while playing. Pinworms can also be transmitted sexually in adults by manual or oral contact with the anus of an infected person. This mode of transmission occurs most commonly among homosexual males. Such sexual practices can also result in the transmission of a one-celled animal (*Entamoeba histolytica*) that causes intestinal **amebiasis**, or amebic dysentery. ■

Pinworms
Small worms (*Enterobius vermicularis*) that live in the large intestine and are generally transmitted through nonsexual contact with the worms' eggs, but which can be transmitted sexually by manual or oral contact with the anus of an infected person.

Amebiasis
Dysentery caused by infestation of amoebae, a one-celled organism.

VAGINITIS

Vaginitis is a general term that refers to any inflammation of the vagina. There are basically three types, and it is rare that a female does not experience at least one of them in her lifetime. Vaginitis has many causes, including hormone imbalances, allergic reactions, chemical irritation, and infection. Symptoms generally include discomfort or pain during urination, along with a vaginal discharge that often has a disagreeable odor.

Vaginitis
A general term that refers to any inflammation of the vagina. There are three general types: trichomoniasis, moniliasis, and bacterial vaginosis.

TRICHOMONIASIS (TRICHOMONAL VAGINITIS)
Only one type of vaginitis, trichomoniasis, is usually contracted by sexual contact. The Centers for Disease Control and Prevention estimates that there will be 3 million new cases of "trich" this year, which is more than gonorrhea, syphilis, and genital herpes combined. Other researchers estimate that there may be as many as 8 million new cases each year (Martens & Faro, 1989).

Trichomoniasis is caused by a one-cell protozoan named *Trichomonas vaginalis* that lives in the vagina and urethra. Symptoms in women generally appear from 4 days to 1 month after exposure and include a copious, foamy, yellowish-green discharge with a foul odor accompanied by severe vaginal itching. However, not all women show symptoms.

Trichomoniasis
A type of vaginitis caused by a one-celled protozoan that is usually transmitted during sexual intercourse.

" About two weeks after becoming sexually involved with my boyfriend, I began to have severe pain during intercourse. Soon I noticed a discharge, itching, and an extremely foul odor. After many weeks of shame I finally went to the infirmary with my roommate who was having urinary problems. Imagine how surprised we were to find out that we both had trichomonia-sis. How could we catch such a thing? The only person she had sex with was her boyfriend and the only person I had sex with was my boyfriend! In the end we found out that our boyfriends went out together one night and had unprotected sex with a girl that they had known less than 6 hours!"

(from the author's files)

T. vaginalis can survive in urine or tap water for hours or sometimes days, so it is possible to pick it up by using a wet toilet seat or by sharing towels. Nonetheless, the vast majority of cases are transmitted by sexual intercourse. Infected males generally show no symptoms, and in those who do, it is usually only a slight urethral discharge. Thus, *men tend to act as asymptomatic carriers*, spreading it to new female partners (just the opposite of what we often see in the early stages of gonorrhea, chlamydia, and syphilis).

Trichomoniasis can be very irritating (due to itching and burning), but until recently most authorities did not believe that there are any serious long-term consequences if it is left untreated and thus regarded trich as a "minor" STD. However, a recent study found that women with trichomoniasis were as likely to develop tubal adhesions leading to infertility as women with gonorrhea (Grodstein, Goldman, & Cramer, 1993). The authors concluded that trich "should be considered a potentially important sexually transmitted disease in women."

The diagnosis of "trich" is made by a microscopic examination of any discharge and then growing the parasite in culture. However, the tests have not been totally reliable. If trichomoniasis is suspected, both the infected person and her male partner (who is usually asymptomatic) should be treated. Otherwise, he will just reinfect her when intercourse resumes. Trich is very easily eradicated by a drug called metronidazole (its trade name is Flagyl), but some authorities worry about treating a non-life-threatening disease with this drug because it is a possible carcinogen.

MONILIASIS (OR CANDIDIASIS)

Moniliasis is caused by an overgrowth of a microorganism (*Candida albicans*) that is normally found in the vagina. It is the fungus or yeast infection that is very common in women. Symptoms include a thick, white, and cheesy discharge accompanied by intense itching. There are about 22 million cases reported every year, but many more cases go unreported. Unfortunately, many women do not realize how common (normal) yeast infections are, and feel alone or dirty when it happens to them.

Moniliasis

Sometimes called candidiasis, a type of vaginitis caused by the overgrowth of a microorganism (*Candida albicans*), which is normally found in the vagina. It is a fungus or yeast infection and usually is a sexually related, rather than a sexually transmitted, disease.

"The first time I got a yeast infection I was terrified. I didn't know what it was. All I knew was that the itching was intolerable and I had this discharge that wasn't normal. . . ."

"The first time I had it was when I was 16. I started to have an uneasy itchy feeling. I took a shower and thought it would go away. It not only continued, but it became worse. The itchiness was now accompanied by a foul smelling discharge. . . . I felt very dirty. . . ."

(from the author's files)

Yeast infections are sometimes transmitted sexually, but the vast majority of cases are not contracted in this manner. *Children, even babies, can get this, too* (Robinson & Ridgway, 1994). Thus, monilial infections are not really considered a sexually transmitted disease, such as trichomoniasis, but are a sexually related disease.

Anything that changes the chemical environment of the vagina can result in an overgrowth, including hormone changes, diabetes, heavy use of antibiotics (which kill off the "friendly" bacteria in the vagina that keep the yeast in check), and even overly zealous hygiene (e.g., the use of perfumy feminine hygiene products). Many women first experience a monilial infection during pregnancy, for example, or when they first start taking oral contraceptives.

"Once when I had an infected tooth, my dentist prescribed an antibiotic. About the third day I developed a yeast infection. No one had ever told me I could get a yeast infection from an antibiotic. When I told some of my friends they told me this had happened to at least two of them before. . . ."

"I had my first yeast infection when I was pregnant with my first child. I was so embarrassed about having this terrible itch in the genital area that I couldn't tell anyone. Finally it was time for my regular prenatal checkup and when the doctor examined me and saw that I had scratched myself raw he wanted to know why I had not called him. I was just too embarrassed to say I had an itch in the genital area."

(from the author's files)

Women with immune deficiencies (e.g., HIV infection and AIDS) are particularly susceptible to yeast infections. Some women have reactions to their partners' semen (this can be prevented by using condoms). The microbe can also invade the mouth (where it is called **thrush**), anus, and skin, as well as internal organs. Some people believe that women can suffer from chronic candidiasis syndrome (also called candidiasis hypersensitivity syndrome or the "yeast connection") characterized by recurrent or chronic yeast infections, severe PMS, gastrointestinal problems, depression and anxiety, and fatigue (Crook, 1983), but this has been challenged by the American Academy of Allergy and Immunology (1986) and treatment to remove the fungus does not reduce internal or psychological symptoms (Dismukes et al., 1990).

Yeast infections are treated with antifungal creams or suppositories. There are over-the-counter drugs that you can purchase in the drugstore (e.g., Monistat and Gyne-Lotrimin). However, if the symptoms do not go away within a few days, see your doctor immediately (for you might have one of the other types of vaginitis).

BACTERIAL VAGINOSIS

This type of vaginitis is caused by the interaction of several vaginal bacteria (most particularly, *Gardnerella vaginalis*) that can also live in the male's urethra. **Bacterial vaginosis** used to be called by a variety of names (haemophilus, Gardnerella, or nonspecific vaginitis), but the new name more correctly reflects what we now know about the microbiology of the disease (Eschenbach, 1993). It is the most common of the three types

Bacterial vaginosis

A type of vaginitis caused by the interaction of several vaginal bacteria (most particularly, *Gardnerella vaginalis*).

of vaginitis. The main complaint of patients is a vaginal odor (sometimes described as fishy), but there is also an abnormal discharge (grayish and nonclumpy). We now know that this type of infection can lead to serious upper genital tract infection as well (Eschen-bach, 1993). Many antibiotics are ineffective; the drugs of choice are metronidazole or clindamycin (Greaves et al., 1988; Lugo-Miro, Green, & Mazur, 1992). To avoid reinfection, the female's partner should also be treated. ∎

BOX 5-A

SEXUALITY AND HEALTH: VAGINAL HEALTH CARE

For women, vaginal infections are probably second in frequency only to the common cold. Here are some hygiene tips to help minimize your chances of getting vaginitis:

1. Bathe regularly, avoiding deodorant soaps and bubble baths, and do not share washcloths and towels.
2. Dry the vulva thoroughly and wear cotton panties (synthetic fabrics retain heat and moisture, conditions in which bacteria thrive).

"I used to get yeast infections several times a year. Every time I would visit or call my doctor . . . I finally figured it out on my own with a little help from one of the hottest days in June. I would always wear silk or polyester blend underpants and nylon hosiery. Does any of these materials allow absorption? Of course not. I ran out and bought cotton underpants and hosiery with garter belts. Five years have passed and not one yeast infection yet."

(from the author's files)

Certainly never wear synthetic underpants to bed. Also, the yeast that results in monilial infections can survive normal laundering in hot waters. As a result, a recent study suggested that women put their laundered, but damp, cotton underwear in a microwave for 5 minutes (do not try this with dry or synthetic fabrics).

3. Avoid feminine hygiene products.
4. After a bowel movement, wipe the anus from front to back, not back to front, as this can spread rectal bacteria to the vagina.
5. Allow time for adequate vaginal lubrication during intercourse, and if you use a lubricant, use a water-soluble one such as K-Y jelly (petroleum-based lubricants cannot only harbor bacteria, but they disintegrate condoms as well).
6. If you and your partner engage in any type of anal stimulation during sex, be sure to wash the hands or penis before touching the vaginal area again.
7. If your partner has sexual relationships with people other than yourself, make sure he uses a condom during intercourse.
8. If you have frequent yeast infections, ask your doctor about douching with a mild acidic solution.
9. Keep stress to a minimum, eat well, and get adequate sleep.
10. See a doctor as soon as you notice any of the previously mentioned symptoms. Remember, vaginal infections are very common and nothing to be ashamed of, and can be treated very easily. ∎

CYSTITIS AND PROSTATITIS

Cystitis refers to a bacterial infection of the bladder. Because the female's urethra is considerably shorter

Cystitis

A bacterial infection of the bladder (often caused by the bacterium *Escherichia coli*).

than the male's (and thus bacteria have a shorter distance to travel), cystitis is much more common in women than men. Many cases are unrelated to sexual activity. The bacterium *Escherichia coli*, for example, is often transmitted from the rectum to the urethral opening by wiping forward from the anus after a bowel movement. Women should always wipe themselves from front to back. Cystitis can also be caused by the *N. gonorrhoeae* and *Chlamydia trachomatis* bacteria, but it is generally not considered a sexually transmitted disease.

Symptoms may include a frequent urge to urinate, painful urination, and lower abdominal pains. It is treated with either sulfa drugs or antibiotics. Vigorous intercourse, especially in women first becoming sexually active, can also result in urinary tract infection (hence the term *"honeymoon cystitis"*) by the inward friction on the urethra allowing nonsexually transmitted bacteria to ascend. For those women who experience postcoital urinary tract infection, trimethoprim and sulfamethoxazole taken together within 2 hours of intercourse prevents infections (Stapleton et al., 1990).

The E. coli bacteria can also be transmitted to a male's prostate during sexual activity, resulting in **prostatitis**. Symptoms may include lower back and/or groin pain, fever, and burning during ejaculation. This, too, is treated with antibiotics. ■

Prostatitis

Inflammation of the prostate gland.

PRACTICING SAFER SEX

Add them up: 4 million new cases of chlamydia per year, at least 3 million new cases of trichomoniasis, nearly 1 million new cases of gonorrhea, one-half million to 1 million new cases of human papillomavirus infection, up to 500,000 new cases of herpes, an unknown number of new HIV infections, plus syphilis, sexually transmitted cases of hepatitis, chancroid, and others. There will be about 12 million new cases of sexually transmitted diseases this year (about 35,000 new cases every day), with most cases occurring within your age group (late teens through 40). Of course, some people who are sexually active will be infected with the same STD two or more times in a single year, or even get two or more different STDs at once. Yes, having one does not prevent you from getting others, so it is possible to hit the jackpot and have more than one at once.

What are you doing to avoid sexually transmitted diseases? It appears that many college students are doing little or nothing. In fact, many continue to engage in high-risk behaviors. There is a strong association between number of sexual partners and having, or having already had, a sexually transmitted disease (e.g., a woman with five or more lifetime partners is eight times more likely to have had an STD than a woman with only one partner; Joffe et al., 1992), yet, according to surveys on college campuses, most students have had multiple lifetime sexual partners. At a midwestern university, for example, females reported an average of 5.6 partners; males reported 11.2 partners (Reinisch et al., 1992). At a heavily Catholic southern university, one fourth of the students had had at least four partners

(King & Anderson, 1994), and at a university in the northeast, over 20 percent of the coeds reported having had three or more sexual partners in the past year (DeBuono et al., 1990). Nationally, over 8 percent of American women report having had two or more partners in the previous 3 months (Seidman, Mosher, & Aral, 1992). A survey of several Canadian colleges found that 21 percent of the men and nearly 9 percent of the women had already had at least 10 sexual partners (MacDonald et al., 1990). These studies and others found that only a minority of college students use condoms on a regular basis.

Why do so many intelligent people continue to engage in high-risk sexual behaviors? (see Box 5-B) According to a 1994 survey by EDK Associates (New York), 78 percent of women who have had multiple sexual partners do not fear getting an STD because they believe "it won't happen to me." We can presume that as many men believe the same. Recall, however, that the Centers for Disease Control and Prevention says that for one in four Americans, it will happen to them. So let's get serious and consider how you can minimize the chances of it ever happening to you.

The absolute best way to avoid STDs, of course, is never to have sex, but few of us wish to live the life of a Tibetan monk. If you are going to have sex, one solution is to *restrict your sexual activity to a long-term, mutually faithful, monogamous relationship*. If neither you nor your

Safer sex

Sexual behaviors with a low risk for contraction of a sexually transmitted disease. These include consistent use of condoms and/or abstaining from sex until one enters a long-term monogamous relationship.

partner have an STD at the start of the relationship, and neither of you have other partners, you do not have to worry about STDs. However, there are problems with this approach. First, while many of us limit our sexual behavior to monogamous relations, most monogamous relationships do not last forever. Many of us have a lifestyle of what is commonly called *serial monogamy*. We break up and eventually enter into another monogamous relationship. You may have been having sex with only one person for a certain period of your life, but how many monogamous relationships have you had in your lifetime? If just one of those partners had an STD, he or she could have transmitted it to you. Whenever we have a new sexual partner, we can rarely be sure of their previous sexual history. A recent study found that many people have lied to new partners about their past sexual experiences (Cochran & Mays, 1990).

"A friend of mine was going out with a guy from . . . They had a sexual relationship and used condoms most of the time. He only recently mentioned that he had tested positive for the AIDS virus in the past. My friend is under tremendous psychological distress. . . ."

(from the author's files)

A second problem is that few of us can be 100 percent certain that our partner will remain monogamous. Read again the personal case histories at the beginning of the chapter.

A second solution is to *always use condoms.* A recent study of 256 heterosexual couples in which one partner was infected with HIV found that for those couples who used condoms consistently, none of the noninfected partners became infected during a total of 15,000 episodes of intercourse (De Vincenzi et al., 1994). It is certainly best to use condoms if you are going to engage in "casual" sex.

"While working in the emergency room one evening a 17-year-old patient came in complaining of spotting. She informed us that she was HIV positive while taking her case history. This has become a common thing so I didn't think too much about it. A nurse took it upon herself to talk about the importance of sexual responsibility. She stated that she knew she had the infection a year ago and had slept with half of her high school football team. When we questioned her on whether condoms were used she said no. We asked her if she had told the boys before hand and she said no. . . ."

(from the author's files)

We would all like to believe that most people would not knowingly give others a sexually transmitted disease, but so many people are asymptomatic during the early stages of various STDs that many people are not even aware that they have an infectious disease. For women whose partners refuse to wear condoms, there are some birth control techniques that reduce the risk of HIV (or other STD) infection. See Box 6-A in the next chapter.

There are problems with condoms (as STD prevention) as well. Even if you and your partner(s) use them consistently and properly, they sometimes tear (see Chapter 6). Even microscopic tears are large enough to allow the passage of viruses. In other words, as was the case with practicing monogamy, condoms cannot guarantee that you will never get a sexually transmitted disease. Which method is better? In a study that used probability modeling to test the amount of risk reduction, the authors concluded that "consistent and careful condom use is a far more effective method of reducing HIV infection than is reducing the number of sexual partners" (Reiss & Leik, 1989).

Whichever behavioral strategy you choose to use—the use of condoms or the practice of monogamy (in a *long-term* relationship)—you will greatly reduce your chances of ever getting a sexually transmitted disease.

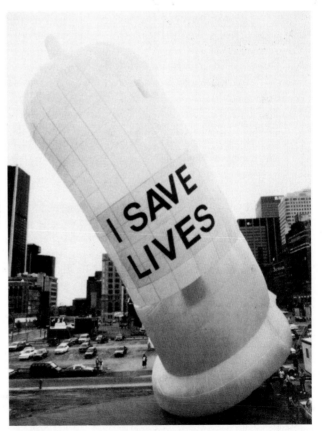

FIGURE 5-12 A GIANT CONDOM DISPLAYED AT THE FIFTH INTERNATIONAL AIDS CONFERENCE IN MONTREAL.

BOX 5-B

SEXUALITY AND HEALTH:
IMPEDIMENTS TO PRACTICING SAFER SEX

Until an effective vaccine is developed, health officials must rely on convincing people to change their behaviors in order to prevent the spread of HIV. For most people in the population, this means convincing them to practice safer sex behaviors. In the 1980s, it was hoped that educating people about AIDS and the transmission of HIV would lead them to practice safer sex. Schools began teaching about HIV; the Surgeon General mailed an informational brochure to all U.S. households; and hardly a day went by that newspapers did not include an article about HIV/AIDS.

Studies in the early 1990s have found that most young people today are, in fact, knowledgable about the transmission of HIV and the consequences of AIDS (Anderson & Christenson, 1991; Ku, Sonenstein, & Pleck, 1992). However, AIDS and sex education programs have had, at best, only a modest effect on convincing people to reduce their number of sexual partners and/or to use condoms regularly (Ku et al., 1992). Even college educational courses have had only a minimal success in convincing students to reduce high-risk sexual behaviors (e.g., Baldwin, Whiteley, & Baldwin, 1990; King & Anderson, 1994). Scare tactics have not even produced behavior change (Ross et al., 1990; Sherr, 1990). In fact, researchers find that there is no relationship at all between people's knowledge of AIDS and their sexual behavior (DiClemente et al., 1990; Gray & Saracino, Klepinger et al., 1993; Ku et al., 1992). This has led many researchers to conclude that by itself, knowledge is ''not sufficient for compliance to safer-sex guidelines'' (Ahia, 1991).

If it is not lack of knowledge that prevents many people from practicing safer sex, what is it? Actually, there are many reasons. We will consider a few of the most important.

The most common reason that college students give for not using condoms is that one was not available when they were in the mood to have sex (Franzini & Sideman, 1994). About one third of heterosexual adults are embarrassed about buying condoms (Choi, Rickman, & Catania, 1994). Condoms are also less likely to be used if the male is ''high'' (from alcohol or drugs) prior to sex (Ku, Sonenstein, & Pleck, 1993; Penkower et al., 1991; Weinstock et al., 1993). People are more likely to have a condom available if they have used them in the past, especially if they are with a partner with whom they have agreed to use condoms.

The major problem is that to have come to an agreement, a couple has to have talked about using condoms, and most people, including college-educated people, do not know ''how to engage in the interpersonal negotiations that have to occur in order for a condom to be used'' (Morrison, quoted in Gladwell, 1992). Practicing safer sex means that you must be able to talk about using condoms with a partner (as well as their previous sexual history), and that you be able to put a stop to sexual activity if he or she will not use one. This requires some degree of assertiveness. Young people who have these behavioral skills are much more likely to practice safer sex (Catania et al., 1989; Fisher & Fisher, 1992; Yesmont, 1992).

One factor that prevents some women from acting in their own best interest is the perceived power difference between men and women. If a woman's predominant experience of male-female relations is of men exerting power over women and always getting their way, they are not likely to insist that a male use a condom if he doesn't want to (Holland et al., 1991). This may be common in cultures that emphasize the ideal of the virile, machismo male (e.g., Hispanic).

Even when there is little or no power difference, communication between a man and a woman about safer sex is often hindered by *cultural double standards* and *sexual scripts* (Ehrhardt, 1992; Metts & Fitzpatrick, 1992; Muehlenhard & Quackenbush, 1988). In American culture, men are given more sexual freedom than are women. Thus, a woman may be viewed negatively (by a partner, and others) if she openly expresses a desire for sex, and may be considered respectable if she refuses a partner's sexual advances. Women who believe that their partners endorse this standard are not likely to provide a condom or suggest that their partner use one. As you will learn in Chapter 15, many woman engage in scripted refusal with new partners—first telling them no (in order to appear respectable) and then consenting (Muehlenhard & McCoy, 1991). Women who engage in this behavior are very unlikely to look after themselves by carrying and providing condoms.

The most common HIV-prevention behavior used by college students is to have sex only with individuals they believe to be ''safe'' (Maticka-Tyndale, 1991). They look for partners who appear to have no symptoms (Baldwin & Baldwin, 1988; Kegeles, Adler, & Irwin, 1988) and then restrict their sexual relations to a monogamous relationship. Many have a lifestyle of what I have previously referred to as serial monogamy. However, sexual scripts often work against the use of condoms when one starts dating a ''respectable'' and ''safe'' partner where the goal is the formation of a relationship (see Metts & Fitzpatrick, 1992). There is a negative relational significance associated with condoms; if they are not being used for birth control, their only other use is for prevention of STDs with an ''unsafe'' partner (Pilkington, Kern, & Indest, 1994). When the focus of ''getting to know you'' is on the other person's suitability as a relational partner, the subject of condoms may be viewed negatively, suggesting promiscuity and possible infection (by oneself or the other) and increasing the likelihood of rejection (see also Choi et al., 1994). In these situations, a couple is likely to avoid directly asking each other about past sexual behaviors or the use of condoms, and just talk about AIDS and safer sex in general rather than in terms of the relationship. People (incorrectly) take a partner's willingness to talk about AIDS as a sign that he or she is safe. Even when condoms are used during early sexual episodes, they are likely to be abandoned once the two individuals perceive themselves as starting a relationship (Ku, Sonenstein, & Pleck, 1994). But without previous explicit, honest discussion about prior sexual experiences, you cannot be certain. Or, put another way, ''You know if you're using a condom or you're not. You don't know if you're picking the right partner'' (Heterosexual AIDS, 1988).

Our culture also has a taboo against seriously discussing any sexual topic (Wight, 1992). For example, dating partners generally do not ask each other directly if the other wishes to have sex, but instead communicate their intentions to one another indirectly via ambiguous body language and other behaviors. Indirect communication also serves as a way of avoiding rejection—cues and signals that go unacknowledged are generally considered to be less rejecting than a direct refusal to verbal requests (O'Sullivan & Byers, 1992). But you can't communicate about the use of condoms with indirect gestures.

In conclusion, the number of individuals practicing safer sex will probably not increase substantially beyond the present levels until health educators begin to teach behavioral skills and address gender issues. In the meantime, you might benefit by engaging in some role playing (Kelly et al., 1989). With a friend (of your particular sexual orientation), pretend that the two of you are on a date and that there is a sexual attraction. Take turns bringing up the subject of condoms and responding to your partner (friend) bringing up the subject of condoms. After you discuss your reactions, try it again, and keep doing so until you are comfortable. This may sound silly, but unless you are already comfortable with the idea of talking about condoms, how do you think you will feel with a date in a real-life situation? ∎

Allow me to review some recommendations for safer sex:

1. Limit the number of sex partners. The more sexual partners you have, the higher your risk of contracting a sexually transmitted disease, because chances increase that sooner or later you will have sex with an infected individual. Indiscriminate promiscuity in this day and age of epidemic STDs and especially AIDS is foolish.

2. Be selective and avoid having sex with anyone who has had lots of other sex partners (e.g., prostitutes, promiscuous individuals). Remember, some people do not tell the truth. You are at high risk of getting an STD if your partner is promiscuous (even if you are not), so take the time to get to know your partner before you start a sexual relationship.

3. Avoid having sex with anyone who uses intravenous drugs or whose partner uses them.

4. When having sex with a new partner leave the lights on and be observant during foreplay, or take a shower together. If you notice anything peculiar (e.g., sores, discharges), it is not too late to change your mind. However, looking for symptoms is not enough by itself. Remember, many people with STDs do not show any symptoms (people with the AIDS virus may not show any symptoms for 5 years or longer).

5. Use a condom or have your partner use one. This is not a 100 percent guarantee that you will not contract an STD (condoms sometimes tear), but it substantially reduces the risk. The risk can be reduced even further by using condoms in combination with spermicides, which kill many of the bacteria and viruses that cause STDs.

6. Wash the genitals before and after sex, and urinate as soon as possible afterwards (this might help to flush out some germs from the urethra).

7. If you are sexually active, have checkups regularly. Remember, women are not usually tested for STDs during their routine pelvic exams unless they ask their doctor to do so. ∎

WHAT TO DO AND WHERE TO GO IF YOU HAVE AN STD

You would think it would be obvious to someone as to what to do if they thought they may have, or thought they were at risk for, a sexually transmitted disease—go to a doctor! Many people hesitate, however, out of fear, shame, guilt, or just plain denial. "Among groups with high-risk behaviors, only 34 percent of sexually experienced teenagers were screened for STD in the past year, as were only 43 percent of women with a positive STD history and 32 percent of women with 10 or more lifetime partners" (Mosher & Aral, 1991). Now that you know the consequences of untreated STDs, I hope that this will not include you. So, if you think you have an STD (or if you have put yourself at high risk of getting one):

1. See a physician immediately. If he or she diagnoses you with having an STD,

2. Abstain from having sex until you are cured (or in the latent stage, if you have herpes), and

3. Tell your partner(s) so that they, too, can be treated and not infect others or yourself again. You do not want to play STD ping pong with your partner.

There are two other reasons that someone might not go to a doctor immediately. Some may not be able to afford the doctor's charges and lab test costs (people such as poor college students, for example), and others might not know where to go even if they had the money (they might not have a doctor, or they may wish to avoid the family doctor). Fortunately, the U.S. Public Health Service provides clinics for the diagnosis and treatment of sexually transmitted diseases— often free of charge! The government is committed to eradicating STDs. So, there is no excuse not to be treated. Contact the Public Health Service clinic in your area.

The Centers for Disease Control and Prevention also have an STD informational National Hotline toll-free number: 1-800-227-8922. ∎

POSITIVE SEXUALITY IN THE ERA OF AIDS

AIDS, human papillomavirus infections, herpes—the attention being given to these and other sexually transmitted diseases is making many people afraid of sex. My intent in this chapter was to educate you about some of the *possible* consequences of sexual behavior, not to scare you so badly that you will want to avoid ever having sexual relations.

There are many activities human beings engage in

*"It's not that I don't trust you, Kevin, I just
don't trust the women who've been with the men who've been
with the women who've been with the men who've
been with the women you've been with."*

(Reproduced by Special Permission of *Playboy* magazine: copyright © 1990 by Playboy.)

that involve risk. Take skiing, for example. No one has to tell us that going down a snow- and ice-covered mountain on a pair of skis is a dangerous activity. If trees, boulders, and other skiers are not avoided, the result can be great bodily injury, yet this doesn't detract from the tremendous enjoyment many people derive from this winter sport. Those who ski learn that there are limitations to how they seek that pleasure. Skiing out of control has its consequences.

The same is true of driving an automobile. Many people own sports cars and many others would like to. They get a certain thrill at accelerating quickly and driving fast. But, again, there are limitations. Taking a corner at too high a speed can be fatal. At high speeds, we must be able to react to unanticipated events (e.g., another car cutting in front of us) in a fraction of a second. Driving while having impaired judgment and motor coordination due to alcohol consumption is certainly an often fatal, high-risk behavior. The fact that each year thousands of people are injured or killed because they foolishly took that risk does not detract from the pleasure that the rest of us often get from driving our cars.

AIDS is not the first sexually transmitted disease, only the most recent. Syphilis and gonorrhea were greatly feared before the discovery of antibiotics. Many millions more have died of syphilis than of AIDS, yet this hasn't stopped people from enjoying sex. Why? Because *sex per se doesn't cause any of these diseases*. Like driving an automobile, if we avoid foolish, high-risk behaviors, we can still enjoy the pleasures of sexual relations. The few seconds it takes to put on a seat belt does not detract from you enjoying your automobile. Similarly, the few seconds it would take you or your partner to put on a condom will not detract from enjoying sex. Similar to drinking and driving, making sexual decisions while under the influence of alcohol is also foolish.

AIDS does not strike randomly—it only affects those who are exposed to the virus. If you make just a few adjustments to reduce the risk of exposure, sex can be as pleasurable and exciting as always.

KEY TERMS

PERSONAL REFLECTIONS

....

1. How do you think you would feel if you found out you had a sexually transmitted disease (or, if you have previously been infected, how did you feel)? Would you feel differently than if you contracted the flu? Why? How would you tell your partners of their possible infection?

2. How would you feel if: (a) your best friend told you that he or she had an STD? (b) your teenaged son told you that he had an STD? (c) your teenaged daughter told you that she had an STD? (d) your partner told you that he or she had an STD acquired from a previous relationship?

3. Many babies are born with sexually transmitted diseases (as a result of their mothers being infected during pregnancy). Is having an STD an indication of immorality, irresponsibility, both, or neither? Explain (you may wish to reconsider your answers to questions 1 and 2 at this point).

4. What do you presently do to protect yourself from sexually transmitted diseases? Now that you have learned more about STDs, what changes in your sexual lifestyle do you plan to make to better protect yourself?

5. Do you and your new partner(s) discuss safer sex? Why or why not?

SUGGESTED READINGS

....

Boston Women's Health Book Collective. (1992). *The new our bodies, ourselves* (4th ed.) New York: Simon & Schuster. The landmark book for women's sexuality and health.

Brandt, A. M. (1985). *No magic bullet: A social history of venereal disease in the United States since 1880.* New York: Oxford University Press.

Gordon, A. N. (1990, February). New STD menace: HPV infection. *Medical Aspects of Human Sexuality.* Discusses the human papillomavirus and its link to cervical and penile cancer.

Langston, D. (1983). *Living with herpes.* Garden City, New York: Doubleday. Comprehensive coverage for those who have herpes.

Leary, W. G. (1988, July 14). Sharp rise in rare sex-related diseases. *The New York Times.*

Planned Parenthood. *Vaginitis: Questions and answers.* 16 pages.

Shilts, R. (1987). *And the band played on: Politics, people, and the AIDS epidemic.* New York: St. Martin's Press. An investigative reporter's look at the incompetence and infighting that prevented an early effective campaign against AIDS.

Ulene, A. (1987). *Safe sex in a dangerous world.* New York: Vintage Books. Discusses how to cope with the threat of AIDS and other STDs.

Zilbergeld, B., and Barbach, L. (1988). *How to talk with your partner about smart sex!* This excellent 1988 tape can be purchased from The Fay Institute, 7242 Ariel Avenue, Reseda, CA 91335 for $9.95.

CHAPTER SIX

BIRTH CONTROL

WHEN YOU HAVE FINISHED STUDYING THIS CHAPTER, YOU SHOULD BE ABLE TO:

1. DISCUSS THE TEENAGE PREGNANCY PROBLEM IN THE UNITED STATES;

2. UNDERSTAND THE WORLDWIDE NEED FOR EFFECTIVE CONTRACEPTIVE TECHNIQUES;

3. LIST SOME CONTRACEPTIVE MYTHS AND RELATIVELY INEFFECTIVE METHODS OF BIRTH CONTROL AND DISCUSS WHY THEY ARE NOT EFFECTIVE;

4. EXPLAIN HOW THE VARIOUS FERTILITY AWARENESS METHODS OF CONTRACEPTION ARE SUPPOSED TO WORK;

5. DESCRIBE HOW SPERMICIDES WORK AND DISCUSS THEIR EFFECTIVENESS AS A METHOD OF BIRTH CONTROL;

6. COMPARE AND CONTRAST THE VARIOUS BARRIER METHODS OF BIRTH CONTROL AND THEIR EFFECTIVENESS;

7. DISCUSS THE LATEST DEVELOPMENTS WITH INTRAUTERINE DEVICES;

8. DESCRIBE THE VARIOUS HORMONAL METHODS OF CONTRACEPTION, HOW THEY WORK, AND THEIR POTENTIAL SIDE EFFECTS;

9. DESCRIBE THE STERILIZATION PROCEDURES AND EXPLAIN THEIR ADVANTAGES AND DISADVANTAGES;

10. DISCUSS THE VARIOUS METHODS OF ABORTION;

11. DISCUSS THE CONTRACEPTIVE METHODS THAT ALSO HELP TO PREVENT SEXUALLY TRANSMITTED DISEASES; AND

12. DETERMINE WHICH CONTRACEPTIVE TECHNIQUE IS RIGHT FOR YOU.

THE TEENAGE PREGNANCY RATE IN THE UNITED STATES HAS REACHED EPIDEMIC PROPORTIONS AND IS OVER twice as high as that found in Canada and most European countries (Jones et al., 1986; Westoff, 1988; see Table 6-1). This is not a recent phenomenon. Teenage births in the United States reached a peak in 1957 and have declined a bit since. What is new is the proportion of births to unwed teens. Only 15 percent of teenage births were out-of-wedlock in 1960, but this rose to 29 percent in 1970 and 49 percent by 1980. In 1990, there was a record high of nearly 1.2 million births to unwed females (National Center for Health Statistics, 1993) and over one-half million of these were to teenagers (a 75 percent increase since 1980). The greatest increase in pregnancy rates was among young teens without a high school education, aged 14 to 17 (Williams, 1991). About 85 percent of births to unwed teens are unintended or unwanted (Forrest & Singh, 1990; Pratt et al., 1984) and over one third are terminated by abortion.

The rate for out-of-wedlock births is much higher for nonwhite teenagers than it is for white teens. In the early 1990s, 92 percent of African-American teenage mothers were single, compared to 61 percent for Hispanics, and 59 percent for whites. However, the most rapid rise during the 1980s was among whites and Hispanics. Moreover, white teens are much more likely than black teens to "hide" an unintended pregnancy by getting married (39 percent versus 7 percent, respectively, of nonmaritally conceived births were legitimated in 1981; Jones et al., 1986). Because the divorce rate for couples married as teenagers is much higher than average, many of these prematurely married white teens end up as young, single parents anyway.

The high pregnancy rate among U.S. teens reflects widespread nonuse of **contraception.** Over a third of U.S. women use no contraceptive method at their first premarital sexual intercourse (Mosher & McNally,

1991). Use of contraception at first intercourse is lowest among young teens, Fundamentalist Protestants, African-Americans, and Hispanics, and is greatest among Jewish women and females whose mothers completed high school. Teen pregnancy rates are particularly high among those who use illicit drugs (perhaps reflecting their greater acceptance of nonconventional behavior; Mensch & Kandel, 1992). Teens' self-esteem, ego development, and educational aspirations also predict whether or not they use contraception (Hayes, 1987).

Contraception
The prevention of conception.

For young teens, ignorance about reproduction and contraception is common.

"As a Paramedic I've delivered more babies than I can count. Once I responded to a person with 'rectal bleeding.' We expected to find a typical older individual and prepared for such. To our surprise a young girl greeted me saying that 'she has something coming out her rectum and she is bleeding all over.' The fifteen-year-old female was scared to death, still clothed in underwear, bleeding, with a large mass between her legs, inside the underwear. Immediately I removed obstructions, assisted with the remainder of the delivery, resuscitated the infant and treated the mother for shock. During this ordeal I gained information from the family that no one (including the patient, who in this case I had adequate reason to believe was totally honest), had any inclination that this fifteen-year-old was even pregnant.

In this case the child and 'child mother' lived. What an education for a fifteen-year-old. Is this really what we want for our children or do we want to provide the availability of more classes such as Human Sexuality. I vote for the latter.''

(from the author's files)

However, most teens know about contraception, and also know that if they have sex without contraception they are taking a chance. But having taken that chance without it resulting in pregnancy, the more likely they are to take the chance again. Eventually, they begin to feel that they can't get pregnant—that it won't happen to them (Luker, 1975).

"I have been having sex since I was 16. I have had different partners and unprotected sex with all of them. I always believed that I couldn't get pregnant. It only happens to bad girls and people who wanted it to hap-

TABLE 6-1 YEARLY TEENAGE PREGNANCY RATE (PER 1000 WOMEN) IN WESTERN NATIONS	
United States	105
England and Wales	58
Norway	45
Canada	41
Finland	38
Sweden	33
Netherlands	15

Source: Westoff, 1988.

pen. There were a couple of late periods and worrying, but it never made me want to try birth control. . . . I found out I was two months pregnant. I was completely shocked."

(from the author's files)

As for the males, those who do poorly in school and lack long-term goals often have the most irresponsible attitudes about reproduction. In fact, many of these men consider getting a woman pregnant as a sign of masculinity. This attitude is more common among African-American men than among whites (Marsiglio, 1993a). Another problem is that many men take no responsibility if their partner is an acquaintance (as opposed to a girlfriend), but often times "girls think they have boyfriends. Boys think they have acquaintances" (L. Smith, 1993).

The teens most likely to have babies are generally the ones least prepared to take care of them (Williams, 1991). The cost to the nation is staggering. The U.S. government spent over $34 billion in 1992 on welfare support for families started by teenagers (Center for Population Options) and the cost would have been even higher if it were not for publicly funded expenditures for contraceptive services (Forrest & Singh, 1990). But the cost to the individual can be even more tragic. Teenage mothers are much more likely to have high-risk babies with health problems, a problem that is often made worse because many pregnant teens never seek prenatal care (Hein, Burmeister, & Papke, 1990). Although some of the problems can be attributed to the socioeconomic status of teen mothers (Makinson, 1985), children born to teenagers are twice as likely to be premature, and three times as likely to have brain or nervous disorders and score significantly lower on achievement and IQ tests. In addition to not being economically or physically ready to have children, teenagers are generally not emotionally ready to have children either. Children of teenage parents are much more likely than other children to be victims of child abuse (Zuravin, 1991).

Being an unwed teenage mother does not guarantee that a girl will be locked into poverty (with no job skills and little education), but most will experience long periods of hardship because of early childbearing (Fursten-

berg et al., 1990). Most daughters of teenaged mothers do not become teenage mothers themselves, but those who do are even more likely to experience economic dependence and inability to escape poverty (Furstenberg et al., 1990; Horwitz et al., 1991). The children of teen parents who later become young teen parents themselves often report that they experienced emotional deprivation at an early age and significant depressive symptoms, and "seek emotional closeness through sexual activity and early parenthood" (Horwitz et al., 1991).

Perhaps the most unfortunate part of all this is that the high rate of births to teens continues to occur in a day and age when highly effective means of birth control are available. This was not always the case. The prevailing attitude during Victorian times and throughout the history of the Christian church, you recall, was that sex was for procreation only and thus birth control was opposed. In many states it was against the law to sell or distribute contraceptive devices. As a result, women generally had several or even numerous children, and many poor women (who worried that they could not feed another child) died during crude and often self-attempted abortions. It was as a result of watching one of these poor tenement women suffer from an abortion attempt in 1912 that Margaret Sanger gave up nursing and founded Planned Parenthood. The work of the reformers and the changing attitude about the role of women in general gradually had its effect.

Two thirds of Americans surveyed in a 1936 Gallup poll said that information about birth control

Margulies/The Journal, VA/Rothco

should be available to those who wanted it. The last of the state laws prohibiting the sale of contraceptive devices was finally repealed in 1965 (by a U.S. Supreme Court decision in the case of *Griswold v. Connecticut*), and by then 81 percent of the public approved of the availability of birth control information. The birth control pill was introduced in 1960, but until recently condoms and other birth control devices that did not require a visit to the doctor were kept behind the counter in drug stores, which inhibited many people from purchasing them. Today, male and female condoms and spermicides are sold openly in most drug stores, yet the number of teenage pregnancies continues to be high. ■

WORLD POPULATION

In addition to personal reasons, there are reasons why a society as a whole should practice birth control. Imagine two shipwrecked couples on a small south Pacific island in the year 1700. The island has a small supply of fresh water, some animal life but no predators, edible vegetation, and a small amount of land suitable for farming. For these four people, the island is Utopia—it has more than they will ever need. Each couple is fertile and have four children (probably a gross underestimate without birth control), and they in turn pair off in their late teens to form four couples, each of which has four more children. Thus, in each generation there would be twice as many people as in the previous generation. If there were no accidental deaths and the people lived until age 65, there would be at least 224 people living on the island by the year 1800. For those people the island is no longer Utopia. The animals have all been killed, the edible plant life is consumed within days of becoming ripe, and there is not nearly enough farm land to support a population of this size. What's worse, even the water supply must be rationed, and the population continues to increase. Soon there will be large-scale death from starvation and dehydration.

Wildlife experts are used to seeing this happen to populations of deer in areas where there are no predators, but is this scenario too far-fetched for humans? The world is really just an island. We have a limited amount of natural resources, including water. Should they become exhausted, we would find ourselves in the same situation

as the inhabitants of our hypothetical island. The world population has been increasing at an alarming rate (see Figure 6-1), and it is now more than 25 times greater than in the year A.D. 1. It was about 800 million in 1760, reached 5 billion in 1987, and reached 5.6 billion in 1993. Each year, 87 million people are born. The United Nations (Population Division) estimates that the world population could rise to 8.5 billion by the year 2025 and reach 10 billion before the middle of the next century. In some countries, such as

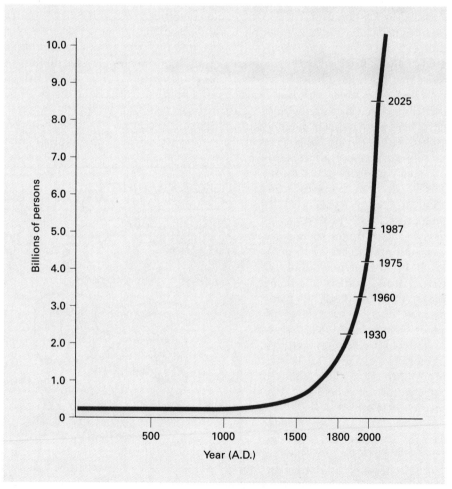

FIGURE 6-1   WORLD POPULATION GROWTH. NOTICE HOW RAPIDLY THE WORLD POPULATION HAS INCREASED SINCE THE BEGINNING OF THIS CENTURY.

Rwanda, the fertility rate is as high as eight children per mother.

Many experts predict that unless this world population explosion is substantially slowed, the end result will be widespread starvation. Robert Repetto of the World Resources Institute estimates that if the present population doubles, all of the current cropland in the world would have to produce 2.8 tons of grain per acre per year, equivalent to the most productive American farms. Paul and Anne Ehrlich, authors of *The Population Explosion* (1990), give the following warning:

We should not delude ourselves: the population explosion will come to an end before very long. The only remaining question is whether it will be halted through the humane method of birth control, or by nature wiping out the surplus. We realize that religious and cultural opposition to birth control exists throughout the world; but we believe that people simply do not understand the choice that such opposition implies. Today, anyone opposing birth control is unknowingly voting to have the human population size controlled by a massive increase in early deaths.

In some parts of the world mass starvation is no longer hypothetical, but already a reality. Most recently, our attention has been focused on Ethiopia and Somalia, where thousands of people have died of starvation because the land can no longer support the population. The sight on TV of little children dying a slow, horrible death is not pretty, and it is not just happening in Somalia and Ethiopia. It is happening in many parts of Africa and Asia, and in Brazil alone there have been an estimated 2 million children abandoned by their parents.

China, the world's most populated country with about 1 billion people, has much less farm land than the United States. There is only one fifth of an acre of land per person, which is just enough to provide food for one person. Any additional increase in the population will mean starvation for millions. As a result, the Chinese government was forced in 1982 to order mandatory birth control. For the next 100 years, couples will not be allowed to have more than one child. Although this will eventually reduce their population by several hundred million, there are presently so many people under the age of 30 that even if the pol-

icy is strictly adhered to, the population will still increase by the amount of the U.S. population by the year 2000. To oversee this policy, each district and town has a Family Planning Council. Birth control courses are given before marriage. Newlywed couples then sign a contract limiting themselves to one child, and those who adhere to the policy earn "model worker" status in their factory, which entitles them to many benefits, including bonus income and free education of their children. Factories with 100 percent participation become "model factories." Older women are assigned to "look after" small groups of females in each neighborhood. If a second pregnancy is detected, tremendous pressure from community leaders is put on the couple to have an abortion and sterilization.

These measures seem very harsh in terms of our own standards of freedom, and with an abundance of farm land in America it is hard for us to imagine such a thing ever happening here. During the "baby boom" years (following the end of World War II through the mid-1950s), there was an average of 3.5 babies born to each American couple. If that rate had continued, the population of the United States today would have been around 500 million, twice what it actually is. Just imagine what the congestion and pollution would have been like. Would our natural resources have been strained? I do not know, but our lifestyle could not possibly have been as good as it is today.

What prevented the United States from having this population explosion? Quite simply, the use of birth control. Reversible birth control devices for couples to postpone having children and sterilization techniques for couples who already have children have made it possible for people to limit the number of children they have. In 1960, only 13 percent of married women aged 25 to 29 were childless, compared to 29 percent in 1985. The birth rate started to fall in the early 1960s, and by 1970, Americans were averaging around two babies per couple. From 1970 to the mid-1980s, the U.S. fertility rate averaged about 1.8 births per woman, below the rate needed to replace their parents' generation. It is presently back to about 2.0 births per woman (see Figure 6-2). As a result, the population of the United States has stabilized, with only a small increase due to immigration. The U.S. Census Bureau predicted in 1989 that the U.S. population would peak at 302 million in the year 2038 and then begin a gradual

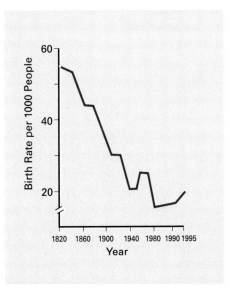

FIGURE 6-2   THE U.S. BIRTH RATE.

decline as people born during the "baby boom" years of 1946–1964 die.

Stop and think about it for a minute. Would you really like to see us in a situation where the U.S. population doubles every generation? We might be able to continue to live comfortably during our lifetime, but what would life be like for our grandchildren? ▪

EVALUATING DIFFERENT BIRTH CONTROL METHODS

If all fertile couples practiced unprotected sexual intercourse (no pills, condoms, diaphragms, etc.) and did not abstain from having sex at any time of the month (no fertility awareness methods), 85 to 90 percent of them would conceive within a year. In judging the effectiveness of the various birth control techniques, we need to know how many couples using a particular contraceptive method would conceive in a year's time. There are actually two figures here that are important: the theoretical effectiveness rate and the actual use effectiveness rate. For a particular contraceptive technique, the **theoretical effectiveness rate** (really a failure rate) is the percentage of couples who would conceive if all couples who were using the technique used it consistently and properly. The **actual use effectiveness rate** is usually worse than the theoretical rate because not all people use a method consistently or properly. The birth control pill, for example, was designed to be taken every day, but not all women remember to do it and this results in some failures. Although all the birth control techniques that you will learn about are better than using nothing at all, some are more effective than others. Ideally, a couple wishing to postpone or prevent pregnancy would like their birth control technique to be 100 per-

Theoretical effectiveness rate

For a particular birth control technique, the percentage of failures during one year of use by couples who use the technique properly and consistently.

Actual use effectiveness rate

For a particular birth control technique, the percentage of failures during one year of use by all couples using the technique, regardless of whether or not they used it properly or consistently.

TABLE 6-2

NUMBER OF PREGNANCIES PER 100 WOMEN DURING THE FIRST YEAR OF CONTINUOUS USE

METHOD	PERFECT USE	TYPICAL USE
Male sterilization	0.1	0.15
Female sterilization	0.2	0.4
Norplant	0.2	0.2
Depo-Provera	0.3	0.3
Combination birth control pill	0.1	3.0
Progestin only (mini) pill	0.5	3.0
IUD (copper)	0.8	1.0
IUD (Progestasert)	1.5	2.0
Male condom (with spermicide)	< 1.0	12.0
Male condom (without spermicide)	3.0	12.0
Female condom	5.0–6.0	12.0–15.0
Diaphragm (with spermicide)	3.0–5.0	15.0
Cervical cap	8.0–10.0 (not given birth)	18.0
Contraceptive sponge	9.0–10.0 (not given birth)	17.0
Spermicides alone	5.0	21.0
Withdrawal	4.0	19.0
Fertility Awareness		
Calendar	9.0	20.0+
BBT	2.0	20.0+
Billings	3.0	16.0+
No Method	85.0	85.0

Source: Various sources cited in text.

cent effective (zero pregnancies in a year's time). Some contraceptive methods approach this, but others do not.

Effectiveness rates are almost always stated in terms of the number of failures that occur *in the first year of use* for every 100 couples using the technique (see Table 6-2). Although I will follow that tradition, you should understand that the chances of an unplanned pregnancy increase with longer use of any contraceptive method. Most young people want to have several years of sexual relations before their first planned birth. If their chosen contraceptive technique has a failure rate of 5 percent in the first year of use, what are the chances of an unplanned pregnancy if they continue to use the technique over a much longer time period?

Estimates differ depending on whether one assumes that the failure rate remains constant or declines over time, but even the most conservative estimates show that over a long period of time the risk of failure is high for most contraceptive techniques (Ross, 1989). For a technique with a first-year failure rate of only 5 percent, for example, the 10-year failure rate is between 23 percent (this assumes the risk declines to zero during that time span) and 40 percent (this assumes the risk remains constant). For a contraceptive technique with a one-year failure rate of 10 percent, the 10-year failure rate is between 40 percent and 66 percent. Some of the contraceptive techniques that we will consider have a first-year failure rate of 20 percent. Over a 10-year time period, the chance of an unplanned pregnancy using these techniques is between 67 percent and 90 percent. Thus, while contraceptive methods reduce the number of unplanned pregnancies, most are far from being 100 percent effective over a long period of time.

In evaluating birth control techniques, we must look at more than just their effectiveness. Some techniques are more suitable for certain subgroups of the population than others. The birth control pill is highly effective, but I would not recommend it for women with diabetes or cardiovascular problems, for example. Some people only wish to postpone pregnancy and therefore require a reversible technique (i.e., one that can be discontinued at any time), while others wish to totally prevent any more pregnancies and require a permanent technique. Factors such as spontaneity and aesthetics sometimes play a role, and some may be looking for simultaneous protection against sexually transmitted diseases. In many cases, religious beliefs must be considered. I will provide as much information about each of the techniques as possible, pro and con, so that whenever you decide to use birth control, you will be able to decide which method is best for you. ■

CONTRACEPTIVE MYTHS

There is a lot of peer pressure to engage in sex during the adolescent years. In addition to the pressure to conform, teens are often given a great deal of misinformation about contraception by friends and potential partners. Some of the information is so incorrect that it can be considered myth. For example, how many of you were told, "You can't get pregnant the first time you have sex," or, "You can't get pregnant if you don't kiss"? Well, it just is not true. A girl is capable of reproduction as soon as she starts having menstrual cycles (recall that in the United States, the first menstrual period occurs at an average age of 12z \ x). This is evidence that she is ovulating, that is, producing eggs. Some of you may have been told that sexual intercourse is safe if the female is on top, or if you have sex while standing up, but these, too, are untrue. Some people believe that a woman must have an orgasm during sex in order to get pregnant, but in fact, the chances may be slightly greater if she does not have one, because the vaginal opening may remain swollen for a longer period of time and thus help to prevent spillage of the sperm. No doubt there are other stories that some of you have heard, but unless they are included in the remainder of the chapter (i.e., they have a basis in fact), chances are they just are not true. ■

RELATIVELY INEFFECTIVE METHODS

Withdrawal (coitus interruptus)

Withdrawal of the male's penis from his partner's vagina before ejaculation to try to avoid conception. It is sometimes ineffective because fluids from the Cowper's glands may contain sperm.

One of the most popular ways in which young people try to prevent pregnancy is **withdrawal** (coitus interruptus), where the male withdraws his penis just before reaching orgasm and ejaculates outside his partner's vagina. In a Gallup poll taken in the early 1990s, 32 percent of college women believed this to be an effective means of birth control. It sounds logical, for if the male does not ejaculate in the female's vagina, there will be no sperm there—right? Wrong! The Cowper's glands, you recall, secrete a few drops of fluid before a man reaches orgasm and this fluid can contain stray sperm. Although a few studies have reported relatively low failure rates (Vessey, Lawless, & Yeates, 1982), most find that nearly 20 out of every 100 couples using this method conceive within the first year of use (see Hatcher et al., 1994).

> "I was one that became pregnant at an early age using the withdrawal method. My boy-friend and I normally used condoms during sexual intercourse but sometimes we wouldn't bother with them."
>
> (from the author's files)

Withdrawal is better than nothing, but ineffective compared to some other types of contraception. What's more, withdrawal may not be very physically or emotionally satisfying to the male or his partner. Even in cases where a couple did not actually begin intercourse, if the male ejaculates on or near his partner's vaginal opening (during heavy petting, for example), it is possible that some sperm could get into the vaginal secretions and make their way into the vagina.

Some women believe that **douching** is an effective method of birth control. Again, it sounds logical. If you wash out the contents of the vagina, there should be no sperm. The problem is that no matter how quickly a woman douches after intercourse, some sperm will have already made it into the cervix. In fact, the pressure caused by douching can actually force sperm into the cervical opening. Over 40 out of every 100 couples who use this as their only means of birth control will conceive in a year's time. Some women have tried douching with ice water or Coca Cola after intercourse with the belief that these will kill sperm, but this, too, is ineffective because of the previously mentioned reasons (and because of the sugars, Coca Cola is likely to cause a fungus or yeast infection as well). Douching should be thought of only as a feminine hygiene practice (and one of questionable value, at that, if used too often).

Douching
A feminine hygiene practice of washing the vagina, usually with specifically prepared solutions.

It is commonly believed that **breast-feeding** a newborn baby protects a woman from getting pregnant. Breast-feeding has been called "nature's contraceptive." There is some truth to this. The sucking response of the baby on the mother's nipple inhibits the release of gonadotropin hormones (FSH and LH) from the pituitary. Before modern contraceptive techniques were introduced, breast-feeding was the major factor that determined the length of the interval between pregnancies. Women normally do not start cycling regularly immediately after giving birth, and one study found that each month of breast-feeding adds, on *average*, about 0.4 months to the birth interval (Jain & Bongaarts, 1981). Studies in rural areas of China and India have found that when breast-feeding is frequent and prolonged, the birth interval is 5 to 10 months longer than for women who do not breast-feed (Jain, 1969; Potter et al., 1965). The failure rate is about 5 percent or less during the first 6 months (Gray et al., 1990). *The risk of ovulation rises if a woman continues breast-feeding beyond six months* (Gray et al., 1990), but if she is not menstruating the method can be very effective for as long as a year (Weis, 1990).

Breast-feeding
In reference to contraception, the sucking response by a baby on the mother's nipple inhibits release of follicle-stimulating hormone, thus preventing ovulation.

The problem is that for this to work the baby must be fed "on demand," that is, whenever it wants to feed at any hour of the day or night. There can be no substituting a bottle (not even with water) and even a pacifier must be avoided as it might satisfy the baby's need to suck. Breast-feeding has been shown to work in less developed countries where women remain at home all the time or can breast-feed in public (Jain, 1969; Potter et al., 1965; Short, 1984), but the actual use failure rate in the United States (where most women cannot feed on demand) is more than 50 pregnancies for every 100 couples per year (Buchanan, 1975). In other words, couples who rely on this method quite often have babies 10 to 12 months apart. ∎

FERTILITY AWARENESS: ABSTAINING FROM SEX DURING OVULATION

Fertility awareness (also called *the rhythm method* or *natural family planning*) may be the only method acceptable to many of you because of your religious beliefs. These are the only birth control methods that are not opposed by the Catholic church and evangelical Protestant denominations. There are three variations to this method, but all are based on pre-

Fertility awareness methods
Methods of birth control that attempt to prevent conception by abstinence from sexual intercourse during ovulation.

dicting when ovulation occurs. *A female can only get pregnant when an egg is present during the first 24 hours or so after ovulation.* After that, the egg is overly ripe and a sperm cannot fertilize it. Rhythm methods involve the identification of "safe days" in a woman's menstrual cycle and the abstinence of sex during the "unsafe period." It would be almost impossible for a woman who is not having regular menstrual cycles to use these techniques. For those who do cycle regularly, they require a great deal of training and motivation.

CALENDAR METHOD

Sperm can live in the Fallopian tubes for 2 or 3 days. Thus, the fertile period in a female's menstrual cycle is from 3 days before ovulation until 1 day afterward (see Chapter 3). In a woman with perfect 28-day cycles, this would be at mid-cycle, and the safest time to have sex to avoid pregnancy would be during menstruation (yet 20 percent of college women in a recent Gallup poll believed it was dangerous to have sex during menstruation). The problem is that few women have the same length cycle month after month. It is normal for a woman's cycle to differ in length over time by several days (see Chapter 3). Most of the differences are due to fluctuations in the preovulatory phase of the cycle. Ovulation generally occurs about 14 days before the start of menstruation, but it doesn't do any good to count back 14 days from the start of menstruation (it is too late by then, anyway). We need to know when ovulation is going to occur.

So the first thing a female must do if she is going to use this method is keep track of the length of her menstrual cycles for a minimum of eight cycles (more would be better). Let us take a hypothetical example of a woman who has kept track of ten cycles and found that although her average cycle length was 28 days, she had one that was only 24 days and another that lasted 32 days. The **calendar method** uses a formula to calculate the unsafe period. Subtract 18 from the length of the shortest cycle (24 − 18 = 6) and 11 from the length of the longest cycle (32 − 11 = 21). The unsafe period would thus be from days 6 through 21 (by the numbering system explained in Chapter 3), a period of over two weeks that she and her partner must abstain from having sexual intercourse. If the woman had had a cycle shorter than 24 days or longer than 32 days, the period of abstinence would have been even longer.

> **Calendar method**
>
> A fertility awareness method of birth control that attempts to determine a woman's fertile period by use of a mathematical formula.

The calendar method has proven to be very unreliable, with some studies reporting an actual use failure rate of as high as 40–45 percent in one year (Ross & Piotrow, 1974). Most studies report that the actual use failure rate is about 20 percent per year (Hatcher et al., 1994; Trussell et al., 1990). It has been called the Russian roulette of birth control: the losers get pregnant right away and the winners get pregnant later and worry in the meantime. In addition to severely testing human motivation, all it takes is just one cycle to be shorter or longer than previously observed. There are two variations of the rhythm method that use biological markers to better identify the time of ovulation.

BASAL BODY TEMPERATURE METHOD

A woman's basal (resting) body temperature rises by a few tenths of one degree Fahrenheit 24 to 72 hours after ovulation. In this method, couples abstain from having sexual intercourse from the end of menstruation until 3 to 4 days after a temperature rise is noted. The **basal body temperature** should be taken at the same time every day, preferably first thing in the morning (before going to the bathroom, eating, drinking, or smoking). Note that this method still involves a long period of abstinence, so it again severely tests human willpower. Even those women who attempt to use it properly often get pregnant, for its success depends on being able to detect a very small temperature increase (and more importantly, the assumption that the increase is due to ovulation). If no increase is noted, a couple must go an entire cycle without sexual relations. What's more, small temperature increases of a few tenths of a degree are often caused by low-grade infections that we are not even aware of, stress, or other factors. Some women have a history of irregular basal body temperatures. The actual use failure rate is about 20 pregnancies per every 100 couples per year (Hatcher et al., 1994; Trussell et al., 1990).

> **Basal body temperature**
>
> The temperature of the body while resting. It rises slightly after ovulation.

BILLINGS METHOD (CERVICAL MUCUS OR OVULATION METHOD)

The fertility awareness method that is most widely used today is the method that attempts to pinpoint the time of ovulation by noting changes in the consistency of a woman's **cervical mucus**. It is named after two Australian doctors who developed it (Billings, Billings, & Catarinch, 1974). Mucus is discharged from the cervix throughout a female's menstrual cycle, and its appearance changes from white (or cloudy) and sticky to clear and slippery (like that of an egg white) a day or two before ovulation. Until recently, the only way to note this change was a finger test, that is, placing a finger in the vagina and then examining the mucus. Women who use this method should not douche, for it makes it more difficult to notice the changes in consistency of the mucus. A couple is instructed to abstain from sexual intercourse from the end of menstruation until 4 days after the mucus changes consistency.

> **Billings method**
>
> A fertility awareness method of birth control in which changes in the consistency and quantity of cervical mucus are used to tell when ovulation has occurred.

> **Cervical mucus**
>
> The slimy secretion of mucous membranes located inside the cervix.

If you wish to use this method, do not rely on the preceding simple instructions. There are organizations that will give you more detailed instructions. Be warned, however, that sometimes these are advocate organizations (i.e., they strongly favor this form of birth control over others), and some may exaggerate the effectiveness of the Billings method. Theoretically, it has only a 2 percent failure rate, but the actual use failure rate is much higher. The Alan Guttmacher Institute reported that the accidental failure rate for married women in 1982 was 16 percent, but most studies have found about 20 pregnancies per year for every 100 couples using this method (Hatcher et al., 1994; Medina et al., 1980; Trussell et al., 1990; Wade et al., 1980). Similar high failure rates obtained in carefully designed studies done in five different countries led the World Health Organization to conclude that the Billings method was "relatively ineffective in general use for preventing pregnancy" (Seventh Annual Report, 1978; see also World Health Organization, 1981).

Advocate groups generally dismiss these high failure rates as due to improper instructions and unmotivated participants (i.e., user failures due to people who have sex during unsafe periods). Most of the pregnancies do, in fact, result from conscious deviations from the rules (World Health Organization, 1981), no doubt because the average period of abstinence is 17 days per cycle. Recent data from a World Health Organization clinical trial indicate that the first-year failure rate is, in fact, only 3.1 percent during *perfect* use (method failure) if women also abstain from sex during stress, but 86.4 percent during imperfect use (Trussell & Grummer-Strawn, 1990). Thus, the Billings method can be very effective if used perfectly, but perfect compliance is difficult for many couples who desire sexual intercourse.

Some couples combine the basal body temperature and Billings method (along with other signs of ovulation, such as ovulatory pain) to enhance the effectiveness of these fertility awareness methods. This is often referred to as the *sympto-thermal method* and has a lower failure rate than any of the other methods used alone (Medina et al., 1980; Wade et al., 1980). However, one of the problems is that perhaps as many as one third of all women do not have the typical mucus pattern. Even in those who do, the finger test is obviously not very scientific.

Sympto-thermal method
A combination of the basal body temperature and Billings fertility awareness methods.

There is real hope for those who want to use the fertility awareness method. Chemical testing kits that will more accurately pinpoint the time of ovulation (by measuring a vaginal mucus enzyme or sodium and potassium levels in saliva) may soon be available in stores for home use. Because sperm can live in the Fallopian tubes for 2 to 3 days, the chemical tests would have to predict ovulation at least 4 to 5 days in advance to be useful as a contraceptive technique (there are already some products available that predict ovulation 12 to 36 hours in advance, but these are useful only for couples who want to conceive).

Fertility awareness methods are usually considered to be safer than other contraception techniques. However, at least two studies have reported abnormally high rates of defective babies born to couples who practice rhythm, possibly due to fertilization of an overly ripe egg once intercourse is resumed (Berger, 1980; Iffy & Wingate, 1970).

FERTILITY AWARENESS METHODS AND SEXUALITY
Perhaps the biggest problem with the various fertility awareness methods is that they all involve a fairly long period of abstinence from sex (*17 days is a long time* for young people who are sexually attracted to each other and living and sleeping together). To make matters worse, many young women in their teens and early twenties still are not cycling regularly. Females who are not yet cycling on a monthly basis would almost never be able to have sex if they tried to use these methods. These methods severely test human willpower, and sexual motivation should not be underestimated (just look at the world population as proof of that). The purpose of birth control is to prevent pregnancy, not sex, but these methods work by doing just that. Not surprisingly, less than 2 percent of all Americans use rhythm for birth control (Peterson, 1995). ∎

SPERMICIDES: SUBSTANCES THAT KILL SPERM

Spermicides are chemicals that kill sperm (nonoxynol-9 or octoxinol-9). They are sold in a variety of forms. Spermicidal foams, jellies, creams, and film (called VCF for *vaginal contraceptive film*, it is a square of film that is placed over the cervix)

Spermicides
Chemicals that kill sperm. In most products, the chemical is nonoxynol-9.

help hold the sperm-killing chemicals in the vagina against the cervix and simultaneously act as a barrier to sperm. Suppositories and tablets are also available. Specific instructions will differ for each type, but they must be placed in the vagina shortly before sexual intercourse begins. They lose their effectiveness over time, so new spermicide must be inserted shortly before each time a woman has intercourse. Be very careful not to confuse spermicidal products with feminine hygiene products. They are often displayed together in drug stores, so if you want the contraceptive material, be sure that the package says spermicide or "kills sperm."

When used alone, foams and suppositories are more effective than jellies and creams. The actual use failure rate is about 21 pregnancies per 100 couples per year (Hatcher et al., 1994; Trussell et al., 1990), but many of the failures are due to improper or inconsistent use (user rather than method failures). When used consistently and properly, the failure rate can be as low as 5 percent (Coleman & Piotrow, 1979). Nevertheless, a woman should consider using spermicides in combination with a blockade or barrier method (diaphragm or condom). The contraceptive sponge and certain brands of condoms already contain a spermicide.

In addition to their contraceptive benefit, spermicides containing nonoxynol-9 reduce the risk of contracting sexually transmitted diseases by killing the bacteria and viruses that cause them (see Box 6-A). This includes HIV, the virus that causes AIDS. A recent study suggested that spermicides were as effective as condoms in preventing sexually transmitted diseases (Rosenberg & Gollub, 1992), but other researchers seriously doubt this and worry also that spermicides can cause vaginal ulcers that would make transmission of HIV easier (e.g., Bird, 1991; Cates, Stewart, & Trussell, 1992). The use of spermicides may also reduce the risk of cervical cancer, probably by helping to kill human papillomavirus (see Chapter 5; Celentano et al., 1987). Although researchers differ in their opinions as to how effective spermicides with nonoxynol-9 are in reducing STDs, all agree that they offer some protection (see Cates & Stone, 1992 a, b for a review).

On the negative side, several studies have found that nonoxynol-9-containing spermicides increase the risk of urinary tract infection (see McGroarty, Reid, & Bruce, 1994). But not using spermicides for this reason must be weighed against the risk of exposure to sexually transmitted diseases and unwanted pregnancy. A few early studies suggested a small increase in the risk of birth defects if spermicides are used at the time of conception or during pregnancy. However, the authors of the most frequently cited study (Jick et al., 1981) repudiated their own results (Watkins, 1986), and most experts believe that spermicides do not cause birth defects (Einarson et al., 1990; Lovik et al., 1987).

Most college women rate spermicides as one of their least preferred types of contraception (Sarvela et al., 1992). The most common complaint is that, like the condom and diaphragm (and sometimes the sponge), inserting the spermicidal material just before intercourse interferes with the spontaneity of sexual relations and detracts from the mood. Others complain that spermicides are messy or detract from oral-genital sex. A few people (one in 20) find that spermicides burn or irritate the vagina or penis. However, as a backup to barrier techniques, and because of their antiviral and antibacterial activity, spermicides have advantages that far outweigh the disadvantages. ■

BARRIER METHODS: PREVENTING SPERM FROM MEETING EGG

Barrier methods of birth control are designed to prevent pregnancy by placing a blockade between the penis and cervix so that sperm cannot reach the egg if ovulation has occurred. Thus, these methods do not require abstaining from sexual intercourse, but they may interfere with spontaneity of sexual relations by requiring you to stop and put something on or put something in.

Blockade or barrier method

General term for contraceptive methods that block the passage of sperm.

Condom

For males, a thin sheath made of latex rubber, lamb intestine, or polyurethane that fits over the penis. For females, a polyurethane intravaginal pouch held in place by two flexible rings. Condoms are effective as contraception and for prevention of sexually transmitted diseases.

MALE CONDOMS

Condoms ("rubbers," "safes," or prophylactics) are thin sheaths made of latex rubber, lamb intestine, or polyurethane that fit over the penis and thus trap the sperm (see Figure 6-3). They also serve as a barrier between the male's membranes and female's membranes, and thus are **also highly effective in preventing the spread of sexually transmitted diseases**. In fact, condoms were originally invented for this purpose in the 1500s. Mass production of condoms became possible in the mid-1800s with the discovery of how to make rubber more flexible and durable. Today, condoms are the most frequently used method of birth control in Japan, England, and some northern European countries, but for a variety of reasons (to be discussed later), American men have been reluctant to use them.

As a birth control technique, condoms are highly effective. They present no major health hazards and are available without a prescription. What's more, their use requires no mathematical calculations and no subjective evaluation of biological processes. There are only a few simple rules to remember:

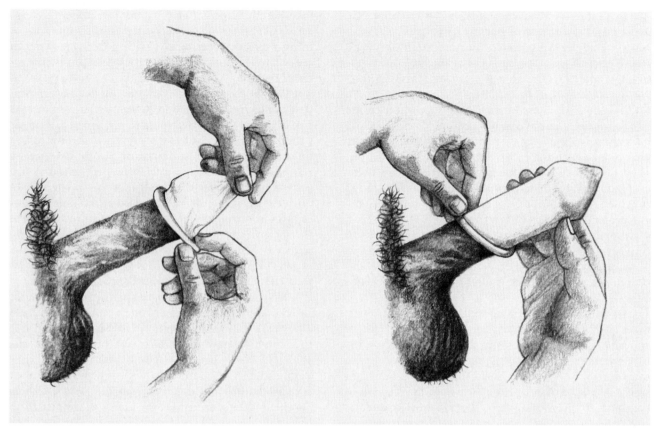

FIGURE 6-3   USE OF THE CONDOM.

1. Put one on before you start having intercourse. Otherwise, its effectiveness is no better than withdrawal. If the condom does not have a nipple tip, leave a little extra space at the tip of the penis to catch the ejaculate. If you are uncircumcised, pull back the foreskin while putting on the condom.

2. Hold on to the base of the condom when you are finished and withdraw. Otherwise, you might leave it and its contents in the female's vagina.

3. Use it only once. If you have intercourse more than one time while having sex, use a new one each time. Some people say that you can wash, dry, powder them with cornstarch, and then roll them up for reuse, but they will eventually tear, so for maximal effectiveness use them only once. After all, even those made from animal membranes are not terribly expensive.

4. Do not store them for long periods of time in a warm place (such as your wallet) or where they are exposed to light. This will eventually deteriorate them. Store them someplace cool, dark, and dry. Also, *do not use rubber condoms in combination with mineral oil, baby oil, vegetable oil, hand lotions, Vaseline, or other petroleum jellies,* for these, too, can damage them.

"During a recent sexual experience, my partner and I used oil from one of those fancy 'bath and body stores' for lubrication in conjunction with a condom. During intercourse, the condom disintegrated."

(from the author's files)

A man should never begin intercourse until his partner is lubricating, but if additional lubricant is needed, use a water-based one (do not confuse with water-soluble) like K-Y jelly or Today Personal Lubricant. Better yet, use a spermicide. (The new polyurethane condoms can be used with oil-based lubricants.)

Condoms come rolled up (dry or lubricated) and, until recently, they came in only one size. However, there is now a jumbo size for men who find the usual type to be too tight. (American manufacturers had been reluctant to make different sized condoms for fear of insulting a male's ego—can you imagine a man asking for a small condom?) A man may wish to practice putting one on his penis if he has never used one before. They are unrolled on the penis, not yanked on like a sock.

If these very simple instructions are followed, the theoretical failure rate is only about 3 percent (Hatcher et al., 1994; Trussell et al., 1990). If always used with a spermicide, the theoretical failure rate is less than 1 percent (Kestelman & Trussell, 1991). However, the actual use failure rate is about 12 pregnancies per 100 couples per year. Most of these failures are due to inconsistent use, and teens are more likely than older persons to use them inconsistently. One study found that the failure rate for women over 30 (almost all of whom used them consistently) was only 1–4 percent, but for women under the age of 25 the failure rate was between 10 percent and 33 percent (Schirm et al., 1982).

Not all failures are due to user failures. *Consumer Reports* (March, 1989) calculated that, on average, one condom in 165 breaks during vaginal intercourse and one in 140 breaks during anal intercourse. However, the laboratory tests must not be realistic enough, because studies find that during human use the breakage rate is about 1–2 percent during vaginal intercourse (see Cates & Stone, 1992 a, b; Grady & Tanfer, 1994). Some studies have reported breakage rates of over 5 percent (Russell-Brown et al., 1992; Steiner et al., 1993; Trussell, Warner, & Hatcher, 1992). Many men have also experienced condoms slipping off during intercourse (this is not caused by use of lubricants, but is often due to penetration beyond the end ring or by improper withdrawal, see rule #2). Condom failure (breakage or slippage) is most common among men who don't use them regularly (Steiner et al., 1993). You should be aware that some brands of condoms are stronger than others—see *Consumer Reports* for a complete ranking.

Remember, the failure rate of condoms can be even further reduced by using them in combination with a spermicide. Many brands of condoms come with a spermicide in their lubricant, but using a vaginal spermicide with condoms is much more effective (*Consumer Reports*). When used with spermicide, condoms are the most effective of the nonprescription birth control techniques.

Condom use by teenagers more than doubled during the 1980s (Sonenstein, Pleck, & Ku, 1989; see also Peterson, 1995), but most American teens and older men still do not use them regularly (Catania et al., 1992).

If condoms are so effective, why aren't all sexually active men using them? Many men will not use condoms because they say condoms reduce their sensitivity ("like taking a shower with a raincoat on").

"Rubbers seem to make getting laid not feel as good as bare skin sex. Is this the price to pay for not having an STD?"

(from the author's files)

Before they have ever tried one, most men have heard many times that condoms will reduce their sensitivity.

Their preconceived notions probably exaggerate the problem. Condoms will reduce a male's sensitivity—slightly—but *Consumer Reports* found that many men eventually find this to be something positive because it makes sex last longer. The new polyurethane condoms are only half as thick as rubber condoms, but we will have to wait and see what men's reactions to them will be.

Others complain that they are allergic to rubber. A few men and women are allergic, but remember, some condoms are made of natural animal membranes and polyurethane. Still others complain about the loss of spontaneity, that is, that it is a nuisance to stop and put a condom on in the middle of having sex. How long does it take to put on a condom? The answer is only a few seconds. These reasons for not wearing condoms are in many cases just excuses. The real reason many men won't use condoms is that they are too embarrassed to go in a store and purchase them.

"During high school, I was actually embarrassed to buy condoms. I only would get them in those bathroom machines. Perhaps if they were discretely available, then more teens would buy them."

(from the author's files)

However, if a man refuses to use condoms or get a vasectomy (usually done only on older men who want no more children), this generally means that his female partner must assume the responsibility for birth control. In fact, 40–50 percent of condoms are purchased by women today. Putting on a condom takes less time than putting in a diaphragm, contraceptive sponge, or cervical cap, and it isn't as messy as most vaginally used spermicides. The latter three must be purchased at a store just like condoms, and use of a diaphragm requires that a woman have a pelvic exam. Although many men may complain about loss of spontaneity and reduced sensitivity, these are just minor annoyances compared to the side effects often associated with use of the pill or IUD. Whatever excuses may be used, there is no excuse for not using a condom if the only alternative is unprotected intercourse, which may result in unwanted pregnancy, not to mention the possible spread of sexually transmitted diseases.

There are certain subgroups of the population for which I highly recommend use of the condom. If you are sexually active and have multiple partners over time, or if your partner has had multiple partners or is an intravenous drug user, you are in a high-risk category for contracting a sexually transmitted disease. STDs are in epidemic proportions today. The walls of latex condoms block the bacteria and viruses that cause sexually transmitted diseases from passing through them. Although skin condoms are stronger (and thus are very effective for contraception), they have small pores that may allow passage of the hepatitis B virus and the virus that causes AIDS. Thus, the latex condom is highly effective for both birth control and STD prevention (see Chapter 5 and Box 6-A for additional information). Perhaps for this reason, the number of women with a favorable opinion about condoms (this includes both users and nonusers) increased from 39 percent in 1982 to 60 percent by the end of the 1980s (Forrest & Fordyce, 1988).

MALE RESPONSIBILITY IN AVOIDING UNWANTED PREGNANCIES

In many countries around the world, male contraceptive techniques are the most popular. Thus, men as well as women take responsibility for birth control. In the United States, however, the responsibility to avoid an unwanted pregnancy has traditionally fallen on women. Recently, the Society for Black Psychologists in New Orleans developed an attitude questionnaire for adolescent males designed to get them to assume more of the responsibility. The students are assembled and given the following statements, to which they respond true or false:

1. Getting a girl pregnant makes you a man.
2. Many adolescent males feel that if a girl becomes pregnant it is her fault and responsibility.
3. Many males believe that if a girl has sex with him she would have sex with other boys.
4. Many males feel that any boy who refuses to have sex with a girl who is willing is a chump.
5. If an adolescent male remains a virgin, his friends think something is wrong with him.
6. All teenage mothers return to school and graduate.
7. A teenage father's education is interrupted as much as the teenage mother's education.
8. Most teenage fathers take care of their babies.
9. Males have the greatest respect for girls who become pregnant.
10. Most teenage males don't care if their teenaged sisters get pregnant.
11. Most teenage males don't care if your teenaged sister gets pregnant.

A response of "true" to any of the statements is then followed by further discussion. Rates for teenage pregnancy will probably remain high as long as males continue to pressure females to engage in sex without any regard for long-term consequences.

THE FEMALE CONDOM

Only recently, in 1993, did we see the introduction of the first woman-controlled barrier method of contraception designed to give simultaneous protection against sexually transmitted diseases (see Gollub & Stein, 1993). The Reality Female condom, as it is called, is actually an intravaginal pouch—a 7-inch long polyurethane bag that is held in place in the vagina by two flexible rings (see Figure 6-4). A woman inserts it with her fingers by pushing the closed-ended ring against the cervix, similar to a diaphragm. It is held in place by the outer ring, which fits on the outside of the vagina, partially covering the labia (see Figure 6-5). It can be inserted up to a few hours before having sexual intercourse.

Many people are put off by its appearance, but it is thinner than male condoms, feels softer than rubber, and transfers heat, and thus many of those who try it say that it feels more like unprotected intercourse than sex with male condoms. As with the diaphragm, the female condom has no major health concerns and does not have adverse effects on the vaginal walls (Soper,

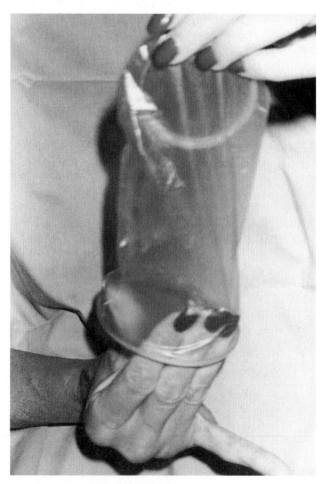

FIGURE 6-4   THE FEMALE CONDOM.

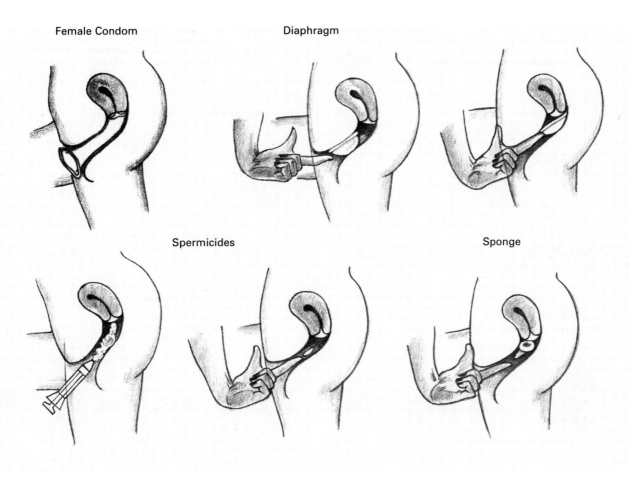

Female Condom   Diaphragm

Spermicides   Sponge

FIGURE 6-5 USE OF THE FEMALE CONDOM, DIAPHRAGM (WITH SPERMICIDE), SPERMICIDES (FOAM AND SUPPOSITORY), AND CONTRACEPTIVE SPONGE.

Brockwell, & Dalton, 1991). However, it is considerably more expensive than male condoms and, like male condoms, is used for only one act of intercourse.

Many people know about HIV and other sexually transmitted diseases, but are nevertheless reluctant to talk about safer sex (e.g., using condoms) on dates. For those women, and for those whose partners refuse to wear a male condom, the female condom provides them with the opportunity to protect their own health. The actual use failure (pregnancy) rate was initially reported to be about 25 percent per year (FDA hearing, 1992), due largely to people who used it improperly. Women apparently are receiving better instructions now, for recent studies have found that the failure rate during typical use was the same as for the diaphragm, sponge, or cervical cap (Farr et al., 1994; Trussell et al., 1994). For those who used it correctly, the 6-month failure rate was 2.6 percent.

The Reality Female condom is just the first of several new female barrier techniques to reach the market. Many others are in various stages of development (see later section).

THE DIAPHRAGM

A **diaphragm** is a large, dome-shaped rubber cup with a flexible rim that fits over the cervix. It thus works by preventing the passage of sperm into the uterus. In Biblical times, women sometimes inserted camel or crocodile dung into the back of the vagina to prevent the sperm's passage. Fortunately for today's women, the rubber cup version was invented in 1882 in Germany. However, because of laws that prohibited the mailing or transportation of "obscene" materials (this included birth control devices), the diaphragm was not used in the United States until the 1920s. By the 1930s, the diaphragm was used by one third of all couples who practiced birth control. With the introduction of the pill in 1960, its use became almost nonexistent. There was a small resurgence in its popularity in the 1970s, but its use among single women declined sharply again in the 1980s (Mosher, 1990).

Diaphragm

A dome-shaped rubber cup with a flexible rim that fits over the cervix and thus acts as a contraceptive device by acting as a barrier to the passage of sperm into the uterus.

A woman has to be fit by a physician or health care worker to properly obtain a diaphragm (the distance between the cervix and pubic bone is measured). She will then be given a prescription for a diaphragm that fits her. It is not something you borrow from a girlfriend for a date. You may have to be refit if your body undergoes any major changes (e.g., pregnancy, weight changes of 10 pounds or more). A woman getting her first diaphragm is also going to need instructions and coaching to learn how to insert it properly and quickly (see Figure 6-5). This may be one reason why there was a decrease in the use of the diaphragm, for it was easier for doctors to prescribe pills than to take time to teach a female how to use a diaphragm.

After you have learned to insert your diaphragm properly, there are only a few simple rules to remember:

1.   I recommended that condoms be used with a spermicidal jelly. This practice is almost universally recommended for diaphragm users as well (Hatcher et al., 1994). Although two studies have found that spermicides do not further reduce the pregnancy failure rate (Craig & Hepburn, 1982; Ferreira et al., 1993), spermicides are nevertheless beneficial in helping to kill bacteria and viruses that cause sexually transmitted diseases (see Box 6-A). Spread spermicidal jelly on the inside part of the diaphragm (the part in contact with the cervix) and rim before insertion.

2.   Insert the diaphragm no more than 2 hours in advance of starting intercourse. Otherwise, the spermicide dissipates and adds little additional protection. For maximal effectiveness, it should be put in immediately prior to intercourse, although this may interfere with spontaneity.

3.   Leave it in for 6–8 hours after intercourse to make sure that there are no more live sperm. If you have intercourse more than once while having sex, place more spermicide in the vagina before each time. Do not remove the diaphragm to do this (sperm may get into the cervix while it is removed), but instead use a plunger or some other means of application. Do not leave it in for more than 12 hours.

When used in combination with a spermicide, the theoretical failure rate is usually stated as about 5–6 percent per year. The actual use failure rate is typically about 15 percent per year (Trussell, Strickler, & Vaughn, 1993). Most of the failures, particularly among young women, are due to inconsistent use. Because of inconsistent use, one study found that the failure rate among women was 21 percent in one year (Kovacs et al., 1986), but in a group of older, married

women the failure rate was well below 5 percent (Vessey, Lawless, & Yeates, 1982). A recent study found that when the diaphragm was used continuously (without spermicide, removing it only during a daily shower to wash it, with immediate re-insertion) the failure rate was only 2.8 percent (Ferreira et al., 1993). Some of the failures are also due to improper insertions or the diaphragm becoming dislodged during vigorous intercourse (this happens most often when the female is on top).

Women with a history of urinary tract infections should not use a diaphragm (Fihn et al., 1986), and it also should not be used during menstruation or periods of abnormal vaginal discharge. A few women may have allergies to rubber or spermicide, but otherwise there are no major health concerns. The most common complaint about the diaphragm is aesthetics. Some complain that insertion is a nuisance (interfering with spontaneity) and that spermicides can be messy and a detractor to such sexual behaviors as oral-genital sexual relations. These complaints are not heard as often, however, in women who are sexually experienced and in a monogamous relationship. The most important thing to consider is that the diaphragm offers an inexpensive, safe, and relatively effective means of birth control when used consistently and properly.

THE CERVICAL CAP

The **cervical cap** is another barrier device that is designed to prevent passage of sperm from the vagina into the uterus. Made of latex rubber, it is smaller and more compact than a diaphragm and resembles a large rubber thimble. *It is used with a small amount of spermicide* (for added effectiveness) and fits over the cervix by suction. Insertion and removal of the cap are more difficult than for the diaphragm, but once in place it is more comfortable than the diaphragm and can be left for 48 hours (*Contraceptive Technology Update*, 1989). Women should check each time after having sexual intercourse to make sure that the cap has not dislodged.

Cervical cap

A contraceptive device that fits over the cervix by suction and thus blocks the passage of sperm into the uterus.

Although the cervical cap has been popular in England for years, it has not been used very much in this country. In fact, it did not receive approval for marketing in the United States until 1988 because of concerns about prolonged exposure to secretions trapped by the cap (including cervical mucus and menstrual flow). However, after a 7-year trial process, the Food and Drug Administration concluded that the cap does not cause toxic shock syndrome. It is presently being recommended that the cap be used only by women who have normal Pap smears (because of possible adverse effects on cervical tissue; Mishell, 1989).

The actual use 1-year failure rate is listed as 18 pregnancies per 100 women, but two studies found the actual use failure rates to be 8 percent and 14 percent (Cagen, 1986; Powell et al., 1986). The cap offers substantially better protection to women who have not yet given birth (Trussell et al., 1993). For these women, when used correctly, the failure rate is only 8–10 percent.

THE CONTRACEPTIVE SPONGE

Note: In early 1995, the manufacturer of the Today Contraceptive Sponge, the only contraceptive sponge available, announced that it would no longer manufacture the product because of problems in upgrading its manufacturing facility (the product itself was not an issue). At the time this book went to press, the sponge was no longer available. However, on the chance that the manufacturer should reverse its decision, I will proceed to provide you with some information about this product.

The polyurethane **contraceptive sponge**, two inches in diameter and an inch thick, contained enough spermicide (nonoxynol-9) to be effective for 24 hours. A woman could have intercourse as many times as she wished without having to insert new spermicide. At the end of 24 hours she simply removed it and threw it away. The sponge worked primarily by killing sperm and blocking the cervical opening.

Contraceptive sponge

A contraceptive device made of polyurethane sponge that contains enough spermicide to be effective for 24 hours after being inserted into the vagina.

The sponge did not require a pelvic exam (as is necessary for a diaphragm). It sold in one size without a prescription. Users reported that it was very easy to insert. A woman simply moistened it with tap water and inserted it deep in the vagina (see Figure 6-5). One side had a concave dimple that fits over the cervix to decrease the chance of dislodgement. The sponge came with a small loop attached to one side for easy removal. Its easy availability (avoiding a doctor) and ease of use is what attracted women to the sponge (Beckman, Harvey, & Murray, 1992). It must be noted, however, that a few users (about 6 percent) occasionally had difficulty removing the sponge.

There were some early concerns that use of the sponge might cause toxic shock syndrome, but studies found that the incidence was extremely low (about one infection in two million uses, only slightly greater than nonusers) and the FDA concluded that it was a safe product (e.g., Faich et al., 1986).

Results of studies of the effectiveness of the sponge differed widely, with an actual use failure rate for all women of about 17 percent (Trussell et al., 1993b). Studies indicated that the sponge was much more effective in preventing pregnancy in women who had not given birth (9–10 percent failure rate, Trussell et al., 1993). As is true for other contraceptive techniques, the failure rate was substantially lower with consistent and proper use.

BARRIER METHODS AND SPONTANEITY

All of us, I suppose, would like our sexual relations to be passionate and spontaneous, with no interruptions. Putting on a condom or inserting a diaphragm, sponge, or spermicide does not take very long for many sexually experienced people (some individuals even integrate the use of barrier methods, e.g., putting on a condom, as part of foreplay), but some couples occasionally take chances (use unprotected intercourse) because they do not want to stop and possibly ruin the mood. This is probably the most common cause of failure for these methods. The following contraceptive techniques (which do not block sperm) get around this problem by not requiring that anything be done at the time when you want to have sex (except getting your partner in the mood, of course). ∎

THE IUD

The **intrauterine device**, like the birth control pill, came on the market in the 1960s and helped to open a new era of what people thought was going to be spontaneous and worry-free sex. However, there were numerous health problems caused by a few of the early IUDs and as a result of the subsequent lawsuits, most were taken off of the market. Before we continue with this part of the story, let us examine how it works.

Intrauterine device (IUD)

A birth control device, usually made of plastic with either a copper or progesterone coating, that is placed in the uterus to prevent conception and implantation.

The IUD is a small plastic and/or metal device (of various shapes) that is placed into the uterus by a physician (see Figure 6-6). This is actually a very ancient idea—camel drivers used to insert a stone into a female camel's uterus to prevent pregnancy (don't ask me how they came up with this idea). It has long been believed that IUDs worked as birth control by preventing implantation of a fertilized egg, and thus it was not acceptable to Roman Catholics and others for moral reasons. However, recent studies have found that *IUDs work primarily by preventing fertilization*, mostly by their effect on sperm transit through the uterus (Bromham, 1993; Senanayake, 1990; Sivin, 1989). The IUDs sold in the United States today have either a copper or progesterone coating as well, both of which further impair the passage of sperm. These IUDs are highly

FIGURE 6-6   AN INTRAUTERINE DEVICE (IUD),
INSERTED.

effective, with actual use failure rates of less than 2 percent per year (Hatcher et al., 1994). The copper T 380 A IUD can be used effectively for 10 years (The Population Council, 1994).

Now back to the story of the early IUDs. Insertion of an IUD requires dilation of the cervical opening, and insertion of some types of IUDs was particularly difficult (the uterus was occasionally punctured during insertion). Once inserted, the woman's uterus often attempted to expel the foreign object. Because some women did not notice that their IUD had been expelled, manufacturers added a thread to the IUD that protrudes from the cervix into the vagina so that women could check to see that their IUD was still in place. However, the thread served as an easy path for bacteria and viruses to follow (Vessey et al., 1981). The spread of gonorrhea and chlamydia into the upper reproductive tract (causing pelvic inflammatory disease)

was especially rapid in women with IUDs. Pelvic inflammatory disease left many women sterile or with an increased chance of a tubal pregnancy. Another major problem with some older types of IUDs was that implantation of a fertilized egg did occasionally occur. Although not as serious, the most common complaint of users of some older types of IUDs was heavier and longer menstrual flow, with more cramps and spotting.

Most of these health risks were limited to one type of IUD, the Dalkon Shield (see Sivin, 1993). The company that manufactured it had no previous experience in contraceptive technology, and despite early warnings from physicians that it was difficult to insert, and complaints from users, the company marketed it anyway. Many pregnancies, infections, and even some fatalities followed. The company filed for bankruptcy after hundreds of millions of dollars in lawsuits were filed. Most of the other IUDs available then were not associated with major health problems, but nevertheless their manufacturers removed them from the market.

The two types of IUDs on the market today are regarded by most physicians and researchers as safe products (e.g., Grimes, 1992; Newton & Tacchi, 1990; Petitti, 1992). The progesterone and copper-coated IUDs used today have a single-filament polyethylene string and are not associated with an increased risk of pelvic inflammatory disease (PID), ectopic pregnancy, infertility, increased bleeding or pain, and there have been no fatalities (Chi, 1993b; Cramer et al., 1985; Daling et al., 1985; Sivin, 1993). They also have a lower expulsion rate. The only real risk of PID associated with the IUD is at insertion (due to bacteria) and this can be eliminated by better sterilization procedures (Farley et al., 1992; Lee et al., 1983). Of those women who use an IUD, 97 percent have a favorable opinion about it, the highest for any contraceptive technique (Forrest & Fordyce, 1988).

To be absolutely safe, many physicians advise that women with multiple sexual partners over time use a contraceptive technique other than the IUD (Mishell, 1989). The IUD cannot protect a woman from her own, or her partner's, sexual behavior. But for women in a stable, monogamous relationship who have completed their families, the IUD is a safe, highly effective method of contraception that also permits spontaneity in sexual relations. ∎

HORMONAL METHODS OF CONTRACEPTION

THE PILL (ORAL CONTRACEPTION)

Of the approximately 35 million women who practice birth control in the United States, nearly 14 million use the pill (Alan Guttmacher Institute), making it by far the most popular of the reversible methods of contraception. It is also the most effective of nonsurgical,

reversible techniques, with a failure rate of close to zero if used correctly. However, the actual use failure rate is three pregnancies per year for every 100 couples using the pill (Hatcher et al., 1994; Trussell et al., 1990). Most of the failures that do occur are due to user, not method, failures. If a woman consistently follows just one simple rule, she really does not need to worry about getting pregnant. What is that? Take the pill every day. However, *the pill is not effective immediately* and a backup method of birth control should be used during the first month of use. After that, even if a woman forgets occasionally, taking two the next day will probably compensate, but any further forgetfulness will certainly result in unprotected intercourse. If you forget to take the pill for a few days, you again must use a backup method of birth control until you have daily taken an entire package of pills. Women, as well as their doctors, should also be aware that *the pill is rendered less effective by simultaneous use of many types of antibiotics, barbiturates, analgesics, and tranquilizers.*

"During our senior year in high school, my cousin came to me because she was afraid that she was pregnant. She was on the pill, and she was taking them correctly. We could not figure out what went wrong . . . About a month before she became pregnant, she went to the doctor for a bad cold. It turned out that the medicine which was prescribed for the cold made the birth control less effective . . . "

(from the author's files)

There is really not just one pill, but several different types. In fact, there are over 30 types marketed in the United States. The most widely used and most effective are the **combination pills**, which contain synthetic estrogen and progesterone (progestins). Most contain a fixed amount of the two hormones in each capsule, but there are also combination pills that adjust the levels of progestins in an attempt to mimic the natural hormonal phases of the menstrual cycle (although the different manufacturers of this type cannot agree on what is "natural"). Regardless of the type, the pill is taken for 21 days and then discontinued for 7 to permit menstrual bleeding. Most companies package the 21 pills containing hormones with seven additional pills that contain no hormones (placebos), so that women will not get out of the habit of taking them every day.

> **Combination pill**
> An oral contraceptive that contains both synthetic estrogen and progesterone.

The combination pill works primarily by preventing ovulation. The hormones in the pill prevent the pituitary from releasing FSH and LH (see Figure 6-7). Without an egg present, it is impossible to get pregnant. Even if ovulation should somehow occur, the progestin inhibits the development of the uterine lining (making implantation difficult) and keeps the cervical mucus thick (making passage of the sperm difficult). When a woman decides to stop using the pill, her menstrual

Inhibition of pituitary hormones

Stimulation of uterus

FIGURE 6-7 HOW ORAL CONTRACEPTIVES WORK.

cycles may not become regular right away, but fertility rates return to normal within one year (Huggins & Cullins, 1990).

There is also a **minipill** that contains only progestins. It works primarily by inhibiting development of the endometrium and by keeping cervical mucus thick. This pill is for women who are breastfeeding (estrogen inhibits milk production) or who cannot tolerate the side effects of the estrogen-containing pill. It is less effective than the combination pill (1.4–4.3 pregnancies per 100

> **Minipill**
> An oral contraceptive that contains only progestins.

women in a year), but just as safe, if not safer (Chi, 1993). However, in some women they may cause menstrual problems.

There was a decline in the use of the combination pill during the 1970s and early 1980s when discoveries of serious health risks were reported (Mosher, 1990). However, many of these studies were conducted with the first-generation, high-dosage pill (containing more than 50 mcg of estrogen). Manufacturers of oral contraceptives stopped marketing high-dosage pills in 1988. All estrogen-containing pills are now low dosage and have less risk associated with them. The pill also has some significant health benefits. Nevertheless, there are specific subgroups of women who should not use the combination pill. Let us examine the risks and benefits in detail.

NEGATIVE SIDE EFFECTS AND HEALTH RISKS.
There were some early reports of a few women showing decreased sex drive as a result of taking the combination pill (Masters & Johnson, 1970). These reports have been questioned and a more recent study found that pill users engage in sex more frequently across the menstrual cycle, and report more sexual satisfaction, than do nonusers (Alexander et al., 1990). Studies with chimpanzees suggest that oral contraceptives might adversely affect sexual desire only in women who already had low sexual desire or preexisting problems in sexual adjustment (Nadler et al., 1993).

It is common for women who are first starting to take the pill to experience some symptoms that mimic those of early pregnancy. These may include nausea, constipation, weight gain, breast tenderness (the bloating feeling is due to water retention), and emotional depression. These responses usually occur only during the first few days of each cycle and usually diminish within a few months. If they continue or are bothersome, the woman's doctor may be able to adjust the dosage of the hormones. Occasionally, use of the pill results in brownish spots on the face (chloasma). Because the hormones in the pill alter the chemical environment of the vagina, there is also an increased susceptibility to yeast infection and increased vaginal secretions. As a result of the lowered dose of hormones in today's pill, breakthrough bleeding (i.e., bleeding during the 21 days of hormone use) sometimes occurs, but it usually disappears during the first 4 months of use. Despite these problems, 95 percent of women who use the pill have a very favorable opinion of it as a contraceptive technique (Forrest & Fordyce, 1988).

The previously mentioned problems may be bothersome, but they are not considered to be serious health risks. However, there are other more serious problems that have been associated with use of the pill. Studies conducted in the 1970s, when the dosage of estrogen in the pill was much higher than today, showed use of the

pill to be associated with (though not necessarily the cause of) high blood pressure (4 percent of users), diabetes (1 percent), migraine headaches (0.5 percent), and liver cancer (rare; Palmer et al., 1989; Rinehart & Piotrow, 1979). The pill was once thought to be the cause of gall bladder disease, but recent studies do not support this (Vessey & Painter, 1994). Prior use of the pill is not associated with birth defects, but a woman should not continue to take it after she is pregnant (Huggins & Cullins, 1990).

Older studies with pills that contained high dosages of estrogen suggested that their use could cause serious cardiovascular problems, such as blood clots, heart attacks, and strokes (Mann & Inman, 1975; Rinehart & Piotrow, 1979; Vessey, 1973). Users of the pill who were in their thirties and smoked, for example, were seven times more likely to have a heart attack than users who did not smoke. More recent studies have shown that other risk factors, primarily smoking, account for most of the cardiovascular problems (Archer, 1990; Goldbaum et al., 1987). If you take the pill and do not smoke, your chances of having a heart attack are actually less than for those who smoke and do not use the pill. Today's low dosage pills carry a much lower risk of cardiovascular problems (e.g., Brill et al., 1991; Lidegaard, 1993). In fact, the Food and Drug Administration voted in late 1989 to allow women over the age of 40 who do not smoke to continue taking the pill (Kaeser, 1989). However, because of the small increased risk of blood clots, women who are about to undergo major surgery should stop taking the pill at least four weeks in advance (Robinson et al., 1991). Prior use of the pill is not associated with any of the previously mentioned cardiovascular disorders, even among long-time users (Stampfer et al., 1988).

Users of the birth control pill may have an increased risk of cervical cancer (Ursin et al., 1994), but there is a great deal of uncertainty as to whether this is due to the pill or other risk factors (see Mishell, 1989). There were also concerns for many years that use of birth control pills containing estrogen increase the risk of breast cancer. Breast cancer is the second most common type of cancer in women, affecting one in eight women some time in their lifetime (see Box 2-A). Although some studies claimed to have found a link between the pill and breast cancer, there have been over 20 studies, including one by the Centers for Disease Control and Prevention (Sattin et al., 1986) that have found that pill users are at no greater risk than nonusers (e.g., Romieu et al., 1989). Studies that claimed to have found a link between breast cancer and oral contraception were recently described as "conflicting and inconsistent" by a subgroup of the Food and Drug Administration. If there is any increased risk, it is small and is limited to long-term users who started taking the pill when they were in their early teens (Rookus et al., 1994; White et al., 1994).

When discussing the health risks associated with use of the pill, you should put things into proper perspective and compare the risks to what would happen if nobody used the pill. The health risks (including deaths) are significantly less than those caused by pregnancy and childbirth (DaVanzo, Parnell, & Forge, 1991; see Table 6-3). We can also substantially reduce the risks by identifying certain groups of women who should not use the pill. These include women with a history of circulatory problems, women in their thirties who smoke (or younger users who are heavy smokers), women with sickle-cell anemia (because of the risk of clots), women with diabetes or high blood pressure or a family history of these disorders, very obese women, women with hepatitis or other liver problems, and those with severe, focal migraine headaches. Young women who do not fall into any of these groups have little to worry

TABLE 6-3
RISK OF DEATH IN A YEAR'S TIME RESULTING FROM SELECTED ACTIVITIES

ACTIVITY	CHANCE OF DYING
Motorcycling	1 in 1000
Automobile driving	1 in 6000
Power boating	1 in 6000
Playing football	1 in 25,000
Using tampons (toxic shock), age 15–44	1 in 350,000
Having sexual intercourse (pelvic infection), age 15–44	1 in 50,000
Using Contraception	
Oral contraception—nonsmoker	1 in 63,000
Oral contraception—smoker	1 in 16,000
Using IUDs	1 in 100,000
Undergoing sterilization	
Laparoscopic tubal ligation	1 in 67,000
Vasectomy	1 in 300,000
Deciding about pregnancy	
Continuing pregnancy	1 in 11,000
Terminating pregnancy	
Illegal abortion	1 in 3,000
Legal abortion	
Before 9 weeks	1 in 260,000
9–12 weeks	1 in 100,000
13–15 weeks	1 in 34,000
After 15 weeks	1 in 10,200

Source: Hatcher et al. (1994). *Contraceptive technology.* New York: Irvington.

about. In fact, some health researchers believe that today's birth control pills are safe enough that they should be available without prescription (Trussell et al., 1993a).

HEALTH BENEFITS. After 35 years of use, it is now known that women who take the pill are at less risk for some health problems than nonusers (see Drife, 1989). Some of these were unexpected and could properly be called fringe benefits. The major benefits include a decreased risk of cancer of the endometrium (only one third as likely compared to nonusers) and cancer of the ovaries (60 percent as likely; Hulka et al., 1982; Rosenberg et al., 1994). (Cautionary note: It has not yet been demonstrated that today's low-dosage oral contraceptives offer the same level of protection against reproductive cancers; see Goldzieher, 1994). Not only is there no reliable evidence that use of the birth control pill is linked to breast cancer, but, in fact, there is a substantial decrease in the number of benign breast tumors (one fourth as likely). Use of the pill also results in reduced rates of ovarian cysts (one fourth as likely), rheuma-

toid arthritis (one-half as likely; Ory, Rosenfeld, & Landman, 1980), and pelvic inflammatory disease (one-half as likely; Kols et al., 1982; Panser & Phipps, 1991). The pill is also known to reduce premenstrual syndrome, reduce menstrual pain and bleeding (anemia is only two thirds as likely; Milsom et al., 1990; Mishell, 1982), and improve acne. In fact, some doctors prescribe the pill to women primarily to reduce menstrual problems, and only secondarily as a contraceptive technique.

" I am now on the birth control pill.... My cramps were minimized a great deal and so was the length and heaviness of my period...."

(from the author's files)

For older women who do not smoke, are not obese, and do not have hypertension or cardiovascular problems, today's low-dosage pills are also being prescribed to regulate menstrual cycle disturbances that are common before menopause (Volpe et al., 1993).

THE "SHOT"

In early 1993, a new type of contraception became available to women in the United States: **Depo-Provera**, an injectable drug containing progestin (a synthetic form of progesterone). The injectable contraceptive was already being used by nearly 4 million women in 90 different countries. The injection is good for 3 months and avoids the problem of pregnancies resulting from missing a daily dose (as with the pill). It works by preventing ovulation (by blocking pituitary hormones) and has a yearly failure rate of less than 1 percent (World Health Organization Task Force, 1983). After a woman stops injections, it takes several months to a year for fertility to return.

> **Depo-provera**
>
> Market name for methylprogesterone, a chemical that when injected suppresses ovulation for 3 months.

Depo-Provera was denied approval by the Food and Drug Administration twice in the 1970s because of concerns of a link to cancers of the breast, cervix, and liver. However, the World Health Organization gave its approval in 1993 after concluding that it did not increase the risk of these cancers, and reduced the risk of cancer of the uterus (Klitsch, 1993a). But there are some possible side effects that might cause some women to choose not to receive additional shots. These include menstrual irregularities (including an increase or decrease in menstrual bleeding), weight gain (an average of 15 pounds), tiredness, weakness, nervousness, dizziness, and/or headaches. Obviously, not all women who use Depo-Provera experience these symptoms, for if they did few would use it.

NORPLANT: THE FIVE-YEAR HORMONE IMPLANT

By now, many of you have heard of **Norplant**, the hormonal implant that offers contraceptive protection for up to 5 years. Approved for use in the United States in 1990, it consists of six flexible silicone tubes, each about the size of a match, that are inserted under the skin in a fanlike pattern on the inside of a woman's upper arm. The procedure takes only 15–30 minutes and costs about the same as a 5-year supply of birth control pills. The tubes contain progestin (levonorgestrel), a synthetic form of progesterone that is slowly released over time and prevents pregnancy by inhibiting ovulation and thickening cervical mucus. The tubes are nonbiodegradable and can be removed at any time.

> **Norplant**
>
> Six flexible silicone tubes containing a progestin that are implanted under the skin to prevent conception for 5 years.

Norplant's failure rate is said to be about 2 in 1,000 (Trussell et al., 1990), compared to 30 in 1,000 for the pill (most of which are user failures). This makes it nearly as reliable as sterilization. Only about 11 to 13 percent of women who decide to use Norplant decide to have it removed by the end of one year, some because they planned to have another child, but many because of unhappiness with side effects (Cullins et al., 1994; Frank et al., 1993). About three fourths of women with Norplant experience side effects in the first year. The most common side effects (as with all progestin forms of contraception) are spotting or irregular bleeding (this can include prolonged menstrual bleeding or no bleeding at all), weight gain, and headaches, but can sometimes include nervousness, dizziness, nausea, breast tenderness, and acne. However, only one third of women who experience side effects are bothered by them. Over two thirds of users are very satisfied (Krueger, Dunson, & Amatya, 1994).

> " I chose the Norplant birth control method after I had my first child at age 20. My life, of course, changed 100 percent, something I was not ready for, mentally or financially. I am now back in school as a single mother. I decided to try Norplant when I was still married and didn't want any more 'accidents.' . . . The in-office procedure lasted only thirty minutes . . . I felt no pain . . . I started to gain a little weight and had some slight dizziness. Then my menstrual periods stopped. Now 10 months later they are normal again and I have no other symptoms. My Norplant will last for 5 years. This is just enough time

BOX 6-A

SEXUALITY AND HEALTH: CONTRACEPTIVE METHODS THAT HELP PREVENT SEXUALLY TRANSMITTED DISEASES

Sexually active individuals who are not in monogamous relationships must (or should) worry about sexually transmitted diseases in addition to pregnancy. Unfortunately, contraceptive development has concentrated almost entirely on preventing pregnancy and ignored STDs. What do we know about the effectiveness of currently available contraceptive devices in preventing STDs?

Fertility awareness methods, sterilization, Norplant, Depo-Provera, the IUD, and the birth control pill offer no protection against STDs (Cates & Stone, 1992b). The IUD, you recall, increases a woman's chances of getting pelvic inflammatory disease should she get a bacterial infection of the lower genital tract (e.g., gonorrhea, chlamydia). The pill offers some protection against pelvic inflammatory disease (e.g., Panser & Phipps, 1991), but increases the risk of cervical infections with chlamydia (e.g., Oriel, Johnson, & Barlow, 1978; also see Cates & Stone, 1992b).

That leaves barrier methods and spermicides. Let us consider spermicides first. The active ingredient in most spermicides, nonoxynol-9, not only kills sperm, but also is effective against most of the bacteria and viruses that cause STDs, including gonorrhea, chlamydia, trichomonas, hepatitis, and HIV (the virus that causes AIDS). There is not enough data to make conclusions about whether spermicides protect against herpes, syphilis, or chancroid. While spermicides reduce the risk, *they do not reduce the risk to zero*. Overall, there is a reduction in risk of about 50 percent. (There are far too many studies for me to cite here; for an excellent review, see Rosenberg & Gollub, 1992; or Howe, Minkoff, & Duerr, 1994, for a review specific to HIV.)

For men, of course, use of rubber condoms will reduce their risk of getting an STD. "Skins" (condoms made of sheep intestine) have pores that are large enough for the passage of HIV and other viruses (Liskin, Wharton, & Blackburn, 1990). However, not all the news is reassuring. Rubber condoms may not have any holes before use, but under conditions that resemble intercourse, about a third of condoms develop very small holes that might be large enough to allow passage of HIV (Carey et al., 1992). What's more, condoms break about 1–2 percent of the time during vaginal intercourse, and more often during anal intercourse (see Cates & Stone, 1992a for a review of numerous studies). Incorrect and inconsistent use also reduces the effectiveness of condoms against STDs. Overall, under actual use conditions, *condoms reduce the rates for STD infection an average of about 50 percent* (Rosenberg, Hill, & Friel, 1991). Of course, we would expect that if condoms were always used correctly and consistently, and always in combination with a spermicide, their effectiveness as STD prevention would be much greater. In one study of 124 serodiscordant couples (one member was HIV-positive) who used condoms consistently, none of the HIV-negative partners became infected during a total of 15,000 acts of intercourse (De Vincenzi et al., 1994).

What about women? What contraceptive methods can they use that will simultaneously reduce the risk of contracting STDs? At first glance an obvious choice might be to have their partners always wear condoms, but this "may be unrealistic because traditional sex roles in most cultures do not encourage a woman to talk about sex or to initiate sexual practices or otherwise control an intimate heterosexual encounter" (Rosenberg & Gollub, 1992). Michael Rosenberg and colleagues (1992) reported that under actual use, women using the contraceptive sponge or diaphragm had lower rates of infection for gonorrhea and trichomonas than women whose partners used condoms. The diaphragm was also more effective than condoms against chlamydia. Other researchers believe that the authors "overstated the scientific case for these methods, especially in comparison with the condom" (Cates, Stewart, & Trussell, 1992). However, there is no question that the barrier contraceptives (diaphragm, sponge, and the new female condom), if used consistently, properly, and with spermicide, offer women *some* protection against many STDs (Cates & Stone, 1992a; Rosenberg & Gollub, 1992). There is not yet enough data to tell whether use of the sponge or diaphragm with spermicides offers any protection against HIV, but some initial results were not promising (Kreiss et al., 1992). We do know, of course, that the male condom helps protect both the male and his partner against this deadly disease. We must wait and see how effective the female condom is in preventing STDs under actual use conditions. ■

for me to finish school. I would recommend this method of birth control to anyone.''

(from the author's files)

Like this student, most women who use Norplant do so as a way to plan their timing of having children (Frank et al., 1992). The Food and Drug Administration and World Heath Organization believe it is a safe form of contraception because it contains no estrogen.

Norplant had already been used by 500,000 women worldwide before it was approved for use in the United States. Nevertheless, Norplant should not be used by women with liver disease or tumors, breast cancer, or a history of blood clots. The television news program "Eye to Eye" reported in 1994 (May 8) that removal of Norplant was difficult and painful in some women, but the manufacturer claims that this was due to improper implantation by doctors who were not qualified for the procedure. ■

VOLUNTARY STERILIZATION

Over one million sterilization procedures are performed in the United States every year. In fact, more Americans rely on sterilization for birth control than any other birth control technique (Peterson, 1995). For a couple to rely on this method, it is not necessary that they both be sterilized, so this figure is derived by adding male and female sterilizations (approximately 30 percent of contraceptive users rely on female sterilization and 12 percent on male sterilization). More than half of all married American couples eventually use sterilization after the birth of their last planned child. The use of sterilization increased most during the decade among less-educated, low-income, African-American, and Hispanic women, especially those who had never married (Mosher, 1990). In many other countries sterilization is even more popular than here (Mumford & Kessel, 1992).

In men, the sterilization procedure is called **vasectomy**. In Western cultures, it has traditionally been done by making a small incision or two in the scrotum (under local anesthesia), then tying off and cutting the vas deferens (see Figure 6-8). The entire procedure takes only about 20 minutes. More recently, "no-scalpel" vasectomy has been introduced from China, where it has been performed safely on over 11 million men (Shun-Quiang, 1988). With this technique the skin of the scrotum is simply pierced with a sharp instrument. It takes less than 10 minutes, produces less bleeding, and fewer infections (Nirapathpongporn et al., 1990). Despite the ease of these procedures, there is some evidence that there may have been a decline recently in the number of men seeking a vasectomy (Adler, 1994).

A vasectomy does not interfere with the production of hormones or sperm in the testicles. New sperm simply cannot get past the point where the vas have been tied and cut and eventually are destroyed by

Sterilization
General term for surgical techniques that render an individual infertile.

Vasectomy
The male sterilization technique in which the vas deferens is tied off and cut, thus preventing passage of sperm through the male's reproductive tract.

FIGURE 6-8   A VASECTOMY AND TUBAL LIGATION.

other cells called phagocytes. Sperm that were already past this point at the time of operation, however, must be eliminated before a man is "safe." Other means of contraception should be used until the man has 12 to 16 ejaculations. Some men are reluctant to get a vasectomy because they think that they will no longer be able to ejaculate (obviously confusing ejaculation with orgasm), but recall from Chapter 2 that nearly all of the fluid in a man's ejaculation comes from the prostate gland and seminal vesicles, which are unaffected by the procedure. A man with a vasectomy will still ejaculate during orgasm, but his ejaculation will contain no sperm.

In women, the term **tubal ligation** is often used for a variety of techniques,

Tubal ligation
A female sterilization technique that originally referred only to the tying of the Fallopian tubes, but which is now often used as a general term for a variety of female sterilization techniques.

but it really refers just to the tying of the Fallopian tubes. More commonly, the procedure involves cutting as well as tying the tubes (see Figure 6-8). Both, of course, prevent passage of the egg and sperm. The egg is absorbed by the woman's body. Both of these procedures require hospitalization, general anesthesia, and large abdominal incisions, but they are being replaced more and more by a procedure in which a laparoscope, a long tubelike instrument that transmits TV pictures, is inserted through a small incision in the navel. Once the tubes are located, surgical instruments are inserted through the laparoscope (or other tiny incisions) and the tubes are cauterized. Many physicians use rings or clips to block the tubes. A **laparoscopy** is usually done with general anesthesia, but does not require lengthy hospitalization. Most women go home the same day. Unlike the male technique, a woman may "safely" engage in sexual intercourse as soon as she feels the desire to do so. Instead of using abdominal incisions, some physicians approach the Fallopian tubes through small incisions in the vagina (a procedure called **culpotomy**). However, minor complications (infection or hemorrhage) are twice as high as with laparoscopies. A nonsurgical female sterilization has been tested on thousands of women around the world and shows much promise (see Mumford & Kessel, 1992). Blockage of the tubes is achieved by inserting a quinacrine pellet through a modified copper T IUD inserter. It is 98–99 percent effective, but has not yet been approved for use in the United States.

Laparoscopy

A technique that involves inserting a slender, tubelike instrument (laparoscope) into a woman's abdomen to examine (via fiberoptics) her reproductive organs or a fetus. The procedure is often used to perform female sterilizations.

Culpotomy

A female sterilization technique in which the Fallopian tubes are approached through a small incision in the back of the vagina and then are cut or cauterized.

COMPLICATIONS. Surgical complications resulting from vasectomy are uncommon (less than 5 percent) and generally minor. However, there have been some concerns about the long-term effects. Rather than being destroyed, some sperm leak into the bloodstream, and as a result at least half of the men who have had a vasectomy produce antibodies to their own sperm. Some initial research with monkeys suggested that this could lead to accelerated arteriosclerosis (hardening of the arteries; Clarkson & Alexander, 1980), and a small study with humans suggested a link between vasectomy and testicular cancer (Cale et al., 1990). But several large studies conducted with thousands of humans have found no link between the surgery and later development of arteriosclerosis or testicular cancer (e.g., Massey et al., 1984; Moller, Knudsen, & Lynge, 1994; Perinn et al., 1984).

More recently, some studies have raised concerns that vasectomy may increase men's risk of prostate cancer (Giovannucci et al., 1993; see Klitsch, 1993b). However, after a scientific panel at the National Institutes of Health met to discuss these findings, they concluded that the evidence was not strong. An editorial accompanying the two reports stated, "There is no known biologic mechanism to explain a causal relationship." Cancer of the prostate is 50 times more common in the United States than in China and other developing countries, and the factors causing this are so poorly understood that it complicates any research about vasectomy as a cause (Farley et al., 1993).

Some physicians have suggested that there is a "post-tubal ligation syndrome" characterized by heavier than normal menstrual bleeding and greater menstrual cramps. One study reported that this occurred in one in every seven to ten cases (Rulin et al., 1989). This has sometimes been used as a justification to perform hysterectomy (Goldhaber et al., 1993), but pathology exams usually reveal nothing abnormal and studies to date have found no support for a biological basis for hysterectomy (Stergachis et al., 1990; Williams Obstetrics, 17th ed.). Studies conducted by the World Health Organization found no increase in menstrual bleeding associated with sterilization (World Health Organization, 1984, 1985), but a replication found a small increase (Richards et al., 1991). A more recent study found that half of sterilized women were experiencing heavy menstrual flow 5 years after surgery (Wilcox et al., 1992). However, most studies find that the large majority of women are satisfied with their choice of surgical contraception. What's more, sterilization in women has some definite health benefits: it substantially decreases their risk of getting cancer of the ovaries (Hankinson et al., 1993). Overall, the long-term benefits outweigh the risks (Kawachi, Colditz, & Hankinson, 1994).

CAN STERILIZATIONS BE REVERSED? Sterilization procedures are highly effective, with failure rates of one to four in 1,000 (Hatcher et al., 1994; Trussell et al., 1990). Today, they should also be considered permanent. Few people who decide to be sterilized ever wish to have it reversed (about 4 percent change their mind), but for those who do there is no guarantee of success. The problem is that the sewing together of the vas deferens or Fallopian tubes requires very skilled microsurgery techniques (the inside diameter of a Fallopian tube, for example, is no greater than a human hair). The success rate for vasectomy reversal has been steadily improving (a new technique using laser surgery appears to be very promising), with some doctors now reporting restored sperm flow in over 50 percent of their patients. However, even with restored sperm flow, the chance of a man impregnating a woman decreases markedly if the reversal is not performed within a year or two, probably due to the increased levels of antibodies to his own sperm. Successful reconstruction of the Fallopian tubes is more difficult because the slightest scarring can impair passage of the egg (and result in tubal pregnancy even if fertilization occurs). Success rates have generally been less than 25 percent. So, while there have been successful reversals in both males and females, the success rates today are still far less than 100 percent and, therefore, only people who are quite sure that they do not want any more children should opt for these procedures.

Most physicians refuse to perform these procedures on young unmarried people, and even married couples with children often are told to consider their decision for a few days to be sure. Some states have a mandatory waiting period (30 days in New York, for example). Sometimes there is more than just the question of children to be considered before making the decision. Anyone who worries about conflicts with their religious beliefs or that they will not be a "whole person" should work these problems out beforehand. Men who have a history of erectile problems are also not good candidates (the procedure might contribute to psychologically caused impotence). Once done, however, many people report an increase in sexual desire because they no longer have to worry about pregnancy or contraceptive side effects, and sexual relations can be completely spontaneous.

WHICH PARTNER SHOULD BE STERILIZED? Remember, if a couple agrees that they do not wish to have any more children and choose sterilization as their contraceptive technique, it requires that only one of them have surgery. Which one should it be, the man or the woman? One study that compared expenses, complication rates, and number of people who regretted their operations, concluded that the male sterilization technique was preferable in every way (Kjersgaard et al., 1989). Whatever the choice may be, it is important that the couple make an educated decision and that both persons are happy with the decision. ∎

UNWANTED PREGNANCIES: THE FINAL OPTIONS

There is no reversible method of contraception that is 100 percent effective (although Norplant, Depo-Provera, and the pill come close); thus, unwanted pregnancies sometimes occur even for couples who are using contraception. If an unwanted pregnancy should occur, a woman (or couple) really has only three options: to continue with the pregnancy and keep the baby, to continue with the pregnancy and put the baby up for adoption, or to terminate the pregnancy (abortion). In many cases, none of these is an easy choice.

The responsibilities involved with **keeping and raising a baby** force many women to drop out of school and remain uneducated and unskilled, locking them into a life of poverty and reliance on state funds and services to raise the child. The rate of child abuse resulting from the emotional frustration in these situations is much higher than normal (Zuravin, 1991).

Some women or couples choose to put an unplanned baby up for **adoption** to others who are better able to care for it. In many cases this may be best for the child, but nevertheless, it often results in long-lasting adjustment problems for those who have surrendered their child. The following is a typical case:

"I was one of the teenage pregnancies. I was 14 years old and was pregnant. My boyfriend, now my husband, was also 14 years old and thought that he could not produce sperm yet, and I believed him. It has caused me a very hard life because of the guilt I feel for having to give up my child. We now have two more children, but it still doesn't fill the void. I only wish we both could have been aware of this then. All of the agony could have been spared."

(from the author's files)

For many women or couples, **abortion** is no less an emotional alternative. Although long-term severe negative reactions are infrequent (Adler et al., 1990), some women and couples go through a period of sadness or guilt.

> Abortion
> Termination of pregnancy. Depending on how far the pregnancy has advanced, this can be done by taking a pill (Ovral or RU486), scraping the uterine lining (dilation and curettage), removing the uterine lining by suction (dilation and evacuation), or inducing labor (by injecting hypertonic saline or prostaglandins).

"At the age of 18 I became pregnant. My boyfriend of four years and I had recently broken up, so I was alone. I suppose I could have told my parents, but I was too scared of their reactions. At three months I terminated my pregnancy. It hurt very badly emotionally. Occasionally I think of how old my baby, boy or girl, would be today."

(from the author's files)

Others feel a sense of relief because of compelling health or economic considerations.

Of these three options, only abortion can be considered a method of birth control. However, many people have strong negative views of abortion used as birth control. Let us discuss this topic in more detail.

ABORTION

There are an estimated 36 to 53 million abortions performed annually throughout the world, of which only about 26 to 31 million are legal (Henshaw, 1990). Abortion is the main form of birth control in China and Russia, with the average Russian woman having six or seven abortions in her lifetime (*Discover*, April, 1986). Although the U.S. abortion rate is well below the worldwide rate (28 versus 37 to 55 per 1,000 women aged 15 to 44), nearly a third of all pregnancies in this country end in abortion. Over 1.5 million abortions are performed in the United States each year (some are done for medical reasons). However, the number of abortions has declined recently to 1.53 million in 1992, the lowest number recorded since 1979 (Alan Guttmacher Institute survey, 1994). According to a 1989 Gallup survey, 9 percent of U.S. college women have had an abortion.

Over three fourths of women who obtain abortions do so within 10 weeks of conception (Koonin et al., 1992). Death resulting from a legal abortion is very uncommon, less than one per 100,000 abortions, and, in fact, is much less common than deaths resulting from childbirth (Grimes & Cates, 1980; Koonin et al., 1992). Modern legal abortions do not increase a woman's subsequent risk of infertility, miscarriage, or low birthweight baby (Frank et al., 1993). Abortions also do not increase the risk of a later ectopic pregnancy (Holt et al., 1989).

What are some of the possible consequences of legalizing abortion? Of abolishing abortion? It has been estimated that adolescent childbearing in New York City is 14.1 percent (white adolescents) to 18.7 percent (African-American adolescents) lower than it would be if abortion were illegal (Joyce & Mocan, 1990). In Romania, the abolishment of legalized abortion led to the highest maternal mortality rate in Europe and the abandonment of tens of thousands of children in institutions (Stephenson et al., 1992).

There are several methods used to terminate a pregnancy:

1. *Emergency birth control:* There are several methods that can be used in emergency situations (rape, incest, etc.) to prevent implantation after unprotected intercourse (see Van Look & Hertzen, 1993). The most commonly used is the *morning-after-pill*. Marketed as Ovral 2+2, this pill contains 50 mcg of ethinyl estradiol and 0.5 mg of dl-norgestrel. When two pills are taken within 72 hours of intercourse followed by two more 12 hours later, they prevent implantation of the fertilized egg in 98 to 99 percent of cases. Ovral tablets are now used in place of an older morning-after pill that contained only a high dose of synthetic estrogen (diethylstilbestrol or DES), which is no longer approved in the United States for this use. The morning-after pill may cause nausea and vomiting, but it has fewer side effects than older pills. However, women who have health problems that disqualify them from use of regular birth control pills should not take the morning-after version either.

   High doses of many presently sold birth control pills reduce the chances of implantation by 75 percent when taken within 72 hours of unprotected intercourse. Although oral contraceptives are sold as emergency birth control in other countries, U.S. companies presently do not sell them for this purpose. Women's health advocates have petitioned the FDA to approve popular birth control pills for this purpose (Neergaard, 1994).

   Insertion of a copper IUD within 5–6 days after intercourse is also a highly effective way of preventing implantation. Recently, it has been reported that if taken within 3 days of unprotected intercourse, the drug RU 486 is more effective than the morning-after pill and causes less nausea (Glasier et al., 1992).

2. *RU 486:* In 1988, the French, Chinese, and Swedish governments approved a pill (called RU 486) made by the French company Roussel-Uclaf that can be used to chemically induce an abortion up to nine weeks after a woman's last menstrual period. Since approved in other countries, it had been used by more than 150,000 women by mid-1994. One third of all abortions performed in France are presently done by this method. It is 99 percent effective when taken in combination with oral prostaglandins, which cause contractions of the uterus (Peyron et al., 1993). RU 486 works by blocking the body's use of progesterone, the hormone necessary for maintaining the endometrium of the uterus, thus causing shedding of the uterine lining (Baulieu, 1989). The main side effects are nausea, cramping, and prolonged uterine bleeding (11–12 days). Contrary to popular belief, it is not taken at home, and must be administered in a clinic. The drug took a step closer to legalization in the United States in 1993 when the French manufacturer licensed

it to the U.S.-based Population Council for eventual distribution.

RU 486 shows tremendous promise in treating a variety of medical problems, including Cushing's disease, breast cancer, fibroid tumors, and osteoporosis. For these reasons, the *Journal of the American Medical Association* in 1990 urged that it be approved for use in the United States.

3. *Dilation and curettage* (D & C): Once the standard procedure for unwanted pregnancies of 15 weeks or less, it is now used less and less for purposes of abortion. Under general anesthesia, a female's cervix is dilated, and the lining of the uterus is scraped with a metal instrument called a curette. In addition to the risk of general anesthesia, it results in more bleeding and discomfort than D & E procedures.

4. *Dilation and evacuation* (D & E): In this procedure, which does not require general anesthesia, a tube is inserted through the cervix and the fetal material is removed by suction. This can be done without anesthesia in the first 4 to 6 weeks of pregnancy, but requires local anesthesia and dilation of the cervix for pregnancies terminated during weeks seven through twelve. Later stage abortions may require gentle scraping of the uterine walls in addition to suction. The older D & C procedure was associated with a risk of subsequent sterility, but early first-trimester abortions performed by the vacuum technique do not appear to have this risk (Frank et al., 1993).

5. *Induced labor*: This is used exclusively for termination of pregnancies that have proceeded beyond 16 weeks (which accounts for only 5 percent of all abortions; Koonin et al., 1992). A solution of hypertonic saline or prostaglandins (hormones which cause smooth muscle contractions) is injected into the amniotic sac and induces labor within 12 to 36 hours. The fetus is born dead.

THE PRESENT STATUS AND FUTURE OF ABORTION IN THE UNITED STATES. Abortion is a subject that has polarized people throughout the nation. Those opposed to abortion ("right-to-lifers") express concerns about protecting human life. "Pro-choicers," on the other hand, wish to retain the right of individuals to make decisions about something that will have a major impact on their own lives. In a 1992 survey conducted by the Gallup Organization, 14 percent of Americans felt that abortion should be illegal under all circumstances, while 31 percent wanted unlimited access to abortion. Fifty-three percent wanted limited access, that is, it depended on the circumstances.

The laws regarding abortion have been in a state of transition for over two decades. Prior to 1973, each state could allow or prohibit abortion as they wished, but in that year a 7–2 Supreme Court decision *(Roe v. Wade)* prohibited the states from interfering with decisions made between a woman and her doctor during the first 3 months of pregnancy. The ruling also prevented states from prohibiting abortion in the second trimester of pregnancy, but did allow for greater regulations designed to protect a woman's health (hospitalization, for example). Antiabortion forces won a victory in 1977 when the Supreme Court upheld the Hyde Amendment, which disallowed the use of federal Medicaid money to pay for abortions. Without public funding, obtaining a legal abortion is difficult for women with limited incomes. Eighty percent of abortions in the United States are given to unmarried women, many of whom have little or no source of income. Nearly two thirds of women who obtain abortions live under the poverty level.

Although the decision in *Roe v. Wade* giving a woman the right to choose is still the law, subsequent court decisions have given states greater leeway in regulating abortion. In 1989, a sharply divided Supreme Court upheld by a 5–4 vote *(Webster v. Reproductive Health Services)* a Missouri law that further restricted public funds and facilities for abortions and that also required physicians to test for fetal viability (the potential for the fetus to survive) at 20 weeks. The earliest point of fetal viability is 24 weeks (the law allowed for a 4-week margin of error in determining the time of conception), and the vast majority of abortions were already performed before the twentieth week. In 1990, the Court voted 6–3 to uphold state laws that ban abortions for girls under age 18 unless a parent is notified. In a 1992 case *(Planned Parenthood v. Casey)*, the Court, in another 5–4 vote, upheld a Pennsylvania law that imposed a 24-hour wait, required doctors to tell women about other options, and also required parental notification for minors. Legal decisions regarding abortion are likely to change when the members of the Supreme Court are replaced, either by more conservative or more liberal justices.

Religious beliefs regarding abortion have often changed as well. Within the Catholic church, for example, the first pope to declare that abortion is murder was Sixtus V in 1588, but that was reversed just 3 years later by Pope Gregory XIV. For the next 300 years, abortion was allowed up to the time of animation by a rational soul (up to 40 days after conception in the case of a male embryo and for the first 80 days in the case of a female fetus; Connery, 1977; Grisez, 1970). In 1869, however, Pope Pius IX again declared that abortion was murder and this has remained the belief of every pope since.

With the diversity of opinion regarding this subject, religious and legal beliefs about abortion will probably continue to change for many decades to come. ■

FUTURE TECHNOLOGY

The female condom became available to women in the United States in 1993. This probably was the first of a whole new generation of female barrier contraceptives. In addition to the condom, there are two other vaginal pouches under development. The *Woman's Choice Female Condomme* is inserted into the vagina with an applicator and has a latex rubber umbrella-like cap that is about a third thicker than the male condom. The *unisex condom garment* is a polyurethane bikini-like item with an attached sheath that can be worn by either men or women (as a vaginal liner or penis cover) for contraception and prevention against sexually transmitted diseases.

Researchers are also testing variations of the cervical cap. The *Lea's Shield* is made of silicone rubber and has a loop that makes it easy to insert and remove. Unlike the present cap, it is intended to be sold over the counter. The *Fem Cap* is also made of silicone rubber. It conforms to the vaginal walls by a surrounding "brim." The *Oves Cervical Cap*, unlike the others, is disposable, and will probably be available across the counter. Other experimental contraceptive devices for women include a small plastic ring that is inserted in a female like a diaphragm and that releases hormones to prevent ovulation (similar to the pill, except that there is less risk of circulatory problems; Sivin et al., 1981).

Research into a *male pill* continues, but do not expect it on the market any time soon (see Comhaire, 1994). The problem is trying to find a pill that inhibits sperm production without simultaneously lowering sexual desire or a man's ability to get and maintain an erection. There was some success with gossypol, a Chinese derivative of cottonseed oil that disables sperm-producing testicular cells, but research was abandoned because as many as 20 percent of men who took it became permanently sterile. Present research is focusing on highly specific aspects of spermatogenesis or, as you will now learn, the use of antibodies.

Perhaps the most promising future means of birth control is *vaccination* (Alexander, 1994). It might be possible to prevent pregnancy the same way you can the flu. Researchers are trying to develop vaccines that will cause the body to produce antibodies to proteins in either sperm or eggs. Scientists in India are already clinically testing a vaccine that stimulates the production of antibodies to HCG (human chorionic gonadotropin), a hormone necessary to maintain pregnancy. A fertilized egg cannot implant and is discharged during menstruation. U.S. scientists are working on a contraceptive vaccine. For example, if women could be inoculated with a vaccine that triggered production of antibodies to a protein found only in sperm, it would prevent fertilization. A booster shot would be needed every couple of years to continue its use.

A report issued in 1990 by the National Research Council's Institute of Medicine warned that the United States is far behind other countries in choices of birth control. The biggest deterrent to new contraceptive methods is not technology or lack of research, but an insurance-product liability problem. Consumers accept that contraceptive methods sometimes fail to prevent pregnancy, but they are less forgiving about side effects. But, as stated by Dr. Carl Djerassi (one of the developers of the pill) before a congressional committee in 1978, "There is no such thing as a wholly safe contraceptive." Some methods, such as Depo-Provera, went through more than 20 years of FDA hearings before final approval, yet were available to people around the world all during that time.

When a legal case involves an individual versus a large corporation, juries often award large settlements to the individual in the belief that the corporation can afford it. A jury awarded $5 million, for example, to a couple who claimed that their child's birth defects were caused by spermicides, even though the authors of the study that claimed to link spermicides with birth defects had repudiated their own results. A few more cases like this and we may see the end of spermicides, the sponge, and the diaphragm. There has never been a contraceptive device that was not associated with some risk, but unless consumers change their attitudes and quit unrealistically expecting perfection, we may retreat to the days when there was nothing available except the condom. ■

CHOOSING A CONTRACEPTIVE METHOD

It is important that men and women choose a method of birth control with which they and their partner are comfortable. A woman may like the diaphragm, but if she is in a relationship it will not be good if her partner resents her stopping in the middle of having sex to put it in. A man may prefer that his female partner take the pill, but it will not be good for the couple's relationship if she resents having to suffer possible side effects. A couple can work these kinds of problems out only by talking about the matter and communicating with each other on a regular basis.

Choosing a particular birth control method does not mean that you have to stick with it if you are unhappy about it for any reason. As you know by now, there are many alternatives. For example, about one out of seven married women attempting to avoid pregnancy decide to abandon their chosen method within the first year of use. Unfortunately, half of these use no type of contraception for at least a month afterwards (Grady, Hayward, & Florey, 1988). If you do not presently wish to have children and are unhappy with the birth control method you use, decide on an alternative method *before* you stop using your present one.

When deciding which type of birth control to use, ask yourself the following questions; they were developed to help you decide whether the method you are considering is a good choice or a poor choice *for you* (from Robert Hatcher et al., *Contraceptive Technology*. New York: Irvington Publishers, 1994).

METHOD OF BIRTH CONTROL YOU ARE CONSIDERING USING: _____

Length of time you used this method in the past: _____

ANSWER YES OR NO TO THE FOLLOWING QUESTIONS:	YES	NO
Have I had problems using this method before?	_____	_____
Have I ever become pregnant while using this method?	_____	_____
Am I afraid of using this method?	_____	_____
Would I really rather not use this method?	_____	_____
Will I have trouble remembering to use this method?	_____	_____
Will I have trouble using this method correctly?	_____	_____
Do I still have unanswered questions about this method?	_____	_____
Does this method make menstrual periods longer or more painful?	_____	_____
Does this method cost more than I can afford?	_____	_____
Could this method cause me to have serious complications?	_____	_____
Am I opposed to this method because of any religious or moral beliefs?	_____	_____
Is my partner opposed to this method?	_____	_____
Am I using this method without my partner's knowledge?	_____	_____
Will using this method embarrass my partner?	_____	_____
Will using this method embarrass me?	_____	_____
Will I enjoy intercourse less because of this method?	_____	_____
If this method interrupts lovemaking, will I avoid using it?	_____	_____
Has a nurse or doctor ever told me NOT to use this method?	_____	_____
Is there anything about my personality that could lead me to use this method incorrectly?	_____	_____
Am I at any risk of being exposed to HIV (the AIDS virus) or other sexually transmitted infections if I use this method?	_____	_____
TOTAL NUMBER OF YES ANSWERS:	_____	

Most individuals will have a few yes answers. Yes answers mean that potential problems may lie in store. If you have more than a few yes responses, you may want to talk to your physician, counselor, partner, or friend. Talking it over can help you to decide whether to use this method, or how to use it so it will really be effective for you. In general, the more yes answers you have, the less likely you are to use this method consistently and correctly.

This chapter only introduced the various contraceptive methods. If additional information is desired, you are urged to contact your local Planned Parenthood organization or your state family planning clinic. The people who work there will be glad to help you.

"Sex is for people who are ready and willing to take a lifetime responsibility for the outcome of sex."

—Sue Finn
(quoted by L. Smith, 1993)

Many parents are opposed to the teaching of contraception in school because they worry it will lead to sexual activity. Research has shown, however, that young people who have had sex education are no more likely to engage in sexual intercourse than those who have not had it, but more importantly, that they are less likely to get pregnant. Look again at the table at the beginning of the chapter. Dutch and Swedish children have sex just as much as American teens, but far fewer get pregnant (or get someone pregnant). In those countries children are taught about contraception at an early age, in an open and frank manner. Family planning programs that include discussion by older students on resisting peer pressure are particularly effective in reducing teen pregnancies (Howard & McCabe, 1990).

KEY TERMS

abortion 150
actual use effectiveness rate 130
basal body temperature method 133
Billings method 133
barrier method 135
breast-feeding 132
calendar method 133
cervical cap 140
combination pill 143
condom 135
contraceptive sponge 141

contraception 126
culpotomy 149
Depo-Provera 146
diaphragm 139
douching 132
female condom 138
fertility awareness method 132
IUD 141
laparoscopy 149
minipill 143
nonoxynol-9 134
Norplant 146

progestins 143
RU 486 151
spermicides 134
sterilization 148
sympto-thermal method 134
theoretical effectiveness rate 130
tubal ligation 148
vasectomy 148
withdrawal (coitus interruptus) 131

PERSONAL REFLECTIONS

1. Are you prepared at the present time to assume the responsibilities of being a parent? Why or why not?

2. How would your life change if you or your partner were pregnant (consider your relationship, finances, career goals, etc.)?

3. If you are having sexual relations, what do you do about contraception?

4. Whose responsibility is it for birth control—your responsibility or your partner's? Why? If you answered that it is your partner's responsibility, do you think that you share *any* of the responsibility for the consequences of engaging in sexual intercourse?

SUGGESTED READINGS

Babies who have babies: A day in the life of teen pregnancy in America. (1994, October 24). *People* magazine. If you want a good idea of what it's like to be a young unwed teenager, read this.

Connell, E. B. (1987, May/June). The crisis in contraception. *Technology Review*. Discusses the problems that politics and lawsuits are causing in contraceptive technology and marketing.

Consumer Reports. (1989, March). Can you rely on condoms? Tests the strength of over 40 types of condoms along with consumer ratings.

Fraser, L. (1988, June). Pill politics. *Mother Jones*. Examines the politics of RU486, the controversial chemically induced abortion technique.

Gordon, L. (1990). *Woman's body, woman's right: A social history of birth control*. New York: Penguin. An excellent history of birth control.

Hatcher, R. et al. (1994). *Contraceptive technology*. New York: Irvington. This is the most comprehensive and technical review of contraceptive methods. It is revised every 2–3 years.

Ismach, J. (1986, July/August). A second look at the pill. *American Health*. Explains how today's pill is safer than in the past, with fewer side effects.

Jarrow, J. P. (1987, December). Vasectomy update: Effects on health and sexuality. *Medical Aspects of Human Sexuality.* Discusses the effects of vasectomy on the endocrine and immune systems.

Ory, H. W. (1982, July/August). The noncontraceptive health benefits from oral contraceptive use. *Family Planning Perspectives,* Vol. 14.

Patient Guide: How to use a condom. (1987, July). *Medical Aspects of Human Sexuality.* Gives instructions on how to use condoms correctly.

Planned Parenthood. (1989). *Facts about birth control.* Easy to understand, it is written at a sixth grade level.

Scales, P. C. (1987, Spring/Summer). How we can prevent teenage pregnancy (and why it's not the real problem). *Journal of Sex Education and Therapy,* Vol. 13. Disputes the myth that sex education leads to promiscuity. Teen sexual activity results from mixed signals.

Wattleton, F. (1989, July 24/31). Teen-age pregnancy: The case for national action. *The Nation.* Discusses the high teen pregnancy rate in the United States and suggests possible causes and solutions.

CHAPTER SEVEN

Human Sexuality Today

PREGNANCY AND CHILDBIRTH

WHEN YOU HAVE FINISHED STUDYING THIS CHAPTER, YOU SHOULD BE ABLE TO:

1. EXPLAIN THE PROCESS OF CONCEPTION, INCLUDING THE TERMS PRIMARY FOLLICLE, GRAAFIAN FOLLICLE, CAPACITATION, AND ZYGOTE;

2. TRACE THE PROCESS OF DEVELOPMENT FROM THE ZYGOTE THROUGH IMPLANTATION, AND DISCUSS SOME PROBLEMS THAT SOMETIMES OCCUR WITH IMPLANTATION;

3. DESCRIBE WHAT OCCURS IN EACH TRIMESTER OF PREGNANCY FOR BOTH MOTHER AND EMBRYO/FETUS;

4. SUMMARIZE THE POSSIBLE EFFECTS OF SMOKING, DRUG USE, ENVIRONMENTAL HAZARDS, DISEASES, AND ANESTHETICS ON THE EMBRYO AND FETUS;

5. COMPARE AND CONTRAST SEVERAL METHODS FOR DETECTING FETAL ABNORMALITIES;

6. DISCUSS TRADITIONAL AND ALTERNATIVE BIRTHING PRACTICES, INCLUDING LAMAZE, LEBOYER, HOME BIRTHS, AND THE USE OF MIDWIVES;

7. EXPLAIN THE THREE STAGES OF LABOR AND THE EVENTS THAT OCCUR IN EACH;

8. IDENTIFY AND EXPLAIN THE PROBLEMS THAT CAN OCCUR DURING BREECH DELIVERIES, CESAREANS, AND PRETERM DELIVERIES;

9. DESCRIBE THE HORMONES NECESSARY FOR MILK FOR BREAST-FEEDING AND DISCUSS THE BENEFITS OF BREAST-FEEDING;

10. DISCUSS RECOMMENDATIONS CONCERNING SEXUAL INTERCOURSE DURING AND FOLLOWING PREGNANCY; AND

11. COMPARE AND CONTRAST THE VARIOUS METHODS FOR DEALING WITH INFERTILITY.

PREGNANCY AND CHILDBIRTH ARE INTENSE EXPERIENCES, REMEMBERED FOR A LIFETIME. THE MOST potent human emotions—hope, fear, love, loneliness, depression, and joy—are often felt at their maximum levels. The first time that a woman feels a baby move inside of her, her first labor contractions, the first time that a child is viewed by its parents after birth—these are often the things that make life worth experiencing. Giving birth means assuming a great responsibility, for the newborn is totally dependent upon his or her parents. Relationships change with the addition of a new life and new responsibilities within a family. This requires that many adjustments in living be made. As you will see, it is important to begin making these adjustments before the baby is born, sometimes before the baby is conceived. ■

CONCEPTION AND IMPLANTATION

As you learned in Chapter 2, the ovaries in females store eggs (**ova**). Each egg is surrounded by a small sac forming what is called a **primary follicle**. As a result of release of FSH from the pituitary gland, one (or more) of these primary follicles matures to become a **Graafian follicle**. About midway through a 28-day menstrual cycle, the Graafian follicle breaks open and the ovum is released into the abdominal cavity, where it is picked up by one of the Fallopian tubes. The ovum moves through the Fallopian tube to the uterus. It will take 3 to 7 days to reach the uterus, *but the ovum can only be fertilized during the first 24 hours after it leaves an ovary* (Moore, 1982). If a sperm does not penetrate the ovum during this time, the ovum becomes overly "ripe" and eventually disintegrates in the uterus, leaving the woman's body during her menstrual flow.

Primary follicle
An immature ovum enclosed by a single layer of cells.

Graafian follicle
A mature follicle.

At orgasm during sexual intercourse, a man will ejaculate 200–400 million **sperm** into the vagina. They then attempt to pass through the cervix and uterus to the Fallopian tubes. This is not an easy journey. Some sperm are stopped by the force of gravity, some by the acidity of the woman's reproductive tract, some by clumping, and some by simply taking wrong turns (because usually only one egg is released, only one Fallopian tube will be the right path for the sperm to follow). Only a few thousand will live long enough to reach the Fallopian tubes. Fewer than 50 reach the egg within the Fallopian tube (Moore, 1982). Most sperm live for only 48 hours inside a woman's reproductive tract, but a few may live for as long as 72 hours (Marieb, 1992). Thus, intercourse can result in conception during only 4 days out of every 28-day menstrual cycle (3 days before ovulation and 1 day afterwards).

Capacitation
A process that sperm undergo, while traveling through the female's reproductive tract, in which their membranes become thin enough so that an enzyme necessary for softening the ovum's membrane can be released.

While the sperm are in the female's reproductive tract, they undergo a process called **capacitation** in which their membranes become thin enough so that an enzyme (called hyaluronidase) can be released to soften the egg's outer layers. Only sperm that undergo capacitation are able to unite with an egg. For capacitation to finish, sperm need to spend several hours in the reproductive tract. The egg sends out tiny projections and pulls one sperm to its surface, the *zona pellucida*. That sperm secretes the enzyme and penetrates the egg's surface, and **conception** takes place. An instantaneous chemical reaction within the ovum then prevents other sperm from penetrating the ovum. Within 24–30 hours, the nuclei of the sperm and the ovum fuse to form a one-celled organism called a **zygote**. This single cell contains the complete genetic code or blueprint for a new human being.

Conception
The union of an egg and a sperm.

Zygote
The one-celled organism created from the fusion of a sperm and egg.

Shortly afterward, the zygote splits into two separate cells, then four, then eight, etc. As cell division occurs, each individual cell gets smaller. This collection of cells is called a **morula**. While cell division is rapidly taking place, the morula is slowly continuing its trip toward the uterus. When the conceptus has about 100 cells, it has a fluid-filled center and is then called a **blastocyst**. After the blastocyst reaches the uterus it may float there for several days. At this point it is still smaller than the head of a pin.

Morula
The collection of cells formed when the zygote begins rapid cell division.

Blastocyst
The fluid-filled sphere that reaches the uterus after fertilization and which was created by the transformation of the morula through continued, rapid cell division.

At about the sixth or seventh day after conception, the blastocyst begins to attempt to attach itself to the wall of the uterus via hairlike roots (villi). The uterine wall at this time has a large supply of blood that serves as a source of nutrients and oxygen. At about 11–12 days after conception the blastocyst burrows into the wall of the uterus, a process called **implantation**. By about 14 days after conception, implantation is usually complete (see Figure 7-1).

Implantation
The process by which the blastocyst attaches itself to the wall of the uterus.

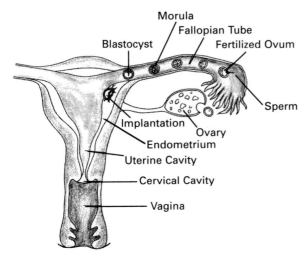

Morula
Fallopian Tube
Blastocyst
Fertilized Ovum
Sperm
Implantation
Ovary
Endometrium
Uterine Cavity
Cervical Cavity
Vagina

FIGURE 7-1   OVULATION, FERTILIZATION, AND IMPLANTATION.

The blastocyst is now called an **embryo**, and is called a **fetus** at about 8 weeks (see Pregnancy section).

The outer cell layers of the embryo are called the **trophoblast** (from the Greek *trophe*, meaning to nourish). The trophoblast begins to grow rapidly and forms four protective layers or membranes, each with a special function. One produces blood cells for the embryo until it can produce its own. Another cell layer forms the **umbilical cord**—the major link between the developing baby and its mother. The third membrane is called the **amnion**. It is a thick-skinned sac filled with water that surrounds the embryo. By surrounding the developing baby with liquid, protection is provided against bumps, sudden movements by the mother, and changes in temperature. The fourth membrane, called the **chorion**, will develop into the lining of the placenta. The **placenta** is an organ that serves as a connection or interface between the embryo's systems and those of the mother. The embryo is connected to the placenta by the umbilical cord. Through it, the embryo receives nourishment from its mother. It also receives antibodies for protection against infection. Wastes from the embryo's system travel from the umbilical cord to the placenta, and from there are taken up by the mother's excretory system.

Trophoblast
The outer-four cell layers of the embryo.

Umbilical cord
The cord that connects an embryo/fetus to the mother's placenta.

Amnion
A thick-skinned sac filled with water that surrounds the embryo/fetus.

Chorion
The fourth membrane of the trophoblast; it develops into the lining of the placenta.

Placenta
An organ that serves as a connection or interface between the fetus's systems and those of the mother.

PROBLEMS WITH IMPLANTATION

It has been estimated that about three fourths of conceptions either fail to implant or are spontaneously aborted within the first 6 weeks (Boklage, 1990). Over 20 percent fail before pregnancy can be detected by chemical tests (Wilcox et al., 1988). Failure to implant may be a means of "weeding out" or preventing the further development of blastocysts that are not completely healthy or normal.

One type of problem with implantation is called **ectopic pregnancy** (from the Greek *ektopos*, meaning "out of place"). In this case, conception is successful, but implantation takes place outside the uterus. In about 96 percent of these cases, implantation occurs in a Fallopian tube. In rarer cases, implantation can occur on an ovary, on the cervix, or in the abdomen. When implantation occurs in a Fallopian tube (often called a "*tubal pregnancy*"), there is simply not enough room for the embryo to grow. Unlike the uterus, the Fallopian tubes are not capable of much expansion. The embryo may be dissolved by the body's immunological system, but if it continues to grow after the eighth week, it may break the tube. This is a serious complication of pregnancy, and it can be fatal. Although the mortality rate has been dropping (due to earlier detection), ectopic pregnancies still account for about 11–15 percent of all maternal deaths (Atrash, Friede, & Hogue, 1987; Koonin et al., 1988).

The rate of ectopic pregnancies increased fourfold from 1970 to the mid-1980s, and they now account for about 1 percent of all pregnancies (Atrash et al., 1987; Centers for Disease Control, 1988). Ectopic pregnancies are caused by conditions that block or slow passage of the conceptus to the uterus. The most common cause is scarring of the Fallopian tubes due to pelvic inflammatory disease resulting from untreated chlamydia or gonorrhea (Chow et al., 1990). Use of condoms reduces the risk of tubal pregnancies in sexually active women. Other factors include anatomical malformations of the tubes, use of (older types of) intrauterine devices, increasing age at time of conception, and douching (Chow et al., 1990). If a woman has an ectopic pregnancy, she has an increased risk of having more ectopic pregnancies in the future, because many of the causes of the original problem, such as scarring, will still be present in later pregnancies.

Ectopic pregnancy
The implantation of a fertilized egg outside of the endometrium of the uterus.

Tubal pregnancy
Implantation of a blastocyst in a Fallopian tube.

"I got pregnant only to learn it was tubular . . . One year later I got pregnant again and again it was tubular. The specialist told me I needed surgery to remove scar tissue that was choking my Fallopian tube . . . "

(from the author's files)

Until recently, women diagnosed with tubal pregnancy always had part of the affected tube surgically removed (thus greatly reducing chances of pregnancy in the future). Today, however, diagnosis can be made within 3 weeks of conception and this has led to procedures that do not require removal of the tube. Initial screening may be done by *ultrasound scan*, which uses sound waves like a radar or sonar device to create a picture of the inside of the woman's reproductive tract. An increasing number of physicians are following this with *laparoscopy*, in which a lighted tube capable of sending TV pictures is inserted into the abdomen for a direct examination of the internal reproductive organs.

(Both of these techniques can also be used to diagnose other problems throughout pregnancy.) If an ectopic pregnancy is confirmed, it can be treated at that time by laparoscopic surgery (rather than tubal sectioning; Maruri & Azziz, 1993). Subsequent successful pregnancies are just as high for the conservative therapy as with the radical therapy (Ory et al., 1993). Alternatively, some physicians are treating ectopic pregnancies by administering a drug called methotrexate (Stovall et al., 1991; Tulandi et al., 1991). This field is undergoing rapid change and there is increasing optimism that more and more women will be treated with these conservative procedures. ■

PREGNANCY

Pregnancy lasts an average of 260–270 days. "Due dates," the dates that the physician sets as the "expected time of arrival" for babies, are rarely the dates of actual birth. This is because the exact date of conception is hard to measure with complete accuracy and because there is great variability among births, even with the same parents. Because pregnancy lasts about nine months, this time is divided into three-month periods called **trimesters** for descriptive purposes.

Trimesters
Three-month periods of pregnancy (months 0–3, 4–6, and 7–9), so labeled for descriptive purposes.

THE FIRST TRIMESTER—THE MOTHER

Recall from Chapter 3 that a missed menstrual period is not a sure sign of the start of pregnancy. There are many things that can cause a missed period, including stress and illness. Women athletes, especially track stars and gymnasts, commonly miss one or more periods in the course of several months. In addition, a period can be missed but a woman may not know it, because implantation of the blastocyst into the uterine wall can cause bleeding that may be mistaken for menstruation.

When a period is missed, women often want quick and accurate information about whether or not they are actually pregnant. To get this information they take a "pregnancy test." These tests are conducted by physicians, medical technicians, and are even sold in drug stores for use at home. They work by determining if a hormone secreted by the placenta (**human chorionic gonadotropin**, or HCG) is present in a woman's urine. To test for HCG, a drop of urine is mixed with chemicals in a tube or glass. If the mixture does not coagulate (lump together), HCG is present and the woman is pregnant. This test is most accurate (95–98 percent) 2 weeks or more after a missed period. Tests that measure HCG in blood can detect if a woman is pregnant even

Human chorionic gonadotropin (HCG)
A hormone secreted by the chorion that stimulates the ovaries during pregnancy.

sooner than this. Even when home pregnancy tests are used properly, their accuracy rate is only 70–90 percent, depending on the brand.

One of the more common or frequent symptoms of pregnancy is nausea (vomiting). It is called "*morning sickness*," though it can occur at any time of the day. It usually goes away by the end of the third month of pregnancy, but it can last longer. Some women eat crackers, drink soda water, and try a variety of other "home remedies" to cope with morning sickness. Although there are several speculations as to its cause, nothing has been proven conclusively. Because the cause of morning sickness is not known, it should come as no surprise that there is no known safe, yet effective, way of treating it. Ask your mother or an older female friend if she had morning sickness (and if she did, how she tried to deal with it). Just remember to tell her that you are asking because the author of this book suggested the idea. Also, ask your father if he ever suffered from it—many men experience some of the same symptoms of pregnancy as their partners. In the United States this is sometimes called "sympathy pains," but the medical term for it is *couvade syndrome*, a French term for the birthing process.

Morning sickness
A symptom of early pregnancy involving nausea.

Couvade syndrome
The experiencing of symptoms of pregnancy by male partners, sometimes called "sympathy pains."

Other symptoms that women *may* exhibit during the first trimester include enlarged and tender breasts, prominent veins on the breasts and darkened areolas, enlarged nipples, increased frequency of urination, and irregular bowel movements. In addition, many women feel tired and "run down."

THE FIRST TRIMESTER—THE EMBRYO/FETUS

In the first trimester of pregnancy, a substantial amount of development takes place (see Figure 7-2).

Embryo
The term given to the blastocyst after it has implanted.

When the blastocyst implants, it is less than ⅓ inch in diameter. After implantation, it is known as an **embryo**. Cell differentiation begins to take place now, and development occurs in orderly ways. Growth in the embryo occurs from the head downward (cephalo-caudal or "head to tail") and from the center (spine) outward (proximal-distal). As mentioned earlier, the outer layers of the blastocyst form structures designed to nourish and protect it. In the embryo, three inner cell layers will form specific parts of the body. The *ectoderm* forms the nervous system, skin, and teeth. The *mesoderm* forms the muscles, skeleton, and blood vessels. The *endoderm* forms the internal organs (lungs, liver, digestive system, etc).

In the third week of pregnancy, a central structure or "neural tube" becomes a dominant feature. This will become the central nervous system. By the end of the fourth week, the umbilical cord, heart, and digestive system begin to form. At 6 weeks, the embryo has a "tail," which will become the tip of the spine. It also has structures that look like gills, but which are actually parts of the neck and face that have not yet fully developed. At 8 weeks, the embryo is about 1⅛ inches long. All organs have begun to develop. The heart is pumping, and the stomach has begun to produce some digestive juices. The embryo, although small, is well on its way toward developing into a unique human being. After 8 weeks and until birth, the developing organism is called a **fetus** (see Figure 7-4).

Fetus
The term given to the embryo after the eighth week of pregnancy.

THE SECOND TRIMESTER—THE MOTHER

In the fourth or fifth month of pregnancy, the movements of the fetus can be felt by its mother. This first experience of movement is called "**quickening**" (Figure 7-3). Although a woman generally knows by this time that she is pregnant, this knowledge is an abstract or "intellectual" thing. Once a woman begins to feel a new life moving inside of her, the fetus begins to be viewed as a person, and an emotional attachment to her unborn baby generally begins to form.

Quickening
The first time a pregnant woman experiences movement of the fetus, usually in the fifth month.

Women generally begin to get over their morning sickness in the second trimester. They respond to quickening, as just described, but they also notice that their figures are changing, and they may worry about no longer being attractive to their partners. As her abdomen expands, red lines, or "stretch marks" may develop on a mother-to-be. The breasts begin to swell and may start to leak *colostrum*, a thick, sticky liquid that is produced before milk starts to flow. Water retention may cause edema (swelling) in the ankles, feet, and hands. As a result, it becomes harder to remove rings from fingers. Women may begin to develop varicose veins and/or hemorrhoids. Interestingly, the loss of morning sickness often brings an increase in appetite, and some women may experience heightened sensuality. Freed of the worry about getting pregnant (it's already happened), some women begin to express their sexuality fully for the first

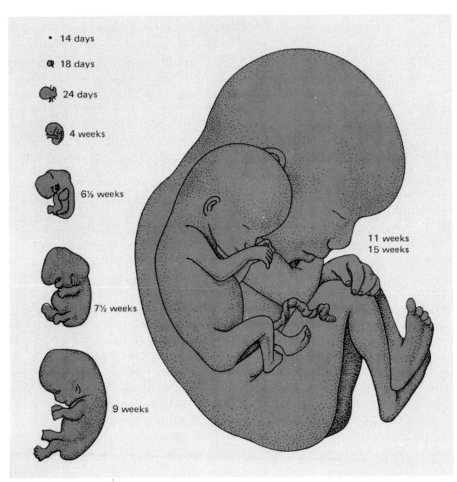

- 14 days
- 18 days
- 24 days
- 4 weeks
- 6½ weeks
- 7½ weeks
- 9 weeks
- 11 weeks 15 weeks

FIGURE 7-2   THE EMBRYONIC PERIOD. THIS IS A LIFE-SIZE ILLUSTRATION OF THE GROWTH OF THE HUMAN EMBRYO AND FETUS FROM 14 DAYS TO 15 WEEKS.

FIGURE 7-3   A WOMAN CAN FEEL HER UNBORN BABY
MOVING FOR THE FIRST TIME (CALLED
QUICKENING) IN THE FOURTH OR FIFTH
MONTH OF PREGNANCY.

time. Masters and Johnson (1966) report that some women experience their first orgasms in the second trimester. I will discuss sexual behavior during pregnancy at length a little later.

THE SECOND TRIMESTER—THE FETUS

At this time, the fetus begins to make sucking motions with its mouth. In the fifth month, the fetus has a detectable heartbeat (see Figure 7-5). It will respond to sound, and it begins to show definite periods of sleep and wakefulness. If born at this time, the fetus has only a one in 10,000 chance of survival. In the sixth month, the fetus can open its eyes. It will suck its thumb and respond to light. At the end of the second trimester, the fetus is about 1 foot long and weighs about 1 pound.

THE THIRD TRIMESTER—THE MOTHER

For the expectant mother, walking, sitting, and rising become more difficult. Pregnant women often have to learn new ways to sit down and to get up out of a chair. Expectant mothers often experience back pain from carrying a new weight load in front of them, thus shifting their center of gravity. The enlarged uterus due to the rapidly growing fetus puts pressure on the bladder and stomach. As a result, urination becomes more frequent—a woman may have to urinate four or five times

a night. Indigestion, heartburn, gas, and constipation are also common complaints. The active movements of the fetus may prevent restful sleep, especially if the fetus develops hiccups. Finding a comfortable sleeping position is not easy, and a woman may have to change positions several times each night. Leg cramps may occur, a condition sometimes treated by taking extra calcium. The woman's navel may push out. Often she experiences a low energy level (Leifer, 1980).

Until recently, most authorities recommended an overall weight gain of 22–27 pounds at term (American College of Obstetricians and Gynecologists, 1985). However, a later study found that 80 percent of women with good pregnancy outcomes had had gains of 22–46 pounds (Abrams & Parker, 1990). In 1990, the Institute of Medicine made new recommendations based on initial weight and height: 28–40 pounds for underweight women, 25–35 pounds for normal-weight women, 15–25 pounds for overweight women, and at least 15 pounds for obese women. If weight gain is too low, there is concern about having proper levels of nourishment for the fetus. If weight gain is too high, blood pressure may rise and there is an increased risk of a difficult labor and emergency cesarean delivery (Johnson, Longmate, & Frentzen, 1992). Also, excess weight may be hard to lose after the baby is born. Weekly checkups by the physician are usual when the due date gets close.

THE THIRD TRIMESTER—THE FETUS

By the end of the seventh month of pregnancy the fetus is about 15 inches long and weighs about 1½ pounds (see Figure 7-6). Fatty tissues begin to develop under the skin. A lack of these tissues is what causes premature infants to look so skinny. In the eighth month, the fetus's weight begins to increase dramatically. At the end of the eighth month, it will weigh about 4 pounds and will be 16–17 inches long. From this point on, the fetus will gain about ½ pound per week. In the ninth month, the fetus will grow to about 20 inches in length and weigh an average of 7–7½, pounds (see Figure 7-7). There is considerable variation in these measurements, however.

The fetus is covered with light hair (lanugo) and a bluish, waxy substance (vernix caseosa). These will make the newborn look very interesting, but they serve as protective devices. Today, the vernix is often allowed to be absorbed into the skin after birth rather than immediately washed off.

Lanugo
Light hair that covers a newborn baby.

Vernix
A bluish, waxy substance that covers a newborn baby.

SEXUAL INTERCOURSE DURING PREGNANCY

Feelings about sexual behavior during pregnancy vary from culture to culture. In some cultures, a man's

3rd Month

5th Month

FIGURE 7-4   THIRD MONTH. THE FETUS IS NOW ABOUT 3 INCHES LONG AND WEIGHS ABOUT 1 OUNCE. IT MAY CONTINUE TO DEVELOP IN THE POSITION SHOWN OR MAY TURN OR ROTATE FREQUENTLY. THE UTERUS BEGINS TO ENLARGE WITH THE GROWING FETUS AND CAN NOW BE FELT EXTENDING ABOUT HALFWAY UP TO THE UMBILICUS.

FIGURE 7-5   FIFTH MONTH. THE FETUS MEASURES ABOUT 10–12 INCHES LONG AND WEIGHS FROM 1/2 TO 1 POUND. IT IS STILL BRIGHT RED. ITS INCREASED SIZE NOW BRINGS THE DOME OF THE UTERUS TO THE LEVEL OF THE UMBILICUS. THE INTERNAL ORGANS ARE MATURING AT ASTONISHING SPEED, BUT THE LUNGS ARE INSUFFICIENTLY DEVELOPED TO COPE WITH CONDITIONS OUTSIDE OF THE UTERUS.

7th Month

9th Month

FIGURE 7-6   SEVENTH MONTH. THE FETUS'S WEIGHT HAS ABOUT DOUBLED SINCE LAST MONTH, AND IT IS ABOUT 3 INCHES LONGER. HOWEVER, IT STILL LOOKS QUITE RED, IS COVERED WITH WRINKLES THAT WILL EVENTUALLY BE ERASED BY FAT. AT 7 MONTHS THE PREMATURE BABY AT THIS STAGE HAS A FAIR CHANCE FOR SURVIVAL IN NURSERIES CARED FOR BY SKILLED PHYSICIANS AND NURSES.

FIGURE 7-7   NINTH MONTH. AT BIRTH OR FULL TERM THE BABY WEIGHS ON AN AVERAGE ABOUT 7¼ POUNDS IF A GIRL AND 7½ IF A BOY. ITS LENGTH IS ABOUT 20 INCHES. ITS SKIN IS COATED WITH A CREAMY COATING. THE FINE DOWNY HAIR HAS LARGELY DISAPPEARED. FINGERNAILS MAY PROTRUDE BEYOND THE ENDS OF THE FINGERS.

penis is seen as intruding on the territory of the fetus if sexual intercourse occurs during pregnancy. In other cultures, pregnancy is closely associated with sexuality, and women may even experience orgasms while giving birth. There is a wide variety of beliefs (many of which are mistaken) about having sexual intercourse during pregnancy.

Many women show a marked decrease of interest in sex during the first trimester of pregnancy due to symptoms of pregnancy, such as morning sickness. In North America, two patterns of sexual activity emerge during pregnancy. The first is a steady decline in sexual activity throughout pregnancy. The second pattern, discussed by Masters and Johnson (1966), is an increase in sexual activity from the first to the second trimester, followed by a decrease in the third trimester (Bogren, 1991; Hart et al., 1991). As you might expect, attitudes about sex during pregnancy are related to attitudes about sex before pregnancy (Fisher & Gray, 1988).

Women list two general reasons for a declining interest in sexual intercourse during pregnancy. The first reason is physical discomfort. The traditional man-on-top position can be increasingly uncomfortable for the woman as pregnancy progresses. This can be alleviated through the use of alternate positions that lessen pressure on the woman's abdomen during intercourse. The female-on-top position is probably most comfortable and it has even been suggested that having sex in this position is a good exercise for women preparing for "natural" childbirth (Bradley, 1981). After the fetus drops, the penis can make contact with an unyielding cervix during sexual intercourse, so shallow penetration is recommended for intercourse late in pregnancy.

The second reason for decreased interest in sex is that women may feel that they no longer appear attractive. They fear that their partners will see them as "ugly," lose interest, and begin to look for new sex partners. Interestingly, men generally do not list this as a cause of decreased sexual activity. More commonly, men list fear of injuring their partner or fetus as a prime reason to stop having sexual intercourse (Masters & Johnson, 1966).

"At about the middle of my pregnancy my husband had a decrease of interest in sex while my interest had increased. I was already feeling fat and ugly and this just made things worse. Many nights I stayed up crying because not only did I think I was fat and ugly, but I thought my husband did too. Then I realized his problem was that he was scared he was going to hurt me or the baby. I tried to convince him that he wouldn't, but I guess he just couldn't stop thinking about it while we were having sex."

(from the author's files)

FIGURE 7-8   IN A POSE FOR *VANITY FAIR* MAGAZINE (AUGUST 1991), ACTRESS DEMI MOORE SHOWS THAT PREGNANCY IS A TIME WHEN A WOMAN CAN STILL BE PROUD OF HER BODY. (© 1995 ANNIE LIEBOVITZ/ CONTACT PRESS IMAGES.)

This leads to an important question: "How far into pregnancy is it safe to engage in sexual intercourse?" There is currently some debate about having sexual intercourse during the last month of pregnancy. Masters and Johnson claim that there is no problem with having sexual intercourse through the ninth month, except for certain cases, which will be discussed shortly. Grudzinskas et al. (1979) compared women who were sexually active in the ninth month of pregnancy with women who were not. Sexual intercourse during this time was associated with more fecal matter (excrement) in the amniotic fluid of fetuses, along with lower scores for newborns on tests of reflexes and development. Naeye (1979) compared similar groups of women and found that sexual intercourse during the ninth month was related to more infections in amniotic fluid, more breathing problems and jaundice in newborns. White and Reamy (1982) cite several flaws in these studies, but it should be remembered that even in the flawed studies no problems were associated with having sexual intercourse before the ninth month of pregnancy. In any case, sexual behavior is not limited to intercourse, and in the latter stages of pregnancy alternative forms of sexual stimulation may be preferred. Hugging, touching, and other displays of affection are important ways of communicating attraction. It is important to speak to a pregnant woman about love and devotion, pride in her, and hope for the future. Telling her that she is beautiful may be a far more effective way of showing that you care than having sexual intercourse (see Figure 7-8).

There are some circumstances that indicate that sexual intercourse should be practiced carefully or avoided altogether during pregnancy. Sexual intercourse with a partner who has a sexually transmitted disease should, of course, be avoided, especially because some of these diseases can be transmitted to the fetus. Intercourse should not occur if there is vaginal bleeding, or if there are signs that the amniotic sac has ruptured. If the cervix is dilated or there are other signs of premature labor, sexual intercourse should be avoided. Herbst (1979) noted that if a woman has had a history of miscarriages, she should not experience orgasms because uterine contractions during orgasms could increase the risk of inducing a new miscarriage. ∎

COMPLICATIONS OF PREGNANCY

Although pregnancy is a complex process, about 97 percent of all births result in a healthy, normal infant (Heinonen et al., 1977). However, complications of pregnancy can occur. Many of these can be prevented if parents-to-be are aware of them.

Substances that can harm an embryo or fetus are called **teratogens** (from the Greek word *tera*, meaning "monster"). The placenta, until recently, was thought to be a perfect filter that kept out all harmful substances. Now we know of hundreds of teratogens that can cross the "placental barrier." Three things determine the harm caused by teratogens—the amount of the teratogen, the duration (amount of time) of exposure to the teratogen, and the age of the embryo or fetus. Each part of the developing body has a time, called a *critical period*, when it is most susceptible to damage. These are the times when they are undergoing most of their formation. During critical periods, body parts are sensitive to "signals" or "messages" about how to develop. Usually, these signals come from the genetic code that guides normal development. However, this sensitivity means that the developing embryo or fetus can be easily influenced by teratogens. Although teratogens should be avoided at all times, most body parts are maximally susceptible to damage during the first 8 weeks of development (see Figure 7-9). Remember that in the first 8 weeks of pregnancy, many women won't be sure if they are pregnant. There is an important lesson to be learned from this. If a woman wants to change her behavior to improve the chances of having a healthy baby (to stop drinking alcoholic beverages, for example), it's better to do this when she is trying to become pregnant rather than after she finds out that she is pregnant. Still, if a woman wants to change, it is better to do so late rather than never. The woman's partner can encourage this by also changing his habits at the same time.

Teratogens
Substances that can harm an embryo or fetus.

Critical period
In relation to teratogens, the time during embryological or fetal development during which a particular part of the body is most susceptible to damage.

DISEASES

Even the "weakened" disease organisms of certain vaccines can be harmful if taken just before or during early pregnancy (O'Brien & McManus, 1978). Some strains of the flu, mumps, chicken pox, and other common diseases can also cause harm to the embryo or fetus. One of the first teratogens to be discovered was the *rubella* virus, or "German measles." A baby exposed prenatally to rubella may be born blind, deaf, and/or intellectually impaired. This is especially true if the mother contracts this virus in the first 3 months of pregnancy. A study by Michaels and Mellin (1960) found that 47 percent of the babies born to mothers who had rubella in the first month of pregnancy were abnormal, compared to 22 percent of the babies whose mother contracted the disease in the second month, and 7 percent of the babies whose mother caught the disease in the third month. In the second trimester, rubella can cause hearing problems and language retardation (Hardy et al., 1969). Rubella is spread by direct contact or through touching droplets from an infected individual. Spring and early summer are times of greatest risk of contraction. During an outbreak in 1964–65, 20,000 women gave birth to abnormal infants, and another 11,000 had abortions after contracting rubella (Franklin, 1984). The use of a rubella vaccine in school children has decreased its prevalence, but this in turn may lead to a decrease in awareness of the disease and a drop in inoculations. The United States may be ripe for another epidemic in the future. A woman can safely be inoculated against rubella any time up to 3 months before becoming pregnant. It is estimated that over 5 million American women are not immune to rubella (Behrman & Vaughan, 1983). Other diseases that can cause harm to the fetus but which can be inoculated against include mumps, polio, and measles.

Rubella
A disease, also known as German measles, caused by a virus. If contracted during pregnancy, it can cause fetal abnormalities.

" . . . Unbeknown to the doctor or myself, I had chlamydia. Since the

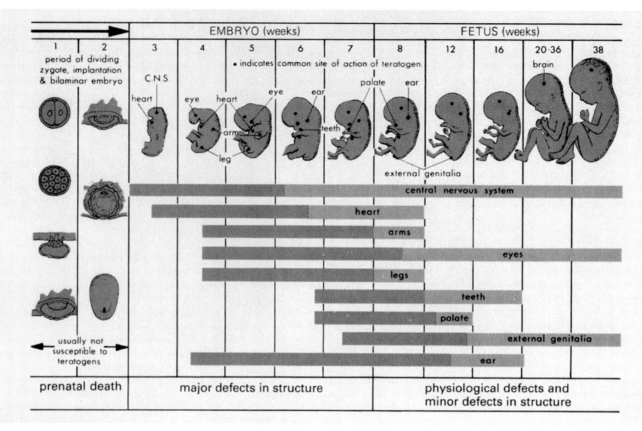

		EMBRYO (weeks)						FETUS (weeks)			
1	2	3	4	5	6	7	8	12	16	20-36	38

period of dividing zygote, implantation & bilaminar embryo

• indicates common site of action of teratogen.

central nervous system

heart

arms

legs

teeth

palate

external genitalia

ear

usually not susceptible to teratogens

prenatal death	major defects in structure	physiological defects and minor defects in structure

FIGURE 7-9   CRITICAL PERIODS IN PRENATAL DEVELOPMENT. BLACK REPRESENTS HIGHLY SENSITIVE PERIODS; WHITE REPRESENTS LESS SENSITIVE PERIODS.

baby was in the birth canal he contracted it in the eyes. It was bad! He almost went blind.''

(from the author's files)

As you learned in Chapter 5, most types of *sexually transmitted diseases* can affect a fetus or newborn baby. There is a one in four chance that a pregnant woman with an HIV infection (the virus that causes AIDS) will pass the virus to the fetus. If a woman has an active case of genital herpes at delivery, you recall, it can result in death or neurological damage in the newborn. Blindness in newborns can result if the mother has either gonorrhea or chlamydia at childbirth. Untreated syphilis is particularly bad, because it can be passed to the fetus, resulting in considerable damage by the time the baby is born.

Toxemia

A disease of pregnancy characterized in its early stage (preeclampsia) by high blood pressure, weight gain, swollen joints, and protein in the urine. Unless it is corrected, it can lead to convulsions and coma.

TOXEMIA OF PREGNANCY

A pregnant woman can also have a disease called **toxemia of pregnancy**. In its early stages, this disease is called *preeclampsia*. Its symptoms include protein in the urine (which allows it to be detected by physicians), high blood pressure, weight gain, and swollen joints due to excessive water retention. In about 5 percent of cases the disease advances to *eclampsia*, characterized by convulsions and coma. In the Western world, eclampsia is one of the major causes of maternal death.

"During my first pregnancy, they discovered that I had toxemia. I was immedi-ately put on a low-sodium diet and had to stay in bed for the rest of my pregnancy. When she was born, my baby weighed only 4 lbs. 10 oz. and her weight then fell to 4 lbs. 1 oz. She had respiratory problems and severe jaundice. They kept her in an incubator for about four weeks. She was a very pretty baby, but took a long time to start crawling, walking, and talking. . . . I didn't get toxemia in my second or third pregnancies.''

(from the author's files)

Toxemia generally occurs in the last trimester of about 6 percent of all pregnancies, but in 20 percent of those who do not get prenatal care (Mabie & Sibai, 1987). It is most likely to occur in younger women, especially if it is the first birth. Women who develop toxemia in their first pregnancy often do not have it again in later pregnancies. Also, women whose partner(s) had used condoms prior to pregnancy have a much higher risk of preeclampsia (Klonoff-Cohen et al., 1989)—in other words, both these findings indicate that the greater the exposure to semen, the less the likelihood a woman will develop preeclampsia. These results suggest that the disease is due to altered immune responses (see Beer, 1989). A low-salt diet and bedrest are the usual treatments. However, if these don't work at reducing the symptoms, labor will be induced prematurely in order to keep the disease from being life-threatening.

SMOKING

About one fifth of all pregnant women smoke (Williamson et al., 1989). However, cigarette smoking during pregnancy is associated with a substantial increase in risk of having a low birthweight baby (see Floyd et al., 1993), and increases the risk of miscarriages, ectopic pregnancies, preterm births, and infant mortality (see DiFranza & Lew, 1995 for a review). Mothers who smoke during pregnancy double (nine cigarettes or less a day) or triple (10 cigarettes or more a day) the risk of their baby dying of sudden infant death syndrome, also known as "crib death" (Haglund et al., 1990). Only about a third of women who smoke quit smoking when they learn that they are pregnant (Fingerhut et al., 1990).

Interestingly, smoking can also influence male sperm production, with men who smoke having higher numbers of abnormal sperm than nonsmokers (Evans et al., 1981). This might be a factor behind higher rates of infertility found in male smokers compared with nonsmokers.

ALCOHOL

Approximately two out of every 1,000 children born in the United States have physical deformities and/or mental retardation because of damage caused by the mother's use of alcohol during pregnancy (*Newsweek*, July 31, 1989). The condition is known as *fetal alcohol syndrome* (FAS) and is six times more common now than in 1979 (CDC, 1995). Children born with FAS are underdeveloped and have facial deformities, abnormally spaced eyes, and small heads. They also have damage to the central nervous system, and occasionally have damage to other organs. FAS is the leading cause of mental retardation in the United States, with an economic impact of over $300 million per year (Abel & Sokol, 1987). Research with animals indicates that alcohol probably has its maximum effect on the developing fetus in the third week of pregnancy (Rossett & Sanders, 1979; Sulik et al., 1981), but it can have neg-

Fetal alcohol syndrome
A condition common to infants born to alcoholic mothers involving physical and nervous system abnormalities.

ative effects throughout pregnancy. Animal research also shows that alcohol can cause the umbilical cord to temporarily collapse, cutting off oxygen to the fetus and causing a condition known as *minimal brain damage* (Mukherjee & Hodgen, 1982), which has been associated with hyperactivity and learning disabilities in humans. Even moderate alcohol consumption can result in children with emotional problems and inability to cope in school (known as *fetal alcohol effect*). These data indicate that *it is probably best to avoid alcohol entirely during pregnancy*. If you wouldn't give your newborn baby an alcoholic drink, why would you give it one before it is even born? In fact, because maximal damage might occur before a woman knows that she is pregnant (the third week), it might be best for a woman to stop drinking if she is trying to become pregnant. Even after the baby is born, a mother should not drink if she is breast-feeding, because this can result in the baby having a low rate of motor development and coordination (Little et al., 1989).

COCAINE

The use of cocaine, especially "crack" cocaine, increased dramatically during the 1980s. Sadly, many of the casualties of this epidemic are children born to women who used cocaine during pregnancy. Ten to 15 percent of babies born in large urban areas are affected by their mothers' use of cocaine—over 100,000 babies a year (Chasnoff et al., 1990; General Accounting Office, 1990; Gomby & Shiono, 1991). The immediate hospital costs alone (at time of delivery) are $5,000 to $12,000 more per child than for unexposed babies (Calhoun & Watson, 1991; Phibbs et al., 1991).

The most widely reported effects of cocaine exposure during pregnancy are diminished growth and preterm birth (both resulting in low birth weight) and decreased head circumference (Bateman et al., 1993; Singer, Minnes, & Arendt, 1993). "Crack babies" have a variety of sensory-motor and behavioral deficits, including irritability and disorientation. Although studies have not yet followed these children long term, there is the real potential of later learning problems and behavioral disorders (see Singer, Farkas, & Kliegman, 1992, for a review). Several states have begun to prosecute women who used cocaine during pregnancy. However, the American Medical Association's Board of Trustees suggests that in most cases rehabilitative treatment and education will be more effective (Cole, 1990).

OTHER DRUGS

Many drugs can cross the placental barrier. These include illegal drugs, prescription drugs, and "over-the-counter" drugs. Women who are addicted to heroin (or methadone) while pregnant will give birth to infants who are already addicted as well. These infants must go through withdrawal after being born, showing symptoms such as fever, tremors, convulsions, and difficulty in breathing. This is extremely painful and can be life-threatening (Brazelton, 1970). Heavy use of marijuana during pregnancy can result in problems that resemble fetal alcohol syndrome (Hingson et al., 1982).

Numerous prescription drugs, such as antibiotics and tranquilizers, are clearly harmful to the fetus. In addition, commonly used drugs, such as antihistamines (in allergy medication and cough medicine) and megadoses of certain vitamins, have proven to have harmful effects. Even aspirin can be harmful. The Food and Drug Administration has issued a warning against taking over-the-counter aspirin products during the last 3 months of pregnancy because it can affect fetal circulation and cause complications during delivery. There is no conclusive evidence that moderate amounts of caffeine (found in coffee, tea, many soft drinks, and chocolate) is harmful to infants, but the amount of data is scarce (see Mills et al., 1993). The best advice, which is being given by increasingly large numbers of physicians, is not to take any drugs during pregnancy if at all possible.

ENVIRONMENTAL HAZARDS

Pollutants, such as heavy metals in drinking water, can cause damage to the fetus. One example of this is the high levels of lead and cadmium that can be found in the drinking water of houses in older neighborhoods. This is caused by the use of old water pipes. If the plumbing in your house is old, it is best to let the water run for a few minutes before a pregnant woman drinks it, especially in the first part of the morning after water has been "sitting still" in the pipes overnight. Mercury-contaminated fish eaten by pregnant women can cause deformities and mental retardation in their children (Milunsky, 1977).

Radiation and X-rays are also powerful teratogens. Radiation from the atomic bombs exploded at Hiroshima and Nagasaki in World War II caused pregnant women exposed to radiation from the bombs to have spontaneous abortions, stillborn children, or severely handicapped children (Haley & Snider, 1962). X-rays are especially damaging to the fetus in the first trimester. The use of X-rays has been linked to increased risk of leukemia (Stewart & Kneale, 1970). Some researchers claim that X-rays given at low dosages late in pregnancy cause no harm to the fetus (for example, giving an emergency X-ray to the mother or giving an X-ray to determine if the baby's head is too large to pass through the mother's birth canal; Moore, 1983). Others feel that ultrasound can give essentially the same information at no risk to the fetus.

ANESTHETICS

Many people reading this book came into the world in a drugged state. This is because anesthetics were used during their mother's labor to relieve pain. Under general anesthesia, a mother is unable to push during contractions. As a result, infants born under these conditions have to be pulled into the world with forceps, which resemble tongs. Anesthetics cross the placental barrier and enter the fetus. Because the fetus's organs are not all fully developed at birth, it cannot get rid of drugs from its system as quickly as its mother. This is one reason why some infants have to be slapped in order to get them to cry and begin breathing. Babies born without the use of anesthetics generally come into the world with eyes open and ready to breathe, without having to be slapped into consciousness. Children whose mothers are given anesthetics may be more susceptible to anoxia, an inability to get enough oxygen to the brain. This problem can influence many aspects of development. Horowitz et al. (1977) found no permanent problems in the children of mothers who were given anesthetics at birth. However, these researchers (studying births in Uganda and Israel) noted that the amount of anesthetic given in their study was generally less than the amount of anesthetic given in the United States. Brackbill (1979) reviewed studies involving the use of anesthetics in labor and concluded that using these drugs was related to lower scores on developmental measures in newborns. Today, most births in which anesthetics are used do not involve general anesthetics. The mother may be anesthetized from the waist down, or any of a number of other possible alternatives. Thus, it is possible to be anesthetized and still be conscious and able to push. These procedures also lessen the effects of anesthetics on the baby. It is important to discuss different anesthetizing procedures with the physician before going into labor, especially to determine the physician's preferred methods.

RH COMPATIBILITY

There is a protein in the blood of a majority of people called the *Rh factor*. It got its name from the Rhesus monkey, the species in which this blood protein was first discovered. If a person has the protein, he or she is "Rh positive." If not, the person is "Rh negative." A blood type of "O positive" means that the person is blood type O and has the Rh factor. Each person has two genes that determine whether or not they have the protein. They receive one of these genes from each parent. The Rh positive gene is dominant, which

Rh factor

A protein in the blood of most individuals. If a mother does not have it and the fetus she carries does, she can develop antibodies against the Rh factor. This is called an Rh incompatibility problem.

means that if a person has one Rh positive and one Rh negative gene, the blood will have this protein. A person can have Rh negative blood only when both genes are Rh negative.

In about 8 percent of all pregnancies in the United States, the mother will be Rh negative and the fetus will be Rh positive. When this occurs, there is an Rh compatibility problem. For the first birth, this situation usually isn't dangerous. But during labor and delivery, blood of the fetus and the mother (kept separate in the placenta during pregnancy) may mix together. If this happens, the mother's blood treats the Rh factor in the baby's blood as if it were a dangerous, foreign substance, forming antibodies that will attack and destroy the "invader" in the future. If the mother then has another Rh positive fetus, these antibodies can cross the placental barrier and attack the fetus's blood supply, causing a miscarriage, possible brain defects in the fetus, or even death. Fortunately, there is an injection that can be given to the mother to prevent these antibodies from forming. The drug used for this is called *Rhogam*. It consists of Rh negative blood that already has these antibodies in it. Since Rhogam already has antibodies, the mother's system doesn't produce very many of its own. The antibodies in Rhogam eventually die off, leaving the mother capable of carrying another Rh positive fetus. It is important that this drug be given immediately after the birth of the first child or after a first miscarriage of a fetus with Rh positive blood. If there is a delay, the mother's body will build up too many antibodies of its own before the drug can be given, making the drug ineffective.

If a child is born with Rh antibodies from its mother, it may survive if given an immediate and complete blood transfusion. It is possible to give a blood transfusion to a fetus in the uterus if it is too small to survive an induced premature birth, but this is a very new, and still experimental, technique.

DETECTION OF PROBLEMS IN PREGNANCY

In addition to X-rays, which are generally only used late in pregnancy, if at all, there are several other techniques for detecting problems in the fetus while it is inside the uterus. The first is called **chorionic sampling** or **chorionic villus biopsy**. As you learned earlier, the chorion sac surrounds the embryo and develops early in pregnancy. In chorionic sampling, a small tube is inserted through the vagina and cervix. Guided by ultrasound (also mentioned earlier), the tube will remove some hairlike cells (villi) from the chorion by gentle vacuum

Chorionic sampling

Technique used for detecting problems in a fetus during the eighth to tenth weeks of pregnancy. Hairlike projections (villi) of the chorion are collected and examined.

suction. These cells can be examined to detect chromosomal problems (such as Down's syndrome) or abnormalities in the fetus, to look for evidence of certain diseases, and even to find out the sex of the fetus. One of the major advantages of chorionic sampling is that it can be used to detect problems early in pregnancy (from the eighth to tenth week of pregnancy), but after 12 weeks of pregnancy all of the villi of the chorion are gone. Initial results indicate that although the safety of chorionic sampling compares favorably with other methods of detecting fetal abnormalities (Green et al., 1988), serious complications (including fetal or neonatal death) can occasionally result (Rosenthal, 1991). Researchers are currently testing a newer, "safer" prenatal technique called **celocentesis** in which a needle is inserted between the placenta and amniotic sac to retrieve cells (Jurkovic et al., 1993).

Another technique that provides similar information is **amniocentesis**. This technique has been in use longer than chorionic sampling. With this method, a hollow needle is inserted through the abdomen and uterus of the mother, through the membrane of the amniotic sac, and into the amniotic fluid surrounding the fetus. Ultrasound is often used to guide the needle. Some of the amniotic fluid is then extracted, and fetal cells that have dropped off and have been floating in the fluid are examined for evidence of abnormalities. This precedure can only be used after the fourteenth week of pregnancy, because before that time there may not be enough fetal cells in the amniotic fluid to make it useful, and the fetus may take up too much room in the amniotic sac for the procedure to be used safely. Finally, there is a 1 percent chance that the procedure will cause a spontaneous abortion.

A relatively new technique being used is called **fetoscopy**. A tube that contains fiber optic strands—wires that can send back "pictures"—is inserted into the amniotic sac. The "fetuscope" can inspect the skin of the fetus and can be used to get a blood sample from the fetus. This technique also carries a risk of damaging the fetus, however.

X-rays, chorionic sampling, amniocentesis, and fetoscopy are called "invasive" techniques, meaning that they invade, or get inside of, the uterus and/or the

Celocentesis

A technique used for detecting fetal abnormalities in which a needle is inserted between the placenta and the amniotic sac to retrieve cells.

Amniocentesis

A technique for detecting fetal problems, involving collection of amniotic fluid after the fourteenth week of pregnancy.

Fetoscopy

A procedure in which a tube containing fiberoptic strands is inserted into the amniotic sac in order to inspect the fetus.

Ultrasound scan

A noninvasive technique for examining internal organs of a fetus, which uses sound waves like a radar or sonar to create a picture.

fetus. **Ultrasound** is thought to be a "noninvasive" technique, because it only bounces sound waves off of the uterus and fetus. Ultrasound can be used to diagnose many problems, though they primarily deal with structural difficulties, such as a malformation of the skeletal system of the mother or fetus. It cannot detect genetic defects like amniocentesis can. Even ultrasound is recommended *only if the expectant mother has an increased risk factor* for a problem with a pregnancy or delivery. Use of ultrasound as a routine screening procedure has no clinical benefits (Ewigman et al., 1993; LeFevre et al., 1993). Detection procedures should never be used simply to find out in advance if the baby will be a boy or a girl. A balance must be found between detecting potential problems versus creating new problems when these procedures are used.

FETAL SURGERY

One of the newest methods in treating a problem pregnancy is **fetal surgery**—performing an operation on the fetus while it is still in the uterus of the mother. Thus far, fetal surgery has been performed primarily for urinary tract obstruction or diaphragmatic hernia. With urinary tract obstruction, urine backs up into the kidneys and damages them. When this problem is detected through ultrasound, the surgeon can insert a needle through the mother's abdomen to help place a little tube (catheter) into the fetus's bladder. Urine then drains through the catheter and bypasses the urinary tract. A newer technique involves making a surgical incision through the fetus's abdomen directly to the bladder. This is done because catheters can get pulled out or plugged, while the surgical incision usually will last until birth, when it can be repaired. The use of surgical incisions rather than catheters is called open fetal surgery. The technological advances in this field have been rapid. In 1989, physicians performed the first successful major surgery on a fetus, repairing a hernia of the diaphragm that if left untreated probably would have resulted in death shortly after birth (Harrison et al., 1990). In 1994, surgeons performed the first endoscopic fetal surgery, using tiny needles guided by miniature cameras without cutting open the mother's uterus.

Fetal surgery

A surgical operation on the fetus while it is still in the uterus.

Several factors must be taken into account when deciding whether to do fetal surgery. This type of surgery involves a risk of causing the uterus to go into labor prematurely (Longaker et al., 1991). Excessive bleeding in the mother's uterus due to surgery is also a risk, because the uterus has a huge blood supply in midpregnancy. However, the procedure does not affect a woman's future reproductive potential. As the technology of fetal surgery evolves, it is expected that risks associated with the procedures will decline and that a greater variety of problems will be remedied in this way.

MISCARRIAGES (SPONTANEOUS ABORTIONS)

Earlier in this chapter you learned that about three fourths of conceptions fail to survive beyond 6 weeks. Of the remaining quarter, about 10 percent fail to survive to term (Boklage, 1990). There are many possible causes for miscarriage, including genetic, anatomic, hormonal (too high levels of luteinizing hormone, for example), infections, and maternal autoimmune responses (Branch, 1990; Regan, Owen, & Jacobs, 1990). But routinely, physicians will not attempt to diagnose causes of miscarriage until the woman has had three of them. *Recurrent miscarriages*, as these are called, occur in 0.5–1.0 percent of women (Alberman, 1988). There are two major reasons for this. The first is that most women who have a miscarriage will carry the next fetus to full term. (Some insurance companies don't want to pay for tests after one or two miscarriages.) The second is that even after three miscarriages have occurred, 60 percent of these women will later have healthy babies, even without treatment. The important thing to remember is that there is almost nothing that a woman can do to make a miscarriage happen (if there were, women with unwanted pregnancies might be doing it in large numbers). Therefore, a woman should never blame herself if she suffers a miscarriage.

Miscarriage

A spontaneous abortion.

For many couples, a miscarriage can be a heavy emotional disappointment:

"I have been married for 14 years. I conceived 7 times and everytime I had a miscarriage at about 4½ months. My doctor diagnosed that my uterus is too weak to carry the baby after 4 months and no matter what and how I try I cannot have a baby of my own. I get very depressed sometimes and cry. Lately I feel very uncomfortable around other people's babies. . . ."

"Some people may think only women are upset because of losing a baby due to miscarriage . . . but this hurt me in ways unimaginable . . . First of all, I felt as if it was my fault for not being there. It hurt the most because a part of us had not yet had a chance to grow and mature into our baby. Our relationship is just now returning to normal . . . ."

(from the author's files)

A close-up photo of sperm on the surface of an ovum

Many sperm attempting to penetrate the membrane of an ovum. Only one will be successful.

A FIBEROPTIC VIEW OF EMBRYONIC AND FETAL DEVELOPMENT

(a) One day (two cells)

(b) 3 1/2 days

(c) 21 days (note the primitive spinal cord)

(d) Four weeks

(e) Eight weeks

(f) Twelve weeks

(g) Sixteen weeks

Stages of prenatal development. The heart and nervous system begin to function by the end of four weeks. The fetus is recognizably human by 16 weeks, but will stand very little chance of survival if born before 24 weeks. Note the umbilical cord connection with the placenta in the photo taken at eight weeks.

The Birth Process

It is important to allow adults who experience miscarriage to express their emotions and grieve (Cole, 1987). It often takes several months to recover.

After reading this section on the possible dangers posed to the fetus, you may begin to believe that it is impossible to protect any unborn baby from these dangers and that most babies will be harmed as a result. At this point I would like to emphasize that hundreds of millions of babies are born without serious problems. A fetus is incredibly resistant to harm. Eating well, avoiding toxic substances, getting early and regular care from a physician with whom you can communicate and who shares your point of view, and preparing for the birth of your child through study and training (which I will describe shortly) all go a long way toward making pregnancy, labor, and birth an enriching, happy experience. ∎

NUTRITION DURING PREGNANCY

One of the best ways to increase the chances of having a healthy baby is to eat well during pregnancy. A poor diet can increase the risk of complications such as toxemia, anemia, and low birth weight.

Remember, if you are pregnant, you are now eating for two. You will need to eat more *good-quality* foods than you usually do. This especially applies if you are a teenager because of the high incidence of low birthweight babies in this age group. Anyone expecting twins must also eat plenty of healthy foods. Here are some suggestions for foods you should eat every day to assure a healthy diet (Brewer & Brewer, 1985):

4 glasses of any kind of milk (e.g., whole, low fat, skim). If you do not like milk, substitute yogurt.

2 eggs

2 servings of meat, including chicken or fish. If you are a vegetarian, substitute beans and rice.

2 servings of green leafy vegetables

1 yellow vegetable (five times a week)

5 servings of whole breads or cereals (part of your milk intake can be with cereal)

1 potato

2 pieces of fresh fruit

While this diet will provide you with most of the necessary nutrients, the U.S. Public Health Service recommends that pregnant women supplement their intake of folic acid through a multivitamin.

Your physician may make additional recommendations for certain conditions (such as adjusting salt intake to ease toxemia). Some women have negative feelings about gaining weight during pregnancy, but remember, this is not only normal but necessary. Never put yourself on a low-calorie diet during pregnancy. ∎

PREPARING FOR CHILDBIRTH

The use of general anesthesia, labor rooms where women waited for hours (usually separated from their male partners) before giving birth, delivery rooms, waiting rooms for men, and other aspects of "modern" birth techniques were all instituted to make it easier for health professionals to deliver their services (Mead, 1975). Women (as well as their male partners) were usually given very little education about what was to come, with only the expectation that it would be painful. For many women, labor and delivery were not positive experiences.

"In 1970 at age 20 I prepared to give birth to my first child. 'Induced labor' was a convenient form of delivery for the physician, and widely practiced in the 70's. At my last visit to his office, he 'broke the water bag,' handed me five Kotex pads and told me to walk across the street to _____ _____ hospital and admit myself. He said he would check on me later that evening. After having called my husband for me at the hospital, the delivery room nurse started a 'drip' to begin contractions. I now know why the old _____ hospital had bars on the labor room windows. I cannot describe that intense pain, especially not having been prepared for natural childbirth. To jump would have been a blessing."

"My experience with childbirth was very traumatic. The pain I had to endure . . . I remember reaching out to punch the nurse because the prepping solution she used on me was so cold. The next thing I knew the gas mask covered my face and I was out cold."

"I woke up in recovery. It was over. 'Ms. G.', the nurse said, 'You had a baby boy.' "

"It is good the way births are being handled now. When I had babies the hospital treated you like the baby belonged to them. My second child wasn't even in the same building with me and I wasn't allowed to see her until the next day. It was torment wondering how she looked.''

(from the author's files)

Fathers were generally the forgotten person when a baby was born. They seldom were allowed to be with their wives during any part of labor or delivery.

"I went out of the room to get a candy bar while the nurse gave my wife an exam (neither I nor my wife had ever heard of Lamaze then). When I returned to her room, I saw my wife being taken away. The nurse explained that my wife was giving birth. I'd been awake for several nights with my wife, so I laid down on her bed to rest and fell asleep. Shortly after 6 P.M., the phone next to the bed rang and the nurse told me I was the father of a baby girl.''

(from the author's files)

In 1932, a British physician named Grantly Dick-Read wrote a book in which he advocated the use of *natural childbirth* (Dick-Read, 1972). He became the founder of a movement away from "modern" techniques, a movement that has become increasingly popular in America. Dr. Dick-Read came to the conclusion that modern birthing techniques in which pregnant women were regarded as "patients" (implying that pregnancy is an illness to be treated) led to a *fear-tension-pain cycle*. He reasoned that women were being put into strange environments, not knowing what was going to happen next, surrounded by strangers, and that this created fear. He believed that fear could cause physiological changes associated with tension, such as tightening muscles. These things were believed to substantially increase the sensation of pain felt by mothers during labor and delivery. Instead, he advocated educating mothers-to-be about pregnancy, labor, birth, and birth procedures to relieve fear of the unknown. He also advocated the training of relaxation techniques to relieve the physiological effects of tension. Drugs were permissible if thought necessary, but should be avoided if possible. Today, people more properly refer to these techniques as **prepared childbirth** rather than natural childbirth.

Fear-tension-pain cycle

According to prepared childbirth advocates, the cycle of events that women experience during labor when they are not properly educated about labor and childbirth.

Prepared childbirth

Courses or techniques that prepare women for labor and childbirth with the goal of making it a positive experience.

THE LAMAZE METHOD

A French physician, Fernand Lamaze, traveled to the Soviet Union in 1951 to study birthing techniques in that country. The Soviets had extended the conditioning techniques of Ivan Pavlov into the area of labor and delivery. They had reasoned that if conditioning could create new association between food and bells, associations between labor and pain could be replaced with new associations. Women were conditioned to learn new, pleasant associations for the sensations of labor and birth. They were also taught relaxation and breathing techniques to aid in making labor easier. Throughout the Soviet Union, Lamaze saw that women were giving birth without either using anesthetics or experiencing great pain. This was a stunning sight to Lamaze. He returned to France, modified the Soviet techniques slightly, and began using this new approach to childbirth in his practice (Lamaze, 1970). An American woman, Marjorie Karmel, used this approach under Lamaze's care and wrote a best-selling book about her experience in 1959 titled *Thank You, Dr. Lamaze*. Since then, the Lamaze method has become increasingly used in this country. Compare the following childbirth experiences from two individuals who went through Lamaze training with the four case histories that were presented at the beginning of this section. Which persons do you think remember giving birth as a positive experience?

Lamaze

A method of prepared childbirth; named after its founder, Fernand Lamaze.

"I have gone through three different ways of giving birth—the first being totally drugged out. I didn't get to see my baby until the next morning. The next two deliveries were natural childbirth using a birthing room and I didn't have any restraints on me. You are given the freedom and dignity of childbirth. I used a birthing chair with my last baby. It was a more natural way of delivery and I found pushing to be less of an effort. The relaxation and breathing techniques taught with Lamaze training really kept me focused and prepared. You know what you want—this is the way you have chosen to give birth . . . When the nurse came to check I was already fully dilated and ready. Unfortunately, the doctor was not, so I was asked to 'choo choo' puff through contractions until the doctor arrived. My husband was there the whole time encouraging me. It was such a joy to see what love had produced. The smile on my husband's face . . . We could hold the baby after its birth—there bonding begins.''

"We had our children using Lamaze. The thing I remember most is how in control my wife was, even at the very end. She had drawn her own focal point a few weeks before and concentrated on it every contraction while doing her breathing and effleurage. You could really tell the women in the labor room who hadn't gone to Lamaze. I remember one in particular—she had just gone into labor and was very frightened and yelling for the doctor with every contraction. My wife was actually trying to comfort her between her own contractions.

The absolutely best thing about the births was both of us being there to see our children the moment they were born. Each of them were so wide awake and looking all around. My wife was yelling, 'It's a girl! It's a girl!' To be able to hold them right away was great. When the last child was born her big brother and big sister were able to put on gowns and hold her after she was born. It was important to be there when my wife was giving birth, to be part of the experience. I cannot remember any other moment when I felt so connected to her and so alive.''

(from the author's files)

The Lamaze approach resembles that of Dr. Dick-Read and other forms of prepared childbirth in that it tries to determine the specific causes of pain and provides methods for dealing with each cause. What are the causes of perceived pain in childbirth? Basically, these break down into (1) anxiety and fear; (2) muscle tension; (3) stretching of muscles; (4) too little oxygen getting to muscles; and (5) pressure on nerves. Here are some ways that Lamaze training deals with each of these.

1. **Anxiety and Fear.** There are a variety of factors that increase the sensation of pain. It is important to remember that pain is a subjective experience. A football player may break an arm or leg and yet be unaware of it and continue to play until after the game is over (when the pain may suddenly become unbearable). Some people, on the other hand, wince and scream when they get a blood test before the needle touches them. These examples illustrate two things that influence the experience of pain. The first is the anxiety and fear associated with the experience, and the second is the attention paid to the source of pain.

In Lamaze training, fear and anxiety are first dealt with through education. The unknown is always frightening, and if a woman in labor does not know what to expect, her anxiety will increase her experience of pain. This is counteracted by teaching expectant mothers about pregnancy and childbirth. They learn about the different stages of labor and medical procedures associated with childbirth. They also are encouraged to pre-register at the hospital (so that this doesn't have to be done later when the mother-to-be has more important things on her mind), and to take a tour of the maternity ward and birthing facilities. In this way the expectant mother knows what to expect and is more familiar with the environment where labor and birth will take place.

Expectant mothers also are not left alone during labor and birth. Throughout their training, labor, and delivery they are accompanied by a "*coach*." The coach is often the father of the baby, but can also be a friend (Figure 7-10). Some women get a second or "back-up" coach just in case the primary coach cannot be available when they go into labor. The coach helps the mother utilize her training. The coach provides support, encouragement, and instruction. It is the coach's responsibility to keep the mother-to-be as comfortable as possible, while at the same time keeping her concentration focused and her spirits up. The coach learns all of the exercises that the expectant mother does, practices with her, and "paces" her during labor.

Another way that the subjective experience of pain is reduced is through learning to focus the expectant mother's attention or concentration. The mother-to-be picks out something outside of her body, such as a favorite doll or a piece of furniture, and learns to focus all of her attention on that thing or "*focal point*." By concentrating on the focal point, she is not concentrating on her pain and so the perception or subjective experience of pain is reduced.

2. **Muscle tension.** When people are anxious or fearful, muscles tighten up. This is a natural reaction and can be adaptive, because it allows quick movement in a "fight or flight" situation. However, over long time periods keeping muscles tense can cause them to ache and be used inefficiently. Labor is just such a situation, lasting several hours with long periods of inactivity between contractions when tense muscles serve no useful purpose. One of the first exercises in Lamaze training involves learning how to know when muscles are tense, and how to relax them. Expectant mothers will

be told to tighten the muscles in one arm, keeping the muscles in the other arm and the legs relaxed. They are told to notice the difference between the "tense" arm and the other limbs. Then, the coach lightly strokes the tensed arm saying "relax, relax" while the mother-to-be slowly relaxes the arm. The coach also learns to distinguish between the relaxed and tensed muscles of the mother. This does two things. First, expectant mothers and coaches learn to control the tension of the woman's muscles so that they can prevent her from tensing up, especially between contractions. Second, through lots of practice and repetition, the woman is conditioned to immediately relax her muscles when the coach says the word "relax."

3. **Stretching of muscles.** The muscles used in labor have to go through many hours of exertion. Like any set of muscles, they will get tired and begin to ache if they are overworked, especially if they are out of condition. The idea that a woman is "sick" when she is pregnant and should "take it easy" and rest as often as possible is a thing of the past if pregnancy is normal. In Lamaze training, women are taught a number of exercises so that muscles to be used in labor and delivery can be toned up and strong when the baby decides to arrive. Though not part of Lamaze training itself, some hospitals are experimenting with weight-lifting programs for pregnant women. Jane Fonda even has a workout video for pregnant women.

4. **Too little oxygen getting to muscles.** If you put down this book now, got up to run 5 miles, and then picked it up again, you would probably have some aching muscles when you resumed your reading. One reason for this is that your muscles use so much energy during vigorous exercise that they often cannot get enough oxygen, and so they begin to ache. The same is true in labor. In order to help deal with this, expectant mothers and coaches learn a variety of breathing techniques. These different types of breathing are generally used during contractions, while the woman's attention is fixed on her focal point, as previously described. During the first part of labor, when contractions are mild and far apart, the expectant mother breathes deeply and slowly (called "low slow" breathing). During transition, she uses a type of breathing called "shallow-chest" or "pant-blow," which keeps the diaphragm (the muscle under the lungs) from pressing down on the top of the uterus during con-

tractions, thus reducing pain. There is even a type of breathing that keeps her from being able to push if the urge to push comes too early or if the physician needs more time.

In addition to helping keep oxygen supplied to muscles, these breathing exercises also force the expectant mother to think about something other than the source of pain. This, like using a focal point, reduces the subjective experience of pain. After labor has been going on for some time, the coach may have to breathe along with the expectant mother, "pacing" her and making her use his (or her) face as the focal point. Coaches are more than cheerleaders and must take command if the mother panics during transition.

5. **Pressure on nerves.** Pressure on nerves caused by the fetus moving through the birth canal is dealt with through the use of *effleurage*, or massage. One type of effleurage involves having the expectant mother lightly touch her abdomen with her fingertips, tracing large ovals on her skin during contractions. This light massage generally is a pleasant sensation, and by continually pairing the discomforts of contractions with a pleasant sensation the subjective experience of pain is reduced. More recently, light massage is being replaced by deep muscle massage. The back, especially the small of the back, is also massaged. If the baby is coming through the birth canal face first rather than crown (back of the head) first, pressure is put on nerves in the lower back (back labor). By applying counterpressure to the lower back, a coach can reduce some of this discomfort.

These techniques are a sample of some of the components of Lamaze training. The shared training and birth experience can help bring a couple closer together. However, while Lamaze's techniques were a major advance, especially in allowing women and their partners more control over an important event in their lives, he is not without his critics. Some, for example, feel that even his methods are too controlling and that the end result is that women give birth "by direction, as if it were a flight plan" (Armstrong & Feldman, 1990). Today, there are several birthing techniques that couples can use in place of the traditional hospital-general anesthesia approach. Here are a few of them.

THE LEBOYER METHOD

Another French physician, Frederick Leboyer, wrote an influential book in 1975 called *Birth Without Violence*. He felt that traditional techniques of delivery were traumatic for babies, and instead advocated "gentle birth." In this technique, the baby is delivered and

FIGURE 7-10   IN RECENT YEARS, THE BIRTH OF A BABY HAS BECOME A FAMILY EVENT, WITH HUSBANDS HELPING THEIR WIVES DURING DELIVERY.

(Nazario, 1990). Of course, home births are also much less expensive. There are also personal considerations. Many couples feel that having a baby in familiar surroundings is more natural than a hospital birth. It also provides an opportunity for the entire family to be present and participate.

To compete with this movement, many hospitals today have "birthing rooms," which are designed to look like bedrooms rather than hospital rooms. Labor and delivery take place in the same bed, and often a crib is present so that the baby can sleep in with the mother after birth. Sometimes even brothers and sisters are allowed to put on hospital gowns and hold the newborn shortly after birth.

immediately placed on the mother's abdomen. The room is dimly lit, to simulate the lighting inside of the mother's body. The umbilical cord is not cut for several minutes, until it stops pulsating. The baby is then put in a warm bath (to simulate the amniotic fluid). The idea behind these procedures is to allow the transition of the baby from life inside of the mother's body to life in the outside world to be as smooth as possible. Leboyer claims that babies born in this manner immediately smile, are calm, and even develop more rapidly. Critics claim that babies at this age are incapable of experiencing trauma, that dim lighting can interfere with the ability of hospital staff to detect problems in the baby or mother, and that there are no data to confirm Leboyer's claims. At present, this birthing method is still controversial, and it is much more difficult to find a physician willing to use this method compared to the Lamaze approach.

HOME BIRTH/BIRTHING ROOMS AND CENTERS/MODERN MIDWIFERY

In 1870, less than 1 percent of women gave birth in hospitals (Tew, 1990). A century later, only about 1–2 percent of women gave birth outside of a hospital. Today, in Europe and the United States, there is a growing movement back to having births in the home. This movement has been driven, in part, by economic considerations. Because of the cost of malpractice insurance, one in eight obstetricians have stopped delivering babies, and one-fourth of the counties in the United States do not have a clinic to provide prenatal care

In many areas a closely related option is *birthing centers*, institutions that offer delivery in a homelike atmosphere with the assistance of skilled individuals such as midwives or physicians. Although new to the United States, birthing centers have been popular in Europe for a long time. They have a low rate for cesarean sections and neonatal mortality (Eakins, 1989), but this may be partly because birthing centers are really an option only to women with no foreseeable complications (Rooks et al., 1989). Should there be an emergency, all centers have procedures for a quick transfer to a (usually nearby) hospital.

Whether the choice is to deliver at home, a birthing center, and increasingly even in hospitals, there is also a growing trend to use **midwives** rather than physicians. In many European countries, over two thirds of babies are delivered by midwives (Nazario, 1990). Midwives are generally registered nurses trained in obstetrical techniques who are well qualified for normal deliveries (and minor emergencies). They are less expensive than physicians, and provide personal care during the latter parts of pregnancy, labor, and delivery. Studies indicate that the outcome for babies (and mothers) is just as good when attended by nurse-midwives as when attended by physicians (Declercq, 1992; Tew, 1990; see also Nazario, 1990). The American College of Obstetricians and Gynecologists officially approved the use of nurse-midwives in 1971. The use of lay-midwives (persons who are not nurses and are

Nurse-midwife

Registered nurses, trained in obstetrical techniques, who deliver babies, often at the expectant mother's home.

generally trained by nurse-midwives) is also increasing in popularity.

Nurse-midwives are certified by the American College of Nurse-Midwives, but in some states there are no certifying agencies. So, it is important to learn about the midwife's background, years of experience, and references. I should point out that a midwife may be either male or female, as evidenced by a man who after practicing this trade for many years officially had his legal name changed to "Mr. Midwife."

Women who have some form of prepared childbirth and who are assisted during labor and delivery by a trained attendant generally require less medication for pain, fewer cesarean sections, and more positive feelings about the experience (Kennell et al., 1991; McNiven et al., 1992). However, a word of caution. Do not start thinking of childbirth as a contest to see if you can get through with the least amount of medical help. This attitude can make the use of anesthetics or a C-section seem like a "failure." That should not be the case. Any birth that results in a healthy mother and baby is a good one, regardless of the technique used. That is always the goal of childbirth, and should not be forgotten. ∎

CHILDBIRTH

Before birth, the fetus will generally rotate its position so that its head is downward. This can happen weeks or hours before birth and is what is meant when people say "the baby dropped." It is also called **"lightening,"** because once the fetus's head (its largest part) has lowered in the uterus, pressure on the mother's abdomen and diaphragm is greatly reduced. Being able to breathe more easily makes a mother feel like the load that she has been carrying (the fetus) weighs less (is "lighter").

Lightening
Rotation of the fetus prior to childbirth so that its head is downward, resulting in decreased pressure on the mother's abdomen.

Shortly before a woman begins to give birth ("goes into labor"), she may experience a burst of energy. A woman may feel better than she has in months, and may start to clean house or do some other type of work as a means of "burning off" this energy. It is probably a good idea to save some of this energy for later, when it certainly will be needed.

True Versus False Labor

Throughout the latter stages of pregnancy, the uterus will undergo contractions—tightenings and relaxations of the muscles of the uterus. These are involuntary, and for most of pregnancy will go unnoticed. The contractions, called *Braxton-Hicks contractions*, are a type of natural "exercise program" for the uterus. Sometimes these contractions become so strong that they are noticed and mistaken for true labor. Parents-to-be sometimes worry and go to a hospital, only to be told that they have had a "false labor" and should return when the woman is in "real" labor. Here are some rules of thumb that help distinguish false labor from true labor.

Braxton-Hicks contractions
Uterine contractions experienced during the last trimester of pregnancy that are often incorrectly interpreted as the beginning of labor (false labor).

False labor
A set of temporary contractions of the uterus that resemble the start of labor.

One important sign of labor is the time between contractions. The uterus is basically a muscle in the shape of a bag. Its job is to push the fetus into the world. Like most muscles engaged in prolonged, heavy labor, it must repeatedly contract or tighten. If contractions are coming 10 minutes apart on a regular basis, this is a good sign that labor has begun. False labor contractions are usually less regular and will eventually cease. The duration of each contraction also should be measured. If contractions are 30 seconds long on a regular basis, this is a good sign that labor has begun. False labor contractions are usually shorter than contractions marking true labor. With true labor, discomfort caused by contractions is usually felt in the back and abdomen. With false labor, discomfort is more likely to be felt in the groin and lower abdomen.

Two important signs of the beginning of labor involve the cervix. In the last month of pregnancy, the cervix will **dilate** to about 1 centimeter in diameter. When a woman goes into labor, the uterine contractions help cause the cervix to dilate more. It must eventually dilate to 10 centimeters (about 4 inches) in diameter before the baby can be born. In the first stage of labor, the cervix will dilate to about 2–3 centimeters. In addition, the cervix must stretch until it is "thinned out" or "**effaced**" so that it won't block the baby's passage into the birth canal (vagina). A good sign of true labor is that the cervix is 70 percent or more effaced. At birth, it will be 100 percent effaced. Although both of these cervical changes are good signs that labor has begun, they also are only general rules of thumb.

Dilate
To make wider or larger.

Effacement
The thinning of the cervix during labor.

Labor for the first child is usually longer than labor for subsequent children. A mother who has had many children may be asked to go to the hospital when contractions are still 20 minutes apart, because she could go directly from 20 minutes apart to a much shorter

FIGURE 7-11   THE STAGES OF CHILDBIRTH.

interval. It is not uncommon for women to wait too long before going to a hospital, and to give birth in taxis, in the hospital parking lot, or in hospital elevators.

False labor can fool even the professionals. I know of one woman who had regular contractions of 30 seconds duration 2 minutes apart for several hours, with 70 percent effacement and 3 centimeters dilation of the cervix. After being examined in the emergency room and admitted, both the nurse and attending physician assured the parents-to-be that labor was in full swing. Ten hours later the couple checked out. Actual labor and birth came 1 week (and two more false alarms) later.

STAGES OF LABOR

Labor is divided into three stages. The initial stage of labor is a **start-up stage**, and involves the woman's body making preparations to expel the fetus from the uterus into the outside world. This stage usually lasts from 6 to 13 hours. At this time, uterine contractions begin to push the fetus downward toward the cervix. The cervix begins to dilate and efface, as described earlier. At first, contractions are far apart (one every 10 to 20 minutes) and don't last long (15 to 20 seconds), but eventually they begin to come closer together (1 to 2 minutes) and last longer (45 to 60 seconds or longer).

During pregnancy, the cervix becomes plugged up with a thick layer of mucus. This prevents the amniotic sac (bag of water) and the fetus from having direct

Start-up stage of labor

Begins with uterine contractions pushing the fetus downward toward the cervix and ends when the cervix is fully dilated.

contact with the outside environment (through the vagina). During labor, this mucous plug will come out. A discharge of mucus and blood (known as a "bloody show") is a sign of labor. However, for some women the mucus comes out a little at a time, so that this sign is not clearly seen. In other women, the plug literally pops out like the cork in a bottle of champagne. As usual, every variation in between is also seen.

For about 10 percent of pregnancies, the amniotic sac will break before labor begins. In some women, the break is a small tear and the fluid seeps out. In other women, the water gushes out. This is what happens when a woman's *water breaks.* Labor usually begins within a day after the amniotic sac breaks. If not, most physicians will induce labor using drugs in order to prevent contact with the outside world from causing infection in the fetus. A woman can also go into labor without the water breaking. Physicians sometimes break the amniotic sac on purpose in order to speed up labor. It is even possible to give birth with the fetus enclosed in an unbroken amniotic sac. Physicians in this country don't allow this to happen and will break the sac first. However, in the Far East, children born in this manner are believed to be blessed with good fortune.

The last part of the first stage of labor is called the **transition phase**. It is called this because it marks the end of the initial stage of labor and the beginning of the next (birth) stage. This phase takes place when the cervix is almost fully dilated (8–10 cm). Contractions are severe, and the woman may feel nauseous, chilled, and very uncomfortable. She will often start to think that there is no end to this process, and many women at this point will announce that they quit and are going home. Fortunately, transition usually lasts 40 minutes or less (compared to the often hours-long duration of the earlier part of the first stage).

During labor, it is important to monitor the fetus's vital signs. A sudden drop in heart rate may indicate a life-threatening situation. Nurses or physicians can monitor heart rate with a stethoscope or by a device called a fetal monitor. With a monitor, a recording device is placed on the expectant mother's abdomen

Transition phase

The last part of the start-up stage of labor, during which the cervix dilates to 10 cm in order for the baby to be able to enter the birth canal.

(or, in the second stage of labor, directly on the fetus's scalp) and heart rate is shown on a machine. Although fetal monitors are no better than stethoscopes in reducing the incidence of perinatal deaths (Shy et al., 1990), they can also be used to show when contractions are beginning, which allows women to prepare for them. The monitor also shows when the most intense or discomforting part of a contraction has passed. Knowing that the worst is over can be a great comfort.

The **second stage** of labor begins when the cervix is fully dilated and the fetus begins moving through the birth canal (Figure 7-11). It ends with birth. Contractions during this stage of labor are accompanied by an intense desire to push or "bear down." The contractions cause the opening of the vagina to expand, and expectant mothers often get a "second wind" because they now can see an end to their work. Expectant mothers (and fathers) begin to get excited about the fact that they will soon be able to see their baby, and this makes the contractions a little easier to bear. This stage lasts from 30 to 80 minutes on the average, depending on whether it is the first child for a woman or a later child. Just before the actual birth, physicians often use a surgical procedure called an episiotomy (see next section).

> **Second stage of labor**
> Begins when the cervix is fully dilated and the fetus begins moving through the birth canal. It ends with birth.

The first sign of the fetus is usually the sight of its head at the opening of the vagina. This is called "*crowning*," because ideally the crown of the head is leading the way. If the head is turned around so that its nose and forehead are leading, it is called a "back labor" because this will cause the crown of the fetus's head to put pressure on nerves in the lower back, making the labor more painful than normal. The person (usually a physician) delivering the baby will tell the expectant mother when and how hard to push during contractions in order to get the baby into the world. The head is delivered first, with the physician reaching beneath the infant's chin to be sure that the umbilical cord is not wrapped around the baby's neck before the head is brought out. Once the head is delivered, suction is applied to the mouth and nose with a small rubber bulb so that the baby can breathe more easily. The head then turns, and the shoulders and rest of the body come out rather quickly. The mouth and nose are suctioned again.

> **Crowning**
> The appearance of the fetus's head at the vaginal opening during childbirth.

A newborn will usually cry at birth. If not, the baby's back will be rubbed to start the baby breathing. The umbilical cord will be clamped and cut about 1z\x inches from the baby's body. This stub will fall off in a few days, leaving the navel. (The navel is either an "inny" or an "outty," but the type of navel you have seems to depend on heredity, not on how the umbilical cord was cut.)

In the **third stage** of labor the placenta detaches from the uterus and leaves the mother's body (along with the other materials). This is what is called the *afterbirth*. This stage usually lasts only from 10 to 12 minutes. The physician examines the afterbirth to make sure that it is one piece, then it is discarded. If even small pieces of the placenta stay in the uterus, infection and bleeding can occur. When this takes place, physicians use a procedure called "D and C" (dilation and curettage), in which the cervix is dilated to allow access to the uterus, which is scraped clean. If any tears in the vagina have occurred, they are repaired at this time.

> **Third stage of labor**
> Detachment and expulsion of the placenta from the uterus after childbirth.

> **Afterbirth**
> The expulsion of the placenta from the uterus after a baby is born.

After the third stage of labor, the uterus should contract and remain constricted. To help this happen, the abdomen is sometimes massaged and/or drugs may be given. This helps prevent excess bleeding (hemorrhage) in the uterus.

EPISIOTOMY AND PREPPING

In the United States, the large majority of women who deliver vaginally in hospitals are given an **episiotomy** just before they give birth. This is an incision made from the bottom of the vagina (through the perineum) toward the anus, thus enlarging the vaginal opening. This is a useful procedure if the baby is in distress, and also reduces tearing of the perineum (which takes longer to heal than an incision). However, many authorities believe that most episiotomies are unnecessary and are done routinely only for the benefit of the physician. Episiotomies are uncommon in midwife-assisted deliveries (see Henriksen et al., 1994). In fact, a recent study found that women having vaginal deliveries who did not have episiotomies had fewer problems than women who were given an episiotomy (Argentine Episiotomy Trial, 1993). When sewing up the incision, a few physicians continue to include a "honeymoon stitch" (or "husband's stitch"), a stitch in the lower part of the vaginal opening. Both of these procedures should be abandoned as routine birthing practices.

> **Episiotomy**
> A surgical procedure performed just before birth to reduce the risk of tearing the perineum.

Another procedure that is used less frequently than in the past is "**prepping**," that is, shaving the pubic hair prior to delivery. Many physicians now think that it is also unnecessary and can even be a source of infection when the hair begins to grow back. ■

> **Prepping**
> The shaving of the pubic hair prior to delivery of a baby.

PROBLEMS WITH CHILDBIRTH

BREECH BIRTHS

Babies, you recall, are generally born head first. This occurs in about 96 percent of all births, and ideally the back of the head or "crown" leads the way. Sometimes, a fetus will try to come through the birth canal feet or buttocks first. This is called a **breech birth** and occurs in 2–4 percent of all births. A fetus can even try to come out back first, shoulder first, or any other conceivable position, but these cases are rare. Sometimes a fetus will spontaneously shift from feet to head first just before delivery. Sometimes during labor a woman will be asked to try lying in new positions, such as on her side, in the hopes that this will cause the fetus to change to a head-first position. A physician can sometimes turn the fetus by grasping the mother's abdomen and manually trying to change the fetus's position.

Breech birth

A birth in which the baby is born feet or buttocks first.

Today, some physicians may try to perform a vaginal ("normal") delivery, even if a breech birth is unpreventable. It will depend on the circumstances and the physician. If the physician feels the risks of a vaginal delivery are too great, he or she may perform a C-section.

PLACENTA PREVIA

The blastocyst normally implants in the upper part of the uterus. However, for about one out of every 200 pregnant women, implantation occurs in the lower uterus (Iyasu et al., 1993). As the placenta grows, it often blocks the cervical opening, a condition called **placenta previa**. This does not affect the fetus, but may prevent a vaginal delivery.

Placenta previa

A condition in which the placenta blocks the cervical opening.

CESAREAN SECTIONS

A **Cesarean section** (also Caesarean, or C-section) is an incision through the abdominal and uterine walls to deliver a baby. Although the name is often attributed to the birth of Julius Caesar, in actuality it is derived from *lex cesarea*, Roman law (715 B.C.) that allowed saving a fetus in the case of its mother's death.

Cesarean section or C-section

The surgical removal of a fetus through the mother's abdomen.

Cesarean sections accounted for 5 percent of live births in the United States in 1970, 14 percent in 1979, 19 percent in 1984, and 24.7 percent in 1988 (Taffel, Placek, & Moien, 1990). The rate has since leveled off (Centers for Disease Control and Prevention, 1995). If this number looks large to you, you are not alone in your perceptions. Many individuals, including many health professionals, have begun to call for changes in the way physicians decide when to use this procedure (National Institutes of Health consensus conference, 1981). Cesareans are supposedly done to reduce the risk to the mother or baby, but most are done on middle- and upper-income women who can afford it (independently or through health insurance; Gould, Davey, & Stafford, 1989). Recall, too, that C-sections are uncommon in deliveries assisted by midwives (Kennell et al., 1991; McNiven et al., 1992). Thus, there has been the suspicion that many C-sections have been performed for the economic benefit of the physician/hospital, or to avoid the risk of malpractice lawsuits in the case of complications during vaginal deliveries.

There are many legitimate reasons for performing a cesarean section. These include *some* cases of breech birth or placenta previa, the baby's head being too big for the mother's pelvis, maternal illness or stress, and fetal stress. It used to be the case that once a woman had a C-section, all later pregnancies would have to end with C-section deliveries (because the cuts were made vertically through the horizontal abdominal muscles and through the contracting part of the uterus). These repeat cesarean sections account for many of the C-sections performed each year. Today, however, incisions are made horizontally through the abdomen and then through the noncontracting part of the uterus, and in most cases it is considered safe for a woman who has previously had a cesarean section to deliver vaginally (Flamm et al., 1990; Rosen et al., 1991). Obstetricians have been slow to respond, but the number of vaginal births after a C-section have doubled since 1988 (Centers for Disease Control and Prevention, 1995). However, C-sections are still the most frequently performed major operation in the United States (966,000 were performed in 1991).

Because C-sections are so common, it is advisable for the pregnant woman to talk with her physician about the techniques he or she uses in considering doing C-sections (and about his or her attitudes regarding normal deliveries with subsequent births) *before* she goes into labor. She should also talk with the physician about episiotomies, use of anesthetics, attitudes about prepared or "natural" childbirth, and all other details of the birth process at this time. This talk should take place when the expectant woman first begins to see the physician. If she doesn't like what she hears, she should find a new doctor.

PRETERM INFANTS

Nine out of every 1000 births in the United States result in the death of the baby after it is delivered. The leading cause of infant mortality is from preterm birth. An infant is considered preterm if it weighs less than 5½ pounds, and the mother was pregnant for less than 37 weeks. Sometimes people use the term "premature infants" to describe such children, but Miller (1985) prefers an alternative term such as "low-birth-weight infants." I will compromise and use the phrase "preterm infants." Preterm births account for about 7 percent of all U.S. births. Conditions such as malnutrition and toxemia increase the risk of having a preterm birth, but in 50 percent of preterm births the cause of the problem is unknown (Hellman & Pritchard, 1971). If a woman goes into labor prematurely, drugs can be given to relax the uterus and postpone labor. This must be done early in labor to be effective, however.

Preterm infant

An infant born weighing less than 5 1/2 pounds and before the 37th week of pregnancy.

Advances in neonatology (the care of newborn babies) have reduced the limit of viability to about 23 to 24 weeks after conception (Allen, Donahue, & Dusman, 1993). One of the biggest problems facing a fetus born at this time is that it has great trouble breathing. Before the age of 23 weeks (around 4 months), the fetus cannot produce a liquid called *surfactin.* Surfactin lets the lungs transmit oxygen from the atmosphere to blood. After 4 months of age, the fetus can produce some surfactin, but it cannot maintain the liquid at the necessary levels until about 8 or 9 months of age. Newborns who cannot maintain proper levels of surfactin develop **respiratory distress syndrome** and die.

"When I was exactly eight months pregnant my amniotic sac broke and labor was induced . . . When I saw my baby in the nursery, she was under oxygen, had all kinds of wires connected to her, an IV in her foot, and she had a lot of trouble breathing. I wasn't ready for this. However, I feel that if I was more informed about premature births I would have understood better."

(from the author's files)

Before 1980, there was little hope of survival for babies born weighing less than 2 pounds. Today, about 17,000 infants per year born weighing less than 2 pounds are placed in *Intensive Care Nurseries* (ICNs), where new techniques and equipment allow these infants a good chance of survival. Infants weighing just over 1 pound have about a 30 percent chance of survival, while those weighing about 2½ pounds have about a 90 percent chance of survival (see Phelps et al., 1991). The cost of such technology is very high. For example, the cost of caring for a 4-month premature baby can be over $300,000. In addition, premature infants run a high risk of having handicaps that can require treatment for many years. Babies born weighing less than 750 grams (a little over 1½ pounds) are much more likely than others to have poor psycho-motor skills, very low IQ scores, and poor performance in school (Hack et al., 1994). Early childhood intervention improves the IQ and verbal performance of preterm infants born weighing 4½ pounds or more, but is of little or no help to very low-birth-weight babies. They still remain cognitively and behaviorally impaired after 5 years (Brooks-Gunn et al., 1994). ■

AFTERWARDS

BREAST-FEEDING THE BABY

Milk production (lactation) begins about 3 days after a woman gives birth (Figure 7-12). Two hormones produced by the pituitary gland are responsible for milk production. **Prolactin** stimulates the breasts to produce milk, while **oxytocin** causes the breasts to eject milk. When the baby sucks on the breasts, a milk flow reflex is created. In fact, over time merely hearing the baby cry can cause the breasts to begin ejecting milk. At first, the breasts give out **colostrum**, mentioned earlier, which is high in protein and also helps immunize the infant against diseases. After about 3 days, milk begins to flow. The average amount of milk produced is 2½–3 cups per day, but there is a lot of variation among individuals. Some women do not produce enough milk and some produce too much.

Prolactin

A hormone that stimulates milk production in the breasts.

Oxytocin

A hormone that causes the breasts to eject milk.

Colostrum

A thick, sticky liquid produced by a mother's breasts before milk starts to flow.

Mothers' milk contains many infection-fighting proteins that protect the infant from gastrointestinal illnesses, respiratory infections, meningitis, skin diseases, and other problems (Howie et al., 1990; Institute of Medicine, 1991; Yolken et al., 1992). There are benefits to mothers as well. When a mother begins nursing, a hormone is released that helps the uterus to contract and helps stop internal bleeding. Nursing mothers may also have a reduced risk of osteoporosis and breast cancer (Institute of Medicine, 1991). Breast-feeding does not interfere with sexual desire (Fisher & Gray, 1988; Masters & Johnson, 1966). Despite these benefits, the number of women in the United States who nurse after childbirth is decreasing. You should know that both the American Academy of Pediatricians and the Institute of Medicine endorse breast-feeding. Keep in mind, however, that drugs and pollutants also can be transmitted to the infant through mothers' milk. Before taking any medication (including birth control pills), therefore, it is important for nursing mothers to consult their physicians or pharmacists.

Nursing does not come naturally to everyone:

" Hospitals have a way to reduce an adult to a child with regard to telling you what is and what is not allowed. I assumed that a nurse would instruct me in the method of breast-feeding. Every feeding the nurse would bring the baby and hand me a baby bottle filled with water and a medicine cup with a watersoaked cotton ball in it.

I had no idea what the cotton ball was used for. For every feeding I gave the baby the water bottle and then dabbed her mouth with the cotton ball afterwards. On the second day after delivery I asked the nurse when did she want me to start breast-feeding? Her expression was priceless! 'You mean you haven't?' she said.

I said, 'No, you didn't tell me to; you just keep bringing me this water bottle and cotton ball.' She wondered why the baby had taken so much supplemental milk 'backstage.' "

(from the author's files)

A mother's breasts and nipples may get sore when she first starts to nurse. Because of reduced estrogen production, her vaginal tissues may also be drier and cause irritation during intercourse (this can be corrected, of course, with use of a lubricant). A nursing mother may not begin her menstrual cycle for several months after birth, giving her some protection against pregnancy (but see Chapter 6). This is especially true when feeding is done "on demand" rather than according to a fixed schedule. It should be remembered, however, that a woman will ovulate and be able to conceive again before she has her next menstrual flow, so this is certainly not a perfect means of contraception.

Despite its benefits, many women choose not to breast-feed their babies, often because of a career outside the home. If a woman stops breast-feeding (or never begins), milk production will stop within days. This can be speeded up by an injection of estrogen. Be aware, however, that human milk is much easier to digest than cow's milk, and if bottle-fed, a baby should be given formula.

Whether a baby is breast-fed or bottle-fed, fathers should not ignore this new responsibility. Fathers can sit with their partner while she breast-feeds

FIGURE 7-12   MOTHER'S MILK CONTAINS MANY INFECTION-FIGHTING PROTEINS AND IS EASIER FOR A BABY TO DIGEST THAN COW'S MILK.

in the middle of the night, or mothers can use breast pumps to extract their milk for a later feeding (allowing tired mothers to sleep while fathers feed the baby).

POSTPARTUM BLUES

The first 3 months after childbirth are called the **postpartum period**. Although most women look forward to having a baby, many experience a period of negative emotions during this time called **postpartum depression**. In some cases it can be extreme:

Postpartum depression

Depression that often occurs in women after giving birth, usually lasting 2 or 3 weeks.

" After I had my son I spent weeks upon weeks of sitting alone on the kitchen floor with him on my lap and crying and crying uncontrollably . . . "

" I was so depressed after giving birth to a little girl. If somebody touched her, I screamed. When my baby was 3 days old I had a fight with my mother-in-law and husband. Actually, they tried to help me out, but I was so depressed that I always fought with them. Things got worse and I thought I was going to get divorced . . . My doctor explained to me it is because of hor-mone changes . . . I am thankful to my husband who always tried to understand me at that time . . . ''

"I can remember being depressed for a couple of months . . . I felt so helpless . . . Sometimes I resented my baby because I felt so bad and was so exhausted. I hated myself for having these feelings . . . ''

(from the author's files)

Biological factors contribute to postpartum depression, particularly hormone changes. The placenta secretes high levels of estrogen and progesterone during pregnancy, but there is a sudden drop in the levels of these hormones after birth. Thyroid disorders have also been implicated in some cases (Harris, 1993). But social and psychological factors also play a role (Gruen, 1990).

Marital unhappiness, for example, can contribute to the depression. Newborn infants need frequent feeding, which can cause mothers to lose lots of sleep. A woman can feel abandoned if she feels she is not receiving support from her partner. The financial responsibilities of being a parent and many other things may also contribute.

Recent studies indicate that if postpartum depression lasts several weeks, it can affect the infant's emotional, behavioral, and cognitive development (Cogill

et al., 1986; Murray, 1992). A simple screening questionnaire has been developed to identify mothers with postpartum depression and is a useful tool to suggest who might need support during this difficult time (Cox, Holden, & Sagovsky, 1987).

SEXUAL INTERCOURSE AFTER BIRTH

"We tried to make love again when our first baby was about 3½ weeks old. The pain from the episiotomy made this impossible and we both wound up very frustrated and wondering if our sex life would ever be back to normal. We finally did succeed at about 6 weeks but still it wasn't very comfortable. After a while we got used to the new normal . . . After my second and third babies were born everything was very different. I didn't have an episiotomy, or tear at all, even though they were both very large. We made love just a few weeks later without any discomfort whatsoever.''

(from the author's files)

Labor often leaves a woman tired and sore for some time, and stitches from an episiotomy may leave her uncomfortable. The loss of estrogen results in vaginal dryness and irritation (during intercourse) for some time. Most physicians advise that sexual intercourse should not be resumed until 4 to 6 weeks after birth.

Women also may worry about their sexuality because of stretch marks, extra weight left over from pregnancy, and "flabby" stomach muscles. The stretch marks soon become paler, and problems with weight and stomach muscles can be helped through exercise. Some women also worry about the size of their vagina being too large after birth. The vaginal muscles generally become firm and tight again, especially if the woman continues to practice Kegel exercises (see Chapter 2).

The best time to resume sexual relations depends on many factors. In all cases, however, a man and a woman must learn to relate to each other as both sexual partners *and* as parents. Making this adjustment to new roles and feelings requires time and patience. Differences in sleep patterns now that an infant must be fed at night, demands on time

"Pretend you're carrying your golf clubs, and you won't mind it."

Reprinted Courtesy of Hoest and Parade Magazine © 1987.

and energy made on parents by children, and difficulty finding periods of privacy all force couples to make adjustments in their sexual behaviors. As you might expect, sexual attitudes in general play a role. Couples who had a positive attitude about sex before pregnancy tend to resume sexual relations earlier than couples with a less than totally positive attitude (Fisher & Gray, 1988).

New Responsibilities

Becoming a parent is like being asked to start a new job with little or no training. Just because someone has given birth or fathered a child does not mean she or he has natural parenting ability. Learning how to deal with children effectively and to provide the right balance of discipline and love is not easy. Although 80 percent of women say they would choose to be a parent again if they had to do it all over (Genevie & Margolies, 1987), most find the demands of new (and multiple) roles in their lives to be stressful (Ventura, 1987). Studies find that after the transition to parenthood, happiness within the marriage is directly related to the sharing of child-care and housekeeping responsibilities (Hackel & Ruble, 1992). Many new fathers, for example, com-

plain about a diminished sex life and their wives' mood swings, yet do little to relieve their partners in their new responsibilities. Men, do you value your relationship enough to share these responsibilities?

It is useful to acquire some training and knowledge about parenting, just as it is useful to acquire training and knowledge about giving birth. Here are some helpful references.

For new parents, the book *Infants and Mothers* by T. B. Brazelton (1969; New York: Delacorte Press/ Seymour Lawrence) is recommended. Read the chapters on the first week of life just before and again immediately after the baby is born.

For child rearing, the book *P.E.T. (Parent Effectiveness Training) in Action* by Thomas Gordon (1976; New York: Banton Books) is widely used.

The Family Resource Coalition has published a listing of programs to improve parenting and strengthen families. To learn about such programs in your area, contact the Family Resource Coalition at 200 S. Michigan Avenue, 16th Floor, Chicago, IL 60604. ■

INFERTILITY

Infertility is usually defined as the inability of a couple to conceive during 12 months or more of sexual intercourse without contraception. This assumes, of course, that the woman is of reproductive age. Most people think of an infertile couple as a couple who have never been able to conceive, called *primary* infertility. However, the inability to conceive after having had one child, called *secondary* infertility, is even more common (Mosher & Pratt, 1990). Many people believe that infertility is increasing and popular magazines make reference to an infertility "epidemic" (e.g., *Newsweek*, September 30, 1991), but statistics show that in actuality there was no increase during the 1980s (Mosher & Pratt, 1991). During this time, about one in 12 couples in the United States had difficulty conceiving. What there has been is a big increase in the number of couples seeking help for infertility, which has led to the perception of an epidemic.

The causes of infertility are many and varied, because so many organs of both sexes must function properly for conception to take place. About 40 percent of the problems involved with infertility are due to the male partner, with another 40 percent to the female. About 20 percent of the cases result from problems in both partners (Hudson, Pepperell, & Wood, 1987; Moore, 1982).

Infertility
The inability of a couple to conceive.

Before we proceed, you should be aware that there is a national organization that offers updated information and support to infertile couples. If interested, contact RESOLVE, 1310 Broadway, Somerville, MA 02144-1731, or call 617-623-0744.

Infertility in Males

As you may remember, only a very few of the millions of sperm cells released during ejaculation survive the trip to the egg. If a man's reproductive system cannot produce enough sperm, and/or if the sperm he produces are too slow or weak, the probability that fertilization can occur is substantially reduced. Low numbers of sperm are caused by a variety of factors, including endocrine problems (low levels of pituitary or gonadal hormones), drugs (including alcohol, and many antibiotics), marijuana, radiation, and infections. If a man gets mumps after puberty, for example, it often spreads to the testicles and causes severe swelling that destroys the seminiferous tubules where sperm are produced. Other infections, including some sexually transmitted diseases, can result in blockage of a male's duct system (just as some STDs can lead to blockage of the Fallopian tubes in women). Varicosity of the veins in the spermatic cord (*varicocele*) can also lead to a low sperm count.

Because sperm can only be produced at a temperature several degrees lower than normal body temperature, sperm count is sensitive to temperature variations. For example, athletes who regularly wear athletic supporters or metal cup protectors for long periods of time (resulting in increased testicular temperatures) risk having a temporary low sperm count. Frequent use of sauna baths or hot tubs can also cause a temporary low sperm count. If a couple is trying to conceive, the male may be told to switch to loose-fitting underwear so that his testes will hang farther from his body and thus have less exposure to body heat. Sperm count also decreases during the summer months (Levine et al., 1990), but we are not yet sure that it is due to the heat (Snyder, 1990).

A recent review of 61 studies conducted worldwide concluded that the average sperm count per ejaculation had dropped by more than half in the last 50 years (Carlsen et al., 1992). What could cause such a dramatic change? Dr. Neils Skakkeback, one of the authors of the paper, said, "It would have to be something in the environment or life style. Changes that occur within a generation could hardly be due to a change in genetic background" (quoted by Epstein in AP release, September 1992). Further evidence is found in the fact that the rates for testicular cancer tripled during the same time period. Could industrial chemical pollutants have such effects? Boys born to (and breast-fed from) mothers exposed to high levels of pollutants have testicular malformations and dramatically undersized penises, and the same is true for many species in the wild (see Begley & Glick, 1994). Many of the suspected pollutants resemble the female sex hormone estrogen in structure. Other scientists who have looked at the same data refute that sperm counts have fallen (Bromwich et al., 1994; Farrow, 1994), though the original authors stick to their conclusions (Keiding et al., 1994). A more recent study also reported that sperm counts had declined over the last few decades (Auger et al., 1995). There will certainly be much research in this area in the future.

Infertility is not just a physical problem; it also affects men emotionally:

"Several months ago we began trying to have kids unsuccessfully. When I was younger I had an . . . operation and my doctor said that because of this I would not be able to have children. My wife and I wanted children, and this situation has really put a strain on our marriage."

"Being sterile is not an easy thing to discuss. On top of diminishing dreams and goals, it has made finding the right girl to begin a life-long relationship with very difficult . . . My future wife and I will never be able to have children of our own . . . I've always wanted to teach my son to play sports or take my daughter to dancing lessons . . . Hopefully someday I will find the right woman and we can adopt."

(from the author's files)

What are the medical treatments for male infertility? Infertility due to varicocele (8–23 percent of cases) can often be corrected with surgery (Takihara et al., 1991). If the cause is hormonal, treatment with pituitary hormones (or brain hormones that cause release of pituitary hormones) or gonadal hormones (androgens) is often successful (Menchini-Fabris et al., 1992). A blocked duct system in men is much easier to correct through surgery than it is to correct blocked tubes in women.

When a man is found to have a low sperm count, a procedure called **artificial insemination** is often used. In this procedure, sperm are collected (via masturbation) and inserted into the female partner's vagina or uterus immediately after ovulation. Several ejaculations are usually collected and stored through freezing (frozen semen is just as effective as fresh). For example, if a man's average ejaculation were found to contain 50 million sperm, six to eight ejaculations (totaling 300 to 400 million sperm) might be collected and frozen. When enough sperm have been collected, they are gathered together for a single insertion. Sperm can be safely preserved for more than 10 years, and some men make deposits in sperm banks before having a vasectomy, undergoing chemotherapy, working a hazardous job, or going off to war (Ames et al., 1991).

Artificial insemination
A method of treating infertility caused by a low sperm count in males. Sperm are collected during several ejaculations and then inserted into the partner's vagina at the time of ovulation.

If a man's sperm count is so low that combining several ejaculations will not help, a couple can choose to use sperm from another, usually anonymous, male. In these cases, artificial insemination is often called *donor insemination*. Donors are usually matched with the physical characteristics of the male. Over 30,000 babies a year are conceived by this method in the United States (see Barratt et al., 1990).

Sperm with X or Y chromosomes can be partially separated (see Chapter 8), and thus artificial insemination also allows couples (who wish so) to attempt to preselect the gender of their child (Beernink et al., 1993).

INFERTILITY IN FEMALES

The discovery that she is infertile can be emotionally devastating to a woman and her partner:

"I used various forms of birth control during the first six years of marriage so that my husband could finish college and medical school. We were so excited when we were finally able to start a family. But then I didn't become pregnant! Each month was pure agony as I would start my period. Most of our close friends were getting pregnant and were always asking us why we weren't, which didn't help at all. It was a very bad time for our marriage, also, as we argued about which one of us might be 'at fault.' We began a series of fertility tests after about a year and a half and they were very degrading . . . After many tests and keeping temperature charts for months, I was given clomid. I'm happy to report that the 2nd month of clomid did the trick . . . "

"My husband and I have been unsuccessful in our attempts to have children. We started trying to have a family 7 years ago. We waited a year and a half before even seeing a doctor. My doctor did the preliminary infertility workup and gave me some low doses of clomid. After 6 months of no success I went to a specialist. He gave me some industrial strength fertility drugs and after about 4 months I got pregnant and miscarried. We tried the same drugs again with no success and finally threw in the towel. All of this took about 5 years.

The experience is terribly isolating. People don't understand what you're upset about—after all, you didn't lose anything that they can see. All of our friends have had their kids. That's a lot of baby showers and first birthday parties that we didn't show up for. The funny thing about new parents is that it is perfectly normal for them to shamelessly go on and on about their new kids and problems—so even when we got together with our friends for other reasons the main topics were breast-feeding and details about their pregnancy and delivery. It was heartbreaking not to be able to be happy for them because at the time we just happened to be in a lot of pain. You can also add to the list the ignorant people who think you are selfish and self-centered for not having any kids. You don't tell them you are having problems because its none of their business and they get to assume the worst. Dr. King—I just think most people don't realize that when you come to realize that you can't have your own kids—is that the couple really does grieve about an imaginary child that everyone has

dreamed about. . . . We plan on adopting this summer."

(from the author's files)

For women, problems with fertilization generally come from two sources—structural problems in the Fallopian tubes or uterus, and failure to release eggs (ova). Probably the most common cause of female infertility is blockage of the Fallopian tubes, accounting for about 40 percent of cases (Paterson & Petrucco, 1987). Blockage can be due to anatomical malformations, growths (e.g., polyps), endometriosis (see below), infections, and scar tissue. Cigarette smoking also increases the risk of infertility (by increasing the risk of pelvic inflammatory disease and blocked tubes; see Scholes et al., 1992). Scar tissue from sexually transmitted diseases, especially chlamydia and gonorrhea (resulting in pelvic inflammatory disease), accounts for at least half the cases of infertility from blocked tubes. About 125,000 women become infertile each year in the United States due to untreated sexually transmitted diseases (*Reproductive Health Digest*, 1988). Given the epidemic levels of these diseases, this will continue to be a primary cause for both ectopic pregnancies and infertility in the near future (Weström et al., 1992; see Chapter 5).

The diameter of the passageway that an egg takes through the Fallopian tube is only about that of a human hair. Sometimes surgeons are able to reopen these tiny structures, but the success rate for microsurgery is less than 50 percent even for the best of physicians (Patton, Williams, & Coulam, 1987). In recent years, laser beams have been used successfully to unblock tubes. An even newer surgical technique to reopen blocked Fallopian tubes involves inserting a small balloon into the tubes and then inflating it (balloon tuboplasty). A similar technique has previously been used to unclog arteries leading to the heart. This technique is less expensive than microsurgery and early results suggest that it may be the most effective of all techniques for women with blocked Fallopian tubes (Confino et al., 1990).

Endometriosis can cause infertility by endometrial tissue growing in the Fallopian tubes and/or around the ovaries. Many women today are postponing pregnancy, but endometriosis is known as the "career women's disease" because it is most common in women in their mid-twenties and over, especially if they have postponed childbirth. Hormone treatment (to control the growth) or surgery (to remove the growth) has commonly been used. Today, laparoscopic surgery (with cautery) is being used with greater frequency for endometriosis-related infertility (Murphy et al., 1991), and use of a drug (pentoxifylline) is presently undergoing clinical trials.

If a woman is having problems becoming pregnant because she is not having regular menstrual cycles, and thus eggs are not being released, her physician may try **fertility drugs**. There are two major types. One type stimulates the pituitary gland to secrete FSH and LH (clomiphene is an example of this type of drug), the hormones necessary to start the cycle (see Chapter 3). A second type stimulates the ovaries directly (HMG, or human menopausal gonadotropins, is an example). The success rate is about 50 to 70 percent in cases where the problem is entirely hormonal.

Fertility drugs
Drugs that enhance the chance of conception in women who are infertile due to hormone deficiencies. The drugs either stimulate the pituitary gland to secrete FSH and LH or stimulate the ovaries directly.

Although often successful, there are two major concerns with the use of fertility drugs. First, they increase the chance of multiple births from 1–2 percent to 10–20 percent. From 1973 to 1990, twin births rose 65 percent, triplet births increased 221 percent, and multiple births of four or more increased over 300 percent, largely because of fertility drugs (Luke et al., 1994; National Center for Health Statistics, 1992). Multiple birth babies have a much greater risk of being born prematurely and of being low birth weight. Second, there has been some concern that fertility drugs may increase the risk of ovarian cancer (Whittemore et al., 1992). However, other physicians, after looking at the same data, caution us that the results are inconclusive and the risk is small at best (Spirtas et al., 1993; see Shoham, 1994 for a review).

ASSISTED REPRODUCTIVE TECHNOLOGY

The techniques for overcoming infertility entered a new era with the development of **in vitro** (in glass) **fertilization (IVF)** in England in the 1970s. Here eggs and sperm are combined in a Petri dish, and after fertilization takes place, several fertilized eggs (usually about the four-cell stage) are placed into the woman's uterus with hopes that at least one will then attach itself to the uterine wall. Fertility drugs are often used to stimulate egg production, which are surgically removed from the ovaries when mature, and sperm is collected via masturbation. The first baby born with use of this technique was Louise Brown of England in 1978 (Steptoe & Edwards, 1978). Children conceived with in vitro fertilization are often called "test tube babies" by the press and others, but as you can see, the procedure does not even use test tubes (Figure 7-13).

In vitro fertilization
A process in which a mature ovum is surgically removed from a woman's ovary, placed in a medium with sperm until fertilization occurs, and then placed in the woman's uterus. This is usually done in women who cannot conceive because of blocked Fallopian tubes.

FIGURE 7-13   A REUNION OF FAMILIES WHO PRODUCED BABIES THROUGH IN VITRO FERTILIZATION.

About 10,000 babies have been born as a result of in vitro fertilization, but the overall success rate is quite low, about 15–20 percent (Society for Assisted Reproductive Technology, 1993). The average cost of a successful delivery is $67,000 to $114,000 (Neumann, Gharib, & Weinstein, 1994). Many institutes were freezing fertilized eggs in case the first attempt failed, but research has shown that the success rate is higher with fresh fertilized eggs (Levran et al., 1990). The major problem, however, is that eggs fertilized outside a woman's Fallopian tubes simply did not attach to the uterine walls as often as eggs fertilized in a normal manner (i.e., within a Fallopian tube).

A major breakthrough came in the mid-1980s when Dr. Ricardo Asch and colleagues simplified and improved the IVF procedure (Asch et al., 1984). They bypassed the Petri dish by putting eggs and sperm into a pipette and inserting them directly into a Fallopian tube. They called the technique **gamete intrafallopian transfer (GIFT)**. The fertilized eggs implanted in the uterus at a higher rate than with IVF and the overall success rate is about 27 percent (40–50 percent in the best clinics; Society for Assisted Reproductive Technology, 1993). But that is not the end of the story. In order to assure fertilization, Asch's group had fertilization take place in a Petri dish (as with IVF) and then placed the fertilized eggs directly into a Fallopian tube, a procedure called **zygote**

Gamete intrafallopian transfer (GIFT)
A procedure for treating female infertility in which sperm and eggs are gathered and placed directly into a Fallopian tube.

Zygote intrafallopian transfer (ZIFT)
A method of treating infertility caused by blocked Fallopian tubes. An ovum taken from the infertile female is fertilized by sperm from her partner and then transferred to the unblocked portion of a Fallopian tube.

intrafallopian transfer (ZIFT). The success rate is presently slightly lower than for GIFT, but with increasing experience of physicians, the success rates are improving yearly (Society for Assisted Reproductive Technology, 1993). The newest technique involves injecting a single sperm directly into the egg. Preliminary evidence indicates that the success rate for implantation by these punctured eggs is five times greater than with IVF (see Blackman, Dolan, & McDowell, 1991). The first U.S. baby conceived by this technique was born in 1993.

These techniques can also be used to screen preembryos for genetic defects. In 1993, for example, 8-cell preembryos were tested for the deadly Tay-Sachs disease (by removing one cell) and three "clean" fertilized eggs were then placed back in the mother. The couple's first child had died of the disease, but they now know that their new baby, born in 1994, is free of the disease.

These techniques are used for a variety of infertility problems (male or female). If it is necessary, donated eggs or sperm can be used for any of the procedures. However, there are some problems. As with fertility drugs, IVF, GIFT, and ZIFT all have an increased chance of multiple births (Bollen et al., 1991). And in the end, at least half of couples who undergo assisted reproductive techniques still will not conceive.

The biggest obstacle to advancement in this field is social-political-legal. Many people oppose these procedures to treat infertility. The Roman Catholic church, for example, rejects both artificial insemination and in vitro fertilization, proclaiming that procreation must be "a physically embodied love act." Many physicians believe that GIFT will be ethically acceptable to most religious groups (see Mastroyannis, 1993), but that remains to be seen. The U.S. government has refused to fund research on IVF for the last 20 years. Joseph Schulman, a former section director at The National Institutes of Health, said "I can think of no other examples where for a decade and a half a whole area of investigation that has in fact proven itself to be of massive value to thousands and thousands of couples has been pigeonholed" (quoted in Baker, 1990). Studies indicate that most people have favorable opinions of infertility treatments that produce a child that is biologically related to both members of the couple (they have less favorable opinions of interventions that use donor eggs, donor sperm, or surrogacy; Halman, Abbey, & Andrews, 1992). How do you feel about this?

Surrogate mother

A woman who carries a fetus to full term for another couple, agreeing to give the infant to the other couple after it is born. The infant generally represents the union of the sperm from the man and either his partner's ovum or the ovum of the surrogate mother.

SURROGATE MOTHERS

One of the most controversial fertility solutions is surrogate motherhood, sometimes used when a woman cannot conceive or carry a fetus during pregnancy. In this case, a couple may create a zygote through in vitro fertilization, and then have the fertilized egg implanted in the uterus of another woman. In a second form, the surrogate mother is impregnated with the male partner's sperm, usually through artificial insemination. The surrogate mother gives birth, and the infant is raised by the infertile couple. The couple will generally pay for the surrogate mother's medical expenses, along with necessary legal fees. They also will pay the surrogate mother a fee for providing this "service" (usually about $10,000). However, some surrogate mothers have changed their minds after delivery, and a 1987 case involved the rights of surrogate mothers to "back out" of such contracts (the judge awarded custody to the infertile couple). Some states have passed laws that allow surrogacy, while others have attempted to outlaw it. Court tests of these laws continue today. This is certainly one area where laws have not kept pace with the new technology.

It is important that couples attempting to deal with infertility receive counseling about the choices they make, the risks of failures (which are high), the consequences of their decisions, and the specific laws of their state. Some parents who use surrogate mothers may pretend that the child was born to them—a decision that could lead to pain and embarrassment later. Women who want to become surrogate mothers should also consider the emotional cost of having to give up a child they have carried through pregnancy and birth.

DELAYED CHILDBEARING AND ASSISTED REPRODUCTIVE TECHNOLOGY

As women grow older, their fertility declines. For most women, this starts happening as young as 31 years of age (van Noord-Zaadstra et al., 1991). After age 30, the chances of having a healthy baby decrease by more than 3 percent per year. The problem is not with the uterus, but with the decreased quality of eggs as they age. At menopause, you recall, the ovaries stop working entirely and women are no longer capable of reproduction—or at least that was what was thought until recently.

As more and more women have entered careers and chosen to delay pregnancy, they have often been faced with fertility difficulties when they do decide they are ready for motherhood. Today, however, in vitro fertilization (and the related procedures) have allowed even some postmenopausal women to become pregnant and have children. Eggs are donated by a young woman (and thus are usually of high quality) and then in vitro fertilization is attempted to achieve fertilization and implantation. The uterus is kept functional with hormone therapy. One of the first women to become pregnant with this technology was a 42-year-old former cancer patient who had lost her ovaries because of chemotherapy (see Sauer, Paulson, & Lobo, 1992).

More recently, postmenopausal women over the age of 50 have elected to have children by egg donation and in vitro fertilization (see Sauer, Paulson, & Lobo, 1993). In 1993, a 59-year-old English woman gave birth to twins by this technique (eggs were donated by a woman in her twenties). In 1994, a 62-year-old Italian woman gave birth after receiving donated eggs. In the words of Dr. Marcia Angell, executive editor of the *New England Journal of Medicine*, "The limits on the childbearing years are now anyone's guess."

Many people, including many physicians, are debating the ethics and health-related issues of assisted delayed childbearing. The older a woman is during pregnancy, the greater the risk of death to the fetus (or shortly after birth) and of very low birth weight (Cnattingius et al., 1992). There are also risks to the woman herself—diabetes and high blood pressure, for example. These problems might be minimized by careful screening, but what about the ethical considerations? For those who oppose it, proponents offer two arguments. First, there is often a double standard, with many people admiring older men who father children. Why shouldn't women have the same opportunity? Second, qualities like love, experience, and responsibility are more important than age in determining who will be a good mother. As stated by the chairperson of the Council of the British Medical Association, it is better to have "a fit, healthy 59-year-old than an unfit, unhealthy 19-year-old" mother. What qualities do you think make a good mother?

ADOPTION

When a couple cannot conceive and medical technology cannot correct the problem, there are still some options available. Many couples become parents by adopting a child. One difficulty with this option is that the demand for children to be adopted is very high. Long waits (sometimes months or even years) may be required before a couple is able to find and adopt a healthy child. Some couples choose not to wait, and adopt children of other nationalities or disabled children. For caring people, adoption benefits everyone—the couple who so badly want a child, and a child who needs a home, love, and affection.

Adoption
Taking a child into one's family by legal process and raising as one's own.

For information about adoption (including a bimonthly magazine called *Ours*) and support, you can contact Adoptive Families of America, 3333 Highway 100 North, Minneapolis, MN 55422, or call 612-535-4829. ■

SUPERFERTILITY

For some women, having children is apparently very easy. According to the *Guinness Book of World Records*, the most prolific mother alive is Leontina Albina of Chile, who gave birth to 59 children—always triplets or twins. She was one of three triplets sent to an orphanage, but while her two brothers were adopted, she was not. She promised herself that if she ever had children, she would never give them away. Leontina married at age 12 and continued to have children into her fifties.

A word of caution: Recent studies show that women who have had six or more pregnancies are at higher risk for coronary heart disease and cardiovascular disease (Ness et al., 1993). Please take this into consideration if you are planning a large family. ■

KEY TERMS

PERSONAL REFLECTIONS

1. What qualities do you possess that will make you a good parent? Do you have any qualities that might not make you a good parent? What things can you do to prepare yourself to be a good parent?

2. How well suited is your partner to be the mother or father of your child?

3. Do you or your partner smoke, drink alcohol, or take drugs? Do you and your partner eat a well-balanced diet and get ample sleep? What decisions about health can you and your partner make to ensure the health of your baby during pregnancy and afterwards?

4. Make a list of all the words that come to your mind when you think of childbirth, labor, and delivery. Examine your list for negative stereotypical concepts. Are there alternatives?

5. Will pregnancy affect the sexual relationship with your partner? How? Why? Will being parents affect your sexual relationship? How? Why? What steps can you and your partner take to ensure that as parents your sexual relationship will continue to be fulfilling?

6. Imagine that you and your partner have tried to conceive for 5 years. You both have gone through innumerable tests, but nothing seems to work. How do you feel? What would you do next? What options would you consider? What options would you never consider? Why?

SUGGESTED READINGS

Andrews, L. B. (1984, December). Yours, mine and theirs. *Psychology Today*. Perhaps a bit dated, but an excellent discussion of the emotional and legal problems involved with using donors.

Beck, M., et al. (1988, 15 August). Miscarriages. *Newsweek*. Discusses the causes of miscarriage and the most recent medical advances to prevent it.

Begley, S. (1995, 4 September). The baby myth, *Newsweek*, An excellent article on reproductive technology for infertile couples and the low success rate.

Bing, E. (1988). Yes, you can. *Childbirth '88*, vol. 5. Discusses sexual intercourse during pregnancy, assuring women that it is okay. If you want more information, see Bing, E., & Coleman, L. (1983). *Making love during pregnancy*, New York, Bantam.

Burns, L. H. (1987, Fall/Winter). Infertility and the sexual health of the family. *Journal of Sex Education and Therapy*. Discusses the effects of infertility on a couple's sexual health.

Eagan, A. B. (1985, December). 200 years of childbirth. *Parents*. Discusses how childbirth procedures have changed, with a new emphasis on the woman's role.

Garfield, E. (1990). Midwifery: Alternative care for pregnancy and childbirth. *Essays of an information scientist: Science literacy, policy, evaluation, and other essays.* Philadelphia: ISI Press, vol. 11, 150–159.

Garner, M. (1986, June). Fragile Fallopian tubes. *Self.* Discusses the functions and problems.

Kitzinger, S. (1989). *The complete book of pregnancy and childbirth.* New York: Knopf. A paperback book that is both comprehensive and sensitive.

Slawson, M. (1982, March). Drugs and pregnancy: What we know today. *Your Life and Health.* Discusses the potentially serious effects of nonprescription drugs on pregnancy.

CHAPTER EIGHT

Human Sexuality Today

BECOMING A WOMAN/ BECOMING A MAN: GENDER IDENTITY AND GENDER ROLES

WHEN YOU HAVE FINISHED STUDYING THIS CHAPTER, YOU SHOULD BE ABLE TO:

1. DEFINE GENDER IDENTITY AND GENDER ROLE;

2. EXPLAIN VARIOUS BIOLOGICAL INFLUENCES ON GENDER AND GENDER IDENTITY;

3. DESCRIBE THE CAUSES OF HERMAPHRODITISM AND PSEUDO-HERMAPHRODITISM;

4. DEFINE AND DIFFERENTIATE THE CONCEPTS TRANSSEXUAL, HOMOSEXUAL, TRANSVESTITE, AND GENDER DYSPHORIA;

5. EXPLAIN THE FREUDIAN, LEARNING, AND COGNITIVE-DEVEL-OPMENTAL THEORIES OF GENDER IDENTITY DEVELOPMENT;

6. CONTRAST THE DIFFERENCES IN EMPHASIS OF THE INDIVID-UALIST AND MICROSTRUCTURAL THEORIES OF GENDER ROLE DEVELOPMENT;

7. DISCUSS THE DUALISTIC AND UNIDIMENSIONAL MODELS FOR MASCULINITY AND FEMININITY AND THE CONCEPT OF ANDROG-YNY;

8. SUMMARIZE THE DEVELOPMENT OF GENDER ROLES IN CHILD-HOOD AND ADULTHOOD; AND

9. DESCRIBE, FROM A MICROSTRUCTURAL VIEWPOINT, HOW GEN-DER ROLES HAVE EVOLVED IN THE UNITED STATES.

HOW DOES A PERSON BECOME A WOMAN OR A MAN? HOW DO WE LEARN THAT WE ARE MALE OR FEMALE? What does it mean to be "masculine" or "feminine"? Is it appropriate for a woman to ask a man for a date? If a father sees his son playing with a doll, what should the father do? Where do our ideas about "acting like a woman" or "acting like a man" come from? Before these questions can be answered, you must learn the distinction between two terms—"gender identity" and "gender role."

Gender identity is your sense of self as being a male or a female, while **gender role** includes everything you feel, think, say and do that shows (to yourself and others) that you are, in fact, a male or female.

Gender identity
One's subjective sense of being a male or a female. This knowledge is usually acquired by the age of 3.

Gender role
Behaviors that one's society considers to be appropriate for males or females.

In other words, gender role is the way you express your gender identity. Gender identity and gender role are not two different things, but rather different aspects of the same thing (Money & Tucker, 1975). Gender identity is the inward experience of your gender role, and gender role is the outward expression of your gender identity.

Kelly and Worell (1977) view gender roles as involving two different traits or sets of characteristics—"masculinity" and "femininity." These two characteristics were once viewed as opposites, and psychological tests for masculinity and femininity measured people along one scale. It was believed that if an individual scored high on masculine traits, he or she would not show any feminine traits (see Spence & Helmreich, 1978).

Today, researchers believe that the characteristics of masculinity and femininity are present in both genders, but to different degrees (Spence, Helmreich, & Stapp, 1974). Bem (1974) developed the Bem Sex Role Inventory to measure the amount of masculinity and femininity dimensions within an individual's gender role. She noted that individuals could be characterized as masculine or feminine if they scored high on one dimension and low on the other. For example, a high score on the femininity dimension and a low score on masculinity would classify a person as "feminine." A person having high scores on both dimensions would be classified as **"androgynous."** The term androgynous comes from the Greek words *andro* for male and *gyn* for female. Some see this combination as socially desirable (Spence et al., 1975). The concept of androgyny implies that it

Androgyny
The ability of an individual to display a variety of personality characteristics, both masculine and feminine, depending on whether a trait or behavior is appropriate for a given situation. It is often viewed as a positive characteristic that gives an individual greater adaptability.

is possible for a person to be both assertive and compassionate, logical and emotional, depending on what is most appropriate for a particular situation. In addition, Bem claimed that some people scored low on both dimensions. Such individuals would be labeled as "*undifferentiated.*" These combinations of femininity and masculinity are summarized in Table 8-1.

Undifferentiated
Individuals who are low on both masculine and feminine traits.

Gender-role stereotypes are oversimplified, rigid beliefs that all members of a particular gender have distinct behavioral, psychological, and emotional characteristics. A person is considered "sex-typed" if he or she endorses a relatively high amount of sex-stereotyped characteristics and claims to not have or to not value the other type of characteristics (Worell, 1978). For example, a man would be sex-typed if he chose only to display masculinity in himself and preferred to not show signs of femininity. In contrast to the sex-typed individual is the androgynous person. An androgynous person is capable of integrating both masculinity and femininity into his or her gender role. A model of androgynous gender roles involves not only the expression of both masculine and feminine behaviors within the same person, but also the belief that this type of gender role would be encouraged (Marecek, 1977).

Stereotypes
Oversimplified, preconceived beliefs that supposedly apply to anyone in a given group.

In this chapter, you will learn about the forces that shape both gender identity and gender roles. These forces are biological and social, internal and external, involving both genetics and learning. Theorists differ in the importance they give to the influence of these different forces. As always, it seems that most theorists agree that it is the interaction of such forces that ultimately determines gender identity and gender role. I will begin the chapter with a discussion of how gender identity is formed, focusing first on biological aspects of this process. The issue of "nature versus nurture" in the formation of gender identity will be explored. You will learn of instances where an individ-

TABLE 8-1
BEM'S SEX ROLE CLASSIFICATIONS

	HIGH FEMININITY	LOW FEMININITY
HIGH MASCULINITY	Androgynous	Masculine
LOW MASCULINITY	Feminine	Undifferentiated

ual's gender identity conflicts with his or her biological sex. Psychological theories of gender identity formation are elaborated upon, including Freudian theory, learning theory, and cognitive-developmental theory. Finally, the development of gender roles and various related theories will be presented, and those forces shaping our concepts of masculinity and femininity will be discussed. ■

BIOLOGICAL INFLUENCES ON GENDER IDENTITY

How do we end up as a boy or girl at birth? Genetics certainly plays an important role, but hormones are equally important.

THE ROLE OF CHROMOSOMES

A human cell normally has 23 pairs of **chromosomes**, rod-shaped structures that determine a person's inherited characteristics. Eggs and sperm have only half the normal genetic material (one chromosome from each of the 23 pairs). Thus, when an egg and sperm unite (called **conception**), the resultant single cell will again have the normal 23 pairs. One of these pairs determines whether a person is anatomically male or female. *Females usually have two X chromosomes (XX), while males usually have one X and one Y chromosome* (XY). Thus, it is the sperm from the male that determines the genetic sex of the child, and this is determined at the moment of conception. However, sometimes individuals with an XX combination are male and other individuals with an XY combination are female. How is this possible? Researchers have determined that a smidgen of the Y chromosome—a gene called SRY (sex-determining region of the Y chromosome)—determines maleness (Sinclair et al., 1990; see Sultan et al., 1991). This piece is missing from XY females' Y, and it is present on XX males' X. More recently, it has been found that a gene on the X chromosome—a gene called DSS (dosage sensitive sex reversal)—may help determine femaleness (Bardoni et al., 1994).

In some cultures it was legitimate for a husband to divorce his wife if she did not have a male baby (e.g., King Henry VIII, King Louis II). Today, some couples attempt to increase their chances of having a boy by having the woman douche with baking soda, by having intercourse as close as possible to the time of ovulation, or even by wearing boots to bed. Needless to say, none of these have proven reliable. More recently, however, preselection of biological sex has been made possible by separating the X and Y sperm by filtering them through liquid albumin (a protein) and then performing artificial insemination (Glass & Ericsson, 1982). This procedure has proven to be very controversial from both ethical and religious viewpoints (e.g., if most couples preferred male offspring, which is the case in

> **Chromosomes**
> Rod-shaped structures containing the genetic material that determines a person's inherited characteristics.

many cultures, there would soon be an oversupply of boys if everyone used this technique), but it appears to be gaining acceptance (Jancin, 1988).

CHROMOSOME DISORDERS

There are over 70 known irregularities involving the sex chromosomes and approximately one in every 426 people is born with sex chromosome abnormalities (Nielson & Wohlert, 1991). For example, in one out of every 500 live male births, there is one or more extra X chromosomes (XXY or XXXY), a condition known as *Klinefelter's Syndrome*. These biological males tend to be tall with long arms, have poor muscular development with enlarged breasts, a small penis with shrunken testes, low sexual desire, and mental and academic impairment (Mandoki et al., 1991). Males can also be born with an extra Y chromosome (XYY). These men are also very tall, tend to be mentally dull, and are less fertile than other males. One study reported that there were more XYY males in prison for violent crimes than would be expected (Jacobs et al., 1965), but subsequent research has questioned this finding.

Turner's Syndrome is a condition in which there is only one X chromosome (XO) and occurs in about one in every 2000 live births (Stratakis & Kennert, 1994). As a result, the ovaries never develop properly, and these women cannot reproduce. Because of the absence of ovarian hormones, they do not menstruate or develop breasts at puberty either. These females are generally short with a webbed neck and broad chest, but are of normal intelligence. *Triple-X Syndrome females* (XXX), on the other hand, may not appear abnormal but are often retarded or mentally disturbed.

One of the most interesting sex chromosome disorders involved Stella Walsh, an internationally renowned athlete who won an Olympic gold medal in the women's 100-meter dash in 1932 and a national pentathlon in 1954 (see Figure 8-1). After her death in 1980, it was found that some of the cells in her body were XX, but others were XY. She had nonfunctional male sex organs, but she had been raised and lived as a female.

Fortunately, the vast majority of us are born with the correct number and combinations of sex chromosomes. However, as you have learned, having an XY chromosome combination does not guarantee that a

FIGURE 8-1   STELLA WALSH WON AN OLYMPIC GOLD
MEDAL IN THE WOMEN'S 100-METER
DASH IN 1932. AFTER HER DEATH, IT
WAS DISCOVERED THAT SHE HAD BOTH XX
AND XY CELLS.

baby will be anatomically a male at birth. Hormones are also critically important in the determination of one's gender.

THE ROLE OF HORMONES

As two researchers put it, "Nature's rule is, it would appear, that to masculinize, something must be added" (Money & Ehrhardt, 1972). This something is **testosterone**, which must be produced at a critical stage of embryological development (i.e., during the first 2 months after conception) in order for an XY combination to result in an anatomically male baby.

Embryos cannot be distinguished as male or female for the first few weeks of development. A pair of primitive gonads develop during the fifth and sixth weeks that have the potential for developing into either ovaries or testes. At this stage, the embryo also has two duct systems: (1) the **Wolffian duct system**, which if allowed to develop will become male structures, and (2) the **Mullerian duct system**, which if allowed to develop will

Wolffian duct system
A primitive duct system found in embryos, which if allowed to develop, becomes the male reproductive system.

Mullerian duct system
A primitive duct system found in embryos, which if allowed to develop, becomes the female reproductive system.

become female structures (see Figure 8-2). If the primitive gonads were to be removed at this stage of development, the baby would always be born anatomically a female, even if it were genetically XY.

Normally, the SRY gene on the Y chromosome triggers the transformation of the primitive gonads into testes during the seventh week of gestation. The newly developed testes begin to secrete testosterone, which promotes the development of the Wolffian duct system into the male internal reproductive system. The masculinizing hormone is also responsible for the development of the external genitalia a few weeks later. What happens to the Mullerian duct system in these male embryos? The testes secrete an additional substance called **Mullerian-inhibiting substance**, which causes these ducts to shrink.

Mullerian-inhibiting substance
Chemical secreted by the testes during embryological development that causes the Mullerian ducts to shrink and disappear.

What happens to embryos with an XX combination (genetically a female)? If there is no Y chromosome (and thus no chemical substance to convert the primitive gonads into testes), the primitive gonads will eventually develop into ovaries. The absence of large levels of testosterone results in the Wolffian duct system shrinking and the Mullerian duct system develops into the female reproductive system.

In summary, it would appear that *unless there are high levels of male hormones at a critical stage of prenatal development, nature has programmed everyone for female development*. In the vast majority of births, the baby's genetic and anatomical sex are matched. Occasionally, however, a different pattern of development may be seen.

ABNORMALITIES IN DEVELOPMENT

Hermaphroditism is a condition in which a person is born with both male and female reproductive systems as a result of the primitive gonads failing to differentiate properly during the embryonic stage (see Blyth & Duckett, 1991). The name is derived from the Greek mythological figure Hermaphroditus, who merged with the nymph Salmacis to form a single body with male and female genitals. Hermaphrodites are usually genetic females, and even though a uterus is almost always present, they often have an ovary and Fallopian tube on one side and a testicle and a vas deferens and/or epididymis on the other (see Figure 8-3). The external genitalia are usually ambiguous in appearance, but because the phallus is often enlarged, nearly two thirds of these individuals are raised as boys, with complications arising at puberty when they begin to develop breasts and men-

Hermaphrodite
A person with both male and female reproductive systems as a result of the primitive gonads failing to differentiate properly during embryological development.

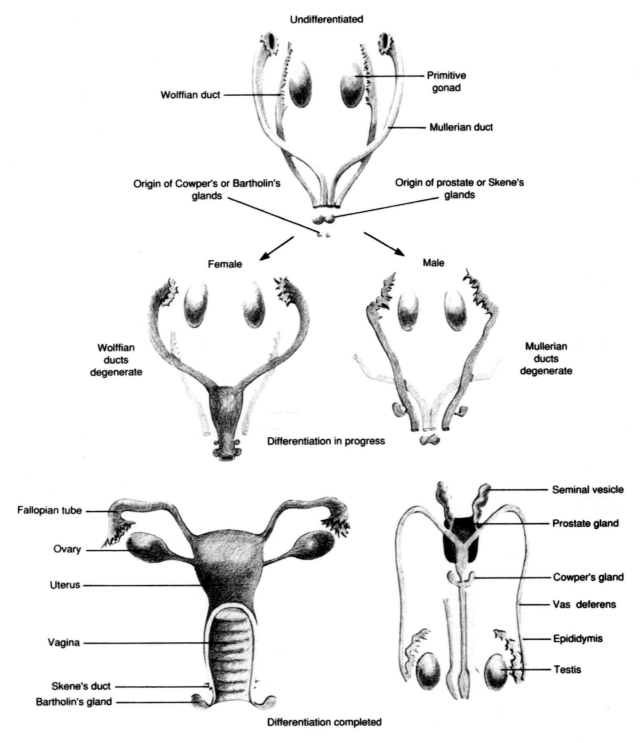

FIGURE 8-2   PRENATAL DIFFERENTIATION OF THE INTERNAL REPRODUCTIVE SYSTEMS IN MALES AND FEMALES.

struate. Fortunately, this is a very rare condition with fewer that 100 recorded cases.

More common is a condition known as **pseudohermaphroditism**, in which a person with an XX or XY chromosome pattern is born with the proper set of gonads (ovaries or testes, respectively), but whose external genitalia are either ambiguous or that of the other sex. In females, the most common cause is known as *adrenogenital syndrome* (AGS, also known as *congenital adrenal hyperplasia*), in which the adrenal glands secrete too much masculinizing hormone during fetal development. The internal organs are normal, but the genitals are masculinized (i.e., the clitoris and labia are enlarged) so that even

Pseudohermaphroditism

A condition in which a person is born with ambiguous genitalia as a result of hormonal abnormalities. (See also adrenogenital syndrome and androgen insensitivity syndrome.)

Adrenogenital syndrome

A condition in females in which the adrenal glands excrete too much testosterone during fetal development, causing masculinization. This includes enlargement of the clitoris and labia, so that the genitals are sometimes mistaken for those of a male.

FIGURE 8-3   HERMAPHRODITISM. THIS GENETIC FEMALE HAS ONE OVARY AND ONE TESTICLE AND HAS ALWAYS LIVED AS A MALE.

physicians sometimes mistake them for boys at birth (see Figure 8-4). If the problem is not recognized and corrected early, the excess adrenal hormones will continue to masculinize the individual during subsequent development.

The first treatment for this condition, developed in the 1950s, included administration of the adrenal hormone cortisone and plastic surgery to correct the appearance of the genitals. Early treatment, combined with being raised as a female, generally leads to masculinized girls developing female gender roles. However, many of them are reported to show tomboyish behavior as children (Ehrhardt & Baker, 1974; Money & Ehrhardt 1972)—of course, tomboyish behavior can be due to other factors as well—and to have fewer fantasies about pregnancy and motherhood during adolescence (Ehrhardt et al., 1984). Nevertheless, the vast majority have a heterosexual orientation as adults, and some who receive treatment later marry and have

FIGURE 8-4   ADRENOGENITAL SYNDROME IN AN INFANT FEMALE.

babies. Many of these women state that the cortisone treatment reduces their sexual desire. Because cortisone reduces the production of androgens (Ehrhardt, Evers, & Money, 1968), it is believed that cortisone was indeed responsible for the decrease in their sexual interest.

The most common cause of pseudohermaphroditism in males is known as *androgen insensitivity syndrome* (sometimes called *testicular feminization syndrome*) in which the testes secrete normal amounts of testosterone, but the body tissues do not respond to it (Kaplan & Owett, 1993). As a result, a clitoris, labia, and short vagina develop, but the internal female structures fail to develop because the testes still secrete Mullerian duct inhibiting substance (see Figure 8-5). These individuals are generally raised as girls. In fact, unless the undescended testes are felt in the groin during infancy, the condition is often not discovered until the individual fails to start menstruating as a teenager. (Undescended testes are a risk factor for the development of cancer and are usually removed by surgery.) These individuals can be very feminine in appearance and behavior, and despite the fact they cannot conceive, they have made excellent adoptive mothers (Money & Ehrhardt, 1972). They are attracted to male sexual partners and clearly have a female gender identity.

Androgen insensitivity syndrome

A condition in which the testes secrete normal amounts of testosterone during male embryologic development, but the tissues do not respond to it. As a result, a clitoris, labia, and a short vagina develop, but the internal female structures do not develop because the testes still secrete Mullerian duct inhibitory substances.

In 1974, 38 genetic males in the Dominican Republic were discovered who suffered from a type of androgen insensitivity syndrome. Prenatally, their testes had produced testosterone and Mullerian duct inhibiting substance so that their internal structures were male. However, because of an inherited enzyme deficiency, the testosterone was not converted into dihydrotestosterone, which is necessary for proper formation of the external genitals (the condition is therefore sometimes called *DHT deficiency*). As a result, they had a very small penis that looked like a clitoris, an incomplete scrotum that looked like labia, undescended testes, and a short closed vaginal cavity.

Eighteen of these children were reared as girls, but at puberty, when their testes started secreting large amounts of testosterone, their voices deepened, muscles developed, the testes descended, and their "clitoris" grew to become a penis. Although the urethral opening was located on the perineum and not the tip of the penis, they were capable of ejaculating sperm.

How do you think you would feel if you were being raised as a girl, but suddenly started growing a penis at puberty? The culture in these remote villages has a strong patriarchal macho bias. Girls are forced to stay home and do chores,

FIGURE 8-5   ANDROGEN INSENSITIVITY SYNDROME IN A GENETIC MALE.

while boys are given considerable freedom, including sexual freedom as adults. Parents of these children generally rejoiced when they discovered that they had an unexpected son. The villagers called them guevote ("penis at twelve"). Under these circumstances, it is probably not surprising that 16 of them decided to become males and subsequently developed a strong sexual interest in girls (Imperato-McGinley et al., 1979). Knowing that other children in the village had the same problem made the transition easier. Do you suppose that the transition would have been so easy in a country like the United States? In fact, most American children with this disorder choose to remain female when their bodies become masculinized (Rubin, Reinisch, & Haskett, 1981). ■

NATURE VERSUS NURTURE IN ACQUIRING GENDER IDENTITY

Is gender identity determined mostly by biology or mostly by teaching the values of society (socialization) through child-rearing practices? Much debate has taken place over this question, although most researchers feel that neither factor by itself can totally account for gender identity development. Consider, for example, the following case history.

Identical twin brothers were circumcised at 7 months of age, but due to a surgical mistake, one of the twins lost his penis. After considerable deliberation, the boy's parents decided to raise the child as a girl. The child's name was changed, and the child was encouraged to play "girls'" games with "girls'" toys. Surgical procedures were begun to reconstruct the genitals to make them female. According to Money (1975), the child readily achieved a female gender identity and gender role. The twin brother developed traditional masculine traits. However, later interviews with the "female" twin revealed many problems as a teenager. Her classmates made fun of her (masculine) appearance and as a result, she had few friends and felt like an outcast (Diamond, 1982). The psychiatrist following her development found that she had great difficulty in her attempt to become a woman (Williams & Smith, 1979). She believed, for example, that boys had a better life than girls and wanted to become a mechanic. Thus, in this case, the effects of both biology and environment

are again apparent. Being reared as female resulted in a successful gender identity reversal, but the individual (who was anatomically and hormonally a male at birth) continued to show interests typically associated with males. After an extensive review of the literature, Money (1987b) reached the conclusion that hormonal forces (both before birth and during puberty) and the effects of socialization are influential in creating an eventual gender identity for each individual.

SEXUAL DIFFERENTIATION OF THE BRAIN

Are male brains different from female brains, and if so, could this account for differences in behavior? In the 1970s, it was discovered that parts of an area of the brain called the hypothalamus (see Chapter 3) were different in male and female rats (Gorski et al., 1978). The difference wasn't noticeable at birth, but became apparent shortly thereafter as a result of differences in testosterone levels (Goy & McEwen, 1980). Destruction of these areas affects male components of sexual behavior in rats (DeJong et al., 1989), though only modestly. Recent studies indicate that other parts of male and female rat brains may also differ.

Studies of humans show that men's and women's hypothalamus also differ (e.g., Swaab, Gooren, & Hofman, 1992). But because these differences are not noticeable in newborns, it raises some interesting questions. Do biological (brain) influences determine behavior, or do social stimuli (e.g., the different manner in which people interact with boys and girls) alter both the psychology and biology of persons (see Breedlove, 1994 for a review)? This is a fascinating new area of research, and we will return to it in the chapter on sexual orientation, but it is too early to make definite conclusions.

TRANSSEXUALISM

A person's gender identity sometimes does not match his or her biological sex. This individual has one biological sex, both internally and externally, and yet feels

Transsexual

A person whose gender identity does not match his or her biological sex.

that he or she is actually a member of the opposite sex. Such a person is a **transsexual**. He or she feels intense distress with his or her anatomy, a condition known as **gender dysphoria** (American Psychiatric Association DSM-IV, 1994; Pauly, 1990). People with gender dysphoria feel that they are "trapped in the wrong anatomic body"

Gender dysphoria

The feeling of being trapped in a body of the opposite gender.

(Pauly, 1985). This feeling of a mismatch between gender identity and anatomy often begins at a very early age (*primary transsexuals*) although in some cases it does not arise until adulthood (*secondary transsexuals*). There is some evidence that even secondary transsexuals begin to develop their mismatched gender identity in their early years (Doorn, Poortinga, & Verschoor, 1994).

Male-to-female transsexuals (who are anatomically male) are three to six times more common than female-to-male transsexuals (Stockard & Johnson, 1980). What are some of the criteria for transsexualism (see Bradley et al., 1991)? Persistent discomfort with their bodies and bodily functions is almost always the case (e.g., boys disgusted with their penises and testicles and distress with facial and body hair, girls not wanting to grow breasts or menstruate or a rejection of urinating in a sitting position). More importantly, there is an intense desire to be the opposite sex. In cases of primary transsexualism, children prefer to cross-dress and participate in the games and pastimes of the opposite sex.

It is important to understand that transsexualism has to do with gender identity, not sexual orientation—it is not the same as homosexuality. Homosexuals have gender identities that agree with their anatomical gender just as often as for heterosexuals. Most transsexuals, in fact, do not regard themselves as homosexual. Most male-to-female transsexuals, for example, are attracted to men because they wish to be desired and loved as a woman by a heterosexual male.

Transsexuality is also not the same as transvestism. A transvestite, as you will learn in Chapter 14, dresses in the clothing of the opposite sex in order to achieve sexual arousal. However, a transvestite does not want to change his or her biological sex and does not experience gender dysphoria. Transsexuals crossdress as a means of attempting to be more comfortable psychologically with their appearance, not for sexual arousal. Some males are sexually aroused by the thought of themselves with female attributes and may even undergo breast augmentation (Blanchard, 1993), but this too is not the same as gender dysphoria.

The cause(s) of transsexualism is not certain. However, given the dissatisfaction that transsexuals feel toward their biological gender and their difficulty in finding comfortable sex partners, what kind of help is available? Traditional psychotherapy has not been successful in alleviating gender dysphoria (Tollison & Adams, 1979). Thus, some individuals have turned to surgery to deal with the problem (Pauly & Edgerton, 1986).

Prior to undergoing *sex reassignment surgery* (a "sex-change operation"), individuals are carefully screened by psychological testing. In addition, they are usually required to live for 1 or 2 years as a member of the "opposite" sex (i.e., living as a member of the opposite anatomical gender) before undergoing surgery (Chong, 1990). For example, a female-to-male transsexual would take on a male identity and wear men's clothing, etc. Sex hormones are also administered to create a growth of secondary sex characteristics of the opposite sex. The male-to-female transsexual is given estrogen, which will result in the development of larger breasts, the formation of fatty deposits in the hips, and a change in skin tone. The female-to-male transsexual is given testosterone, which will cause a deeper voice, increase facial and body hair, and inhibit menstruation.

During this period, the transsexual can prepare family, friends, and acquaintances for the planned gender change. It is common for there to be a great deal of anxiety, apprehension, and discomfort in the way that family members and friends react to the idea of transsexual surgery. It is best for these feelings to be confronted and dealt with before the surgery. Likewise, obtaining legal recognition of a gender change can be attempted during this try-out period. Many courts in the United States have refused to recognize individuals as really being the other gender (different from their chromosomal or anatomical gender) after a sex reassignment operation (Hurley, 1984). Marriages following the operation may also not be legally recognized if the marriage partner is the same gender as the transsexual was before the surgery.

In male-to-female transsexual surgery, the penis and testes are removed first. Next, a vagina is created using pelvic tissue. Sensory nerves in the skin of the penis are relocated inside the new vagina. Sexual intercourse is possible after the operation, though lubricants may have to be used. There are also reports that a full range of sexual responses, including orgasm, have been achieved after surgery (Money & Walker, 1977), although greater proof of these claims is needed. Male-to-female surgery is a much simpler procedure than that of female-to-male.

In female-to-male surgery, the uterus, ovaries, and breasts are removed. Some individuals have no further changes made, while others decide to have an artificial penis created. The new organ is made using flaps of skin and muscle (from the groin, forearm, or other places) or by clitoral enlargement (Hage, Bloem, & Suliman, 1993). The new penis is incapable of normal erection, although artificial means of creating erections are possible, such as those used in treating erectile dysfunctions (Hage et al., 1993).

One of the most famous cases of sexual reassignment was that of an ophthalmologist named Richard Raskind (Richards & Ames, 1983). Richard Raskind had attended college and medical school, became a highly ranked tennis player, and married. He hated his maleness and genitalia and reported the agony that he felt in his presurgery dilemma. "As a child . . . I would pray every night that I could be a girl. I knew then that I wanted Renee as my name. It means reborn" (*People* magazine, 1976). He eventually decided to have a sex-change operation and become Renee Richards (Figure 8-6).

After the operation, Renee felt more comfortable with her gender identity, but found that female tennis players did not want to let her compete in the top professional tournaments. They claimed that Renee's physical abilities gave her an unfair advantage. However, a judge ruled that Renee could compete on the professional women's circuit. She did so for several years and later became a tennis coach, most notably for Wimbledon tennis champion Martina Navratilova. In a more recent case (Docter, 1985), a man decided to undergo transsexual surgery at the age of 74. He had been happily married for 37 years, but had had lifelong fantasies of becoming a woman. He finally decided to become a woman after his wife had been dead for several years.

The purpose of sex reassignment surgery is to lessen the feeling of gender dysphoria in the transsexual and to contribute to his or her emotional health and well-being. Some researchers claim that the surgery does not result in psychological benefits (Lindemalm et al., 1986; Meyer & Reter, 1979), while others indicate that

FIGURE 8-6   TENNIS PLAYER RENEE RICHARDS AS SHE APPEARED AFTER A SEX-REASSIGNMENT OPERATION (RIGHT) AND BEFORE AS DR. RICHARD RASKIND (LEFT).

the vast majority of transsexuals achieve satisfactory results with the procedure (Blanchard et al., 1985; Pauly & Edgerton, 1986). In a more recent study, none of the biological females or 36 homosexual males interviewed regretted having had a sex-change operation, and only four of 14 heterosexual males regretted it (Blanchard et al., 1989). In male-to-female transsexuals, adjustment after surgery is sometimes made difficult by scars on the breasts and other physical reminders that the person is "not a real woman" (Ross & Need, 1989). Kockott and Fahrner (1988) compared male-to-female and female-to-male transsexuals. They found that female-to-male transsexuals more often had close ties to siblings and parents, established lasting relationships more frequently with partners of the same biological sex, and were more sexually satisfied compared to male-to-female transsexuals. These differences in partnership behaviors were not changed as a result of surgery.

More information is needed before we have a complete understanding of the impact of transsexual surgery. It is important to remember that *the surgery is used to help confirm an individual's previously established gender identity* (Edgerton, 1984). Such gender confirmation can be heavily influenced by the society within which the transsexual lives. The need for external validation of a person's sense of self varies from individual to individual, with the social acceptance of transsexuality varying across settings and times. It seems reasonable to state that surgery will help those most who can find both internal and external confirmation of their gender identities after the operation. ■

PSYCHOLOGICAL THEORIES OF GENDER IDENTITY DEVELOPMENT

Three major psychological theories of development claim that the parent is an important role model who influences the development of gender identity.

FREUDIAN THEORY

Freud believed that psychological development was influenced primarily by sexual development. He called sexual energy *libido* and thought that the location of the libido (the area of the body responsible for sexual pleasure) changes over time. The part of the body where the libido is focused is called an "erogenous zone." The primary erogenous zone, according to Freud, depends on which *stage of psychosexual development* the individual has reached. In the first year of life, the mouth is the primary erogenous zone, so Freud called this the *oral stage*. Pleasure is derived from sucking and from exploring things with the mouth.

The second stage is called the *anal stage*, which lasts from age 1 1/2 to about age 3. According to Freud, the primary source of pleasure in this stage comes from holding in and expelling feces. Conflicts arise when parents attempt to teach their children to control their bowel movements in ways that are socially acceptable. Children at this time may fight parental control and toilet training.

The third stage, called the *phallic stage*, lasts from about age three to five. Freud believed that gender identity is learned at this time. It is during this stage, according to Freud, that boys begin to derive pleasure through masturbation and as they do so, they begin to sexually desire their mothers and come to view their fathers as powerful rivals who might punish them for these desires by taking away their penises. This fear is called "castration anxiety," and is based on the fact that previous sources of pleasure have already been taken away through weaning and toilet training. In addition, because girls and women do not have a penis, this further suggests that the penis may be taken away. Gender identity formation for boys takes place by resolving these conflicts, known as the *male Oedipus complex*. This was named after the principal character in the Greek play *Oedipus Rex*, in which a man kills the king of a city and then marries his queen, who turns out to be his own mother. Following the rule, "If you can't beat them, join them," boys try to become like their fathers and adopt their fathers' gender identity. This process occurs unconsciously and is called **identification**. In this way, boys try to assure that for the future, they, too, will be able to fulfill their sexual desires, just like their fathers.

Identification

The adoption of the sex roles of the same-sexed parent by a child. In Freudian theory, identification resolves the Oedipus complex.

Freud has a more complicated explanation for how gender identity is learned in girls. In the *female Oedipus complex*, according to Freud, when a girl realizes that she has no penis, she feels envious and angry, a state which he referred to as "penis envy." The girl blames her mother for this, and wants to possess her father in order to replace the mother. Once she realizes that this cannot happen, she unconsciously identifies with her mother as a means of ensuring that she, too, will be able to fulfill her sexual desires in the future.

Most psychologists do not believe that Freud's theories are accurate descriptions of development. Many feel that his ideas are blatantly sexist and were the result of thinking founded on Victorian ideas of morality and sex roles (e.g., Balmary, 1982; Lerman, 1986). Nevertheless, he was one of the first modern thinkers to discuss the possibility that children are sexual and to relate this to gender identity development (see Figure 8-7).

LEARNING THEORY

Learning theory emphasizes the acquisition of new associations. An important type of learning that may be involved in acquiring gender roles is that of **operant conditioning**, which is a type of learning similar to training. For example, a boy may be praised by a parent for not crying after he falls down and "acting like a man"; he may be yelled at or punished for putting on his mother's lipstick; or he may be allowed to stop doing his homework in order to help his father fix the car. In each of these three examples, the boy is being "trained" to behave in a "masculine manner." He is learning a gender identity and a gender role, as he will associate good things with "masculine behavior" and negative associations (or even punishment) with "feminine behavior." For a girl, encouragement and praise may follow the display of "feminine behavior," while "boyish behavior" may result in being ignored or being shown disapproval by parents. Thus, behaviors that are rewarded will continue, and behaviors that are not rewarded will eventually stop.

Operant conditioning

According to learning theory, a type of training thought to be responsible for acquiring sex roles by rewarding "masculine" behavior in boys and "feminine" behavior in girls and not rewarding behaviors associated with the opposite sex.

Research with children shows that they do not always actually have to perform a behavior to learn it (Bandura & Walters, 1963; Mischel, 1970). Most young boys observe their mothers putting on lipstick,

Girls

1. Penis envy

Desire for father

2. Identification with mother

3. Gender identity

Psychoanalytic Theory

1. Attachment to mother as main rewarder and punisher

2. Identification with mother through modeling

3. Gender identity

Behavioral Theory

1. Gender identity

2. Modeling of mother

3. Attachment to mother

Cognitive Theory

Boys

1. Desire for mother

Fear of father's retaliation

2. Identification with father

3. Gender identity

Psychoanalytic

1. Attachment to father as major rewarder (and punisher-controller)

2. Identification modeling of father

3. Gender identity

Behavioral Theory

1. Gender identity

2. Modeling of father

3. Attachment to father

Cognitive Theory

FIGURE 8-7   DEVELOPMENT OF GENDER IDENTITY IN GIRLS (TOP) AND BOYS (BOTTOM), ACCORDING TO FREUDIAN, LEARNING, AND COGNITIVE-DEVELOPMENTAL THEORIES.

but may never do it themselves because they learn from observing others that the behavior is met with ridicule or other punishment.

Another type of learning described by social learning theory involves **imitation**. Children love to imitate their parents and learn what "daddy" and "mommy" do simply by watching their parents. It is always interesting to ask children, "What kinds of things are daddies supposed to do?" and "What kinds of things do mommies do?" "Do daddies wash dishes?" "Do mommies use a saw and hammer nails?" Answers to these questions will tell a lot about the gender roles that children learn from their parents. (How did you answer these questions?) Children also will try to do the things that their parents do (i.e., imitate them), although the amount of time between when the behavior is observed and when they eventually imitate it can be quite long (Figure 8-8).

> **Imitation**
>
> Following the behaviors of someone taken on as one's model.

Operant conditioning and social learning theory do not have to be competing theories. Imitation may cause a child to first try a specific behavior, but the rewards or punishments that follow that behavior will determine if the child attempts the behavior again (B. F. Skinner, personal communication).

COGNITIVE-DEVELOPMENTAL THEORY

Cognitive theory views infants as "information seekers." Rather than talking about an "oral stage of psychosexual development" to explain why crawling infants put things into their mouths, cognitive theory claims that this is done because infants can "know" things and acquire information about the world this way. To a crawling infant without language, the world can be divided into things that can and cannot be put in the mouth. It can also be known in terms of things that taste good, bad, or have no taste. Gender is another category into which children can sort themselves.

This theory (Kohlberg, 1966) states that the concept of "male" is first learned by observing others. For example, father is a male and because he is more like father than mother, boys begin to think of themselves and their fathers as males. Boys become motivated to seek out information about what a male should do and how he should behave, imitating a ready source of information about male conduct from their fathers. The mother becomes the prime source of information about what is appropriate "female behavior" for girls.

At this early age, children's idea of gender is "concrete," based on physical cues like hairstyle and dress. Cognitive theorists say that while most children have learned that they are a "boy" or a "girl" by the age of three, they do not yet have an understanding of **gender constancy**. Gender constancy is the knowledge that one's sex is constant and will not change. For example, a 4-year-old boy may think that if girls have long hair, and he lets his hair grow long, he will change into a girl. A 4-year-old girl may believe that when she wears jeans and a football helmet, she is a boy, but when she takes them off, she may believe that she changes back into a girl again. Because they do not yet have an understanding of gender constancy, young boys may say that they will become mamas when they grow up and girls may say they'll be daddies. This is a natural thing to believe until gender constancy has been acquired, which *usually happens by age 6 or 7.*

> **Gender constancy**
>
> The knowledge that one's gender identity is constant and will not change. This is usually acquired by age 6 or 7.

Stagnor and Ruble (1987) point out that cognitive theory is similar to psychoanalytic theory in that both describe development as occurring in stages (see Figure 8-7). Both describe a "motivation" to complete development. In psychoanalytic theory, identification is driven by the need to reduce anxiety and maintain a good self-image. In cognitive theory, the motiva-

FIGURE 8-8   CHILDREN OFTEN LEARN GENDER ROLES AND A GENDER IDENTITY BY OBSERVING AND IMITATING THEIR PARENTS.

tion is a need to attain mastery over the behaviors typical of one's gender.

Both cognitive theory and social learning theory claim that imitation is extremely important in development. But social learning theory states that behavior is done because of the rewards that follow. Cognitive theory claims that behaviors are done because just doing the behavior is rewarding by itself. In other words, social learning theory states that gender understanding occurs because of the learning process. Cognitive theory states that a need to understand one's gender causes a child to want to learn (Stagnor & Ruble, 1987). ∎

GENDER ROLES

THEORIES OF GENDER ROLE

Our sexual anatomy is biologically determined, but what about our behaviors and emotions? Are differences between men and women biologically determined? Males are often considered to be more active and aggressive than females. Is this perhaps due to higher levels of the male hormone testosterone or is it because aggression in males is tolerated more than in females (see Lips, 1992)? One point of view, called *biological essentialism*, holds that biological influences establish predetermined limits to the effects of cultural influences. But how strong is the evidence?

One of the most frequently cited series of studies involved women who had been exposed before birth to diethylstilbestrol (DES)—a masculinizing hormone that used to be given to pregnant women who were at risk for miscarriage. The hormone does not noticeably masculinize the body (and thus children would not be treated differently from other children), but in non-human species, prenatal exposure to this hormone has a masculinizing or defeminizing influence on behavior (for example, on rough-and-tumble play). Early studies with DES-exposed women were inconsistent, with some reporting increased masculinity and lessened orientation toward parenting, and others finding no effect (Ehrhardt et al., 1989; Hines, 1982; Lish et al., 1991). However, later studies by some of the same researchers led them to conclude that prenatal exposure to DES in human females did not cause behavioral masculinization or defeminization of childhood play and adult gender-role behavior (Lish et al., 1992). Recall, too, the Dominican Republic children who were raised as girls until 12 years old, but then made a successful transition to male gender identity and gender roles when they "grew" a penis. Money's (1987a) studies of the twin boy whose penis was amputated and who was then raised as a girl suggest that both biological and cultural effects are important, but for the moment, there is considerably more evidence for cultural influences (Lips, 1992). With this in mind, I will follow Mirra Komarovsky's (1992) usage of the term **gender** to "refer to the social construction of femininity and masculinity."

A **gender role** is a set of norms about the behavior and attitudes of men and women. Gender roles vary from culture to culture (see Box 8-A), a strong indication of the importance of the socialization process. How, then, are gender roles acquired?

Risman and Schwartz (1989) describe two major perspectives on gender role development: individualist versus microstructural theory. **Individualist theory** is based on the idea that an individual's personality is created relatively early in life. There is a set of personality traits developed early on that do not change much over the life cycle; these traits then determine an individual's expression of masculine or feminine behavior. Thus, an adult female may choose not to enter a "masculine" career, such as welding, because she cannot be motivated to start such a career. Her personality structure and self-concept prevent her from making such a choice.

> **Individualist theory**
>
> The theory that personality traits develop early in life and do not change much over the life cycle; these traits then determine an individual's expression of masculine or feminine behavior.

Microstructural theory, on the other hand, is based on the notion that it is society's expectations of male and female behavior that predict how they will behave. Thus, rather than believing that masculinity or femininity is expressed because of internal forces such as rigid personality traits, microstructural theory indicates that men and women would behave identically if society had identical expectations of them. Gender role differences are therefore constructed by the way men and women interact within their environment and with each other. Furthermore, the nature of these interactions can change over time and in different settings.

> **Microstructural theory**
>
> Stresses the role of the external environment in shaping gender roles.

In the introduction to this chapter, you learned that prior to the 1970s masculinity and femininity were viewed as opposite ends of a unidimensional continuum (Hathaway & McKinley, 1943; Strong, 1936; Terman & Miles, 1936). In this bipolar model, a person who was high in masculinity would have to be low in femininity, and vice versa.

This conceptualization of masculinity and femininity was revolutionized in 1973 by Anne Constantinople, who proposed that masculinity and femininity were independent constructs. This led to the theory of androgyny, which said that a person could be both

BOX 8-A

CROSS-CULTURAL PERSPECTIVES: GENDER ROLES

Today in the United States, boys and girls are often treated differently beginning at birth. Consider, for example, the blue or pink name tags that many hospitals use to designate a boy or girl baby. However, this was not always the case. Until the early part of this century, infant boys and girls were treated very much alike in things like dress (both wore gowns) and hair style (long curls). The socialization process of emphasizing masculine or feminine qualities did not begin until the age of 2 or 3 (Garber, 1991).

Some other cultures do not emphasize differences between boys and girls for several years after birth. Some African cultures even have nonmasculine titles (e.g., ``woman-child'') for boys (Whiting, 1979). In these cultures there is usually a ritualized initiation ceremony for boys (generally between the ages of 7 to 12) to eliminate any identification with female gender roles and emphasize male alliance and gender roles (Munroe, 1980). These rituals often include painful practices such as circumcision of the penis (see Box 2-C). Some of these cultures have rituals for girls as well, and usually focus on their role in fertility (Schlegel & Barry, 1979, 1980). However, there are other cultures that allow even adult males to express their ``feminine'' side, often in a practice called couvade in which males are secluded (like women) and act out giving birth (Paige & Paige, 1981; Whiting, 1979).

Whether it begins in infancy or later in childhood, the large majority of cultures emphasize nurturant behavior in females and achievement and self-reliance in males (Barry, Bacon, & Child, 1957). But even this is not universal. In fact, completely opposite gender roles can be found in cultures living in close proximity to one another. Margaret Mead (1935, 1975), for example, described a tribe in New Guinea, the Tchambuli, in which men were considered too weak to do hard physical labor, were emotional, gossipy, easily embarrassed, and were primarily artistic in their activities. In that culture, women were independent, aggressive, and made all the important tribal decisions. In another New Guinea culture, the Arapesh, qualities that many Americans would consider ``feminine'' are reinforced in both males and females. As a result, Arapesh men and women are peaceful, cooperative, and nurturing. Just 80 miles away in the Mundugumor society, ``Both men and women are expected to be violent, competitive, aggressively sexed, jealous, and ready to see and avenge insult, delighting in display, in action, in fighting.''

Notice that one of the characteristics expected of Mundugumor women is that they be sexually aggressive. This is generally true for women in many cultures in the South Pacific. Recall the Mangaians, for example (Marshall, 1971; see Chapter 1). In Western culture, Victorian morals and ideals stressed that women be passive in sexual nature.

What can be concluded from cross-cultural studies such as these? Mead concluded:

> ``Many, if not all, of the personality traits which we have called masculine or feminine are as lightly linked to sex as are the clothing, the manners, and the form of head-dress that a society at a given period assigned to either sex . . . . The evidence is overwhelmingly in favor of social conditioning.''

masculine and feminine, and that this was the healthiest of all gender roles (Bem, 1974; Block, 1976; Spence, Helmreich, & Stapp, 1975). According to Bem (1974), "Both historically and cross-culturally, masculinity and femininity seem to have represented two complementary domains of positive traits and behaviors, a cognitive focus on 'getting the job done' (a masculine or *instrumental* orientation) and 'an affective concern for the welfare of others' (a feminine or *expressive* orientation)."

Androgynous individuals are viewed by these researchers as being healthy because of their flexibility, demonstrating instrumental or expressive orientations as the situation demands:

"...behaviorally flexible with respect to all manner of gender related phenomena. As such, they are willing and able to exhibit masculine behaviors, feminine behaviors, or both as situationally appropriate. Individuals with sex-typed personalities, on the other hand, will tend to avoid or exhibit lower levels of cross-sex-typed behaviors."

(Helmreich, Spence, & Holahan, 1979)

Recently, there have been some challenges to the dualistic theory of gender and questions about androgyny. A recent study, for example, found support for both the dualistic and unidimensional models. Biernat (1991) studied the development of gender stereotypes when making social judgments of others and concluded that young children view gender in dualistic terms, but as they grow older come to view gender as a unidimensional construct. Others have even questioned the Bem Sex Role Inventory, the most popular measure of androgyny. One study found that while the items on the Inventory did, in fact, measure two different personality characteristics, the two characteristics no longer had anything to do with masculinity and femininity—they suggested the terms "instrumental" and "expressive" (Ballard-Reisch & Elton, 1992). One possibility is that people's perceptions of gender roles have changed over the last 20 years. Interestingly, Bem (1979) predicted the destruction of the concept of androgyny:

"If there is a moral to the concept of psychological androgyny, it is that behavior should have no gender. But there is an irony here, for the concept of androgyny contains an inner contradiction and hence the seeds of its own destruction. Thus, as the etymology of the word implies, the concept of androgyny necessarily presupposes that the concepts of femininity and masculinity themselves have distinct and substantive content. But to the extent that the androgynous message is absorbed by the culture, the concepts of femininity and masculinity will cease to have such content and the distinctions to which they refer will blur into invisibility. Thus, when androgyny becomes a reality, the concept of androgyny will have been transcended."

GENDER ROLE DEVELOPMENT DURING CHILDHOOD

Regardless of the particular theory that researchers support on how gender identity and gender roles are acquired, they do agree that this process occurs and that society's expectations become a part of the individual's own set of attitudes and behaviors. The process of internalizing society's beliefs is called **socialization**, which begins at birth (e.g., different colors are used to represent a baby boy or a baby girl).

Socialization
The process of internalizing society's beliefs.

What kinds of attitudes do children learn from our society about gender roles? Cognitive theory, described earlier, shows that young children have difficulty understanding complex concepts. Their early learning often consists of dual categories, such as "good and bad" or "big and small." It is not surprising, then, that young children's ideas about gender roles reflect concrete, simple ideas, dividing behaviors or traits into either "masculine" or "feminine." In our society, there are stereotypes regarding gender roles. **Stereotypes**, you recall, are oversimplified, preconceived beliefs that supposedly apply to anyone in a given group.

The stereotype for the female gender role is that of a person who nurtures and cares for others (Figure 8-9), is passive and dependent, cooperative, seeks social approval, and is expressive in showing her emotions. The male gender role stereotype emphasizes independence, dominance, competition, aggression, success, achievement, and emotional repression ("big boys don't cry" or "the strong, silent type"). Research done many years ago showed that most people at that time believed men and women differ in these ways (Broverman et al., 1972).

Harvard psychologist Jerome Kagan said, "If I showed you a hundred kids aged 2, and you couldn't tell the sex by the haircuts, you couldn't tell if they were boys or girls" (quoted in Shapiro, 1990). If this is true, when do gender roles start developing and what (or who) is responsible?

Parents who assume "traditional" (stereotypic) gender roles behave differently toward their children (McHale & Huston, 1984). In these families, mothers act as the caregivers, while the fathers act as a playmate

However, in another condition boys were asked to play with dolls or kitchen sets the way girls would, while girls were asked to play with army war games or cowboy outfits the way boys would. This was done while parents were out of the room. The experimenters were interested in studying how the parents would react when they entered the room and saw the types of toys the children were playing with. Mothers reacted similarly, regardless of whether the toys fit gender role stereotypes or not; but fathers showed much greater negative reactions when they found their children playing with toys that did not fit gender roles. This was especially true when boys were playing with "girls'" toys, as the fathers often interfered with play or showed other signs of negative emotions in those situations (Langlois & Downs, 1980) (see Figure 8-10).

"My Godson, Mikey, will definitely grow up with the idea that men are the head of the households and that women are 'under' them. My uncle encourages Mikey to play football and run around in the house, yet when he and his sister dance around it is not acceptable. Mikey is only allowed to play 'boy' games. He is not allowed to cook, because that is what a girl does. . . . ''

"For as far back as I can remember my father only allowed us to do 'masculine' type things. Sports, cars, outdoor activities, etc. He never allowed us to play with girls. On one occasion I distinctly remember playing with two girl neighbors. My father came looking for me and found his son playing with dolls. For quite a while after that I was known as his 'faggot son.' I couldn't have been more than 10. I never became the 'faggot' son, but I did leave that day with a low self-esteem that I carried with me for quite some time.''

(from the author's files)

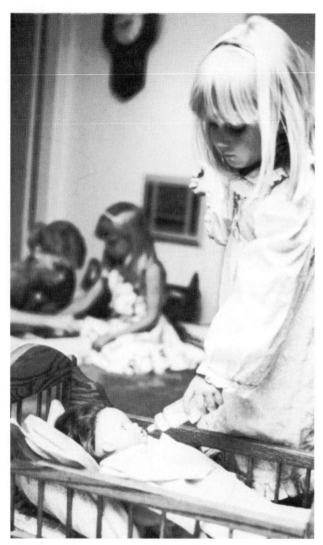

FIGURE 8-9   CHILDREN BEGIN LEARNING ROLES IN INFANCY. THEY OFTEN SHOW GENDER STEREOTYPED BEHAVIOR EVEN BEFORE THEY HAVE A FIRM GRASP OF GENDER IDENTITY OR GENDER CONSTANCY.

to their infants (Lamb, 1986; Parke & O'Leary, 1976). Fathers, however, may be more likely to treat their children in gender-stereotyped ways (Etaugh, 1983; Fagot & Leinbach, 1987). Fathers emphasize strength and coordination of newborn sons and the beauty and softness of newborn daughters (Krieger, 1976; Rubin, Provenzano, & Luria, 1974). This is done in spite of there being little difference between the behavior of newborn boys and girls. Fathers are also more likely to offer toys that are stereotypically male to their newborn sons (Jacklin & Maccoby, 1983).

In one study, preschoolers were presented with stereotypic gender-role toys. In one condition, children were given toys that matched stereotypic gender toys.

Other adults treat male and female children in different ways as well. In another study, individuals were shown an infant and asked to make observations about its appearance and behavior. The types of comments made were very different, depending on whether they were told the infant was a boy or a girl (Condry & Condry, 1977). The socialization process in gender role development is seen everywhere in the child's environment. The toys available for boys are often action-oriented, while girls are given more passive playthings. Take a walk through a toy store and look at the toys being offered. It is interesting to see how toys are packaged. Many have pictures of children playing with the

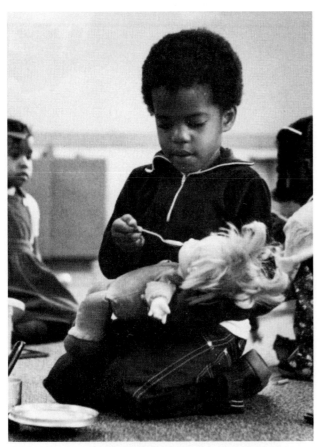

FIGURE 8-10   HOW WOULD YOU REACT IF YOU FOUND YOUR YOUNG SON PLAYING WITH A DOLL? DO YOU THINK THAT PLAYING WITH DOLLS CAN TEACH BOYS BEHAVIORS THAT WILL BE USEFUL WHEN THEY BECOME ADULTS?

product on the front of the box. How many toys have pictures of both boys and girls playing with the same toy? (Very few.) Have you ever wondered why boys' bicycles have to be different from girls' bicycles? (They don't.)

Here is a little experiment that you can try on your own. Ask a boy playing with a toy soldier or a plastic model of a superhero if he is playing with dolls. He probably will say "no." (Boys in our culture don't often play with dolls, but they do play with "action figures.") Give the boy a toy soldier and a male "fashion figure," such as the one who usually serves as a "boyfriend" to a famous female doll, and then ask the boy to point to the toys that are dolls. He will probably point to the "fashion figure." Now give the soldier's clothes (and weapons) to the "fashion figure" and make the soldier wear the other toy's clothes (and accessories). Then ask the question again. Which one will the boy now think is the doll? What do you think? Why? Some psychologists think that boys should learn at an early age how to care for infants by playing with baby dolls. Learning

at an early age how to put on diapers, etc., can help make a man respond in a more useful way after a real baby is born. Some fathers refuse to change diapers because (1) it is disgusting work, and (2) it is "women's work." It is true that changing diapers can sometimes be disgusting, but it is also necessary. It is not true that this is "women's work." If a man can change the dirty oil in his car, he should be able to manage changing a dirty diaper. Women should also remember that the same holds true for them. Girls can learn to use tools and change the car oil just as easily as they can learn to change diapers. Dirty oil and dirty diapers are neither masculine nor feminine. They just need to be changed.

Picture books, stories, and television all contribute to the development of gender roles. For example, children's stories often depict boys or men as being adventuresome and courageous, while girls or women are often in need of rescue or are in charge of keeping the house and fulfilling "domestic" duties (Weitzman et al., 1972). Very few girls or women are the central characters in cartoons, with female cartoon characters usually taking passive roles or playing the part of comforter and supporter to male characters. This is true for most television shows as well ("Roseanne" being one noted exception) and thus it should not be surprising that people who watch a lot of TV generally believe in more stereotyped gender roles (Lips, 1992).

The socialization process begins at an early age. In one study, it was found that boys aged 2 1/2 believed that girls don't fight and that they like to clean house. Girls of the same age believed that boys don't cry and that they like to fight. Boys and girls aged 2 and 3 believed that boys like to help their dads, like to hit, and to break the rules. They thought that girls liked to help their moms and didn't hit (Kuhn, Nash, & Brucken, 1978). As early as 14 months of age, infants play with toys that are gender stereotyped more often than with other toys (O'Brien & Huston, 1985). Thus, children show gender stereotyped behavior even before they have a firm grasp of gender identity or gender constancy.

Bem (1981, 1983) has proposed that children cognitively organize the world according to gender. She calls this **gender schema**—ideas about gender roles that children create from their interactions with their environment. Objects in the environment are often treated as masculine or feminine. Why, for example, do we often regard dogs as masculine and cats as feminine? Languages such as French or Spanish classify all nouns as either masculine or feminine. Gender schemas can influence decisions about what activities to take part in or learn about, including things like affection, which really has nothing

Gender schemas

Ideas about gender roles that children create from their interactions with their environment.

to do with one's sexual anatomy. Unfortunately, many American men regard displays of affection as effeminate, even toward their own children (see Salt, 1991):

> **"**I know my father cares about his children, but he never displays any kind of affection toward me (male) or my brother, only to my sisters. I think that is one big experience that I missed during my childhood. . . . ''

> (from the author's files)

Children organize their world according to gender starting at ages 2 or 3 (Hort, Leinbach, & Fagot, 1991). In fact, it may be the first social category used by children (Kohlberg & Ullian, 1974). Bem (1983) concludes that "gender has come to have cognitive primacy over many other social categories because the culture has made it so."

When children reach school age, peers and teachers become powerful influences on the process of socialization and gender role development (Moller, Hymel, & Rubin, 1992). Children quickly identify individuals who act "different." Boys or girls who do not display behaviors similar to the gender roles adopted by most of their peers may be singled out for teasing or ridicule. Interestingly, "tomboy" behavior in girls is usually far more tolerated by peers, teachers, and parents than "effeminate" behavior in boys. It is much easier to carry the label of a "tomboy" than that of a "sissy." Peers will apply great social pressure against boys who show "girlish" behavior (Birns & Sternglanz, 1983). Physical play at recess is tolerated more in boys than girls, who may be asked to keep clean and stay "ladylike." Girls may cry more quickly than boys and use it as a means of getting help. Crying is "okay" for girls and may be a reaction to hurt and frustration as well as a call for assistance. Boys may be encouraged to "act like a man" by crying as little as possible. Textbooks and history books in particular have emphasized the central, dominant role of men and the supporting role of women. Even the activities and chores that teachers assign to children in the classroom are often determined by stereotypic gender roles (Wynn & Fletcher, 1987). As boys and girls approach junior high school age, they tend to participate less in girl-dominated activities and more in male-dominated activities (Sandberg & Meyer-Bahlburg, 1994).

Gender roles in adolescents have begun to change in recent years. It is now more common for girls to ask boys out. One study, for example, found that while it was once uncommon (and considered improper) for girls to call boys on the telephone, it is now very common (Anderson et al., 1995). The authors were able to identify 1965–1980 as the period in which this gender role changed (Figure 8-11). However, there are still

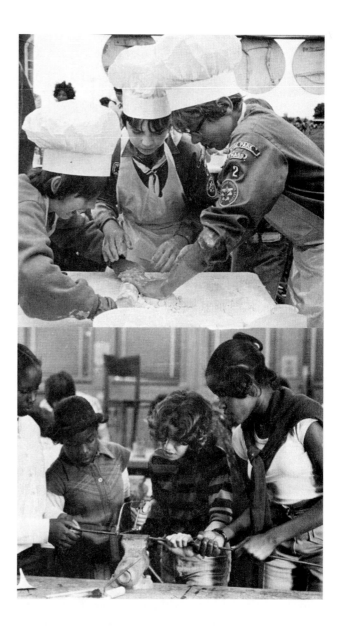

FIGURE 8-11   IN THE PAST, TRADITIONAL GENDER ROLE EXPECTATIONS WOULD NEVER HAVE ALLOWED THESE BOYS AND GIRLS TO ENJOY THESE EXPERIENCES.

some double standards regarding sexual aggressiveness. Many people, for example, continue to view sexually active females as "sluts" and sexually active males as "studs."

In spite of some changes away from the traditional gender role expectations, stereotypic gender roles are often still in force during puberty and are reinforced by peer pressure (Doyle, 1985). For example, many teenage girls still view being popular and attractive to boys as the primary way to enhance their self-worth. For many teenage boys, achievement in athletics and/or in career-related activities is the primary means of gaining self-esteem (Offer & Offer, 1975).

I will refer to two recent studies to help summarize what we know about the development of gender roles in childhood and adolescence. There may be little noticeable difference between boys and girls before the age of 2, but there is no question that most children have embraced gender stereotypes by the age of 4. By three or four, children know sex stereotypes about clothing, toys, games, and work, and by the age of 4 or 5 most have stereotyped occupational goals (Huston, 1983). According to Yale psychiatrist Kyle Pruett, "There are rules about being feminine and there are rules about being masculine. You can argue until the cows come home about whether those are good or bad societal influences, but when you look at the children, they love to know the differences. It solidifies who they are" (quoted in Shapiro, 1990).

However, Pruett's own work shows that children don't necessarily have to develop strongly stereotyped views (see Shapiro, 1990 for a review). He followed the development of children in 16 families where the mothers worked full time and the fathers were mostly responsible for caring for the children. The children had strong gender identities of being male or female, but more relaxed views of gender roles than their friends. Pruett commented, "I saw the boys really enjoy their nurturing skills. They knew what to do with a baby, they didn't see that as a girl's job, they saw it as a human job. I saw the girls have very active images of the outside world and what their mothers were doing in the workplace . . . " (quoted in Shapiro, 1990).

Pruett also feels that fathers benefit by assuming more responsibility in raising their children. He says, "The more involved father tends to feel differently about his own life. A lot of men, if they're on the fast track, know a lot about competitive relationships, but they don't know much about intimate relationships. Children are experts at intimacy. After a while the wives in my study would say, 'He's just a nicer guy' " (Shapiro, 1990).

The second study investigated how, and to what extent, young children and adolescents use gender stereotypes to make judgments about the characteristics of individual males and females (Biernat, 1991). It was found that young people rely on gender labels as judgment cues to the same degree from kindergarten to college years, but, as they grow older, they increasingly rely on more individuating information as well. In other words, as people grow older, they are more able to rely on information about an individual to make judgments, even when the information is not consistent with stereotyped gender roles.

GENDER ROLE DEVELOPMENT IN CHILDREN RAISED IN SINGLE-PARENT HOUSEHOLDS

The traditional American family has been declining in number since the 1960s. In 1970, 85 percent of chil-dren lived with two parents, but by the early 1990s less than three fourths did so (U.S. Census Bureau). This was especially true among African-Americans. Fewer than a third of black children lived with one parent in 1970, but by the early 1990s nearly 60 percent lived with one parent—their mothers in all but a few cases.

What happens to the development of sex roles in children raised by a single parent? Several early studies concluded that a critical factor in sex role development was the identification of children with their fathers, by either interacting with their fathers or by watching their parents interact (Biller, 1969; Biller & Bahm, 1971; Roberts et al., 1987). Recall, too, that it is fathers more than mothers who are concerned that their children act in gender stereotyped ways (Etaugh, 1983; Fagot & Leinbach, 1987). So, what happens to children raised in a household in which the father is absent? In short, children who are raised in single-parent households are more likely than those raised in "intact" households to become androgynous (Russell & Ellis, 1991). This is true not only for boys, but for girls as well (Biller & Weiss, 1970; Covell & Turn-bull, 1982; Stephens & Day, 1979).

Androgyny is generally considered to be a positive characteristic (see next section). If so, one study concluded "that parents who model adaptive yet nontraditional roles may play an important role in the healthy development of their children" (Russell & Ellis, 1991).

GENDER ROLE DEVELOPMENT IN ADULTHOOD

Among adults today, gender roles are in transition (Figure 8-12). Women have not only entered the work force in larger numbers, but they have gained entry into careers and attained access to higher level positions previously dominated by males. In 1960, fewer than 20 percent of women with children under the age of 6 were employed outside the home, but by the late 1980s over half of women with young children were in the labor force and three fourths of mothers with school-age children had jobs outside the home (Bureau of Labor Statistics). Thus, the idea that being a mother means giving up having a career is no longer true and is not influencing women to the extent it did in the past (Gerson, 1989). Nonetheless, gender stereotypes may not have changed much during the 1970s and 1980s (Bergen & Williams, 1991) and double standards often still exist even in two-career families. For example, even if a woman works outside of the home, she generally assumes more responsibility for house cleaning, meals, and child care than does her male partner (Berk, 1985). Men with traditional stereotyped attitudes are likely to evaluate their marriages negatively if "forced" into egalitarian roles (McHale & Crouter, 1992). Women are also more likely to encounter sexual harassment, at work (see Chapter 15). Many women in the workplace must be able to balance a feminine

FIGURE 8-12 WHAT IS CONSIDERED TO BE
MASCULINE AND FEMININE IN ADULT
GENDER ROLES IS FAR LESS RIGID
TODAY THAN IN PAST GENERATIONS.

appearance with a businesslike appearance, while men are far less concerned with how they dress for work.

Women who work in the home may not have the same chance for self-gratification or self-fulfillment as men, who often serve as both breadwinners and heads of households. Many people still consider work in the home to be "not as important" as work outside the home. In 1990, for example, students at Wellesley College objected to then First-Lady Barbara Bush giving the commencement address because she had been a stay-at-home wife and mother. According to a 1990 survey conducted for *Time* magazine, 86 percent of young men wanted a mate who was hardworking and ambitious. While the same survey found that nearly half of young men wanted to spend more time at home to raise their children, the number of "househusbands," whose primary responsibility is work in the home, remains small, as career achievement is still used to determine the worth of individuals, rather than the ability to maintain a home and care for others.

What is considered to be masculine and feminine in adult gender roles is becoming far less rigid or distinct than was seen in past generations. Some research-

ers see these trends as a movement toward **androgyny**. As you recall, this is the ability of individuals, regardless of gender, to display a variety of personality characteristics where one can be both assertive and compassionate, both instrumental and expressive, and both masculine and feminine, depending on whether a trait or behavior is appropriate for a given situation. Thus androgyny is often viewed as a positive characteristic that gives an individual greater adaptability (Spence et al., 1975). Taylor and Hall (1982) concluded that in American society, androgynous or masculine individuals show greater social adaptation and adjustment, regardless of their gender. They believe, for example, that women who show masculine characteristics may initially not be rewarded for acting that way, but those who continue to do so are eventually given greater rewards and prestige than women with mostly feminine characteristics. In a now classic study, Spence and Helmreich (1972) found that people (including liberal women and constructive men) liked women best who were competent and doing "masculine" things.

Nevertheless, the push for gender equality has taken its toll on some individuals. Rotheram and Weiner (1983) found that among dual-career couples, dual-career status increased relationship satisfaction, but also increased personal stress. By 1990, 80 percent of people believed that it was difficult or very difficult to balance marriage, children, and a career (the 1980s "superwoman" ideal) and, in a shift from previous surveys, many women rated a happy marriage as more important to them than a successful career (*Time* magazine survey). It is obvious that different women can have the same roles (mother, wife, worker), yet have different experiences in the quality of each (Baruch & Barnett, 1986).

Some researchers have noted that as individuals develop as adults, they acquire more complex sets of gender roles. For example, the fact of fatherhood may force men to acquire more experience being nurturing, while working outside of the home may force women to be more assertive and independent. Labouvie-Vief (1990) further states that with more complexity in gender role patterns of behavior comes a greater chance for the integration of gender roles. Labouvie-Vief, Hakim-Larson, and Hobart (1987) found that both men and women who were more developmentally complex also were less likely to approve of immature coping strategies. Although men and women arrive at developmental complexity by different routes, the adaptive end point for both genders is an integration of gender roles, that is, gender roles tend to converge in adulthood (see Blanchard-Fields and Suhrer-Roussel, 1992). Thus, gender role development extends well into adulthood with cross-gender role (i.e., behavior of the opposite sex) characteristics often emerging among both older men and women. This has been referred to as a *transcendent model* of gender role development, rather than a *traditional model* of gender role development (Fischer & Narus, 1981). Individuals with a large number of both masculine and feminine characteristics will then be better able to cope with a wide range of life challenges and social situations than will those individuals with a more rigid or narrow range of gender role patterns of behavior.

GENDER ROLES AND SEXUAL RELATIONS

Victorian-era physicians and sexologists such as Freud and Havelock Ellis believed that male and female sexuality were very different. Female sexuality was viewed as more passive, weaker, and less fulfilling than was male sexuality. Many Victorian physicians did not even believe that women had orgasms, you recall (see Chapter 4). More recently, Kinsey's surveys (1948, 1953) and the physiological studies by Masters and Johnson (1966) have emphasized that male and female sexuality are very similar. Although some feel that socio-political influences may also have contributed to the conclusion that male and female sexuality are similar (Irvine, 1990), a recent study found that there were, in fact, no gender differences in sexual satisfaction (Oliver & Hyde, 1993).

However, there are still some gender differences. As a general rule, men have considerably more permissive attitudes about casual sex than do women (Oliver & Hyde, 1993). The authors of this study suggest that this gender difference helps explain why the same behavior may be interpreted as reasonable by a man, but as harassment by a woman. Also, if people have stereotypic views that men ought to be more sexual than women, this can result in negative labeling of those who don't conform. If a man does not appear to engage in sex as often as others, he may be viewed as inadequate and "unmanly." Conversely, if a woman demonstrates that she really enjoys sex and likes having sex frequently, she may be considered by some to be "easy" or a "slut." Clearly, there is a wide range of individual differences in the way both men and women feel and act with regard to sex. There is no "right" amount of sex drive and/or sexual activity for either men or women.

One commonly held stereotype is that women should be nurturant, loving, and accepting, while men should not express deep feelings and emotions.

"Recently I was involved in a relationship with a very 'sex-typed' guy.... Every time I would try to talk to him about how I felt about things or let him know how my emotional needs were going unfulfilled, he would change the subject or dismiss the whole discussion as being 'sissified.'"

(from the author's files)

All people of both genders need to express their feelings and emotions and be able to communicate them. The image of man as "strong and silent" robs him of a fundamental part of his humanity and robs his partner of a true companion. Goldberg (1979), author of the book *The New Male*, has written extensively about the harmful effects of men trying to live up to the so-called male role. He states that the entire male socialization process is contrary to the human needs of men and is hazardous to their health and well-being. Good communication leads to happier, healthier, and often more satisfying sexual relations and greater intimacy (Rubin et al., 1980). Men and women are first and foremost human beings, and we need to strive to live up to human roles rather than rigid male or female roles. It is this shared humanity that should be the focus of our relationships and the strong foundation upon which they are built.

In Chapter 10 you will learn that many parents deny (by hiding) their sexuality to their children. As a result, some people view parents, and parenthood, as less sexual than others. For people with extreme stereotyped views of gender roles, this can create a conflict when their own partner becomes a parent:

"My husband and I were in what seemed an ideal marriage. Not only was our coupling wonderful, but we also shared an extremely intense sexual relationship as well. 2½ years into our marriage we were informed that we were going to be parents. My husband was great; he was so attentive and supportive during the time I carried our child. . . .

He was a proud father. However, things were never the same between us after the birth of our daughter. My husband insisted I stay home and raise her as he did not want her brought up in nurseries or with baby sitters. Soon, he was obsessed with work. . . . He was working 18–20 hrs. a day 6 days a week. . . . There had been little sex between us since the baby, but I attributed it to his long hours. . . .

I started sensing that my husband was distant. I told him he was growing away from us instead of with us. I asked him what was wrong. . . . He said that ever since I became a mother that he no longer could see me as a sexual partner. I was a mom and that was something sacred that should be put on a pedestal. He said it was impossible to think of me in a sexual way anymore. . . ."

(from the author's files)

Recall from Chapter 4 that in some cultures, females' genitals are mutilated, in part because males view female sexual desire as being inconsistent with their roles as wives and mothers. In our own culture, childbearing often symbolizes the acceptance of traditional gender roles (Nock, 1987). An androgynous person is less likely to have conflicting gender views about sexuality and parenthood, and to view his or her partner as both nurturant (whether female or male) and sexual.

MICROSTRUCTURAL THEORIES OF GENDER ROLE DEVELOPMENT

Many adults today were raised with traditional role expectations through socialization in their childhood and adolescence, but are currently being influenced by recent trends in society toward more androgynous gender roles. Such "mixed signals" can result in confusion about what is truly masculine or feminine, with some people claiming that even making such a distinction is unnecessary. In order to better understand how individuals react to times of transition and major social changes that influence traditional gender roles, we shall examine the research based on microstructural theory within the sociological literature.

Sociologists are interested in the processes of group dynamics and change. Microstructural theory, like learning theory in psychology, stresses the role of the external environment in shaping attitudes and behavior. The focus of this type of research is less on the individual and more on large-scale social institutions. In looking at how gender roles have evolved in our country's past, we may better understand what is happening today.

Cancian (1989) and Kimmel (1989) have examined the way in which gender roles have evolved in America. Cancian (1989) argues that love became feminized during the 1800s when the United States was becoming industrialized. Early American society did not have different gender roles for the expression of love, nurturance, or dependency. According to Cancian (1989), this was because the home was the center of the educational, economic, and social activities of the family, where both men and women shared in all aspects of family life. The Church admonished men and women to be nurturant and loving to each other, as this ensured a stable home environment. However, with increased industrialization men began to earn their living away from home, and the economic activities of men and women began to split. Men were viewed as breadwinners who left the home to compete in a harsh outside world filled with competition and danger. Women continued to stay at home, and the home began to be viewed as a retreat for the husband after finishing his day's labors. The home became an idealized place of peace and affection, in contrast to the business world. Because the woman maintained the home, the qualities of nurtu-rance, love, and devotion became associated with being feminine. The work that a wife did at home was either ignored or not considered to be as important or meaningful as work done outside the home. Perhaps this was due to the fact that women failed to receive monetary compensation for their labors within the household. Independence, success, achievement, competition, and self-control came to be valued as masculine characteristics as the male pursued work outside the home.

Cancian (1989) believes that our present gender roles evolved as a means of achieving control. Workers in industrial settings were dependent upon companies for their wages, while the individual male was viewed as being independent, tough-minded, and thriving in an impersonal, affection-free business world. This fostered the illusion that the individual male still had control over his life through the display of masculine characteristics, especially in the home. Women were dependent upon wage-earning husbands, but this dependency was hidden by the feminine gender role of women in the form of being nurturant, emotional, passive, and physically weak, although morally pure. Women who worked outside of the home were almost always single, and once married would retire to do the housework of the feminine wife and/or mother. It should be noted that the 1800s saw the opening of the American frontier, and this was seen as a man's job, calling for independence, self-reliance, and the ability to do without female influence.

Kimmel (1989) indicated that the end of the 1800s saw a great amount of challenge to traditional masculine and feminine gender roles. Kimmel argues that social changes in the late 1800s gave rise to the "New Woman," who was single, economically independent, and highly educated, and who did not believe that a woman should have to become dependent on a man in order to be feminine. The New Woman was part of a growing women's movement, which attempted to challenge traditional gender roles and create a more equal distribution of power within American society. In an attempt to combat traditional gender roles, some women tried to act and dress in a less restrictive manner.

According to Kimmel (1989), men reacted to the rise of the women's movement in one of three ways. The first way was an antifeminist response, with an emphasis on the need to return the woman to the home. A second reaction was a pro-male reaction, which involved segregating boys and girls into separate schools and other social institutions in order to "preserve" boys' masculinity from the corrupting influence of feminism. The third reaction was pro-feminist. Some men joined with feminists to promote equality among the sexes. Kimmel notes that past definitions of masculinity and femininity help reproduce power relationships between the sexes, and when those power relationships are challenged, gender roles are questioned as well and may begin to change.

We have similar forces at work in our society today. Women are seeking more control over job opportunities, the same amount of pay as men receive for comparable work, more freedom in the conduct of their personal affairs, and in general, more equality between the sexes. Reactions to today's feminist movement are similar to the ones described at the turn of the century, for gender roles are still being seriously questioned and redefined within our society. Qualities that are believed to characterize men and women appear to be undergoing a dramatic change. The initial force behind the changes has come from the women's movement, which asserts that the traditional system of sex-role differentiation is outmoded and destructive (Marecek, 1977). Pleck (1976), a leading authority on the male gender role, notes that women are challenging their traditional gender-role patterns and redefining their roles and their place in society. In turn, men in our society have begun to reexamine their own gender roles. This can cause a conflict within a man between what he was taught to be appropriate for his gender role when he was a boy versus society's current expectations for the "New Man."

Pleck (1976) refers to this as the *gender* or *sex-role strain perspective*. This perspective contends that the problem for the male gender role is that men in our society are confronted by contradictory demands and expectations in their early socialization process and their adult life experience. For example, men are conditioned to control their emotions and be unexpressive in order to be strong and to be a so-called real man, while the adult male role (i.e., marital role, parental role) calls for the ability to express feelings and to share affection with their spouses and children.

Perhaps it is more difficult for men to adopt non-traditional role behaviors, as it is harder for men who wish to act in ways that may be labeled feminine. In order for men to move away from traditional gender role behavior, it has been noted that men need not only to feel such change is desirable and beneficial as far as improving the quality of their lives, but they also need to receive support from their spouses, other men, and the workplace (Canavan & Haskell, 1977). Pleck (1976) believes that in redefining their gender roles, men need to make changes in their relationships to women, other men, their children, and to their work environment.

The rise in the divorce rate, the availability of contraceptives, the large number of women in the work force (especially working mothers), increased sensitivity to civil rights and personal freedoms in the 1960s, and many other forces have contributed to challenging such traditional attitudes as "a woman's place is in the home" and "a man's home is his castle." Despite the many gains women have made personally and professionally, feminists are sometimes still considered radical by those individuals satisfied with gender roles received from previous generations. Additionally, women often still get paid less to do the same work as men, have fewer opportunities for higher level leadership roles in corporate or government settings, and must contend many times with conflicting sets of expectations from parents, friends, bosses, etc., about what is appropriate feminine behavior.

Microstructural theories see gender roles as based on gender relationships and power. Reactions to attempts to redistribute power are similar, whether at the turn of the century or today. Risman and Schwartz (1989) argue that the way to change gender roles is not to retrain individuals, but to restructure the social environment. Women will become assertive if their jobs demand it and when they are rewarded for acting assertively. Men will become nurturant when they are held responsible for taking care of others (Chodorow, 1978).

KEY TERMS

PERSONAL REFLECTIONS

1. In your opinion, what traits (other than physical characteristics) make a man masculine? A woman feminine? Why?

2. Compare your answers for Question 1. Were there any traits shared by both men and women? Why or why not? Can a man be gentle, caring, affectionate/emotional, nurturing to his children, and still be masculine? Why or why not? Can a woman be assertive, independent, ambitious in a career, and still be feminine? Why or why not?

3. Do you consider yourself to be sex-typed or androgynous? Why?

4. Have you ever considered marriage? If so, what traits do you want in a husband or wife? Are these the same traits you will want after you become parents? Is your answer consistent with your answers to the previous questions?

5. Men: Your wife has decided to resume postgraduate studies leading to a career. This will require that she be away from home more than before and that you assume more responsibilities for care of the house and children. Your reaction?

6. Women: Your husband has decided to pass up a career opportunity (leading to higher rank and salary) to spend more time at home with the children. Your reaction?

7. How would you react if you found your young son playing with Barbie dolls? Why? How would you react if you found your young daughter playing with toy soldiers and footballs? Why?

8. How would you react if your teenaged son wanted to take home economics instead of machine shop or auto mechanics? Why? How would you react if your teenaged daughter wanted to take machine shop or auto mechanics instead of home economics? Why?

9. Look through popular magazines or watch several television shows. Notice the gender roles that are presented for men and for women. What do you feel should be changed, if anything?

10. Visit your local toy store and look at the toys that are displayed. Do manufacturers present different toys in ways that appeal more to girls or more to boys? Do these toys help create stereotypes or do they result from societal stereotypical ideas? Would you change anything?

SUGGESTED READINGS

Laqueur, T. (1992). *Making sex: Body and gender from the Greeks to Freud.* Cambridge, MA: Harvard University Press (paperback).

Laying, A. (1989, May). What keeps women "in their place"? *USA Today* Magazine (Society for the Advancement of Education). An anthropological examination of why there is still inequality between the sexes.

Lips, H. (1992). *Sex and gender.* Mountain View, CA: Mayfield. This is an easy-to-read, good introduction to gender roles.

Merlin, K. (1987, February). When men and women think about sex: Ways they differ. *Cosmopolitan.* Discusses how men and women differ in the ways they think about love and sex.

Morris, J. *Conundrum* (1974). New York: Harcourt, Brace, & Jovanovich. The story of a transsexual's experiences.

Segell, M. (1989, January/February). The American man in transition. *American Health.* 1989. Discusses the results of a new survey that shows that most people believe that men need to change.

Shapiro, L. (1990, May 28). Guns and dolls. *Newsweek.* An excellent article on the development of gender roles during childhood.

Welbourne-Moglia, A., and Calderwood, D. (1984, November). Gender, gender role, and sexual health. *SIECUS Report.* Compares and contrasts male and female sexual health throughout the lifespan.

CHAPTER NINE

SEXUAL ORIENTATION

WHEN YOU HAVE FINISHED STUDYING THIS CHAPTER, YOU SHOULD BE ABLE TO:

1. DEFINE THE TERMS SEXUAL ORIENTATION, HETEROSEXUAL, HOMOSEXUAL, AND BISEXUAL;

2. SUMMARIZE WHAT WE KNOW ABOUT THE PREVALENCE OF HOMOSEXUALITY AND BISEXUALITY IN THE UNITED STATES;

3. UNDERSTAND THE DIFFERENCE BETWEEN SEXUAL ORIENTATION, GENDER IDENTITY, AND GENDER ROLES;

4. DISCUSS THE ORIGINS OF SEXUAL ORIENTATION, INCLUDING PSYCHOANALYTIC, SOCIAL LEARNING, AND BIOLOGICAL EXPLANATIONS;

5. TRACE THE HISTORY OF ATTITUDES ABOUT HOMOSEXUALITY IN WESTERN CULTURE;

6. COMPARE OUR ATTITUDES ABOUT HOMOSEXUALITY WITH THOSE IN OTHER CULTURES;

7. UNDERSTAND WHAT IT INVOLVES FOR AN INDIVIDUAL TO "COME OUT";

8. UNDERSTAND HOMOSEXUAL LIFESTYLES AND THEIR ABILITY TO PARENT; AND

9. DISCUSS THE CAUSES OF HOMOPHOBIA.

ARE YOU SEXUALLY ATTRACTED TO MEN? TO WOMEN? TO BOTH MEN AND WOMEN? THESE ARE QUESTIONS about **sexual orientation**—one's sexual attraction to members of the opposite gender, same gender, or both genders. Attraction to members of the opposite sex is called **heterosexuality**, while attraction to same-gender individuals is called **homosexuality**. **Bisexuality** refers to sexual attraction to people of either sex.

Heterosexual
An individual with a sexual orientation primarily to members of the opposite gender.

Homosexual
An individual with a sexual orientation primarily to members of the same gender.

At one time it was believed that people were either one or the other: heterosexual or homosexual (Gordon & Snyder, 1989). Today, sexual orientation is viewed as a continuum, with people who are exclusively heterosexual at one end and those who are exclusively homosexual at the other end. Kinsey and his colleagues (1948) devised a 7-point rating scale to measure sexual orientation, with 0 representing people who are exclusively heterosexual and 6 representing people who are exclusively homosexual (see Table 9-1). Kinsey's group regarded anyone as bisexual who had a rating of 2, 3, or 4. Kinsey's scale relied heavily on overt behavior, but there are problems with defining heterosexuality-homosexuality only in terms of behavior. However, before we address these problems let us examine the results by Kinsey and others regarding behavior. ∎

Bisexual
An individual with a sexual orientation to members of both genders.

PREVALENCE OF HOMOSEXUALITY AND BISEXUALITY

The large-scale surveys by Kinsey and his associates discussed in Chapter 1 (Kinsey et al., 1948, 1953) were the first source of information about the prevalence of homosexuality in this country. They found that 4 percent of their sample of white males had been exclusively homosexual for life, 10 percent had been exclusively homosexual for at least a 3-year period in their lives, and 37 percent had had at least one homosexual experience to orgasm. This last figure shocked America, and Kinsey's survey was attacked as either biased or totally false (for example, see Reisman & Eichel, 1990). An associate of Kinsey's later claimed that the 37 percent figure was, in fact, too high, but only lowered the estimate to 25–33 percent (Pomeroy, 1972). For women, Kinsey's group found that 13–19 percent had had at least one homosexual experience, and 1–3 percent were predominantly or exclusively homosexual after age 15.

A survey taken over 20 years later by Morton Hunt (1975) for *Playboy* magazine found that 20–25 percent of males had had at least one homosexual experience in their lifetimes. However, only 12–13 percent had had a homosexual experience after age 15, and only 2–3 percent were found to be predominantly or exclusively homosexual after that age. A survey taken by the Kinsey Institute at about the same time (1970) found that 3.3 percent of adult males had homosexual experiences "occasionally" or "fairly often" (Fay et al., 1989). Hunt found that 20 percent of single women reported having had at least one homosexual experience in their lifetime, but only 10–12 percent had done so after age 15. About 2 percent of single women were predominantly homosexual. For married women, 10–11 percent of Hunt's sample said that they had had at least one homosexual experience, but only 3 percent of them after age 15, and fewer

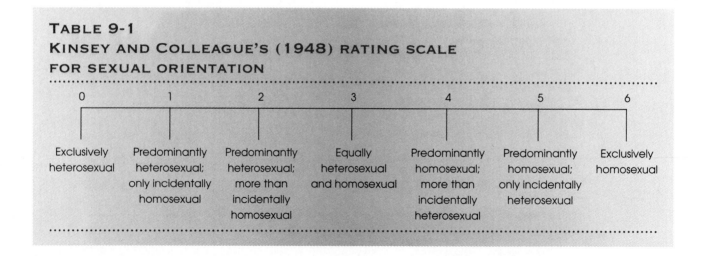

TABLE 9-1
KINSEY AND COLLEAGUE'S (1948) RATING SCALE FOR SEXUAL ORIENTATION

0	1	2	3	4	5	6
Exclusively heterosexual	Predominantly heterosexual; only incidentally homosexual	Predominantly heterosexual; more than incidentally homosexual	Equally heterosexual and homosexual	Predominantly homosexual; more than incidentally heterosexual	Predominantly homosexual; only incidentally heterosexual	Exclusively homosexual

than 1 percent were predominantly homosexual. Thus, for both men and women most people who said that they had had a homosexual experience(s) had done so as adolescents, but were exclusively heterosexual as adults.

> "At the age of about 12, I experienced an act of homosexuality. My cousins and I performed anal intercourse with each other. It never occurred to me that I might be gay when I got older. I am now grown up and am not a homosexual. . . . . Maybe because it was just a game to me or exploring different functions."
>
> (from the author's files)

Hunt, like many others, felt that Kinsey overestimated the prevalence of homosexuality in the United States, but at the same time he felt that his survey may have underestimated the number of homosexual people. What do more recent surveys indicate?

In a national cross-sectional survey, Janus and Janus (1993) found that 22 percent of men and 17 percent of women said that they had had homosexual ex-periences, and that for 9 percent of men and 5 percent of women the experiences were either "frequent" or "ongoing." However, a survey done for *Parade* magazine found that only 3 percent of men and 1 percent of women identified themselves as homosexual, and another 3 percent of men and 0.4 percent of women said they were bisexual (Clements, 1994). Another survey found that only 2 percent of men reported having had a homosexual experience within the last 10 years (Billy et al., 1993). In perhaps the best sexual survey to date, Laumann and colleagues (1994) found that 2.8 percent of men and 1.4 percent of women identified themselves as homosexual or bisexual. This was consistent with behavior: 2.7 percent of the men and 1.3 percent of the women in the survey said that they had had sex with someone of their own gender in the past year. However, in large urban areas more than 9 percent of men identified themselves as homosexual.

Two recent reviews are especially relevant here. One reviewed three surveys conducted by the National Opinion Research Center in 1988, 1989, and 1990 (Rogers & Turner, 1991). The other relied on seven surveys, including five conducted after 1987 (Seidman & Rieder, 1994). What did they conclude? As many as 20 percent of men have had a homosexual experience, but only about 5 percent since the age of 18, and only

FIGURE 9-1   MILLIONS OF AMERICAN MEN AND WOMEN ARE EITHER PREDOMINANTLY OR EXCLUSIVELY HOMOSEXUAL.

1–6 percent have done so in the last 12 months (most of the surveys put this last figure at around 2 percent).

After all this research, what is the overall conclusion? About 3–5 percent of adult American men and about 1 percent of adult American women are predominantly or exclusively homosexual (Figure 9-1). Many more people, however, have had sexual experiences with individuals of the same sex. ■

DEFINING SEXUAL ORIENTATION: ANOTHER LOOK

As I implied earlier, we must look at more than behavior when characterizing people as heterosexual, homosexual, or bisexual. For example, what about sexual fantasies? Most heterosexuals have had fantasies of homosexual experiences (and vice versa; Bell & Weinberg, 1978). Although this does not mean that they are homosexual or bisexual, what sexual orientation is a person who has been exclusively heterosexual in behavior, but whose sexual fantasies are *predominantly* homosexual in content?

What about a person's sexual self-identity—how someone *feels* about himself or herself? In fact, you do not have to have ever had sex to consider yourself as heterosexual or homosexual. Also, some people who are predominantly heterosexual in behavior may feel that they are homosexual or bisexual, but limit themselves because of perceived social constraints and engage in same-gender sexual experiences only on an occasional basis. For example, Laumann et al. (1994) found that more than twice as many people (5.5 percent of women and 6 percent of men) said that they found the idea of having sex with someone of their own gender appealing than had actually engaged in same-gender sex in the past year or who identified themselves as homosexual or bisexual. Another study found that 12 percent of predominantly heterosexuals reported awareness of some homosexual feelings (McConaghy et al., 1994).

Sexual orientation

Distinct preferences for sexual partners of a particular gender in the presence of clear alternatives.

How, then, shall we define **sexual orientation**? I will use a modification of the definition by Ellis and Ames (1987):

distinct preferences consistently made after adolescence in the presence of clear alternatives.

Preferences can be reflected in desire and/or behavior, and, as noted by Ellis and Ames, "isolated instances of sexual behavior may or may not reflect one's sexual orientation."

Perhaps the biggest confusion, and controversy, is with the term bisexual. Many people still insist on viewing sexual orientation as a dichotomous choice (either/or) and have difficulty accepting a third orientation. Many homosexuals (as well as heterosexuals) view people who have engaged in bisexual behavior as really homosexuals who have not yet "come out of the closet" (Gordon & Snyder, 1989).

Is bisexuality a behavior, a feeling, or an identity? In a study of nearly 7,000 men who acknowledged sexual experiences with both men and women, it was found that 2 percent described themselves as homosexual, 69 percent as heterosexual, and only 29 percent as bisexual (Lever et al., 1992). In the survey by Janus and Janus (1993), 22 percent of men said that they had had a homosexual experience, but only 4 percent regarded themselves as homosexual and another 5 percent as bisexuals. Thus, most people who have had sexual experiences with both opposite- and same-gender individuals do not regard themselves as bisexual. For example, in an interesting study, Humphreys (1970) examined a behavior called "tearoom trade." This involves men giving oral sex to other men in public bathrooms, often without exchanging names. He found that a majority of those who allowed oral sex to be performed on them viewed themselves as heterosexual (54 percent were married and had children) and many did not believe that they had engaged in a homosexual act because they had only been the passive partner. In the study by Lever et al. (1992), those men who identified themselves as bisexual said that they were predominantly or sometimes homosexual, whereas those who identified themselves as heterosexual were predominantly heterosexual in behavior. Similar results were found in a smaller study (Doll et al., 1992). These studies point out the shortcomings of relying exclusively on either behavior or self-identity as a definition.

A commonly used definition of bisexuality was suggested by MacDonald (1981, 1982):

"To be bisexual means that a person can enjoy and engage in sexual activity with members of both sexes, or recognizes a desire to do so. Also, although the strength and direction of preference may be constant for some bisexuals, it may vary considerably for others with respect to time of life and specific partners."

Recall that by Kinsey's definition (1948) the sexual behavior (or desire to behave) must be more than incidental. However, Kinsey's scale implies that the farther away an individual gets from one of the extremes (exclusively heterosexual or exclusively homosexual), the weaker that orientation becomes. A bisexual person, therefore, would have only moderate degrees of both orientations. This may not be true. One study found that bisexuals had the same amount of oppo-site-sex fantasies as heterosexuals and the same amount of same-sex fantasies as homosexuals (Storms, 1980). In conclusion, most researchers today agree that bisexuality is a legitimate classification of sexual orientation, distinct from both heterosexuality and bi-sexuality. ∎

SEXUAL ORIENTATION, GENDER IDENTITY, AND GENDER ROLES

It has been my experience that many students are un-certain (or mistaken) about the relationship between a person's sexual orientation and his or her gender iden-tity and gender roles. The latter two are independent of sexual orientation (Lips, 1992). The gender identity of the vast majority of homosexuals and bisexuals is just as strong and consistent with their anatomical gender as is found among heterosexuals. Homosexuality and bisexuality are not the result of gender dysphoria, and homosexual is not the same as transsexual (see Chapter 8). Also, do not confuse homosexuality or bisexuality with transvestism; as you will learn in Chapter 14, most transvestites are heterosexual males.

The real misunderstanding concerns sexual orien-tation and gender roles. Early sexologists like Freud and Havelock Ellis thought that homosexuality resulted from reversed gender roles (Ross, 1983). Many people today still hold to this belief (De Cecco & Elia, 1993), which is reinforced often by the media portraying male homosexuals as effeminate and female homosexuals as masculine. While many homosexuals do not conform to gender roles that society considers "normal" for their sex (Snyder, Weinrich, & Pillard, 1994), that is also true for many heterosexuals (Bell, Weinberg, & Hammersmith, 1981). Whether a person conforms or does not conform to gender stereotypes does not always predict sexual orientation.

However, because of these beliefs, many people are quick to label others who do not appear to be "typical." For example, people are much more likely to assume that a man is homosexual if he works as a nurse or secretary, or if his face has some "feminine" features (Deaux & Lewis, 1983; Dunkle & Francis, 1990). Conversely, many people are quick to attribute femi-nine characteristics to a man they are told is (but in actuality is not) homosexual (Weissbach & Zagon, 1975).

Probably the major reason for beliefs like these is that for many people masculinity and femininity are basic assumptions of heterosexuality: men are mascu-line and attracted to women, women are feminine and attracted to men. If you believe this, then it follows that the less "masculine" a male is the more likely that he will be perceived as homosexual, and if a man is homosexual the more likely he will be perceived as "feminine" (Ross, 1983). However, as you learned in the previous chapter, gender roles change over time, and this is true within the homosexual community as well as the heterosexual community. Before the 1970s, for example, effeminate qualities were emphasized in the male homosexual community, but since then mas-culinity has been emphasized (Garber, 1991). Con-sider, too, the butch and femme roles assumed by many female homosexuals (most prevalent prior to 1960)—their behaviors were quite different but their sexual orientation was the same. Again, there is no strong evidence that a homosexual or bisexual orientation must be associated with atypical gender roles. A great many homosexuals and bisexuals do not walk, talk, dress, or act any differently than anyone else (Kirk & Madsen, 1989). Consider the following:

He had attended a Catholic high school, was a star athlete on school teams, and was engaged to be married to his high school sweetheart. They had been going steady for several years. He was handsome, masculine looking, well-liked—an "All American" type of young man. Raised in a supportive family environment along with a younger brother and sister, he had come from as normal a back-ground as could be imagined. He, too, had al-ways thought of himself as normal.

His first awareness of his attraction to men came in adolescence. . . . He felt as if he was the only person in the world with this "problem." He loved his girlfriend, but he knew that some-thing wasn't right and after high school he broke off the engagement. . . . He does not apologize for his homosexuality, for he feels that there is absolutely nothing to apologize for (it would be like apologizing for breathing or the color of his eyes).

He does not explain his homosexuality as the result of following role models, for he had none. He felt that he alone had these feelings during his adolescence. He does not think that he acted out of rebellion against his parents. They were a close, warm family and his parents treated his brother and sister in a similar manner. Neither of them are homosexual. He knows of no close relative who is homosexual. He was just like everyone else in high school and today is indistinguishable from any of the other male students in college. . . .

(from the author's files) ∎

THE ORIGINS OF SEXUAL ORIENTATION

Why are some people heterosexual, others homosexual, and still others bisexual? Researchers and clinicians used to direct their efforts to the question "What causes homosexuality?" However, any study of the causes of homosexuality is inevitably about the causes of heterosexuality, and vice versa—you can't consider one without considering the other (Friedman, 1992).

Is sexual orientation biologically determined? Is it the result of the environment (family background, peers, etc.) shaping individuals? There are probably few topics in the study of human characteristics in which the nature-versus-nurture question has been so strongly debated. I will review this work and then come to two conclusions, which I give in advance: (1) neither heterosexuality, nor homosexuality, nor bisexuality have a single cause; and (2) biological, psychological, and social/cultural influences interact to produce sexual orientation (see Byne & Parsons, 1993; De Cecco & Elia, 1993; Friedman, 1992).

PSYCHOANALYTIC EXPLANATIONS

Freud viewed all people as capable of becoming either heterosexual or homosexual—neither was assumed to be innate. He believed that a person's sexual orientation depended on how the Oedipus complex was resolved (see Chapter 8) and that heterosexuality was the "normal" outcome. Homosexuality was the result of fixation at (or regression to) this stage of development when a particular set of circumstances occurred.

More specifically, Freud believed that male homosexuality resulted when a boy had a domineering, rejecting mother and turned to his father for love (and later to men in general) or, in other circumstances, if the boy's fear of castration anxiety (by his father) was so great that he shunned his mother (and later all women) as an object of sexual desire. According to Freud, female homosexuality develops when a girl loves her mother and identifies with her father and becomes fixated at this stage. As an adult, the woman continues to seek the love of women (mother figures). Freud also felt that some individuals managed to keep their homosexual tendencies hidden from their conscious mind, or "repressed," until these tendencies emerged sometime later. He called these persons latent homosexuals.

In support of Freud, Bieber and colleagues (1962) studied male homosexuals and claimed that they typically had domineering, overly protective mothers and weak, detached fathers who did not provide masculine models. The mothers were seductive (in that they were jealous of, and discouraged, any interest their boys had in girls) and destroyed their boys' masculine behavior. Bieber claimed that the boys became fearful of heterosexual relations and turned to men for the love that they never received from their fathers. In a related study in support of Freud, Wolff (1971) claimed that female homosexuals came from homes with absent fathers and cold and rejecting mothers. The girls then spent the remainder of their lives searching for the love that their mothers never gave them by having other women as sexual partners.

These studies were done with a small number of people who were in therapy. While some other studies have found similar results (Evans, 1969), a later, much larger study of better adjusted persons failed to support their findings. Bell, Weinberg, and Hammersmith (1981) could find little evidence that male homosexuals had dominant mothers and weak fathers, or that female homosexuals had chosen their fathers as role models.

What can we conclude? Although there is some evidence that persons with a family background like those described by Bieber or Wolf "have a greater than average likelihood of becoming homosexual" (Marmor, 1980), it is important to keep in mind that homosexuals have all kinds of parents, both good (reread the previous case history) and bad, caring and cold (Masters & Johnson, 1979). The same is true of heterosexuals. The psychoanalytic theories cannot possibly begin to explain the sexual orientation of all individuals.

Interestingly, although Freud's followers viewed homosexuality as a mental illness (see section on homosexuality), he apparently had a less harsh attitude, as evidenced by this letter to the mother of a homosexual son:

Dear Mrs. _____,
I gather from your letter that your son is a homosexual. . . . Homosexuality is assuredly no advantage, but it is nothing to be ashamed of, no vice, no degradation, it cannot be classified as an illness; we consider it to be a variation of the sexual function produced by a certain arrest of sexual development.

Many highly respectable individuals of ancient and modern times have been homosexuals, several of the greatest men among them (Plato, Michelangelo, Leonardo da Vinci, etc.).

It is a great injustice to persecute homosexuality as a crime, and cruelty, too. . . .

OTHER PSYCHOSOCIAL EXPLANATIONS

Social learning theory explains homosexuality and heterosexuality as learned behaviors (Gagnon & Simon, 1973; Masters & Johnson, 1979). This theory would therefore treat homosexuality and heterosexuality similarly, with each type of sexual orientation being dependent on the learning history of an individual. Homosexuals would be expected to have had good or rewarding experiences with same-sexed individuals and bad experiences with members of the opposite sex in their early social experiences. Once initiated, the sexual act itself, being pleasurable, becomes rewarding. Over time, they would therefore learn to associate homosexuality with more pleasure than heterosexuality. Also, they may have had role models to pattern themselves after in their youth.

What is the evidence in support of this explanation? Many people assume that homosexuals are people who are not attractive (or masculine or feminine) enough to "make it" with the opposite sex. However, the data do not support this. Most female homosexuals, for example, have had pleasurable sexual relations with men. They simply prefer sexual relations with women (Martin & Lyon, 1972). In their study, Bell, Weinberg, and Hammersmith (1981) found that "homosexual orientation among females reflects neither a lack of heterosexual experience nor a history of particularly unpleasant heterosexual experiences." However, there is some evidence that an extremely bad negative experience, such as being the victim of rape, can result in an individual avoiding heterosexual relations (Grundlach, 1977).

There is also some evidence that if a person's first adolescent (or preadolescent) sexual experiences, such as mutual masturbation, are with a same-sexed individual, then there is a greater than usual chance that the person's sexual orientation will be homosexual (Van Wyk, 1984, but see Box 9-A). Storms (1980) has suggested that children who begin puberty early are particularly more likely than others to experiment with adolescent homosexual experiences (for which there are more opportunities than heterosexual experiences), and these early pleasurable experiences make it more than likely that a homosexual orientation will develop. However, there is no evidence to support the myth that adolescents became homosexual because they were seduced by an older homosexual (Bell et al., 1981).

Even if the studies about adolescent homosexual experimentation are true, that still leaves the question of which came first: Did homosexual experimentation lead to a homosexual orientation, or did homosexual tendencies lead to homosexual experimentation? Bell, Weinberg, and Hammersmith (1981) found that a person's sexual orientation was usually well established by adolescence, and that gender (role) nonconformity during childhood was often, but not always, associated later with a homosexual orientation. Similar results have been reported by others (Philips & Over, 1995; Saghir & Robins, 1973; Whitam, 1977a).

The relation between childhood gender nonconformity and later homosexuality is greater for boys than it is for girls ("tomboyish" behavior by girls is accepted more than "sissy" behavior by boys). One study found that for boys, the absence of masculine traits was a better predictor of later homosexuality than was the presence of feminine traits (Hockenberry & Billingham, 1987). Another study found that for boys who persistently play with girls' dolls and display other stereotypically feminine traits, there is about a 75 percent chance of them being homosexual as an adult (Bailey & Zucker, 1995).

Richard Green (1987) studied a small sample of extremely effeminate boys (who he called "sissy boys") over a 15-year period. A few families reinforced the behavior, but most of the families simply maintained (rather than initiated) it. The boys had poor relations with their fathers, but this could be the result of the boys' "unmasculine" behavior rather than a cause. Most of the boys engaged in homosexual fantasizing and behavior as adolescents, but others developed a clear heterosexual orientation. Thus, even in cases of extreme childhood gender role nonconformity, one cannot absolutely predict future sexual orientation. Also, keep in mind that homosexual males who were "sissies" as boys comprise only a portion of homosexuals; many showed typical gender-role behavior as children (Bell et al., 1981; see section on gender roles).

Green's subjects had been different since early childhood. Bell et al. (1981) suggested that the results by them, Green (1987), and others indicated a possible biological basis for sexual orientation. Let's now consider the evidence for that.

BIOLOGICAL EXPLANATIONS

There is no question that males and females are structurally different. In Chapter 8, you learned that there are also some differences in male and female brains. Is it possible that brain difference could account for differences in sexual orientation?

GENETIC FACTORS. In 1952, Kallman found nearly 100 percent concordance for homosexual orientation in identical twins (i.e., if one twin was homosexual the other almost always was too). The concordance for fraternal (nonidentical) twins was only about 10 percent. Similar results were found by a German researcher (Schlegel, 1962), and together these findings challenged the prevailing view that homosexuality was determined by social influences.

The results of these first studies with twins were questioned when several reports appeared in the 1960s and 1970s of single cases or small numbers of identical twins who were discordant for homosexual orientation (see Whitam, Diamond, & Martin, 1993 for a review). However, several recent larger-scale studies have reestablished a possible genetic basis for sexual orientation. Bailey and Pillard (1991) studied 167 pairs of brothers and found that 52 percent of identical twin brothers of homosexual males were also homosexual, compared with 22 percent of nonidentical twins, and 11 percent of adoptive brothers. In another study of 143 pairs of sisters, they found that 48 percent of identical twins of homosexual females were also homosexual, compared to 16 percent of nonidentical twins, and six percent of adoptive sisters (Bailey et al., 1993). Another study found a 65.8 percent concordance rate for homosexual orientation in identical twin brothers, compared to 30.4 percent in nonidentical twins (Whitam et al. 1993). Still another group of researchers found that 33 of 40 pairs of homosexual brothers shared the identical DNA pattern on the tip of one arm of their X chromosomes (inherited from the mother; Hamer et al., 1993), but another group of scientists could not duplicate Hamer's findings.

More recently, a researcher has presented evidence that male homosexuality is determined by a gene in a specific region of the X chromosome (Turner, 1995). Although it is far removed from human studies, research with flies indicate that sexual orientation can be altered by inserting an extra gene (Odenwald & Zhang, 1995).

What does all this mean? Although the studies suffered from several methodological flaws (Baron, 1993), they leave little doubt of a biological contribution to sexual orientation. But how much? Remember, not all of the identical twins were homosexual, and in the study by Hamer et al. (1993), seven pairs of homosexual brothers did not share the same gene pattern. Michael Bailey, author of several twin studies, concluded that "the degree of the genetic contribution (to homosexuality) could range from 30 percent to 70 percent depending on the assumptions used. . . ." Even if his upper estimate is correct, that still leaves a lot of room for the influence of social/environmental factors. Social interactions might well mediate aspects of any genetic role in sexual orientation (Byne & Parsons, 1993). For example, even if the

extreme gender nonconformity displayed by children in the "sissy boy" syndrome (see previous section) was the result of genetics, if the children were treated differently from other children that could reinforce later nonconformity in gender roles (Hines & Green, 1991).

ANATOMICAL FACTORS. At about the same time that researchers were finding a genetic component to sexual orientation, others were reporting differences in the brains of heterosexuals and homosexuals. Simon LeVay, a neuroscientist and an avowed homosexual with both a homosexual brother and a lover who had died of AIDS, performed autopsies on the brains of 19 homosexual men and 16 heterosexual men. He found that a part of the hypothalamus (at the base of the brain) known to influence sexual behavior (specifically, the interstitial nucleus of the anterior hypothalamus-3, or INAH-3) was more than twice as large in heterosexuals (LeVay, 1991). This area of the hypothalamus is affected by sex hormones (see next section). These results do not prove causation; it is possible that behavioral differences cause anatomical differences.

LeVay's study followed a report that another part of the hypothalamus, the suprachiasmatic nucleus, had twice as many cells in homosexual men than in heterosexual men (Swaab & Hofman, 1990). A subsequent study found that a major fiber bundle that connects the two halves of the brain (the anterior commissure) was 34 percent larger in homosexual males than in heterosexual males, but no different from heterosexual females (when brain weight differences between men and women were adjusted; Allen & Gorski, 1992).

What do the anatomical findings mean, and how are they related to the genetic research? Dr. Dean Heimer of the National Institutes of Health concluded, "The simplest interpretation would be that there is a gene, or genes, that control the growth of (the INAH-3 and other brain structures). Both point to the same idea, that there is a biological component of sexual orientation" (cited by Maugh in the *Los Angeles Times,* 1991).

HORMONAL FACTORS. How might genes affect brain anatomy, and if that can be determined, when? Before birth? Shortly after birth? During childhood? At puberty?

It is likely that the critical link is hormones. Gorski and colleagues (1978) were the first to show differences in brain (hypothalamus) structure between male and female rats. Gorski's group later manipulated the levels of sex hormones in newborn rats and, as a result, were able to get male rats that showed female rat sexual behavior. Several studies with nonhuman species have shown that treatment with hormones prenatally (before birth) can result in homosexual behavior (Dorner, 1968; Money & Ehrhardt, 1972).

In humans, one thing we do know is that the level of circulating male sex hormones (testosterone) does not differ between adult heterosexual and homosexual males (see Gladue, 1988). Furthermore, giving sex hormones to adult homosexuals (testosterone to homosexual males, for example) does not change their sexual orientation. However, there is evidence for differences in hormonal responses. When injected with the female hormone estrogen, women show an elevation of the pituitary hormone LH (luteinizing hormone; see Chapter 3), while men normally show no elevation. Studies have found that male homosexuals show an intermediate elevation in LH after an injection of estrogen (Dorner et al., 1975; Gladue, Green, & Hellman, 1984). Does this mean that homosexual men have a "female" hypothalamus? These and other studies suggest that if hormones do cause a difference in brain structure, it would have to be caused early in life.

Ethical considerations do not allow manipulation of hormones in human fetuses or infants, but there is some evidence that what has been found in nonhuman species is also true in humans. For example, studies have found that women who were exposed to high levels of masculinizing hormones before birth (see congenital adrenal hyperplasia in Chapter 8) are much more likely than others to prefer boys' toys and activities as children (Berenbaum & Snyder, 1995) and develop a homosexual or bisexual orientation as adults (Ehrhardt, Evers, & Money, 1968; Meyer-Bahlburg et al., 1995; Money & Schwartz, 1977).

Ellis and Ames (1987), in an extensive review of both human and animal research, concluded that sexual orientation is primarily determined before birth. According to their theory, all mammals begin life with a single sexual orientation. It is the presence of certain (although yet undetermined) amounts of hormonal factors that direct sexual development and create a variety of sexual orientations, heterosexuality being the most frequent orientation. The presence of testosterone during the second month of embryological development, you recall, is critical for determining one's sexual anatomy (see Chapter 8). Ellis and Ames claim that the critical period for the development of sexual orientation comes between the middle of the second month and the middle of the fifth month of pregnancy. Others claim that hormones have their effect in the first year or two after birth (recall the work by Gorski), but notice that all agree that the effect (on sexual orientation) occurs very early. Ellis and Ames list several

potential factors that could influence an unborn child's development of sexual orientation, including genetic-hormonal factors, drugs, stress in the mother, and immune system dysfunctions.

CONCLUSIONS

Although there is a growing body of evidence for a biological contribution to sexual orientation, this does not mean that one's sexual orientation is destined by biology (Byne & Parsons, 1993; Gladue, 1994). Most researchers agree that biological and social influences *both* contribute to the development of sexual orientation. The question is no longer nature versus nurture, but to what extent each influences orientation. They certainly interact in some complex, yet undetermined, manner. At the moment, the most we can say for biological factors is that they probably *predispose* (this is not the same as "cause") an individual to a particular sexual orientation. What this means is that given a certain genetic background and a particular set of social/environmental influences, it is more likely than not that a person will assume a heterosexual or homosexual orientation.

The recent genetic and anatomical findings have created debate in the homosexual community. On the one hand, there are those who feel that proof of a biological determinant of sexual orientation will lead to greater tolerance. As stated by Dr. Richard Pillard, coauthor of the twin studies, "A genetic component in sexual orientations says, 'This is not a fault, and it's not your fault'" (quoted in Gelman et al., 1992). Or, as stated by George Neighbors Jr. of the Federation of Parents and Friends of Lesbians and Gays, "It may help people look at this as a genetic issue. . . . If you believe in God or nature, that's what homosexuality develops from" (quoted by Recur, 1993).

On the other hand, Neighbors and others worry that if a biological basis can be found, some people with an antihomosexual bias will press for medical changes in sexual orientation, as was tried in the recent past (see next section). Perhaps the best perspective was presented by David Barr, assistant director of policy for the Gay Men's Health Crisis in New York, who said, "It doesn't really matter why people are gay or not gay. That's not the important question. What's really important is how they're treated. I haven't spent that much time thinking about where my sexuality comes from. I've spent a lot more time thinking about how I fit into this world I have to live in" (quoted by Angier, 1991).

It is certainly the case that homosexual men and women are often treated negatively by others. Let us examine what it means to be homosexual in our culture. ■

HOMOSEXUALITY

Homosexuality is a word derived from the Greek *homo*, meaning "same" (do not confuse this with the Latin *homo*, meaning "man"). The term was first used by a Hungarian physician in a pamphlet published in Germany in 1869 (Gregersen, 1982), and was popularized in the English language two decades later by Havelock Ellis. The prefix *hetero*, by the way, is also derived from a Greek word and means "different."

Homosexual behavior has been reported in nearly all cultures throughout the world (see Box 9-A). Homosexual behavior (male-male or female-female mounting) has also been observed and studied in a variety of nonhuman species, including many primates and dolphins. Among male animals, it is often done as a display of dominance, and otherwise generally serves as a social (reinforcing relations) rather than a sexual function (see Denniston, 1980; Ford & Beach, 1951; and Linden, 1992). However, in some cases sexual arousal may also serve as a stimulus (Srivastava, Borries, & Sommer, 1991).

Over the years there have been many derogatory terms used to describe homosexuals (e.g., faggot, queer, fairy, dyke). Most homosexuals prefer the term **gay** for a male homosexual (although in some places the term is used for homosexuals of either sex) and **lesbian** for a female homosexual (derived from the Greek island Lesbos, where, in about 600 B.C., the poetess Sappho led a circle of young female disciples). Heterosexuals are often referred to as **"straights."** Among some gay and lesbian organizations, the term *homophile* is preferred when referring to a homosexual person.

Gay
A term generally used to refer to male homosexuals, although in some places it is used to refer to homosexuals of either gender.

Lesbian
A female homosexual.

Straight
A term used by homosexuals for a heterosexual.

HISTORY OF ATTITUDES ABOUT HOMOSEXUALITY

Western attitudes about homosexuality have varied considerably throughout history. In ancient Greece, homosexuality was widely accepted as an alternative to heterosexuality (Boswell, 1980). Plato praised homosexual relations in his *Symposium*. Homosexual relations between Greek scholars (e.g., Socrates, Plato) and their students were considered to be a natural part of a young boy's education. Marriage between same-gender individuals was legal and commonly accepted among the upper class during the Roman Empire.

Homosexual activities were practiced (often as part of religious rituals) by many groups of Hebrews prior to the seventh century B.C. As part of a reformation movement designed to unify the many Hebrew groups, homosexuality was thereafter condemned (along with other acts that had been part of older rituals) and was punishable by death:

> If a man lies with a male as with a woman, both of them have committed an abomination; they shall be put to death, their blood is upon them.

> (Leviticus 20:13, Revised Standard Version)

Female homosexuality was dealt with less harshly by the Jews because it didn't involve "spillage of seed" or violation of male property rights.

European Christians, following the Roman tradition, initially were tolerant of homosexuality (Boswell, 1980). It wasn't until the time of St. Thomas Aquinas (A.D. 1225–1274), who emphasized the views of St. Augustine that the only purpose of sex was procreation, that homosexuality came to be viewed as unnatural or "against the laws of nature." However, Boswell (1980) notes that while same-gender sex was considered a sin in the Middle Ages, people who committed the sin were not then viewed as a *type* of person who was different from others. This remained true during the 1600s and 1700s when homosexual acts became a crime as well as a sin.

It wasn't until the late 1800s and the rise of modern medicine (particularly psychiatry) that people who engaged in homosexual acts came to be viewed as a particular class of people—people with a mental illness. As a result, there has never been a period in Western culture with as much intolerance of homosexuality as there has been in the twentieth century. Because they were viewed as mentally ill, the medical profession subjected homosexuals to frontal lobotomies, forced castrations or hysterectomies, electric shock treatments, hormone injections, and endless hours of psychotherapy (Katz, 1976; also, see James Harrison's 1992 documentary film *Changing Our Minds*).

Until the 1960s, homosexuals had never been studied outside of a medical or prison setting. Then, in 1957, Evelyn Hooker published a paper showing that nonclinical heterosexual and homosexual males could not be distinguished by the best psychological tests (i.e., the homosexual males were as well adjusted as the heterosexual males). Finally, in 1973, the American Psychiatric Association decided to discontinue classifying homosexuality as a mental illness (see Hooker, 1993 for a review of some of the events leading to this decision). The decision was not unanimously applauded; 37 percent of APA members were opposed to change.

BOX 9-A

CROSS-CULTURAL PERSPECTIVES: HOMOSEXUALITY IN OTHER CULTURES

Homosexuality is viewed very differently in different cultures. Because there has been very little study of female homosexuality in other cultures, we will restrict ourselves here to attitudes about male homosexuality.

In a review of anthropological studies of 294 societies, Gregersen (1982) found that of 59 societies that had a clear opinion of homosexuality, 69 percent approved of it and only 31 percent condemned it. In an earlier study that included 76 societies in which homosexuality was noted, Ford and Beach (1951) found that 64 percent approved and 36 percent did not. Among major Western industrialized countries, only the United States and Britain bar known homosexuals from the military (Walsh, 1992). Canada, Australia, Germany, France, and the Netherlands all display less discrimination. In Russia and China, on the other hand, homosexuality is still a crime.

Recall that in ancient Greece sexual relations between men was highly idealized (Plato's *Symposium*) and it was believed that a boy could acquire knowledge by swallowing semen from an intellectual tutor. Homosexual *activity* with an older male during childhood and adolescence is common in many Melanesian (part of South Pacific islands) societies. In perhaps the most studied group, the Sambians (Herdt, 1981, 1987; Stoller & Herdt, 1985), boys are separated from their mothers about the age of 7 and live with males only. They regularly perform oral sex on older (but not yet adult) males; swallowing semen is a practice that the Sambians believe will make them strong, virile, and good warriors and hunters. The boys continue this for 6–8 years and then reverse roles, becoming semen donors to younger males. At 16 years of age, a Sambian boy marries and for the next year or two is given oral sex by his new bride as well as younger boys. Once he has sexual intercourse with his wife, however, the homosexual behavior stops and the new Sambian adult male is exclusively heterosexual (in desire as well as behavior) thereafter. Similar practices have been observed in the Ku Ku Ku Ku tribe of New Guinea and the Bataak of Indonesia (Money & Ehrhardt, 1972).

Several important points can be learned from these cross-cultural studies. First, we must distinguish between homosexual practices and a homosexual orientation. For example, although all Sambian males engage in homosexual practices during a specified time of their lives, Herdt (1981) estimates that fewer than 5 percent have a homosexual orientation as an adult. In Mexico, Brazil, Morocco and other northern African countries, Turkey, and Greece, it is not uncommon for males to engage in oral-genital sex or anal intercourse, but only the passive partner is regarded as homosexual (Carrier, 1980). Thus, what is considered homosexuality is, in part, culturally defined. The fact that fewer than 5 percent of Sambian males develop a homosexual orientation as an adult also says much about the role of the environment and biology. If environment were more important than biological factors, you would certainly expect to see a larger proportion of homosexual adults.

The percentage of homosexuals across cultures that have been extensively studied is about the same: from 1 to 7 percent (Diamond, 1993; Whitam, 1983). Homosexuals in different cultures greatly resemble one another in lifestyle as well, further evidence for a biological basis (Whitam & Mathy, 1986). What does vary from culture to culture are attitudes about homosexuality. That is a learned response, and what is learned depends on the time and the place in which a person is raised. ∎

The APA decision has had far-reaching implications. If homosexuality is no longer considered an illness, there is no need to cure it. As you can see, the way individuals deal with homosexuality is based on what they believe. However, attitudes often change very slowly. Simply *being* homosexual is no longer a criminal offense, but many states still have old laws on the books that prohibit the sexual expression of homosexuality. For example, in over 20 states there are laws against anal or oral sex that are used usually only to prosecute homosexuals (see Chapter 16). A police raid on the Stonewall Inn in Greenwich Village in 1969 led to 3 days of public demonstrations, an event that many say was the beginning of the gay rights movement.

Similarly, the Catholic church no longer considers homosexuality *per se* a sin, but it continues to condemn homosexual behavior. A letter to bishops worldwide written by Cardinal Joseph Ratzinger and approved by Pope John Paul II stressed that homosexual acts are sins. Homosexuals instead were urged to lead "a chaste life." In another letter to U.S. Catholic bishops in 1992, the Vatican called homosexuality "an objective disorder" and encouraged discrimination against homosexuals in public housing, family health benefits, and the hiring of teachers. The June 1988 convention of Southern Baptists adopted a resolution that said that homosexuals, "like all sinners, can receive forgiveness through personal faith in Jesus Christ," but added that homosexuality ". . . is not a normal life style and is an abomination in the eyes of God." The Catholic church and Southern Baptists are not alone. While there are some exceptions, most Christian churches continue to have a rejecting-punitive attitude toward homosexuality (J. Nelson, 1980).

At the present time, many individuals still have a harsh or negative attitude about homosexuality. Almost 75 percent of individuals surveyed in 1984 thought that sexual relations between adults of the same sex are always wrong (Davis & Smith, 1984). If anything, attitudes have worsened in the past 10 years because many heterosexuals incorrectly blame homosexuals for AIDS. In a more recent survey, for example, 89 percent of 15–19-year-old males believed that sex between two men was "disgusting" (Marsiglio,

FIGURE 9-2 SOCRATES. THIS GREEK PHILOSOPHER AND TEACHER BELIEVED THAT ANY EVIL COMMITTED BY HUMAN BEINGS IS DONE OUT OF IGNORANCE. HE DEVOTED HIS LIFE COMPLETELY TO SEEKING TRUTH AND GOODNESS.

1993b). Only 12 percent said they could be friends with a gay person.

Today, these widespread negative attitudes are spilling over into the voting booth. While more than 130 states, countries, or cities had passed laws to protect gays and lesbians against discrimination (by 1993), there has been a backlash. Oregon voters narrowly rejected an antihomosexual measure in 1992, but a similar ballot measure in Colorado passed in the same year (the Colorado Supreme Court subsequently overturned it). In 1994 alone, there were 134 antihomosexual measures introduced in Congress, state, or local governments.

The U.S. military has always banned and discharged homosexuals. At the urging of President Clinton, a "compromise" was enacted in 1993: new recruits can no longer be asked if they are homosexual, but they can still be discharged for engaging in homosexual acts.

For people with a homosexual orientation, the battle for acceptance continues.

COMING OUT

With so many people in our society having negative attitudes about homosexuality, it should come as no surprise that acknowledging to oneself that one is homosexual, and then publicly declaring it, is often very difficult. The process of disclosing one's homosexuality is called **coming out**. There are several stages to this process (Boston Women's Health Book Collective, 1984).

Coming out
Disclosing to others one's homosexual orientation.

The first stage is *admitting to oneself of a homosexual orientation*. Some researchers believe that sexual orientation is established by the age of 4 (Gordon & Snyder, 1989), and many homosexuals knew that they were "different" at a very young age. Attraction to same-gender individuals generally occurs well before sexual activity begins (Bell et al., 1981).

> " I discovered my sexuality at a surprising six years old. Naturally I didn't know at that young age that I was a lesbian, but I can remember having 'crushes' on my teachers and female upperclassmen."

"I think that the most important thing you lectured on was the predisposition of sexual orientation before birth. I, too, felt different as a child as early as by 10."

(from the author's files)

For others, self-recognition is often a confusing and anxiety-producing discovery. Some do not recognize their sexual orientation until well into adolescence, or even later (recall the case history in the section on gender roles).

Dear Ann Landers:... I am a married woman in my late 20s. (We have children.) I never had a homosexual experience until after I was married. I sought counseling, and I am trying to keep my head together.

The feelings I have toward a certain woman are more surprising to me than to anyone. They are more intense than just the physical desire. This is the deepest friendship I have ever known. . . .

I'm sure millions of women who are reading this are thinking "How gross!" "How sick!" A year ago I would have been one of them. I did not go looking for this. It just happened. . . . I am not prepared to throw away my marriage and family, but this new relationship has certainly changed my life. My husband doesn't know about it and hopefully he never will. Most of all I would hate to do anything that would hurt my kids. . . . Please give me some insight.

(Staying in the Closet
for Now, Illinois)
(Reprinted with permission
of Ann Landers and
Creators Syndicate.)

Because so many people have a negative opinion of it, recognizing that one is homosexual is often a lonely and painful experience.

"As a young gay person, you feel all of the things every other young person feels. You feel all of the normal doubts, uncertainties, questions and frustrations common to that time of life. And you also begin to have feelings and thoughts as precious and deep as any can be: of self, and worth, and love, and life, and purpose. But when you are young *and gay*, you also face a world of pain and isolation few people have to face.

We all know how vulnerable and fragile a life can be in those early years. And yet few people seem ready or willing to consider how it must feel to be young and gay. In a time when nurturing and affirmation are so important, the young gay person is told by his church that he is evil. The law says that she is a criminal. Society says that they are misfits. The media displays freaks. And the world seems to say they are less than a whole person. And so, when you are young and gay, you can feel so much hatred, so much rejection, so unwanted, so unwelcome, so worthless, so unaccepted and so misunderstood.

Other people throughout time have known the kind of pain and persecution which reaches deep into a person's heart. There have always been people who were made to feel hated and demeaned because of their color, their religion, their heritage, or their gender. But as much pain and suffering as these people have known, they also knew they were not alone. They always had someone else they could see who was just like them; someone to identify with. And most important of all, they had someone to talk to; someone to share the pain with.

When you are young and gay, you feel the same terrible depth of pain. But you look around and there is no one to talk to; no one to share the pain with. There is no one who has feelings like yours or who understands how deeply you hurt. You feel so isolated and so alone. And at times, that vulnerability and pain and isolation can be so terribly overwhelming."

(Steve L., New Orleans)

In the next stage, the individual *gets to know other homosexuals*, thus ending the sense of isolation. It is easier to come out if the individual finds acceptance in others, and those most likely to be accepting are other homosexuals. Most homosexuals were raised in the same antihomosexual environment as others and by coming into contact with other homosexuals these negative stereotypes may be replaced by a more positive attitude about homosexuality—and about themselves.

"As I was growing up, I heard all of the jokes and stories about the lives gays lived. I saw all of the negative images that the media could dish up for public consumption. . . . I wanted to find someone I could share the rest of my life with.

And then I looked for that life and tried to find it. . . . The only place society had allowed gays to meet was in one small bar-filled pocket of the city. And so I turned to where I was accepted and where I could breathe. But then I heard society condemn me because of the life style I 'chose' to lead.

In time, I grew to learn that there was more of a life to be had than just the narrow world which society tries to impose upon gays. I met many happy and healthy gay people who helped me to understand and learn and grow.''

(Steve L., New Orleans)

Once contact is made with other homosexuals, a new way of expressing sexuality has to be developed. In many ways, what happens next is quite similar to what happens when heterosexuals begin to date. There are initial relationships, breakups, and often lasting relationships are eventually formed. Contact with other homosexuals may also lead to an increased interest in gay rights and other political activities to support the rights of homosexuals.

In the third, very difficult, stage, the individual *tells family and friends of his or her sexual orientation.* Many hide their sexual orientation from others for long periods.

"But as bad as you hurt, you keep the pain to yourself. You fear being discovered by the people you love and need the most; for everything your world has taught you makes you afraid you will lose their love and friendship if they find out you are gay. The world gives you the pain, and then makes it impossible for you to talk about it because of fear.

So not only does the world isolate you from learning about your feelings and others who are like you, but you begin to isolate a part of yourself from family and friends. You begin to develop techniques of telling half-truths and skirting around questions. You learn how to hide inside of yourself and smother feelings. You learn how to be around other people without letting them get too close. You learn how to survive.

And then, you grow tired of hiding. You grow tired of not being able to share the beauty as well as the pain that fills your life. You grow tired of not being as close as you want to be to the people you care most about.

But the fear is still very strong. You find it is easier to avoid the questions by just staying away more often. And you don't have to find as much strength to hide and be silent. So you drift further and further from the people you love the most and you feel the pain and isolation building up inside.''

(Steve L., New Orleans)

Some, because of social constraints and possible punitive actions, feel that they must keep their orientation a secret.

"I've come to terms with my sexuality and live with it. However, I don't choose to show that side of me. I am in the military and must remain discrete. As a matter of fact, I'm in charge of a number of troops. Some members of my unit are in this class, which keeps me from relaxing. Although the new policy in the military is 'Don't ask,' 'Don't tell,' 'Don't pursue,' if found to be gay I would be discharged.''

(from the author's files)

Others may choose not to disclose because they are parents (Green & Clunis, 1988). When an individual does finally disclose his or her homosexuality to family, it often creates a crisis (Cramer & Roach, 1988; Zitter, 1987).

"My parents became aware of my sexual preference when I was eighteen. Since that time, I have endured numerous nasty conflicts with them. My mother told me that she would rather me be a prostitute, and my father told me I would never be anyone as long I was a 'faggot.' They threw me out immediately after graduation from high school and forbade me to enter their house. They took me back on their terms—that I would go straight and live what is in their opinion a good, decent, moral life style. I agreed and abided for a few months, but found myself extremely unhappy. I ended up moving out after a fight with my father.

The continual attempts to persuade me to change drove me to a feeling of no self worth. My parents do not understand that my life style is not something I can just change—turn on and off like a light switch. They think that if they make me miserable enough, that I'll want to change.''

(from the author's files)

In most cases the family eventually adjusts and accepts their family member's homosexuality (Holtzen & Agresti, 1990). Usually, after the family has been told, the next step is to tell friends, but this too is often met with different reactions.

"I am a 25-year-old female. I've been close friends with 'Darla' since 7th grade. 'Darla' and I used to talk about girl things all the time (boys, dating, sex). I felt there was nothing we couldn't discuss.

Two years after high school graduation, 'Darla' and I along with another mutual friend got together for pizza and to catch up on old times. 'Darla' then said she had something very important to tell us. She told us she was gay. She said she had those feelings since she was a child and only recently acted on them. I handled her news supportively, but our other friend told 'Darla' that she was 'disgusting' and 'gross.' I'm sure without a doubt that was the hardest day in 'Darla's' life.''

(from the author's files)

The emotional issue of revealing one's homosexuality to family recently received national attention in the newspaper cartoon comic strip series "For Better or For Worse" (by Lynn Johnston, March 1993), in which the 17-year-old character Lawrence, after much agonizing, tells his parents that he is gay. The series is normally carried by 1,400 newspapers, but, not surprisingly, some rejected it during that episode. For those of you who are homosexual and have not yet revealed your orientation to your family, Weinberg (1973) has some excellent suggestions.

The final stage is *complete openness about one's homosexuality*. This includes telling people at work and completes the process, making one's homosexuality a total lifestyle. The important task for all adults, regardless of their sexual orientation, is to develop an acceptance of their sexuality (i.e., of themselves), to find acceptable ways to express it, and to learn to incorporate their sexuality into their total lifestyle and personality.

Homosexual Lifestyles and Relations

Finding companions and sexual partners can be difficult for many homosexuals, especially in rural areas and small towns, where there may be little tolerance of homosexuals meeting together in public. In large urban areas there is usually a much larger number of people who are homosexual, as well as a much greater acceptance of their lifestyle. Prior to the 1970s, gays and lesbians met in "secret" bars, bathhouses, or public bathrooms. But gay bars became more than places in which to have sex. Because homosexuality was not openly tolerated, the bars provided an atmosphere where one's sexual orientation was accepted without criticism.

Over the last three decades, the homosexual urban community has grown from a small collection of bars and bathhouses to entire neighborhoods of gay and lesbian stores, restaurants and coffeehouses, churches, and counseling and activity centers. The typical member of the gay community today is well-educated, in a professional career position, and openly homosexual. In San Francisco, homosexuals have achieved positions of

political leadership as well (Shilts, 1987). This description, however, fits only those who are openly homosexual. For homosexual individuals who have not yet come out, homosexual relations are still dominated by secret meetings in bars and bathrooms, often with strangers (see Humphreys, 1970 for a description of this "tearoom trade" lifestyle).

In a 1978 study of gays and lesbians in the San Francisco Bay area, Bell and Weinberg found that 71 percent of homosexual lifestyles fell into one of the following five categories:

1. *Close-coupled* (male—10 percent, female—28 percent): In this relationship, individuals have only one partner and generally report that they are happy with their sexual orientation.
2. *Open-coupled* (male—18 percent, female—17 percent): In this relationship there is a primary partner but additional sexual partners are sought outside the relationship. They are generally happy with their sexual orientation.
3. *Functional* (male—15 percent, female—10 percent): This relationship resembles the "swinging single." Individuals are comfortable with their homosexuality, enjoy their independence, and have multiple partners.
4. *Dysfunctional* (male—12 percent, female—5 percent): These people are sexually active, but are not happy with their homosexuality and often have sexual problems.
5. *Asexual* (male—16 percent, female—11 percent): These people are single, have few partners, and are not interested in seeking partners.

The types of relationships found by Bell and Weinberg for homosexuals are similar to the types of relationships found among heterosexuals. Many heterosexuals believe that homosexual couples are less committed than heterosexual couples, but studies have found no differences in the amount of love and satisfaction between cohabiting heterosexuals and cohabitating homosexuals (Peplau 1981, 1988). In fact, homosexual couples may be better at being "best friends" than heterosexual couples (Peplau, 1988). The smaller number of close-coupled pairs (in the Bell and Weinberg study) compared to married heterosexuals may be a function of the negative attitudes that our society often has regarding homosexual couples. How would you feel if a homosexual couple, who were openly affectionate to each other, moved next door to you? Many people would have negative or even hostile reactions. Also, young gays are not likely to see role models of monogamous, close-coupled relationships in gay bars (just as married heterosexual couples are rarely seen in "swinging singles" bars together). Furthermore, TV and the other communications channels of our society do not give such monogamous homosexual relationships much coverage or encouragement.

We will now focus specifically on the sexual relations of gays and lesbians. Before we begin, let me put things in proper perspective. The term "homosexual" tends to focus attention only on a person's sex life. However, gays and lesbians spend only a very small part of their lives engaged in sexual activities. The same is true of heterosexuals. Homosexuals and heterosexuals alike spend the large majority of their lives pursuing careers, enjoying recreational activities with family and friends, and exploring social-cultural-political interests. Most heterosexuals would not want to be judged solely on their sexual behavior! The same is true for homosexuals.

Let us consider males first. Bell and Weinberg (1978) found that over 50 percent of their sample of openly homosexual men living in San Francisco had had at least 500 sexual partners in their lifetimes and 28 percent said that they'd had over 1000 partners. Their data have been criticized for not being representative of all homosexuals and, in fact, two earlier studies found that only 22 percent (Kinsey et al., 1948) or 8 percent (Hunt, 1975) of gays had had more than 11 sexual partners in their lifetimes. Still, the sexual lifestyle reported by Bell and Weinberg may not have been atypical for openly homosexual males living in a large urban homosexual community in 1978 (*before* we knew about AIDS). Many researchers have found that males, as a general rule, seek physical gratification and do not place as high a value on monogamy as do women. When large numbers of male homosexuals share this set of beliefs and have easy opportunities to meet, the large numbers of partners reported by Bell and Weinberg may not seem surprising. However, Bell and Weinberg's study (1978) was before anyone knew about AIDS. Studies conducted since then indicate that gay men now place far greater emphasis on relationships (Carl, 1986; Levine, 1992). Young gay men today tend to value emotional aspects of their relationship more than older gay men (Deenen, Gijs, & Naerssen, 1994). This change was observed as early as 1983; in that year a survey of 600 gay men in San Francisco by McKusick and colleagues found an increased interest in forming long-term rela-

FIGURE 9-3   LEONARDO DA VINCI. THIS ITALIAN RENAISSANCE PAINTER (*MONA LISA, THE LAST SUPPER*), ANATOMIST, ASTRONOMER, AND ENGINEER WAS ONE OF THE MOST VERSATILE GENIUSES IN HISTORY.

tionships, with a majority stating that they now felt that a monogamous relationship would be best for them (Meredith, 1984). AIDS emphasized the importance of relationships, and, as one researcher put it, "The relational ethos fostered new erotic attitudes. Most men now perceived coupling, monogamy, and celibacy as healthy and socially acceptable" (Levine, 1992).

The Kinsey (1953) survey found that only 4 percent of the lesbians sampled had had more than 11 partners, and the Hunt survey found only 1 percent. Even in the Bell and Weinberg survey (1978), a majority (70 percent) of lesbians reported having fewer than ten partners, while 50 percent said that they did not like to have one-night stands. Females, whether straight or lesbian, seem to value commitment and romantic love. This is reflected in the longer-lasting relationships and the fewer number of partners they have compared to men (Leigh, 1989; Tuller, 1988). As usual, males and females are very different in their sexual behaviors and attitudes, regardless of their sexual orientations.

In their sexual relations, homosexual couples do everything that heterosexual couples do (Blumstein & Schwartz 1983; Masters & Johnson, 1979). They kiss, caress, engage in oral-genital sex, and, in the case of men, engage in anal intercourse (very few lesbians practice this). Lesbian couples generally take a great deal more time touching and caressing one another than heterosexual couples, for whom sexual relations are often dominated by the goal-oriented male (Hite, 1976; Masters & Johnson, 1979). Manual stimulation of the genitals and oral-genital sex are the preferred ways of reaching orgasm for lesbians (Bell & Weinberg, 1978; Masters & Johnson, 1979). Many lesbians engage in tribadism, the rubbing of genitals against another's genitals or other body parts, but very few use dildos (objects shaped like a penis). Perhaps because they take more time and understand each other's body better, lesbians have orgasms far more regularly during sex than do married heterosexual women (Kinsey et al., 1953). Among gays, oral-genital sex was once the most common sexual practice, followed by manual stimulation; anal intercourse was least common (Bell & Weinberg, 1978). Today, because of AIDS, there are fewer gays than in the past engaging in sexual practices that involve exchange of body fluids (Martin, 1987).

A common stereotype that many heterosexuals have of homosexuals is that they adopt a single role in a sexual relationship, with one being the "masculine" partner and the other being the "feminine" partner. This, of course, is based on their own heterosexual relations, but, in fact, is not true. Most homosexuals change positions and roles or use simultaneous stimulation during sex (McWhirter & Mattison, 1984). Hooker (1965) found, for example, that only 20 percent of male homosexuals preferred only one sexual role.

Homosexuals and Marriage

Studies estimate that one fifth of gay men and one third of lesbians have been married (Bell & Weinberg, 1978; Masters & Johnson, 1979). Millions of bisexual men and women are partners in heterosexual marriages (Gochros, 1989; I. Hill, 1987). While some of these men and women were not aware of their sexual orientation when they married, many others were aware. Why would someone who knows they are homosexual or bisexual choose to marry a heterosexual? There are many possible reasons, including societal or family pressures, affection for the partner, desire to have children, or even negative feelings about leading a homosexual lifestyle (Bozett, 1987; Coleman, 1981).

Of those married people who are consciously aware of their homosexuality or bisexuality, very few admit it to their partners (Gochros, 1989). Many experts find that there is little chance of a married homosexual or bisexual person being monogamous with a heterosexual partner (Clark, 1987; Masters, Johnson, & Kolodny, 1992). The secret life led by the homosexual or bisexual partner can cause them considerable anxiety and stress. When the partner does discover the truth, he or she often experiences considerable pain and anger, which is heightened by feeling stupid and deceived. Most say they would have never married had they known the truth (Hays & Samuels, 1989).

Many gays and lesbians establish long-lasting relationships. Should they be allowed to legally marry? Polls indicate that most Americans oppose the idea of homosexual marriage. Why? Many heterosexuals say there is no point to it because homosexual couples can't have children (but see next section). Is the only purpose of marriage to have children?

In 1993, Hawaii's Supreme Court ruled that state's ban against homosexual marriages may be unconstitutional and sent the case back to a lower court (the case was still pending when this book went to press). The Constitution requires that states honor each other's laws, but it also holds that exceptions can be made when there are strong contrary points of view—and over 20

FIGURE 9-4   GERTRUDE STEIN (LEFT) WITH ALICE B. TOKLAS. STEIN INTRODUCED A UNIQUE STYLE OF WRITING THAT INFLUENCED A WHOLE GENERATION OF WRITERS.

states have laws that outlaw sodomy (see Chapter 16). Several western states are attempting to pass legislation that specifically excludes same-sex marriages. No doubt, there will also be legal issues raised about spousal health-plan and retirement coverage. The next few years will probably see many legal challenges, both pro and con, about this issue.

Homosexuals as Parents

There are, of course, several million married or formerly married homosexual (or bisexual) people who also are parents. Once the "secret" is unveiled, should an openly gay or lesbian person and his or her partner be allowed to raise a child? Should an openly homosexual couple be allowed to adopt a child? Before we continue, read the following real-life story:

This is the story of Kerry and Val, a lesbian couple. It is told in Kerry's own words.

"Val and I have been together for six years. We have two children, a daughter 5, Nicole, and a son 2, Nicholas. We both wanted a family but were a little afraid of the effects that our life style would have on the children. We finally decided that in spite of our sexual orientation, we would still be loving, caring parents with much to offer our children.

Next arose the problem of how to go about it. (We could not very well do it on our own.) We ended up choosing a mutual friend of ours to father the children. This took much understanding on Val's part to have her lover sleep with someone else. We were stable enough in our relationship that this did not cause us problems. The man we chose is divorced with three children. We wanted someone who already had children so that we would not have any custody problems. He already knew that we were gay and we were honest with him about our plans and wishes. He and I were both checked medically beforehand and the most opportune time for conception was determined.

I got pregnant easily both times. Val and I went to the doctor together from the beginning. We paid for all the expenses. Val took care of me while I was pregnant. We experienced all of the changes together: hearing the unborn baby's heartbeat, feeling it move, staying up with me when it was too uncomfortable to sleep. Val was with me all through labor and delivery. She got to see the babies being born and was the first to hold them. She was there from beginning to end. It was a wonderful experience for us to share and it brought us much closer.

We both believe that a lot of love and a lot of time spent with our children is the key. We try to never be too busy to listen to them. We both are involved with Nicole's school (Val especially, she is a room parent for Nicole's class), friends, and activities. This is very difficult because we both work. I am self-employed and attend school full time and Val is planning to return to school next semester. We also spend a lot of time involved in family activities such as going to the park or zoo, bike riding, camping, etc. We almost always include the kids in everything we do.

We both share all the responsibilities for the children, the house (cooking, cleaning, etc.,), and finances. Val helps me tremendously with my work so I can devote more effort to school. We are very happy together and can't imagine life without one another. We both wish that legally we could be recognized as a couple. It would be nice to be able to get insurance as a family, file taxes together, etc., but most importantly are the kids. If anything ever happens to me, what will happen to them? Val loves them as if they were her own and they love her and are very attached to her. I would want them to stay with her, but there is nothing I can do legally.

My parents both know my wishes (they are divorced and both remarried). My dad adores Val and is very proud of the life we have made together and the stable home we have provided for our children. He would do his best to assure that the children remain with Val. On the other hand, my mom hates my life style. She refuses to have anything to do with Val and because of this we rarely speak. If anything ever happened to me, she would try her best to take the children from Val and would raise the children to hate me (she has told me this). She is not proud of me at all, regardless of how well I have done. She doesn't accept the fact that without Val, I would be nothing. Yet, she is proud of my sisters who are bums. . . .

Val and I believe that as far as the children are concerned, we will never lie or hide any information about our life style or their pasts. Along with their everyday education, we will also include the information about our life style as they are able to understand it. We do not sexually do anything in front of the children—no parents should. We do hug, hold hands and kiss goodbye. It is healthy for the children to see people displaying affection for each other.

We are honest with everyone about our life style. Our friends, families, and employers and

FIGURE 9-5   WALT WHITMAN. MANY SCHOLARS CONSIDER HIS *LEAVES OF GRASS* TO BE THE GREATEST COLLECTION OF POEMS EVER WRITTEN BY AN AMERICAN.

co-workers all know we are gay. To us honesty is the best policy. We do not flaunt anything in front of them or do anything to embarrass anyone, nor would we, but we don't lie about it either. For the most part we have gotten nothing but respect from our straight friends. Sometimes they are curious, but that is natural. Mostly they respect our privacy and admire our honesty. Once people really get to know us they realize that we are no different from anyone else. At first we were a little worried about the reception that we would get from other parents that our children were associated with. Would they shun our children because of how we live? We wanted to be honest with them because their children were involved and we didn't want them to find out later and think badly of us because we lied. As it turns out honesty was best.

Val and I plan to grow old together. We are working together for the future. We have plans and dreams for the future as all couples do. We have and are continuously fighting to better ourselves and be accepted. We want to be treated normal just as everyone else. We are good people. The only difference is what we do behind closed doors. We do the best we can for our children. We want them to grow up normal, happy, and healthy. We are not pushing our life style on our kids nor do we want them to grow up gay. We want them to have good careers and families of their own. We want grandchildren who will visit us in our old age. But, no matter what they choose, we will always love them.''

(from the author's files)

The topic of homosexuals as parents is viewed very negatively by most heterosexuals. A 1989 *Time* magazine/CNN poll found that 75 percent of Americans opposed the idea, while a 1994 *Newsweek* poll found that 65 percent were opposed. This negativity has been reflected in court custody cases as well. In 1993, for example, a Virginia woman lost custody of her 2-year-old son because the judge called her lesbian relationship with another woman "immoral." Many other gays and lesbians have had similar experiences in court. Why the negativity? According to child psychiatrist Betty Ann June Muller, who debated on the subject at the 1994 annual meeting of the American Bar Association, "Judges often have cited long-held stereotypes in justifying awarding custody to the heterosexual parent. Those myths include the view that gays and lesbians are mentally ill, have weak parental instincts or are more

likely to raise children who will be homosexual or be sexually abused" (Theim, 1994).

What does the scientific literature show? I have already reviewed the literature on mental illness; most homosexuals are as well adjusted as heterosexuals. As for sexual abuse, several studies have found that very few cases of parental sexual abuse are committed by homosexuals; most are committed by heterosexuals (Barrett & Robinson, 1990; Cramer, 1986; Newton, 1978). What about openly homosexual parents serving as role models for their children's gender identity and gender role development? Children raised in a household where the parent is openly homosexual do not show gender identity conflicts, do not have poor relations with their peers, and have a heterosexual orientation as often as children raised by heterosexual parents (Bailey et al., 1995; see Patterson, 1992 for a review of many studies). (This last finding is perhaps further evidence that biology is more important than environment in determining sexual orientation.) Openly homosexual parents also generally have positive relationships with their children (Turner et al., 1985).

Perhaps when the public becomes educated about these findings the negativity will subside. Meanwhile, the controversy continues. When the New York City school board proposed a "Children of the Rainbow" curriculum in 1992 that included the young children's books *Daddy's Roommate* (about a boy who spends weekends with his father and his male lover) and *Heather Has Two Mommies*, it ignited a public outcry. Should good parenting be based on sexual orientation, or are there other qualities that make a person a good or bad parent? ■

FIGURE 9-6   MARTINA NAVRATILOVA. THIS CZECHOSLOVAKIAN-BORN TENNIS PLAYER WAS PERHAPS THE GREATEST FEMALE ATHLETE OF THE 1980s.

HOMOPHOBIA

"During my junior year in high school I made a new male friend. The more I got to know him the more I began to suspect that he was gay. This scared me. As a result of my growing fears I discontinued our friendship."

"When I was in high school I worked at a flower shop. I didn't realize the owner's son was gay until my junior year. He acted totally normal. . . . One afternoon I saw him driving somewhere with his boy friend. Ever since that day I am kind of afraid and don't like to even have conversation with him. I don't know why I fear him so much because he has never done any harm to me."

". . . I don't even want to be near them or share the same things. . . . I feel like I might catch their 'gay' germs. . . ."

(from the author's files)

Many people are prejudiced against others who they perceive to be different. People discriminate on the basis of skin color, gender, and religion, but hostility toward homosexuals is probably far more accepted among Americans than any other type of bias (Goleman, 1990). Recall, for example, the study that found that 89 percent of young males consider male homosexuality to be disgusting (Marsiglio, 1993b). AIDS, who many believe (incorrectly) is a homosexual disease, has increased prejudice against homosexuals (Lewes, 1992). The National Gay and Lesbian Task Force reported 817 incidents of antigay physical assaults (usually by groups of heterosexual males) in 1992. Over 90 percent of gay men have been verbally abused or threatened (Herek, 1989). In such a harsh world, is it any wonder that 30 percent of suicides committed each year by people aged 15 to 24 are by homosexuals (Health and Human Services Department, 1989)?

Homophobia is an irrational fear of homosexuality (some researchers prefer the term "anti-gay prejudice"; Haaga, 1991). It is greater among males than it is among females (Van de Ven, 1994; Whitley & Kite, 1995; but see Oliver & Hyde, 1993). Why do some people have such fear and/or hostility of homosexuals? Studies find that among males, homophobic views are greatest in men with stereotypic male gender role attitudes, a religious fundamentalist attitude, and little education (Marsiglio, 1993; Van de Ven, 1994). But this tells us nothing of the psychological basis of homophobia.

Some psychologists believe that it stems from "self-righteousness in which homosexuals are perceived as contemptible threats to the moral universe" (Goleman, 1990). However, there is a major inconsistency with this explanation. Many sexually explicit male-oriented magazines regularly devote several pages to female-on-female sexual activity and female homosexual sex scenes are often shown in hard core porno films made for male heterosexual audiences. Surveys in my own course indicate that few male students are disturbed by female-on-female sex scenes, but are greatly bothered by male-on-male scenes. Why is it that many males have such a negative attitude toward male homosexuality in particular (Herek, 1984)?

> ### Homophobia
> An irrational fear of homosexual individuals and homosexuality.

Reprinted by permission: Tribune Media Services

Obviously, male homosexuality must be more threatening to many men than female homosexuality. Some of Freud's followers believe that it is the result of remnants of homosexuality in the "normal" (i.e., heterosexual) resolution of the Oedipal complex—identification with one's father involves love for one's father (de Kuyper, 1993).

Most researchers have a slightly different explanation. For most people, adolescence is a confusing time period as they try to establish their own identity and orientations. Most heterosexuals have homosexual fantasies on occasion (see Chapter 11) and lack of understanding of this and other aspects of sexuality enhance the confusion. Gregory Herek, the leading authority on homophobia, believes that antigay prejudice is an attempt to suppress any attraction to the same sex (see Herek, 1988). He says, "The teens and early 20's is a time of identity consolidation, struggling with issues of manhood and masculinity, how one becomes a man. By attacking a gay man or a lesbian, these guys are trying symbolically to affirm their manhood" (Associated Press, July 1993).

Homophobia affects relations among heterosexuals as well. Many Americans were probably shocked at seeing eastern European and Asian male athletes hug and kiss each other in international competitions (such as the Olympics). This is normal in these countries, where they have learned to differentiate affection from sex. Here, homophobia is so widespread that it prevents many same-sex family members (most commonly, fathers and sons) and friends from being affectionate with one another (Britton, 1990; Garnets et al., 1990). It prevents many people, especially men, from enjoying intimate relations with others. Are you able to hug your same-sexed parent? Good friends of the same sex? If not, examine what fears prevent you from doing so. Homophobia hurts everyone, including those who display it.

NATIONAL SUPPORT GROUPS

You can find the addresses and phone numbers of several organizations in the Resource section of the appendix. Also, be sure to contact local support group organizations. Most college campuses, for example, have gay and lesbian alliances. ■

CAN (SHOULD) SEXUAL ORIENTATION BE CHANGED?

Recall that in the not too distant past homosexuality was viewed by the psychiatric field as psychopathology that required medical treatment. Many homosexuals were involuntarily subjected to "treatments" such as lobotomies, castration, and electric shock treatment. Rejection of the psychopathology model of homosexuality led to the abandonment of the idea that all homosexuals should be "cured," whether voluntarily or involuntarily. There are still therapists who attempt to convert homosexuals to heterosexuals, but the only legitimate reason today is personal choice (see Murphy, 1992).

One study found that when homosexuals were asked if they would choose to take a "magic heterosexual pill" to change their sexual orientation, 14 percent of gays and 5 percent of lesbians said that they would do so (Bell & Weinberg, 1978). Note that these results also indicate that the large majority of homosexuals feel comfortable with their sexual orientation and do not wish to change. It is a myth held by heterosexuals that most homosexuals want to change.

For those homosexual individuals who choose to change their orientation, there are therapists who practice a variety of techniques including psychoanalysis (Bieber, 1965; Marmor, 1980) and behavioral therapy (Cautela & Kearney, 1986; Masters & Johnson, 1979, see Murphy, 1992 for a review). However, others charge that changing an individual's sexual orientation is not possible (Acosta, 1975; Marciano, 1982). This conclusion has gained strength with the recent findings of a possible biological (particularly hereditary) role in sexual orientation.

Although homosexuals no longer have to fear unwanted medical treatment, it is still questionable whether those gays and lesbians who seek reorientation truly do so "voluntarily" (Halleck, 1976; Murphy, 1992). Most probably do so because of years of dealing with family pressure, job discrimination, legal hassles, etc., resulting in self-loathing. According to Murphy (1992), "If this is true, it would appear that 'treating' the 'homosexual' would still be a form of blaming the victim, i.e., treating the person who suffers rather than ameliorating those social forces which devalue homoeroticism."

In 1994, the American Medical Association finally reversed a long-standing policy of recommending that physicians make efforts to turn unhappy homosexuals into heterosexuals. The new policy states that most of homosexuals' emotional problems "is due more to a sense of alienation in an unaccepting environment" and that "through psychotherapy, gay men and lesbians can become comfortable with their sexual orientation and understand the social responses to it" (AMA, 1994).

KEY TERMS

bisexual   216, 218
coming out   226
gay   224
gender identity   192, 219

gender roles   192, 219
heterosexual   216
homophobia   234
homosexual   216

lesbian   224
Oedipus complex   200, 220
sexual orientation   218
straight   224

PERSONAL REFLECTIONS

1. Are you comfortable with your sexual orientation? If not, why? What steps can you take to become more comfortable?

2. Homosexuals and bisexuals: Have you told your family and friends of your sexual orientation? Why or why not?

3. How would you react if someone at work told you that he or she was homosexual? What if your best friend told you that he or she was homosexual? Your brother or sister? Your teenaged son or daughter? Why?

4. Heterosexuals: Do you ever judge others exclusively, or almost exclusively, by their sexual orientation? How do you suppose you would feel if others ignored your accomplishments in school, your career, sports/hobbies, and in your community, and judged you exclusively on some aspect of your sex life?

SUGGESTED READINGS

Bendet, P. (1986, August/September). Hostile eyes. *Campus Voice*. Discusses homophobia on college campuses.

Burr, C. (1993, March). Homosexuality and biology. *The Atlantic Monthly*. An excellent article on the biology of sexual orientation.

Clark, D. H. (1987). *The new loving someone gay*. Berkeley, CA: Celestial Arts. Written for parents of gays.

De Cecco, J. (Ed.). (1988). *Gay relationships*. New York: Haworth Press. Essays on many aspects of gay relations.

Fairchild, B., and Hayward, N. (1979). *Now that you know: What every parent should know about homosexuality*. New York: Harcourt Brace Jovanovich. Sensitively written for parents.

Gelman, D., Foote, D., Barett, T., and Talbot, M. (1992, February 24). Born or bred? *Newsweek*. An excellent article on the possible biological bases of homosexuality.

Gladue, B. A. (1994, October). The biopsychology of sexual orientation. *Current Directions in Psychological Science, 3*. An excellent review of the biology of sexual orientation.

Leland, J. (1995, July 17). Bisexuality. *Newsweek*.

Leland, J., Rosenberg, D., and Miller, M. (1994, February 14). Homophobia. *Newsweek*.

Loulan, J. (1984). *Lesbian sex*. San Francisco: Spinsters Ink. Examines the lesbian lifestyle and sexual relationships.

Meredith, N. (1984, January). The gay dilemma. *Psychology Today*. How many gays have changed their sexual lifestyles as a result of AIDS.

Peplau, L. A. (1981, March). What homosexuals want in relationships. *Psychology Today*.

Remafedi, G. (1989, May/July). The healthy sexual development of gay and lesbian adolescents. *SIECUS Report*. Discusses characteristics of healthy homosexual development.

Toufexis, A. (1992, August 17). Bisexuality: What is it? *Time*. A short introduction to a very misunderstood subject.

CHAPTER TEN

LIFE-SPAN SEXUAL DEVELOPMENT

WHEN YOU HAVE FINISHED STUDYING THIS CHAPTER, YOU SHOULD BE ABLE TO:

1. EXPLAIN INFANTS' EXPLORATION OF THEIR BODIES AND THEIR NEED FOR CLOSE PHYSICAL COMFORT;

2. DISCUSS MASTURBATION AND SEX PLAY IN YOUNG CHILDREN;

3. DISCUSS THE DEVELOPMENT OF MODESTY AND INHIBITIONS DURING THE EARLY SCHOOL-AGED YEARS;

4. SUMMARIZE THE CHANGES THAT OCCUR IN BOYS' AND GIRLS' BODIES AT PUBERTY AND IDENTIFY THE HORMONES THAT ARE RESPONSIBLE;

5. DISCUSS SEXUAL BEHAVIOR AMONG ADOLESCENTS AND THE EFFECTS OF PEER PRESSURE;

6. EXPLAIN HOW THE SEXUAL BEHAVIOR OF YOUNG ADULTS OFTEN DIFFERS FROM THAT OF YOUNGER AND OLDER AGE GROUPS;

7. DISCUSS THE SEXUAL LIFESTYLES OF ADULTS, INCLUDING MARRIAGE, COHABITATION, AND EXTRAMARITAL SEX;

8. DESCRIBE THE CHARACTERISTICS THAT MEN AND WOMEN LOOK FOR WHEN CHOOSING A SHORT-TERM OR LONG-TERM MATE;

9. DESCRIBE THE SEXUAL BEHAVIOR OF MIDDLE-AGED INDIVIDUALS AND THE PHYSICAL CHANGES THAT COME WITH AGING; AND

10. EXPLAIN THE REALITIES OF AGING THAT CAN DIRECTLY AFFECT SEXUALITY IN THE ELDERLY, AND DISCUSS THE PREVALENCE OF SEXUAL RELATIONS AMONG HEALTHY ELDERLY COUPLES.

PEOPLE ARE SEXUAL BEINGS. TO DENY OUR SEXUALITY IS TO DENY OUR HUMANITY. IT SHOULD COME AS no surprise, therefore, that our sexuality begins from the moment of our birth (and perhaps before) until our death (even if we live a very long life). ∎

EARLY INFANCY (Age 0—1)

Sexuality apparently starts in the womb. Ultrasound recordings have discovered that male fetuses have erections months before they are born (Calderone, 1983b). After birth, male babies often have erections before the umbilical cord is cut. Similarly, female babies can have vaginal lubrication in the first 24 hours after birth (Langfeldt, 1981; Masters, 1980).

An important part of sexual development involves the amount of hugging and cuddling that an infant has with its caregivers. Many physicians and psychologists strongly encourage parents to hold their babies immediately after birth and to continue to give large amounts of hugging and cuddling throughout childhood. Some psychologists and physicians believe that lots of hugging and cuddling between parent and infant allows a strong attachment to be formed between them, which is a process called "bonding." Monkeys raised in isolation and deprived of the opportunity of close physical comfort have difficulty forming relationships later. The same seems to be true for children (Harlow & Harlow, 1962; Money, 1980). Fifty years ago a physician reported that one in three human infants in foundling homes died during the first year of life, even though they were well-fed and provided with adequate medical care. What these babies were not receiving was cuddling, hugging, fondling, and kissing—they apparently died from emotional neglect (Spitz, 1945, 1946). Today, some hospitals are recruiting volunteers to hold and talk to babies (especially premature ones) so that they will not be deprived of early physical contact if their parents cannot provide it. When nursing, infant boys may get an erection and infant girls may display vaginal lubrication. These are reflexive reactions and are normal, and parents should not be alarmed when they happen.

As soon as infants gain sufficient control over their movements, they begin to touch all parts of their bodies. As part of this exploration infants sometimes touch their genitals. They can feel pleasure from this and may continue to stimulate themselves. This happens because the nerve endings in the genitals are already developed at birth and transmit sensations of pleasure when stimulated. However, it is important to remember that infants do not comprehend adult sexual behavior. Their behavior is aimed at finding pleasurable physical sensations, not expressing sexual desire. Although the initial sexual self-stimulation of children may be random, once they discover its pleasurable component, such stimulation quickly becomes purposeful. Taking a child's hand away from his or her genitals may cause the child to make a disagreeable face or noises, and the child may quickly try to resume self-stimulation (Bakwin, 1974). Kinsey and his colleagues reported that 32 percent of boys less than 1 year of age were able to have orgasms (though ejaculation during orgasm is not possible until puberty is reached). He also reported a number of cases of girls 3 years old or younger masturbating to orgasm (Kinsey et al., 1948, 1953). ∎

EARLY CHILDHOOD (Age 2—6)

Before age 2, children are highly egocentric, a term coined by psychologist Jean Piaget in his theory of cognitive development (the growth of knowledge in human beings). This means that they cannot consider other people's points of view. Egocentric children do not play games together, because most play requires cooperation, and cooperation in turn requires respecting or anticipating someone else's point of view. Bodily exploration during this time is confined mainly to self-exploration (Figure 10-1). After the age of 2, however, children increasingly play together and their natural curiosity now extends not only to their own bodies, but to those of others.

Studies have shown that sexualized behaviors increase dramatically in children after age 2 and reach a peak in the 3- through 5-year age period, and then decrease until puberty (Friedrich et al., 1991; Rutter, 1971). Interest in the genitals is very common for boys and girls in this age group, as is undressing and sexual exploration games (that involve showing one's body and genitals to others, or vice versa). Let us examine some of the common, normal behaviors frequently observed in young children.

As just mentioned, by the age of 2 children are very interested in their bodies. Because of this they will try to watch their siblings and parents bathing and urinating.

"When I was a very young girl, my parents brought me with them to visit some friends of theirs who had two young boys. One boy was my age and one was a couple of years older. I went to the bathroom with them and watched them urinate. My mother got very, very angry. This totally surprised, shocked, and confused me. Maybe if she had had a course like this one, she could have handled the situation a little better.''

(from the author's files)

The fact that boys stand and girls sit while urinating is fascinating to children. They will also take their clothes off together and will play games such as "playing doctor" and "playing house" that allow for sexual exploration. Most of the time, these games are limited to viewing and touching genitals. More aggressive sexual behaviors like oral-genital contact and inserting objects into the vagina or anus are uncommon (Friedrich et al., 1991) and may be an indication of abuse. Sexual exploration games will not harm a child's development. What may be harmful is if parents react too strongly when they "catch" their children engaging in sex play.

" I can still remember the day my mother caught me playing 'doctor' with my neighbor. I was five years old. She got so mad at me that she locked me up in the bathroom. I don't remember how long I was in there. I didn't understand what I had done wrong. I ended up crying myself to sleep on the bathroom floor.''

" When I was 4, my cousin (age 5) and sister (age 3) had a slumber party. When we were all laying down we started asking questions and being curious. We then started 'playing doctor.' Well, my parents caught us and I was spanked and punished for a long time. I have very vivid memories of this event and now I do not have very positive feelings about sex or my sexuality.''

" When I was about 4 or 5 years old I got caught playing doctor with a little boy and girl. My mom was *very* angry and she put me on my knees with no pants or underwear. She made me stay there with no clothes on until my dad came home, so that he could see me like this. I believe

that this really has affected me in a negative way towards sex even now.''

(from the author's files)

Sexual exploration games are often played with playmates of the same sex. This is probably more common than sexual contact between sexes, because even at this age children usually play more with playmates of the same sex. Engaging in homosexual contact at this age does not mean that a child will become homosexual as an adult. Adult homosexuals may or may not have been involved in homosexual play in early childhood. The same is true of heterosexual adults.

Recall that Freud said the genitals were the focus of children's pleasure during the phallic stage (approximately ages 3–7) of psychosexual development (see Chapter 8). It is true that nearly all young children touch and explore their genitals, although young boys engage in masturbatory behavior more often than young girls (probably because the male genitals are more visible; Friedrich et al., 1991). Here, too, the way parents respond is very important.

" My sister has a five-year-old little boy. . . . She was all worried that something was wrong with him. He would constantly play with his penis. She scolded him one day and told him that if little boys play with themselves like that it would fall off. . . . I am afraid that this could scar him for life. . . . ''

" I was raised in a strict Catholic family. I remember distinctly how my initially unhealthy attitude towards my sexuality and that of others began. As a small child, I used to masturbate. My mother would hit the ceiling when she would catch me because my favorite time to do this was at nap time. She would yell and scream and slap my hands and tell me that it was nasty. Her contempt for my actions was so obvious that I could not help but develop a negative attitude towards my sexuality. I worried for a long time that I was the only person who did this and felt very guilty about it. . . . ''

(from the author's files)

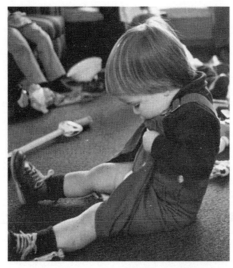

FIGURE 10-1   IT IS NORMAL FOR CHILDREN TO EXPLORE THEIR OWN BODIES.

Most parents respond negatively to finding their young child masturbating (Gagnon, 1985).

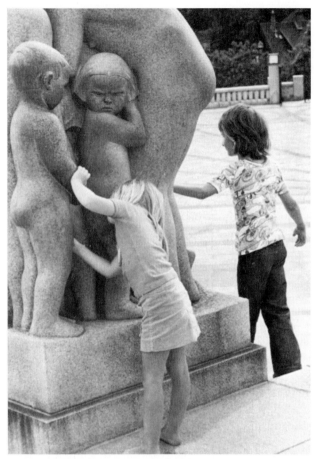

FIGURE 10-2 CHILDREN WILL ATTEMPT TO SATISFY THEIR NATURAL CURIOSITY ABOUT THE HUMAN BODY WHENEVER THEY GET A CHANCE. IF THIS WERE YOUR CHILD, WOULD YOU PULL HER AWAY, OR WOULD YOU LET HER EXPLORE AND TRY TO ANSWER ANY QUESTIONS SHE MIGHT HAVE ABOUT THE DIFFERENCE BETWEEN BOYS AND GIRLS?

& Johnson, 1970; Money, 1980). It is okay to teach your children that it is not appropriate (as opposed to "bad") to touch their genitals in certain situations; in public, for example. According to one child expert, "The attitude of the parent should be to socialize for privacy rather than to punish or forbid" (Calderone, 1983a). If your child touches herself or himself at home, the best thing to do is ignore it. If you feel that you have to stop it (because it bothers you), do not scold; simply distract your child by getting her (or him) involved in another activity.

By now, you should understand that parents' responses to normal behaviors are very important for later sexual development and attitudes about one's body. According to one group of researchers, "From the earliest period in life, the child's family will reciprocally influence the sexual characteristics of the child. The family establishes a 'psychosexual equilibrium' that is a function of the parents' sexual adjustment, the child's developing sexuality, and the impact of the child's sexual development on parental sexual development. . . . " (Friedrich et al., 1991). The way parents react to the sexuality of their children is often an indication of the way they feel about their own sexuality.

It is important that parents be comfortable with their own sexuality, because parents are the major source of sexual information for young children. By age 4, for example, children often have asked parents where babies come from. They may also ask other frankly sexual questions. At this point, parents have a decision to make. Children will either learn about sex from parents or from other people. Generally, those "other people" will be other children who may not share your values and who may give bad advice or misinformation. Moreover, schools, and even those with sex education courses, may not always deal with values. Sex education is largely absent in schools before puberty (except for lessons like "Don't get into a car with strangers," or "Don't let strangers touch you in your private places"). Chapter 17 describes *how to talk to children of different ages about sexuality*—both your sexuality and theirs. The ability to communicate with your children about sex and other topics is a critical part of good parenting. ■

However, when you become a parent try not to overreact. Allowing children to explore and satisfy their curiosity enables them to become comfortable with their bodies, both as a child and as an adult (Renshaw, 1988). Punishment or negative messages may lead to a poor body image and later sexual problems (Masters

THE INITIAL SCHOOL-AGE YEARS (Age 7–11)

Freud believed that this time of life was a period of "latency" when children were not concerned with sexuality. Studies have found that children in fact do engage in less overt sexual behavior at this time (Friedrich et al., 1991; Money & Ehrhardt, 1972). This is probably due to learning cultural standards. By

the time they begin kindergarten or first grade, children generally have developed a sense of modesty and inhibitions about exposing their bodies in public (Money & Ehrhardt, 1972). They may be very shy about undressing in front of parents, and for the first time start demanding privacy in the bathroom.

FIGURE 10-3   WHEN THEY ENTER KINDERGARTEN
OR FIRST GRADE, CHILDREN ARE STILL
CURIOUS ABOUT SEXUALITY, BUT ARE
ALSO DEVELOPING A SENSE OF MODESTY
AND INHIBITIONS ABOUT EXPOSING
ONE'S BODY IN PUBLIC.

FIGURE 10-4   BOYS AND GIRLS OFTEN PLAY
TOGETHER DURING EARLY CHILDHOOD,
BUT TEND TO SEGREGATE BY GENDER
BY AGE 9.

Some researchers believe that the amount of sex play does not slow down at this stage, but that it is simply hidden more from parents (Goldman & Goldman, 1982; Kinsey, Pomeroy, & Martin, 1948; Kinsey et al., 1953). Children tend to segregate by gender by age 9 and thus much of the sexual play is with same-sexed children (Elias & Gebhard, 1969). This is a normal part of growing up and parents should not interpret it as homosexual activity in the same manner as between two adults.

When caught engaging in sexual exploration games, girls are often treated more harshly than boys. This establishes a double standard—as a general rule, boys are allowed more freedom to explore their sexuality than girls. Consider the following: What if the principal of your child's school called and said that your son had been caught telling a female classmate, "You can touch my thing, if I can touch yours." How would you react? Would you react differently if your daughter had said this to a boy? Why?

Although the amount of overt sexual play may decrease during the initial school-age years, curiosity about sex does not, and children will ask their parents questions such as "Where do babies come from?" Bernstein (1976) claimed that most children in the United States have learned about sexual intercourse and its connection to pregnancy by the age of 8 or 9. However, many continue to have rather strange ideas about sex and birth. Goldman and Goldman (1982) found that at least 50 percent of children 11 years of age or younger in their North American sample believed that children were born through the anus. Many children believed that sex is primarily carried out by insertion of the penis into the anus. Again, how parents respond will affect their children's responses (and willingness to ask questions of their parents about sex) in the future.

Unfortunately, many parents are evasive or even negative.

My mother damaged my attitude about sexuality by responding to my question about the origins of babies by telling me that when a man and a woman kiss, it's called making love and this is where babies come from.

Even today, she still refuses to discuss sex or sexuality. . . . ''

(from the author's files)

After this period of relatively restrained sexuality, sexual exploration increases dramatically again just before or during puberty. ∎

PUBERTY

Puberty (from the Latin *puber*, meaning of ripe age, adult) is the time of life when we become capable of reproduction. It does not happen overnight, but instead is *a process lasting several years*. The pituitary gland begins to secrete FSH in high doses, stimulating the production of sperm in seminiferous tubules in boys and the maturation of ova in girls (see Chapter 3). Prior to this time, boys do not ejaculate (though they can have orgasms) and girls do not have menstrual cycles. In girls, the maturing ovary produces estrogen and progesterone, while increased levels of the hormone ICSH from a boy's pituitary stimulates production of testosterone in the testes. The increased levels of hormones lead to a variety of physiological changes in girls and boys (e.g., breast development, facial hair).

> **Puberty**
> The time in life when an individual becomes capable of reproduction.

> **Secondary sex characteristics**
> Bodily changes that occur during puberty which differentiate males and females.

These are often referred to as **secondary sex characteristics**. These changes in physical appearance create psychological changes in the way children think about themselves and others. Let us examine these changes in more detail and discuss how they affect adolescents' behavior.

CHANGES IN GIRLS

One of the first noticeable changes in girls is a growth spurt starting at about the age of 12. Many sixth- and seventh- grade boys suddenly realize one day that a lot of the girls in their classroom are taller than they are (a fact they may not discover until those first school dances). The reason for this is that the growth spurt in boys does not start, on average, until about age 14. Most of the boys eventually catch up with and pass the girls, because girls generally stop growing by age 16 and boys keep growing until about 18; but those first couple of years can be awkward.

The development of breasts in girls during puberty (a result of increased levels of estrogen) is viewed with great attention by both girls and boys. Breast buds generally start developing at about age 11, but can start as early as 8. Many girls rush out to purchase training bras, which probably do nothing except make them feel mature. Girls worry that if they are not as "stacked" as their friends, they will be left behind in the rush to be popular with boys. Not all girls develop at the same rate, so insecurities may develop early. Some decide to speed things up on their own, as eleven-year-old Margaret did in Judy Blume's novel, *Are You There God? It's Me, Margaret* (Bradbury Press, 1970):

> I tiptoed back to my room and closed the door. I stepped into my closet and stood in one corner. I shoved three cotton balls into each side of my bra. Well, so what if it was cheating! Probably other girls did it too. I'd look a lot better, wouldn't I? So why not!
> I came out of the closet and got back up on my chair. This time when I turned sideways I looked like I'd grown. I liked it!''

The increase in estrogen levels also causes an increase in fatty deposits in the hips and buttocks.

Pubic hair generally starts to appear shortly after breast development begins, followed in a couple of years by the appearance of axillary (underarm) hair. The growth of hair on new parts of the body results from increased levels of male hormones (mainly from the adrenal gland). These hormones also cause the sweat glands to develop, so that body odor and acne (caused by clogged glands) often become a new source of concern.

Puberty may be a process that takes several years, but in many people's minds, a girl's first menstruation marks a turning point in her maturity. The vagina and uterus begin to enlarge about the time that pubic hair appears, and the first menstrual period (called **menarche**) occurs at an average age of about 12.5 for American girls. There is considerable variability, however, and it is normal for the cycles to be very irregular during the first couple of years after menarche. The rise in estrogen levels causes the vaginal walls to become thicker and more elastic and also results in lubrication during sexual arousal.

> **Menarche**
> The term for a female's first menstrual period.

The average age for menarche has been dropping

over the last few centuries. A study of New York City females in 1934 found that the average age was 13.5 years, while the average age in Western Europe in the early 1800s was at least 14.5 years (Bullough, 1981) and perhaps as high as 17 in some places (Tanner, 1962). Many researchers believe that the reason for this decline is better nutrition resulting in an earlier acquisition of some minimally required amount of body fat (the putative signal that tells the brain to start releasing FSH). Women suffering from anorexia nervosa (an eating disorder in which a person has an aversion to food) never menstruate, and very irregular cycles are common in female long-distance joggers who have lower than normal levels of body fat.

The reaction of a young woman to her first menstrual cycle will be influenced primarily by what she has been told. Menarche can be viewed as something very positive (a "sign of becoming a woman"), "a simple fact of nature," or a "curse" or something disgusting. Mothers generally discuss menstruation with their daughters, and pass on mothers' attitudes and beliefs about it.

"My mother told me that menstruation was a 'nasty' experience. As a result, I always did my utmost to totally hide the fact that I was menstruating. I didn't even want other women to know that I was having my period. I would refuse to purchase sanitary products out of the machines in restrooms if anyone else was in the restroom. . . . "

". . . Then when my big moment came, instead of treating me as though something natural and exciting were happening, my mother reacted with embarrassment. I was very hurt when she told me to get my sister to show me how to wear a sanitary napkin. We never talked about any of these things. The sanitary napkins were even kept locked . . . and whenever any of us needed one we would slip it under our shirt and scurry into the bathroom. Menstrual periods were regarded as a shameful secret in our home."

"My mother told me when I was very young that I would have a period around age 13 or so. . . . Finally, one month before my 15th birthday I started my period. I remember being so excited 'it' finally came. I called my mom in the bathroom and told her. Well, she was so excited she started calling my grandmothers and her friends. When my dad came home he got all excited too. They were so proud I'd finally 'become a woman.' "

(from the author's files)

Which of these girls do you suppose began adolescence with good self-esteem about her body?

Older sisters, friends, sex education courses in schools, and fathers may also give information about menstruation. As you can see from the previous case histories, for some parents the subject is still a taboo, and some girls are never told anything until it happens. This is especially true among African-American girls (Scott et al., 1989). In a study done by the Tampax Corporation, it was found that one fourth of all people surveyed felt that menstruation was an unacceptable topic for discussion even in the home (Tampax, Inc., 1981). Thus, some girls experience menarche with no prior knowledge, which makes it a frightening experience.

For boys, menarche is rarely a topic of discussion with their parents. Most learn about it "on the street," and it seems to be another mysterious difference between men and women. Menarche often is viewed as the topic of crude jokes, though most boys remain ignorant about the basic facts regarding menstruation until they reach adulthood (if then).

CHANGES IN BOYS

As mentioned earlier, pubertal development in boys lags about 2 years behind development in girls. The first noticeable change in boys is usually growth of the testes and scrotum, the result of increased levels of testosterone. Testosterone then stimulates growth of the penis, prostate gland, and seminal vesicles. The growth of the genitals begins, on average, about the age of $11Z \backslash x$ and is completed, on average, by about the age of 15. Boys generally become capable of ejaculation about a year after the penis begins to grow.

The first experience many males have with ejaculation is a nocturnal emission, or "wet dream." Some boys have nocturnal emissions frequently, while others have only a few experiences. Fewer fathers prepare their sons for nocturnal emissions than mothers prepare girls for menstruation, and as a result many boys are ashamed, or even frightened, by these experiences.

"When I was 13 years old, I had a 'wet dream' for the first time. I was shocked to later find out that I did not have a disease. I honestly thought I had one. . . . "

(from the author's files)

Because they are ashamed, some boys may hide their underwear and sheets or try other ways to "hide the evidence." Because nocturnal emissions are not under voluntary control, there is no reason for shame. It is therefore important to educate children about nocturnal emissions (and all other aspects of puberty) *before* they begin to occur.

Many boys may also be initially frightened by the emission of a strange fluid from the penis that now occurs during masturbation. A case cited by sex therapist Bernie Zilbergeld (1978) is probably not unusual:

``. . . I kept stroking, my penis got hard, and the sensations felt better and better. Then I was overcome with feelings I had never before felt and, God help me, white stuff came spurting out the end of my cock. I wasn't sure if I had sprung a leak or what. I was afraid but calmed down when I thought that since it wasn't red it couldn't be blood. I kept on stroking and it hurt. I didn't know if the hurt was connected with the white stuff (had I really injured myself?) or if the event was over and my penis needed a rest. But I decided to stop for the moment. Of course, I returned the next day and did it again. . . .''

Many boys also develop temporarily enlarged breasts during puberty, called **gynecomastia**. This results from increased levels of estrogen (from the testes).

Gynecomastia
Excessive development of the male breasts.

"When I was about 13-years-old something started to happen to my chest. It seemed as though I was beginning to grow breasts. I went to my mother and showed her so she brought me to the doctor. I was a wrestler in middle school and all I could think about was how could I avoid taking off my shirt in public for one to two years. . . .''

(from the author's files)

Gynecomastia usually disappears by the mid-teens, but unless boys are told why this is happening and that it is a normal, temporary condition, they may feel confused, embarrassed, and/or ashamed. Some fear that they are turning into girls. Some will stop swimming in public because they are too modest to display their male "breasts."

Pubic hair starts to grow about the same time as the genitals start to develop, the result of increasing testosterone levels, but underarm and facial hair generally do not appear for another 2 years. The amount of body hair, however, is also determined by heredity. As in girls, testosterone also causes development of the sweat glands with all their accompanying problems (acne, body odor).

The appearance of facial hair is often as important to boys as the development of breasts is to young girls, for it is one of the few outward signs that they are becoming men. They often start shaving long

FIGURE 10-5   PUBERTY AND THE DEVELOPMENT OF SECONDARY SEX CHARACTERISTICS MARK DRAMATIC INCREASES IN INTEREST IN SEXUALITY.

before it is necessary, only to wish a few years later that they could avoid it altogether. Another change that is obvious to others is a deepening of the voice, a result of testosterone stimulating the growth of the larynx (voice box). This occurs today at an average age of about 13Z\x, but it may have occurred at a later age in past centuries. It was not uncommon in Europe at one time for boys who sang in the great church choirs to be castrated before puberty (with parental approval) in order to preserve their soprano voices. (If castration is done after puberty, by the way, it does not substantially raise a male's voice because the larynx has already undergone its change.)

For Better or For Worse

Precocious Puberty

Although the changes that occur during puberty generally begin about the age of 11 or 12, they have been

> **Precocious puberty**
> A condition in which the events of puberty begin before the age of 9.

known to occur much earlier. When sexual development begins before the age of nine, it is called **precocious puberty**. This occurs in about one out of every 10,000 children. The youngest girl known to have given birth was only 5 years old: a Peruvian Indian girl who delivered a baby by cesarean section in 1939. This means, of course, that she was ovulating and having menstrual periods by the age of 4 or 5. The youngest couple on record who became parents was a Chinese boy and girl, aged 9 and 8, respectively.

In recent years, there have been isolated outbreaks around the world of very young children developing breasts. This has happened to boys and girls as young as 6 months old. The most recent cases have occurred in Puerto Rico, where 2000 to 3000 children have been affected. Experts believe the cause to be illegal use of high amounts of estrogens by poultry farmers. The hormone is used to fatten the chickens, but it can cause undesired effects when the chicken is eaten frequently by people.

Sexual Exploration

After the relative restraint of the initial school-age years, interest in sex as well as sexual exploration increase dramatically at puberty. In a review of studies of sexual development, Rutter (1971) found that masturbation, and both heterosexual and homosexual play, were common in 13 year olds. For example, while only 10 percent of children were masturbating at age 7, about 80 percent do so at age 13. The sexual exploration games (such as "spin the bottle" and "post office") also have a greater erotic content than the games of early childhood. ∎

ADOLESCENCE (Age 13–18)

Adolescence (from the Latin *adolescens*) refers to the time of life between puberty and adulthood. The term

> **Adolescence**
> The time of life between puberty and adulthood.

was first used in the English academic literature in 1904 by psychologist G. Stanley Hall. In our culture this is a transition period before adulthood, and a rather extended one at that, but in many nonindustrial cultures individuals are considered to be adults when they reach puberty.

For most adolescent boys and girls, the most important issue in their lives is self-identity (Erikson, 1968). Because of their rapidly changing bodies, the search for self-identity first focuses on body image and physical characteristics. According to Maddock et al. (1983), "There is an intensification of body aware-

ness . . . based upon the fact that the body is a primary 'symbol of self' in which feelings of personal worth, security, and competence are rooted." An adolescent's self-esteem is generally based on his or her physical attractiveness. Broad-based self-esteem derived from one's accomplishments develops later. Thus, in the adolescent world there is usually a strong relationship between one's physical attractiveness and one's social acceptance (Kleck, Richardson, & Ronald, 1974). For those adolescents who fit the football star or prom queen image, adolescence is often a positive experience. For the rest of us, it is a difficult time, and more and more so if you fall farther and farther away from what is considered attractive. We will return to this issue shortly.

MASTURBATION

For most (but certainly not all) people, the first experience with orgasm occurs during masturbation (for others it occurs during mutual touching, petting, sexual intercourse, or dreams). The first data on masturbation during adolescence came from Kinsey's group (1948, 1953). He found that by age 15, 82 percent of boys and 20 percent of girls had masturbated to orgasm. By the age 20, these figures had risen to 92 percent for males and 33 percent for females. The frequency of masturbation by age 15 was 1.8 times per week on the average for boys and 0.5 times per week on the average for girls. Seventeen percent of the boys interviewed had masturbated from four to seven times per week. Haas (1979) interviewed individuals aged 16 to 19 and found that more than two thirds of the males and one-half of the females masturbated to orgasm at least one time per week or more.

What do these numbers tell us? For one thing, most adults have masturbated and started doing so during adolescence. This is more true for men than women, but there seems to be a trend indicating that more and more women also are masturbating to orgasm during adolescence. Kolodny (1980) interviewed women aged 18 to 30 and found that 75 percent reported masturbating during adolescence. Nevertheless, males still have more experience with orgasm by the time they become adults, as a result of higher frequency of masturbation. There may be cultural differences as well. Some studies indicate, for example, that masturbation is more common among white adolescents than among African-American or Latino teens (Belcostro, 1985; Cortese, 1989).

These numbers also may indicate a greater willingness to admit to having masturbated. Santrock (1984) states that only 15 percent of adolescents believe that masturbation is wrong. However, this does not prevent many adolescents from experiencing guilt and other negative feelings about masturbation. Sorenson (1973) reported that 57 percent of adolescent girls and 45 percent of adolescent boys occasionally experienced negative feelings about masturbating. More recently, Laumann and colleagues (1994) found that about half of men and women who masturbated felt guilty about it. Even those who show little guilt and talk about masturbating in front of their peers may not want to let their parents know about it. The data indicate that this may be even truer for girls than boys.

Many sex therapists believe that masturbation serves important functions in adolescence. Because sexual activity among adolescents is not condoned in our society, masturbation can serve as an outlet for sexual tensions. It is interesting that we also live in a society where teenagers are constantly exposed to more and more sexually explicit episodes in movies, on TV, and in advertising. The typical teenager, you recall, sees over 2,000 references to sex a year on TV (Greenberg et al., 1987). Thus, our society sends an interesting double standard message to adolescents—sex is great, but not for you. Masturbation also can serve as a way to sexually experiment, gain sexual self-confidence, and control sexual impulses (Barbach, 1980). Kinsey thought that masturbation to orgasm was especially important for girls. He felt that familiarity with orgasm during masturbation made it easier for them to experience orgasm during sexual intercourse as an adult. Sexual intercourse does not always automatically result in orgasm for women, and therefore, a lack of awareness of their bodily or physical responses to erotic stimulation (or the fear of such responses) may further impede the ability to experience orgasm during intercourse. We will discuss this in Chapter 13.

John Gagnon (1977), a sociologist and psychologist who studies communication between generations, notes that masturbation is the single most powerful predictor of adult sexuality. People who masturbated during adolescence generally engage in sexual activity more frequently and have more positive attitudes about sex than people who did not. However, there are few programs or parents attempting to communicate anything positive about masturbation or other forms of sexual expression. Most communication about sex is negative ("don't do this; don't let this happen to you"). Gagnon's point is that parents should at least stop attaching guilt to the practice of masturbation in their children (an attitude that reflects the negative Victorian attitudes toward sex described in Chapter 1). If nothing else, it is surely the "safest" sexual outlet available. However, attitudes are hard to change; former Surgeon General Joycelyn Elders was fired for expressing similar views about masturbation. Masturbation as a normal adult behavior will be discussed in Chapter 11.

SEXUAL FANTASIES

Sexual fantasies in adolescence become very focused and explicit, compared to fantasies in childhood. Male fantasies are often focused on specific sexual activities (e.g., an orgy, having sex with a movie star or cheerleader), while sexual fantasies of females are more likely to involve romance and be socially oriented. Fantasies often accompany masturbation (Hass, 1979). Sexual fantasies can serve many useful purposes, including substituting for unavailable experiences, allowing mental rehearsal of sexual techniques, inducing arousal, and enhancing pleasure. Because many adults use mental imagery to enhance sexual pleasure, fantasizing in adolescence can be a useful prelude to adults' use of sexual imagery (see Chapter 11). Sexual fantasy is only part of the increased use of all types of fantasy in adolescence. By fantasizing, teenagers can experience things that are denied to them in real life. Sex is only one such experience.

PETTING

Kinsey's team of researchers defined petting as physical contact between males and females attempting to produce erotic stimulation without sexual intercourse. Such a definition would include a variety of behaviors, such as kissing, deep (French) kissing, stimulation of the female's breasts, touching of the genitals, and oral-genital sex. Many sex researchers today define *petting* as noncoital sexual contact below the waist. Any other physical contact is called *necking*. Kinsey et al. (1953) found that by age 18, over 80 percent of the boys and girls in their sample had engaged in petting. Twenty-one percent of boys and 15 percent of girls had petted to orgasm by this age. Typically, adolescents' sexual experiences proceed through the following sequence: holding hands, embracing, necking, feeling breasts (through clothing and then directly), feeling genitals (through clothing first, usually by the male first), and for many, sexual intercourse (Miller, Christopherson, & King, 1993; Smith & Udry, 1985).

Sorenson (1973) surveyed 13- to 19-year-olds. Seventy-two percent of the boys had felt a girl's breasts by age 15; 68 percent of the girls had had their breasts fondled by boys by age 15.

More recently, Kolodny (1980) interviewed first-year college students about their sexual experiences in high school. Kolodny found that 82 percent had engaged in genital touching. Fifty percent of the men and 40 percent of the women had petted to orgasm during adolescence.

Haas (1979) sampled 15- to 19-year-olds and found that 55 percent of the boys and 43 percent of the girls in the sample had engaged in genital touching. About one third of both boys and girls had engaged in oral sex. Among girls, experience with oral sex often precedes their first experience of intercourse (Newcomer & Udry, 1985). These numbers tell us that teenagers are engaging in most forms of sexual activity at an earlier age than in the past. What is extremely interesting about the Haas study is that for genital touching, 95 percent of the boys and 83 percent of the girls surveyed said that they approved of this behavior, while 90 percent of the boys and 70 percent of the girls indicated approval of oral sex. Thus, data indicate that acceptance of these behaviors exceeds the actual numbers of adolescents engaging in these behaviors. Attitudes are also changing with regard to relationships between the sexes in general. Murstein (1980) claims that older patterns of interaction, such as "going steady," are now sometimes replaced by less formal and less structured types of relationships.

SEXUAL INTERCOURSE

The number of unmarried adolescents engaging in sexual intercourse has risen in recent years, and the average age at which they first have intercourse has been steadily declining. Kinsey's group, in 1953, found that only 3 percent of 15-year-old girls had engaged in sexual intercourse. Twenty years later, Sorenson (1973) found that 26 percent of 15-year-old girls had had intercourse, and by age 19, 55 percent were nonvirgins. Jessor and Jessor (1975) found that 55 percent of high school senior girls reported that they had engaged in intercourse. Zelnik and Kantner (1979) reported 69 percent of the teenage girls in their survey were nonvirgins. According to the recent survey by Laumann and colleagues (1994), over one half of American teenagers have engaged in sexual intercourse before their seventeenth birthday (by age 15 for African-American males).

Yearly surveys conducted by the Centers for Disease Control and Prevention and others have confirmed that for both boys and girls, most have had sexual intercourse by age 17, and nearly three fourths by the twelfth grade (CDC, 1992; see Seidman & Rieder, 1994). The figures were slightly higher for African-American teens than for white teens. However, the latest surveys by the CDC (1995) show that the number of sexually active teens is leveling off, and other studies show that the level of sexual activity is relatively moderate—for males, an average of 1.9 partners in the last year, with an average frequency of intercourse of 2.7 times in the last month (Sonenstein, Pleck, & Ku, 1991).

A recent study found that women who had engaged in premarital sex were much more likely to have their marriages end in divorce than virgin brides (Kahn & London, 1991). The authors of the study attributed the higher divorce rate to a greater willingness to break traditional norms. Another study found that boys and girls who had had sexual intercourse when aged 12 to 16 were much more likely than others to have used alcohol and smoked marijuana (Orr, Beiter, & Ingersol, 1991).

How do teenagers feel about their first experiences of sexual intercourse? Weis (1983) found that women experience a range of emotions during their first experience of sexual intercourse. About one third had strongly negative emotional reactions (e.g., guilt, anxiety, shame, fear, regret), while another third had highly positive emotional experiences. For the final third, their experience was neither positive nor negative, but a "Is that all there is?" response (e.g., disappointment, boredom). A later study found that about one third of women had experienced severe physical pain at first intercourse, while 28 percent had experienced no pain (Weis, 1985). Women with positive experiences and minimal pain generally had an extensive childhood and adolescent history of sex play (kissing, petting, masturbation, and often oral sex), had positive attitudes about their sex play, and had their first intercourse in a

FIGURE 10-6   THE BIOLOGICAL CHANGES THAT OCCUR IN ADOLESCENCE LEAD TO AN INTEREST IN AND THE DEVELOPMENT OF SEXUAL BEHAVIOR AND SEXUAL IDENTITY.

safe environment (no fear of discovery) with a caring partner. Those who had experienced negative reactions and pain had little previous experience with sex play, had not planned it, and "gave in" to the male's pressure (see also Thompson, 1990). Interestingly, more American women have had negative emotional reactions to their first experience of sexual intercourse than women in Sweden, a sexually more permissive culture (Schwartz, 1993).

PEER PRESSURE

Half of males are motivated by curiosity the first time they have sex, while nearly a third of females say they "went along" with it (Laumann et al., 1994). Although many teens engage in sex because they have positive feelings about it, many others who are sexually active are motivated by desires to boost self-esteem and a desire for acceptance (Hajcak & Garwood, 1988). For most teens there is enormous peer pressure to engage in sex. What is

peer pressure? It is the expectations (of one's peer group) of how you are supposed to behave. If a teenager believes that most of his or her friends are having sex, there can be intense pressure (internally as well as externally) to conform. Some researchers believe that television shows with sexual content add to the likelihood that teens will engage in sex (Brown & Newcomer, 1991), but others are uncertain (Peterson, Moore, & Furstenberg, 1991).

Peer pressure
The expectations by one's peer group about how one is supposed to behave.

In Lakewood, California in 1993, a group of high school male athletes calling themselves the "Spur Posse" received a lot of national attention when they told investigators, and then the media (including TV talk shows), that they had a contest of who could "bed" the most girls. Several of these teens had already had sex with over 50 girls, some of whom were greatly underaged (thus the investigation). To be part of the group, these males were more concerned about scoring than they were about sex. According to sociologist Donna Elder, "There's quite a bit of research that adolescent males use sex as another arena to achieve and score. They take the competitive sense and move it into the realm of sexuality" (quoted in Gelman & Rogers, 1993).

Gender roles tend to be very rigid in adolescence, and peer pressure makes failure to conform even more difficult. What about those males who don't wish to become sexually active yet?

"You were right about the fact that there is great pressure to engage in sex. I didn't have sex until I got married at the age of 22. My friends thought it was dumb for me to want to wait so I lied to them and told them that I had sex and made up a bunch of lies about it. I realize now it was dumb of me. If they were really my friends they would have understood my decision to wait."

"I am a 19-year-old sophomore and I have not yet had sexual relations. I made a promise to myself long ago that I would not have sex until I am married. I made this promise because of my own moral convictions and I am content with it. I have been the target of a great deal of laughter and ridicule because of this decision. . . . I have been accused of being gay by some and of being sexually repressed by others. I don't see what the fuss is all about. If I am content with my sexuality and I decide to wait until I'm married to have sex, why should I be considered abnormal?"

(from the author's files)

Many teenaged girls also feel pressured to engage in sex:

``. . . I had sex at 17 in my senior year. . . . So many of my girlfriends would talk about doing it with and for their boyfriends, and would ask me about my experience. I was so ashamed for never having done anything throughout my entire life. . . . I was pressured by myself, him, and all my friends to do it, so I did. For no other reason than curiosity, I went through pain. . . .''

"My first sexual experience was when I was 15. Everyone else was 'doing it' so I figured I should too. When it was over I cried. I wish I would have waited. Maybe not till I was married, but until I was more mature.''

"I had my first sexual relationships at 14. . . . I realize now that my reason for these relationships was to be accepted, wanted, have a boyfriend and pleasing him to keep him.''

(from the author's files)

For many girls, the need for emotional intimacy is an important part of finding their self-identity (see Shaughnessy & Shakesby, 1992). Unfortunately, many confuse and mistake sexual intimacy for emotional intimacy. It should not be surprising, therefore, that far fewer teenage girls than boys (fewer than half of sexually active girls, in fact) find sex to be a pleasurable experience (survey by Roper Starch Worldwide, 1994). In many peer groups there is a double standard that also results in a negative sexual experience for many girls. While men worldwide enjoy female promiscuity, in most cultures males prefer women (as mates) who are virgins (Buss & Schmitt, 1993, see Box 10-A).

``. . . I would let some of the guys from school touch my breasts because of the attention I got from them. I only got a bad reputation instead. . . .''

"Please talk about labelling women. When I was 15, I had some experiences with some older guys around 17. Well, I did some things that I regret. Word got around at my all-girl Catholic high school that I was a slut. You don't know what it is like to walk down a hall and have girls call you a slut. Guys wanted to go out with me for just one thing. I was depressed and paranoid of what people thought. I even thought of killing myself. I am 21 and have a 'steady' boyfriend who does not know what I did six years ago. I still feel guilty. When I see girls from my high school, some of them still call me a slut. I am very hurt. Please mention this. It is hard to imagine the six years of hurt.''

(from the author's files)

Just as is the case with some teenaged boys, many teenaged girls decide not to have sexual relations until they are older and are content with their decision:

"I am writing this letter to let others like myself know that it is okay to be a virgin. I am a 19-year-old college student and a virgin. There is nothing wrong or strange about it. . . . You do not have to give in to sex just to please others or to simply fit in. . . . You should feel good about yourself, whatever and whenever you decide. When the moment is right, so will you be ready. . . .''

(from the author's files)

If you engage in sex it should be for the right reasons and you should feel good about yourself afterwards. Dr. Elizabeth Allgeier (1985) modified an eight-question list (Lieberman & Peck, 1982) that is designed to get teens to think about whether they are engaging (or about to engage) in sex for the right reasons. You are ready for sex if:

1. You feel guiltless and comfortable about your present level of involvement.
2. You are confident that you will not be humiliated and that your reputation will not be hurt.
3. Neither partner is pressuring the other for sex.
4. You are not trying to:
   a. prove your love for the other person;
   b. increase your self-worth;
   c. prove that you are mature;
   d. show that you can attract a sexual partner;
   e. get attention, affection, or love;
   f. rebel against parents, society, etc.
5. It will be an expression of your current feelings rather than an attempt to improve a poor relationship or one that is growing cold.
6. You can discuss and agree on an effective method of contraception and share the details, responsibilities, and costs of the use of the method.
7. You can discuss the potential of contracting or transmitting sexually transmitted diseases.
8. You have discussed and agreed on what both of you will do if conception occurs, because no contraception method is 100% effective.

Sex educator Carol Cassell has recommended that teens be taught to say, "Not now" rather than "No" to partners pressuring them to engage in unwanted sexual relations. She feels that saying "No" is often viewed by others as denying sexual feelings (which may be considered abnormal) and that it also ignores the reality of teen sexuality. According to Cassell, "We owe it to young people to own up to the facts that sexual feelings are normal, that desire can be very strong because sex is pleasurable, and that these feelings ought to be a part of their lives." So, the next time someone wants to have sexual relations and you don't, say "Not now."

Teenage Pregnancy

You learned about the problem of teenage pregnancy in the United States in Chapter 6. As you recall, over 1 million teenage girls become pregnant in the United States every year. Eighty to 90 percent of these pregnancies are unplanned, and about 40 percent of them end in abortion (Forrest & Singh, 1990b; Henshaw, 1990). Few teen pregnancies lead to marriage (Robinson, 1988), yet fewer than 5 percent of unwed teenage mothers give their children up for adoption (Voydanoff & Donnelly, 1990). With all the responsibilities involved in raising a child, teenage mothers have a high risk for dropping out of school (and therefore becoming low wage earners). Teenage marriages that are the result of unwanted pregnancies often end in divorce or desertion, and the suicide rate among teenage girls in this group is high (Furstenberg et al., 1981).

There are two approaches that have been suggested to deal with this problem. The first is to encourage teenagers to say "no" to sex under any circumstances, pointing out the dangers, hazards, and responsibilities associated with teenage pregnancy. Nearly three fourths of parents do, in fact, tell their children to wait until they are older before having sex. Sixty percent tell their daughters to wait until marriage (*Time*/CNN poll, 1993). Although this approach appeals to most parents it generally does not work (e.g., Christopher & Roosa, 1990). Attempts to frighten teenagers into becoming safe drivers by showing bloody films in driver's education classes have not caused a dramatic increase in teenage driving safety. (If you don't believe this, try to buy car insurance for a teenage driver.) The same would probably be true for any mass campaign to deal with the teenage pregnancy rates using scare tactics. Most teenagers now believe that premarital sex is not immoral if the couple deeply care for each other. To accept this argument against having sex would mean denying something that most teenagers already "know" is the truth. Challenging deeply held beliefs is not the way to influence people.

The second approach is to better educate both male and female adolescents in the use of contraceptives. This isn't nearly as appealing to parents as the first approach, but the number of teenage pregnancies is reaching epidemic proportions. A telecast of the TV show "60 Minutes" showed a high school that dispenses free contraceptives to its students. The reason behind this was that the high school already had to set up a day care center for the students' babies. Three hundred of the school's 1000 female students were either pregnant or already mothers.

Dear Abby: My telephone just rang. It was a doctor telling me that my 16-year-old daughter was just in his office asking for birth control pills. Abby, what are these young people doing to us mothers?

I knew she had a steady boyfriend, but I never dreamed they were in need of anything like that. I am heartsick. I tried to raise the girl right. Where have I failed?

(Ashamed to Sign My Name)

Dear Ashamed: You haven't failed, and if you tried to raise her right you should not be ashamed. I am not in favor of premarital sex for teenagers, but once a girl has gone all the way it is unrealistic to think she will stop simply because she is denied the pill. So then what? She risks becoming pregnant. And if she does, what has the doctor accomplished? He will have been responsible for (a) an unwanted baby, (b) an abortion, or (c) a hasty marriage. Which would you choose for your daughter?

If you are among those mothers who say, "If that's the way she is going to act, then let her suffer the consequences," please consider the baby. Don't you think every child should come into this world wanted by its natural mother? I do.

(Taken from the "Dear Abby" column by Abigail Van Buren. Copyright 1981, Universal Press Syndicate. Reprinted with permission. All rights reserved.)

Few teenage boys use condoms; thus young women are often forced to assume the responsibility for contraception. If pregnancy does occur, it is common for the boy to blame the girl. This situation will only begin to improve when young men begin to assume greater responsibility for their sexual behavior, and particularly for their role in birth control—it takes two to tango. Young men will change their attitudes and behaviors only when their parents begin to assume the responsibility of honestly communicating with their sons and daughters about sexuality and relationships. ■

YOUNG ADULTHOOD (Age 19—24)

The average age at marriage has increased dramatically in recent decades. The U.S. Census Bureau reported that the median age at which people first got married in 1993 was 24.5 for women and 26.5 for men, the highest levels in this century. This is an increase of more than 2 years of age since 1980 and more than 4 years since 1960. As a result, some psychologists and sociologists think that a new stage of life has developed in today's society—*young adulthood*. This is an extended period of being a single adult, which occurs between adolescence and parenthood. Young adults have more freedom from parental restraints and more opportunity for privacy than in the past.

According to Seidman and Rieder (1994), who reviewed the results of numerous recent sexual surveys, the sexual activity of young adults is generally different from younger and older age groups. By the age of 20, approximately 90 percent of young adults are sexually experienced and having sex regularly, and most young adults have had multiple, serial sexual partners during their young lifetimes. Let us review some of these studies.

Kinsey and his colleagues (1948) found that 68 percent of men surveyed with a college education, 85 percent of men with a high school education, and 98 percent of men with only an elementary school education had had premarital sex. The numbers for females were much lower, but more recent data indicate a striking increase in the number of women who have had premarital sex. Hunt (1975), for example, found that 81 percent of married women in the 18- to 24-year-old group in his survey had had premarital sex. Surveys conducted in the late 1980s and early 1990s found that among unmarried persons aged 18–24, 84 percent of the men and 81 percent of the women had engaged in premarital sex with a heterosexual partner (Anderson & Dahlberg, 1992; Gagnon, Lindenbaum, & Martin, 1989; unpublished data from 1988–1990 General Social Surveys). Janus and Janus (1993) found that 91 percent of men and 83 percent of women had had premarital sex. Males are much more likely than females to have permissive attitudes about premarital sex, especially "casual" sex (Oliver & Hyde, 1993). Interestingly, Janus and Janus also found that the relation with education level had reversed since Kinsey's time. According to their findings, college students are more likely to have had premarital sex than people with only a high school education. How religious one was did not appear to be a major factor.

As previously mentioned, the sexual activity of young adults often includes multiple partners. As many as one third of young women and one half of young men aged 18 to 19 have had two or more partners in the past year (Forrest & Singh, 1990b) and probably 10 percent or more of young unmarried women have had two or more sexual partners in the past 3 months (Seidman, Mosher, & Aral, 1992). As for college students, a study at a private New England university found that three fourths of the coeds had had multiple sexual partners, and over one quarter had had three sexual partners in the last year (DeBuono et al., 1990). At a midwestern college, coeds reported an average of 5.6 sexual partners and males, an average of 11.2 partners (Reinisch et al., 1992). Over 20 percent of college undergraduates at a Southern university reported having four or more sexual partners (King & Anderson, 1994). Among Canadian undergraduates, over 20 percent of the men and nearly 9 percent of the

FIGURE 10-7   YOUNG ADULTHOOD IS AN EXTENDED PERIOD OF BEING A SINGLE ADULT. THE LARGE MAJORITY OF YOUNG ADULTS ARE SEXUALLY EXPERIENCED AND HAVE SEX REGULARLY.

women had already had at least 10 sexual partners in their lifetime (MacDonald et al., 1990).

Many of these surveys focused on women in particular. These studies find that the earlier a female becomes sexually experienced, the more likely she will have had multiple sexual partners. Also, the more experienced she becomes, the less time she spends between sexual relationships (Seidman et al., 1992; Tanfer & Schoorl, 1992). Less religious women are more likely to have had multiple partners than religious women, especially Catholic women, and less educated women were found to have had more lifetime partners than college-educated women (except for divorced or separated white women, for whom the reverse was true). Young adult white women were more likely to have had multiple sexual partners during their lifetime than young adult black women. For all people with fewer than 20 lifetime partners, the number of partners reported by men is only slightly higher than the number of partners reported by women (Morris, 1993).

In summary, for adolescents and young adults the number of sexual partners steadily increases the longer the individual has been sexually experienced (see Tanfer & Schoorl, 1992). For some young adults, this is a period of sexual experimentation in which they engage in "one-night stands" or even group sex:

"After going out and becoming wasted, me and my boyfriend decided to have kinky sex. His 2 roommates were supposed to be sleeping, so I agreed. He tied me up spreadeagle to the bedposts and blindfolded me. After having sex on and off for about 30 minutes, I was untied and unblindfolded. I saw his 2 roommates standing in the room wearing underwear. I was then told it was planned to happen this way. They had all 'done me.' I admitted I enjoyed it, and still have group sex to this day."

"In high school there was a girl who would sleep with about five of us at a time. She was very pretty, popular, and intelligent. I never could figure out why she did it. She used to make us wear condoms, but I still worry. I saw in the paper yesterday that she got married. . . . "

(from the author's files)

However, many adolescents and young adults probably begin a sexual relationship with the hope and expectation that it will last. Reiss (1981) found that most people limited their premarital sexual activity to "serious relationships." More recently, Clements (1994) reported that 86 percent of women and 71 percent of men said that it was difficult for them to have sex without emotional involvement.

"Dates often leave me feeling bad that I don't engage in the one night stand scenes. . . . I prefer to make love. Sex is not a sport to me. Personally, it's too emotional to take it that lightly. . . . "

(from the author's files)

Thus, for many young adults their sexual lifestyle can be called **serial monogamy**—a series of relationships in which sex is reserved for just the one other person.

> **Serial monogamy**
> Having a series of monogamous, sexual relationships.

The period of young adulthood is also a time in which most people gradually are less influenced by peer pressure and gain a better understanding of their own sexual motivations.

" . . . I now make my own choices and give my opinions without being intimidated about what someone else might think. But most of all I have stopped confusing sex for the attention I was thriving for. For example, I used to think that if I give him sex then that means he must like me or is my friend. . . . "

(from the author's files) ■

ADULTS AGED 25–39

In their review of sexual surveys, Seidman and Rieder (1994) concluded that relatively long-lasting monogamy was the norm for most adults aged 25 and older. For people in this age group, about 80 percent of sexually active heterosexual men and 90 percent of sexually active heterosexual women report having had only one sex partner within the last year (data largely from the National Surveys of Family Growth and the General Social Surveys). Nearly identical findings were reported by Laumann's group (1994).

For this age group, the best predictors of having multiple partners are marital status, gender, age, and race. Not only are men, particularly younger unmarried men, more likely than women to have had multiple partners in the preceding year, but for unmarried women abstinence becomes more common with increasing age (see Seidman & Rieder review). African-

Americans are less likely to marry than whites and thus are more likely to have had multiple partners recently (Billy et al., 1993; Laumann et al., 1994; Seidman et al., 1992; Tanfer & Schoorl, 1992).

Marriage

As mentioned in the introduction to this section, many people today are postponing marriage. Still others never marry. In 1993, 19 percent of women and 30 percent of men aged 30–34 had never been married. This is much truer for African-Americans than it is for Americans in general (Saluter, 1994; Tucker, Taylor, & Mitchell-Kernan, 1993). However, because of the history of negative attitudes about sexuality in Western culture (see Chapter 1), for many people sexual relations are legitimized only within marriage.

The frequency of sexual intercourse in the first year of marriage is usually high, an average of about 15 times a month in the first year (Greenblatt, 1983). The frequency of sexual relations generally declines thereafter. However, for the entire population, the frequency of sexual relations is highest for married couples in their mid-twenties to mid-thirties (Clements, 1994; Janus & Janus, 1993; Laumann et al., 1994). Married women are also more likely than single women to have orgasms during sexual intercourse (Laumann et al., 1994).

The decrease in sexual relations after the first year or two of marriage occurs for a variety of reasons. Sex has to compete with other time demands, such as career advancement. Parenthood means less privacy, more demands, and often results in exhaustion at the end of the day. It is also normal for sexual relations to decrease somewhat as the novelty wears off and individuals within a relationship become accustomed to one another (Blumstein & Schwartz, 1983).

Studies find that married couples today are more likely to use a variety of sexual techniques than in the past. This is true for positions of sexual intercourse and for oral-genital sex (Hunt, 1975). Hunt found that a majority of young people also continue to masturbate after getting married. In fact, people with sexual partners are much more likely to masturbate than people who do not have a partner (Laumann et al., 1994; see Chapter 11). For men, Hunt found that the average rate was about twice a month, while for women, the average rate was about once a month. However, a majority of both men and women report marital sex to be very satisfying, more so than do singles (Clements, 1994; Laumann et al., 1994). I will have more to say about marriage and sex in a later section of the chapter.

Living Together (Cohabitation)

A 1990 Census Bureau survey showed that 2.9 million unmarried heterosexual couples were living together. This represents an increase of 80 percent since 1980 and well over a 500 percent increase since the 1970 census. Forty percent of couples who live together have children. The increase in the number of couples living together may be one reason for the older age of couples today who marry for the first time.

Living together can be a test or trial period before marriage (there is much more to living together happily and successfully than simply enjoying sex). Fifty-six percent of college students interviewed in a 1989 Gallup survey said that they approved of living together in trial marriage. Living together can also be an alternative to marriage. The amount of commitment that couples make to each other while living together can vary a great deal (Bumpass, Sweet, & Cherlin, 1991). Many people

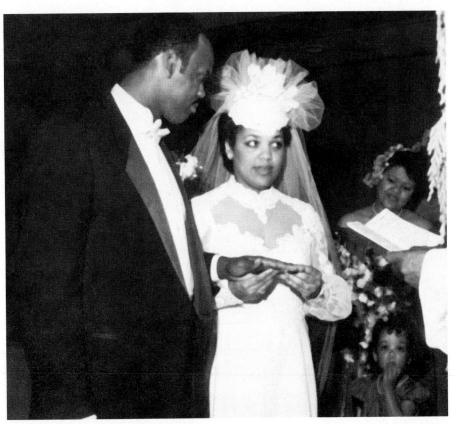

FIGURE 10-8   RELATIVELY LONG-LASTING MONOGAMY IS THE NORM FOR MOST ADULTS AGED 25 AND OLDER.

BOX 10-A

CROSS-CULTURAL PERSPECTIVES: HOW DO PEOPLE SELECT A MATE?

The boxes on cross-cultural perspectives presented throughout this book generally show cultures to differ widely in their attitudes and behaviors regarding sexuality. Recently, however, David Buss and David Schmitt (1993) surveyed people throughout the world, from Zambia to China, and found that people's mating preferences and attitudes were very much alike. The only major differences were between men's and women's desires, and whether or not people were interested in a short-term relationship (casual sex) or a long-term mate.

Short-term relationships dominate human mating patterns, but men and women engage in short-term liaisons for different reasons, according to the authors of the study. Men tend to engage in casual sex to test their virility, while a woman's short-term relationships are largely experimental in nature, either to test her market value (to see how desirable she is) or to determine what her desires are. On the average, men wanted about 18 women as sexual partners in their lifetime, while the average woman wanted four men.

Other studies confirm that, as a general rule, men are much more likely than women to engage in casual sex with someone they hardly know, or don't know at all (see Oliver & Hyde, 1993). In one study, for example, researchers had an attractive man or an attractive woman approach college students and ask them if they would have sex with him or her (Clark & Hatfield, 1989). Three fourths of the men said yes, but none of the women agreed to have sex with an attractive stranger. Buss and Schmitt found that most men were willing to have sex with a woman after knowing her for only a week, whereas the typical woman preferred to wait 6 months.

Buss and Schmitt found that in all cultures the idealistic goal was a lasting relationship. Across all cultures, over 90 percent of people eventually marry (Buss, 1985; Epstein & Guttman, 1984). However, this does not mean that people spend their lives with one partner. About 80 percent of all societies allow men to have multiple wives or mistresses (although only about 20 percent of men actually do so; Ford & Beach, 1951; Murdock, 1967). According to Buss and Schmitt, Western cultures may have outlawed polygyny, but people get around it by having serial marriages (divorce and remarriage) and by having extramarital affairs. In the United States, the divorce rate is around 50 percent (H. Fisher, 1987) and from 25 to 75 percent of people are estimated to have engaged in adultery (H. Fisher, 1987; Hite, 1987; Kinsey et al., 1948, 1953; Symons, 1979).

Buss and Schmitt believe that for males promiscuity is a primal instinct that maximizes reproduction potential. How do men balance their short- and long-term desires? Buss says, ''If a man could have his fantasy, he would sequester and monopolize all the attractive women in the country. Indeed, men who are in a position to get what they want—kings, tycoons, celebrities—often do things like that'' (quoted by Gura, 1994). Men may enjoy female promiscuity in a short-term relationship, but when looking for a long-term mate they seek a chaste woman, someone who has not yet had sex. Of 37 countries studied by Buss and Schmitt, in more than two thirds the men valued chastity in choosing a mate more than the women. This was especially true among Palestinian Arabs, Iranians, and male Indonesians.

''I am of Mexican descent. In our culture, it is 'okay' for boys to engage in sex before marriage. In fact, it is encouraged. Girls, however, are not to have sex until after marriage. We are made to believe that a man will not want to marry a girl who is not a virgin. In most cases, it turns out to be true.''

(from the author's files)

Remember from Box 4-A that in large parts of northern Africa and the Middle East, girls' genitals are sewn together to assure chastity at the time of marriage. Chastity at marriage was not important to most men in Scandinavia and the Netherlands. Regardless of culture, men also placed a high value on physical attractiveness in choosing a long-term mate (Buss, 1989; Buss & Barnes, 1987) and prefer mates who are younger than they are (Buss, 1989; Kendrick & Keefe, 1992). Zambian men preferred wives who are at least 7 years younger, while Italian men preferred an age difference of 3 years, and U.S. men a difference of about 2 years.

Women's mating strategies are different from men's, according to Buss and Schmitt. Because a woman has a limited number of reproductive years and must invest time and energy in childbearing, women prefer mates who can offer them economic and physical protection. Women, more so than men, prefer men who are good financial prospects (Buss, 1989). Some researchers believe that dating and marriage frequently involve an exchange of sex for financial support (e.g., Muehlenhard & Schrag, 1990). Factors like a promising career, ambition, and education are important factors in women's decisions across all cultures. Women prefer older mates, but are not as concerned about physical attractiveness as are men. Chastity of a potential mate is important to women only in some Oriental cultures.

Buss and Schmitt believe that there is evolutionary value for what men and women seek in a relationship. Whether or not you agree with this, one thing is clear from this large cross-cultural study—love is not really blind. ■

who live together do not see their relationship as a planned attempt at a trial marriage (Macklin, 1978), but most expect to marry their partner (Bumpass et al., 1991). Studies show that in cohabitation there is generally less certainty about the relationship than in marriage (Bumpass et al., 1991). One advantage people claim for living together over marriage is that since there has been no formal contract, such as a marriage license, it is easy to simply walk away from a relationship that does not seem to be working. One disadvantage in living together is that it is easy to walk out on a relationship that does not seem to be working. (Think about it.)

Although most people think that cohabitation is something done mostly by college students, cohabitation is most common among the least educated people in the population, particularly those from less religious families (Bumpass et al., 1991; Thornton, Axinn, & Hill, 1992). On the average, the level of sexual activity is slightly higher among couples who live together than among either married couples or unmarried noncohabitants (Bachrach, 1987; Risman et al., 1981).

Interestingly, studies find that couples who live together before getting married are more likely than others to get divorced (Axinn & Thornton, 1992; Bumpass & Sweet, 1989). The higher divorce rate is not due to the greater time that cohabitors have spent together (DeMaris & Rao, 1992). Axinn and Thornton (1992) believe that cohabitation "may reinforce the idea that intimate relationships are fragile and temporary" and

this might "reduce the expectation that marriage is a lifetime relationship." Living together, they said, "probably attracts people who are, on average, more accepting of the termination of intimate relationships." Other studies support their conclusion (Booth & Johnson, 1988; Thomas & Colella, 1992). However, a later study failed to confirm that cohabitors have a higher divorce rate because of unconventional attitudes about family ideology (DeMaris & MacDonald, 1993). Although more research is needed to determine why people who live together premaritally are more likely than others to divorce when married, we are able to conclude that cohabitation is not the answer to a stable relationship that many have hoped it would be.

SINGLE PARENTHOOD

In 1993, there were 10.9 million single parents raising children (9.3 million women and 1.6 million men), nearly triple the number in 1970 (U.S. Census Bureau). Nearly 25 percent of white children and 63 percent of black children lived with a single parent. Some adults become single parents through divorce or separation, but nearly 25 percent of never-married women are also mothers. This trend involves all socioeconomic groups. For example, among never-married managerial or professional women, the proportion who were mothers increased from 3.1 percent in 1981 to 8.2 percent in 1992.

I discussed the effects of single parenthood on children's gender identities and gender roles in Chapter 8.

There has been very little research on the sexual behavior of single parents as a group.

EXTRAMARITAL SEX—IN SUPPOSEDLY MONOGAMOUS MARRIAGES

In their original surveys (1948, 1953), Kinsey and his colleagues found that at least 50 percent of married men and 24 percent of married women had engaged in extramarital sex on at least one occasion. Surveys by magazines such as *Cosmopolitan, Playboy, Woman's Day,* and *Redbook* have found equally high, and often higher (especially for women), percentages. However, the Kinsey surveys have been criticized for being nonrepresentative, and magazine surveys are almost always nonrepresentative (see Chapter 1).

What do current, more scientifically conducted, surveys indicate? In their 1990 "New Report on Sex," the Kinsey Institute found that 37 percent of husbands and 29 percent of wives had had at least one extramarital affair. Janus and Janus (1993) found that 35 percent of married men (and 56 percent of divorced men) and 26 percent of married women (and 59 percent of divorced women) admitted to extramarital affairs. Some therapists believe the figure is even higher (see Mehren, 1991), but some other recent surveys find a lower percentage of people who admit to having been unfaithful to their spouse (Choi, Catania, & Dolcini, 1994; Clements, 1994; Laumann et al., 1994). Laumann's group found that 25 percent of men and 15 percent of women admitted to having had an affair. Extramarital affairs are generally very secretive and it is possible, of course, that these latter surveys were not as probing as the others. Choi's group, for example, used a telephone survey and found that only 22 percent of their respondents admitted to having had an affair in the previous year. Would you admit to such behavior over the telephone? By the way, the rate of extrarelational affairs is just as high for cohabiting couples as it is for married couples (Blumstein & Schwartz, 1983).

These statistics on adultery refer to extramarital *sexual* relations. But, according to psychologist Shirley Glass, "That's a male definition (of adultery). If you look at emotional involvement and sexual involvement short of intercourse, you add another 20 percent" (quoted in Mehren, 1991). Indeed, Thompson (1984) found that extramarital affairs that involved a deep emotional involvement (but nonsexual) were about half as common as sexual affairs.

Reiss et al. (1980) found that almost 75 percent of married people felt that sex outside of marriage was always wrong. A 1989 Kinsey Institute survey found that 87 percent of people believed that extramarital sex was "always wrong" or "almost always wrong." Thus, many people who claim to believe that extramarital affairs are wrong do it anyway—in other words, there is a great deal of hypocrisy regarding this issue.

Most individuals view extramarital relationships by their spouses as being destructive to the marital relationship. Interestingly, Kinsey and his colleagues found that though men were more likely to engage in extramarital sex than women, they were also more likely to rate affairs as harmful to a relationship—if their wives were unfaithful to them. Men are more upset at the idea of their partner getting physical with someone else than they are about an emotional attachment. Women, on the other hand, are more concerned about emotional infidelity by their mates and are much more likely than men to forgive a partner for sexual infidelity (Buss, 1994).

Why do so many people engage in extramarital sex (or sex outside of any supposedly monogamous relationship)? Some are simply curious to see what sex with another person would be like, while some want more variety in their lives. Some people have affairs to seek revenge on their spouse (who also may be having an affair). Some also seek out other partners in order to prove that they are still desirable or young (the famous "mid-life crisis" or "middle-aged crazy" cause of extramarital sex), while others may be looking for the companionship no longer found in their marriages. And, of course, there is the excitement factor. As described by John Gagnon (1977):

> "Most people find their extramarital relationships highly exciting, especially in the early stages. This is a result of psychological compression: the couple gets together; they are both very aroused (desire, guilt, expectation); they have only three hours to be together. . . . Another source of attraction is that the other person is always seen when he or she looks good and is on best behavior, never when feeling tired or grubby, or when taking care of children, or when cooking dinner. . . . Each time, all the minutes that the couple has together are special because they have been stolen from all these other relationships. The resulting combination of guilt and excitement has a heightening effect."

Blumstein and Schwartz (1983) found that men generally look for casual sex and have more extramarital partners than women. Women are more likely to seek an emotional attachment with their new partner. Still, in most cases affairs are primarily short-term or "one-night stands" (Gagnon, 1977).

There is very little relationship between social background and whether or not one engages in extramarital affairs, including political leaning (ultraconservative vs. ultraliberal) and whether or not one is religious (Janus & Janus, 1993; Thompson, 1983). Whitehurst (1972) indicates two things that contribute to having "outside sex." The first is simply opportunity. For example, Levin and Levin (1975) found that while

27 percent of all housewives surveyed reported having had an extramarital affair, 47 percent of married women who worked at least part-time away from home had had sex outside of marriage. College-educated women are more likely to have an extramarital affair than women with just a high school education (Janus & Janus, 1993). Women who work have more opportunity to meet other men and to have affairs than women who stay at home all day. As put by psychotherapist Marcella Weiner, "Women are in the work force to stay now, and they have many more opportunities (to meet men). It has always been okay with men, but it is becoming more and more a phenomenon with women" (quoted in Mehren, 1991). With the rising number of wives entering the work force outside of the home, the number of women having extramarital sex may continue to increase. The second thing mentioned by Whitehurst is alienation. People can grow apart and develop different interests over time. Thus, if you meet someone else who shares your interests, seems attractive, and seems attracted to you, it can lead to sharing other parts of your life as well (see Chapter 12). An interesting thing about Whitehurst's argument is that situational factors are seen as responsible for the likelihood of extramarital sex, rather than some personality flaw. This would also explain why married individuals generally have affairs in the day—it is simply easier to get away and cover one's tracks during the day than at night.

EXTRAMARITAL SEX—CONSENSUAL ARRANGEMENTS

Some couples agree to have sex outside of the marital relationship. One such arrangement is **open marriage**, where both partners agree that it is okay to have sex with others. Even here, however, there are usually some agreed upon restrictions such as not having sex with a mutual friend or not having sex with the same person twice (Blumstein & Schwartz, 1983). Couples make these restrictions so that their primary commitment is to the marriage and thus the nonmarital partner will not be viewed as competition. According to Nena and

Open marriage
A marital relationship in which the couple agrees that it is permissible to have sexual relations outside of the marriage.

George O'Neill, authors of the 1972 best seller *Open Marriage*, this type of marriage challenges the idea that a single partner can meet all of a person's needs, and allows personal growth for both individuals. Blumstein & Swartz (1983) found that perhaps as many as 26 percent of married couples had some sort of "understanding" that allowed for extramarital sexual relations. Although this type of extramarital arrangement is supposed to add role equality and flexibility to a marriage (O'Neill & O'Neill, 1972), the divorce rate among open-marriage couples is just as high as for sexually monogamous couples (Rubin & Adams, 1986). However, for those open-marriage couples that did break up, sexual jealousy was rarely the reason.

Another arrangement that allows consensual extramarital sex is **swinging** (often called "wife swapping") where a married couple has extramarital relations together. Couples get together by answering ads in newspapers or swingers' magazines, or by going to commercial clubs that encourage recreational sex. In some cases, several couples get together for swinging parties. The sexual activity often includes sex between the women (while the husbands watch), but male homosexual activity is much less common, and in many cases forbidden. It's been estimated that 2–4 percent of married couples have engaged in swinging on at least an occasional basis (Hunt, 1975; Weiss, 1983). Some couples abandon swinging after giving it a short try, usually because they find it creates (for them) feelings of jealousy, sexual inadequacy, or rejection (Masters & Johnson; 1976; Murstein, 1978). Except for the fact that they tend to be less religious than others and to have had more premarital sexual experience, swingers are no different from others, and many are middle class and conservative (Jenks, 1985; Murstein, 1978; Weiss, 1983).

Swinging
A type of open marriage relationship in which a couple has extramarital relations together.

At this point it should be emphasized that unless a person *always* uses condoms, anytime a person has sexual partners outside of a monogamous relationship (whether consensual or nonconsensual) it increases his or her chances of contracting a sexually transmitted disease; see Chapter 5. ■

MIDDLE AGE (Age 40—59)

Many students believe that their own parents and grandparents love each other, but how many students think of their parents and grandparents as being sexually active? Studies have found that many college students have difficulty accepting their parent's sexuality and underestimate how often their parents have sex by about half (Allgeier & Murnen, 1985; Pocs & Godow,

1977). Here are a variety of responses from students in my course:

" I was about 14 when my mom told me she and my dad have sex. I was shocked and thought it was disgusting. I didn't want to hear it any more."

"My parents don't have sex. They have other things to do."

"The thought of my parents actually possessing sexuality or having sex mortified me."

"...the thought of my parents having sex made me sick, not because of their age, but because of the fact that they were *my* parents."

"...and plus they are in their late 40's and early 50's—I just can't imagine them having sex."

"When I was a teenager, it would make me uncomfortable when they would go in their room and shut and lock the door because I knew what they were going to be doing and I just felt it was weird because to me, they were 'old.' Now that I'm in my twenties, it makes me feel good to know that my parents still love and care about each other, and it helps me to believe that I will have a positive sexual attitude well into my 40's and 50's."

"...Sometimes I tease them a little when I catch my dad home late in the morning because I know he stayed home so they could have sex. I think it's great that they still love each other and express themselves sexually after being married for 25 years."

(from the author's files)

Pocs and Godow (1977) concluded that "... many parents may appear to be non-sexual because they hesitate to discuss the topic of sexuality in any way with their children or because they are not inclined to exhibit loving, affectionate responses, let alone sexual behavior, in the presence of their children." Allgeier and Murnen (1985) later found that students whose parents had dis-

"Actually, Dad knows quite a bit about sex for a man his age."
(Reprinted from Good Housekeeping *by permission of Rex May.)*

(Reprinted from *Good Housekeeping* by permission of Rex May.)

cussed sex with them gave more accurate estimates of their parents' sexual frequency.

Ask yourself these questions: "Do my parents enjoy sexual intercourse? How often? Do they enjoy using different positions? Do they enjoy oral-genital sex? Do my grandparents enjoy sex? How often? Do they enjoy using different positions? Do they enjoy oral-genital sex?"

Think about how you answered these questions, and then ask yourself: "What are my attitudes about sex? Is it something good that two people share?" For those of you who are sexually experienced, also ask yourself, "Do I like sex? How often do I enjoy it?" If you enjoy sex, why wouldn't your parents or grandparents? Sex therapists have found that the way that you feel about sex now is the best estimate of how you will feel about it in the future (Masters & Johnson, 1966). If you enjoy sex now, why should you stop enjoying sex later in life? *Adults of all ages are sexual beings.* Sex can be healthy and enjoyable throughout life. Problems with fully enjoying sex are more often due to one's beliefs and attitudes than to physiological changes (Kellett, 1991). If you want to have a good healthy sex life in the future, you need to be aware now that older adults are still enjoying the pleasurable aspects of sex.

If you think that your parents have no sex lives or have dull sex lives at best, what will you expect for yourself when you become a parent? People often act out "roles" that are based on their expectations of what people in those roles are supposed to do. If you view the role of parent as essentially devoid of healthy, fun, and fulfilling sex, then you may come to expect a dull sex life for yourself when you take on this role. These negative beliefs can become self-fulfilling prophecies (ideas that become true because you expect them to become true). From the previous case histories, which students do you think will enter parenthood with more positive attitudes about sexuality?

Negative attitudes about sexual activity in older adults can create many unnecessary barriers for people. Today, for example, people are not surprised when two young people decide to live together without getting married. However, the same young people might be shocked if a widowed parent or grandparent decided to move in with an older adult. Barring a tragedy, we will all grow old someday. These negative attitudes must change if today's young people want to be treated decently when they are older.

FREQUENCY OF SEXUAL INTERCOURSE

It is a common belief that sexual activity is highest for young people. As mentioned earlier, two recent national cross-sectional surveys found that sexual activity was highest for people in their mid-twenties to mid-thirties (Clements, 1994; Janus & Janus, 1993). Is there a sharp dropoff after that? Not really. Although most recent surveys do show a decline in sexual activity for people in their forties, and a further decline in the fifties, the dropoff is very gradual (Bachrach & Horn, 1987; Blumstein & Schwartz, 1983; Clements, 1994; Smith, 1991; see Seidman & Rieder, 1994). At most, the frequency of sexual intercourse for married couples decreases by only a couple of times a month from the thirties through the fifties (from 7–8 times a month to 5–6 times a month). In fact, Janus and Janus (1993) recently found very little evidence of any decline in sexual activity up through the early sixties. People in all age groups say that they would like to have sex more often (an average of 13 times a month; Clements, 1994), but lack of time or being physically tired prevent them from doing so (Blumstein & Schwartz, 1983).

A lot of people also believe that the sex lives of older married people are dull compared to singles. Actually, the surveys indicate that married people have sex more often than singles (never married or divorced) and are happier with their sex lives than are singles (Clements, 1994; Laumann et al., 1994; Smith, 1991). When asked if sex is important to them, more people in their thirties, forties, and early fifties say yes than do people in their late teens or early twenties (Clements, 1994).

Older couples who have sex frequently are also generally found to have the happiest marriages. Of course, we can't know what came first, the chicken or the egg. According to Andrew Greeley, "Their sex lives may be better because their lives are more satisfying, or the other way around" (cited in Coleman, 1992). We do know that as people grow older, they tend to regard behaviors as hugging and kissing as much more important and pleasurable than when they were younger (Clements, 1994).

Loss of a Mate (by Divorce or Death)

Over half of all marriages in the United States now end in divorce (Martin & Bumpass, 1989). Other people become single again as a result of their partners' death. When this happens, reentry into the singles world and dating are often difficult, particularly if the relationship had been a long-lasting one. Many divorced and widowed persons have no idea of what the current expectations are in dating, and thus learning how to interact with potential partners may take some time and at first may be very awkward (Spanier & Thompson, 1987). New rules have to be created or discovered. For example, should a 42-year-old divorced woman have sex with her date (a) on the first date, (b) after they've gone out a few times, (c) only after she thinks they love each other, or (d) not at all?

The early sex surveys by Kinsey and colleagues (1953) and Hunt (1974) reported that divorced individuals were very sexually active. However, more recent studies have found that while some people become

FIGURE 10-9   THE RESPONSIBILITIES OF RAISING CHILDREN AND CAREERS MAY RESULT IN FEWER OPPORTUNITIES TO HAVE SEXUAL RELATIONS, BUT SEXUAL INTEREST DOES NOT DECLINE. DO YOU BELIEVE THAT YOUR PARENTS STILL ENJOY SEX? WHEN YOU BECOME A PARENT, WILL YOU BE EMBARRASSED IF YOUR CHILDREN KNOW THAT YOU AND YOUR PARTNER ENJOY SEXUAL RELATIONS?

more sexually active after divorce, about one fourth to one third show a decrease (Simenauer & Carroll, 1982). Three fourths of divorced persons have either a single sexual partner or no partner in the first year (Stack & Gundlach, 1992). Still, almost all divorced men and women will return to an active sex life eventually. Resuming sexual activity is an important part of letting go of the former bonds. For men in particular, the resumption of sexual activity is associated with their well-being and self-confidence (Spanier & Thompson, 1987).

Many divorced or widowed men and women remarry, but there are more opportunities for men. By the time people reach early forties in age, there are over 200 single women for every 100 single men (Blumstein & Schwartz, 1983). There is also a double standard in our society. While many people frown upon women having sexual relationships with men much younger than themselves, most feel that it is okay for men to have relationships with younger women. Have you ever noticed that whenever Hollywood puts a middled-aged leading man in a romantic role it is almost always with a woman 10–20+ years younger than he is? Because of the male-female ratio and double standard, women over age 40 generally have a more difficult time finding new partners than older men. For example, about one half of widowers, but only one quarter of widows, remarry (Lown & Dolan, 1988).

About three fourths of divorced people remarry, usually within 3 to 4 years (Coleman & Ganong,

1991; Lown & Dolan, 1988), but do they do a better job of choosing a partner? Apparently not, for half or more of second marriages also end in divorce (Blumstein & Schwartz, 1983; Ganong & Coleman, 1989). Since the early 1970s, the percentage of people who have married three or more times has doubled, from 4 percent to 8 percent (National Center for Health Statistics). For some, marriage is just another form of serial monogamy.

FEMALE SEXUALITY: PHYSICAL CHANGES WITH AGE

As a woman grows older, her ovaries do not respond as well to the pituitary hormones FSH and LH (see Chapter 3), so that menstrual cycle irregularities are common after the age of 35 (cycles become more frequent or less frequent than before). Eventually her ovaries atrophy (wither) and she quits having menstrual cycles entirely, thus ending her ability to have children.

Menopause

A female's last menstrual period.

Climacteric

The changes that occur in women in the few years that precede and follow menopause.

The cessation of menstruation is referred to as **menopause** and usually occurs in a woman's late forties or early fifties (Note: menopause is defined differently in some other cultures—see Lock, 1994). The changes that occur in the few years that precede and follow menopause are called the **climacteric**. How a woman and her partner react to these changes can affect other aspects of a relationship, so it is important that everyone understand their physical basis (see Nachtigall, 1994 for a review).

As the ovaries atrophy, they produce less and less gonadal hormones, and eventually produce no progesterone and only minute amounts of estrogen. Most women will experience some symptoms as a result of these hormonal changes. Estrogen and progesterone, you recall, inhibited release of FSH and LH from the pituitary. At menopause, these pituitary hormones are no longer inhibited and are released in large amounts. In addition to their reproductive role, these hormones affect the diameter of blood vessels, causing them to dilate. Subjectively, this physiological change is perceived as a *hot flash*, a sudden sensation of warmth or intense heat that spreads over the upper body, face, and head (see Kronenberg, 1994). It is usually accompanied by flushing and sweating and is often followed by a feeling of being chilled. Pressure in the head or chest, nausea, or feelings of suffocation can also be experienced during a hot flash. The sensations last from a few seconds to 15 minutes or more and are very common at night, thus interfering with sleep. Hot

Hot flashes

A warm feeling over the upper body experienced by postmenopausal women as a result of increased levels of FSH and LH.

flashes generally disappear within a few years, but 20 percent of affected women may experience hot flashes for 5 years or longer. Interestingly, while a majority of American and European women experience hot flashes after menopause, hot flashes (as well as other "symptoms" of menopause) are relatively uncommon among postmenopausal women in some other cultures (e.g., Japanese and Mayan women), suggesting that cultural differences (in diet, or perhaps attitudes toward older persons) play a role (Kronenberg, 1994; Lock, 1994).

The loss of estrogen also causes the vagina to become thinner and less elastic, with a marked *decrease in the amount of vaginal lubrication* during sexual arousal. If the vagina is not properly lubricated, sexual intercourse will be painful, so that some postmenopausal women may start avoiding sexual relations (see Sherwin, 1991). This is unnecessary, however, if a woman and her partner accept vaginal dryness after menopause as a normal physiological response and not as an indication of lack of desire. The dryness can be countered with estrogen-based cream (Fonda, 1994). In addition, a water-based lubricant, such as K-Y jelly, is recommended.

A lot of attention has recently been given to the role of decreased estrogen levels in *osteoporosis*, a condition in which the bones become more brittle with age (see Rozenberg et al., 1994). There are over 250,000 hip fractures a year due to osteoporosis, resulting in up to 50,000 premature deaths in women (National Institutes of Health Consensus Panel).

Today, the medical profession treats osteoporosis, hot flashes, vaginal dryness, and other less common problems associated with menopause (e.g., decreased clitoral sensitivity, recurrent urinary tract infections), with estrogen replacement therapy (in pill, cream, or skin patch form). However, there have been some concerns that estrogen replacement therapy might increase the risks of breast and endometrial cancer. A review by the Centers for Disease Control and Prevention found that women who used estrogen for 5 years had no increased risk of breast cancer (Steinberg et al., 1991). Prolonged use (15 years or more) was associated with a slight increase in risk. Two very recent studies reported conflicting results, with one finding a slight increase in risk of breast cancer and the other finding no increased risk (Colditz et al., 1995; Stanford et al., 1995). Progestins are presently given with estrogen to protect against endometrial problems, and recent studies indicate that estrogen therapy reduces the risk of cardiovascular disease (Nabulsi et al., 1993; Stampfer et al., 1991).

When considering estrogen therapy, a woman must weigh the risks against the benefits. The overall death rate for elderly women taking estrogen is lower

BOX 10-B

SEXUALITY AND HEALTH: SEX AND HEART ATTACKS

Victorian-era physicians, you recall, believed that sex was harmful to one's health (see Chapter 1). Even Freud believed that loss of semen was as detrimental to a man's health as loss of blood (Haller & Haller, 1977). We now know, of course, that this is not true, but are there other sex-related health problems? An article in a 1986 issue of *National Safety and Health News* startled many, particularly older, people. The article reported the results of a Japanese study in which investigators looked at the autopsies of 5000 people who had died suddenly. Thirty-four died during intercourse. Are people with heart disease, especially former heart attack victims, putting themselves at risk by having sex?

Many people apparently think so. About one quarter of men who have had heart attacks never resume sexual activity and half do so only occasionally (Kolodny et al., 1979). However, physicians and sex therapists say the greatest barrier is not the physical condition of the heart patient, but anxiety and fear. Wives of former heart attack victims also worry that sex might cause another attack (Gould, 1989). The anxiety and stress can cause sexual problems. Female heart patients are less likely than men to cease sexual activity or develop sexual problems (Kolodny, Masters, & Johnson, 1979; Schover & Jensen, 1988).

During sex with one's usual partner, the maximum heart rate increases to about 120 beats per minute (Tobis, 1977). This is no greater, and perhaps less, of an increase than one would experience during a brisk walk or some other form of moderate exercise (Masur, 1979; McLane, Krop, & Mehta, 1980). Extreme stress (physical or emotional), and things like alcohol or drugs, might be a risk and so might sex involving emotional tension or extreme physical exertion. It must be noted, therefore, of the 34 people that the Japanese study found to have died during sexual intercourse, all were intoxicated or near intoxication and 30 were having extramarital relations with a partner who, on average, was 18 years younger.

Most physicians believe that sexual activities can be resumed within a few weeks after a heart attack (see Tardif, 1989). Generally, masturbation can be resumed first. A general rule of thumb used by some physicians is that sexual activity should not be resumed until the patient can engage in moderate physical exercise (such as climb two flights of stairs) without exhaustion.

For most people, daily exercise in moderate amounts is recommended for strengthening cardiovascular endurance. A daily brisk walk of at least 20 minutes is highly recommended for older people (Kligman & Pepin, 1992). Regular exercise also improves mental health (Taylor, Sallis, & Needle, 1985). The American College of Sports Medicine recommends any physical activity that raises heart rate at least to 60 to 80 percent of your range. Sexual activity with one's usual partner produces heart rate changes like this. It is very possible, therefore, that regular sexual activity is beneficial in maintaining cardiovascular endurance. Sounds like a lot more fun to me than a stationary bike. ■

partner (Blumstein & Schwartz, 1983). There is no decline with age in the number of erections men experience at night (see Pesmen, 1993).

For those middle-aged and elderly men who are showing physiological changes, such as a longer time to become fully erect, there is a positive side—more time spent in foreplay, which generally translates into greater sexual happiness for the partner. If age interferes with quantity, however, there is no reason it has to interfere with quality. Sexual relations involve more than just using the penis and include the lips, tongue, hands, and other body parts, as well as one's emotional responsivity. Many men who experience declining erectile capacity with age report that their overall sex life is still just as good (Rowland et al., 1993). Good sexual communication is a total human sexual response.

As a parting thought, here is a quiz (Pesmen, 1993):

Question: What is the most powerful sex organ?
Answer: The brain.

Question: What, then, is the second most powerful sex organ?
Answer: The skin.

As stated by Pesmen, "Fortunately for most men, the brain and the skin are stable, healthy partners in mid-life and beyond. Setting penis power aside, no matter what normal changes beset a man's sex organs later in life, a continuing capacity for sexual pleasure remains." ∎

THE ELDERLY YEARS (Age 60 +)

....

"I didn't think that elderly people thought about sex. I thought when you got older you just lost all interest. . . ."

(from the author's files)

In our culture elderly people are regarded as asexual human beings—neuters. Sex is something enjoyed only by the young and healthy (Gochros, Gochros, & Fisher, 1986). According to Rose and Soares (1993), "Evidence of sexuality among the aged is often joked about, dismissed, or defined as troublesome behavior. A sexually active older man is seen as a 'dirty, old man' and a sexually active older woman is considered preposterous or embarrassing. This culturally embedded denial may be rooted in people's difficulty accepting the sexuality of their own parents."

In the 1980s, some behavioral scientists and physicians began to challenge our culture's stereotype of old people as over the hill and sexless. Several studies showed elderly people continuing to enjoy sex well into their sixties, seventies, eighties, and beyond. Andrew Greeley recently reported, for example, that over one third of married couples aged 60 and over have sex at least once a week. In another study, over half of white and African-American married couples aged 60 and over were having sexual intercourse an average of once a week (Marsiglio & Donnelly, 1991). One fourth of couples older than 76 were still having sexual intercourse regularly. In a *Consumer Reports* magazine survey (caution: only 0.2 percent of readers responded), two thirds of women (including 81 percent of married women) and 80 percent of men aged 70 and older said that they were still sexually active (Brecher, 1984). They all had intercourse with their partners and over half engaged in oral-genital sex. Most sexually active elderly people say that their sexual pleasure is as good or better than when they were younger (Starr & Weiner, 1981). Similar results have been reported for elderly homosexual individuals (e.g., Berger, 1982, Raphael & Robinson, 1980). In addition to the scientific literature, popular television series such as "The Golden Girls"

and "In the Heat of the Night" have helped to portray the elderly as sexual human beings.

Is there any age at which sexual activity must stop? Well, in a study of 202 *healthy* men and women aged 80 to 102, Bretschneider and McCoy (1988) found that three fourths of them still fantasized about sexual relations and enjoyed touching and caressing their partners. Nearly half were having sexual intercourse and a third were engaging in oral-genital sex. Sexual activity was limited by living arrangements and availability of partners, not a lack of interest. Consistent with results of other studies (see last section), present enjoyment of sexual activities was highly correlated with attitudes about sex earlier in life.

The conclusion reached by the behavioral scientists who conducted these studies is a very positive one—sexuality does not have to end at any given age (Figure 10-10). In the words of Myrna Lewis and Robert Butler (1994), authors of *Love and Sex After 60*, "Relatively healthy older people who enjoy sex are capable of experiencing it often until very late in life."

So, which is correct, the cultural stereotype of the aged as sexless, or the optimistic picture painted by the recent surveys of the elderly as a still sexually active group? The truth may be somewhere in between. One recent report, for example, accused the earlier reports and their conclusions of sounding like "pep talks," trying to convince everyone that there will be no loss of sexual pleasure with aging (Rose & Soares, 1993). The authors said the earlier reports "glossed over certain realities of aging which directly affect sexuality": the much greater number of women to men, the greater number of people suffering from chronic illness and disability, and the greater number of people dependent on others for daily personal care. Let us consider these problems.

The earlier studies were largely of married men and women—older people who had partners. The ratio of single women to single men that we discussed in the section on middle age becomes even more unfavorable to women over 60. In the United States, women outlive men by an average of 8 years. For peo-

FIGURE 10-10   FROM THE MOMENT OF BIRTH TO THE DAY WE DIE, WE ARE ALL SEXUAL BEINGS.

ple over 65, there are 100 single women for every 27 single men (Robinson, 1983). Thus, many women are faced with involuntary sexual retirement. The recent survey by Laumann and colleagues (1994) found that seven out of 10 women in their seventies were no longer having partnered sex. Other studies find that one third to one half of women in their sixties and seventies masturbate (Brecher, 1984; Starr & Weiner, 1981), although these are mainly women who masturbated when they were young as well, and again we cannot be sure whether the results are representative of all elderly women.

In addition to having partners, most of the respondents in the sex surveys (reporting elderly people having sexual relations) were people in good health. However, many people experience serious medical problems and disabilities as they grow older. Problems like heart disease, stroke, arthritis, diabetes, prostate problems, and problems due to alcohol, smoking, or overeating are common. By age 65, about a third of men are experiencing erectile difficulties, mostly due to medical problems, and by age 70 more than half have erectile dysfunctions (Diokno, Brown, & Herzog, 1990; Mulligan et al., 1988; Weizman & Hart, 1987; see Chapter 13).

Opportunities for sexual relations become very limited for elderly people with disabilities that require dependency on others for their care. For example, administrators and staff in many nursing homes do not allow their elderly residents to have sexual relations, requiring married couples to live in separate rooms (when both are institutionalized) or denying privacy when the healthy partner of an institutionalized spouse

comes to visit (Starr & Weiner, 1981; Wasow & Loeb, 1979).

What can we conclude about sexuality in the elderly years? Sexual opportunities are limited for single women, but for healthy men and women with healthy partners, sexual activity will probably continue throughout life if they had a positive attitude about sex when they were younger. Sexual interests may continue even for those with serious medical problems and disabilities. Sex surveys tend to measure sexual behavior in terms of physical acts such as sexual intercourse and oral sex, but there is more to sexuality than this. Elderly people often report great sexual satisfaction with emotionally erotic experiences (Shaw, 1994). Sexual pleasure, for example, includes touching, caressing, physical closeness, and intimacy. These can often be achieved even in the most extreme cases:

"Mr. N was deaf, blind, and unable to talk due to a recent laryngotomy. He was quite dependent on Mrs. N who had severe arthritis and had a mastectomy years ago. They typically sat close together, in part to aid communication due to Mr. N's impairments. But the way they held hands revealed great tenderness and affection. They slept in twin beds and indicated they no longer engaged in intercourse. Yet, they had a nightly ritual in which Mr. N helped his wife bathe and then gave her a massage in bed, which they described with some embarrassment and blushing. Interestingly, through this sensual routine, Mr. N, usually the more dependent of the two, was able to offer something of value to his wife."

(from Rose and Soares, 1993)
(Reprinted by permission. ©1993, The Haworth Press, Binghamton, NY. Journal of Gerontological Social Work, Vol. 19(3/4), p. 170.)

Perhaps the biggest problem for elderly people interested in physical relations is our culture's negative stereotypes of the aged as sexless (Barrow & Smith, 1992). Many people poke fun at, or discriminate against, other people who are different from themselves, and this often includes the elderly. But, unless there is a tragedy, all of us will be elderly some day. Do you enjoy sexual relations now? Do you ever want to give it up? If not, how do you think you will feel if one day younger people think you are silly, preposterous, or even lecherous or perverted for wanting the pleasure of someone else's touch? The time to address these attitudes is now, not later. We are all sexual human beings, from birth to death.

KEY TERMS

adolescence   245
climacteric   260
cohabitation   253
egocentric   238
gynecomastia   244
hot flashes   260
menarche   242

menopause   260
necking   247
nocturnal emission   243
open marriage   257
peer pressure   248
petting   247
phallic stage   200, 239

precocious puberty   245
puberty   242
secondary sex
     characteristics   242
serial monogamy   252
swinging   257
young adulthood   251

PERSONAL REFLECTIONS

1. Does the thought of young children examining and touching their own genitals make you uncomfortable? If so, why? How would you feel if you found your 5-year-old boy with his pants down playing "doctor"? Why? Would your reaction be any different if you found your 5-year-old girl with her pants down playing "doctor"? Why?

2. Try to recall the feelings you experienced during puberty as your body changed. Would better understanding of these events (via parents or sex education classes) have made it a more positive experience?

3. What kinds of pressure to engage in sex have you experienced (from dates, friends, the media, etc.)? Have you ever engaged in sex because of pressure (to please a boyfriend/girlfriend, to feel older, to be "like everyone else," etc.)? How have you dealt with the pressure? How could you deal better with the pressure?

4. What would you tell a young teenager about sex? Why? Pretend you have an adolescent child who has just told you he/she is considering having sexual intercourse. What is your reaction? Does your answer change depending on the sex of the child? Why?

5. Does the thought of your parents *enjoying* sexual relations make you comfortable or uncomfortable? Why? If you have difficulty viewing your parents as sexual human beings, what effect do you think that will have on your own sexual relationship when you and your partner become parents (and view one another as parents)? Do you think it is healthy or unhealthy for parents to hide their sexuality from their children? Why?

6. Does the thought of elderly people *enjoying* sexual relations make you comfortable or uncomfortable? Why? Do you hope to still enjoy sexual relations when you are in your fifties and older? If not, at what age do you think that you will stop enjoying sex? Why?

SUGGESTED READINGS

Allgeier, E. R. (1985, March). Perceptions of parents as sexual beings: Pocs and Godow revisited. *SIECUS Report.* Discusses how many children view their parents as married and asexual.

Beck, M., et al. (1992, May 25). Menopause: The search for straight talk and safe treatment. *Newsweek. Newsweek's* cover story covers both the medical and feminist perspectives on menopause.

Brecher, R. M. (1984). *Love, sex, and aging.* Boston: Little, Brown . Excerpts in *Connecticut* magazine, November, 1984. Elderly men and women enjoy sexual relations well into their sixties, seventies, and eighties.

Bulcroft, K., and O'Conner-Roden. (1986, June). Never too late. *Psychology Today.* Concludes that dating patterns of people over 65 are similar to those of younger adults.

Goodman, E. (1983, July). The turmoil of teenage sexuality. *MS.* Discusses what teens are doing sexually and how parents often send mixed signals.

Gordon, S. (1986, October). What kids need to know. *Psychology Today.* Discusses some topics about sexuality that children need to know and gives advice to parents and schools about how to teach these subjects.

Janus, S., and Janus, C. (1993). *The Janus report.* New York: John Wiley & Sons. Results of a nationwide survey of sexual behavior.

Kiester, E., Jr. (1988, July). Good sex makes good marriages. *50 Plus.* Interview with a noted authority on how life after fifty can be a time of great sexual fulfillment.

Laumann, E., et al. (1994). *Sex in America.* Boston: Little, Brown. Results of one of the most scientifically conducted surveys ever done.

Pesmen, C. (1993, March). The last orgasm. *GQ.* A short but informative article on the effects of aging on sexual response in males.

Seidman, S. N., and Rieder, R. O. (1994, March). A review of sexual behavior in the United States. *The American Journal of Psychiatry.* An excellent review of the numerous sex surveys.

Willis, J. (1986, July/August). Demystifying menopause. *FDA Consumer.* Discusses the normal experiences of menopause.

CHAPTER ELEVEN

ADULT SEXUAL BEHAVIORS AND ATTITUDES

WHEN YOU FINISH STUDYING THIS CHAPTER, YOU SHOULD BE ABLE TO:

1. EXPLAIN WHAT IS MEANT BY "NORMAL" SEXUAL BEHAVIORS;

2. IDENTIFY THE MAJOR HISTORICAL, AS WELL AS CURRENT, SOURCES OF NEGATIVE ATTITUDES TOWARD MASTURBATION, AND DISCUSS RECENT FINDINGS ABOUT THIS SEXUAL ACTIVITY;

3. DESCRIBE WHAT OCCURS DURING THE NORMAL SLEEP CYCLE THAT CAN RESULT IN NOCTURNAL ORGASMS;

4. SUMMARIZE THE RESEARCH FINDINGS ABOUT THE FREQUENCY, QUALITY, AND ROLE OF SEXUAL FANTASIES IN ENHANCING SEXUAL EXPRESSION;

5. EXPLAIN WHY DIFFERENT CULTURES, AS WELL AS INDIVIDUALS WITHIN A CULTURE, USE DIFFERENT POSITIONS OF SEXUAL INTERCOURSE;

6. DISCUSS WAYS TO KEEP THE SEXUAL ASPECTS OF A RELATIONSHIP FROM BECOMING RITUALIZED;

7. DEFINE FELLATIO AND CUNNILINGUS AND DESCRIBE THE CURRENT RESEARCH FINDINGS ON THESE ACTIVITIES; AND

8. DEFINE A SEXUALLY HEALTHY PERSON.

FOR THE HUMAN SPECIES TO SUR-
VIVE, IT REQUIRES THAT MALES AND
FEMALES HAVE SEXUAL INTER-
course. We need only to look at the large number of
people in the world to know that this is not an uncommon sexual practice. But what about other behaviors,
that is, behaviors that are not necessary for procreation?

How many people engage in oral-genital sex? Is your
partner unusual for wanting to try different positions?
Is it normal to have sexual fantasies? Is masturbation
unnatural and bad for your health? Many people are
unsure about the answers to these questions, and thus
may have anxieties about whether the sexual behaviors
they, or their partners, wish to engage in are "normal." ■

WHAT IS NORMAL?

Just what is "normal" sexual behavior? The answer is: it
depends. Many factors are involved, including the age
of the individual and the society and period in history
in which the person lives. What is considered normal
changes over the life-span of an individual and from
generation to generation.

In this chapter you will read about several sexual
behaviors that can be considered normal from a statistical point of view. If a behavior is normal statistically,
it means that a large number of people engage in it.
However, you should not consider yourself to be "abnormal" if you have not engaged in all of the behaviors
discussed here. It is best to think of normal behavior as
including a *range of behaviors*. Today, sexual intercourse, masturbation, oral-genital sex, homosexuality,
and other behaviors are considered to be within the
range of behaviors labeled normal for adults by mental
health professionals, while masturbation might be considered the only normal behavior for a child.

For any particular behavior, there is also the question of how frequently people engage in it. How often
is normal? Averages can be (and are) computed, but you
should not interpret "normal" as meaning only
the average value. Again, normal involves a *range of
values*. For example, what is the normal number of
times per month that married women masturbate? The
answer is a range (from 0 to some higher number). Most
behaviors are considered normal as long as the
individual does not suffer physical and/or psychological
damage, does not inflict physical and/or psychological
damage on others, and the behavior does not interfere
with being able to cope in dealing with the activities of
daily life.

The incidence and frequency of the various sexual
behaviors you will read about in this chapter were obtained by taking sex surveys. Be sure to review the
section on surveys and sampling procedures in Chapter 1. ■

MASTURBATION

"Until I became sexually active with a partner, I masturbated every day. Even after
marriage, I continue to masturbate." (male)

"The guilt I feel right after masturbating is so
painful that I cry at times." (male)

"I have a steady girlfriend who satisfies my sexual needs. But sometimes I am not able to
satisfy hers. This is the primary reason why I enjoy
masturbating—because I don't have to worry
about trying to satisfy anyone but me." (male)

"I didn't masturbate until after I was sexually
active, which was in college. In between
sex with my boyfriends, I didn't know there
were ways I could 'pleasure' myself with sex—
and without a partner. Now, after finding it, I
truly enjoy it." (female)

"I had masturbated long before I became sexually active and, as long as I kept it to myself,
I never seemed to have a problem with it. Now,
when my boyfriend asks me if I ever masturbated, I can't help but feel guilty." (female)

"I've masturbated since about the age of
14. I still do, with and without my husband
present. I have no guilty feelings about it, not
even when I was younger. There are times
when I would rather masturbate than make
love. Not that I would give up intercourse. It's
just nicer sometimes." (female)

"All through my childhood I thought that
masturbation was something only guys
could do. But *Cosmo* started printing all kinds of
articles telling women to masturbate so they can
show their partner what to do, and I got confused. I know I shouldn't be ashamed of my body,
but I still can't bring myself to do it." (female)

"I am 36 years old and never in my wildest
dreams would I have thought I would be

masturbating, but I did and I think its great because I can stimulate parts that a male partner would not have the slightest idea about.'' (female)

"When my boyfriend and I engage in sexual activities, I get absolutely aroused when he masturbates in front of me. . . .'' (female)

(from the author's files)

ATTITUDES ABOUT MASTURBATION

When you were growing up, what kind of things did you hear might happen to you if you masturbated?

Masturbation
Self-stimulation of one's genitals.

Many of us were told (by friends, acquaintances, and sometimes parents) that masturbation could cause us to go blind or deaf, have nosebleeds, heart murmurs, acne, painful menstruation, cause hair to grow on the palms of our hands, and finally, if we didn't stop, insanity. Others of us were simply told that we had better not do it to excess. The consequences of doing it to excess were never quite spelled out, but the possibilities that it was bad for our health or could lead to insanity were always implied. And scarier yet, what was considered excessive? Whatever it was, most of us convinced ourselves that it was more than we did it.

It is obvious that masturbation is considered bad by some people, but where did these stories come from? The negative attitudes about masturbation have, in fact, been handed down from generation to generation for centuries. The Greek physician Hippocrates believed that overindulging in sex was harmful to one's health. Ancient Chinese cultures condemned male masturbation as a waste of "yang" (male essence), while the Biblical Hebrews considered it "spillage of seed," punishable by death (recall from the Bible, the divine slaying of Onan for spilling his seed). The early Roman Catholic church, you recall, considered the only legitimate purpose of sex to be for procreation (St. Augustine called intercourse an unpleasant necessity), and sexual behaviors that did not have this as a goal (i.e., were done for pleasure) were considered immoral. Many scholars believe that the word masturbation is derived from the Latin words *manus* (hand) and *sturpore* (to defile) or *tubare* (to disturb).

In 1758, a Swiss physician named Tissot published a book entitled *Onania, or a Treatise Upon the Disorders Produced by Masturbation.* In his book, Tissot claimed that excessive sex, and especially masturbation, was dangerous because it deprived vital tissues of blood and led to insanity. As proof of this, he said, one only had to look at the many men in insane asylums who sat around openly masturbating. Tissot's views were accepted by many physicians. In Victorian times (1800s and early 1900s), many physicians also believed that loss of semen was as detrimental to a male's health as loss of blood. Freud, for example, believed that the loss of one ounce of semen produced the same degree of fatigue as the loss of 40 ounces of blood. The Victorians, you recall, vehemently denied any pleasurable component of sex and were particularly concerned about masturbation (see Hall, 1992). Children were not only forced to wear chastity belts and metal gloves to bed (see Figure 1-3), but castration, circumcision, and clitoridectomy became popular during this time as a means by which parents tried to prevent their children from masturbating. As an example of the extreme Victorian beliefs, read the following passages from a book written in 1903 by an M.D., Ph.D. (*Perfect Womanhood,* by Mary Melendy) as advice to women about their male children and masturbation:

Impress upon him that if these organs are abused, or if they are put to any use besides that for which God made them . . . they will bring disease and ruin upon those who abuse . . . he will not grow up happy, healthy and strong.

Teach him that when he handles or excites the sexual organs, all parts of the body suffer, because they are connected by nerves that run throughout the system, this is why it is called "self-abuse." . . .

. . . The sin is terrible, and is, in fact, worse than lying or stealing!

If the sexual organs are handled it brings too much blood to these parts, and this produces a diseased condition, it also causes disease in other organs of the body, because they are left with a less amount of blood than they ought to have. . . .

It lays the foundation for consumption, paralysis and heart disease. It weakens the memory, makes a boy careless, negligent and listless.

It even makes many lose their minds; others when grown, commit suicide.

Similarly, Dr. J. W. Kellogg (1882) wrote the following about the effects of masturbation in girls:

Wide observations have convinced us that a great many of the backaches, sideaches, and other aches and pains of which girls complain, are attributable to this injurious habit. Much of the nervousness, hysteria, neurolgia, and general worthlessness of girls originates in this cause alone.

The period of puberty is one at which thousands of girls break down in health. The constitution, already weakened by a debilitating, debasing vice, is not prepared for the strain, and the poor victim drops into a premature grave.

He wrote the following about masturbation in boys:

> In solitude he pollutes himself, and with his own hand blights all his prospects for both this world and the next. Even after being solemnly warned, he will often continue this worse than beastly practice, deliberately forfeiting his right to health and happiness for a moment's mad sensuality.
>
> (J. W. Kellogg, Plain Facts for Old and Young)

This is the same J. W. Kellogg associated with the breakfast cereals. He invented corn flakes to be used as a breakfast food that would curb youthful lust. Graham crackers were invented by Dr. Sylvester Graham for much the same purpose (Money, 1985).

Although not all cultures have had negative attitudes about masturbation (e.g., the ancient Egyptians believed that the world was created when the God Atum ejaculated), negative attitudes are still widely found in Western societies (Gregersen, 1982). For example, the Catholic church called it an "intrinsically and seriously disordered act" in 1975, and Orthodox Jews regard it as one of the worst sins included in the Torah.

When former surgeon general Joycelyn Elders was fired in 1994 for talking about masturbation, sociologist John Gagnon was quoted as saying, "It remains a puzzle for me why a relatively innocuous behavior evokes tides of anxiety and fear in otherwise well-adjusted people."

INCIDENCE OF MASTURBATION

With this long history of scare tactics, you would expect, then, that very few people masturbate. In fact, the large majority of human beings masturbate. Kinsey and colleagues (1948, 1953) found that 92 percent of the men he surveyed had masturbated by age 20. It was generally the first sexual experience to orgasm for adolescent males. Only a third of the women in Kinsey's study reported that they had masturbated by age 20, but another third had done so by age 40 (a total of 62 percent). Nearly identical results were found 20 years later by Hunt (1975). In other words, men are more likely to start masturbating before they experience sexual intercourse, whereas many women do not start masturbating until after they start engaging in intercourse (Gagnon, 1977).

Not all people who have masturbated continue to do so regularly. Laumann and colleagues (1994) found that for Americans under the age of 60, only 60 percent of men and 40 percent of women masturbated in the past year. Kinsey found that the better educated a person was, the more likely it was that he or she mastur-

bated. Among today's college students, about twice as many men as women masturbate (Atwood & Gagnon, 1987; Leitenberg, Detzer, & Srebnik, 1993), again reflecting the gender-age differences found by Kinsey (1948, 1953). On the average, men who masturbate do so two or three times more frequently than women who masturbate (Kinsey et al., 1953; Hunt, 1975; Leitenberg et al., 1993). Interestingly, in a recent review of many studies, it was found that although women report a much lower incidence of masturbation than do males, their attitudes toward masturbation do not differ from men's (Oliver & Hyde, 1993).

Are all of these people risking their health or sanity? No. Masturbation, whether done once a month or three times a day, does not cause any of the problems mentioned previously, and few doctors today, if any, would make such a claim. *It is a perfectly normal human behavior.* How can I be so confident to call it normal when historically it has been so condemned? Just look at the statistics—when the vast majority of people engage in a particular behavior, it has to be considered normal. It is a behavior engaged in by a great many other species as well (Ford & Beach, 1951). Still, there are some who continue to feel guilty or wrong about it (one in six young people according to Hunt). Among college students, for example, 40 percent of those who do not masturbate say it is because they believe it is immoral (Atwood & Gagnon, 1987).

METHODS OF MASTURBATION

People differ in the way they masturbate, but men display less variation than do women. Almost all men masturbate by rhythmically stroking up and down the body

"Now they tell us masturbation is harmless!"

(*Reproduced by Special Permission of PLAYBOY Magazine. Copyright © 1971 by PLAYBOY.*)

(Reproduced by special permission of *Playboy* magazine. Copyright © 1971 by *Playboy*.)

and glans of the penis with one hand (Hite, 1981). They may differ in how much of the penis they stimulate, and in the rhythm and pressure applied, but it is generally still a stroking motion. Very few thrust. Many men simultaneously stimulate their testicles and other parts of their bodies as well. In order to enhance arousal, many males fantasize and/or look at sexually explicit pictures while masturbating. Hunt (1975) found, for example, that 75 percent of men had fantasies of sexual intercourse with a loved person during masturbation.

Some individuals (mostly adolescent males) try to make their orgasms more intense by hanging or other activities that deprive them of oxygen (Saunders, 1989). This is called *autoerotic asphyxiation.* Although masturbation per se does not cause health problems, these behaviors are dangerous and 500 to 1000 people die each year while engaging in them (Hazelwood et al., 1983). Other than simply holding your breath, you should not engage in any behavior that deprives you of oxygen (during sex or any other time).

Most women who masturbate do so by stimulating their clitoris, labia minora, and/or the entire vulva. Only 20 percent or fewer insert a finger or anything else into their vagina while masturbating (Hite, 1976; Kinsey et al., 1953). Those who do should not consider themselves to be abnormal; for remember, "normal" encompasses a wide range of behaviors, not a single behavior. The manner in which women stimulate themselves is quite diverse. Many prefer to lie on their backs while masturbating, while some prefer a facedown position, with considerable individual preferences in the position of the legs. Some use a single finger, while others use their entire hand to apply pressure to a wider area. Kinsey's group (1953) found that about 11 percent of women stimulate their breasts during masturbation. Although only a few women in his sample reported using a vibrator, the number who do so today has substantially increased because of the easy availability of these products now.

> "In the masturbation section I believe you should emphasize the importance of a vibrator for women. Methods of masturbation seem apparent to males, but I think women need more guidance in this area. In my experience a vibrator is the most intensely pleasurable way to masturbate."
>
> (from the author's files)

Like men, most women enhance their arousal by fantasizing during masturbation (Hunt, 1975).

FUNCTIONS OF MASTURBATION

Why do people masturbate? Quite simply, because it feels good. The genitals, you recall, have lots of nerve endings and are thus very sensitive to touch. As you learned in the chapter on development, almost all young children touch their genitals when they have an opportunity (e.g., in the bathtub) and do so because it gives them physical pleasure. By the early teens, however, genital touching is not just physical. It is often accompanied by erotic thoughts. Although it also allows for sexual release when a partner is not available, masturbation does not necessarily cease when one forms a sexual relationship with someone. Hunt (1975) found that 72 percent of men and 68 percent of women continued to masturbate after marriage. More recently, Janus and Janus (1993) reported that 66 percent of men and 67 percent of women agreed or strongly agreed that "masturbation is a natural part of life and continues on in marriage." In fact, Laumann et al. (1994) found that more people with sexual partners masturbate than people living alone, and that the more sex a person has the more likely he or she is to masturbate. In other words, masturbation is not so much an outlet for lack of sex as it is a reflection of a sexually active lifestyle.

Why do people with sexual partners masturbate? *Variety*—it is a sexual experience that is different (not necessarily better) than sex with their partner.

> "I masturbated a lot when I was without a partner, and now I still do. The orgasm is so different than those I get during intercourse. . . . My boyfriend doesn't understand . . . , but I love making love with him. . . ."
>
> (from the author's files)

Freud thought that adult masturbation was immature. Even today, some people argue that it may be habit-forming and prevent development of "normal" adult sexual relations. However, Kinsey's group (1953) found that women who were able to masturbate to orgasm without guilt or shame during adolescence generally had the least difficulty in making the transition to enjoying sex with a partner. More recent studies report that not only is masturbation during adolescence not harmful to sexual adjustment in young adulthood (Leitenberg, Detzer, & Srebnik, 1993), but that masturbation during marriage is often associated with a greater degree of marital and sexual satisfaction (Hurlbert & Whittaker, 1991). So, if you suspect your partner of masturbating occasionally, do not assume that he or she is unhappy with his or her sex life. There would only be a problem if your partner is masturbating (indicating a need for a sexual outlet), but showing little or no interest or sexual desire for you.

Today, some therapists prescribe masturbation as part of treatment for overcoming orgasm problems in women and for greater ejaculatory control in men (Barbach, 1980; Kaplan, 1974; LoPiccolo & Lobitz,

1972; LoPiccolo & Stock, 1986). Thus, what was once a taboo is now often used as part of sexual therapy. This is not to imply, however, that everyone should masturbate, particularly if they are comfortable with their sexuality. Just as it was once wrong to make people feel bad because they masturbated, it would be equally wrong to make people feel abnormal if they did not. The important point is that those who have a desire to masturbate should be able to do so without feelings of guilt or worries about their health. ■

NOCTURNAL ORGASMS

"During wet dreams I always seem to wake up when I reach climax and am greeted with a puddle of sperm. I am not embarrassed by such occurrences—it just forces me to wash my sheets." (male)

"I was 17 years old, and one morning I woke up finding my sheets wet. I thought I urinated in bed at first until I realized it wasn't urine. I was ashamed and didn't want anyone to know what happened. I quickly changed my sheets and took a bath." (male)

"I experience nocturnal orgasms 5–6 times a month on the average. They are always corresponding to a sexual dream I am having. The orgasm wakes me up. I consider it a blessing." (female)

"I heard, when I was growing up, about 'wet dreams' but thought that only applied to males. It wasn't until recently I awoke from a deep sleep, very sexually aroused, my heart beating rapidly, my body sweating, and vaginal lubrication had already begun. I don't remember the dream I was having." (female)

(from the author's files)

Many people have orgasms in their sleep. There are five stages of sleep. Stages I and II are light sleep and stages III and IV are deep sleep. Adults enter a fifth stage about every 90 minutes. This is called REM or paradoxical sleep. REM stands for rapid eye movements (our eyes move all around under the eyelids during this stage), and our EEG (a measure of the activity of the brain) is paradoxically identical to that of an awake, alert individual. But we are asleep! Many physiological events normally occur in this stage of sleep, including penile erection in males and vaginal lubrication in females. In fact, when people do not show these responses, it is an indication that something physiologically is wrong. This is also the stage of sleep in which we have our most vivid dreams, but do not as-

Nocturnal orgasm

An orgasm that occurs during sleep (sometimes called "wet dreams" in males).

sume that the dreams have a sexual theme just because people are experiencing erection or lubrication. Remember, unless there is something physiologically wrong, people are going to have these responses regardless of what they are dreaming. An orgasm may result merely from the rubbing of the genitals against the sheets and have nothing to do with dream content.

Similar to attitudes about masturbation, there is a long history of negative opinions about nocturnal orgasms as well. In the early 1800s, a French physician named Claude Francois l'Allernand believed that male nocturnal emissions ("wet dreams") were caused by the same thing that caused gonorrhea. Thus, in the Victorian era, nocturnal emissions were called "spermatorrhea." Some Victorian parents made their male children wear spiked "spermatorrhea rings" to bed at night to prevent emissions (see Figure 1-3).

A lot of unfortunate Victorian boys must have experienced punctures. Kinsey et al. (1948) found that 83 percent of men reported having had nocturnal emissions. This occurs most frequently during the teen years and declines substantially after that, but they can occur at any age. Many teenage boys are embarrassed by the wet spot on the sheets, especially if they have not been told in advance by their parents that this may (and is likely to) occur (see Chapter 10 for a more detailed discussion). Parents should not embarrass or ridicule their teenaged boys for having wet dreams, particularly since it is a behavior over which they have no control (they occur during sleep). In fact, many males do not remember having an orgasm in their sleep and are only aware that they did because of the wet spot.

Forty percent of the women in Kinsey's sample (1953) and 37 percent in a more recent sample (Wells, 1988) also reported having nocturnal orgasms. However, the disparity between the response of the two sexes may not really be this great. Females do not have a wet spot on the sheets in the morning as proof of a nocturnal orgasm, so only those women who are awakened by the orgasmic contractions can report them.

It is also normal for people to have sexually explicit dreams. Nearly 100 percent of the men and 70 percent of the women in Kinsey's studies reported having such dreams, although in some cases it caused distress. Keep in mind, however, that dreaming about something is not the same as doing it. ■

SEXUAL FANTASIES

"My sister, who was much older than I, would always have friends over and I would fantasize about making love to them while masturbating." (male)

"... they (fantasies) almost always include my wife. It may also include another female. . . . " (male)

"I enjoy being male, but have occasionally fantasized about what it is like to be female during lovemaking." (male)

"During sex I have sexual fantasies about making love to a woman. . . . I would view my husband as a woman." (female)

"My sexual fantasy has been the same since age 16. The man uses me, sometimes beats me, and bring his other female partners around me. This fantasy bothers me." (female)

"I have sexual fantasies while making love to my husband, usually about men I'm attracted to from work. I think about how it would be and when I come, it's stronger and harder than it usually is." (female)

(from the author's files)

Nearly everyone has sexual fantasies from time to time. Sometimes the fantasy may be a warm thought of a romantic interaction with a special person, but many times the fantasies are very sexually explicit. It was once thought that only men had sexual fantasies (because women were thought to be less interested in sex), but this is not true. While most men think about sex more often than women (54 percent of men say they do so every day compared to 19 percent of women; Laumann et al., 1994), the large majority of women do have sexual fantasies. Kinsey et al. (1953) found that nearly two thirds of women who masturbated used fantasy to enhance sexual arousal. Two decades later, Hunt (1975) reported that three fourths of men and 80 percent of women fantasized during masturbation. Crépault et al. (1977) reported that 94 percent of women used fantasies for sexual arousal. Similarly, Masters, Johnson, and Kolodny (1992) found that 86 percent of women had erotic fantasies. A recent survey of college women reported that 97 percent said they had sexual fantasies (Pelletier & Harold, 1988). Although women's sexual fantasies tend to be more romantic and emotional than men's fantasies, they are also very explicit and detailed (Crépault et al., 1977; Leitenberg & Henning, 1995; Masters, Johnson, & Kolodny, 1992). The length and explicitness of an individual's sexual fantasies are related to his or her level of sexual experience (Gold & Chick, 1988; Pelletier & Harold, 1988).

Sexual fantasies can occur at any time. One study found that 72 percent of women and 71 percent of men enhanced their sexual arousal by using fantasy (Zimmer et al., 1982). It is also common for people to fantasize while having sexual intercourse, and the most common type at this time is the replacement fantasy, where one imagines him or herself having sex with someone other than his or her sexual partner (Cado & Leitenberg, 1990). If you have ever felt guilty about having these fantasies, as some people do (believing them to be immoral or socially unacceptable), you should be aware that they are so common that chances are your partner has had them, too (Cado & Leitenberg, 1990; Crépault et al., 1977). The fantasized partner can be a friend, neighbor, former partner, celebrity (e.g., movie star, musician), or anyone else. Sharing fantasies with one's partner may enhance intimacy and sexual interest in some cases, but may lead to jealousy and self-doubt in other cases. Most people prefer that their fantasies be kept private.

The content of sexual fantasies is almost limitless. Other common fantasy themes are experimentation of never-before-tried experiences, watching others having sex (including their spouse with another person), idyllic romantic encounters with a stranger under near-perfect conditions, group sex, being conquered, homosexual encounters, and rape or sadomasochistic fantasies (Masters & Johnson, 1979). Dominance fantasies are common for men, while submission fantasies of being overpowered are common for women (Leitenberg & Henning, 1995).

The content of sexual fantasies does not indicate sexual unhappiness and/or personality or psychological problems (Davidson & Hoffman, 1986; Hariton & Singer, 1974; Leitenberg & Henning, 1995). In fact, sexual fantasies are most common in those individuals who have the fewest number of sexual problems (Leitenberg & Henning, 1995). Most sex therapists view sexual fantasies as something positive and to be enjoyed rather than as bad for one's sexual health. Sexual fantasies often serve to satisfy our curiosity about something unattainable or not yet experienced (fantasizing about group sex, for example). Having a sexual fantasy, however, does not mean that a person actually wants to experience it in real life. Many heterosexuals occasionally have fantasies of a homosexual encounter, for example, but Masters and Johnson have found that this is not a strong indicator that they are latent homosexuals. Fantasies also provide a safe and private outlet for thoughts that, if actually engaged in, might be considered improper and/or illegal. In fact, in most cases where people have acted out their fantasy, the result has been disappointment. One reason for this is that we are totally in control of the sequence of events in our fantasies, so that they proceed just to our liking; but this is seldom true in real life, where partners can cause distractions and have desires and demands of their own.

Although generally viewed as positive, sexual fantasies can sometimes cause such guilt and distress that counseling is necessary (because the behaviors fantasized about are not in tune with a person's self-image). For the most part, however, they are harmless. And because the vast majority of people have them, they are also in the range of normal behavior. ■

COITAL POSITIONS AND LOCATIONS

"**B**efore I became sexually active, I believed that everyone who engaged in sexual intercourse did so in the missionary position in the privacy of their own bedroom. Now I look forward to new positions." (female)

" . . . was boring me. We always used the same position—his favorite one." (female)

"**M**y boyfriend has the concept that men should be in control of sex. Well, I say 'What about my pleasure?' My favorite position is 'me on top' because I'm guaranteed to receive an orgasm." (female)

" . . . and also I like having sex standing up with my legs wrapped around the male's waist and walking around at the same time." (female)

"**I** am a mature, responsible, middle-aged female. I am also an experienced diver with a mate who is equally comfortable under water. In my opinion, the most stimulating, exciting, and extraordinary sex on earth happens beneath the surface of the water. Complete sex beyond the grasp of gravity in a quiet, sensuous, foreign world is beyond our limited language to describe." (female)

(from the author's files)

Missionary position

A face-to-face position of sexual intercourse in which the female lies on her back and the male lies on top with his legs between hers. It was called this because Christian missionaries instructed people that other positions were unnatural.

For most Americans, the first experience with sexual intercourse is in the *missionary position*, that is, a face-to-face position in which the female lies on her back and the male lies on top with his legs between hers. It is called the missionary position because Christian missionaries in foreign countries used to instruct natives that this was the only "proper" way to have sexual intercourse. St. Paul, you may recall, believed that women should be subordinate to men during intercourse (i.e., on the bottom), while St. Augustine said that any other position was unnatural and a sin against nature (see Chapter 1).

Coitus
Sexual intercourse.

For many couples, male-on-top may be the only position in which they ever have sex. Kinsey et al., (1948) found, for example, that over two thirds of the population had never attempted any other position. The preference for this position by many American couples, however, appears to be culturally rather than biologically determined. The female-on-top position is most popular in some other cultures, especially those in which women enjoy high status (see Box 11-A). In most nonhuman primate species, the male inserts his penis into the female's vagina from the rear.

More recent surveys suggest that American couples are practicing a greater variety of sexual positions during intercourse than in Kinsey's time. Hunt (1975), for example, found that of the married people he surveyed, 75 percent had tried female-on-top, 50 percent had tried side-by-side, 40 percent had tried rear vaginal entry, and 25 percent had had intercourse while sitting.

Why do couples experiment with different positions? After all, the missionary position is perfectly adequate for procreational purposes. Well, to answer this, let's first examine the advantages and disadvantages of the missionary position. Perhaps the nicest thing about this position is that it allows for intimacy while having sex. A couple is face-to-face. But for most women, the benefits stop right there. In most couples, the man is considerably heavier than the woman, which means that she has to support a great deal of weight in the male-on-top position (and more and more so as the male gets tired). Some women may even have trouble breathing in this position. Women in my class have additionally pointed out that they receive very little touching or fondling in this position because their male partners are too busy supporting themselves. With a woman's hips "pinned to the mat," the man is in total control (probably the major reason

FIGURE 11-1

FIGURE 11-2

276

Figure 11-3

Figure 11-4

that American men like this position), and it is often difficult to fully enjoy sex when you have little or no control over the movement or tempo.

There are other positions that still involve eye-to-eye contact, but allow greater freedom and involvement for the female. As you will see in a later chapter, female-on-top is a position that is recommended by many therapists for optimal sexual arousal in both people. It is generally a lot easier for the male to support the female, and it is also a position in which it is easy for the man or the woman herself to manually stimulate the clitoris during intercourse. Some couples enjoy rear vaginal entry because in this position the penis stimulates the front wall of the vagina (where some women have a small area of sensitivity called the Grafenberg spot, or G spot, you recall).

Although these considerations are important, probably the main reason that most couples have sexual intercourse in different positions is to bring variety to their sex lives. Many a sexual relationship has become stale and boring by allowing it to become *ritualized,* that is, by only having sex at the same time of day, in the same place, in the same position.

Even the manner in which many couples have sex is highly ritualized. Therapists report that it often proceeds in the following predictable manner: a few fleeting moments of kissing followed very quickly by the man touching and/or kissing the woman's breasts, followed directly by genital touching, followed by intercourse as soon as vaginal lubrication is detected.

Couples try different positions to keep their sex lives exciting, fresh, and fun—the way it was at the beginning of the relationship. There are sex manuals that show drawings of couples in what appears to be hundreds of different positions, but if you boil them all down, there are really just a few major variations that a couple can try: they can face each other or the female can turn her back, and they can lie down, sit, or stand up. However, couples should try different positions only because they want to, and not because they feel obliged to do so.

Whether or not a couple ever tries different sexual positions while having intercourse, it is important that they not allow their sex life to become a standardized ritual. The secret to that is to allow your sexual relations to be spontaneous, creative, and fun whenever possible. Some people get locked into a habit of never having sex until right before they go to sleep at night. If you and your partner are in the mood in the morning or afternoon, have sex then. Don't postpone it until later, when you might be tired. It is also normal for couples to have sex in a variety of places, for example, the couch, on the rug, different rooms, or any other place. There is no rule that states you can only have sex in bed.

Dear Ann Landers: My wife and I have been married 20 years. We have two sweet children and consider ourselves very fortunate. The problem is one we cannot discuss with our minister.

My wife believes that sex anywhere but in the bedroom is sinful according to the Bible. I say a change of setting can add extra pleasure, and so long as there is complete privacy, it is perfectly moral.

The place I have in mind is the car. We have a garage with a sturdy lock on the door. No one could possibly get in.

We are good Christians and want to know what the Bible says about this. Can you contact a religious scholar?

(Strictly Confidential in Kentucky)

Dear Strictly: Since the Bible predates the automobile by a couple of thousand years, there is no point in bothering a Christian scholar.

If you will settle for my opinion, here it is: It is perfectly all right for a married couple to make love anywhere they choose, providing it is private, safe, and reasonably comfortable.

(Reprinted with permission of Ann Landers and Creators Syndicate)

If you and your partner are on the couch and get in the mood to have sex, there is nothing immoral, sinful, or indecent to spontaneously do so right there (assuming, of course, that the shades are pulled, there are no children around, and you are using contraception if pregnancy is unwanted). One of Ann Landers' readers felt compelled to respond to the letter by "Strictly Confidential":

Dear Ann Landers: I was interested in the letter from the man who enjoyed making love in the car. His wife felt guilty and wanted to know if it was the "Christian" thing to do. You said so long as it was private, not dangerous, and reasonably comfortable, it was nobody's business.

I married one in a million. She was totally uninhibited, willing, and eager to make love any place at any time. I must say, we dreamed up some mighty unusual situations. We traveled quite a bit, and it was not unusual for us to pull off the road in the middle of the day if we ran into a wooded area, a vacant house, a sandy beach, a calm lake, or an inviting motel. On

Box 11-A

CROSS-CULTURAL PERSPECTIVES: POSITIONS OF SEXUAL INTERCOURSE

The males of other primate species always mount the female from behind during sexual intercourse. The buttocks of the females become swollen and red when she is sexually receptive, which acts as a sexual stimulant to the males. With evolution of the two-legged stance in humans, mating occurred primarily face-to-face, with greater opportunity for emotional interaction and communication via facial gestures and vocalization (Lambert, 1995). Some researchers believe that one of the reasons many men find female breasts to be sexually arousing is that breasts mimic the round contour of the buttocks (Diamond & Karlen, 1980).

Face-to-face is the preferred manner of sexual intercourse in all known cultures, but not necessarily man-on-top. In many African cultures the most common position is with the partners lying side by side, while in Polynesian and many Asian cultures the most common position is with the woman lying on her back and the man squatting or kneeling between her legs (Gregersen, 1982). (By the way, it was the Polynesians who originally called the male-on-top position taught to them by European missionaries the ``missionary position.'') Actually, in most cultures there is more than one preferred position. Mangaians, for example, practice a variety of positions while preferring some variety of male-on-top, but use the male-from-behind position when their partner is pregnant (Marshall, 1971).

Some researchers believe that a culture's preferred position of intercourse is a reflection of women's social status (Goldstein, 1976). In cultures where a woman's sexual satisfaction is considered to be as important as the man's, female-on-top is usually preferred. The ancient Romans preferred this position. In male-dominated cultures, however, the reverse is true (Langmyhr, 1976). There may be no better reflection of the relation between women's social status and coital position than in our own culture. Here, women's gender roles have changed dramatically since World War II. In the 1940s, you recall, Kinsey et al. (1948) found that over two thirds of couples had never attempted any position other than male-on-top. More and more women began to enter the work force after that and women's rights evolved rapidly in all areas. Twenty-five years later, Hunt (1975) found that the large majority of couples in the United States had tried the female-on-top position. ■

occasion, when the mood came upon us and none of the above was available, we just used the car.

This kept up until we were in our 60s, when my beloved wife passed away. I always felt as if we had the healthiest sex life of anyone I knew because we never stopped turning each other on. Sex was always unpredictable, imaginative, and fun. Our sexual compatibility spilled over into all areas of our life and we were divinely happy.

You can print this letter if you want to but no name or city, please. Just call me. . . .

(Beautiful Memories)

Dear Beautiful: How lucky you were to find each other. It was a perfect match. Lots of readers will be envious.

(Reprinted with permission of Ann Landers and Creators Syndicate)

However, whenever, and wherever you decide to do it, try to make your sexual relations spontaneous, exciting, enjoyable, and fulfilling. A healthy and satisfying sex life can contribute to our overall physical and emotional well-being. ■

ORAL-GENITAL SEX

" I was highly against oral sex because I thought it was so nasty and demeaning. But when I experienced it, my attitude changed. I didn't realize what I was against could feel so damn good." (female)

" ... what did surprise me was the fact that I enjoyed giving more than receiving. I think it is a great way for two people to share very intimate moments." (male)

" It is a great way to relax, feel unpressured and not worry about pregnancy or how good you perform." (male)

" I do engage in oral-genital sex, but really prefer it as foreplay. I don't like the idea of a guy coming in my mouth—it gags me!" (female)

" Oral sex is by far the most pleasurable sexual experience I have ever engaged in. It has produced some of the most intense orgasms that I have ever experienced, especially in the 69 position. I also very much enjoy orally stimulating my partner individually as much as being stimulated myself." (female)

(from the author's files)

Sexual relations generally include a great deal of oral stimulation. One of the first sexual behaviors that most people engage in is kissing, which, of course, involves mouth-to-mouth stimulation. This usually progresses from "dry" kissing (lip to lip) to "wet" kissing (also known as "French" or "soul" kissing, involving the tongue) within a short time. It is also normal while having sex for people to kiss and lick other parts of their partner's body (the neck, for example). For many people, this includes their partner's genitals.

Oral stimulation of the penis is called **fellatio** (from Latin meaning "to suck"), and oral stimulation of the vulva (clitoris, labia, vaginal opening) is called **cunnilingus** (from Latin meaning "one who licks the vulva") (Figures 11-5, and 11-6). These can be done either as part of foreplay or as the preferred sexual behavior, individually or at the same time (sometimes referred to as "69"). Although the slang term for fellatio is "blow job," the large majority of men prefer a sucking action to blowing. Many women report oral stimulation of the area around the clitoris to be more pleasurable than intercourse (the vaginal walls, you recall, have few nerve endings), and even many men find fellatio (particularly orgasm during fellatio) to be more intense than intercourse (Janus & Janus, 1993). The pleasure, however, is not always reserved entirely for the recipient. While it is true that many people prefer receiving oral sex to giving it (Laumann et al., 1994), many others enjoy orally stimulating their partner (and observing their reaction) nearly or equally as much as being stimulated themselves. For many people, it represents a moment of extreme intimacy.

How common are these behaviors? Kinsey's group (1948, 1953) found that about 50 to 60 percent of married people had engaged in oral-genital sex. However, only 15 percent of singles and only 10 percent of adolescents reported having engaged in it. More recent surveys indicate that about 75 to 90 percent of young adults eventually engage in oral-genital relations (e.g., Billy et al., 1993; Hunt, 1975;

Fellatio
Oral stimulation of a male's genitals.

Cunnilingus
Oral stimulation of a female's genitals.

FIGURE 11-5

FIGURE 11-6

Janus & Janus, 1993; Laumann et al., 1994). Nearly 50 percent of adolescents report having engaged in oral-genital sex today, with some girls preferring this behavior to intercourse (Newcomer & Udry, 1985).

Although no other behavior has increased as much in popularity since Kinsey's time as oral-genital stimulation (Gagnon & Simon, 1987), there are some notable differences among socioeconomic groups. Oral-genital sex is mostly practiced among white, college-educated individuals (e.g., Kinsey et al., 1948; Laumann et al., 1994). In Kinsey's time, oral-genital sex was so uncommon among African-Americans that it was almost a taboo, and still today only about 50 percent of African-Americans have done it (Laumann et al., 1994).

Some individuals consider oral-genital sex to be disgusting, and no one should feel pressured to engage in a behavior just because a lot of other people do it. On the other hand, if you expect your partner to do it for you, then you should not have a double standard about doing it for him or her. Double standards in sexual relations can lead to serious problems in other aspects of the relationship.

"My girlfriend refuses to have oral sex with me, but thinks that it is just fine for me to do it to her! Even though I enjoy doing this to her, I don't think it is fair that she would not even try it." (male)

"There are people out there who are sexually selfish. I was seeing someone for 7 months . . . I'll never forget our last encounter. His favorite sexual act was fellatio, so naturally I obliged. After I had done so, I wanted to kiss him. He had a very negative (and immature) reaction. I think if I could have castrated him, I would have!" (female)

"For almost 18 months I have been involved in what many of my friends consider the 'healthiest' relationship on campus. My boyfriend and I are compatible emotionally, physically, and intellectually. But there is one flaw that tortures me daily: our oral-genital sex relations to this point have been very one-sided, and I am bewildered. My personal hygiene is wonderful but when I finally got the courage to ask him to give me cunnilingus he was mortified. Yet from the beginning I have not hesitated to give him fellatio when he requests. I felt like his pleasure was my reward. When he refused me I felt insulted and I cried for an hour. I just can't lose the feeling of very deep, very personal humiliation." (female)

(from the author's files)

People often become more accepting of a sexual behavior when they learn that it is not abnormal (or that their partner is not abnormal or kinky for wanting to try it). As an example, try to remember your reaction when you first heard about French kissing. For many of us it seemed disgusting, but we later learned to enjoy it. Nevertheless, some people may have reservations about engaging in oral-genital sex because of cleanliness. Certainly, people ought to bathe regularly if they expect their partners to give them oral-genital stimulation (or engage in sexual relations of any kind for that matter).

Even if a couple has good hygiene habits, however, there may be reservations about the cleanliness and odors of genital secretions. As discussed in the chapter on anatomy, the odor of a healthy vagina is not offensive. Some women do not like the taste of semen, but it, too, is relatively clean. In fact, mouth-genital contact is no less hygienic than mouth-to-mouth contact (the mouth harbors as many germs as the genital orifices). This assumes, of course, that neither person has a sexually transmitted disease, for these can be transmitted during oral-genital stimulation as well as during intercourse. On the other hand, there are no health benefits to swallowing genital secretions (e.g., curing acne, prolonging youthfulness), as some individuals mistakenly believe.

Finally, there are even some people who worry that these are homosexual acts. It is true that the vast majority of homosexuals engage in oral-genital sex, but so do heterosexuals, just as both groups kiss or hold hands. It is not the behaviors that determine whether one is heterosexual or homosexual, but with whom you regularly practice them. ■

ANAL STIMULATION

"The first time I had ever heard of anal sex was in 1981. A girl I worked with told me that she and her boyfriend had used this. I knew that male homosexuals had intercourse in that manner, but it never once occurred to me that heterosexuals did also!" (female)

"Last summer my boyfriend decided he wanted to try some of the different types of things . . . I will never try sex again in the anus because it was so painful. . . . " (female)

"I do very much enjoy anal stimulation, if done properly. For me, anal stimulation during oral sex has produced the 'ultimate' orgasm . . . if it is done gently and not forcefully." (female)

"I like anal sex, probably a lot more than most females. When I first had anal sex, I didn't like it. . . . The difference is in how fast or slow the guy is in penetrating and also how turned on I am before he goes in. . . . " (female)

"My boyfriend and I sometimes use a mini-vibrator while making love. While we're in the missionary position, I insert the vibrator through the anus. At the same time, he continues to penetrate. I receive the ultimate feeling in sexual pleasure." (female)

(from the author's files)

The anus has numerous nerve endings and is very sensitive to touch. Many people enjoy having their anus manually stimulated (i.e., using fingers) by their partner during sexual intercourse. The anal sphincter muscle undergoes rhythmic muscular contractions during orgasm in both males and females, and thus anal stimulation can further enhance the pleasure. Although there is a physical basis for this, many other people feel very negatively about anal sex, and consider it to be abnormal, perverted, or kinky (Janus & Janus, 1993).

Anal intercourse is common among male homosexuals, but how common is it among heterosexual couples? Kinsey et al. (1948) found that 11 percent of the people he surveyed had attempted this behavior (only 8 percent successfully), but surveys conducted more recently indicate that about 20 to 25 percent of young adults have tried anal intercourse (Billy et al., 1993; Hunt, 1975; Laumann et al., 1994; Reinisch et al., 1992). One in 10 heterosexual couples engage in anal intercourse somewhat regularly (Voeller, 1991). When asked why they participate in this behavior, many women say that it is their least favorite activity (but occasionally engage in it for variety), but as you can see from the personal testimonials at the beginning of this section, others enjoy it.

For those who engage in this behavior, some words of caution are necessary. First, the anal sphincter muscle contracts in response to attempted penetration, and attempts to force the penis into the anus can result in injury. A water-soluble lubricant (like K-Y jelly) should be used if you engage in this behavior. The muscle spasms do not relax for 30 to 60 seconds after penetration, so the woman often experiences some initial discomfort, even if her male partner proceeds slowly and gently. Even so, this behavior will almost certainly result in rupturing of small capillaries (unlike the vagina, the rectum does not readily accommodate this kind of stimulation, Agnew, 1986). Anal intercourse itself does not cause AIDS, but the ruptured capillaries maximize the chances of contracting HIV (the virus that causes AIDS) from an *infected* partner. In addition, bacteria that are normally found in the anus can easily cause infection if introduced into the vagina. Couples who engage in anal stimulation, therefore, should never put anything (i.e., finger, penis, objects) in the vagina that has been in contact with the anus unless it has been washed first. ∎

PREFERRED SEXUAL BEHAVIORS

What are the preferred behaviors for most Americans? In their recent, well-conducted study, Laumann and colleagues (1994) found that most Americans were rather traditional. All but 5 percent of the people in their survey had engaged in vaginal intercourse the last time they had sex. It was by far the most preferred behavior. Oral-genital sex ranked a distant third, and anal intercourse was far below that. What was the second most preferred behavior? A rather large proportion of men and women said that it was watching their partner undress. ∎

THE SEXUALLY HEALTHY PERSON

You have now read about several sexual behaviors that a large number of people engage in. They are normal from a statistical perspective. Does this mean that you should try all these behaviors just because a large number of other people practice them? Do we judge sexual normalcy by the variety of sexual experiences or number of partners a person has had? No, not at all. Sexual health should not be judged like a decathlon event in the Olympics. A **sexually healthy person** is someone who (a) feels comfortable with his or her sexuality (i.e., does not view sex as something naughty, bad, improper, or sinful, and can engage in it without feeling guilty or anxious), and (b) feels free to choose whether or not he or she wishes to try a variety of sexual behaviors. "Feels free" means free of peer pressure, partner pressure, and/or social pressure. In today's world of epidemic sexually transmitted diseases, sexual health also means freedom from life-threatening diseases. Individuals should not engage in sex simply because they are being pressured by peers or a potential partner. A person can be sexually healthy and still say "no." Always saying "yes" does not prove that one is sexually healthy any more than it proves one is a "real man" or a "real woman."

By this definition, someone who has engaged in a wide variety of behaviors with numerous partners, but who gets little fulfillment from his or her sexual relations or who regards it as dirty, would not be considered sexually healthy. Sometimes we can tell people's real attitude about sex by how they regard their partner(s). For example, some people claim to have a positive attitude about sex, but they view their partner(s) as dirty or bad for engaging in sex with them. On the other hand, a person could be sexually inexperienced and still be considered sexually healthy if he or she regards sex as something good and positive and was choosing not to engage in it for other reasons (e.g., saving sexual relations for someone he or she loves or cares for).

There are many behaviors that a couple can engage in that have not even been mentioned. This chapter discussed only the most common ones. (I am reminded of the couple who told Dr. Ruth Westheimer [*Playboy*, 1986] that among their favorite practices was having the woman toss onion rings over her partner's erect penis from various distances.) If a couple views their sexual relationship as something good and satisfying and wants to experiment with different techniques, should they or anyone else have any concerns? Remember, most therapists take the view that any behavior between consenting adults done in private that does not cause physical, emotional, and/or psychological harm to anyone involved is okay.

> **Sexually healthy person**
>
> Someone who feels comfortable with his or her sexuality and who feels free to choose whether or not he or she wishes to try a variety of sexual behaviors.

KEY TERMS

PERSONAL REFLECTIONS

1. What was your emotional reaction, if any, when you first saw the drawings for this chapter? If your reaction was anxiety or disgust, why? Do you regard the behaviors shown as normal?

2. What sexual behaviors do you enjoy the most? The least? Why?

3. Try to recall your reactions when someone first told you about French kissing (also called wet kissing and soul kissing). Was your reaction somewhat negative? Could you really imagine allowing someone else putting his or her tongue in your mouth? How did your attitude change as you began to realize that most people engage in this behavior? Might this same process eventually change your attitude about any of the behaviors discussed in this chapter to which you presently have negative reactions?

4. Do you have sexual fantasies (most people do)? Are you comfortable or uncomfortable (i.e., do they cause anxiety or guilt) with your fantasies? If your partner told you that he or she fantasized while having sex with you, what would your feelings be? Analyze the nature of your fantasies (e.g., content, when they occur). What purpose do you think your fantasies serve?

5. What are your feelings about masturbation? If they are negative, why? Do you have negative feelings when you pleasure yourself by touching (i.e., rubbing, massaging, scratching) other parts of your body? Consider masturbation in context of a larger question: Is use of the genitals reserved only for procreation (to have children), or are they also a source of pleasure?

6. Are you a sexually healthy person? Explain.

7. How do you expect to keep your sexual relationship from becoming ritualized after 6 months, 6 years, 20 years, 60 years? The brain is your largest sex organ. Make sure you continue to use it to your advantage.

SUGGESTED READINGS

Atwood, J. D., and Gagnon, J. (1987, Fall/Winter). Masturbatory behavior in college youth. *Journal of Sex Education and Therapy.*

Blumstein, P., and Schwartz, P. (1983). *American couples.* New York: William Morrow and Co. An excellent survey of married, unmarried, and cohabitating couples.

Comfort, A. (1972). *The joy of sex.* New York: Crown. A nicely illustrated, well-written sex manual. A best-seller since its publication.

Friday, N. (1973). *My secret garden.* New York: Simon and Schuster. All about female sexual fantasies.

Friday, N. (1980). *Men in love.* New York: Delacorte Press. All about male sexual fantasies.

Goleman, D., and Bush, S. (1977, October). The liberation of sexual fantasy. *Psychology Today.* Discusses the positives and negatives of fantasy.

Janus, S., and Janus, C. (1993). *The Janus report.* New York: John Wiley & Sons. Results of a nationwide survey of sexual behavior.

Kaplan, H. S. (1985, September). Talking frankly about oral sex. *Redbook.* Discusses the myths and problems about oral-genital sexual relations.

Laumann, E., et al. (1994). *Sex in America: A definitive survey.* Boston: Little, Brown. The thinner, public version of the results of what is probably the most scientifically conducted sex survey ever.

CHAPTER TWELVE

LOVE AND RELATIONSHIPS

When you have finished studying this chapter, you should be able to:

1. Describe the characteristics that romantic love and friendship have in common, and the characteristics that distinguish romantic love from friendship;
2. Describe companionate love and its relation to romantic love;
3. Discuss the prerequisites for love;
4. Explain what causes jealousy and how best to deal with it;
5. Differentiate between feelings of sexual desire and those of love;
6. Evaluate the place of love without sex in your system of values;
7. Discuss Sternberg's triangular theory of love and how different combinations of three components lead to liking and loving;
8. Describe Lee's different styles of love and his explanation for how to find a compatible love relationship;
9. Discuss love in other cultures;
10. Explain how a couple can maintain a loving relationship; and
11. Discuss how couples can achieve greater intimacy.

POETS WRITE WORDS TO RHYME WITH IT. NOVELISTS GLORIFY IT IN PROSE. LYRICISTS PRAISE IT IN SONG. PHIlosophers wonder about its meaning, and politicians all support it.

What is this ubiquitous subject? Why, it's love, of course. Have I exaggerated? Think about it for a moment. How many popular songs that you hear on the radio are about love (e.g., first love, new love, broken hearts)? In fact, you may have to listen for quite a while before you find one that is not about love. When was the last time that you read a novel that didn't include at least one romantic subplot?

Love is obviously an emotion that most humans consider to be extremely important to their lives. But what is love? There have probably been as many definitions and thoughts about love as there have been philosophers, behavioral scientists, theologians, and biologists. Freud believed that the repression of sexuality from infancy through childhood is part of a developmental process that results in the adult's ability to experience love. Others have viewed love as a social instinct that satisfies a need for companionship with others. In *The Origins of Love and Hate* (1952), Ian Suttie expressed the belief that, "The specific origin of love, in time, was at the moment the infant recognizes the existence of others." In contrast, others, including some noted psychologists, have expressed the belief that love results from conditioning, that is, that it is a learned response. By this account, a person comes to be desired or loved when others have positive experiences in their presence. Love has also been viewed as a mania (Plato, in *Phaedrus*), a neurosis (Askew, 1965), an addiction (Peele, 1988), a disease (Burton, 1951/1963), and the enshrinement of suffering and death (de Rougement, 1969).

Christian ideals of love are found in St. Augustine's definition: "Love means: I want you to be." Viewing love simply as a desire for another person "to be" honors his or her existence. It transcends sexual desire and acknowledges that this emotion can be felt for a lover, parent, child, or friend of the opposite or same sex. Noted psychoanalyst Erich Fromm has echoed similar beliefs about love:

> I want the loved person to grow and unfold for his own sake, and in his own ways, and not for the purpose of serving me.

(Erich Fromm, 1956, pp. 23–24) ∎

FRIENDSHIP VERSUS ROMANTIC LOVE

Studies conducted nearly 1600 years after St. Augustine confirm his belief that the structure of love is very similar for various types of close relationships (Sternberg & Grajek, 1984). Let us first ask what distinguishes love from friendship. Nearly 2000 years ago, the Roman statesman and philosopher Seneca wrote, "Friendship always benefits; love sometimes injures." Is this true? Are love and friendship qualitatively different feelings, or is love just a more intense form of the emotion felt in friendship?

Studies by Keith Davis (1985) of the University of South Carolina have revealed several characteristics that are essential for **friendship**: (1) *enjoyment* of each other's company most of the time (although periods of temporary annoyance or anger may occur); (2) *acceptance of one another* as they are; (3) a *mutual trust* that each will act in his or her friend's best interest; (4) a *respect for each other* (an assumption that each will use good judgment in making life choices); (5) *mutual assistance* of one another during times of need; (6) *confiding* in one another; (7) an *understanding* of each other's behavior; and (8) rather than playing a role, each feels free to be himself or herself (*spontaneity*).

Friendship

A relationship that includes (a) enjoyment of each other's company, (b) acceptance of one another, (c) mutual trust, (d) respect for one another, (e) mutual assistance when needed, (f) confiding in one another, (g) understanding, and (h) spontaneity.

Davis found that people rated their "spouse/lover" and best friend nearly the same for all these characteristics except enjoyment, for which more people listed a lover rather than their best friend. What about close friends (rather than best friends)? People tended to rate spouses and lovers higher for enjoyment, respect, mutual assistance, and understanding. Still, close friends also generally fared well for these characteristics.

Are there some characteristics unique to spouses and lovers? Davis found that people generally rated **romantic love** relationships much higher (compared to friends) in *fascination* (a preoccupation with the other person, even when they should be doing other things), *exclusiveness* (not having the same relationship with another person), *sexual desire* (a desire for physical intimacy), and *giving the utmost* (when the other is in need) (Figure 12-1). These feelings can be extremely intense. The loved one is perceived as able (and often solely able) to satisfy needs, fulfill expectations, and provide rewards and pleasure.

Romantic love

The combination of passion and liking (intimacy). Romantic love relationships have high levels of fascination (with one another), exclusiveness, sexual desire, and giving the utmost when the other is in need.

Davis and others report that most lovers find that their mood depends on reciprocation of their feelings

FIGURE 12-1   COMPARED TO FRIENDSHP, ROMANTIC LOVE RATES HIGH IN FASCINATION (A
PREOCCUPATION WITH THE OTHER PERSON), EXCLUSIVENESS, SEXUAL DESIRE, AND
GIVING THE UTMOST (WHEN THE OTHER IS NEEDED.)

more so than in friendships. Lovers tend to view their relationships as more under control of social rules and expectations. Romantic relationships also rate much higher in ambivalence (mutually existing feelings) than friendships. Thus, while romantic relationships are generally more rewarding than friendships, they are also more volatile and frustrating than friendships. ■

HOW DO I KNOW IF THIS IS REALLY LOVE?

In addition to a preoccupation with the loved person, it has been argued that *romantic* love involves physiological arousal and the cognitive interpretation of that as being caused by the other person (Berscheid & Walster, 1974). Consider, for example, the following hypothetical scenario:

Susan was in her first year of college. She had gone out a few times, but too many weekend nights had been spent with girlfriends, and she generally felt lonely and bored. She was surprised when David, a handsome junior who had sat next to her in sociology class, called and asked her to go to a movie Friday night. They had a good time and studied together on Sunday. However, David didn't sit next to her in class on Tuesday, and Susan worried all that day and the next if he would call again. She could hardly contain herself when he called Wednesday evening and asked her to a big party at his fraternity.

Susan and David spent a lot of time together during the next two weeks. She was no longer lonely or bored, and, in fact, her girlfriends let her know that they envied her. On the other hand, she worried when they were apart (if and when David would call), and her growing sexual attraction to David was keeping her aroused and agitated.

Is Susan in love? She has feelings of extreme happiness (sometimes elation), periods of anxiety and frustration, sexual desire, and finds herself thinking about David when she should be concentrating on other things. David fulfills needs and satisfies desires (sexual, physical, and ego). There is no question that she is better off than before. But is this really love, or just infatuation?

Romantic love almost always includes certain *physiological responses*, such as heavy breathing, a pounding heart and increased blood pressure, sweaty palms, and a dry mouth when we are close to or thinking about the loved one. Dr. Michael Liebowitz (1983) has found that feelings of romantic love are associated with an increase in three brain chemicals called dopamine, norepinephrine, and phenylethylamine, the last of which is chemically similar to amphetamines. Falling in love, with the release of these chemicals, literally gives the person a natural high. (Some people are known to eat large amounts of chocolate, which is high in phenylethylamine, when suffering the heartache of a broken romance.) Hormones are also involved. Oxytocin, a hormone that sensitizes nerves and stimulates muscle contractions, is released in large amounts (Fisher, 1992).

The problem is, of course, almost any kind of excitement or stress will cause a pounding heart and the other just-mentioned physiological responses. A *cognitive component* is necessary to interpret these responses as a particular type of emotion. To prove this, psychologists Stanley Schacter and Jerome Singer (1962) administered adrenalin, which causes increased heart rate and other signs of physiological arousal, to volunteer subjects who were told it was a vitamin shot. The subjects were then instructed to wait in another room with a fellow subject. This other subject, however, was really working for the researchers, and in half the cases acted very happy and in the other half very angry. The real subjects were experiencing strange physiological responses of arousal due to the adrenalin, but it was the environmental cues that determined how they interpreted them. The subjects with the happy person acted happy, while those with the angry person acted angry. When subjects were warned in advance of the physiological changes they would experience, they were not affected by the phony subject's behavior.

If Susan's friends are having similar experiences and say they are "in love," the chances are good that Susan, too, will interpret her newly aroused state as love. Under other circumstances, she might not.

Will Susan's feelings of love for David last? Initially, Susan certainly loves the way David makes her feel. But as many of you have discovered, that initial high usually doesn't last, at least not at the peak it first was at. Just as with amphetamines, the body builds up resistance to phenylethylamine, so that it takes larger amounts to experience the same "high." Some people, call them "love junkies" if you'd like, go from relationship to relationship, ending each one as the initial high (passion) begins to subside. If love is to last for Susan, she must come to love David for who he is, and not just for what he causes her to experience.

COMPANIONATE LOVE

Companionate love has been defined as "the affection we feel for those with whom our lives are deeply entwined" (Hatfield & Walster, 1978). It is based on togetherness, trust, sharing, affection, and a concern for the welfare of the other (more so than passion). When there is love between parents and children, it is usually what we call "companionate." It is also a stable kind of love that is characteristic of lasting adult relationships, for few relationships can sustain the initial level of excitement and sexual passion.

Companionate love
Love based on togetherness, trust, sharing, and affection rather than passion.

> Young love is a flame; very pretty, often very hot and fierce but still only light and flickering. The love of the older and disciplined heart is as coals, deep burning, unquenchable. . . .
>
> (Henry Ward Beecher)

Scientists have discovered that the continued presence of a partner increases the production of endorphins, natural opiate-like chemicals found in the brain (Fisher, 1992; see Toufexis, 1993). Perhaps it is these that give long-term lovers a sense of calm, peace, and security (in contrast to the high produced by the initial surge of amphetamine-like chemicals).

Companionate love, however, does not always come later in a relationship, for some people do not consider romance to be their most important goal when establishing a relationship. Some people desire companionship more than anything else. Companionate love very often includes a good, satisfying sexual relationship as well. This is understandable in that a good, overall relationship often leads to a healthy and good sexual relationship. Many people refer to this type of relationship as *realistic love*, because it is not based on the fantasies and ideals of romantic love. The predictability (and avoidance of extreme highs and lows) of companionate love offers security, so that people may enjoy their lives outside of the relationship as well as in.

A drab, mundane form of companionship might be called **attachment** (Berscheid, 1982), where one's partner gives few positive rewards for remaining in the relationship other than predictability (a different use of the term attachment is given in the

Attachment
A drab, mundane form of companionship where one's partner gives few positive rewards, other than predictability, for remaining in the relationship.

next section). For most people, familiarity is comforting, and this can also be true even when all other aspects of a relationship are poor.

> **"I** confronted my boyfriend about growing up before we were supposed to get married. I said to him what he had ignored for 29 years of his life—he needs to leave mom and move out on his own. He acted as though I had spoiled all of his high hopes when I told him this. I, like five women before me, chose to confront the issue, yet he is totally bewildered about why his longest relationship with a woman has been merely 3 months long. No matter what confidences I shared with him, he would always have to spill the beans to mom. Any time there was a problem he would slip back into his comfort zone with mom there to cuddle him.''

(from the author's files)

Knowing what to expect may cause less anxiety for some than the thought of leaving and venturing into an unknown future. An extreme example of this is the devotion displayed by some battered wives toward abusing husbands on whom they are economically dependent (the fear of having to support themselves on their own may seem worse than the abuse). ∎

PREREQUISITES FOR LOVE

SELF-ACCEPTANCE

In order for someone to love another, it is first necessary that he or she be able to love himself or herself. Erich Fromm once stated that "if an individual is able to love productively, he loves himself, too; if he can love only others, he cannot love at all" (1956, p. 60). The first prerequisite for a loving relationship, therefore, is a **positive self-concept** (good self-esteem).

Self-esteem
The feeling one has about oneself.

Why is a positive self-concept so important? Comedian Woody Allen once said, "I wouldn't want to be a member of any organization that would let me be a member." If you cannot accept and love yourself, it will be impossible for you to accept that someone else may love you. Like Woody Allen, people who cannot accept themselves generally reject other people.

A positive self-concept does not necessarily mean that someone is self-centered or believes that they are always correct, good, and moral and can do no wrong. To accept oneself is to accept one's shortcomings as well as one's strengths, that is, "to accept myself for what I am" (Coutts, 1973). *The manner in which one is raised is important for acquiring a positive self-concept.*

> **"I** think the reason I don't like myself is because of all the problems I had in the past. ... the absence of mom and dad, and when they were around so was abuse. I feel that since my parents couldn't accept me, why should I? I felt like a failure, the ugliest person alive, and basically trash. I had tried to kill myself. . . .''

(from the author's files)

It is not unusual for children who have been neglected or abused to have negative self-concepts as adults and sometimes be unable to be loving to others (in fact, abused children often become abusive parents). Having loving, caring parents during infancy and childhood teaches us not only that other people do nice things that make us feel good (and, thus, they are good), but that we are worthy of someone else caring about us. The trust that is gained by this experience generalizes to other people as we grow older.

Hazan and Shaver (1987) have extended these ideas into what they call an *attachment theory of love.* They claim that the quality of the attachment between parents and child greatly affects the child's ability to form romantic relations as an adult. As adults, people are either *secure lovers* (who don't fear abandonment and find it easy to get close to others), *avoidant lovers* (who have difficulty trusting a partner and letting someone get close to them), or *anxious-ambivalent lovers* (who are insecure in their relations and try desperately to get close to their partners, often resulting in scaring them away). These researchers found that slightly more than half of adults could be called secure, while about one fourth were avoidant, and one fifth were anxious-ambivalent (Shaver, Hazan, & Bradshaw, 1988).

SELF-DISCLOSURE

Self-acceptance and trust in ourselves give us the potential to trust and love others, but for love to really develop, there must be **self-disclosure** by both parties, resulting in an exchange of vulnerabilities (Masters & Johnson, 1975). You cannot really love a person whom you do not really know, and, of course, the same is true for the other person. He or she cannot really love you until they get to know the real you. This is what distinguishes love from infatuation.

Self-disclosure
Revealing one's thoughts, feelings, and emotions to another.

Letting others get to know the real you is not always easy. In fact, for some people, emotional intimacy may be more difficult than sexual intimacy. We initially try to look and act our best, but for the other person to really get to know you requires that you reveal your needs, feelings, emotions, and values. Unfortunately, some people go through life with a mask on, never allowing themselves to be known by others. A study conducted in the 1950s found that women were much more willing than men to disclose personal information to friends or strangers under laboratory conditions (Jourard & Lasakow, 1958). This is what might be expected in a society where gender roles have traditionally favored emotional repressiveness for men and emotional expressiveness for women, but as you learned in Chapter 8, gender roles have been changing. Nevertheless, a review of 205 studies of self-disclosure found that there was still a gender difference in disclosure—women disclose slightly more than men in relationships (Dindia & Allen, 1992).

People may be reluctant to reveal what they really think or feel out of fear that other people might judge them or might have less respect for them, or even worse, no longer want them as a lover or friend. This requires trust, and sometimes that trust is misplaced. Some people may even use another person's trust to fulfill their own selfish desires. If John, for example,

feels lust for Joanne, he may show her a lot of attention with the goal of having sex with her. Joanne, on the other hand, may actually be fond of John and interpret his attention for her as love and subsequently reveal her feelings. John may then say, "I love you" to Joanne just to fulfill his own selfish sexual goal. After satisfying his sexual curiosity, John may dump Joanne to pursue other sexual conquests, leaving Joanne emotionally devastated. She may also be more reluctant to trust again.

All of us need the perceptive ability to avoid placing our trust in those who would abuse it, but for love to develop, we must occasionally take that chance or risk. Relationships develop best when two people self-disclose to one another at about the same time. If Joe reveals some of his true thoughts and feelings to Mary, for example, it is expected that she will reciprocate. Well-timed self-disclosure makes a person more likeable to his or her partner (Archer, Berg, & Runge, 1980; Collins & Miller, 1994). Emotional intimacy is achieved only after a couple has shared a reasonable level of self-disclosure (an exchange of vulnerabilities), and each has accepted his or her partner's state of awareness. At this point, they can be said to be interdependent. ∎

JEALOUSY

Shakespeare, in *Othello*, described it as "the green-eyed monster which doth mock the meat it feeds on." He was referring, of course, to the emotion we call jealousy. How would you feel if your partner appeared to be forming an emotional attachment to another person? How would you feel if your partner and another person appeared to be sexually interested in one another? These are situations that typically cause many people to feel jealous. **Jealousy** is an emotional "state that is aroused by a perceived threat to a valued relationship or position and motivates behavior aimed at countering the threat" (Daly, Wilson, & Weghorst, 1982; see also Salovey, 1991; White & Mullen, 1989). The perceived threat can involve more than the actual loss of a partner, and include loss of face, loss of self-esteem, and loss of feeling special (Buunk & Bringle, 1987). Jealousy is a negative emotion that is hard to describe, but usually involves anger, humiliation, anxiety, and depression (Clanton & Smith, 1977).

Some people become jealous if their partner has even casual interactions with other persons. What type of person is most likely to become jealous? Research has shown that people with low self-esteem and who are personally unhappy with their lives (Bringle et al., 1977; Pines & Aronson, 1983), or who place great

Jealousy
An emotional state that is aroused by a perceived threat to a valued relationship or position.

value on things like popularity, wealth, fame, and physical attractiveness are more likely than others to be jealous individuals (Salovey & Rodin, 1985). However, cultural factors also play a role. Jealousy is most likely to occur in cultures that emphasize marriage for guilt-free sex, security, and social recognition, and which value personal ownership of property (Hupka, 1981). This is true of U.S. culture (as well as many others), where sexual jealousy by men is the leading cause of beating and murder of wives (Daly & Wilson, 1988). In societies that allow polygyny, jealousy is far less common (Laughlin & Allgeier, 1979).

There are important gender differences in jealousy as well. Men are much more likely to become jealous to the perception of a partner's sexual infidelity, whereas women are much more likely to experience jealousy to a partner's emotional infidelity (Buss et al., 1992). Men's and women's reactions to jealousy also tend to differ (Bryson & Shettel-Neuber, 1978; White, 1981 a, b). Women tend to experience jealousy when feeling inadequate, and respond by making themselves more attractive to their partner. Men, on the other hand, tend to initially experience jealous feelings and then have feelings of inadequacy, and tend to seek solace in outside relationships.

Paradoxically, while jealousy is an emotional reaction to a perceived threat to a relationship and self-esteem, expression of jealousy is likely to further damage both (Buunk & Bringle, 1987). Withdrawing from or attacking one's partner, for example, may cause him or her to withdraw or attack, thus increasing the fear of loss which, in turn, may increase or prolong the feeling of jealousy. How, then, should you deal with occasional bouts of jealousy? Acknowledge your feelings to your partner and describe what caused them. (Conversely, never purposely try to make your partner jealous, as a few people do in order to get attention; White, 1980a, 1981). Establish mutual trust, while at the same time respecting your partner's need for some personal freedom. If you can do this, your chances are good of keeping that green-eyed monster at bay. ■

SEX WITHOUT LOVE

Is it possible to have a lifestyle of sex without love and still be happy? In the movie *Annie Hall*, Diane Keaton says to Woody Allen, "Sex without love is an empty experience." Woody responds, "Yes, but as empty experiences go, it's one of the best." In his book *Sex without Love* (1980), Russell Vannoy argues that love is unnecessary and that sex should be enjoyed for its own sake. Masters and Johnson report that they have worked with hundreds of people who weren't in love, but who deeply enjoyed sex. In fact, throughout history there have been many famous people who were noted for their sexual relations with hundreds, often thousands, of partners (e.g., Cleopatra, Empress Theodora, Catherine the Great, Sarah Bernhardt, King Solomon, King Ibn-Saud).

Love and sex share many things in common, including the fact that both may be intensely exciting experiences involving physiological changes that may be expressed in many ways. Feelings of love, however, tend to be more selective than sexual desires, and while the experience of being in love is generally felt all over, sexual sensations are generally confined to a few body parts.

In the United States, most people feel that sexual relations should be reserved for strongly affectionate relationships (Laumann et al., 1994; McCabe, 1987). Women in particular are apt to find sex unenjoyable unless it is within a loving relationship (Christopher & Cate, 1984; McCabe, 1987; Ubell, 1984):

❝ I find it much more pleasurable and rewarding to make love with my partner. We have times when we have sex but I enjoy making love much more. My partner caresses me and makes me feel more special and loved."

(from the author's files)

Men, on the other hand, are much more likely than women to enjoy sex without emotional involvement (Carroll, Volk, & Hyde, 1985; Leigh, 1989; Quadagno & Sprague, 1991). In a recent study of people's private wishes (Ehrlichman & Eichenstein, 1992), many more men than women wished "to have sex with anyone I choose." Even so, this represented a minority of men. A large majority of women, and a small majority of men, wished "to deeply love a person who deeply loves me."

Some people who engage in casual or recreational sex may actually be searching for intimacy. Many people, particularly men, never learn how to express or receive affection (e.g., hug, cuddle) and mistakenly believe that sex and intimacy are synonymous (see Chapter 10). However, this doesn't mean that a person cannot enjoy a lifestyle of sex without love. Some people may simply prefer their independence rather than emotional involvement. And remember, the emphasis in the United States of sex within a loving relationship is a culturally learned value. In some other cultures, people put considerable more emphasis on sexual pleasure (and think that Americans' attitude of love first is peculiar) and encourage sexual relations with many partners (see Chapter 1). ■

LOVE WITHOUT SEX

Keith Davis (1985), you recall, included sexual desire as one of the characteristics that distinguished romantic love from friendship. Is it possible for people to experience romantic love without engaging in sexual relations?

Although sexual deprivation will not kill you (like lack of water or food), there is strong evidence that physical contact is important for human beings. Babies who are deprived of physical contact may sicken and die or show arrested social development. Researcher Harry Harlow (1959) raised Rhesus monkey babies in isolation with make-believe, terrycloth mothers. They were well-fed and clung to the terrycloth models as they would their real mother. When they matured, however, and were placed in cages with other monkeys, they were antisocial and refused to mate and perform sexually. Nearly 50 years ago, a physician similarly reported that one in three human infants in foundling homes died during the first year of life, even though they were well-fed and provided with adequate medical care. What these babies were not receiving was cuddling, hugging, fondling, and kissing—they apparently died from emotional neglect (Spitz, 1945, 1946). We never outgrow the need to be held and touched, but these needs can be fulfilled without actually engaging in sex.

Love is a feeling, not an act. Therefore, people who have a loving relationship may or may not choose to express their closeness with sex. Although attitudes toward premarital or nonmarital sexual relations are not as stringent as in previous generations, many couples still prefer to reserve their sexuality for marriage (Laumann et al., 1994). This period of voluntary celibacy allows them to devote time and energy to other aspects of their relationship (and allows the intimacy component to grow), perhaps resulting in their finding many nonsexual ways to express their love for one another. Even in sexually consummated relationships, sexual relations may have to be interrupted, sometimes for long periods of time, because of illness or physical separation (due to military duty, etc.), but this doesn't mean that feelings of love are also interrupted.

UNCONDITIONAL LOVE

So far, most of our discussion about love has centered on romantic love, which tends to be **conditional love**, or what Maslow (1968) called *deficiency love* (or *D-love*). We fall in love with someone and remain in love because he or she satisfies certain needs, fulfills desires, and because it is positively reinforcing to be with him or her. We tend to fall out of love when our expectations and needs are no longer met. Our feelings for the other person depend to some extent, perhaps to a large extent, on how he or she makes us feel and contributes to our happiness.

Distinguished from conditional love is **unconditional love** (what Maslow called *being love* or *B-love*), in which one's feelings do not depend on the loved one meeting certain expectations and desires (Fromm, 1956). People love out of choice, not out of need. Unconditional love is the type of love that many mothers feel for their children (Fromm believed that father-love is conditional in most cases), that many grown-up children continue to feel for their parents, and that many people feel for other individuals of the same or opposite sex. How one feels about his or her romantic partner can also eventually transcend the ability of the partner to satisfy needs and fulfill expectations. This is perhaps most closely approximated by what is called companionate love and which is expressed so well in St. Augustine's definition of love, "I want you to be." ■

> **Conditional love**
> Feelings of love that depend on the loved one satisfying needs and fulfilling desires.

> **Unconditional love**
> Feelings of love that do not depend on the loved one meeting certain expectations and desires.

THEORIES OF LOVE

Any textbook that includes the topic of love must, as an obligation I suppose, present some coverage of the theories of love. But which ones? There are as many theories of love as there are definitions, maybe more. Many, as pointed out by philosopher Alan Soble (1989), "only seem to say various things about love, hardly ever supporting their claims with valid and sound arguments. The reader might conclude the area is a mess, the idea is a mess, probably love itself is a mess." Pop literature treatises on love (such as Leo Buscaglia's *Love*, M. Scott Peck's *The Road Less Traveled*, or Ben Dominitz's *How to Find the Love of Your Life: 90 Days to a Permanent Relationship*) seldom support their claims with any real evidence. The works of some of the great thinkers (Plato, Aristotle, Kant), on the other hand, treat love as an academic subject and are often lacking in sensitivity. Experimental social psychologists have now joined the list of those analyzing love, although their contribution may be no better than previous attempts (Soble, 1989). As examples of this approach to love, I have selected the works of two pioneers in the field: Robert Sternberg and John Lee. Other texts may have chosen different theories, but these will give you a good idea of how social psychologists perceive this complex topic we call love. ■

ROBERT STERNBERG'S TRIANGULAR THEORY OF LOVE

Although most people rate their spouse/lover higher for some characteristics than they do their friends (Davis, 1985), this still does not tell us whether liking and loving are qualitatively different emotions or different regions along a single continuum of emotions. Robert Sternberg (1987) has proposed a **triangular theory of love** in which he takes a broader view of liking and loving. He suggests that all the different positive emotions that people can have for other individuals can be understood by the combination of

FIGURE 12-2   STERNBERG'S TRIANGULAR MODEL OF LOVE. ALL THE DIFFERENT POSITIVE EMOTIONS THAT PEOPLE CAN HAVE FOR OTHERS ARE UNDERSTOOD BY THE COMBINATION OF INTIMACY, PASSION, AND DECISION/COMMITMENT.

three components. In his model, each component is viewed as the vertex of a triangle as shown in Figure 12-2. The triangle should not be viewed as a geometric model, but as a useful metaphor for visualizing the way in which the three components are related.

The top vertex of the triangle is **intimacy**. Intimacy refers to those feelings in a relationship that promote closeness or bondedness and the experience of warmth. There are many signs of intimacy, including a desire to promote the welfare of the other, experiencing happiness with and having a high regard for the other, receiving and giving emotional support, mutual understanding, and valuing the other person in your life (Sternberg & Grajek, 1984). The left-hand vertex represents the experience of **passion**, or those drives leading to physical attraction, sexual relations, and romance. The right-hand vertex is **decision/commitment**, which includes the decision that one loves another person and the commitment to maintain it over time.

Sternberg says that the different combinations of these three components result in different kinds of emotions. When all three components are absent, the result is *nonlove*. This characterizes most of our casual relationships, where there is no love or friendship in

Intimacy
Those feelings in a relationship that promote closeness or bondedness and the experience of warmth.

Passion
The drive leading to physical attraction, sexual relations, and romance.

Decision/commitment
One of the three basic components in Sternberg's theory of love; the decision that one loves another person and the commitment to maintain it.

any meaningful way. If the intimacy component is expressed alone without passion or decision/commitment, it results in *liking*. Liking is not used in a trivial manner to refer to casual acquaintances, but instead refers to the feelings of closeness, bondedness, and warmth in true friendships. When passion is felt in the absence of the other two components, the result is *infatuated love*, or what we call "love at first sight." A person feeling passion alone is obsessed with the other person as an ideal, rather than the individual as he or she is in reality. The decision and commitment to love another person without intimacy or passion is experienced as *empty love*. In our society, empty love often occurs at the end of long-term, stagnant relationships, but in other cultures where marriages are arranged, it may be the first stage in a long-term relationship.

If you look at the triangle, you can see that there are four possible combinations of the components. If you add passionate arousal to liking (the intimacy component alone, you recall), the result is *romantic love*. It results from two people being drawn together both physically and emotionally. There is no commitment, and the lovers may even know that a permanent relationship is not possible, such as in "summer love." This is the Romeo and Juliet type of love that poets, playwrights, and novelists are so fond of writing about.

The combination of intimacy and decision/commitment without passion leads to *companionate love*, a long-term committed friendship. Sternberg (1988) believes that most romantic love relationships that survive do so by eventually turning into a companionate love relationship.

When a commitment is made on the basis of passion without the experience of intimacy, the result is *fatuous love*. This leads to whirlwind romances, the type we often read about involving Hollywood stars. Without intimacy, there is a high risk of the relationship ending once the passion starts to fade (the romances are often over so quickly that there has been no chance for the intimacy component to develop).

Sternberg believes that complete love, what he calls *consummate love*, is found only in relationships that include all three components—passion, intimacy, and commitment. It is his belief that this is the type of love that most of us strive for in our romantic relationships. Thus, other types of relationships are viewed as lacking something (i.e., one or more of the three components). ■

JOHN LEE'S MANY COLORS OF LOVE

The English language gives us only one word—love—to describe a number of interpersonal relationships. Words such as liking, affection, and infatuation are not used synonymously with love. As a result, our different

experiences of love tend to be measured as differences in quantity: "Tell me *how much* you love me," and, "I love you *more* than I've ever loved anybody." In our search for a partner, we hope to find someone who loves us *as much* as we love them. When relationships do not work out, we often deny any experience of love (e.g., "After a while, I realized I really didn't love Suzy," or "Suzy really didn't love me"). It's as if our experiences of love are measured in black and white and shades of gray.

Sociologist John Lee (1974, 1976, 1988) believes that there is more than one type of partnering love, with no one of them being singled out as "true love." He suggests that our different experiences are not due to whether or not two persons' feelings are of the same intensity, but how well one person's style of loving matches with another's style. Rather than black and white, Lee uses the analogy of colors to explain love. Different styles of love are portrayed by different colors. Sternberg (1988) believes that his theory of love is most akin in spirit to that of Lee's. However, there is a major difference between the two of them. Sternberg's theory implies that there is only one type of true love (consummate love) and that all the others are not really love. Lee's model, on the other hand, does not suggest that one style of love is superior or better than another, but only that there are many different styles. According to Lee, mutual love results from two styles or colors (not intensities) that make a good match.

Just as different colors result from blending red, yellow, and blue, the three primary colors, Lee proposes that different styles of loving arise from blending three primary love-styles—eros, storge, and ludus. Let us first look at each of these and their various combinations and then we will see what makes a good match.

The Primary Colors

Eros (named after the Greek mythological figure) is a highly idealized love based on physical beauty.

> **Eros**
> A highly idealized type of romantic love that is based mainly on physical beauty. Erotic lovers look for physical perfection.

According to Lee, every erotic lover has a specific physical type that turns him or her on. They look for physical perfection, knowing it is rare, and when they find him or her, they quickly feel a strong physical attraction and emotions they feel as love. It is as if they have always known this person that they have just met—their romantic ideal. Thus, the erotic lover is inclined to feel "love at first sight." Perhaps the most important thing in an erotic lover's life is to find and live with their romantic ideal. However, erotic lovers are usually quick to find flaws and shortcomings in their new partners, so that many of their relationships are quick to fizzle out (because the partner cannot live up to their unrealistic ideal). Therefore, erotic love is generally very transient, and erotic lovers tend to fall in love very often. Erotic lovers desire to have an exclusive relationship with their partners, but they do not try to possess them.

Lee's eros, by the way, has little in common with the eros of Plato's *Symposium*, which was altogether good and healthy. Lee's choice of terms here is perhaps unfortunate.

Ludus (from Latin meaning "play" and pronounced loo-dus) is a self-centered type of love. The ludic lover avoids commitment and treats love like a game, often viewing the chase as more pleasurable than the prize.

> **Ludus**
> A self-centered type of love. Ludic lovers avoid commitment and treat love as a game, often viewing the chase as more pleasurable than the prize.

> " 'm a 23 year old male in your MWF Sex Class. . . . I first had intercourse at age 13 . . . As of this writing, I have had intercourse with 508 women. I have done it 1,823 times in the last 9½ years. My goal is 2,000 times by 1989. I've devoted a notebook strictly for recording names, dates, and places of sexual encounters. . . . I can say that I honestly love all women. . . .''
>
> (from the author's files)

Ludic lovers have no romantic ideal and never see any one person often enough to become dependent on them (or vice versa). Sex is had for fun, not for expressing commitment, for ludic lovers do not have feelings of falling in love. They avoid jealous partners who might spoil the fun and see nothing wrong with having more than one partner at the same time. They are also more likely than people with other love-styles to use verbal coercion to obtain sex (Sarwer et al., 1993). Ludic lovers can be deceptive with their partners like a Don Juan, but many play the game honestly to avoid feelings of guilt (and thus their partners know exactly what they are getting). This promiscuous type of love-style may seem empty to people with other love-styles, but most ludic lovers look back on their relationships with pleasure.

Storge (from Greek and pronounced stor-gay) is an affectionate type of love that develops from friendship slowly over time. The storgic lover does not have a physical ideal and does not go looking for love, but instead develops feel-

> **Storge**
> An affectionate type of love that grows from friendship.

ings of affection and commitment with a partner through experiencing activities that they both enjoy. Storgic lovers generally cannot recall a specific point in time when they fell in love. They are more practical than emotional, and their relationships lack the passionate emotional highs (but also avoid the dramatic downturns). In fact, storgic lovers would be embarrassed by having to say "I love you," or by excessive shows of emotion from their partners. They are more interested in talking about their shared interests than their mutual love. A true storgic lover would probably find this whole chapter very silly.

The Secondary Colors

How many different love-styles are there? You can get numerous colors by blending red, yellow, and blue, and the same is true for mixing the primary love-styles. Look at the color wheel in Figure 12-3. The apexes of the large triangle within the circle represent the three primary colors. Each pair can be combined by either going around the circle or along the edge of the triangle. When you combine two things, new properties may emerge (and others may be lost). No one, for example, could have predicted the properties of water by looking at the properties of hydrogen and oxygen. Let us now look at a few of the numerous combinations that can result from mixing the primary love-styles.

Pragma (from Greek for pragmatic) is a rational or practical style of loving resulting from combining ludus and storge. The pragmatic lover has the manipulative confidence of a ludic lover and consciously looks for a compatible mate. They are not looking for an exciting romance or affair, but instead are trying to find a sensible, storgic partnership (a "good match"). The person with a pragmatic love-style has a shopping list of qualities he or she is looking for in a mate and consciously and carefully sorts candidates to see if they have all the desired qualities. Women, for example, give more weight than men to socioeconomic status, ambitiousness, and intelligence in choosing a mate (Feingold, 1992). If a suitable mate cannot be found at work or in the community, the pragmatic lover may join organizations (e.g., church, club), or even try computer dating ser-

> **Pragma**
> A rational or practical type of love. Pragmatic lovers actively look for a "good match."

vices, to find a compatible partner. Pragmatic lovers want their partners to reciprocate signs of thoughtfulness and commitment, but do not like excessive displays of emotion or jealousy. Sexual compatibility is not unimportant, but it is treated more as a technical skill that can be improved upon if need be, rather than the result of chemistry. A person with this love-style views herself or himself as "in love" and tends to remain loyal and faithful as long as the partner continues to be a good match.

Mania (from Greek meaning love that hits like a lightning bolt) is a love-style characterized by an intense emotional dependency on the attention and affection of one's partner. Dorothy Tennov (1979) coined the term *limerance* to describe extreme "head over heels" love in which one is obsessed with the loved one (e.g., extreme preoccupation and acute longing for exclusivity). The manic lover is intensely jealous and repeatedly needs to be assured of being loved. The feelings are so intense that it can be likened to addiction, with the manic lover at the same time often not even liking the partner, but unable to break it off. As a result, the manic lover rides an emotional roller coaster: extreme highs when the partner is showing them attention, and extreme lows when he or she is not. This love-style results from mixing eros and ludus. The manic lover wants an intense, physically stimulating relationship, but usually chooses inappropriate partners and madly projects desired qualities onto the partner. Everyone but he or she can see that the partner does not really have those qualities. The manic lover attempts to manipulate the relationship (by pulling back and not calling the partner, for example), but is too dependent on his or her partner's love to remain confidently detached like the ludic lover (guess who ends up breaking down and calling first?). Because the manic lover is unable to break off the relationship, it is usually the partner who does so, leaving the manic lover devastated. Although many people have had an experience of manic love, the true manic lover is apt to repeat the same type of relationship again and again.

> **Mania**
> A type of love characterized by an intense emotional dependency on the attention and affection of one's lover.

Agape (from Greek and pronounced ah-gah-pā) is a selfless, altruistic love-style that puts the interest of the loved person ahead of his or her own, even if it means great sacrifice. Agape was Jesus' love—he sacrificed himself for all humans. This is the style of loving proposed by St. Augustine ("love means: I want you to be") as a goal for all Christians and strived for by Fromm (1956). It is the result of combining eros and storge. Rather than yearning to find the perfect partner, the

> **Agape**
> A type of romantic love that puts the interest of the loved person ahead of one's own, even if it means great sacrifice.

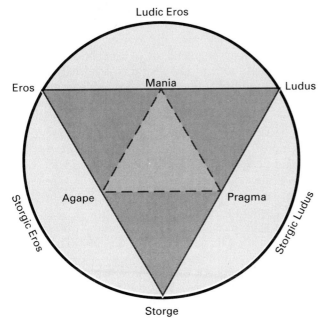

FIGURE 12-3   JOHN LEE'S COLOR WHEEL OF LOVE-STYLES.

agapic lover submits to the perfect will of God and becomes the devoted friend of those who need his or her love. Agapic lovers believe it is their duty to love, but the feelings are often not directed toward a specific person, but instead to all who need their love.

Lee believes that agape is the least common love-style, and he is probably correct. In fact, there is a theoretical question as to whether humans are capable at all of true agape, which is selfless (see Nygren's *Agape and Eros*, 1982; Singer's trilogy *The Nature of Love*, 1984, 1987, or Soble, 1989). An example that is often given is found in Charles Dickens' novel *A Tale of Two Cities*, a love story which takes place during the French Revolution. The hero, Sidney Carton, is in love with Lucie Manette, who is in love with Charles Darnay. At the end of the story, Charles Darnay is sentenced to die in the guillotine. Sidney's love for Lucie is so strong that he takes Darnay's place and dies in the guillotine so that Lucie can be with the man she loves. However, Sidney would not have sacrificed himself for Mary or Sue, for whom he felt no passion. Or perhaps Sidney couldn't bear the pain of seeing Lucie in distress. In any case, there is no passion or any other type of self-interest in agape. Humans can, however, strive to achieve a love-style that approaches agape.

OTHER COMBINATIONS

Lee's theory has received support from the results of a large-scale study (Hendrick & Hendrick, 1986). Over 1300 students were asked to agree or disagree with various statements about love. Their responses clustered into six different groups that closely fit the six categories just reviewed. There were some interesting gender and ethnic differences as well. Men tended to be more ludic than women, who tended to be more pragmatic, storgic, and manic. Asian-Americans tended to be more pragmatic and storgic than other ethnic groups.

Pragma, mania, and agape, however, are not the only possible outcomes of mixing the primary colors. Lee's analogy is mixing flour and water. Try mixing them when the water is hot, and then try it again when the water is cold. You are mixing the same ingredients, but the results are different.

Like agape, **storgic eros** results from the combination of eros and storge. Storgic eros lovers feel that the act of loving is the most important thing in life, even more than the partner for whom it is expressed. Thus, they feel fulfilled even if their love is not reciprocated. They do not prefer any particular type, do not attempt to possess their beloved, and have no feelings of jealousy. Storgic eros lovers will even step aside if they feel that another person can better fulfill the partner's needs. Love is seen as a duty, and sexual intimacy is not emphasized. The act of loving itself is all that is needed to lead a fulfilling life.

Ludic eros lovers (resulting from the same primaries as mania) want a variety of experiences of love and enjoy different body types, and though they do not want to become too involved, they want each partner to enjoy it too. Love is treated like an art form to be enjoyed by everyone. Feelings are never expressed in a manner that would suggest exclusivity, and the ludic eros lover attempts to avoid possessiveness and jealousy by his or her partner. The relationship is ended if it is no longer found to be enjoyable.

Storgic ludus results from combining the same primaries as pragma. There is no emphasis on finding a permanent mate and, in fact, storgic ludus lovers usually already have one. Instead, the emphasis is on finding partners for discreet affairs. The liaisons are to be enjoyed when it is mutually convenient, but there is no need to be "in love." There is no commitment and the storgic ludus lover avoids possessiveness and jealousy by his or her partner, from whom they expect self-restraint, breaking off the affair if it threatens their permanent relationship.

FINDING A GOOD MATCH

Did you recognize your love-style from the preceding list? There are tests you can take to determine your love-style preference (Hendrick & Hendrick, 1986; Laswell & Lobsenz, 1980), but Lee (1988) suggests that you just review your own experiences. When doing this, keep in mind that love-styles are not necessarily fixed. We are not born with a particular love-style that we are stuck with for life, but instead we can learn from our experiences and change preferences (we cannot learn from our experiences if we look at love as black and white and dismiss failed love as due simply to differences in intensity of feelings). Thus, you may have experienced more than one of the preceding styles. It is not unusual, for example, for a person's first love-style to be mania, or to experience mania for the first time in mid-life after a storgic marriage has become dull and uninteresting (conversely, one may prefer a comfortable, storgic relationship after experiencing mania). Once over mania, it is a mistake to dismiss it as infatuation (something other than love), for it demonstrates how intense your feelings can be for another person, and this can help you in a later love-style. Rather than accusing your partner of "not really loving me," it is more realistic to tell him or her that "your style of loving is not what I want."

Lee believes that the secret to finding mutual love is to find a good match, not in the amount of love each person gives, but in the style of loving. There are some obvious bad matches—a manic lover with a ludic lover, for example. The ludic lover's vanity will enjoy all the attention given by the manic lover, but the possessiveness and jealousy of the manic lover are not desired. Manic lovers thrive on problems, and the ludic lover is

BOX 12-A

CROSS-CULTURAL PERSPECTIVES: LOVE AND MARRIAGE

Romantic love is not something new; there are references to it throughout history. In Western culture it became idealized during the Middle Ages with the rise of courtly love (a young man devoting himself to a noblewoman). Even so, romantic love was not considered to be a good reason to enter into marriage until the 1800s. Prior to that, colonial Americans agreed to marry as more or less an arrangement, with the main purpose being to have children (Rothman, 1984). In fact, in a study conducted in the early to middle 1960s, about one third of U.S. men and three fourths of women indicated that being ``in love'' was not a necessity for marriage (Kephart, 1967). By 1976, this had changed; all but about 15 percent of men and women said that romantic love was a necessary prerequisite for marriage, and the same results were found in 1984 (Simpson, Campbell, & Berscheid, 1986). The change in attitude, mostly by women, was attributed to the better economic status of people—financial independence allowed them to make relationship decisions based on romance.

Is romantic love a creation of highly industrialized cultures where people have much leisure time and many comforts? Anthropologists have found that rules about marriage are, in fact, influenced by economics and politics (Barry & Schlegel, 1984; Hsu, 1981). In industrialized countries, where importance is attached to individuals, monogamy is the standard. In simpler societies, where less importance is given to individuals and more to situations, *polygyny* (a man is allowed to have more than one wife) is often the rule. In a study of 862 cultures, 83 percent permitted polygyny and only 16 percent were monogamous (Murdock, 1967). Polygyny is very common in societies with strong fraternal interests (with brides-wealth payments), or where there is warfare for capture of women, or where there are no constraints on expansion into new lands (White & Burton, 1988).

There are many differences among cultures in the relationship between a husband and wife. In a great many cultures marriages are arranged by parents (sometimes at birth). In contrast to the highly romantic beginnings of marriages in the United States, Japanese arranged marriages start off with very little love, but there is no difference in the amount of love within the two types of marriages after 10 years (due largely to the decrease in romantic love over time in American marriages; Blood, 1967). Marriages in India are arranged by caste, age, and other factors. Many Islamic societies require that a young man marry his father's brother's daughter (first cousin), and husband-wife relations are generally without affection, and are often very hostile (Lindholm & Lindholm, 1980). Pacific islanders and people in southeast Asia are often required to marry their mother's brother's daughter. Some cultures require that a male capture a wife from an enemy village, as in the case of the Gusii of Kenya (Levine, 1974), who rape their wives whenever they wish to have sex. A male of the Marind Anim of New Guinea must first share his newlywed wife with all the other males of his clan before he is allowed to consummate the marriage (Money & Ehrhardt, 1972).

Does all this mean that romantic love is restricted to a few highly industrialized cultures? No, say William Jankowiak and Edward Fischer (1992), who recently studied love in 166 cultures, and found evidence of romantic love in at least 147 of them. Even in cultures where marriages are arranged and rules of marriage are highly structured, romantic love often flowers in clandestine forms (as is often the case for extramarital affairs in our own culture). Romantic weddings may not be universal, but love is apparently ``a very primitive, basic human emotion, as basic as fear, anger, or joy'' (anthropologist Helen Fisher, quoted by Gray, 1993), one that escapes all the restrictions and barriers imposed by numerous cultures. ∎

guaranteed to provide them. It is not uncommon, however, to find this pairing, and while not very happy and ultimately doomed, a manic-ludic relationship is always interesting.

With the exception of mania and ludus love-styles, *a good match generally results from two styles that are close on the chart* (see Figure 12-3). A pragmatic love-style and storgic love-style make a good match, for example. Some difference is usually needed to maintain interest, so identical love-styles are probably not as good. The further apart two love-styles are, the less likely they would make a good match. The erotic or manic lover, for example, is likely to find the storgic love-style to be dull and regard it as friendship without passion and not love at all. The storgic lover will similarly accuse the behavior of the erotic or manic lover as not being love. A relationship between two

people with these two styles is probably doomed within a short time. In the end both may accuse the other of not having really loved, but in reality both will have loved in his or her own way. It simply was not a good match in love-styles.

Studies have shown that whether or not a relationship is successful can, in fact, be partially predicted by the compatibility in Lee's love-styles (Hendrick et al., 1988). So, the next time you find yourself attracted to someone, do not ask yourself how much this person loves you, but how (what style of love) they love you and whether or not your colors make a good match. Lee (1988) warns us, however, not to define mutual love in terms of longevity. Two people may have a mutually satisfying relationship, but just because it ends because one of them had a change in love-style does not mean it wasn't wonderful while it lasted. ∎

MAINTAINING A RELATIONSHIP

There is hardly any activity, any enterprise, which is started with such tremendous hopes and expectations and yet which fails so regularly as love.

(Erich Fromm, 1956)

The divorce rate is so high not because people make foolish choices, but because they are drawn together for reasons that matter less as time goes on.

(Robert Sternberg, 1985)

Many factors play a role in the initiation of a relationship. These include: (a) physical attractiveness—men generally attach more importance to this than women (Buss, 1989; Dion & Dion, 1987; Hatfield & Sprecher, 1986; Walster et al., 1966); (b) proximity—people are most likely to fall in love with someone they interact with often (at work, school, etc.) (Berscheid & Walster, 1978); (c) similarity—people tend to be attracted to others who have similar interests, values, intellectual abilities, and degrees of attractiveness (there is no evidence to support the old saying that "opposites attract")(Byrne, Clore, & Smeaton, 1986; Wetzel & Insko, 1982; White, 1980b); and (d) reciprocity—we tend to like people who show that they like us (no one likes rejection)(Berscheid & Walster, 1978; Byrne et al., 1986; Curtis & Miller, 1988).

Let us return for a moment to our hypothetical example of Susan and David (see "How do I know if this is really love?"). All four factors played a role in these two people beginning a relationship. Susan, and David let's suppose, have experienced physiological arousal in each other's presence and have interpreted their responses as "being in love." The relationship continues to develop if there is mutual self-disclosure, equity in what each wishes to gain from (and give to) the relationship, and finally, commitment. But will it last?

If there is anything that is unavoidable in life it is change. Couples will be faced with a variety of new challenges in life, including parenthood, financial crises, career-related stress, and, inevitably, aging. Two people who believe themselves to be in complete harmony during the dating, passion, and romantic loving period are often surprised to find themselves in disagreement on how to handle these matters. Many couples, for example, report the child-rearing years to be the most stressful and least satisfying in a marriage (Hendrick & Hendrick, 1983). Fixed gender roles, or conversely, changing gender roles, may contribute to this (see Chapter 8). Today, there are the added challenges of two-job families and job-related moves far away from family and friends.

THE DECLINE OF PASSION

The challenges in life are not the only things that change. People also change over time. One of the things that normally occurs in a relationship leading to changes in how we interact with our partners is **habituation**. Think of your favorite food. What makes it your favorite food? The taste and smell are no doubt important, but I am willing to bet that another factor is that you do not have it very often. If you were

Habituation

Responding less positively to a stimulus with repeated exposure.

served your favorite food every day for a month, do you still think it would be your favorite? Would we look forward to Thanksgiving turkey if we ate turkey every week? It's doubtful. When organisms, including humans, are repeatedly exposed to a stimulus that is initially very positive, it becomes less positive over time. This is why popular, weekly TV shows eventually go off the air and why hit songs eventually drop off the Billboard "top 10" list. We grow tired of seeing and hearing them. The same is true of the ability of other people to stimulate us—socially, emotionally, intellectually, and alas, sexually. Of all the challenges that a couple face in a relationship, habituation is certainly one of the greatest ones (Byrne & Murnen, 1988).

The decline of passion is almost inevitable, for a large component of passion is novelty and fantasy. A new partner cannot continue to arouse strong emotions, and with the passage of time it takes greater and greater stimulation to cause the same response that once was brought about by a mere glance or touch. As the passion subsides and fantasy is replaced with reality, the result is often disappointment. In a study of 62 cultures, Fisher (1992) found that the divorce rate peaked around the fourth year of marriage (seven years if a couple has another child two or three years after the first). The reason most frequently given by couples in the process of divorce is that they had "fallen out of (romantic) love" (see Roberts, 1992) and were bored (Hill, Rubin, & Peplau, 1976). Marital therapy has traditionally focused on improving communication and the development of rational skills, and only recently have therapists realized the importance of addressing emotional problems—the loss of sexual attraction and romantic love (Roberts, 1992). Many couples make the mistake of allowing their sex lives to become ritualized, but even when the passion has subsided a sexual relationship can remain exciting, fun, and fulfilling if the couple works for variety and spontaneity (see Chapter 11).

Although passion will decline with time due to familiarity and habituation, there is no need for *intimacy* (those feelings and experiences that promote closeness and bondedness) to decline. The key to maintaining a relationship is replacing passion with those things that lead to companionate love.

Growing Together/Growing Apart: Will Companionate Love Develop?

To maintain their relationship, therefore, Susan and David must simultaneously deal with the need for similarity in the relationship, the inevitable changes that occur (for example, they will not always be in school together), and the natural process of habituation. Similarity, so important in establishing their relationship, can be maintained and habituation can be kept to a minimum by embarking on new activities together (Byrne & Murnen, 1988). For example, they may find it stimulating to engage in new sports and games together, share new hobbies, *try new sexual experiences together* (see Chapter 11), join dinner groups, plan vacations together, and/or seek new educational opportunities together. One of the major predictors of marital success is the number of shared pleasurable activities (Ogden & Bradburn, 1968). Couples in long-lasting, happy relationships frequently say that they regard their partner as their best friend (Lauer & Lauer, 1985). Couples who are unhappy in their relationships often report that their children are their only or greatest source of satisfaction together (Luckey & Bain, 1970). Whether or not Susan and David develop intimacy and companionate love will depend, of course, on their commitment (the third component necessary in Sternberg's model for consummate love). Couples who successfully accomplish this grow together; those who do not grow apart.

> Married lovers grow within love; they develop into better human beings.
>
> (Erich Fromm, 1965)

What is meant by growing together or growing apart? I will try to demonstrate this with the use of intersecting circles (Levinger, 1988). Each person in the relationship is represented by a circle; the degree of intimacy shared is shown by the amount of overlap. The amount of passion felt by one person for the other is represented by plus (+) signs within the circle at the periphery of the intersection.

Look now at Figure 12-4. At the beginning of Susan and David's relationship (two circles at top), both are going to college. Their interests are shown within the circles, and each have their own set of friends: C, D, E, F, and G for Susan, and H, I, J, K, L, M for David. Susan and David met and began to date, you recall, while taking the same course. Because they have a great deal in common, they have a lot to talk about when they are together: their college courses, their good, bad, and peculiar professors, their campus activities and sporting events, and, of course, their career goals. Let us suppose that they both play tennis, and dancing is their favorite activity on dates. David even goes bowling with Susan even though he doesn't like it much. Over time they establish a mutual set of friends, including other couples (C-D and K-L) and singles (N). They each still have their own set of friends as well (each has lost contact with some, retained some, and gained some new ones and enjoy some activities not shared by the other—bridge and reading for Susan and golf for David). There is a great deal of passion felt by both Susan and David, and before long they tell one another that they are in love (decision). Dating is now more than just a good time, for there is a romantic component to being together. They realize that they share a great deal of their lives together (i.e., there is a strong intimacy component as shown by the amount of overlap in the circles in the middle), and neither can imagine life without the other. They make the commitment to have a lifelong relationship.

Let us now jump several years ahead and see what has happened to our imaginary couple. They no longer have the opportunity to spend most of the day together, for college is now just a distant memory. Instead, one of them is pursuing a career and spends 8 to 10 hours a day in an office (in today's world, it could be either Susan or David, but let us assume here that it is David), while the other is a full-time house and child caretaker. Yes, our imaginary couple now has children, and they only see each other briefly in the morning, in the evening before they go to sleep, and on the weekends (assuming that our career person does not work then, as well). How they adjust to this big change will determine whether the relationship remains positive or turns negative.

Unfortunately, many couples **grow apart** over time. Let's assume, for example, that Susan now goes to bowling league, plays bridge and tennis

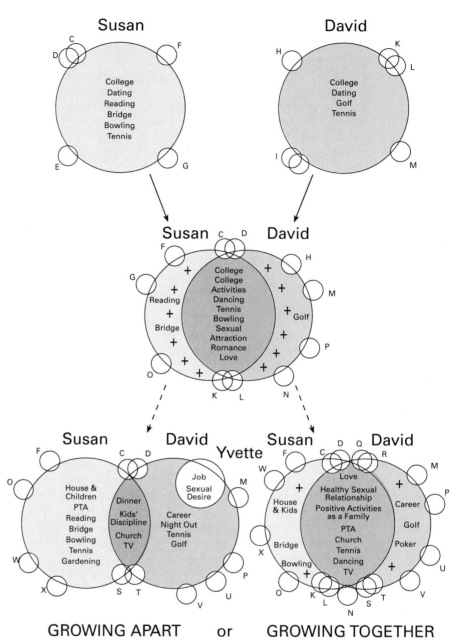

FIGURE 12-4   AN EXAMPLE OF GROWING APART OR GROWING TOGETHER.

Growing apart

Having fewer common interests over time.

with friends, and enjoys reading and gardening, all without David. David, on the other hand, plays golf and tennis with friends and enjoys an occasional night out with friends, all without Susan. They rarely go dancing anymore, and most of their time together is spent watching TV (with a minimal amount of conversation). Susan and David have children, but they do very little together as a family either. David considers it Susan's duty to go to the PTA and drive the children to and from all their activities even when he is

home. Susan and David and their children eat dinner together (quickly) and go to church together, but most of Susan and David's conversations about their children involve school and discipline problems. Raising their children is treated more as a responsibility than as a blessing. Although Susan and David live together and have children, they actually share less together now than when they were dating (there is less intimacy, indicated by less overlap in their circles). There is no passion left and very little affection (e.g., hugging, kissing, holding hands) is ever displayed between them. They have grown apart. This is not uncommon.

"I am married, yet feel as if I do not have a husband. He goes hunting every weekend during hunting season, and goes fishing a lot too. Between his softball league and poker games at the club, most weeknights are taken as well. Most of my time is taken up by the kids' activities and what social life I have is spent with other wives. Most of the time I am too tired to make love when my husband is in the mood, which is not very often. A friend recently described our marriage as 'married singles.' . . . "

"My boyfriend and I rapidly grew apart in our relationship. We did the same things over and over and did not feel comfortable enough to express our feelings towards one another. We did not accept each other for who we were; we kept trying to change things about each other. . . . "

(from the author's files)

People generally grow apart very slowly and by the time they realize it, they may have little left in common. At this point some people may think that it is easier to form a new relationship than work at their present one. For example, let us suppose that David spends a great deal of time with Yvette while at work (see Figure 12-4). They are together all day at least 5 days a week. They talk about the boss, fellow workers, job-related problems, and career goals. They even start telling each other about their personal problems at home. Add sexual attraction and feelings of passion, and David may conclude that he has as much in common with Yvette as he once had with Susan when they were in college together. David may decide to have an affair with Yvette, or leave Susan for Yvette. Unless David learns to work at keeping a relationship strong, however, this will just be a short-term solution, for over time David's passionate feelings for Yvette will subside as well and they, too, will grow apart.

Let us now look at another possible outcome for David and Susan. People change over time, but a couple who **grows together** substitutes new common interests as old ones drop out (see Figure 12-4). In place of college, which once gave them both a great deal to talk about together, our couple views their children and family activities as something very positive. They go to movies as a family, have picnics together, go to the zoo together, and both parents are involved in Little League, swimming team, Boy Scouts and Girl Scouts, PTA, and church and church social activities. Because they view their children's activities as positive experi-

Growing together
Maintaining common interests (although not necessarily the same ones) over time.

ences, it gives our two adults a great deal to talk about. They have substituted new shared activities for some of the ones they used to do together. They still find time (or *make time*) to play tennis on the weekends, go to movies, and they still enjoy dancing together as they did when they were dating. They also have a large number of mutual friends. It is not necessary that Susan and David do everything together in order to be happy. In addition to being apart during weekdays, David still plays golf regularly and enjoys an evening of poker with friends, while Susan has joined a bowling league (David refuses to bowl anymore) and plays bridge with friends. They are different from when they were dating, but the amount of shared interests is just as great as then. Their feelings of passion for one another have declined, of course (hearts don't beat faster, breathing doesn't get heavier, and palms don't sweat when they see each other), but their sexual interest for one another remains strong. They enjoy each other's body and seek variety in the way they stimulate one another. There has been no decline in intimacy. They have grown together.

BECOMING MORE INTIMATE

For most couples, the passion component is generally greatest early in a relationship and then declines over time. Therefore, one of the most important things in maintaining a relationship is developing and maintaining intimacy. Sternberg (1986, 1988) defined **intimacy** as those feelings in a relationship that promote closeness or bondedness and the experience of warmth. Similarly Elaine Hatfield (1984) defines it as "a process in which people attempt to get close to another; to explore similarities (and differences) in the way they think, feel, and behave." It is easy to share our similarities and positive feelings, but what about our differences and negative feelings? In order to become really intimate with someone, you must share your differences as well. Hatfield has made several suggestions designed to teach couples to become more intimate (Hatfield, 1988). Let us briefly examine these.

1. Both individuals in a relationship need to *accept themselves as they are*. I have previously discussed this in the chapter, but the need for self-acceptance bears repeating. Your best may not be *the* best, but it is all that anyone, including yourself, can ask of you. Learn to accept your ideas and feelings as legitimate.
2. Each individual in a relationship needs to *recognize his or her partner for what they are*. As hard as we may be on ourselves, we are often harder on our partners because they are not everything we would want them to be and we cannot understand why they will not change. Intimacy is not possible with an imaginary,

"perfect" partner. It can only occur when one recognizes his or her mate for what they really are—their weaknesses as well as their strengths.

3. Each individual must *feel comfortable to express himself or herself.* People are often hesitant to express any doubts, irritations, or anger to their partners in a loving relationship. To do so requires that an individual be capable of independence, for independence and intimacy go hand in hand (Hatfield, 1988). An individual who is totally dependent on his or her mate is unlikely to express any anxieties or fears. It is important that we express positive responses to our partners, for the ratio of positive to negative interactions is a key factor in maintaining a happy relationship (Byrne & Murnen, 1988). Positive responses for one's partner can and should be communicated in many ways (for example, by eye contact, holding hands and other physical closeness, thoughtful phone calls, cards or gifts, as well as sexual interest and verbal responses). However, we must also be able to express our anxieties, fears, and anger to our partners. If we cannot, then we are not really intimate.

4. Learn to *deal with your partner's reactions.* If you express your feelings to your partner, he or she may not like what they hear. Your partner may become angry or feel very hurt, but you must learn not to automatically back up or apologize for expressing feelings. Instead, keep calm and keep reminding yourself that your feelings are legitimate and that you are entitled to express them. In other words, keep trying. Only when both of you can express your own feelings and allow the other to do the same is there a chance for real intimacy.

The more intimate two people become, the greater the chance that the relationship will be maintained.

Love is an active power in man; a power which breaks through the walls which separate man from his fellow men . . . In love the paradox occurs that two beings become one yet remain two.

(Erich Fromm, 1956)

KEY TERMS

agape   295
attachment   288
attachment theory of love   289
companionate love   288, 293
conditional love   292
consummate love   293
decision/commitment   293
empty love   293
eros   294
fatuous love   293
friendship   286
growing apart   300

growing together   301
habituation   298
infatuated love   293
intimacy   293, 301
jealousy   290
liking   293
limerance   295
ludic eros   296
ludus   294
mania   295
nonlove   293
passion   293

polygyny   297
pragma   295
romantic love   286, 293
self-acceptance (self-esteem)   289
self-disclosure   289
storge   294
storgic eros   296
storgic ludus   296
triangular theory of love   292
unconditional love   292

PERSONAL REFLECTIONS

1. How do you define love? Which of Lee's love-styles best describes you in your present or last relationship? Do you think that you are locked in this love-style in future relationships? Why? Are there changes you need to make so that you can be happy and healthy in your relationships?

2. How important is loving and being loved to you? Do you believe that you could enjoy sex without love? Why or why not? Could you enjoy being in a romantic love relationship for an extended period of time if the relationship did not include sex? Why or why not?

3. Do you have a positive self-concept? Why or why not? If your self-concept is less than totally positive, what effects do you think this has on your ability to participate in a loving relationship?

4. Do you reveal your true needs, feelings, emotions, and values to your partner? Why or why not? Do you think that your partner reveals his or her true needs, feelings, emotions, and values to you? Why or why not? Do you deal with your partner's reactions when he or she does not like you expressing your true feelings, or do you back up and/or apologize? Why or why not?

5. Do you ever have feelings of jealousy? Are they so strong that they interfere with your relationship(s)? What are the conditions that usually cause you to become jealous? Does your partner ever try to make you jealous? What things might you do to control these feelings?

6. For those presently in a long-lasting relationship: Have the activities you share with your partner changed since you first began dating? Have new shared activities replaced old ones? Are you growing together or growing apart? If you feel that you are growing apart, what can you do to change this?

SUGGESTED READINGS

Avery, C. S. (1989, May). How do you build intimacy in an age of divorce? *Psychology Today.*

Davis, K. E. (1985, February). Near and dear: Friendship and love compared. *Psychology Today.*

Fromm, E. (1956). *The art of loving.* New York: Harper & Row. An oldie, but a classic.

Gray, P. (1993, 15 February). What is love?; Toufexis, A. The right chemistry. *Time* magazine.

Rubenstein, C. (1983, July). The modern art of courtly love. *Psychology Today.* Results of a reader survey regarding romance, love, and sexuality reveal some interesting differences between men and women.

Seider, S. (1991). *Romantic longings: Love in America, 1830–1980.* New York: Routledge.

Singer, I. (1984, 1987). *The nature of love.* Chicago: University of Chicago Press. A three-volume set for the serious student.

Thayer, S. (1988, March). Close encounters. *Psychology Today.* Discusses the importance of touch in establishing intimacy and examines some gender and cultural differences.

Trotter, R. J. (1986, September). The three faces of love. *Psychology Today.* An easy-to read review of Sternberg's triangular theory of love.

CHAPTER THIRTEEN

HST
Human Sexuality Today

SEXUAL PROBLEMS AND THERAPY

WHEN YOU HAVE FINISHED STUDYING THIS CHAPTER, YOU SHOULD BE ABLE TO:

1. DISCUSS THE COMMON SEXUAL DIFFERENCES COUPLES MAY ENCOUNTER IN THEIR RELATIONSHIP;

2. DESCRIBE SOME COMMONLY USED SEXUAL THERAPY TECHNIQUES (THE MEDICAL HISTORY, THE SEXUAL HISTORY, SYSTEMATIC DESENSITIZATION, SENSATE FOCUS, SELF-AWARENESS, PSYCHOSEXUAL THERAPY, AND THE PLISSIT MODEL OF THERAPY);

3. DESCRIBE SEXUAL PROBLEMS THAT CAN AFFECT BOTH MALES AND FEMALES (HYPOACTIVE SEXUAL DESIRE, HYPERSEXUALITY, AND DYSPAREUNIA);

4. DESCRIBE THE SEXUAL PROBLEMS THAT OCCUR ONLY IN MALES (ERECTILE DISORDER, PREMATURE EJACULATION, ORGASMIC DISORDER, BENIGN COITAL CEPHALALGIA, AND PRIAPISM);

5. EXPLAIN THE SEXUAL DYSFUNCTIONS THAT OCCUR ONLY IN FEMALES (ORGASMIC DISORDER AND VAGINISMUS); AND

6. EXPLAIN SOME SIMILARITIES AND DIFFERENCES IN THE TYPES OF SEXUAL PROBLEMS EXPERIENCED BY HOMOSEXUALS.

In the fantasy world of sex, nothing ever hurts, nothing rubs or chafes, nobody is anxious, no one is tired, there are no menstrual cramps, strange viruses, or pregnancy fears, nothing bad ever happens and everything fits perfectly; in the fantasy world of sex, erections function, orgasms are easy, desire surges, birth-control methods don't interfere with spontaneity, and bodies melt. In the real world, it doesn't always happen this way.

(From What Really Happens in Bed by Steven Carter and Julia Sokol. Copyright © 1989 by Steven Carter and Julia Sokol. Reprinted with permission of the publisher, M. Evans and Company, Inc., New York.)

SEVERAL STUDIES HAVE FOUND THAT ONE HALF OR MORE OF ALL COUPLES HAVE HAD, OR WILL EVENTUALLY have, sexual problems at some time in their relationships (Ende, Rockwell, & Glasgow, 1984; Frank, Anderson & Rubenstein, 1978; Nathan, 1986). In this chapter you will learn about the types of sexual problems that men and women may experience. In some cases, individuals have sexual problems regardless of who their partner is. Within a relationship, however, sexual problems frequently arise simply because of individual differences—people are different in what they want and how often they want it. I will begin with a discussion of the types of differences that can lead to sexual problems within a relationship. ■

INDIVIDUAL DIFFERENCES

DIFFERENT EXPECTATIONS

Men and women often have different ideas about sex and love and therefore often differ on why they have sex. Many women are looking for affection and are interested in what their partner thinks, while most men engage in sex because of their partner's looks, body, and sexual attractiveness (Randolf & Winstead, 1988). Many men equate intimacy with sex. When asked to give six responses to the question, "What things do you personally like best in a lover?" for a survey in my course, most males listed specific anatomical characteristics (e.g., "nice ass," "big breasts," "sexy legs") or behaviors (e.g., positions, oral sex, no inhibitions). Women, on the other hand, were less concerned about anatomy ("attractive" and "good build" were the only two responses) and specific behaviors and much more concerned about being in a relationship in which they felt cared for, loved, and/or respected. Nearly every woman expressed the desire that her male partner take his time. In fact, this was often expressed as a complaint—the male partners were not taking their time. These different expectations about a sexual relationship can lead to problems.

" I got married at a very early age. Sex to me was usually just wifely duties because it was demanded. I used to make up excuses just so I didn't have to do it. Our marriage finally broke up. . . . "

(from the author's files)

Dear Ann Landers: Two years ago I found out that my wife of 27 years was having an affair with another man. She was driving 40 miles to a motel twice a week to meet him for "lunch."

When I learned what was going on, I asked her, "Why? It seemed to me you were getting more than enough sex at home."

Her reply was, "What I am getting at home is just that. SEX. And sex is no substitute for love."

Her answer made me stop and think. I had to admit she was right.

I am writing this letter to all you husbands out there who are making the same mistake. Ask yourselves this question, "Am I making love to my wife, or am I just having sex with her?"

Glad I Got Smart
(Reprinted with permission of Ann Landers and Creators Syndicate.)

Kinsey's group (1948, 1953) found that foreplay for most couples lasted no more than a few minutes. In a later study, Hunt (1975) found that couples averaged 15 minutes of foreplay. This may mean that men are becoming more aware that women are more likely to enjoy sexual intercourse if they take their time.

DIFFERENT ASSUMPTIONS

Men and women often have different initial sexual experiences, which can lead to incorrect assumptions about the opposite sex. The first sexual experience to orgasm for most males is masturbation. Most males masturbate by moving a hand up and down the penis at a continually accelerating rate as they approach orgasm (Masters & Johnson, 1966). Kinsey (1948) found that, on average, men took only 2 to 3 minutes to reach orgasm during masturbation (extremely orgasm-oriented). Women are more variable in their masturbation techniques, but most prefer indirect stimulation of the clitoris (a circular motion or up and down one side). Kinsey found that only 20 percent of women masturbated by inserting a finger in the vagina, while Hite (1976) reported that only 1.5 percent of the women she surveyed did so. It takes women longer to masturbate to orgasm on the average than it does for men (Kinsey et al., 1953).

Without any evidence to the contrary, it is logical for people to assume that what feels best for them must feel best for others as well. Men often assume, therefore, that women greatly enjoy having their clitoris and other genitals vigorously stimulated (including rapid thrusting of a finger in and out of the vagina) during foreplay, when, in fact, this may not be the case. Based on her own masturbatory experiences, a woman might assume that her male partner prefers gentle indirect stimulation (Masters & Johnson, 1970), when, in fact, this may not be the case.

DIFFERENCES IN DESIRE

One of the most common types of problems that a couple might encounter is a difference in the frequency with which sex is desired (Zilbergeld & Kilmann, 1984). In the early 1980s movie *Annie Hall* there is a scene where a man, played by Woody Allen, and a woman, played by Diane Keaton, are shown talking to their respective therapists. Woody says that he and his girlfriend (Diane Keaton) hardly ever have sex, perhaps three times a week. Diane Keaton tells her therapist that they have sex all the time, maybe three times a week. Who has the problem? Is the woman played by Diane Keaton undersexed and to blame, or is the problem that Woody is oversexed? Suppose that Woody, who wants sex once a day, was instead having a relationship with another woman, who wanted sex at least three times a day. Now who is to blame? Would Woody now be considered undersexed, or is his new partner oversexed? It does no good to point the finger and put the blame on one person or the other. People are generally only oversexed or undersexed relative to their partners' desires. When actress Rita Hayworth was married to an Arab prince, she accused him of being oversexed. His response was that he had cut down his level of activity for her. *It is the couple that has the problem.* If the woman played by Diane Keaton had instead had a relationship with someone who also wanted sex once or twice a week, there would be no problem; and the same would be true if Woody had a relationship with someone who also wanted sex every day.

Sexual desire is not necessarily set at a fixed level. An individual's desire for sex often varies depending on the circumstances. For example, stress and fatigue can greatly affect our interest in sex. If your partner is showing less interest in sex than he or she once did, it may be due to other things happening in his or her life. Our understanding of our partner's feelings would be greatly enhanced, of course, if we could only switch places for a little while.

"When I stayed home and my husband worked, I did not understand his seeming lack of desire. Not that he didn't enjoy it, but it could be placed low on a list of priorities.

He would say things like, 'Wait, let me finish watching the ball game,' or 'I don't feel well,' or, 'I'm tired.' He would tell me about his problems at work, and I was really interested in making love then. I didn't want to hear how obnoxious, rude, or unintelligent his boss could be.

I took all of these 'excuses' as a personal put down. I would say, 'You're home now, forget what happened in the day.' Little did I realize then, he could not separate them. A bad day could not be erased by a few hugs and kisses. At that time, though, I tried to persuade him, which may have turned into a contest of who was going to win.

After a while, he started telling me that maybe he would be more interested if I didn't push him. After that, I began to let up and things went along fair. I still felt as though I wanted more than he was willing to give. Whenever I would tell him so, he would answer with, 'quality, not quantity.' Then I would get mad and say, 'You don't understand me and what I need.'

This period was heightened by his decision to quit his job of 25 years. When he finally decided to do this, I said I would go out to work and became a Kelly Girl. I really only wanted temporary work, but I'd go on short assignments of two or three weeks and stay three or four months with maybe only two or three days off in between. So, it was almost like working at one full time job.

I started with feeling the pressures of coping with a job. Even though I did not have to stay at a place I did not like, I never turned down an assignment and gave it my all. Now I am receiving tension, problems with bosses, and plain being physically and mentally tired.

When I came home from work, I'd look for dinner, make remarks about the house, or want to know if he checked on the children's homework. He would be ready to be cuddly and kiss and I had a barrage of questions. I'd also start telling him about problems I had during the day. At first, I realized these were things he said to me, and I didn't say any more. Finally, I told him, 'I can't believe I'm doing and saying the same things you did to me.'

After a while it became a joke, and I'd say these things and we'd laugh about it. He then knew how it felt and so did I. Well this same attitude spilled over to the bedroom. I realized I was now telling him, 'I'm tired,' 'I have to get up early,' 'Why didn't you start this earlier?' all things he had said to me. I knew how he was feeling and he knew how I was feeling. It was not that we didn't want to make love, but we used other issues to cloud our minds. We now are more understanding of each other's feelings, because we know where they are coming from. Even though I'm in school now, my time is even more used up, because of studying, but we are conscious of each other's needs.

Every so often my mother takes care of the two younger ones and we get away for a few days without any responsibilities or pressures. Just like two lovers on a lost weekend.''

(from the author's files)

DIFFERENCES IN PREFERRED BEHAVIORS

Differences in the type of sexual activities each person wants to engage in can also lead to problems. Suppose, for example, that person A (who can be either a man or a woman) wants to have sex only in the missionary position and is in a relationship with person B who wants to have sexual intercourse in a variety of positions and locations.

"My girlfriend and I are sexually active. I am tired of doing the same old missionary position. Whenever I mention a new position, she doesn't want to do it. I am so tired of the same old position I lose interest in sex. I don't want to even have sex sometimes.''

(from the author's files)

Who is to blame for the problem here? Is A inhibited or repressed, or is B perverted? Once again, it is all relative. It does no good to point a finger. Suppose that instead of having a relationship with A, person B was in a relationship with person C who wanted to try bondage and anal intercourse (which B does not want to try). Should person B now be viewed as inhibited? *It is the couple that has the problem*, not any one individual. ∎

WHO NEEDS THERAPY?

In summary, there are many differences that two people can have that can cause sexual problems. When this happens, it is far too common for one person to get upset and blame the other. It is generally best, however, that a couple view these types of problems as *their* problem, rather than a particular individual's problem. This means working together to resolve it.

Sexual relations, of course, are only part of a couple's overall relationship. As you learned in the last chapter, if a couple's overall relationship is good and positive, this generally carries over to sexual relations. Conversely, if a couple is experiencing relationship problems, this generally will affect sexual relations as well.

To work out sexual differences or relationship problems requires that a couple be able to talk

FIGURE 13-1   STUDIES HAVE SHOWN THAT ONE HALF OR MORE OF COUPLES HAVE HAD, OR EVENTUALLY WILL HAVE, SEXUAL PROBLEMS AT SOME TIME IN THEIR RELATIONSHIPS.

about their differences or problems. Most people do not know how to talk about sex comfortably, and Chapter 17 provides you with some guidelines. When couples cannot work out individual differences or relationship problems by themselves, they may need the aid of a counselor. When choosing a counselor, it is important to check his or her credentials. Be sure that you pick one who is properly trained and certified. In addition, just as you should do when choosing a doctor, shop around until you find one that you like. Some couples may prefer male and female cotherapists.

The names and addresses of certified marriage and family therapists in your area can be obtained by writing the American Association for Marriage and Family Therapy (AAMFT), 1100 17th Street, N.W., 10th Floor, Washington, DC 20036.

Not all sexual problems are the result of individual differences within a relationship. Rather than focusing exclusively on behavioral criteria (e.g., frequency of intercourse), we must also look at a person's basic beliefs, self-concept, and inner feelings and emotions. If a particular sexual behavior is causing an individual a great deal of stress and anxiety (sometimes interfering with his or her ability to function in a relationship), then that person may be regarded (and probably regards himself or herself) as having a problem. In this case, the individual would probably benefit by seeing a sex therapist. However, as you will soon see, again it is often beneficial to consider the individual and his or her partner as needing sex therapy together rather than focusing on either one of them. ■

SEXUAL THERAPY

What is a sex therapist? What do they do? My experience in class has been that many students giggle and laugh when asked this, and some have expressed the mistaken belief that sex therapists have sex with their clients. When you have a toothache you go to a dentist, but does the dentist drill his or her own teeth while you're there? When you have an eye infection you go to an ophthalmologist, and when you have a chest pain you go to a cardiologist. Just as many physicians specialize in different kinds of medical problems, therapists often specialize as well. A sex therapist is someone who specializes in helping people with sexual problems. Like any other specialist, a sex therapist has had several years of training before beginning practice.

Sex therapists consider it highly unethical for a therapist to have sex with a client (Lazarus, 1992). The following is an example of an unethical therapist. If anything like this ever happens to you, leave immediately and report the therapist.

"Six years ago I willingly went to a psychiatrist feeling that I needed someone to talk to that could maybe relinquish some of the thoughts I had about sex that were very disturbing. After two visits the doctor proceeded to show me different sexual positions in his books. The next visit he showed me the positions using me as his partner. I never went back. Two years after this, a friend of mine confided in me and told me she was once a victim of incest (her uncle). She told me the psychiatrist she went to made her opinion of men even worse. That doctor was the same one I went to and he did the same thing to her."

(from the author's files)

Sex therapy is a relatively new field. In fact, the American Psychiatric Association's *Diagnostic and Statistical Manual* (DSM-IV, 1994) did not even list psychosexual disorders until 1980. Until the pioneering work by Masters and Johnson, which was published in 1966, most people with a sexual problem went to their family doctor, a urologist, or, if they could afford one, a psychoanalyst. Most physicians were not prepared to deal with such problems. In fact, sex education was not even offered in most medical schools at that time. Psychoanalysis generally involved long-term treatment (sometimes years) and attempts to "cure" the problem by resolving childhood conflicts (believed to be unconscious). The behavioral problem is viewed as merely a symptom of some other deeper conflict.

Masters and Johnson (1970) originally believed that most sexual problems were the result of faulty learning and could be undone in a relatively short time period (often 2 weeks) by using **cognitive-behavioral therapy**. These procedures focus on the specific behavioral problems, and most therapists work with couples rather than individuals. People with a sexual problem are often very distressed and do not want to wait months or years for help. Psychoanalysts often charge, however, that behavioral therapies only treat the symptoms and, if the underlying cause is not determined, the problem will eventually manifest itself in another manner. No one can deny, however, that behavioral approaches have been enormously successful in treating sexual problems like erectile problems in men and orgasmic problems in women.

This relatively new field of therapy is still refining its techniques, and in the years since Masters and

Cognitive-behavioral therapy
Therapy that views problems as resulting from faulty learning and which focuses on specific behavioral problems.

Johnson began their clinical practice it became clear that **psychosexual therapy**, designed to give insight into the historical cause of clients' problems, was often more successful for some types of problems (e.g., low sexual desire or sexual aversion; Kaplan, 1974, 1983). More recently, LoPiccolo (1992) has added what he calls *systems therapy* to provide insight to the client about the function of his or her problem in the current relationship.

Sexual therapy programs generally have many things in common. Most follow what is called the **PLISSIT model** (Annon, 1974). PLISSIT is an acronym for permission, limited information, specific suggestions, and intensive therapy—the four levels of therapy. Each represents a successively more in-depth level of therapy. In the first level, the therapist "gives permission" for the client to feel and behave sexually. This is important, because many people and institu-

tions cause people to suppress or repress their sexuality while growing up (e.g., parents, some religions). In the second level, the therapist gives information to the client (educates him or her) about the sexual problems (e.g., information about clitoral stimulation, the effects of alcohol). This is done in a manner so that the client continues to acquire a positive attitude about sexuality. At the specific suggestion (third) stage, the therapist gives exercises (to be done at home) to help with the specific problem. If the client is still experiencing problems after completing the specific suggestions, then intensive (psychosexual) therapy will be used. Only about 10 percent of people who go to sex therapy require this last step.

If you ever think that you may need the help of a sex therapist, be sure to check the credentials of therapists first. In some places, almost anyone can advertise themselves as a "counselor."

The names and addresses of certified sex counselors and therapists in your area can be obtained by writing the American Association of Sex Educators, Counselors and Therapists (AASECT), 435 North Michigan Avenue, Suite 1717, Chicago, IL 60611-4065. ■

SEXUAL THERAPY TECHNIQUES

MEDICAL HISTORY

Sexual problems are sometimes caused by physical or medical problems (Kolodny et al., 1979). Circulatory problems (e.g., arteriosclerosis), hormone abnormalities (e.g., low testosterone levels), or anything that causes central nervous system damage (e.g., diabetes, spinal cord injury) can cause a sexual problem. Alcohol and drugs often cause sexual impairment as well. One common cause of impotence in men, for example, is some prescription medications used to treat hypertension and heart disease (Segraves & Segraves, 1992; Smith & Talbert, 1986). It is important, therefore, that a therapist have a complete medical history of the patient (and possibly have a physician do a medical exam) before beginning therapy in order to rule out any physiologic basis for the presenting problem. Behavioral therapy would do little good, of course, if the problem had an organic cause.

SEXUAL HISTORY

Nearly all sex therapists will take a complete sexual history of the client before treatment begins. These histories are very thorough, and the length of time devoted to this will depend on how candid the client is about his or her past experiences. Some therapists, like Masters and Johnson, prefer to work with couples because "there is no such thing as an uninvolved partner." A person's partner(s) is involved in the problem in some manner, and even when they are not the ini-

tial cause (in those cases where the problem existed before the relationship started, for example), it is common when one member of a couple has a sexual problem for the partner to develop one as well.

SYSTEMATIC DESENSITIZATION

Many patients have severe anxieties about sex in certain situations. Therapists often attempt to reduce this anxiety through muscle relaxation exercises or stress reduction techniques. A series of anxiety-producing scenes is presented to the patient, and he or she is told to try to imagine the scene. If this causes anxiety, the relaxation exercises are used until the scene can be imagined without anxiety. They then proceed to the next scene and repeat the procedure until the entire series can be completed without anxiety. Imagining a scene, of course, is not the same as a real-life situation, so a series of homework exercises is usually given as well.

SELF-AWARENESS AND MASTURBATION

As you learned in Chapter 2, some people have never explored their own bodies. As a result, they are totally out of touch with their own physical responses. If you don't know what your body looks like and how it responds, it will be difficult to communicate your needs and feelings to a partner. For those who are not in touch with their bodies, therapists are likely to tell them to spend time examining themselves. Some therapists give their clients instructions on how to masturbate (LoPiccolo, 1978; LoPiccolo & Stock, 1986). Many therapists consider it helpful to have a couple masturbate in each other's presence to show what each finds most arousing and pleasurable. Isn't it interesting that what once was taboo is now sometimes used as a therapeutic technique?

Sensate Focus

Many people are too goal- and/or performance-oriented during sexual relations (e.g., focusing on orgasm). Others have guilt or anxieties about enjoying sex. As a result, many people never really learn how to give or receive physical pleasure. Most therapists, therefore, instruct couples to use *nondemand mutual pleasuring techniques* when touching each other. They are instructed to go home, get undressed, and take turns touching each other without it immediately leading to the goal of having intercourse or having an orgasm. Touching of the breasts and genitals is forbidden at first, but all other areas of the body are to be explored

(see Figure 13-2). The receiver is instructed to focus on the sensations produced by the giver and to produce feedback as to what feels good and what does not. The giver learns what makes his or her partner feel good while simultaneously learning the pleasure of touching. The couple learns to be sensual in a nondemanding situation. Ask yourself, when was the last time you gave your partner a massage without asking or expecting anything in return?

Masters and Johnson, who created these **sensate focus exercises**, often have patients spend several days doing this nongenital-oriented touching. The purpose is to reduce anxiety and teach nonverbal communication skills. Eventually, the couple is instructed to include breast and genital stimulation in their touching, but to avoid orgasm-oriented touching. More and more is slowly added, including mutual touching and *hand-riding techniques* in which the receiver places his or her hand over the giver's hand and guides it over their own body (touching the hand lightly at body spots where they like gentle stimulation and pressing harder at spots where they like firm pressure).

Sensate focus
Exercises designed to reduce anxiety and teach mutual pleasuring through nongenital touching in nondemanding situations.

FIGURE 13-2   SENSATE FOCUS IS A NONDEMAND MUTUAL PLEASURING TECHNIQUE IN WHICH A COUPLE LEARNS HOW TO TOUCH AND BE TOUCHED WITHOUT WORRYING ABOUT PERFORMING OR REACHING A GOAL.

SEXUAL SURROGATES

These sensate focus exercises require a cooperative partner who is willing to devote a great deal of time (and also be willing to postpone intercourse and orgasm). What about the client who has no steady partner? What does he or she do? Remember, sexual contact between therapist and client is considered unethical by professional standards, and most prostitutes are not likely to show much sympathetic interest. Some sex therapists, therefore, employ surrogate partners who are trained and skilled in sensate focus techniques (as well as being cooperative and sympathetic). The surrogate's services can cost up to $125 per hour (the legal status of surrogates has still not been determined in many states). Although trained surrogates can provide a useful and necessary service, Masters and Johnson and some other therapists have discontinued their use because of emotional attachments that often form between the client and surrogate.

SPECIFIC EXERCISES

After the sensate focus exercises are successfully completed, therapists generally assign specific exercises to help with the problem for which the person came for treatment. These will be described as we discuss some of the most common types of problems. These exercises usually precede sexual intercourse. When the therapist does allow sexual intercourse, it is almost always in a female-on-top or side-by-side position where neither partner is in total control. Therapists believe that these positions have much more erotic potential than the missionary position that is frequently used by many couples. ∎

SEXUAL PROBLEMS AFFECTING BOTH MALES AND FEMALES

HYPOACTIVE SEXUAL DESIRE AND SEXUAL AVERSION

"I am 35 years old, my wife is 25, and we have been married for 6 years. From the outside we look like the perfect couple—clean cut, church-going, the works. The problem is my wife. She devotes all her time to cleaning, cooking, and doing volunteer work for the church. However, we have had sex 3 times in the last 12 months. She says that I should be happy with everything else she does for me. It has even gotten to the point where she wants separate vacations because a hotel room with me is too much pressure for her to stand. I love my wife but can't continue to live this way."

(from the author's files)

The DSM-IV (American Psychiatric Association, 1994) defines a lack of interest in sex as a problem when there is persistent or recurrent absence of sexual fantasies and sexual desire. People with **hypoactive** (or inhibited) **sexual desire** show decreased frequencies of sexual arousal, self-initiated sexual activity, and sexual fantasy (Segraves & Segraves, 1992). First reported in the 1970s (Kaplan, 1977; Lief, 1977), today many therapists believe that it is the most common problem of couples going to sex therapy (Leiblum & Rosen, 1989). One survey found it to be the most common problem mentioned by women reporting sexual difficulties (Clements, 1994). In another recent survey, 16 percent of married couples had been sexually inactive during the previous month (Donnelly, 1993). Some therapists put the es-

Hypoactive sexual desire
A sexual problem characterized by a persisting and pervasive inhibition of sexual desire.

timate as high as 20 percent of the population (Schover & LoPiccolo, 1982; *Time*, April 14, 1983). There are at least just as many men in therapy with this problem as there are women (Spector & Carey, 1990).

The problem in defining hypoactive sexual desire, of course, is defining what is meant by "persistent." What is the normal frequency for sexual desire? "Inhibited" is a relative term that must take into account the partner's frequency of desire (see the section on Individual Differences) and the level of desire of other people in the community. Some therapists classify a person as having hypoactive desire if he or she *initiates* an average of two or fewer sexual experiences a month (Schover et al., 1982). This does not have to mean intercourse and can include masturbation and sex play. It is more than just a lack of sexual activity, however. These individuals do not desire sex and avoid it even when there is an opportunity to engage in it. Sexually hypoactive persons display less physiological and subjective sexual arousal to erotic stimuli than do normal people (Palace & Gorzalka, 1992). Therapist Helen Kaplan's studies (1979) suggest that on some level inhibited persons suppress their desire because they do not want to feel sexual. Another therapist has called it "sexual anorexia nervosa." In its most extreme form, the avoidance of sex becomes phobic in nature and is called **sexual aversion** (Kaplan, 1987). The anticipation of any kind of sexual interaction (even conversation about sex), or, in some cases, touch, causes great anxiety, so persons with sexual aversion simply "turn it off" at a very early stage (Ponticas, 1992). Masters, Johnson, and

Sexual aversion
An extreme form of hypoactive sexual desire in which an individual's avoidance of sex becomes phobic.

Kolodny (1992) believe that sexual aversion is uncommon, but Helen Kaplan (1987) feels that it is underreported.

It is difficult for people who enjoy sex to imagine that others find it unpleasant. What could cause such a lack of interest in sex? *Primary asexuality* (people who have never had sexual feelings) is uncommon, but can result from mental illness and some diseases. *Secondary* or *acquired inhibited sexual desire* can be attributed to organic factors such as hormone deficiencies or tumors, in some cases, but the vast majority of cases are believed to be due to psychological factors (Leiblum & Rosen, 1988). Some cases may be due to a past trauma, such as rape or sexual molestation during childhood (see Chapter 15 on sexual abuse). A person doesn't have to have been a victim of sexual abuse, however, to acquire a negative attitude about sex. Some people simply may never have learned to associate sex with pleasure because of a selfish partner(s).

> "My husband was drunk on our wedding night. He could hardly walk and practically tore my clothes off. I wanted to kiss and hug and feel like I was loved, but all he wanted was to screw. I wasn't ready and it hurt real bad. He made me do things I didn't want to do. Afterwards he threw up in the bathroom and passed out. I cried all night. Now I still don't want him to touch me."
>
> (from the author's files)

Sometimes, an unwanted pregnancy or contracting (or fear of contracting) a sexually transmitted disease can cause a person to have a negative attitude about sex.

> "When I was 15 I had sex with a prostitute. My friends encouraged me to do so. One week later I noticed two sores on my penis. I couldn't tell my parents, they would kill me. I couldn't sleep. I asked a friend for help. I remember how he looked at me. I felt rejected. . . . I was horrified. . . . His father was a doctor and he treated me. I remember the anxiety when he told me I had chancroid. I didn't know if it was curable. . . . Today, I'm afraid of having sex with anyone. I have not had relations with a woman in nearly five years."
>
> (from the author's files)

Hypoactive sexual desire is also often associated with depression, life stresses, a sexually repressive upbringing, or aversions to female genitals or common types of sexual behaviors such as masturbation and oral-genital sex (Donahey & Carroll, 1993; LoPiccolo, 1980).

Interestingly, many females with anorexia or other eating disorders have very low sexual functioning and satisfaction (Rothschild et al., 1991).

Today, many therapists believe that relationship factors are one of the most important factors contributing to hypoactive sexual desire (Schwartz & Masters, 1988; Verhulst & Heiman, 1988). Hypoactive women are generally very unhappy in the quality of their relationship with their partner, particularly with the expression of affection, while hypoactive men tend to be overly reliant emotionally on their partners and have anxieties about finding the right combinations of sexual passion and emotional intimacy for their partner (Apt, Hurlbert, & Powell, 1993; Donahey & Carroll, 1993; Kaplan, 1988). In probably half or more of couples who go to therapy for sexual desire problems, one or the other partner has a coexisting sexual problem (see Leiblum & Rosen, 1988). In some cases, hypoactive sexual desire may be a way of avoiding the sexual failure due to the other problem (Kolodny, Masters, & Johnson, 1979).

Hypoactive sexual desire is probably the most difficult sexual problem to treat (DeAmicis et al., 1985; Hawton et al., 1991; Kaplan, 1987). Masters and Johnson once reported an 80 percent success rate in treating hypoactive clients with conventional, short-term therapy used for other problems, but this claim was severely criticized by other therapists, some of whom reported only a 10–20 percent success rate with conventional techniques. Today, most begin with the short-term, behavioral and cognitive techniques (used for other problems) that are designed to increase pleasure and communication and decrease anxiety, but add couples' therapy to resolve relationship problems and individual psychosexual therapy to help the person understand what it is that is causing anxieties about sex (e.g., LoPiccolo & Friedman, 1988; Schwartz & Masters, 1988; Zilbergeld & Hammond, 1988).

HYPERSEXUALITY: COMPULSION, ADDICTION, OR MYTH?

In the beginning of the chapter, you learned that two people in a relationship frequently differ in their frequency of sexual desire, but that ordinarily neither one should be considered hyposexual or hypersexual. By how much one's sexual desire would have to differ from most others before he or she would be considered extraordinary is a matter of subjective judgment, which (as usual) varies across different cultures and times. However, as you have just read, some people can be classified as having hypoactive (inhibited) sexual desire. Can we make the same distinction at the other extreme? Can people be classified as "hypersexual"? Many therapists say no. In fact, the American Psychiatric Association's manual DSM-IV (1994) has no such category. Let us explore this controversial issue further.

History is full of stories of famous people who reportedly had hundreds of sexual partners and often had sex many times a day: Cleopatra, Empress Theodora, Casanova, Catherine the Great, Rasputin, and King Solomon, to name a few. Terms like *nymphomania* and *satyriasis* have long been used to describe people with seemingly insatiable sexual appetites. However, those therapists who favor a new classification for hypersexuality say that it is more than just numbers. Patrick Carnes (1983, 1991) was the first to use the designation **sexual addiction**. Many therapists objected to this term, saying that there is no evidence of physical addiction as in the case of alcohol or drugs. Goodman (1992) recently redefined sexual addiction as follows:

"A disorder in which a behavior that can function both to produce pleasure and to provide escape from internal discomfort is employed in a pattern characterized by (1) recurrent failure to control the behavior, and (2) continuation of the behavior despite significant harmful consequences."

This definition includes aspects of both dependency ("behavior motivated by an attempt to achieve a pleasurable internal state") and compulsivity ("behavior motivated by an attempt to evade or avoid an unpleasurable/aversive internal state") and is similar to the definition in DSM-IV for psychoactive substance addiction.

Opponents of a designation "sexual addiction" argue that it is repressive morality that can be used against anyone engaged in nonmonogamous sex (Barth & Kinder, 1987; Coleman, 1986; Levine & Troiden, 1988). Coleman (1986), for example, stated "this concept can potentially be used to oppress sexual minorities . . . because they do not conform to the moral values of the prevailing culture (or therapist) . . . Mental health professionals using such conceptualizations have become simply instruments of such conservative political views and have made people who do not fit into a narrow, traditional sexual life style feel bad, immoral, and, now mentally ill." These therapists prefer to regard people who show a lack of sexual control as having a *sexual compulsion*.

Note that there is some common ground: both sides admit that it is possible to engage in sex compulsively. I will use the purely descriptive term hypersexual to describe such individuals.

Hypersexuality
A term reserved for people who engage in sex compulsively, with little or no emotional satisfaction. Sometimes called sexual addiction.

A **hypersexual individual** is distinguished from other people by the compulsiveness with which he or she engages in sex. Hypersexuals engage in sex repeatedly and compulsively, usually finding little or no emotional satisfaction.

They feel driven to have sex, looking for something in sex that they can never find. If they fall in love and establish a relationship, they often cannot stop their promiscuous behavior. Hypersexuality interferes with the ability to carry out normal daily living and results in unhappiness, unfulfillment, and an inability to break a pattern of compulsive behavior. The threat of possibly contracting a sexually transmitted disease, including HIV infection and possibly AIDS, does not stop them. Although the term sexual addiction may be controversial, it has been found that some hypersexual individuals also display excessive use of alcohol, drugs, and/or food to satisfy emotional needs. It is not uncommon, for example, for people who display cocaine abuse to engage in high-risk sexual behaviors (e.g., new partners) when taking the drug (Washton, 1989). The dual addiction becomes a vicious cycle with one addiction leading to the other.

Coleman (1986) believes that hypersexuality ("sexual compulsivity") results from "intimacy dysfunction" during childhood. This can occur, for example, if a child is neglected or abused. Such children often have low self-esteem and feelings of inadequacy and unworthiness as adults. They are often very lonely, and their emotional pain causes them to engage in behaviors (e.g., alcohol, drugs, food, sex) that give pleasure and evade the internal discomfort. The relief is only momentary and is followed by a need to engage in the behavior again. However, engaging in the behavior results in greater feelings of unworthiness and shame, which makes it more likely that the person will engage in the behaviors in order to avoid the negative feelings felt at present.

How would one distinguish hypersexuality from a healthy interest in sex? Remember, it is not so much the frequency as it is one's lifestyle. Ask yourself some questions as guidelines. Do you *frequently* use sex to alleviate depression or anxiety? Is your sexual behavior abusive or injurious (physically or emotionally) to yourself or others? Could it possibly damage your relationship, your career, your health, or your self-respect? Have you ever wanted to stop, but found yourself unable to do so? A positive response to these questions may make you a candidate for therapy.

Therapy is often twofold: (1) treating the internal discomfort (perhaps initially with antidepressants or stabilizing drugs), and (2) helping the individual find healthy, adaptive ways of dealing with his or her emotions and needs (psychotherapy will probably be used here). Those therapists favoring the addictive viewpoint probably will also teach cognitive-behavioral strategies to help the individual abstain from the addictive behavior (Goodman, 1992). While therapists continue to argue the validity of sexual addiction, a number of self-help organizations similar to Alcoholics Anonymous (e.g., Sexaholics Anonymous, Sex Addicts Anonymous) have been created for people who think they need help.

PAINFUL INTERCOURSE

Painful intercourse is called **dyspareunia**. It usually, but not always, is caused by a physical problem. In men, the most common causes are a prostate, bladder, or urethral infection (Davis & Noble, 1991), or the foreskin of the penis being too tight (a condition called *phimosis*). In rare cases, fibrous tissue deposits around the corpora cavernosa of the penis cause curvature of the penis (known as *Peyronie's disease*) and pain during erection (Ansell, 1991; Gregory & Purcell, 1989). In a very rare condition, some men experience persistent and recurring pain in the genitals during or immediately after ejaculation. This is called *postejaculatory pain syndrome* and is caused by involuntary spasms of the genitals that are triggered by psychological conflicts (Kaplan, 1993).

Dyspareunia

Painful intercourse, usually resulting from organic factors (e.g., vaginal, prostate, or bladder infections).

Phimosis

A condition in uncircumcised males in which the foreskin of the penis is too tight, causing pain during erection.

Painful intercourse is much more common in women than men. It has been estimated that 1–2 percent of women suffer from chronic dyspareunia, with perhaps as many as 15 percent occasionally experiencing problems (Brody, 1988). One of the most common causes is vaginal dryness. If a woman is not fully lubricated when intercourse begins, the thrusting of the penis will severely irritate the dry vaginal walls. Lack of sufficient lubrication can be due to a partner who doesn't take his time, but it can also be the result of fear or anxiety, which interferes with the vasocongestive process (vaginal lubrication, you recall, is the result of the walls of the vagina becoming engorged with blood). Vaginal dryness can also result from hormonal changes (which occur at menopause), use of antihistamines and other medications, and even tampons. Use of a water-soluble lubricant can often substantially alleviate this problem.

Dyspareunia in women can also be caused by endometriosis (growth of the endometrium outside the uterus), pelvic inflammatory disease, yeast and other vaginal infections, Bartholin's gland infections, and urinary tract infections. Allergies to semen, feminine hygiene products (deodorants and scented douches), powders, and spermicides can also make sexual intercourse painful (Erard, 1988).

If the physical factors responsible for dyspareunia are not quickly taken care of, it can lead to other sexual problems. The anticipation of pain, for example, can become so great that it can lead to erectile problems in men, vaginismus in women, or loss of sexual desire in either sex. The resultant psychological stress can also damage relationships. Remember, pain during intercourse is generally an indication that there is something physically wrong, so see a physician immediately before it leads to greater problems. ■

MALE SEXUAL PROBLEMS

ERECTILE DISORDER

An **erectile disorder** refers to a man's inability to attain or maintain an erection. This condition was once called impotency, but this is an unfortunate term because it has negative connotations about a male's manhood. Therapists now prefer the purely descriptive term (NIH Consensus Statement, 1992). Erectile disorders can be *primary* (i.e., a male who has never had an erection) or *secondary* (i.e., the individual has not had erectile problems in the past), and *global* (i.e., it happens in all situations) or *situational* (e.g., a man who cannot get an erection with his usual partner, but can with other women or during masturbation).

Erectile disorder

A sexual problem in which a male has difficulty or an inability to get and maintain an erection.

Historically, and in many cultures, an erect phallis has been a symbol of male power and fertility. Having an erectile problem can therefore be psychologically devastating. As one male put it, "I felt I wasn't a full man anymore" (*Newsweek*, June 18, 1984). But the disorder can affect more than the male. It often destroys the self-esteem of the female partner as well, because she often feels like she is doing something wrong.

Billy and Karen were in their mid-thirties and had been married for three years. They had no children and both worked full-time; he as the manager of a small insurance office and she as a lab technician in a hospital. Their sexual relationship, which began while they were dating, had always been "wonderful."

In their third year of marriage, Karen was promoted to a job selling hospital equipment. About six months later, Billy began to have erectile difficulties. At first, Billy would lose his erection after intercourse had begun, but after about two months he began to have difficulty during foreplay as well. Sometimes he couldn't get an erection at all. He was embarrassed by this (calling himself a ``failure'') and began reacting by rolling over and going to sleep.

When the problem started, Karen tried to be supportive and didn't say anything, but as Billy's problem worsened she became angered at his silent withdrawal and lack of attempts to satisfy her through other means. As things progressed, Karen, who had been regularly orgasmic in the past, found that she could no longer reach orgasm. Now when they had sex Karen worried so much that Billy would get upset that she, too, lost all focus on sexual pleasure. Billy also began to rush her through foreplay to try and see if he would be able to perform in the "main event." Karen not only missed the intercourse and her own orgasms, but also the tenderness and closeness. Both felt inadequate because they both had sexual difficulty and could not figure out what was causing it.

(Case history courtesy of
Dr. David M. Schnarch, Ph.D.,
New Orleans, LA)

How common are erectile problems? It is a rare male who will not experience an erectile problem at least once in his life. An erection results from the spongy-like tissues of the corpora cavernosa and corpus spongiosum of the penis becoming engorged with blood (the penile arteries dilate and valves in the veins close). This response is under reflexive control by two centers in the spinal cord (the lower one responds to touch and the upper one responds to erotic thoughts). They normally work together, and depend on the presence of testosterone (the male hormone) and other chemicals. Any number of things can upset the balance and impair functioning, including fatigue, stress, alcohol, and drugs. A drink or two loosens our inhibitions, but most men are unaware that alcohol is also a central nervous system depressant, and it is quite common to experience erectile problems after drinking too much (which sometimes may be only a couple of drinks; R. C. Rosen 1991).

So should we say that all men have erectile problems? No, but it is somewhat arbitrary as to where we draw the line. Masters and Johnson (1970) classify a man as having an erectile dysfunction if he is having problems in at least 25 percent of his sexual encounters, but others add that the problem must exist for at least 6 weeks to be considered chronic erectile dysfunction. By these definitions, it is estimated that perhaps 10 million American men have an erectile disorder. Erectile problems are much more common in elderly men, with only 7 percent of males aged 25 to 55 experiencing such problems, compared to 27 percent for men over 70 (Kravis & Molitch, 1990). However, erectile problems are *not* inevitable with advancing age (i.e., age alone is not the cause), and the problem can be treated with a variety of therapies (NIH Consensus Statement, 1992).

What is responsible for so many men having an erectile disorder? Masters and Johnson once argued that as many as 80 percent of cases are due to psychological factors, but physicians and therapists now estimate that a majority of cases have a physical basis (NIH Consensus Statement, 1992; Sullivan, 1987). Causative factors include diet, diabetes, aging, medications, alcohol, and smoking. One study of 188 dysfunctional men aged 40 to 70 (Morley, 1986) found that all but 14 percent were due, at least in part, to an organic cause. Circulatory problems (e.g., arteriosclerosis, sickle-cell anemia), neurological disorders (e.g., accidents, pelvic surgery), and hormone imbalances (primary abnormalities or secondary complications due to diabetes) often result in erectile dysfunction (Kravis & Molitch, 1990). One fourth of erectile problems are due to medications prescribed for other conditions (such as beta-blocking medications used to treat blood pressure and heart disease; NIH Consensus Statement, 1992). Eighty percent of alcoholics are impaired. Smokers are 50 percent more likely than nonsmokers to suffer from erectile problems (Mannino et al., 1994; see also M. P. Rosen et al., 1991). It is important, therefore, that a client with an erectile problem have a complete medical exam before treatment begins.

Actually, there is an easy test that can often (but not always) determine whether the cause of an erectile disorder is physical or psychological. Males, you remember, get erections at night during REM sleep. If a man gets normal erections during REM sleep, then the problem is most likely psychological. If not, then it is physical.

Organically caused erectile disorder can often be reversed if the cause is medications or hormone deficiencies (although many still need sexual therapy because of the anxieties it has produced). Self-injections of phentolamine and papaverine hydrochloride, drugs which cause expansion of vessels that supply blood to the penis and constriction in vessels that carry blood away from the penis, have proven to be very successful in many men to reverse erectile problems due to circulatory problems (Althof et al., 1991; Lakin & Montague, 1988). Another option is vacuum devices that force blood into the penis, thus causing it to become erect (Witherington, 1990). Scientists have identified the chemical that causes the smooth muscles of the penis to relax and allow blood vessels to enlarge and fill (nitric oxide), and use of this chemical may prove to be an effective treatment in the future (Rajfer et al., 1992). In 1995, the Food and Drug Administration gave their first approval of a drug to relieve erectile disorders. The drug (Caverject or olprostadil, a naturally occurring form of the hormone prostaglanin) is injected into the penis and is effective in 80 percent of cases.

For those men for whom there is no cure (e.g., they suffer permanent nerve or vascular damage), *penile implants* can be used. There are three types. One is made of semirigid plastic rods and is inserted in the erectile chambers of the penis. It is stiff enough to permit intercourse, but flexible enough that it can be bent downward during daily activity. A second, more sophisticated, type of implant is made of two soft tubes that are implanted in the erectile chambers. They are connected by tubes to a small pouch containing a saline solution that is implanted under the muscles in the pubic region. The pouch, in turn, is connected to a tiny pump located inside the scrotum. When a man wants to have sex, he gently presses the pump, which forces the saline solution into the tubes in the penis and causes an erection. Squeezing a valve in the pump reverses the process. A third type is a silicone sack that is also inflated by a pump. Over 30,000 American men are presently using these implants, and, although postsurgical levels of sexual satisfaction do not always match presurgical expectations, a large majority of the patients and their partners are satisfied with the results (McCarthy & McMillan, 1990).

Quite often it is not easy to attribute an erectile problem to solely organic or psychological factors. If a man has a problem due to a physical cause (or a temporary problem due to medications), he can become so apprehensive that he becomes completely impaired (Buvat et al., 1990; NIH Consensus Statement, 1992).

If the cause of an erectile problem is determined to be psychological, the success rate during therapy depends largely on whether it is primary or secondary. Men with primary (psychological) erectile disorders are often found to have had a strict religious upbringing in which sex was equated with sin and guilt (Masters & Johnson, 1970).

> "I was raised a _____ throughout my life. . . . I do remember in the 8th or 9th grade my father and I were talking about sex and he told me not to have sex until I was married or I would go to hell—I thought that for the longest time. Then when I discovered masturbation I felt terribly guilty so I went to talk to a priest. He told me how wrong it was and gave me some

SEX ISN'T AN OLYMPIC EVENT, LET'S MAKE LOVE!!

(Cartoon by Everett Moore.)

prayers to say. From that time on I felt very guilty every time I did it. . . . I haven't had a full erection in 10 years (I'm 26). . . ."

(from the author's files)

An early traumatic experience might also result in long-term erectile problems:

> "At 16 years old . . . my best friend thought it was a shame I was still a virgin. . . . In a drunken stupor I was goaded into going downtown to pick up a hooker with my friend. The next day I walked tall and proud (although I felt no different), that is until I noticed a week later a greenish-yellow discharge on my underwear. A doctor diagnosed gonorrhea. I brought it up with my father, who became enraged, and to this day he still teases me about it. My brother laughed at me. . . . I did not date anyone for 3 years. Once I began, it took me 3 or 4 years to have sex. . . . I would get to the point of intercourse then I would lose my erection. . . ."

(from the author's files)

Therapists find that these primary disorders are much more difficult to treat than secondary disorders. Masters and Johnson report a 60 percent success rate, but many other therapists feel that only about 20 percent can be successfully treated (Kaplan, 1979). Men with a primary psychological disorder may be treated by having a penile implant.

Situational erectile disorders are quite clearly psychological in origin.

"My husband doesn't stay hard when we make love. Everything is OK at the start, but then he gets soft in a minute or two. He stays hard when I give him oral sex or masturbate him."

(from the author's files)

If this man's erectile problem was caused by something physically wrong with him he would be unable to maintain an erection with any type of sexual activity.

Performance anxiety

A fear of failure during sexual relations. This can lead to erectile disorder in males and inhibited orgasm in females.

For men with a secondary erectile disorder due to psychological factors, the most common cause is **performance anxiety**. Performance anxiety is a fear of failure.

"My girlfriend and I are sexually active. Since we first started having sex, I would have an orgasm but she wouldn't. She still hasn't had one, and we have had sex plenty of times. I feel that I am not doing my job as a man. I also feel embarrassed. It makes me feel I do not know much about sex. Lately . . . I have trouble getting an erection. . . ."

(from the author's files)

Men who judge their sexual experiences like Olympic events (eg., they are unhappy unless their partner has multiple orgasms) put enormous pressure on themselves. The same is true of men who feel they are competing with a real or imagined suitor. In both these cases the man is likely to become distracted by observing his partner's or his own responses, resulting in an erectile disorder.

As you learned previously, nearly all males will experience an erectile problem sometime in their life, often due to fatigue, drugs, or too much too drink. One of the most common causes is a life change. For example, the stress caused by unemployment frequently leads to erectile problems (Morokoff & Gilliland, 1993). According to Levine and Althof (1991), "Typically, the man does not fully appreciate his response to these life changes, for example, his affects, defenses, coping devices, and adaptational shifts. Neither does he fully realize that the trigger mechanism for his arousal problem is contained in these responses. He avoids recognizing what these affect-laden events mean to him and only focuses on his loss of sexual confidence—that is, performance anxiety. He remains baffled by how he became dysfunctional."

Recall, for example, the case history of Billy and Karen. Let us continue with their story:

When Billy and Karen started therapy, they still had no idea what was causing the problem. They felt they were doing everything the same as before. In actuality, Billy was threatened by Karen's impressive career enhancement. Although he tried hard to be a liberated male, he was threatened by her increased income and status and the time she spent entertaining the various physicians and hospital administrators in her territory.

During sexual relations, Billy had begun to worry if Karen found him as appealing as she had when she was more "naive and unworldly." He also had the secret fear that Karen was having an affair, and although she wasn't, he had begun to compete with his own fantasy of Karen's other partner. As with many men, this was sufficient to produce Billy's initial difficulty in maintaining an erection. Once the difficulty began, Billy's anticipation of it happening made it begin to occur earlier in each subsequent sexual encounter.

(case history courtesy of Dr. David Schnarch)

Although erectile problems in any of the previously mentioned situations is normal, many men are not aware of that and begin to worry about being "impotent." The next time they have sex the anxiety caused by fear of failure can result in what is called **spectatoring**—observing and evaluating their own responses rather than experiencing the sexual pleasures. Spectatoring is distracting (a loss of intimacy) and can lead to loss of erection, which results in even greater anxiety the next time. The behavior becomes a vicious cycle, and what started as a normal response to fatigue, alcohol, drugs, or other factors can become a chronic psychological disorder.

Spectatoring

Observing and evaluating one's own sexual responses. This generally causes distraction with subsequent erectile and/or orgasm problems.

What is the best therapy for a man with a psychologically caused erectile problem (performance anxiety)? Today, many therapists are emphasizing the importance of the couple's dynamics and interpersonal issues in the cause and treatment of erectile problems: "Clinical experience suggests that couples with strong, committed and supportive relationships generally develop effective coping strategies in the face of even the most severe sexual problems. In contrast uncommitted couples with unresolved marital conflicts appear to derive little or no benefit from even the most advanced medical, surgical or psychological interventions" (Leiblum & Rosen, 1991). Initial assessment of a couple's motivation and interactions is important for choosing a therapy approach (Hawton, Catalan, & Fagg, 1992).

After their medical and sexual history is taken, men with an erectile disorder are assigned sensate focus exercises. Many men are amazed to find that they are able to get a full erection during these initial sessions. The reason, of course, is that the touching in sensate focus exercises involves nondemand pleasuring—the man does not have to perform, but instead learns (or relearns) how to experience pleasure. When genital touching is allowed, the female partner is instructed to stop fondling the penis after the male gets an erection (see Figure 13-3). This is intended to teach the man that he does not have to use his erection immediately (many men with erection problems rush their performance for fear that they will lose their erection). With this *"teasing" procedure*, the male's erection comes and goes, and thus he also learns that loss of erection does not mean that he has failed (for it will come back again). When intercourse is finally allowed, it is always in a female-on-top or side-by-side position, and the female inserts the penis. Thus, the male is not put in a position of feeling that he has to perform.

Erectile problems can be so psychologically devastating that many men try to deal with their problem alone. However, there is now an organization called Impotents Anonymous, with 19 chapters nationwide that offer information and support. Wives of men with erectile problems are also welcome to attend meetings.

PREMATURE EJACULATION

"... I have a problem with premature ejaculation. As soon as I start to have sex I ejaculate. I feel like the whole world is laughing at me.... All my other friends are having sex and doing it right."

(from the author's files)

When many people think of someone who prematurely ejaculates, they think of a male who reaches orgasm before intercourse even begins. Although this does sometimes happen, it is more often the case that a male ejaculates shortly after the couple begins intercourse. Masters and Johnson believe that as many as 15 to 20 percent of American men ejaculate prematurely on a regular basis, making it the most common male sexual problem. Men who are concerned only with their own orgasm, of course, may not regard it as a problem. In fact, in some cultures around the world where men are very dominant and the sexual pleasure of women is denied, the ability to ejaculate quickly is considered

FIGURE 13-3   A COMMONLY USED MALE TRAINING TECHNIQUE.

very masculine. It is estimated that only 20 percent of premature ejaculators in the United States ever seek therapy.

How, then, do we define **premature ejaculation**?

The American Psychiatric Association (DSM-IV,

Premature ejaculation

A recurrent and persistent absence of reasonable voluntary control of ejaculation.

1994) says that the essential feature is "the persistent or recurrent onset of orgasm and ejaculation with minimal sexual stimulation before, on, or shortly after penetration and before the person wishes it." How long does a man have to continue in intercourse without being classified as a premature ejaculator? At various times in the past, premature ejaculation has been defined by a specified minimal number of thrusts, a minimal amount of time engaged in intercourse, or in terms of whether or not the female partner reaches orgasm at least 50 percent of the time. The problem with the first two types of definitions is that they do not consider the partner. Suppose a man always reaches orgasm in only a minute and a half after beginning intercourse, but that his female partner always reaches orgasm within that time period as well. Should he be considered as having a problem? The trouble with the last definition is that it depends exclusively on the partner's responses. What if the partner has difficulties reaching orgasm regardless of who her partner is? A man could continue intercourse until he's blue in the face and still be classified as a premature ejaculator. Most therapists choose to view premature ejaculation in terms of *absence of reasonable voluntary control* of ejaculation (Kaplan, 1974). By this definition, orgasm should not be a totally involuntary event, and a man should be able to have some control over when it occurs. A man who regularly reaches orgasm before he wants to, therefore, would be a candidate for sexual therapy.

A man who is disturbed by his own inability to exert any control over when he ejaculates may develop low self-esteem and performance anxiety (Kaplan, 1989). This, in turn, can lead to an erectile problem (and commonly does). Others may avoid dating new partners because of fear of embarrassment. Some males have attempted to maintain an erection after orgasm by wearing a tight-fitting ring around the base of the penis (a "cockring") to trap the blood, but this can cause damage to the penile tissues and blood vessels.

What causes some men to ejaculate too quickly? In a few cases it may be because they are physically overly sensitive to sexual stimulation (Assalian, 1994; Strassberg et al., 1987). However, it is believed that in most cases it is due to psychological or interpersonal (e.g., anger at one's partner) factors. In addition, many therapists believe that the early sexual experiences of many males actually teach them to rush during sex. Male masturbatory behavior is generally orgasm-oriented anyway, but a male may hurry it even more in situations where he fears being caught. Early heterosexual experiences often occur in places like a car, a parent's or friend's house, or some other place where there is a possibility of discovery, and thus sexual intercourse is hurried. The following therapeutic exercises are designed to teach a man not to hurry during sexual relations. (Premature ejaculation, however, may sometimes result from an attitude of viewing women as sex objects; such men probably would not seek therapy.)

After a couple has completed the sensate focus exercises described earlier in this chapter, the woman is instructed to manually stimulate the man's penis until he gets close to orgasm. She then squeezes his penis firmly between her thumb and index and second fingers for three to five seconds and discontinues stimulation until he calms down. She repeats this three to four times before finally bringing him to orgasm. This *"squeeze technique"* was developed by Masters and Johnson (1970) and is still regarded as the most effective treatment (St. Lawrence & Madakasira, 1992). In a variation of this, called *"stop-start,"* the female partner simply stops manual stimulation and then starts again after the feeling of impending ejaculation has diminished (Semans, 1956). Both these techniques teach the man that he can delay ejaculation, which he can also practice during masturbation. When intercourse resumes, it is in a side-by-side or female-on-top position (it generally takes longer to reach orgasm if you are not in total control).

MALE ORGASMIC DISORDER

This problem can be thought of as just the opposite of premature ejaculation. **Male orgasmic disorder** (formerly called inhibited male orgasm or inhibited ejaculation) refers to a difficulty reaching orgasm and ejaculating in a woman's vagina, and it can be either *primary* or *secondary*. It used

Male orgasmic disorder

A persistent or recurrent delay in, or absence of, orgasm following a normal sexual excitement phase.

to be thought that only 1–2 percent of men suffered with this problem (Apfelbaum, 1980; Masters & Johnson, 1970), but more recent studies indicate that perhaps as many as 4–9 percent of men have this problem on more than just an occasional basis (Spector & Carey, 1990). It is often referred to as **ejaculatory incompetence** if a man is totally unable to ejaculate in a woman's vagina. Although a few cases can be traced to organic causes (e.g., drugs, alcohol, neurological disorders; Munjack & Kanno, 1979), most of these

Ejaculatory incompetence

A condition in which a man is totally unable to ejaculate in a woman's vagina during sexual intercourse.

men are able to reach orgasm either during masturbation or during manual or oral stimulation by the partner (Kaplan, 1979), which indicates that the usual cause is psychological and not physical.

Masters and Johnson (1970) reported that primary inhibited ejaculation is often associated with a strict religious upbringing, a fear of getting a woman pregnant, negativity and hostility toward the partner, and/or maternal dominance. Secondary problems are less common and are often associated with some kind of previous trauma.

Inhibited ejaculation is often treated by what's called a *"bridge maneuver."* The man is first taught to masturbate to orgasm while alone, and then in the presence of the partner. Once this is successfully completed, the partner manually stimulates the male to orgasm. When this is consistently successful, the female partner stimulates the man until he is very close to orgasm and then quickly inserts his penis into her vagina. The idea is that if this can be done several times, the male will overcome his fears of ejaculating inside her vagina.

Headaches After Orgasm

Recently, several studies have brought attention to a problem suffered by some men during sex: severe headaches that start during or slightly after orgasm (see Diamond & Maliszewski, 1992 for several articles). This condition is called **benign coital cephalalgia** (alternative spelling: cephalgia). This is not a new problem, and, in fact, was first reported by Hippocrates, the father of modern medicine, in the fifth century B.C. It has been estimated that as many as 250,000 Americans may presently suffer from this problem. Most are men who are middle-aged, mildly obese, and somewhat hypertensive. The severe headaches may last for minutes or hours. They are not related to exertion or type of sexual activity, and al-

Benign coital cephalalgia
Severe headaches that start during or slightly after orgasm in males.

though physicians sometimes mistake the pains as the sign of an imminent stroke, they are usually not associated with any other serious disorder. The headaches are generally caused by contraction of muscles and/or blood vessels in the head, neck, or upper body during intercourse. For reasons that are not understood, the headaches often disappear for weeks or months at a time and then suddenly reappear. A recent study found that the headaches eventually stop recurring in men who do not also suffer tension headaches or migraines (Ostergaard & Kraft, 1992). Treatment may include the teaching of relaxation techniques or medications for high blood pressure.

Priapism

`" . . . sometimes my erection will stay for hours, which is kind of uncomfortable. . . . "`

(from the author's files)

To many men, the idea of having a *long-lasting erection* might seem appealing. **Priapism** is a rare condition in which the penis remains erect for prolonged periods of time, sometimes days. It results from damage to the valves regulating penile blood flow and can be caused by tumors, infection, or chemical irritants (such as Spanish fly; see Chapter 4). It is not usually accompanied by a desire for sex. Priapism is often painful, not to mention inconvenient, and men with this condition would gladly trade it for a normal erection. Many different treatments have been tried, ranging from ice packs to general anesthesia, but a recent study suggests that administration of the beta-agonist drug terbutaline is most effective (Shantha, Shantha, & Bennett, 1990). ∎

Priapism
A condition in which the penis remains erect for a prolonged period of time (sometimes days).

FEMALE SEXUAL PROBLEMS

Vaginismus

Vaginismus refers to pain experienced during attempted sexual intercourse (intromission). It is caused by *involuntary contractions* of the muscles that surround the outer third of the vagina. Sometimes it is situational and occurs only during attempted intercourse, but in many cases it occurs at attempts to insert anything into the vagina (e.g., a finger or tampon). A pelvic examination may be impossible for women with this condition. To a man attempting intercourse, it feels like his penis is

Vaginismus
A sexual problem in females in which pain is experienced during attempted intercourse because of involuntary muscle spasms in the muscles surrounding the outer third of the vagina.

hitting a wall, and forceful attempts at penetration can be quite painful for the woman.

About 2 percent of women have vaginismus (Renshaw, 1990). The cause is usually *psychological* (Kaplan, 1974). It is normal for inexperienced women to have anxieties before intercourse that may result in some degree of involuntary muscle contraction, but the vast majority of women soon learn to relax (and even gain voluntary control over these muscles). Persistent and recurrent involuntary muscle spasms are often associated with past trauma (e.g., rape, abortion) or negative sexual experiences, religious upbringing (where sex is equated with sin), hostility or fear toward men, or even medical reasons (Masters & Johnson, 1970; Van de

Wiel et al., 1990). Treatment usually consists of sensate focus relaxation exercises followed by *gradual dilation of the vagina* (with a set of dilators, or increasing from one to three fingers). The use of dilators in an atmosphere that is free of sexual demand (so there is no performance anxiety) allows the female to slowly overcome her anxieties about having an object in her vagina. Masters and Johnson (1970) report a 100 percent success rate in treating this problem.

FEMALE ORGASMIC DISORDER

The vast majority of women who go to sexual therapy do so because of problems in reaching orgasm. As with erectile problems, **orgasmic disorder** can be *primary* or

Female orgasmic disorder

A persistent or recurrent delay in, or absence of, orgasm following a normal sexual excitement phase.

absolute (i.e., never had one under any circumstances), *secondary* (i.e., were once regularly orgasmic), or *situational* (e.g., can reach orgasm during masturbation, but not during intercourse). Some men use the term "frigid" to describe such women, but this is an unfortunate term because it has negative connotations about a woman's emotional responsivity. Most women who have orgasm problems are emotionally responsive to sexual stimulation and otherwise enjoy sex.

One of the very first questions to ask, of course, is whether a woman with problems reaching orgasm during sexual intercourse is receiving sufficient stimulation from her partner. Has there been enough time and foreplay?

"My problem seems like one that some of my friends have—short foreplay. It takes me a long time to reach orgasm. When we take a long time and work up slowly to lovemaking, I have intense orgasms. It is wonderful for both of us. But this happens very rarely. Because 'John' works a nine hour work day and usually comes home exhausted, our lovemaking is short and to the point. He's satisfied and I lay there feeling nothing because I faked an orgasm for him. Then, when I insist on continuing, I start to feel guilty for wasting his time."

"I have no trouble reaching climax with my husband, but it takes a long time. How can I get him interested in foreplay so we both can experience enjoyment before intercourse? I don't want him to get bored with me."

(from the author's files)

These responses are apparently not unusual. Remember that in response to a survey question asked in my course ("What things do you personally like best in

a lover?"), well over half of the women who indicated that they were sexually experienced included as one of their answers that they wanted their partner(s) to take his time. Here are some examples:

"Doesn't rush, and takes his time."

"Lover takes his time and is as concerned with fondling and foreplay as he is intercourse."

"Unhurried attitude toward sex and lovemaking in general."

"Be willing to take his time, not hurry."

"Partner who likes to take time with foreplay and not rush into intercourse. A caring and sensitive person who is not out just to get a 'piece of ass.'"

(from the author's files)

A man's first physiological sexual response, you recall, is erection of the penis, which allows him to perform sexually almost immediately, even if he is experiencing very little emotionally. It generally takes women longer to reach orgasm than men (Gebhard, 1966; Kinsey, 1953), and many need additional emotional involvement as well, so that lengthy foreplay is very important for most women.

Even if her partner takes his time, many women may still have difficulties reaching orgasm during intercourse. The key for many women is the degree of stimulation to the clitoris, for most women prefer clitoral stimulation to reach orgasm (with or without vaginal stimulation; Darling, Davidson, & Cox, 1991). During sexual intercourse, the penis only indirectly stimulates the clitoris by causing the clitoral hood to rub back and forth over the clitoral glans. Helen Kaplan (1974) and Shere Hite (1976) have estimated, however, that fewer than half of all women are capable of reaching orgasm regularly during intercourse without more direct stimulation of the clitoris. I have seen numerous letters to magazine advisor columns, for example, written by women who were concerned about their lack of physical sensations during intercourse, particularly in the missionary position. None could reach orgasm during intercourse, but had no trouble during masturbation (with more clitoral stimulation), which indicates that there was nothing physically wrong. A recent letter to the *Playboy* Advisor was written by a woman whose partner refused to give her any type of clitoral stimulation so that she could "learn" how to have a vaginal orgasm.

Unfortunately, many men take the attitude that what feels good to the gander must feel good to the goose—if it feels good to the man to have his penis in his partner's vagina, then it must also feel equally good to the woman to have his penis in her vagina. The stimulation provided by the vaginal walls to the penis during intercourse is similar to that experienced by men during masturbation, but the reverse is not true for women. The inner two thirds of the vagina, you recall, has relatively few nerve endings. Most women who masturbate do so by stimulating their clitoris. Men should not feel inadequate if their female partner requires manual stimulation of the clitoris during intercourse to reach orgasm.

"Your class has also taught me how to talk to my boyfriend about sex. By stimulation of the clitoris manually it has brought great joy to my sex life. I now even reach orgasm from it during sex."

(from the author's files)

If a man cares for his partner, he will do (or let her do) whatever she says feels best, not what he believes ought to feel best. Therapists agree that *clitoral stimulation during intercourse is not cheating.*

Not all cases of female orgasm problems can be blamed on insufficient stimulation. Sex is more than the physical rubbing together of tissues. A healthy positive attitude about sex and pleasure is also very important. Some cases of primary orgasmic dysfunction, for example, are associated with a very strict religious upbringing, where sexual feelings are associated with sin and guilt rather than something positive (Masters & Johnson, 1970; Purcell, 1985).

"I grew up sexually in marriage. In those days no one discussed sex, and my husband and I both only knew bits and pieces. I understood it to be very natural for women not to have orgasms, therefore, if I did, my private Catholic girl school upbringing made me feel ashamed of my own natural desires and pleasures."

"I was a Catholic girl all my life. Throughout school there was always a hidden notion that sex was bad and dirty. Those views and ideas were always instilled in me. It made me feel as if I would die if I engaged in any sexual behavior."

(from the author's files)

Even if not associated with sin, it is a fact that most parents allow less sexual freedom for their daughters than their sons during adolescence. Female sexuality is more likely to be suppressed during this time period than is male sexuality.

"I was told my whole life as a child and as an adolescent that because I was a woman, I was not supposed to feel sexual, or be sexual. My daddy told me that good women who wanted to be loved by a man did not feel sexual. A good man did not look for a woman who was sexual."

(from the author's files)

Sexual suppression generally leads to passivity in sexual relations with a partner. But studies have found that sexually assertive women—those who are active in initiating sex, communicate with their partners about their likes and dislikes and direct sexual activity, and concentrate on themselves—have higher frequencies of sexual activity and orgasms than less assertive women (Hurlbert, 1991). They also generally report greater satisfaction in their relationships. Multi-orgasmic women are generally more explorative in their sexual activities, and more aware of pleasurable sensations of the clitoris via masturbation, than are other women (Darling, Davidson, & Jennings, 1991).

In addition, sex involves sweating, underarm and vaginal odors (and often, vaginal noises), and facial grimaces that many women were taught are unfeminine. To fully enjoy sex and experience the pleasures of orgasm, one must "let go." Simply telling a young woman that sex is now okay is not going to change these attitudes overnight. It may take years to overcome inhibitions about sex.

"I was raised as good girls don't, and if you do you are used property. After getting married, the morals were supposed to change. I had great difficulty in the transition of why it is OK now, after marriage. I am now divorced. I wish I would have had your class prior to marriage. It would have made the transition a lot easier."

(from the author's files)

Kinsey's group (1953), you recall, found that half of all women who masturbated did not start doing so until after the age of 20 (and thus probably after they were sexually experienced). More recent studies have found that married women who have masturbated to orgasm have more orgasms and greater marital and sexual satisfaction than married women who have not masturbated to orgasm (Hurlbert & Whittaker, 1991). In fact, some therapists now include masturbation therapy as a first step in the treatment of inhibited female orgasm in order to make a woman more aware of her own body (Barbach, 1976; LoPiccolo, 1978; LoPiccolo & Stock, 1986).

Performance anxiety can also contribute to orgasm problems. This can easily happen if a woman's partner expects or demands that she have an orgasm during sex. The subsequent spectatoring then makes the problem even worse.

"About orgasms: this is a subject I have trouble with. Almost every guy I've been with tries his hardest to make me have one once he finds out I haven't. They want to be the 'first.' Sex can be repulsive when it is done as a forced series of steps."

(from the author's files)

Just as with erectile dysfunctions, it sometimes takes only a few instances of a woman being unable to reach orgasm for performance anxiety to develop.

"My husband and I have a really good sex life, but I don't reach climax every time. This doesn't bother me, but it really bothers him. I've started worrying about it so much

that I'm now having fewer orgasms and starting to fake more."

(from the author's files)

Women (and their partners) should not expect to reach orgasm with every experience of sexual intercourse. This is an unrealistic expectation that can lead to unnecessary feelings of guilt (Davidson & Moore, 1994).

What are the procedures used in therapy to help a woman become more orgasmic? As explained before, if a woman has always had difficulty reaching orgasm (and particularly if she has never masturbated), the first thing that a therapist is likely to suggest is self-exploration. You don't necessarily need a therapist, but if you have never explored your body and responses before, some type of instruction will probably be necessary. Two books, one by Barbach (1976) and another by Heiman and LoPiccolo (1988), are listed at the end of the chapter as good references.

The next step is exploration with a partner—the widely used and popular sensate focus exercises. These nondemand exercises allow the woman and her partner to relax and learn what gives each maximum pleasure. The hand-riding technique is particularly useful here

FIGURE 13-4   A COMMONLY USED FEMALE TRAINING TECHNIQUE.

BOX 13-A

CROSS-CULTURAL PERSPECTIVES: SEX THERAPY

The model of sex therapy presented in this chapter is based primarily on Western, middle-class values (Lavee, 1991). The two most important assumptions in the model are that people engage in sex primarily for (physical) pleasure, and that men and women are viewed as equals. It assumes also that men and women want to know about sex and that better communication makes for better sex.

Not all cultures share these attitudes. Recall from Box 4-A, for example, that in large parts of northern Africa and the Middle East (primarily Islamic populations) sexual pleasure is reserved for the males and women's pleasure is denied by clitoral circumcision and genital mutilation (Giorgis, 1981; Hosken, 1989). Many Latin countries are also male-dominant to the point of denying females' sexual feelings (Guerrero Pavich, 1986). In these cultures, a woman's difficulty in reaching orgasm is not considered to be important, and certainly no grounds for therapy. Even painful intercourse (dyspareunia, vaginismus) is considered unimportant unless it interferes with a woman's ability to engage in sex. For women, the only purpose of sex is procreation and the pleasure of their husband. For men, ``premature'' ejaculation is not regarded as a problem. Men do regard difficulty in getting and maintaining an erection as a problem, but both men and women refuse the very idea of engaging in sensate focus exercises as a solution, for this is a mutual pleasuring technique (Lavee, 1991).

In sharp contrast to these attitudes (and our own) about sex, are those held by many Hindu and Buddhist societies (Voigt, 1991). Tantric scriptures urge people to strive for the goal of transcendent unity and harmony, and thus sex is viewed as an opportunity for spiritual growth. While Western therapists emphasize mutual physical pleasures of sex, these Asian societies emphasize the spiritual union. For example, in this chapter orgasm is presented as resulting from proper physical stimulation and effective technique. Those who follow Tantrism, on the other hand, ``understand orgasm as a product of deep relaxation and a profound level of contact between partners.'' Western culture emphasizes doing, stimulation, activation, and outcome-focus, while Tantrism emphasizes being, stillness, meditation, and process-immersion. Good sex is not achieved by focusing on one or the other partner, but by focusing on the *between*. Couples might be urged to follow five exercises (Voigt, 1991): (1) creation of a ceremonial sex ritual (a simple ceremony that sets the tone for shared sexual expression—for example, candles, flowers, a special room, massage, chanting together or joint meditation); (2) synchronized breathing while embracing or touching; (3) sustained, steady eye contact; (4) becoming motionless at the peak sensual experience during intercourse; and (5) refraining from orgasm at times in order to intensify the sexual-spiritual energy.

Sex therapy as we know it is geared, obviously, for our particular cultural beliefs, and perhaps for only part of our society. Nonwhite people, for example, are much less interested in going to sex therapy for an acknowledged sex problem than are white people (Perez, Mulligan, & Wan, 1993). This may be due, in part, to a distrust of mental-health professionals (Wilson, 1986), but may also reflect different cultural attitudes about sex. Lavee (1991) has suggested that rather than trying to teach all people what healthy sex is (based on Western, middle-class values), therapists would be wiser to fit the treatment to the individuals' cultural values. ∎

(Masters & Johnson, 1970). After several days of this, the therapist will probably instruct the partner to manually explore the woman's genitals, usually while both are sitting in the position shown in Figure 13-4. (Some therapists may first have the woman stimulate her own genitals in front of her partner, but this often requires that she get over a great deal of inhibitions.)

When the couple is finally instructed that they may resume sexual intercourse, they will almost always be told to use a position that allows the woman a great deal of control, such as woman-on-top. She will decide when intromission begins and initiate pelvic movements once they start. By this point in therapy, both she and her partner will be comfortable with manual stimulation of the clitoris during intercourse. Helen Kaplan (1974) has suggested that couples at first interrupt intercourse with periods of additional foreplay, but contrary to advice given in a recent popular book (Eichel & Nobile, 1992), no particular technique of intercourse can guarantee orgasms (Kaplan, 1992b). The couple will have to try different techniques. With some practice, for example, the woman might be able to reach orgasm without manual stimulation by rubbing her clitoris against her partner's pubic bone, or vice-versa (in a "high-ride" position).

What you have just read is the standard therapy program. However, at this point I should also mention another exercise that is sometimes used in addition to (not as a substitute for) the above steps. Recall from Chapter 2 that women with weak pubococcygeus (PC) muscles (the muscle that surrounds the vagina and bladder) generally have little or no vaginal sensations during intercourse, while women with strong PC muscles generally report pleasurable vaginal

sensations (Kegel, 1952). As a result, some sex therapists have advocated daily exercises, called **Kegel exercises**, to strengthen these muscles in order to enhance orgasmic responsiveness (Barbach, 1976; Graber, 1982; Perry & Whipple, 1981), although others have expressed doubt (Sultan & Chambles, 1982; Trudel & Saint Laurent, 1983). These are the same exercises that physicians advise women to do after childbirth in order to regain bladder control; so learning them will be useful to most women even if many find they do not enhance orgasmic responsiveness. Instructions for how to do Kegel exercises are given in Chapter 2.

If at this point you are thinking that female orgasm problems have been treated rather mechanically, as if the solution is nothing more than finding the correct manner of physical stimulation, you are probably right. For many women, sexual satisfaction is closely related to how emotionally involved they are with their partners and how happy they are in their overall relationships (Hurlbert & Whittaker, 1991; Newcomb & Bentler, 1983). These things are better predictors of women's sexual satisfaction than are frequency of sex and number of orgasms (Hurlbert, Apt, & Rabehl, 1993). Conversely, the better a woman regards her emotional relationship with her partner, the more likely she will judge her sex life to be satisfying (Darling et al., 1991; Rosenzweig & Dailey, 1989). In other words, for many women the therapy steps outlined in this section may do little good if the emotional aspects of their relationships are not satisfying. ∎

> **Kegel excercises**
> Exercises that are designed to strengthen the pubococcygeus muscle that surrounds the bladder and vagina.

SEXUAL PROBLEMS AMONG HOMOSEXUALS

Like some heterosexuals, homosexuals sometimes suffer from sexual problems, and they also seek sex therapy to deal with them. However, the types of problems and the focus of therapy is often different for homosexual men and women. Heterosexuals generally go to therapy for problems related to sexual intercourse, but homosexuals seeking sex therapy often have problems that arise from dealing with HIV and AIDS and/or homophobic attitudes within society, which in some cases become internalized (Friedman, 1991; Margolies et al., 1988; Nichols, 1988; Reece, 1988; Shannon & Woods, 1991). These can lead to depression (or in the case of internalized homophobia, repression of sexuality) and consequent loss of sexual desire. Orgasm problems are not common among lesbians, but many lesbians who go to therapy have nega-

tive feelings about engaging in cunnilingus (Margolies et al., 1988). Similarly, many gay men in therapy have negative feelings about anal sex (Reece, 1988).

Masters and Johnson (1979) reported a 93 percent success rate for treating erectile disorders in male homosexuals as well as anorgasmia in lesbians. Sensate focus exercises used with heterosexuals are similarly used with homosexuals. In fact, the success rate for homosexuals is generally higher than that for heterosexuals. This may be due to the fact that members of the same sex may be more understanding of the needs and pleasurable experiences of homosexual partners. In any case, an understanding partner who is sympathetic, willing to communicate, and not overly demanding is crucial to successful sex therapy for both heterosexual and homosexual individuals. ∎

AVOIDING SEXUAL PROBLEMS

What have you learned in this and previous chapters that you could apply to your own life to minimize the chance of occurrence of sexual problems?

First, establish an open, honest line of communication with your partner. Although you should learn to accentuate and reinforce the positive aspects of your relationship, this does not mean that you cannot say "no." A sexually heathy person, you remember, is free to make choices, but you must work any differences out with your partner.

In order to communicate, we must be properly educated. Sexual therapy, in fact, is really just sex education combined with a medical exam and counseling. Why did you have to wait until your age to receive a sex education? When you have children, teach them the proper names for their body parts and instruct them about sexuality in such a way that they will grow up to think of the human body as something beautiful and good. A good sex life can contribute to a healthy and satisfying life. You can treat sexuality as something positive while at the same time teaching morals and sexual responsibility. Whatever you do, never equate sex with sin and guilt.

In the relationship with your partner, try to learn and grow together. Remember, a good relationship with your partner (e.g., sharing and caring) often carries over into sexual relations. Keep your sexual relations spontaneous and fun and do *not* set goals as if sex were an Olympic event. Do not focus on orgasm. Enjoy touching for touching's sake—it doesn't always have to immediately lead to sexual intercourse.

KEY TERMS

benign coital cephalalgia   320
cognitive-behavioral
    therapy   308
dyspareunia   314
ejaculatory incompetence   319
erectile disorder   314
female orgasmic disorder   321
hypersexuality   313
hypoactive sexual desire   311
Kegel exercises   35, 325
male orgasmic disorder   319

medical history   309
performance anxiety   317
phimosis   314
PLISSIT model   309
premature ejaculation   318
priapism   320
primary sexual problem   314, 321
psychosexual therapy   309
secondary sexual
    problem   314, 321
self-awareness   309

sensate focus   310
sexual addiction   313
sexual aversion   311
sexual history   309
sexual surrogate   311
situational sexual problem   314
spectatoring   317
systematic desensitization   309
vaginismus   320

PERSONAL REFLECTIONS

1. Are you able to comfortably communicate your sexual values and needs to your sexual partner or potential partner? If not, what barriers are preventing you from doing so? Do you create any barriers that may prevent your partner from comfortably communicating his or her sexual values and needs to you?

2. What do you do when your partner desires sex and you are not in the mood? What would you expect your partner to do if you desired sex and he or she wasn't in the mood? Why? Have you ever pretended to be tired or feeling poorly to avoid sex with your partner? Have you ever faked an orgasm? If so, why? Do you think that responses like these are the best way to communicate with your partner about sexual needs?

3. Stop and reflect on the physical interactions you have with your partner(s). In most of your interactions, are you able to engage in extended nongenital touching and caressing of your partner, or are you usually in a hurry to achieve some immediate genital/breast touching? Is your partner able to caress your arms, legs, neck, etc. without you quickly attempting to steer the behavior toward sexual play? Why or why not?

4. Almost all people experience sexual dysfunction at some point in their lives. If you were in an ongoing relationship and were consistently experiencing a problem, would you go to a sex therapist? Why? How

long would you wait before you decided to go? Most therapists believe that the earlier therapy is initiated, the better the chance for a cure.

5. Have you ever experienced performance anxiety during sexual relations (e.g., anxiety about pleasing your partner, maintaining erection, reaching orgasm)? If so, what do you think is the cause of the anxiety?

6. Are you able to "let go" totally during sex (i.e., no anxieties about nudity, sweat, odors, noises, facial expressions, etc.)? If not, why?

7. If you are in an ongoing sexual relationship, what do you do to ensure against the boredom that can arise if sex is allowed to fall into a predictable routine (Saturday night, after the news, same position, etc)?

SUGGESTED READINGS

Barbach, L. G. (1975). *For yourself: The fulfillment of female sexuality.* Garden City, NY: Doubleday. Discusses orgasmic problems in women.

Barbach, L. G. (1982). *For each other: Sharing sexual intimacy.* New York: Anchor/Doubleday.

Belliveau, F., and Richter, L. (1970). *Understanding human sexual inadequacy.* New York: Bantam. An easy-to-read review of Masters and Johnson's work.

The Boston Women's Health Book Collective. (1984). *The new our bodies, ourselves: A book by and for women.* New York: Simon & Schuster.

Cohen, S. S. (1987, April). The power of touch. *New Woman.* Discusses the importance of touching for enhancing intimacy.

Heiman, J., and LoPiccolo, J. (1988). *Becoming orgasmic: A sexual growth program for women.* Englewood Cliffs, NJ: Prentice Hall.

Kaplan, H. (1975). *The illustrated manual of sex therapy.* New York: Quadrangle-New York Times. Easy to read and tastefully written.

Kaplan, H. S. (1989). *PE: How to overcome premature ejaculation.* New York: Bruner/Mazel.

Masters, W. H., Johnson, V. E., and Kolodny, R. C. (1986, July). Masters and Johnson's new guide to better loving. *Redbook.* Sixteen tips to improve your sexual relations.

Schnarch, D. (1991). *Constructing the sexual crucible: An integration of sexual and marital therapy.* New York: W. W. Norton. Written for the professional, this book has had an amazing crossover success with the general public.

Switzer, E. (1984, November). Orgasm—beyond the myths. *Ladies Home Journal.* Discusses the physiological, psychological, and sociological aspects of female orgasm as well as therapy.

Thayer, S. (1988, March). Close encounters. *Psychology Today.* Explores the role of touching in intimate relationships and examines gender and cultural differences.

Zilbergeld, B. (1978). *Male sexuality: A guide to sexual fulfillment.* Boston: Little, Brown. A readable book about male sexuality and overcoming problems.

CHAPTER FOURTEEN

PARAPHILIAS AND SEXUAL VARIANTS

WHEN YOU HAVE FINISHED STUDYING THIS CHAPTER, YOU SHOULD BE ABLE TO:

1. DESCRIBE THE VARIOUS WAYS ONE CAN DEFINE A BEHAVIOR AS BEING UNCONVENTIONAL (I.E., STATISTICAL, SOCIOLOGICAL, AND PSYCHOLOGICAL APPROACHES);

2. EXPLAIN THE DIFFERENCE BETWEEN A SEXUAL VARIANT AND A PARAPHILIA;

3. DEFINE AND DISCUSS THE FOLLOWING PARAPHILIAS: FETISHISM, TRANSVESTISM, EXHIBITIONISM AND OBSCENE PHONE CALLS, VOYEURISM, ZOOPHILIA, PEDOPHILIA, SADISM, MASOCHISM, UROPHILIA, COPROPHILIA, MYSOPHILIA, FROTTEURISM, KLISMAPHILIA, AND NECROPHILIA;

4. DISCUSS THE VARIOUS THEORIES OF HOW PARAPHILIAS DEVELOP; AND

5. DISCUSS THE TREATMENT (THERAPY) FOR INDIVIDUALS WITH A PARAPHILIA.

THERE ARE ENORMOUS INDIVIDUAL DIFFERENCES AMONG PEOPLE IN EVERY ASPECT OF HUMAN BEHAVIOR. It should be obvious from the many references to other cultures in previous chapters that this includes sexual behavior as well. Variety in behavior is usually considered to be good. We enjoy wearing different clothing, eating different foods, listening to different kinds of music, and as you learned in Chapter 11, most of us enjoy practicing a variety of sexual behaviors.

What determines whether a behavior is designated "normal" or "conventional" versus "abnormal" or "unconventional"? What is normal or conventional is not always easy to define. Most of us would probably agree that someone who ate beetles was abnormal, but this is common in some African cultures. Obviously, cultural factors must be considered. Even within the same culture, what is believed to be normal today may not have been viewed as normal in the past, and may not be viewed as normal in the future. Here's an example. If a woman wears a string bikini on the beach today, she is considered normal. But if a woman living in 1900 had worn that outfit to a beach, she would have been arrested. The kindest treatment that she might have received would have been treatment for an illness. On the other hand, if a woman wore a full-length swimsuit with bloomers to the beach today (the typical swimwear for American women in 1900), she might be considered sexually inhibited. Similarly, a man or woman can walk naked in New Orleans' French Quarter on Mardi Gras day and get pinched a lot, but not arrested. However, if he or she walked naked down the same streets the day before or the day after Mardi Gras, the person would be arrested.

Even at the same point in time, normal behavior might be a matter of where it is observed. If someone tried to sunbathe in the nude at the local public swimming pool, he or she would probably be arrested. If this same person was sunning himself or herself on certain beaches on the West or East coasts, on the other hand, he or she could walk in naked splendor alongside a whole beach full of other naked people. When does such behavior start being normal—before getting to the beach, after getting to the beach, never, or always? Again, the point is that "normal" is not an absolute thing. It can be determined by many factors, including where you are and when you are there.

Researchers have generally attempted to define "normal" or "abnormal" in one of three ways. One way is called the *statistical approach*, in which a behavior is considered normal or conventional if a large number of people engage in it, and abnormal or unconventional if only a few people do it (Pomeroy, 1966). Some professionals who use the statistical approach do not use the terms "abnormal" or "uncon-

ventional" to describe behaviors, and instead use the label "sexual minorities" (Gagnon, 1977). There are, of course, some rather large minorities, and there are some behaviors that are so different that they represent a minority of one. However, the fact that only a minority of people have engaged in a behavior does not necessarily make that behavior bad or wrong, or the individuals disturbed or sick. Probably only a small minority of people in our culture, for example, have ever had sex outdoors (in private) at night under the stars, but most would agree that doing so would certainly not be a sign of mental illness. Because of the limitations of this approach—defining normal and abnormal purely in terms of numbers—others have preferred a sociological or psychological approach.

The *sociological approach* calls a behavior unconventional if it is not customary within a society. Customs vary not only from culture to culture, but also within subcultures at the same time. Followers of this approach are concerned with the social conditions that give rise to abnormal behavior as well as the interaction of people labeled abnormal with the rest of society.

The *psychological approach* focuses on the psychological health of the individual and the impact that behaviors have on this health (Buss, 1966). A sexual activity is considered to be a problem behavior if it makes an individual feel distressed or guilty, or causes problems functioning efficiently in ordinary social and occupational roles.

This chapter will focus primarily on the psychological approach. Let us now take a look at how the psychiatric/psychological profession has dealt with the subject of sexual abnormalities.

HISTORICAL PERSPECTIVE

In the Victorian era, sexual behaviors that were considered abnormal were referred to as "perversions" and later as "deviations." The first classification of sexual deviations was made by Richard von Krafft-Ebing in 1886 (*Psychopathia Sexualis*). His work was based on genetic predisposition, and although it is now discredited, his case histories are still widely cited.

Sigmund Freud believed that any type of sexual behavior that took precedence over heterosexual vaginal intercourse was an indication of impaired psychosexual development. A person's sexual behavior was considered deviant if it was not directed toward an appropriate object (heterosexual partner) and/or the aim was not sexual intercourse. By this system, masturbation and oral-genital sex were considered very disturbed. (This is another, excellent example of how what is considered abnormal depends on the time and culture.)

Today, the American Psychiatric Association's handbook *Diagnostic and Statistical Manual of Mental Disorders* (DSM-IV, 1994) refers to psychosexual

Paraphilias

General term for a group of unusual behaviors upon which a person's sexual arousal and gratification depend almost exclusively.

disorders (of the type considered in this chapter) as **paraphilias**, derived from the Greek *para* (meaning "besides," "beyond," or "amiss") and *philia* ("love"). Not all statistically or sociologically unusual behaviors are paraphilias. For a person's behavior to be called a paraphilia, the distinguishing feature is that *the person's sexual arousal and gratification must depend almost exclusively* on engaging in or thinking (fantasizing) about the behavior. The essential features of a paraphilia are that the fantasies and behaviors are recurrent (American Psychiatric Association DSM-IV, 1994). As you read through the chapter, there will probably be one or more behaviors covered that you have either fantasized about or engaged in yourself (e.g., voyeurism, exhibitionism, S & M). This does not mean you have a paraphilia. It is a paraphilia if that is the preferred way in which you become sexually aroused. Otherwise, behaviors and fantasies are generally referred to as **sexual variants** (Stoller, 1977).

Some of the paraphilias covered in this chapter can result in physical harm to oneself (e.g., masochism) or physical or psychological harm to others (e.g., sadism, exhibitionism, voyeurism, pedophilia). Others can lead to arrest and prosecution. However, some would appear to be harmless: transvestism (cross-dressing) in the privacy of one's own home, for example. Some clinicians argue that harmless behaviors (this assumes that the behavior is engaged in without feelings of guilt, shame, or remorse) should not have a negative label, but others say that no paraphilia is harmless because, as the only source of sexual gratification, it deprives the individual of physically affectionate relations with others.

The following sections cover many, but not all, paraphilias. The chapter concludes with a discussion of causes and treatments. ■

Sexual variant

For an individual, statistically or sociologically unusual behaviors that are engaged in for variety and not as one's preferred manner of becoming sexually aroused.

FETISHISM

In anthropology, a fetish is an object that is believed to have magical powers (usually by capturing or embodying a powerful spirit). The term **erotic fetishism**

Fetishism

A condition in which sexual arousal occurs primarily when using or thinking about an inanimate object or a particular part of the body (such as the feet).

was devised by Alfred Binet (inventor of the first standardized intelligence test) in 1888. It refers to achieving sexual arousal and gratification *almost exclusively* by handling or fantasizing about an inanimate object or a particular part of the body. Some of the more common fetishes involve women's undergarments (panties, bras, or stockings), shoes (usually high-heeled) or boots, hair, objects made of leather or rubber, and feet. Fetishes to hard objects (such as boots, leather or rubber objects) are often associated with sadomasochistic practices and fantasies. Heterosexual male fetishists are aroused by the theme of "femininity" in their preferred object, while homosexual male fetishists are aroused by the theme of "masculinity" in the preferred objects (Weinberg, Williams, & Calhan, 1994).

The large majority of known fetishists are men, and when their fetish involves clothing or shoes they greatly prefer articles that have been used and have an odor. A man with a panty fetish, for example, would become highly aroused by a used pair of panties that retained vaginal odor, but would probably find little arousal with the same panties if they were clean.

❝ I work at a department store. One night I was folding towels when a man came over and started asking silly questions like, 'How often do you put rugs on sale?' I noticed that while he was talking, he kept glancing at my feet. He asked me where I got my shoes and if the inside was soft. He also asked if they held an odor. Not thinking, I said 'no' and took off a shoe. By this time, he had knelt down, picked up the shoe, and smelled it several times. He then gave it back and immediately left the store. Since my experience, he has been back in the store twice and has done the same thing to two other girls.❞

❝ I know a married man in his late twenties who has a fetish. He goes around asking women (the ones he has affairs with) for a pair of their dirty underwear.❞

(from the author's files)

I chose to cover fetishism first because it provides an excellent example of the difference between a paraphilia and a variant. Most heterosexual males are aroused by female panties, and many men have purchased sheer, lacy lingerie items for their partners from places like Victoria's Secret. Most men have preferences about a partner's anatomy (breasts, buttocks, legs, shoulders), and many have sucked their partner's toes. For the large majority of men, none of these are the end goal; they are used to enhance sexual activity with their partners, not to compete with them. Thus, these activities are considered normal variants—they fall within the normal range of behavior. The fetishist, on the other hand, is focused exclusively on the object (e.g., panties) or body part (e.g., toes). The partner's personality or body (as a whole) cannot sustain arousal; her only role is to serve as a vehicle to enact the fantasy. In its most extreme form, the fetishist doesn't need (or desire) the partner at all. The extreme panty fetishist, for example, is completely gratified by stealing (from a laundromat perhaps) and masturbating with used pairs of women's panties.

Sexual arousal to specific objects or body parts is often explained in terms of classical conditioning (other explanations will be considered later).Consider, for example, heterosexual males' arousal by female panties. Most males' first exposure to female panties comes during early necking or petting experiences, at which time they are highly sexually aroused. A few associations of panties with this emotional state, and panties themselves, elicit some degree of arousal. A demonstration of this process was provided several years ago (Rachman, 1966). Under laboratory condi-tions, males were shown pictures of women's boots paired with pictures of nude women. After many pairings, pictures of the boots alone elicited sexual arousal (measured by penile blood volume). Some clinicians have suggested that sexual arousal to an object (or body part) could develop into a fetish by a person repeatedly including the object in fantasies during mas-turbation. Many men with fetishes were first attracted to their desired objects at an early age (e.g., Gosselin & Wilson, 1980; Tollison & Adams, 1979), perhaps as a result of the object being associated with some of their first experiences of sexual arousal.

How common is fetishism? We don't really know; fetishists rarely are arrested or seek therapy on their own. However, in a recent survey by Janus and Janus (1993) of people's attitudes about fetishes, 22 percent of men and 18 percent of women said that they thought fetishes were either "very normal" or "all right" (as opposed to "unusual," "kinky," or "never heard of it"). Fewer than 2 percent said that this was their preferred way to achieve orgasm. ∎

TRANSVESTISM

"He was an officer in the army (respected by his fellow officers and men), a devoted hus-band, and a father. He also wore women's clothing at home, often passing as a female rel-ative, and was known as "aunt" to his child when he assumed his womanly role." (cited in Hirschfeld, 1948, pp. 174–78)

Transvestism (from the Latin *trans*, meaning "across," and *vestia*, meaning "dress") refers to dressing as a member of the opposite sex *in order to achieve sexual arousal and gratification*. Most researchers regard it as very similar to a cloth-ing fetish, except that the clothing is worn rather than just held and looked at (Pomeroy, 1975). Cross-dressing is not considered to be an example of transvestism if it is done for fashion (as in the case of most women who dress in "men's" clothing), as a party costume or as an act (fe-male impersonators, for example), or as part of trans-sexualism (in which case individuals cross-dress not for sexual arousal, but because they believe themselves to be members of the opposite sex). It also is not con-sidered transvestism if it is done for the purpose of at-tracting members of the same sex. (Men who have a sexual interest in cross-dressed men constitute a much less common, lesser known, paraphilia called *gynandromorphophilia*; Blanchard & Collins, 1993.)

Two surveys of transvestites, one of subscribers to a magazine for transvestites (Prince & Bentler, 1972) and the other of members of a transvestite club (Buhrich, 1976), found that the large majority were heterosexual men and most were married. Similar results have been found in smaller, clinical studies (Talamini, 1982; Wise & Meyer, 1980). A few men completely cross-dress as women and walk about in public for short periods of time, but most transvestites cross-dress in the privacy of their own homes. Many wear only female undergarments during their cross-dressing. The transvestite may masturbate during a cross-dressing episode or during fantasies of cross-dressing, or may use the experience to become aroused enough to have sex with a partner. Although a few wives of transvestites support their husbands' behav-iors, most only tolerate it and many are distressed and resent it (Brown & Collier, 1989; Weinberg & Bul-lough, 1988, Wise, Dupkin, & Meyer, 1981).

Transvestism

> A condition in which sexual arousal is achieved primarily by dressing as a member of the opposite sex.

FIGURE 14-1   HENRY HYDE, GOVERNOR OF NEW YORK (1702–1709), CHOSE TO HAVE HIS PORTRAIT PAINTED WHILE DRESSED IN FEMALE CLOTHING.

BOX 14-A

CROSS-CULTURAL PERSPECTIVES: THE NATIVE AMERICAN TWO-SPIRIT

Berdache

In North American Indian tribes of past centuries a person, usually a male, who assumed the dress, occupations, and behavior of the other sex in order to effect a change in gender status. The term two-spirit is now preferred over berdache.

Two-spirit

The term preferred by Native Americans and anthropologists for berdache.

Before the influence of Western culture led to their disappearance, there existed among many North American Indian tribes individuals, known until recently as berdaches, who had special gender status. According to Callender and Kochems (1987), a *berdache* was ``a person, usually male, who was anatomically normal but assumed the dress, occupations, and behavior of the other sex to effect a change in gender status.'' Accounts of berdaches date back to the 1500s (Katz, 1976) and they existed in at least 113 groups that extended from California to the Mississippi Valley and upper Great Lakes (list compiled by Callender and Kochems, 1987).

Early observations were heavily influenced by Western values and perceptions and focused primarily on the homosexuality or bisexuality of many of the berdaches. In fact, the word berdache is not an Indian term, but is a medieval French term meaning ``male homosexual.'' According to Callender and Kochems, homosexuality didn't bestow the status of berdache on an individual, but many berdaches became homosexual. Translation of the Indian terms give ``halfman-halfwoman'' or ``man-woman,'' with no insinuation about sexuality. Native Americans, as well as anthropologists, are presently urging that scholars use the term **"two-spirit"** or terms within native languages when referring to these individuals (see Jacobs & Thomas, 1994).

The two-spirits were held in awe and highly revered, but were not chiefs or religious leaders (they were not shamans). Individuals became two-spirits by showing a strong interest in the work of the opposite sex during childhood and/or (and more commonly) by having a supernatural vision during adolescence that confirmed the change in gender status. In almost all groups, a male two-spirit dressed and fixed his hair like women and assumed their occupations, at which he excelled—part of the reason he was admired. On certain occasions, he dressed like and assumed the role of a man. He was generally responsible for burial rituals, but because he could cross back and forth between genders, he was especially valued as a go-between for men and women. It was these exceptional gender-mixing abilities that led to him being greatly admired. But, as noted, Western values intervened. Lurie (1953), who studied the Winnebago Indians, reported, for example, that ``most informants felt that the two-spirit was at one time a highly honored and respected person, but that the Winnebago had become ashamed of the custom because the white people thought it was amusing or evil.'' ■

How many transvestites are there in the United States? Enough so that there exists an entire transvestite subculture with clubs, magazines, and newsletters (transvestites generally identify themselves in underground newspapers by the abbreviation TV). In a recent survey, 2 percent of men felt that cross-dressing was "very normal" and 6 percent thought it was "all right" (Janus & Janus, 1993).

Why do some men dress in women's clothing? Transvestites are a very diverse group. What they have in common is a "comforting fantasy of the self as a girl or woman" (Levine, 1993). Most transvestites started cross-dressing by the time they were 9 years old (Buhrich, 1976; Croughan et al., 1981), but then most children have experiences of cross-dressing (remember, children do not acquire the concept of gender constancy until about age 7—see Chapter 8—so most young boys will dress up as both mom and dad). Is there anything that distinguishes the early childhood cross-dressing experiences of transvestites from those of others? Some transvestites report that they were punished by being made to dress as girls (Stoller,

1977), while some were encouraged to dress as girls (Bullough, Bullough, & Smith, 1983). Some clinicians believe that transvestism arises at an early age through association of opposite-sex clothing with sexual arousal (in the same manner as fetishes are acquired). However, explanations for transvestism (or for why there are many more male transvestites than female ones) range from the psychoanalytic (an attempt to conquer castration fears), to anthropological-economic (Munroe, 1980), to neurological (right-brain, left-brain differences; Flor-Henry, 1987), to the sociobiological (Wilson, 1987). ∎

"Sometimes I think you married me for my clothes!"

(Cartoon by Bill Hoest ©1987. Reprinted courtesy of Bill Hoest and *PARADE* Magazine.)

EXHIBITIONISM

"One day at sunset, I was walking back to my car in the . . . parking lot. As I was opening my car door I glanced over at the car facing mine. . . . This man was almost in a back-bend over his driver seat masturbating at full speed. For a moment I was stunned and shocked. I just got in my car and drove off."

(from the author's files)

In today's society, exposure of the body is highly glamorized and commercialized--in movies and television, books and magazines, and advertisements. Many people, including many celebrities, have posed naked for magazines, and some even star in sexually explicit films or "topless-bottomless" stage shows. Some of you may have gone to a nudist colony at one time or another. However, none of these are examples of exhibitionism because they involve willing observers. **Exhibitionism** (or "indecent exposure") is defined as exposing one's genitals to *involuntary* observers in order to obtain sexual arousal and gratification. Some of you may have even "mooned" someone on occasion or participated in streaking (at one time, a popular college prank). Although these involve involuntary observers, these acts are also generally considered apart from exhibitionism, for another characteristic of exhibitionists is that they engage in the behavior *compulsively*.

Exhibitionism

Exposing one's genitals compulsively in inappropriate settings to obtain sexual gratification.

Most victims of exhibitionists ("flashers") are women or children. Some studies have found that as many as 33 to 44 percent of women have been the victim of exhibitionism on at least one occasion (Cox, 1988; Gittelson, Eacott, & Melita, 1978). One fifth of the victims found the experience to be very distressing (one can only assume that a greater percentage of children would be distressed).

Although there have been a few reported cases of females exposing their genitals (Grob, 1985; Hollender, Brown, & Roback, 1977), almost all exhibitionists are men. Most are in their twenties or thirties and half or slightly more either are or have been married (Gebhard et al., 1965). The large majority of these men are described as shy and/or personally immature, but otherwise without serious emotional or mental disorders. They typically feel inadequate and insecure, fear rejection, and have problems forming close, intimate (including sexual) relations (Blair & Lanyon, 1981; Marshall, 1989; Marshall, Eccles, & Barbaree, 1991).

Lance Rentzel was a star wide receiver for the Dallas Cowboys professional football team and had recently married one of the top, young actresses in Hollywood. The Cowboys were headed to the Superbowl in 1970, but on November 19 while in the middle of a slump, Lance exposed himself to a ten-year-old girl. The media soon discovered that he had been arrested for the same thing four years earlier while playing for the Minnesota Vikings—and in the midst of another personal slump. Lance had always been a hero on the football field and felt that he had to be highly successful to please his family. In his autobiography and account of his exhibitionism, Lance says that he felt pressure to prove his masculinity over and over again, and as part of this he avoided close, intimate relations with women (and instead, proved his masculinity to himself by sexual conquests of women). During times of stress, when he wasn't a "winner," Lance resorted to exposing himself as a way to prove his masculinity.

(Summarized from Rentzel, 1972,
*When All the Laughter Died
in Sorrow*)

Although most exhibitionists are of normal or above-normal intelligence, some cases of exhibitionism occur among people who are intellectually impaired, by birth, neurological disorder, or age. In these cases, the cause is usually an inability to distinguish what society considers (or the individual previously considered) to be right and wrong.

Only about half of exhibitionists have erections while exposing themselves, and they may or may not masturbate during the act (Langevin et al., 1979). But they usually do masturbate shortly afterwards while fantasizing about the experience, and their erotic turn-on is directly related to the victim's reaction of shock, disgust, and fear (Blair & Lanyon, 1981). Exhibitionists rarely attempt to molest their victims (American Psychiatric Association, DSM-IV, 1994); thus, the best response (if you are ever a victim) is to give no facial or verbal reaction while leaving the scene and then report it immediately. Interestingly, many exhibitionists compulsively expose themselves in the same location; perhaps the danger

FIGURE 14-2   WALKING ON THE BEACH NAKED MIGHT SEEM UNUSUAL AND UNACCEPTABLE TO YOU, BUT IF IT IS NOT DONE IN FRONT OF OBSERVERS, IT IS A SEXUAL VARIANT, NOT A PARAPHILIA.

of being caught increases the arousal (Stoller, 1977). As a result, they are the most frequently caught paraphiliac offender, comprising about one third of all arrests for sexual offense. ∎

OBSCENE PHONE CALLS

" . . . The calls came three to four times a night. The caller would make obscene suggestions about his penis, oral sex, and bondage, and say that he was 'masturbating to the sound of my voice and the thought of my pussy.' Then he would start moaning. I was very shocked and disgusted. . . . "

(from the author's files)

Many of you may have made an obscene telephone call as a prank during adolescence. Although inappropriate, this is different from the paraphiliac phone caller who makes obscene calls as his primary source of sexual arousal and gratification. **Telephone scatologia**, as it is called, is considered a kind of exhibitionism (unique to the twentieth century, of course; Matek, 1988). Similar to exhibitionists, the scatologist's arousal is proportionate to the victim's reaction of disgust, shock, and fear and the sense of control it gives him.

Telephone
scatologia

A condition in which sexual arousal is achieved primarily by making obscene telephone calls.

In April, 1990, the president of American University resigned after police traced obscene phone calls to his office phone. His victims were women who had advertised home day-care services in the local newspaper. He had degrees from Ivy League schools and was a well-known civic activist who had appeared on television hundreds of times as a spokesman for higher education.

(*Newsweek*, May 7 and
June 11, 1990)

What can explain behavior like this on the part of an intelligent (and in this case, prominent) individual? Telephone scatologists feel inadequate and insecure and have difficulty keeping normal sexual relations, much like exhibitionists, you recall (Nadler, 1968). They compulsively use the telephone for sexual interactions —it is safe (until recently anyway), distant, and avoids intimacy. Of those who have been caught, a rather high proportion were sexually abused as children, as was the case for the university president (Gelman, 1990).

There are over one million obscene phone calls reported to the phone companies or police each year in the United States. Some callers boast about themselves, some just breathe heavily, while others express their sexual intentions, sometimes in the form of threats. Some use the guise of taking a survey to get the victim to talk about herself. Many obscene callers know the name of their victims, which can make the experience particularly frightening to the victim. It is rare, however, for scatologists to molest (or even approach) their victims. They prefer to keep their distance and masturbate either during or after the call.

If you should ever be a victim, the best advice is to say nothing and hang up *immediately* (remember, the scatologist is aroused by your reactions; even slamming the phone down can give him reinforcement). If the calls persist, your telephone company will cooperate in helping the police trace calls. Ask your phone company about Call Trace, a new technology that allows the phone company to instantly record the source of a call made to you. Today, telephone caller ID machines are making obscene phone calls an increasingly risky behavior. When the caller is identified, do not be surprised if he turns out to be someone you know or have met; that is often the case. ∎

VOYEURISM

" Last month, I was sitting on my bed and I saw a shadow move across my window. I reluctantly peeked through the blinds and there was this man stroking his penis. . . . Last night I got a phone call from a neighbor telling me someone was looking in my window. I reported it. Apparently, they've been trying to catch this guy for a while. I'm very frightened right now."

(from the author's files)

What is a voyeur (from the French *voir*, meaning "to see")? Are men who like to look at naked women in magazines or at topless shows voyeurs? What about people who go to nudist colonies, or men who enjoy looking at women in string bikinis at the beach? What if a man sneaks a peak up a woman's skirt as she is sitting down, or if he was innocently walking down the street and noticed a woman undressing in her room and stopped to watch? Although the description "voyeur" is often used to describe such behavior, these are really just more examples of normal variants.

Voyeurism

Repeatedly seeking sexual arousal by observing nude individuals without their knowledge or consent.

To be a **voyeur** (a paraphiliac), one must *repeatedly* seek sexual arousal by observing people undress or in the nude *without their consent or knowledge.* The voyeur is aroused by the risk of discovery and thus is not interested in going to nudist colonies or other places where people know that they are being watched (Sagarin, 1977; Tollison & Adams, 1979). A variation of voyeurism is **scoptophilia**, defined as repeatedly seeking sexual arousal by secretly watching sexual acts. In either case, it is the preferred means of sexual arousal. A man was arrested in Mandeville, Louisiana, in 1992, for example, for 341 cases of peeping in women's windows.

Scoptophilia

Repeatedly seeking sexual arousal by secretly observing genitals and sexual intercourse.

The great majority of voyeurs are males (thus the term *Peeping Tom* applies). Most are young with characteristics that resemble those of exhibitionists: feelings of inadequacy and insecurity, shyness with poor social skills, and a history of great difficulty in heterosexual relations (Gebhard et al., 1965; Tollison & Adams, 1979; Yalom, 1960).

" I often 'do it' (masturbate) in my car while parked in areas where I can watch women. My social skills are poor, and I do not get on well with people easily."

(from the author's files)

Voyeurs may masturbate while observing their victims, or masturbate later while fantasizing about the incident. The large majority are not dangerous, preferring to keep their distance, but there are exceptions (Gebhard et al., 1965; Langevin, 1985; Yalom, 1960). If you are ever a victim, you should consider a voyeur to be potentially dangerous if he either tries to draw attention to the fact that he is watching, or if he attempts to approach you or enters your building. ∎

BESTIALITY AND ZOOPHILIA

"In my early teens my cousins and I penetrated a horse. I did it because of a dare. I've grown up now and have 3 children and a wife. Every now and then I think about what I've done and it makes me want to throw up."

"One night several years ago myself and a few acquaintances were sharing some college experiences. One of the group stated that to become a member of . . . he had to have sexual intercourse with a goat."

(from the author's files)

Bestiality is the act of having sexual contact with an animal. Greek mythology provides many stories of gods disguising themselves as animals and having sex with goddesses or humans. But is this type of sexual contact common for humans? Kinsey and his colleagues (1948, 1953) reported that about 8 percent of the men in his sample and over 3 percent of the women had had sexual contact with an animal on at least one occasion. Seventeen percent of boys raised on a farm admitted to such experiences. Fantasies of having sex with an animal are very common. For males, bestiality usually involves a farm animal, while household pets are more common for women. Males are most likely to engage in intercourse with the animal; women usually have the animal lick their genitals or they masturbate a male animal.

For the large majority of people who have engaged in bestiality, it was only one or a few experiences, often during adolescence when no partner was available (Tollison & Adams, 1979). It might have happened as a dare, as an initiation stunt, or out of curiosity. Bestiality becomes a paraphilia, called **zoophilia**, only when it is the preferred means of sexual arousal (Perretti & Rowan, 1983). Zoophilia, however, is very rare and is usually a sign of severe psychological problems. ∎

Bestiality
The act of having sexual contact with an animal.

Zoophilia
Using sexual contact with animals as the primary means of achieving sexual gratification.

PEDOPHILIA

He was a man loved by children. He played a clown at birthday parties, and little ones loved to see him coming into their homes. Then he was caught molesting a child at a party where he had been hired to entertain. Interviews were conducted with children at parties he had worked before. They revealed that he had used his job as a means to repeatedly engage in sexual behavior with children. He was a pedophiliac.

(summarized from news articles)

Pedophilia
A condition in which sexual arousal is achieved primarily and repeatedly through sexual activity with children who have not reached puberty.

Pedophilia (from Greek meaning "love of children") is a condition in which an adult's sexual arousal and gratification depends primarily (or exclusively) on having sex with children. Although legal definitions of a minor differ from state to state (ranging from 16 to 21 years), sex researchers generally define a child as someone who is younger than 13 years old (Gebhard et al., 1965). Thus, we are discussing sexual relations by an adult with prepubertal children. To be considered an example of pedophilia, the adult must be at least 16 years old and at least 5 years older than the child (American Psychiatric Association, DSM-IV, 1994).

An isolated act of child molestation, although reprehensible, does not necessarily qualify as pedophilia. Remember, to be designated a pedophile, the molester must *repeatedly* seek sexual relations with children.

This is the most serious of the paraphilias, each year resulting in many thousands of victims who suffer long-term emotional and psychological problems. This section is intended only as an introduction to the concept of pedophilia. To learn about pedophiles, and the effects that their behavior has on the victims, see Chapter 15 (Sexual Abuse). ∎

SADOMASOCHISM

Sadism refers to the infliction of pain on another person for sexual arousal and gratification. The term is named after the Marquis de Sade (1740–1814), a French aristocrat and novelist who wrote stories, supposedly based on his own experiences, of beating and torturing women while being sexually stimulated himself (his works include the novels *Justine* and *120 Days of Sodom*). **Masochism** refers to achieving sexual arousal by experiencing pain. It is named after Leopold von Sacher-Masoch (1835–1895), a practicing masochist who wrote novels (e.g., *Venus in Furs*) about people getting sexual pleasure by having pain inflicted on them. If the partner of a sadist participates willingly, as is usually the case, then he or she is, of course, a masochist, and the linkage of the two behaviors is indicated in the term **sadomasochism** (S & M). The terms sadism and masochism were coined by Krafft-Ebing, who also was one of the first to report clinical cases:

Sadists
Individuals who repeatedly and intentionally inflict pain on others in order to achieve sexual arousal.

Masochists
Individuals who obtain sexual pleasure primarily from having pain and/or humiliation inflicted on them.

There was a man who habitually attacked young girls on the street with a knife, wounding them in the upper arm. When arrested, he said that he did it because he would have an ejaculation at the moment he cut them. (cited in Krafft-Ebing, 1951, p. 223)

A 28-year-old man would have a woman tie him up with straps he brought for that purpose. Then he would have the woman take whips (which he had also brought) and beat him on the soles of his feet, the calves, and backside until he ejaculated. (cited in Krafft-Ebing, 1951, p. 261)

In a particularly bizarre form of masochism, called **stigmatophilia**, individuals inflict pain on themselves (Ryken, Henderson, & Merrell, 1990). These persons are sexually aroused by such behaviors as inserting wires and other foreign objects into their urethra or through their genitals or nipples, marking their own bodies, and performing surgery on themselves.

Stigmatophilia
Sexual arousal by marking one's own body or inserting foreign objects into the urethra, genitals, or nipples.

How common are sadism and masochism? In its mildest forms, it is probably very common. Many people, for example, enjoy being bitten, slapped (e.g., on the buttocks), pinched, scratched, or pinned down during sex.

"I consider myself to be a normal sexual person. . . . I love to be spanked. . . . " (female)

" . . . I figured I could ask you if it's 'normal' if you like to be bitten during sex? My arousal does not depend exclusively on biting nor does my boyfriend have to bite me hard, I just love it."

(from the author's files)

Kinsey and his associates (1948, 1953) found that over one fourth of the men and women in their survey had erotic responses to being bitten during sex. Some people are sexually aroused by inflicting or experiencing pain that goes beyond love bites or spanking:

"My best friend always talked about how he wanted to have anal sex with his girlfriend. All he really talked about was how he wanted to hear her let out a cry when he finally got to."

(from the author's files)

Janus and Janus (1993) reported that 16 percent of men and 12 percent of women agreed or strongly agreed that "pain and pleasure really go together in sex." However, only half as many felt that S & M was very normal or all right, indicating that many people do not regard their own behaviors as S & M. Where then do we draw the line as to what characterizes S & M?

To qualify as a paraphilia, sadomasochism must be the *preferred* means of sexual arousal. Until the 1980s, most of what was known about sadists and masochists was obtained from clinical case studies (such as Krafft-Ebing's) of individuals who had inflicted or experienced tremendous physical pain and harm (in the case of sadists, often with unwilling partners). Sadomasochism was thus viewed as a psychological abnormality, practiced by people with severe personality disorders. In its extreme form, sadism is less common than masochism (Gebhard et al., 1965) and male sadists far outnumber female sadists (Fiester & Gay, 1991). Sadists who act out their aggressive impulses share many features with other sexual aggressors (Langevin et al., 1988). Some of these features include: abuse of alcohol and drugs, poor socialization, frequent history of abuse as children, tendency toward committing nonsexual crimes as well as sexual crimes, and long histories of antisocial behavior. Most experts feel that sadomasochistic activities involving severe pain are relatively uncommon.

Recent studies by sociologists and psychologists in nonclinical settings reveal that the majority of people who participate in sadomasochism differ substantially from individuals who have come to the attention of clinicians. Weinberg and associates (Weinberg, 1987; Weinberg, Williams, & Moser, 1984) found that the distinctive feature in most sadomasochistic relations is not pain, but **domination** and **submission**, in which humiliation, more so than extreme pain, is what is inflicted or experienced. Dominators ("master," "mistress," "tops") and submissives ("slaves," "bottoms") act out roles in highly structured scenarios (often involving *bondage*). It is usually done with a trusted partner (thus allowing them to explore dominance and submission safely), with both agreeing beforehand on the set of activities that follow.

Domination

Ruling over and controlling another individual. In sexual relations, it generally involves humiliation of the partner as well.

Submission

Obeying and yielding to another individual. In sexual relations, it generally involves being humiliated by the partner as well.

" My most favorite sexual activity is bondage. This is usually done with a partner with whom I have had sex enough times to develop a feeling of trust. I explain that I will tie her spread eagle to the bed and do anything to her that I want. After doing so, communication is active and only things that bring pleasure are done. At no time is fear or physical abuse implied. There has never been a bad experience to me or my partner during these adventures."

"... The dominatrix (female dominator) commands me to clean a toilet, then 'rewards' me by allowing me to chew on one of her dirty socks...."

(from the author's files)

The scenarios often include special clothing (e.g., leather garments, high-heeled shoes or boots) and gadgets (e.g., leashes, collars, whips, chains), but pain-inducing behaviors are more symbolic than real. Sadomasochists may go to S & M establishments and pay to experience dominance or submission in structured role-playing.

Dominators and submissives generally are not interested in injury or extreme pain, and pain is erotically arousing *only* when it is part of the agreed-upon ritual (Gosselin & Wilson, 1980). (Male homosexual S & M tends to be more violent than heterosexual S & M; Breslow et al., 1986.) Activities preferred by a majority of both men and women include (in order) spanking, master–slave relationships, oral sex, masturbation, bondage, humiliation, erotic lingerie, restraint, and

FIGURE 14-3   S & M DEVICES FOR SALE IN A SEX SHOP.

anal sex (Breslow et al., 1985; Moser & Levitt, 1987). People who participate in dominance and submission have a strong desire to control their environment (Breslow et al., 1986), and the acting out of the highly structured S & M scenarios can become the preferred means of sexual arousal:

" Growing up I had fantasies about having a partner that would enjoy being on the submissive end of S & M. Well I found one and . . . I never knew my tendencies for that could become so everyday. We both fed on that behavior . . . ."

(from the author's files)

Most nonclinical sadomasochists are male (2 to 1 ratio over females), heterosexual, and well educated (Breslow et al., 1985; Moser & Levitt, 1987). Most have a preference for dominant or submissive roles, but many are able to switch between the two. Many female participants do so to please their male partners (Breslow et al., 1985). They, too, tend to be well educated, and while most prefer the submissive role, a sizable minority prefer the dominant role or have no preference (Levitt, Moser, & Jamison, 1994). Although most people who engage in S & M are socially well adjusted, close to a third report extreme nervous anxieties, and many have concerns that their participation in S & M could eventually become dangerous (Breslow et al., 1985).

Psychoanalytic explanations of sadism often focus on unconscious anger directed at one's mother, while masochism is sometimes explained as sadism directed at oneself. Behavior therapists, on the other hand, contend that S & M results from early associations of pain with orgasm. One study found that 80 percent of male sadomasochists and 40 percent of females attributed their interest in S & M to childhood or adolescent experiences (Breslow et al., 1985), but in another study only 20 percent could recall such experiences (Moser, 1979). Weinberg (1987) believes that sadomasochism (dominance-submission) can be understood as a social phenomenon. Most men involved in S & M are submissives and many are not only well educated, but successful and prominent, and the highly structured scripts with a trusted partner allow them to safely play a role that contradicts what our society says is appropriate for males (also see Money, 1984). The dominator role, on the other hand, may be preferred by those who normally have little or no influence or power. ∎

OTHER PARAPHILIAS

The sexual behaviors that have been discussed to this point represent only the most common paraphilias. There are less common, more bizarre, paraphilias and I introduce a few of them here. For a description of others, see Money (1984).

Some of these paraphilias might be considered specific types of fetishes (urophilia, coprophilia, mysophilia, klismaphilia) as they involve sexual arousal by specific body discharges (Money, 1986). Behaviors such as urophilia and coprophilia are sometimes included in sadomasochistic acts as well.

" I personally know someone that was a urophiliac. He used to talk to one of my friends. She told me that every time they were together, he used to ask if he could urinate on her belly."

" My boyfriend likes to watch as I urinate. I even let him taste it one time."

(from the author's files)

Urophiliacs are sexually aroused by the act of urination. They enjoy watching others urinate, and many are sexually aroused by urinating on their partner or having their partner urinating on them (often called "golden showers"). Some even drink urine. The noted sexologist Havelock Ellis (see Chapter 1) admitted that he developed a mild form of urophilia during adolescence after witnessing his mother suffer several bouts of urinary incontinence.

Urophilia
Sexual arousal caused by urine or the act of urination.

Coprophiliacs are sexually aroused by excrement. They may play with, masturbate with, or even eat (*coprophagia*) feces. In some brothels around the world, coprophiliac patrons can pay to watch from under a glass as prostitutes defecate. Although you might think that urophilia and coprophilia are extremely rare, they are common enough that there is a market for video cassettes showing people engaged in these behaviors. Janus and Janus (1993) found that 6 percent of men in

Coprophilia
Sexual arousal caused by feces or the act of defecation.

their survey, and 3 percent of women, believed that golden showers was very normal or all right. Three percent of men and 1 percent of women said that being defecated on was very normal or all right.

Closely related is **mysophilia**, sexual arousal caused by filth. For example, there are documented cases of people who for their sexual arousal and gratification prefer (and eat) vomit or nasal mucus.

One of the more unusual paraphilias is **klismaphilia**, obtaining sexual arousal by being given an enema. Some men pay a prostitute not for sexual intercourse or oral-genital sex, but to lay them across their lap and give them an enema.

Mysophilia
Condition in which sexual arousal is caused primarily by filth or filthy surroundings.

Klismaphilia
A condition in which sexual arousal is achieved primarily by being given an enema.

" A year ago I went with a small group of friends from my high school to London. Well, we were on a very crowded tube (subway) and were packed in so tight that we could barely move. But the guy behind me was able to move. He kept rubbing up and down against me the whole ride. I just thought that someone kept pushing him against me. My friends told me that he looked like he was 'getting off' by doing that. I never wore those pants again because I felt used and dirty."

(from the author's files)

Frotteurism involves rubbing one's genitals against other people in public while fully clothed. Frotteurists seek out crowded buses or other places where "bumping" into strangers is less likely to cause them to be arrested. Again, it isn't unusual to get aroused by close physical contact with someone (such as when you are dancing and holding your partner close to you). However, most people hope that they will get together after the

Frotteurism
A condition in which sexual arousal is achieved primarily by rubbing one's genitals against others in public places.

dance for more intimate forms of contact. A frotteurist would not be interested in this, and prefers to escape before he is confronted.

Perhaps the most bizarre paraphilia is **necrophilia**—obtaining sexual arousal and gratification by sex with dead bodies. Almost all known cases involve men, although a few cases of female necrophiles have been reported

Necrophilia
Sexual arousal by having sex with a dead body.

(see *San Francisco Chronicle*, April 25, 1982, p. 2). Janus and Janus (1993) found that only 1 percent of men, and no women, thought that this behavior was all right. Most experts consider these people to be severely emotionally disturbed or psychotic. Necrophiles often seek employment in mortuaries or morgues in order to have access to their "partners." Many pay prostitutes to pretend that they are dead (e.g., white powder, lying very still) while having sex with them. ■

MULTIPLE PARAPHILIAS

Many sexual offenders do not wish to describe their "private" lives. However, a study was conducted with outpatient sexual offenders in which the participants were guaranteed immunity from prosecution for any crimes they described in the research interviews (Abel et al., 1987, 1988a). In this study, 62 percent admitted to having committed a previously concealed deviant sexual behavior. Over half reported that they had engaged in more than one type of the previously described deviant behaviors, with the average being three to four types. Most had developed their sexual interests and fantasies by age 12 or 13, but were afraid to discuss their arousal patterns with their parents.

Other studies have also found that individuals in treatment for one type of paraphilia often engage in other paraphilias (Bradford, Boulet, & Pawlak, 1992; Flor-Henry, 1987; Langevin, 1985). In fact, some types of paraphilias tend to cluster together more often than others. People clinically diagnosed as sadists (and confined in a psychiatric hospital), for example, are frequently associated with exhibitionism, voyeurism, frotteurism, and/or telephone scatologia as well (Fedora et al., 1992; the reverse is not necessarily true; most exhibitionists, voyeurs, frotteurists, and scatologists, you recall, are not dangerous). These studies indicate that the incidence of multiple paraphilias in individuals may be greater than previously believed, and explanations of the paraphilias must take this into account. ■

WHAT CAUSES PARAPHILIAS?

What causes people to become paraphiliacs? *Freudian* (psychoanalytic) *theorists* believe that paraphilias are the result of arrested psychosexual development, often due to a failure to resolve emotional conflicts. In this theory, paraphilias serve as defense mechanisms to reduce anxiety. A recent explanation of transvestism, for example, is that the behavior "functions to comfort, soothe, and alleviate unpleasant emotions" (Levine, 1993). Although Freudian theory has the advantage of being very flexible, the effectiveness of psychoanalysis as a therapy for paraphiliacs is very debatable, and is seldom used.

Learning theorists (behaviorists) attribute paraphilias to (usually early) learned associations. Recall, for example, the study by Rachman (1966) regarding acquisition of a "fetish" to boots. Some individual case studies also lend credence to this explanation. A man's fetish for plaster casts, for example, was traced to an experience he had at age 11 after he broke his leg (Tollison & Adams, 1979). He got an erection as the nurse held his leg, and later masturbated while fantasizing about it. His repeated fantasy/masturbation episodes led to the fetish.

Although both of these approaches have their advocates, an interesting question still remains: Why are most paraphiliacs males? Of the nearly 88,000 arrests for sexual offenses other than forcible rape and prostitution in 1993, over 90 percent were men. Most paraphiliacs describe themselves as heterosexual, but they generally have poor social skills, low self-esteem, histories of childhood abuse or neglect (or were raised in families where sex was thought of as evil and normal erotic development was inhibited), and anger at women. As a result, paraphiliacs have difficulties with intimacy, especially when they attempt to have sexual relationships. Conventional sexual relationships are too complex and threatening for most paraphiliacs, who need to have a great deal of control in order to become sexually aroused. Think for a minute—what do a pair of panties, a dead body, an animal, a person being secretly watched, and a young child have in common (all of them objects of paraphiliacs' fantasies)? These objects are quiet, passive, and nonrejecting. Consider, for example the following case history of necrophilia:

"Two males worked with me at _____ . There we worked in the morgue and they used to always want me to watch one morgue while they watched another. Well, one day I went to their morgue after hearing about a young Puerto Rican female body which had been delivered after she died of a drug overdose. There was one guy on top of her and the other was waiting his turn. After talking with them, I found out that they had done this many times before. They tried to get me to do it but I refused, saying they were crazy. They said, 'No, you're crazy because this is the best. We have them any way we want, how we want and do whatever we want to them without any back talk!' "

(from the author's files)

In a *social systems perspective*, the need for some men to dominate women might encourage or sustain attempts to utilize unusual means of becoming sexually aroused in order to ensure against failure. Our society's often subtle but powerful expectations for males to be masculine and dominant may make it difficult for some men to form caring, normal relationships.

Did you notice a common element in all three explanations? In all three, childhood or early adolescent experiences play an important role. The manner in which one is raised is very important for healthy sexual development. John Money (1986) explains the impact of childhood experiences in terms of *lovemaps*. Lovemaps, according to Money, depict an idealized lover, love scene, and erotic activities, and develop and are rehearsed during adolescence. For children whose rehearsal has been severely punished or restricted the lovemaps become distorted, with one outcome being the paraphilias.

Today, many researchers are recognizing the similarity between paraphilias and other obsessive-compulsive disorders. Recall from Chapter 13 the cycle of events that drives the individual who is hypersexual (or the sex addict, as some prefer). The individual is first preoccupied with obsessive thoughts, which leads to ritualistic behaviors (causing further sexual excitement) that eventually lead to the sexual act. The act, however, produces despair; and in order to reduce the anxieties the individual becomes preoccupied again (Carnes, 1983, 1991). Hypersexuality is not recognized as a paraphilia in the American Psychiatric Association's diagnostic manual (DSM-IV, 1994), but the fact that a great many paraphiliacs engage in their behaviors compulsively cannot be denied. As explained by sexologist Eli Coleman, the paraphiliac's behavior "may initially be driven by the sexual excitement. . . . But the primary motivation is the reduction of stress and anxiety. There is usually a short-lived feeling of relief, followed by the recurrence of the anxiety" (quoted by Thompson, 1991; see also Coleman & Edwards, 1986). Although the similarities between obsessive-compulsive disorder and paraphilias have some merit, preliminary evidence from therapeutic drug studies suggests that the two conditions are not entirely identical (Kruesi et al., 1992). ∎

THERAPY

No one type of therapy has proven successful in treating paraphiliacs. For behaviors that cause harm to others (e.g., pedophilia, sadism), *medical approaches* to reduce the sex drive are sometimes used. These include antiandrogen drugs (e.g., cyproterone acetate) that reduce testosterone levels (Bradford & Pawlak, 1993a, b; Cooper, 1986; Emmanuel et al., 1991; Rousseau et al., 1990; Wincze et al., 1986). However, these are not cures; they are used to curb the urge to engage in the behaviors while other therapies can be tried. Drugs used for obsessive-compulsive disorders or generalized anxiety disorders (e.g., Prozac, clomipramine, buspirone) have also proved to be promising in treatment of specific paraphilias such as transvestism, exhibitionism, and fetishism (e.g., Fedoroff, 1992; Kafka, 1991; Kruesi et al., 1992).

Therapy often takes a multifaceted approach. Traditional *psychotherapy* or *group therapy* may be tried to get the individual to become aware of his feelings, while confrontational approaches are sometimes used to force the individual to see the effect his behavior has on others. Behavioral approaches often include *aversion therapy* in which unpleasant stimuli are presented or associated with the undesired behavior, or *orgasmic reconditioning* where pleasant stimuli (fantasies) are associated with orgasm.

Therapy is not completed once the paraphiliac's inappropriate urges have been controlled. Remember, paraphiliacs usually have anxieties about intimate relations and poor social skills. Unless these problems can be resolved, the inappropriate behaviors will eventually return. For the anxieties, the most successful approach is *desensitization*. Here, the anxiety-causing stimulus (relations with women in this case) are slowly introduced to the subject. Fantasies of normal relations with women are attempted first. Once this can be done in a relaxed state, thoughts of normal relations are gradually replaced with actual behaviors (for example, being alone in a room with a woman, sitting next to a woman, and talking to a woman may be introduced in succession). *Social skills training* teaches these men skills (how to carry on a conversation and how to cope with rejection) that most of us, but not the paraphiliac, learned during adolescence.

No type of therapy, for any problem (not just paraphilias), has a high success rate unless the individual wants to change. This is one reason that therapy ordered by criminal courts of law are often unsuccessful; the individual does not come to therapy on his own. For many paraphiliacs, the urge to engage in the behavior is so strong that it never seriously occurs to them to give it up (Money, 1986).

The social systems perspective advocates a different approach to dealing with paraphilias. Rather than trying to change individuals, those who believe in this perspective advocate changing society's stereotypes about male dominance over females. A prediction of the social system perspective is that an early socialization process that did not place heavy expectations on males to control or dominate sexual relationships would lead to a sharp decline in the amount of paraphilia in our society. What do you think?

KEY TERMS

berdache   332
bestiality   336
coprophilia   339
domination   338
exhibitionism   333
fetishism   330
frotteurism   339
klismaphilia   339

masochism   337
mysophilia   339
necrophilia   340
paraphilia   330
pedophilia   336
sadism   337
scoptophilia   335
sexual variant   330

stigmatophilia   337
submission   338
telephone scatologia   334
transvestism   331
two-spirit   332
urophilia   339
voyeurism   335
zoophilia   336

PERSONAL REFLECTIONS

1. Do you engage in sexual practices that may be physically or psychologically harmful to yourself or others (e.g., exhibitionism, obscene telephone calls, voyeurism, sadomasochism, pedophilia)? If so, have you sought therapy to help with your behavior? If you have not sought therapy, why?

2. If you are ever victimized by a person with a paraphilia, what do you think you would do? Would you talk about it? To whom? Would you report it? To whom?

3. Do you believe that it is okay for consenting adults to engage in any sexual behavior in private as long as it does not cause physical and/or emotional injury and does not interfere with normal social and occupational activities? Why or why not?

SUGGESTED READINGS

Brown, G. R. (1990, June). The transvestite husband. *Medical Aspects of Human Sexuality.*
Garber, M. (1992). *Vested interests: Cross-dressing and cultural anxiety.* New York: Routledge. Interesting and provocative.
Gebhard, P. H., Pomeroy, W. B., Gagnon, J., and Christenson, C. V. (1967). *Sex offenders: An analysis of types.* New York: Bantam Books. Discusses the psychological and social factors leading to unconventional sexual behaviors.
Money, J., and Lamacz, M. (1989). *Vandalized lovemaps.* New York: Prometheus Books. Excellent case histories.
Stoeller, R. J. (1977). Sexual deviations. In F. A. Beach (Ed.), *Human sexuality in four perspectives.* Baltimore: John Hopkins University Press. An easy-to-read review of the paraphilias.
Weinberg, T., and Kamel, G. W. (Eds.). (1983). *Studies in sadomasochism.* Buffalo, NY: Prometheus Books. Eighteen articles about sadomasochism.

CHAPTER FIFTEEN

SEXUAL ABUSE

WHEN YOU HAVE FINISHED STUDYING THIS CHAPTER, YOU SHOULD BE ABLE TO:

1. DISCUSS, FROM AN HISTORICAL PERSPECTIVE, ATTITUDES ABOUT RAPE AND VICTIMS OF RAPE;

2. UNDERSTAND THE PREVALENCE OF RAPE AND DESCRIBE SOME CHARACTERISTICS OF RAPISTS AND THEIR VICTIMS;

3. DESCRIBE ACQUAINTANCE RAPE, DATE RAPE, SEXUAL COERCION, MARITAL RAPE, GANG RAPE, STATUTORY RAPE, AND THE FREQUENCY OF EACH;

4. DISCUSS WHY RAPE IS COMMON IN SOME CULTURES AND RARE IN OTHERS;

5. COMPARE AND UNDERSTAND THE PSYCHODYNAMIC, CULTURAL, SOCIAL LEARNING, AND INTERPERSONAL FACTORS THAT CONTRIBUTE TO RAPE;

6. IDENTIFY SEVERAL MYTHS ABOUT RAPE AND APPRECIATE WHY THEY ARE NOT TRUE;

7. DESCRIBE RAPE TRAUMA SYNDROME AND OTHER REACTIONS TO RAPE;

8. DISCUSS AND EVALUATE THREE APPROACHES TO RAPE PREVENTION;

9. DESCRIBE SEXUAL HARASSMENT IN THE WORKPLACE AND IN THE CLASSROOM AND WAYS TO DEAL WITH IT;

10. DESCRIBE THE DIFFERENT TYPES OF CHILD MOLESTERS AND THE SITUATIONS IN WHICH SEXUAL ABUSE OF CHILDREN IS MOST LIKELY TO OCCUR;

11. DISCUSS THE VARIOUS FORMS OF INCEST AND DESCRIBE THE FAMILY DYNAMICS THAT ARE TYPICALLY FOUND IN CASES OF FATHER-CHILD INCEST; AND

12. UNDERSTAND THE DEVASTATING LONG-TERM EFFECTS THAT CAN RESULT FROM SEXUAL ABUSE OF CHILDREN.

RAPE

In the United States, 16 rapes are attempted every hour; on average, another woman is raped every 6 minutes.

On average, another woman is beaten every 18 seconds in the United States; three out of four American women will be victims of at least one violent crime during their lifetime.

The number of rape cases is increasing at four times the rate of other crimes (only a third of this increase can be attributed to better crime reporting).

The United States has a rape rate nearly four times higher than in Germany, 13 times higher than in England, and more than 20 times higher than in Japan.

(Source: 1990 Senate Judiciary Committee hearings on violent crimes against women)

Historical Perspective

The word rape comes from the Latin word *rapere*, meaning to steal or carry off. A story about the founding of Rome describes how the early Romans abducted women from a neighboring tribe in order to get wives ("the rape of the Sabine women"). Many cultures have ritualized the abduction of the bride-to-be by the groom as part of the marriage ceremony. In our own culture, for example, the practice of carrying a new bride across the threshold is a ceremonial re-creation of the Roman legend.

In Western culture long ago (and still true in many parts of the world today), women were treated as if they were property belonging to their father or husband, and fathers and husbands could do as they wished with their property. For example, the Old Testament (Genesis 19:1–8) tells of Lot, who lived in the town of Sodom. Two angels disguised as men came to Sodom and Lot invited them to his house, but the men of Sodom surrounded Lot's house and demanded that he send them outside. Lot instead offered to give the crowd his two virgin daughters to do with as they pleased if only the men would leave his guests alone. In Biblical times, rape was viewed as a crime against a man's property rather than against a person (the woman).

The Old Testament (Deuteronomy 22:23–28) also describes different punishments for rape. If a married woman was raped, it was assumed that she had wanted it (and thus violated her husband) and both she and the rapist were put to death. If a betrothed virgin was raped inside the city walls, both the rapist and victim were to be stoned to death, because it was assumed that the young woman could have cried out for help and been heard if she had wanted to resist. If a young woman was raped outside the city walls, the punishment was based on whether or not the woman was engaged. If she was, only the rapist was killed because it was assumed that the woman's cries for help could not have been heard. If she was not engaged, the rapist had to pay a fine to the young woman's father (it was his "property" that was damaged) and marry the woman (for who would want to marry "damaged goods"?).

It was not until the thirteenth century that English law dropped its distinction between raping a married woman versus raping a virgin, and also dropped the practice of forcing the rapist and victim to marry (Brownmiller, 1975). The idea that a wife was property of her husband, and a husband could therefore do as he pleased with her, continued for many centuries. You will learn of recent changes in the law regarding this in the section on marital rape.

Throughout history, men of victorious armies have raped the women of defeated nations. When the Japanese army invaded China in 1937, for example, the soldiers raped virtually every woman and girl in the wartime capital of Nanking. They later rounded up tens of thousands of Korean women to serve as sex slaves, with most of the women forced to have sex with dozens of soldiers every day. In the 1990s in Bosnia, Serbian troops have raped tens of thousands of Muslim women as part of their "ethnic cleansing" war. Wartime rapes generally are vicious gang rapes, and reports of American soldiers participating in such rapes appear in the court-martial records during the Vietnam war.

Why do soldiers, men, engage in such atrocious behavior? It is done to demonstrate power, to destroy the national pride, the manhood, and the honor of the vanquished country. In the words of Susan Brownmiller (1993), " . . . to give vent to his submerged rage against all women *who belong to other men* . . . In one act of aggression, the collective spirit of women and of the nation is broken, leaving a reminder long after the troops depart. And if she survives the assault . . . symbol of her nation's defeat. A pariah. Damaged property."

Rape Statistics

FBI records show that there were 104,806 reported cases of rape in the United States in 1993. Although this is a large number, everyone agrees that the actual number of rapes committed each year is much higher than the number reported. The Justice Department (Bureau of Justice Statistics, 1995) estimates that there are 170,000 rapes and 140,000 attempted rapes committed each year in the United States, while the National Victims Center estimates that there are as many as 683,000 rapes of adult women a year. Other recent surveys have found that the percentage of women who have been the victim of rape or an attempted rape is somewhere between 15 percent (Koss et al., 1987) and 30 percent (Ward et al., 1991). Russell and Howell (1983) estimated that a woman living in the United States has a one in four chance of being raped in her lifetime.

Women between 16 and 24 years of age are the most frequently reported victims of rape (Bureau of Justice Statistics, 1991). However, the records show that anyone can be a victim of rape, including young children, elderly women, and men. For example, my grandmother was raped by a teenager when she was 85 years old:

B y the age of 80, Hazel's failing health no longer allowed her to make the trip next door to her daughter's house to prepare the family dinner. She was hunched over due to osteoporosis, and her hands were so arthritic that she had to give up playing the organ at church. Her face was heavily wrinkled, and her hair was gray and thin.

When she was 85, a man in his late teens or early twenties broke into her room one night. He forced her to display herself, and he made her lean over his knees while he spanked her. This went on for two or three hours. He beat her up, permanently damaged one of her eyes, and raped her.

There was no known motive. The rapist was a stranger and was never caught. The police said that she had apparently been picked at random.

(from the author's files)

The Bureau of Justice Statistics reported that in 1992, 51 percent of rape victims were girls under age 18. However, these are reported rapes. A study by the National Victims Center, which included both reported and unreported rapes, found that nearly 62 percent of victims were under age 18; 29.3 percent were under age 11. Karen Hanna of the National Victims Center says that young people are frequently the target of rape because "the youngest are the least likely to fight back and often don't realize they are victimized" (quoted by Sniffen, 1994).

Even infants can be the victims of rape:

E ight-month-old "Susan" was placed in the care of her mother's boyfriend "Joe" for a few hours. Upon returning home, her mother found Susan hemorrhaging badly. The baby was rushed to the emergency room of a local hospital, where evidence of vaginal penetration was found. Susan had to have an immediate operation, in which all of her reproductive organs except the vagina were removed in order to stop the bleeding. There were many vaginal lacerations, but the surgeons were able to stitch them up. This was an eight-month-old girl who would not be able to have children in the future and who would have to undergo repetitive reconstructive surgery. She was a victim of rape.

Police found that Joe had abused Susan before, but without vaginal penetration. Susan's mother had refused to contact police because Joe was her boyfriend. After the near death of Susan, her mother reported Joe to the police. He was then arrested for aggravated rape. Because of her failure to report Joe after his first abuse of Susan, the baby was taken from her mother and placed in a child protection center. Anyone can be a victim of rape.

(summarized from news releases)

The younger the rape victim, the more likely it is that the attacker is an acquaintance or relative (Bureau of Justice Statistics for 1992). For rapes of girls under 12 years old, 96 percent were committed by a family member or acquaintance; 67 percent for women 18 or older. Women are much more likely to report a rape if raped by a stranger; thus, most men convicted of rape were strangers to their victims. If prior to taking this course you had been asked to describe a "typical" rape, chances are you, too, would have described a scenario in which a victim was raped by a stranger. However, *most rapes are committed by someone the victim knows* (Bureau of Justice Statistics; National Victims Center). The rapist can be a friend or acquaintance, but can also be a husband or boyfriend (or ex-) or a relative (including father or stepfather).

Some rapes are spontaneous, but rapists generally plan their assaults to some degree (Amir, 1971; Chappell & James, 1976). Even in rape cases committed by a stranger, the rapist often picks a particular place and/ or time, with the victim simply being the first person to come along. Thus, being victim of rape can simply be a matter of being in the wrong place at the wrong time. Rapists, however, often look for vulnerable women, such as those living alone or who live in a place that can be easily entered (Selkin, 1975). One way that rapists may test for vulnerability is by asking a woman for help (e.g., asking the time, asking for directions). Selkin (1975) found that in 25 percent of the rape cases committed by a stranger, the woman had responded to a request for help. The first interactions between rapists and victims occur indoors as often as outdoors (Amir, 1971), and about a third take place in the victim's home (Bureau of Justice Statistics).

SOME CHARACTERISTICS OF RAPISTS

Most rapists are young men who repeat the crime (Cohen et al., 1971). In fact, roughly half of convicted rapists are rearrested within 3 years (Bureau of Justice Statistics). The large majority of rapists have no history of psychiatric illness and do not have any lower IQs than men convicted of other crimes (Ruff et al., 1976; Vera et al., 1979). One study found that 15 percent of college men reported committing an act that met the legal definitions of rape (Rapaport & Burkhart, 1984).

There is no compelling evidence to show that rapists, in general, are oversexed. Some studies have found higher than normal levels of testosterone in sex offenders, but this appears to be true only in the most aggressive of offenders (Rada et al., 1983). But, of course, not all men with high testosterone levels are rapists. Moreover, studies have found that most rapists have sexual partners (wives or girlfriends) they live with (e.g., Groth, 1979). One study, for example, found that one third of their sample of rapists were married and having sexual intercourse regularly with their wives (Groth & Burgess, 1977). Kinsey and his colleagues (1953) found that rape is just as common in places where prostitution is available as in places where it is forbidden. Groth and Burgess (1977) examined 101 men convicted of rape and found that 27 percent had erectile difficulties during the rape, 5 percent had premature ejaculation, and 26 percent had ejaculatory incompetence. These men did not have problems in their sexual relations with consenting partners, indicating that something was wrong with their arousal and that their primary motivation for rape was not sexual desire.

Are rapists highly aroused by rape-related stimuli? Two early studies suggested so, finding that rapists became sexually aroused while listening to audiotapes of rape. Nonrape sex offenders did not (Abel et al., 1977; Barbaree et al., 1979). In these studies both groups responded the same to tapes of consenting sex, but another study found that rapists were less aroused by listening to tapes of consenting sex than were nonrapists (Quinsey et al., 1984). However, in a recent review of many studies, Marshall (1992) concluded that these findings hold true only for the subgroup of rapists that use a great amount of violence in their attacks. A more recent study found that rapists with a low level of physical violence during their attacks are not abnormally aroused while listening to audiotapes of physically violent rapes, but are much more aroused than normal by listening to rape involving humiliation (Proulx et al., 1994).

What about the developmental history of rapists? Studies have found that an unusually high number of sexual offenders were themselves physically and sexually abused as children (Groth, 1979; Seghorn et al., 1987). Even if not abused themselves, the family environment in which they were raised often included a great deal of verbal or physical abuse by the father directed at the mother. With this type of family history, a child may well come to view aggression toward women as normal. Psychologist Eugene Porter was quoted as saying, "I haven't seen a rapist who didn't have a childhood horror story" (Newsweek, July 23, 1990). As a result of this history, rapists may not have internal controls, such as fear, guilt, or sympathy, or they may have learned to overcome them, as opposed to nonrapists. For example, an in-depth study of rapists found that some had fantasized about rape and violence toward women and had committed other sex crimes long before actually committing rape (Abel, 1981), suggesting that the violent behavior escalated over time as their internal controls broke down. The majority of arrested rapists were drinking prior to the assault (Ladouceur & Temple, 1985; Muehlenhard & Linton, 1987), thus further releasing any inhibitions or internal controls. Although many sexually coercive males have normal social skills (Koralewski & Conger, 1992; Segal & Marshall, 1985), there is some support that many are unable to deal with any type of stress except by anger and aggression (Panton, 1978). Men who force sex on women tend to have adversarial relationships with women in general. According to Dr. Neil Malamuth, "These men feel they have to be in control of their relationships with women, even in conversation" (quoted by Goleman, 1992).

One thing that is clear is that most rapists lack empathy—the ability to see things from the victim's perspective. Most are convinced that their victims wanted to have sex with them, or deserved to be raped. As an example, psychiatrist Gene Abel, one of the foremost experts on rapists, relayed the story of a rapist (a patient) with a long arrest record for rape who said that he had never raped anyone. When asked how he knew when a woman wanted to have sex with him, Abel's patient responded that he knew a woman wanted sex if she spoke to him (cited in Gelman et al., 1990).

This section was intended only as a general introduction to rapists. Keep in mind that much of what we know comes from studies of convicted rapists, most of whom were strangers to their victims. You will learn more about what makes some men rape in later sections. First, let us look at some specific types of rape.

DATE RAPE AND SEXUAL COERCION

One way to classify rapes is by the relationship that exists between the rapist and victim. I will use the term

Stranger rape

Rape committed by someone who is not known by the victim.

Acquaintance rape

A rape committed by someone who is known by the victim.

Date rape

A type of acquaintance rape, committed during a social encounter agreed to by the victim.

stranger rape to refer to a rape committed by someone the victim does not know. But remember, most rapes are committed by someone the victim knows, and thus are often called **acquaintance rape**. Acquaintance rape is called **date rape** if the rape occurs during a social encounter agreed to by the victim. The term "date rape," although purely descriptive in intent, has turned out to be an unfortunate term because many people believe that it is somehow different from rape by a stranger. Many people attribute more blame, and are less sympathetic, to victims of date rape than they are to victims of rape by a stranger (Barnett et al., 1992; Bridges & McGrail, 1989; Coller & Resick, 1987; L'Armand & Pepitone, 1982). This holds true for police, medical, and social service personnel as well (Holmstrom & Burgess, 1978). *Rape by a date or an acquaintance is no less real than rape by a stranger* and we should simply refer to it as rape. Here are two examples:

"How many times have we heard our friends say, 'Go out with him, he is such a nice guy?' Well, I'm writing this letter to tell about a terrible occurrence that happened to me by a 'nice guy.'

I met this guy in one of my college classes. We had four very fun dates. We would go to movies, dancing, parties, and he would always act like a perfect gentleman. He even told me that he did not date many girls at the university because they were only interested in sex. We had a great relationship, and I began to care for him. But my feelings soon changed.

On our fifth date, he had a little too much to drink. Our friends dropped us at his apartment because he did not want to drive. I knew I was there for the night. I was not worried because he had always treated me with such respect. But that was soon to change. He became very aggressive with me. He told me he wanted to have sex with me because he cared for me so much. I begged him to leave me alone. I tried to fight him off, but I was not strong enough. That turned out to be the worst night of my life, because I was raped.

I did not think I was leading him on by being in his apartment. I was in shock that such a 'nice guy' could do such a horrible thing to me.''

"Robby (a grad student teacher at this university) lived around the corner while I was growing up. I thought of him like a brother, so when I was 17 and he asked me if I was still a virgin, I was not embarrassed to tell him that I was. About a month later a bunch of us went out and after too much to drink, I passed out. I thought I was safe since I was with friends, but he made them leave and I woke up with his fat 270 pound body on top of me. It was horrible and I passed out again. There went 5½ years of friendship and trust. . . .''

(from the author's files)

How commonly are women forced into unwanted sexual activity on a date (or during a mutually agreed upon social interaction)? Koss and Oros (1982) surveyed a group of university women and asked if they had ever been raped. Six percent answered "yes" to this question. They were then asked if any of them had had sex with men when they didn't want to, but were pressured into it. Twenty-one percent answered "yes" to this question. In a later study, Koss, Gidycz, and Wisniewski (1987) found that 25 percent of a national sample of college women had been pressured into sexual intercourse when they didn't want to have it. Others have reported similar results (e.g., Muehlenhard & Linton, 1987; Russell, 1984; see Benson et al., 1992 and Berkowitz, 1992 for reviews). The rate for consent to unwanted sex by women in the United States is far greater than for women in Japan or Russia (Sprecher et al., 1994).

Only about 5 percent of such rapes are ever reported to the police and nearly half of the victims have never told anyone (Koss et al., 1988; Muehlenhard & Linton, 1987). Victims of rape often blame themselves (see later section), and this is particularly true when the rape was committed by a date or close acquaintance (Katz & Burt, 1986). Women who accept extreme stereotypic gender roles often continue in relationships with their violators (Murnen, Perot, & Byrne, 1989).

"When I was 16 I was raped by four guys at a college frat party. In a way I still blame myself for being put in that position. . . . It was my fault for getting drunk. Especially at the age of 16. Guys take advantage of young 16-year-old girls.''

"Exactly six months ago today, I was 'date raped.' Though before taking your course, I blamed myself, now I see it was him and not me who was in the wrong. I actually felt responsible and as if I had provoked it.''

(from the author's files)

Laumann and colleagues (1994) found that 22 percent of women said that they had been forced into unwanted sex at some time, nearly always by someone they knew, but that only 3 percent of men felt that they had ever forced a woman into having sex. However, another study found that 15 percent of a sample of college men admitted that they had had forced intercourse on a date (Rapaport & Burkhart, 1984). Still another study found that one third of college men had, on at least one occasion, used physical force or threatened to use it to have sex with a date (Mosher & Anderson, 1986). Men often try to rationalize date rape and may claim that "she got me aroused and I couldn't stop," or "she came to my apartment, so she must have wanted it." Just because a woman goes out with a man, goes to his home or apartment, or engages in necking or petting, does NOT mean that she wants to (or has to) engage in sexual intercourse.

Most people have no difficulty defining sex without consent of the partner as rape if the act involved physical force, violence, or use of a weapon. But what about physical coercion? What about getting a partner heavily intoxicated (to the point of offering little or no resistance, as in the "Robby" case history) to have sex? What about verbal coercion (e.g., verbal pressure, anger, use of psychological power, or lying)?

" **M**any times my boyfriend forced me into having sex when I didn't want to. He thought that kissing always led to sex and when I said 'No,' he would become very angry."

(from the author's files)

Koss and colleagues have been criticized for calling these experiences rape (Gilbert, 1991; Roiphe, 1993), and fewer than half of the victims in Koss' studies viewed their own experiences as rape (Koss et al., 1988). (Women with an exaggerated adherence to stereotypic feminine gender roles are not only the most likely to date men who use force to obtain sex, but also the most likely to rationalize the behavior of these men; McKelvie & Gold, 1994). A national survey taken for *Time*/CNN found that while over three fourths of women *and* men considered sex with an intoxicated partner rape, over half did not classify a male's use of verbal or emotional pressure to have sex as rape (*Time*, June 3, 1991, p. 50). The question of what defines a rape has recently been addressed (Muehlenhard et al., 1992). However, whether or not these behaviors are rape is not the real issue. The real issue is whether or not it is right to have sex with someone against their will, and the answer to that is "No!"

I will refer to cases in which a person is forced into unwanted sexual activity by physical or verbal coercion as **sexual coercion**. Some instances of coercive sex avoid the label rape only because the victims, fearing that they might be raped, "consent" to having sex. Studies have found that about two thirds of college men admit to having used sexual coercion of some type in order to have sex with a date (Mosher & Anderson, 1986; Rapaport & Burkhart, 1984). Sexual coercion is also quite common in male gay relations (Waterman et al., 1989). However, studies have found that women, too, sometimes use sexual coercion with a partner. In a study conducted at the University of Northern Iowa, for example, 14.2 percent of women said that they had forced sexual activity on a partner (Story, 1986). At a west coast university, 8.1 percent of women admitted to such activity (Gwartney-Gibbs et al., 1987), while at Texas A & M University, 13.4 percent said that they had used verbal coercion and 6.5 percent physical coercion to pressure a male into sex (Muehlenhard & Cook, 1986). In a study of several colleges in the New York-New Jersey area, Anderson (1989) found that over 15 percent of women admitted to having abused a partner (e.g., deliberately inducing intoxication) to have sex.

> **Sexual coercion**
> The act of forcing another person into unwanted sexual activity by physical or verbal coercion (restrain or constrain).

In a series of studies, Muehlenhard and her colleagues found that nearly as many men as women have been the victims of sexual coercion (Muehlenhard, 1989; Muehlenhard et al., 1985; Muehlenhard & Long, 1988). However, there was an important difference: the coercion used by males was often physical, whereas the coercion used by women was generally verbal. Verbal coercion often includes tactics such as persuasion, threat of love withdrawal, and bribery, but a few women include physical restraint and intimidation as well (Struckman-Johnson & Struckman-Johnson, 1994). Anderson (1991) adds that there is also "the question of whether the male partners in the above studies can properly be viewed as 'victims' in the same manner as female victims of sexual abuse. Even if a female is using verbal or physical force, it requires that he become aroused to engage in sexual intercourse."

Several of the previously cited researchers believe that *some* unwanted sexual experiences with social partners are due to poor communication skills. When it comes to giving or interpreting sexual intentions, too many people rely on subtle cues (e.g., gestures, body language) that might be misunderstood. Without clear verbal intent in advance, some men misinterpret a woman's desire to engage in kissing and necking to mean that she wants "to go all the way." On the other hand, Muehlenhard and colleagues found that over one third of college women admit to having engaged in

Token resistance to sex

Saying "no" to sex when one means "yes."

token resistance—saying "no" when they mean "yes"—during such encounters (Muehlenhard & Hollabaugh, 1989). In the survey for *Time/*CNN, 54 percent of women indicated that "some women like to be talked into having sex" (*Time*, June 3, 1991, p. 50). Men who have had experiences with women who offer token resistance are likely to push ahead with another partner when she says "no." Some men may even use it as a rationale to force sex on a partner.

Recent studies have found that just as many, or more, men as women have engaged in token resistance to sex and that men may do so more frequently than women (Muehlenhard, Giusti, & Rodgers, 1993; Muehlenhard & Rodgers, 1993; O'Sullivan & Allgeier, 1995; Sprecher et al., 1994). Most instances of token resistance occur in ongoing relationships, are done as expressive game-playing to increase sexual arousal (not for manipulative reasons), and are perceived as pleasant interactions by both partners. Nevertheless, there is still the danger that men who have had experience with a partner engaging in token resistance may misinterpret sincere resistance by a future partner.

The use of alcohol no doubt further complicates interpersonal communication. One study found that approximately three fourths of date rapists *and* their victims had been drinking or taking drugs before the attack (Copenhaver & Grauerho, 1991).

Unfortunately, many people, including many women, believe that it is okay for a male to force a female into unwanted sexual intercourse in some circumstances (Goodchilds & Zellman, 1984; Kanin, 1967; Muehlenhard & Linton, 1987; *Time/*CNN poll, 1991). These attitudes about relationships and appropriate sexual behaviors are learned early in life. For example, a survey was taken of 1700 seventh to ninth graders who attended an assault awareness program presented by the Rhode Island Rape Crisis Center at schools throughout the state (Kikuchi, 1988). Answers about male behavior toward a woman on a date included the following:

1. Twenty-nine percent of the boys and 20 percent of the girls said that a male has a right to force his date to have sexual intercourse if she has had sexual intercourse with other men.
2. Twenty-two percent of the boys and 10 percent of the girls said that a man has the right to sexual intercourse against the woman's consent if he had spent a lot of money on her.
3. Forty-eight percent of the boys believed that it was okay for a man to force a date to have

sexual intercourse if she let him touch her above the waist.
4. Fifty-seven percent of the boys and 38 percent of the girls believed it was okay for a man to force a date to have sexual intercourse if they had done it before.
5. Sixty-seven percent of the boys and 59 percent of the girls said that a husband has the right to force his wife to have sexual intercourse against her will.

Is it any wonder that about one fifth of young teenage girls have been forced into unwanted sexual activity (often forced intercourse) by a boyfriend or first date (Small & Kerns, 1993)?

It would be best to make a firm decision about your sexual behavior (for that social occasion) *before* you begin (and before you start to drink alcohol) and then communicate your sexual intentions clearly and verbally to your partner. This will stop some unwanted sexual experiences. It will not, of course, stop someone who would use force to have sex, or who would take advantage of a defenseless (e.g., intoxicated) person. When this occurs it is rape, and no less real than any other type of rape.

RAPE IN MARRIAGE

In the seventeenth century, a chief justice of England named Sir Matthew Hale wrote, "The husband cannot be guilty of rape committed by himself upon his lawful wife. For by their mutual consent and contract, the wife hath given herself up in this kind." There were two ideas in Hale's statement that found their way into the American system of justice (which is based on British common law). The first idea is that when two people marry, the marriage contract implies that the husband has a right to have sex with his wife even if she does not consent to it. The second idea is that this is justified because the wife is the property of the husband.

"In the 5th year of my marriage I was raped by my husband after a violent, physical attack. He blamed me for the attack and also said it was my obligation to provide sex whenever he desired it. . . . my marriage ended quite bitterly. For the last 3½ years I was blaming myself for what happened. . . . "

"My only form of sexual abuse was a one-time rape by my husband. I remember well; I thought that dying at the moment would be a blessing, anything to get me out of the situation I was in. After ten years, the mental anguish and hurt still remain. Often the memory resurfaces. To think that the man who promised to love, honor, and protect me was capable of such a violent act! How humiliating to have him stand there laughing at me while I lay crying. As far as I am concerned, the man belongs in jail.''

(from the author's files)

Today, citizens and legislatures realize that laws based on such unfair and antiquated ideas must be changed. In 1978, John Rideout was prosecuted in Oregon for the rape of his wife. Although he was found "not guilty," the trial inspired several states to change their laws to allow for prosecution of **marital rape**. Today, all 50 states make marital rape a crime, but about half require that there be extraordinary violence for prosecution. Only a third provide the same legal protection to wives as in other types of rape (Muehlenhard et al., 1992).

Marital rape
Rape of a wife by her husband.

A 1992 report by the National Victims Center estimated that 9 percent of women had been raped by their husbands or ex-husbands. Other studies have put the estimate even higher (Russell, 1990). Marital rape is often accompanied by severe beatings and other forms of physical abuse (Finkelhor & Yllo, 1985). Frieze (1983) reported that out of 137 women beaten by their husbands, 34 percent were also raped as part of their "punishment." Russell (1990) sees marital rape as being motivated by the same things as any other type of rape—power, anger, and sadism. There is no excuse for marital rape or abuse of a spouse—any rape is real rape regardless of who the rapist is.

GANG RAPE

Seven teenagers were arrested in 1989 in Glen Ridge, New Jersey for forcing a 17-year-old mentally impaired girl to perform sex acts while other teens watched. In April 1989, a 12-year-old girl was kidnapped in Los Angeles and assaulted for 4 days by teenage members of a gang called the Rolling 40s Crips. In 1994, five men were charged with raping a woman in a bar after she

BOX 15-A

CROSS-CULTURAL PERSPECTIVES: RAPE

Rape of women is common in many societies throughout the world. For example, there is a warlike tribe in Africa called the Gusii in which it is the custom for males to obtain brides by stealing young women from neighboring tribes. On the wedding night, the Gusii warrior rapes his new bride as many times as possible to prove his manhood to the others (Levine, 1959). Some tribes use rape to punish women (Chappell, 1976). In the Mangaian culture in the South Pacific, for example, women who violate the sanctity of male-only gathering areas are taken into the forest and gang raped (Marshall, 1971). Throughout history, mass rapes during wartime have routinely been committed by victorious soldiers to punish the defeated nation (see historical perspective section).

However, rape is not common in all cultures. Rape is unheard of, for example, among the Arapesh, who raise males to be caring, gentle, and nurturant (Mead, 1935). Anthropologist Peggy Sanday (1981) found over 40 societies that were free of rape. What do these societies have in common that results in this lack of violence by men toward women? Like the Arapesh, boys are raised to be nurturant, not aggressive, and to view women as equals who share power and responsibility within the society.

Rape of women is several hundred times more common in the United States than in these societies, but we are not alone; Sanday (1981) found over 50 ''rape-prone'' societies. Do these cultures have anything in common? The answer is yes. Sanday found that rape-prone societies like the United States promote and glorify male aggression, treat women as inferior and demean their nurturant roles (from which men remain aloof), view relationships between men and women as adversarial, and, to make matters worse, instill these attitudes beginning early in development.

The fact that rape is almost nonexistent in some societies proves that it can be eliminated, but for that to happen here we will have to raise boys to have different values than in the past. What type of values will you teach your sons? ■

passed out from having too much to drink. In a highly publicized case, six teenagers in Manhattan attacked a lone 26-year-old jogger in Central Park. She was raped, beaten unconscious, and left for dead. This rape was not connected with drugs, robbery, or racial hatred. The only reason given was that it was "something to do" to escape boredom. The youths called their escapade "wilding."

Gang rape refers to incidences in which a victim is assaulted by more than one attacker. There are several forms of gang rape. In prisons, weaker men are often gang raped by other male inmates. For female victims, some cases of gang rape can begin as a date rape (O'Sullivan, 1991). On college campuses as many as 90 percent of gang rapes are committed by fraternity members (for whom there is often emphasis on heavy drinking and acting machismo; Ponce, 1994). In other instances, the victim may be chosen at random. In a study by Amir (1971), 43 percent of rape victims had been attacked by more than one assailant. Of the rapists studied, 71 percent had taken part in rapes with more than one assailant involved. Gang rapes were usually planned, though the specific victim was not always selected in advance. Victims usually lived in the same neighborhood as the rapists.

Gang rape
Rape in which a victim is assaulted by more than one attacker.

What motivates individuals to participate in gang rapes? Some of the reasons are the same reasons that single rapes are committed—power and attempts at achieving control over others, anger, and the view (often reinforced by movies, television, and society in general) that men are the hunters or aggressors and that sexual relations involve conquering female victims. However, gang rapes often have a dynamic of their own. The individuals may not be capable of sexual assault if acting alone, but being a member of a group creates special circumstances (O'Sullivan, 1991). As a group member, individuality is lost. This also means that individual responsibility for things a person does can be forgotten or diffused while committing a rape as a member of a group. Furthermore, taking part in gang rape may be a way of demonstrating loyalty in the eyes of group members, and hesitant individuals may decide to take part in order not to be seen as cowards (Sanday, 1990). Gang rapes are usually more violent than rapes committed by individuals because each member of the group is challenged to outdo the other (Gidyez & Koss, 1990). They may even bait one another into hideously shocking acts. In the Glen Ridge case, for example, the victim was sexually assaulted with a stick, a broom handle, and a miniature baseball bat.

Individuals who participate in gang rape tend to be younger than rapists who act alone—62 percent are under age 21, compared to only 20 percent for single-offender rapes (United States Bureau of Justice Statistics). The number of 13- and 14-year-old boys accused of rape doubled between 1976 and 1986 (National Center for Juvenile Justice). Peer pressure is intense for teenagers. In a society where common teenage entertainment involves axe murder and slasher movies, and where violence is a commonly seen means of interaction between men and women, it is not surprising that gang rapes occur. It is only when the expectations of society are a *lack* of violence and the establishment of equality in relations between men and women that gang rape and other forms of rape will begin to diminish in frequency.

STATUTORY RAPE

Most states have laws involving the crime **statutory rape**, sometimes referred to as **carnal knowledge of a juvenile**. These laws make it illegal for an adult to have sexual intercourse with anyone under a certain age, even if that person consented to having sex. The legal "age of consent" varies from state to state, ranging from 12 to 18. Some states also add provisions about the difference in ages between the adult and minor, such as stating that a male must be 17 or older and be at least 2 years older than the female. The idea behind these laws is that underaged individuals are not capable of giving informed consent (i.e., that they are not capable of fully understanding the meaning and consequences of sexual relations).

Statutory rape
Sexual intercourse by an adult with a (consenting) partner who is not yet at the legal "age of consent." Sometimes called carnal knowledge of a juvenile.

The mentally handicapped are often protected by these laws as well. A landmark case was the Glen Ridge gang rape (see gang rape). Although the 17-year-old victim allegedly agreed to have sex and had been sexually active since age 12, the defendants were convicted after the prosecution showed that she had an IQ of 64 and the social skills of an 8-year-old, and thus could not fully understand her actions. Thus, in some cases, a person can be found guilty of rape even if the victim was consenting.

MALE RAPE

The FBI's Uniform Crime Report doesn't even acknowledge that rape of males exists. Yet it does exist. For example, approximately 1 in 30 rape victims who consult the Rape Crisis Center in New Orleans are male (Read, 1993).

Male rape
Rape in which the victim is a male.

Can a man be raped by a woman? Many people have difficulty believing that a man could get an erection while feeling great fear or terror, but it does happen. Sarrell and Masters (1982) reported 11 instances in which men had been kidnapped by a woman or a group of women who then forced them (often with use of a weapon) to engage in sexual intercourse. Anderson

(1989) reported that some college women admitted to having used physical force or a weapon to have sex with a man. Others have also reported cases where men were victims of female sexual assault (Smith, Pine, & Hawley, 1988). These male victims of rape suffered long-term problems similar to female victims of rape (see section on Reactions to Rape) and generally felt guilt, or that something was wrong with them, because they were able to respond sexually under the circumstances (Masters, 1986; Sarrel & Masters, 1982).

Most men who are raped are victimized by other men, and many people assume that it occurs only in prison. Indeed, from 0.5 percent to 3 percent of male inmates are sexually assaulted by other inmates (Moss, Hosford, & Anderson, 1979). The victims are usually gang raped by men who otherwise consider themselves to be heterosexual (Cotton & Groth, 1982; Lockwood, 1980). However, males are also raped by other men outside of prison.

> "I am a student in your class. I am a 24-year-old male. I am writing this because I feel it can help others in my situation. At 9 years of age, I was raped by three friends. They invited me in their house to play 'strip poker.' I didn't know how to play, so I lost my shirt. Last, but not least, my underwear came off. At this point, the oldest, aged 16, told me to play with his penis. I refused and he punched me in the face. I started to cry and he hit me over and over. I still remember the look on his face. Well, anyway, they all took their penises and proceeded to rape me. They then took turns and at one point they made me perform oral sex on them. I still have nightmares about it. I still remember the blood, the pain, and the shame. What happened to them? Nothing. I never told anyone until this year."

(from the author's files)

Grown men are also victims of rape by other men:

> On a stopover in St. Louis, he decided to stroll from the bus station to the Mississippi River. He was standing by the waves looking out at the water when a man approached and asked if he wanted to smoke some marijuana. Senter accepted the offer.
>
> He followed the man, then suddenly found himself being pushed into an empty tractor-trailer rig. . . . "He had his arm on my shoulder and his hand on my belt," Senter said. "I tried to get away once. He slammed me up on the side of the truck and told me not to do that again."

At first, Senter tried to protest. His attacker told him that if he kept quiet, it would be over sooner. So Senter bit down on his thumb to keep from crying out. He bit so hard his thumb was left without feeling for days afterward.

Inwardly, though, his feelings exploded. (Read, 1993, p. E-3)

Most rapes go unreported, but this is particularly true when men are raped by other men. However, two groups have recently published several accounts of male rapes committed outside of prison (Lipscomb et al., 1992; Mezey & King, 1989, 1992). Weapons were used in most of the assaults, and in many cases the assailants were total strangers. One study found that there was nothing that distinguished the victims from other men, and concluded that "all men are potential victims" (Lipscomb et al., 1992).

In the previous examples the victims, and often the perpetrators, were heterosexual. However, gay men can also be the victims, and perpetrators, of male rape, and the nonconsensual sex sometimes involves men currently having, or who previously had, consensual activity (similar to the nonconsensual sex that occurs in some heterosexual relationships; Hickson et al., 1994).

EXPLANATIONS OF RAPE

Many years ago it was believed that men raped because of an overpowering sexual urge which women released by their looks, dress, or behavior. Then the pendulum swung so that rape was considered as violence or anger at women which was merely expressed by a sexual act. Today, the prevailing view is that there are many types of rapists and that violence and sexual desires work to differing degrees in the different types. Let us review some of the explanations of rape.

PSYCHODYNAMIC THEORIES. Psychodynamic theories view sexually deviant behavior as psychopathology—a character disorder that is very resistant to change. In the 1970s, two such theories for rapists were proposed that have had a substantial impact over the last two decades. Both attempted to classify rapists by the psychology (motivation) of the offender. The first was by Cohen et al. (1971) and classified rapists according to whether their aim was aggression, sexual, or sadism. I will focus on the second theory, that by Groth, Burgess, and Holmstrom (1977). The two theories, however, have much in common.

The authors describe three types of rapists. **Power rapists** commit premeditated attacks in order to overcome personal feelings of insecurity and inadequacy. The "rape is the means by which he reassures himself of his sexual

Power rapists
Rapists who commit their attacks in order to overcome personal feelings of insecurity and inadequacy. Their rapes give them a sense of mastery and control.

adequacy and identity, of his strength and potency" (p. 1240). The rapes give them a sense of mastery and control. Power rapists seek to humiliate and degrade their victims through language and acts. Power rapists use whatever force is required to overcome the will of their victims, including threats and weapons, and while this sometimes can lead to injury, there is usually little physical harm to the victim beyond the act itself. The rape may last for an extended time. Power rapists usually have great difficulty in relating to women and are often very awkward in their interpersonal relations. Groth (1979) estimates that 55 percent of all rapes are power rapes. A second type commit what are called **anger rapes**. An anger rapist generally commits unplanned assaults in an attempt to show his hostility or anger toward some wrong he feels has been done to him—by life or by his victim. His anger is often directed at women in general. Anger rapists often use more physical abuse than is necessary to commit the rape in an effort to punish their victims. The attack usually is of short duration. Groth estimates that 40 percent of all rapes are anger rapes. Finally, there is the **sadistic rape**. Sadistic rapists are erotically aroused by physical force and derive pleasure from inflicting physical pain on their victims. They may not be sexually satisfied if the victim does not resist and may torture or even murder their victims to satisfy themselves. The attacks usually are of extended duration. Groth estimates that only 5 percent of all rapes are sadistic rapes.

Anger rapists
Rapists who commit their attacks out of hostility or anger directed at their victim or at women in general.

Sadistic rapists
Rapists who are aroused by physical force and who derive pleasure by harming their victims.

Groth et al. (1977) concluded that although rape involves a sexual act, first and foremost it is an act of violence. According to Groth, "We look at rape as the sexual expression of aggression, rather than as the aggressive expression of sexuality" (*Newsweek*, 1990). There are many ways in which rape can be used to display dominance or power. In one case, a man known as the "ski mask rapist" committed several rapes in Texas and Louisiana. He always chose a female victim who lived with a male (husband or boyfriend). He would stake out her home, wait until the man left, and then break in when the woman was alone. He would then tie her up, wait until the man returned, and then tie up the man and force him to watch while the woman was raped. If sexual release had been the rapist's primary motivation, he would not have waited until the male partner returned home. In this case, the primary motive was clearly to dominate and humiliate both the woman and her male partner. Gang rapes (of either women or men) provide another example of rape being used to demonstrate power or domination.

There are many examples of anger rape as well. The following letter illustrates a clear case of rape being used to act out the rapist's hostility toward women.

Dear Ann Landers: You have printed letters from bartenders, secretaries, lawyers, musicians, housewives, lovesick teenagers . . . , but I have never seen a letter from a rapist. This may be your first, if you have the guts to publish it.

I am 32 years old and started on this rotten road when I was 20. As of last week, I have raped 25 women, mostly in Oklahoma, Arizona, and California. I've never been caught. The system I use is virtually risk-free. I am highly intelligent—a college graduate from an Ivy League school.

I am writing in the hope that you will print the letter and educate the public. They need to know why men rape. Perhaps if the reason were known, today's mothers of young children will do a better job and prevent another generation from growing up to be rapists who terrorize women of all ages. I hate what I am; but I know what caused me to be like this, and hope you will give my views as much coverage as possible.

I have read repeatedly in your column, "Rape is not an act of lust. It is an act of violence." You are so right. Actually, rape has very little to do with sex. It has a lot to do with the way a male relates to females. Almost always, if you put it all together it spells M-O-T-H-E-R.

I came from a well-to-do family and was raised by a domineering, overpowering mother (divorced). My miserable, cruel grandmother lived with us. Almost every day since I can remember, I was slapped, punched, kicked, beaten with a belt or a hairbrush. Once I suffered three broken ribs from being pushed down a flight of stairs. When I was taken to the doctor (Mom thought I might have a broken leg), I was instructed to say I fell off my bike.

I have never had a girlfriend because I despise all women. I know I am sick in the head, but I have this uncontrollable urge to punish all females, and rape is the best way to get even.

Please tell young mothers to love their little boys. If they can't, then do the kid a favor and put him in a foster home or give him in adoption to a family that will treat him like a human being. Children who are whipped and knocked around have the need to get even. . . .

(No Name, No City, and No Fingerprints)
(Reprinted with permission of Ann Landers and Creators Syndicate)

Groth et al.'s (1977) classification was based on in-depth research of convicted rapists. But, recall that most convicted rapists are stranger rapists, who commit a minority of all rapes. Based on what we now know about acquaintance (including date) rapes, some researchers have proposed a fourth type of rapist—the **opportunistic rapist** (Prentky, 1988). Here, the primary motivation is sex. These men rape impulsively when there is an opportunity, such as on a date. They use only enough force to commit the act and their only anger is to the victim's resistance. Opportunistic rapists probably account for the majority of date rapes.

Opportunistic rapists
Rapists motivated by sex who rape impulsively when there is an opportunity.

Recent research has made it clear that rape cannot be explained only by psychopathology of individuals, for rape is far more common in some cultures than others (see Box 15-A). Cultural, social learning, and interpersonal factors all play a role.

CULTURAL THEORIES. Look again at the rape statistics at the very beginning of the chapter. Why is the incidence of rape so much higher in the United States than in many other countries? Studies have found that rape is most common in societies that glorify violence by men, particularly when the society is also sexually repressive (Prescott, 1975; Sanday, 1981). These societies not only encourage boys to be aggressive (see Box 15-A), but have distinct gender roles for men and women, with men regarding women's roles as inferior. Allgeier and Allgeier (1988) believe that when both men and women conform to extremely stereotypic gender roles (e.g., men are aggressive, women are passive), men are more likely to use force to overcome women. In fact, men who commit rape or engage in sexual coercion are much more likely than men who do not to believe in stereotypic gender roles, to view men as dominant and consider relations with women to be adversarial (very competitive), and to have male friends who are sexually aggressive and who believe that the use of physical force to have sex is okay in some situations (Alder, 1985; Cate & Lloyd, 1992; Harney & Muehlenhard, 1991; Kanin, 1985; Malamuth, 1984, 1986; Rapaport & Burkhart, 1984).

It has also been found that the amount of sexual violence toward women in a society is greater in cultures that support legitimate violence (e.g., movies and magazines that glorify male violence), particularly in times of cultural disorganization (e.g., high unemployment; Baron, Straus, & Jaffee, 1987). You will learn about the effects of pornography in the next chapter. One of the conclusions of research in this area is that men who look at scenes of aggression toward women—and the scenes do not need to be sexually explicit—become less sensitive to the victims of rape and more accepting of sexual violence (Donnerstein & Linz, 1984; Linz, 1989; Malamuth & Check, 1981). Non-sexually explicit rape scenes are exactly the type that are commonly shown on television, despite the warnings of leading researchers in the field (Linz, Wilson, & Donnerstein, 1992).

One study, which found a strong positive correlation between men's attitudes about sexual relations (whether or not they held callous attitudes) and their use of sexual coercion with partners, concluded by stating that "the socialization of the macho man, if it does not directly produce a rapist, appears to produce calloused sex attitudes toward women and rape and proclivities toward forceful and exploitive tactics to gain sexual access to reluctant women" (Mosher & Anderson, 1986).

SOCIAL LEARNING THEORIES. These theories have much in common with cultural explanations. You have already read much of the social learning research in previous sections, so this will serve mainly as a review. Recall that many rapists were either themselves abused as children or witnessed it within the family (Groth, 1979; Seghorn et al., 1987). Whatever type of family life a child experiences while growing up and accepts as "normal," it is likely that he or she will model the same behavior as an adult (Bernard & Bernard, 1983). Interestingly, women with a childhood experience of sexual abuse are more likely than others to be revictimized as adults (White & Humphrey, 1991), perhaps because the experience often affects self-esteem (lowering it) and makes these women more vulnerable to being easily pressured into sex (Skelton, 1984). Thus, for both men and women a past experience of sexual abuse (or physical to a lesser extent) is predictive of the likelihood of inflicting or receiving such abuse when they are adults (Gwartney-Gibbs et al., 1987; Petrovich & Templer, 1984; Story, 1986).

Learned gender roles are also important. Men who have learned extremely conservative stereotypes and who also believe that relationships between men and women are adversarial, tend to believe the myths about rape that legitimize violence against women (see next section) (Burt, 1980; Koss et al., 1985; Muehlenhard & Falcon, 1990). These men are more likely than others to be sexually violent or aggressive (also see Scully & Marolla 1984).

INTERPERSONAL THEORIES. Much of this section, too, will be review. Recall that a lack of shared meaning between men and women can lead to unwanted sexual aggression by men (Perper & Weis, 1987). Recall also that many men (and women) believe that rape is justified under some situations, including if a man spends money on the date, or if he feels that she has "led him on" (e.g., engaging in necking or petting, going to his apartment; Goodchilds & Zellman, 1984; Kikuchi, 1988; Muehlenhard, 1988). Men who accept extreme gender stereotypes of women are most likely to misinterpret behaviors like these to be an invitation for sex (Muehlenhard & Cook, 1988). The fact that some women engage in token resistance (initially saying "no" when they want the male to continue) compounds the misinterpretation of intentions (Muehlenhard & Hollabaugh, 1989), not only on that date but on future dates with other women as well.

(Feiffer © 1989 Jules Feiffer. Reproduced with permission of Universal Press Syndicate.)

Now recall the research that found that convicted rapists, but not nonrapists, were sexually aroused by listening to tapes of, or viewing, rape scenes (see section on characteristics of rapists). Are there any situations in which normal men might also respond to rape scenes—become aroused like a rapist? Barbaree and Marshall (1991) found that many men could become aroused by rape scenes when they had been drinking, and, you remember, most date rapes occur when the male or both people have been drinking (Copenhaver & Grauerho, 1991; Muehlenhard & Linton, 1987). Barbaree's team also found that normal men's arousal to rape scenes became more like that of rapists if a woman had made them angry (this was done purposely as part of the research) just before testing. How might these men behave if they (incorrectly) believed that a woman had "led them on?" Dr. Barbaree concluded, "with the right combination of factors, most men can be aroused by violent sex" (cited in Goleman, 1992).

Misconceptions about Rape

By this point in the chapter you have probably learned some facts about rapes and rapists that have challenged the beliefs you held before enrolling in the course. Mistaken beliefs about rape are widespread, so widespread that they are often referred to as *rape myths* (Burt, 1980). These myths work to place the blame on the victims. In general, men are more accepting of these myths than women (Brady et al., 1991; Quackenbush, 1991), particularly young males (Blumberg & Lester,

Rape myths
Widespread, mistaken beliefs about rape.

1991). This is particularly true of men who accept conservative gender role stereotypes, and this combination (belief in stereotypes and rape myths), you recall, is commonly found in men who engage in sexually coercive behavior (see cultural and social learning theories of rape). It is important, therefore, that we dispel of these myths in our society. Let us examine some of them.

MYTH #1: WOMEN WHO ARE RAPED USUALLY PROVOKED IT BY THEIR DRESS AND BEHAVIOR.
Read again the results of the study by Kikuchi (1988) at the end of the section on date rape. Many junior high school boys and girls believed that date rape was okay if the woman had engaged in certain behaviors. Many adults continue to hold these beliefs. One third to one half of people believe that a woman is at least partially to blame for rape if she wore a short skirt or went braless, went to the man's home or room, or was drinking alcohol (Burt, 1980; Holcomb et al., 1991; *Time*/CNN poll, 1991). For example, in 1989 a jury in Ft. Lauderdale, Florida acquitted a drifter on trial for rape because his victim was wearing a lace miniskirt at the time (the jury foreman was quoted as saying "she asked for it . . ."). The man was a serial rapist who was later convicted of another rape. As a result of this case, the Florida legislature enacted a law that prevents discussion of a rape victim's clothing during court trials. Other states are now passing similar laws. Many women also blame female victims of rape, and mistakenly believe that they can prevent themselves from ever being raped by behaving differently (for example, by dressing conservatively).

When others put the blame for rape on the victim, it makes the emotional trauma all the worse:

"I lost my virginity through rape at age 15. Even my parents thought it must have been my fault because I was at a party. Needless to say, this made matters worse. I had difficulty having a productive relationship until recently."

(from the author's files)

Why is rape the only crime for which we have a tendency to blame the victims? Consider the following hypothetical scenario:

Steve wore his finest Italian suit and shoes to the company's reception. He was particularly proud of his new Rolex watch and felt sure it would make an impression on the brunette in accounting. At the party he had two or three drinks. Steve enjoyed a drink on these occasions because it made him feel more sociable, but he often found that he had one more than he wanted because of peer pressure—others made him feel like an outcast if he didn't have a drink in his hand. He intermingled freely and toward the end of the evening finally struck up a conversation with the woman in accounting. They made plans to get together for lunch the next day, so by the time Steve left, around midnight, he was feeling really good.

On the way home Steve remembered he was out of bread and eggs, so he stopped at a convenience store, parking his BMW slightly off to the side. When he went to get back in his car, he was stopped by a man who said that he had a gun under his coat and that Steve had better give him his Rolex, wallet, and ring. Steve wanted to avoid injury and quickly handed over his valuables while pleading with the man not to hurt him. The man took the valuables and ran.

Steve called the police immediately, hoping to catch the robber. But when the police arrived, rather than asking for a description of the robber, they started to act suspicious about him. One asked why he was out so late. Didn't he know this is when most muggings take place? The other wanted to know how much he'd had to drink and made him take a breathalyzer test. When Steve finally got to tell them what the robber took they were not sympathetic, but instead made comments that insinuated that he had invited the robbery by dressing so well and wearing a Rolex in public.

When Steve got home, his two male roommates couldn't believe that he hadn't resisted. They would have put up a fight, they said; it would never have happened to them.

Steve went to bed feeling ashamed and guilty. The next day he didn't mention it at the office. . . .

You probably found this scenario to be ridiculous, and well you should. So, if you have ever thought that it is women's faults that they are raped because of their behavior, stop for a moment and re-examine your attitude.

MYTHS #2 AND 3: WOMEN SUBCONSCIOUSLY WANT TO BE RAPED; NO WOMAN CAN BE RAPED IF SHE TRULY DOES NOT WANT IT. These two closely related ideas are also widely believed (Burt, 1980; Holcomb et al., 1991). Although many women have had fantasies of rape, and most are aroused by watching eroticized rape scenes (Stock, 1982, 1983), this does not mean that they actually wish to be raped. Most of us have fantasized about things we would never do in real life; the difference between fantasy and reality is that we are in control of our fantasies. Real rape involves someone else taking away all of your control. Women, unlike many men, are not sexually aroused by watching *realistic* rape scenes.

Most rapists are bigger and stronger than their victims, and many assaults involve more than one male. In our culture, most males are reinforced for their physical aggressiveness while growing up, while many females are reinforced for being passive. The end result is that most women wouldn't even know how to fight back if they were attacked. Nearly a third of rapists use some kind of weapon (Bureau of Justice Statistics). The use of force and threats can result in anyone being raped. If the myth were true, then we would certainly never expect men to be raped, but it happens every day (out of prison as well as in).

MYTH #4: WOMEN FREQUENTLY MAKE FALSE ACCUSATIONS OF RAPE. This myth is based on the idea that a woman uses the accusation of rape to get even with a man—revenge. Many men believe this (Holcomb et al., 1991). However, FBI statistics show that the percentage of reported rapes that are false is actually lower (2 percent) than for most other crimes. (When false accusations do occur, it is usually to provide an alibi, seek revenge, or obtain sympathy; Kanin, 1994.) We do not automatically doubt people when they claim that they were the victim of some other type of crime. So why do you suppose some people are so quick to doubt a woman's accusation of rape?

REACTIONS TO RAPE

In their initial reactions and long-term coping strategies, female victims of rape go through what is called **rape trauma syndrome**

Rape trauma syndrome

Reactions of a rape victim, including an acute phase (involving initial physical and psychological recovery from the attack) and longterm reorganization (involving attempts to deal with the long-term effects of the attack and to prevent a future rape).

(Burgess & Holmstrom, 1974; Burt & Katz, 1988). For most victims, it can be considered a form of post-traumatic stress disorder (Foa & Riggs, 1995). First, there is an *acute phase*, which begins right after the rape and continues for several weeks. During this phase, the victim's body has to recover from the physical damage that may have been caused by the rape. About one fourth of rape victims suffer minor injuries and about 4 percent are seriously injured (National Victim Center, 1992). In addition, the victim must begin to recover from the psychological damage that was done (Duddle, 1991; Rynd, 1987). Some victims become very expressive about their feelings and may cry and experience severe depression, become angry or fearful, and/or experience great anxiety. Others may have what is called a controlled reaction, as if they were trying to deny that the rapist had affected them in any way. However, these victims must also work through a great deal of anguish and may become expressive later. Many rape victims experience dissociative symptoms (restricted affect, detachment from other people, concentration problems), and the presence of these symptoms is associated with long-term posttraumatic stress syndrome (Foa & Riggs, 1995). Many rape victims still display symptoms of posttraumatic stress syndrome three months after the attack. Most victims will also experience headaches, sleeplessness, and/or restless behaviors as well in the acute phase. Many victims believed rape myths prior to the rape, and as a result experience guilt and self-blame, which makes the depression even worse (Frazier, 1991). Because the trauma for many victims is long term, rape victims may well be referred to as rape survivors.

> "The lectures on rape were traumatic for me because I could remember everything so vividly. But I stuck with the lecture so I could find out if it was my fault. Now I don't feel as dirty."
>
> (from the author's files)

Next, the victim enters a *period of long-term reorganization*. In this stage, the rape victim attempts to regain control of her or his life (including steps to prevent rape from occurring again) and may move or change jobs. Each of us wants to believe that our world is a relatively safe, secure, and predictable place to live in and to feel that we have control over our lives and what happens to us. This belief allows us to reduce our fears and anxieties about the world we live in, so that we can function efficiently and effectively in it. However, when a violent crime such as rape is committed, our belief system is surely shaken and our security is threatened. Rape victims often feel as if they no longer have any control over what is going to happen to them (Santiago et al., 1985). Many of the reactions to rape are attempts by victims to reassert control over their lives. A basic sense of trust in the goodness of people and society has been damaged, and this damage takes a long time to heal.

Many victims lose their desire for sex and have trouble becoming sexually aroused (Becker et al., 1984; Burgess & Holmstrom, 1979; Gilbert & Cunningham, 1987). Some show a decreased frequency of sexual relations that lasts for years.

Victims who seek help shortly after being raped generally suffer fewer long-term emotional problems (Duddle, 1991; Stewart et al., 1987). The reactions of the victim's family is very important in this respect. For example, women whose partners respond warmly and sympathetically, and do not pressure them to reestablish sexual relations, have fewer long-term sexual problems (Howard, 1980). For rape victims who initially suppress their feelings, it is not unusual for symptoms to emerge months or even years after the incident.

> "The first thing I went and did after your class today was run to my car and cry for a half hour. Fourteen years ago I was raped. . . ."
>
> (from the author's files)

Just like female victims, men who are the victims of rape suffer long-term problems (Mezey & King, 1989). They frequently have sexual problems, difficulties forming close relationships, and a damaged self-image. Unlike women who are victims, they are also likely to have doubts about their sexual self-identity and question whether the experience means that they are homosexual. Recovery is made more difficult because male victims are even less likely than female victims to tell anyone else, and thus are less likely to seek counseling.

The rates for child molestation, incest, and rape are high in our society, and thus, unfortunately, some victims of sexual abuse are later revictimized.

> "When growing up, I was raped by five males in my neighborhood. . . . The speaker and your lectures helped me to realize that it wasn't my fault. . . . Recently, I was raped again . . . and it was very traumatic to me. When I told a close friend of mine, she reacted as if I had done it, asking questions like 'how did you enjoy it?' She just couldn't understand how it could happen to me twice, and to be honest, neither can I."
>
> (from the author's files)

Perhaps as many as 21–35 percent of rape victims have been sexually assaulted before (Cohen & Roth, 1987; Ellis et al., 1982; Miller et al., 1978). Studies have found that some (but not all) people attribute greater fault to a repeat victim than to a first-time victim, regarding her as the type of person to get herself into rape situations (Kanakar, Pinto, & Mazumdar, 1985; Schult & Schneider, 1991). Counseling to eliminate self-blame will be very important for repeat victims. While rape victims often have sexual problems afterwards, women who have suffered *both* childhood sexual abuse and rape as an adult often have sexual problems that are different from other rape victims. Many have histories of brief sexual relations with multiple partners, which often results in unintended pregnancies and abortions. For victims with this history, treatment includes help with decision making (about sexual relations and contraception) as well as help with self-esteem and self-blame (Wyatt et al., 1992).

Reactions of the Partner

A rape victim's partner and family must also deal with their reactions and emotions. When a woman is raped, some male partners blame themselves for not being there to protect her, but it is important that the male put this aside and direct his attention and emotions to the real victim. He should let her recover from the assault at her own pace and allow her to make her own decisions. After all, one of the biggest steps on the road to recovery is regaining control of one's own life.

Perhaps the most devastating thing that can happen to a rape victim *after* the attack is if her partner and/or family believe in rape myths and blame her. This will make recovery all the more difficult (Davis et al., 1991).

FIGURE 15-1   THIS SELF-PORTRAIT BY A VICTIM OF SEXUAL ABUSE SHOWS THE EMOTIONAL SUFFERING THAT IS OFTEN EXPERIENCED LONG AFTER THE CRIME.

"My girlfriend . . . about 1 year ago (3 years into the relationship) was walking alone on her college campus and was violently raped. I somehow held her responsible for 'letting' this happen to her. Both her parents also blamed her. I know I treated her with a little less respect after this happened. Now I feel like a complete schmuck. I realize that she had no control over what happened. Fortunately, her therapist convinced her that it was not her fault."

(from the author's files)

If your partner is ever the victim of rape, do not ask questions such as, "Why did you have to go there?" or "Why were you out so late?" or "What were you wearing?" Questions like these imply that the rape must have somehow been the victim's fault. Both the victim *and* partner often find counseling very useful in learning how to cope with rape.

What Happens If You Report a Rape?

In most metropolitan areas, the police department has special units for dealing with the sexual abuse of children and rape victims. If a rape is reported, uniformed officers will arrive on the scene and determine if a case of sexual abuse has occurred. They will search for the attacker, but the investigation of the case will be carried out by a detective from the special Rape Investigation Unit, who will be next on the scene. These detectives are specially trained to deal with victims of rape. Most large cities now have *rape victim advocate programs* as well. These programs provide a specially trained counselor to be with the woman from the initial investigation through the prosecution. After the initial investigation, the victim is referred to a hospital for a medical exam.

To maximize the chance of a successful prosecution, it is very important to get a medical exam as soon as possible after a rape. It is crucial not to wash, douche, or change clothing after being raped, as doing so may destroy vital evidence (such as semen in the vagina) needed by the police to catch the rapist and prove that the crime was committed. Some victims are initially reluctant to prosecute, but later change their minds. If a medical exam has taken place, this option is still available. Without such medical attention, a successful prosecution (or even an attempted prosecution) is less likely.

Most hospitals today are much more sensitive to the trauma experienced by rape victims than they were in the past. Their emergency units are educated and trained to deal with rape victims, who are given the second highest priority for treatment (only life and death situations are given higher priority). The hospital staff recognizes the need to be very supportive. In addition to possible physical injury, rape also carries the risk of an unwanted pregnancy and/or getting a

BOX 15-B

SEXUALITY AND HEALTH: SEXUAL ABUSE AND SEXUALLY TRANSMITTED DISEASES

In addition to the immediate physical trauma that may occur during rape, the victim of sexual abuse is also burdened with the fear of possible pregnancy and/or sexually transmitted disease. The risk of pregnancy resulting from rape is actually low, about one pregnancy in 100 assaults of women of reproductive age (Davies & Clay, 1992), but STDs are another matter. Although one of the first studies reported that the prevalence of STDs in rape victims was also low (Groth & Burgess, 1977), recent studies have found that many rape victims have infections. Between 2 percent and 13 percent of female rape victims have gonorrhea, while 8–26 percent have chlamydia and 6–22 percent have trichomoniasis (Davies & Clay, 1992; Estreich et al., 1990; Glaser et al., 1989, 1991; Jenny et al., 1990; Schwarcz & Whittington, 1990). Fewer than 2 percent have syphilis.

STDs are very common, so not all of the infected victims in the above studies contracted the diseases during rape. In some, the infections existed before the assault, while others were acquired from new partners in the interval between the assault and the medical examination. STDs that are found in the first 24 hours after the assault probably represent pre-existing conditions (Blackmore et al., 1982). Nevertheless, recent studies have verified that many rape victims do, in fact, acquire STDs at the time of the rape (Glaser et al., 1991; Jenny et al., 1990). In child sexual abuse cases, 3 percent to 16 percent of victims contract sexually transmitted diseases (Bays & Chadwick, 1993; Paradise, 1990). As a result, authorities are saying that *all* rape victims should be treated with a variety of medications shortly after the rape (e.g., Glaser et al., 1991).

What about the possibility of becoming infected with HIV, the virus that causes AIDS, during a rape? Recall from Chapter 5 that the test for HIV (actually, antibodies to HIV) cannot confirm the presence of the virus until many weeks after initial infection. So why not test the rapist if he's caught? In most states, victims and prosecutors are not allowed to see the results of rapists' AIDS tests because of a defendant's right to privacy. This seems very unfair to victims (and most others), for the worry about the possibility of AIDS adds to the trauma of many rape victims. At least one has allowed her attacker to have a reduced sentence in exchange for his AIDS test results (see Salholz et al., 1990). However, remember that it is difficult to spread HIV from person to person—the odds of becoming infected during one act of unprotected vaginal intercourse with an *infected* partner is only about 1 in 500 (Hearst & Hulley, 1988). Thus, AIDS experts believe that the chance of getting HIV during a rape is extremely low. ■

---

sexually transmitted disease (see Box 15-B). Rape victims can be given an injection or pills to prevent unwanted pregnancy if they seek medical help shortly after the attack. At most hospitals social workers are also available to help rape victims (in areas that do not have an advocate program).

Almost half of all reported rapes are dismissed before trial (U.S. Senate Judiciary Committee report, May 1993). Most of the dismissed cases are acquaintance rapes, for which prosecutors have traditionally been hesitant to bring cases to trial. However, with increased education (of the public, police, and courts) there have been dramatic changes in the manner in which rape victims are treated by the courts. For example, the U.S. Supreme Court has upheld broad **rape-shield laws** that make prosecution easier and prevent the victim from feeling like she (or he) is on trial. In 1991, the court ruled that states can enact laws that bar an accused (acquaintance) rapist from introducing evidence that he and his victim had previously had consensual sex. In addition, a victim's past sexual history is no longer allowed to be introduced during trial, but the accused rapist's past sexual offenses can be. Because many women delay reporting their rapes and many others appear calm and relaxed afterward—two common behaviors associated

Rape-shield laws

Laws that make prosecution of rapists easier and that also prevent the victims from feeling like they are on trial.

with rape trauma—many juries in the past have refused to believe victims' stories. Many states now allow expert testimony about rape trauma syndrome to educate jurors about these behaviors. Previously, evidence of emission of semen had to be found before an assault could be called a rape. Today, many states no longer require evidence of ejaculation for rape to be charged. The attacker can be charged and convicted of assault, even if he is not charged with rape. In a landmark 1993 case, a rapist was sentenced to 40 years in prison by a jury that disregarded his claim that she consented because she asked him to wear a condom.

However, prosecution of rape is made easier when semen (in the vagina or on pubic hair or clothing) is found during the medical examination, especially now that there is genetic fingerprinting. In the past, semen could only reveal an attacker's blood type, but recent scientific discoveries now make it possible to identify a person from fragments of DNA in their body cells, including semen and blood, much like a fingerprint. This new identification procedure was first used in a criminal case in England in 1987. A man the police had arrested for two rapes and murders was freed after DNA from semen found on the victims did not match his own. The police then took blood samples from 4000 men who lived in the area and the real rapist was arrested and convicted when it was found that his DNA matched that found on the victims (see Joseph Wambaugh's *The Blooding*, 1989).

With increasing public awareness of the myths surrounding rape, it is hoped that more attackers will be charged and convicted of rape. If people do not report a rape, it means that someone else will likely be victimized by the same rapist. Even if you choose not to prosecute the crime, the information you provide may be valuable to the police and may prevent future rapes.

PREVENTING RAPE

In general, there are three basic perspectives or approaches suggested for the prevention of rape. The **first approach focuses on the rapist**. Malamuth and colleagues (1980, 1981) found that many men indicated they would commit rape if they were certain they would not get caught. It was noted that watching films that showed violence toward women increased this attitude. (See Chapter 16, "Sex and the Law.") Surely some legal form of deterrent is necessary to prevent rape. This perspective calls for more policemen on patrol, more lights in dark parking lots, tougher laws that are more rigorously enforced, more arrests, and longer prison sentences for rapists. During its 1994 session, for example, Congress passed The Violence Against Women Act which, among other things, increased penalties for sex offenses. About half of the 50 sates have recently passed laws requiring that sex criminals released from prison register their addresses with police.

This first approach attempts to use deterrents to prevent rape. Almost everyone is in favor of strict law enforcement and a speedy and just court system. However, this approach deals with the symptom only (rape behavior) and not the cause (why does a man want to commit rape?). A law and order approach, by itself, may only make rapists more cautious in choosing the time, place, and victim.

THE SECOND PERSPECTIVE FOCUSES ON THE POTENTIAL VICTIM. The first part of this approach involves decreasing the chance that a woman will be the target of a rape. Women are often urged to avoid settings or people that might increase the likelihood of rape (e.g., dark alleys, picking up hitchhikers). They are also taught to keep dead bolts on doors, to avoid advertising the fact they might live alone, not to trust door chains as a means of identifying strangers, etc. When going to their cars, women are encouraged to look under and around the vicinity of their cars from a distance, as well as to check the back seat before getting in their cars.

This approach also involves reacting to an attempted rape. Women are urged to learn at least a little bit about self-defense. Women who resist decrease the chance of the rape being completed by about 80 percent (Marchbanks, Kung-Jong, & Mercy, 1990). Surveys of victims of attempted rape have found that resistance is related to an increased chance of escape without serious harm (Bart, 1980; McIntyre, 1980; Ullman & Knight, 1991). In our culture, most women are not raised to be physically aggressive and it has been my experience from talking to women about rape prevention that many at first are uneasy about defending themselves in a manner that might cause physical harm to the rapist. Self-defense courses (such as are widely offered through the YWCA) prepare women both mentally and physically for how to defend themselves.

Verbal assertiveness or aggression can also help prevent an attack, especially if used when a woman is first approached (Warner, 1980). Brodsky (1976) reported that being assertive and fighting back is most likely to be successful when the rapist initially is polite, hesitant, or precedes the attack with conversation. Some women even get themselves to urinate, vomit, defecate, or tell their attacker that they have a sexually transmitted disease in order to make themselves repulsive to an attacker. Other forms of trickery include trying to talk the rapist into going to a place where someone can recognize what's going on and help.

" I was once approached by a rapist, who dragged me off into an alley. A part of me somehow remained calm. I simply told him that I would rather go to a motel, and that I would pay for it. It blew his mind at first, and he started to choke me. I pushed him away from me and calmly informed him that my husband was a Mafia hit man and that he often checked up on me and would kill us if he found us together. A motel would be the only place where we would be safe alone. And if we went to the phone company where I worked at the time, I would get my check and take the day off. He fell for it.

I kept calmly talking to him and assuring him how nice it was going to be and how lucky I was to be getting away from my husband. (Any and every lie I could conceive of, I verbalized casually.) At the phone company there was a guard with a gun. When I saw the guard, I began running in circles and screaming for help. The guard quickly pulled out his gun. What amazed me was that the rapist made no attempt to run, but instead told the guard we were going to a motel. His voice had degenerated into blubbering in anticipation. When the police came, he told them he was going to give me a baby in the alley, and I suggested a motel.

He was a notorious child molester, who had put eight little girls (aged 8 to 11 years old) in the hospital. I was the only one old enough to go to court against him—the kids were too young."

(from the author's files)

There are some problems with this approach to rape prevention as well. The first problem is that by placing the responsibility for preventing rape in the hands of the victim, women who are raped may feel that they have somehow failed and that the rape was their fault. As stated before, a woman should never feel guilty for being raped, as she did not instigate or cause the action. Screaming, whistles, mace, vomiting, or talking sometimes work very well, but they may not work in every case. Techniques that may work to drive away one rapist may do the reverse and anger another. There is no perfect defense against rape. Finally, these attempts to prevent rape do not deal with the underlying causes of rape.

A final approach comes from a **social systems perspective**. From this point of view, rape is caused by our society's belief that males should be sexually aggressive and dominant. The explanation of rape as a form of social pathology (mentioned earlier) fits this point of view. In a society where violence has become both commonplace and acceptable (look at our TV and movie heroes), it should come as no surprise that men use violence as a means of subjugating women. From this perspective, rape can best be prevented by changing social attitudes toward the way that men and women relate to each other. Even though this approach attempts to deal directly with the cause of rape, it may be the most difficult to change. Nonetheless, changing the values and attitudes of a society is hard, but certainly not impossible. Traditional sex role stereotypes have, in fact, been changing over the past two decades in the United States to the benefit of both men and women. In Mead's (1935) writings about a culture in which males were expected to be nurturant rather than dominant and aggressive toward women, she reported that rape was unknown. Recall, too, that rape is much less common in many other civilized countries.

What do you think? Is a tougher law-and-order approach to rape needed? Should more women become prepared to deal with attempted rape? Is this enough? Will rape ever stop being a serious problem in our society? Why or why not? ∎

SEXUAL HARASSMENT

Anita Hill's accusation of sexual harassment by Supreme Court nominee Clarence Thomas, and similar charges against U.S. Senator Bob Packwood by several of his female staff and interns, brought attention to an issue in the early 1990s that many people (particularly men) had not taken seriously. Was sexual harassment something new? Of course not. Many surveys taken during the 1980s found that a large proportion of women (generally from 40 to 60 percent) in all sorts of occupations felt that they had been the victim of sexual harassment while at work (e.g., Duldt, 1982; Gutek, 1985; Loy & Stewart, 1984; Tangri, Burt, & Johnson, 1982; U.S. Merit Systems Protection Board, 1988). Seven to eight percent of women in the work force have experienced direct bribes in return for sex, or negative consequences for not cooperating (Gold, 1987). Although not as common, men too can be the victims of sexual harassment at work (Janus & Janus, 1993; Tangri et al., 1982).

What is sexual harassment? The Equal Employment Opportunity Commission (EEOC) established a legal definition of **sexual harassment** in the workplace in 1980:

> Unwelcome sexual advances, requests for sexual favors, and other verbal or physical conduct of a sexual nature constitute unlawful sexual harassment when (a) submission to such conduct is made either explic-

Sexual harassment
Unwelcome sexual advances that persist after the recipient has indicated that it is unwanted. See text for an expanded definition.

itly or implicitly a term or condition of an individual's employment, (b) submission to or rejection of such conduct by an individual is used as the basis for employment decisions affecting such individual, or (c) such conduct has the purpose or effect of unreasonably interfering with an individual's work performance or creating an intimidating, hostile, or offensive working environment.

Behavior is considered harassment when it *persists* after the recipient has indicated that it is unwanted. In 1986, the U.S. Supreme Court expanded the definition by ruling that harassment based on sex, which creates a hostile or offensive work environment, is also illegal (*Meritor Savings Bank* v. *Vinson*, 1986). In other words, a victim *does not have to prove that sexual favors were demanded in exchange for job benefits*. A hostile or offensive work environment can include such things as nude calendars, lewd jokes, touching, and obsessive staring. This interpretation of sexual harassment was reaffirmed in a 1993 ruling.

The EEOC and courts have also ruled that a company can be held liable for sexual harassment by its employees if it doesn't take "immediate and appropriate corrective action." Today, many large businesses have explicit policies against sexual harassment, as well as educational programs for their employees. Charges of sexual harassment are usually prosecuted as civil suits (rather than criminal cases) under Title VII of the Civil Rights Act of 1964, which bans discrimination in employment based on sex. The Civil Rights Act of 1991 expanded the limit of punitive and compensatory damages.

Here are two examples of sexual harassment in the workplace provided to me by students:

"My boss started off saying nasty jokes. Then he began to relate the jokes to his own personal experiences. Next he started making comments about how big my breasts were or how my butt looked in jeans. At this time I got real scared. . . ."

"I started working as a legal assistant at the second largest law firm in New Orleans. I was assigned to two young associates. One of the associates was 28, engaged to be married, and took interest in helping me learn how the trial process is handled. I began to notice little things that 'Rich' did that were making me feel uncomfortable. First, compliments or personal remarks about my looks. Then he would make insinuations in front of others about how late we worked the night before, and how well we worked together. All of these were said in a manner that made me extremely uncomfortable.

The last straw was the touching. At first on the back as I was typing or reading; but later on the thighs and calves. I went to my superior and we met with the head of personnel and the Director of our law department. I quit that day without pressing charges or causing a big fuss. Why? Because the department I worked in was the Labor Department. 'Rich' defended sexual harassment cases and won. He actually defended employees against sexual harassment—he knew better.''

(from the author's files)

It is obvious from this last case history that "some men just don't get it." Many more men than women feel that the problem of sexual harassment has been greatly exaggerated (Dietz-Uhler & Murrell, 1992; Safran, 1981; Tangri et al., 1982), and many men believe that women should not be so quickly offended when men show sexual interest in them (Dietz-Uhler & Murrell, 1992). Although men recognize overt behaviors as harassment (e.g., offering favors in return for sex), many men don't view less overt behaviors (e.g., sexual jokes and remarks) as harassment (Dietz-Uhler & Murrell, 1992; Gutek et al., 1980; Powell, 1986). Many men even blame the women for being sexually harassed (Jensen & Gutek, 1982). Thus, men generally take the issue of sexual harassment less seriously than women.

Why is this a serious issue to women? Sexual harassment usually occurs in a relationship where there is unequal power, such as employer-employee or teacher-student (MacKinnon, 1979). This makes the victims of harassment very vulnerable, especially if they are economically dependent on their jobs. Victims may feel that there is no recourse. Who do you complain to if it is the boss who is doing the harassing? If a woman refuses sexual advances or objects to an offensive work environment, she might be the target of retaliation (e.g., passed over for raises or promotions, poor ratings, or even fired). If she quits she may be ineligible for unemployment compensation. Whether she is fired or she quits, she will be unable to ask for references from this employer in the future because he will no doubt invent reasons for her termination (having to do with poor performance). The end result is that victims of sexual harassment often are left with feelings similar to other victims of sexual abuse—a feeling of helplessness (Safran, 1976). In addition, victims often feel humiliation, shame, and anger (Hamilton et al., 1987; Loy & Stewart, 1984).

SOME CAUSES OF SEXUAL HARASSMENT

Carlota Bustelo, of the United Nations Committee on the Elimination of Discrimination against Women, said that sexual harassment "defines an ancient phenomenon that is frequent in the workplace but that remained undiscussed until the 1970s. Its disclosure, which began in the U.S., was due to changes taking place in the power relationships between men and women in society at large and, more particularly, on the job . . . " (in *World Press Review*, February 1992). Research has shown that the more a male believes in traditional stereotypical roles for men and women, the more accepting he is of sexual harassment (Dietz-Uhler & Murrell, 1992).

Gender roles have changed considerably as more and more women have entered the work force over the last few decades, and in Chapter 8 you learned that our society has slowly evolved from stereotypical roles to a more androgynous state. Lately, however, there has been a disturbing increase in sexual harassment by young males, which many of them view as an appropriate gender role. For example, many teenage boys try to "demonstrate their manhood" and gain popularity by yelling explicit propositions to girls or fondling them as they walk by (Henneberger & Marriott, 1993). A survey of teenagers commissioned by the American Association of University Women (conducted by Louis Harris & Associates) in 1993 found that more than two thirds of girls (and a fair proportion of boys) had been fondled, grabbed, or pinched in an explicitly sexual manner. This behavior among young males portends a dim outlook for correcting sexual harassment in the workplace in the future. "Raising awareness among men," according to one expert, "may be more important than getting women to complain" (Michelle Paludi, quoted in *New York Times*, Oct. 22, 1991, p. C1).

Even in social situations the signals between men and women are often ambiguous and the possibility of misunderstanding is great. A man may misinterpret how a woman is dressed or behaving as interest in him. Some men, however, construe every smile, gesture, or pleasantry as sexual interest. In our culture, men are also expected to be sexually aggressive, so if a man interprets a behavior as interest (correctly or incorrectly) he is likely to pursue it. Many men accept initial resistance on the part of a woman to be part of the "game," reinforced perhaps by the fact that some women first say "no" even when they want to be pursued (Muehlenhard & Hollabaugh, 1988). When, then, does sexual interest become sexual harassment? When a woman has made it clear that sexual advances, or comments, are unwanted, then *any* persistence on the part of the male is clearly harassment. This should be true anywhere, but it is particularly true in the workplace.

Sexual Harassment of College Students

Sexual harassment can occur in any setting in which there are power differences between people. College campuses are certainly an example of this. In 1994, the president of a state university in Arkansas was dismissed on grounds of sexual harassment and inappropriate sexual activity. Several studies have found that many college women (17 to 33 percent, depending on the study) have been sexually harassed by their instructor (Adams et al., 1983; Benson & Thompson, 1982; Fitzgerald et al., 1988; McCormack, 1985; Popovich & Licata, 1986; Reilly et al., 1986). Female students are likely targets of harassment regardless of their ethnicity, or marital status (Hughes et al., 1995). On college campuses, males also are often the target of sexual harassment (Baier, 1990; Mazer & Percival, 1989; Roscoe et al., 1987).

The harassment can be direct (offering an "A for a lay" or threatening to lower a grade unless the student agrees to sex) or less obvious (e.g., crude comments, hugs, insistence on seeing the student alone). As can happen in the workplace, an instructor can create an offensive environment for a student even if there are no direct propositions or threats:

"It was during my second semester in college when I became the target of sexual harass-ment from my instructor. The ordeal started when he began to stare at me in class for long periods of time. I grew uncomfortable and more importantly, self-conscious. I couldn't figure out why he was staring at me. He then began to approach me and make small talk. In between 'hello' and 'how are you?' he would squeeze in a compliment. Eventually his compliments became suggestive, and before long, he was making blatant sexual innuendoes to me in front of the class. He would say 'I can't concentrate on my lectures with you sitting in the front row looking like that,' or, 'You sure do make it hard (emphasis on hard) on a guy.'

Once when I wore a skirt to class, he asked, 'Did you wear this for me?' as he fixed his eyes on my legs. On another occasion as I was picking up my school bag he tapped me on the shoulder and said, 'Don't bend over in those jeans like that.' Once he said he'd like to take me to lunch and have me for dessert.

I finally had enough and I began to sit in the back of the lecture hall. He would come to me after class and tell me he 'missed me in the front row.' That was when I quit going altogether. I had four friends in class who knew what was going on and they insisted after about two weeks of absences that I come back to class. They begged me to press charges against him.

The day I returned, my professor asked me where I'd been and told me that 'if I knew what he was thinking I could charge him with sexual harassment.' The next week I wore a tie to class and he touched my tie and commented, 'I'd like to tie you up.' A girl I didn't know approached me after class and offered herself as a witness if I wanted to file a formal complaint. I wanted to do just that. However, I was and still am very concerned about my grades; I was sure that if I charged him with this behavior he would have penalized me through my grade.

This happened two years ago, and I saw this man again last week. (We haven't seen each other since I had his class.) The first thing he said to me—in front of my other professor and many students was 'Hi honey, my place or yours?' This was the first impression my new professor had of me. This time I'm angry. I don't deserve to be talked to this way, nor does anyone else. My friends were right—he should be stopped!!''

(from the author's files)

It is *never* appropriate for an instructor to give sexual, or even romantic, overtures to a student presently enrolled in his class or under his supervision (such as thesis advisor). Because of the difference in power, all such cases should be regarded as harassment. As in the workplace, students who are the victims of sexual harassment may feel that there is no recourse, and the experience often results in negative emotional effects (Satterfield & Muehlenhard, 1990). Some victims feel so compromised that they change majors or drop out of school (Dziech & Weiner, 1984). Today, most colleges and universities have firm guidelines about harassment and grievance procedures that can be used by victims, and the U.S. Supreme Court recently ruled that under Title IX of the Education Amendment of 1972, schools can be held liable for not taking action (*Franklin* v. *Gwinnett County Public Schools*, 1992). Do you know if your campus has established a policy about sexual harassment?

How to Deal with Sexual Harassment

The number of sexual harassment cases reported to the EEOC doubled during the 1980s (Faludi, 1991). Still, only 5 percent of victims ever decide to take formal action (U.S. Merit Systems Protection Board, 1988).

Sexual harassment can often be prevented if the recipient is assertive at the first sign of inappropriate behavior. Unfortunately, some women are uneasy about being assertive for fear that they will appear "unfriendly" or "impolite." Keep in mind that you are not the one who has behaved improperly. Telling the harasser a firm "no" (or that you will not tolerate being talked to like that) is expressing your right for personal dignity. If you are not assertive, some men may misinterpret that as a sign of interest.

If the harasser continues his behavior after you have delivered a clear message that it is not appreciated, then you will have to take other steps to deal with it. Most women choose to avoid it passively (e.g., ignoring it, dropping the class, quitting the job) or defuse it by stalling tactics or making a joke out of it (Gruber, 1989).

When the harassment is blatant, persistent, and highly offensive, as in the example of the university professor in the case history, stronger measures are necessary. Talk to the harasser, or write a letter to him, relaying the facts and again expressing clearly and firmly that the behavior must stop. Document all the episodes of harassment (dates, places) and list all witnesses. The very next time the behavior continues, follow the grievance procedure of your company or school and report it. Those companies and schools that have implemented grievance procedures will protect you against retaliation. If you should be treated unjustly, report it to the EEOC or file a civil suit (remember, companies and schools can now be held liable for not taking action).

I urge you not to deal with harassment passively, but instead to take assertive actions. Why? Because if you deal with harassment by simply avoiding the harasser, he will start harassing someone else. Case in point: the university professor in the case study continues to teach and continues to treat other coeds in the same manner. Behavior like this will be stopped only when someone decides to press charges.

For more information on how to deal with sexual harassment, contact one of the organizations listed in the Resource Section of the appendix. ■

SEXUAL ABUSE OF CHILDREN

In 1992, a former priest was convicted of sexually molesting 32 children aged 10 to 14, some allegedly in church. In the same year, a former national teacher of the year was sentenced to a year in jail for molesting young boys at his cabin home. In separate cases in the state of Washington, two men with long histories of sexual abuse were convicted of raping numerous young children and killing several of them, leading that state to pass a "sexual predator" law which requires that career molesters be confined for life.

Our culture has a long history of denial about sexual abuse of children (Olafson, Corwin, & Summit, 1993), but an abundance of research in the past few decades has made it clear that this is a serious, widespread problem. How common is sexual abuse of children? In a comprehensive review of many studies, Peters, Wyatt, and Finkelhor (1986) found that estimates of sexual abuse of girls ranged from 6 percent to 62 percent, and from 3 percent to 31 percent for boys. One of the problems is how we define sexual abuse. Within psychology and psychiatry, "children" refers to *prepubescent* children (before age 13), and most professionals also stipulate that the abuse must be by someone at least 5 years older (DSM-IV, 1994). Kinsey et al. (1953) found that 24 percent of the women in their survey qualified as victims of sexual abuse by this definition. A more recent review estimates that 10 to 15 percent of children experience at least one incident of sexual abuse (Mrazek, 1984). In the recent survey by Laumann and colleagues (1994), 17 percent of women and 12 percent of men reported being victims of sexual touching (or worse) by an older person when they were younger than 13. The YWCA Rape Crisis Program says that *one out of every four girls and one out of every seven boys will be victims of some form of sexual abuse before they reach the age of 18* (Becker & Coleman, 1988; Wolfe et al., 1988).

As the above data show, twice as many girls as boys are targeted as victims (Mrazek, 1984). Kinsey's group found that in 80 percent of cases only one incident of molestation occurred, but a 1985 *Los Angeles Times* poll found that for about 15 percent of victims the abuse continues for more than a year. Other studies have found that at least 10 to 15 percent of victims are abused by more than one adult (Conte et al., 1986; Tufts New England Medical Center, 1984).

Gebhard et al. (1965) found that sexual contact with children usually involved fondling the genitals, and that children, especially young ones, usually did not understand the sexual significance of these behaviors. Although Gebhard et al.'s and Kinsey et al.'s studies found that sexual intercourse with children was uncommon, more recent studies have found an increasingly greater proportion of child molestation cases that involve vaginal or anal intercourse, or oral-genital sex (Conte et al., 1986; Erickson et al., 1988; Leventhal, 1988; Moore, Nord, & Peterson, 1989).

Who Molests Children?

The stereotype of a child molester is often that of a dirty old man who hangs around playgrounds offering candy to young boys and girls, and who snatches the children away when their parents are not present. However, this is usually not the case. Studies have found that in the majority of molestation cases, the molester is an adult known to the victim, and often a relative (Bureau of Justice Statistics for 1992; Gebhard et al., 1968; Leventhal, 1988; Mohr et al., 1964). In fact, the YWCA Rape Crisis Program estimates that *about 80 percent of all molesters are known by their victims* (Kikuchi, 1988; Starr, 1988).

"When I was 12 years old I was sexually molested by my sister's boyfriend. My mother and sister earlier that day had a doctor's appointment and he had offered to keep an eye on me while they were gone. . . . He dared me to do sexual things. If I refused he would then get forceful toward me and out of being scared I went along with it. He forced me to have oral sex on him. Finally, some one knocked at the door and they saved me from having to go through any more. . . . "

"When I was little (ages 5–7), I was molested. My parents worked but let me stay with our elderly neighbors. The old man did this to me. He taught me how to kiss and touch his penis. He did this when his wife would either go to the store or leave out of the room. I hated it. He didn't like it when I'd fight him away from me. What I can't understand is why: why me. . . . "

(from the author's files)

Researchers have attempted to classify molesters in many different ways. For example, Groth, Hobson, and Gary (1982) proposed that molesters could be distinguished as *fixated* (arrested psychosexual development) or *regressed* (under stress, after normal development). Howells (1981), Lanyon (1986), and others prefer the distinction **preference molesters** (they have a primary sexual orientation to children and are relatively uninterested in adult partners) and **situational molesters** (primary interests are toward adults and they consider their urges toward children, often done impulsively during stress, as abnormal). This last classification has much in common with that in the American Psychiatric Association's manual DSM-IV (1994), which classifies molesters as pedophiles or nonpedophiles. You were introduced to the topic of pedophilia (from Greek meaning "love of children") in Chapter 14. A **pedophile** is a man for whom children provide the "repeatedly preferred or exclusive method of achieving sexual excitement." Thus, if a man were

Preference molesters

Child molesters who have a primary sexual orientation to children and who are relatively uninterested in adult partners.

Situational molesters

Child molesters who have a primary sexual orientation to adults. They have sex with children impulsively and regard their behavior as abnormal.

Pedophilia

A condition in which sexual arousal is achieved primarily and repeatedly through sexual activity with children who have not reached puberty.

to commit an act of child molestation, but was not repeatedly attracted to children, he would not be considered a pedophile (here the term *situational molester* is appropriate).

The older classification of incestuous molesters versus nonincestuous molesters, which assumed that the former limited their offenses to family members and were not a threat to the general community, is no longer regarded as a useful distinction. Both groups have similar sexual preference patterns (Abel et al., 1981) and nearly half of incestuous fathers and step-fathers have sexually abused other children during the same time period they were abusing their own children (Abel et al., 1988b).

> "I am a victim of child sexual abuse. I was six years old and my godmother's fiance was the predator. . . . He made me do everything from vaginal penetration to oral genital sex. . . . Later it was found that he did this to four of his six children, myself, two of my cousins and six other children. . . ."

(from the author's files)

Pedophiles have been further classified according to their psychological characteristics (Cohen, Seghorn, & Calmas, 1969). The *personally immature pedophile* is the most common. He is attracted to children because he has never developed the social skills necessary to initiate and maintain a sexual relationship with an adult. A relationship with a child allows this individual to be in control, which he cannot achieve with an adult. Notice that the primary motivation here, control, is similar to the motivation in many rape cases. The *regressive pedophile*, on the other hand, is likely to engage in sexual relations in an impulsive manner, often with a child who is a stranger. They describe their acts as the result of an uncontrollable urge. Unlike the personally immature pedophile, the regressed pedophile has a history of normal adult sexual relations. They begin turning to children as a result of developing feelings of sexual inadequacy, often due to stress, and the problem is often complicated by additional abuse of alcohol (Gebhard et al., 1965), which they often use as an excuse for their behavior (MacNamara & Sagarin, 1977). A third, and fortunately the least common type, is the *aggressive pedophile*. They are not satisfied with just having sex with their young victims, but are aroused by inflicting physical injury. Here, too, notice that the primary motivation, sadistic acts, is similar to that in one of the classifications of rape discussed earlier. In fact, these men can be called child rapists (Groth et al., 1982), and often show a variety of other antisocial behaviors. Seven to 15 percent of child molestation cases include physical harm to the victims (Conte, 1991; Mrazek et al., 1981).

Pedophiles typically have molested many children before they are caught, if they are caught at all. For example, in one study of male pedophiles who were undergoing treatment, nonincestuous offenders who targeted girls had averaged 20 victims each, while those targeting boys had averaged nearly 200 victims each (Abel et al., 1987). Child molestation committed by men who are not pedophiles is usually within a father-daughter (or stepdaughter) relationship and generally involves only one child (Freund, Watson, & Dickey, 1991). Women are sometimes involved in acts of sexual molestation, but pedophilia among women is rare (Finkelhor, 1984).

Only a small minority of male sex offenders target both boys and girls (Groth & Birnbaum, 1978). Heterosexual males account for 95 percent of sexual abuse of girls, while "homosexual" males account for most cases involving boys (Finkelhor & Russell, 1984; homosexual was placed in quotes because most molesters of boys do not have homosexual attractions to adults; Freund & Langevin, 1976). Although the ratio of female to male victims is 2 to 1, because male offenders who target boys generally have many more victims, the ratio of heterosexual pedophiles to homosexual pedophiles has been estimated to be approximately 11 to 1 (Freund & Watson, 1992).

What is the child molester like personally? Most are respectable and otherwise law-abiding citizens (Lanyon, 1986). Many are shy, passive, and unassertive (Langevin, 1983), although incestuous fathers are generally very domineering and controlling within their own families (Meiselman, 1978). However, for the most part there are no reliable personality characteristics correlated with pedophilia (Lanyon, 1986; Okami & Goldberg, 1992). In short, there is no single personality profile; child molesters are a very heterogeneous group (McAnulty, Adams, & Wright, 1994).

We do know that, unlike normal people, child molesters have the capacity to be sexually aroused by young children (Abel et al., 1981; Finkelhor & Araji, 1986; Marshall et al., 1986). This ability is generally acquired when molesters rehearse and fantasize what they will do to children while they masturbate, and this type of rehearsal often goes on for years. A majority of pedophiles were themselves the victims of sexual abuse as children (this is not true of sex offenders against adults; Freund & Kuban, 1994; Groth, 1979), and thus may never have learned that it is wrong to have sex with children. However, some experts believe that the molesters' sexual behaviors are primarily motivated by nonsexual needs (e.g., affection, control; Groth et al., 1982; Lanyon, 1986). The pedophile, unlike most other paraphiliacs, usually does not display other paraphilias (Fedora et al., 1992).

One thing that is well established is that the deviate behavior often begins early in life (Becker & Abel,

1985). One study found that the median age for the first offense was 16 (Groth et al., 1982). In 1992 in Buckley, Washington, a 9-year-old boy was found to have raped or molested eight younger children at knifepoint over a 2-year period. Adolescents may be responsible for as many as 30 to 50 percent of child sexual abuse cases (Davis & Leitenberg, 1987; Groth & Loredo, 1981; see Murphy et al., 1992). A recent study found that pedophiles recall having a much greater than normal curiosity in their own childhood to seeing naked children, without such curiosity about adults (Freund & Kuban, 1993).

Tragically, the true pedophile, in order to satisfy his sexual urges, often finds positions where he has access to children. In New Orleans, a man who worked as a clown at children's birthday parties was convicted of molesting dozens of children who attended the parties. In a neighboring city, an officer in the child molestation unit was arrested for having sex with the children he was supposed to protect. Pedophiles have been found in positions as teachers, scout leaders, camp counselors, and even ministers or priests.

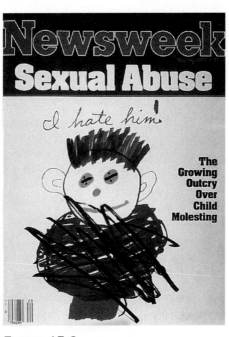

FIGURE 15-3

"I attended a very respectable summer camp during my junior high summers. Every session, about midway through the camp, the camp director took us to creek to go on the sliding rock. He would tell the kids if they slid down the rock 'skinny sliding' (nude) they would get to be in line first for the dinner buffet. The counselors were sharply divided on this. Some thought it was just funny and others thought it was odd. Two years ago, the director was caught for child molestation. He was convicted and served time in jail."

"I entered a monastery for boys. . . . As a novice I was told to go to confession daily and the Father Superior would counsel me in both Christian education and my personal life. Confessions were very informal. The Father Superior heard them from 7:30 P.M. until midnight in his room. . . . One night he said, 'and do you know how they took oaths in the Old Testament? One would put his hand on the other man's genitals. But there was no sexual connotation intended. The Jews viewed sex differently than we do.' I was a little puzzled and didn't ask any questions.

About a week later I went to see one of the brothers for confession, but he told me that the Father Superior wanted to see me. . . . He said, 'Do you want to take an oath like in the Old Testament?' I was stunned and didn't really know what he meant. Finally he took my hand and placed it under his robe on his penis. I was shocked and pulled my hand away immediately, but he said, 'Don't be afraid, there is no sexual intent here. You are keeping a very ancient form of taking an oath.' As he was saying this he took my hand again and placed it on his penis. I wanted to pull back, but I was afraid he would go into another temper tantrum. . . . He didn't do anything else that night, but he talked to me about how much we had to be obedient children. He often stressed obedience—total obedience. (This was how he set us up. We must be totally obedient.)

Then it happened. One night we were talking and he said, 'Do you want to kiss my penis?'—I was so naive. I didn't know what he was talking about. He said, 'Do you want me to kiss your penis? That's how much I love you.' I said no, but then he said, 'Don't you think I love you? There is no sexual intent. It is a pure act of platonic love.' (He defined platonic love as love without passion—including sexual contact. He emphasized this: *without* passion. Passion is wrong. All passions. This passionless sex, he explained, could only be between him and his children.) Then he drew me closer to him, he opened my robe, unzipped my pants, put his hands into my underwear, brought my penis into the open and kissed it.

It later turned into fellatio. . . . He taught me what he wanted done to him. He had orgasms every time that 'I went for confession.' I was instructed never to have orgasm. Never! 'That would not be good for me spiritually.'

I have some very deep scars and am now receiving therapy."

(Author's note: This young man later found out that many other boys had been victimized by the same man.)

(from the author's files)

Effects on the Children

Because of the strong social stigma against sexual relations between adults and children in our culture, it has traditionally been assumed that the effects on the child were always very negative and long-lasting. Considerable research has now shown, however, that there is no single "post-sexual-abuse-syndrome" with a specific course or outcome (e.g., Beitchman et al., 1991, 1992; Lipovsky & Kilpatrick, 1992). In fact, some "victims" recall their experiences as having been positive or pleasurable, leading some investigators to question whether the sexual behavior in these cases can be called "abuse" (e.g., Havgaard & Emery, 1989; Okami, 1991; Sandfort, 1992). Those children reporting positive sexual relations must have had a different experience than the many others who report anxiety, fear, depression, panic disorder, sexual dysfunctions and other negative reactions (Beitchman et al., 1991, 1992; Friedrich, 1990; Murrey et al., 1993). At least 60 percent of girls and over a third of boys report their reactions to sex with an adult as very negative (Elvik et al., 1986). It would appear that the effects of adult-child sexual relations represent a continuum of experiences.

Several factors contribute to the particular response of a child. The greatest harm in terms of long-lasting negative effects are seen in cases where the abuse is frequent or long-lasting; the abuse involves penetration, force, threats, or violence; the abuser is the father or stepfather; and where there is little support from the mother (Beitchman et al., 1992; Kendall-Tackett, Williams, & Finkelhor, 1993). In these cases, the most frequent symptoms include fears, poor self-esteem, inappropriate sexual behavior, greater tendency for homosexual experiences, depression, and a greater likelihood to be revictimized. Some victims of severe sexual abuse later show increased sexual behavior themselves (Friedrich, 1993), confusing sex with love or becoming sexually preoccupied or aggressive. They are also more likely to report their own children to have been abused (Boyer & Fine, 1992). Some victims of "serious" sexual abuse show no apparent symptoms (Kendall-Tackett et al., 1993), but in some cases this might be due to the denial or emotional suppression displayed by many victims (Leitenberg, Greenwald, & Cado, 1992).

Only about a third of child victims inform their parents or another adult of the abuse (Finkelhor, 1979), and reactions that are perceived by the child as less than supportive can greatly add to the negativity of the experience. Consider, for example, the following three cases:

"When I was younger, I was sexually abused by one of my father's good friends. I told my mother . . . but they acted like they did not believe me. I felt very embarrassed." (female)

"At the age of 9, I was molested by a man right outside of my neighborhood. I told my mother what had happened. I was very hurt and scared, but instead of talking to me, my mother refused to talk about it and acted as if it was my fault. Years later I discovered the man had done the same thing to other children. By then it was too late, I was already emotionally scarred." (female)

"I was about 8 years old when I was sexually abused by a friend of my father. I refused, but he beat me up and made me have sexual intercourse with him. Later the same night I told my father, but my father instead of going to the police, as I thought, beat me very harshly with a wood stick." (male)

(from the author's files)

Similar to victims of rape, victims of child molestation have a tendency for self-blame, which can greatly affect self-esteem.

"I was sexually abused for 9 years as a child by my older sister's husband. For years I believed it had happened because there was something wrong with me."

(from the author's files)

A recent review of many studies concluded that about two thirds of victims of child sexual abuse show substantial recovery during the first 12 to 18 months (Kendall-Tackett et al., 1993). The same has been found for a group of preschoolers who were ritualistically abused (Waterman et al., 1992). Even for these individuals, however, some symptoms such as sexual preoccupation and aggressiveness may worsen (Friedrich & Reams, 1987; Gomes-Schwartz et al., 1990). From 10 to 24 percent of abused children not only fail to improve over time, but actually get worse (see Kendall-Tackett et al., 1993).

Recently, there have been an increasing number of adults who, while undergoing therapy for other problems (e.g., depression), have been guided by therapists into "remembering" childhood sexual abuse. "Recovered memory" of childhood abuse, as it is called, is very controversial. No doubt in some cases it is legitimate, but others worry that therapists can "create" false memories. According to Harvard psychiatrist Harrison Pope, "There are a certain number of therapists who see sexual abuse in every patient they see. And they can lead a patient by a thousand suggestions and implications, and by reinforcing what they do and don't listen to" (quoted by Cole, 1994).

For both sides of this controversy, see Morfit (1994) and Althof (1994).

PREVENTING AND DEALING WITH CHILD SEXUAL ABUSE

The first thing to do to minimize the chance of your child being a victim of sexual abuse is to **educate yourself.** You should be able to talk openly and candidly about sexual matters, including sexual abuse, with your children. You should be aware of the fact that children who tell about being molested are almost never making the stories up. Remember that most molesters are known to their victims, so do not doubt your child if he or she tells you that the molester was someone you know.

The next thing to do is to **educate your child.** As I have indicated in previous chapters, it is important that children know the correct names of their anatomies (e.g., penis, vagina). If molested, they will then be able to describe to you where they were touched. What words do you use in front of your children to describe body parts? What do your children learn if you refuse to mention certain body parts or functions, or use slang terms?

Dear Ann Landers: I have just spent a week on jury duty, hearing evidence in a sexual battery case. One victim was an 11-year-old girl in the sixth grade. She had difficulty describing what had happened because the poor child did not know the names of the parts of the human body. . . . When asked if she had ever seen a diagram of the human body, she replied, ''No, we don't even get that till next year.''

(Reprinted with permission of Ann Landers and Creators Syndicate)

Children should not be ashamed of their bodies, but they should also know which parts of their bodies are personal or private and which should not be touched by other people. You must teach your children to be assertive and to know that it is all right to say "No!" to an adult who attempts to touch them in the genital area or on their breasts or buttocks. Your child must also know that he or she won't be punished for talking about being molested, no matter what the molester might say. Similarly, they must know that although some molesters will threaten to hurt their parents, these threats are lies. Play "what if" games, letting your child act out what to do if approached by a molester. Treat this as a serious topic and be matter of fact, just like when teaching traffic safety. Finally, it is crucial that your child know that he or she can communicate with you about sexual matters in general. If you are

always open to discussion about sex, your child will be more likely to confide in you.

Know what to do if your child is molested or approached by a molester. Reassure him or her that talking to you about it was the right thing to do. Let your child know that it was not his or her fault if they were molested and that the adult was wrong. Don't confront the molester in front of your child, and if the molester is a family member or friend, let your child know that you want to help the molester get well. Let your child know that he or she will not be harmed by the molester. Finally, contact the police, even if you don't intend to press charges. The police can put you in contact with support groups and give useful information as well. In reporting the case to the police, you also may help them in preventing further child abuse.

There are certain signs to look for that may indicate that a child has been a victim of sexual abuse. A victim may suddenly begin to have episodes of depression, crying, or other out-of-character changes in mood or personality. He or she may begin to want to be alone or become afraid to go to a certain place or see a certain person. A victim may suddenly start to have problems at school or with discipline. Remember, if abuse is occurring, a victim may be unwilling or fearful to ask for help (abusers often threaten their victims). If you are a parent, do not write off these types of behaviors as a phase. Something serious might be hurting your child.

Even if you are not the parent, you can still help. Most states have a special office that someone can contact if there is a suspected case of sexual abuse of a child. Staff answering the phone will ask for information, determine if an emergency exists, and will have a social worker sent to investigate if action seems necessary. There are often several areas of specialization within these offices, for example, Abuse and Neglect, Sexual Abuse, and Abuse within Institutions (e.g., suspected abuse within a child day care center). Investigators from this office generally provide services for the families and children involved, and in extreme cases can have a child removed from a home and put in foster care.

In a case that went before the United States Supreme Court, the court stated, "child abuse is one of the most difficult crimes to detect and prosecute, in large part because there often are no witnesses except the victim" (*Pennsylvania* v. *Ritchie*, 1987, p. 60, cited in Myers, 1993). One of the greatest difficulties was that the Sixth Amendment of the United States Constitution guarantees that in all criminal cases, the accused has the right to confront all witnesses against him. Face-to-face confrontations were often very traumatic for children, who, in addition, were no match for shrewd and manipulative defense lawyers. However, in 1990 the Supreme Court ruled that individuals being prosecuted for child abuse have no guaranteed right to face-to-face confrontations with their young accusers if the children would suffer emotional trauma as a result. The court upheld state laws that allowed use of videotaped testimony and testimony by one-way closed-circuit television. Most states have eliminated the corroboration rule as well. Courts are also allowing minors to testify using anatomically correct dolls so that they might show what happened to them, although there are still some unanswered questions as to the reliability of this method of assessment (Elliott, O'Donohue, & Nickerson, 1993). (See Whitcomb, 1992 for a review of the legal changes.)

Myths and stereotypes about child abuse are also being refuted by movies, TV, and media stories. As the general public becomes more informed on the topic of child sexual abuse, individuals will feel more inclined to report such cases. In order to focus public attention on this matter, television celebrity Oprah Winfrey, Michael Reagan (Ronald Reagan's son), and U.S. Senator Paula Hawkins have revealed that they were sexually molested as children by an adult. We can all hope that improved communications between children and their parents about human sexuality will result in more widespread knowledge about child molestation (to prevent it), as well as a greater willingness to talk about it and deal with it if a child is molested.

THE MOLESTER: TREATMENT OR IMPRISONMENT?

Every state has laws that make it illegal to involve children in sexual activity, or to fail to protect a child from sexual abuse. The goal of these laws is to protect the child and to see to it that the adult does not repeat the offense (see Conte, 1991). The goals would be best served by a coordinated effort among the police, the courts, and child welfare and community mental health programs, but attitudes among these four components often differ with regard to what to do about victims and offenders (Trute, Adkins, & MacDonald, 1992). As the extent of sexual abuse of children has become better known, it has become increasingly controversial as to what to do about known molesters. Meanwhile, without a coordinated effort, many accused adults "fall

out of the system" and receive little therapy or confinement, and many victims receive little or no treatment after the initial child protection interview (Conte, 1991).

As for the nonpedophile (situational) molester, whose sexual attraction is primarily to adults, many experts believe that society is best served by seeing to it that he receives therapy. Behavioral approaches, such as covert sensitization (where aversive stimuli are paired with the deviant sexual fantasies) and orgasmic reconditioning (to reestablish sexual responsiveness to adults) have shown much promise (see Kelly, 1982, and Lanyon, 1986).

The outcome of therapy for pedophiles is less certain. For these men, sexual orientation is primarily and repeatedly directed to children, with little or no sexual interest in adults. As you have already learned, many of these men have victimized dozens, and in some cases hundreds, of children (Abel et al., 1987), yet they typically display considerable denial and defensiveness (Grossman, Haywood, & Wasyliw, 1992). The antiandrogen drugs cyproterone acetate and medroxyprogesterone acetate have proven effective in lowering the sex drive, thus allowing clinicians to attempt therapy while the subject is not driven to commit his crimes (Bradford & Pawlak, 1993b; Bye, 1990; Cooper et al., 1992). However, the judicial system is full of examples of pedophiles who have been caught, confined, and undergone therapy, time and time again. These types are often referred to as career pedophiles (McCaghy, 1971), or more recently, as career sexual predators. Washington passed its sexual predator law (which, you recall, requires that molesters identified as career predators be confined for life) after two career pedophiles with long arrest records escalated their crimes to include murdering the victims, and admitted that they would continue to have sex with children if ever set free. Our society will no doubt continue to debate this sensitive issue, weighing rights of offenders versus rights of victims and future victims, for many years to come. What do you think is best? ■

INCEST

The term incest comes from a Latin word meaning "impure." **Incest** refers to sexual activity between relatives (who are too closely related to marry) and is illegal in all 50 states. One reason it is illegal is because this type of mating has the highest probability of defective offspring (Baird & MacGillivray, 1982; Thornhill, 1992). Until recently, many people thought that incest was rare, but it happens much more often than people might (or want to) believe. Gebhard et al.

Incest

Sexual contact between two closely related persons.

(1965), for example, reported that 4 percent of their sample had experienced incest. Hunt (1974) found that 14 percent of males and 9 percent of females had had sexual contact with a relative. Most of these cases were between cousins and often involved just light petting. Sexual abuse of nieces by uncles is also a very common type of incest (Kinsey et al., 1953; Russell, 1986). Nearly 4 percent of Hunt's sample reported having had sex with a brother or sister, and 0.5 percent had been involved in father-daughter sexual relations. Another study found that 1 percent of college coeds had been victimized by their fathers (Finkelhor, 1979). A more recent study found that 3.3 percent of men and 4.5 percent of women reported having been molested by a relative as a child, and in about 60 percent of these cases the molestation was "often" or "ongoing" (Janus & Janus, 1993). Only about 2 percent of adult-child incestuous relations ever get reported to authorities (Russell, 1984) and some victims do not understand that what happened to them was abuse (Kikuchi, 1988).

Although they have received little attention by researchers, **polyincestuous families** are not uncommon (Faller, 1991). In these families, there are both multiple abusers and multiple victims, both across generations and within the same generation. Victims often become abusers, and in many cases view the activity as acceptable, or even expected. Unlike other cases of child molestation, many of the abusers in polyincestuous families are female (Faller, 1987; McCarty, 1986). In over half of such families, there are also abusers and victims from outside the family (Faller, 1991).

Polyincestuous family

Families in which there are both multiple incestuous abusers and multiple victims, across generations and within the same generation.

Much more is known about specific types of incest. After you have read about these, we will return to a discussion of family dynamics in incest.

INCEST BETWEEN SIBLINGS

Brother-sister incest, or in some cases **brother-brother incest**, is believed to be five times more common than parent-child incest (Cole, 1982; Gebhard et al., 1965; Smith & Israel, 1987). Finkelhor (1980) surveyed college undergraduates and found that 15 percent of the women and 10 percent of the men in his sample had had some type of sexual experience with a sibling. This usually involves fondling, but sometimes includes sexual intercourse as well (Meiselman, 1978). In families in which sibling sexual activity occurs, the parents are often distant or inaccessible and/or stimulate a sexual climate in the home (Smith & Israel, 1987).

"I was a victim from age four until thirteen. My two brothers continually cornered me and forced me. My mother worked and was much too busy or tired to observe. She did not believe me when I tried to tell her. To this day, I still have problems sexually, emotionally, and mentally. My way of solving it was to move away (1200 miles away)."

(from the author's files)

There is considerable debate among professionals about the long-term effects of sibling incest. Some be-

lieve that *if* the experience occurs between siblings of nearly the same age (less than a 4- to 5-year age difference), *if* there is no betrayal of trust, and *if* the children are not traumatized by adults in cases where their activity is discovered, then it is just "sex play" and a "part of growing up" (Finkelhor, 1980; Forward & Buck, 1978; Pittman, 1987; Steele & Alexander, 1981). However, as you can see from the previous case history, the effects can sometimes be quite negative. This is particularly the case when the incest involves coercion, threats, force, or betrayal of trust (Bank & Kahn, 1982; Canavan et al., 1992; Courtois, 1988). Only about 12 percent of people with childhood sibling incest experiences have ever told anyone, and "the pain of secrecy" adds to the negative experience (Finkelhor, 1980). In cases where physical pleasure is experienced in exploitative or abusive incest, the result can be confusion and guilt regarding sexuality (Canavan et al., 1992). Other long-term effects can include distrust of men in general, poor self-concept, depression, and confusing intimacy and sex (resulting in sex as the only way to relate to men; Canavan et al., 1992; Cole, 1982; Russell, 1986).

PARENT-CHILD INCEST

"At the age of five, I was the oldest of two children (my little sister was one year old). My mom would go to church and leave me in the care of my father. He would take out his penis and have me look at it and touch it, but I didn't know what was happening. It stopped for a while, but then he would try to put his tongue into my mouth. At the age of eight, after my mom had another baby, he would touch my vagina and lay on top of me (all 195 lbs.). At the age of 11, he got into my bed trying to take off my panties. I put up a fight but they were removed. He then took out his penis and tried to have sex, but I moved continuously trying to wake up my sister who shared by my bed (unsuccessfully). I began to cry; he got up and said he was sorry. I thought 'this bastard!' I was so afraid. I thought if I told he would do it again, and everyone would hate me for breaking up the family. Mothers! Please watch out for your kids. I am 19 years old; I am a sophomore here at UNO, and it still hurts. I try to get over the hating of my father, but I don't really care what he thinks about me." (female)

"My father began to molest me when I was 12—on the night after my mother's funeral. I am an only child and he explained that since my mother was gone I was going to have to function as the 'woman' of the house. At first I was only required to function as a woman in the evenings (and most mornings too) sharing his bed as my mother had. As I grew older additional chores were added such as cooking and cleaning. It was always explained that if I truly loved him I would never hesitate to do his bidding—oral and anal sex, giving him showers, dressing him, etc. Finally I managed to get the courage to leave my father. . . . Throughout my entire adult life I have never had a successful re-lationship. I'm not gay, but I don't know how a man should act. I only know how to function as the 'lady of the house.' '' (male)

(from the author's files)

Of all the types of incest, parent-child incest probably evokes the greatest emotional response in people. After all, most people believe that it is the role of parents to nurture, provide for, and protect their children,

Box 15-c

CROSS-CULTURAL PERSPECTIVES: INCESTUOUS INBREEDING: A UNIVERSAL TABOO?

Incest has often been called the universal taboo, and there are many theories as to why it is supposedly banned throughout the world. One of the major theories comes from Freud (1913), who believed that most people prefer close kin as mating partners:

'' . . . (B)eyond the possibility of doubt that an incestuous love choice is in fact the first and regular one . . . '' (Freud, 1953, pp. 220–221)

But inbreeding can lead to serious genetic defects in offspring (Thornhill, 1992) and eventually ruin a society if it were practiced widely. Freud believed it was for this reason that societies make rules against incest.

A second, much different, theory was proposed by Edward Westermarck in 1891. He believed that close, physical contact between two people during childhood naturally results in loss of sexual attraction. Findings of several anthropological studies have been used as support for this theory (e.g., McCabe, 1983; Pastner, 1986; Shepher, 1971; Wolf, 1970). However, Nancy Thornhill (1991) has proposed that incest rules are not aimed at close family members (because of the Westermarck effect), but instead are directed at more distant kin (cousins) and special kinds of adultery (e.g., a man and his father's wife). Inbreeding between cousins, she says, ''can concentrate wealth and power within families to the detriment of the powerful positions of (male) rulers in stratified societies.''

Claude Levi-Strauss (1969) offered yet a fourth explanation. His ''alliance theory'' says that the incest taboo exists not to prohibit marriage within the family, but is ''a rule obliging the mother, sister, or daughter to be given to others.'' It ensures that women be exchanged between groups. According to Levi-Strauss, ''The incest taboo is where nature transcends itself. It brings about and is the advent of a new order.''

There is no question that incestuous inbreeding is viewed very negatively in Western cultures (Ford & Beach, 1951). In the United States, marriage between first cousins is illegal in most states (Bratt, 1984). Fewer than one-half percent of marriages in North America and Western Europe are between first cousins (Lebel, 1983). But what about elsewhere—is inbreeding viewed with equal negativity in non-Western societies? In times past in some cultures (e.g., Egypt, Incas, Hawaii) brothers and sisters married within royal families (Gregersen, 1982). For example, Egyptian pharaoh Ramesses II's wives included his younger sister and three of his daughters. Today, in areas that are primarily Muslim (northern Africa, western and southern Asia, middle Asian republics of the former Soviet Union, and northern, eastern, and central India), one fourth to one half of all marriages are between persons who are second cousins or closer (see Bittles et al., 1991, for a review). Marriages between parallel first cousins (with a father's brother's daughter) are particularly preferred. Among the Hindus of southern India, 20–45 percent of marriages are between close relatives, with the preferred unions being uncle-niece or cross first cousins (mother's brother's daughter). One third to one half of marriages in sub-Saharan Africa are believed to be between relatives, and the practice is also thought to be very common in China.

Are there sociological or economic factors that might predict the acceptance of incestuous inbreeding? Yes: in those areas of the world where it is practiced, it is most common among either (a) rural, poor, uneducated people, or (b) in very rich land-owning families (again, see Bittles et al., 1991, for references).

In conclusion, mother-son incestuous inbreeding is unheard of in any culture and with rare exception all cultures similarly frown upon father-daughter and brother-sister relations. However, outside of Western culture, marriages between first cousins or uncles and nieces is widely practiced. ■

not turn them into sexual objects for their own selfish needs. Yet adults who commit incest with their children come from all walks of life. Former Miss America Marilyn Van Derbur focused much attention on this issue when she revealed that she had been repeatedly assaulted sexually beginning at age 5 by her father, a millionaire businessman, socialite, and philanthropist —a pillar of the community.

Although parent-child incest accounts for only 10 percent of all incest cases (Finkelhor, 1979), nearly 80 percent of arrests involve **father(stepfather)—daughter incest** (Francoeur, 1982). Stepfathers are more likely to victimize their children than are biological fathers (Finkelhor, 1979; Renshaw, 1983), but both types of cases are common. Fathers who commit incest are generally shy and publicly devoted family men who appear to be quite average, but in their own home they are very dominating and authoritarian—"King of their castle" (Meiselman, 1978; Rosenfeld, 1979). They tend to be impulsive, but generally are not psychotic. In relations with their children, they are often overprotective, selfish, and jealous (Hinds, 1981).

Incestuous fathers, obviously, have the capacity to become sexually aroused by children (remember, nearly half of incestuous fathers also molest other children; Abel et al., 1988b). Some incestuous fathers try to rationalize that they are teaching their children in a loving way about life (Hinds, 1981). Virginia Johnson (of Masters and Johnson) has found that incestuous fathers are often very religious and feel that incest is less of a sin than masturbation (*New York Times*, November, 1986).

Incestuous fathers who are caught often claim that the influence of alcohol or drugs caused them to commit incest, or that *he* was seduced. Many of us have had too much to drink at times, but we didn't molest children while under the influence of alcohol. An incestuous father may have a drinking problem, but first and foremost he has a sexual problem.

The role of the mother in father-child incest is critical, and her response, or rather her lack of any, is often as traumatizing to the child as is the molestation. Consider, for example, the responses of the following four victims:

`` . . . (M)y mother didn't believe me. Even at age 19, I still feel resentment for her for not protecting me and for not believing me. At the time she was totally dependent on him (stepfather) and the thought of losing him was unthinkable. . . . ''

`` . . . I thought every father did that to their daughter. I thought it was a part of growing up, especially because my mom knew about it. . . . ''

`` . . . I eventually told my mother and she told me that it was nothing, that he probably thought it was her and she didn't mention it again. . . . ''

`` . . . I grabbed onto her leg saying— screaming, crying—'Don't leave me please. I don't want to be here with him!' She said I had to behave and then left without even looking at me. From this moment on I knew she was not going to listen to me, let alone protect me. This is why I am angry today. . . . ''

(from the author's files)

Some mothers do call authorities when they become aware of the incest, but more than two thirds do not try to protect their daughters (Herman & Hirschman, 1977). Although some mothers of incest victims have normal personalties (Groff, 1987), many are emotionally distant from their children and dependent on their husbands. They fear abandonment more than living with the fact that their children are victims of incest (Finkelhor, 1984; Rosenfeld, 1979). Many were victims of child abuse themselves (Summit & Kryso, 1978), and continue to suffer physical abuse within the marriage (Truesdell et al., 1986). Some even force their daughters to assume the role of sex partner in order to avoid having sexual contact with their husbands (Justice & Justice, 1979).

In some cases, the mother is the abuser. **Mother-son incest** has generally been regarded as rare (see Finkelhor, 1986). However, others believe that it may be underreported because surveys rarely ask specific questions about this type of incest (Lawson, 1993). Mother-son incest typically occurs in disrupted families where the mother seeks emotional support and physical closeness from her son rather than adults (Krug, 1989). It generally starts by sharing the boy's bed and may progress to sexual intercourse. Contrary to earlier reports (Meiselman, 1978), most of these mothers are not psychotic or suffering from severe psychological damage (Krug, 1989).

Grandparents as incest perpetrators has also been found to be uncommon (e.g., Cupoli & Sewell, 1988; Kendall-Tackett & Simon, 1987; Russell, 1986), but may be on the increase because of the increased number of working parents leaving their children with the grandparents.

> `` . . . I only had to see him when we visited in the summer. He would get me downstairs in the cellar alone. . . . He would touch my vagina and I remember it hurting all of the time. He would sometimes take his penis out of his pants. . . . I never talked to anyone about it. One time I briefly talked to my sister about it at his funeral. She asked me why I did not seem sad. . . . She said it happened to her also. If it happened to me and my sister, it must have happened to all of the other grandchildren. I wonder if my mother was sexually abused as a child. I wonder if she knew or my grandmother knew. . . . ''

(from the author's files)

A recent large study of incestuous grandparents found that nearly all cases were **grandfather-granddaughter incest** (Margolin, 1992). Stepgranddaughters were at a higher risk than biological granddaughters. *Most of the abusive grandfathers had also been sexually abusive fathers.* One has to wonder what kind of mother would leave her children with an adult who had sexually abused her when she was a child? Contrary to earlier studies which typically described the abuse as "gentle," many of the incestuous grandfathers used threats, physical assault, or suddenly grabbed the grandchildren's genitals.

EFFECTS ON CHILDREN

In this section, I will focus on the effects of father-child incest, although much of what you learn is true of victims of other types of incest as well. Father-child incest generally involves frequent, long-term abuse, and in many cases there is vaginal and/or anal penetration. These are precisely the factors that often cause the greatest long-term harm in child molestation cases (Beitchman et al., 1992; Kendall-Tackett et al., 1993). A lack of support from the mother also substantially adds to the victims' outcome.

Another important factor that leads to long-term problems in victims of father-child incest is that many victims blame themselves (often with encouragement from the father; Morrow, 1991). Thus, victims of incest are similar to rape victims in this respect. Consider, for example, the feelings of the following two victims:

> `` . . . I am 18 now and I believe that it was my fault. No matter how I look at it, I feel as though I could have prevented it. . . . ''

> `` . . . (S)till question myself about if there was something I could have done to prevent it, or worse yet, if there was, somehow, something I did to cause it. . . . ''

(from the author's files)

Victims can be very confused if they experienced any degree of physical pleasure during the abuse:

> `` . . . In my mind, I blamed me, not him. To make matters worse, somewhere along the way my 12-year-old adolescent body had my first orgasm. I hated it, hated myself, hated him. . . . I couldn't understand something I hated feeling good. Heavy, heavy guilt trip. . . . ''

(from the author's files)

Sadly, studies have found that many people, particularly men, also *incorrectly* attribute blame to victims, especially if the victims were adolescents at the time of the abuse (Collings & Payne, 1991; Waterman & Foss-Goodman, 1984). If a victim tells someone of his or her experience and is met with this kind of response, this too contributes to the long-term negativity.

Children who are victims of incest often have a variety of long-term problems besides self-blame (Lindberg & Distad, 1985; Scott & Stone, 1986). However, as with other types of child molestation, there is no definite or typical "incest syndrome" (Kinzl & Biebl, 1992). As adults, victims may have feelings of anxiety, helplessness, and powerlessness. Many victims suffer from low self-esteem and poor self-image (including a sense of separate selves or a loss of memory about self; Cole & Putnam, 1992).

> "I've always felt alone, disassociated. Even when I'm with friends I don't feel like a part of the group. In class, I've never felt like I belonged...."

> "...(B)ut deep down I feel really disgusted about my body...."

(from the author's files)

Some victims later develop eating disorders (Hall et al., 1989; Hambridge, 1988), while others suffer from major depressive episodes and alcohol or drug abuse (Burnam et al., 1988).

> "...By the time I was 13, I had found alcohol and drugs as a safe haven from the immense pain inside me. By the age of 17, I was a full-blown alcoholic experiencing blackouts...."

(from the author's files)

Victims of child incest may also suffer from a variety of sexual problems. Some abused children may even victimize other children in an attempt to work out the distressing events (Johnson, 1989). As adults, they may be unable to form close, trusting relationships because they expect to be betrayed, rejected, and further abused (Cole & Putnam, 1992). This can lead to avoidance of relationships, or, at the other extreme, promiscuity. Victims are also a likely target for revictimization.

> "...I find I cannot have open relationships with guys. It is hard for me to trust anyone. For the one time I tried to open up to a guy, I ended up even more hurt. I am 20 years old and I cannot even kiss a guy, much less give a simple hug to someone...."

> "...My relationships with men have all been abusive, even to the point that I have been battered and raped on several occasions....I choose men that are very similar to my Dad...mainly because that's all I know...."

(from the author's files)

Boys who are victims of incestuous mothers often experience such anxiety and disgust that they emotionally reject all women as adults (Krug, 1989).

In one study of the background of women in prison, it was found that over half of the prostitutes, over a third of the felons, and one quarter of the child molesters had been incest victims (Hinds, 1981). In a more recent study of imprisoned serial rapists (males), nearly half had been victims of father(stepfather)-son incest (McCormack et al., 1992).

FAMILY DYNAMICS AND TREATMENT

Father(stepfather)-child incest (and in many cases sibling incest) typically occurs in certain family contexts (Canavan et al., 1992; Larson & Maddock, 1986; Finkelhor, 1978). We have considered some of their characteristics, but let us review them here.

Within the home there is an all-powerful, authoritarian male (who may appear shy, but otherwise normal to others) who sets hard, fixed gender roles for everyone, and establishes an isolated, rigid system with strong external boundaries that separates the family from the outside world. However, boundaries within the family become blurred, and all emotional needs are met within the family. Independent thoughts and feelings are considered destructive as the family becomes isolated and family members become overdependent on one another. Although marital problems are common, the mother fails to protect her children, adding to their sense of abandonment and fear. Themes associated with insecure parent-child incest (rejection, role reversal, fear) are common within incestuous families (Alexander, 1992). Children who grow up in an environment like this may view it as normal and repeat the pattern when they become parents.

For these incestuous families, a family-systems approach is often chosen as therapy. Here, therapy for each family member is combined with therapy for each pair within the family, and followed by therapy for the family together (Lanyon, 1986). Group therapy is also often included. For positive change to occur, the father must accept responsibility for what he has done and the mother must also accept responsibility (often for what she has not done). The child, on the other hand, must learn to believe that he or she is not responsible. The father must also give up his complete authoritarian rule and each family member learns to become more independent.

Sex is the closest form of communication between two people and can be one of life's most beautiful experiences. It is extremely important, therefore, for a person to get counseling and support from professionals and organizations if he or she is still feeling the effects of incest as an adult. Everyone should have the ability to enjoy sex in ways that are open, honest, and that allow them to form healthy, intimate relationships. Teach your own children about sex in a manner so that they, too, can learn to enjoy their own sexuality in ways that enable them to grow, to love, to relate to others in a healthy and meaningful way. It is my hope that this text will help you in realizing these goals. ∎

RESOURCES FOR HELP

For counseling, contact the **YWCA Rape Crisis Centers** nearest you. Services include: 24-hour rape crisis line; adult and child sexual assault and incest victims; families/friends of victims; crisis, long-term counseling; weekly support group; victim advocacy; information and referral; training for hospital/medical personnel and police; agency consultation; community education including assault prevention programs for ages two through senior citizens; court monitoring.

For a more extensive list, see the Resource section at the end of the text.

KEY TERMS

acquaintance rape 347
aggressive pedophile 366
anger rapists 353
date rape 347
gang rape 351
incest 370
male rape 351
marital rape 350
opportunistic rapists 354

pedophilia 336, 365
personally immature pedophile 366
polyincestuous family 371
power rapists 352
preference molester 365
rape myths 355
rape-shield laws 359
rape trauma syndrome 356

regressive pedophile 366
sadistic rapist 353
sexual coercion 348
sexual harassment 361
situational molester 365
statutory rape 351
stranger rape 347
token resistance 349

PERSONAL REFLECTIONS

1. Do you ever use sex to express power, dominance, control, and/or anger? If so, under what circumstances? Why do you use sex as an outlet for these desires/emotions?

2. Have you ever been the victim of sexual abuse? If so, has it affected how you feel about yourself or your relations with others? If it has affected you in any way (including any sense of self-blame), have you ever sought counseling? If you have not sought counseling, why not?

3. Is a man entitled to sexual intercourse when a woman agrees to go out with him, or because he spent money on her, or because she went to his house or apartment, or because his date engaged in necking? Men: If you answered yes, do you communicate these expectations to your dates *before* you go out?

4. Have you ever used sexual coercion to have sex with someone when he or she did not want to? This includes (but is not limited to): (a) purposely getting someone drunk to have sex; (b) physical coercion (e.g., persistent and relentless touching, holding, grabbing); and (c) verbal coercion (e.g., anger and/or threats to break up, other threats, put downs). If so, why do you suppose you act like this? What effects might your behavior have on those you coerce?

5. Men: Have you ever ignored a date or acquaintance saying "no" to your sexual advances? Why? Women: Have you ever said "no" to a man's sexual advances when you did not mean it? Why? If you answered yes, what are some possible repercussions of your behavior? Is there a better way that you might communicate with others about your sexual desires?

6. Have you ever been the victim of sexual harassment by a supervisor (or employer) or an instructor? Did you report it? If not, why? Are you familiar with your campus' procedures for dealing with sexual harassment? If you are not familiar with the procedures, where can you go to find out?

7. Are you ever sexually aroused by children? If so, have you ever sought counseling? If you have not sought counseling, why not? Would it be better to seek counseling before you acted on an urge, or afterwards?

SUGGESTED READINGS

Bass, E., and Davis, L. (1988). *The courage to heal: A guide for women survivors of child sexual abuse.* New York: Harper & Row.

Brownmiller, S. (1975). *Against our will: Men, women, and rape.* New York: Simon & Schuster. A key book in changing our society's attitudes about rape.

Crewdson, J. (1988). *By silence betrayed: Sexual abuse of children in America.* Boston: Little, Brown.

Finkelhor, D. (1984). *Child sexual abuse.* New York: Free Press.

Gelman, D. et al., (1990, July 23). The mind of the rapist. *Newsweek.* Examines the motivations of rape.

Gilbert, B., and Cunningham, J. (1987, October). Women's postrape sexual functioning: Review and implications for counseling. *Journal of Counseling and Development.* Discusses the effects of having been raped on long-term sexual functioning.

Groth, A. N. (1979). *Men who rape.* New York: Plenum Press. An excellent psychological and motivational profile of rapists.

Journal of Social Issues. (1992). Volume 48, no. 1. A special issue devoted to sexual aggression.

Kohn, A. (1987, February). Shattered innocence. *Psychology Today.* Discusses sexual abuse of girls and boys in the United States.

Lew, M. (1988). *Victims no longer: Men recovering from incest and other sexual child abuse.* New York: Nevraumont.

Moskal, B. S. (1989, July 3). Sexual harassment, '80's-style. *Industry Week.* Discusses and identifies sexual harassment and its consequences. Includes self-tests.

Newsweek. (1993, October 25). Several articles and essays on date rape and sexual harassment.

Parrot, A., and Bechofer, L. (Eds.). (1991). *Acquaintance rape: The hidden crime.* New York: John Wiley & Sons. Many scholarly articles.

Powell, E. (1991). *Talking back to sexual pressure: What to say, to resist pressure, to avoid disease, to stop harassment, to avoid acquaintance rape.* Minneapolis, MN: Comp Care Publishers. An excellent book; Ms. Powell gives many suggestions on how to resist unwanted sexual behavior, and devotes much space to behavioral rehearsals.

Sanday, P. R. (1990). *Fraternity gang rape.* New York: University Press. Analysis of a seldom discussed type of sexual violence.

Senter, J. (1988, Spring/Summer). Male rape: The hidden crime. *Changing Men.* A victim of male rape discusses the occurrence and consequences of this crime.

Volkman, E., and Rosenberg, H. L. (1985, June). The shame of the nation. *Family Weekly.* Discusses child pornography and its link to child abuse.

Yegidis, B. L. (1986, Fall/Winter). Date rape and other forced sexual encounters among college students. *Journal of Sex Education and Therapy 12.* Discusses date rape from both the victim's and rapist's point of view.

CHAPTER SIXTEEN

SEX AND THE LAW

WHEN YOU HAVE FINISHED STUDYING THIS CHAPTER, YOU SHOULD BE ABLE TO:

1. DEFINE AND DESCRIBE THE DIFFERENT TYPES OF PROSTITUTION;

2. DESCRIBE THE CHARACTERISTICS OF PROSTITUTES AND THEIR CUSTOMERS;

3. EVALUATE THE PROS AND CONS OF PROSTITUTION FROM A LEGAL AS WELL AS A MORAL POINT OF VIEW;

4. TRACE THE HISTORY OF SEXUALLY EXPLICIT MATERIAL IN THE UNITED STATES AND THE LEGAL ACTIONS TAKEN TO CONTROL IT;

5. DISCUSS THE USES OF SEXUALLY EXPLICIT MATERIAL;

6. COMPARE AND EVALUATE THE EFFECTS OF NONVIOLENT AND VIOLENT SEXUALLY EXPLICIT MATERIAL; AND

7. EXPLAIN SODOMY LAWS AND THEIR IMPLICATION FOR HETEROSEXUAL AND HOMOSEXUAL INDIVIDUALS.

Sex is an important part of most people's lives. Sex provides physical pleasure, it can be given and received as an expression of love and affection, and it can make us feel more masculine or feminine. People engage in a wide variety of sexual behaviors. In Chapter 11 you learned that most therapists take the view that any behavior between consenting adults which is done in private and does not cause physical, emotional, and/or psychological harm is okay. This text has treated sexual relations between consenting adults as something healthy, good, and positive, but there can be serious consequences if people do not act in a mature, responsible manner (e.g., unwanted pregnancies or sexually transmitted diseases).

There are laws to prevent the sexual abuse of children and nonconsenting adults, as there should be (you learned about these in Chapter 15), but there are also laws that are designed to prevent or regulate sexual activity between consenting adults. As you might

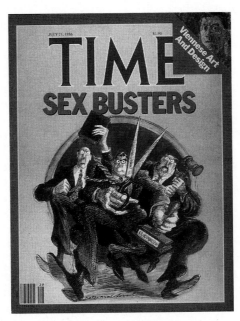

FIGURE 16-1

suspect, these laws are controversial, with many people objecting to others attempting to regulate their private lives. Some of these laws were proposed and passed by politicians who were concerned about health-related issues (the spread of STDs, for example), but some appear to be attempts by individuals to force the public to conform to their own moral standards. Many states, for example, once had laws that forbade the sale or distribution of contraceptive devices (these laws were finally ruled unconstitutional by the U.S. Supreme Court in *Griswold* v. *Connecticut*, 1965).

In this chapter, you will read about three topics for which there has been a long history of individuals attempting to regulate the sexual activity of others. I have purposely attempted not to show my own bias regarding these issues and have tried to take a neutral stand. My intent is to stimulate your own thinking by presenting both sides of an issue. You be the judge as to whether or not there should be laws regulating these activities. ■

PROSTITUTION

Prostitution is often referred to as "the world's oldest profession." While this may or may not be true, the trade of sex for money or other favors has been around for as long as the recorded history of human beings. In the ancient Hebrew culture it was not a crime for a father to prostitute his daughter, but if a daughter freely chose to have sex with a man (thus depriving her father of income), she could be put to death. Prostitution was very common in Roman society. In fact, the word **fornication** (sexual intercourse between a man and a woman who are not married to one another) is derived from *cellae fornicae*, the Latin term for the vaulted underground dwellings where prostitutes took their partners after the theater, circus, or gladiator contests.

In the Bible, Jesus told Mary Magdalene to "go, and sin no more," but prostitution flourished in Europe during the Middle Ages, and the Church had a somewhat tolerant attitude about it. St. Thomas Aquinas reasoned that just as the palace would become polluted without sewers, the world would become

Fornication
Sexual intercourse between a man and a woman who are not married to one another.

immersed in lust without prostitution. Parisian prostitutes even adopted Mary Magdalene as their own patron saint.

In Victorian times (middle nineteenth century to early twentieth century), the upper class maintained a public attitude of purity and prudery, but prostitution was a common sexual outlet for husbands. The poverty and squalor among the lower class pushed many young women into prostitution, and it has been estimated that there were as many as 80,000 prostitutes in London at any one time. Prostitution was legalized and regulated by an act of the British Parliament in 1860.

Northern Puritanism and the availability of slaves in the South kept prostitution to a minimum in colonial and early America. Immigration and industrialization, however, resulted in larger urban areas, and prostitution flourished in the last half of the nineteenth century. Houses of prostitut (brothels) were commonplace, especially in the West where men greatly outnumbered women. Ship captains imported thousands of women from the Orient and Central and South America to be forced into prostitution. San Francisco's population reached 25,000 in the early

1850s, and this included 3,000 prostitutes (Tannahill, 1980).

Opposition to prostitution in the United States began to grow during the first part of this century. Illinois became the first state to pass laws against prostitution in 1908. Federal laws passed at the start of World War I shut down many of the houses of prostitution that had existed near service bases (there were no cures for gonorrhea or syphilis at that time, and many men were being rejected for service because of infections).

These laws did not put a stop to prostitution. Kinsey and his colleagues (1948) found that 69 percent of white males had had at least one experience with a prostitute. Twenty-five percent of college-educated men and 54 percent of high school-educated men had had intercourse with a prostitute before marriage. Fewer men have their first sexual experience with prostitutes today than in the past. Hunt's survey taken in the early 1970s found that only 19 percent of men under 35 years of age with some college education had had premarital sex with a prostitute. This was not due to a decrease in the availability of prostitutes, but instead probably reflected changed attitudes and behaviors regarding premarital sex. In a recent survey, 20 percent of the male respondents indicated that they had paid for sex on at least one occasion (Janus & Janus, 1993). The percentage was the same for all income groups and most of the men said that they did this occasionally.

Definition and Types of Prostitution

We generally think of a prostitute as someone who exchanges sex for money. However, by this definition we would have to include people who allow someone else to have sex with them for a job or career promotion, to gain a favor, or in return for a trip to Cancun or some other vacation spot. Some prostitutes bitterly complain that what they do is no different from a woman who remains married to and has sex with a man she cannot stand, just for the security. To get around these problems, legal definitions generally distinguish **prostitution** from other activities on the basis of the indiscrimination with which it occurs. The Oregon Supreme Court, for example, ruled that: "The feature which distinguishes a prostitute from other women who engage in illicit intercourse is the indiscrimination with which she offers herself to men for hire."

Prostitute
A person who exchanges sex for money. The feature that distinguishes a prostitute from other people who engage in illicit sexual intercourse is the indiscrimination with which she or he offers herself or himself to others for hire.

How common is prostitution in the United States today? There are generally about 84,000 women a year working as full-time prostitutes (Potterat et al., 1990), not counting the women who have sex in exchange for

drugs at crackhouses and other such places. However, in a recent cross-sectional national survey, Janus and Janus (1993) found that over 4 percent of women responded "yes" to the question "Have you ever had sex for money?" In other words, there are many women who have engaged in prostitution part- or short-time. Estimates of young teenage prostitutes, for example, range from 100,000–200,000 to over 2 million (U.S. General Accounting Office, 1982).

Prostitution in the United States was transacted primarily in brothels until the turn of the century, but today it occurs in a variety of settings. Prostitutes can be divided roughly into three types according to status. On the lowest tier are **streetwalkers**, who solicit in public. Almost all of these women become prostitutes for financial reasons (e.g., to escape poverty or to support a drug habit) and not because of pathological sexual needs. Very few are forced into it as in past centuries, but some are often recruited. Most streetwalkers are protected by a pimp, who often takes a large share of the earnings. The sexual activity generally takes place in a room in a cheap hotel or apartment where the manager is aware of what is occurring. The typical streetwalker has sex with 4–5 men a day and the sexual activity usually involves giving oral-genital sex (Freund et al., 1989).

Streetwalker
A prostitute who solicits in public.

The once-common house of prostitution is now legal only in some counties in Nevada. The Chicken Ranch, that best little whorehouse in Texas (later moved to Nevada) made famous by the Broadway play and Hollywood movie, once did such a booming business that it had its own FAA-approved airplane strip and operated the Chicken Ranch Airline from Las Vegas. However, business at these legalized houses declined substantially during the 1980s, perhaps due to the fear of AIDS, but probably also due to the increase in popularity of escort services.

Elsewhere, the **brothel prostitute** has been replaced by **B-girls**, who work in bars and hotels, generally with the approval of the ownership (who may take a cut of the profits or else benefit by the customers they attract). Open solicitation, however, is generally frowned upon, so nonverbal messages are often used. The price is usually higher than for a streetwalker's services, and the sexual activity generally takes place in the customer's room.

Brothel prostitute
Prostitutes who work in houses of prostitution.

B-girls
Prostitutes who work in bars and hotels, generally with the approval of the ownership.

"Candy" (her own fictitious name) is an attractive 33-year-old African-American B-girl. She solicits customers in New Orleans

French Quarter bars along Bourbon, Chartres, and Decatur Streets. Her minimum charge for sex is $50 for 15 minutes or $200 for a night. The vast majority of her customers are white males in town for a convention. She says that 75 percent of them are married. The sexual activity takes place either in the john's hotel room or a neutral hotel. Whenever possible, however, she robs her customers rather than having sex with them. Candy says this is usually easy to do before they ever get out of the bar. She rubs their genitals and in their state of excitement they rarely notice that she is pickpocketing them with the other hand. She doesn't worry about returning to the bar in a few days, because by then the ''score'' has left New Orleans. If she does have sex with a customer, afterward she tries to relax them to sleep and then robs them of all their money and valuables.

Candy has four children and is on welfare. After high school she worked as a housekeeper and at other minimum wage jobs. When she was 27, a pimp showed her the expensive nightclubs around town and said that she, too, could enjoy this life style. After some deliberation, she paid him $300 to be ''his lady'' and now lives with him (her children live with her mother). She turns all the money that she makes as a prostitute and thief over to him. In return, he gives her protection and buys her nice clothing and jewelry and lets her drive a Cadillac Seville.

Candy doesn't think about the future. She has been arrested 22 times on various charges in the past seven years, and if convicted of prostitution again, she could be sentenced to two years in prison. She doesn't worry very much about AIDS or other sexually transmitted diseases either. Although she sometimes makes $3,000 to $4,000 in a month, none of it has been saved for when the time comes that she can not prostitute anymore. She just enjoys the life style that the money will buy now.

(from the author's files)

More recently, sexual services have increasingly been offered through thinly disguised store fronts such as *massage parlors* (it should be noted, however, that some of these are legitimate). Women who work in massage parlors are often called "hand whores" because toward the end of the massage (often given in the nude) they generally rub the thighs and groin area and let it be known that for a "tip" they will massage the genitals.

The highest status prostitutes are the **call girls**. New customers are screened (recommendations from trusted sources are often required), and appointments are generally made by telephone. The call girl generally works out of her own apartment, but often provides company for dinner and social occasions in addition to sexual services. The services do not come cheaply, however, with some of the most attractive ones charging $1,000 per night or more. A more commercialized, and somewhat less expensive, variety of call girl prostitution today is offered through *escort services*, which advertise in newspapers. Judging by the increase in these advertisements, escort service prostitution increased by over 400 percent in the 1980s (Janus & Janus, 1993, p. 132).

> **Call girls**
> The highest status prostitutes, who generally work out of their own apartments by appointment only.

Prostitution is not limited to females catering to heterosexual males. Although not nearly as common as female prostitution, males sometimes sell their bodies to women as well. These males, called **gigolos**, are the male counterpart of call girls and often work as part of an escort service (generally used by older, single, wealthy women).

> **Gigolos**
> Male prostitutes who cater to females.

In today's society, homosexual prostitution is nearly as common as heterosexual prostitution in some large urban areas. Male prostitutes are called **hustlers** and are similar to female streetwalkers in that they generally solicit their customers on the street. Many hustlers do not regard themselves as homosexual (Earls & David, 1989; Lloyd, 1976), because in America the male prostitute generally plays a passive role, that is, the customers pay to give oral sex to the prostitute and not vice versa. As many as 70 percent of hustlers do this only part-time (Allen, 1980), with the primary motivation being financial and not sexual (Earls & David, 1989).

> **Hustler**
> A male prostitute who caters to males.

CHARACTERISTICS OF PROSTITUTES

The primary reason given by persons engaging in prostitution is economics (Bess & Janus, 1976; Earls & David, 1989; Rio, 1991; Weisberg, 1985). Most prostitutes come from financially poor families, have little education, or are young runaways with few or no skills (Bell, 1987; Lloyd, 1976). However, even for call girls or middle-class housewife (working part-time) prostitutes, the main attraction is still money—their income is higher compared to other women matched for age and education (Exner et al., 1977).

Prostitution, and the need for money, is often fueled by drug use. The large majority of prostitutes are habitual users of addictive drugs such as heroin and crack cocaine (Feucht, 1993; James et al., 1979;

Simon et al., 1992). Pimps often see to it that their prostitutes become addicted just so they will remain economically dependent. For the typical streetwalker or B-girl, prostitution does not turn out to be the goldmine it may have seemed at first, for most end up turning over most of their earnings to the pimp.

Economics may be the main motivation, but many prostitutes are attracted to the thrill and the danger of "the life" (Janus & Bess, 1977; Potterat et al., 1985). In fact, Janus and Bess (1977) found that for some prostitutes the lifestyle itself was addicting. Most people believe that prostitutes do not really enjoy sex with their customers (and perform the sex acts mechanically), but one study found that many prostitutes do, in fact, enjoy sex with their customers (including giving fellatio) at least sometimes (Savitz & Rosen, 1988).

Beyond the economic explanations, aside from the frequent drug dependency, is the fact that most prostitutes had very sad backgrounds. Many prostitutes, including the large majority of teenage prostitutes, were sexually abused as children (Earls & David, 1989; Janus & Bess, 1977; Rio, 1991; Satterfield & Listiak, 1982). Physical abuse by parents, and alcohol or drug abuse by parents, are also common backgrounds (Hersch, 1988). Many prostitutes had trouble in school, had few friends, and just generally felt rejected (Davis, 1978; Lloyd, 1976; Price et al., 1984). As a result, many grew up with severe self-esteem and self-identity problems, and generally are just less psychologically healthy (Gibson-Ainyette et al., 1988).

With this background, it is not surprising that most teenaged prostitutes are runaway or throwaway (not wanted even if they return) children who, with no other job options, have turned their first trick by the time they are 14 (Weisberg, 1985).

"Jean" looks like most other 15-year-old girls. In fact, when her hair is in a ponytail she is often mistaken for 13 or 14 years old. The men, most of whom are married with daughters as old or older than she is, like her very young looks. They want to have sex with a "schoolgirl." Jean fulfills their fantasy by telling them that she is a sophomore at one of the local high schools. She charges them $30 to $50 depending on what they want (oral sex in their car is least expensive). Jean doesn't really go to school at all. She is a runaway. She ran away the last time at age 14 and found herself in New Orleans alone and hungry. That's when she met "Frank." He bought her a hamburger and offered her a place to stay. There were two other girls about her same age staying with Frank. He was particularly nice to Jean and bought her nice dresses. She felt wanted and cared for, and after a few days she and Frank

had sex (her first time). He also introduced her to drugs. He told her that she was his special girl. Two weeks later he told her he needed money and asked her to go to bed with another man. The other girls told her it was easy. Jean was surprised to find out how easy it was, and within a short time she was having sex with up to six men a day. All she had to do was stand on a corner and within a short while older men would stop and talk to her.

(from the author's files)

Rejected by parents and schoolmates, runaway teens often find a sense of belonging with the pimp and others with similar backgrounds. Unfortunately, there are some people who prefer to have sex with young teens, and thus this sexual exploitation of children will continue as long as there is a demand for and supply of young, destitute, runaway, and throwaway children. The following organizations are devoted to helping these children get off the street:

Covenant House 1-800-999-9999
Provides counseling, shelter, and other referral services.
National Network of Runaway and Youth Services
Department P, P.O. Box 8283
Washington, DC 20024
1-800-448-4663
They will put you in touch with the nearest shelter program.
National Runaway Switchboard
1-800-621-4000
They encourage runaway children to reestablish contact with their families.

A recent study of adult male street prostitutes found that nearly all had serious problems with feelings of personal inadequacy, loneliness and social alienation (most said they had no friends), mistrust of others, and depression (Simon et al., 1992). All were drug users and felt that they were locked into their deviate careers. While the authors acknowledge that the psychological problems may reflect the prostitutes' dangerous and chaotic environment (and probably their past), they also suggest that this psychological functioning leads them to this particular lifestyle.

THE CUSTOMER

Prostitution has continued to flourish for centuries despite laws, penalties, and the protests of outraged citizens. Part of the reason it has continued with unabated frequency is the fact that it is perceived as easy income by unskilled, financially destitute women; but without the demand for their services, of course, prostitution could not exist. In order for it to flourish as it has, the demand for sexual services must be great.

Customers are called *johns, tricks,* or *scores* by prostitutes. Most are white, middle class, middle-aged, and married (James, 1982; Velarde & Warlick, 1973). There are many reasons why males pay for sex (see Stein, 1977). A few are able to function sexually only with prostitutes (Bess & Janus, 1976), but the reasons for most include lack of a part-

John

A street term for a male who pays for sex with a prostitute; also called tricks or scores.

ner (e.g., due to military service, traveling, or an inability to find a partner because of physical or social handicaps), the desire for a new partner or a novel sexual act, or the extra excitement of doing something naughty with a "bad" girl. Many prostitutes report that their customers want companionship and conversation just as much as physical gratification, and, in some cases, they even report never having had sexual intercourse with some customers. Another major reason that many men pay for a prostitute's services is to enjoy sex without the time or effort required of an emotional involvement. Some men feel that they have to perform (i.e.,

BOX 16-A

SEXUALITY AND HEALTH: PROSTITUTION AND THE AIDS VIRUS

You learned about the human immunodeficiency virus (HIV) and AIDS in Chapter 5. HIV infection, you recall, is the leading cause of death of young adults in at least 64 large U.S. cities (Selik, Chu, & Buchler, 1993). This applies to women as well as men—AIDS is the leading cause of death of young women in at least nine cities. Although once uncommon, heterosexual transmission is now the major cause of most new AIDS cases in women (Centers for Disease Control and Prevention, 1995).

Because of their sexual relations with multiple partners, as well as a high percentage who use drugs intravenously, prostitutes are at high risk for contracting HIV and are high-risk sexual partners for those who use them (Des Jarlais et al., 1989; Morse et al., 1991). Fewer than 1 percent of U.S. citizens are infected with HIV, but what about prostitutes? Here are some examples of results of recent studies: over half the female prostitutes in northern New Jersey are HIV-positive (Turner, Miller, & Moses, 1989), over one quarter are infected in Miami (Turner et al., 1989), and 6.7 percent tested positively for HIV in a national study (Khabbaz et al., 1990). Among male prostitutes, 17.5 percent tested positive in New Orleans (Simon et al., 1992), while 27 percent in Atlanta tested positive (Elifson et al., 1989). A recent study reported that in some urban areas the rate for male prostitutes is 50 percent or higher (Boles & Elifson, 1994). Several of these studies found high rates of infection for hepatitis B and syphilis as well.

You might think that men engaging in high-risk sexual behavior, such as sex with a prostitute, would use condoms. Regular use of condoms does substantially reduce the risk of getting HIV. In legalized brothels in Nevada where condom use is required, for example, none of the prostitutes had tested positive for HIV by the end of the 1980s, and low rates of infection have also been found among African prostitutes who regularly use condoms (Mann et al., 1987; Ngugi et al., 1988). Condom use by men in the general population is quite low (Catania et al., 1992), but two European studies found that use of condoms was much higher among men who have sex with prostitutes (Barnard et al., 1993; Hooykaas et al., 1989). However, this may not be true in this country (Leonard, Fruend, & Pratt, 1989), and even in the European studies there were many clients of prostitutes who did not use condoms. What's more, the clients in one of the studies reported that their condoms tore over 10 percent of the time (Barnard et al., 1993). Alcohol or drug use beforehand may also make it less likely that a client will use a condom with a prostitute (Weinstock et al., 1993b).

What can we conclude? By their use of prostitutes, especially when condoms are not used, many men are putting themselves *and their noncommercial partners* at high risk for infection with HIV. ■

please their partner) in their usual relationship, but sex with a prostitute allows them to receive pleasure without having to reciprocate. The majority of men who go to streetwalker prostitutes pay to have oral-genital sex performed on them (Leonard, Freund, & Platt, 1989).

Men who pay to have sex with male prostitutes come from all walks of life (Fisher et al., 1982; Kamel, 1983; Lloyd, 1976; Morse et al., 1992). Most describe themselves as heterosexual or bisexual, and are married. They are not part of the open gay community and use prostitutes in order to conceal their homosexual activities. Despite their married status, very few use condoms, although they engage in a variety of high-risk sexual behaviors (for sexually transmitted diseases).

Prostitution and the Law

Opponents of prostitution argue that it is often accompanied by drug addiction, the high risk of spread of sexually transmitted diseases [which the john can then spread to his wife or girlfriend(s)], and assault and battery by the prostitute and her pimp (what do you suppose the chances are of a victimized john filing charges?). Recent studies in some cities, for example, found that many prostitutes are infected with the virus (HIV) that causes AIDS (see Box 16-A). The primary concern of many people, however, is the moral issue. They believe that it is sinful and a degrading sexual activity for both the individuals involved and society as a whole. As a result, there has been a renewed effort by some residents of Nevada to close the legalized houses of prostitution in that state.

Many people, on the other hand, argue that prostitution is a victimless crime (see Rio, 1991). It is certainly true that very few prostitutes are reported by complainants. Instead, most are caught by undercover vice squad policemen posing as johns. Proponents of decriminalization or legalization of prostitution argue that local governments spend a great deal of money on a continually losing battle against prostitution. They propose the licensing and regulation of prostitutes, including regular required health checks for sexually transmitted diseases. This is already done in Nevada's legalized houses of prostitution, where customers are also now required to use condoms. Not one of Nevada's licensed prostitutes has tested positive for HIV infection. If prostitution were legalized everywhere, proponents say, pimps and organized crime would become less influential and the taxes collected on prostitutes' fees could be used to fight more serious crimes. Prostitution is legal and regulated in many other countries.

The United States seems to have very ambivalent attitudes about prostitution. It is illegal in some places and legal in others. Although illegal in most places, many only halfheartedly prosecute it. While all states prosecute the sellers (prostitutes), very few seriously go after the buyers (johns who patronize them). Prostitution is the only sexual offense for which more women than men are prosecuted. If society does not curb the demand, the supply of prostitution will always be there, and thus our society's present treatment of prostitution probably assures that it will continue unabated. What do you think we should do to solve this problem: push for greater enforcement (including arrest and severe prosecution of johns), or require the licensing and regulation of prostitutes? ∎

PORNOGRAPHY

Sexually explicit material seems to be everywhere today: on TV, at the movies, in books and magazines, over the telephone, and even available on computers. This was not always the case, however. There has always been sexually explicit art, pictures, or literature available for those who wanted it. But only in the last few decades has there been such an eruption in the quantity of this material that even those who don't seek it out have difficulty avoiding it. Magazines with sexually explicit covers, for example, are often displayed right behind the cash register at drugstores where children and anyone else cannot help but see them.

How did this all happen? The United States for a long time was a very puritanical country (and believe it or not, still is, compared to some other countries). The first real erotic literature by an American was Walt Whitman's *Leaves of Grass*, written in 1855. However, the **Comstock law**, passed in 1873, made the mailing of this or any other material considered to be obscene or lewd a felony. Even information about birth control was not allowed to be mailed. Importation of James Joyce's novel *Ulysses* was banned when it was first published in 1922. The ban was lifted in 1933, but other novels such as D. H. Lawrence's *Lady Chatterley's Lover* and Henry Miller's *Tropic of Cancer* were banned in the United States and most other English-speaking countries until the late 1950s.

Censorship in movies was also very strict during the era. The movie industry was banned from using erotica in 1935. Clark Gable's final words to Vivien Leigh (who played Scarlet O'Hara) in the movie *Gone with the Wind* ("Quite frankly, my dear, I don't give a damn!") were shocking to many people. The brief love scene on the beach (with bathing suits on) in the 1950s movie *From Here to Eternity* was considered

Comstock law
A law passed in 1873 that made it a felony to mail any material regarded to be obscene or lewd.

scandalous. Because it came into people's living rooms, TV was censored even more heavily than movies during the 1950s and 1960s. Even comedy shows carefully avoided the subject of sex until the 1970s. Rock and roll was opposed by many parents in the 1950s, not only for its "suggestive" words (e.g., "Whole Lot of Shakin' Going On," "Let Me Be Your Teddy Bear"), but because of the performers' gyrations. Elvis Presley was shown only from the waist up when he appeared on the Ed Sullivan Show in 1956.

What about sexually explicit magazines? In the 1950s and 1960s there was really only *Playboy* (on a large scale, anyway). Hugh Hefner spent $600 in 1953 to publish the first issue, which featured nude photos of Marilyn Monroe, selling it on the street himself. He turned it into a multimillion dollar publishing empire. Hefner really didn't have any competitors until the late 1960s and early 1970s, about the same time that movies and TV became more explicit.

Why the move toward more permissiveness in the middle and late 1960s? The story of Hugh Hefner's success pretty much tells the answer. It became obvious that despite efforts at censorship, there was a large demand for sexually oriented material. As a result, other magazines started to compete for a share of the market (e.g., *Penthouse, Hustler, Playgirl*), and in an effort to outdo one another, the borders of sexual license were continually expanded. At the same time, Americans flocked to see erotic European movies starring actresses like Brigitte Bardot, and their box office success led Hollywood to explore sexual boundaries as well.

So, where are we in the 1990s? One can easily buy magazines that show hetero- or homosexual couples (or groups of people) having every imaginable kind of sex, using every position, oral or anal sex, sex with violent themes or with animals, and much more that is probably beyond your imagination. There is a booming $8 billion a year market in XXX-rated movies and video rentals (see Figure 16-2). The XXX-rated movie *Deep Throat* cost only $24,000 to make, but it has earned over $25 million in profits. Sexually explicit material has even kept up with technological advances. Today, computer software allows you to watch sex on home computers (including "virtual reality" programs that allow some interaction). Sex has become a hot topic on the Internet.

You no longer have to turn to X-rated material for full frontal nudity and torrid sex scenes. R-rated movies such as 1992's *Body of Evidence* with Madonna and William Dafoe or *Basic Instinct* with Sharon Stone were clearly designed to shock us. But with all the sexually explicit material available, it takes a lot to shock us today, so much so that Madonna's book of photographs, *Sex*, hardly made a ripple when it came out in 1992. Even our ears are being bombarded with explicit material in the 1990s. The 2 Live Crew's

FIGURE 16-2 SEXUALLY EXPLICIT MOVIES AND BOOKS ARE READILY AVAILABLE IN MOST PARTS OF THE UNITED STATES.

album "As Nasty as They Wanna B" in 1990 led to calls for rating CDs, just as is done with movies. New York based "shock" jock Howard Stern has been fined hundreds of thousands of dollars for his explicitness on the radio. For hard-core fans, there's dial-a-porn (telephone sex). Yes, explicit sex is everywhere today, and you would have to be a hermit living without radio, TV, or magazines to avoid it.

Do we want it? Well, apparently many Americans do. Every year Americans rent over 200 million X-rated videos. A 1985 Gallop poll found that 40 percent of all VCR owners had watched an X-rated movie in their home within the last year. In fact, when asked if they had seen an X-rated movie in the last year, about a third of all Americans questioned since 1982 said yes (Laumann et al., 1994). Nearly all college men and women have looked at an explicit magazine such as *Playboy* or *Playgirl* by the time they leave high school, and 85–90 percent have done so in junior high school (Bryant & Brown, 1989). The average college man spends about 6 hours a month looking at sexually explicit material, and the average college woman, about 2 hours (Padgett, Brislutz, & Neal, 1989).

USES OF SEXUALLY EXPLICIT MATERIAL

Why do people look at, read, or listen to sexually explicit material? Bryant and Brown (1989) have identified four major reasons. Some people, they say, turn to sexually explicit material to learn about sex. In fact, many college students use sexually explicit material as a source of sexual information (Duncan & Donnelly, 1991; Duncan & Nicholson, 1991).

"My boyfriend, when I first started dating him, was *very* misinformed about females, what they like/disliked and about how a woman's anatomy should look like. He now has a more accurate view of things. He got his info from porno movies."

(from the author's files)

A second reason is that it allows people to rehearse sexual behaviors, much like fantasy does. A third, related reason is that today many people consider fantasy and masturbation while looking at or listening to explicit material as a form of safe sex (safe from sexually transmitted diseases, for example).

Probably the foremost reason many people use sexually explicit material, however, is that they enjoy the sexual arousal it produces. Many people masturbate while using sexually explicit material. Many couples watch sexually explicit videos together to heighten their arousal, although in a few cases this results in people becoming dissatisfied with their own partner's sexual attraction and performance (Zillmann & Bryant, 1988). In short, most people regard sexually explicit material as a form of fantasy, and use it to escape from the monotony of their daily routines (Davis, 1983).

EFFECTS OF NONVIOLENT SEXUALLY EXPLICIT MATERIAL

As you will learn shortly, there have been many attempts to ban or censor sexually explicit material. People would not be concerned, of course, if they didn't believe that exposure to sexually explicit material has a negative effect on behavior. In order to determine if this were true, President Lyndon Johnson in 1968 appointed an 18-member commission which spent 2 years collecting and studying evidence. The findings of the President's Commission on Obscenity and Pornography were released in 1970 and stimulated a decade of research (much of it originally funded by the Commission). Here are some of the major conclusions from that era:

1. Looking at, reading, or listening to sexually explicit material (movies, pictures, books, tapes) produces physiological arousal in a majority of both men and women (Report of the Commission, 1970; Englar & Walker, 1973; Heiman, 1977; Henson, Rubin, & Henson, 1979; McConaghy, 1974; Schmidt & Sigusch, 1970; Wincze, Hoon, & Hoon, 1976). It was once believed that only men

were aroused by sexually explicit material, but similar physiological responses were observed in both sexes. Many women may actively avoid sexually explicit material, but nevertheless do respond to it when they see or hear it. (A recent study found that women's subjective arousal was greater during female-initiated, female-centered erotic films than it was during the typical male-initiated, male-centered erotic films; Laan et al., 1994).

2. People are more aroused by looking at sexual behaviors they consider to be normal than they are by unconventional behaviors. Sexually explicit material does not seem to create desires that were not already there (Report of the Commission, 1970).

3. When exposed to sexually explicit material, some people show an increase in sexual behavior, a smaller proportion show a decrease, but the majority of people report no change in their behaviors. Increases (almost always expressed as masturbation or intercourse with the usual partner) are short-lived and disappear within 48 hours (Report of the Commission, 1970).

4. Continued exposure to sexually explicit material leads to a marked decrease in interest (indifference, boredom) in these materials (Report of the Commission, 1970; Lipton, 1983).

5. Contrary to many people's belief that sex offenders are generally obsessed with pornography, convicted sex offenders in prisons (e.g., rapists, child molesters) were found to have actually had less exposure to sexually explicit materials (sex education as well as pornography) during adolescence than nonoffenders (Report of the Commission, 1970).

6. Consistent with the previous findings, it was found that when Denmark legalized the sale of hard-core pornographic material to adults in the mid-1960s, there was a lot sold at first as people satisfied their curiosity, but then sales dropped off considerably. There was over a 30 percent drop in sex crimes in the first few years after legalization, suggesting that pornography served as an outlet for some people who might otherwise commit sex crimes. (Report of the Commission, 1970; Kutchinsky, 1973).

The Commission concluded that there was no significant link between exposure of adults to sexually explicit materials and sex crimes or other deviant or harmful behavior. They recommended the repeal of obscenity and pornography laws and that sex education be taught in the public schools:

> "Failure to talk openly and directly about sex has several consequences. It overemphasizes sex, gives it a magical, non-natural quality, making it more attractive and fascinating. It diverts the expression of sexual interest out of more legitimate channels, into less legitimate channels. . . . The Commission believes that interest in sex is normal, healthy, good."

Richard Nixon was president when the Commission's Report was released in 1970. He dismissed it as "morally bankrupt" and rejected its findings.

The conclusion that sex offenders have had less exposure to sexually explicit material has proven to be somewhat controversial. Although most of the studies examined by the Commission found that there was no reliable difference between imprisoned sex offenders and nonoffenders in their rate of exposure to pornography (Cook & Fosen, 1970; Gebhard et al., 1965; Walker, 1970), there was a study that disagreed (Davis & Braught, 1970). A subsequent study supported the Commission's conclusion (Goldstein, 1973), but a still later study found that sex offenders had used sexually explicit material more during adolescence than had nonoffenders (Marshall, 1988). A more recent study found that child molesters were exposed to sexually explicit material at a later age than were nonoffenders, and that adult sex offenders and nonoffenders did not differ in how often they looked at such material (Nutter & Kearns, 1993). The large majority of sex offenders in these studies believed that sexually explicit material did not cause them to commit their crimes, and a recent study found that looking at nonviolent sexually explicit material had no effect on men's attitudes about women (Padgett et al., 1989).

Although there is no evidence that nonviolent sexually explicit material causes harm or incites men to commit sex crimes (none of the Commission members committed a sex crime after looking at hard-core pornography for 2 years), some feminists nevertheless oppose it on the grounds that it causes men to view women as sex objects and leads to sex discrimination (e.g., Dworkin, 1989). Today's sexually explicit movies do, in fact, emphasize the sexual desires and prowess of men while portraying women as sexually willing and available (Brosius, Weaver, & Staab, 1993). However, other feminists worry that attempts to ban sexually explicit material on the grounds of discrimination reinforce a double standard. "It reasserts that women are sexually different from men and in need of special protection. Yet special protection inadvertently reinforces the ways in which women are legally and socially said

to be different from men" (Vance, 1988; also see A. M. Smith, 1993).

EFFECTS OF VIOLENT AND DEGRADING SEXUALLY EXPLICIT MATERIAL

In the years since the President's Commission of 1970, there have been concerns that the amount of sexually explicit material showing women being bound, chained, raped, and tortured has increased (e.g., Check, 1984; Donnerstein & Linz, 1984; Malamuth & Spinner, 1980). Although sexual themes that include violence have actually never accounted for more than a very small proportion (generally less than 10 percent) of sexually explicit videotapes and magazines (Scott & Cuvelier, 1993; Slade, 1984), it is nevertheless an important question as to whether violent sexually explicit material is related to sex offenses. The President's Commission did not specifically examine this issue. Can looking at violent pornography cause some men to rape women?

In numerous scientifically conducted studies designed to answer this question, volunteer subjects were shown films or heard tapes of either mutually consenting erotic behavior, scenes of aggression toward women, or scenes with both sexual explicitness and aggression. In many of the studies, violent sexually explicit material was found to cause arousal in male subjects (Malamuth et al., 1980, 1981). In fact, they were often more aroused by violent sexually explicit scenes (e.g., of naked women bound and distressed) than they were by scenes of women enjoying sex (Heilbrun & Seif, 1988; Malamuth, 1981). After watching violent sexually explicit films, many of the subjects became less sympathetic toward female rape victims, showed greater belief in rape myths (viewing rape victims as more responsible for their assaults), displayed increased hostility to women in the lab, and indicated a greater likelihood that they would commit rape themselves if they were certain that they would not get caught (Donnerstein, 1982, 1983; Donnerstein & Berkowitz, 1981; Donnerstein & Linz, 1984; Malamuth, 1981; Rosen & Beck, 1988; see Linz, 1989 or Malamuth & Donnerstein, 1984 or Donnerstein, Linz, & Penrod, 1987 for reviews). Donnerstein (1983) was startled to find that by the last day of looking at sexually explicit films showing violence toward women, many men found the material "less debasing and degrading of women, more humorous, more enjoyable, and claimed a greater willingness to see this type of film again." Similar results were found when men looked at *degrading sexually explicit material* (nonviolent material showing women as sex objects and where there is a clear unequal balance of power; Linz, 1985; Zillmann & Bryant, 1982). However, not all studies have found that violent pornography causes men to have antiwoman thoughts or attitudes, and we are still not certain what the precise conditions are that cause some men to react in such a manner (see Fisher & Granier, 1994).

Violent sexually explicit films are often highly eroticized—the female victims are often portrayed as enjoying forced sex after putting up some initial resistance. Interestingly, laboratory studies have shown that many women also are aroused by watching erotic rape scenes (Stock, 1982, 1983). Unlike many men, women are not aroused by watching realistic rape scenes, but childhood exposure to sexually explicit material results in many women having attitudes more supportive of sexual violence against women (Corne, Briere, & Esses, 1992).

Arousal by fantasies of rape is not the same as actually committing a rape. None of the previous studies proved that looking at violent pornography really causes sex crimes to be committed (as far as we know, none of the volunteer subjects committed a rape after leaving the lab). To explore whether there really is a causal relationship between violent pornography and sex crimes, Edwin Meese, then the Attorney General of the United States, appointed an 11-member Commission on Pornography in 1985. They released their conclusions in the spring of 1986, less than a year after they were formed (see Figure 16-3). Their conclusion: a "causal relationship" exists between sexually violent pornography and violence toward women. They stated that these materials help foster the myth that women enjoy being raped and that "sexually explicit materials featuring violence [are] on the whole harmful to society." In contrast to the recommendations of the 1970 Commission, they advocated stronger government enforcement of present obscenity laws and additional laws that would result in greater restrictions of sexually explicit material.

The 1986 Commission funded no original research, but instead relied heavily on the findings of the previously conducted laboratory experiments. However, the scientists who conducted that research accused the Commission of drawing conclusions and making legal recommendations that did not follow

FIGURE 16-3   WITH THE BARE-BREASTED *SPIRIT OF JUSTICE* IN BACK OF HIM, U.S. ATTORNEY EDWIN MEESE ACCEPTS THE REPORT OF THE 1986 COMMISSION ON PORNOGRAPHY. WHAT IS EROTICA TO SOME PEOPLE IS PORNOGRAPHY TO OTHERS.

from their data (see Linz, Donnerstein, & Penrod, 1987; Mulvey & Havgaard, 1986). Even some of the Commission members were critical of the report. Ellen Levine, editor of *Woman's Day* magazine, and Judith Becker, a clinical psychologist from New York State Psychiatric Institute, issued a formal statement of dissent. They both said that while they found pornography objectionable and offensive to women, the panel's report was flawed and rushed. Others questioned the objectivity of some of the Commission's members, six of whom had previously called for greater government enforcement against pornographic materials. The Commission's chairman, for example, was a U.S. attorney from Virginia who had made his reputation by prosecuting adult bookstores. In summary, it would appear that some of the panelists were unable to distinguish between their own personal views and objective research.

The behavioral scientists conducting work in this area were brought together in their own conference in 1986. They agreed with the 1970 Commission's conclusion that exposure to nudity alone has no detrimental effects on adult behavior (see Linz et al., 1987). They suggested that the real focus of concern should be depictions of violence toward women, regardless of whether or not it was in a sexually explicit context. Donnerstein (1986), for example, was quoted as saying, "These conclusions (by the 1986 Commission) seem bizarre to me. It is the violence more than the sex—and negative messages about human relationships—that are the problem. And these messages are everywhere" (*The New York Times*, May 17, p. A6). Subsequent studies showed that it is violence-toward-women themes more than sexual explicitness that result in potentially harmful attitude and behavioral changes (Linz et al., 1987; Scott & Schwalm, 1988).

This type of potentially harmful material (violence toward women without sexual explicitness) is precisely the type of material that is common in R-rated movies and on TV today. Overall, one out of eight Hollywood films show a rape scene (National Coalition on Television Violence, 1990). In fact, it is much more common in R-rated movies, TV shows, and detective magazines than in X-rated movies or magazines like

Playboy (Dietz et al., 1986; Palys, 1986; Scott, 1986). Studies have consistently found, for example, that viewing nonexplicit movies with violence toward women results in many men becoming less sensitive toward rape victims (Linz, 1989). So, what is the conclusion of the leading behavioral scientists in the field?

"The most clear and present danger . . . is all violent material in our society, whether sexually explicit or not, that promotes violence against women"

(Donnerstein & Linz, 1986).

In order to eliminate possible detrimental effects on society, we would have to suppress all materials showing violence toward women, not just sexually explicit material with violent themes. Scientists suggest that rather than imposing stricter laws, it might be easier to educate the public about the effects of viewing violence so that they can make better choices about what programs, movies, and books to which they expose themselves and their children.

SEXUALLY EXPLICIT MATERIAL INVOLVING CHILDREN

"Directly after high school I worked at a photo developing store. One day while sorting some pictures I noticed that the first six shots were of boys that looked to be no older than 10 having fellatio and sodomy with each other. The last eight pictures introduced an older man of about 40 years old. I, of course, showed my manager and he called the police. When the man's wife came to pick up the pictures she was arrested. She was charged with passing pornographic material through our store. Her husband was given a heavier sentence—20 years. He was a prestigious teacher at an uptown school and a career pedophile. In that year alone he had molested 12 boys."

(from the author's files)

The President's Commission of 1970 found no evidence that pornography was harmful to adults and suggested the repeal of laws prohibiting the sale and distribution of sexually explicit material. But what about photographs or films that show children nude or having sex (with an adult or with another child)?

"I can watch as much crime and violence as I like as long as they keep their clothes on."

Could looking at child pornography cause someone to molest children, or does this type of pornography provide an outlet for those who might otherwise abuse children? We cannot answer this, because for obvious ethical reasons there has been very little research in this area (Jarvie, 1992). Nevertheless, this is one type of pornography that nearly everyone feels should be banned. How can we do this and still protect First Amendment rights?

One way is to ask whether the "stars" of kiddie porn are capable of making informed consent. Many are runaways who are coerced into participating by financial or other reasons. Some participants are so young that they could not possibly have any idea of what they are doing. They are obviously being exploited by adults (sometimes by their own parents or guardians). Children who are used in this manner generally grow up to feel like objects rather than people and often suffer a variety of emotional and sexual problems (Burgess et al., 1984). The U.S. Supreme Court ruled unanimously in 1982 that publishers and distributors of child pornography could be prosecuted for child abuse without having to prove that the material was obscene, thus avoiding arguments about First Amendment rights. The passage of the Protection of Children Against Sexual Exploitation Act in 1977, the Child Protection Act in 1984, and the Child Protection and Obscenity Enforcement Act in 1988 made it a federal crime to ship or receive in interstate or foreign commerce, or mails, pictures of nude children or children (defined as any person under the age of 18) engaged in sexual acts. The maximum punishment for the first offense is 10 years in jail and a fine of $100,000 (except for participating parents and guardians, who can be sentenced to 20 years to life in prison). As a result of the legislation, prosecutions of child pornography increased more than 250 percent in the first few years after the Child Protection Act was passed. Adults who participate in any capacity in child pornography can be prosecuted. In 1990, the Supreme Court upheld an Ohio law which made it a crime to even possess pornography showing children under the age of 18.

This is presently the only type of sexually explicit material that is legally banned. The U.S. Customs Service has established a hotline of the National Center for Missing and Exploited Children to receive tips about pornography: 1-800-843-5678.

Even with this material, however, there is a question of where we should draw the line. What is child pornography? Authorities in programs for sex offenders have noted that there are men who become sexually aroused by watching diaper advertisements on TV. Should we ban all pictures of naked or partially clothed babies and children?

COMPLETE LEGALIZATION OR CENSORSHIP?

What should we do about sexually explicit material? Should we remove all restrictions to the sale and distribution of hard-core material to adults (i.e., make it completely legal), or should we attempt to ban all such material? There are good arguments for both cases.

The Presidential Commission of 1970, you recall, found substantial evidence that sexually explicit material serves as an outlet to people with sexually criminal tendencies and may actually reduce sex crimes. It is probably difficult for you to believe that material that you find offensive and repugnant may actually do some good, but that is because you are normal and have no deviant tendencies. Therapist John Money of the Johns Hopkins University has noted that patients in sex offender clinics often say that they use pornography to fantasize about abnormal sexual activity so that they will not have to act out their desires in real life. In fact, most sex therapists still believe that socially unacceptable sexual behaviors often result from attempts to severely repress sexuality. Father Bruce Ritter, founder of Covenant House, is a possible example of this. A Meese commission member and outspoken opponent of both pornography and sex for purposes of pleasure, even within a marriage ("It wastes the seed," he said), Father Ritter resigned from Covenant House after being accused of sexual molestation by several male residents of the shelter for runaway children. The Attorney General's Commission attempted to show that violent sexually explicit material had harmful effects, but their investigation was heavily criticized; and it may be the case that it is material with violent themes, with or without sex, that provokes violent crimes.

Even if it should eventually be proven that hard-core explicit material reduces sex crimes, it nevertheless is true that many people find it highly offensive and degrading and do not want themselves or their children exposed to it. This is particularly true for women, who are generally shown only as sex objects.

A recent survey found that over half of Americans feel that there is too much sexually explicit material in their neighborhood stores (Janus & Janus, 1993) and there have been numerous attempts by citizens, school boards, and local governments to ban some sexually oriented materials that they considered to be offensive. The producers or distributors of the materials (or others) invariably protest on the grounds of First Amend-

ment rights, and many cases have reached the U.S. Supreme Court. The First Amendment of our Constitution guarantees, among other things, that Congress "shall make no law . . . abridging the freedom of speech, or of the press. . . . " I suspect that the founding fathers never intended this to apply to explicit pictures of couples having anal sex, but the problem is deciding where to draw the line. Guess which of the following magazines and books have been targets of censorship by some communities in recent years:

The American Heritage Dictionary	*Huckleberry Finn*
the *Bible*	*Hustler* magazine
Brave New World	*Macbeth*
The Catcher in the Rye	*Penthouse* magazine
Cinderella	*Playboy* magazine
Club magazine	*Romeo and Juliet*
The Diary of Anne Frank	*Sports Illustrated* (swimsuit issues)
Gorillas in the Mist	Stories about dinosaurs
The Grapes of Wrath	*The Wizard of Oz*

If you guessed all of them, you were correct. Yes, there are some people who believe that parts of the *Bible* are too explicit for others to read. *The American Heritage Dictionary* was banned in some places because it included "bad words." High school teachers in Erie, Pennsylvania blacked out passages in *Gorillas in the Mist* (by naturalist Dian Fossey) describing mating habits of apes. Not all of the above materials were banned because they were sexually explicit, however. *Cinderella*, for example, was banned from public schools in a Tennessee community in 1986 because it mentioned witchcraft, and *Macbeth* was banned by the same community because it mentioned magic (this was overturned by a decision of the U.S. Supreme Court). Attempts to censor or ban sexually explicit material continue today. The record album "As Nasty as They Wanna B" by the rap group 2 Live Crew became the first ever (in 1990) to be ruled obscene in Federal Court. In July 1990, the curator of Cincinnati's Contemporary Art Center was ordered to go to trial on obscenity charges for putting on an exhibit of homoerotic photos by photographer Robert Mapplethorpe. In 1995, the United States Senate Commerce Committee proposed the Communications Decency Act, which would make it a crime to transmit obscene images through electronic media (the Internet).

With regard to sexually explicit material, the problem the Supreme Court has had to deal with (in cases appealed on First Amendment rights) is trying to distinguish between erotica and pornography. **Erotica** (from the

Erotica
Any literature or art that has a sexual theme. This is a morally neutral term.

JIM MEDDICK reprinted by permission of Newspaper Enterprise Association, Inc.

peals to prurient interest (lustful craving or interests) in sex.

Even the Supreme Court justices recognized problems with this definition, however. For example, in the following year (*Jenkins* v. *Georgia*, 1974) the court ruled that local communities do not have "unbridled discretion" to decide what is obscene (a Georgia community had decided that the Hollywood movie *Carnal Knowledge* was obscene). Who determines what is patently offensive or what art or literature lacks serious value? Former Supreme Court Justice Potter Stewart admitted that he could not come up with a good definition of hard-core pornography, but said, "I know it when I see it" (*Jacobelis* v. *Ohio*, 1965). We all see things differently, however. You know what you find to be obscene, but do you want someone else to make that decision for you?

Greek word *erotikos* meaning love poem) is any literature or art with a sexual theme, while **pornography** (from the Greek words *porne*, which means prostitute, and *graphos*, meaning depicting) is literature or art with a sexual theme that is designed to cause arousal. Many people use the terms pornography and obscenity interchangeably, while others feel that obscenity is a more limited term (see Penrod & Linz, 1984, for a history of this subject). The key, therefore, is how we define obscene. What is erotica to one person is pornography to another. The Venus de Milo may be regarded as a great work of art by most people (erotica), but to some it is just a statue of a nude woman (obscene and pornographic). Why are old paintings of nude persons or nude couples making love generally considered art, but modern photos of the same thing often considered pornographic? (see Figure 16-4). Why are drawings of couples having sex considered educational if they appear in sexuality textbooks (such as those in Chapter 11 in this book), but pornographic if the same thing is found in magazines (see King & Lococo, 1990)?

After grappling with this issue for many years, the Supreme Court finally came up with a three-part definition of obscenity in 1973 (*Miller* v. *California*). Material was considered **obscene** if: (1) by contemporary community standards it depicts patently offensive sexual conduct; (2) it lacks "serious literary, artistic, political, or scientific value"; and (3) it ap-

Pornography

Literature or art with a sexual theme that is designed to cause arousal and excitement and which is considered to be obscene.

Obscene

In legal cases, refers to material that by contemporary community standards depicts patently offensive sexual conduct, lacks serious value, and appeals to prurient interests.

FIGURE 16-4   WHY ARE MANY PAINTINGS WITH SEXUALLY EXPLICIT THEMES CONSIDERED GREAT ART WHEN MODERN PHOTOS WITH THE SAME THEME ARE OFTEN REGARDED TO BE PORNOGRAPHIC? (BOUCHER'S *HERCULES AND OMPHALE*—1730S)

We are one of the few countries in the world whose people have freedom of expression. Most people are offended by at least some of the sexually explicit material that is published or filmed today, but many worry that allowing others to have the power to ban certain materials might eventually infringe on their own presently enjoyed freedom of expression (after all, there are those who would ban passages in the *Bible,* you recall). What do you think should be done? ■

SODOMY LAWS

What do you do behind closed and locked doors in your own home or apartment? You're right, it is none of my business. Is it anyone else's business either? Well, you might be surprised to find out then that many states have laws prohibiting certain sexual acts, even if done by consenting adults (including married couples) in private.

Sixteen states and the District of Columbia have laws that make fornication and/or cohabitation a crime (see Table 16-1). The maximum penalty is generally 3 to 6 months in jail and/or a fine. Adultery, which is a crime in 26 states, has historically been considered a more serious offense because it violates the sanctity of the family. Also, past attitudes held that women were property belonging to their husbands (and thus adultery was a violation of property rights). Are people ever prosecuted under these laws? Yes; in states that have laws forbidding adultery, for example, it is not uncommon for one member of a quarreling married couple to press charges against the other to gain an advantage during the settlement, or perhaps just for revenge (Sachs, 1990). In these cases, it is usually a husband who presses charges against his wife.

More recently, there has been much attention devoted to **sodomy laws**, which ban specific behaviors between consenting adults. Twenty-two states have laws that forbid oral or anal sex (see Table 16-1), which are often referred to as "crimes against nature" even though a large number of couples (the vast majority, as far as oral-genital sex is concerned) engage in them (see Chapter 11). To some degree these laws reflect the early Judeo-Christian attitude that the only natural sexual act is heterosexual intercourse, because it is the only sexual behavior that can result in reproduction.

Sodomy laws
Laws that prohibit oral and/or anal sex.

In six states the sodomy laws are aimed specifically at homosexuals, but in 16 others they do not distinguish between heterosexual or homosexual couples. The existence of sodomy laws means then, of course, that millions of married American couples are committing crimes for which they could potentially be put in jail (up to 5 years or more in 13 states). However, when the laws are enforced, which isn't too often, they are generally enforced only against homosexuals. Homosexuals regard these laws as "legalized fag bashing" and have legally challenged a number of them.

Does the U.S. Constitution guarantee us the right to privacy? Apparently not. A Virginia law that forbids oral and anal sex between either hetero- or homosexual individuals was upheld by both a state and federal court in 1975. The U.S. Supreme Court refused to grant a hearing on the case (*Doe* v. *Commonwealth's Attorney*) in 1976 and thus upheld the right of states to regulate the private activity of its citizens. Basically, the ruling was that states have the right to regulate sexual behaviors just as they have the right to require you to use seat belts or anything else if it is "for your own good."

The case of a Georgia man focused national attention on the legality of sodomy laws. Michael Hardwick was arrested for having oral sex with another man in the privacy of his own bedroom (the arresting officer had come to the house about a traffic violation and was let in by another person). Hardwick, who could have served up to 20 years for this crime, sued the state of Georgia, but the case was thrown out by a U.S. district judge on the basis of the 1976 Virginia ruling. The U.S. 11th Circuit Court of Appeals reinstated the suit (*Bowers* v. *Hardwick*), and the U.S. Supreme Court this time agreed to hear arguments. The Supreme Court upheld the Georgia law by a 5-4 vote in June, 1986. Writing for the majority, Justice Byron White stated, "The proposition that any kind of private sexual conduct between consenting adults is constitutionally in-

WAIT...I THINK WE'D BETTER HAVE OUR LAWYER PRESENT.

(Reprinted by permission of United Features Syndicate, Inc.)

TABLE 16-1
LAWS REGULATING SEXUAL BEHAVIOR BETWEEN CONSENTING ADULTS

STATE	FORNICATION AND/OR COHABITATION PUNISHABLE OFFENSE	MAXIMUM PENALTY
Arizona	"Open and notorious cohabitation"	30 days and/or $500
District of Columbia	Fornication	6 months and/or $300
Florida	Cohabitation	60 days and/or $500
Georgia	Fornication	1 year and/or $1000
Idaho	Fornication/Cohabitation	6 months and/or $300
Illinois	Fornication/Cohabitation	6 months or $500
Massachusetts	Cohabitation	3 months or $300
Michigan	Cohabitation	1 year and/or $500
Minnesota	Fornication	90 days and/or $700
Mississippi	Fornication/Cohabitation	6 months or $500
North Carolina	Fornication/Cohabitation	6 months and/or $500
North Dakota	Cohabitation	30 days and/or $500
Rhode Island	Fornication	$10
South Carolina	Fornication/Cohabitation	1 year and/or $500
Utah	Fornication	6 months or $299
Virginia	Fornication	$100
West Virginia	Fornication/Cohabitation	$20 minimum/6 months or $50 minimum

STATE	ORAL OR ANAL SEX (AS OF JANUARY 1994) PUNISHABLE OFFENSE	MAXIMUM PENALTY
Alabama	Oral or anal sex with someone other than your spouse	1 year
Arizona	"Infamous crime against nature"	30 days and/or $500
Arkansas	Oral or anal sex with anyone of the same sex	1 year and/or $1000
Florida	"Unnatural and lascivious act"	60 days and/or $500
Georgia	Oral or anal sex	20 years
Idaho	"Infamous crime against nature"	Minimum of 5 years
Kansas	Oral or anal sex with anyone of the same sex	6 months and/or $1000
Louisiana	"Unnatural carnal copulation"	5 years and/or $2000
Maryland	Oral or anal sex with anyone of the same sex	10 years and/or $1000
Massachusetts	Sodomy and buggery	
Michigan	Abominable and detestable crime against nature	15 years or $2500
Minnesota	Oral or anal sex	1 year and/or $3000
Mississippi	Detestable and abominable crime against nature	10 years
Missouri	Oral or anal sex with anyone of the same sex	1 year and $1000
Montana	Sexual contact with anyone of the same sex	10 years and/or $50,000
North Carolina	Crime against nature	10 years
Oklahoma	Detestable and abominable crime against nature	10 years
Rhode Island	Abominable and detestable crime against nature	20 years (7 yrs. min.)
South Carolina	Abominable crime of buggery	5 years and/or $500
Tennessee	Crime against nature with anyone of the same sex	15 years
Utah	Oral or anal sex with anyone other than your spouse	6 months or $299
Virginia	Oral or anal sex	5 years or $1000

Source: National Gay and Lesbian Task Force

sulated from state proscription is unsupportable." In a dissenting opinion, Justice Harry Blackmun said, "What the court really has refused to recognize is the fundamental interest all individuals have in controlling the nature of their intimate associations."

In their ruling, the Court avoided the larger issue of whether sodomy laws could be used to prosecute heterosexuals—the ruling was limited to "consensual homosexual sodomy." However, there was nothing in the language to cast doubt on the constitutionality of laws that forbid oral or anal sex between married heterosexual individuals. In 1992, Kentucky's Supreme Court struck down that state's sodomy law, which was aimed specifically at homosexuals, stating, "We need not sympathize, agree with, or even understand the sexual preference of homosexuals in order to recognize their right to equal treatment before the bar of criminal justice." Other states are expected to follow.

Interestingly, the American Law Institute's Model Penal Code recommended as far back as 1962 that sexual behaviors between consenting adults (excluding prostitution) be decriminalized. Legislators tend to view *decriminalization* as a safer political route to take than legalization. They worry that any attempt to legalize sexual behaviors will be interpreted by voters as condoning them. Decriminalization simply means either that the acts will no longer be defined as criminal or that they will no longer be subject to penalties, and it is thus a morally neutral term.

Several states have followed the American Law Institute's recommendations and have decriminalized sexual acts between consenting adults. However, legislators in some states are still proposing restrictive laws. A bill proposed in the state of Washington in 1990, for example, would have made it a prosecutable offense (90 days in jail and a $5,000 fine) for anyone under the age of 18

BOX 16-B

CROSS-CULTURAL PERSPECTIVES: ILLEGAL SEX AROUND THE WORLD

In the last part of this chapter you learned that many states prohibit and punish sexual behaviors such as fornication, cohabitation, adultery, and oral or anal sex. However, we are not the only country for which this is true. In fact, most countries make it illegal for consenting adults to engage in some forms of sex. The United States is more restrictive than some countries and more permissive than others. Here is a list of some of the countries around the world and the sexual activities that they consider to be illegal.

	Fornication	Cohabitation	Adultery	All anal sex	All oral sex	Homosexual oral or anal sex
Mexico	—	—	✓	—	—	✓
Brazil	—	—	✓	—	—	—
Argentina	—	—	✓	—	—	—
Chile	—	—	✓	—	—	✓
England	—	—	—	—	—	—
France	—	—	—	—	—	—
Germany	—	—	—	—	—	—
Sweden	—	—	—	—	—	—
Italy	—	—	—	—	—	—
Russia	—	—	✓	—	—	—
China	✓	✓	✓	✓	✓	—
Japan	—	—	—	—	—	—
India	—	—	✓	✓	—	✓
Australia	—	—	✓	—	—	✓
Saudi Arabia	✓	✓	✓	✓	✓	—
Iran	✓	✓	✓	✓	✓	—
Egypt	✓	✓	✓	✓	✓	—
Zaire	—	—	—	✓	✓	—
Kenya	—	—	✓	✓	✓	—
South Africa	—	—	✓	✓	✓	—

to engage in necking or petting. Which approach do you believe is more correct? Do you believe that a couple should have the right to decide for themselves what sexual behaviors they engage in (assuming, of course, that it is done with mutual consent and does not cause physical or emotional harm to either person), or that a state should serve as a higher moral authority and regulate the private consensual sexual activities of its citizens?

KEY TERMS

B-girls   380
brothel prostitute   380
call girls   381
Comstock law   384
degrading sexually explicit
   material   387
erotica   390

fornication   379
gigolos   381
hustlers   381
johns   383
nonviolent sexually explicit
   material   386
obscene   391

pornography   391
prostitution   380
sodomy laws   392
streetwalkers   380
violent sexually explicit
   material   387

PERSONAL REFLECTIONS

1. How do you feel about prostitution: should it remain illegal or should we attempt to legalize and regulate it? Why? If you feel it should be illegal, should the "clients" be prosecuted?

2. Are you ever physically aroused by looking at sexually explicit photos or movies? What is your emotional reaction to this material and any arousal it causes? Why? Have you ever learned anything from photos of naked persons or by watching R-rated or X-rated sex scenes? If you had the power, would you ban this material, or allow unrestricted distribution to adults? Why?

3. How would you respond if someone told you that this textbook was obscene and pornographic?

4. Do you think that state legislatures, which represent large groups of people, should have the right to regulate the private (and physically nonharmful) sexual behaviors of consenting adults? Why or why not?

5. If you answered "no" to question 4, do you think that you or any other individual should pass judgment on others for their private, consensual, sexual behaviors?

SUGGESTED READINGS

Baxter, M. (1990, 5 May). Flesh and blood. *New Scientist.* A short article on the studies of the effects of violent pornography.
Donnerstein, E. J., and Linz, D. G. (1986, December). The question of pornography. *Psychology Today.* Authors of pornography research challenge the conclusions of the Attorney General's Commission and say that we should be more concerned with violence in the media.
Final Report of the Attorney General's Commission on Pornography. (1986). Nashville, Tennessee: Rutledge Hill Press. A paperback edition of the controversial conclusions of the Commission headed by former Attorney General Meese.
Kelly, G. F. (1984). Is it time for sexologists to clarify a position on pornography? *Journal of Sex Education and Therapy 10*(2).
Millett, K. (1976). *The prostitution papers.* New York: Ballantine. Reviews and discusses the role of prostitutes in the United States and possible legal solutions.
Report of the Commission on Obscenity and Pornography. (1970). New York: Bantam Books. A paperback edition of the results and conclusions of the 1970 Commission.
Volkman, E., and Rosenberg, H. L. (1985, June). The shame of the nation. *Family Weekly.* Discusses the problem of child pornography and the factors leading to it.

CHAPTER SEVENTEEN

Human Sexuality Today

COMMUNICATING ABOUT SEX

WHEN YOU HAVE FINISHED STUDYING THIS CHAPTER, YOU SHOULD BE ABLE TO:

1. TAKE STEPS THAT ENABLE YOU AND YOUR PARTNER TO BECOME MORE COMFORTABLE TALKING ABOUT YOUR SEXUAL RELATIONSHIP (INCLUDING AGREEMENT ON A SEXUAL VOCABULARY);

2. TAKE RESPONSIBILITY FOR YOUR OWN SEXUAL PLEASURE;

3. UNDERSTAND THE IMPORTANCE OF POSITIVE REINFORCEMENT AND "I" LANGUAGE;

4. BECOME A BETTER LISTENER;

5. UNDERSTAND THE IMPORTANCE OF NONVERBAL COMMUNICATION;

6. UNDERSTAND WHY THE SEX EDUCATION OF CHILDREN SHOULD BE AN ONGOING PROCESS RATHER THAN A SINGLE "BIRDS AND BEES" TALK;

7. KNOW AT WHAT AGE PARENTS SHOULD DISCUSS CERTAIN SEXUALITY-RELATED TOPICS WITH THEIR CHILDREN; AND

8. KNOW HOW TO SPEAK TO YOUR CHILDREN IN A MANNER SO THAT THEY ARE LIKELY TO VALUE YOUR OPINION.

YOU HAVE NOW NEARLY COMPLETED A COMPREHENSIVE COURSE IN HUMAN SEXUALITY. I HAVE CHOSEN TO end this text with a chapter on communication skills. Why at the end? **Communication** is the act of making known (information); the exchange of thoughts or ideas (*American Heritage Dictionary*). Prior to now, you may have lacked factual information about a wide variety of topics in human sexuality. However, when it comes to talking about the topic of sex, it is not enough to have factual information. Many people have trouble talking about sex, even with their partner (Barbach, 1982).

> **Communication**
>
> The exchange of information, thoughts, ideas, or feelings.

In this chapter I will present some guidelines to help you communicate better about sexual matters. There are a variety of situations in which people might communicate about sexually related matters, including interactions with a new or short-term partner (dating, initiating sexual activities, contraception and safer sex), conveying needs and desires to a long-term partner, and conveying information and values to children. Because I cannot possibly cover them all, I have chosen to limit this chapter to sexual communication between long-term partners and communication between parents and their children about sexuality. In Chapter 5 you can find some advice on initiating discussions about safer sex with a dating partner.

The first half of this chapter deals with communication between two people who have made a commitment to a long-term relationship. It assumes that each person genuinely cares for the other; that there is trust and intimacy. As you learned in Chapter 13, most couples are going to experience sexual differences or problems in their relationship (Ende, Rockwell, & Glasgow, 1984; Frank, Anderson, & Rubenstein, 1978; Nathan, 1986). How they work those problems out—how they communicate with one another about their differences and problems—will affect the overall relationship. Good communication leads to better relationships, and a better relationship generally leads to better sex (Cupach & Metts, 1991; Cupach & Comstock, 1990). The last half of the chapter is designed to help parents (and future parents) take what they have learned in this course and teach it to their children.

In order to better communicate with you about communication, I have elected to abandon the normal academic style of textbook writing. I present to you a few guidelines about improving your communication skills in a question-and-answer format. ■

TALKING WITH YOUR PARTNER ABOUT SEXUAL DIFFERENCES AND PROBLEMS

Why Is It Difficult to Talk about Sex?

Intercourse means communication (*Webster's Dictionary*), but there are few topics that people have more difficulty talking about than sex. One of the major reasons for this is that most people have little experience talking about sex in an intelligent and mature manner. Recall that surveys in my own course consistently indicate that fewer than a third of the 1000 students per semester have ever had a serious discussion with their parents about sex. Very few ever had a course in sex education during junior high or high school. This means, of course, that most people's only experience with discussing sex is locker room conversation and jokes, usually with individuals of the same sex. Much of this is crude and vulgar and contains misinformation. As adolescents, talking to members of the opposite sex about sex is often avoided because of fears that it will be interpreted as an invitation or come on. Thus, males generally have some experience talking about sex with other males, and females with other females, but many people reach adulthood with little or no experience with talking to the opposite sex. Even conversations with the same sex may be limited to nonthreatening sexual topics, for to talk about a sexual problem is to admit that you have one. Many people, particularly adolescents, are unwilling to do this because of worries that their friends might think less of them and tell others. As adults, some people are afraid to talk with their partner about a sexual problem because they are afraid it will threaten the relationship.

Communication about sex is also often hampered when a couple is locked into stereotypic gender roles. For example, one harmful stereotype is that men are experts at sex. This is simply not true. Women and men both *learn* about sex. Individuals differ greatly in the types of sexual experiences that they enjoy. Each person must explore and learn about what brings the greatest pleasure to his or her sexual partner. Because sexual behaviors are learned, anyone can become an "expert" if they are willing to read, try new behaviors, listen to feedback and direction from a partner, and be willing to learn as well as to teach.

Another harmful stereotype is that men should not express their feelings and emotions (including sexual feelings), while women do. All people of both genders need to express their feelings and emotions and be able to communicate them. The image of a man as "strong and silent" robs him of a fundamental part of his humanity and robs his partner of a true companion (see Goldberg's *The New Male*, 1979).

Finally, power differences in a relationship can affect communication. We are most likely to express our opinion, particularly a difference of opinion, to those persons we perceive as having equal status. In some relationships there is a power imbalance (in heterosexual relationships, it is usually in favor of the male). Although the following suggestions for improving communication should be helpful to everyone, they will be most useful to individuals in an egalitarian relationship. (To resolve a major power imbalance in a relationship may require professional counseling.)

How Can My Partner and I Get Used to Talking about Sex?

One of the best ways to get used to talking with your partner about sex is to discuss together any sexuality-related topics in your daily newspaper. Hardly a day goes by when there isn't at least one article (and there are often many) in the paper about sexuality—AIDS, birth control, fertility research, and, best of all, results of sex surveys. Columns by Dear Abby and Ann Landers often are about sexually related matters. Show your partner some selected topic in this book and start off with a statement like, "I didn't know this," or "This is really interesting."

When you both become more comfortable talking about sex together, then you can more safely talk about your own sexual relationship. Often a good place to start is to talk about why it is difficult for you both to talk about sex. If, for example, your parents had a negative attitude about talking about sex, talk about that and how you would like to be different. Next, you might talk about normal bodily functions related to sexuality and how they affect your sexual relationship. Try talking about menstruation, for example. Many people have *learned* (and thus can unlearn) negative attitudes about that (see Chapter 3 for an extensive discussion of learned negative attitudes about menstruation and how it affects sexual relations).

When you and your partner are comfortable enough to talk about sexual differences (in attitudes, preferred behaviors, etc.), you might begin by discussing when and how to talk about such matters. For couples interested in exploring their attitudes about different sexual behaviors, looking at a sex manual together might be helpful (e.g., Alex Comfort's *The Joy of Sex*).

What If I Am Uncomfortable with the Language of Sex—What Words Should I Use?

Many of the commonly used words for our sexual anatomy and their functions reflect the negativity that has prevailed in Western culture since early Christianity. Words like "prick," "cock," "cunt," "pussy," "screw," and "fuck" may be common in conversations among men (Sanders & Robinson, 1979), but many women (as well as many men) might feel uncomfortable using such words with their partner, particularly if they wish to express positive emotions. Medically correct terms

such as "penis," "vagina," and "sexual intercourse" may avoid any negative connotations, but are so unerotic that they, too, may seem inappropriate in conversations between two people in a deeply emotional relationship. Euphemisms such as "go to bed with," "sleeping with," and "making love" may seem more erotic to some, and convey that there is a relationship, but are often inappropriate as well—do we always "make love" when we have sex? Some couples develop a private vocabulary for body parts that is used only in conversations between themselves.

It is not for me to tell you what words to use with your partner when talking about sex. However, it is important that you *both* be comfortable with a sexual vocabulary. Therefore, as part of the process of getting used to talking about sex (previous section), be sure to discuss this with your partner until you both agree on a vocabulary that is explicit and specific enough to convey your feelings and desires and that you also find to be nonoffensive (yet still erotic).

When (and Where) Should I Try to Talk to My Partner?

When is a good time to tell your partner that you prefer different behaviors, or wish to be touched or made love to in a different manner (or any other difference)? If you do it right after sex, you run the risk of making it sound like a report card or performance rating (and perhaps not a very good one at that). If you do it during sex, you might distract or frustrate your partner, and if you express your dissatisfaction before you start, it might cause performance anxiety.

Perhaps a neutral time would be best. Recall from the previous section that one of the general topics you and your partner might first discuss is when to talk about sexual differences. Whenever you do it, make sure you are not frustrated, angry, or highly emotional at the time. It is not so much when you discuss your differences, but how you go about it, and your concerns may not be well received if you begin in a negative emotional state (see following sections). Try to judge when your partner would be most receptive to talking about your concerns.

Finally, if you have most of your sexual relations in the bedroom, never worry about or discuss your sexual problems while in bed. If you do this too often, the bed can become a stimulus for sexual tension and anxiety; that is, just being in bed can cause you to start worrying. Save the bed for pleasant experiences and pick a neutral site (like the living room) for worrying about problems.

How Should I Approach My Partner about Concerns with Our Sexual Relationship?

Because of their inexperience talking about sex (particularly sexual problems), many people say nothing and allow the problem to continue, with the end result often being increasingly greater frustration and/or anger. When they finally do get around to saying something, many people begin with statements like, "I don't like it when you . . . ," or "You don't . . ." These types of statements accentuate the negative and are often met with defensive reactions and counter-accusations (Zimmer, 1983). This can quickly result in a full-scale argument.

There are few things that as easily insult a person's ego as criticizing his or her sexual expression or interaction. Nearly everyone would like to believe that they are a good sexual partner. To try to solve your own frustrations by criticizing your partner, therefore, is asking for trouble. Sometimes people ask for it and then get upset with the response. Some people, for example, ask questions like, "How was it?" "Did you like it?" or "Wasn't that great?" after having sex. Sometimes they are really looking for a pat on the back or ego reinforcement rather than an honest answer, so this is really not a good time to express any negative reactions. Whenever possible, accentuate the positive rather than the negative. This is the most important advice that I can give you. Rather than beginning the conversation with "I don't like it when you . . . ," try "I like it when you . . ." Your partner must do something that you like while having sex, so give him or her some positive reinforcement. Thousands of studies have shown that behaviors increase when they are reinforced, and praise is generally a powerful reinforcer for human beings.

WHAT IF I THINK THAT MY PARTNER IS TO BLAME—CAN I EVER COMPLAIN?

If you haven't expressed your concerns to your partner in a clear, specific manner (because you are uncomfortable talking about sex or for any other reason), do not lay the blame entirely on your partner. The problem has continued because you have allowed it to. Your partner cannot know what you want unless you tell him or her. It is wrong for you to think, or expect, that your partner should know what you want or how to please you. *You must take the responsibility for your own pleasure*, and you can do this only if you tell your partner of your needs and desires.

Although I emphasized the use of positive reinforcement in the previous section, that does not mean that you can never complain or express anger. However, when angry, learn to control it. Express your anger only after you have calmed down (remember, highly emotional, negative accusations will probably be met with similar responses on the part of your partner). Ask yourself what your motivation is for expressing complaints. Is it to hurt your partner, or is it for constructive change? Couples with good relationships accept that there will be differences, and sometimes even conflict, but they resolve those conflicts in constructive ways, not destructive ways. If you criticize your partner, make sure you criticize his or her behavior, not his or her character. There is a big difference between saying, "You don't show me often enough how much you care," and saying "You are an uncaring person." If you must criticize your partner's behavior, be sure to praise other aspects of his or her behavior as well.

HOW SHOULD I EXPRESS MY NEEDS AND DESIRES?

Most communications experts suggest that individuals use "I" language when expressing their desires to their partner. That means begin sentences with "I," followed by *your* feelings, desires, or thoughts. There are some important advantages to this. By directly stating your feelings, you are taking the responsibility for your own well-being (see previous section). In addition, "I" sentences avoid a blaming or accusatory tone common in statements that begin with "You." Statements such as "You don't like to hug me anymore," or "You don't love me," attack the other person's character and may well be met with a defensive response. The statement "I would like you to hug me more often" more directly expresses your feelings and desires and is less likely to elicit a defensive, negative response.

Questions that begin with "Why" (don't you . . .) are also often used to criticize a partner. Avoid those as well. Even sentences that begin with "we" can cause problems because they make assumptions about your partner's desires, moods, thoughts, or feelings. Don't talk for your partner.

Dr. Harold Bloomfield and Sirah Vettese, marriage partners and co-authors of *Lifemates: The Love Fitness Program for a Lasting Relationship* (1989), suggest "sexual heart talks" to enhance sexual intimacy. They ask couples to take turns completing the following statements with their spouse:

> "The best thing about our sex life is . . ."
> "What I find sexually attractive about you is . . ."
> "A sexual delight I would like to indulge with you is . . ."
> "A sexual fantasy I would like to act out with you is . . ."
> "The way I would like to be touched is . . ."
> "When I would like to be sexually romantic and you don't respond I . . ."
> "I feel like withdrawing from sex when . . ."
> "Three sexual fears I have are . . ."
> "I feel sexually frustrated when . . ."

HOW CAN I FIND OUT ABOUT MY PARTNER'S DESIRES AND NEEDS?

Yes, it's important that you know and understand your partner's sexual desires and needs, but as a preliminary step be sure that you are aware of your own. Once you are certain, a good place to start is with self-disclosure. Reveal to your partner (using "I" language) your thoughts, feelings, desires, and needs. This creates an environment of trust and understanding, and most people will self-disclose in return. Compare and discuss how each of you feel about different behaviors. Learn each other's preferences. Here, again, a sex manual might be helpful.

Of course, you can also ask your partner about his or her preferences, but make sure that you ask questions that are open-ended (e.g., "How do you like me to touch you when . . ."). Avoid questions that can be answered with one word ("yes" or "no" questions such as "Did you like it?" or "Do you like me to kiss your neck?").

Is Listening Important? If So, How Can I Become a Better Listener?

Effective communication is what holds close relationships together and enables them to grow. However, many people forget that communication requires not just talking, but listening as well. This is as true for sexual relations as it is for any other behavior. How well do you listen?

We may hear with our ears, but we show how attentive we are with body language—body position (Do you face your partner while he or she talks to you?), eye contact, facial expressions. Be supportive of your partner's attempts to communicate with you. In addition to positive body language, interact with him or her in a constructive manner. Make comments or paraphrase what your partner is saying so that you both are sure what the other is trying to say (not everyone conveys their messages clearly).

To improve your listening skills, try giving your partner a massage. Giving one another a massage strengthens relationships by promoting better communication (Comiskey, 1989). Use some oil and make it a good massage. When starting the massage, it is normal to assume that what feels best to you will feel best to others as well. If you like your shoulders and neck massaged with a lot of pressure, for example, it is only natural that you will start off attempting to please your partner in this manner. However, not everyone else likes the same things you do. Your partner may prefer gentle massaging of the lower back. How will he or she communicate this to you? He or she may tell you, but it is important to realize that a person does not have to use words to communicate. When a massage really feels good, most people emit little noises like "ooh" and "aah." These responses should be just as effective as words in letting you know that what you are doing feels good.

When giving your partner a massage, vary the pressure and explore different areas of your partner's body. Avoid touching genitals and breasts, for the purpose of the massage is not for your own sexual pleasure, but to learn how to listen (you may discover, however, that massage is a great form of foreplay and you may want to use it for that purpose in the future). Listen to your partner's responses while massaging. If you listen well and care about your partner, you can modify your behavior and give a massage that pleases him or her instead of giving one that might please only you.

If you are a good enough listener to adjust a massage to please your partner, you can easily do the same while having sex. All of us want to believe we are (or will be) a good sexual partner, but to be one we must first be a good listener.

Is It Possible to Communicate Nonverbally?

The answer, of course, is yes. Actually, I already partially answered this for the last question. Things like eye contact, facial expressions, and interpersonal distance (how close you stand or sit next to someone) all express messages. Single persons commonly use these type messages to convey interest, or lack of interest, in another person. Silence can convey a message (e.g., anger, anxiety). Touch, in particular, is a very powerful nonverbal means of communication. As put by one person who studies communication and intimacy, "If intimacy is proximity, then nothing comes closer than touch, the most intimate knowledge of another" (Thayer, 1986). For the exercise in the previous question, for example, the manner in which you and your partner go about giving the other a massage may well reflect how much you care about the other.

Perhaps the biggest problem with nonverbal signals is that, because they are not as precise as verbal messages, they can be misinterpreted. This frequently happens in the singles' world.

For two people communicating verbally, it is important that there be agreement between the verbal and nonverbal aspects of the communication. How do you suppose your partner would feel if while telling him or her how much you care, you were inattentive, with little or no eye contact?

If I Want My Partner to Change and I Follow These Guidelines, How Soon Can I Expect to See a Change?

Even when there is good communication, neither you nor your partner can be expected to change overnight. It is important to keep in mind that if there are several things about your partner's attitude or behavior that bother you, do not address them all at once. Attempt to change only one thing at a time. If you present your partner with a long list of criticisms all at once it will probably be met with defensiveness and retaliatory criticism.

What If We Cannot Agree?

No one person will always be able to satisfy all the needs and desires of another. That is true even in the best of relationships. People simply have differences in opinions and different preferences. When this happens, good communication can only lead to an understanding of those things that the two of you disagree about. It is often helpful to agree that you disagree. However, if either you or your partner is greatly bothered because your needs and desires are going unfulfilled, then it would be wise to seek professional counseling. Chapter 13 provides the names and addresses of two organizations that will help you locate qualified professionals in your area. ■

IN THE FUTURE: TALKING WITH YOUR CHILDREN ABOUT SEX

When asked where he received his education, Mark Twain answered, "Throughout my life, except for the years I attended school." This is generally true for most people when it comes to learning about sexually related matters as well. **Sex education** courses are really just an intervention—a *formal* attempt to provide knowledge. For those few people who take a comprehensive sex education course, it generally does not occur until they are in high school or college. However, **sexual learning** begins in infancy and is ongoing throughout childhood and adolescence. It is informal and is received from family, friends, the media, and the rest of the general environment.

Sexual learning
Knowledge about sex that is received (usually informally) from family, friends, the media, and society in general.

During the preadolescent years, a child's parents are the most powerful influence on his or her beliefs and behavior. Even if parents never discuss sex with their children—and most do not—their behaviors and attitudes still serve as role models from which children learn.

As children approach their teenage years, their peer groups come to have as much, and often greater, influence on behaviors and attitudes as their parents. Parents must also contend with the influence of TV and other media. The average child watches several hours of TV every day and is exposed to over 2,000 references to sex in a year (Greenberg et al., 1986, 1987). Between the amount of time that their children spend with peers and watching TV, it is obvious that parents have a difficult time competing as a source of sexual knowledge and values. Unfortunately, the peer group is often misinformed, and TV and movies often display irresponsible sex (e.g., couples having sex without any mention of birth control).

Today, with the threat of AIDS, there has never been a better reason to teach our children responsibility about their health and their bodies. Yet, despite all the public debate about AIDS and other sexually related matters, most parents continue to remain silent (*Time/CNN* poll, 1993).

> "Sex was *never* a topic in my home when I was growing up. It led to embarrassment when I finally had to ask questions, but I could only ask my friends, never my parents. It shouldn't be like that, it shouldn't be embarrassing and I should have been able to talk to my parents."
>
> (from the author's fiiles)

Surveys show that the vast majority of Americans favor sex education in schools (e.g., 1991 Gallup survey; Janus & Janus, 1993). So why is there reluctance to teach it at home? Probably because most parents never received sex education themselves and are thus uncomfortable with their own sexual knowledge and feelings. Some parents will not discuss sex because they do not want to think about the possibility of their children being sexually active. I even know of some parents who have never talked to their children about sex because of fear that the children would then suspect that they have sexual relations, as if it were wrong for parents to do.

With the completion of this book, you should be ready to put an end to the cycle of noncommunication that has existed between parents and each new generation of children. I realize, however, that while you have learned the necessary information, you may still feel uncomfortable about discussing sex with someone else.

(Photo courtesy of Planned Parenthood of Hawaii.)

(courtesy of Planned Parenthood of Hawaii)

This part of the chapter is intended to help you initiate discussions of sexuality with your children, so that they too may acquire factual information. I will try to answer some of the questions that often concern parents.

WHY SHOULD I TALK TO MY CHILD ABOUT SEX?

Unless you are willing to keep your children locked up in a closet until they reach adulthood, *there is no avoiding their learning about sex.* As I have already said, even if they stay home all the time and do nothing but watch TV and listen to the radio, your children will still see and hear thousands of references to sex every year. Do you really want to leave it to the soap operas and "shock" disc jockeys to educate your children about this important subject? What kind of values do you suppose they will learn? Also, do not fool yourself. Children (and in all likelihood your own child as well) do talk about sex with their friends. Not only may your child's friend be misinformed, but do you want to leave it to your child's peer group to teach sexual values? Even formal sex education courses are generally value-free. By assuming the primary responsibility for your children's sex education, you can make certain that they are not only getting factual information, but at the same time you can stress the social and emotional aspects of sex and teach them values that you consider to be important. June Reinisch, former director of the Kinsey Institute, said, "If parents are comfortable and have good information, they can be wonderful sex educators. They can contextualize the sexual information into the fabric of family values, ethics, morals and religious beliefs. Sex is embedded in all of these" (quoted by Henderson, 1990).

DOES TELLING CHILDREN ABOUT SEX LEAD THEM TO DO IT?

Some of you may worry that if you educate your child about sex, she or he will try it and get pregnant or get someone else pregnant. Does drivers' education cause automobile accidents? Surveys show that the majority of people engage in premarital sex. The average age of first intercourse today is 16, and in some large metropolitan areas it is much younger (Centers for Disease Control and Prevention, 1991; Laumann et al., 1994). Most of these teens never had a formal sex education, at school or at home, so sex education can hardly be blamed. Studies have shown, you may recall, that children who have had sex education are no more likely to have sexual relations than those who have not, and they are much less likely to get pregnant (Zelnik & Kim, 1982). In fact, children whose parents take an active role in their sex education are the most likely to follow traditional moral values (Lewis, 1973). Do you need a better reason to talk to your child about sex?

WILL A SINGLE "BIRDS AND BEES" TALK SUFFICE?

Do you really believe that one talk will prepare your child for a lifetime of sexual relations and problems? The answer is no! Experts say that it is a mistake to think that talking about sex means sitting down for one long, serious conversation (see Roan, 1993). Even if you could fit all the necessary information and values into one talk, that one talk can hardly compete with the hundreds of hours of exposure to sexually related matters your child will receive while growing up. As Mark Twain said, education is a lifelong thing. Communication between parents and children about sex and anything else should also be lifelong.

WHEN SHOULD I START TALKING WITH MY CHILD ABOUT SEXUALITY?

When asked why she had not yet begun talking to her 13-year-old daughter about sex, a mother said, "I kept waiting for the right time. But I'm just too afraid to bring it up. I'm not sure what to say" (Roan, 1993).

As I hope you have learned by now, sex education is more than just explaining sexual intercourse. Children should be properly educated about their bodies, for example, and this means teaching them the correct anatomical terms for their genitals at the same time you teach them the names of the other parts of their bodies. "Penis" and "vagina" are not too difficult for young children to pronounce. American parents are notoriously silent about this. One study found that only 23 percent of 9-year-old North American children knew the physical sex differences of newborn baby boys and girls (Goldman & Goldman, 1982). This was a much lower percentage than found for children in some other countries where sex education is provided in school. The following comments were written by a student in my course:

> "I disagree strongly with teaching children about sexuality starting from preschool to third grade. Kids at this age don't even know the ABC's.... I just don't believe that kids under grade 4 should be told the terms 'penis' and 'vagina.' I do feel that kids under the age of 10 should be taught to know when a stranger is touching them wrong."
>
> (from the author's files)

Think about this for a moment. How will this woman tell her children about inappropriate touching without using the proper words? Will she use cutesy words (e.g., "pee-wee," "weenie") or make vague references (e.g., "Don't let anyone touch your bottom")? Either of these approaches may convey an attitude to the child that these parts of his or her body are naughty or dirty and eventually help lead to an attitude that the functions of these body parts are also dirty. Teaching boys that they have a penis and girls that they have a vagina is honest and helps them attain a healthy attitude about sexuality.

It is also very important to discuss with your children the physiological changes that start at puberty *before* they begin puberty. Some parents don't talk to their daughters about the menstrual cycle or to their sons about "wet dreams" until after they occur (see Chapter 10). This is very wrong. These changes can be frightening to children, who may think that they are sick or dying.

"There is one thing I would personally put more emphasis on (in the book). That is the importance of explaining menstruation in advance. From personal experience, I feel this is critical. I had no idea what was happening to me when I started menstruating for the first time. I can remember that I couldn't stop the bleeding and was scared to death and was afraid and embarrassed to tell anyone. I finally told a friend who was in the dark just as I was. She then told her mother. Her mother gave me a pad and said this would happen every month. That was the extent of communication on the subject."

(from the author's files)

It is also important to explain the changes associated with puberty in females to boys and the changes in males to girls. Men should be able to relate to women with empathy and understanding (and vice versa). Ignorance about the physiological (and emotional) changes being experienced by the opposite sex is not a good basis on which to build relationships.

Children, themselves, are often the best guides as to when to initiate talks about a particular topic. It is common, for example, for young children to ask where babies come from. If they are curious enough to ask questions about some sexually related matter, don't avoid discussing it. Never brush them off. If you do, they may avoid coming to you in the future and may rely instead on getting their information from somewhere else.

FIGURE 17-1   THE GOALS OF TEACHING ABOUT SEXUALITY ARE DIFFERENT FOR CHILDREN AT DIFFERENT AGES. AT ANY AGE, HOWEVER, BE TRUTHFUL. DON'T TELL YOUR YOUNG CHILD THAT THE BABY IS IN MOMMY'S "TUMMY." USE CORRECT TERMS WHILE EXPLAINING THE BODY.

Some guidelines for when to start talking about specific topics within human sexuality and family living are presented on p. 404. The guidelines are a condensed composite of those suggested by the Sex Information and Education Council of the U.S. (SIECUS National Guidelines Task Force, 1991) and Planned Parenthood (1991). These are only general guidelines for only a few of the many things your child may want to know about. Remember, if your child asks questions before the age level indicated here, don't wait to respond.

WHAT SHOULD I TELL MY CHILDREN ABOUT AIDS AND OTHER STDs?

The AIDS epidemic, more than anything else, has provided the impetus for bringing frank, explicit discussions about human sexuality to children, both at home and at school. Former U.S. Surgeon General C. Everett Koop, you recall, advocated teaching sex education, including information about AIDS, to children beginning in grade school. Most experts agree that this should begin no later than junior high school.

With all the attention devoted to AIDS by the media today, children are naturally going to be curious about it. The first question about sexuality that my son ever asked me was about AIDS. If you hear your child mention AIDS, be sure to take the opportunity to ask what he or she knows about it. Clear up any myths or misunderstandings. If your child should never mention AIDS, do not ignore the subject, for this is a very serious disease that everyone needs to be educated about. Initiate the discussion yourself. Remember, however, that you must teach your child about sexuality on a level that he or she can understand. Whatever their age, teach them respect for individual differences and acceptance of others.

Most parents fear that in order to explain about AIDS, they must explain behaviors like anal and oral sex. This is really not necessary for preschool and elementary school children. Most preadolescent children are not going to understand anal and oral sex. Young children can be taught to be in charge of their own bodies—sexual responsibility—without telling them what anal sex is.

What kind of questions is your child likely to ask? Valentich and Gripton (1989) have listed many questions about AIDS that are frequently asked by chil-

AGE (SCHOOL) LEVEL	CONCEPTS TO BE LEARNED
3–5 (preschool)	Correct names for body parts (e.g., ``penis,'' ``vagina''); differences between boys and girls; both boys' and girls' bodies are special and each of us can be proud of our special body; adults kiss and hug each other to show how much they care; respect for the privacy of others; their bodies belong to themselves and they have a right to say ``no'' if they don't want to be touched; how to respond if a stranger offers candy or a ride
6–9 (early elementary)	Continue to use a proper vocabulary when talking about body parts; continue to promote self-esteem (their bodies are special); people have body parts that feel good when touched; touching those body parts should be done in private; ``sex talk'' is done at home; the basics of reproduction and that our genitals and reproductive organs enable this; a fetus is inside the uterus and a baby usually comes out the vagina; milk comes from breasts; people can have babies only after puberty; meaning of heterosexual and homosexual; awareness of sexuality of people of all ages (parents and grandparents); understanding that there are different types of caring homes and families (e.g., single-parent families); promote nonstereotyped gender roles both inside and outside the home (both mothers and fathers have important jobs and there are no jobs just for boys or just for girls); good hygiene
9–13 (upper elementary)	Changes in *both* boys and girls during puberty (e.g., girls menstruate, boys ejaculate and have wet dreams) and that the changes occur at different ages in different people; the idea that human sexuality is natural and that sexual feelings are normal; sex is not just for reproduction, but is also pleasurable; masturbation (many people do it, it's not harmful, often a child's first experience with sexual pleasure); intercourse can cause pregnancy and having children is a long-term responsibility that should be planned (include basics on contraception); children are not ready for sexual intercourse; physical appearance does not determine a person's value—liking yourself; communication and assertiveness skills; people can disagree and have different values but still be friends; men and women have equal talents and strengths; recognition of the potential of sexual abuse (including that it is most often committed by someone the child knows) and how to react to it; continued encouragement of good hygiene; encouragement that it is okay to talk to parents about sexuality (*even if our opinions differ*)
13–15 (junior high school)	It is normal to have sexual feelings, desires, and fantasies; sex is pleasurable; the size of one's penis or breasts does not determine whether one will be a good sexual partner; people of all body shapes (including the disabled) have sexual feelings and desire; understanding the differences in sexual behavior (sexual orientation, abstinence, marriage); love is not the same as sexual attraction or desire; understanding the possible consequences of unprotected sexual intercourse (pregnancy); contraception; young teens are not yet ready for sexual intercourse; dating (why, when, how) and relationships (e.g., going steady); peer pressure and your right to say ``no'' and your right to disagree with your friends; respecting the limits that are set by your partners; awareness of exploitive relationships (psychological coercion, alcohol, physical force, date rape); physical health (e.g., breast and testicular self-exams); establishing a value system (and consideration of the above topics within that system)
15–18 (high school)	People of all ages are sexual beings; sexuality is only one part of your total personality; integration of sexuality into your value system; feeling good about your body, sexuality, and sexual orientation; how to express your sexual feelings in appropriate ways; communicating your sexual feelings, desires, and limits to partners in an open and honest manner; expressing your sexual feelings without intercourse; further understanding of sexual exploitation among adolescents; for those who engage in sexual intercourse, choosing a method of contraception that will be used consistently; knowledge of the responsibilities of parenthood and child care; understanding that long-term commitments (including marriage and parenthood) require work and that people's sexual and emotional needs change over time

dren. Early elementary school-aged children may want to know answers to questions like: What is AIDS? Can I get AIDS? Can I get it by playing with friends or by touching someone at school? Will it make me sick? Is there medicine I can take to make it go away?

Elementary school children aged 9–12 will want to know more about how AIDS is transmitted (e.g., whether they can get AIDS by holding hands, hugging, kissing, having sexual intercourse, or by being in the same classroom with someone who has AIDS) and how they can tell if someone has it. Children at this age can also be taught about STDs such as gonorrhea, chlamydia, syphilis, and herpes (and that they are caused by bacteria and viruses) (SIECUS, 1991). Teenagers will probably want answers to more explicit questions about transmission (e.g., whether they can get AIDS by French kissing, masturbation, genital touching, or sexual intercourse) and prevention (including the use and reliability of condoms). Be sure to include further discussion of other sexually transmitted diseases at this time as well.

You should prepare yourself for questions like these so that you can give your child factual information appropriate for his or her age. When answering their questions, you can also discuss values with your child (including means of transmission, prevention, and treatment).

No matter what their age, *you should not deny the pleasures of sex and resort to scare tactics.* Teaching children that sex is something good and pleasurable is as important as teaching that it must be used responsibly.

How Detailed Should the Discussions Be?

Your discussions should be frank and explicit. Children do not want "birds and bees" analogies—they want factual information using real terms. In fact, euphemisms and analogies will only confuse them. At the same time, do not make things so detailed they cannot understand at their age level. *Make your answer age-appropriate.* Always check to see if your child understands what you have said. You may have to give your answer again in a different way to make it clear. Sometimes we give great answers, but not to the question the child asked (or thought they asked). Remember, a child

FIGURE 17-2   WHEN A PET GIVES BIRTH, PARENTS HAVE A GREAT OPPORTUNITY TO TEACH ABOUT SEX.

may not know what to ask or how to ask it correctly. When a 6 year old asks where babies come from, for example, many parents worry that they must explain intercourse in detail. Your 6 year old is not really asking about that. Keep your answer uncomplicated and tell the child only what he or she wants to know. In this case, you could explain that the baby is in a special part of the mother called a uterus (do not avoid explicitness by saying "tummy"—this is incorrect anyway), and when it is ready to be born it comes out an opening called the vagina.

Remember that young children are curious about *everything*, and that sex is only one part of their world. Also, children don't think about sex the way adults do. Children have not had sexual intercourse (unless they were molested), have not had babies, and may not look at sex as a special topic of conversation. (In fact, chances are you are making a bigger deal about it than your child.) When the 6 year old son of one of my colleagues asked how babies were born, his father apprehensively explained about the uterus, the entry of the baby into the world through the vagina, etc. After giving detailed, accurate information, the father asked, "Do you have any more questions?" His son yawned and said, "Can we talk about something else now?"

What If I Feel Embarrassed?

Many of you will not be able to avoid embarrassment sometimes, but the result—your child's education—is worth the discomfort of using real terms and direct language. Be honest. Let them know that you are a bit embarrassed, but that you are glad they asked to talk with you, that you'll be happy to answer all of their questions, and that it's okay to talk to you about the subject. What you say to your children is important, but it's more important to let them know that you are willing to (and want to) listen to their questions.

How Should I Talk with My Child?

Most important, *discuss—never lecture*. Also, be sure not to grill your child about his or her behavior or attitudes. Allow your child to have his or her input. Your tone of voice is particularly important, for your child learns attitudes from your tone. Try to sound calm and relaxed at all times. Sol Gordon, author of *Raising Your Child Conservatively in a Sexually Permissive World* (1989), says, "The most important message is that nothing a child does will be made worse by talking to the parent about it. There is no way of dealing with sexuality unless the parent has created the atmosphere of love and caring. Unless that atmosphere is there, nothing works. The child will lie" (quoted by Roan, 1993).

Also, it is not necessary to always have formal talks; this may create tension. You can break the ice by briefly explaining and discussing sexually related matters that your child sees on TV (try watching "Beverly Hills, 90210" with your teenaged child), hears on radio, reads in "Dear Abby," etc.

Remember, *avoid scare tactics*. You must teach sexual responsibility without making your child afraid of sex—children should learn that sex is something good and positive and not something to feel ashamed or guilty about. Scare tactics probably will not work anyway, and they may cause emotional and psychological problems.

What about Morals? Aren't They Important Too?

Most formal sex education is value-free and that is why it is so important for parents to assume some responsibility for their child's education, even if their child is receiving sex education at school. Sex is more than a biological function. If you want your child to share your beliefs and values about sex, you must talk about them. However, when discussing moral values with your child, there are some important guidelines you should follow.

Most important, *you can emphasize your values, but don't preach*. It is not wrong for you to say how you feel, but if your child has developed some values that are different from yours, you must learn to discuss your differences rather than dictate. Remember, you want to create an atmosphere that allows your

child to be comfortable so that he or she will come to you when they have questions. If you always preach and pass judgment, your child may be reluctant to discuss sexuality with you at all, and then you will have no input.

One of the biggest dilemmas facing parents when discussing sexuality with their children is whether to emphasize global moralities or situational ethics. *Global moralities* are values that are supposed to apply to all people under all circumstances. An example is when parents tell their children that sexual relations should be reserved for marriage. As you recall, however, surveys show that well over half of all adolescents engage in premarital intercourse. Can you safely assume that your children will never have premarital sexual relations, and thus you can avoid the topic of birth control? Many parents are reluctant to talk about birth control with their children because they think that it promotes promiscuity. The consequences of not talking about it, however, can be devastating (e.g., unwanted pregnancies and/or sexually transmitted diseases).

Situational ethics emphasize the proper thing to do in particular situations (i.e., "We prefer that you don't do it, but if you're going to do it anyway, then . . ."). In this case, for example, it could be explained to an adolescent child how condoms substantially reduce the risk of both an unwanted pregnancy and sexually transmitted diseases. I cannot tell you which of these two approaches to use. Only you can make that choice.

Can My Behavior Affect My Child's Attitudes and Behavior?

You should also be aware that *your own behavior can play a role* in your child's sexuality and moral values. It is important that children learn that their parents share affection for each other. Hugging between parents and between parents and children teaches youngsters that the open display of affection is appropriate and appreciated.

"My husband and I have always tended to be very private about showing affection. I guess that's because our parents were that way. However, as a result of what I've learned in this class we've been hugging and kissing in front of our kids—who are both teenagers. They've noticed the changes and have even asked us about it, which has given us wonderful opportunities for open and frank discussions with them. Hopefully, it's not too late."

(from the author's files)

Parents who wait until they are alone to kiss or hug are teaching their children that there is something wrong about physical contact between the sexes. *Don't confuse affection with sex.*

At the same time, we live in a day when many parents are divorced and have boyfriends and girlfriends of their own. You must avoid appearing to be hypocritical. If you want your child to abstain from premarital sexual relations, for example, you must avoid premarital sexual relations or be very discreet yourself. What message do you suppose you are sending your child if you tell him or her it is wrong to engage in sex and they know that you are having premarital sexual relations?

Even if you never discuss sexuality with your children, your behavior will still serve as a role model. Unfortunately, many children acquire negative attitudes about sexuality by watching and listening to their parents. Many adults, for example, enjoy "dirty" jokes. What attitude do you suppose is conveyed when children overhear their parents laughing and snickering at jokes involving sex and/or body parts? Learning that there are "clean" and "dirty" jokes can lead to beliefs that sex is dirty, especially if other sources of information about sex are unavailable.

Children become interested in jokes by the time they reach kindergarten. Although they may not understand the meaning of jokes, they are eager to use them as a source of information. They also want to act older, and seeing older children use obscenities or tell and laugh at dirty jokes will lead to imitation. Laughing at the child's use of obscenity or joking about it will only reinforce the behavior, making it increase in frequency (remember, you are a role model). If your child uses an obscenity, don't go overboard. Calmly explain what the word means. Often the child will not know. Reacting calmly tells the child that they can discuss anything with you.

How do you feel about dirty jokes? What makes it dirty? Is sex dirty? When comedian Woody Allen, who has a bizarre sense of humor, was asked if sex was dirty, he responded, "Only if it's done right." Let's hope your children won't grow up believing this.

How Do I Know if I Have Succeeded?

You really can judge the success of your attempts to educate your children about sexuality only by their willingness to come to you when they have questions and problems.

> "I am a non-traditional student with three kids. I didn't know that I should start talking with them about sex at such a young age. My boys are 7 and 9 and my daughter is 5-years-old. They are very receptive to our talks. And now they always want to talk to me about anything. 'Open lines of communications.' Thanks."
>
> (from the author's files)

All normal adolescents will have an interest in sex and will continue to need information about their sexuality as long as they live. They will want to know about dating, courtship, marriage, living together, starting a family, and many different things at different times in their lives. They will seek information about these and other matters from a variety of sources, and you will want to be one of them. This will only happen, however, if communication between children and parents is open and continuous. ∎

HOPE FOR THE FUTURE

At the beginning of the book, I said that fewer than a third of the more than 1000 students per semester who have taken my course had ever had a serious discussion with their parents about sex. For those who had, in many cases it was just a single "birds and bees" talk explaining sexual intercourse. You have learned how this lack of knowledge has been costly to both individuals and society in terms of out-of-wedlock births, sexually transmitted diseases, and sexual abuse. Misinformation about sexual matters is often a contributing factor in sexual dysfunctions and relationship problems as well.

I hope that by enhancing people's knowledge, courses like this will result in greater sexual responsibility and fewer of the previously mentioned problems. I hope, too, that this book has helped you feel more comfortable with your sexuality so that you are not ashamed of your body or embarrassed by its functions. Most of all, I hope that when you have children you will be able to discuss sexual matters with them. I recently found that students who had completed my course were much more likely to discuss sexuality with their children than were former college students who had not taken a comprehensive human sexuality course (King, Parisi, & O'Dwyer, 1993).

Let us hope that in the years to come when I ask my students on the first day of class if they have had discussions with their parents about sex, most of them will say yes.

KEY TERMS

communication,   397
global moralities,   406

"I" language,   399
nonverbal communication,   400

sexual learning,   401
situational ethics,   406

PERSONAL REFLECTIONS

1. Suppose that you are in a long-term monogamous relationship that includes sexual relations. Suppose also that your partner often does not take as much time during foreplay as you would like and does not spend as much time holding and touching you afterwards, which often leaves you sexually unfulfilled and frustrated. How would you go about correcting this situation? Be as specific as possible.

2. Suppose that you are unsure of your partner's sexual desires and preferences, and you are unsure whether he or she is totally aware of yours. How might you communicate with one another? Suppose your desires and preferences are not exactly the same?

3. Some day you will probably be a parent (if you aren't already). Do you plan to educate your child about sexuality? If so, how? When will you begin?

4. How do you suppose you will react if:
   (a) your 5-year-old child asks you where babies come from,
   (b) your 9-year-old child asks you what sex is,
   (c) your 10-year-old child asks you what "French kissing" is,
   (d) your 12-year-old son comes home from school saying that he had to watch a gross movie about girls having their period,
   (e) your 15-year old son asks you about birth control, and
   (f) your 15-year-old daughter asks you about birth control?

5. Would your reactions to any of the situations in question 4 discourage your child from coming to you in the future and talking to you about sex?

SELECTED READINGS FOR COUPLES

A Couple's Guide to Communication by John Gottman. The most recommended book by members of the Society for the Scientific Study of Sex (Althrop & Kingsberg, 1992). Champaign, IL: Research Press, 1976.

For Each Other: Sharing Sexual Intimacy by Lonnie Barbach. New York: Anchor/Doubleday, 1982.

The Love Fitness Program for a Lasting Relationship by Harold Bloomfield and Sirah Vettese. This married couple suggests "sexual heart talks" to enhance sexual intimacy. New York: New American Library, 1989.

Messages: The Communication Book by Matthew McKay, Martha Davis, and Patrick Fanning. Oakland, CA: New Harbinger Publications.

The New Peoplemaking by Virginia Satir. Easy to read, it covers both communication and family relationships. Palo Alto, CA: Science and Behavior Books, 1988.

Self-Disclosure by Valerian Derlega and others. Newbury Park, CA: Sage Publications, 1993.

SELECTED SEX EDUCATION REFERENCES TO HELP PARENTS

How to Talk with Your Child about AIDS by Planned Parenthood, 1988. (16 pages)

How to Talk with Your Child about Sexuality: A Parent's Guide by Planned Parenthood: Faye Wattleton with Elizabeth Keiffer. New York: Doubleday & Co., 1986.

How to Teach Your Children about Sex by Dr. Grace Ketterman. Grand Rapids, MI: Revell, 1981.

Raising Your Child Conservatively in a Sexually Permissive World by Sol Gordon. New York: Fireside, 1989.

Talking with TV by The Center for Population Options (1025 Vermont Avenue, NW, Suite 210, Washington, DC 20005). An excellent guide for adults and kids on how to make TV a conversation starter on relationships, values, and sexuality. Updated yearly.

Talking with Your Child about Sex: Questions and Answers for Children from Birth to Puberty by Mary Calderone and James Ramey. New York: Random House, 1983.

What We Told Our Kids about Sex by Betsy and Michael Weisman. Gives answers to 102 questions asked by preadolescent children. New York: Harcourt, Brace Jovanovich, 1987.

SELECTED SEX EDUCATION REFERENCES FOR CHILDREN

(Selections are listed in age-appropriate order.)

Where Did I Come From? by P. Mayle, A. Robins, and P. Walter, is for young children. Secaucus, NJ: Lyle Stuart, 1973.

Where Did I Come From? by Peter Mayle is a 27-minute animated videocassette version of the book. New World.

Babies Come from People by George and Ann Carpenter is for preschoolers. Salt Lake City, Utah: Coldstream, 1975.

What's Happening To Me? by Peter Mayle is for children approaching puberty. Secaucus, NJ: Lyle Stuart, 1975.

Are You There God? It's Me, Margaret by Judy Blume is an educational story about a girl going through puberty. Englewood Cliffs, NJ: Bradbury Press, 1970.

Having Your Period by Planned Parenthood (16 pages).

Dr. Ruth Talks to Kids by Dr. Ruth Westheimer is aimed at children aged 8 through 14. *Time* magazine (May 24, 1993) says that Dr. Ruth's book provides an excellent middle ground between those sex educators who want to teach abstinence only and those who favor a more comprehensive approach.

What Every Teen-ager Ought to Know by Dear Abby. Send a check or money order for $2.50 and a long, stamped (50 cents), self-addressed envelope to: Dear Abby, Teen Booklet, P.O. Box 447, Mount Morris, IL 61054.

Teensex? It's OK to Say: No Way! by Planned Parenthood. (16 pages, also available on VHS video cassette.)

Talk About Sex by SIECUS. For teens, this 46-page booklet "offers clear, honest, straightforward information and instruction about relationships, communication skills, and safer sex behaviors in a very engaging, youth-friendly" manner. 1–4 copies/$2 each. SIECUS, 130 West 42nd Street, Suite 2500, New York, NY 10036.

GLOSSARY

A

abortion Termination of pregnancy. Depending on how far the pregnancy has advanced, this can be done by taking a pill (Ovral or RU486), scraping the uterine lining (dilation and curettage), removing the uterine lining by suction (dilation and evacuation), or inducing labor (by injecting hypertonic saline or prostaglandins). (Ch. 6)

acquaintance rape A rape committed by someone who is known by the victim. (Ch. 15)

actual use effectiveness rate For a particular birth control technique, the percentage of failures during one year of use by all couples using the technique, regardless of whether or not they used it properly or consistently. (Ch. 6)

adolescence (ad″ ʼl es′ ʼns) The time of life between puberty and adulthood. (Ch. 10)

adoption Taking a child into one's family by legal process and raising as one's own. (Ch. 6 and 7)

adrenal (ad- re′ nal) **glands** Endocrine glands located near the kidneys that secrete small amounts of gonadal hormones. (Ch. 3)

adrenogenital (ah-dre″ no-jen′ y-tal) **syndrome** A condition in females in which the adrenal glands excrete too much testosterone during fetal development, causing masculinization. This includes enlargement of the clitoris and labia, so that the genitals are sometimes mistaken for those of a male. (Ch. 8)

afterbirth The expulsion of the placenta from the uterus after a baby is born. (Ch. 7)

agape (ah′ gah pā″) A type of romantic love that puts the interest of the loved person ahead of one's own, even if it means great sacrifice. (Ch. 12)

aggressive pedophile A pedophile who is aroused by inflicting physical injury on victims. (Ch. 15)

AIDS (Acquired Immunodeficiency Syndrome) A fatal disease caused by a virus (HIV) that destroys the immune system. It is spread by intimate sexual activity (the exchange of bodily fluids) or contaminated blood. (Ch. 5)

AIDS related complex (ARC) *See* symptomatic HIV infection. (Ch. 5)

amenorrhea (ah-men″ o-re′ ah) The absence of menstruation. (Ch. 3)

amebiasis (am″ e-bi′ ah-sis) Dysentery caused by infestation of amoebae, a one-celled organism. (Ch. 5)

amniocentesis (am″ ne-o-sen-te′ sis) A technique for detecting fetal problems, involving collection of amniotic fluid after the fourteenth week of pregnancy. (Ch. 7)

amnion (am′ ne-on) A thick-skinned sac filled with water that surrounds the fetus. (Ch. 7)

ampulla (am-pul′ lah) The expanded end of the vas deferens where sperm are stored prior to ejaculation. (Ch. 2)

anabolic (an″ ah-bol′ ik) **steroids** Synthetic steroid hormones that combine the growth (anabolic) effects of adrenal steroids with the masculinizing effects of androgenic steroids. (Ch. 3)

anal intercourse Insertion of the penis into the anus and rectum of a sexual partner. (Ch. 11)

anaphrodisiac (an″ af-ro-dĭz′ e-ak) Substances that suppress sexual functioning. (Ch. 4)

androgen insensitivity syndrome A condition in which the testes secrete normal amounts of testosterone during male embryologic development, but the tissues do not respond to it. As a result, a clitoris, labia, and a short vagina develop, but the internal female structures do not develop because the testes still secrete Mullerian duct inhibitory substances. (Ch. 8)

androgens (an′ dro-jens) Hormones that possess masculinizing activities. (Ch. 2)

androgyny (an-droj′ ĭ-ne) The ability of an individual to display a variety of personality characteristics, both masculine and feminine, depending on whether a trait or behavior is appropriate for a given situation. It is often viewed as a positive characteristic that gives an individual greater adaptability. (Ch. 8)

anger rapists Rapists who commit their attacks out of hostility or anger directed at their victim or at women in general. (Ch. 15)

anoxia (ah-nok′ se-ah) An inability to get enough oxygen to the brain. (Ch. 7)

aphrodisiac (af″ ro-dĭz′ e-ak) Substance that enhances sexual desire or performance. (Ch. 4)

areola (ah-re′ o-lah) The darkened ring surrounding the nipple of a breast. (Ch. 2)

artificial insemination A method of treating infertility caused by a low sperm count in males. Sperm are collected during several ejaculations and then inserted into the partner's vagina at the time of ovulation. (Ch. 7)

ascetic (ah set′ ik) **philosophy** A philosophy that originated among the ancient Greeks. It emphasized that from wisdom came virtue and that these could only be achieved by avoiding strong passions. (Ch. 1)

asymptomatic Showing no symptoms. (Ch. 5)

attachment A drab, mundane form of companionship where one's partner gives few positive rewards, other than predictability, for remaining in the relationship. (Ch. 12)

attachment theory of love   The theory that the quality of the attachment between parents and child greatly affects the child's ability to form romantic relations as an adult. (Ch. 12)

autoerotic asphyxiation   Depriving oneself of oxygen during masturbation-induced orgasm. (Ch. 11)

autoinoculation   Infecting oneself. (Ch. 5)

B

bacteria   Small, single-celled organisms that lack a nuclear membrane, but have all the genetic material (RNA and DNA) to reproduce themselves. (Ch. 5)

bacterial vaginosis (vaj″ ĭ-no′ sis)   A type of vaginitis caused by the interaction of several vaginal bacteria (most particularly, *Gardnerella vaginalis*). (Ch. 5)

Bartholin's (bar′ to-linz) **glands**   Glands located at the base of the labia minora in females that contribute a small amount of an alkaline fluid to their inner surfaces during sexual arousal. (Ch. 2)

basal body temperature   The temperature of the body while resting. It rises slightly after ovulation. (Ch. 6)

baseline mammogram   Low-radiation X-ray used to detect breast tumors. (Ch. 2)

benign coital cephalalgia (sef″ ah-lal′ je-ah)   Severe headaches that start during or slightly after orgasm in males. (Ch. 13)

berdache (bar dash′)   In North American Indian tribes of past centuries, a person, usually a male, who assumed the dress, occupations, and behavior of the other sex in order to effect a change in gender status. The term two-spirit is now preferred over berdache. (Ch. 14)

bestiality (bes-te-al′ĭ-te)   The act of having sexual contact with an animal. (Ch. 14)

beta-endorphins   Natural pain killers produced by the body. (Ch. 7)

B-girls   Prostitutes who work in bars and hotels, generally with the approval of the ownership. (Ch. 16)

Billings method   A fertility awareness method of birth control in which changes in the consistency and quantity of cervical mucus are used to tell when ovulation has occurred. (Ch. 6)

biological essentialism   The belief that biological influences establish predetermined limits to the effects of cultural influences. (Ch. 8)

bisexual   An individual with a sexual orientation to members of both genders. (Ch. 9)

blastocyst (blas′ to-sist)   The fluid-filled sphere that reaches the uterus after fertilization and which was created by the transformation of the morula through continued, rapid cell division. (Ch. 7)

blockade or **barrier method**   General term for contraceptive methods that block the passage of sperm. (Ch. 6)

Braxton-Hicks contractions   Uterine contractions experienced during the last trimester of pregnancy that are often incorrectly interpreted as the beginning of labor (false labor). (Ch. 7)

breast-feeding   In reference to contraception, the sucking response by a baby on the mother's nipple inhibits release of follicle stimulating hormone, thus preventing ovulation. (Ch. 6)

breasts (brests)   In females, located on the front of the chest, providing milk for infants. (Ch. 2)

breech birth   A birth in which the baby is born feet or buttocks first. (Ch. 7)

brothel prostitutes   Prostitutes who work in houses of prostitution. (Ch. 16)

bulb   The expanded inner end of the spongy body of the penis. (Ch. 2)

bulbocavernosus (bul″ bo-kav″ er-no′sus) **muscle**   A ring of sphincter muscles that surround the vaginal opening in females or the root of the penis in males. (Ch. 2)

bulbourethral (bul″ bo-u-re′ thral) **glands**   *See* Cowper's glands. (Ch. 2)

C

calendar method   A fertility awareness method of birth control that attempts to determine a woman's fertile period by use of a mathematical formula. (Ch. 6)

call girls   The highest status prostitutes, who generally work out of their own apartments by appointment only. (Ch. 16)

candidiasis (kan″ dĭ-di′ ah-sis)   *See* moniliasis. (Ch. 5)

capacitation   A process that sperm undergo, while traveling through the female's reproductive tract, in which their membranes become thin enough so that an enzyme necessary for softening the ovum's membrane can be released. (Ch. 7)

carnal knowledge of a juvenile   *See* statutory rape.

celocentesis (se″ lo-sen-te′ sis)   A technique used for detecting fetal abnormalities in which a needle is inserted between the placenta and the amniotic sac to retrieve cells. (Ch. 7)

cephalalgia   *See* benign sexual cephalalgia. (Ch. 13)

cervical cap   A contraceptive device that fits over the cervix by suction and thus blocks the passage of sperm into the uterus. (Ch. 6)

cervical mucus   The slimy secretion of mucous membranes located inside the cervix. (Ch. 6)

cervicitis (ser″ vĭ-si′ tis)   Inflammation of the cervix. (Ch. 5)

cervix (ser′ viks)   The lower, narrow end of the uterus that projects into the vagina. (Ch. 2)

cesarean (se-sa′ re-an) **section** or **C-section**   The surgical removal of a fetus through the mother's abdomen. (Ch. 7)

chancre (shang′ ker) The painless sore that is the main symptom of the primary stage of syphilis. (Ch. 5)

chancroid (shang′ kroid) A sexually transmitted disease caused by the *Hemophilus ducreyi* bacterium, that is characterized by small, painful bumps. (Ch. 5)

child molestation Sexual contact between an adult and a child. (Ch. 15)

chlamydia (klah-mid′ e-ah) A sexually transmitted disease caused by the *Chlamydia trachomatis* bacterium, which lives on mucous membranes. (Ch. 5)

chorion (ko′ re-on) The fourth membrane of the trophoblast; it develops into the lining of the placenta.

chorionic sampling A technique used for detecting problems in a fetus during the eighth to tenth weeks of pregnancy. Hairlike projections (villi) of the chorion are collected and examined. (Ch. 7)

chromosomes (kro′ mo-somz) Rod-shaped structures containing the genetic material that determines a person's inherited characteristics. (Ch. 8)

circumcision (ser″ kum-sizh′ un) In males, the removal of all or part of the foreskin of the penis. In females, the removal of the clitoral hood. (Ch. 2)

climacteric (kli-măk′ ter-ik) The changes that occur in women in the few years that precede and follow menopause. (Ch. 10)

clitoral hood The part of the labia minora that covers the clitoris in females. (Ch. 2)

clitoridectomy (klĭ″ to-rĭ-dek′ to-me) Removal of the clitoris, often accompanied by removal of the labia minora. In an extreme form, called **infibulation**, the labia majora are also removed and the sides of the vulva are then sewn together. (Ch. 4)

clitoris (klĭ′ to-ris) A small, elongated, erectile structure in females that develops from the same embryonic tissue as the penis. It has no known reproductive function other than to focus sexual sensations. (Ch. 2)

coach In the Lamaze birthing technique, an individual (usually the woman's partner) who works with the expectant mother during labor to help her use her training and provide support and encouragement. (Ch. 7)

cognitive-behavioral therapy Therapy that views problems as resulting from faulty learning and which focuses on specific behavioral problems. (Ch. 13)

cohabitation Living together in an unmarried relationship. (Ch. 10)

coitus (ko′ ĭ-tus) Sexual intercourse. (Ch. 11)

coitus interruptus *See* withdrawal. (Ch. 6)

colostrum (ko-los′ trum) A thick, sticky liquid produced by a mother's breasts before milk starts to flow. (Ch. 7)

colpotomy (kol-pot′ o-me) A female sterilization technique in which the Fallopian tubes are approached through a small incision in the back of the vagina and then are cut or cauterized. (Ch. 6)

combination pill An oral contraceptive that contains both synthetic estrogen and progesterone. (Ch. 6)

coming out (of the closet) Disclosing to others one's homosexual orientation. (Ch. 9)

communication The exchange of information, thoughts, ideas, or feelings. (Ch. 17)

companionate love Love based on togetherness, trust, sharing, and affection rather than passion. (Ch. 12)

Comstock law A law passed in 1873 that made it a felony to mail any material regarded to be obscene or lewd. (Ch. 16)

conception The union of an egg and a sperm. (Ch. 7)

conditional love Feelings of love that depend on the loved one satisfying needs and fulfilling desires. (Ch. 12)

condom For males, a thin sheath made of latex rubber, lamb intestine, or polyurethane that fits over the penis. For females, a polyurethane intravaginal pouch held in place by two flexible rings. Condoms are effective as contraception and for prevention of sexually transmitted diseases. (Ch. 6)

consummate love According to Sternberg, the complete love found in relationships that include passion, intimacy, and commitment. (Ch. 12)

contraception The prevention of conception. (Ch. 6)

contraceptive sponge A contraceptive device made of polyurethane sponge that contains enough spermicide to be effective for 24 hours after being inserted into the vagina. (Ch. 6)

coprophilia (kop″ ro-fil′ e-ah) Sexual arousal caused by feces or the act of defecation. (Ch. 14)

copulation (kop″ u-la′ shun) Sexual intercourse. (Ch. 11)

corona (ko-ro′ nah) The rounded border of the glans of the penis. (Ch. 2)

corpora cavernosa (kor′ po-rah kav″ er-no′ sah) The two cavernous bodies of the penis or clitoris that fill with blood during sexual arousal. (Ch. 2)

corpus luteum (kor′ pus lew′ te-um) The follicular cells that remain in the ovary after the follicle expels the ovum during ovulation. They begin to secrete progesterone in large quantities in the postovulatory stage. (Ch. 3)

corpus spongiosum (kor′ pus spun″ je-o′ sum) The spongy body of the penis that fills with blood during sexual arousal and through which the urethra travels. (Ch. 2)

couvade (koo-vahd′) **syndrome** The experiencing of symptoms of pregnancy by male partners, sometimes called "sympathy pains." (Ch. 7)

Cowper's (kow' perz) **glands**   Two pea-shaped structures located beneath the prostate gland in males that secrete a few drops of an alkaline fluid prior to orgasm. (Ch. 2)

critical period   In relation to teratogens, the time during embryological or fetal development during which a particular part of the body is most susceptible to damage. (Ch. 7)

crowning   The appearance of the fetus's head at the vaginal opening during childbirth. (Ch. 7)

crura (kroo' rah)   The leglike ends of the cavernous bodies that attach to the pubic bone. (Ch. 2)

cryptorchidism (krip-tor' kĭ-dizm)   A defect in which the testes fail to descend into the scrotum. (Ch. 2)

cunnilingus (kun" ĭ-ling'gus)   Oral stimulation of a female's genitals. (Ch. 10)

cystitis (sis-ti' tis)   A bacterial infection of the bladder (often caused by the bacterium *Escherichia coli*). (Ch. 2 and 5)

D

date rape   A type of acquaintance rape, committed during a social encounter agreed to by the victim. (Ch. 15)

decision/commitment   One of the three basic components in Sternberg's theory of love; the decision that one loves another person and the commitment to maintain it. (Ch. 12)

degrading sexually explicit material   Nonviolent sexually explicit material that shows women as sex objects and where there is a clear unequal balance of power. (Ch. 12)

depo-provera   Market name for methylprogesterone, a chemical that when injected suppresses ovulation for 3 months. (Ch. 6)

desensitization   A therapy technique used to reduce anxiety by slowly introducing elements of the anxiety-producing theme. (Ch. 13 and 14)

desire   ". . . is experienced as specific sensations which move the individual to seek out, or become receptive to, sexual experiences" (Kaplan, 1979). Kaplan and others have suggested that desire precedes excitement as the first stage of the sexual response cycle. (Ch. 4)

detumescence (de" tu-mes' ens)   Loss of erection. (Ch. 4)

DHT deficiency   A type of androgen insensitivity syndrome in which, because testosterone is not converted into dihydrotestosterone, boys' external genitals do not develop properly. Development occurs at puberty with the rise in testosterone.

diaphragm   A dome-shaped rubber cup with a flexible rim that fits over the cervix and thus acts as a contraceptive device by acting as a barrier to the passage of sperm into the uterus. (Ch. 6)

dilate   To make wider or larger. (Ch. 7)

domination   Ruling over and controlling another individual. In sexual relations, it generally involves humiliation of the partner as well. (Ch. 14)

douching (doosh-ing)   A feminine hygiene practice of washing the vagina, usually with specifically prepared solutions. (Ch. 6)

dualism   The belief that body and soul are separate and antagonistic. (Ch. 1)

dyke   A slang term for a masculine lesbian. This is a stereotype that generally does not reflect how most lesbians look or behave. (Ch. 9)

dysmenorrhea (dĭs" men-o-re' ah)   Painful menstruation. (Ch. 3)

dyspareunia (dĭs' pah-roo' ne-ah)   Painful intercourse, usually resulting from organic factors (e.g., vaginal, prostate, or bladder infections). (Ch. 13)

E

eclampsia (e-klamp' se-ah)   An advanced case of toxemia of pregnancy, characterized by convulsions and coma. (Ch. 7)

ectoderm   A layer of the embryo that forms the nervous system, skin, and teeth. (Ch. 7)

ectopic (ek-top' ik) **pregnancy**   The implantation of a fertilized egg outside of the endometrium of the uterus. (Ch. 7)

edema   Swelling.

effacement   The thinning of the cervix during labor. (Ch. 7)

effleurage (ef-loo-rahzh')   In the Lamaze birthing technique, a light self-massage of the abdomen that is used to counter the discomfort of labor contractions. (Ch. 7)

egocentric   A term used by Jean Piaget in his theory of cognitive development. It refers to the idea that young children cannot consider other people's points of view. (Ch. 10)

ejaculation   The expulsion of semen from the body. (Ch. 4)

ejaculatory duct   One-inch-long paired tubes that pass through the prostate gland. The third part of the duct system that transports sperm out of a male's body. (Ch. 2)

ejaculatory incompetence   A condition in which a man is totally unable to ejaculate in a woman's vagina during sexual intercourse. (Ch. 13)

embryo (em' bre-o)   The term given to the blastocyst after it has implanted. (Ch. 7)

emission   The first stage of an orgasm in males. Rhythmic muscular contractions in the vas deferens, prostate gland, and seminal vesicles force the sperm and prostate and seminal fluids into the ejaculatory ducts, thus forming semen. (Ch. 4)

empty love According to Sternberg, the emotion felt when there is decision and commitment to love another person, but no intimacy or passion. (Ch. 12)

endocrine system A network of ductless glands that secrete their chemical substances, called hormones, directly into the bloodstream, where they are carried to other parts of the body to exert their effect. (Ch. 3)

endoderm A layer of the embryo that forms the internal organs of the fetus. (Ch. 7)

endometriosis (en″ do-me″ tre-o′ sis) The growth of endometrial tissue outside of the uterus. (Ch. 3)

endometrium (en-do-me′ tre-um) The inner, mucous membrane of the uterus where a fertilized egg implants. Its thickness varies with the phase of the menstrual cycle. (Ch. 2 and 3)

epididymis (ep″ ĭ-did′ ĭ-mis) The elongated cordlike structure on the back of a testicle. It is the first part of the duct system that transports sperm out of a male's body. (Ch. 2)

episiotomy (e-piz″ e-ot′ o-me) A surgical procedure performed just before birth to reduce the risk of tearing the perineum. (Ch. 2 and 7)

erectile disorder A sexual problem in which a male has difficulty or an inability to get and maintain an erection. (Ch. 13)

erection (of the penis) The state of the penis during sexual arousal (i.e., hard and elongated) due to vasocongestion of tissues. (Ch. 4)

erogenous zone According to psychoanalytic theory, the part of the body where sexual energy is focused. (Ch. 8)

eros A highly idealized type of romantic love that is based mainly on physical beauty. Erotic lovers look for physical perfection. (Ch. 12)

erotica Any literature or art that has a sexual theme. This is a morally neutral term. (Ch. 16)

estrogen (es′ tro-jen) A hormone that is produced by the ovaries (and in very small amounts by the testes and adrenal glands). (Ch. 3)

estrous cycle The cycle of hormonal events that occurs in most nonhuman mammals. The females are sexually receptive ("in heat" or estrus) to males only during ovulation. (Ch. 3)

excitement The first stage of the sexual response cycle as proposed by Masters and Johnson. The first signs are erection in the male and vaginal lubrication in the female. (Ch. 4)

exhibitionism Exposing one's genitals compulsively in inappropriate settings to obtain sexual gratification. (Ch. 14)

expulsion The second stage of an orgasm in males. Contractions in the urethra and muscles at the base of the penis force the semen from the penis (ejaculation). (Ch. 4)

F

Fallopian (fal-lo′ pe-an) **tubes** The passageway that the egg follows on the way to the uterus. (Ch. 2)

false labor A set of temporary contractions of the uterus that resemble the start of labor. (Ch. 7)

fatuous love According to Sternberg, the emotion felt when a commitment is made on the basis of passion without the experience of intimacy. (Ch. 12)

fear-tension-pain cycle According to prepared childbirth advocates, the cycle of events that women experience during labor when they are not properly educated about labor and childbirth. (Ch. 7)

fellatio (fe-la′ she-o) Oral stimulation of a male's genitals. (Ch. 11)

female orgasmic disorder A persistent or recurrent delay in, or absence of, orgasm following a normal sexual excitement phase. (Ch. 13)

fertility awareness methods Methods of birth control that attempt to prevent conception by abstinence from sexual intercourse during ovulation. (Ch. 6)

fertility drugs Drugs that enhance the chance of conception in women who are infertile due to hormone deficiencies. The drugs either stimulate the pituitary gland to secrete FSH and LH or stimulate the ovaries directly. (Ch. 7)

fertilization Impregnation; the fusion of a sperm with an ovum. (Ch. 7)

fetal alcohol syndrome A condition common to infants born to alcoholic mothers involving physical and nervous system abnormalities. (Ch. 7)

fetal monitor A device attached to the expectant mother's abdomen during labor to monitor the heart rate of the fetus and the contractions of the uterus. (Ch. 7)

fetal surgery A surgical operation on the fetus while it is still in the uterus. (Ch. 7)

fetishism (fet′ ish-ĭ-zum) A condition in which sexual arousal occurs primarily when using or thinking about an inanimate object or a particular part of the body (such as the feet). (Ch. 14)

fetoscopy A procedure in which a tube containing fiberoptic strands is inserted into the amniotic sac in order to inspect the fetus. (Ch. 7)

fetus The term given to the embryo after the eighth week of pregnancy. (Ch. 7)

fibrocystic (fi″ bro-sis′ tik) **disease** Benign overgrowth of fibrous tissue in the breast. (Ch. 2)

fimbria (fim′ bre-ah) The fingerlike processes at the ovarian end of the Fallopian tubes. (Ch. 2)

focal point   In the Lamaze birthing technique, a point outside of the woman's body on which she focuses her concentration during labor contractions. (Ch. 7)

follicle (fol' lǐ-k'l)   Found in the ovary, a sac containing an ovum and surrounding follicular cells. (Ch. 2 and 3)

follicle stimulating hormone (FSH)   A gonadotropin hormone released by the pituitary gland that stimulates the development of a follicle in the ovary and the production of sperm in the testicles. (Ch. 3)

follicular phase   The preovulatory, or proliferative, phase of the menstrual cycle, lasting from about day 5 to day 13 in a 28-day cycle. (Ch. 3)

fornication (for' nǐ ka' shun)   Sexual intercourse between a man and a woman who are not married to one another. (Ch. 16)

foreskin   The loose skin of the penis that folds over the glans and which is sometimes cut away in a procedure known as circumcision. (Ch. 2)

friendship   A relationship that includes (a) enjoyment of each other's company, (b) acceptance of one another, (c) mutual trust, (d) respect for one another, (e) mutual assistance when needed, (f) confiding in one another, (g) understanding, and (h) spontaneity. (Ch. 12)

frigidity   The common term used by males for females who have orgasm problems, but which is generally not used by therapists because it has negative connotations about emotional responsivity. (Ch. 13)

frotteurism (fro-tur' izm)   A condition in which sexual arousal is achieved primarily by rubbing one's genitals against others in public places. (Ch. 14)

fundus (fun' dus)   The broad end of the uterus. (Ch. 2)

G

galactorrhea (gah-lak" to-re' ah)   The spontaneous flow of milk. (Ch. 2)

gamete intrafallopian transfer (GIFT)   A procedure for treating female infertility in which sperm and eggs are gathered and placed directly into a Fallopian tube. (Ch. 7)

gang rape   Rape in which a victim is assaulted by more than one attacker. (Ch. 15)

gay   A term generally used to refer to male homosexuals, although in some places it is used to refer to homosexuals of either gender. (Ch. 9)

gender constancy   The knowledge that one's gender identity is constant and will not change. This is usually acquired by age 6 or 7. (Ch. 8)

gender dysphoria (dis-fo' re-ah)   The feeling of being trapped in a body of the opposite gender. (Ch. 8)

gender identity   One's subjective sense of being a male or a female. This knowledge is usually acquired by the age of 3. (Ch. 8)

gender role   Behaviors that one's society considers to be appropriate for males or females. (Ch. 8)

gender schemas (ske' mahs)   Ideas about gender roles that children create from their interactions with their environment. (Ch. 8)

genital herpes   Herpes infection in the genital region. It can be caused by herpes simplex virus types I or II. (Ch. 5)

genital warts (*condyloma-acuminata*)   Warts in the genital (and anal) region caused by human papillomaviruses (mainly types 6 and 11). The warts look like cauliflower-like growths. (Ch. 5)

genitalia (jen" ǐ-ta' leah)   The reproductive organs of the male or female. (Ch. 2)

gigolos (jig-ah-los)   Male prostitutes who cater to females. (Ch. 16)

glans (glanz)   The rounded end of the penis or clitoris. (Ch. 2)

global moralities   Values that are supposed to apply to all people under all circumstances. (Ch. 17)

gonadotropin (gon" ah-do-tro' pin)   A hormone that has a stimulating effect on the ovaries or testicles. (Ch. 3)

gonococcus (gon" o-kok' us)   Common name for the bacterium that causes gonorrhea. (Ch. 5)

gonorrhea (gon" o-re' ah)   A sexually transmitted disease caused by the *Neisseria gonorrhoeae* bacterium (often referred to as the gonococcus), which lives on mucous membranes. (Ch. 5)

Graafian (graf' e-an) **follicle**   A mature follicle. (Ch. 7)

Grafenberg (graf' en-burg) **spot**   A small, sensitive area on the front wall of the vagina found in about 10 percent of women. (Ch. 2 and 4)

granuloma inguinale (gran" u-lo' mah ing' gwǐ-nah le)   A rare (in the United States) sexually transmitted disease that is characterized by ulceration of tissue. (Ch. 5)

growing apart   Having fewer common interests over time. (Ch. 12)

growing together   Maintaining common interests (although not necessarily the same ones) over time. (Ch. 12)

G-spot   *See* Grafenberg spot.

gumma (gum' ah)   A soft, gummy tumor that occurs in late (tertiary) syphilis. (Ch. 5)

gynecomastia (jin" ě-ko-mas' te-ah)   Excessive development of the male mammary glands. (Ch. 2 and 10)

H

habituation   Responding less positively to a stimulus with repeated exposure. (Ch. 12)

hand-riding   A technique used to teach people how to touch, in which the receiver places his or her hand over the giver's hand and guides it over the receiver's body. This is often included as part of sensate focus exercises. (Ch. 13)

HCG   *See* human chorionic gonadotropin.

hepatitis (hep″ah-ti′ tis)   **A, B,** and **C** Liver infections caused by a virus. Type A is spread by direct or indirect contact with contaminated feces. Type B is transmitted by infected blood or body fluids, with 25 to 50 percent of the cases contracted during sex. Type C is spread mainly by contaminated blood, but is possibly spread during sexual intercourse in some cases. (Ch. 5)

hermaphrodite (her-maf′ ro-dīt″)   A person with both male and female reproductive systems as a result of the primitive gonads failing to differentiate properly during embryological development. (Ch. 8)

herpes (her′ pez)   Painful blisters usually found on the mouth (fever blisters; cold sores) or genitals that are caused by a virus (herpes simplex virus types I or II). Genital herpes is almost always contracted by intimate sexual activity, but oral herpes may be spread by casual kissing. (Ch. 5)

heterosexual   An individual with a sexual orientation primarily to members of the opposite gender. (Ch. 9)

HIV   *See* human immunodeficiency virus.

homophobia   An irrational fear of homosexual individuals and homosexuality. (Ch. 9)

homosexual   An individual with a sexual orientation primarily to members of the same gender. (Ch. 9)

hormones   Chemical substances that are secreted by ductless glands into the bloodstream. They are carried in the blood to other parts of the body where they exert their effects on other glands or target organs. (Ch. 3)

hot flashes   A warm feeling over the upper body experienced by postmenopausal women as a result of increased levels of FSH and LH. (Ch. 10)

HPV   *See* human papillomaviruses.

human chorionic (ko″re-on′ik) **gonadotropin (HCG)**   A hormone secreted by the chorion that stimulates the ovaries during pregnancy. (Ch. 3 and 7)

human immunodeficiency virus (HIV)   A virus that kills CD4 cells, eventually resulting in AIDS. (Ch. 5)

human papillomaviruses (HPV) (pap″ĭ-lo′ mah)   Viruses that cause abnormal growths in epithelial cells. There are over 70 types. A few (types 6 and 11) cause genital warts, while others (types 16, 18, 31, 33, and 45) can lead to cancer of the cervix. (Ch. 5)

hustler   A male prostitute who caters to males. (Ch. 16)

hyaluronidase (hi″ah-lu-ron′ĭ-das)   An enzyme secreted by a sperm that allows the sperm to penetrate the surface of an ovum. (Ch. 7)

hymen (hi′ men)   The thin membrane that partially covers the vaginal opening in many sexually inexperienced women. Its presence or absence, however, is really a very poor indicator of prior sexual experience. (Ch. 2)

hypersexuality   A term reserved for people who engage in sex compulsively, with little or no emotional satisfaction. Sometimes called sexual addiction. (Ch. 13)

hypoactive sexual desire   A sexual problem characterized by a persisting and pervasive inhibition of sexual desire. (Ch. 13)

hysterectomy (his″ tĕ-rek′ to-me)   Surgical removal of the uterus. (Ch. 2)

I

ICSH   *See* interstitial cell-stimulating hormone.

identification   The adoption of the sex roles of the same-sexed parent by a child. In Freudian theory, identification resolves the Oedipus complex. (Ch. 8)

"I" language   Communicating your desires to another person by beginning sentences with "I," followed by your feelings, desires, or thoughts. (Ch. 17)

imitation   Following the behaviors of someone taken on as one's model. (Ch. 8)

immune system   Refers to bodily mechanisms involved in the production of antibodies in response to bacteria, viruses, and cancerous cells. (Ch. 5)

implantation   The process by which the blastocyst attaches itself to the wall of the uterus. (Ch. 7)

impotence   A common term for erectile disorders in males, but generally not used by therapists because it has negative connotations about a male's manhood. (Ch. 13)

incest   Sexual contact between two closely related persons. (Ch. 15)

incontinence   A term used to refer to the inability to control one's bladder. (Ch. 4)

individualist theory   The theory that personality traits develop early in life and do not change much over the life cycle; these traits then determine an individual's expression of masculine or feminine behavior. (Ch. 8)

infatuated love   According to Sternberg, the emotion felt when there is passion in the absence of intimacy and commitment. (Ch. 12)

infertility   The inability of a couple to conceive. (Ch. 7)

infibulation   *See* clitoridectomy. (Ch. 2)

inhibited ejaculation   *See* male orgasmic disorder. (Ch. 13)

inhibited female orgasm   *See* female orgasmic disorder. (Ch. 13)

interstitial cell-stimulating hormone (ICSH)   A hormone produced in the anterior pituitary gland that stimulates the testicles to produce male hormones. In females the same hormone triggers ovulation and is called luteinizing hormone. (Ch. 3)

intimacy   Those feelings in a relationship that promote closeness or bondedness and the experience of warmth. (Ch. 12)

intrauterine device (IUD)   A birth control device, usually made of plastic with either a copper or progesterone coating, that is placed in the uterus to prevent conception and implantation. (Ch. 6)

introitus (in-tro′ ĭ-tus)   The entrance to the vagina. (Ch. 2)

in vitro fertilization   A process in which a mature ovum is surgically removed from a woman's ovary, placed in a medium with sperm until fertilization occurs, and then placed in the woman's uterus. This is usually done in women who cannot conceive because of blocked Fallopian tubes. (Ch. 7)

IUD   *See* intrauterine device.

J

jealousy   An emotional state that is aroused by a perceived threat to a valued relationship or position. (Ch. 12)

john   A street term for a male who pays for sex with a prostitute; also called tricks or scores. (Ch. 16)

K

Kaposi's sarcoma (kap′-o-sez sar-ko′mah)   A cancer of the capillary system that often occurs in people with AIDS. (Ch. 5)

Kegel exercises   Exercises that are designed to strengthen the pubococcygeus muscle that surrounds the bladder and vagina. (Ch. 2 and 13)

Klinefelter's Syndrome   A condition in males in which there is one or more extra X chromosomes. (Ch. 8)

klismaphilia (kliz″ mah-fil′ e-ah)   A condition in which sexual arousal is achieved primarily by being given an enema. (Ch. 14)

L

labia majora (la′ be-ah majo′ rah)   Two outer elongations extending from the mons to the perineum in females. Its outer surfaces become covered with pubic hair during puberty. (Ch. 2)

labia minora (la′be-ah mino′rah)   Two hairless elongations located between the labia majora in females. They meet at the top of the vulva to form the clitoral hood. (Ch. 2)

Lamaze   A method of prepared childbirth; named after its founder, Fernand Lamaze. (Ch. 7)

lanugo (lah-nu′ go)   Light hair that covers a newborn baby. (Ch. 7)

laparoscopy (lap″ ah-ros′ko-pe)   A technique that involves inserting a slender, tubelike instrument (laparoscope) into a woman's abdomen to examine (via fiberoptics) her reproductive organs or a fetus. The procedure is often used to perform female sterilizations. (Ch. 6 and 7)

lesbian (lez′ be-an)   A female homosexual. (Ch. 9)

Leydigs (li′ digz), **interstitial cells of**   The cells in the testes that produce male hormones. (Ch. 2)

libido (lĭ-be′ do)   In psychoanalytic theory, the sexual energy of an individual. (Ch. 8)

lightening   Rotation of the fetus prior to childbirth so that its head is downward, resulting in decreased pressure on the mother's abdomen. (Ch. 7)

liking   According to Sternberg, the emotion felt when there is intimacy without passion or commitment. (Ch. 12)

limerance   "Head over heels" love in which one is obsessed with the loved one. (Ch. 12)

love   There are many possible definitions, and, according to researchers, many different types. For example, *see* agape, companionate love, eros, ludus, mania, pragma, and storge. (Ch. 12)

ludic eros   According to Lee, the love-style that results from combining ludus and eros styles. (Ch. 12)

ludus   A self-centered type of love. Ludic lovers avoid commitment and treat love as a game, often viewing the chase as more pleasurable than the prize. (Ch. 12)

lumpectomy   Surgical procedure in which only a breast tumor and a small bit of surrounding tissue is removed. (Ch. 2)

luteal (lu′ te-al) **phase**   The postovulatory, or secretory, phase of the menstrual cycle, lasting from about day 15 to day 28 in a 28-day cycle. (Ch. 3)

luteinizing (lu′ te-in″ i-zing) **hormone** or **LH**   A gonadotropin hormone that is released by the pituitary. A large increase in LH signals the onset of ovulation. Also see interstitial cell-stimulating hormone. (Ch. 3)

lymphogranuloma venereum (lim″ fo-gran″ u-lo′ mah vene′ reum) or **LGV**   A sexually transmitted disease that is common in tropical countries and which is caused by chlamydia. If left untreated, it causes swelling of the inguinal lymph nodes, penis, labia, or clitoris. (Ch. 5)

M

male orgasmic disorder A persistent or recurrent delay in, or absence of, orgasm following a normal sexual excitement phase. (Ch. 13)

male rape Rape in which the victim is a male. (Ch. 15)

mammary glands Milk-producing glands of the breast. (Ch. 2)

mania A type of love characterized by an intense emotional dependency on the attention and affection of one's lover. (Ch. 12)

marital rape Rape of a wife by her husband. (Ch. 15)

masochists (mas′ o-kists) Individuals who obtain sexual pleasure primarily from having pain and/or humiliation inflicted on them. (Ch. 14)

mastectomy (mas-tek′ to-me) Surgical removal of a breast. (Ch. 2)

masturbation Self-stimulation of one's genitals. (Ch. 10 and 11)

meatus (me-a′ tus) General term for an opening or passageway, as in urinary meatus. (Ch. 2)

medical history One of the first steps used by most sex therapists. A complete medical history or exam is important because many sexual problems have an organic basis. (Ch. 13)

menarche (mě-nar′ ke) The term for a female's first menstrual period. (Ch. 3 and 10)

menopause (men′ o-pawz) A female's last menstrual period. (Ch. 3 and 10)

menstrual cycle The monthly cycle of hormonal events in a female that leads to ovulation and menstruation. (Ch. 3)

menstrual taboos Incorrect, negative attitudes about menstruating females. (Ch. 3)

menstruation (men″ stroo-a′ shun) The monthly discharge of endometrial tissue, blood, and other secretions from the uterus that occurs when an egg is not fertilized. (Ch. 3)

mesoderm A layer of the embryo that forms the muscles, skeleton, and blood vessels. (Ch. 7)

microstructural theory Stresses the role of the external environment in shaping gender roles. (Ch. 8)

midwife *See* nurse-midwife

minipill An oral contraceptive that contains only progestins. (Ch. 6)

miscarriage A spontaneous abortion. (Ch. 7)

missionary position A face-to-face position of sexual intercourse in which the female lies on her back and the male lies on top with his legs between hers. It was called this because Christian missionaries instructed people that other positions were unnatural. (Ch. 1 and 11)

Mittelschmerz (mit′ el-shmārts) Abdominal pain at the time of ovulation. (Ch. 3)

molluscum contagiosum (mo-lus′ kum contagio′ sum) A sexually transmitted virus with symptoms that look like small pimples filled with kernels of corn. (Ch. 5)

moniliasis (mon-ĭ-lī′ ah-sis) Sometimes called candidiasis, a type of vaginitis caused by the overgrowth of a microorganism (*Candida albicans*), which is normally found in the vagina. It is a fungus or yeast infection and usually is a sexually related, rather than a sexually transmitted, disease. (Ch. 5)

mons veneris (monz ven′ eris) The soft layer of fatty tissue that overlays the pubic bone in females. It becomes covered with pubic hair during puberty. (Ch. 2)

morning sickness A symptom of early pregnancy involving nausea. (Ch. 7)

morula (mor′ u-lah) The collection of cells formed when the zygote begins rapid cell division. (Ch. 7)

Mullerian (mil-e′ re-an) **duct system** A primitive duct system formed in embryos, which if allowed to develop, becomes the female reproductive system. (Ch. 8)

Mullerian-inhibiting substance Chemical secreted by the testes during embryological development that causes the Mullerian ducts to shrink and disappear. (Ch. 8)

multiple orgasms Having two or more successive orgasms without falling below the plateau level of physiological arousal. (Ch. 4)

myotonia (mi′ o-to′ ne-ah) A build-up of energy in nerves and muscles, resulting in involuntary contractions. (Ch. 4)

mysophilia (mi″ so-fil′ e-ah) Condition in which sexual arousal is caused primarily by filth or filthy surroundings. (Ch. 14)

N

necking Noncoital sexual contact above the waist. (Ch. 10)

necrophilia (nek″ ro-fil′ e-ah) Sexual arousal by having sex with a dead body. (Ch. 14)

nipple The protuberance on the breast that consists of smooth muscle fibers. In females, it contains the outlets for the milk ducts. (Ch. 2)

nocturnal emission An ejaculation that occurs during sleep in males; a "wet dream." (Ch. 10)

nocturnal orgasm An orgasm that occurs during sleep (sometimes called "wet dreams" in males). (Ch. 11)

nongonococcal (nonspecific) urethritis or **NGU** Refers to any inflammation of the urethra that is not caused by the *Neisseria gonorrhoeae* (gonococcus) bacterium. (Ch. 5)

nonlove According to Sternberg, the emotion felt in the absence of intimacy, passion, and commitment. (Ch. 12)

nonoxynol-9 The active chemical in most spermicides. (Ch. 6)

nonverbal communication Communicating with another person without using words. (Ch. 17)

nonviolent sexually explicit material Sexually explicit material that does not show violent interactions between individuals. (Ch. 16)

Norplant Six flexible silicone tubes containing a progestin that are implanted under the skin to prevent conception for 5 years. (Ch. 6)

nurse-midwife Registered nurses, trained in obstetrical techniques, who deliver babies, often at the expectant mother's home. (Ch. 7)

O

obscene In legal cases, refers to material that by contemporary community standards depicts patently offensive sexual conduct, lacks serious value, and appeals to prurient interests. (Ch. 16)

Oedipus (ed′ i-pus) **complex** According to psychoanalytic theory, this is the sexual desire that a boy feels toward his mother (male Oedipus complex) or the sexual attraction that a girl feels toward her father (female Oedipus complex) during the phallic stage of psychosexual development. (Ch. 8)

open marriage A marital relationship in which the couple agrees that it is permissible to have sexual relations outside of the marriage. (Ch. 10)

operant conditioning According to learning theory, a type of training thought to be responsible for acquiring sex roles by rewarding "masculine" behavior in boys and "feminine" behavior in girls and not rewarding behaviors associated with the opposite sex. (Ch. 8)

opportunistic diseases Term used to refer to a variety of diseases that occur in individuals with a very weakened immune system, as occurs in AIDS. (Ch. 5)

opportunistic rapists Rapists motivated by sex who rape impulsively when there is an opportunity. (Ch. 15)

oral contraceptive The birth control pill. (Ch. 6)

oral herpes Herpes infection in or around the mouth. It can be caused by herpes simplex virus types I or II. (Ch. 5)

orchiectomy (or″ ke-ek′ to-me) Removal of one or both testicles. (Ch. 3)

orgasm The brief, but intense, sensations (focused largely in the genitals but really a whole body response) experienced during sexual arousal. At this time, rhythmic muscular contractions occur in certain tissues in both the male and female. The third stage of the sexual response cycle, as proposed by Masters and Johnson. (Ch. 4)

orgasmic platform The engorgement and consequent swelling of the outer third of the vagina during the plateau stage, causing the vaginal opening to narrow by 30–50 percent. (Ch. 4)

os The opening of the cervix. (Ch. 7)

ovary (o′ vah-re) The female gonad in which ova are produced. (Ch. 2)

ovulation (o″ vu-la′ shun) The expulsion of an egg from one of the ovaries. (Ch. 3)

ovum An egg; the female reproductive cell. (Ch. 2 and 7)

oxytocin (ok″se-to′sin) A hormone that causes the breasts to eject milk. (Ch. 7)

P

Pap smear Named for Dr. Papanicolaou, who developed it; a test for cancer of the cervix in females. (Ch. 2)

paraphilias (par″ ah-fil′ e-ahs) General term for a group of unusual behaviors upon which a person's sexual arousal and gratification depend almost exclusively. (Ch. 14)

passion The drive leading to physical attraction, sexual relations, and romance. (Ch. 12)

pedophilia (pe″ do-fil′ e-ah) A condition in which sexual arousal is achieved primarily and repeatedly through sexual activity with children who have not reached puberty. (Ch. 14 and 15)

peer pressure The expectations by one's peer group about how one is supposed to behave. (Ch. 10)

pelvic exam A necessary part of female health care to check for cervical and vaginal infections; it includes a Pap smear. (Ch. 2)

pelvic inflammatory disease or **PID** A bacterially caused inflammation of a female's reproductive tract, particularly the Fallopian tubes, that can result in sterility. The most common (though not the only) cause is untreated gonorrhea and/or chlamydia. (Ch. 5)

penis (pe′ nis) The male organ for sexual intercourse and the passageway for sperm and urine. (Ch. 2)

penis envy According to psychoanalytic theory, the anger and envy that a girl feels during the phallic stage of psychosexual development, when she realizes that she has no penis (and will never have one). This supposedly causes her to become angry at her mother, whom the girl blames for this condition. (Ch. 8)

performance anxiety A fear of failure during sexual relations. This can lead to erectile disorder in males and inhibited orgasm in females. (Ch. 13)

perineum (per″ i-ne′ um) Technically refers to the entire pelvic floor, but more commonly is used to mean the hairless bit of skin between the anus and either the vaginal opening (in females) or scrotum (in males). (Ch. 2)

personally immature pedophile A pedophile who is attracted to children because he never developed the social skills necessary to initiate and maintain a sexual relationship with an adult. (Ch. 15)

phallic stage (fal′ ik) According to psychoanalytic theory, the third stage of psychosexual development in which children's sexual desire for the opposite-sexed parent emerges and is resolved through the process of identification. (Ch. 8)

petting Noncoital sexual contact below the waist. (Ch. 10)

pheromones (fer′ah monz) Chemical substances secreted externally by animals that convey information to, and produce specific responses in, members of the same species. (Ch. 3)

phimosis (fi-mo′ sis) A condition in uncircumcised males in which the foreskin of the penis is too tight, causing pain during erection. (Ch. 2 and 13)

PID *See* pelvic inflammatory disease. (Ch. 5)

pill *See* oral contraceptive. (Ch. 6)

pinworms Small worms (*Enterobius vermicularis*) that live in the large intestine and are generally transmitted through nonsexual contact with the worms' eggs, but which can be transmitted sexually by manual or oral contact with the anus of an infected person. (Ch. 5)

pituitary (pǐ-tu′ ǐ-tār″ e) **gland** A gland located at the base of the brain that secretes eight hormones, including follicle-stimulating hormone and luteinizing hormone. (Ch. 3)

placenta (plah-sen′tah) An organ that serves as a connection or interface between the fetus's systems and those of the mother. (Ch. 7)

placenta previa A condition in which the placenta blocks the cervical opening. (Ch. 7)

plateau The second stage of the sexual response cycle as proposed by Masters and Johnson. Physiologically, it represents a high state of arousal. (Ch. 4)

PLISSIT model An acronym for the four levels of treatment in sexual therapy: permission, limited information, specific suggestions, and intensive therapy. (Ch. 13)

PMS *See* premenstrual syndrome. (Ch. 3)

pneumocystis carinii (nu″ mo-sis′ tis cari′ nii) **pneumonia** A rare respiratory infection that often occurs in people with AIDS. (Ch. 5)

polygyny The practice of having two or more wives at the same time. (Ch. 12)

polyincestuous family Families in which there are both multiple incestuous abusers and multiple victims, across generations and within the same generation. (Ch. 15)

pornography Literature or art with a sexual theme that is designed to cause arousal and excitement and which is considered to be obscene. (Ch. 16)

postpartum depression Depression that often occurs in women after giving birth, usually lasting 2 or 3 weeks. (Ch. 7)

power rapists Rapists who commit their attacks in order to overcome personal feelings of insecurity and inadequacy. Their rapes give them a sense of mastery and control. (Ch. 15)

pragma A rational or practical type of love. Pragmatic lovers actively look for a "good match." (Ch. 12)

precocious puberty A condition in which the events of puberty begin before the age of 9. (Ch. 10)

preeclampsia (pre″ e-klamp′se-ah) The early stage of toxemia of pregnancy, characterized by high blood pressure, weight gain, and swollen joints. (Ch. 7)

preference molesters Child molesters who have a primary sexual orientation to children and who are relatively uninterested in adult partners. (Ch. 15)

premature ejaculation A recurrent and persistent absence of reasonable voluntary control of ejaculation. (Ch. 13)

premenstrual syndrome (PMS) A group of physical and/or emotional changes that many women experience in the last 3–14 days before the start of their menstrual period. (Ch. 3)

prepared childbirth Courses or techniques that prepare women for labor and childbirth with the goal of making it a positive experience. (Ch. 7)

prepping The shaving of the pubic hair prior to delivery of a baby. (Ch. 7)

preterm infant An infant born weighing less than $5Z \backslash x$ pounds and before the 37th week of pregnancy. (Ch. 7)

priapism (pri′ ah-pizm) A condition in which the penis remains erect for a prolonged period of time (sometimes days). (Ch. 13)

primary follicle An immature ovum enclosed by a single layer of cells. (Ch. 2 and 7)

primary sexual problem A problem that has existed throughout an individual's life. (Ch. 13)

procreation To produce offspring. (Ch. 1)

progesterone (pro-jes tě-ron) A hormone that is produced in large amounts by the ovaries after ovulation. It prepares the endometrium of the uterus to nourish a fertilized egg. (Ch. 3)

progestin (proj-jes′ tin) A synthetic form of progesterone. (Ch. 6)

prolactin (pro-lak′ tin) A hormone that stimulates milk production in the breasts. (Ch. 7)

proliferation phase The preovulatory, or follicular, phase of the menstrual cycle, lasting from about day 5 to day 13 in a 28-day cycle. (Ch. 3)

prophylactic *See* condom. (Ch. 6)

prostaglandins (pros″ tah-glan′ dinz) Chemical substances in the body that cause uterine contractions. (Ch. 3 and 6)

prostate (pros′ tat) **gland**   A gland in males that surrounds the urethra and neck of the bladder and which contributes many substances to the seminal fluid. (Ch. 5)

prostatitis (pros″tah-ti′ tis)   Inflammation of the prostate gland. (Ch. 5)

prostitute   A person who exchanges sex for money. The feature that distinguishes a prostitute from other people who engage in illicit sexual intercourse is the indiscrimination with which she or he offers her or himself to others for hire. (Ch. 16)

pseudohermaphroditism (su″ do-her-maf′ ro-di-tizm″)   A condition in which a person is born with ambiguous genitalia as a result of hormonal abnormalities. (*See also* adrenogenital syndrome and androgen insensitivity syndrome.) (Ch. 8)

psychosexual therapy   Therapy designed to provide insight into the historical cause of a client's problem. (ch. 13)

puberty (pu′ ber-te)   The time in life when an individual becomes capable of reproduction. (Ch. 10)

pubic (pu′ bik) **hair**   Hair that grows in the genital region starting at puberty; a secondary sex characteristic. (Ch. 2)

pubic (pu′ bik) **lice**   Also known as "crabs," an infestation of the parasite *Pediculosis pubis*, which attach themselves to pubic hair and feed on blood. (Ch. 5)

pubococcygeus (pu″ bo-kok-sij′ e-us) **muscle**   The major muscle in the pelvic region. Voluntary control over this muscle (to aid in preventing urinary incontinence or to enhance physical sensations during intercourse) is gained through Kegel exercises. (Ch. 2)

Q

quickening   The first time a pregnant woman experiences movement of the fetus, usually in the fifth month. (Ch. 7)

R

random sampling   A sampling procedure in which observations are drawn so that each possible sample of that size has an equal chance of being selected. (Ch. 1)

rape myths   Widespread, mistaken beliefs about rape. (Ch. 15)

rape-shield laws   Laws that make prosecution of rapists easier and that also prevent the victims from feeling like they are on trial. (Ch. 15)

rape trauma syndrome   Reactions of a rape victim, including an acute phase (involving initial physical and psychological recovery from the attack) and long-term reorganization (involving attempts to deal with the long-term effects of the attack and to prevent a future rape). (Ch. 15)

Reformation   The sixteenth-century religious movement that was directed at reforming the Roman Catholic church. (Ch. 1)

refractory period   In males, the period of time after an orgasm in which their physiological responses fall below the plateau level, thus making it impossible for them to have another orgasm (until the responses build back up to plateau). (Ch. 4)

regressive pedophile   A pedophile with a past history of normal adult sexual relations. (Ch. 5)

resolution   The fourth and final stage of the sexual response cycle as proposed by Masters and Johnson. It refers to a return to the unaroused state. (Ch. 4)

respiratory distress syndrome   An illness commonly found in premature infants, caused by insufficient levels of surfactin. (Ch. 7)

retarded ejaculation   *See* inhibited male orgasm.

retrograde ejaculation   Refers to an abnormal condition experienced by some males during orgasm in which the semen is forced into the bladder instead of out of the body. (Ch. 4)

Rh factor   A protein in the blood of most individuals. If a mother does not have it and the fetus she carries does, she can develop antibodies against the Rh factor. This is called an Rh incompatibility problem. (Ch. 7)

Rhogam   A drug used to treat Rh incompatibility problems consisting of Rh negative blood that already had Rh antibodies. (Ch. 7)

rhythm   *See* fertility awareness methods. (Ch. 6)

romantic love   The combination of passion and liking (intimacy). Romantic love relationships have high levels of fascination (with one another), exclusiveness, sexual desire, and "giving the utmost" when the other is in need. (Ch. 12)

root (of the penis)   This consists of the crura and the bulb. (Ch. 2)

RU486   A pill that chemically induces an abortion by blocking progesterone. (Ch. 6)

rubella (roo-bel′ ah)   A disease, also known as German measles, caused by a virus. If contracted during pregnancy, it can cause fetal abnormalities. (Ch. 7)

S

sadistic rapists   Rapists who are aroused by physical force and who derive pleasure by harming their victims. (Ch. 15)

sadists (sad′ ists)   Individuals who repeatedly and intentionally inflict pain on others in order to achieve sexual arousal. (Ch. 14)

safer sex   Sexual behaviors with a low risk for contraction of a sexually transmitted disease. These include consistent use of condoms and/or abstaining from sex until one enters a long-term monogamous relationship. (Ch. 5)

sample A subset of a population of subjects. (Ch. 1)

scabies (ska′ bez) A contagious infestation of parasitic mites (*Sarcoptes scabiei*) that burrow under the skin and lay their eggs. (Ch. 5)

schemas *See* gender schemas. (Ch. 8)

scoptophilia (skop″ to-fil′ e-ah) Repeatedly seeking sexual arousal by secretly observing genitals and sexual intercourse. (Ch. 14)

scrotum (skro′ tum) The pouch beneath the penis that contains the testicles. (Ch. 2)

secondary sex characteristics Bodily changes that occur during puberty which differentiate males and females. (Ch. 10)

secondary sexual problem A sexual problem that has occurred in an individual who has not had the problem in past sexual relations. (Ch. 13)

second stage of labor Begins when the cervix is fully dilated and the fetus begins moving through the birth canal. It ends with birth. (Ch. 7)

secretory phase The postovulatory, or luteal, phase of the menstrual cycle, lasting from about day 15 to day 28 in a 28-day cycle.

self-awareness In sexual therapy, this refers to getting in touch with one's own physical responses. (Ch. 13)

self-disclosure Revealing one's thoughts, feelings, and emotions to another. (Ch. 12)

self-esteem The feeling one has about oneself. (Ch. 12)

semen (se′ men) The fluid expelled from a male's penis during orgasm consisting of sperm and fluids from the prostate gland and seminal vesicles. (Ch. 4)

seminal vesicles (sem′ ĭ-nal ves′ ĭ-k'lz) Two structures in the male that contribute many substances to the seminal fluid. (Ch. 2)

seminiferous (se″ mĭ-nif′ er-us) **tubules** The tubules in the testes that produce sperm. (Ch. 2)

sensate focus Exercises designed to reduce anxiety and teach mutual pleasuring through nongenital touching in nondemanding situations.

sensuality The state of being sensual. It encompasses all of our senses and who we are as a total person. (Ch. 2)

serial monogamy Having a series of monogamous, sexual relationships. (Ch. 10)

sex roles Behaviors that are associated with being stereotypically masculine or feminine. (Ch. 8)

sex-tension flush The rash that appears on the skin (due to vasocongestion) in 50–75 percent of women and 25 percent of men during the plateau stage of the sexual response cycle. (Ch. 4)

sexual addiction *See* hypersexuality. (Ch. 13)

sexual aversion An extreme form of hypoactive sexual desire in which an individual's avoidance of sex becomes phobic. (Ch. 13)

sexual coercion The act of forcing another person into unwanted sexual activity by physical or verbal coercion (restrain or constrain). (Ch. 15)

sexual harassment Unwelcome sexual advances that persist after the recipient has indicated that it is unwanted. See text for an expanded definition. (Ch. 15)

sexual history One of the first steps in most sexual therapy programs. (Ch. 13)

sexuality All of the sexual attitudes, feelings, and behaviors associated with being human. The term does not refer specifically to a person's capacity for erotic response or to sexual acts, but to a dimension of one's personality. (Ch. 1)

sexual learning Knowledge about sex that is received (usually informally) from family, friends, the media, and society in general. (Ch. 17)

sexually healthy person Someone who feels comfortable with his or her sexuality and who feels free to choose whether or not he or she wishes to try a variety of sexual behaviors. (Ch. 11)

sexually related diseases A disease of the reproductive system or genitals that is not contracted through sexual activity. Often refers to overgrowths of bacteria, yeasts, viruses, or fungal organisms that are found naturally in sexual or reproductive organs. (Ch. 5)

sexually transmitted diseases Term used to refer to diseases that can be, but are not necessarily always, transmitted by sexual contact. This term is generally preferred to the term "venereal diseases." (Ch. 5)

sexual orientation Distinct preferences for sexual partners of a particular gender in the presence of clear alternatives. (Ch. 9 and 10)

sexual response cycle The physiological responses that occur during sexual arousal, which many therapists and researchers have arbitrarily divided into different stages. (Ch. 4)

sexual revolution A period in U.S. history, beginning in about 1960, of increased sexual permissiveness. (Ch. 1)

sexual surrogate *See* surrogate. (Ch. 13)

sexual variant For an individual, statistically or sociologically unusual behaviors that are engaged in for variety and not as one's preferred manner of becoming sexually aroused. (Ch. 14)

shaft The long body of the penis or clitoris. (Ch. 2)

shigellosis (she″ gel-lo′ sis) A disease that can be contracted during sexual activity by exposure to feces containing the *Shigella* bacterium. (Ch. 5)

situational ethics Values or ethics that emphasize the proper thing to do in particular situations. (Ch. 17)

situational molesters Child molesters who have a primary sexual orientation to adults. They have sex with children impulsively and regard their behavior as abnormal. (Ch. 15)

situational sexual problem   A sexual problem that occurs only in specific situations. (Ch. 13)

Skene's (skenz) **glands**   Glands located in the urethra of some women that are thought to develop from the same embryological tissue as the male prostate, and which may be the source of a fluid emitted by some women during orgasm. (Ch. 4)

smegma (smeg′mah)   The cheesy secretion of sebaceous glands that can cause the clitoris to stick to the clitoral hood or the foreskin of the penis to stick to the glans. (Ch. 2)

socialization   The process of internalizing society's beliefs. (Ch. 8)

sodomy (sod′ o-me) **laws**   Laws that prohibit oral and/or anal sex. (Ch. 16)

spectatoring   Observing and evaluating one's own sexual responses. This generally causes distraction with subsequent erectile and/or orgasm problems. (Ch. 13)

sperm   The germ cell of a male. (Ch. 2 and 7)

spermatic (sper-mat′ ik) **cord**   The cord that suspends a testicle in the scrotum. (Ch. 2)

spermatorrhea (sper″ mah-to-re′ ah)   The Victorian name for male nocturnal emissions (wet dreams), so named because Victorian physicians believed it was caused by the same thing that caused gonorrhea. (Ch. 1 and 11)

spermicides   Chemicals that kill sperm. In most products, the chemical is nonoxynol-9. (Ch. 6)

start-up stage of labor   Begins with uterine contractions pushing the fetus downward toward the cervix and ends when the cervix is fully dilated. (Ch. 7)

statistically normal   A range of behaviors or values that encompasses a large number of individuals. (Ch. 11)

statutory rape   Sexual intercourse by an adult with a (consenting) partner who is not yet at the legal "age of consent." Sometimes called carnal knowledge of a juvenile. (Ch. 15)

stereotypes   Oversimplified, preconceived beliefs that supposedly apply to anyone in a given group. (Ch. 8)

sterilization   General term for surgical techniques that render an individual infertile. (Ch. 6)

stigmatophilia (stig″ mah to-fil′ e-ah)   Sexual arousal by marking one's own body or inserting foreign objects into the urethra, genitals, or nipples. (ch. 14)

storge (stor′ ga)   An affectionate type of love that grows from friendship. (Ch. 12)

storgic eros   According to Lee, the love-style that results from combining storge and eros styles. (Ch. 12)

storgic ludus   According to Lee, the love-style that results from combining storge and ludus styles.

(Ch. 12)

straight   A term used by homosexuals for a heterosexual. (Ch. 9)

stranger rape   Rape committed by someone who is not known by the victim. (Ch. 15)

streetwalker   A prostitute who solicits in public. (Ch. 16)

submission   Obeying and yielding to another individual. In sexual relations, it generally involves being humiliated by the partner as well. (Ch. 14)

surfactin   A liquid that lets the lungs transmit oxygen from the atmosphere to the blood. (Ch. 7)

surrogate   A person, usually a female, trained and skilled in sensate focus techniques who works under the direction of a therapist with a single partnerless client undergoing sexual therapy. (Ch. 13)

surrogate mother   A woman who carries a fetus to full term for another couple, agreeing to give the infant to the other couple after it is born. The infant generally represents the union of the sperm from the man and either his partner's ovum or the ovum of the surrogate mother. (Ch. 7)

survey   A study of people's attitudes, opinions, or behaviors. (Ch. 1)

swinging   A type of open marriage relationship in which a couple has extramarital relations together. (Ch. 10)

swish   A slang term for an effeminate gay. This is a stereotype that generally does not reflect how most gays look or behave. (Ch. 9)

symptomatic HIV infection   Formerly called AIDS related complex (ARC); the early symptoms of HIV infection that can lead to AIDS. (Ch. 5)

sympto-thermal method   A combination of the basal body temperature and Billings fertility awareness methods. (Ch. 6)

syphilis (sif′ i-lis)   A sexually transmitted disease caused by the *Treponema pallidum* bacterium (spirochete), which can also pass directly through any cut or scrape into the bloodstream. (Ch. 5)

systematic desensitization   *See* desensitization. (Ch. 13)

T

telephone scatologia (skat″ o-lo′ge-ah)   A condition in which sexual arousal is achieved primarily by making obscene telephone calls. (Ch. 14)

teratogens (teh rat′ ojinz)   Substances that can harm an embryo or fetus. (Ch. 7)

testicles (tes′ ty-k'ls)   The male gonads that produce sperm and male hormones. (Ch. 2)

testicular torsion   An uncommon condition in which the spermatic cord twists and cuts off the blood supply to the testicles. (Ch. 2)

testosterone (tes-tos′ te-ron)   A hormone that is produced by the testicles (and in very small amounts by the ovaries and adrenal glands). (Ch. 2 and 3)

theoretical effectiveness rate   For a particular birth control technique, the percentage of failures during one year of use by couples who use the technique properly and consistently. (Ch. 6)

third stage of labor   Detachment and expulsion of the placenta from the uterus after childbirth. (Ch. 7)

thrush   A yeast infection (candidiasis) of the mouth. (Ch. 5)

token resistance to sex   Saying "no" to sex when one means "yes." (Ch. 15)

toxemia   A disease of pregnancy characterized in its early stage (preeclampsia) by high blood pressure, weight gain, swollen joints, and protein in the urine. Unless it is corrected, it can lead to convulsions and coma. (Ch. 7)

toxic shock syndrome   A syndrome (e.g., high fever, vomiting, diarrhea, dizziness) caused by toxins produced by the *Staphylococcus aureus* bacterium. (Ch. 3)

transition phase   The last part of the start-up stage of labor, during which the cervix dilates to 10 cm in order for the baby to be able to enter the birth canal. (Ch. 7)

transsexual   A person whose gender identity does not match his or her biological sex. (Ch. 8)

transvestism   A condition in which sexual arousal is achieved primarily by dressing as a member of the opposite sex. (Ch. 14)

triangular theory of love   Sternberg's theory of love that says that all of our different positive emotions are the result of different combinations of intimacy, passion, and decision/commitment. (Ch. 12)

trichomoniasis (trik″ o-mo-ni′ ah-sis)   A type of vaginitis caused by a one-celled protozoan that is usually transmitted during sexual intercourse. (Ch. 5)

trimesters   Three-month periods of pregnancy (months 0–3, 4–6, and 7–9), so labeled for descriptive purposes. (Ch. 7)

Triple-X Syndrome   A condition in which females have an extra X chromosome. (Ch. 8)

trophoblast (trof′o-blast)   The outer-four cell layers of the embryo. (Ch. 7)

tubal ligation   A female sterilization technique that originally referred only to the tying of the Fallopian tubes, but which is now often used as a general term for a variety of female sterilization techniques. (Ch. 6)

tubal pregnancy   Implantation of a blastocyst in a Fallopian tube. (Ch. 7)

Turner's Syndrome   A condition in which females have only one X chromosome, and as a result their ovaries never develop properly. (Ch. 8)

two-spirit   The term preferred by Native Americans and anthropologists for berdache. (Ch. 14)

U

ultrasound scan   A noninvasive technique for examining internal organs of a fetus, which uses sound waves like a radar or sonar to create a picture. (Ch. 7)

umbilical (um-bil′ ĭ-kal) **cord**   The cord that connects an embryo/fetus to the mother's placenta. (Ch. 7)

unconditional love   Feelings of love that do not depend on the loved one meeting certain expectations and desires. (Ch. 12)

undifferentiated   Individuals who are low on both masculine and feminine traits. (Ch. 8)

urethra (u-re′ thrah)   The passageway from the bladder to the exterior of the body. In males, it also serves as a passageway for semen during ejaculation. (Ch. 2)

urophilia (u″ ro-fil′ e-ah)   Sexual arousal caused by urine or the act of urination. (Ch. 14)

uterus (u′ ter-us)   The womb. The hollow, muscular organ in females where the fertilized egg normally implants. (Ch. 2)

V

vagina (vah-ji′ nah)   The sheathlike canal in the female that extends from the vulva to the cervix and that receives the penis during intercourse. (Ch. 2)

vaginal lubrication   The first sign of sexual arousal in females; the result of the vaginal walls becoming engorged with blood. (Ch. 4)

vaginismus (vaj″ ĭ-niz′ mus)   A sexual problem in females in which pain is experienced during attempted intercourse because of involuntary muscle spasms in the muscles surrounding the outer third of the vagina. (Ch. 13)

vaginitis (vaj″ ĭ-ni′ tis)   A general term that refers to any inflammation of the vagina. There are three general types: trichomoniasis, moniliasis, and bacterial vaginosis. (Ch. 5)

vas deferens (vas def′ er-enz)   The second part of the duct system that transports sperm out of a male's body. (Ch. 2)

vasectomy (vah-sek′ to-me)   The male sterilization technique in which the vas deferens is tied off and cut, thus preventing passage of sperm through the male's reproductive tract. (Ch. 2 and 6)

vasocongestion (vas′ okunjeschun)   Refers to tissues becoming engorged (filled) with blood. (Ch. 4)

venereal diseases   Term originally used to refer to gonorrhea, syphilis, and three other diseases that are spread almost exclusively by sexual contact. (Ch. 5)

venereal warts   *See* genital warts. (Ch. 5)

vernix   A bluish, waxy substance that covers a newborn baby. (Ch. 7)

vestibular (ves-tǐb′ u-lar) **area**   A term sometimes used to refer to the area between the two labia minora. (Ch. 2)

vestibular (ves-tib′ u-lar) **bulbs**   These surround the vaginal opening and fill with blood during sexual arousal, resulting in swelling of the tissues and a narrowing of the vaginal opening. (Ch. 2)

Victorian era   The period during the reign of Queen Victoria of England (1819–1901). With regard to sexuality, it was a time of great public prudery (the pleasurable aspects of sex were denied) and many incorrect medical beliefs. (Ch.1)

violent sexually explicit material   Sexually explicit material that shows violence, almost always males treating females violently. (Ch. 16)

virus   A protein shell around a nucleic acid core. They have RNA or DNA, but not both, and thus cannot reproduce themselves. They invade host cells that provide the material to manufacture new virus particles. (Ch. 5)

voyeurism (voi′ yer-izm)   Repeatedly seeking sexual arousal by observing nude individuals without their knowledge or consent. (Ch. 14)

vulva (vul′ vah)   A term for the external female genitalia, which includes the mons veneris, labia majora, labia minora, clitoris, vaginal opening, and urethral opening. (Ch. 2)

W

wet dream   An involuntary, nocturnal emission of semen. This type of ejaculation often is the first experience with ejaculation for a boy, as wet dreams generally begin at the onset of puberty. (Ch. 10 and 11)

withdrawal (coitus interruptus)   Withdrawal of the male's penis from his partner's vagina before ejaculation to try to avoid conception. It is sometimes ineffective because fluids from the Cowper's glands may contain sperm. (Ch. 6)

Wolffian duct system   A primitive duct system found in embryos, which if allowed to develop, becomes the male reproductive system. (Ch. 8)

Z

zona pellucida (zo′nah pellu′ cǐda)   The surface of an ovum. (Ch. 7)

zoophilia (zo″ ofil′ e-ah)   Using sexual contact with animals as the primary means of achieving sexual gratification. (Ch. 14)

zygote (zi′ got)   The one-celled organism created from the fusion of a sperm and egg. (Ch. 7)

zygote intrafallopian transfer (ZIFT)   A method of treating infertility caused by blocked Fallopian tubes. An ovum taken from the infertile female is fertilized by sperm from her partner and then transferred to the unblocked portion of a Fallopian tube. (Ch. 7)

RESOURCES

General

American College Health Association
P.O. Box 28937
Baltimore, MD 21240-8937
(410) 859-1500

National Self-Help Clearinghouse
25 West 43rd Street
New York, NY 10036
(212) 354-8525
They will help you locate a self-help organization in your area.

SIECUS (Sex Information and Education Council of the U.S.)
130 West 42nd Street, Suite 350
New York, NY 10036
(212) 819-9770

Society for the Scientific Study of Sex
P.O. Box 208
Mount Vernon, IA 52314

Abortion

National Abortion and Reproductive Rights Action League
1156 15th Street, N.W.
Suite 700
Washington, DC 20005
(202) 973-3000
The leading pro-choice abortion group.

National Right to Life Committee
419 7th Street, N.W.
Suite 500
Washington, DC 20004
(202) 626-8800
The leading anti-abortion group.

Birth Control

Alan Guttmacher Institute
120 Wall Street, Floor 21
New York, NY 10005
(212) 248-1111

Association for Voluntary Surgical Contraception (AVSC)
79 Madison Avenue
New York, NY 10016
(212) 561-8000

Planned Parenthood Federation of America
810 Seventh Avenue
New York, NY 10019
(212) 541-7800
You can contact the national headquarters to get the address and phone number of the clinic closest to you.

Cancer

American Cancer Society
19 West 56th Street
New York, NY 10019
(212) 586-8700
Local units can be found in your telephone directory.

National Cancer Institute Cancer Information Service
1(800) 4-CANCER

Child Sexual Abuse/Incest

CHILDHELP National Child Abuse Hotline
1(800) 422-4453
Provides information, crisis intervention, and referrals to local services if you wish to report abuse.

Children's Defense Fund
25 E Street, N.W.
Washington, DC 20001
(202) 628-8787
Provides information about child abuse prevention.

Incest Survivors Anonymous
P.O. Box 17245
Long Beach, CA 90807-7245
(310) 428-5599
For incest victims.

Incest Recovery Services of the Family Place
4211 Cedar Springs
Suite 100
Dallas, TX 75219
(214) 559-2170
For incest victims.

Looking up
P.O. Box K
Augusta, ME 04330
(207) 626-3402
For adult incest survivors.

National Center for Missing and Exploited Children
2101 Wilson Blvd.
Suite 550
Arlington, VA 22201
1(800) 843-5678
(703) 235-3900 (office)
For parents who wish to report missing children, and others who may have information about missing children.

National Resource Center on Child Sexual Abuse Information Service
106 Lincoln Street
Huntsville, AL 35801
1(800) 543-7006

RAINN (Rape, Abuse, and Incest National Network)
1(800) 656-HOPE
Contact them for the number and address of the rape crisis program nearest to you.

Voices in Action
P.O. Box 148309
Chicago, IL 60614
(312) 327-1500
For incest victims.

YWCA Rape Crisis Program
Check your telephone directory for a program nearest to you, or call RAINN (see above).

HIV/AIDS

AIDS Action Council
1875 Connecticut Avenue, N.W.
Suite 700
Washington, DC 20009
(202) 986-1300

AIDS Information
U.S. Public Health Services
Office of Public Affairs,
    Room 721-H
200 Independence Avenue, S.W.
Washington, DC 20201
(301) 443-3087

AIDS Information Exchange
U.S. Conference of Mayors
1620 Eye Street, N.W.
Washington, DC 20006
(202) 293-7330

American Red Cross AIDS Public
    Education Program
2025 E Street, N.W.
Washington, DC 20003
(202) 728-6400

ACLU Lesbian and Gay Rights/
    AIDS Project
American Civil Liberties Union
132 W. 43rd Street
New York, NY 10036
(212) 944-9800, ext. 545

American Foundation for AIDS
    Research
733 Third Avenue
12th Floor
New York, NY 10017
(212) 682-7440

National HIV/AIDS Hotline
    (Centers for Disease Control and
    Prevention)
1(800) 342-AIDS

National AIDS Information
    Clearinghouse
1(800) 458-5231
    Service provided by the Centers
    for Disease Control and Preven-
    tion.

National Association of People with
    AIDS
1413 K Street, N.W.
Seventh Floor
Washington, DC 20005
(202) 898-0414

See also listings under
    homosexuality.

Homosexuality

ACLU Lesbian and Gay Rights/
    AIDS Project
American Civil Liberties Union
132 West 43rd Street
New York, NY 10036
(212) 944-9800, ext. 545

Federation of Parents and Friends of
    Lesbians and Gays (PFLAG)
1101 14th Street, N.W.
Suite 1030
Washington, DC 20005
(202) 638-4200

Gay Men's Health Crisis
129 W. 20th Street
New York, NY 10011-3629
AIDS Hotline: (212) 807-6655

Hetrick-Martin Institute
401 West Street
New York, NY 10014
(212) 674-2400
    Gay, lesbian, and bisexual youth
    service agency.

Lambda Legal Defense and
    Education Fund, Inc.
666 Broadway
Suite 1200
New York, NY 10012
(212) 995-8585

National Gay and Lesbian Task Force
2320 17th Street, N.W.
Washington, DC 20009-2702
(202) 332-6483

National Lesbian and Gay Health
    Association
P.O. Box 65472
Washington, DC 20035
(202) 797-3708
(202) 939-7880

Infertility/Adoption

Adoptive Families of America
3333 Highway 100 North
Minneapolis, MN 55422
(612) 535-4829

American Society for Reproductive
    Medicine
1209 Montgomery Highway
Birmingham, AL 35216
(205) 978-5000
    Formerly called the American
    Fertility Society

National Council for Adoption
1930 17th Street, N.W.
Washington, DC 20009
(202) 328-1200
    Contact them for information
    about adoption services in your
    area

Resolve, Inc.
1310 Broadway
Somerville, MA 02144-1731
(617) 623-0744

Pregnancy/Childbirth

American College of Nurse-Midwives
818 Connecticut Avenue, N.W.
Suite 900
Washington, DC 20006
(202) 728-9860

American College of Obstetricians
    and Gynecologists
409 12th Street, S.W.
Washington, DC 20024
(202) 638-5577

ASPO/Lamaze (American Society for
    Psychoprophylaxis in Obstetrics/
    Lamaze)
1200 19th Street, N.W.
Suite 300
Washington, DC 20036-2401
1(800) 368-4404
    Contact them for the name and
    address of a certified Lamaze in-
    structor in your area.

La Leche League International
1400 North Meacham Road
Schaumburg, IL 60173-4840
(708) 519-7730
    Advice about breast-feeding.

March of Dimes Birth Defects
Foundation
1275 Mamaroneck Avenue
White Plains, NY 10605
(914) 428-7100
Provides information on birth defects and gives referrals to genetic
counseling and services in your
area.

Rape

Center for the Prevention of Sexual
and Domestic Violence
936 North 34th Street
Suite 200
Seattle, Washington 98103
(206) 634-1903

National Clearinghouse on Marital
and Date Rape
(510) 524-1582

National Resource Center on
Domestic Violence
1(800) 537-2238

National Victims Center
2111 Wilson Blvd.
Suite 300
Arlington, VA 22201
(703) 276-2880

RAINN (Rape, Abuse, and Incest
National Network)
1(800) 656-HOPE
Contact them for the number and
address of the rape crisis program
nearest to you.

U.S. Department of Justice
Office of Violence Against Women
10th and Constitution Avenue,
N.W.
Room 5302
Washington, DC 20530

YWCA Rape Crisis Program
Check your telephone directory
for a program nearest to you, or
call RAINN (see above).

Runaway Children

Covenant House (Crisis Intervention
Hotline)
1(800) 999-9999
Provides counseling, shelter, and
other referral services.

National Network of Runaway and
Youth Services (Youth Crisis
Hotline)
Department P
P.O. Box 8283
Washington, DC 20024
1(800) 448-4663
They will put you in touch with
the nearest shelter program.

National Runaway Switchboard
1(800) 621-4000
They encourage runaway children
to reestablish contact with their
families.

Sex/Marital Therapy

AAMFT (American Association for
Marriage and Family Therapy)
1100 17th Street, N.W.
10th Floor
Washington, DC 20036-4601
They will provide names and addresses of certified marriage and
family therapists in your area.

AASECT (American Association of
Sex Educators, Counselors and
Therapists)
435 North Michigan Avenue
Suite 1717
Chicago, IL 60611-4065
They will provide names and ad-
dresses of certified sex counselors
and therapists in your area.

Sexual Harassment

Center for Women in Government
State University of New York at
Albany
Draper Hall, Room 302
135 Western Avenue
Albany, NY 12222
(518) 442-3900

National Organization for Women
1000 16th Street, N.W.
Suite 700
Washington, D.C. 20036
(202) 331-0066

Women's Legal Defense Fund
1875 Connecticut Avenue, N.W.
Suite 710
Washington, D.C. 20009
(202) 887-0364

*Sexually Transmitted Diseases (other
than HIV/AIDS)*

American Social Health Association
P.O. Box 13827
Research Triangle Park, NC 27709

Herpes Resource Center (hotline)
(919) 361-8488
Service provided by the American
Social Health Association.

STD National Hotline
1 (800) 227-8922
Service provided by the American
Social Health Association, and
funded by the Centers for Disease
Control and Prevention.

PHOTO AND ART CREDITS

AARONSON, I. A. (1994). Micropenis: Medical and surgical implications. *Journal of Urology, 152*, 4–14.

ABEL, E. L., & SOKOL, R. J. (1987). Incidence of fetal alcohol syndrome and economic impact of FAS-related anomalies. *Drug and Alcohol Dependency, 19*, 51–70.

ABEL, G. G. (1981 October 15). *The evaluation and treatment of sexual offenders and their victims.* Paper presented at St. Vincent Hospital and Medical Center, Portland, OR.

ABEL, G. G., BARLOW, D. H., BLANCHARD, E. B., & GUILD, D. (1977). The components of rapists' sexual arousal. *Archives of General Psychiatry, 34*, 895–903.

ABEL, G. G., BECKER, J. V., MURPHY, W. D., & FLANAGAN, B. (1981). Identifying dangerous child molesters. In R. B. Stuard (Ed.), *Violent behavior: Social learning approaches to prediction, management, and treatment* (pp. 116–137). New York: Brunner/Mazel.

ABEL, G. G. et al. (1987). Self-reported sex crimes of non-incarcerated paraphiliacs. *Journal of Interpersonal Violence, 2*, 3–25.

ABEL, G. G. et al. (1988a). Multiple paraphiliac diagnoses among sex offenders. *Bulletin of the American Academy of Psychiatry and the Law, 16*, 153–168.

ABEL, G. G. et al. (1988b). Predicting child molesters' response to treatment. *Annals of the New York Academy of Sciences, 528*, 223–234.

ABRAMS, B., & PARKER, J. D. (1990). Maternal weight gain in women with good pregnancy outcome. *Obstetrics and Gynecology, 76*, 1–7.

ABU-EL-FUTUH SHANDALL, A. (1967). Circumcision and infibulation of females: A general consideration of the problem and a clinical study of the complications in Sudanese women. *Sudan Medical Journal, 5*(4), 178–212.

ACOSTA, F. (1975). Etiology and treatment of homosexuality: A review. *Archives of Sexual Behavior, 4*, 9.

ADAMS, J. W., KOTTKE, J. L., & PADGITT, J. S. (1983). Sexual harassment of university students. *Journal of College Student Personnel, 24*, 484–490.

ADDIEGO, F. et al. (1981). Female ejaculation: A case study. *Journal of Sex Research, 17*, 13–21.

ADDUCCI, C., & ROSS, L. (1991, October). Common urethral injuries in men. *Medical Aspects of Human Sexuality,* pp. 32–34.

ADLER, E. (1994, March 4). Vasectomies cheaper, easier—and dropping. *New Orleans Times-Picayune,* pp. E–10.

ADLER, N. E. et al. (1990). Psychological responses after abortion. *Science, 248*, 41–44.

ADOLFSSON, J., STEINECK, G., & WHITMORE, W. F., JR. (1993). Recent results of management of palpable clinically localized prostate cancer. *Cancer (Philadelphia), 72*, 310–322.

AGNEW, J. (1986). Hazards associated with anal erotic activity. *Archives of Sexual Behavior, 15*, 307–314.

AHIA, R. N. (1991). Compliance with safer-sex guidelines among adolescent males: Application of the health belief model and protection motivation theory. *Journal of Health Education, 22*, 49–52.

ALBERMAN, E. (1988). The epidemiology of repeated abortion. In R. W. Beard & F. Sharp (Eds.), *Early pregnancy loss: Mechanisms and treatment* (pp. 9–17). London: Royal College of Obstetricians and Gynaecologists.

ALDER, C. (1985). An exploration of self-reported sexually aggressive behavior. *Crime and Delinquency, 31*, 306–331.

ALEXANDER, C. J., SIPSKI, M. L., & FINDLEY, T. W. (1993). Sexual activities, desire, and satisfaction in males pre-and post-spinal cord injury. *Archives of Sexual Behavior, 22*, 217–228.

ALEXANDER, G. M., & SHERWIN, B. B. (1993). Sex steroids, sexual behavior, and selection attention for erotic stimuli in women using oral contraceptives. *Psychoneuroendocrinology, 18*, 91–102.

ALEXANDER, G. M., SHERWIN, B. B., BANCROFT, J., & DAVIDSON, D.W. (1990). Testosterone and sexual behavior in oral-contraceptive users and nonusers: A prospective study. *Hormones and Behavior, 24*, 388–402.

ALEXANDER, N. J. (1990). Sexual transmission of human immunodeficiency virus: Virus entry into the male and female genital tract. *Fertility and Sterility, 54*, 1–18.

ALEXANDER, N. J. (1994). Vaccines for contraception: A summary. *Reproduction Fertility Development, 6*, 417–419.

ALEXANDER, P. C. (1992). Application of attachment theory to the study of sexual abuse. *Journal of Consulting and Clinical Psychology, 60*, 185–195.

ALLEN, D. M. (1980). Young male prostitutes: A psychosocial study. *Archives of Sexual Behavior, 9*, 399–426.

ALLEN, L. S., & GORSKI, R. A. (1992). Sexual orientation and the size of the anterior commissure in the human brain. *Proceedings of the National Academy of Sciences of the U.S.A., 89*, 7199–7202.

ALLEN, M. C., DONAHUE, P. K., & DUSMAN, A. E. (1993). The limit of viability—neonatal outcome of infants born at 22 to 25 weeks gestation. *New England Journal of Medicine, 329*, 1597–1601.

ALLGEIER, A. R., & ALLGEIER E. R. (1988). *Sexual interactions* (2nd ed.). Lexington, MA: D.C. Heath.

ALLGEIER, E. R. (1985, July). Are you ready for sex?: Informed consent for sexual intimacy. *SIECUS Report, 13*, 8–9.

ALLGEIER, E. R., & MURNEN, S. K. (1985, March). Perception of parents as sexual beings: Pocs and Godow revisited. *SIECUS Report, 4*, 11–12.

AL SAMARAI, A. M. et al. (1989). Sequential genital infections with herpes simplex virus types 1 and 2. *Genitourin Medicine, 65*, 39–41.

ALTER, M. J. et al. (1989). Importance of heterosexual activity in the transmission of hepatitis B and non-A, non-B hepatitis. *Journal of the American Medical Association, 262*, 1201–1205.

ALTHOF, S. E. (1994). A therapist's perspective on the false memory controversy. *Journal of Sex Education and Therapy, 20*, 246–254.

ALTHOF, S. et al. (1991). Sexual, psychological, and marital impact of self-injection of papaverine and phentolamine: A long-term prospective study. *Journal of Sex and Marital Therapy, 17*, 101–112.

ALZATE, H., & HOCH, Z. (1986). The "G-spot" and "female ejaculation": A current appraisal. *Journal of Sex and Marital Therapy, 12*, 211–220.

ALZATE, H., & LONDONO, M. L. (1984). Vaginal erotic sensitivity. *Journal of Sex and Marital Therapy, 10*, 49–56.

AMERICAN ACADEMY OF ALLERGY AND IMMUNOLOGY. (1986). Candidiasis hypersensitivity syndrome. *Journal of Allergy and Clinical Immunology, 78*, 271–273.

AMERICAN ACADEMY OF PEDIATRICS AND AMERICAN COLLEGE OF OBSTETRICIANS AND GYNECOLOGISTS (1983). *Guidelines For Perinatal Care.* Evanston, IL.

AMERICAN COLLEGE OF OBSTETRICIANS AND GYNECOLOGISTS. (1985). *Standards for obstetric-gynecologic services.* Washington, DC: Author.

AMERICAN COLLEGE OF PHYSICIANS AND INFECTIOUS DISEASES SOCIETY OF AMERICA. (1994). Human immunodeficiency virus (HIV) infection. *Annals of Internal Medicine, 120*, 310–319.

AMERICAN MEDICAL ASSOCIATION (AMA) (1994). *Health care needs of gay men and lesbians in the U.S. Policy paper adopted December 6.* Chicago: Author.

AMERICAN PSYCHIATRIC ASSOCIATION. (1994). *Diagnostic and statistical manual of mental disorder (DSM-IV)* (4th ed.). Washington, DC: Author.

AMES, K., GORDON, J., & MASON, M. (1991, February 18). Savings plan for a generation. *Newsweek,* p. 71.

AMIR, M. (1971). *Patterns in forcible rape.* Chicago: University of Chicago Press.

AMMAR, H. (1954). *Growing up in an Egyptian village.* London: Routledge & Kegan Paul.

ANDERSCH, B. et al. (1986). Premenstrual complaints: I. Prevalence of premenstrual symptoms in a Swedish urban population. *Journal of Psychosomatic Obstetrics and Gynecology, 5*, 39–49.

ANDERSON, D., & CHRISTENSON, G. (1991). Ethnic breakdown of AIDS related knowledge and attitudes from the national student health survey. *Journal of Health Education, 22*, 30–34.

ANDERSON, J. E., & DAHLBERG, L. L. (1992). High-risk sexual behavior in the general population. *Sexually Transmitted Diseases, 19*, 320–325.

ANDERSON, P. B. (1989). *Adversarial sexual beliefs and past experience of sexual abuse of college females as predictors of their sexual aggression toward adolescent and adult males.* Unpublished doctoral dissertation, New York University, New York.

ANDERSON, P. B. (1991). Can men be the victim of unwanted sexual intercourse? In B. M. King, C. J. Camp, & A. Downey (Eds.), *Human sexuality today* (p. 370). Englewood Cliffs, NJ: Prentice Hall.

ANDERSON, P. B. et al. (1995). Changes in the telephone calling patterns of adolescent girls. *Adolescence,* in press.

ANDERSON-HUNT, M., & DENNERSTEIN, L. (1994). Increased female sexual response after oxytocin. *British Medical Journal, 309*, 929.

ANGELL, M. (1991). A dual approach to the AIDS epidemic. *New England Journal of Medicine, 324*, 1498–1500.

ANGIER, N. (1991, September 1). The biology of what it means to be gay. *New York Times,* Sect. 4, p. 1.

ANGIER, N. (1992). A male menopause? Jury is still out. *New York Times.*

ANNON, J. (1974). *The behavioral treatment of sexual problems.* Honolulu, HI: Enabling Systems.

ANSELL, J. (1991, September). The crooked penis: Causes and treatment. *Medical Aspects of Human Sexuality,* pp. 32–38.

APFELBAUM, B. (Ed.). (1980). *Expanding the boundaries of sex therapy.* Berkeley, CA: Berkeley Sex Therapy Group.

APT, C., HURLBERT, D. F., & POWELL, D. (1993). Men with hypoactive sexual desire disorder: The role of interpersonal dependency and assertiveness. *Journal of Sex Education and Therapy, 19,* 108–116.

ARAL, S. O., & HOLMES, K. K. (1991). Sexually transmitted diseases in the AIDS era. *Scientific American, 264,* 62–69.

ARAL, S. O., MOSHER, W. D., & CATES, W. (1991). Self-reported pelvic inflammatory disease in the United States, 1988. *Journal of the American Medical Association, 266,* 2570–2573.

ARAL, S. O., MOSHER, W. D., & CATES, W. (1992). Vaginal douching among women of reproductive age in the United States: 1988. *American Journal of Public Health, 82,* 210–214.

ARCHER, D. F. (1990, February). Cardiovascular disease and oral contraceptives. *Medical Aspects of Human Sexuality,* pp. 26–33.

ARCHER, R. L., BERG, J. H., & RUNGE, T. E. (1980). Active and passive observer's attraction to a self-disclosing other. *Journal of Experimental Social Psychology, 16,* 130–145.

ARGENTINE EPISIOTOMY TRIAL COLLABORATIVE GROUP. (1993). Routine vs. selective episiotomy: A randomized controlled trial. *Lancet, 342,* 1517–1518.

ARMSTRONG, P., & FELDMAN, S. (1990). *A wise birth.* New York: William Morrow.

ARRILLAGA, A., ERSEK, R. A., BARICOS, W. M., & RYAN, R. F. (1977, November). Method for the prevention of firm breasts from capsular contraction. *Plastic and Reconstructive Surgery,* pp. 752–754.

ASCH, A., & ROUSSO, H. (1985). Therapists with disabilities: Theoretical and clinical issues. *Psychiatry, 48,* 1–12.

ASCH, R. H., ELLSWORTH, L. R., BALMACEDA, J. P., & WONG, P. C. (1984). Pregnancy after translaparoscopic gamete intra-fallopian transfer [Letter]. *Lancet, 2,* 1034–1035.

ASCHER, M. S. et al. (1993). Does drug use cause AIDS? *Nature (London), 362,* 103–104.

ASKEW, M. W. (1965). Courtly love: Neurosis as institution. *Psychoanalytic Review, 52,* 19–29.

ASSALIAN, P. (1994). Premature ejaculation: Is it psychogenic? *Journal of Sex Education and Therapy, 20,* 1–4.

ATHANASIOU, R., SHAVER, P., & TAVRIS, C. (1970, July). Sex. *Psychology Today,* pp. 37–52.

ATRASH, H. K., FRIEDE, A., & HOGUE, C. J. R. (1987). Ectopic pregnancy mortality in the United States, 1970–83. *Obstetrics and Gynecology, 70,* 817–822.

ATWOOD, J. D., & GAGNON, J. (1987). Masturbatory behavior in college youth. *Journal of Sex Education and Therapy, 13,* 35–42.

AUGER, J., KUNSTMANN, J. M., CZYGLIK, F., & JOUANNET, P. (1995). Decline in semen quality among fertile men in Paris during the past 20 years. *New England Journal of Medicine, 332,* 281–285.

AXINN, W. G., & THORNTON, A. (1992). The relationship between cohabitation and divorce: Selectivity or causal influence? *Demography, 29,* 357–374.

AYOOLA, E. A. (1988). Viral hepatitis in Africa. In A. J. Zuckerman (Ed.), *Viral hepatitis and liver disease.* New York: Alan R. Liss.

BACCHETTI, P., & MOSS, A. R. (1989). Incubation period of AIDS in San Francisco. *Nature (London), 338,* 251–253.

BACHMAN, G. A. (1989). Brief sexual inquiry in gynecologic practice. Part 1. *Obstetrics and Gynecology, 73,* 425–427.

BACHMANN, G. (1992). Using androgens to increase libido. *Medical Aspects of Human Sexuality, 26,* 6.

BACHRACH, C. A. (1987). Cohabitation and reproductive behavior in the U.S. *Demography, 24,* 623–637.

BACHRACH, C. A., & HORN, M. C. (1987). Married and unmarried couples—United States, 1982: Data from the National Survey of Family Growth. *Vital Health Statistics, 23,* 1–52.

BAIER, J. L. (1990). Sexual harassment of university students by faculty members at a Southern research university. *The College Student Affairs Journal, 10* (2), 4–11.

BAILEY, J. M., BOBROW, D., WOLFE, M., & MIKACH, S. (1995). Sexual orientation of adult sons of gay fathers. *Developmental Psychology, 31,* 124–129.

BAILEY, J. M., & PILLARD, R. C. (1991). A genetic study of male sexual orientation. *Archives of General Psychiatry, 48,* 1089–1096.

BAILEY, J. M., PILLARD, R. L., NEALE, M. C., & AGYEI, Y. (1993). Heritable factors influence sexual orientation in women. *Archives of General Psychiatry, 50,* 217–223.

BAILEY, J. M., & ZUCKER, K. J. (1995). Childhood sex-typed behavior and sexual orientation: A conceptual analysis and quantitative review. *Developmental Psychology, 31,* 43–55.

BAIRD, P. A., & MacGILLIVRAY, B. (1982). Children of incest. *Journal of Pediatrics, 101,* 854–858.

BAKER, B. (1990). Birth control. *Common Cause Magazine, 16*(3), 11–14.

BAKWIN, H. (1974). Erotic feelings in infants and young children. *Medical Aspects of Human Sexuality, 8,* 200–215.

BALDWIN, J. D., & BALDWIN, J. I. (1988). Factors affecting AIDS-related sexual risk-taking behavior among college students. *Journal of Sex Research, 25,* 181–196.

BALDWIN, J. I., WHITELEY, S., & BALDWIN, J. D. (1990). Changing AIDS- and fertility-related behavior: The effectiveness of sexual education. *Journal of Sex Research, 27,* 245–262.

BALLARD-REISCH, D., & ELTON, M. (1992). Gender orientation and the Bem sex role inventory: A psychological construct revisited. *Sex Roles, 27,* 291–306.

BALMARY, M. (1982). *Psychoanalyzing psychoanalysis.* Baltimore: Johns Hopkins University Press.

BANCROFT, J. (1980). Endocrinology of sexual function. *Clinical Obstetrics and Gynecology, 7,* 253–281.

BANCROFT, J. (1984). Hormones and human sexual behavior. *Journal of Sex and Marital Therapy, 10,* 3–21.

BANCROFT, J. et al. (1983). Mood, sexuality, hormones, and the menstrual cycle: III. Sexuality and the role of androgens. *Psychosomatic Medicine, 45,* 509–524.

BANDURA, A., & WALTERS, R. H. (1963). *Social learning and personality development.* New York: Holt, Rinehart & Winston.

BANK, S. P., & KAHN, M. (1982). *The sibling bond.* New York: Basic Books.

BARBACH, L. G. (1976). *For yourself: The fulfillment of female sexuality.* New York: Anchor/Doubleday.

BARBACH, L. G. (1980). *Women discover orgasm.* New York: Free Press.

BARBACH, L. G. (1982). *For each other: Sharing sexual intimacy.* Garden City, NY: Anchor Press/Doubleday.

BARBAREE, H. E., & MARSHALL, W. L. (1991). The role of male sexual arousal in rape: 6 models. *Journal of Consulting and Clinical Psychology, 59,* 621–630.

BARBAREE, H. E., MARSHALL, W. L., & LANTHEIR, R. (1979). Deviant sexual arousal in rapists. *Behavior Research and Therapy, 17,* 215–222.

BARBIERI, R. L., & GORDON, A. M. C. (1991). Hormonal therapy of endometriosis: The estradiol target. *Fertility and Sterility, 56,* 820–822.

BARDONI, B. et al. (1994). A dosage sensitive locus at chromosome XP21 is involved in male to female sex reversal. *Nature Genetics, 7,* 497–501.

BARNARD, M. A., McKEGANEY, N. P., & LEYLAND, A. H. (1993). Risk behaviors among male clients of female prostitutes. *British Medical Journal, 307,* 361–362.

BARNETT, M. A. et al. (1992). Factors affecting reactions to a rape victim. *Journal of Psychology, 126,* 609–620.

BARON, L., STRAUS, M., & JAFFEE, D. (1987). Legitimate violence, violent attitudes, and rape: A test of the cultural spillover theory. *Annals of the New York Academy of Sciences, SR121,* 1–23.

BARON, M. (1993). Genetics and human sexual orientation. *Biological Psychiatry, 33,* 759–761.

BARRATT, C. L. R., CHAUHAN, M., & COOKE, J. D. (1990). Donor insemination—a look to the future. *Fertility and Sterility, 54,* 375–387.

BARRETT, R. L., & ROBINSON, B. E. (1990). *Gay fathers.* Lexington, MA: Lexington Books.

BARROW, G., & SMITH, T. (1992). Aging, ageism, and society. St. Paul, MI: West.

BARRY, H., III, BACON, M. K., & CHILD, I. L. (1957). A cross-cultural survey of some sex differences in socialization. *Journal of Abnormal and Social Psychology, 55,* 327–332.

BARRY, H., III, & SCHLEGEL, A. (1984). Measurements of adolescent sexual behavior in the standard sample of societies. *Ethnology, 23,* 315–329.

BARSON, M. (1984, March). Penis size: A sexual or political issue? *Cosmopolitan,* pp. 224–226.

BART, P. (1980). *Avoiding rape: A study of victims and avoiders.* Final Report. Rockville, MD: National Institute of Mental Health. (MH29311)

BART, P. B. (1971). Depression in middle-aged women. In V. G. Gornick & B. K. Moran (Eds.), *Women in sexist society.* New York: Basic Books.

BARTH, R. J., & KINDER, B. N. (1987). The mislabeling of sexual impulsivity. *Journal of Sex and Marital Therapy, 13,* 15–23.

BARUCH, G. K., & BARNETT, R. (1986). Role quality, multiple role involvement, and psychological well-being in midlife women. *Journal of Personality and Social Psychology, 51,* 578–585.

BATEMAN, D. A., NG, S. K. C., HANSEN, C. A., & HEAGARTY, M. C. (1993). The effects of intrauterine cocaine exposure in newborns. *American Journal of Public Health, 83*, 190–193.

BAUER, H. M., et al. (1991). Human papillomavirus infection in female university students as determined by a PCR-based method. *Journal of the American Medical Association, 265*, 472–477.

BAULIEU, E.-E. (1989). Ru-486 as an antiprogesterone steroid. *Journal of the American Medical Association, 262*, 1808–1814.

BAYS, J., & CHADWICK, D. (1993). Medical diagnosis of the sexually abused child. *Child Abuse & Neglect, 17*, 91–110.

BECK, M. et al. (1992). Menopause: The search for straight talk and safe treatment. *Newsweek*, May 25, 71–79.

BECKER, J. V., & ABEL, G. G. (1985). Methodological and ethical issues in evaluating and treating adolescent sex offenders. In E. M. Otey & G. D. Ryan (Eds.), *Adolescent sex offenders: Issues in research and treatment* (pp. 109–129). Rockville, MD: USDHHS.

BECKER, J. V., & COLEMAN, E. M. (1988). Incest. In V. B. Van Hasselt, R. L. Morrison, A. S. Bellack, & M. Hersen (Eds.), *Handbook of family violence*. New York: Plenum.

BECKER, J. V. et al. (1984). Sexual problems of sexual assault survivors. *Women and Health, 9*, 5–20.

BECKMAN, L. J., HARVEY, S. M., & MURRAY, J. (1992). Perceived contraceptive attributes of current and former users of the vaginal sponge. *Journal of Sex Research, 29*, 31–42.

BEER, A. E. (1989). Immunology, contraception, and preeclampsia. *Journal of the American Medical Association, 262*, 3184.

BEERNINK, F. J., DMOWSKI, W. P., & ERICSSON, R. J. (1993). Sex preselection through albumin separation of sperm. *Fertility and Sterility, 59*, 382–386.

BEGLEY, S., & GLICK, D. (1994, March 21). The estrogen complex. *Newsweek*, pp. 76–77.

BEHRMAN, R. E., & VAUGHAN, V. C., III. (1983). *Pediatrics*. Philadelphia: Saunders.

BEITCHMAN, J. H. et al. (1991). A review of the short-term effects of child sexual abuse. *Child Abuse & Neglect, 15*, 537–556.

BEITCHMAN, J. H. et al. (1992). A review of the long-term effects of child sexual abuse. *Child Abuse & Neglect, 16*, 101–118.

BELCASTRO, P. (1985). Sexual behavior differences between black and white students. *Journal of Sex Research, 21*, 56–67.

BELL, A. P., & WEINBERG, M. S. (1978). *Homosexualities*. New York: Simon & Schuster.

BELL, A. P., WEINBERG, M. S., & HAMMERSMITH, S. K. (1981). *Sexual preference: Its development in men and women*. Bloomington: Indiana University Press.

BELL, L. (Ed.). (1987). *Good girls/bad girls: Sex trade workers confront feminists*. Seattle, WA: Seal Press.

BELL, T. A. et al. (1992). Chronic chlamydia trachomatis infections in infants. *Journal of the American Medical Association, 267*, 400–402.

BELZER, G. (1981). Orgasmic expulsions of women: A review and heuristic inquiry. *Journal of Sex Research, 17*, 1–12.

BEM, S. L. (1974). The measurement of psychological androgyny. *Journal of Consulting and Clinical Psychology, 42*, 155–162.

BEM, S. L. (1979). Theory and measurement of androgyny: A reply to Pedhazur-Tetenbaum and Locksley-Colten critiques. *Journal of Personality and Social Psychology, 37*, 1047–1054.

BEM, S. L. (1981). Gender schema theory: A cognitive account of sex typing. *Psychological Review, 88*, 354–364.

BEM, S. L. (1983). Gender schema theory and its implications for child development: Raising gender-aschematic children in a gender schematic society. *Signs, 8*, 598–616.

BENSON, D., CHARLTON, C., & GOODHART, F. (1992). Acquaintance rape on campus: A literature review. *Journal of American College Health, 40*, 157–165.

BENSON, D., & THOMPSON, G. (1982). Sexual harassment on a university campus: The confluence of authority relations, sexual interest, and gender stratification. *Social Problems, 29*, 236–251.

BENSON, R. (1985). Vacuum cleaner injury to penis: A common urologic problem? *Urology, 25*, 41–44.

BENTLER, P. M., & PEELER, W. H. (1979). Models of female orgasm. *Archives of Sexual Behavior, 8*, 405–424.

BERENBAUM, S. A., & SNYDER, E. (1995). Early hormonal influences on childhood sex-typed activity and playmate preferences: Implications for the development of sexual orientation. *Developmental Psychology, 31*, 31–42.

BERGEN, D. J., & WILLIAMS, J. E. (1991). Sex stereotypes in the United States revisited: 1972–1988. *Sex Roles, 24*, 413–423.

BERGER, C. J. (1980). Medical risks associated with "natural" family planning. *Advances in Planned Parenthood, 15*, 1.

BERGER, G. S., WESTRÖM, L. V., & WOLNER-HANSSEN, P. (1992). Definition of pelvic inflammatory disease. In G. S. Berger & L. V. Weström (Eds.), *Pelvic inflammatory disease*. New York: Raven Press.

BERGER, R. M. (1982). The unseen minority: Older gays and lesbians. *Social Work, 27*, 236–242.

BERGLER, G., & KROGER, W. S. (1954). *Kinsey's myth of female sexuality*. New York: Grune & Stratton.

BERGSTRÖM, R. et al. (1993). Detection of preinvasive cancer of the cervix and the subsequent reduction in invasive cancer. *Journal of the National Cancer Institute, 85*, 1050–1057.

BERK, F. (1985). *The gender factory: The apportionment of work in American households*. New York: Plenum.

BERKLEY, S. (1993). AIDS in the developing world: An epidemiologic overview. *Clinical Infectious Diseases, 17*, S329–S336.

BERKLEY, S. et al. (1990). AIDS and HIV infection in Uganda—are more women infected than men? *AIDS, 4*, 1237–1242.

BERKOWITZ, A. (1992). College men as perpetrators of acquaintance rape and sexual assault: A review of recent research. *Journal of American College Health, 40*, 175–181.

BERNARD, M. L., & BERNARD, J. L. (1983). Violent intimacy: The family as a model for love relationships. *Family Relations, 32*, 282–286.

BERNSTEIN, A. C. (1976, January). How children learn about sex and birth. *Psychology Today, 9*, 31–35, 66.

BERNSTEIN, L. et al. (1994). Physical exercise and reduced risk of breast cancer in young women. *Journal of the National Cancer Institute, 86*, 1403–1408.

BERSCHEID, E. (1982). Interpersonal attraction. In E. Aronson & G. Lindzey (Eds.), *Handbook of social psychology* (3rd ed.). Reading, MA: Addison-Wesley.

BERSCHEID, E., & WALSTER, E. (1974). A little bit about love. In T. L. Huston (Ed.), *Foundations of interpersonal attraction* (pp. 355–381). New York: Academic Press.

BERSCHEID, E., & WALSTER, E. (1978). *Interpersonal attraction* (2nd ed.). Reading, MA: Addison-Wesley.

BESS, B. E., & JANUS, S. S. (1976). Prostitution. In B. Sadock et al. (Eds.), *The sexual experience*. Baltimore: Williams & Wilkins.

BIEBER, I. (1965). Clinical aspects of male inversion. In J. Marmor (Ed.), *Sexual inversion* (pp. 248–267). New York: Basic Books.

BIEBER, I. et al. (1962). *Homosexuality: A psychoanalytic study*. New York: Basic Books.

BIERNAT, M. (1991). Gender stereotypes and the relationship between masculinity and femininity: A developmental analysis. *Journal of Personality and Social Psychology, 61*, 351–365.

BILLER, H. (1969). Father absence, maternal encouragement, and sex role development in kindergarten-age boys. *Child Development, 40*, 539–545.

BILLER, H., & BAHM, R. (1971). Father absence, perceived maternal behavior, and masculinity of self-concept among junior high school boys. *Developmental Psychology, 4*, 178–181.

BILLER, H., & WEISS, S. (1970). The father-daughter relationship and the personality development of the female. *Journal of Genetic Psychology, 116*, 79–93.

BILLINGS, E. L., BILLINGS, J. J., & CATARINCH, M. (1974). *Atlas of the ovulation method*. Collegeville, MN: Liturgical Press.

BILLY, J. O. G., TANFER, K., GRADY, W. R., & KLEPINGER, D. H. (1993). The sexual behavior of men in the United States. *Family Planning Perspectives, 25*, 52–60.

BINKIN, N. J., & ALEXANDER, Z. R. (1983). Neonatal herpes: How can it be prevented? *Journal of the American Medical Association, 250*, 3094–3095.

BIRD, K. D. (1991). The use of spermicide containing nonoxynol-9 in the prevention of HIV infection. *AIDS, 5*, 791–796.

BIRNS, B., & STERNGLANZ, S. H. (1983). Sex-role socialization: Looking back and looking ahead. In M. B. Liss (Ed.), *Social and cognitive skills: Sex roles and children's play*. New York: Academic Press.

BISHOP, P., & LIPSITZ, A. (1988, November). *Sexual behavior among college students in the AIDS era: A comparative study*. Paper presented at the annual meeting for the Scientific Study of Sex, San Francisco.

BITTLES, A. H., MASON, W. M., GREENE, J., & RAO, N. A. (1991). Reproductive behavior and health in consanguineous marriages. *Science, 252*, 789–794.

BLACKMAN, A., DOLAN, B. & McDOWELL, J. (1991, September 30). Making babies. *Newsweek*, pp. 56–63.

BLACKMORE, C. A., KEEGAN, R. A., & CATES, W., JR., (1982). Diagnosis and treatment of sexually transmitted diseases in rape victims. *Review of Infectious Diseases, 4*(Suppl), S877– S882.

BLAIR, C. D., & LANYON, R. I. (1981). Exhibitionism: Etiology and treatment. *Psychological Bulletin, 89*, 439–463.

BLANCHARD, R. (1993). The she-male phenomenon and the concept of partial autogynephilia. *Journal of Sex and Marital Therapy, 19,* 69–76.

BLANCHARD, R., & COLLINS, R. I. (1993). Men with sexual interest in transvestites, transsexuals, and she-males. *Journal of Nervous and Mental Disease, 181,* 570–575.

BLANCHARD, R., STEINER, B., & CLEMMENSEN, L. (1985). Gender dysphoria, gender reorientation, and the clinical management of transsexualism. *Journal of Consulting and Clinical Psychology, 53,* 295–304.

BLANCHARD, R. et al. (1989). Prediction of regrets in postoperative transsexuals. *Canadian Journal of Psychiatry, 34,* 43–45.

BLANCHARD-FIELDS, F., & SUHRER-ROUSSEL, L. (1992). Adaptive coping and social cognitive development of women. In E. E. Guice (Ed.), *Women and aging: Now and the future?* Westport, CT: Greenwood Press.

BLANCHE, S. et al. (1994). Relation of the course of HIV infection in children to the severity of the disease in their mothers at delivery. *New England Journal of Medicine, 330,* 308–312.

BLOCK, J. (1976). Issues, problems, and pitfalls in assessing sex differences. *Merrill-Palmer Quarterly, 22,* 283–308.

BLOOD, R. O., JR. (1967). *Love match and arranged marriage.* New York: Free Press.

BLOOMFIELD, H., & VETTESE S. (1989). *Lifemates: The love fitness program for a lasting relationship.* New York: New American Library.

BLUMBERG, M. L., & LESTER, D. (1991). High school and college students' attitudes toward rape. *Adolescence, 26,* 727–729.

BLUME, J. (1970). *Are you there God? It's me, Margaret.* Englewood Cliffs, NJ: Bradbury Press.

BLUMSTEIN, P. W., & SCHWARTZ, P. (1983). *American couples.* New York: William Morrow.

BLYTH, B., & DUCKETT, J. W. (1991). Gonadal differentiation: A review of physiological process and influencing factors based on recent experimental evidence. *Journal of Urology, 145,* 689–694.

BOGREN, L. (1991). Changes in sexuality in women and men during pregnancy. *Archives of Sexual Behavior, 20,* 35–46.

BOHLEN, J. G., HELD, J. P., & SANDERSON, M. D. (1980). The male orgasm: Pelvic contractions measured by anal probe. *Archives of Sexual Behavior, 9,* 503–521.

BOHLEN, J. G., HELD, J. P., SANDERSON, M. O., & AHLGREN, A. (1982). The female orgasm: Pelvic contractions. *Archives of Sexual Behavior, 11,* 367–386.

BOKLAGE, C. E. (1990). Survival probability of human conceptions from fertilization to term. *International Journal of Fertility, 35,* 75–94.

BOLES, J., & ELIFSON, K. W. (1994). Sexual identity and HIV: The male prostitute. *Journal of Sex Research, 31,* 39–46.

BOLLEN, N. et al. (1991). The incidence of multiple pregnancy after in vitro fertilization and embryo transfer, gamete, or zygote intrafallopian transfer. *Fertility and Sterility, 55,* 314–318.

BONGAARTS, J., REINING, P., WAY, P., & CONANT, F. (1989). The relationship between male circumcision and HIV infection in African populations. *AIDS, 3,* 373–377.

BOOTH, A., & JOHNSON, D. (1988). Premarital cohabitation and marital success. *Journal of Family Issues, 9,* 255–272.

BOSTON WOMEN'S HEALTH BOOK COLLECTIVE. (1984). *The new our bodies, ourselves.* New York: Simon & Schuster.

BOSWELL, J. (1980). *Christianity, social tolerance, and homosexuality.* Chicago: University of Chicago Press.

BOYER, D., & FINE, D. (1992). Sexual abuse as a factor in adolescent pregnancy and child maltreatment. *Family Planning Perspectives, 24,* 4–11.

BOZETTE, F. W. (Ed.). (1987). *Gay and lesbian parents.* New York: Praeger.

BRACKBILL, Y. (1979). Obstetrical medication and infant behavior. In J. D. Osofsky (Ed.), *Handbook of infant development.* New York: Wiley(Interscience).

BRADFORD, J. M. W., BOULET, J., & PAWLAK, A. (1992). The paraphelias: A multiplicity of deviant behaviors. *Canadian Journal of Psychiatry, 37,* 104–107.

BRADFORD, J. M. W., & PAWLAK, A. (1993a). Double-blind placebo crossover study of cyproterone acetate in the treatment of the paraphelias. *Archives of Sexual Behavior, 22,* 383–402.

BRADFORD, J. M. W., & PAWLAK, A. (1993b). Effects of cyproterone acetate on sexual arousal patterns of pedophiles. *Archives of Sexual Behavior, 22,* 629–641.

BRADLEY, R. A. (1981). *Husband coached childbirth.* New York: Harper & Row.

BRADLEY, S. J. et al. (1991). Interim report of the DSM-IV Subcommittee on Gender Identity Disorders. *Archives of Sexual Behavior, 20,* 333–343.

BRADY, E. C. et al. (1991). Date rape: Expectations, avoidance, strategies, and attitudes toward victims. *Journal of Social Psychology, 131,* 427–429.

BRANCH, D. W. (1990). Autoimmunity and pregnancy loss. *Journal of the American Medical Association, 264,* 1453–1454.

BRANDT, E. N., JR. (1982). Physicians and sexually transmitted disease: A call to action. *Journal of the American Medical Association, 248,* 2032.

BRATT, C. S. (1984). Incest statutes and the fundamental right of marriage: Is Oedipus free to marry? *Family Law Quarterly, 18,* 257–309.

BRAZELTON, T. B. (1969). *Infants and mothers.* New York: Delacorte Press/ Seymour Lawrence.

BRAZELTON, T. B. (1970). Effect of prenatal drugs on the behavior of the neonate. *American Journal of Psychiatry, 126,* 1261–1266.

BRECHER, E. M. (1984). *Love, sex, and aging.* Mount Vernon, NY: Consumers Union.

BREEDLOVE, S. M. (1994). Sexual differentiation of the human nervous system. *Annual Review of Psychology, 45,* 389–418.

BRESLOW, N., EVANS, L., & LANGLEY, J. (1985). On the prevalence and roles of females in the sadomasochistic subculture. *Archives of Sexual Behavior, 14,* 303–317.

BRESLOW, N., EVANS, L., & LANGLEY, J. (1986). Comparisons among heterosexual, bisexual, and homosexual sadomasochists. *Journal of Homosexuality, 13,* 83–107.

BRETSCHNEIDER, J. G., & McCOY, N. L. (1988). Sexual interest and behavior in healthy 80-to 102-year-olds. *Archives of Sexual Behavior, 17,* 109–129.

BREWER, S. S., & BREWER, T. (1985). *What every pregnant woman should know: The truth about diet and drugs in pregnancy.* New York: Penguin Press.

BRIDGES, J. S., & McGRAIL, C. A. (1989). Attributions of responsibility for date and stranger rape. *Sex Roles, 21,* 273–286.

BRILL, K., NORPOTH, T., SCHNITKER, J., & ALBRING, M. (1991). Clinical experience with a modern low-dose oral contraceptive in almost 100,000 users. *Contraception, 43,* 101–110.

BRINGLE, R. G., ROACH, S., ADLER, C., & EVENBECK, S. (1977). *Correlates of jealousy.* Paper presented at the annual meeting of the Midwestern Psychological Association, Chicago.

BRINTON, L. et al. (1989). The male factor in the etiology of cervical cancer among sexually monogamous women. *International Journal of Cancer, 44,* 199–203.

BRITTON, D. M. (1990). Homophobia and homo sociality: An analysis of boundary maintenance. *Sociological Quarterly, 31,* 423–439.

BRODSKY, S. L. (1976). Prevention of rape: Deterrence by the potential victim. In M. J. Walker & S. L. Brodsky (Eds.), *Sexual assault.* Lexington MA: D. C. Heath.

BRODY, J. E. (1988, March 10). Personal health. *New York Times,* p. 16.

BROMHAM, D. R. (1993). Intrauterine contraceptive devices—A reappraisal. *British Medical Bulletin, 49,* 100–123.

BROMWICH, P., COHEN, J., STEWART, I., & WALKER, A. (1994). Decline in sperm counts: An artifact of changed reference range of "normal"? *British Medical Journal, 309,* 19–22.

BROOKS, J., RUBLE, D. N., & CLARKE, A. E. (1977). College women's attitudes and expectations concerning menstrual-related changes. *Psychosomatic Medicine, 39,* 288–298.

BROOKS-GUNN, J. et al. (1994). Early intervention in low-birth-weight premature infants. *Journal of the American Medical Association, 272,* 1257–1262.

BROSIUS, H.-B., WEAVER, J. B., III, & STAAB, J. F. (1993). Exploring the social and sexual "reality" of contemporary pornography. *Journal of Sex Research, 30,* 161–170.

BROUDE, G. J., & GREENE, S. J. (1976). Cross-cultural codes on twenty sexual attitudes and practices. *Ethnology, 15,* 409–429.

BROVERMAN, J. K. et al. (1972). Sex-role stereotypes: A current appraisal. *Journal of Social Issues, 28,* 59–78.

BROWN, D. (1990). The penis pin. In V. Sutlive (Ed.), *Female and male in Borneo: Contributions and challenges to gender studies* (pp. 435–454). Borneo: Borneo Research Council.

BROWN, G. R., & COLLIER, L. (1989). Transvestites' women revisited: A nonpatient sample. *Archives of Sexual Behavior, 18,* 73–83.

BROWN, J. D., CHILDERS, K. W., & WASZAK, C. (1990). Television and adolescent sexuality. *Journal of Adolescent Health Care, 11,* 62–70.

BROWN, J. D., & NEWCOMER, S. F. (1991). Television viewing and adolescents' sexual behavior. *Journal of Homosexuality, 21,* 77–91.

BROWNMILLER, S. (1975). *Against our will: Men, women, and rape.* New York: Simon & Schuster.

BROWNMILLER, S. (1993, January 4). Making female bodies the battlefield. *Newsweek,* p. 37.

BRUNHAM, R. C. et al. (1988). Etiology and outcome of acute pelvic inflammatory disease. *Journal of Infectious Diseases, 158,* 510–517.

BRYANT, H., & BRASHIER, P. (1995). Breast implants and breast cancer—Reanalysis of a linkage study. *New England Journal of Medicine, 332,* 1535–1539.

BRYANT, J., & BROWN, D. (1989). Uses of pornography. In Z. Dolf & B. Jennings (Eds.), *Pornography: Research advances and policy considerations.* Hillsdale, NJ: Erlbaum.

BRYNER, C. (1989). Recurrent toxic shock syndrome. *American Family Physician, 39,* 157–164.

BRYSON, J., & SHETTEL-NEUBER, J. (1978, February). Unbalanced relationships: Who becomes jealous of whom. Cited by James Hasset in *Psychology Today, 11,* 26–29.

BUCHANAN, R. (1975, July). Breast-feeding: Aid to infant health and fertility control. *Population Reports, Series* J.

BUCHBINDER, S. P. et al. (1994). Long-term HIV-1 infection without immunologic progression. *AIDS, 8,* 1123–1128.

BUCKLEY, W. E. et al. (1988). Estimated prevalence of anabolic steroid use among male high school seniors. *Journal of the American Medical Association, 260,* 3441–3445.

BUFFUM, J. (1988). Substance abuse and high-risk sexual behaviors: Drugs and sex—the dark side. *Journal of Psychoactive Drugs, 20,* 165–168.

BUFFUM, J. et al. (1981). Drugs and sexual function. In H. Lief (Ed.), *Sexual problems in medical practice.* Monroe, WI: American Medical Association.

BUHRICH, N. (1976). A heterosexual transvestite club: Psychiatric aspects. *Australian and New Zealand Journal of Psychiatry, 10,* 331–335.

BULLOUGH, V., BULLOUGH, B., & SMITH, R. (1983). Comparative study of male transvestites, male to female transsexuals, and male homosexuals. *Journal of Sex Research, 19,* 238–257.

BULLOUGH, V. L. (1981). Age at menarche: A misunderstanding. *Science, 213,* 365–366.

BUMPASS, L. L., & SWEET, J. A. (1989). Childrens' experience in single-parent families: Implications of cohabitation and marital transitions. *Family Planning Perspectives, 21,* 256–260.

BUMPASS, L. L., SWEET, J. A., & CHERLIN, A. (1991). The role of cohabitation in declining rates of marriage. *Journal of Marriage and the Family, 53,* 913–927.

BURGER, M. P. M. et al. (1993). Cigarette smoking and human papillomavirus in patients with reported cervical cytological abnormality. *British Medical Journal, 306,* 749–755.

BURGESS, A. W., HARMAN, C., McCAUSLAND, M., & POWERS, P. (1984). Response patterns in children and adolescents exploited through sex rings and pornography. *American Journal of Psychiatry, 141,* 656–662.

BURGESS, A. W., & HOLMSTRÖM, L. L. (1974). Rape trauma syndrome. *American Journal of Psychiatry, 131,* 981–986.

BURGESS, A. W., & HOLMSTRÖM, L. L. (1979). Rape: Sexual disruption and recovery. *American Journal of Orthopsychiatry, 49,* 648–657.

BURKE, R. L. (1993). Current status of HSV vaccine development. In B. Roizman, R. J. Whitley, & C. Lopez (Eds.), *The human herpesviruses.* New York: Raven Press.

BURNAM, M. A. et al. (1988). Sexual assault and mental disorders in a community population. *Journal of Consulting and Clinical Psychology, 56,* 843–850.

BURT, M. R. (1980). Cultural myths and supports for rape. *Journal of Personality and Social Psychology, 38,* 217–230.

BURT, M. R., & KATZ, B. L. (1988). Coping strategies and recovery from rape. *Annals of the New York Academy of Sciences, 528,* 345–358.

BURTON, R. (1963). The anatomy of melancholy. In A. M. Witherspoon & F. Warnke (Eds.), *Seventeenth-century prose and poetry* (pp. 132–133). New York: Harcourt Brace Jovanovich. (Original work published in 1651.)

BUSCH, M. P. et al. (1991). Evaluation of screened blood donations for human immunodeficiency virus type-1 infection by culture and DNA amplification of pooled cells. *New England Journal of Medicine, 325,* 1–5.

BUSS, A. (1966). *Psychopathology.* New York: Wiley.

BUSS, D. M. (1985). Human mate selection. *American Scientist, 73,* 47–51.

BUSS, D. M. (1989). Sex differences in human mate selection: Evolutionary hypotheses tested in 37 cultures. *Behavioral and Brain Sciences, 12,* 1–49.

BUSS, D. M. (1994, August). *Evolution of desire: Person, environment, interaction and human mating.* Paper presented at the annual convention of the American Psychological Association, Los Angeles.

BUSS, D. M., & BARNES, M. F. (1987). Preferences in human mate selection. *Journal of Personality and Social Psychology, 50,* 559–570.

BUSS, D. M., LARSEN, R. J., WESTEN, D., & SEMMELROTH, J. (1992). Sex differences in jealousy: Evolution, physiology, and psychology. *Psychological Science, 3,* 251–255.

BUSS, D. M., & SCHMITT, D. P. (1993). Sexual strategies theory: An evolutionary perspective on human mating. *Psychological Review, 100,* 204–232.

BUTLER, C. A. (1976). New data about female sexual response. *Journal of Sex and Marital Therapy, 2,* 40–46.

BUUNK, B., & BRINGLE, R. (1987). Jealousy in love relationships. In D. Perlman & S. Duck (Eds.), *Intimate relationships.* Newbury Park, CA: Sage.

BUVAT, J. et al. (1990). Recent developments in the clinical assessment and diagnosis of erectile dysfunction. In J. Bancroft (Ed.), *Annual review of sex research,* (Vol. 2). (pp. 265–308). Mount Vernon, IA: The Society for the Scientific Study of Sex.

BYE, P. S. T. (1990). Hypersexuality and aggression. In *Male hypersexuality: Aspects of assessment and treatment.* UK: Schering Health Care.

BYNE, W., & PARSONS, B. (1993). Human sexual orientation: The biologic theories reappraised. *Archives of General Psychiatry, 50,* 228–239.

BYRNE, D., CLORE, G., & SMEATON, G. (1986). The attraction hypothesis: Do similar attitudes affect anything? *Journal of Personality and Social Psychology, 51,* 1167–1170.

BYRNE, D., & MURNEN, S. K. (1988). Maintaining loving relationships. In R. J. Sternberg & M. L. Barnes (Eds.), *The psychology of love.* New Haven, CT: Yale University Press.

CACERES, C. F., & VAN GRIENSVEN, G. J. P. (1994). Male homosexual transmission of HIV-1. *AIDS, 8,* 1051–1061.

CADO, S., & LEITENBERG, H. (1990). Guilt reactions to sexual fantasies during intercourse. *Archives of Sexual Behavior, 19,* 49–64.

CAGEN, R. (1986). The cervical cap as a barrier contraceptive. *Contraception, 33,* 487–496.

CALDERONE, M. S. (1983a). Childhood sexuality: Approaching the prevention of sexual disease. In G. Albee et al. (Eds.), *Promoting sexual responsibility and preventing sexual problems.* Hanover, NH: University Press of New England.

CALDERONE, M. S. (1983b). Fetal erection and its message to us. *SIECUS Report, 11* (5/6), 9–10.

CALE, A. R. J. et al. (1990). Does vasectomy accelerate testicular-tumor? Importance of testicular examinations before and after vasectomy. *British Medical Journal, 300,* 370.

CALHOUN, B. C., & WATSON, P. T. (1991). The cost of maternal cocaine abuse: I. Perinatal cost. *Obstetrics and Gynecology, 78,* 731–734.

CALLE, E., MIRACLE-McMAHILL, H. L., THUN, M. J., & HEATH, C. W. (1994). Cigarette smoking and risk of fatal breast cancer. *American Journal of Epidemiology, 139,* 1001–1007.

CALLENDER, C., & KOCHEMS, L. (1987). The North American Berdache. *Current Anthropology, 24,* 443–456.

CAMPOSTRINI, S., & McQUEEN, D. V. (1993). Sexual behavior and exposure to HIV infection: Estimates from a general-population risk index. *American Journal of Public Health, 83,* 1139–1143.

CANAVAN, M. M., MEYER, W. J., III, & HIGGS, D. C. (1992). The female experience of sibling incest. *Journal of Marital and Family Therapy, 18,* 129–142.

CANAVAN, P., & HASKELL, J. (1977). The great American male stereotype. In C. Garney & S. McMahon (Eds.), *Exploring contemporary male/female roles: A facilitator's guide.* LaJolla, CA: University Associates.

CANCIAN, F. M. (1989). Love and the rise of capitalism. In B. J. Risman & P. Schwartz (Eds.), *Gender in intimate relationships: A microstructural approach.* Belmont, CA: Wadsworth.

CANNISTRA, S. A. (1993). Cancer of the ovary. *New England Journal of Medicine, 329,* 1550–1559.

CAPITANO, J. P., & LERCHE, N. W. (1991). Psychosocial factors and disease progression in Simian AIDS: A preliminary report. *AIDS, 5,* 1103–1106.

CAREY, R. F. et al. (1992). Effectiveness of latex condoms as a barrier to human immunodeficiency-sized particles under conditions of simulated use. *Sexually Transmitted Diseases, 19,* 230–234.

CARL, D. (1986). Acquired immune deficiency syndrome: A preliminary examination of the effects on gay couples and coupling. *Journal of Marital and Family Therapy, 12,* 241–247.

CARLSEN, E., GIWERCMAN, A., KEIDING, N., & SKAKKEBACK, N.E. (1992). Evidence for decreasing quality of semen during past 50 years. *British Medical Journal, 305,* 609–613.

CARNES, P. J. (1983). *Out of the shadows: Understanding sexual addiction.* Minneapolis, MN: Compeare Publishers.

CARNES, P. J. (1991). *Don't call it love.* New York: Bantam Books.

CARRIER, J. M. (1980). Homosexual behavior in cross-cultural perspective. In J. Marmor (Ed.), *Homosexual behavior* (pp.100–122). New York: Basic Books.

CARROLL, J., VOLK, K., & HYDE, J. (1985). Differences between males and females in motives for engaging in sexual intercourse. *Archives of Sexual Behavior, 14,* 131–139.

CARTER, S., & SOKOL, J. (1989). *What really happens in bed: A demystification of sex.* New York: M. Evans.

CASTRO, B. A. et al. (1991). Persistent infection of baboons and rhesus monkeys with different strains of HIV-2. *Virology, 184,* 219–226.

CASTRO, K. G. et al. (1988). Transmission of HIV in Belle Glade, Florida: Lessons for other communities in the United States. *Science, 239,* 193–197.

CATALONA, W. et al. (1991). Measurement of prostate-specific antigen in serum as a screening test for prostate cancer. *New England Journal of Medicine, 324,* 1156–1161.

CATANIA, J. A. et al. (1989). Predictors of condom use and multiple partnered sex among sexually active adolescent women: Implications for AIDS-related health interventions. *Journal of Sex Research, 26,* 514–524.

CATANIA, J. A. et al. (1992). Prevalence of AIDS-related risk factors and condom use in the United States. *Science, 258,* 1101–1106.

CATANIA, J. A. et al. (1993). Changes in condom use among Black, Hispanic, and white heterosexuals in San Francisco: The AMEN cohort study. *Journal of Sex Research, 30,* 121–128.

CATE, R. M., & LLOYD, S. A. (1992). *Courtship.* Newbury Park, CA: Sage.

CATES, W., JR., ROLFS, R. T., & ARAL, S. O. (1990). Sexually transmitted diseases, pelvic inflammatory disease and infertility: An epidemiologic update. *Epidemiology Reviews, 12,* 199–220.

CATES, W., JR., STEWART, F. H., & TRUSSELL, J. (1992). Commentary: The quest for women's prophylactic methods—hopes vs. science. *American Journal of Public Health, 82,* 1479–1482.

CATES, W., JR., & STONE, K. M. (1992a). Family planning, sexually transmitted diseases and contraceptive choice: A literature update. Part I. *Family Planning Perspectives, 24,* 75–84.

CATES, W., JR., & STONE, K. M. (1992b). Family planning, sexually transmitted diseases and contraceptive choice: A literature update. Part II. *Family Planning Perspectives, 24*(3), 122–128.

CATOTTI, D. N., CLARKE, P., & CATOE, K. E. (1993). Herpes revisited: Still a cause of concern. *Sexually Transmitted Diseases, 20,* 77–80.

CATTERALL, R. D. (1974). *A short textbook of venereology.* Philadelphia: Lippincott.

CAUTELA, J., & KEARNEY, A. J. (1986). *The covert conditioning handbook.* New York: Springer.

CELENTANO, D. D., KLASSEN, A. C., WEISMAN, C. S., & ROSENSHEIN, N. B. (1987). The role of contraceptive use in cervical cancer: The Maryland cervical cancer case-control study. *American Journal of Epidemiology, 126,* 592–604.

CENTERS FOR DISEASE CONTROL. (1988). Ectopic pregnancies—United States, 1984 and 1985. *Morbidity and Mortality Weekly, 37,* 637–639.

CENTERS FOR DISEASE CONTROL AND PREVENTION. (1992). Revised classification system for HIV infection and expanded surveillance case definitions for AIDS among adolescents and adults. *Morbidity and Mortality Weekly, 41,* 1–19.

Cervical cap: A birth control method with several advantages. (1989). *Contraceptive Technology Update, 10,* 2.

CHAN, D. W. (1990). Sex knowledge, attitudes, and experiences of Chinese medical students in Hong Kong. *Archives of Sexual Behavior, 19,* 73–93.

CHAPPELL, D. (1976). Cross-cultural research on forcible rape. *International Journal of Criminology and Penology, 4,* 295–304.

CHAPPELL, D., & JAMES, J. (1976). *Victim selection and apprehension from the rapist's perspective: A preliminary investigation.* Paper presented at the Second International Symposium on Victimology, Boston.

CHASNOFF, I. J., LANDRESS, H., & BARRETT, M. (1990). The prevalence of illicit drug or alcohol use during pregnancy and discrepancies in mandatory reporting in Pinellas County, Florida. *New England Journal of Medicine, 322,* 1202–1206.

CHECK, J. (1984, August). *Mass media sexual violence: Content analysis and counteractive measures.* Paper presented at the annual meeting of the American Psychological Association, Toronto.

CHI, I.-C. (1993a). Safety and efficacy issues of progestin-only oral contraceptives—An epidemiologic approach. *Contraception, 47,* 1–21.

CHI, I.-C. (1993b). What we have learned from recent IUD studies: A researcher's perspective. *Contraception, 48,* 81–108.

CHIAPPA, J. A., & FORISH, J. J. (1976). *The VD book.* New York: Holt, Rinehart & Winston.

CHIASSON, M. et al. (1990). Risk factors for human immunodeficiency virus type 1 (HIV-1) infection in patients at a sexually transmitted disease clinic in New York City. *American Journal of Epidemiology, 131,* 208–220.

CHIAZZE, R., JR. et al. (1968). The length and variability of the human menstrual cycle. *Journal of the American Medical Association, 203*(6), 89–92.

CHIN, J. (1990). Current and future dimensions of the HIV/AIDS pandemic in women and children. *Lancet, 336,* 221–224.

CHIPOURAS, S. et al. (1979). *Who cares? A handbook on sex education and counseling services for disabled people.* Washington, DC: George Washington University.

CHITWOOD, D. D. et al. (1990). HIV seropositivity of needles from shooting galleries in South Florida. *American Journal of Public Health, 80,* 150–152.

CHODOROW, N. (1978). *The reproduction of mothering: Psychoanalysis and the sociology of gender.* Berkeley: University of California Press.

CHOI, K.-H., CATANIA, J. A., & DOLCINI, M. M. (1994). Extramarital sex and HIV risk behavior among US adults: Results from the National AIDS Behavioral Survey. *American Journal of Public Health, 84,* 2003–2007.

CHOI, K.-H., & COATES, T. J. (1994). Prevention of HIV infection. *AIDS, 8,* 1371–1389.

CHOI, K.-H., RICKMAN, R., & CATANIA, J. A. (1994). What heterosexual adults believe about condoms. *New England Journal of Medicine, 331,* 406–407.

CHONG, J. M. (1990). Social assessment of transsexuals who apply for sex reassignment therapy. *Social Work in Health Care, 14,* 87–105.

CHOW, J. M. et al. (1990). The association between chlamydia trachomatis and ectopic pregnancy. *Journal of the American Medical Association, 63,* 3164–3167.

CHOW, Y.-K. et al. (1993). Use of evolutionary limitations of HIV-1 multidrug resistance to optimize therapy. *Nature (London), 361,* 650–654.

CHRISTENSON, C. V., & GAGNON, J. H. (1965). Sexual behavior in a group of older women. *Journal of Geriatrics, 20,* 351–356.

CHRISTOPHER, F. S., & CATE, R. (1984). Factors involved in premarital decision making. *Journal of Sex Research, 20,* 363–376.

CHRISTOPHER, F. S., & ROOSA, M. W. (1990). An evolution of an adolescent pregnancy prevention program: Is 'just say no' enough? *Family Relations, 39,* 68.

CHU, S. Y. et al. (1992). AIDS in bisexual men in the United States: Epidemiology and transmission to women. *American Journal of Public Health, 82,* 220–224.

CLANTON, G., & SMITH, L. G. (1977, March). The self-inflicted pain of jealousy. *Psychology Today, 10,* 44–47.

CLARK, D. (1987). *The new loving someone gay.* Berkeley, CA: Celestrial Arts.

CLARK, J. T., SMITH, E. R., & DAVIDSON, J. M. (1984). Enhancement of sexual motivation in male rats. *Science, 224,* 847–849.

CLARK, R. D., & HATFIELD, E. (1989). Gender differences in receptivity to sexual offers. *Journal of Psychology and Human Sexuality, 2,* 39–55.

CLARKE, E., HATCHER, J., McKEOWN-EYSSEN, G., & LICKRISH, G. (1985). Cervical dysplasia: Association with sexual behavior, smoking, and oral contraceptive use? *American Journal of Obstetrics and Gynecology, 151,* 612–616.

CLARKE, J. (1994). The meaning of menstruation in the elimination of abnormal embryos. *Human Reproduction, 9,* 1204–1207.

CLARKSON, T. B., & ALEXANDER, N. J. (1980). Long-term vasectomy: Effects on the occurrence and extent of atherosclerosis in rhesus monkeys. *Journal of Clinical Investigation, 65,* 15–25.

CLEARY, P. D. et al. (1991). Behavior changes after notification of HIV infection. *American Journal of Public Health, 81,* 1586–1590.

CLEAVER, E. (1968). *Soul on ice.* New York: Dell.

CLEMENTS, M. (1994, August 7). Sex in America today. *Parade Magazine,* pp. 4–6.

CLUMECK, N. et al. (1989). A cluster of HIV infection among heterosexual people without apparent risk factors. *New England Journal of Medicine, 321,* 1460–1462.

CNATTINGIUS, S., FORMAN, M. R., BERENDES, H. W., & ISOTALO, L. (1992). Delayed childbearing and risk of adverse perinatal outcome. *Journal of the American Medical Association, 268,* 886–890.

COBLEIGH, M. A. et al. (1994). Estrogen replacement therapy in breast cancer survivors: A time for change. *Journal of the American Medical Association, 272,* 540–545.

COCHRAN, S. D., & MAYS, V. M. (1990). Sex, lies, and HIV. *New England Journal of Medicine, 322,* 774–775.

COCORES, J., DACKIS, C., & GOLD, M. (1986). Sexual dysfunction secondary to cocaine abuse. *Journal of Clinical Psychiatry, 47,* 384–385.

COGILL, S. et al. (1986). Impact of maternal postnatal depression on cognitive development of young children. *British Medical Journal, 292,* 1165–1167.

COHEN, L. J., & ROTH, S. (1987). The psychological aftermath of rape: Long-term effects and individual differences in recovery. *Journal of Social and Clinical Psychology, 5,* 525–534.

COHEN, M. L., GAROFALO, R., BOUCHER, R., & SEGHORN, T. (1971). The psychology of rapists. *Seminars in Psychiatry, 3,* 307–327.

COHEN, M. L., SEGHORN, T., & CALMAS, W. (1969). Sociometric study of the sex offender. *Journal of Abnormal Psychology, 74,* 249–255.

COHEN, S. (1979). The volatile nitrates. *Journal of the American Medical Association, 241,* 2077–2078.

COLDITZ, G. A. et al. (1995). The use of estrogens and progestins and the risk of breast cancer in postmenopausal women. *New England Journal of Medicine, 332,* 1589–1593.

COLE, D. (1987, July). It might have been: Mourning the unborn. *Psychology Today,* pp. 64–65.

COLE, E. (1982). Sibling incest: The myth of benign sibling incest. *Women and Therapy, 5,* 79–89.

COLE, H. M. (1990). Legal interventions during pregnancy. *Journal of the American Medical Association, 264,* 2663–2670.

COLE, P. M., & PUTNAM, F. W. (1992). Effect of incest on self and social functioning: A developmental psychopathology perspective. *Journal of Consulting and Clinical Psychology, 60,* 174–184.

COLE, R. (1994, March 26). Lawsuit challenges daughter's memory of sexual abuse. *New Orleans Times-Picayune,* p. A2.

COLEMAN, B. C. (1992, November 1). Sex after 60 makes for happier marriages. *New Orleans Times-Picayune,* p. E-1.

COLEMAN, C. N., & KAPLAN, I. D. (1993). Prostate cancer: Technology versus biology. *Cancer (Philadelphia), 72,* 305–309.

COLEMAN, E. (1981–1982). Developmental stages of the coming out process. *Journal of Homosexuality, 7,* 31–43.

COLEMAN, E., & EDWARDS, B. (1986, July). Sexual compulsion vs. sexual addiction: The debate continues. *SIECUS Report,* pp. 7–10.

COLEMAN, M., & GANONG, L. (1991). Remarriage and stepfamily research in the 1980s: Increased interest in an old form. In A. Booth (Ed.), *Contemporary families: Looking forward, looking back.* Minneapolis, MN: National Council on Family Relations.

COLEMAN, S., & PIOTROW, P. (1979). Spermicides: Simplicity and safety are major assets. *Population Reports, Series H,* No. 5.

COLLER, S. A., & RESICK, P. A. (1987). Women's attributions of responsibility for date rape: The influence of empathy and sex-role stereotyping. *Violence and Victims, 2,* 115–125.

COLLINGS, S. J., & PAYNE, M. F. (1991). Attribution of causal and moral responsibility to victims of father-daughter incest: An exploratory examination of five factors. *Child Abuse & Neglect, 15,* 513–521.

COLLINS, N. L., & MILLER, L. C. (1994). Self-disclosure and liking: A meta-analytic review. *Psychological Bulletin, 116,* 457–475.

COMHAIRE, F. H. (1994). Male contraception: Hormonal, mechanical and other. *Human Reproduction, 9,* 586–590.

COMISKEY, K. M. (1989). Relationship workshops: How "good marriages" can be strengthened. *Contemporary Sexuality, 1,* 10.

COMMISSION ON OBSCENITY AND PORNOGRAPHY. (1970). *The report of the Commission on Obscenity and Pornography.* Washington, DC: U.S. Government Printing Office.

CONCORDE COORDINATING COMMITTEE. (1994). Concorde: MRC/ANRS randomised double-blind controlled trial of immediate and deferred zidovudine in symptom-free HIV infection. *Lancet, 343,* 871–881.

CONDRA, J. H. et al. (1995). In vivo emergence of HIV-1 variants resistant to multiple protease inhibitors. *Nature (London), 374,* 569–571.

CONDRY, J., & CONDRY, S. (1977). Sex differences: A study of the eye of the beholder. *Child Development, 47,* 812–819.

CONFINO, E. et al. (1990). Transcervical balloon tuboplasty: A multicenter study. *Journal of the American Medical Association, 264,* 2079–2082.

CONNERY, J. (1977). *Abortion: The development of the Roman Catholic perspective.* Chicago: Loyola University Press.

CONSTANTINOPLE, A. (1973). Masculinity-femininity: An exception to a famous dictum. *Psychological Bulletin, 80,* 389–407.

CONTE, J. R. et al. (1986). Child sexual abuse and the family: A critical analysis. *Journal of Psychotherapy and the Family, 2,* 113–126.

CONTE, J. R. (1991). The nature of sexual offenses against children. In C. R. Hollin & K. Howells (Eds.), *Clinical approaches to sex offenders and their victims* (pp. 11–34). New York: Wiley.

COOK, A. S., & ROCK, J. A. (1991). The role of laparoscopy in the treatment of endometriosis. *Fertility and Sterility, 55,* 663–680.

COOK, L. S., KOUTSKY, L. A., & HOLMES, K. K. (1994). Circumcision and sexually transmitted diseases. *American Journal of Public Health, 84,* 197–201.

COOK, R., & FOSEN, R. (1970). Pornography and the sex offender: Patterns of exposure and immediate arousal effects of pornographic stimuli. In *Technical report of the Commission on Obscenity and Pornography* (Vol. 7). Washington, DC: U.S. Government Printing Office.

COOPER, A. J. (1986). Progestogens in the treatment of male sex offenders: A review. *Canadian Journal of Psychiatry, 31,* 73–79.

COOPER, A.J., & CERNOVSKY, Z. (1992). The effects of cyproterone acetate on sleeping and waking penile erections in pedophiles: Possible implications for treatment. *Canadian Journal of Psychiatry, 37,* 33–37.

COOPER, A. J., CERNOVSKY, Z., & MAGNUS, R. V. (1992). The long-term use of cyproterone acetate in pedophilia: A case study. *Journal of Sex and Marital Therapy, 18,* 292–302.

COOPER, T. G. (1990). In defense of a function for the human epididymis. *Fertility and Sterility, 54,* 965–975.

COPENHAVER, S., & GRAUERHO, E. (1991). Sexual victimization among sorority women: Exploring the link between sexual violence and institutional practices. *Sex Roles, 24,* 31–41.

COREY, L. (1988). Atypical HSV lesions underscore importance of laboratory diagnosis. *Obstetrics and Gynecology News, 23,* 10A.

COREY, L. et al. (1983). Genital herpes simplex virus infections: Clinical manifestations, course, and complications. *Annals of Internal Medicine, 98,* 958–972.

CORNE, S., BRIERE, J., & ESSES, L. M. (1992). Women's attitudes and fantasies about rape as a function of early exposure to pornography. *Journal of Interpersonal Violence, 7,* 454–461.

CORTESE, A. (1989). Subcultural differences in human sexuality: Race, ethnicity,and social class. In K. McKinney & S. Sprecher (Eds.), *Human sexuality: The societal and interpersonal context.* Norwood, NJ: Ablex.

COSTE, J. et al. (1994). Sexually transmitted diseases as major causes of ectopic pregnancy: Results from a large case-control study in France. *Fertility and Sterility, 62,* 289–295.

COTTON, D., & GROTH, A. (1982). Innate rape: Prevention and intervention. *Journal of Prison and Jail Health, 2,* 45–57.

COURTOIS, C. A. (1988). *Healing the incest wound.* New York: Norton.

COUTINHO, R. A. (1994, March/April). Epidemiology of sexually transmitted disease. *Sexually Transmitted Diseases,* pp. S51–S52.

COUTTS, R. L. (1973). *Love and intimacy: A psychological approach.* San Ramon, CA: Consensus.

COVELL, K., & TURNBULL, W. (1982). The long-term effects of father absence in childhood on male university students' sex-role identity and personal adjustment. *Journal of Genetic Psychology, 141,* 271–276.

COX, A. D., HOLDEN, J.M., & SAGOVSKY, R. (1987). Detection of postnatal depression: Development of the 10 item Edinburgh postnatal depression scale. *Journal of Personality and Social Psychology, 150,* 782–786.

COX, D. J. (1988). Incidence and nature of male genital exposure behavior as reported by college women. *Journal of Sex Research, 24,* 227–234.

CRAIG, S., & HEPBURN, S. (1982). The effectiveness of barrier methods of contraception with and without spermicide. *Contraception, 26,* 347–359.

CRAMER, D. (1986). Gay parents and their children: A review of research and practical implications. *Journal of Counseling and Development, 64,* 504–507.

CRAMER, D., & ROACH, A. (1988). Coming out to mom and dad: A study of gay males and their relationships with their parents. *Journal of Homosexuality, 14,* 77–88.

CRAMER, D. W. et al. (1985). Tubal infertility and the intrauterine device. *New England Journal of Medicine, 31,* 941–947.

CRÉPAULT, C. et al. (1977). Erotic imagery in women. In R. Gemme & C. C. Wheeler (Eds.), *Progress in sexology* (pp. 267–283). New York: Plenum.

CROOK, W. G. (1983). *The yeast connection: A medical breakthrough.* Jackson, TN: Professional Books.

CROUGHAN, J. L., SAGHIR, M., COHEN, R., & ROBINS, E. (1981). A comparison of treated and untreated male cross-dressers. *Archives of Sexual Behavior, 10,* 515–523.

CROWE, L. C., & GEORGE, W. H. (1989). Alcohol and human sexuality: Review and integration. *Psychological Bulletin, 105,* 374–386.

CULLINS, V. E. et al. (1994). Comparison of adolescent and adult experiences with Norplant levonorgestrel contraceptive implants. *Obstetrics and Gynecology, 83,* 1026–1032.

CUMMING, D. C., CUMMING, C. E., & KIEREN, D. K. (1991). Menstrual mythology and sources of information about menstruation. *American Journal of Obstetrics and Gynecology, 164,* 472–476.

CUPACH, W. R., & COMSTOCK, J. (1990). Satisfaction with sexual communication in marriage. *Journal of Social and Personal Relationships, 7,* 179–186.

CUPACH, W. R., & METTS, S. (1991). Sexuality and communication in close relationships. In K. McKinney & S. Sprecher (Eds.), *Sexuality in close relationships.* Hillsdale, NJ: Erlbaum.

CUPOLI, J. M., & SEWELL, P. M. (1988). One thousand fifty-nine children with a chief complaint of sexual abuse. *Child Abuse & Neglect, 12,* 151–162.

CURTIS, R., & MILLER, K. (1988). Believing another likes or dislikes you:

Behavior making the beliefs come true. *Journal of Personality and Social Psychology, 51,* 284–290.

CUTLER, W. B. et al. (1986). Human axillary secretions influence women's menstrual cycles: The role of donor extract from men. *Hormones and Behavior, 20,* 463.

DAAR, E. S., MOUDGIL, T., MEYER, R. D., & HO, D. D. (1991). Transient high levels of viremia in patients with primary human immunodeficiency virus Type 1 infection. *New England Journal of Medicine, 324,* 961–964.

DALING, J. et al. (1992). Cigarette smoking and the risk of anogenital cancer. *American Journal of Epidemiology, 135,* 180–189.

DALING, J. R. et al. (1985). Primary tubal infertility in relation to the use of an intrauterine device. *New England Journal of Medicine, 312,* 937–941.

DALTON, K. (1959, January 17). Menstruation and acute psychiatric illness. *British Medical Journal,* pp. 148–149.

DALTON, K. (1960). Menstruation and accidents. *British Medical Journal, 2,* 1425–1426.

DALTON, K. (1964). *The premenstrual syndrome.* Springfield, IL: Charles C. Thomas.

DALTON, K. (1980). Cyclical criminal acts in premenstrual syndrome. *Lancet, 2,* 1070–1071.

DALY, M., & WILSON, M. (1988). Evolutionary social psychology and family violence. *Science, 242,* 519–524.

DALY, M., WILSON, M., & WEGHORST, S. J. (1982). Male sexual jealousy. *Ethology and Sociobiology, 3,* 11–27.

DARLING, C. A., DAVIDSON, J. K., & CONWAY-WELCH, C. (1990). Female ejaculation: Perceived origins, the Grafenberg spot/area, and sexual responsiveness. *Archives of Sexual Behavior, 19,* 29–47.

DARLING, C. A., DAVIDSON, J. K., & COX, R. P. (1991). Female sexual response and the timing of partner orgasm. *Journal of Sex and Marital Therapy, 17,* 3–21.

DARLING, C. A., DAVIDSON, J. K., & JENNINGS, D. A. (1991). The female sexual response revisited: Understanding the multiorgasmic experience in women. *Archives of Sexual Behavior, 20,* 527–540.

DATTA, P. et al. (1994). Mother-to-child transmission of human immunodeficiency virus type I: Report from the Nairobi study. *Journal of Infectious Diseases, 170,* 1134–1140.

DA VANZO, J., PARNELL, A. M., & FOEGE, W. H. (1991). Health consequences of contraceptive use and reproductive patterns. *Journal of the American Medical Association, 265,* 2692–2696.

DAVIDSON, J. K., & HOFFMAN, L. E. (1986). Sexual fantasies and sexual satisfaction: An empirical analysis of erotic thought. *Journal of Sex Research, 22,* 184–205.

DAVIDSON, J. K., & MOORE, N. B. (1994). Guilt and lack of orgasm during sexual intercourse: Myth versus reality among college women. *Journal of Sex Education and Therapy, 20,* 153–174.

DAVIDSON, J. M. (1984). Response to "Hormones and human sexual behavior" by John Bancroft. *Journal of Sex and Marital Therapy, 10,* 23–27.

DAVIDSON, J. M. et al. (1983). Hormonal changes and sexual function in aging men. *Journal of Clinical Endocrinology and Metabolism, 57,* 71–77.

DAVIES, A. G., & CLAY, J. C. (1992). Prevalence of sexually transmitted disease infection in women alleging rape. *Sexually Transmitted Diseases, 19,* 298–300.

DAVIS, B., & NOBLE, M. (1991, April). Putting an end to chronic testicular pain. *Medical Aspects of Human Sexuality,* pp. 26–34.

DAVIS, G. E., & LEITENBERG, H. (1987). Adolescent sex offenders. *Psychological Bulletin, 101,* 417–427.

DAVIS, J. A., & SMITH, T. (1984). *General social surveys, 1972-1984: Cumulative data.* New Haven, CT: Yale University, Roper Center for Public Opinion Research.

DAVIS, K. E. (1985, February). Near and dear: Friendship and love compared. *Psychology Today,* pp. 22–28.

DAVIS, K. E., & BRAUGHT, G. N. (1970). Exposure to pornography, character, and sexual deviance: A retrospective study. In *Technical report of the Commission on Obscenity and Pornography* (Vol. 7). Washington, DC: U.S. Government Printing Office.

DAVIS, M. S. (1983). *Smut: Erotic reality/obscene ideology.* Chicago: University of Chicago Press.

DAVIS, N. J. (1978). Prostitution: Identity, career, and legal-economic enterprise. In J. M. Henslin & E. Sagarin (Eds.), *The sociology of sex: An introductory reader.* New York: Schocken Books.

DAVIS, R. C., BRICKMAN, E., & BAKER, T. (1991). Supportive and unsupportive responses of others to rape victims: Effects on concurrent victim adjustment. *American Journal of Community Psychology, 19,* 443–451.

DE AMICIS, L. et al. (1985). Clinical follow-up of couples treated for sexual dysfunction. *Archives of Sexual Behavior, 14,* 467–489.

DEAUX, K., & LEWIS, L. L. (1983). Components of gender role stereotypes. *Psychological Documents, 13,* 25.

DEBUONO, B. A., ZINNER, S. H., DAAMEN, M., & McCORMACK, W.M. (1990). Sexual behavior of college women in 1975, 1986, and 1989. *New England Journal of Medicine, 322,* 821–825.

DE CECCO, J. P., & ELIA, J. P. (1993). A critique and synthesis of biological essentialism and social constructionist views of sexuality and gender. Introduction. *Journal of Homosexuality, 24,* 1–26.

DECLERCQ, E. R. (1992). The transformation of American midwifery: 1975 to 1988. *American Journal of Public Health, 82,* 680–684.

DECOCK, K. M. et al. (1990). AIDS—The leading cause of adult death in the west African city of Abidjan, Ivory Coast. *Science, 249,* 793–796.

DEENEN, A. A., GIJS, L., & VAN NAERSSEN, A. X. (1994). Intimacy and sexuality in gay male couples. *Archives of Sexual Behavior, 23,* 421–431.

DE JONG, F. H. et al. (1989). Lesions of the SDN-POA inhibit sexual behavior of male Wistar rats. *Brain Research Bulletin, 23,* 483–492.

DE KUYPER, E. (1993). The Freudian construction of sexuality: The gay foundations of heterosexuality and straight homophobia. In *If you seduce a straight person, can you make them gay?* (pp. 137–144). New York: Haworth Press.

DELANEY, J., LUPTON, M. J., & TOTH, E. (1988). *The curse: A cultural history of menstruation.* Urbana and Chicago: University of Illinois Press.

DeMARIS, A., & MacDONALD, W. (1993). Premarital cohabitation and marital instability: A test of the unconventionality hypothesis. *Journal of Marriage and the Family, 55,* 399–407.

DeMARIS, A., & RAO, K. V. (1992). Premarital cohabitation and subsequent marital stability in the United States: A reassessment. *Journal of Marriage and the Family, 54,* 178–190.

DE MAURO, D. (1989–1990, December/January). Sexuality education 1990: A review of state sexuality and AIDS education curricula. *SIECUS Report, 18*(2), 1–9.

DENIS, L. et al. (1992). Alternatives to surgery for benign prostatic hyperplasia. *Cancer (Philadelphia), 70,* 376–378.

DENNISTON, R. H. (1980). Ambisexuality in animals. In J. Marmor (Ed.), *Homosexual behavior* (pp.25–40). New York: Basic Books.

DE ROUGEMENT, D. (1969). *Love in the western world.* New York: Fawcett.

DE SADE, D., THE MARQUIS. *Justine.* (R. Seaver & A. Wainhouse, Trans.). (1965). New York: Grove Press.

DES JARLAIS, J. C. et al. (1989). HIV-1 infection among intravenous drug users in Manhattan, New York City, from 1977–1987. *Journal of the American Medical Association, 261,* 1008.

DESROSIERS, R. C. (1990). A finger on the missing link. *Nature (London), 345,* 288–289.

DE VILLIERS, E.-M. (1989). Heterogeneity of the human papillomavirus group. *Journal of Virology, 63,* 4898–4903.

DE VINCENZI, I., AND THE EUROPEAN STUDY GROUP (1994). A longitudinal study of human immunodeficiency virus transmission by heterosexual partners. *New England Journal of Medicine, 331,* 341–346.

DIAMOND, A., DIAMOND, A. L., & MAST, M. (1972). Visual sensitivity and sexual arousal levels during the menstrual cycle. *Journal of Nervous and Mental Disease, 155,* 170–176.

DIAMOND, M. (1982). Monozygotic twins reared in discordant sex roles and the BBC follow-up. *Archives of Sexual Behavior, 11,* 181–186.

DIAMOND, M. (1993). Homosexuality and bisexuality in different populations. *Archives of Sexual Behavior, 22,* 291–310.

DIAMOND, M., & KARLEN, A. (1980). *Sexual decisions.* Boston: Little, Brown.

DIAMOND, S., & MALISZEWSKI, M. (Eds.). (1992). *Sexual aspects of headaches.* Madison, CT: International University Press.

DICKINSON, G. M. et al. (1993). Absence of HIV transmission from an infected dentist to his patients. *Journal of the American Medical Association, 269,* 1802–1806.

DICK-READ, G. (1972). *Childbirth without fear* (4th ed.). New York: Harper & Row. (1st ed. 1932)

DiCLIMENTE, R. J. et al. (1989). Evaluation of school-based AIDS education curricula in San Francisco. *Journal of Sex Research, 26,* 188–198.

DiCLIMENTE, R. J. et al. (1990). College students' knowledge and attitudes about AIDS and changes in HIV-preventive behaviors. *AIDS Education and Prevention, 2,* 201–212.

DIETZ, P. E., HARRY, B., & HAZELWOOD, R. R. (1986). Detective magazines: Pornography for the sexual sadist? *Journal of Forensic Sciences, 31,* 197–211.

DIETZ-UHLER, B., & MURRELL, A. (1992). College students perceptions of sexual harassment: Are gender differences decreasing? *Journal of College Student Development, 33,* 540–546.

DiFranza, J. R., & Lew, R. A. (1995). Effect of maternal cigarette smoking on pregnancy complications and sudden infant death syndrome. *Journal of Family Practice, 40,* 385–394.

Dindia, K., & Allen, M. (1992). Sex differences in self-disclosure: A meta-analysis. *Psychological Bulletin, 112,* 106–124.

Diokno, A. C., Brown, M. B., & Herzog, A. R. (1990). Sexual function in the elderly. *Archives of Internal Medicine, 150,* 197–200.

Dion, K. L., & Dion, K. K. (1987). Belief in a just world and physical attractiveness stereotyping. *Journal of Personality and Social Psychology, 52,* 775–780.

Dismukes, W. E. et al. (1990). A randomized, double-blind trial of nystatin therapy for the candidiasis hypersensitivity syndrome. *New England Journal of Medicine, 323,* 1717–1723.

Docter, R. F. (1985). Transsexual surgery at 74: A case report. *Archives of Sexual Behavior, 14,* 271–277.

Doering, C. et al. (1978). Plasma testosterone levels and psychologic measures in men over a 2-month period. In R. R. Friedman et al. (Eds.), *Sex differences in behavior.* Huntington, NY: Krieger.

Doll, L. S. et al. (1992). Homosexually and nonhomosexually identified men who have sex with men: A behavioral comparison. *Journal of Sex Research, 29,* 1–14.

Donahey, K. M., & Carroll, R. A. (1993). Gender differences in factors associated with hypoactive sexual desire. *Journal of Sex and Marital Therapy, 19,* 25–40.

Donnelly, D. A. (1993). Sexually inactive marriages. *Journal of Sex Research, 30,* 171–179.

Donnerstein, E. (1982). Pornography: Its effect on violence against women. In N. M. Malamuth & E. Donnerstein (Eds.), *Pornography and sexual aggression.* (pp. 53–81). Orlando, FL: Academic Press.

Donnerstein, E. (1983). Massive exposure to sexual violence and desensitization to violence and rape. Paper presented at the 26th annual meeting of the society for the scientific study of sex, Chicago, November 20.

Donnerstein, E., & Berkowitz, L. (1981). Victim reactions in aggressive erotic films as a factor in violence against women. *Journal of Personality and Social Psychology, 41,* 710–724.

Donnerstein, E., & Linz, D. (1984). Sexual violence in the media: A warning. *Psychology Today, 18,* 14–15.

Donnerstein, E., & Linz, D. (1986, December). The question of pornography. *Psychology Today,* pp. 56–59.

Donnerstein, E., Linz, D., & Penrod, S. (1987). *The question of pornography: Research findings and policy implications.* New York: Free Press.

Donovan, B., Bassett, I., & Bodsworth, N. J. (1994). Male circumcision and common sexually transmissible diseases in a developed nation setting. *Genitourin Medicine, 70,* 317–320.

Doorn, C. D., Poortinga, J., & Verschoor, A. M. (1994). Cross-gender identity in transvestites and male transsexuals. *Archives of Sexual Behavior, 23,* 185–201.

Dorner, G. (1968). Hormonal induction and prevention of female homosexuality. *Journal of Endocrinology, 42,* 163–164.

Dorner, G. et al. (1975). A neuroendocrine predisposition for homosexuality in men. *Archives of Sexual Behavior, 4,* 1–8.

Douglas, M. (1966). *Purity and danger: An analysis of concepts of pollution and taboo.* New York: Praeger.

Douglass, W. C. (1988). *WHO murdered Africa?* Circulated booklet.

Doyle, J. (1985). *Sex and gender.* Dubuque, IA: W. C. Brown.

Drife, J. (1989). The benefits of combined oral contraceptives. *British Journal of Obstetrics and Gynaecology, 96,* 1255–1258.

Dryfoos, J. (1985, November). What the United States can learn about prevention of teenage pregnancy from other developed countries. *SIECUS Report, 14,* 1–7.

Duddle, M. (1991). Emotional sequelae of sexual assault. *Journal of the Royal Society of Medicine, 84,* 26–28.

Duesberg, P. H. (1989). Human immunodeficiency virus and acquired immunodeficiency syndrome: Correlation but not causation. *Proceedings of the National Academy of Sciences of the U.S.A., 86,* 755–764.

Duesberg, P. H. (1990). AIDS: Non-infectious deficiencies acquired by drug consumption and other risk factors. *Research Immunology, 141,* 5–11.

Duldt, B. W. (1982, June). Sexual harassment in nursing. *Nursing Outlook,* pp. 336–343.

Duncan, D. F., & Donnelly, J. W. (1991). Pornography as a source of sex information for students at a private northeastern university. *Psychological Reports, 68,* 782.

Duncan, D. F., & Nicholson, T. (1991). Pornography as a source of sex information for students at a southeastern state university. *Psychological Reports, 68,* 802.

Dunkle, J. H., & Francis, P. L. (1990). The role of facial masculinity/femininity in the attribution of homosexuality. *Sex Roles, 23,* 157–167.

Dunn, M. E., & Trost, J. E. (1989). Male multiple orgasms: A descriptive study. *Archives of Sexual Behavior, 18,* 377–387.

Dworkin, A. (1989). *Pornography: Men possessing women.* New York: Dutton.

Dziech, B. W., & Weiner, L. (1984). *The lecherous professor: Sexual harassment on campus.* Boston: Beacon Press.

Eakins, P. S. (1989). Free-standing birth centers in California. *Journal of Reproductive Medicine, 34,* 960–970.

Earls, C. M., & David, H. (1989). A psychosocial study of male prostitution. *Archives of Sexual Behavior, 18,* 401–419.

Edgerton, M. (1984). The role of surgery in the treatment of transsexualism. *Annals of Plastic Surgery, 13,* 473–476.

Ehrhardt, A. A. (1992). Trends in sexual behavior and the HIV pandemic. *American Journal of Public Health, 82,* 1459–1461.

Ehrhardt, A. A., & Baker, S. W. (1974). Fetal androgens, human nervous system differentiation, and behavioral sex differences. In R. C. Friedman, R. M. Richart, & R. Van de Wiele (Eds.), *Sex differences in behavior.* New York: Wiley.

Ehrhardt, A. A., Evers, K., & Money, J. (1968). Influence of androgen on some aspects of sexually dimorphic behavior in women with the late-treated androgenital syndrome. *Johns Hopkins Medical Journal, 123,* 115–122.

Ehrhardt, A. A., Meyer-Bahlburg, H., Feldman, J., & Ince, S. (1984). Sex-dimorphic behavior in childhood subsequent to prenatal exposure to exogenous progestogens and estrogens. *Archives of Sexual Behavior, 13,* 457–477.

Ehrhardt, A. A. et al. (1989). The development of gender-related behavior in females following prenatal exposure to diethylstilbestrol (DES). *Hormones and Behavior, 23,* 526–541.

Ehrlich, P. R., & Ehrlich, A. H. (1990). *The population explosion.* New York: Simon & Schuster.

Ehrlichman, H., & Eichenstein, R. (1992). Private wishes: Gender similarities and differences. *Sex Roles, 26,* 399–422.

Eichel, E. W., & Nobile, P. (1992). *The perfect fit: How to achieve mutual fulfillment and monogamous passion through the new intercourse.* New York: Donald Fine.

Einarson, T. P. et al. (1990). Maternal spermicide use and adverse reproductive outcome: A meta-analysis. *American Journal of Obstetrics and Gynecology, 162,* 655–660.

Ekstrand, M., Coates, T. J., & McKusick, L. (1988). *AIDS: Its impact on gay male relationships in San Francisco.* Paper presented at the 96th annual meeting of the American Psychological Association, Atlanta, GA.

Elias, J., & Gebhard, P. (1969). Sexuality and sexual learning in childhood. *Phi Delta Kappan, 50,* 401–405.

Elifson, K. W. et al. (1989). Seroprevalence of human immunodeficiency virus among male prostitutes. *New England Journal of Medicine, 321,* 822–833.

Elliot, A. N., O'Donohue, W. T., & Nickerson, M. A. (1993). The use of sexually anatomically detailed dolls in the assessment of sexual abuse. *Clinical Psychology Review, 13,* 207–221.

Ellis, E. M., Atkeson, B. M., & Calhoun, K. S. (1982). An examination of differences between multiple and single incident victims of sexual assault. *Journal of Abnormal Psychology, 91,* 221–224.

Ellis, L., & Ames, M. A. (1987). Neurohormonal functioning and sexual orientation: A theory of homosexuality-heterosexuality. *Psychological Bulletin, 101,* 223–258.

Elvik, S. L., Berkowitz, C. D., & Greenberg, C. S., (1986). Child sexual abuse: The role of the NP. *Nurse Practitioner, 11*(1), 15–22.

Elwin, U. (1968). *The kingdom of the young.* Oxford: Oxford University Press.

Emmanuel, N., Lydiard, R., & Ballenger, J. (1991). Fluoxetine treatment of voyeurism. *American Journal of Psychiatry, 148,* 950.

Ende, J., Rockwell, S., & Glasgow, M. (1984). The sexual history in general medicine practice. *Archives of Internal Medicine, 44,* 558–561.

Englar, R. C., & Walker, C. E. (1973). Male and female reactions to erotic literature. *Psychological Reports, 32,* 481–482.

Epstein, E., & Guttman, R. (1984). Mate selection in man: Evidence, theory, and outcome. *Social Biology, 31,* 243–278.

Erard, J. R. (1988). Vaginal discharges: Diagnosis and therapy. *Diagnosis, 10*(6), 47.

Erickson, W. D., Walbek, N. H., & Seely, R. K. (1988). Behavior patterns of child molesters. *Archives of Sexual Behavior, 17,* 77–86.

ERIKSON, E. (1968). *Identity: Youth and crisis*. New York: Norton.

ESCHENBACH, D. A. (1993). History and review of bacterial vaginosis. *American Journal of Obstetrics and Gynecology, 169*, 441–445.

ESTREICH, S., FORSTER, G. E., & ROBINSON, A. (1990). Sexually transmitted diseases in rape victims. *Genitourin Medicine, 66*, 433–438.

ETAUGH, C. (1983). Introduction: The influence of environment factors on sex differences in children's play. In M. B. Liss (Ed.), *Social and cognitive skills: Sex roles and children's play*. New York: Academic Press.

EUROPEAN COLLABORATIVE STUDY. (1991). Children born to women with HIV-1 infection: Natural history and risk of transmission. *Lancet, 337*, 253–260.

EUROPEAN COLLABORATIVE STUDY. (1992). Risk factors for mother-to-child transmission of HIV-1. *Lancet, 339*, 1007–1012.

EUROPEAN COLLABORATIVE STUDY. (1994a). Cesarean section and risk of vertical transmission of HIV-1 infection. *Lancet, 343*, 1464–1467.

EUROPEAN COLLABORATIVE STUDY. (1994b). Perinatal findings in children born to HIV-infected mothers. *British Journal of Obstetrics and Gynaecology, 101*, 136–141.

EUROPEAN STUDY GROUP ON HETEROSEXUAL TRANSMISSION OF HIV. (1992). Comparison of female to male and male to female transmission of HIV in 563 stable couples. *British Medical Journal, 304*, 809–813.

EVANS, H. J., FLETCHER, J., TORRANCE, M., & HARGREAVE, T. B. (1981). Sperm abnormalities and cigarette smoking. *Lancet, I*, 627–629.

EVANS, R. B. (1969). Childhood parental relationships of homosexual men. *Journal of Counseling and Clinical Psychology, 33*, 129–135.

EWIGMAN, B. G. et al. (1993). Effect of prenatal ultrasound screening on perinatal outcome. *New England Journal of Medicine, 329*, 821–827.

EXNER, J. F., WYLIE, J., LEURA, A., & PARRILL, T. (1977). Some psychological characteristics of prostitutes. *Journal of Personality Assessment, 41*, 474–485.

FAGOT, B., & LEINBACH, M. (1987). Socialization of sex roles within the family. In D. B. Carter (Ed.), *Current conceptions of sex roles and sex typing*. New York: Praeger.

FAICH, G., et al. (1986). Toxic shock syndrome and the vaginal contraceptive sponge. *Journal of the American Medical Association, 255*, 216–218.

FALLER, K. C. (1987). Women who sexually abuse children. *Victims and Violence, 2*(4), 23–27.

FALLER, K. C. (1991). Polyincestuous families: An exploratory study. *Journal of Interpersonal Violence, 6*, 310–321

FALLOWFIELD, L. J., & HALL, A. (1991). Psychosocial and sexual impact of diagnosis and treatment of breast cancer. *British Medical Bulletin, 47*, 388–399.

FALUDI, S. C. (1991, October 18). Women lost ground in 1980s, and EEOC didn't help. *Wall Street Journal*, p. B4.

FARKAS, G. M., & ROSEN, R. C. (1976). Effect of alcohol on elicited male sexual response. *Journal of Studies on Alcohol, 37*, 265–272.

FARLEY, T. M. M. et al. (1992). Intrauterine devices and pelvic inflammatory disease: An international perspective. *Lancet, 339*, 785–788.

FARLEY, T. M. M., MEIRIK, O., MEHTA, S., & WAITES, G. M. H. (1993). The safety of vasectomy: Recent concerns. *Bulletin of the World Health Organization, 71*, 413–419.

FARR, G., GABELNICK, H., STURGEN, K., & DORFLINJER, L. (1994). Contraceptive efficacy and acceptability of the female condom. *American Journal of Public Health, 84*, 1960–1964.

FARROW, S. (1994). Falling sperm quality: Fact or fiction? *British Medical Journal, 309*, 1–2.

FAUCI, A. S. (1993). CD4 + T-Lymphocytopenia without HIV infection—No lights, no cameras, just facts. *New England Journal of Medicine, 328*, 429–430.

FAUSTO-STERLING, A. (1985). *Myths of gender*. New York: Basic Books.

FAY, R. E. et al. (1989). Prevalence and patterns of same-gender sexual contact among men. *Science, 243*, 338–348.

FEDORA, O. et al. (1992). Sadism and other paraphilias in normal controls and aggressive and nonaggressive sex offenders. *Archives of Sexual Behavior, 21*, 1–15.

FEDOROFF, J. P. (1992). Buspirone hydrochloride in the treatment of an atypical paraphilia. *Archives of Sexual Behavior, 21*, 401–406.

FEINGOLD, A. (1992). Gender differences in mate selection preferences: A test of the parental investment model. *Psychological Bulletin, 112*, 125–139.

FERGUSSON, D. M., LAWTON, J. M., & SHANNON, F. T. (1988). Neonatal circumcision and penile problems: An 8-year longitudinal study. *Pediatrics, 81*, 537–540.

FERREIRA, A. E. et al. (1993). Effectiveness of the diaphragm, used continuously, without spermicide. *Contraception, 48*, 29–35.

FEUCHT, T. E. (1993). Prostitutes on crack cocaine: Addiction, utility, and marketplace economics. *Deviant Behavior: An Interdisciplinary Journal, 14*, 91–108.

FIESTER, S. J., & GAY, M. (1991). Sadistic personality disorder: A review of data and recommendations for DSM-IV. *Journal of Personality Disorders, 5*, 376–385.

FIFE, D., & MODE, C. (1992). AIDS prevalence by income group in Philadelphia. *Journal of Acquired Immune Deficiency Syndromes, 5*, 1111–1115.

FIHN, S. D. et al. (1986), Association between diaphragm use and urinary tract infection. *Journal of the American Medical Association, 254*, 240–245.

FINGERHUT, L. A., KLEINMAN, J. C., & KENDRICK, J. S. (1990). Smoking before, during, and after pregnancy. *American Journal of Public Health, 80*, 541–544.

FINKELHOR, D. (1978). Psychological, cultural and family factors in incest and family sexual abuse. *Journal of Marriage and Family Counseling, 4*, 41–49.

FINKELHOR, D. (1979). *Sexually victimized children*. New York: Free Press.

FINKELHOR, D. (1980). Sex among siblings: A survey on prevalence, variety, and effects. *Archives of Sexual Behavior, 9*, 171–194.

FINKELHOR, D. (1984). *Child sexual abuse: New theory and research*. New York: Free Press.

FINKELHOR, D., & ARAJI, A. (1986). Explanations of pedophilia: A four-factor model. *Journal of Sex Research, 22*, 145–161.

FINKELHOR, D., & RUSSELL, D. (1984). The gender gap among perpetrators of child sexual abuse. In D. Russell (Ed.), *Sexual exploitation: Rape, child sexual abuse, and workplace harassment* (pp. 215–231). Beverly Hills, CA: Sage.

FINKELHOR, D., & YLLO, K. (1985). *License to rape: Sexual abuse of wives*. New York: Holt, Rinehart & Winston.

FISCHER, G. J. (1989). Sex words used by partners in a relationship. *Journal of Sex Education and Therapy, 15*(1), 50.

FISCHER, J. L., & NARUS, L. R., JR. (1981). Sex-role development in late adolescence and adulthood. *Sex Roles, 7*, 97–106.

FISCHL, M. A. et al. (1989). Prolonged zidovudine therapy in patients with AIDS and advanced AIDS-related complex. *Journal of the American Medical Association, 262*, 2405–2410.

FISHER, B. et al. (1989). Eight-year results of a randomized clinical trial comparing total mastectomy and lumpectomy with or without irradiation in the treatment of breast cancer. *New England Journal of Medicine, 320*, 822–828.

FISHER, B. et al. (1993). Lumpectomy compared with lumpectomy and radiation therapy for the treatment of intraductal breast cancer. *New England Journal of Medicine, 328*, 1581–1586.

FISHER, B., WEISBERG, D., & MAROTTA, T. (1982). *Report on adolescent male prostitution*. San Francisco: Urban and Rural Systems Associates.

FISHER, H. E. (1987). The four year itch. *Natural History, 10*, 22–29.

FISHER, H. E. (1992). *Anatomy of love: The natural history of monogamy, adultery and divorce*. New York: Norton.

FISHER, J. D., & FISHER, W. A. (1992). Changing AIDS-risk behavior. *Psychological Bulletin, 11*, 455–474.

FISHER, S. (1973). *The female orgasm*. New York: Basic Books.

FISHER, T. D. (1987). Family communication and the sexual behavior and attitudes of college students. *Journal of Youth and Adolescence, 16*, 481–495.

FISHER, W., & GRAY, J. (1988). Erotophobia-erotophilia and sexual behavior during pregnancy and postpartum. *Journal of Sex Research, 25*, 379–396.

FISHER, W. A., BRANSCOMBE, N. R., & LEMERY, C. R. (1983). The bigger the better? Arousal and attributional responses to erotic stimuli that depict different size penises. *Journal of Sex Research, 19*, 337–396.

FISHER, W. A., & GRENIER, G. (1994). Violent pornography, antiwoman thoughts, and antiwoman acts: In search of reliable effects. *Journal of Sex Research, 31*, 23–38.

FITZGERALD, L. F., SHULLMAN, S. L., BAILEY, N., & RICHARDS, M. (1988). The incidence and dimensions of sexual harassment in academia and the workplace. *Journal of Vocational Behavior, 32*, 152–175.

FLAMM, B. L. et al. (1990). Vaginal birth after cesarean delivery: Results of a 5-year multicenter collaborative study. *Obstetrics and Gynecology, 76*, 750–754.

FLEMING, C. et al. (1993). A decision analysis of alternative treatment strategies for clinically localized prostate cancer. *Journal of the American Medical Association, 269*, 2650–2658.

FLOR-HENRY, P. (1987). Cerebral aspects of sexual deviation. In G. D. Wilson (Ed.), *Variant sexuality: Research and theory*. Baltimore: Johns Hopkins University Press.

FLOYD, R. L. et al. (1993). A review of smoking in pregnancy: Effects on pregnancy outcomes and cessation efforts. *Annual Review of Public Health, 14,* 379–411.

FOA, E. B., & RIGGS, D. S. (1995). Posttraumatic stress disorder following assault: Theoretical considerations and empirical findings. *Current Directions in Psychological Science, 4,* 61–65.

FONDA, G. (1994). Local oestrogen replacement for local symptoms in older community dwelling women. *Gerontology, 40*(Suppl.), 9–13.

FORD, C. S., & BEACH, F. A. (1951). *Patterns of sexual behavior.* New York: Harper & Brothers.

FORREST, J. D., & FORDYCE, R. R. (1988). U.S. women's contraceptive attitudes and practices: How have they changed in the 1980's? *Family Planning Perspective, 20,* 112–118.

FORREST, J. D., & SILVERMAN, J. (1989). What public school teachers teach about preventing pregnancy, AIDS and sexually transmitted diseases. *Family Planning Perspectives, 21,* 65–72.

FORREST, J. D., & SINGH, S. (1990a). Public-sector savings resulting from expenditures for contraceptive services. *Family Planning Perspectives, 22,* 6–15.

FORREST, J. D., & SINGH, S. (1990b). The sexual and reproductive behavior of American women, 1982-1988. *Family Planning Perspectives, 22,* 206–214.

FORREST, K. A. et al. (1989). Vaginal douching as a risk factor for pelvic inflammatory disease. *Journal of the National Medical Association, 81,* 159–165.

FORWARD, S., & BUCK, C. (1978). *Betrayal of innocence: Incest and its devastation.* Los Angeles: J. P. Tarcher.

FRANCOEUR, R. T. (1982). *Becoming a sexual person.* New York: John Wiley.

FRANK, E., ANDERSON, C., & RUBENSTEIN, D. (1978). Frequency of sexual dysfunction in "normal" couples. *New England Journal of Medicine, 299,* 111–115.

FRANK, M. L., POINDEXTER, A. N., JOHNSON, M. L., & BATEMAN, L. (1992). Characteristics and attitudes of early contraceptive implant acceptors in Texas. *Family Planning Perspectives, 24,* 208–213.

FRANK, M. L. et al. (1993). One-year experience with subdermal contraceptive implants in the United States. *Contraception, 48,* 229–243.

FRANK, P. et al. (1993). The effect of induced abortion on subsequent fertility. *British Journal of Obstetrics and Gynaecology, 100,* 575–580.

FRANKLIN, D. (1984). Rubella threatens unborn in vaccine gap. *Science News, 125,* 186.

FRANZINI, L. R., & SIDEMAN, L. M. (1994). Personality characteristics of condom users. *Journal of Sex Education and Therapy, 20,* 110–118.

FRAZIER, P. A. (1991). Self-blame as a mediator of postrape depressive symptoms. *Journal of Social and Clinical Psychology, 10,* 47–57.

FREEMAN, E., RICKELS, K., SONDHEIMER, S. J., & POLANSKY, M. (1990). Ineffectiveness of progesterone suppository treatment for premenstrual syndrome. *Journal of the American Medical Association, 264,* 349–353.

FREUD, S. (1913). *Totem and taboo.* New York: Vintage Books.

FREUD, S. (1943). *A general introduction to psychoanalysis.* Garden City, NY: Garden City Publishing.

FREUND, K., & KUBAN, M. (1993). Toward a testable developmental model of pedophilia: The development of erotic age preference. *Child Abuse & Neglect, 17,* 315–324.

FREUND, K., & KUBAN, M. (1994). The basis of the abused abuser theory of pedophilia: A further elaboration on an earlier study. *Archives of Sexual Behavior, 23,* 553–563.

FREUND, K., & LANGEVIN, R. (1976). Bisexuality in homosexual pedophilia. *Archives of Sexual Behavior, 5,* 415–423.

FREUND, K., & WATSON, R. J. (1992). The proportions of heterosexual and homosexual pedophiles among sex offenders against children: An exploratory study. *Journal of Sex and Marital Therapy, 18,* 34–43.

FREUND, K., WATSON, R., & DICKEY, R. (1991). Sex offenses against female children perpetrated by men who are not pedophiles. *Journal of Sex Research, 28,* 409–423.

FREUND, M., LEONARD, T. L., & LEE, N. (1989). Sexual behavior of resident street prostitutes with their clients in Camden, New Jersey. *Journal of Sex Research, 26,* 460–478.

FRIEDLAND, G. H. et al. (1990). Additional evidence for lack of transmission of HIV infection by close interpersonal (casual) contact. *AIDS, 4,* 639–644.

FRIEDLAND, G. H. et al. (1991). Survival differences in patients with AIDS. *Journal of Acquired Immune Deficiency Syndromes, 4,* 144–153.

FRIEDMAN, R. (1947). The story of scabies (Vol. I). New York: Froben Press.

FRIEDMAN, R. C. (1991). Couple therapy with gay couples. *Psychiatric Annals, 21,* 485–490.

FRIEDMAN, R. C. (1992). Neuropsychiatry and homosexuality: On the need for biopsychosocial interactionism. *Journal of Neuropsychiatry and Clinical Neurosciences, 4,* 1–2.

FRIEDRICH, W. N. (1990). *Psychotherapy of sexually abused children and their families.* New York: Norton.

FRIEDRICH, W. N. (1993). Sexual victimization and sexual behavior in children: A review of recent literature. *Child Abuse & Neglect, 17,* 59–66.

FRIEDRICH, W. N., & REAMS, R. A. (1987). Course of psychological symptoms in sexually abused young children. *Psychotherapy, 24,* 160–170.

FRIEDRICH, W. N. et al. (1991). Normative sexual behavior in children. *Pediatrics, 88,* 456–464.

FRIEZE, I. H. (1983). Investigating the causes and consequences of marital rape. *Signs, 8,* 532–553.

FROMM, E. (1956). *The art of loving.* New York: Harper & Row.

FUMENTO, M. (1990). *The myth of heterosexual AIDS: How a tragedy has been distorted by the media and partisan politics.* New York: Basic Books.

FURSTENBERG, F. F., LEVINE, J. A., & BROOKS-GUNN, J. (1990). The children of teenage mothers: Patterns of early childbearing in two generations. *Family Planning Perspectives, 22*(2), 54–61.

FURSTENBERG, F. F., MENCKEN, J., & LINCOLN, R. (1981). *Teenage sexuality, pregnancy, and childbearing.* Philadelphia: University of Pennsylvania Press.

GABRIEL, S. E. et al. (1994). Risk of connective-tissue diseases and other disorders after breast implantation. *New England Journal of Medicine, 330,* 1697–1702.

GAGNON, J. H. (1985). Attitudes and responses of parents to preadolescent masturbation. *Archives of Sexual Behavior, 14,* 451–466.

GAGNON, J. H. (1977). *Human sexualities.* Glenview, IL: Scott, Foresman.

GAGNON, J. H., LINDENBAUM, S., & MARTIN, J. L. (1989). Sexual behavior and AIDS. In C. F. Turner, H. G. Miller, & L. G. Moses (Eds.), *AIDS, sexual behavior, and intravenous drug use.* Washington, DC: National Academy Press.

GAGNON, J. H., & SIMON, W. (1973). *Sexual conduct: The social origins of human sexuality.* Chicago: Aldine.

GAGNON, J. H., & SIMON, W. (1987). The sexual scripting of oral genital contacts. *Archives of Sexual Behavior, 16,* 1–25.

GAIL, M. H. et al. (1989). Projecting individualized probabilities of developing breast cancer for white females who are being examined annually. *Journal of the National Cancer Institute, 81,* 1879–1886.

GALLAGHER, W. (1986, February). The etiology of orgasm. *Discover,* pp. 51–59.

GALLOWAY, D. A. (1994). Human papillomavirus vaccines: A warty problem. *Infectious Agents and Disease, 3,* 187–193.

GANONG, L., & COLEMAN, M. (1989). Preparing for remarriage: Anticipating the issues, seeking solutions. *Family Relations, 38,* 28–33.

GAO, F. et al. (1992). Human infection by genetically diverse SIV$_{SM}$-related HIV-2 in West Africa. *Nature (London), 358,* 495–499.

GARBER, L. (1991). Vested interests. Boston: Little, Brown.

GARNETS, L. et al. (1990). Violence and victimization of lesbians and gay men: Mental health consequences. *Journal of Interpersonal Violence, 5,* 366–383.

GAUVREAU, K., DEGRUTTOLA, U., PAGANO, M., & BELLOCCO, R. (1994). The effect of covariates on the induction time of AIDS using improved imputation of exact seroconversion times. *Statistics in Medicine, 13,* 2021–2030.

GEBHARD, P. H. (1966). Factors in marital orgasm. *Journal of Social Issues, 22,* 88–95.

GEBHARD, P. H., GAGNON, J. H., POMEROY, W. B., & CHRISTENSON, C. V. (1965). *Sex offenders: An analysis of types.* New York: Harper & Row.

GEBHARD, P. H., GAGNON, J. H., POMEROY, W. B., & CHRISTENSON, C. V. (1968). Child molestation. In E. Sagarin & D. E. J. MacNamara (Eds.), *Problems of sex behavior.* New York: Crowell.

GELMAN, D. (1990, June 11). Was it illness or immorality? *Newsweek,* p. 55.

GELMAN, D. et al. (1990, July 23). The mind of the rapist. *Newsweek,* pp. 46–52.

GELMAN, D., FOOTE, D., BARRETT, T., & TALBOT, M. (1992, February 24). Born or bred? *Newsweek,* pp. 46–53.

GELMAN, D., & ROGERS, P. (1993, April 12). Mixed messages. *Newsweek,* pp. 28–29.

GENEVIE, L., & MARGOLIES, E. (1987). *The Motherhood report: How women feel about being mothers.* New York: Macmillan.

GEORGE, J. R. et al. (1992). Prevalence of HIV-1 and HIV-2 mixed infections in Cote d'Ivoire. *Lancet, 340,* 337–339.

GERSHON, R. R. M., VLAHOV, D., & NELSON, K. E. (1990). The risk of transmission of HIV-1 through non-percutaneous, non-sexual modes—a review. *AIDS, 4,* 645–650.

GERSON, K. (1989). Reluctant mothers: Employed women in the 80's. In B. J. Risman & P. Schwartz (Eds.), *Gender in intimate relationships: A microstructural approach* (pp. 205–219). Belmont, CA: Wadsworth.

GERTIG, D. M., MARION, S. A., & SCHECHTER, M. T. (1991). Estimating the extent of underreporting in AIDS surveillance. *AIDS, 5,* 1157–1164.

GIBSON-AINYETTE, I., TEMPLER, D. I., BROWN, R., & VEACO, L. (1988). Adolescent female prostitutes. *Archives of Sexual Behavior, 17,* 431–438.

GIDYEZ, C. A., & KOSS, M. P. (1990). A comparison of group and individual sexual assault victims. *Psychology of Women Quarterly, 14,* 325–342.

GILBERT, B., & CUNNINGHAM, J. (1987). Women's post rape sexual functioning: Review and implications for counseling. *Journal of Counseling and Development, 65,* 71–73.

GILBERT, N. (1991). The phantom epidemic of sexual assault. *The Public Interest, 103,* 54–65.

GIORGIS, B. (1981). *Female circumcision in Africa.* Addis Ababa, Ethiopia: United Nations Economic Commission for Africa.

GIOVANNUCCI, E. et al. (1993a). A prospective cohort study of vasectomy and prostate cancer in United States men. *Journal of the American Medical Association, 269,* 873–877.

GIOVANNUCCI, E. et al. (1993b). A retrospective cohort study of vasectomy and prostate cancer in United States men. *Journal of the American Medical Association, 269,* 878–882.

GITTELSON, N. L., EACOTT, S., & MELITA, B. (1978). Victims of indecent exposure. *British Journal of Psychiatry, 132,* 61–66.

GLADUE, B. A. (1988). Hormones in relationship to homosexual/bisexual/heterosexual gender orientation. In J. M. A. Sitesen (Ed.), *Handbook of sexology: Vol. 6. The pharmacology and endocrinology of sexual function.* Amsterdam: Elsevier.

GLADUE, B. A. (1994). The biopsychology of sexual orientation. *Current Directions in Psychological Science, 3,* 150–154.

GLADUE, B. A., GREEN, R., & HELLMAN, R. E. (1984). Neuroendocrine response to estrogen and sexual orientation. *Science, 225,* 1496–1498.

GLADWELL, M. (1992, May 24). Safer-sex campaign is not slowing AIDS epidemic. *The Washington Post.*

GLASER, J. B., HAMMERSCHLAG, M. R., & McCORMACK, W. M. (1989). Epidemiology of sexually transmitted diseases in rape victims. *Review of Infectious Diseases, 11,* 246–254.

GLASER, J. B. et al. (1991). Sexually transmitted diseases in postpubertal female rape victims. *Journal of Infectious Diseases, 164,* 726–730.

GLASIER, A. et al. (1992). Mifepristone (Ru 486) compared with high-dose estrogen and progestogen for emergency postcoital contraception. *New England Journal of Medicine, 327,* 1041–1044.

GLASS, R., & ERICSSON, R. (1982). *Getting pregnant in the 1980s.* Berkeley: University of California Press.

GOCHROS, H., GOCHROS, J. S., & FISHER, J. (Eds.). (1986). *Helping the sexually oppressed.* Englewood Cliffs, NJ: Prentice Hall.

GOCHROS, J. S. (1989). *When husbands come out of the closet.* New York: Harrington Park Press.

GOERGEN, D. (1975). *The sexual celibate.* New York: Seabury.

GOLD, S. R., & CHICK, D. A. (1988). Sexual fantasy patterns as related to sexual attitude, experience, guilt and sex. *Journal of Sex Education and Therapy, 14,* 18–23.

GOLD, Y. (1987). *The sexualization of the workplace: Sexual harassment of white, blue, and pinkcollar women.* Paper presented at the annual meeting of the American Psychological Association, New York.

GOLDBAUM, G. et al. (1987). The relative impact of smoking and oral contraceptive use on women in the United States. *Journal of the American Medical Association, 258,* 1339–1342.

GOLDBERG, D. C. et al. (1983). The Grafenberg spot and female ejaculation: A review of initial hypotheses. *Journal of Sex and Marital Therapy, 9,* 27–37.

GOLDBERG, H. (1979). *The new male.* New York: William Morrow.

GOLDBERG, L. H. et al. (1993). Long-term suppression of recurrent genital herpes with acyclovir. *Archives of Dermatology, 129,* 582–587.

GOLDHABER, M. K. et al. (1993). Long-term risk of hysterectomy among 80,007 sterilized and comparison women at Kaiser Permanente, 1971–1987. *American Journal of Epidemiology, 138,* 508–521.

GOLDMAN, B., BUSH, P., & KLATZ, R. (1987). *Death in the locker room: Steroids, cocaine, and sports.* Tucson, AZ: The Body Press.

GOLDMAN, R., & GOLDMAN, J. (1982). *Children's sexual thinking: A comparative study of children aged 5 to 15 years in Australia, North America, Britain, and Sweden.* London: Routledge & Kegan Paul.

GOLDSTEIN, B. (1976). *Human sexuality.* New York: McGraw-Hill.

GOLDSTEIN, M. J. (1973). Exposure to erotic stimuli and sexual deviance. *Journal of Social Issues, 29,* 197–220.

GOLDZIEHER, J. W. (1994). Are low-dose oral contraceptives safer and better? *American Journal of Obstetrics and Gynecology, 171,* 587–590.

GOLEMAN, D. (1990, July 10). Homophobia: Scientists find clues to its roots. *New York Times,* pp. C1, C11.

GOLEMAN, D. (1992). New studies map the mind of the rapist. *New York Times.*

GOLLUB, E. L., & STEIN, Z. A. (1993). Commentary: The new female condom—Item 1 on a women's AIDS prevention agenda. *American Journal of Public Health, 83,* 498–500.

GOMBY, D., & SHIONO, P. H. (1991). Estimating the number of substance-exposed infants. *Future Child, 1,* 17–25.

GOMES-SCHWARTZ, B., HOROWITZ, J. M., CARDARELLI, A. A., & SAUZIER, M. (1990). The aftermath of child sexual abuse: 18 months later. In B. Gomes-Schwartz, J. M. Horowitz, & A. P. Cardarelli (Eds.), *Child sexual abuse: The initial effects* (pp. 132–152). Newbury Park, CA: Sage.

GOODCHILDS, J., & ZELLMAN, G. (1984). Sexual signaling and sexual aggression in adolescent relationships. In N. Malamuth & E. Donnerstein (Eds.), *Pornography and sexual aggression.* Orlando, FL: Academic Press.

GOODE, E. (1972). Sexual marijuana. *Sexual Behavior, 2,* 45–51.

GOODMAN, A. (1992). Sexual addiction: Designation and treatment. *Journal of Sex and Marital Therapy, 18,* 304–314.

GOODMAN, M. J. (1991). Breast cancer in multi-ethnic populations: The Hawaii perspective. *Breast Cancer Research and Treatment, 18,* 55–59.

GORDIS, R. (1978). *Love and sex: A modern Jewish perspective.* New York: Farrar Straus Giroux.

GORDON, A. N. (1990). New STD menace: HPV infection. *Medical Aspects of Human Sexuality,* February, 20.

GORDON, S. (1989). *Raising your child censervatively in a sexually permissive world.* New York: Fireside.

GORDON, S., & SNYDER, C. W. (1989). *Personal issues in human sexuality: A quidebook for better sexual health* (2nd ed.). Boston: Allyn and Bacon.

GORDON, T (1976). *P.E.T. (Parent Effectiveness Training) in action.* New York: Bantam Books.

GORMLEY, G. J. et al. (1992). The effect of finasteride in men with benign prostatic hyperplasia. *New England Journal of Medicine, 327,* 1185–1191.

GORSKI, R., GORDON, J., SHRYNE, J., & SOUTHAM, A. (1978). Evidence for a morphological sex difference within the medial preoptic area of the rat brain. *Brain Research, 148,* 333–346.

GOSSELIN, C., & WILSON, G. (1980). *Sexual variations: Fetishism, sadomasochism, transvestism.* New York: Simon & Schuster.

GOULD, J. B., DAVEY, B., & STAFFORD, R. S. (1989). Socioeconomic differences in rates of cesarean section. *New England Journal of Medicine, 321,* 233–239.

GOULD, L. (1989, April). Impact of cardiovascular disease on male sexual function. *Medical Aspects of Human Sexuality,* pp. 24–27.

GOY, R. W., & McEWEN, B. S. (1980). *Sexual differentiation in the brain.* Cambridge, MA: MIT Press.

GRABER, B. (Ed.). (1982). *Circumvaginal musculature and sexual function.* New York: Karger.

GRADY, W. R., HAYWARD, M. D., & FLOREY, F. A. (1988). Contraceptive discontinuation among married women in the United States. *Studies in Family Planning, 19,* 227–235.

GRADY, W. R., & TANFER, K. (1994). Condom breakage and slippage among men in the United States. *Family Planning Perspectives, 26,* 107–112.

GRAFENBERG, E. (1950). The role of the urethra in female orgasm. *International Journal of Sexology, 3,* 145–148.

GRAHAM, N. M. H. et al. (1992). The effects on survival of early treatment of human immunodeficiency virus infection. *New England Journal of Medicine, 326,* 1037–1042.

GRAHAM, S. et al. (1982). Sex patterns and herpes simplex virus type 2 in the epidemiology of cancer of the cervix. *American Journal of Epidemiology, 115,* 729–735.

GRAM, I., AUSTIN, H., & STALSBERG, H. (1992). Cigarette smoking and the incidence of cervical intraeptihelial neoplasia, grade III, and the cancer of the cervix uteri. *American Journal of Epidemiology, 135,* 341–346.

GRAY, L. A., & SARACINO, M. (1989). AIDS on campus: A preliminary study of college students' knowledge and behaviors. *Journal of Counseling and Development, 68,* 199–202.

GRAY, P. (1993, February 15). What is love? *Time,* pp. 46–49.

GRAY, R. H. et al. (1990). Risk of ovulation during lactation. *Lancet, 335,* 25–29.

GREAVES, W. et al. (1988). Clindamyein versus metronidazole in the treatment of bacterial vaginosis. *Obstetrics and Gynecology, 72,* 799–802.

GREEN, G., & CLUNIS, D. (1988). Married lesbians. *Women and Therapy, 8,* 41–49.

GREEN, J. E. et al. (1988). Chorionic villus sampling: Experience with an initial 940 cases. *Obstetrics and Gynecology, 71,* 208–212.

GREEN, R. (1987). *The "sissy boy syndrome" and the development of homosexuality.* New Haven, CT: Yale University Press.

GREENBERG, B. S. et al. (1986). *Sex content on soaps and primetime television series most viewed by adolescents* (Projects CAST Report No. 2). East Lansing: Michigan State University: Department of Telecommunication.

GREENBERG, B. S. et al. (1987). *Adolescents and their exposure to television and movie sex* (Projects CAST Report No. 4). East Lansing: Michigan State University, Department of Telecommunication.

GREENBLATT, C. S. (1983). The salience of sexuality in the early years of marriage. *Journal of Marriage and the Family, 45,* 289–299.

GREENDALE, G. A. et al. (1993). The relationship of Chlamydia trachomatis infection and male infertility. *American Journal of Public Health, 83,* 996–1001.

GREER, D. M. et al. (1982). A technique for foreskin reconstruction and some preliminary results. *Journal of Sex Research, 18,* 324–330.

GREGERSEN, E. (1982). *Sexual practices.* New York: Franklin Watts.

GREGORY, J. G., & PURCELL, M. M. (1989). Penile curvature: Assessment and treatment. *Medical Aspects of Human Sexuality, 23,* 64.

GRIMES, D. A. (1992). The intrauterine device, pelvic inflammatory disease, and infertility: The confusion between hypothesis and knowledge. *Fertility and Sterility, 58,* 670–673.

GRIMES, D. A., & CATES, W., JR. (1980). Abortions: Methods and complications. In E. S. Hofiz (Ed.), *Human reproduction: Conception and contraception* (pp. 796–813). New York: Harper & Row.

GRISEZ, G. G. (1970). *Abortion: The myths, the realities, and the arguments.* New York: Corpus Books.

GROB, C. S. (1985). Female exhibitionism. *Journal of Nervous and Mental Disease, 173,* 253.

GRODSTEIN, F., GOLDMAN, M. B., & CRAMER, D. W. (1993). Relation of tubal infertility to history of sexually transmitted diseases. *American Journal of Epidemiology, 137,* 577–584.

GROFF, M. G. (1987). Characteristics of incest offenders' wives. *Journal of Sex Research, 23,* 91–96.

GROSSMAN, L. S., HAYWOOD, T. W., & WASYLIW, O. E. (1992). The evaluation of truthfulness in alleged sex offenders' self-reports: 16 PF and MMPI validity scales. *Journal of Personality Assessment, 59,* 264–275.

GROTH, A. N. (1979). *Men who rape.* New York: Plenum.

GROTH, A. N., & BIRNBAUM, H. J. (1978). Adult sexual orientation and attraction to underage persons. *Archives of Sexual Behavior, 7,* 175–181.

GROTH, A. N., & BURGESS, A. W. (1977). Sexual dysfunction during rape. *New England Journal of Medicine, 297,* 764–766.

GROTH, A. N., BURGESS, A. W., & HOLMSTROM, L. (1977). Rape: Power, anger, and sexuality. *American Journal of Psychiatry, 134,* 1239–1243.

GROTH, A. N., HOBSON, W. F., & GARY, T. S. (1982). The child molester: Clinical observations. In J. Conte & D. A. Shore (Eds.), *Social work and child sexual abuse* (pp. 129–144). New York: Haworth Press.

GROTH, A. N., & LOREDO, C. M. (1981). Juvenile sexual offenders: Guidelines for assessment. *International Journal of Offender Therapy and Comparative Criminology, 25,* 31–39.

GRUBER, J. E. (1989). How women handle sexual harassment: A literature review. *Sociology and Social Research, 74,* 3–7.

GRUDZINKAS, J. F., WATSON, C., & CHARD, T. (1979). Does sexual intercourse cause fetal distress? *Lancet, 29,* 692–693.

GRUEN, D. (1990). Postpartum depression: A debilitating yet often unassessed problem. *Health and Social Work, 15,* 261–269.

GRUNDLACH, R. (1977). Sexual molestation and rape reported by homosexual and heterosexual women. *Journal of Homosexuality, 2,* 367–384.

GRUPPO ITALIANO PER LO STUDIO DELL ENDOMETRIOS. (1994). Prevalence and anatomical distribution of endometriosis in women with selected gynaecological conditions: Results from a multicentric Italian study. *Human Reproduction, 9,* 1158–1162.

GUERRERO PAVICH, E. (1986). A Chicana perspective on Mexican culture and sexuality. In L. Lister (Ed.), *Human sexuality, ethnoculture, and social work.* New York: Haworth Press.

GUILLEMIN, R. (1980). Hypothalamic hormones: Releasing and inhibiting factors. In D. T. Krieger & J. C. Hughes (Eds.), *Neuroendocrinology.* Sunderland, MA: Sinauer Associates.

GURA, T. (1994, July 31). Mating study: Men seek variety, women security. *New Orleans Times-Picayune,* pp. A–7.

GUTEK, B. A. (1985). *Sex and the workplace.* San Francisco: Jossey-Bass.

GUTEK, B. A. et al. (1980). Sexuality and the workplace. *Basic and Applied Psychology, 1,* 225–265.

GWARTNEY-GIBBS, P., STOCKARD, J., & BOHMER, S. (1987). Learning courtship aggression: The influence of parents, peers, and personal experience. *Family Relations, 36,* 276–282.

GWINN, M. et al. (1991). Prevalence of HIV infection in childbearing women in the United States. *Journal of the American Medical Association, 265,* 1704–1708.

HAAGA, D. A. (1991). Homophobia? *Journal of Behavior and Personality, 6,* 171–174.

HAAS, A. (1979). *Teenage sexuality: A survey of teenage sexual behavior.* New York: Macmillan.

HACK, M. et al. (1994). School-age outcomes in children with birth weights under 750g. *New England Journal of Medicine, 331,* 753–759.

HACKEL, L. S., & RUBLE, D. N. (1992). Changes in marital relationship after the first baby is born: Predicting the impact of expectancy disconfirmation. *Journal of Personality and Social Psychology, 62,* 944–957.

HAGE, J. J., BLOEM, J. J. A. M., & BOUMAN, F. G. (1993). Obtaining rigidity in the neophallus of female-to-male transsexuals: A review of the literature. *Annals of Plastic Surgery, 30,* 327–333.

HAGE, J. J., BLOEM, J. J. A. M., & SULIMAN, H. M. (1993). Review of the literature on techniques for phalloplasty with emphasis on the applicability in female-to-male transsexuals. *Journal of Urology, 150,* 1093–1098.

HAGLUND, B. et al. (1990). Cigarette smoking as a risk factor for sudden infant death syndrome: A population-based study. *American Journal of Public Health, 80,* 29–32.

HAHN, B. (1990). Biologically unique, SIV-like HIV-2 variants in healthy west African individuals. In M. Girard & L. Valette (Eds.), *Proceedings of the Fifth Colloque des Cent Gandes,* Lyon, France.

HAJCAK, F., & GARWOOD, P. (1988). Quick-fix sex: Pseudosexuality in adolescents. *Adolescence, 23,* 755–760.

HAJJAR, D. (1993). Paper presented at the annual conference of the American Heart Association.

HALEY, T. J., & SNIDER, R. S. (Eds.). (1962). *Response of the nervous system to ionizing radiation.* New York: Academic Press.

HALL, L. A. (1992). Forbidden by God, despised by men: Masturbation, medical warnings, moral panic, and manhood in Great Britain, 1850–1950. *Journal of the History of Sexuality, 2,* 365–387.

HALL, R. C. et al. (1989). Sexual abuse in patients with anorexia nervosa and bulimia. *Psychosomatics, 30,* 73–79.

HALLECK, S. L. (1976). Another response to "Homosexuality: The ethical challenge." *Journal of Consulting and Clinical Psychology, 44,* 167–170.

HALLER, J. S., & HALLER, R. M. (1977). *The physician and sexuality in Victorian America.* New York: Norton.

HALMAN, L. J., ABBEY, A., & ANDREWS, F. M. (1992). Attitudes about infertility interventions among fertile and infertile couples. *American Journal of Public Health, 82,* 191–194.

HALLSTRÖM, T. (1979). Sexuality in the climacteric. *Clinical Obstetrics and Gynecology, 4,* 227–239.

HAMBRIDGE, D. M. (1988). Incest and anorexia nervosa: What is the link? *British Journal of Psychiatry, 152,* 145–146.

HAMER, D. H. et al. (1993). A linkage between DNA markers on the X chromosome and male sexual orientation. *Science, 261,* 321–327.

HAMILTON, J., ALAGNA, S., KING, L., & LLOYD, C. (1987). The emotional consequences of gender-based abuse in the workplace: New counseling programs for sex discrimination. *Women and Therapy, 6,* 155–182.

HAMILTON, J. D. et al. (1992). A controlled trial of early versus late treatment with zidovudine in symptomatic human immunodeficiency virus infection. *New England Journal of Medicine, 326,* 437–443.

HANDSFIELD, H. H. (1990). Old enemies: Combating syphilis and gonorrhea in the 1990s. *Journal of the American Medical Association, 264,* 1451–1452.

HANDSFIELD, H. H., & SCHWEBKE, J. (1990). Trends in sexually transmitted diseases in homosexually active men in King County, Washington, 1980-1990. *Sexually Transmitted Diseases, 17,* 211–215.

HANKINS, C. A., & HANDLEY, M. A. (1992). HIV disease and AIDS in women: Current knowledge and a research agenda. *Journal of Acquired Immune Deficiency Syndromes, 5,* 957–971.

HANKINSON, S. E. et al. (1993). Tubal ligation, hysterectomy, and risk of ovarian cancer: A prospective study. *Journal of the American Medical Association, 270,* 2813–2818.

HARDY, J. B., MCCRACKEN, G. H., JR., GILKESON, M. R., & SEVER, J.L. (1969). Adverse fetal outcome following maternal rubella after the first trimester of pregnancy. *Journal of the American Medical Association, 207,* 2414–2420.

HARITON, E. B., & SINGER, J. L. (1974). Women's fantasies during sexual intercourse: Normative and theoretical implications. *Journal of Consulting and Clinical Psychology, 42,* 313–322.

HARLAP, S. (1992). The benefits and risks of hormone replacement therapy: An epidemiologic overview. *American Journal of Obstetrics and Gynecology, 166,* 1986–1992.

HARLOW, H. F. (1959). Love in infant monkeys. *Scientific American, 200* (6), 68–74.

HARLOW, H. F., & HARLOW, M. (1962). The effect of rearing conditions on behavior. *Bulletin of the Menninger Clinic, 26,* 213–224.

HARNEY, P., & MUEHLENHARD, C. (1991). Rape. In E. Graverholz & M. Korlewski (Eds.), *Sexual coercion: A sourcebook on its nature, causes, and prevention.* Lexington, MA: Lexington Books.

HARNISH, S. (1988, July). Congenital absence of the vagina: Clinical issues. *Medical Aspects of Human Sexuality,* pp. 54–60.

HARPER, E. B. (1964). Ritual pollution as an integrator of caste and religion. *Journal of Asian Studies, 23,* 151–197.

HARRIS, B. (1993). A hormonal component to postnatal depression. *British Journal of Psychiatry, 163,* 403–405.

HARRIS, R. (1994). Breast cancer among women in their forties: Toward a reasonable research agenda. *Journal of the National Cancer Institute, 86,* 410–412.

HARRISON, M. R. et al. (1990). Successful repair in utero of a fetal diaphragmatic hernia after removal of herniated viscera from the left thorax. *New England Journal of Medicine, 322,* 1582–1584.

HART, J., COHEN, E., GINGOLD, A., & HOMBURG, R. (1991). Sexual behavior in pregnancy: A study of 219 women. *Journal of Sex Education and Therapy, 17,* 86–90.

HARVEY, S. (1987). Female sexual behavior: Fluctuations during the menstrual cycle. *Journal of Psychosomatic Research, 31,* 101–110.

HASSETT, J. (1978). Sex and smell. *Psychology Today, 11,* 40–42,45.

HATCHER, R. A. et al. (1994). *Contraceptive technology* (16th ed.). New York: Irvington Publishers.

HATFIELD, E. (1984). The dangers of intimacy. In V. Derlaga (Ed.), *Communication, intimacy, and close relationships* (pp. 207–220). New York: Academic Press.

HATFIELD, E. (1988). Passionate and companionate love. In R. J. Sternberg & M. L. Barnes (Eds.), *The psychology of love* (pp. 191–217). New Haven, CT: Yale University Press.

HATFIELD, E., & SPRECHER, S. (1986). *Mirror, mirror... The importance of looks in everyday life.* Albany: State University of New York Press.

HATFIELD, E., & WALSTER, G. W. (1978). *A new look at love.* Lantham, MA: University Press of America.

HATHAWAY, S. R., & MCKINLEY, J. C. (1943). *The Minnesota multiphasic personality inventory.* New York: Psychological Corporation.

HAVGAARD, J. J., & EMERY, R. E. (1989). Methodological issues in child sexual abuse research. *Child Abuse & Neglect, 13,* 89–100.

HAWTON, K., CATALAN, J., & FAGG, J. (1991). Low sexual desire: Sex therapy results and prognostic factors. *Behavior Research and Therapy, 29,* 217–224.

HAWTON, K., CATALAN, J., & FAGG, J. (1992). Sex therapy for erectile dysfunction: Characteristics of couples, treatment outcome, and prognostic factors. *Archives of Sexual Behavior, 21,* 161–175.

HAYES, C. D. (Ed.). (1987). *Risking the future: Adolescent sexuality, pregnancy, and childbearing* (Vol. I). Washington, DC: National Academy Press.

HAYNES, B. F. (1993). Scientific and social issues of human immunodeficiency virus vaccine development. *Science, 260,* 1279–1286.

HAYS, D., & SAMUELS, A. (1989). Heterosexual women's perceptions of their marriages to bisexual or homosexual men. *Journal of Homosexuality, 18,* 81–100.

HAZAN, C., & SHAVER, P. (1987). Love conceptualized as an attachment process. *Journal of Personality and Social Psychology, 52,* 511–524.

HAZELWOOD, R. R., DIETZ, P. E., BURGESS, A. W., & LANNING, K. V. (1983). Autoeroticism and the public visibility of autoerotic asphyxia. In R. R. Hazelwood, P. E. Dietz, & A. W. Burgess (Eds.), *Autoerotic fatalities* (pp. 1–12). Lexington, MA: Lexington Books.

HEARST, N., & HULLEY, S. B. (1988). Preventing the heterosexual spread of AIDS: Are we giving our patients the best advice? *Journal of the American Medical Association, 259,* 2428–2432.

HEATH, D. (1984). An investigation into the origins of a copious vaginal discharge during intercourse—"enough to wet the bed"—that "is not urine." *Journal of Sex Research, 20,* 194–215.

HEILBRUN, A., & SEIF, D. (1988). Erotic value of female distress in sexually explicit photographs. *Journal of Sex Research, 24,* 47–57.

HEIMAN, J. (1975). The physiology of erotica: Women's sexual arousal. *Psychology Today, 8*(11), 90–94.

HEIMAN, J. (1977). A psychophysiological exploration of sexual arousal patterns in females and males. *Psychophysiology, 14,* 266–274.

HEIMAN, J., & LOPICCOLO, J. (1988). *Becoming orgasmic: A sexual growth program for women.* Englewood Cliffs, N.J.: Prentice Hall

HEIN, H. A., BURMEISTER, L. F., & PAPKE, K. R. (1990). The relationship of unwed status to infant mortality. *Obstetrics and Gynecology, 76,* 763–768.

HEINONEN, O. P., SLONE, D., & SHAPIRO, S. (1977). *Birth defects and drugs in pregnancy.* Littleton, MA: Publishing Sciences Group.

HELLINGER, F. J. (1993). The lifetime cost of treating a person with HIV. *Journal of the American Medical Association, 270,* 474–478.

HELLMAN, L. M., & PRITCHARD, J. A. (1971). *Williams obstetrics* (14th ed.). New York: Appleton-Century-Crofts.

HELMREICH, R., SPENCE, J., & HOLAHAN, C. (1979). Psychological androgyny and sex role flexibility: A test of two hypotheses. *Journal of Personality and Social Psychology, 37,* 1631–1644.

HENDERSON, B. E., & BERNSTEIN, L. (1991). The international variation in breast cancer rates: An epidemiological assessment. *Breast Cancer Research and Treatment, 18,* 511–517.

HENDERSON, R. (1990, November 22). Parents need right words, right time to tell kids about sex. *Los Angeles Times,* p. X1.

HENDRICK, C., & HENDRICK, S. (1983). *Liking, loving and relating.* Monterey, CA: Brooks/Cole.

HENDRICK, C., & HENDRICK, S. (1986). A theory and method of love. *Journal of Personality and Social Psychology, 50,* 392–402.

HENDRICK, C., HENDRICK, S., & ADLER, N. (1988). Romantic relationships: Love, satisfaction, and staying together. *Journal of Personality and Social Psychology, 54,* 980–988.

HENNEBERGER, M., & MARRIOTT, M. (1993). What teens call flirting, adults call sex harassment. *New York Times.*

HENRIKSEN, T. B., BEK, K. M., HEDEGAARD, M., & SECHER, N. J. (1994). Methods and consequences of changes in use of episiotomy. *British Medical Journal, 309,* 1255–1258.

HENSHAW, S. K. (1990). Induced abortion: A world review, 1990. *Family Planning Perspectives, 22*(2), 76–89.

HENSON, C., RUBIN, H. B., & HENSON, D. E. (1979). Women's sexual arousal concurrently assessed by three genital measures. *Archives of Sexual Behavior, 8,* 459–479.

HERBST, A. L. (1979). Coitus and the fetus. *New England Journal of Medicine, 301,* 1235–1236.

HERDT, G. H. (1981). *Guardians of the flute.* New York: McGraw-Hill.

HERDT, G. H. (1987). *The Sambia.* New York: Holt, Rinehart, & Winston.

HERDT, G. H. (1993). Semen transactions in Sambia culture. In D. N. Suggs & A. W. Miracle (Eds.), *Culture and human sexuality* (pp. 298–327). Pacific Grove, CA: Brooks/Cole.

HEREK, G. M. (1984). Beyond homophobia: A social psychological perspective on attitudes toward lesbians and gay men. *Journal of Homosexuality, 10,* 1–21.

HEREK, G. M. (1988). Heterosexuals' attitudes toward lesbian and gay men: Correlates and gender differences. *Journal of Sex Research, 25,* 451–477.

HEREK, G. M. (1989). Hate crimes against lesbian and gay men: Issues for research and policy. *American Psychologist, 44,* 948–955.

HEREK, G. M., & CAPITANIO, J. P. (1993). Public reactions to AIDS in the United States: A second decade of stigma. *American Journal of Public Health, 83,* 574–577.

HERMAN, J., & HIRSCHMAN, L. (1977). Father-daughter incest. *Journal of Women in Culture and Society, 2,* 735–756.

HERSCH, P. (1988, January). Coming of age on city streets. *Psychology Today, 22,* 28–37.

HERZOG, L. (1989). Urinary tract infections and circumcision. *American Journal of Diseases of Children, 143,* 348–350.

HESSOL, N. A. et al. (1992). Impact of HIV infection on mortality and accuracy of AIDS reporting on death certificates. *American Journal of Public Health, 82,* 561–564.

HETEROSEXUAL AIDS: SETTING THE ODDS. (1988). *Science, 240,* 597.

HICKSON, F. C. I. et al. (1994). Gay men as victims of nonconsensual sex. *Archives of Sexual Behavior, 23,* 281–294.

HILL, C. T., RUBIN, Z., & PEPLAU, L. A. (1976). Breakups before marriage: The end of 103 affairs. *Journal of Social Issues, 32,* 147–168.

HILL, E. (1987). Premalignant and malignant disorders of the uterine cervix. In M. Pernoll & R. Benson (Eds.), *Current obstetric and gynecologic diagnosis and treatment 1987* (6th ed.). Los Altos, CA: Appleton & Lange.

HILL, I. (1987). *The bisexual spouse.* McLean, VA: Barlina Books.

HINDS, M. C. (1981, June 15). The child victim of incest. *New York Times.*

HINES, M. (1982). Prenatal gonadal hormones and sex differences in human behavior. *Psychological Bulletin, 92,* 56–80.

HINES, M., & GREEN, R. (1991). Human hormonal and neural correlates of sex-typed behaviors. *Review of Psychiatry, 10,* 536–555.

HINGSON, R. et al. (1982). Effects of maternal drinking and marijuana use on fetal growth and development. *Pediatrics, 70,* 539–546.

HINGSON, R. W., STRUNIN, L., BERLIN, B. M., & HERREN, T. (1990). Beliefs about AIDS, use of alcohol and drugs, and unprotected sex among Massachusetts adolescents. *American Journal of Public Health, 80,* 295–299.

HIRA, S. et al. (1990). Genital ulcers and male circumcision as risk factors for acquiring HIV-1 in Zambia. *Journal of Infectious Diseases, 161,* 584–585.

HIRSCHFELD, M. (1948). *Sexual anomalies.* New York: Emerson.

HITE, S. (1976). *The Hite report.* New York: Macmillan.

HITE, S. (1981). *The Hite report on male sexuality.* New York: Knopf.

HITE, S. (1987). *Women and love: A cultural revolution in progress.* New York: Knopf.

HOCH, Z. (1986). Vaginal erotic sensitivity by sexological examination. *Acta Obstetricia et Gynecologica Scandinavica, 65,* 767–773.

HOCKENBERRY, S. L., & BILLINGHAM, R. (1987). Sexual orientation and boyhood gender conformity. *Archives of Sexual Behavior, 16,* 475–493.

HOLCOMB, D. R. et al. (1991). Gender differences among college students. *College Student Journal, 25,* 434–439.

HOLLAND, J. et al. (1991). Between embarrassment and trust: Young women and the diversity of condom use. In P. Aggleton, P. Davies, & G. Hart (Eds.), *AIDS: Responses, intervention and care.* Basingstoke, England: Falmer Press.

HOLLENDER, M. H., BROWN, C. W., & ROBACK, H. B. (1977). Genital exhibitionism in women. *American Journal of Psychiatry, 134,* 436–438.

HOLMSTROM, L. L., & BURGESS, A. W. (1978). *The victim of rape: Institutional reactions.* New York: Wiley.

HOLT, V. L. et al. (1989). Induced abortion and the risk of subsequent ectopic pregnancy. *American Journal of Public Health, 79,* 1234–1238.

HOLTZEN, D. W., & AGRESTI, A. A. (1990). Parental responses to gay and lesbian children. *Journal of Social and Clinical Psychology, 9,* 390–399.

HOOFNAGLE, J. H. (1989). Toward universal vaccination against hepatitis B virus. *New England Journal of Medicine, 321,* 1333–1334.

HOOKER, E. (1957). The adjustment of the male overt homosexual. *Journal of Projective Techniques, 21,* 18–31.

HOOKER, E. (1965). An empirical study of some relations between sexual patterns and gender identity in male homosexuals. In J. Money (Ed.), *Sex research: New developments.* New York: Henry Holt.

HOOKER, E. (1993). Reflections of a 40-year exploration: A scientific view on homosexuality. *American Psychologist, 48,* 1–4.

HOOVER, D. R. et al. (1995). Long-term survival without clinical AIDS after CD4+ cell counts fall below 200 x 10⁶/l. *AIDS, 9,* 145–152.

HOOYKAAS, C. et al. (1989). Heterosexuals at risk for HIV: Differences between private and commercial partners in sexual behavior and condom use. *AIDS, 3,* 525–532.

HOROWITZ, F. D. et al. (1977). The effects of obstetrical medication on the behavior of Israeli newborn infants and some comparisons with Uruguayan and American infants. *Child Development, 48,* 1607–1623.

HORT, B. E., LEINBACH, M. D., & FAGOT, B. I. (1991). Is there coherence among the cognitive components of gender acquisition? *Sex Roles. 24,* 195–207.

HORWITZ, S. M., KLERMAN, L. V., KUO, H. S., & JEKEL, J. F. (1991). Intergenerational transmission of school-age parenthood. *Family Planning Perspectives, 23,* 168–177.

HOSKEN, F. (1989, July/August). Female genital mutilation—strategies for eradication. *The Truth Seeker,* pp. 22–30.

HOWARD, C. R., HOWARD, F. M., & WEITZMAN, M. L. (1994). Acetaminophen analgesia in neonatal circumcision: The effect on pain. *Pediatrics, 93,* 641–646.

HOWARD, E. (1980, November). Overcoming rape trauma. *Ms.,* p. 35.

HOWARD, M., & McCABE, J. B. (1990). Helping teenagers postpone sexual involvement. *Family Planning Perspectives, 22,* 21–26.

HOWE, J. E., MINKOFF, H. L., & DUERR, A. C. (1994). Contraceptives and HIV. *AIDS, 8,* 861–871.

HOWELLS, K. (1981). Adult sexual interest in children: Considerations relevant to theories of etiology. In M. Cook & K. Howells (Eds.), *Adult sexual interest in children* (pp. 55–94). New York: Academic Press.

HOWIE, P. W. et al. (1990). Protective effect of breast feeding against infection. *British Medical Journal, 300,* 11–16.

HSU, F. L. K. (1981). *Americans and Chinese: Passage to difference* (3rd ed.). Honolulu: University Press of Hawaii.

HUDSON, B., PEPPERELL, R., & WOOD, C. (1987). The problem of infertility. In R. Pepperell, B. Hudson, & C. Wood (Eds.), *The infertile couple.* Edinburgh: Churchill-Livingstone.

HUGGINS, G. R., & CULLINS, V. E. (1990). Fertility after contraception or abortion. *Fertility and Sterility, 54,* 559–573.

HUGHES, J., JENKINS, P., SEYDLITZ, R., & DAY, C. (1995). *Sexual harassment in a university setting: A multivariate analysis.* Manuscript submitted for publication.

HULKA, B. et al. (1982). Protection against endometrial carcinoma by combination-product oral contraceptives. *Journal of the American Medical Association, 247,* 475–477.

HUMPHREYS, L. (1970). *Tearoom trade: Impersonal sex in public places.* Chicago: Aldine.

HUNT, M. (1974). *Sexual behavior in the 1970s.* Chicago: Playboy Press.

HUPKA, R. B. (1981, August). Cultural determinants of jealousy. *Alternative Life Styles,* p. 4.

HURLBERT, D. F. (1991). The role of assertiveness in female sexuality: A comparative study between sexually assertive and sexually nonassertive women. *Journal of Sex and Marital Therapy, 17,* 183–190.

HURLBERT, D. F., APT, C., & RABEHL, S. M. (1993). Key variables to understanding female sexual satisfaction: An examination of women in nondistressed marriages. *Journal of Sex and Marital Therapy, 19,* 154–165.

HURLBERT, D. F., & WHITTAKER, K. E. (1991). The role of masturbation in marital and sexual satisfaction: A comparative study of female masturbators and nonmasturbators. *Journal of Sex Education and Therapy, 17,* 272–282.

HURLEY, T. (1984). Constitution implications of sex-change operations. *Journal of Legal Medicine, 5,* 633–664.

HUSTON, A. C. (1983). Sex-typing. In E. M. Hetherington (Ed.), *Handbook of child psychology: Vol. 4. Socialization, personality, and social development* (pp. 387–468). New York: Wiley.

IFFY, L., & WINGATE, M. D. (1970). Risks of rhythm method of birth control. *Journal of Reproductive Medicine, 5*(3), 11–17.

IMPERATO-MCGINLEY, J., PETERSON, R. E., GAUTIER, T., & STURLA, E. (1979). Androgens and the evolution of male-gender identity among male pseudohermaphrodites with 5-reductase deficiency. *New England Journal of Medicine, 300,* 1233–1237.

INSTITUTE OF MEDICINE. (1990). *Nutrition during pregnancy.* Washington, DC: National Academy of Sciences, Subcommittee on Nutritional Status and Weight Gain during Pregnancy.

INSTITUTE OF MEDICINE. (1991). *Nutrition during lactation.* Washington, DC: National Academy Press.

IRVINE, J. M. (1990). From difference to sameness: Gender ideology in sexual science. *Journal of Sex Research, 27,* 7–24.

IYASU, S. et al. (1993). The epidemiology of placenta previa in the United States, 1979 through 1987. *American Journal of Obstetrics and Gynecology, 168,* 1424–1429.

JACKLIN, C. N., & MACCOBY, E. E. (1983). Issues of gender differentiation in normal development. In M. D. Levine, W. B. Carey, A. C. Crocker, & R. T. Gross (Eds.), *Developmental-behavioral pediatrics.* Philadelphia: Saunders.

JACOBS, P. A. et al. (1965). Aggressive behavior, mental subnormality, and the XYY male. *Nature (London), 208,* 1351–1352.

JACOBS, S.-H., & THOMAS, W. (1994). Native American two-spirits. *Anthropology Newsletter, 35*(8), 7.

JACQUEZ, J. A. et al. (1994). Role of the primary infection in epidemics of HIV infection in gay cohorts. *Journal of Acquired Immune Deficiency Syndromes, 7,* 1169–1184.

JAIN, A. K. (1969). Pregnancy outcome and the time required for next conception. *Population Studies, 23,* 421–433.

JAIN, A. K., & BONGAARTS, J. (1981). Breastfeeding: Patterns, correlates and fertility effects. *Studies in Family Planning, 12*(3), 79–99.

JAMES, J. (1982). The prostitute as a victim. In M. Kirkpatrick (Ed.), *Women's sexual experience.* New York: Plenum.

JAMES, J., GOSHO, C., & WOHL, R. W. (1979). The relationship between female criminality and drug use. *International Journal of the Addictions, 14,* 215–229.

JAMISON, P. L., & GEBHARD, P. H. (1988). Penis size increase between flaccid and erect states: An analysis of the Kinsey data. *Journal of Sex Research, 24,* 177–183.

JANCIN, B. (1988). Prenatal gender selection appears to be gaining acceptance. *Obstetrics and Gynecology News, 23,* 30.

JANKOWIAK, W. R., & FISCHER, E. F. (1992). A cross-cultural perspective on romantic love. *Ethnology, 31,* 149–155.

JANUS, S. S., & BESS, B. (1977, May 5). *Prostitution: Option or addiction?* Paper presented at the National Convention of the American Psychiatric Association, Toronto, Canada.

JANUS, S. S., & JANUS, C. L. (1993). *The Janus report on sexual behavior.* New York: Wiley.

JARVIE, I. C. (1992). Child pornography and prostitution. In W. O'Donohue & J. H. Geer (Eds.), *The sexual abuse of children: Theory and research* (Vol. 1, pp. 307–328). Hillsdale, NJ: Erlbaum.

JENKS, R. (1985). Swinging: A replication and test of a theory. *Journal of Sex Research, 21,* 199–210.

JENNY, C. et al. (1990). Sexually transmitted diseases in victims of rape. *New England Journal of Medicine, 322,* 713–716.

JENSEN, J. W., & GUTEK, B. A. (1982). Attributions and assignment of responsibility in sexual harassment. *Journal of Social Issues, 38,* 121–136.

JESSOR, S. L., & JESSOR, R. (1975). Transition from virginity to nonvirginity among youth: A social-psychological study over time. *Developmental Psychology, II*, 473–484.

JICK, H. et al. (1981). Vaginal spermicides and congenital disorders. *Journal of the American Medical Association, 245*, 1329–1332.

JOFFE, G. P. et al. (1992). Multiple partners and partner choice as risk factors for sexually transmitted disease among female college students. *Sexually Transmitted Diseases, 19*, 272–278.

JOHNSON, J. W. C., LONGMATE, J. A., & FRENTZEN, B. (1992). Excessive maternal weight and pregnancy outcome. *American Journal of Obstetrics and Gynecology, 167*, 353–372.

JOHNSON, T. C. (1989). Female child perpetrators: Children who molest other children. *Child Abuse & Neglect, 13*, 571–585.

JONES, E. F. et al. (1986). *Teenage pregnancy in industrialized countries*. New Haven, CT: Yale University Press.

JOURARD, S. M., & LASAKOW, P. (1958). Some factors in self-disclosure. *Journal of Abnormal and Social Psychology, 56*, 91–98.

JOYCE, T. J., & MOCAN, N. H. (1990). The impact of legalized abortion on adolescent childbearing in New York City. *American Journal of Public Health, 80*, 273–278.

JURKOVIC, D. et al. (1993). Coelocentesis: A new technique for early prenatal diagnosis. *Lancet, 341*, 1623–1624.

JUSTICE, B., & JUSTICE, R. (1979). *The broken taboo: Sex in the family*. New York: Human Sciences Press.

KAESER, L. (1989). Reconsidering the age limits on pill use. *Family Planning Perspectives, 21*, 273–274.

KAFKA, M. P. (1991). Successful antidepressant treatment of nonparaphiliac sexual addictions and paraphilias in men. *Journal of Clinical Psychiatry, 52*, 60–65.

KAHN, J. R., & LONDON, K. A. (1991). Premarital sex and the risk of divorce. *Journal of Marriage and the Family, 53*, 845–855.

KALICHMAN, S. C., & SIKKEMA, K. J. (1994). Psychological sequelae of HIV infection and AIDS: Review of empirical findings. *Clinical Psychology Reviews, 7*, 611–632.

KALLMAN, F. J. (1952). Comparative twin study on the genetic aspects of male homosexuality. *Journal of Nervous and Mental Disease, 115*, 283–298.

KAMEL, H. (1983). *Downtown street hustlers: The role of dramaturgical imaging practices in the social construction of male prostitution*. San Diego: University of California.

KAMINSKI, P. F., SOROSKY, J. J., PEES, R. C., & PODCZASKI, E. S. (1993). Correction of massive vaginal prolapse in an older population: A four-year experience at a rural tertiary care center. *Journal of the American Geriatric Society, 41*, 42–44.

KANAKER, S., PINTO, N. J. P., & MAZUMDAR, D. (1985). Causal and moral responsibility of victims of rape and robbery. *Journal of Applied Social Psychology, 15*, 622–637.

KANIN, E. (1967). Reference groups and sex conduct norms. *Sociological Quarterly, 8*, 495–504.

KANIN, E. J. (1985). Date rapists: Differential sexual socialization and relative deprivation. *Archives of Sexual Behavior, 14*, 219–231.

KANIN, E. J. (1994). False rape allegations. *Archives of Sexual Behavior, 23*, 81–92.

KAPLAN, H. S. (1974). *The new sex therapy*. New York: Bruner/Mazel.

KAPLAN, H. S. (1977). Hypoactive sexual desire. *Journal of Sex and Marital Therapy, 3*, 3–9.

KAPLAN, H. S. (1979). *Disorders of desire*. New York: Bruner/Mazel.

KAPLAN, H. S. (1983). *The evaluation of sexual disorders: Psychological and medical aspects*. New York: Bruner/Mazel.

KAPLAN, H. S. (1987). *Sexual aversion, sexual phobias, and panic disorders*. New York: Brunner/Mazel.

KAPLAN, H. S. (1988). Intimacy disorders and sexual panic states. *Journal of Sex and Marital Therapy, 14*, 3–12.

KAPLAN, H. S. (1989). *How to overcome premature ejaculation*. New York: Brunner/Mazel.

KAPLAN, H. S. (1992a). A neglected issue: The sexual side effects of current treatments for breast cancer. *Journal of Sex and Marital Therapy, 18*, 3–19.

KAPLAN, H. S. (1992b). Does the CAT technique enhance female orgasm? *Journal of Sex and Marital Therapy, 18*, 285–291.

KAPLAN, H. S. (1993). Post-ejaculatory pain syndrome. *Journal of Sex and Marital Therapy, 19*, 91–103.

KAPLAN, H. S., & OWETT, T. (1993). The female androgen deficiency syndrome. *Journal of Sex and Marital Therapy, 19*, 3–24.

KARMEL, M. (1959). *Thank you Dr. Lamaze*. Philadelphia: Lippincott.

KATLAMA, C., & DICKINSON, G. M. (1993). Update on opportunistic infections. *AIDS, 7*, S185–S194.

KATZ, B. L., & BURT, M. R. (1986, August). Effects of familiarity with the rapist on postrape recovery. Paper presented at the meeting of the American Psychological Association, Washington, DC.

KATZ, J. (1976). *Gay American history: Lesbian and gay men in the U.S.A.* New York: Crowell.

KAWACHI, I., COLDITZ, G. A., & HANKINSON, S. (1994). Long-term benefits and risks of alternative methods of fertility control in the United States. *Contraception, 50*, 1–16.

KEET, I. P. M. et al. (1994). Predictors of disease progression in HIV-infected homosexual men with CD4 + cells < 200 > $10^6/1$ but free of AIDS-defining clinical disease. *AIDS, 8*, 1577–1583.

KEGEL, A. (1952). Sexual functions of the pubococcygeus muscle. *Western Journal of Surgery, Obstetrics, and Gynecology, 60*, 521–524.

KEGELES, S. M., ADLER, N. E., & IRWIN, C. E. (1988). Sexually active adolescents and condoms: Changes over one year in knowledge, attitudes and use. *American Journal of Public Health, 78*, 460–461.

KEIDING, N., GIWERCMAN, A., CARLSEN, E., & SKAKKEBACK, N. E. (1994). Importance of empirical evidence. *British Medical Journal, 309*, 22.

KELEN, G. D. et al. (1988). Unrecognized human immunodeficiency virus infection in emergency department patients. *New England Journal of Medicine, 318*, 1645–1650.

KELLETT, J. M. (1991). Sexuality and the elderly. *Sexual and Marital Therapy, 6*, 147–155.

KELLOGG, J. W. (1882). *Plain facts for old and young*.

KELLY, J. A., ST. LAWRENCE, J. S., HOOD, H. V., & BRASFIELD, T. L. (1989). Behavioral intervention to reduce AIDS risk activities. *Journal of Consulting and Clinical Psychology, 57*, 60–67.

KELLY, J. A., & WORELL, J. (1977). New formulations of sex roles and androgyny: A critical review. *Journal of Consulting and Clinical Psychology, 45*, 1101–1115.

KELLY, R. J. (1982). Behavioral reorientation of pedophiles: Can it be done? *Clinical Psychology Review, 2*, 387–408.

KENDALL-TACKETT, K. A., & SIMON, A. F. (1987). Perpetrators and their acts: Data from 365 adults molested as children. *Child Abuse & Neglect, 11*, 237–245.

KENDALL-TACKETT, K. A., WILLIAMS, L. M., & FINKELHOR, D. (1993). Impact of sexual abuse on children: A review and synthesis of recent empirical studies. *Psychological Bulletin, 113*, 164–180.

KENDRICK, D. T., & KEEFE, R. C. (1992). Age preferences in mates reflect sex differences in reproductive strategies. *Behavioral and Brain Sciences, 15*, 75–133.

KENNELL, J. et al.(1991). Continuous emotional support during labor in a U. S. hospital. *Journal of the American Medical Association, 265*, 2197–2201.

KENNEY, A. M., GUARDAD, S., & BROWN, L. (1989). Sex education and AIDS education in the schools. *Family Planning Perspectives, 21*, 56–64.

KEPHART, W. M. (1967). Some correlates of romantic love. *Journal of Marriage and the Family, 29*, 470–474.

KERLIKOWSKE, K. et al. (1995). Efficacy of screening mammography: A meta-analysis. *Journal of the American Medical Association, 273*, 149–154.

KESTELMAN, P., & TRUSSELL, J. (1991). Efficacy of the simultaneous use of condoms and spermicides. *Family Planning Perspectives, 23*, 226–232.

KETTL, P. et al. (1991). Female sexuality after spinal cord injury. *Sexuality and Disability, 9*, 287–295.

KEY, N. S. et al. (1990). Infection of vascular endothelial cells with herpes simplex virus enhances tissue factor activity and reduces thrombomodulin expression. *Proceedings of the National Academy of Sciences of the U.S.A., 87*, 7095–7099.

KEYE, W. R. (1983). Update: Premenstrual syndrome. *Endocrine and Fertility Forum, 6*, 1–3.

KHABBAZ, R. F. et al. (1990). Seroprevalence and risk factors for HTLV-I/II infection among female prostitutes in the United States. *Journal of the American Medical Association, 263*, 60–64.

KIECOLT-GLASER, J., & GLASER, R. (1988). Major life changes, chronic stress, and immunity. *Advances in Biological Psychiatry, 44*, 217–224.

KIESSLING, A. A. (1992). Semen transmission of human immunodeficiency virus. *Fertility and Sterility, 58*, 667–669.

KIKUCHI, J. J. (1988, Fall). Rhode Island develops successful intervention program for adolescents. *NCASA News*, p. 26.

KILMANN, P. R., WANLASS, R. L., SABALIS, R. F., & SULLIVAN, B. (1981). Sex education: A review of its effects. *Archives of Sexual Behavior, 10*, 177–205.

KIMMEL, M. S. (1989). From separate spheres to sexual equality: Men's responses to feminism at the turn of the century. In B. J. Risman &

P. Schwartz (Eds.), *Gender in intimate relationships: A microstructural approach.* Belmont, CA: Wadsworth.

KING, B. M., & ANDERSON, P. B. (1994). A failure of HIV education: Sex can be more important than a long life. *Journal of Health Education, 25,* 13–18.

KING, B. M., & LOCOCO, G. C. (1990). Effects of sexually explicit textbook drawings on enrollment and family communication. *Journal of Sex Education and Therapy, 16,* 38–53.

KING, B. M., PARISI, L. S., & O'DWYER, K. R. (1993). College sexuality education promotes future discussions about sexuality between former students and their children. *Journal of Sex Education and Therapy, 19,* 285–293.

KINSEY, A. C., POMEROY, W., & MARTIN, C. (1948). *Sexual behavior in the human male.* Philadelphia: Saunders.

KINSEY, A. C., POMEROY, W., MARTIN, C., & GEBHARD, P. (1953). *Sexual behavior in the human female.* Philadelphia: Saunders.

KINZL, J., & BIEBL, W. (1992). Long-term effects of incest: Life events triggering mental disorders in female patients with sexual abuse in childhood. *Child Abuse & Neglect, 16,* 567–573.

KIRBY, D. (1984). *Sexuality education: An evaluation of programs and their effects.* Santa Cruz, CA: Network Publications.

KIRK, M., & MADSEN, H. (1989). *How America will conquer its fear and hatred of homosexuals in the '90s.* New York: Doubleday.

KJERSGAARD, A. G. et al. (1989). Male or female sterilization: A comparative study. *Fertility and Sterility, 51,* 439–443.

KLECK, R. E., RICHARDSON, S. A., & RONALD, L. (1974). Physical appearance cues and interpersonal attraction in children. *Child Development, 45,* 305–310.

KLEPINGER, D. H., BILLY, J. O. G., TANFER, K., & GRADY, W. R. (1993). Perception of AIDS risk and severity and their association with risk-related behavior among U.S. men. *Family Planning Perspectives, 25,* 74–82.

KLIGMAN, E. W., & PEPIN, E. (1992). Prescribing physical activity for older patients. *Geriatrics, 47*(8), 33–47.

KLITSCH, M. (1993a). Injectable hormones and regulatory controversy: An end to the long-running story. *Family Planning Perspectives, 25,* 37–40.

KLITSCH, M. (1993b). Vasectomy and prostate cancer: More questions than answers. *Family Planning Perspectives, 25,* 133–135.

KLONOFF-COHEN, H. S., SAVITZ, D. A., CEFALO, R. C., & McCANN, M. F. (1989). An epidemiologic study of contraception and preeclampsia. *Journal of the American Medical Association, 262,* 3143–3147.

KOCKOTT, G., & FAHRNER, E. M. (1988). Male-to-female and female-to-male transsexuals: A comparison. *Archives of Sexual Behavior, 17,* 539–546.

KOESKE, R. (1983). Lifting the curse of menstruation: Toward a feminist perspective on the menstrual cycle. *Women and Health, 8,* 1–16.

KOHLBERG, L. (1966). A cognitive-developmental analysis of children's sex-role concepts and attitudes. In E. E. Maccoby (Ed.), *The development of sex differences* (pp. 82–173). Stanford, CA: Stanford University Press.

KOHLBERG, L., & ULLIAN, D. Z. (1974). Stages in the development of psychosexual concepts and attitudes. In R. C. Friedman, R. M. Richart, & R. L. Van de Wiele (Eds.), *Sex differences in behavior* (pp. 209–222). New York: Wiley.

KOLATA, G. (1995). Drug group promising in HIV fight. *New York Times.*

KOLODNY, R. C. (1980, November). *Adolescent sexuality.* Paper presented at the Michigan Personnel and Guidance Association annual convention, Detroit.

KOLODNY, R. C. (1981). Effects of marijuana on sexual behavior and function. Paper presented at the Midwestern Conference on drug use, St. Louis, MO.

KOLODNY, R. C., MASTERS, W. H., & JOHNSON, V. E. (1979). *Textbook of sexual medicine.* Boston: Little, Brown.

KOLODNY, R. C., MASTERS, W. H., KOLODNY, W. H., & TORO, G. (1974). Depression of plasma testosterone levels after chronic intensive marijuana use. *New England Journal of Medicine, 290,* 872–874.

KOLS, A. et al. (1982, May-June). Oral contraceptives in the 1980's. *Population Reports,* Series A, No. 6.

KOMAROVSKY, M. (1992). The concept of gender role revisited. *Gender and Society, 6,* 301–313.

KOONIN, L. M., ATRASH, H. K., ROCHAT, R. W., & SMITH, J. C. (1988). Maternal mortality surveillance, United States, 1980-1985. *Morbidity and Mortality Weekly, 37*(Suppl. ss-5), 19–29.

KOONIN, L. M. et al. (1992). Abortion surveillance—United States, 1989. *Morbidity and Mortality Weekly, 41* (Spec. Suppl. 5).

KORALEWSKI, M. A., & CONGER, J. C. (1992). The assessment of social skills among sexually coercive college males. *Journal of Sex Research, 29,* 169–188.

KOSS, M. P., DINERO, T. E., SEIBEL, C. A., & COX, S. L. (1988). Stranger and acquaintance rape: Are there differences in the victim's experience? *Psychology of Women Quarterly, 12,* 1–23.

KOSS, M. P., GIDYCZ, C. A., & WISNIEWSKI, N. (1987). The scope of rape: Incidence and prevalence of sexual aggression and victimization in a national sample of higher education students. *Journal of Consulting and Clinical Psychology, 55,* 162–170.

KOSS, M. P., LEONARD, K., BEEZLEY, D., & OROS, C. (1985). Nonstranger sexual aggression: A discriminant analysis of the psychological characterists of undetected offenders. *Sex Roles, 12,* 981–982.

KOSS, M. P., & OROS, C. J. (1982). Sexual experiences survey: A research instrument investigating sexual aggression and victimization. *Journal of Consulting and Clinical Psychology, 50,* 455–457.

KOUTSKY, L. A. et al. (1992a). Underdiagnosis of genital herpes by current clinical and viral-isolation procedures. *New England Journal of Medicine, 326,* 1533–1539.

KOUTSKY, L. A. et al. (1992b). A cohort study of the risk of cervical intraepithelial neoplasia grade 2 or 3 in relation to papillomavirus infection. *New England Journal of Medicine, 327,* 1272.

KOVACS, G. T. et al. (1986). The contraceptive diaphragm: Is it an acceptable method in the 1980's? *Australian & New Zealand Journal of Obstetrics and Gynaecology, 26,* 76–79.

KOVACS, J. A. et al. (1995). Increases in CD4 T lymphocytes with intermittent courses of interleukin-2 in patients with human immunodeficiency virus infection. *New England Journal of Medicine, 332,* 567–575.

KRAFFT-EBING, R. V. (1978; originally 1886). *Psychopathia sexualis.* New York: Stein & Day.

KRAUS, S. J., & STONE, K. M. (1990). Management of genital infection caused by human papillomavirus. *Reviews of Infectious Diseases, 12,* S620–S632.

KRAVIS, D., & MOLITCH, M. E. (1990, February). Endocrine causes of impotence. *Medical Aspects of Human Sexuality,* pp. 62–67.

KREBS, H. B. (1989). Management of human papillomavirus-associated genital lesions in men. *Obstetrics and Gynecology, 73,* 312–316.

KREISS, J. et al. (1992). Efficacy of nonoxynol 9 contraceptive sponge use in preventing heterosexual acquisition of HIV in Nairobi prostitutes. *Journal of the American Medical Association, 268,* 477–482.

KRIEGER, L. M. (1993, May). Gay youths ignoring AIDS threat, health study says. *San Francisco Examiner.*

KRIEGER, W. G. (1976). Infant influences and the parent sex by child sex interaction in the socialization process. *JSAS Catalogue of Selected Documents in Psychology, 6,* 36.

KRITCHEVSKY, D. (1990). Nutrition and breast cancer. *Cancer (Philadelphia), 66,* 1321–1325.

KRONENBERG, F. (1994). Hot flashes. In R. A. Lobo (Ed.), *Treatment of the postmenopausal woman: Basic and clinical aspects* (pp. 97–117). New York: Raven Press.

KRUEGER, S. L., DUNSON, T. R., & AMATYA, R. N. (1994). Norplant contraceptive acceptability among women in five Asian countries. *Contraception, 50,* 349–361.

KRUESI, M. J. P. et al. (1992). Paraphilias: A double-blind crossover comparison of clomipramine versus desipramine. *Archives of Sexual Behavior, 21,* 587–593.

KRUG, R. S. (1989). Adult male report of childhood sexual abuse by mothers: Case descriptions and long-term consequences. *Child Abuse & Neglect, 13,* 111–119.

KU, L. C., SONENSTEIN, F. L., & PLECK, J. H. (1992). The association of AIDS education and sex education with sexual behavior and condom use among teenage men. *Family Planning Perspectives, 24,* 100–106.

KU, L. C., SONENSTEIN, F.L., & PLECK, J. H. (1993). Young men's risk behaviors for HIV infection and sexually transmitted diseases, 1988 through 1991. *American Journal of Public Health, 83,* 1609–1615.

KU, L. C., SONENSTEIN, F. L., & PLECK, J. H. (1994). The dynamics of young men's condom use during and across relationships. *Family Planning Perspectives, 26,* 246–251.

KUHN, D., NASH, S., & BRUCKEN, L. (1978). Sex role concepts of two- and three-year olds. *Child Development, 49,* 445–451.

KULHANJIAN, J. A. et al. (1992). Identification of women at unsuspected risk of primary infection with herpes simplex virus type 2 during pregnancy. *New England Journal of Medicine, 326,* 16–20.

KUSHI, L. H. et al. (1992). Dietary fat and postmenopausal breast cancer. *Journal of the National Cancer Institute, 84,* 1092–1099.

KUTCHINSKY, B. (1973). The effect of easy availability of pornography on the incidence of sex crimes. *Journal of Social Issues, 29,* 163–182.

KUTCHINSKY, B. (1992). A case for testing: The roles of safer sex and HIV testing in AIDS prevention. In P. B. Anderson, D. de Mauro, & R. J. Noonan (Eds.), *Does anyone still remember when sex was fun?* (2nd ed.). (pp. 46–96) Dubuque, IA: Kendall/Hunt.

LAAN, E., EVERAERD, W., VAN BELLEN, G., & HANEWALD, G. (1994). Women's sexual and emotional responses to male- and female-produced erotica. *Archives of Sexual Behavior, 23*, 153–169.

LABOUVIE-VIEF, G. (1990). Modes of knowledge and the organization of development. In M. L. Commons, C. Armon, L. Kohlberg, S. A. Richards, T. A. Gropzer, & J. Sannott (Eds.), *Adult development models and methods in the study of adolescents and adult thought.* New York: Praeger.

LABOUVIE-VIEF, G., HAKIM-LARSON, J., & HOBART, C. J. (1987). Age, ego level, and the life-span development of coping and defense processes. *Psychology and Aging, 2*, 286–293.

LADAS, A. K., WHIPPLE, B., & PERRY, J. D. (1982). *The G spot and other recent discoveries about human sexuality.* New York: Holt, Rinehart & Winston.

LADOUCEUR, P., & TEMPLE, M. (1985). Substance abuse among rapists: A comparison with other serious felons. *Crime and Delinquency, 31*, 269–294.

LAFFERTY, W. E. et al. (1987). Recurrences after oral and genital herpes simplex virus infection: Influence of site of infection and viral type. *New England Journal of Medicine, 316*, 1444–1449.

LAGA, M., MEHEUS, A., & PIOT, P. (1989). Epidemiology and control of gonococcal ophthalmia neonatorum. *Bulletin of the World Health Organization, 67*, 471–478.

LAKIN, M. M., & MONTAGUE, D. K. (1988). Intracavernous injection therapy in post priapism cavernosal fibrosis. *Journal of Urology, 140*, 828–829.

LAMAZE, F. (1970). *Painless childbirth.* Chicago: H. Regnery. (1st ed., 1956).

LAMB, M. E. (1986). *The Father's role: Cross-cultural perspectives.* Hillsdale, NJ: Erlbaum.

LAMBERT, J. D. (1995). A legacy of pleasure. In P. B. Anderson, D. de Mauro, & R. J. Noonan (Eds.), *Does anyone still remember when sex was fun?* (3rd ed.) (pp. 13–30). Dubuque, IA: Kendall/Hunt.

LANG, A. et al. (1980). Expectancy, alcohol, and sex guilt as determinants of interest in and reaction to sexual stimuli. *Journal of Abnormal Psychology, 89*, 644–653.

LANG, W. et al. (1989). Patterns of T lymphocyte changes with human immunodeficiency virus infection: From seroconversion to the development of AIDS. *Journal of Acquired Immune Deficiency Syndromes, 2*, 63–69.

LANGEVIN, R. (1983). *Sexual strands.* Hillsdale, NJ: Erlbaum.

LANGEVIN, R. (1985). An overview of the paraphelias. In M. H. Ben-Aron, S. J., Hucker, & C. D. Webster (Eds.), *Clinical criminology: The assessment and treatment of criminal behavior* (pp. 177–190). Toronto: M & M Graphics and Clarke Institute of Psychiatry.

LANGEVIN, R. et al. (1979). Experimental studies of the etiology of genital exhibitionism. *Archives of Sexual Behavior, 8*, 307–332.

LANGEVIN, R. et al. (1988). Sexual sadism: Brain, blood, and behavior. *Annals of the New York Academy of Sciences, 528*, 163–171.

LANGFELDT, T. (1981). Sexual development in children. In M. Cook & K. Howells (Eds.), *Adult sexual interest in children.* London: Academic Press.

LANGLOIS, J. H., & DOWNS, A. C. (1980). Mothers, fathers, and peers as socialization agents of sex-typed play behaviors in young children. *Child Development, 51*, 1237–1247.

LANGMYHR, G. J. (1976, June). Varieties of coital positions: Advantages and disadvantages. *Medical Aspects of Human Sexuality*, pp. 128–139.

LANYON, R. I. (1986). Theory and treatment in child molestation. *Journal of Consulting and Clinical Psychology, 54*, 176–182.

L'ARMAND, K. L., & PEPITONE, A. (1982). Judgements of rape: A study of victim-rapist relationship and victim sexual history. *Personality and Social Psychology Bulletin, 8*, 134–139.

LARSON, N. R., & MADDOCK, J. W. (1986). Structural and functional variables in incest family systems: Implications for assessment and treatment. *Journal of Psychotherapy and the Family, 2*, 27–44.

LARUE, G. A. (1989, July/August). Religious traditions and circumcision. *The Truth Seeker*, pp. 4–8.

LASSWELL, M. E., & LOBSENZ, N. M. (1980). *Styles of loving.* New York: Ballantine.

LAUER, J., & LAUER, R. (1985, June). Marriages made to last. *Psychology Today*, pp. 22–26.

LAUGHLIN, C. D. J. R., & ALLGEIER, E. R. (1979). *Ethnography of the So of Northeastern Uganda.* New Haven, CT: Human Relations Area Files, Inc.

LAUMANN, E., MICHAEL, R., GAGNON, J., & MICHAELS, S. (1994). *The social organization of sexuality: Sexual practices in the United States.* Chicago: University of Chicago Press.

LAURENCE, J. et al. (1992). Acquired immunodeficiency without evidence of infection with human immunodeficiency virus types 1 and 2. *Lancet, 340*, 273–274.

LAVEE, Y. (1991). Western and non-Western human sexuality: Implications for clinical practice. *Journal of Sex and Marital Therapy, 17*, 203–213.

LAWRENCE, D. H. (1930). *Lady Chatterley's lover.* New York: W. Faro.

LAWSON, C. (1993). Mother-son sexual abuse: Rare or underreported? A critique of the research. *Child Abuse & Neglect, 17*, 261–269.

LAZARUS, J. A. (1992). Sex with former patients almost always unethical. *American Journal of Psychiatry, 149*, 855–857.

LEBEL, R. R. (1983). Consanguinity studies in Wisconsin. 1. Secular trends in consanguineous marriage, 1843-1981. *American Journal of Medical Genetics, 15*, 543–560.

LEBOYER, F. (1975). *Birth without violence.* New York: Knopf.

LEE, H. H. et al. (1995). Diagnosis of chlamydia trachomatis genitourinary infection in women by ligase chain reaction assay of urine. *Lancet, 345*, 213–216.

LEE, J. A. (1974, October, 8). The styles of loving. *Psychology Today*, pp. 43–50.

LEE, J. A. (1976). *The colors of love.* Englewood Cliffs, NJ: Prentice Hall.

LEE, J. A. (1988). Love-styles. In R. J. Sternberg & M. L. Barnes (Eds.), *The psychology of love* (pp. 38–67). New Haven, CT: Yale University Press.

LEE, N. C., RUBIN, G. L., ORY, H. W., & BURKMAN, R. T. (1983). Type of intrauterine device and the risk of pelvic inflammatory disease. *Obstetrics and Gynecology, 62*, 1–6.

LEE-FELDSTEIN, A., ANTON-CULVER, H., & FELDSTEIN, P. J. (1994). Treatment differences and other prognostic factors related to breast cancer survival. *Journal of the American Medical Association, 271*, 1163–1168.

LEFEVRE, M. L. et al. (1993). A randomized trial of prenatal ultrasonagraphic screening: Impact on maternal management and outcome. *American Journal of Obstetrics and Gynecology, 169*, 483–489.

LEIBLUM, S. R., & ROSEN, R. C. (Eds.). (1988). *Sexual desire disorders.* New York: Guilford.

LEIBLUM, S. R., & ROSEN, R. C. (1989). *Principles and practice of sex therapy: An update for the 1990s.* New York: Guilford.

LEIBLUM, S. R., & ROSEN, R. C. (1991). Couples therapy for erectile disorders: Conceptual and clinical considerations. *Journal of Sex and Marital Therapy, 17*, 147–159.

LEIBLUM, S R.. et al. (1983). Vaginal atrophy in the post menopausal woman. The importance of sexual activity and hormones. *Journal of the American Medical Association, 249*, 2195–2198.

LIEF, H. J. (1977). Inhibited sexual desire. *Medical Aspects of Human Sexuality, 7*, 94–95.

LEIFER, M. (1980). *Psychological effects of motherhood: A study of first pregnancy.* New York: Praeger.

LEIGH, B. (1989). Reasons for having and avoiding sex: Gender, sexual orientation, and relationship to sexual behavior. *Journal of Sex Research, 26*, 199–208.

LEITENBERG, H., DETZER, M. J., & SREBNIK, D. (1993). Gender differences in masturbation and the relation of masturbation experience in preadolescence and/or early adolescence to sexual behavior and sexual adjustment in young adulthood. *Archives of Sexual Behavior, 22*, 87–98.

LEITENBERG, H., GREENWALD, E., & CADO, S. (1992). A retrospective study of long-term methods of coping with having been sexually abused during childhood. *Child Abuse & Neglect, 16*, 399–407.

LEITENBERG, H., & HENNING, K. (1995). Sexual Fantasy. *Psychological Bulletin, 117*, 469–496.

LEMP, G. F. et al. (1990). Projection of AIDs morbidity and mortality in San Francisco. *Journal of the American Medical Association, 263*, 1497–1501.

LEMP, G. F. et al. (1992). Survival for women and men with AIDS. *Journal of Infectious Diseases, 166*, 74–79.

LENDERKING, W. R. et al. (1994). Evaluation of the quality of life associated with zidovudine treatment in asymptomatic human immunodeficiency virus infection. *New England Journal of Medicine, 330*, 738–743.

LEONARD, T. L., FREUND, M., & PLATT, J. J. (1989). Behavior of clients of prostitutes. *American Journal of Public Health, 79*, 903.

LERMAN, H. (1986). *A mote in Freud's eye: From psychoanalysis to the psychology of women.* New York: Springer.

LEVAY, S. (1991). A difference in hypothalamic structure between heterosexual and homosexual men. *Science, 253*, 1034–1037.

LEVENTHAL, J. M. (1988). Have there been changes in the epidemiology of sexual abuse of children during the 20th century? *Pediatrics, 82*, 766–773.

LEVER, J. et al. (1992). Behavior patterns and sexual identity of bisexual males. *Journal of Sex Research, 29*, 141–167.

LEVIN, R. J., & LEVIN, A. (1975, September). Sexual pleasure: The surprising performances of 100,000 women. *Redbook*, p. 51.

LEVIN, R. J., & WAGNER, G. (1985). Orgasm in women in the laboratory—Quantitative studies on duration, intensity, latency, and vaginal blood flow. *Archives of Sexual Behavior, 11*, 367–386.

LEVINE, M. P. (1992). The life of gay clones. In G. Herdt (Ed.), *Gay culture in America: Essays from the field*. Boston: Beacon Press.

LEVINE, M. P., & TROIDEN, R. R. (1988). The myth of sexual compulsivity. *Journal of Sex Research, 25*, 347–363.

LEVINE, R. A. (1959). Gussi sex offenses: A study in social control. *American Anthropologist, 61*, 965–990.

LEVINE, R. A. (1974). Gussi sex offenses: A study in social control. In N. N. Wagner (Ed.), *Perspectives on human sexuality* (pp. 308–352). New York: Behavioral Publishers.

LEVINE, R. J. et al. (1990). Differences in the quality of semen in outdoor workers during summer and winter. *New England Journal of Medicine, 323*, 12–16.

LEVINE, S. B. (1993). Gender-disturbed males. *Journal of Sex and Marital Therapy, 19*, 131–141.

LEVINE, S. B., & ALTHOF, S. E. (1991). The pathogenesis of psychogenic erectile dysfunction. *Journal of Sex Education and Therapy, 17*, 251–266.

LEVINGER, G. (1988). Can we picture "love"? In R. J. Sternberg & M. L. Barnes (Eds.), *The psychology of love* (pp. 139–158). New Haven, CT: Yale University Press.

LÉVI-STRAUSS, C. (1969). *The elementary structures of kinship*. Boston: Beacon Press.

LEVITT, E. E., MOSER, C., & JAMISON, K. V. (1994). The prevalence and some attributes of females in the sadomasochistic subculture: A second report. *Archives of Sexual Behavior, 23*, 465–473.

LEVRAN, D. et al. (1990). Pregnancy potential of human oocytes—The effect of cryopreservation. *New England Journal of Medicine, 323*, 1153–1156.

LEWES, K. (1992). Homophobia and the heterosexual fear of AIDS. *American Imago, 49*, 343–356.

LEWIS, D. K., WATTERS, J. K., & CASE, P. (1990). The prevalence of high-risk sexual behavior in male intravenous drug users with steady female partners. *American Journal of Public Health, 80*, 465–466.

LEWIS, M., & BUTLER, R. (1994). *Love and sex after 60*. New York: Ballantine.

LEWIS, R. A. (1973). Parents and peers: Socialization agents in the coital behavior of young adults. *Journal of Sex Research, 9*, 156–170.

LIDEGAARD, O. (1993). Oral contraception and risk of a cerebral thromboembolic attack: Results of a case-controlled study. *British Medical Journal, 306*, 956–963.

LIDEGAARD, O., & HELM, P. (1990). Pelvic inflammatory disease: The influence of contraceptive, sexual, and social life events. *Contraception, 41*, 475–483.

LIEBERMAN, E. J., & PECK, E. (1982). *Sex and birth control*. New York: Schocken.

LIEBOWITZ, M. (1983). *The chemistry of love*. Boston: Little, Brown.

LIFSON, A. R. et al. (1990). HIV seroconversion in two homosexual men after receptive oral intercourse with ejaculation: Implications for counseling concerning safe sexual practices. *American Journal of Public Health, 80*, 1509–1511.

LIGHTFOOT-KLEIN, H. (1989). *Prisoners of ritual: An odyssey into female genital circumcision in Africa*. Binghamton, NY: Haworth Press.

LIGHTFOOT-KLEIN, H., & SHAW, E. (1991). Special needs of ritually circumcised women patients. *Journal of Obstetrics, Gynecology and Neonatal Nursing, 20*, 102–107.

LIN, J.-S. L. et al. (1992). Underdiagnosis of Chlamydia trachomatis infection. *Sexually Transmitted Diseases, 19*, 259–265.

LINDBACK, S., BROSTRÖM, C., KARLSSON, A., & GAINES, H. (1994). Does symptomatic primary HIV-1 infection accelerate progression to CDC stage IV disease, CD4 count below 200 x 10⁶/l, AIDS, and death from AIDS? *British Medical Journal, 309*, 1535–1537.

LINDBERG, F. H., & DISTAD, L. J. (1985). Post-traumatic stress disorders in women who experienced childhood incest. *Child Abuse & Neglect, 9*, 329–334.

LINDEMALM, G. et al. (1986). Long-term follow-up of "sex change" in 13 male-to-female transsexuals. *Archives of Sexual Behavior, 15*, 187–210.

LINDEN, E. (1992, August 17). Apes that swing many ways. *Time Magazine*, pp. 50–51.

LINDHOLM, C., & LINDHOLM, C. (1980, Summer). Life behind the veil. *Science Digest Special*.

LINZ, D. (1985). *Sexual violence in the media: Effects on male viewers and implications for society*. Doctoral thesis, University of Wisconsin, Department of Psychology, Madison.

LINZ, D. (1989). Exposure to sexually explicit materials and attitudes toward rape: A comparison of study results. *Journal of Sex Research, 26*, 50–84.

LINZ, D., DONNERSTEIN, E., & PENROD, S. (1987). The findings and recommendations of the Attorney General's Commission on Pornography: Do the psychological "facts" fit the political fury? *American Psychologist, 42*, 946–953.

LINZ, D., WILSON, B., & DONNERSTEIN, E. (1992). Sexual violence in the mass media: Legal solutions, warnings, and mitigation through education. *Journal of Social Issues, 48*, 145–171.

LIPOVSKY, J. A., & KILPATRICK, D. G. (1992). The child sexual abuse victim as an adult. In W. O'Donohue & J. H. Geer (Eds.), *The sexual abuse of children: Clinical issues* (Vol. 2). Hillsdale, NJ: Erlbaum.

LIPS, H. (1992). *Sex and gender*. Mountain View, CA: Mayfield Publishing.

LIPSCOMB, G. H., MURAM, D., SPECK, P. M., & MERCER, B. M. (1992). Male victims of sexual assault. *Journal of the American Medical Association, 267*, 3064–3066.

LIPTON, M. A. (1983). The problem of pornography. In W. E. Fann et al. (Eds.), *Phenomenology and treatment of psychosexual disorders* (pp. 113–134). New York: Spectrum.

LISH, J. D. et al. (1991). Gender-related behavior development in females exposed to diethylstilbestrol in utero: An attempted replication. *Journal of the American Academy of Child and Adolescent Psychiatry, 30*, 29–37.

LISH, J. D. et al. (1992). Prenatal exposure to diethylstilbestrol (DES): Childhood play behavior and adult gender-role behavior in women. *Archives of Sexual Behavior, 21*, 423–441.

LISKIN, L., WHARTON, C., & BLACKBURN, R. (1990). Condoms—now more than ever. *Population Reports, Series H, 8*, 1–36.

LITTLE, R. E. et al. (1989). Maternal alcohol use during breastfeeding and infant mental and motor development at one year. *New England Journal of Medicine, 321*, 425–430.

LITWIN, M. (1993). *Side effects of prostate treatment (impotency & incontinence)*. Paper presented at the meeting of the American Urological Association.

LLOYD, R. (1976). *For money or love: Boy prostitution in America*. New York: Vanguard Press.

LO, B., & STEINBROOK, R. (1992). Health care workers infected with the human immunodeficiency virus. *Journal of the American Medical Association, 267*, 1100–1105.

LO, S. C. et al. (1989). A novel virus-like infectious agent in patients with AIDS. *American Journal of Tropical Medicine and Hygiene, 40*, 213–226.

LOCK, M. (1994). Menopause in cultural context. *Experimental Gerontology, 29*, 307–317.

LOCKWOOD, D. (1980). *Prison sexual violence*. New York: Elsevier.

LONARDO, A. D., VENUTI, A., & MARCANTE, M. L. (1992). Human papillomavirus in breast cancer. *Breast Cancer Research and Treatment, 21*, 95–100.

LONDON, S. J., CONNOLLY, J. L., SCHMITT, S. J., & COLDITZ, G. A. (1992). A prospective study of benign breast disease and the risk of breast cancer. *Journal of the American Medical Association, 267*, 941–944.

LONGAKER, M. T. et al. (1991). Maternal outcome after open fetal surgery. *Journal of the American Medical Association, 265*, 737–741.

LONGNECKER, M. P., NEWCOMB, P. A., MITTENDORF, R. et al. (1992). Risk of breast cancer in relation to past and recent alcohol consumption. *American Journal of Epidemiology, 136*, 1001.

LOPICCOLO, J. (1978). Direct treatment of sexual dysfunction. In J. LoPiccolo & L. LoPiccolo (Eds.), *Handbook of sex therapy* (pp. 1–17). New York: Plenum.

LOPICCOLO, J. (1992). Postmodern sex therapy for erectile failure. In R. Rosen & S. Leiblum (Eds.), *Erectile disorders*. New York: Guilford.

LOPICCOLO, J., & FRIEDMAN, J. (1988). Broad-spectrum treatment of low sexual desire: Integration of cognitive, behavioral, and systemic therapy. In S. R. Leiblum & R. C. Rosen (Eds.), *Sexual desire disorders*. New York: Guilford.

LOPICCOLO, J., & LOBITZ, W. C. (1972). The role of masturbation in the treatment of orgasmic dysfunction. *Archives of Sexual Behavior, 2*, 163–171.

LOPICCOLO, J., & STOCK, W. (1986). Treatment of sexual dysfunction. *Journal of Consulting and Clinical Psychology, 54*, 158–167.

LOPICCOLO, L. (1980). Low sexual desire. In S. R. Leiblum & L. A. Pervin (Eds.), *Principles and practice of sex therapy* (pp. 29–64). New York: Guilford.

LOVIK, C. et al. (1987). Maternal exposure to spermicides in relation to certain birth defects. *New England Journal of Medicine, 317*, 474–476.

LOWN, J., & DOLAN, E. (1988). Financial challenges in remarriage. *Lifestyles: Family and Economic Issues, 9*, 73–88.

LOWY, D. R., KIRNBAUER, R., & SCHILLER, J. T. (1994). Genital human papillomavirus infection. *Proceedings of the National Academy of Sciences, of the U.S.A., 91*, 2436–2440.

Loy, P. H., & Stewart, L. P. (1984). The extent and effects of the sexual harassment of working women. *Sociological Focus, 17*, 31–43.

Luckey, E. B., & Bain, J. K. (1970). Children: A factor in marital satisfaction. *Journal of Marriage and the Family, 32*, 43–44.

Luger, A. (1993). The origin of syphilis. *Sexually Transmitted Diseases, 20*, 110–117.

Lugo-Miro, V. I., Green, M., & Mazur, L. (1992). Comparison of different metronidazole therapeutic regimens for bacterial vaginosis. *Journal of the American Medical Association, 268*, 92–95.

Luke, B. (1994). The changing pattern of multiple births in the United States: Maternal and infant characteristics, 1973 and 1990. *Obstetrics and Gynecology, 84*, 101–106.

Luker, K. (1975). *Taking chances.* Berkeley: University of California Press.

Lurie, N. O. (1953). Winnebago berdache. *American Anthropologist, 55*, 708–712.

Lu-Yao, G. L., McLerran, D., Wasson, J., & Wennberg, J. E. (1993). An assessment of radical prostatectomy. *Journal of the American Medical Association, 269*, 2633–2636.

Lynch, H. T., & Lynch, J. F. (1992). Hereditary ovarian carcinoma. *Hematology/Oncology Clinics of North America, 6*, 783–811.

Mabie, W. C., & Sibai, B. M. (1987). Hypertensive states of pregnancy. In M. Pernoll & R. Benson (Eds.), *Current obstetric and gynecologic diagnosis and treatment.* Los Altos, CA: Appleton & Lange.

MacDonald, A. P. (1981). Bisexuality: Some comments on research and theory. *Journal of Homosexuality, 6*, 21–35.

MacDonald, A. P. (1982). Research on sexual orientation: A bridge which touches both shores but doesn't meet in the middle. *Journal of Sex Education and Therapy, 8*, 9–13.

MacDonald, N. E. et al. (1990). High-risk STD/HIV behavior among college students. *Journal of the American Medical Association, 263*, 3155–3159.

Mac Kenzie, W. R. et al. (1992). Multiple false-positive serologic tests for HIV, HTLV-1, and hepatitis C following influenza vaccination, 1991. *Journal of the American Medical Association, 268*, 1015–1017.

MacKinnon, C. A. (1979). *Sexual harassment of working women.* New Haven, CT: Yale University Press.

Macklin, E. D. (1978). Review of research on non-marital cohabitation in the U.S. In B. I. Murstein (Ed.), *Exploring intimate lifestyles* (pp. 197–243). New York: Springer.

MacNamara, D., & Sagarin, E. (1977). *Sex, crime, and the law.* New York: Free Press.

Maddock, J. W. et al. (1983). *Human sexuality and the family.* New York: Haworth Press.

Maddox, J. (1989). Sexual behavior unsurveyed. *Nature (London), 341*, 181.

Maj, M. (1990). Organic mental disorders in HIV-1 infection. *AIDS, 4*, 831–840.

Makinson, C. (1985). The health consequences of teenage fertility. *Family Planning Perspectives, 17*, 132–139.

Malamuth, N. (1981). Rape proclivity among males. *Journal of Social Issues, 37*, 138–157.

Malamuth, N. (1984). Aggression against women: Cultural and individual causes. In N. Malamuth & E. Donnerstein (Eds.), *Pornography and sexual aggression.* New York: Academic Press.

Malamuth, N. (1986). Predictors of naturalistic sexual aggression. *Journal of Personality and Social Psychology, 50*, 953–962.

Malamuth, N., & Check, J. (1981). The effects of mass media exposure on acceptance of violence against women: A field experiment. *Journal of Research in Personality, 15*, 436–446.

Malamuth, N., & Donnerstein, E. (Eds.) (1984). *Pornography and sexual aggression.* New York: Academic Press.

Malamuth, N., & Spinner, B. (1980). A longitudinal content analysis of sexual violence in the best-selling erotic magazines. *Journal of Sex Research, 16*, 226–237.

Malatesta, V. J. (1979). Alcohol effects on the orgasmic-ejaculatory response in human males. *Journal of Sex Research, 15*, 101–107.

Malatesta, V. J. et al. (1982). Acute alcohol intoxication and female orgasmic response. *Journal of Sex Research, 18*, 1–17.

Malone, K. E., Daling, J. R., & Weiss, N. S. (1993). Oral contraceptives in relation to breast cancer. *Epidemiologic Reviews, 15*, 80–97.

Malotte, C. K., Wiesmeier, E., & Gelineau, K. J. (1990). Screening for chlamydial cervicitis in a sexually active university population. *American Journal of Public Health, 80*, 469–471.

Mandoki, M. W., Sumner, G. S., Hoffman, R. P., & Riconda, D. L. (1991). A review of Klinefelter's Syndrome in children and adolescents. *Journal of the American Academy of Child and Adolescence Psychiatry, 30*, 167–172.

Mann, J. et al. (1987). Condom use and HIV infection among prostitutes in Zaire. *New England Journal of Medicine, 316*, 345.

Mann, J. J., & Inman, W. H. (1975). Oral contraceptives and death from myocardial infarction. *British Medical Journal, 2*, 245–248.

Manniche, L. (1987). *Sexual life in ancient Egypt.* London: KPI.

Mannino, D. M., Klevens, R. M., & Flanders, W. D. (1994). Cigarette smoking: An independent risk factor for impotence? *American Journal of Epidemiology, 140*, 1003–1008.

Marchbanks, P. A., Kung-Jong, L., & Mercy, J. A. (1990). Risk of injury from resisting rape. *American Journal of Epidemiology, 132*, 540–549.

Marciano, T. D. (1982). Four marriage and family texts: A brief (but telling) array. *Contemporary Sociology, 11*, 150–153.

Marecek, J. (1977). Psychological androgyny and positive mental health: A biosocial perspective. In G. Garney & McMahon (Eds.), *Exploring contemporary male/female roles: A facilitator's guide.* LaJolla, CA: University Associates.

Margolies, L., Becher, M., & Jackson-Brewer, K. (1988). Internalized homophobia: Identifying and treating the oppressor within. In Boston Lesbian Psychologies Collective (Eds.), *Lesbian psychologies.* Urbana: University of Illinois Press.

Margolin, L. (1992). Sexual abuse by grandparents. *Child Abuse and Neglect, 16*, 735–742.

Marieb, E. N. (1992). *Human anatomy and physiology* (2nd ed.). Redwood City, CA: Benjamin/Cummings.

Marks, G., Richardson, J. L., & Maldonado, N. (1991). Self-disclosure of HIV infection to sexual partners. *American Journal of Public Health, 81*, 1321–1323.

Marmor, J. (Ed.). (1980a). *Homosexual behavior.* New York: Basic Books.

Marmor, J. (1980b). Clinical aspects of male homosexuality. In J. Marmor (Ed.), *Homosexual behavior: A modern reappraisal* (pp. 267–279). New York: Basic Books.

Marshall, D. S. (1971). Sexual behavior on Mangaia. In D. S. Marshall & R. C. Suggs (Eds.), *Human sexual behavior* (pp. 103–162). New York: Basic Books.

Marshall, W. L. (1989). Intimacy, loneliness, and sexual offenders. *Behavior Research and Therapy, 27*, 491–503.

Marshall, W. L., Eccles, A., & Barharee, H. (1991). The treatment of exhibitionists: A focus on sexual deviance versus cognitive and relationship features. *Behavior Research and Therapy, 29*, 129–135.

Marshall, W. L. (1992). Pornography and sex offenders. In D. Zillman & J. Bryant (Eds.), *Pornography: Recent research, interpretation, and policy considerations.* Hillsdale, NJ: Erlbaum.

Marshall, W. L. (1988). The use of sexually explicit stimuli by rapists, child molesters, and nonoffenders. *Journal of Sex Research, 25*, 267–268.

Marshall, W. L., Barbaree, H. E., & Christophe, D. (1986). Sexual offenders against female children: Sexual preferences for age of victims and type of behavior. *Canadian Journal of Behavioral Science, 18*, 424–439.

Marsiglio, W. (1993a). Adolescent males' orientation toward paternity and contraception. *Family Planning Perspectives, 25*, 22–31.

Marsiglio, W. (1993b). Attitudes toward homosexual activity and gays as friends: A national survey of heterosexual 15- to 19-year-old males. *Journal of Sex Research, 30*, 12–17.

Marsiglio, W., & Donnelly, D. (1991). Sexual relations in later life: A national study of married persons. *Journal of Gerontology, 46*, S338–S344.

Martens, M. G., & Faro, S. (1989). Update on trichomoniasis: Detection and management. *Medical Aspects of Human Sexuality, 23*, 73–79.

Martin, D., & Lyon, P. (1972). *Lesbian-women.* New York: Bantam Books.

Martin, D. H. et al. (1992). A controlled trial of a single dose of azithromycin for the treatment of chlamydial urethritis and cervicitis. *New England Journal of Medicine, 327*, 921–925.

Martin, J. L. (1987). The impact of AIDS on gay male sexual behavior patterns in New York City. *American Journal of Public Health, 77*, 578–581.

Martin, T. C., & Bumpass, L. L. (1989). Recent trends in marital disruption. *Demography, 26*, 37–51.

Maruri, F., & Azziz, R. (1993). Laparoscopic surgery for ectopic pregnancies: Technology assessment and public health implications. *Fertility and Sterility, 59*, 487–498.

Maslow, A. H. (1968). *Toward a psychology of being* (2nd ed.). Princeton, NJ: Van Nostrand.

Massey, F. J., Bernstein, G. S., & O'Fallon, W. M. (1984). Vasectomy health: Results from a large cohort study. *Journal of the American Medical Association, 252*, 1023–1029.

MASTERS, W. H. (1980, October 20). *Update on sexual physiology.* Paper presented at the Masters & Johnson Institute's Postgraduate Workshop on Human Sexual Function and Dysfunction, St. Louis, MO.

MASTERS, W. H. (1982, June 12). *Update on sexual physiology.* Paper presented at the Masters & Johnson Institute's Advanced Workshop on Human sexuality, St. Louis, MO.

MASTERS, W. H. (1986). Sexual dysfunction as an aftermath of sexual assault of men by women. *Journal of Sex and Marital Therapy, 12,* 35–45.

MASTERS, W. H., & JOHNSON, V. E. (1966). *Human sexual response.* Boston: Little, Brown.

MASTERS, W. H., & JOHNSON, V. E. (1970). *Human sexual inadequacy.* Boston: Little, Brown.

MASTERS, W. H., & JOHNSON, V. E. (1976). *The pleasure bond.* New York: Bantam Books.

MASTERS, W. H., & JOHNSON, V. E. (1979). *Homosexuality in perspective.* Boston: Little, Brown.

MASTERS, W. H., JOHNSON, V. E., & KOLODNY, R. C. (1988). *Crisis: Heterosexual behavior in the age of AIDS.* New York: Grove Press.

MASTERS, W. H., JOHNSON, V. E., & KOLODNY, R. C. (1992). *Human sexuality* (4th ed.). New York: Harper Collins.

MASTROYANNIS, C. (1993). Gamete intrafallopian transfer: Ethical considerations, historical development of the procedure, and comparison with other advanced reproductive technologies. *Fertility and Sterility, 60,* 389–402.

MASUR, F. T. (1979). Resumption of sexual activity following myocardial infarction. *Sexuality and Disability, 2,* 98–114.

MATEK, O. (1988). Obscene phone callers. *Journal of Social Work and Human Sexuality, 7,* 113–130.

MATICKA-TYNDALE, E. (1991). Sexual scripts and AIDS prevention: Variations in adherence to safer-sex guidelines by heterosexual adolescents. *Journal of Sex Research, 28,* 45–66.

MATTHEWS, K. A. et al. (1990). Influences of natural menopause on psychological characteristics and symptoms of middle-aged healthy women. *Journal of Consulting and Clinical Psychology, 58,* 345–351.

MAZER, D. B., & PERCIVAL, E. F. (1989). Students' experiences of sexual harassment at a small university. *Sex Roles, 20,* 1–22.

MCANULTY, R. D., ADAMS, H. E., & WRIGHT, L. W., JR. (1994). Relationship between MMPI and penile plethysmograph in accused child molesters. *Journal of Sex Research, 31,* 179–184.

MCCABE, M. (1987). Desired and experienced levels of premarital affection and sexual intercourse during dating. *Journal of Sex Research, 23,* 23–33.

MCCABE, S. (1983). FBD marriage: Further support for the Westermarck hypothesis of the incest taboo? *American Anthropologist, 85,* 50–69.

MCCAGHY, C. H. (1971). Child molesting. *Sexual Behavior, 1,* 16–24.

MCCARTHY, J., & MCMILLAN, S. (1990). Patient/partner satisfaction with penile implant surgery. *Journal of Sex Education and Therapy, 16*(1), 25.

MCCARTY, L. (1986). Mother-child incest: Characteristics of the offender. *Child Welfare, 6,* 447–458.

MCCLINTOCK, M. (1971). Menstrual synchrony and suppression. *Nature (London), 229,* 244–245.

MCCLURE, D. (1988, May). Men with one testicle. *Medical Aspects of Human Sexuality,* pp. 22–32.

MCCONAGHY, N. (1974). Penile volume responses to moving and still pictures of male and female nudes. *Archives of Sexual Behavior, 3,* 566–570.

MCCONAGHY, N., BUHRICH, N., & SILOVE, D. (1994). Opposite sex-linked behaviors and homosexual feelings in the predominantly heterosexual male majority. *Archives of Sexual Behavior, 23,* 565–577.

MCCORMACK, A. (1985). The sexual harassment of students by teachers: The case of students in science. *Sex Roles, 13,* 21–32.

MCCORMACK, A., ROKOUS, F. E., HAZELWOOD, R. R., & BURGESS, A. W. (1992). An exploration of incest in the childhood development of serial rapists. *Journal of Family Violence, 7,* 219–228.

MCGROARTY, J. A., REID, G., & BRUCE, A. W. (1994). The influence of nonoxynol-9-containing spermicides on urogenital infection. *Journal of Urology, 152,* 831–833.

MCHALE, S. M., & CROUTER, A. C. (1992). You can't always get what you want: Incongruence between sex-role attitudes and family work roles and its implications for marriage. *Journal of Marriage and the Family, 54,* 537–547.

MCHALE, S. M., & HUSTON, T. L. (1984). Men and women as parents: Sex role orientations, employment and parental roles with infants. *Child Development, 55,* 1349–1361.

MCINTYRE, J. (1980). *Victim responses to rape: Alternative outcomes.* Final report, ROIMH29043. Rockville, MD: National Institute of Mental Health.

MCKEGANEY, N. P. (1994). Prostitution and HIV: What do we know and where might research be targeted in the future? *AIDS, 8,* 1215–1226.

MCKELVIE, M., & GOLD, S. R. (1994). Hyperfemininity: Further definition of the construct. *Journal of Sex Research, 31,* 219–228.

MCLANE, M., KROP, H., & MEHTA, J. (1980). Psychosexual adjustment and counseling after myocardial infarction. *Annals of Internal Medicine, 92,* 514–519.

MCNEELY, T., & WAHL, S. (1995). Paper presented at a meeting of the American Society for Microbiology.

MCNEIL, J. G. et al. (1991). Trends of HIV seroconversion among young adults in the U.S. Army, 1985 to 1989. *Journal of the American Medical Association, 265,* 1709–1714.

MCNIVEN, P., HODNETT, E., & O'BRIEN-PALLAS, L. (1992). Supporting women in labor: A work sampling study of the activities of labor and delivery nurses. *Birth, 19,* 3–8.

MCWHIRTER, D. P., & MATTISON, A. M. (1984). *The male couple: How relationships develop.* Englewood Cliffs, NJ: Prentice Hall.

MEAD, M. (1935). *Sex and temperament in three primitive societies.* New York: William Morrow.

MEAD, M. (1975). *Male and female.* New York: William Morrow.

MEDINA, J. E. et al. (1980). Comparative evaluation of two methods of natural family planning in Columbia. *American Journal of Obstetrics and Gynecology, 138,* 1142–1147.

MEHREN, E. (1991, June 2). What we really think about adultery. *Los Angeles Times,* pp. E1, E8.

MEINKING, T. L., & TAPLIN, D. (1990). Advances in Pediculosis, scabies, and other mite infestations. *Advances in Dermatology, 5,* 131–152.

MEISELMAN, K. (1978). *Incest: A psychological study of causes and effects with treatment recommendations.* San Francisco: Jossey-Bass.

MELENDY, M. R. (1903). *Perfect womanhood: For maidens-wives-mothers.* Philadelphia: K. T. Boland.

MELNICK, S. L. et al. (1993). Changes in sexual behavior by young urban heterosexual adults in response to the AIDS epidemic. *Public Health Reports, 108,* 582–588.

MELNICK, S. L. et al. (1994). Survival and disease progression according to gender of patients with HIV infection. *Journal of the American Medical Association, 272,* 1915–1921.

MENCHINI-FABRIS, G. F., TURCHI, P., & CANALE, D. (1992). Medical treatment of male infertility. *International Journal of Fertility, 37,* 330–334.

MENSCH, B., & KANDEL, D. B. (1992). Drug use as a risk factor for premarital teen pregnancy and abortion in a national sample of young white women. *Demography, 29,* 409–429.

MEREDITH, N. (1984, January). The gay dilemma. *Psychology Today, 18,* 56–62.

MESSENGER, J. (1971). Sex and repression in an Irish folk community. In D. Marshall & R. Suggs (Eds.), *Human sexual behavior* (pp. 3–37). New York: Basic Books.

METTS, S., & FITZPATRICK, M. A. (1992). Thinking about safer sex: The risky business of "Know your partner" advice. In T. Edgar, M. A. Fitzpatrick, & V. S. Freimuth (Eds.), *AIDS: A communication perspective.* Hillsdale, NJ: Erlbaum.

MEUWISSEN, I., & OVER, R. (1992). Sexual arousal across phases of the human menstrual cycle. *Archives of Sexual Behavior, 21,* 101–119.

MEYER, J., & RETER, C. (1979). Sex assignment: Follow-up. *Archives of General Psychiatry, 36,* 1010–1015.

MEYER-BAHLBURG, H. F. L. et al. (1995). Prenatal estrogens and the development of homosexual orientation. *Developmental Psychology, 31,* 12–21.

MEZEY, G., & KING, M. (1989). The effects of sexual assault on men: A survey of 22 victims. *Psychological Medicine, 19,* 205–209.

MEZEY, G., & KING, M. (1992). Male victims of sexual assault. *AIDS Care, 5,* 247.

MICHAELS, D., & LEVINE, C. (1992). Estimates of the number of motherless youth orphaned by AIDS in the United States. *Journal of the American Medical Association, 268,* 3456–3461.

MICHAELS, R. H., & MELLIN, G. W. (1960). Prospective experience with maternal rubella and the associated congenital malformations. *Pediatrics, 26,* 200–209.

MILLER, B. C., CHRISTOPHERSON, C. R., & KING, P. K. (1993). Sexual behavior in adolescence. In T. P. Gullott et al. (Eds.), *Adolescent sexuality.* Newbury Park, CA: Sage.

MILLER, C. A. (1985). Infant mortality in the U.S. *Scientific American, 235,* 31–37.

MILLER, J. et al. (1978). Recidivism among sex assault victims. *American Journal of Psychiatry, 135,* 1103–1104.

MILLS, J. L. et al. (1993). Moderate caffeine use and the risk of spontaneous abortion and intrauterine growth retardation. *Journal of the American Medical Association, 269,* 593–597.

MILLS, S. V. (1988). Stress and PMS severity. *Cycles, 4,* 3.

MILSOM, I., SUNDELL, G., & ANDERSCH, B. (1990). The influence of different combined oral contraceptives on the prevalence and severity of dysmenorrhea. *Contraception, 42,* 497–506.

MILUNSKY, A. (1977). *Know your genes.* Boston: Houghton Mifflin.

MINIUM, E. W., KING, B. M., & BEAR, G. (1993). *Statistical reasoning in psychology and education* (3rd ed.) New York: Wiley.

MIRKIN, G., & HOFFMAN, M. (1978). *The sportsmedicine book.* Boston: Little, Brown.

MISCHEL, W. (1970). Sex-typing and socialization. In P. H. Musses (Ed.), *Carmichael's manual of child psychology* (Vol. 2, pp. 3–72). New York: Wiley.

MISHELL, D. R., JR. (1982). Non-contraceptive health benefits of oral steroidal contraceptives. *American Journal of Obstetrics and Gynecology, 142,* 809–816.

MISHELL, D. R., JR. (1989). Medical progress: Contraception. *New England Journal of Medicine, 320,* 777–787.

MISHU, B. et al. (1990). A surgeon with AIDS: Lack of evidence of transmission to patients. *Journal of the American Medical Association, 264,* 467–470.

MOEN, M. H. (1995). Is mild endometriosis a disease? *Human Reproduction, 10,* 8–12.

MOHR, J. W., TURNER, R. E., & JERRY, M. B. (1964). *Pedophilia and exhibitionism.* Toronto: University of Toronto Press.

MOLLER, H., KNUDSEN, L. B., & LYNGE, E. (1994). Risk of testicular cancer after vasectomy: Cohort study of over 73,000 men. *British Medical Journal, 209,* 295–299.

MOLLER, L. C., HYMEL, S., & RUBIN, K. H. (1992). Sex typing in play and popularity in middle childhood. *Sex Roles, 26,* 331–335.

MONEY, J. (1970). Clitoral size and erotic sensation. *Medical Aspects of Human Sexuality, 4,* 95.

MONEY, J. (1975). Ablatio penis: Normal male infant sex-reassigned as a girl. *Archives of Sexual Behavior, 4,* 65–72.

MONEY, J. (1980). *Love and love sickness.* Baltimore: Johns Hopkins University Press.

MONEY, J. (1984). Paraphelias: Phenomenology and classification. *American Journal of Psychotherapy, 38,* 164–179.

MONEY, J. (1985). *The destroying angel.* Buffalo, NY: Prometheus Books.

MONEY, J. (1986). *Lovemaps: Clinical concepts of sexual/erotic health and pathology, paraphilia, and gender transposition in childhood, adolescence, and maturity.* New York: Irvington.

MONEY, J. (1987a). Human sexology and psychoneuroendocrinology. In D. Crews (Ed.), *Psychobiology of reproductive behavior: An evolutionary perspective* (pp. 323–344). Englewood Cliffs, NJ: Prentice Hall.

MONEY, J. (1987b). Sin, sickness, or status? Homosexual gender identity and psychoneuroendocrinology. *American Psychologist, 42,* 384–399.

MONEY, J. (1987c). Treatment guidelines: Antiandrogen and counseling of paraphiliac sex offenders. *Journal of Sex and Marital Therapy, 13,* 219–223.

MONEY, J., & EHRHARDT, A. E. (1972). *Man & woman, boy & girl.* Baltimore: Johns Hopkins University Press.

MONEY, J., & SCHWARTZ, M. (1977). Dating, romantic and nonromantic friendships, and sexuality in 17 early-treated adrenogenital females, aged 16-25. In P. A. Lee et al. (Eds.), *Congenital adrenal hyperplasia.* Baltimore: University Park Press.

MONEY, J., & TUCKER, P. (1975). *Sexual signatures.* Boston & Toronto: Little, Brown.

MONEY, J., & WALKER, P. (1977). Counseling the transsexual. In J. Money & H. Musaph (Eds.), *Handbook of sexology* (pp. 1287-1301). Amsterdam: Elsevier/North-Holland.

MOORE, K. (1982). *The developing human: Clinically oriented embryology* (3rd ed.). Philadelphia: Saunders.

MOORE, K. A., NORD, C. W., & PETERSON, J. L. (1989). Nonvoluntary sexual activity among adolescents. *Family Planning Perspectives, 21,* 110–114.

MOORE, M. L. (1983). *Realities in childbearing* (2nd ed.). Philadelphia: Saunders.

MORAN, J. S., & ZENILMAN, J. M. (1990). Therapy for gonococcal infections: Options in 1989. *Reviews of Infectious Diseases, 12,* S633–S644.

MORFIT, S. H. (1994). Challenge to psychotherapy: An open letter to psychotherapists concerning clinical practice as seen through the lens of the "recovered" or "false memory" debate. *Journal of Sex Education and Therapy, 20,* 234–245.

MORLEY, J. E. (1986). Impotence. *American Journal of Medicine, 80,* 897–905.

MOROKOFF, P. J., & GILLILLAND, R. (1993). Stress, sexual functioning, and marital satisfaction. *Journal of Sex Research, 30,* 43–53.

MORRIS, M. (1993). Telling tails explain the discrepancy in sexual partner reports. *Nature (London), 365,* 437–440.

MORRIS, N. M., & UDRY, J. R. (1978). Pheromonal influences on human sexual behavior-experimental search. *Journal of Biosocial Science, 10,* 147–159.

MORROW, K. B. (1991). Attributions of female adolescent incest victims regarding their molestation. *Child Abuse & Neglect, 15,* 477–483.

MORSE, E. V. et al. (1991). The male street prostitute: A vector for transmission of HIV infection into the heterosexual world. *Social Science and Medicine, 32,* 535–539.

MORSE, E. V., SIMON, P. M., BALSON, P. M., & OSOFSKY, H. J. (1992). Sexual behavior patterns of customers of male street prostitutes. *Archives of Sexual Behavior, 21,* 347–357.

MOSER, C. (1979). *An exploratory-descriptive study of a self-defined S/M (sadomasochistic) sample.* Unpublished manuscript, Institute for the Advanced Study of Human Sexuality, San Francisco.

MOSER, C., & LEVITT, E. (1987). An exploratory-descriptive study of a sadomasochistically oriented sample. *Journal of Sex Research, 23,* 322–337.

MOSHER, D., & ANDERSON, R. (1986). Macho personality, sexual aggression, and reactions to guided imagery of realistic rape. *Journal of Research in Personality, 20,* 77–94.

MOSHER, D. C. (1980). In J. Mahood & K. Wenburg (Eds.), *The Mosher survey: Sexual attitudes of 45 Victorian women.* New York: Arno Press.

MOSHER, W. D. (1990). Contraceptive practice in the United States, 1982-1988. *Family Planning Perspectives, 22,* 198–205.

MOSHER, W. D., & ARAL, S. O. (1991). Testing for sexually transmitted diseases among women of reproductive age: United States, 1988. *Family Planning Perspectives, 23,* 216–221.

MOSHER, W. D., & MCNALLY, J. W. (1991). Contraceptive use at first premarital intercourse: United States, 1965-1988. *Family Planning Perspectives, 23,* 108–116.

MOSHER, W. D., & PRATT W. F. (1991). Fecundity and infertility in the United States: Incidence and trends. *Fertility and Sterility, 56,* 192–193.

MOSS, C., HOSFORD, R., & ANDERSON, W. (1979). Sexual assault in prison. *Psychological Reports, 44,* 823–828.

MOSS, H. B., PANZAK, G. L., & TARTER, R. E. (1993). Sexual functioning of male anabolic steroid abusers. *Archives of Sexual Behavior, 22,* 1–12.

MRAZEK, F. J. (1984). Sexual abuse of children. In B. Lahey & A. E. Kazdin (Eds.), *Advances in child clinical psychology* (Vol. 6, pp. 199–215). New York: Plenum.

MRAZEK, P. B., LYNCH, M., & BENTOUIM, A. (1981). Recognition of child sexual abuse in the United Kingdom. In P. B. Mrazek & C. H. Kempe (Eds.), *Sexually abused children and their families* (pp. 35–49). Oxford: Pergamon.

MUEHLENHARD, C. L. (1989, April). Young men pressured into having sex with women. *Medical Aspects of Human Sexuality,* pp. 50–62.

MUEHLENHARD, C. L., & COOK, S. (1986, June). *"Real men" don't say no: Do men have sex when they don't want to?* Paper presented at symposium (Miscommunication and date rape: causes and consequences) conducted at the annual Midcontinent meeting of the Society for the Scientific Study of Sex, Madison, WI.

MUEHLENHARD, C. L., & COOK, S. W. (1988). Men's self-reports of unwanted sexual activity. *Journal of Sex Research, 24,* 58–72.

MUEHLENHARD, C. L., & FALCON, P. (1990). Men's heterosexual skill and attitudes toward women as predictors of verbal and sexual coercion and forceful rape. *Sex Roles, 23,* 241–259.

MUEHLENHARD, C. L., FELTS, A., & ANDREWS, S. (1985, June). *Men's attitudes toward the justifiability of date rape: Intervening variables and possible solutions.* Paper presented at the annual Midcontinent meeting of the Society for the Scientific Study of Sex, Chicago.

MUEHLENHARD, C. L., GIUSTI, L. M., & RODGERS, C. S. (1993, November 7). *The social construction of "token resistance to sex": The nature and function of the myth.* Paper presented at the annual meeting of the Society for the Scientific Study of Sex, Chicago.

MUEHLENHARD, C. L., & HOLLABAUGH, L. (1988). Do women sometimes say no when they mean yes? The prevalence and correlates of women's token resistance to sex. *Journal of Personality and Social Psychology, 54,* 872–879.

MUEHLENHARD, C. L., & LINTON, M. (1987). Date rape and sexual aggression in dating situations: Incidence and risk factors. *Journal of Consulting Psychology, 34,* 186–196.

MUEHLENHARD, C. L., & LONG, P. (1988, May). *Men's versus women's reports of pressure to engage in unwanted sexual intercourse.* Paper presented at the Western Region meeting of the Society for the Scientific Study of Sex, Dallas, TX.

MUEHLENHARD, C. L., & MCCOY, M. L. (1991). Double standard/double blind: The sexual double standard and women's communication about sex. *Psychology of Women Quarterly, 15,* 447–461.

MUEHLENHARD, C. L., POWCH, I. G., PHELPS, J. L., & GIUSTI, L. M.

(1992). Definitions of rape: Scientific and political implications. *Journal of Social Issues, 48*, 23–44.

MUEHLENHARD, C. L., & QUACKENBUSH, D. M. (1988, November). *Can the sexual double standard put women at risk for sexually transmitted diseases? The role of the double standard in condom use among women.* Paper presented at the annual meeting of the Society for the Scientific Study of Sex, San Francisco.

MUEHLENHARD, C. L., & RODGERS, C. S. (1993, August 23). *Narrative descriptions of "token resistance" to sex.* Paper presented at the annual meeting of the American Psychological Association, Toronto.

MUEHLENHARD, C. L., & SCHRAG, J. (1990). Nonviolent sexual coercion. In A. Parrot & L. Bechhofer (Eds.), *Hidden rape: Sexual assault among acquaintances, friends, and intimates.* New York: Wiley.

MUKHERJEE, A. B., & HODGEN, G. D. (1982). Maternal ethanol exposure induces transient impairment of umbilical circulation and fetal hypoxia in monkeys. *Science, 218*, 700–702.

MULLIGAN, T., RETCHIN, S. M., CHINCHILLI, V. M., & BETTINGER, C.B. (1988). The role of aging and chronic disease in sexual dysfunction. *Journal of the American Geriatrics Society, 36*, 520–524.

MULVEY, E. P., & HAVGAARD, J. L. (1986). *Report of the Surgeon General's workshop on pornography and public health.* Washington, DC: U.S. Department of Health and Human Services, Office of the Surgeon General.

MUMFORD, S. D., & KESSEL, E. (1992). Sterilization needs in the 1990s: The case for quinacrine nonsurgical female sterilization. *American Journal of Obstetrics and Gynecology, 167*, 1203–1207.

MUNJACK, D. J., & KANNO, P. H. (1979). Retarded ejaculation: A review. *Archives of Sexual Behavior, 8*, 139–150.

MUNROE, R. L. (1980). Male transvestism and the couvade: A psychocultural analysis. *Ethos, 8*, 49–59.

MURDOCK, G. P. (1964). Cultural correlates of the regulation of premarital sex behavior. In R. A. Manners (Ed.), *Process and pattern in culture* (pp. 339–410). Chicago: Aldine.

MURDOCK, G. P. (1967). *Ethnographic atlas.* Pittsburgh: University of Pittsburgh Press.

MURNEN, S. K., PEROT, A., & BYRNE, D. (1989). Coping with unwanted sexual activity: Normative response, situational determinants, and individual differences. *Journal of Sex Research, 26*(1), 85–106.

MURPHY, A. A. et al. (1991). Laparoscopic cautery in the treatment of endometriosis-related infertility. *Fertility and Sterility, 55*, 246–251.

MURPHY, T. F. (1992). Redirecting sexual orientation: Techniques and justifications. *Journal of Sex Research, 29*, 501–523.

MURPHY, W. D., HAYNES, M. R., & PAGE, I. J. (1992). Adolescent sex offenders. In W. O'Donohue & J. H. Geer (Eds.), *The sexual abuse of children: Clinical issues* (Vol. 2, pp. 394–429). Hillsdale, NJ: Erlbaum.

MURRAY, L. (1992). The impact of postnatal depression on infant development. *Journal of Child Psychology and Psychiatry, 33*, 543–561.

MURREY, G. J. et al. (1993). History of childhood sexual abuse in women with depressive and anxiety disorders: A comparative study. *Journal of Sex Education and Therapy, 19*, 13–19.

MURSTEIN, B. I. (1978). Swinging, or comarital sex. In B. I. Murstein (Ed.), *Exploring intimate life styles* (pp. 109–130). New York: Springer.

MURSTEIN, B. I. (1980). Mate selection in the 1970s. *Journal of Marriage and the Family, 42*, 777–792.

MYERS, G., MACINNES, K., & KORBER, B. (1992). The emergence of simian/human immunodeficiency viruses. *AIDS Research and Human Retroviruses, 8*, 373–386.

MYERS, J. E. B. (1993). A call for forensically relevant research. *Child Abuse & Neglect, 17*, 573–579.

MYERS, L., ET AL. (1990). Effects of estrogen, androgen, and progestin on sexual psychophysiology and behavior in postmenopausal women. *Journal of Clinical Endocrinology and Metabolism, 70*, 1124–1131.

NABRINK, M., BIRGERSSON, L., COLLING-SALTIN, A.-S., & SOLUM, T. (1990). Modern oral contraceptives and dysmenorrhea. *Contraception, 42*, 275–283.

NABULSI, A. A. et al. (1993). Association of hormone-replacement therapy with various cardiovascular risk factors in postmenopausal women. *New England Journal of Medicine, 328*, 1069–1075.

NACHTIGALL, L. E. (1994). Sexual function in menopause and postmenopause. In B. A. Lobo (Ed.), *Treatment of the postmenopausal woman: Basic and clinical aspects* (pp. 301–306). New York: Raven Press.

NADLER, R. (1968). Approach to psychodynamics of obscene telephone calls. *New York Journal of Medicine, 68*, 521–526.

NADLER, R. D., DAHL, J. F., GOULD, K. G., & COLLINS, D. C. (1993). Effects of an oral contraceptive on sexual behavior of chimpanzees (Pan troglodytes). *Archives of Sexual Behavior, 22*, 477–500.

NAEYE, R. L. (1979). Coitus and associated amniotic-fluid infections. *New England Journal of Medicine, 301*, 1198–2000.

NATHAN, S. (1986). The epidemiology of the DSM-III psychosexual dysfunctions. *Journal of Sex and Marital Therapy, 12*, 267–281.

NATIONAL INSTITUTES OF HEALTH (NIH). (1981). *Cesarean childbirth: Report of the NICHD Task Force on Cesarean Childbirth,* (DHHS publication No. (NIH) 82–2067). Bethesda, MD: Author.

NATIONAL INSTITUTES OF HEALTH (NIH). (1992). Impotence. *NIH Consensus Statement, 10*(4), 1–33.

NAZARIO, S. L. (1990, September 9). Midwifery is staging revival as demand for prenatal care, low-tech births rises. *Wall Street Journal*, pp. B1, B4.

NEERGAARD, L. (1994, December 16). Pill can work the morning after. AP release. *New Orleans Times-Picayune*, pp. A–13.

NELSON, J. (1980). Gayness and homosexuality: Issues for the church. In E. Batchelor, Jr. (Ed.), *Homosexuality and ethics.* New York: Pilgrim Press.

NESS, R. B. et al. (1993). Number of pregnancies and the subsequent risk of cardiovascular disease. *New England Journal of Medicine, 328*, 1528–1533.

NEUMANN, P. J., GHARIB, S. D., & WEINSTEIN, M. C. (1994). The cost of a successful delivery with in vitro fertilization. *New England Journal of Medicine, 331*, 239–243.

NEWCOMB, M. D., & BENTLER, P. M. (1983). Dimensions of subjective female orgasmic responsiveness. *Journal of Personality and Social Psychology, 44*, 862–873.

NEWCOMER, S. F., & UDRY, R. (1985). Oral sex in an adolescent population. *Archives of Sexual Behavior, 14*, 41–46.

NEWTON, D. E. (1978). Homosexual behavior and child molestation: A review of the evidence. *Adolescence, 13*, 29–42.

NEWTON, J., & TACCHI, D. (1990). Long-term use of copper intrauterine devices. *Lancet, 335*, 1322–1323.

NGUGI, E. N. et al. (1988). Prevention of transmission of human immunodeficiency virus in Africa: Effectiveness of condom promotion and health education among prostitutes. *Lancet, 2*, 887–890.

NICHOLS, M. (1988). Bisexuality in women: Myths, realities, and implications for therapy. *Women and Therapy, 7*, 235–252.

NICOLOSI, A. et al. (1994). The efficiency of male-to-female and female-to-male sexual transmission of the human immunodeficiency virus: A study of 730 stable couples. *Epidemiology, 5*, 570–575.

NIELSON, J., & WOHLERT, M. (1991). Chromosome abnormalities found among 34,910 newborn children: Results from a 13-year incidence study in Arhus, Denmark. *Human Genetics, 87*, 81–83.

NIRAPATHPONGPORN, A., HUBER, D. H., & KRIEGER, J. H. (1990). No-scalpel vasectomy at the King's birthday vasectomy festival. *Lancet, 335*, 894–895.

NOCK, S. (1987). The symbolic meaning of childbearing. *Journal of Family Issues, 8*, 373–393.

NORDIC MEDICAL RESEARCH COUNCIL'S HIV THERAPY GROUP. (1992). Double blind dose-response study of zidovudine in AIDS and advanced HIV infection. *British Medical Journal, 304*, 13–17.

NUTTER, D. E., & KEARNS, M. E. (1993). Patterns of exposure to sexually explicit material among sex offenders, child molesters, and controls, *Journal of Sex and Marital Therapy, 19*, 77–85.

NYGREN, A. (1982). *Agape and eros.* Chicago: University of Chicago Press.

O'BRIEN, M., & HUSTON, A. C. (1985). Development of sex-typed play behavior in toddlers. *Developmental Psychology, 21*, 866–871.

O'BRIEN, T. E., & MCMANUS, C. E. (1978). Drugs and the fetus. A consumer's guide by generic and brand name. *Birth and the Family Journal, 5*, 58–86.

O'CAMPO, P. et al. (1992). Prior episode of sexually transmitted disease and subsequent sexual risk-reduction practices: A need for improved risk-reduction interventions. *Sexually Transmitted Diseases, 19*, 326.

O'CARROLL, R., & BANCROFT, J. (1984). Testosterone therapy for low sexual interest and erectile dysfunction in men: A controlled study. *British Journal of Psychiatry, 145*, 146–151.

ODDONE, E. Z. et al. (1993). Cost effectiveness analysis of early zidovudine treatment of HIV infected patients. *British Medical Journal, 307*, 1322–1325.

OFFER, D., & OFFER, J. B. (1975). *From teenage to young manhood.* New York: Basic Books.

OGDEN, S. R., & BRADBURN, N. M. (1968). Dimensions of marriage happiness. *American Journal of Sociology, 73*, 715–731.

OKAMI, P. (1991). Self-reports of "positive" childhood and adolescent sexual contacts with older persons: An exploratory study. *Archives of Sexual Behavior, 20*, 437–457.

OKAMI, P., & GOLDBERG, A. (1992). Personality correlates of pedophilia: Are they reliable indicators? *Journal of Sex Research, 29*, 297–328.

OLAFSON, E., CORWIN, D. L., & SUMMIT, R. C. (1993). Modern history of child sexual abuse awareness: Cycles of discovery and suppression. *Child Abuse & Neglect, 17*, 7–24.

OLIVER, M. B., & HYDE, J. S. (1993). Gender differences in sexuality: A meta-analysis. *Psychological Bulletin, 114,* 29–51.

O'NEILL, N., & O'NEILL, G. (1972). *Open marriage: A new life style for couples.* New York: M. Evans and Co.

ORIEL, J. D., JOHNSON, A. L., & BARLOW, D. (1978). Infection of the uterine cervix with chlamydia trachomatis. *Journal of Infectious Diseases, 147,* 443–451.

ORR, D. P., BEITER, M., & INGERSOL, G. (1991). Premature sexual activity as an indicator of psychosocial risk. *Pediatrics, 87,* 141–147.

ORY, H. W., ROSENFELD, A., & LANDMAN, L. C. (1980). The pill at 20: An assessment. *Family Planning Perspectives, 12,* 278–283.

ORY, S. J. et al. (1993). Fertility after ectopic pregnancy. *Fertility and Sterility, 60,* 231–235.

OSMOND, D. H. et al. (1993). Risk factors for hepatitis C virus seropositivity in heterosexual couples. *Journal of the American Medical Association, 269,* 361–365.

OSTERGAARD, J., & KRAFT, M. (1992). Natural course of benign coital headache. *British Medical Journal, 305,* 1129.

O'SULLIVAN, C. S. (1991). Acquaintance gang rape on campus. In A. Parrot & L. Bechhofer (Eds.), *Acquaintance rape: The hidden crime.* New York: Wiley.

O'SULLIVAN, L. F., & ALLGEIER, E. R. (in press). Disassembling a stereotype: Gender differences in the use of token resistance. *Journal of Applied Social Psychology.*

O'SULLIVAN, L. F., & BYERS, E. S. (1992). College students' incorporation of imitation and restrictor roles in sexual dating interactions. *Journal of Sex Research, 29,* 435–446.

OU, C.-Y. et al. (1992). Molecular epidemiology of HIV transmission in a dental practice. *Science, 256,* 1165–1171.

PADGETT, V. R., BRISLUTZ, J. A., & NEAL, J. A. (1989). Pornography, erotica, and attitudes toward women: The effects of repeated exposure. *Journal of Sex Research, 26,* 479–491.

PADIAN, N. S., SHIBOSKI, S. C., & JEWELL, N. P. (1990). The effect of number of exposures on the risk of heterosexual HIV transmission. *Journal of Infectious Diseases, 161,* 883–887.

PADIAN, N. S., SHIBOSKI, S. C., & JEWELL, N. P. (1991). Female-to-male transmission of human immunodeficiency virus. *Journal of the American Medical Association, 266,* 1664–1667.

PAIGE, K. E. (1978a). The declining taboo against menstrual sex. *Psychology Today, 12*(7), 50–51.

PAIGE, K. E. (1978b). The ritual of circumcision. *Human Nature, 1,* 40.

PAIGE, K. E., & PAIGE, J. M. (1981). *The politics of reproductive ritual.* Berkeley: University of California Press.

PALACE, E. M., & GORZALKA, B. B. (1992). Differential patterns of arousal in sexually functional and dysfunctional women: Physiological and subjective components of sexual response. *Archives of Sexual Behavior, 21,* 135–159.

PALMER, J. R. et al. (1989). Oral contraceptive use and liver cancer. *American Journal of Epidemiology, 130,* 878–882.

PALYS, T. S. (1986). Testing the common wisdom: The social content of video pornography. *Canadian Psychology, 27,* 22–35.

PANSER, L. A., & PHIPPS, W. R. (1991). Type of oral contraceptive in relation to acute, initial episodes of pelvic inflammatory disease. *Contraception, 43,* 91–99.

PANTON, J. H. (1978). Personality differences appearing between rapists of adults, rapists of children, and nonviolent sexual molesters of female children. *Research Communications in Psychology, Psychiatry, and Behavior, 3,* 385–393.

PAPE, J. W. et al. (1990). Prevalence of HIV infection and high-risk activities in Haiti: *Journal of Acquired Immune Deficiency Syndromes, 3,* 995–1001.

PAPE, J. W., & WARREN, W. D., JR. (1993). AIDS in Haiti, 1982-1992. *Clinical Infectious Diseases, 17,* S341–S345.

PAPINI, D. R., FARMER, F. L., CLARK, S. M., & SNEL, W. E. (1988). An evaluation of adolescent patterns of sexual self-disclosure to parents and friends. *Journal of Adolescent Research, 3,* 387–401.

PARADISE, J. E. (1990). The medical evaluation of the sexually abused child. In R. M. Reece (Ed.), *The pediatric clinics of North America: Child abuse* (pp. 839–862). Philadelphia: Saunders.

PARKE, R. D., & O'LEARY, S. E. (1976). Father-mother, -infant interaction in the newborn period: Some findings, some observations and some unresolved issues. In K. F. Riegel & J. A. Meacham (Eds.), *The developing individual in a changing world: Vol 2. Social and environment issues* (pp. 653–663). Chicago: Aldine.

PASTNER, C. M. (1986). The Westermarck hypothesis and first cousin marriage: The cultural modification of negative imprinting. *Journal of Anthropological Research, 24,* 573–586.

PATERSON, P., & PETRUCCO, A. (1987). Tubal factors and infertility. In R. Pepperell, B. Hudson, & C. Woods (Eds.), *The infertile couple.* Edinburgh: Churchill-Livingstone.

PATTERSON, C. J. (1992). Children of lesbian and gay parents. *Child Development, 63,* 1025–1042.

PATTON, P. E., WILLIAMS, T. J., & COULAM, C. B. (1987). Microsurgical reconstruction of the proximal oviduct. *Fertility and Sterility, 47,* 35–39.

PAULY, I. B. (1985). Gender identity disorder. In M. Farber (Ed.), *Human sexuality: Psychosexual effects of disease* (pp. 295–316). New York: Macmillan.

PAULY, I. B. (1990). Gender identity disorders: Evaluation and treatment. *Journal of Sex Education and Therapy, 16,* 2–24.

PAULY, I. B., & EDGERTON, M. (1986). The gender identity movement: A growing surgical-psychiatric liason. *Archives of Sexual Behavior, 15,* 315–327.

PEANO, G. M. et al. (1992). Heterosexual transmission of hepatitis C virus in family groups without risk factors. *British Medical Journal, 305,* 1473–1474.

PEELE, S. (1988). Fools for love: The romantic ideal, psychological theory, and addictive love. In R. J. Sternberg & M. L. Barnes (Eds.), *The psychology of love* (pp. 159–188). New Haven, CT: Yale University Press.

PELLETIER, L., & HAROLD, E. (1988). The relationship of age, sex guilt, and sexual experience with female sexual fantasies. *Journal of Sex Research, 24,* 250–256.

PENKOWER, L. et al. (1991). Behavioral, health and psychosocial factors and risk for HIV infection among sexually active homosexual men: The multicenter AIDS cohort study. *American Journal of Public Health, 81,* 194–196.

PENLAND, L. R. (1981, April). Sex education in 1900, 1940, and 1980: A historical sketch. *Journal of School Health,* pp. 274–281.

PENROD, S., & LINZ, D. (1984). Using psychological research on violent pornography to inform legal change. In N. M. Malamuth & E. Donnerstein (Eds.), *Pornography and sexual aggression* (pp. 247–275). Orlando, FL: Academic Press.

PEPLAU, L. A. (1981, March). What homosexuals want in relationships. *Psychology Today,* pp. 28–38.

PEPLAU, L. A. (1988). Research on homosexual couples. In J. De Cecco (Ed.), *Gay relationships.* New York: Haworth Press.

PEREZ, E. D., MULLIGAN, T., & WAN, T. (1993). Why men are interested in an evaluation for a sexual problem. *Journal of the American Geriatric Society, 41,* 233–237.

PERINN, E. B. et al. (1984). Long-term effect of vasectomy on coronary heart disease. *American Journal of Public Health, 74,* 128–132.

PERPER, T., & WEIS, D. (1987). Proceptive and rejective strategies of U. S. and Canadian college women. *Journal of Sex Research, 23,* 455–480.

PERRETTI, P. O., & ROWAN, M. (1983). Zoophilia: Factors related to its sustained practice. *Panminerva Medicine, 25,* 127.

PERRILLO, R. P. et al. (1990). A randomized, controlled trial of interferon alfa-2b alone and after prednisone withdrawal for the treatment of chronic hepatitis B. *New England Journal of Medicine, 323,* 295–301.

PERRY, J. D., & WHIPPLE, B. (1981). Pelvic muscle strength of female ejaculators: Evidence in support of a new theory of orgasm. *Journal of Sex Research, 17,* 22–39.

PERSKY, H. et al. (1982). The relation of plasma androgen levels to sexual behavior and attitudes of women. *Psychosomatic Medicine, 44,* 305–319.

PERSSON, G., DAHLOF, L. G., & KRANTZ, J. (1993). Physical and psychological effects of anogenital warts on female patients. *Sexually Transmitted Diseases, 20,* 10–13.

PESMEN, C. (1993, March). The last orgasm. *GQ,* pp. 266–270.

PETER, J. B., BRYSON, Y., & LOVETT, M. A. (1982, March–April). Genital herpes: Urgent questions, elusive answers. *Diagnostic Medicine,* pp. 71–74, 76–78.

PETERS, S. D., WYATT, G. E., & FINKELHOR, D. (1986). Prevalence. In D. Finkelhor (Ed.), *A sourcebook on child sexual abuse* (pp. 15–59). Beverly Hills, CA: Sage.

PETERSEN, L. R. et al. (1992). No evidence for female-to-female HIV transmission among 960,000 female blood donors. *Journal of Acquired Immune Deficiency Syndromes, 5,* 853–855.

PETERSON, J. L., MOORE, K. A., & FURSTENBERG, F. F., JR. (1991). Television viewing and early initiation of sexual intercourse: Is there a link? In *Gay people, sex, and the media.* Binghamton, NY: Haworth.

PETERSON, L. S. (1995, February 14). Contraceptive use in the United States: 1982-1990. *Advance Data, from Vital and Health Statistics* (No. 260). Hyattsville, MD: National Center for Health Statistics.

PETITTI, D. B. (1992). Reconsidering the IUD. *Family Planning Perspectives, 24,* 33–35.

PETITTI, D. B., & REINGOLD, A. L. (1988). Tampon characteristics and menstrual toxic shock syndrome. *Journal of the American Medical Association, 259,* 686–687.

PETROVICH, M., & TEMPLER, D. (1984). Heterosexual molestation of children who later become rapists. *Psychological Reports, 54,* 810.

PEYRON, R. et al. (1993). Early termination of pregnancy with mifepristone (RU486) and the orally active prostaglandin misoprostol. *New England Journal of Medicine, 328,* 1509–1513.

PFUTZNER, A. et al. (1992). HIV-1 and HIV-2 infections in a high-risk population in Bombay, India: Evidence for a spread of HIV-2 and presence of a divergent HIV-1 subtype. *Journal of Acquired Immune Deficiency Syndromes, 5,* 972–977.

PHELPS, D. L. et al. (1991). 28-day survival rates of 6676 neonates with birth weights of 1250 grams or less. *Pediatrics, 87,* 7–17.

PHIBBS, C. S., BATEMAN, D. A., & SCHWARTZ, R. M. (1991). The neonatal costs of maternal cocaine use. *Journal of the American Medical Association, 266,* 1521–1526.

PHILLIPS, G., & OVER, R. (1995). Differences between heterosexual, bisexual, and lesbian women in recalled childhood experiences. *Archives of Sexual Behavior, 24,* 1–10.

PIATUK, M. P., LUK, K.-C., WILLIAMS, B., & LIFSON, J. D. (1993). Quantitative competitive polymerase chain reaction of accurate quantitation of HIV DNA and RNA species. *BioTechniques, 14,* 70–77.

PILKINGTON, C. J., KERN, W., & INDEST, D. (1994). Is safer sex necessary with a "safe" partner? Condom use and romantic feelings. *Journal of Sex Research, 31,* 203–210.

PINES, A., & ARONSON, E. (1983). Antecedents, correlates, and consequences of sexual jealousy. *Journal of Personality, 51,* 108–136.

PITTMAN, F. (1987). *Turning points: Treating families in transition and crisis.* New York: Norton.

PLANNED PARENTHOOD. (1991). *Human sexuality: What children should know and when they should know it.* New York: Author.

PLASMA-MEDIATED ANTIMICROBIAL RESISTANCE IN NEISSERIA GONORRHOEA. (1990). *Morbidity and Mortality Weekly, 39,* 284.

PLATT, R., RICE, P. A., & McCORMICK, W. M. (1983). Risk of acquiring gonorrhea and prevalence of abnormal adnexal findings among women recently exposed to gonorrhea. *Journal of the American Medical Association, 250,* 3205–3209.

PLECK, J. H. (1976). The male sex role: Definitions, problems and sources of change. *Journal of Social Issues, 32*(3), 155–164.

POCS, O., & GODOW, A. G. (1977). Can students view parents as sexual beings? *The Family Coordinator, 26,* 31–36.

POLAND, R. L. (1990). The question of routine neonatal circumcision. *New England Journal of Medicine, 322,* 1312–1315.

POLYSON, J., LASH, S., & EVANS, K. (1986). Human sexuality courses: Where and how many. *Teaching of Psychology, 15*(4), 221–222.

POMEROY, W. B. (1966). Normal vs. abnormal sex. *Sexology, 32,* 436–439.

POMEROY, W. B. (1972). *Dr. Kinsey and the Institute for Sex Research.* New York: Harper & Row.

POMEROY, W. B. (1975). The diagnosis and treatment of transvestites and transsexuals. *Journal of Sex and Marital Therapy, 1,* 215–224.

PONCE, P. (1994, April 10). Fraternities working to be campus rape solution. *New Orleans Times-Picayune,* p. A-4.

PONTICAS, Y. (1992). Sexual aversion versus hypoactive sexual desire: A diagnostic challenge. *Psychiatric Medicine, 10,* 273–281.

POPE, H. G., JR., & KATZ, D. L. (1988). Affective and psychotic symptoms associated with anabolic steroid use. *American Journal of Psychiatry, 145,* 487–490.

POPOVICH, P. M., & LICATA, B. J. (1986). Assessing the incidence and perceptions of sexual harassment behaviors among American undergraduates. *Journal of Psychology, 120,* 387–396.

POPULATION COUNCIL (1994, September 27). Copper T380A Intrauterine Device is effective for 10 years [News release].

POTTER, R. G. et al. (1965). Applications of field studies to research on the physiology of human reproduction: Lactation and its effects upon birth intervals in eleven Punjab villages, India. In M. Sheps & J. Ridley (Eds.), *Public health and population change.* Pittsburgh: University of Pittsburgh Press.

POTTERAT, J. J., PHILLIPS, L, ROTHENBERG, R. B., & DARROW, W. V. (1985). On becoming a prostitute: An explanatory case-comparison study. *Journal of Sex Research, 21,* 329–335.

POTTERAT, J. J., WOODHOUSE, D. E., MUTH, J. B., & MUTH, S. Q. (1990). Estimating the prevalence and career longevity of prostitute women. *Journal of Sex Research, 27,* 233–243.

POWELL, G. N. (1986). Effects of sex role identity and sex on definitions of sexual harassment. *Sex Roles, 14,* 9–19.

POWELL, M. G., MEARS, B. J., DEBER, R. B., & FERGUSON, D. (1986). Contraception with the cervical cap: Effectiveness, safety, continuity of use, and user satisfaction. *Contraception, 33,* 215–232.

PRATT, W. F. et al. (1984). Understanding U. S. fertility: Findings from the National Survey of Family Growth, III. *Population Bulletin, 39*(5), 31.

Pregnancy + alcohol = problems. (July 31, 1989). *Newsweek,* p. 57.

PRENTKY, R. A., KNIGHT, R. A., & ROSENBER, R. (1988). Validation analysis on a taxonomic system for rapists: Disconfirmation and reconceptualization. *Annals of the New York Academy of Sciences, 528,* 21–40.

PRESCOTT, J. W. (1975). Body pleasure and the orgins of violence. *The Futurist,* April, 64–74.

PRETI, G. et al. (1986). Human axillary secretions influence women's menstrual cycles: The role of donor extract of females. *Hormones and Behavior, 20,* 474–482.

PRICE, V., SCANLON, B., & JANUS, M.-D. (1984). Social characteristics of adolescent male prostitution. *Victimology, 9,* 211–221.

PRINCE, V., & BENTLER, P. M. (1972). Survey of 504 cases of transvestism. *Psychological Reports, 31,* 903–917.

PRIOR, J., & VIGNA, Y. (1991). Ovulation disturbances and exercise training. *Clinical Obstetrics and Gynecology, 34,* 180–190.

PROFET, M. (1993). Menstruation as a defense against pathogens transported by sperm. *Quarterly Review of Biology, 68,* 335–381.

PROULX, J., AUBUT, J., McKIBBEN, A., & CÔTÉ, M. (1994). Penile responses of rapists and nonrapists to rape stimuli involving physical violence or humiliation. *Archives of Sexual Behavior, 23,* 295–310.

PURCELL, S. (1985, August 25). *Relation between religious orthodoxy and marital sexual functioning.* Paper presented at a meeting of the American Psychological Association, Los Angeles.

QUACKENBUSH, R. L. (1991). Attitudes of college men toward women and rape. *Journal of College Students Development, 32,* 376–377.

QUADAGNO, D., & SPRAGUE, J. (1991, June). Reasons for having sex. *Medical Aspects of Human Sexuality,* p. 52.

QUINSEY, V., CHAPLIN, T., & UPFOLD, D. (1984). Sexual arousal to nonsexual violence and sadomasochistic themes among rapists and non-sex-offenders. *Journal of Consulting and Clinical Psychology, 52,* 651–657.

RABOCH, J., & RABOCH, J. (1992). Infrequent orgasms in women. *Journal of Sex and Marital Therapy, 18,* 114–120.

RACHMAN, S. (1966). Sexual fetishism: An experimental analogue. *Psychological Record, 16,* 293–296.

RADA, R. T. et al. (1983). Plasma androgens in violent and nonviolent sex offenders. *Bulletin of the American Academy of Psychiatry and the Law, 11,* 149–158.

RAJFER, J. et al. (1992). Nitric oxide as a mediator of relaxation of the corpus cavernosum in response to noradrenergic, noncholinergic neurotransmission. *New England Journal of Medicine, 326,* 90–94.

RANDOLF, B. H., & WINSTEAD, B. (1988). Sexual decision making and object relations theory. *Archives of Sexual Behavior, 17,* 389.

RAO, M., WILKINSON, J., & BENTON, D. (1991). Screening for undescended testes. *Archives of Disease in Children, 66,* 934–937.

RAPAPORT, K., & BURKHART, B. R. (1984). Personality and attitudinal characteristics of sexually coercive college males. *Journal of Abnormal Psychology, 93,* 216–221.

RAPHAEL, S., & ROBINSON, M. (1980). The older lesbian: Love relationships and friendship patterns. *Alternate Lifestyles, 3,* 207–229.

READ, K. (1993, April 27). Male rape: One of the last taboo topics. *The Times-Picayune,* pp. E-1, E-3.

RECUR, R. (1993, July 17). Study: Male homosexual gene pattern is found. *New Orleans Times-Picayune,* p. G-20.

REECE, R. (1988). Special issues in the etiologies and treatments of sexual problems among gay men. *Journal of Homosexuality, 15,* 43–57.

REEVES, W. C. et al. (1994). Risk factors for genital papillomavirus infection in populations at high and low risk for cervical cancer. *Journal of Infectious Diseases, 170,* 753–758.

REGAN, L., OWEN, E. J., & JACOBS, H. S. (1990). Hypersecretion of luteinizing hormone, infertility, and miscarriage. *Lancet, 336,* 1141–1144.

REILLY, M. E., LOTT, B., & GALLOGLY, S. M. (1986). Sexual harassment of university students. *Sex Roles, 15,* 333–358.

REIN, M. F. (1977). Epidemiology of gonococcal infections. In R. B. Roberts (Ed.), *The gonococcus* (pp. 1–31). New York: Wiley.

REINGOLD, A. L. (1983). Nonmenstrual toxic shock syndrome: The growing picture. *Journal of the American Medical Association, 249,* 932.

REINISCH, J. M. (1990). *The Kinsey Institute new report on sex.* New York: St. Martin's Press.

REINISCH, J. M., SANDERS, S. A., HILL, C. A., & ZIEMBA-DAVIS, M. (1992). High-risk sexual behavior among heterosexual undergraduates at a midwestern university. *Family Planning Perspectives, 24,* 116–121, 145.

REISMAN, J. A., & EICHEL, E. W. (1990). *Kinsey, sex and fraud: The indoctrination of a people.* Lafayette, LA: Huntington House.

REISS, I. L. (1981). Some observations on ideology and sexuality in America. *Journal of Marriage and the Family, 43,* 271–283.

REISS, I. L., ANDERSON, R. E., & SPONAUGLE, G. C. (1980). A multivariate model of the determinants of extramarital sexual permissiveness. *Journal of Marriage and the Family, 42,* 395–411.

REISS, I. L., & LEIK, R. K. (1989). Evaluating strategies to avoid AIDS: Number of partners versus use of condoms. *Journal of Sex Research, 4,* 411–433.

RENSHAW, D. (1983). *Incest-understanding and treatment.* Boston: Little, Brown.

RENSHAW, D. (1990). Short-term therapy for sexual dysfunction: Brief counseling to manage vaginismus. *Clinical Practice in Sexuality, 6(5),* 23–29.

RENSHAW, D. C. (1988). Young children's sex play: Counseling the parents. *Medical Aspects of Human Sexuality, 22,* 68–72.

RENTZEL, L. (1972). *When all the laughter died in sorrow.* New York: Saturday Review Press.

Report of the Commission on Obscenity and Pornography (1970). New York: Bantam Books.

RESNICK, R. H., & KOFF, R. (1993). Hepatitis C-related hepatocellular carcinoma: Prevalence and significance. *Archives of Internal Medicine, 153,* 1672–1677.

RICCI, J. M., FOJACO, R. M., & O'SULLIVAN, M. J. (1989). Congenital syphilis: The University of Miami/Jackson Memorial Medical Center experience, 1986–1988. *Obstetrics and Gynecology, 74,* 687–693.

RICE, P. A., & SCHACHTER, J. (1991). Pathogenesis of pelvic inflammatory disease. *Journal of the American Medical Association, 266,* 2587–2593.

RICHARDS, J. M., KOHLER, C. L., RYAN, W. G., JACKSON, J. R., & GOLDENBERG, R. L. (1991). Contraceptive female sterilization in Alabama: A replication of the WHO study. *Contraception, 43,* 325–333.

RICHARDS, R., & AMES, J. (1983). *Second serve.* New York: Stein & Day.

RICHMAN, K. M., & RICKMAN, L. S. (1993). The potential for transmission of human immunodeficiency virus through human bites. *Journal of Acquired Immune Deficiency Syndromes, 6,* 402–406.

RIEVE, J. E. (1989). Sexuality and the adult with acquired physical disability. *Nursing Clinics of North America, 24,* 265–276.

RINEHART, W., & PIOTROW, P. T. (1979, January). OCs: Update on usage, safety, and side effects. *Population Reports,* Series A.

RIO, L. (1991). Psychological and sociological research and the decriminalization or legalization of prostitution. *Archives of Sexual Behavior, 20,* 205–217.

RISMAN, B. J., HILL, C., RUBIN, Z., & PEPLAU, L. A. (1981). Living together in college: Implications for courtship. *Journal of Marriage and the Family, 43,* 77–83.

RISMAN, B. J., & SCHWARTZ, P. (1989). Being gendered: A microstructural view of intimate relationships. In B. J. Risman & P. Schwartz (Eds.), *Gender in intimate relationships: A microstructural approach.* Belmont, CA: Wadsworth.

ROAN, S. (1993, February 16). Beyond the birds and the bees. *Los Angeles Times,* pp. E1, E8.

ROBBINS, M., & JENSEN, G. (1978). Multiple orgasm in males. *Journal of Sex Research, 14,* 21–26.

ROBERTS, C., GREEN, R., WILLIAMS, K., & GOODMAN, M. (1987). Boyhood gender identity development: A statistical contrast of two family groups. *Developmental Psychology, 23,* 544–557.

ROBERTS, T. W. (1992). Sexual attraction and romantic love: Forgotten variables in marital therapy. *Journal of Marital and Family Therapy, 18,* 357–364.

ROBINSON, A. J., & RIDGWAY, G. L. (1994). Sexually transmitted diseases in children: Non viral including bacterial vaginosis, *Gardnerella vaginalis,* mycoplasmas, *Trichomonas vaginalis, Candida albicans,* scabies and pubic lice. *Genitourinary Medicine, 70,* 208–214.

ROBINSON, B. (1988). Teenage pregnancy from the father's perspective. *American Journal of Orthopsychiatry, 58,* 46–51.

ROBINSON, G. E. et al. (1991). Changes in haemostasis after stopping the combined contraceptive pill: Implications for major surgery. *British Medical Journal, 302,* 269–271.

ROBINSON, P. (1976). *The modernization of sex.* New York: Harper & Row.

ROBINSON, P. (1983). The sociological perspective. In R. Weg (Ed.), *Sexuality in the later years: Roles and behavior.* New York: Academic Press.

ROEHRBORN, C. G., & McCONNELL, J. D. (1991). *Benign prostatic hyperplasia guideline panel,* 1991. Agency for Health Care Policy and Research.

ROGERS, A. S. et al. (1993). Investigation of potential HIV transmission to the patients of an HIV-infected surgeon. *Journal of the American Medical Association, 269,* 1795–1801.

ROGERS, D. E. (1992). Report card on our national response to the AIDS epidemic—some A's, too many D's. *American Journal of Public Health, 82,* 522–524.

ROGERS, E. M., & STROVER, S. L. (1980). Peer communication and sexuality. In E. J. Roberts (Ed.), *Childhood sexual learning.* Cambridge, MA: Ballinger.

ROGERS, S. M., & TURNER, C. F. (1991). Male-male sexual contact in the U.S.A.: Findings from five sample surveys, 1970-1990. *Journal of Sex Research, 28,* 491–519.

ROIPHE, K. (1993). *The morning after: Sex, fear, and feminism on campus.* Boston: Little, Brown.

ROLFS, R. T., GALAID, E. I., & ZAIDI, A. A. (1992). Pelvic inflammatory disease: Trends in hospitalizations and office visits, 1988. *American Journal of Obstetrics and Gynecology, 166,* 983–990.

ROLFS, R. T., & NAKASHIMA, A. K. (1990). Epidemiology of primary and secondary syphilis in the United States, 1981 through 1989. *Journal of the American Medical Association, 264,* 1432–1437.

ROMIEU, I. et al. (1989). Prospective study of oral contraceptive use and risk of breast cancer in women. *Journal of the National Cancer Institute, 81,* 1313–1321.

ROMIEU, I., BERLIN, J. A., & COLDITZ, G. (1990). Oral contraceptives and breast cancer: Review and meta-analysis. *Cancer (Philadelphia), 66,* 2253–2263.

ROOKS, J. et al. (1989). Outcomes of care in birth centers. *New England Journal of Medicine, 321,* 1804–1811.

ROOKUS, M. A. et al. (1994). Oral contraceptives and risk of breast cancer in women aged 20-54 years. *Lancet, 344,* 844–851.

ROSCOE, B., GOODWIN, M., REPP, S., & ROSE, M. (1987). Sexual harassment of university student and student-employees: Findings and implications. *College Student Journal, 12,* 254–273.

ROSE, M. K., & SOARES, H. H. (1993). Sexual adaptations of the frail elderly: A realistic approach. *Journal of Gerontological Social Work, 19,* 167–178.

ROSEBURY, T. (1971). *Microbes and morals: The strange story of venereal disease.* New York: Viking Press.

ROSEN, M. G., DICKINSON, J. C., & WESTHOFF, C. L. (1991). Vaginal birth after cesarean: A meta-analysis of morbidity and mortality. *Obstetrics and Gynecology, 77,* 465–470.

ROSEN, M. P. et al. (1991). Cigarette smoking: An independent risk factor for atherosclerosis in the hypogastric-cavernous arterial bed. *Urology, 145,* 759–763.

ROSEN, R. C. (1991). Alcohol and drug effects on sexual response: Human experimental and clinical studies. In J. Bancroft (Ed.), *Annual review of sex research,* (Vol. 2). Mount Vernon, IA: The Society for the Scientific Study of Sex.

ROSEN, R. C., & ASHTON, A. K. (1993). Prosexual drugs: Empirical status of the "new aphrodisiacs." *Archives of Sexual Behavior, 22,* 521–540.

ROSEN, R. C., & BECK, J. (1988). *Patterns of sexual arousal.* New York: Guilford.

ROSENBERG, L. et al. (1994). A case-control study of oral contraceptive use and invasive epithelial ovarian cancer. *American Journal of Epidemiology, 139,* 654–661.

ROSENBERG, M. J. et al. (1992). Barrier contraceptives and sexually transmitted diseases in women: A comparison of female-dependent methods and condoms. *American Journal of Public Health, 82,* 669–674.

ROSENBERG, M. J., & GOLLUB, E. L. (1992). Methods women can use that may prevent sexually transmitted disease, including HIV. *American Journal of Public Health, 82,* 1473–1478.

ROSENBERG, M. J., HILL, H. A., & FRIEL, P. J. (1991, October 7). *Spermicides and condoms in prevention of sexually transmitted diseases: A meta-analysis.* Presented at the meeting of the International Society for Sexually Transmitted Disease Research, Banff, Canada.

ROSENFELD, A. (1979). Endogamic incest and the victim perpetrator model. *American Journal of Diseases of Children, 133,* 406.

ROSENTHAL, E. (1991). Technique for early prenatal test comes under question in studies. *New York Times.*

ROSENZWEIG, J. M., & DAILEY, D. M. (1989). Dyadic adjustment/sexual satisfaction in women and men as a function of psychological sex role self-perception. *Journal of Sex and Marital Therapy, 15,* 42–56.

ROSS, C., & PIOTROW, P. T. (1974). Periodic abstinence: Birth control with contraceptives. *Population Reports,* Series I, No. L.

ROSS, J. A. (1989). Contraception: Short-term vs. long-term failure rates. *Family Planning Perspectives, 21,* 275–277.

ROSS, M. W. (1983). Homosexuality and sex roles: A re-evaluation. *Journal of Homosexuality, 9,* 1–6.

ROSS, M. W., & NEED, J. A. (1989). Effects of adequacy of gender reassignment surgery on psychological adjustment: A follow-up of fourteen male-to-female patients. *Archives of Sexual Behavior, 18,* 145–153.

Ross, M. W. et al. (1990). The effect of a national campaign on attitudes toward AIDS. *AIDS Care, 2,* 339–346.

Rossett, H. L., & Sanders, L. W. (1979). Effects of maternal drinking on neonatal morphology and state regulation. In J. D. Osofsky (Ed.), *Handbook of infant development.* New York: Wiley (Interscience).

Rossi, A. S., & Rossi, P. E. (1980). Body time and social time: Mood patterns by menstrual cycle phase and day of the week. In J. E. Parsons (Ed.), *The psychobiology of sex differences and sex roles* (pp. 269–304). New York: McGraw-Hill.

Rossignol, A. M., Zhang, J., Chen, Y., & Xiang, Z. (1989). Tea and premenstrual syndrome in the People's Republic of China. *American Journal of Public Health, 79,* 67–69.

Rotheram, M. J., & Weiner, N. (1983). Androgyny, stress, and satisfaction: Dual-career and traditional relationships. *Sex Roles, 9,* 151–158.

Rothman, E. K. (1984). *Hands and hearts: A history of courtship in America.* New York: Basic Books.

Rothschild, B. S., Fagan, P. J., Woodall, C., & Anderson, A. E. (1991). Sexual functioning of female-disordered patients. *International Journal of Eating Disorders, 10,* 389–394.

Rotolo, J., & Lynch, J. (1991, June 15). Penile cancer: Curable with early detection. *Hospital Practice,* pp. 131–138.

Rousseau, L. et al. (1990). Effect of combined androgen blockade with LHRH agonist and flutamide in one severe case of male exhibitionism. *Canadian Journal of Psychiatry, 35,* 338–341.

Rowland, D. L. et al. (1987). Endocrine, psychological and genital response to sexual arousal in men. *Psychoneuroendocrinology, 12,* 149–158.

Rowland, D. L., Greenleaf, W. J., Dorfman, L. J., & Davidson, J.M. (1993). Aging and sexual function in men. *Archives of Sexual Behavior, 22,* 545–557.

Rozenbaum, W. et al. (1988). HIV transmission by oral sex. *Lancet, 1,* 1395.

Rozenberg, S. et al. (1994). Osteoporosis prevention with sex hormone replacement therapy. *International Journal of Fertility, 39,* 262–271.

Rubin, A. M., & Adams, J. R. (1986). Outcomes of sexually open marriages. *Journal of Sex Research, 22,* 311–319.

Rubin, J., Provenzano, F., & Luria, Z. (1974). The eye of the beholder: Parents' views on sex of newborns. *American Journal of Orthopsychiatry, 44,* 512–519.

Rubin, R. T., Reinisch, J. M., & Haskett, R. F. (1981). Postnatal gonadal steroid effects on human behavior. *Science, 211,* 1318–1324.

Rubin, Z. (1980). Self-disclosure in dating couples: Sex roles and the ethic of openness. *Journal of Marriage and the Family, 42,* 305.

Rubinow, D. R. et al. (1988). Changes in plasma hormones across the menstrual cycle in patients with menstrually related mood disorder and in control subjects. *American Journal of Obstetrics and Gynecology, 158,* 5–11.

Ruff, C. F., Templer, D. I., & Ayers, J. L. (1976). The intelligence of rapists. *Archives of Sexual Behavior, 5,* 327–329.

Rulin, M. C. et al. (1989). Changes in menstrual symptoms among sterilized and comparison women: A prospective study. *Obstetrics and Gynecology, 74,* 149–154.

Russell, C. D., & Ellis, J. B. (1991). Sex-role development in single parent households. *Social Behavior and Personality, 19,* 5–9.

Russell, D. E. H. (Ed.). (1984). *Sexual exploitation: Rape, child sexual abuse and workplace harassment.* Beverly Hills, CA: Sage.

Russell, D. E. H. (1986). *The secret trauma: Incest in the lives of girls and women.* New York: Basic Books.

Russell, D. E. H. (1990). *Rape in marriage* (rev. ed.). Bloomington: Indiana University Press.

Russell, D. E. H., & Howell, N. (1983). The prevalence of rape in the United States revisited. *Signs, 8,* 688–695.

Russell-Brown, P. et al. (1992). Comparison of condom breakage during human use with performance in laboratory testing. *Contraception, 45,* 429–437.

Rutherford, G. W. et al. (1990). Course of HIV-1 infection in a cohort of homosexual and bisexual men: An 11 year follow up study. *British Medical Journal, 301,* 1183–1188.

Rutter, M. (1971). Normal psychosexual development. *Journal of Child Psychology and Psychiatry, 11,* 259–283.

Ryken, T. C., Henderson, S. T., & Merrell, A. N. (1990, January). Stigmatophilia. *Medical Aspects of Human Sexuality,* pp. 50A–50B.

Rynd, N. (1987). Incidence of psychosomatic symptoms in rape victims. *Journal of Sex Research, 24,* 155–161.

Sachs, A. (1990, October 1). Handing out scarlet letters. *Time,* p. 98.

Safran, C. (1976, November). What men do to women on the job: A shocking look at sexual harassment. *Redbook,* pp. 148–150, 156.

Safran, C. (1981. March). Sexual harassment: The view from the top. *Redbook,* pp. 47–51.

Sagarin, E. (1977). Power to the peephole. *Sexual Behavior, 3,* 2–7.

Saghir, M. T., & Robins, E. (1973). *Male and female homosexuality: A comprehensive investigation.* Baltimore, MD: Williams & Wilkins.

Salholz, E., Springen, K., de la Peña, N., & Witherspoon, D. (1990, July 23). A frightening aftermath: Concern about AIDS adds to the trauma of rape. *Newsweek,* p. 53.

Salovey, P. (Ed.). (1991). *The psychology of jealousy and envy.* New York: Guilford.

Salovey, P., & Rodin, J. (1985, September). The heart of jealousy. *Psychology Today,* pp. 22–29.

Salt, R. E. (1991). Affectionate touch between fathers and preadolescent sons. *Journal of Marriage and the Family, 53,* 545–554.

Saluter, A. F. (1994). Marital status and living arrangements: March 1993. *Current Population Reports, 20,* 478.

Samuel, M. C. et al. (1991). Changes in sexual practices over 5 years of follow-up among heterosexual men in San Francisco. *Journal of Acquired Immune Deficiency Syndrome, 4,* 896–900.

Samuels, S. (1989, December). Chlamydia: Epidemic among America's young. *Medical Aspects of Human Sexuality, 23,* 16–24.

Sanchez-Guerrero, J. et al. (1995). Silicone breast implants and the risk of connective-tissue diseases and symptoms. *New England Journal of Medicine, 332,* 1666–1670.

Sanday, P. (1981). The socio-cultural context of rape: A cross-cultural study. *Journal of Social Issues, 37,* 5–27.

Sanday, P. (1990). *Fraternity gang rape: Sex, brotherhood and privilege on campus.* New York: New York University Press.

Sandberg, D. E., & Meyer-Bahlburg, H. F. L. (1994). Variability in middle childhood play behavior: Effects of gender, age, and family background. *Archives of Sexual Behavior, 23,* 645–663.

Sanders, J., & Robinson, W. (1979). Talking and not talking about sex: Male and female vocabulary. *Journal of Communication, 29,* 22–30.

Sandfort, T. G. M. (1992). The argument for adult-child sexual contact: A critical appraisal and new data. In W. O'Donohue & J. H. Geer (Eds.), *The sexual abuse of children: Theory and research* (Vol. 1). Hillsdale, NJ: Erlbaum.

Santiago, J. M., McCall-Perez, F., Gorcey, M., & Beigel, A. (1985). Long-term psychological effects of rape in 35 rape victims. *American Journal of Psychiatry, 142,* 1338–1340.

Santrock, J. W. (1984). *Adolescence: An introduction* (2nd ed.). Dubuque, IA: W. C. Brown.

Sarrel, P., & Masters, W. (1982). Sexual molestation of men by women. *Archives of Sexual Behavior, 11*(2), 117–131.

Sarvela, P. D. et al. (1992). Connotative meanings assigned to contraceptive options. *Journal of American College Health, 41,* 91–97.

Sarwer, D. B. et al. (1993). Sexual aggression and love styles: An exploratory study. *Archives of Sexual Behavior, 22,* 265–275.

Sattar, S. A., & Springthorpe, V. S. (1991). Survival and disinfectant inactivation of the human immunodeficiency virus: A critical review. *Reviews of Infectious Diseases, 13,* 430–447.

Satterfield, A., & Muehlenhard, C. (1990, November). *Flirtation in the classroom: Negative consequences on women's perceptions of their ability.* Paper presented at the annual meeting of the Society for the Scientific Study of Sex, Minneapolis, MN.

Satterfield, S., & Listiak, A. (1982, May 15–21). *Juvenile prostitution: A sequel to incest.* Paper presented at the 135th meeting of the American Psychiatric Association, Toronto.

Sattin, R. W. et al. (1986). Oral-contraceptive use and the risk of breast cancer: the Cancer and Steroid Hormone Study of the Centers for Disease Control and the National Institute of Child Health and Human Development. *New England Journal of Medicine, 315,* 405–411.

Sauer, M. V., Paulson, R. J., & Lobo, R. A. (1992). Reversing the natural decline in human fertility. *Journal of the American Medical Association, 268,* 1275–1279.

Sauer, M. V., Paulson, R. J., & Lobo, R. A. (1993). Pregnancy after age 50: Application of oocyte donation to women after natural menopause. *Lancet, 341,* 321–323.

Saunders, E. J. (1989). Life-threatening autoerotic behavior: A challenge for sex educators and therapists. *Journal of Sex Education and Therapy, 15*(2), 77–81.

Savitz, L., & Rosen, L. (1988). The sexuality of prostitutes: Sexual enjoyment reported by streetwalkers. *Journal of Sex Research, 24,* 200–208.

Schachter, J. et al. (1986). Prospective study of perinatal transmission of chlamydia trachomatis. *Journal of the American Medical Association, 255,* 3374–3377.

SCHACHTER, J. et al. (1992). Nonculture tests for genital tract chlamydial infection. *Sexually Transmitted Diseases, 19,* 243–244.

SCHACHTER, M., & SHOHAM, Z. (1994). Amenorrhea during the reproductive years—is it safe? *Fertility and Sterility, 62,* 1–16.

SCHACHTER, S., & SINGER, J. (1962). Cognitive, social and physiological determinants of emotional state. *Psychological Review, 69,* 379–399.

SCHECHTER, M. T. et al. (1993). HIV-1 and the aetiology of AIDS. *Lancet, 341,* 658–659.

SCHIAVI, R. C. (1990). Sexuality and aging in men. In J. Bancroft (Ed.), *Annual review of sex research* (Vol. 1). (pp. 227–249). Mount Vernon, IA: The Society for the Scientific Study of Sex.

SCHIRM, A. L., TRUSSELL, J., MENKEN, J., & GRADY, W. R. (1982). Contraceptive failure in the United States: The impact of social, economic and demographic factors. *Family Planning Perspectives, 14*(2), 68–75.

SCHLEGEL, A., & BARRY, H., III. (1979). Adolescent initiation ceremonies: Cross-cultural codes. *Ethnology, 18,* 199–210.

SCHLEGEL, A., & BARRY, H., III. (1980). The evolutionary significance of adolescent initiation ceremonies. *American Ethnologist, 7,* 696–715.

SCHLEGEL, W. S. (1962). Die konstitutionbiologischen grundlagen der homosexualitat. *Zeitschrift fuer Menschliche Vererbungs und Konstitutionslehre, 36,* 341–364.

SCHMID, G. P. (1990). Treatment of chancroid, 1989. *Reviews of Infectious Diseases, 12,* S580–S619.

SCHMIDT, G., & SIGUSCH, V. (1970). Sex differences in responses to psychosexual stimulation by films and slides. *Journal of Sex Research, 6,* 268–283.

SCHMIDT, P. J. et al. (1991). Lack of effect of induced menses on symptoms in women with premenstrual syndrome. *New England Journal of Medicine, 324,* 1174–1179.

SCHNEIDER, A. (1993). Pathogenesis of genital HPV infection. *Genitourin Medicine, 69,* 165–173.

SCHOEN, E. J. (1990). The status of circumcision of newborns. *New England Journal of Medicine, 322,* 1308–1312.

SCHOLES, D., DALING, J. R., & STERGACHIS, A. S. (1992). Current cigarette smoking and risk of acute pelvic inflammatory disease. *American Journal of Public Health, 82,* 1352–1355.

SCHOOLNIK, G. (1988). *Sex and cancer: Human papilloma virus—the sexually transmitted disease of the 90's.* Paper presented at the seventh annual American Medical Association Science Reporters Conference, San Francisco.

SCHOVER, L. R. (1988). *Sexuality & cancer: For the woman who has cancer, and her partner.* New York: American Cancer Society.

SCHOVER, L. R. et al. (1982). Multiaxial problem-oriented system for sexual dysfunctions. *Archives of General Psychiatry, 39,* 614–619.

SCHOVER, L. R., & JENSEN, S. B. (1988). *Sexuality and chronic illness: A comprehensive approach.* New York: Guilford.

SCHOVER, L. R., & LOPICCOLO, J. (1982). Treatment effectiveness for dysfunctions of sexual desire. *Journal of Sex and Marital Therapy, 8,* 179–197.

SCHULT, D. G., & SCHNEIDER, L. J. (1991). The role of provocativeness, rape history, and observer sex in attributions of blame in sexual assault. *Journal of Interpersonal Violence, 6,* 94–101.

SCHULTZ, W. C. M. et al. (1989). Vaginal sensitivity to electric stimuli: Theoretical and practical implications. *Archives of Sexual Behavior, 18,* 87–95.

SCHWARTZ, S. K. et al. (1990). National surveillance of antimicrobial resistance in Neisseria gonorrhoeae. *Journal of the American Medical Association, 264,* 1413–1417.

SCHWARCZ, S. K., & WHITTINGTON, W. L. (1990). Sexual assault and sexually transmitted diseases: Detection and management in adults and children. *Reviews of Infectious Diseases, 12*(Suppl. 6), S682–S690.

SCHWARTZ, I. M. (1993). Affective reactions of American and Swedish women to their first premarital coitus: A cross-cultural comparison. *Journal of Sex Research, 30,* 18–26.

SCHWARTZ, M., & MASTERS, W. (1988). Inhibited sexual desire: The Masters and Johnson Institute treatment model. In S. R. Leiblum & R. C. Rosen (Eds.), *Sexual desire disorders.* New York: Guilford.

SCHWEIGER, U. (1991). Menstrual function and luteal-phase deficiency in relation to weight changes and dieting. *Clinical Obstetrics and Gynecology, 34,* 191–197.

SCOTT, C. S., ARTHUR, D., PANIZO, M. I., & OWEN, R. (1989). Menarche: The Black American experience. *Journal of Adolescent Health, 10,* 363–368.

SCOTT, J. E. (1986). An updated longitudinal content analysis of sex references in mass circulation magazines. *Journal of Sex Research, 22,* 385–392.

SCOTT, J. E., & CUVELIER, S. J. (1993). Violence and sexual violence in pornography: Is it really increasing? *Archives of Sexual Behavior, 22,* 357–371.

SCOTT, J. E., & SCHWALM, L. (1988). Rape rates and the circulation rates of adult magazines. *Journal of Sex Research, 24,* 241–250.

SCOTT, R. L., & STONE, D. A. (1986). MMPI measures of psychological disturbance in adolescent and adult victims of father-daughter incest. *Journal of Clinical Psychology, 42,* 251–259.

SCULLY, D., & MAROLLA, J. (1984). Convicted rapists' vocabulary of motives: Excuses and justifications. *Social Problems, 31,* 530–544.

SEAMAN, B. (1972). *Free and female.* New York: Coward, McGann & Geoghegan.

SEGAL, Z., & MARSHALL, W. (1985). Heterosexual social skills in a population of rapists and child molesters. *Journal of Consulting and Clinical Psychology, 53,* 55–63.

SEGHORN, T. K., PRENTKY, R. A., & BOUCHER, R. J. (1987). Childhood sexual abuse in the lives of sexually aggressive offenders. *Journal of the American Academy of Child and Adolescent Psychiatry, 26,* 262–267.

SEGRAVES, R. T. (1991). Pharmacological enhancement of human sexual behavior. *Journal of Sex Education and Therapy, 17,* 283–289.

SEGRAVES, R. T., & SEGRAVES, K. (1992). Aging and drug effects on male sexuality. In R. Rosen & S. Leiblum (Eds.), *Erectile disorders.* New York: Guilford.

SEIDLIN, M. et al. (1993). Heterosexual transmission of HIV in a cohort of couples in New York city. *AIDS, 7,* 1247–1254.

SEIDMAN, S. N., MOSHER, W. D., & ARAL, S. O. (1992). Women with multiple sexual partners: United States, 1988. *American Journal of Public Health, 82,* 1388–1394.

SEIDMAN, S. N., & RIEDER, R. O. (1994). A review of sexual behavior in the United States. *American Journal of Psychiatry, 151,* 330–341.

SELIK, R. M., CHU, S. Y., & BUCHLER, J. W. (1993). HIV infection as leading cause of death among young adults in US cities and states. *Journal of the American Medical Association, 269,* 2991–2994.

SELKIN, J. (1975). Rape. *Psychology Today, 8,* 70–76.

SEMANS, J. H. (1956). Premature ejaculation: A new approach. *Journal of Southern Medicine, 79,* 353–361.

SENANAYAKE, P. (1990). IUDs: A global review. XVIIth Current Fertility Control Symposium. *British Journal of Family Planning, 15*(Suppl.), 8–12.

SENANAYAKE, P. (1992). Positive approaches to education for sexual health with examples from Asia and Africa. *Journal of Adolescent Health, 13,* 351–354.

SESSION, D. R., KELLY, A. C., & JEWELEWICZ, R. (1993). Current concepts in estrogen replacement therapy in the menopause. *Fertility and Sterility, 59,* 277–284.

SEVELY, J. L., & BENNETT, J. W. (1978). Concerning female ejaculation and the female prostate. *Journal of Sex Research, 14,* 1–20.

SHANGOLD, M. (1985). Causes, evaluation, and management of athletic oligamenorrhea. *Medical Clinics of North America, 69,* 83–95.

SHANNON, J. W., & WOODS, W. J. (1991). Affirmative psychotherapy for gay men. *Counseling Psychologist, 19,* 197–215.

SHANTHA, T. R., SHANTHA, D. T., & BENNETT, J. K. (1990, April). Priapism. *Medical Aspects of Human Sexuality,* pp. 63–67.

SHAPIRO, L. (1990, May 28). Guns and dolls. *Newsweek,* pp. 54–65.

SHAUGHNESSY, M. F., & SHAKESBY, P. (1992). Adolescent sexual and emotional intimacy. *Adolescence, 27,* 475–480.

SHAVER, P., HAZAN, C., & BRADSHAW, D. (1988). Love as attachment. In R. J. Sternberg & M. L. Barnes (Eds.), *The psychology of love* (pp. 68–99). New Haven, CT: Yale University Press.

SHAW, J. (1994). Aging and sexual potential. *Journal of Sex Education and Therapy, 20,* 134–139.

SHEPHER, J. (1971). Mate selection among second generation kibbutz adolescents and adults: Incest avoidance and negative imprinting. *Archives of Sexual Behavior, 1,* 293–307.

SHERMAN, K. J. et al. (1990). Sexually transmitted diseases and tubal pregnancy. *Sexually Transmitted Diseases, 17,* 115–121.

SHERR, L. (1990). Fear arousal and AIDS: Do shock tactics work? *AIDS, 4,* 361–364.

SHERWIN, B. B. (1988). A comparative analysis of the role of androgens in human male and female sexual behavior: Behavior specificity, critical thresholds and sensitivity. *Psychobiology, 16,* 416–425.

SHERWIN, B. B. (1991). The psychoendocrinology of aging and female sexuality. In J. Bancroft (Ed.), *Annual review of sex research* (Vol. 2) (pp. 181–198). Mount Vernon, IA: The Society for the Scientific Study of Sex.

SHERWIN, B. B., GELFAND, M., & BRENDER, W. (1985). Androgen enhances sexual motivation in females: A prospective crossover study of sex steroid administration in the surgical menopause. *Psychosomatic Medicine, 47,* 339–351.

SHILTS, R. (1987). *And the band played on.* New York: St. Martin's Press.

SHOHAM, Z. (1994). Epidemiology, etiology, and fertility drugs in ovarian epithelial carcinoma: Where are we today? *Fertility and Sterility, 62,* 433–448.

SHORT, R. V. (1984). Breast-feeding. *Scientific American, 250*(4), 35–41.

SHOSTAK, M. (1981). *Kalahari hunter-gatherers.* Cambridge, MA: Harvard University Press.

SHUN-QUIANG, L. (1988). *Vasal sterilization techniques: Teaching material for the national standard workshop.* Chong quing, China: Scientific and Technical Literature Press.

SHY, K. et al. (1989). Papanicolaou smear screening interval and risk of cervical cancer. *Obstetrics and Gynecology, 74,* 838–843.

SHY, K. et al. (1990). Effects of electronic fetal-heart-rate monitoring as compared with periodic auscultation, on the neurologic development of premature infants. *New England Journal of Medicine, 322,* 588–593.

SIECUS NATIONAL GUIDELINES TASK FORCE. (1991). *Guidelines for comprehensive sexuality education.* New York: Author.

SIEGEL, B. S. (1989). *Love, medicine & miracles.* New York: Perennial/ Harper & Row.

SIEGEL, D. et al. (1991). AIDS knowledge, attitudes, and behavior among inner city, junior high school students. *Journal of School Health, 61,* 160–165.

SILBER, M. (1994). Menstrual cycle and work schedule: Effects on women's sexuality. *Archives of Sexual Behavior, 23,* 397–404.

SIMENAUER, J., & CARROLL, D. (1982). *Singles: The new Americans.* New York: Simon & Schuster.

SIMON, P. M. et al. (1992). Psychological characteristics of a sample of male street prostitutes. *Archives of Sexual Behavior, 21,* 33–44.

SIMPSON, J. A., CAMPBELL, B., & BERSCHEID, E. (1986). The association between romantic love and marriage: Kephart (1967) twice revisited. *Personality and Social Psychology Bulletin, 12,* 363–372.

SINCLAIR, A. H. et al. (1990). A gene from the human sex-determining region encodes a protein with homology to a conserved DNA binding motif. *Nature (London), 346,* 240–244.

SINGER, I. (1984-1987). *The nature of love* (Vols. 1–3). Chicago: University of Chicago Press.

SINGER, J., & SINGER, I. (1972). Types of female orgasm. *Journal of Sex Research, 8,* 255–267.

SINGER, L., ARENDT, R., & MINNES, S. (1993). Neurodevelopmental effects of cocaine. *Clinics in Perinatology, 20*(1), 245–262.

SINGER, L., FARKAS, K., & KLIEGMAN, R. (1992). Childhood medical and behavioral consequences of maternal cocaine use. *Journal of Pediatric Psychology, 17,* 389–406.

SINICCO, A. et al. (1993). Risk of developing AIDS after primary acute HIV-1 infection. *Journal of Acquired Immune Deficiency Syndromes, 6,* 575–581.

SIVIN, I. (1989). IUDs are contraceptives, not abortifacients: A comment on research and belief. *Studies in Family Planning, 20,* 355–359.

SIVIN, I. (1993). Another look at the Dalkon Shield: Meta-analysis underscores its problems. *Contraception, 48,* 1–12.

SIVIN, I. et al. (1981). A multicenter study of levonorgestrel-estradiol contraceptive vaginal rings. I. Use effectiveness. *Contraception, 24,* 341–358.

SKELTON, C. (1984). *Correlates of sexual victimization among college women.* (No. DER 84–26609). Unpublished doctoral dissertation, Auburn University, Auburn, AL.

SLADE, J. (1984). Violence in the hard-core pornographic film: A historical survey. *Journal of Communication, 34,* 148–163.

SLATTERY, M. L. et al. (1989). Sexual activity, contraception, genital infections, and cervical cancer: Support for a sexually transmitted disease hypothesis. *American Journal of Epidemiology, 130,* 248–258.

SLOB, A. K., ERNSTE, M., & TENBOSCH, J. J. (1991). Menstrual cycle phase and sexual arousibility in women. *Archives of Sexual Behavior, 20,* 567–577.

SMALL, S. A., & KERNS, D. (1993). Unwanted sexual activity among peers during early and middle adolescence: Incidence and risk factors. *Journal of Marriage and the Family, 55,* 941–952.

SMITH, A. M. (1993). 'What is pornography?': An analysis of the policy statement of the campaign against pornography and censorship. *Feminist Review, 43,* 71–87.

SMITH, E. A., & UDRY, J. R. (1985). Coital and non-coital sexual behaviors of white and black adolescents. *American Journal of Public Health, 75,* 1200–1203.

SMITH, H., & ISRAEL, E. (1987). Sibling incest: A study of the dynamics of 25 cases. *Child Abuse & Neglect, 11,* 101–108.

SMITH, L. (1993, January 6). Saying no to birth control. *Los Angeles Times,* pp. A1, A12.

SMITH, P. I., & TALBERT, R. L. (1986). Sexual dysfunction with antihypertensive and antipsychotic agents. *Clinical Pharmacy, 5,* 373–384.

SMITH, R., PINE, C., & HAWLEY, M. (1988). Social cognitions about adult

male victims of female sexual assault. *Journal of Sex Research, 24,* 101–112.

SMITH, T. W. (1991). Adult sexual behavior in 1989: Number of partners, frequency of intercourse, and risk of AIDS. *Family Planning Perspectives, 23,* 102–107.

SNIFFEN, M. J. (1994, June 23). Study: Most rape victims young. *New Orleans Times-Picayune,* p. A-9.

SNYDER, J. L. (1989, July/August). The problem of circumcision in America. *The Truth Seeker,* pp. 39–42.

SNYDER, P. J. (1990). Fewer sperm in the summer: It's not the heat, it's . . . *New England Journal of Medicine, 323,* 54–56.

SNYDER, P. J., WEINRICH, J. D., & PILLARD, R. C. (1994). Personality and lipid level differences associated with homosexual and bisexual identity in men. *Archives of Sexual Behavior, 23,* 433–451.

SOBLE, A. (1989). Analyzing love. *Philosophy of the Social Sciences, 19,* 493–500.

SOCIETY FOR ASSISTED REPRODUCTIVE TECHNOLOGY, THE AMERICAN FERTILITY SOCIETY. (1993). Assisted reproductive technology in the United States and Canada: 1991 results from the Society for Assisted Reproductive Technology generated from The American Fertility Society Registry. *Fertility and Sterility, 59,* 956–962.

SOLOMON, D. (1993). Screening for cervical cancer: Prospects for the future. *Journal of the National Cancer Institute, 85,* 1018–1019.

SONENSTEIN, F. L., PLECK, J. H., & KU, L. C. (1989). Sexual activity, condom use and AIDS awareness among adolescent males. *Family Planning Perspectives, 21,* 152–158.

SONENSTEIN, F. L., PLECK, J. H., & KU, L. C. (1991). Levels of sexual activity among adolescent males in the United States. *Family Planning Perspectives, 23,* 162–167.

SOPER, D. E., BROCKWELL, N. J., & DALTON, H. P. (1991). Evaluation of the effects of a female condom on the female lower genital tract. *Contraception, 44,* 21–29.

SORENSON, R. C. (1973). *Adolescent sexuality in contemporary America.* New York: World Publishing Co.

SPANIER, G. B., & THOMPSON, L. (1987). *Parting: The aftermath of separation and divorce.* Newbury Park, CA: Sage.

SPARLING, P. F., ELKINS, C., WYRICK, P. B., & COHEN, M. S. (1994). Vaccines for bacterial sexually transmitted infections: A realistic goal. *Proceedings of the National Academy of Sciences of the U.S.A., 91,* 2456–2463.

SPECTOR, I., & CAREY, M. (1990). Incidence and prevalence of the sexual dysfunctions: A critical review of the empirical literature. *Archives of Sexual Behavior, 19,* 389–408.

SPENCE, J. T., & HELMREICH, R. L. (1972). Who likes competent women? Competence, sex-role congruence of interests, and attitudes towards women as determinants of interpersonal attraction. *Journal of Applied and Social Psychology, 2,* 197–213.

SPENCE, J. T., & HELMREICH, R. L. (1978). *Masculinity & femininity: Their psychological dimensions, correlates, and antecedents.* Austin: University of Texas Press.

SPENCE, J. T., HELMREICH, R. L., & STAPP, J. (1974). The personal attributes questionnaire: A measure of sex role stereotypes and masculinity-femininity. *JSAS Catalog of Selected Documents in Psychology, 4,* 43.

SPENCE, J. T., HELMREICH, R. L., AND STAPP, J. (1975). Ratings of self and peers on sex role attributes and their relation to self-esteem and conceptions of masculinity and femininity. *Journal of Personality and Social Psychology, 32,* 29–39.

SPIRTAS, R., KAUFMAN, S. C., & ALEXANDER, N. J. (1993). Fertility drugs and ovarian cancer: Red alert or red herring? *Fertility and Sterility, 59,* 291–293.

SPITZ, R. A. (1945). Hospitalism: An inquiry into the genesis of psychiatric conditioning in early childhood. In D. Fenschel & A. Freud (Eds.), *Psychoanalytic studies of the child* (Vol. 1). New York: International Universities Press.

SPITZ, R. A. (1946). Hospitalism: A follow-up report. In D. Fenschel, P. Greenacre, & A. Freud (Eds.), *Psychoanalytic studies of the child* (Vol. 2). (pp. 113–117). New York: International Universities Press.

SPITZER, P., & WEINER, N. (1989). Transmission of HIV infection from a woman to a man by oral sex. *New England Journal of Medicine, 320,* 251.

SPRECHER, S. et al. (1994). Token resistance to sexual intercourse and consent to unwanted sexual intercourse: College students' dating experiences in three countries. *Journal of Sex Research, 31,* 125–132.

SRIVASTAVA, A., BORRIES, C., & SOMMER, V. (1991). Homosexual mounting in free-ranging female Hanuman Langurs *(Presbytis entellus). Archives of Sexual Behavior, 20,* 487–512 .

STACK, S., & GUNDLACH, J. H. (1992). Divorce and sex. *Archives of Sexual Behavior, 21,* 359–368.

STAFFORD, R. S., SULLIVAN, S. D., & GARDNER, L. B. (1993). Trends in cesarean section use in California, 1983 to 1990. *American Journal of Obstetrics and Gynecology, 168,* 1297–1302.

STAGNOR, C., & RUBLE, D. N. (1987). Development of gender knowledge and gender constancy. In L. S. Lieben & M. L. Signorella (Eds.), *Children's gender schemata.* San Francisco: Jossey-Bass.

STALL, R. et al. (1990). Relapse from safer sex: The next challenge for AIDS prevention efforts. *Journal of Acquired Immune Deficiency Syndromes, 3,* 1181–1187.

STAMEY, T. A. (1992). Diagnosis of prostate cancer: A personal view. *Journal of Urology, 147,* 830–832.

STAMPFER, M. J. et al. (1988). A prospective study of past uses of oral contraceptive agents and risk of cardiovascular diseases. *New England Journal of Medicine, 319,* 1313–1317.

STAMPFER, M. J. et al. (1991). Postmenopausal estrogen therapy and cardiovascular disease. *New England Journal of Medicine, 325,* 756–762.

STANFORD, J. L. et al. (1995). Combined estrogen and progestin hormone replacement therapy in relation to risk of breast cancer in middle-aged women. *Journal of the American Medical Association. 274,* 137–142.

STANG, H. J. et al. (1988). Local anesthesia for neonatal circumcision: Effects and distress and cortisol response. *Journal of the American Medical Association, 259,* 1507–1511.

STAPLETON, A., LATHAM, R. H., JOHNSON, C., & STAMM, W. E. (1990). Postcoital antimicrobial prophylaxis for recurrent urinary tract infection. *Journal of the American Medical Association, 264,* 703–706.

STARK, R. (1982). *The book of aphrodisiacs.* New York: Stein & Day.

STARR, B. D., & WEINER, M. B. (1981). *The Starr-Weiner report on sex and sexuality in the mature years.* New York: Stein & Day.

STARR, R. H., JR. (1988). Physical abuse of children. In V. B. Van Hasselt, R. L. Morrison, A. S. Bellack, & M. Hersen (Eds.), *Handbook of family violence.* New York: Plenum.

STD-related infertility finds 125,000 victims a year in U.S. (1988). *Reproductive Health Digest 2*(4).

STEELE, B. F., & ALEXANDER, H. (1981). Long-term effects of sexual abuse in childhood. In P. B. Mzazek & C. H. Kempe (Eds.), *Sexually abused children and their families* (pp. 223–233). New York: Pergamon.

STEIN, M. L. (1977). Prostitution. In J. Money & H. Musaph (Eds.), *Handbook of sexology.* Amsterdam: Elsevier/North-Holland.

STEINBERG, K. K. et al. (1991). A meta-analysis of the effect of estrogen replacement therapy on the risk of breast cancer. *Journal of the American Medical Association, 265,* 1985–1990.

STEINEM, G. (1983). *Outrageous acts and everyday rebellions.* New York: Holt, Rinehart & Winston.

STEINER, M., PIEDRAHITA, C., GLOVER, L., & JOANIS, C. (1993). Can condom users likely to experience condom failure be identified? *Family Planning Perspectives, 25,* 220–223, 226.

STEINER, M. et al. (1995). Fluoxetine in the treatment of premenstrual dysphoria. *New England Journal of Medicine, 332,* 1529–1534.

STELLATO, G. (1992). Intralesional recombinant alpha 2B interferon in the treatment of human papillomavirus-associated cervical intraepithelial neoplasia. *Sexually Transmitted Diseases, 19,* 124–126.

STEPHENS, M., & DAY, H. D. (1979). Sex-role identity, parental identification, and self-concept of adolescent daughters from mother-absent, father-absent, and intact families. *Journal of Psychology, 103,* 193–202.

STEPHENSON, P., WAGNER, M., BADEA, M., & SERBANESCU, F. (1992). Commentary: The public health consequences of restricted induced abortion—lessons from Romania. *American Journal of Public Health, 82,* 1328–1331.

STEPTOE, P. C., & EDWARDS R. G. (1978). Birth after the implantation of a human embryo (letter). *Lancet, 2,* 366.

STERGACHIS, A. et al. (1990). Tubal sterilization and the long-term risk of hysterectomy. *Journal of the American Medical Association, 264,* 2893–2898.

STERNBERG, R. J. (1986). A triangular theory of love. *Psychological Review, 93,* 119–135.

STERNBERG, R. J. (1987). Liking vs. loving: A comparative evaluation of theories. *Psychological Bulletin, 102,* 331–345.

STERNBERG, R. J. (1988). Triangulating love. In R. J. Sternberg & M. L. Barnes (Eds.), *The psychology of love* (pp. 119–138). New Haven, CT: Yale University Press.

STERNBERG, R. J., & GRAJEK, S. (1984). The nature of love. *Journal of Personality and Social Psychology, 47,* 312–329.

STEWART, A., & KNEALE, G. W. (1970). Radiation dose effects in relation to obstetric X-rays and childhood cancers. *Lancet, 1,* 1185–1188.

STEWART, B. et al. (1987). The aftermath of rape. Profiles of immediate and delayed treatment seekers. *Journal of Nervous and Mental Disorders, 175,* 90–94.

ST. LAWRENCE, J. S., & MADAKASIRA, S. (1992). Evaluation and treatment of premature ejaculation: A critical review. *International Journal of Psychiatry in Medicine, 22,* 77–97.

STOCK, W. E. (1982, November). *The effect of violent pornography on women.* Paper presented at the national meeting of the Society of the Scientific Study of Sex, San Francisco.

STOCK, W. E. (1983). *Effects of exposure to violent pornography.* Presented at the 26th annual meeting of the Society for the Scientific Study of Sex, Chicago.

STOCKARD, J., & JOHNSON, M. M. (1980). *Sex roles, sex inequality and sex role development.* Englewood Cliffs, NJ: Prentice Hall.

STOLLER, R. J. (1977). Sexual deviations. In F. Beach (Ed.), *Human sexuality in four perspectives* (pp. 190–214). Baltimore: Johns Hopkins University Press.

STOLLER, R. J., & HERDT, G. H. (1985). Theories of origins of male homosexuality. *Archives of General Psychiatry, 42,* 399–404.

STONE, K. M. et al. (1989). National surveillance for neonatal herpes simplex virus infections. *Sexually Transmitted Diseases, 16,* 152–160.

STORMS, M. (1980). Theories of sexual orientation. *Journal of Personality and Social Psychology, 38,*783–792.

STORY, M. (1986). *Factors affecting the incidence of partner abuse among university students.* Unpublished manuscript, University of Northern Iowa, Home Economics Department, Waterloo.

STOVALL, T. G. et al. (1991). Methotrexate treatment of unruptured ectopic pregnancy: A report of 100 cases. *Obstetrics and Gynecology, 77,* 749–753.

STRASSBERG, D. S., KELLY, M. P., CARROLL, C., & KIRCHER, J. C. (1987). The psychophysiological nature of premature ejaculation. *Archives of Sexual Behavior, 16,* 327–336.

STRATAKIS, C. A., & RENNERT, O. M. (1994). Turner syndrome: Molecular and cytogenetics, dysmorphology, endocrine, and other clinical manifestations and their management. *Endocrinologist, 4,* 442–453.

STRAUSS, R. H. (1991). Anabolic steroids in the athlete. *Annual Review of Medicine, 42,* 449–457.

STRONG, E. K. (1936). Interests of men and women. *Journal of Social Psychology, 7,* 49–67.

STROUSE, J., & FABES, R. A. (1985). Formal versus informal sources of sex education: Competing forces in the sexual socialization of adolescents. *Adolescence, 20,* 251–262.

STRUCKMAN-JOHNSON, C., & STRUCKMAN-JOHNSON, D. (1994). Men pressured and forced into sexual experience. *Archives of Sexual Behavior, 23,* 93–114.

SULIK, K. K., JOHNSON, M. C., & WEBB, M. A. (1981). Fetal alcohol syndrome: Embryogenesis in a mouse model. *Science, 214,* 936–938.

SULLIVAN, W. (1987, December 29). Sexual potency saved after surgery to remove prostate. *New York Times,* p. 16.

SULTAN, C. et al. (1991). SRY and male sex determination. *Hormone Research, 36,* 1–3.

SULTAN, F. E., & CHAMBLES, D. L. (1982). Pubococcygeal function and orgasm in a normal population. In B. Graber (Ed.), *Circumvaginal musculature and sexual function* (pp. 74–87). New York: Karger.

SUMMIT, R., & KRYSO, J. (1978). Sexual abuse of children: A clinical spectrum. *American Journal of Orthopsychiatry, 48,* 237–251.

SUTTIE, I. D. (1952). *The origins of love and hate.* New York: Julian Press.

SWAAB, D. F., GOOREN, L. J. G., & HOFMAN, M. A. (1992). The human hypothalamus in relation to gender and sexual orientation. *Progress in Brain Research, 93,* 205–219.

SWAAB, D. F., & HOFMAN, M. A. (1990). An enlarged suprachiasmatic nucleus in homosexual men. *Brain Research, 537,* 141–148.

SWINKER, M. (1986). Chlamydia trachomatic genital infections in college women. *Journal of American College Health, 34,* 207.

SYMONS, D. (1979). *The evolution of human sexuality.* New York: Oxford University Press.

TADDIO, A. et al. (1995). Effect of neonatal circumcision on pain responses during vaccination in boys. *Lancet, 345,* 291–292.

TAFFEL, S. M., PLACEK, P. J., & MOIEN, M. (1990). 1988 cesarean-section rate at 24.7 per 100 births—a plateau? *New England Journal of Medicine, 323,* 199–200.

TAKIHARA, H., SAKATOKU, J., & COCKETT, A. T. (1991). The pathophysiology of varicocele in male infertility. *Fertility and Sterility, 55,* 861–868.

TALAMINI, J. T. (1982). *Boys will be girls: The hidden world of the heterosexual male transvestite.* Washington, DC: University Press of America.

TANFER, K., GRADY, W. R., KLEPINGER, D. H., & BILLY, J. O. G. (1993). Condom use among U. S. men, 1991. *Family Planning Perspectives, 25,* 61–66.

TANFER, K., & SCHOORL, J. J. (1992). Premarital sexual careers and partner change. *Archives of Sexual Behavior, 21,* 45–68.

TANGRI, S., BURT, M., & JOHNSON, L. (1982). Sexual harassment at work: Three explanatory models. *Journal of Social Issues*, 38(4), 33–54.

TANNAHILL, R. (1980). *Sex in history*. New York: Stein & Day.

TANNER, J. M. (1962). *Growth at adolescence*. Oxford: Blackwell.

TAPLIN, D. et al. (1991). Community control of scabies: A model based on use of permethrin cream. *Lancet*, 337, 1016–1018.

TARDIF, G. S. (1989). Sexual activity after a myocardial infarction. *Archives of Physical Medicine and Rehabilitation*, 70, 763–766.

TAYLOR, C. V., SALLIS, J. F., & NEEDLE, R. (1985). The relation of physical activity and exercise to mental health. *Public Health Reports*, 100, 195–201.

TAYLOR, M. C., & HALL, J. A. (1982). Psychological androgyny: Theories, methods, and conclusions. *Psychological Bulletin*, 92, 347–366.

TENNOV, D. (1979). *Love and limerence*. New York: Stein and Day.

TERMAN, L., & MILES, C. C. (1936). *Sex and personality*. New York: McGraw-Hill.

TEW, M. (1990). *Safer childbirth? A critical history of maternity care*. London: Chapman & Hall.

THAYER, L. (1986). *On communication*. Norwood, NJ: Ablex.

THEIM, R. (1994, August 6). Gay parents' custody rights debated by lawyers. *New Orleans Times-Picayune*, p. A-7.

THOMAS, E., & COLELLA, V. (1992). Cohabitation and marital stability: Quality or commitment? *Journal of Marriage and the Family*, 54, 259–267.

THOMPSON, A. (1983). Extramarital sex: A review of the research literature. *Journal of Sex Research*, 19, 1–22.

THOMPSON, A. (1984). Emotional and sexual components of extramarital relations. *Journal of Marriage and the Family*, 46, 35–42.

THOMPSON, L. (1991). Paraphilia spans extremes of sexual disorders. *The Washington Post*.

THOMPSON, R. (1990). Is routine circumcision indicated in the newborn? An opposing view. *Journal of Family Practice*, 31, 189–196.

THOMPSON, S. (1990). Putting a big thing into a little hole: Teenage girls' accounts of sexual initiation. *Journal of Sex Research*, 27, 341–361.

THORNBURG, H. D. (1981). Adolescent sources of information on sex. *Journal of School Health*, 51, 274–277.

THORNHILL, N. W. (1991). An evolutionary analysis of rules regulating human inbreeding and marriage. *Behavioral and Brain Sciences*, 14, 247–293.

THORNHILL, N. W. (1992). Human inbreeding. In N. W. Thornhill (Ed.), *The natural history of inbreeding and outbreeding: Theoretical and empirical perspectives*. Chicago: University of Chicago Press.

THORNTON, A., AXINN, W. G., & HILL, D. H. (1992). Reciprocal effects of religiosity, cohabitation, and marriage. *American Journal of Sociology*, 98, 628–651.

TIEFER, L. (1991). Historical, scientific, clinical and feminist criticisms of "The human sexual response" model. In J. Bancroft, C. M. Davis, & H. J. Ruppel (Eds.), *Annual review of sex research* (Vol. 2). (pp. 1–23). Mount Vernon, IA: The Society for the Scientific Study of Sex.

TIME/CNN POLL. (1993, May 24). pp. 62–63.

TOBIS, J. (1977). Cardiovascular patients and sexual dysfunctions. In R. Marinelli & A. Dell Orto (Eds.), *The psychological and social impact of physical disability*. New York: Springer.

TOLLISON, C. D., & ADAMS, H. E. (1979). *Sexual disorders: Treatment, theory, and research*. New York: Gardner Press.

TONIOLO, P. G. et al. (1995). Prospective study of endogenous estrogens and breast cancer in postmenopausal women. *Journal of the National Cancer Institute*, 87, 190–197.

TOUFEXIS, A. (1993, February 15). The right chemistry. *Time*, pp. 49–51.

TRUDEL, G., & SAINT LAURENT, S. (1983). A comparison between the effects of Kegel's exercises and a combination of sexual awareness relaxation and breathing on situational orgasmic dysfunction in women. *Journal of Sex and Marital Therapy*, 9, 204–209.

TRUDGILL, E. (1976). *Madonnas and Magdalens: The origins and development of Victorian sexual attitudes*. New York: Holmes & Meier.

TRUESDELL, D., MCNEIL, J., & DESCHNER, J. (1986). Incidence of wife abuse in incestuous families. *Social Work*, 31, 138–140.

TRUSSELL, J., & GRUMMER-STRAWN, L. (1990). Contraceptive failure of the ovulation method of periodic abstinence. *Family Planning Perspectives*, 2(2), 65–75.

TRUSSELL, J. et al. (1990). Contraceptive failure in the U.S.: An update. *Studies in Family Planning*, 21(1), Table 1.

TRUSSELL, J. et al. (1993a). Should oral contraceptives be available without prescription? *American Journal of Public Health*, 83, 1094–1099.

TRUSSELL, J., STRICKLER, J., & VAUGHAN, B. (1993b). Contraceptive efficacy of the diaphragm, the sponge and the cervical cap. *Family Planning Perspectives*, 25, 100–105, 135.

TRUSSELL, J., STURGEN, K., STRICKLER, J., & DOMINIK, R. (1994). Comparative contraceptive efficacy of the female condom and other barrier methods. *Family Planning Perspectives*, 26, 66–72.

TRUSSELL, J., WARNER, D. L., & HATCHER, R. A. (1992). Condom slippage and breakage rates. *Family Planning Perspectives*, 24, 20–23.

TRUTE, B., ADKINS, E., & MACDONALD, G. (1992). Professional attitudes regarding the sexual abuse of children: Comparing police, child welfare and community mental health. *Child Abuse & Neglect*, 16, 359–368.

TUCKER, M. B., TAYLOR, R. J., & MITCHELL-KERNAN, C. (1993). Marriage and romantic involvement among aged African Americans. *Journal of Gerontology*, 48, S123–S132.

TUFTS NEW ENGLAND MEDICAL CENTER. (1984). *Sexually exploited children: Services and research project*. Boston: Author.

TULANDI, T., BRET, P., ATRI, M., & SENTERMAN, M. (1991). Treatment of ectopic pregnancy by transvaginal methotrexate administration. *Obstetrics and Gynecology*, 77, 627–630.

TULLER, N. R. (1988). Couples: The hidden segment of the gay world. In J. De Cecco (Ed.), *Gay relationships*. New York: Haworth.

TURNER, C. F., MILLER, H. G., & MOSES, L. E. (Eds.). (1989). *AIDS: Sexual behavior and intravenous drug use*. Washington, DC: National Academy Press.

TURNER, P. H. et al. (1985, March). *Parenting in gay and lesbian families*. Paper presented at the first meeting of the Future of Parenting Symposium, Chicago.

TURNER, W. J. (1995). Homosexuality, type 1: An X$_q$28 phenomenon. *Archives of Sexual Behavior*, 24, 109–134.

TYLER, D. C. (1988). Pain in the neonate. *Pre- and Peri-Natal Psychology Journal*, 3, 53–59.

UBELL, E. (1984, October 28). Sex in America today. *Parade*, pp. 11–13.

UDRY, J., BILLY, J., MORRIS, N., GROFF, T., & RAJ, M. (1985). Serum androgenic hormones motivate sexual behavior in adolescent boys. *Fertility and Sterility*, 43, 90–94.

ULLMAN, S. E., & KNIGHT, R. A. (1991). A multivariate model for predicting rape and physical injury outcomes during sexual assaults. *Journal of Consulting and Clinical Psychology*, 59, 724–731.

ULLRICH, H. E. (1992). Menstrual taboos among Havik Brahmin women: A study of ritual change. *Sex Roles*, 26, 19–40.

URSIN, G. et al. (1994). Oral contraceptive use and adenocarcinoma of cervix. *Lancet*, 344, 1390–1394.

U.S. ATTORNEY GENERAL'S COMMISSION ON PORNOGRAPHY. (1986). *Final Report of the Attorney General's Commission on Pornography*. Washington, DC: U.S. Justice Department.

U.S. DEPARTMENT OF JUSTICE. *Uniform crime reports for the United States 1993*. Washington, DC: U.S. Government Printing Office.

U.S. GENERAL ACCOUNTING OFFICE. (1982). *Sexual exploitation of children—A problem of unknown magnitude*. Gaithersburg, MD: Author.

U.S. GENERAL ACCOUNTING OFFICE. (1990). *Drug exposed infants: A generation at risk*. Washington, DC: Author (Publication GAO/HRD-90-138.)

VALENTICH, M., & GRIPTON, J. (1989). Teaching children about AIDS. *Journal of Sex Education and Therapy*, 15(2), 92.

VANCE, C. S. (1988). Ordinances restricting pornography could damage women. In R. T. Francoeur (Ed.), *Taking sides: Clashing views on controversial issues in human sexuality*. Guilford, CT: Dushkin Publishing Group.

VANCE, E. B., & WAGNER, N. N. (1976). Written descriptions of orgasm: A study of sex differences. *Archives of Sexual Behavior*, 5, 87–98.

VAN DEN HOEK, A., VAN HAASTRECHT, H. J. A., & COUTINHO, R. A. (1990). Heterosexual behavior of intravenous drug users in Amsterdam: Implications for the AIDS epidemic. *AIDS*, 4, 449–453.

VAN DE PERRE, P., LEPAGE, P., HOMSY, J., & DABIS, F. (1992). Mother-to-infant transmission of human immunodeficiency virus by breast milk: Presumed innocent or presumed guilty? *Clinical Infectious Diseases*, 15, 502–507.

VAN DE VELDE, T. H. (1930). *Ideal marriage: Its physiology and technique*. New York: Couici-Friede Publishers.

VAN DE VEN, P. (1994). Comparisons among homophobic reactions of undergraduates, high school students, and young offenders. *Journal of Sex Research*, 31, 117–124.

VAN DE WIEL, H., JASPERS, J., WEIJMAR-SCHULTZ, W., & GAL, J. (1990). Treatment of vaginismus: A review of concepts and treatment modalities. *Journal of Psychosomatic Obstetrics and Gynecology*, 11, 1–18.

VAN LOOK, P. F. A., & VON HERTZEN, H. (1993). Emergency contraception. *British Medical Bulletin*, 49, 158–170.

VAN NOORD-ZAADSTRA, B. et al. (1991). Delaying childbearing: Effect of age on fecundity and outcome of pregnancy. *British Medical Journal*, 302, 1361–1365.

VANNOY, R. (1980). *Sex without love: A philosophical exploration*. Buffalo, NY: Prometheus Books.

VAN WYK, P. (1984). Psychosocial development of heterosexual, bisexual, and homosexual behavior. *Archives of Sexual Behavior, 13*, 505–544.

VEITH, J. et al. (1983, August 27). *Exposure to men influences the occurrence of ovulation in women*. Paper presented at the 91st Convention of the American Psychological Association, Anaheim, CA.

VELARDE, A., & WARLICK, M. (1973). Massage parlors: The sensuality business. *Society, 11*, 63–74.

VENTURA, J. N. (1987). The stresses of parenthood reexamined. *Family Relations, 36*, 26–29.

VERA, H., BARNARD, G. W., & HOLZER, C. (1979). The intelligence of rapists: New data. *Archives of Sexual Behavior, 8*, 375–378.

VERHULST, J., & HEIMAN, J. R. (1988). A systems perspective on sexual desire. In S. R. Leiblum & R. C. Rosen (Eds.), *Sexual desire disorders*. New York: Guilford.

VESSEY, M. P. (1973). Oral contraceptives and stroke. *New England Journal of Medicine, 288*, 906–907.

VESSEY, M. P., LAWLESS, M., & YEATES, D. (1982). Efficacy of different contraceptive methods. *Lancet, 1*, 841–842.

VESSEY, M. P., & PAINTER, R. (1994). Oral contraceptive use and benign gallbladder disease; revisited. *Contraception, 50*, 167–173.

VESSEY, M. P. et al. (1981). Pelvic inflammatory disease and the intrauterine device. *British Medical Journal, 282*, 855–857.

VEUGELERS, P. J. et al. (1993). Differences in time from HIV seroconversion to CD4+ lymphocyte end-points and AIDS in cohorts of homosexual men. *AIDS, 7*, 1325–1329.

VOELLER, B. (1991). AIDS and heterosexual anal intercourse. *Archives of Sexual Behavior, 201*, 233–269.

VOIGT, H. (1991). Enriching the sexual experience of couples: The Asian traditions and sexual counseling. *Journal of Sex and Marital Therapy, 17*, 214–219.

VOLBERDING, P. A. et al. (1990). Zidovudine in asymptomatic human immunodeficiency virus infections. *New England Journal of Medicine, 322*, 941–949.

VOLLMAN, R. F. (1977). *The menstrual cycle*. Philadelphia: Saunders.

VOLPE, A., SILFERI, M., GENAZZANI, A. D., & GENAZZANI, A. R. (1993). Contraception in older women. *Contraception, 47*, 229–239.

VOYDANOFF, P., & DONNELLY, B. (1990). *Adolescent sexuality and pregnancy*. Newbury Park, CA: Sage.

WADE, M. E. et al. (1980, September). *A randomized prospective study of the use-effectiveness of two methods of natural family planning*. Paper presented at the International Federation for Family Life Promotion Second International Congress, Navan, Ireland.

WALKER, C. E. (1970). Erotic stimuli and the aggressive sexual offender. In *Technical report of the Commission on Obscenity and Pornography* (Vol. 7, pp. 91–147). Washington, DC: U.S. Government Printing Office.

WALSH, M. W. (1992, October 29). Canada far ahead of U. S. in recognizing gay rights. *Los Angeles Times*, pp. A1, A8.

WALSTER, E., ARONSON, V., ABRAHAMS, D., & ROTTMAN, L. (1966). Importance of physical attractiveness in dating behavior. *Journal of Personality and Social Psychology, 4*, 508–516.

WAMBAUGH, J. (1989). *The blooding*. New York: Bantam Books.

WARD, M. C. (1989). *Nest in the wind: Adventures in anthropology on a tropical island*. Prospect Heights, IL: Waveland Press.

WARD, S. et al. (1991). Acquaintance rape and the college social scene. *Family Relations, 40*, 65–71.

WARNER, C. G. (Ed.). (1980). *Rape and sexual assault*. Germantown, MD: Aspen Systems Corp.

WASHINGTON, A. E., CATES, W., & WASSERHEIT, J. N. (1991). Preventing pelvic inflammatory disease. *Journal of the American Medical Association, 266*, 2574–2580.

WASHINGTON, A. E., & KATZ, P. (1991). Cost of and payment source for pelvic inflammatory disease: Trends and projects, 1983 through 2000. *Journal of the American Medical Association, 266*, 2565–2569.

WASHTON, A. M. (1989, December). Cocaine abuse and compulsive sexuality. *Medical Aspects of Human Sexuality, 23*, 32–39.

WASOW, M., & LOEB, M. (1979). Sexuality in nursing homes. *Journal of the American Geriatrics Society, 27*, 73–79.

WASSERHEIT, J. N. (1991). Epidemiological synergy: Interrelationships between HIV infection and other STDs. In L. C. Chen et al. (Eds.), *AIDS and women's reproductive health*. New York: Plenum.

WASSERHEIT, J. N. (1992). Epidemiological synergy: Interrelationships between human immunodeficiency virus infection and other sexually transmitted diseases. *Sexually Transmitted Diseases, 19*, 61–77.

WASSON, J. H. et al. (1995). A comparison of transurethral with watchful waiting for moderate symptoms of benign prostatic hyperplasia. *New England Journal of Medicine, 332*, 1995.

WATERMAN, C. K., DAWSON, L. J., & BOLOGNA, M. J. (1989). Sexual coercion in gay male and lesbian relationships: Predictors and implications for support services. *Journal of Sex Research, 26*, 118–125.

WATERMAN, C. K., & FOSS-GOODMAN, D. (1984). Child molesting: Variables relating to attribution of fault to victims, offenders and nonparticipating parents. *Journal of Sex Research, 20*, 329–349.

WATERMAN, J., KELLY, R. J., MCCORD, J., & OLIVERI, M. K. (1992). *Behind the playground walls: Sexual abuse in preschools*. New York: Guilford.

WATKINS, R. N. (1986). Vaginal spermicides and congenital disorders: The validity of a study. *Journal of the American Medical Association, 256*, 3095.

WAY, P. O., & STANECKI, K. (1993). How bad will it be? Modelling the AIDS epidemic in Eastern Africa. *Population and Environment, 14*, 265–278.

WEBER, M. (1993). Images in clinical medicine: Pinworms. *New England Journal of Medicine, 328*, 927.

WEINBERG, G. (1973). *Society and the healthy homosexual*. New York: Anchor.

WEINBERG, M. S., WILLIAMS, C. J., & CALHAN, C. (1994). Homosexual foot fetishism. *Archives of Sexual Behavior, 23*, 611–626.

WEINBERG, M. S., WILLIAMS, C., & MOSER, C. (1984). The social constituents of sadomasochism. *Social Problems, 31*, 379–389.

WEINBERG, T. (1987). Sadomasochism in the United States: A review of recent sociological literature. *Journal of Sex Research, 23*, 50–69.

WEINBERG, T., & BULLOUGH, V. (1988). Alienation, self-image, and the importance of support groups for the wives of transvestites. *Journal of Sex Research, 24*, 262–268.

WEINSTOCK, H. S., BOLAN, G., REINGOLD, A. L., & POLISH, L. B. (1993a). Hepatitis C virus infection among patients attending a clinic for sexually transmitted diseases. *Journal of the American Medical Association, 269*, 392–394.

WEINSTOCK, H. S. et al. (1993b). Factors associated with condom use in a high-risk heterosexual population. *Sexually Transmitted Diseases, 20*, 14–20.

WEIS, D. L. (1983). Affective reactions of women to their initial experience of coitus. *Journal of Sex Research, 19*, 209–237.

WEIS, D. L. (1985). The experience of pain during women's first sexual intercourse: Cultural mythology about female sexual initiation. *Archives of Sexual Behavior, 14*, 421–428.

WEIS, P. (1990). The contraceptive potential of breastfeeding in Bangladesh. *Studies in Family Planning, 24*(2), 100–108.

WEISBERG, D. K. (1985). *Children of the night: A study of adolescent prostitution*. Lexington, MA: Lexington Books.

WEISS, D. (1983). Open marriage and multilateral relationships: The emergence of nonexclusive models of the marital relationship. In E. Macklin & R. Rubin (Eds.), *Contemporary families and alternative lifestyles*. Newbury Park, CA: Sage.

WEISS, H. (1978). The physiology of human penile erection. In A. Comfort (Ed.), *Sexual consequences of disability*. Philadelphia: Stickley.

WEISSBACH, T. A., & ZAGON, G. (1975). The effect of deviant group membership upon impression of personality. *Journal of Social Psychology, 95*, 263–266.

WEITZMAN, L. J. et al. (1972). Sex role socialization in picture books for pre-school children. *American Journal of Sociology, 77*, 1125–1150.

WEIZMAN, R., & HART, J. (1987). Sexual behavior in healthy married elderly men. *Archives of Sexual Behavior, 16*, 39–44.

WELLER, A., & WELLER, L. (1993). Menstrual synchrony between mothers and daughters and between roommates. *Physiology and Behavior, 53*, 943–949.

WELLS, B. L. (1986). Predictors of female nocturnal orgasms. *Journal of Sex Research, 22*, 421–437.

WESTERMARCK, E. A. (1891). *The history of human marriage*. New York: Macmillan.

WESTOFF, C. F. (1988). Unintended pregnancy in America and abroad. *Family Planning Perspectives, 20*, 254.

WESTRÖM, L. (1980). Incidence, prevalence, and trends of acute pelvic inflammatory disease and its consequences in industrialized countries. *American Journal of Obstetrics and Gynecology, 138*, 880.

WESTRÖM, L. et al. (1992). Pelvic inflammatory disease and fertility. *Sexually Transmitted Diseases, 19*, 185–192

WETZEL, C., & INSKO, C. (1982). The similarity-attraction relationship: Is there an ideal one? *Journal of Experimental Social Psychology, 18*, 253–276.

WHALEN, R. (1977). Brain mechanisms controlling sexual behavior. In

F. A. Beach (Ed.), *Human sexuality in four perspectives*. Baltimore: Johns Hopkins University Press.

WHIPPLE, B., OGDEN, G., & KOMISARUK, B. R. (1992). Physiological correlates of imagery-induced orgasm in women. *Archives of Sexual Behavior, 21*, 121–133.

WHITAM, F. L. (1977a). Childhood indicators of male homosexuality. *Archives of Sexual Behavior, 6*, 89–96.

WHITAM, F. L. (1977b). The homosexual role: A reconsideration. *Journal of Sex Research, 13*, 1–11.

WHITAM, F. L. (1983). Culturally invariable properties of male homosexuality: Tentative conclusions from cross-cultural research. *Archives of Sexual Behavior, 12*, 207–226.

WHITAM, F. L., DIAMOND, M., & MARTIN, J. (1993). Homosexual orientation in twins: A report on 61 pairs and three triplet sets. *Archives of Sexual Behavior, 22*, 187–205.

WHITAM, F. L., & MATHY, R. M. (1986). *Male homosexuality in four societies: Brazil, Guatemala, the Philippines, and the United States*. New York: Praeger.

WHITCOMB, D. (1992). Legal reforms on behalf of child witnesses: Recent developments in the American courts. In H. Dent & R. Flin (Eds.), *Children as witnesses* (pp. 151–165). Chichester, England: Wiley.

WHITE, D. R., & BURTON, M. L. (1988). Causes of polygyny: Ecology, economy, kinship, and warfare. *American Anthropologist, 90*, 871–887.

WHITE, E., MALONE, K. E., WEISS, N. S., & DALING, J. R. (1994). Breast cancer among young U.S. women in relation to oral contraceptive use. *Journal of the National Cancer Institute, 86*, 505–513.

WHITE, G. L. (1980a). Inducing jealousy: A power perspective. *Personality and Sexual Psychology Bulletin, 6*, 222–227.

WHITE, G. L. (1980b). Physical attractiveness and courtship progress. *Journal of Personality and Social Psychology, 39*, 660–668.

WHITE, G. L. (1981a). Some correlates of romantic jealousy. *Journal of Personality, 49*, 129–147.

WHITE, G. L. (1981b). Relative involvement, inadequacy, and jealousy: A test of a causal model. *Alternative Lifestyles, 4*, 291–309.

WHITE, G. L., & MULLEN, P. E. (1989). *Jealousy: Theory, research, and clinical strategies*. New York: Guilford.

WHITE, J., & HUMPHREY, J. (1991, August). Victims of rape, resistance, revictimization, and acknowledgment. Paper presented at the annual meeting of the American Psychological Association, Washington, DC.

WHITE, S. E., & REAMY, K. (1982). Sexuality and pregnancy: A review. *Archives of Sexual Behavior, 11*, 429–444.

WHITEHURST, R. N. (1972). Extramarital sex: Alienation or extension of normal behavior. In J. N. Edwards (Ed.), *Sex and society*. Chicago: Rand McNally.

WHITING, B. (1979). Contributions of anthropology to the study of gender identity, gender role, and sexual behavior. In H. Katchadourian (Ed.), *Human sexuality: A comparative and developmental perspective*. Berkeley: University of California Press.

WHITLEY, B. E., JR., & KITE, M. E. (1995). Sex differences in attitudes toward homosexuality: A comment on Oliver and Hyde (1993). *Psychological Bulletin, 117*, 146–154.

WHITTEMORE, A. S., HARRIS, R., ITNYRE, J. & THE COLLABORATIVE OVARIAN CANCER GROUP. (1992a). Characteristics relating to ovarian cancer risk: Collaborative analysis of 12 U.S. case-control studies. II: Invasive epithelial ovarian cancers in white women. *American Journal of Epidemiology, 136*, 1184–1203.

WHITTEMORE, A. S., HARRIS, R., ITNYRE, J., & THE COLLABORATIVE OVARIAN CANCER GROUP. (1992b). Characteristics relating to ovarian cancer risk: The pathogenesis of epithelial ovarian cancer. *American Journal of Epidemiology, 136*, 1212–1220.

WHITTLE, H. et al. (1994). HIV-2 infected patients survive longer than HIV-1 infected patients. *AIDS, 8*, 1617–1620.

WIDSTRAND, C. G. (1964). Female infibulation. *Studia Ethnographica Upsaliensia, 20*, 95–122.

WIEST, W. (1977). Semantic differential profiles of orgasm and other experiences among men and women. *Sex Roles, 3*, 399–403.

WIGHT, D. (1992). Impediments to safer heterosexual sex: A review of research with young people. *AIDS Care, 4*, 11–23.

WILCOX, A. J. et al. (1988). Incidence of early loss of pregnancy. *New England Journal of Medicine, 319*, 189–194.

WILCOX, D., & HAGER, R. (1980). Toward realistic expectation for orgasmic response in women. *Journal of Sex Research, 16*, 162–179.

WILCOX, L. W. et al. (1992). Menstrual function after tubal sterilization. *American Journal of Epidemiology, 135*, 1368–1381.

WILLIAMS, L. B. (1991). Determinants of unintended childbearing among ever-married women in the United States: 1973-1988. *Family Planning Perspectives, 23*, 212–221.

WILLIAMS, N., CHELL, J., & KAPILA, L. (1993). Why are children referred for circumcision? *British Medical Journal, 306*, 28.

WILLIAMS, P., & SMITH, M. (1979). Interview. In *The first question* [Department film]. London: British Broadcasting System Science and Features.

WILLIAMSON, D. F., et al. (1989). Comparing the prevalence of smoking in pregnant and nonpregnant women, 1985 to 1986. *Journal of the American Medical Association, 261*, 70.

WILLSON, J., & CARRINGTON., E. (1991). *Obstetrics and gynecology* (9th ed.). St. Louis, MO: Mosby.

WILSON, G. D. (1987). An ethological approach to sexual deviation. In G. D. Wilson (Ed.), *Variant sexuality: Research and theory*. Baltimore: Johns Hopkins University Press.

WILSON, P. (1986). Black culture and sexuality. *Journal of Social Work and Human Sexuality, 4*, 29–46.

WINCZE, J. P., BANSAL, S., & MALAMUD, M. (1986). Effects of medroxyprogesterone acetate on subjective arousal, arousal to erotic stimulation, and nocturnal penile tumescence in male sex offenders. *Archives of Sexual Behavior, 15*, 293–305.

WINCZE, J. P., HOON, E. F., & HOON, P. W. (1976). Physiological responsivity of normal and sexually dysfunctional women during erotic stimulus exposure. *Journal of Psychosomatic Research, 20*, 445–451.

WISE, T., DUPKIN, C., & MEYER, J. K. (1981). Partners of distressed transvestites. *American Journal of Psychiatry, 138*, 1221–1224.

WISE, T., & MEYER, J. (1980). Transvestism: Previous findings and new areas for inquiry. *Journal of Sex and Marital Therapy, 6*, 116–128.

WISWELL, T. E., ENZENAUER, R. W., CORNISH, J. D., & HANKINS, C.T. (1987). Declining frequency of circumcision: Implications for changes in the absolute incidence and male to female sex ratio of urinary tract infections in early infancy. *Pediatrics, 79*, 338–342.

WITHERINGTON, R. (1990). External penile appliances for management of impotence. *Seminars in Urology, 8*, 124–128.

WOLF, A. P. (1970). Childhood association and sexual attraction: A further test of the Westermarck hypothesis. *American Anthropologist, 72*, 503–515.

WOLFE, A. A., WOLFE, V. V., & BEST, C. L. (1988). Child victims of sexual abuse. In V. B. Van Hasselt, H. R. L. Morrison, A. S. Bellack, & M. Hersen (Eds.), *Handbook of family violence*. New York: Plenum.

WOLFF, C. (1971). *Love between women*. New York: Harper & Row.

WOLFF, M. S. et al. (1993). Blood levels of organochlorine residues and risk of breast cancer. *Journal of the National Cancer Institute, 85*, 648–652.

WOLNER-HANSSEN, P., KIVIAT, N. K., & HOLMES, K. K. (1989). Atypical pelvic inflammatory disease: Subacute, chronic, or subclinical upper genital tract infection in women. In K. K. Holmes et al. (Eds.), *Sexually transmitted diseases* (2nd ed.). New York: McGraw-Hill.

WOLNER-HANSSEN, P. et al. (1990). Association between vaginal douching and acute pelvic inflammatory disease. *Journal of the American Medical Association, 263*, 1936–1941.

WORELL, J. (1978). Sex roles and psychological well being: Perspectives on methodology. *Journal of Consulting and Clinical Psychology, 46*, 777–791.

WORLD HEALTH ORGANIZATION (W.H.O.). (1978). *Special Programme of Research, Development and Research Training: Seventh annual report*. Geneva: Author.

WORLD HEALTH ORGANIZATION (W.H.O.). (1981). A prospective multicentre trial of the ovulation method of natural family planning. II. The effectiveness phase. *Fertility and Sterility, 36*, 591–598.

WORLD HEALTH ORGANIZATION (W.H.O.). (1984). Mental health and female sterilization: Report of a WHO collaborative prospective study. *Journal of Biosocial Sciences, 16*, 1–21.

WORLD HEALTH ORGANIZATION (W.H.O.). (1985). Mental health and female sterilization: A follow-up. *Journal of Biosocial Sciences, 17*, 1–18.

WORLD HEALTH ORGANIZATION CONSENSUS STATEMENT. (1989). Sexually transmitted diseases as a risk factor for HIV transmission. *Journal of Sex Research, 26*, 272–275.

WORLD HEALTH ORGANIZATION TASK FORCE ON LONG-ACTING AGENTS FOR THE REGULATION OF FERTILITY (1983). Multinational comparative clinical trial of long-acting injectable contraceptives: Norethisterone enanthate given in two dosage regimens and depotmedroxyprogesterone acetate: final report. *Contraception, 28*, 1–20.

WRIGHT, K. (1990). Mycoplasmas in the AIDS spotlight. *Science, 248*, 682–683.

WURTMAN, J. J., BRZEZINSKI, A., WURTMAN, R. J., & LAFERRERE, B. (1989). Effect of nutrient intake on premenstrual depression. *American Journal of Obstetrics and Gynecology, 161*, 1228–1234.

WYATT, G. E., GUTHRIE, D., & NOTGRASS, C. M. (1992). Differential effects of women's child sexual abuse and subsequent sexual revictimization. *Journal of Consulting and Clinical Psychology, 60*, 167–173.

Wynn, R., & Fletcher, C. (1987). Sex role development and early educational experiences. In D. B. Carter (Ed.), *Current conceptions of sex roles and sex typing*. New York: Praeger.

Yalom, I. D. (1960). Aggression and forbiddenness in voyeurism. *Archives of General Psychiatry, 3*, 305–319.

Yesalis, C. E., Kennedy, N. J., Kopstein, A. N., & Bahrke, M. S. (1993). Anabolic-androgenic steroid use in the United States. *Journal of the American Medical Association, 270*, 1217–1221.

Yesmont, G. A. (1992). The relationship of assertiveness to college students' safer sex behaviors. *Adolescence, 27*, 253–272.

Yolken, R. H. et al. (1992). Human milk mucin inhibits rotavirus replication and prevents experimental gastroenteritis. *Journal of Clinical Investigation, 90*, 1984–1991.

Zaviacic, M., & Whipple, B. (1993). Update on the female prostate and the phenomenon of female ejaculation. *Journal of Sex Research, 30*, 148–151.

Zaviacic, M., Zaviacicova, A., Holoman, I. K., & Molcan, J. (1988). Female urethral expulsions evoked by local digital stimulation of the G-spot: Differences in the response patterns. *Journal of Sex Research, 24*, 311–318.

Zelnik, M., & Kantner, J. F. (1979). Reasons for nonuse of contraception by sexually active women aged 15-19. *Family Planning Perspectives, 11*, 289–296.

Zenker, P. N., & Rolfs, R. T. (1990). Treatment of syphilis, 1989. *Reviews of Infectious Diseases, 12*, S590–S609.

Zilbergeld, B. (1978). *Male sexuality: A guide to sexual fulfillment*. Boston: Little, Brown.

Zilbergeld, B., & Ellison, C. R. (1980). Desire discrepancies and arousal problems in sex therapy. In S. R. Leiblum & L. A. Pervin (Eds.), *Principles and practice of therapy*. New York: Guilford.

Zilbergeld, B., & Hammond, D. (1988). The use of hypnosis in treating desire disorders. In S. R. Leiblum & R. C. Rosen (Eds.), *Sexual desire disorders*. New York: Guilford.

Zilbergeld, B., & Kilmann, P. (1984). The scope and effectiveness of sex therapy. *Psychotherapy, 21*, 319–326.

Zillmann, D., & Bryant, J. (1982, Autumn). Pornography, sexual callousness, and the trivialization of rape. *Journal of Communication*, pp. 10–21.

Zillmann, D., & Bryant, J. (1988). Pornography's impact on sexual satisfaction. *Journal of Applied Social Psychology, 18*, 438–453.

Zillmann, D., Schweitzer, K. J., & Mundorf, N. (1994). Menstrual cycle variation of women's interest in erotica. *Archives of Sexual Behavior, 23*, 579–597.

Zimmer, D. (1983). Interaction patterns and communication skills in sexually distressed, maritally distressed, and normal couples: Two experimental studies. *Journal of Sex and Marital Therapy, 9*, 251–265.

Zimmer, D., Borchardt, E., & Fischle, C. (1982). Sexual fantasies of sexually distressed and nondistressed men and women: An empirical comparison. *Journal of Sex and Marital Therapy, 9*, 38–50.

Zimmerman, H. L. et al. (1990). Epidemiologic differences between chlamydia and gonorrhea. *American Journal of Public Health, 80*, 1338–1342.

Zitter, S. (1987). Coming out to mom: Theoretical aspects of the mother-daughter process. In Boston Lesbian Psychologies Collective (Eds.), *Lesbian psychologies: Explorations and challenges* (pp. 177–194). Urbana: University of Illinois Press.

Zuckerman, A. J. (1982, November/December). Viral hepatitis. *Practical Gastroenterology, 16*, 21–27.

Zuravin, S. J. (1991). Unplanned childbearing and family size: Their relationship to child neglect and abuse. *Family Planning Perspectives, 23*, 155–161.

INDEX

STUDENT STUDY GUIDE

Assessing Your Risk for Getting HIV/AIDS and Other Sexually Transmitted Diseases

This year there will be close to 12 million newly diagnosed cases of sexually transmitted diseases in the United States. One in four Americans between the ages of 15 and 55 will have at least one STD sometime in their lifetime (Centers for Disease Control). Ask yourself, "Am I at risk of getting a sexually transmitted disease?" What precautions do you take to prevent it from ever happening? Surveys conducted on college campuses indicate that most students do nothing more than look for symptoms in potential new partners. However, many infected individuals, including those with the virus that causes AIDS, do not show any symptoms. We must, therefore, do more than just look for symptoms. As a first step you should have some idea of your level of risk. Everyone who has sexual relations is at some risk, some more than others. The following questions are designed to help you assess your own level of risk. Be honest when you answer the questions; the questionnaire cannot be of any use to you if you have not answered each item truthfully.

1. How many sexual partners (intercourse or oral-genital sex) have you had: a) in the last seven years if you have not had an HIV antibody test, or b) since your last HIV antibody test that proved negative?

   4 points ___ 42 or more (an average of 6 or more per year)
   3 points ___ 8-41
   2 points ___ 2-7
   1 point ___ 1
   0 points ___ none

2. Do you use drugs intravenously?

   4 points ___ yes
   0 points ___ no

   Note: If you scored zero on the first two questions, you are at extremely low risk of being infected with the human immunodeficiency virus or any other virus, bacterium, or parasite discussed in Chapter 5. You may stop here. If you scored greater than zero, complete the questionnaire.

3. How many sexual partners have you had in the last year?

   4 points ___ 6 or more
   3 points ___ 3-5
   2 points ___ 2
   1 point ___ 1
   0 points ___ none

4. What kinds of sexual contacts have you had? (Note: Working from top to bottom, give yourself the points *only* for the *first* category you check.)

   4 points ___ "one night stands" with relative strangers, sex with a prostitute, or group sex
   3 points ___ "casual sex" (i.e., sex with acquaintances or friends with whom you do not have a "steady" relationship)
   2 points ___ steady relationship(s), but have "cheated" on at least one occasion
   1 point ___ steady relationship(s) without cheating during relationship
   0 points ___ you have not yet had sexual intercourse or oral-genital sex

5. What is your sexual orientation?

   4 points ___ male homosexual, male bisexual, or male heterosexual with occasional male homosexual experiences (Note: Homosexuality does not cause STDs, but STDs are very prevalent in these groups.)
   1 point ___ a) exclusively male or female heterosexual, or b) female homosexual
   0 points ___ you have not yet had sexual intercourse or oral-genital sex

6. Have you been a victim of forced sexual activity in the last seven years?

   4 points ___ yes, and you have not been tested for STDs (including an HIV antibody test)
   1 point ___ yes, but subsequent STD tests, including an HIV antibody test, were negative
   0 points ___ no

7. What kinds of sexual activities do you usually engage in? (Note: Working from top to bottom, give yourself the points only for the first category you check.)

   4 points ___ anal intercourse, fisting, oral-anal, or any other activities involving contact with feces or urine
   3 points ___ unprotected (no condom) vaginal intercourse
   2 points ___ unprotected oral-genital sex
   1 point ___ protected (condom) vaginal and/or oral-genital sex
   0 points ___ kissing, caressing, massage, masturbation

8. How often have you had sex after using alcohol or drugs?

   4 points ___ very often
   3 points ___ usually at parties only
   2 points ___ sometimes
   1 point ___ hardly ever
   0 points ___ never

9. Where do most of your sexual partners live?

1 point ____ in a large city or immediate suburb
0 points ____ in a small city or town
0 points ____ you have not yet had sexual intercourse or oral-genital sex

10. In the last year, how often have you or your sexual partners used condoms?

4 points ____ never or rarely, and you have had more than one partner
3 points ____ usually, but sometimes you have taken chances
2 points ____ never or rarely, but you have had only one steady partner
1 point ____ **every** time (for each act of penetration), including the first time with a new partner
0 points ____ a) you have not yet had sexual intercourse or oral-genital sex, or
b) you are exclusively female homosexual

11. How many sexual partners has your current (or last) partner had prior to you?

4 points ____ many
3 points ____ several
2 points ____ one or a few
1 point ____ none (you think)
0 points ____ you have not yet had sexual intercourse or oral-genital sex

12. How certain are you that your current (or last) sexual partner has not had sex with anyone else since you and he or she started having sex?

4 points ____ you are certain your partner has had sex with others during your relationship

3 points ____ you suspect your partner of having sex with others during your relationship
2 points ____ you are uncertain
1 point ____ you are relatively certain that he or she has not (Note: No one can be 100 percent certain.)
0 points ____ you have not yet had sexual intercourse or oral-genital sex

(Answer question 13 only if you are not male homosexual or bisexual.)

13. Have any of your sexual partners had male homosexual experiences or had sex with someone who has? (Note: Homosexuality per se does not cause STDs.)

4 points ____ definitely yes
3 points ____ possibly
1 point ____ do not know
0 points ____ you are relatively certain that he or she has not

14. Have any of your sexual partners used drugs intravenously?

4 points ____ yes
2 points ____ you do not know
0 points ____ no

15. Do you and your sexual partner(s) discuss sexually transmitted diseases and "safer sex"?

2 points ____ rarely
1 point ____ yes, but you have not been tested
0 points ____ a) yes, and you have both been tested, or
b) you have not yet had sexual intercourse or oral-genital sex

HOW TO SCORE

If you use condoms every time during vaginal or anal intercourse (be honest–it must be **every** time), for questions 3, 4, 5, 8, 11, 12, and 13 subtract 1 point for each question you scored a "2," and subtract 2 points for each question you scored a "3" or a "4." If you and your partner are in a monogamous relationship (neither of you has ever cheated) lasting several years, you may subtract 2 points if you scored a "2" or greater for question 7.

Add up your adjusted total points for the 15 questions (a maximum of 4 points on questions 1–8 and 10–14; 2 points on question 15; and 1 point on question 9).

15 points or less   Unless you take drugs intravenously (an automatic high risk), you are at low risk of contracting a sexually transmitted disease.

16–29 points   You are at moderate risk and should adjust your lifestyle.

30 points or more   You are at high risk. You are strongly advised to change your lifestyle. If you take drugs intravenously, you are at high risk regardless of your point total.

If you are at moderate or high risk, how can you adjust your lifestyle? Look back at the questions and see where simple changes would result in subtracting points. The easiest way is to limit the number of sexual partners and/or by always using condoms. Think about it–it could save your life.

CHAPTER 1 INTERACTIVE REVIEW

Some people feel that sex education should be the responsibility of parents, yet fewer than a third of college students have ever had a meaningful discussion about sex with their parents. Most young people turn to (1)_____ and (2)_____ for information about sex, but much of what they learn is incorrect. The best alternative would be for children to receive factual information in school. Surveys indicate that approximately (3)_____ percent of Americans favor sex education in school, but only half or less of junior high schools, high schools, and colleges in the United States presently offer such courses.

Sex is only a part of (4)_____, which encompasses all of the sexual attitudes, feelings, and behaviors associated with being human. Sexual behaviors and attitudes (such as what is considered to be sexually attractive) vary from culture to culture, and can even change within a culture over time. American sexual attitudes are both permissive and repressed, and as a result many people in the United States have ambivalent feelings about sex.

In order to understand how we arrived at our current values we must examine the history of sexual attitudes in our culture. The idea that the primary purpose of sex is for procreation (to have children) originally came from (5)_____, but they also had a very positive attitude about their bodies and sexual pleasure between husbands and wives. The early (6)_____ kept the procreational purpose of sex, but completely denied the pleasurable aspects of sex. Sexual desire, even within marriage, was now associated with guilt. The two biggest proponents of this view within Christianity were (7)_____ and (8)_____. Negative attitudes (in Western culture) about sex reached their zenith during the reign of (9)_____ of England. During this time, the medical profession contributed many negative, incorrect beliefs about engaging in sex, including the belief that excess sex, particularly masturbation, could lead to serious medical problems and eventually insanity.

The industrial revolution slowly changed Americans' lives, including their sex lives. With shorter work days (and shorter work weeks) and greater mobility (e.g., automobiles) than was available in past generations, people now had more free time to spend together. With the discovery of (10)_____ during World War II, and the marketing of (11)_____ in 1960, the United States entered the sexual revolution.

Because of the antisexual attitudes of the Victorian era, scientific study of human sexuality was slow to develop. (12)_____, who emphasized the sexuality of all people, including children, and (13)_____, who published seven volumes about the psychology of sex, were two Victorian-era individuals who attempted to counter antisexual attitudes. However, it has only been within the last 30 to 40 years that the scientific and medical community has accepted sex as a subject for serious discussion and research. The first large-scale surveys were done by (14)_____ in the 1940s and early 1950s. (15)_____ published their physiological investigations of human sexual behavior in 1966. Even today, however, there is some resistance by governmental agencies to fund research of human sexual behavior.

Surveys are conducted by taking samples from the population. The way in which a sample is drawn, as well as the manner in which the survey is constructed, determines to what extent results can be correctly generalized to the population.

CHAPTER 1 SELF-TEST

A. TRUE OR FALSE

- [T] [F] 16. The Old Testament presents a positive view of sex within marriage.
- [T] [F] 17. American sexual behaviors are considered to be the norm by the rest of the world.
- [T] [F] 18. Because of AIDS, all states now require that public schools offer sex education.
- [T] [F] 19. The larger the number of people in a survey, the more accurate it always is.
- [T] [F] 20. All cultures consider female breasts to be highly erotic.
- [T] [F] 21. Puritan sexual values were a major influence on current American values.
- [T] [F] 22. Kissing is one sexual behavior that is done worldwide.
- [T] [F] 23. One method of obtaining a random sample is to randomly pick names from a phone book.
- [T] [F] 24. Each year in the United States, one in ten teenaged girls gets pregnant and one in seven sexually active teens gets a sexually transmitted disease.
- [T] [F] 25. Over half of American teenagers have had sexual intercourse before their seventeenth birthday.
- [T] [F] 26. The era of permissiveness known as the "sexual revolution" started during the Victorian era.

T ☐   F ☐   27. About one fourth of societies in the world encourage or openly tolerate children engaging in sex.

T ☐   F ☐   28. A small survey conducted by Dr. Celia Mosher in 1892 shows that most Victorian women did not desire or enjoy sex.

T ☐   F ☐   29. Kinsey's surveys are a good example of the use of random sampling techniques.

B.   MATCHING

_____ 30. A Victorian-era physician who emphasized the sexuality of children and adults

_____ 31. He viewed sex for procreation as an unpleasant necessity and equated guilt with sexual desire

_____ 32. Conducted the first large-scale physiological study of human sexual behavior

_____ 33. He systematized Christian thoughts during the Middle Ages

_____ 34. Believed that the purpose of sex was for procreation, but had a very positive attitude about sexual relations between a husband and wife

_____ 35. Reformation leader who said that priests and nuns should be allowed to marry

_____ 36. Proved their worthiness not by denying the pleasurable aspects of marital sex, but by living frugal and industrious lives

_____ 37. Believed in an ascetic philosophy: wisdom and virtue come from denying physical pleasures

_____ 38. Conducted first large-scale survey of American sexual attitudes and behaviors

_____ 39. First major influence on Christian sexual values; regarded bodily pleasures as evil and thought it "well for a man not to touch a woman"

_____ 40. A Victorian-era sex researcher with a tolerant attitude about sexuality

_____ 41. Held antisexual attitudes that were reinforced by the mistaken medical beliefs of that time

a. Havelock Ellis
b. Edwardians
c. St. Paul
d. ancient Greeks
e. Jesus
f. Sigmund Freud
g. Masters and Johnson
h. Biblical Hebrews
i. Puritans
j. Victorians
k. Morton Hunt
l. St. John
m. Martin Luther
n. St. Thomas Aquinas
o. Alfred Kinsey
p. St. Augustine

C.   FILL IN THE BLANKS

42. Anthropologists believe the most sexually repressive society in the world to be the _____ .

43. Name four important influences that led to the "sexual revolution": a. _____ , b. _____ , c. _____ , and d. _____ .

44. A random sample is properly defined as a sample drawn from a population in a manner so that _____ has an equal chance of being selected.

45. _____ believed that intellectual love could lead to immortality.

46. The _____ had a positive view of sex within the marriage and brought this view over to the colonies in the New World.

47. In the United States, the average child sees over _____ references to sex a year on television alone.

48. A major influence on early Christian thought was the Greek philosophy of dualism which separated _____ and _____ .

49. Freud referred to sexual energy as _____ .

50. Victorian physicians called nocturnal emissions _____ because they believed it was caused by the same thing that causes gonorrhea.

CHAPTER 2 INTERACTIVE REVIEW

When referring to their genitals or breasts, many people feel more comfortable using slang terms than the correct anatomical names. The use of sexual slang often reflects (1)_____ feelings about sex and may lead to misinformation.

The external female genitalia are collectively known as the (2)_____. This includes the (3)_____, (4)_____, (5)_____, (6)_____, (7)_____, and (8)_____. The (9)_____ and (10)_____ become covered with hair at puberty. The (11)_____ has no known function other than to focus pleasurable sensations. It is most similar in structure to the male's (12)_____. The (13)_____ meet at top to form the clitoral hood. The area between the labia minora is called the (14)_____. Many sexually inexperienced females have a thin membrane, called the (15)_____, that partially covers the vaginal opening. It has no known physiological function, but its presence or absence is used by men in many cultures to tell whether or not their partner is a virgin. In actuality, it is a (16)_____ indicator of prior sexual experience.

A woman's breasts are not part of her reproductive anatomy, but in cultures where men consider them to be erotic they are part of her sexual anatomy. One in (17)_____ women will get breast cancer sometime in their lifetime.

A female's internal reproductive system includes the (18)_____, (19)_____, (20)_____, and (21)_____. The (22)_____ is the depository for sperm, the birth canal, and the exit route for menstrual fluids. It is a self-cleansing organ and its odor is generally not offensive. The walls of the inner two thirds of the (23)_____ are relatively insensitive to touch, but about 10 percent of women have an area of heightened sensitivity on the front wall called the (24)_____. When a mature ovum (egg) is released from an (25)_____, it is picked up by a (26)_____, which then transports it to the (27)_____. If fertilized by a sperm, the egg usually implants in the (28)_____ of the uterus. The female's urinary system is not related to her reproductive system except for the fact that the urethral opening is located between the (29)_____ and (30)_____. Women should have an annual pelvic exam and Pap smear to test for (31)_____.

The male's external anatomy consists of the penis and the (32)_____, which contains the (33)_____. Erection of the penis occurs when the two (34)_____ and the (35)_____ become engorged with blood. The rounded end of the penis, called the (36)_____, is covered by the (37)_____ unless this excess skin has been surgically removed in an operation called (38)_____. There is great debate today about the merits of routine circumcision of males.

The male's internal reproductive system includes the (39)_____, which produce sperm and the male hormone (40)_____, and a four-part duct system (starting from the testicles): (41)_____, (42)_____, (43)_____, and (44)_____, to transport sperm out of the body. During an ejaculation, sperm are mixed with fluids from the (45)_____ and (46)_____ to form (47)_____. A small amount of fluid is released by the (48)_____ before a male reaches orgasm. Cancer of the (49)_____ is the most common type of cancer in men aged 20 to 35. The most common cancer (other than skin cancer) among all men in the United States is cancer of the (50)_____.

CHAPTER 2 SELF-TEST

A. TRUE OR FALSE

T F 51. The testicles in adult males normally produce millions of new sperm every day.

T F 52. It is normal for one testicle to hang lower in the scrotum than the other.

T F 53. Most of the fluid in a male's ejaculation comes from the prostate gland.

T F 54. Sperm can only be produced in an environment that is several degrees lower than normal body temperature.

T F 55. Most doctors routinely check for sexually transmitted diseases when they perform pelvic exams.

T F 56. Most women have a G spot.

T F 57. The American Cancer Society advises that women should have baseline mammograms, starting with one between the ages of 35 and 40.

T F 58. The ovaries produce hundreds of new eggs every month during a woman's reproductive years.

| T | F | 59. | The American Academy of Pediatrics presently favors the routine circumcision of males for health reasons. |

☐ T ☐ F 59. The American Academy of Pediatrics presently favors the routine circumcision of males for health reasons.

☐ T ☐ F 60. The use of feminine hygiene sprays and douches is a recommended part of normal feminine hygiene.

☐ T ☐ F 61. Females can reduce their chances of getting a urinary tract infection (cystitis) by wiping themselves from front to back after a bowel movement.

☐ T ☐ F 62. There is no direct, physical pathway between the ovaries and the Fallopian tubes.

☐ T ☐ F 63. The majority of older men experience prostate problems as a result of their prostates becoming smaller with age.

☐ T ☐ F 64. The labia majora are hairless and meet at the top to form the clitoral hood.

☐ T ☐ F 65. The vagina is an open orifice that is always ready to accommodate insertion of a penis.

☐ T ☐ F 66. Deep, pleasurable vaginal sensations during intercourse are due to sensitive vaginal walls.

☐ T ☐ F 67. It is not uncommon for adolescent males to have enlarged breasts due to increased estrogen levels.

☐ T ☐ F 68. Erections in men are due in part to a bone that protrudes into the penis.

☐ T ☐ F 69. The hymen is a good indicator of whether or not a woman has had sexual intercourse.

☐ T ☐ F 70. A woman's sexual responsiveness is related to breast size.

B. MATCHING

_____ 71. areola

_____ 72. os

_____ 73. mammogram

_____ 74. mons veneris

_____ 75. cystitis

_____ 76. perineum

_____ 77. introitus

_____ 78. corpora cavernosa

_____ 79. bulbocavernosus muscle

_____ 80. corona

_____ 81. fimbria

_____ 82. glans

_____ 83. Bartholin's glands

_____ 84. smegma

_____ 85. pubococcygeus muscle

_____ 86. circumcision

_____ 87. vestibular bulbs

a. an inflammation of the bladder

b. a term used to refer to the vaginal opening

c. the darkened area around the nipple

d. the opening to the cervix

e. X-ray procedure used for early detection of breast cancer

f. hairless area of skin between the vaginal opening and the anus

g. the cheesy substance secreted by glands in the foreskin and clitoral hood

h. soft layer of fatty tissue overlaying the pubic bone

i. two spongy cylinders in the penis

j. large muscle that surrounds the vagina and the bladder

k. the raised ridge where the glans and shaft of the penis meet

l. tiny fingerlike endings of the Fallopian tubes

m. the smooth rounded end of the penis

n. two glands located at the base of the labia minora

o. the surgical removal of the foreskin

p. ring of sphincter muscles that surround the vaginal opening and root of the penis

q. located on both sides of the vaginal opening and become engorged with blood during sexual arousal

C. FILL IN THE BLANK

88. The American Cancer Society advises all women aged 18 or over to have regular pelvic exams and _____ tests to check for _____ cancer.

89. All men over the age of 40 should have an annual examination to check for cancer of the _____.

90. In females, the two outer, elongated folds of skin that extend from the mons to the perineum are called the _____ .

91. The innermost layer of the uterus, which is sloughed off and discharged from the female's body during menstruation, is called the _____ .

92. In human males, an erection results from the spongy tissues of the penis becoming engorged with _____ .

93. When a male becomes sexually aroused, a few drops of a clear fluid produced by the _____ may appear at the tip of the penis.

94. The soft layer of fatty tissue overlaying the pubic bone in females is called the _____ .

95. Breast size in women is determined by _____ .

96. The best time for most women to examine their breasts for abnormal lumps is _____ .

97. After an egg is released from an ovary, it travels through one of the _____ on the way to the uterus.

98. The sac beneath the penis is called the _____ .

99. After sperm travel through the vas deferens, they enter the paired _____ .

100. Most of the fluid in an ejaculation comes from the _____ .

101. The best time for a man to examine his testicles for abnormal lumps is _____ .

102. Two glands that secrete small amounts of alkaline fluid into ducts at the base of the labia minora are called _____ .

103. Sperm are produced in the _____ of the testicles.

104. Male hormone testosterone is produced by the _____ in the testicles.

105. Both the penis and the _____ have corpora cavernosa.

106. The muscle surrounding the vagina and bladder is called the _____ muscle.

107. In women who have a G spot, it is located on the _____ wall of the vagina.

108. _____ is a condition in which the spermatic cord becomes twisted and cuts off the blood supply to the testicles.

109. The corpora cavernosa expand and fan out to form _____ , which attach to the pubic bone.

CHAPTER 3 INTERACTIVE REVIEW

....

Hormones are chemical substances that are released into the bloodstream by ductless (1)_____ glands. The ovaries and testicles are part of this system. The testicles produce the "male hormone" (2)_____ and the ovaries produce the "female hormones" (3)_____ and (4)_____ . Hormones from the (5)_____ cause the ovaries and testicles to produce their hormones.

    In adult females, an egg matures on an average of every (6)_____ days. The pituitary hormone that starts the menstrual cycle is called (7)_____ . This hormone stimulates the development of a (8)_____ in the ovary. During the preovulatory phase of the menstrual cycle (also called the (9)_____ phase), estrogen from the follicle promotes growth of the (10)_____ , inhibits release of (11)_____ , and stimulates release of (12)_____ . The (13)_____ surge signals the onset of (14)_____ , at which time the ovum is expelled into the (15)_____ and is picked up by a (16)_____ . During the postovulatory phase of the cycle (also called the (17)_____ phase), the (18)_____ secretes progesterone in large amounts. If the egg is fertilized by a sperm, it normally implants in the (19)_____ . If the egg is not fertilized, the corpus luteum degenerates and the (20)_____ is shed and discharged in a normal physiological process called (21)_____ . Although the average length of the menstrual cycle is 28 days, the large majority of women have cycles that vary in length by (22)_____ . In most nonhuman mammalian species this cycle of hormonal events is called the (23)_____ cycle. One difference is that, unlike women, females of species with this type of cycle are sexually receptive to males only during (24)_____ . Some cultures have menstrual (25)_____ that prohibit contact with a menstruating woman, and even in our own culture many women and their partners avoid sexual intercourse during menstruation, but this generally reflects inaccurate information and/or negative culturally learned responses. Menstrual discharge consists simply of (26)_____ , (27)_____ , and (28)_____ .

    In males, FSH stimulates (29)_____ . LH, which is often called (30)_____ in men, stimulates the production of (31)_____ in the testicles. Misuse of anabolic steroids, derivatives of testosterone, can cause serious harmful effects such as (32)_____ (name three effects).

    Some women experience menstrual-related problems. The absence of menstruation is called (33)_____ . Emotional and/or physical changes (34)_____ days before the start of menstruation is referred to as (35)_____ . The thing that distinguishes this condition from other emotional states is that it ends (36)_____ . The major cause of (37)_____ , painful menstruation, is an overproduction of (38)_____ . Endometriosis refers to a condition in which (39)_____ . Women who use tampons, but do not change them frequently, are at a higher risk of getting a serious bacterial infection called (40)_____ .

    In men, sexual desire appears to be related to circulating levels of (41)_____ . Studies of women after menopause, or after surgical removal of the ovaries, suggest that women's sexual desire is not strongly affected by the hormones (42)_____ or (43)_____ . Other studies indicate that the hormone (44)_____ does influence sexual desire in women.

CHAPTER 3 SELF-TEST

....

A. TRUE OR FALSE

- [T] [F] 45. Hormones are important for women's sexual desire, but not for men's.
- [T] [F] 46. Testosterone is found only in males, and estrogen is found only in females.
- [T] [F] 47. All female mammals have menstrual cycles.
- [T] [F] 48. Most women's menstrual cycles are 28 days in length.
- [T] [F] 49. It is medically safe for a man to have sexual intercourse with a menstruating woman.
- [T] [F] 50. Premenstrual syndrome refers only to women who have emotional, but not physical, changes before the start of menstruation.
- [T] [F] 51. Women who use tampons should change them 3 or 4 times a day, even if the tampons are advertised as long lasting.
- [T] [F] 52. Large doses of anabolic steroids can cause mental disorders.
- [T] [F] 53. Men can no longer have an interest in sex after castration.
- [T] [F] 54. Women show maximal sexual desire around the time of ovulation.

T ☐ F ☐   55. Females produce new eggs throughout their lifetimes.

T ☐ F ☐   56. Cervical mucus changes during ovulation.

T ☐ F ☐   57. Near the end of the postovulatory phase of the menstrual cycle there is an LH surge.

T ☐ F ☐   58. Ovulation almost always occurs 14 days before the start of menstruation.

T ☐ F ☐   59. There is some evidence that suggests that the female menstrual cycle can be altered by certain smells.

T ☐ F ☐   60. Women with PMS generally have normal hormone levels.

T ☐ F ☐   61. Only women can get toxic shock syndrome.

T ☐ F ☐   62. Estrogen, according to most research, is the primary hormone responsible for sexual desire in women.

B.   MATCHING

_____ 63. endocrine system

_____ 64. testosterone

_____ 65. luteinizing hormone

_____ 66. estrogen

_____ 67. FSH

_____ 68. follicular phase

_____ 69. corpus luteum

_____ 70. amenorrhea

_____ 71. luteal phase

_____ 72. dysmenorrhea

_____ 73. Mittelschmerz

_____ 74. ovulation

_____ 75. prostaglandins

_____ 76. premenstrual syndrome

_____ 77. endometriosis

a. substances that cause muscle contractions of the uterus

b. cells surrounding the ovum that are left behind at ovulation

c. emotional and/or physical changes that precede menstruation

d. male hormone produced in testicles, ovaries, and adrenal glands

e. cramps experienced for about a day during ovulation

f. postovulatory phase when the corpus luteum begins to secrete large amounts of progesterone

g. endometrial tissue growing outside the uterus

h. network of ductless glands

i. rupture of the mature ovum into the abdominal cavity

j. female hormone produced in ovaries, testicles, and adrenal glands

k. preovulatory phase when the pituitary secretes FSH and the follicle secretes estrogen

l. pituitary hormone that stimulates production of sperm and maturation of ova

m. absence of menstruation

n. pituitary hormone that triggers ovulation in women and the production of testosterone in males

o. painful cramps during menstruation

C.   FILL IN THE BLANK

78. The gland located at the base of the brain that secretes follicle-stimulating hormone and luteinizing hormone is the _____ gland.

79. Natural body scents that can affect the behavior of other members of the same species are called _____.

80. The release of FSH from the pituitary stimulates _____ in the ovary.

81. Female gonadotropin and gonadal hormone levels show cyclic fluctuations referred to as _____.

82. Each immature ovum is surrounded by other cells within a thin capsule of tissue to form what is called a _____ .

83. During ovulation, the cells that surround the ovum in the follicle remain in the ovary, and are then referred to as the _____ .

84. After ovulation, there is a large increase in circulating levels of the hormone _____ .

85. A woman's first menstrual cycle is called _____ .

86. The removal of the testicles is known as castration or _____.

87. Once people have become sexually experienced, the _____ plays an equal, if not greater, role than hormones in our level of sexual desire.

88. _____ is the hormone most influential in affecting sexual desire in women.

89. Toxic shock syndrome is caused by _____.

90. If the egg is fertilized by a sperm and implantation occurs, the corpus luteum is maintained by a hormone from the developing placenta called _____.

CHAPTER 4 INTERACTIVE REVIEW

(1)_____ observed and recorded physiological responses from hundreds of people engaged in sexual activity. This work led them to conclude that males and females are (2)_____ in their responses than previously believed. They divided the physiological responses during sex into four phases: (3)_____, (4)_____, (5)_____, and (6)_____ . This pattern of responses is often referred to as the (7)_____ . Other researchers have organized the responses into fewer or more phases, and this chapter agrees with sex therapist (8)_____ and includes (9)_____ as the first phase.

The first response in the excitement phase for both males and females is a (10)_____ response, which results in (11)_____ in men and (12)_____ in women. During the (13)_____ phase in women, the tissues of the outer third of the vagina become swollen with blood, causing the vaginal opening to narrow. This response is referred to as the (14)_____ . Also during this phase the clitoris (15)_____ . Early in the plateau phase (16)_____ percent of women and about 25 percent of men experience a rash on the skin called the (17)_____ .

At the time of orgasm, both men and women have (18)_____ in specific tissues that initially occur every 0.8 seconds. However, recent studies indicate that the real essence of orgasm is not in the genitals, but in (19)_____ . Men's and women's descriptions of orgasm are (20)_____ . Male orgasms occur in two stages, (21)_____ and (22)_____ . The expulsion of semen from the penis is called (23)_____ . After males have an orgasm, their physiological responses generally dip below plateau, during which time they cannot have another orgasm. This period of time is called the (24)_____ . Unlike most men, some women can have (25)_____ —two or more orgasms in quick succession without dropping below the plateau level. The return to the unaroused state is called (26)_____ .

By most estimates, only (27)_____ percent of adult women experience orgasm regularly during intercourse. Masters and Johnson claim that all women in good health are capable of reaching orgasm during intercourse, but Helen Kaplan and others believe that many women are incapable of reaching orgasm during intercourse without simultaneous (28)_____ stimulation.

Freud believed that there were two types of female orgasms, one caused by (29)_____ stimulation and another by (30)_____ sensations. Masters and Johnson originally claimed that all female orgasms were identical and were focused in the (31)_____ . However, some women report having experienced different types of orgasms, and work conducted in the 1980s revealed that many of these women had a sensitive area on the (32)_____ wall of the vagina called the (33)_____ . Stimulation of this area sometimes resulted in (34)_____ during orgasm. In some women the fluid was identified as urine, but in others it contained an enzyme found in secretions from the male's (35)_____ .

Most women say that the size of a partner's penis is (36)_____ for their pleasure during intercourse. Many people have tried to enhance their sexual desire or performance by taking substances called (37)_____ , but there is little evidence that they have any real effect. In many places in the world, sexual pleasure is denied to females by mutilating their genitals in procedures called (38)_____ and (39)_____ . The World Health Organization has had little luck in stopping these ancient cultural practices.

CHAPTER 4 SELF-TEST

A. TRUE OR FALSE

[T] [F] 40. Once a person has sexual desire, stimulation of any of the five senses can lead to excitement.

[T] [F] 41. The sexual responses caused by touching are the same as those caused by fantasy.

[T] [F] 42. The first physiological signs of arousal in men occur within seconds, but take several minutes to begin in women.

[T] [F] 43. Vaginal lubrication is actually superfiltered blood plasma.

[T] [F] 44. The presence of vaginal lubrication means that a woman is ready to begin sexual intercourse.

[T] [F] 45. Both men and women can experience nipple erection during the excitement phase.

[T] [F] 46. When the clitoris pulls back and disappears beneath the clitoral hood, it means that a woman is less sexually aroused than before.

[T] [F] 47. The secretion of fluids from the vaginal walls may slow down if the plateau phase is prolonged.

[T] [F] 48. The Bartholin's glands secrete a small amount of fluid during the initial excitement phase.

T   F   49. Changes that occur during the plateau phase in males are not as distinct as the changes that occur in females.

T   F   50. Generally speaking, descriptions of orgasm written by women can be easily distinguished from those written by men.

T   F   51. Orgasm and ejaculation occur at the same time in men and are actually the same event.

T   F   52. The rhythmic muscular contractions during orgasm recorded by Masters and Johnson are not strongly related to a person's subjective sensations of pleasure.

T   F   53. A full orgasm for the male, with ejaculation, is almost always followed by a refractory period.

T   F   54. Some people who are paralyzed, with no sensations from the genitals, can experience orgasm.

T   F   55. The walls of the inner two thirds of the vagina are very sensitive to touch, thus making penis length an important factor during intercourse.

T   F   56. There is more variation in penis length in the unaroused condition than in the erect state.

T   F   57. Alcohol excites the central nervous system and enhances sexual performance.

T   F   58. Regular, long-term use of marijuana can lower testosterone levels and decrease sperm production.

T   F   59. A man's penis size is related to his height, weight, or race.

T   F   60. Regular use of cocaine often leads to erectile problems and difficulties reaching orgasm.

B.   MATCHING (SOME QUESTIONS HAVE MULTIPLE ANSWERS)

_____ 61. desire

_____ 62. excitement phase

_____ 63. plateau phase

_____ 64. orgasm phase

_____ 65. resolution phase

_____ 66. a vasocongestive response

a. Cowper's glands secrete a few drops of clear fluid
b. penis starts to become erect
c. labia minora become engorged with blood
d. specific sensations cause the individual to seek out, or become receptive to, sexual experiences
e. rhythmic muscular contractions in outer vagina, uterus, and anal sphincter muscles
f. clitoris pulls back against the pubic bone
g. vaginal lubrication begins
h. blood drains from breasts, outer third of the vagina, labia minora, and clitoris
i. the sex-tension flush appears
j. nipples become erect
k. clitoris is most prominent at this time
l. scrotum thickens and helps pull the testicles toward the body
m. blood drains from penis and testicles
n. walls of the inner two thirds of the vagina begin to balloon out
o. return to the unaroused state
p. rhythmic muscular contractions in vas deferens, prostate gland, urethra, and anal sphincter muscles
q. outer third of the vagina becomes engorged with blood
r. nipples appear to be less erect
s. labia majora flatten and spread apart
t. testicles increase in size by 50-100 percent
u. in males, emission of a fluid from the urethra

C.   FILL IN THE BLANKS

67. The two basic physiological responses that occur during sexual arousal are called _____ and _____ .

68. Sperm, prostate fluids, and seminal fluids combine to form _____ .

69. _____ started the controversy about clitoral versus vaginal orgasms.

70. Some women emit a fluid during orgasm that comes from the _____.

71. Most women and many men get a skin rash called the _____ when they become highly sexually aroused.

72. Substances that suppress sexual functioning are called _____.

73. _____ refers to the buildup of energy in nerves and muscles resulting in involuntary contractions.

74. The first stage of orgasm in males is called _____.

75. A medical problem in which the sphincter muscles dysfunction and force semen into the bladder is called _____.

76. The engorgement and swelling of the outer third of the vagina was named the _____ by Masters and Johnson.

77. A sensitive area that is found on the front wall of the vagina in about 10 percent of women is called the _____.

78. After ejaculating, most men have a period of time called the _____ during which it is impossible to have another orgasm.

79. In women, the _____ become greatly engorged with blood during the plateau phase, resulting in a doubling or tripling in their thickness and a vivid color change.

80. The type of female orgasm resulting from clitoral stimulation and characterized by the buildup and discharge of myotonia in the orgasmic platform and the pubococcygeus muscles is called _____.

CHAPTER 5 INTERACTIVE REVIEW

There are about 35,000 new cases of sexually transmitted diseases in the United States every day. For Americans under the age of 55, about one in (1)_____ will have at least one STD sometime in their life.

Sexual behavior does not cause STDs. The behavior is merely the mode of transmission for (2)_____, (3)_____, and/or (4)_____ that must be present for the diseases to be transmitted. These causative agents are nondiscriminating—anyone having sex with an infected partner can get a sexually transmitted disease.

The three most common STDs (in the U.S.) caused by bacteria are (5)_____, (6)_____, and (7)_____ . In the early stages of (8)_____ and (9)_____, most women and many men show no symptoms. If they are not treated, the bacteria that cause these two STDs can invade the upper reproductive tract and cause prostatitis and epididymitis in men and (10)_____ in women. (11)_____ passes through several stages, and if left untreated, can cause organ damage and death. These types of STDs can be cured with (12)_____.

Sexually transmitted diseases caused by viruses are generally incurable because the viruses live inside normal body cells. Herpes has been around since Biblical times and is spread by direct (13)_____ -to- _____ contact. Genital herpes is almost always transmitted by genital-to-genital or mouth-to-genital contact; oral herpes is often spread by more casual contact. After the primary attack, many herpes sufferers experience (14)_____ attacks when the virus replicates and sheds. The virus is most easily transmitted during active attacks, but can be transmitted at other times.

Hepatitis is an inflammation of the (15)_____ and can be caused by contact with contaminated (16)_____ (hepatitis A) or infected (17)_____ (hepatitis B). One fourth to one half the cases of hepatitis B are sexually transmitted.

Warts in the genital and anal area are caused by a few types of the (18)_____ virus. Other types of the virus are associated with cancer of the cervix and penis. Physicians can attempt to remove the warts or abnormal cervical cells, but they cannot attack the viruses directly, thus in many cases the condition reappears.

AIDS is caused by the (19)_____. HIV invades and destroys (20)_____ (also called helper T) cells, white blood cells that are a critical part of the body's (21)_____ system. Most people infected with HIV remain asymptomatic for several years. HIV infection is not called AIDS until the immune system is so weakened that the individual's life is threatened. People with AIDS eventually die from a variety of (22)_____ infections. About half of all individuals who become infected with HIV will develop AIDS within (23)_____ years. HIV probably originated in Africa from simian (nonhuman primate) immunodeficiency viruses. It is transmitted by (24)_____ and exposure to infected (25)_____ (including mother-to-fetus). It is not spread by (26)_____. HIV infection is a true pandemic, with at least 40 million cases expected worldwide by the year 2000. Worldwide, most cases are spread by sexual activity between (27)_____ . Presently, there is no cure, but there are several anti-viral drugs that slow the progression of the infection.

Pubic lice and scabies are not really diseases, but (28)_____. Pubic lice attach themselves to pubic hair and feed on blood. Scabies is caused by a mite that burrows under the skin to lay its eggs.

Vaginitis is a general term that refers to any inflammation of the vagina. There are three types. (29)_____ is caused by a one-celled protozoan that is transmitted during sexual intercourse. The other two types of vaginitis are not considered STDs because most cases are not acquired during sexual relations. (30)_____ vaginitis is the fungus or yeast infection that is very common in females. Anything that changes the chemical environment of the vagina can cause a yeast infection. Probably the most common type of vaginitis is (31)_____, caused by an interaction of several vaginal bacteria. Vaginal infections are very common and nothing to be ashamed of.

STDs do not strike randomly—they only affect those who are exposed to the bacteria or viruses. You can greatly reduce your chance of ever contracting a sexually transmitted disease by practicing safer sex. This means making one of two choices: (1) using condoms (preferably with spermicide) properly and consistently, or (2) abstaining from sexual relations until you are reasonably confident that you are in a long-term, monogamous relationship. See the self-assessment questionnaire at the beginning of the study guide.

CHAPTER 5 SELF-TEST

A. TRUE OR FALSE

[T] [F]   32. People who have had a sexually transmitted disease in the past are immune to getting that type of STD again.

[T] [F]   33. Untreated chlamydia results in serious complications more often than untreated gonorrhea.

[T] [F]   34. Cold sores and fever blisters are symptoms of herpes.

[T] [F]   35. Homosexuality is one of the causes of AIDS.

[T] [F]   36. This century, more people have died from syphilis than from AIDS.

[T] [F]   37. If left untreated, gonorrhea can turn into syphilis.

[T] [F]   38. Yeast infections (monilial vaginitis) can usually be prevented by using feminine hygiene products.

[T] [F]   39. A person with a cold sore on the mouth can give his or her partner genital herpes during oral-genital sex.

[T] [F]   40. If neither person had an STD to begin with, a monogamous heterosexual or homosexual couple can engage in oral-genital or anal sex without fear of getting an STD, including AIDS.

[T] [F]   41. Gonorrhea, chlamydia, and syphilis are often contracted by people using toilet seats previously used by infected individuals.

[T] [F]   42. Having a sexually transmitted disease is a sign of promiscuity.

[T] [F]   43. Chlamydia is more common than gonorrhea.

[T] [F]   44. Syphilis is caused by a bacterium.

[T] [F]   45. It is possible to contract HIV by hugging, touching, or being close to an infected person.

[T] [F]   46. The large majority of women do not show any symptoms in the early stages of gonorrhea or chlamydia.

[T] [F]   47. Herpes can sometimes be cured with antibiotics.

[T] [F]   48. A person can have only one type of sexually transmitted disease at a time.

[T] [F]   49. HIV, the virus that causes AIDS, is sometimes spread by mosquitoes.

[T] [F]   50. Viruses lack the genetic material necessary to reproduce themselves.

[T] [F]   51. Pelvic inflammatory disease can be caused by infections that were not contracted during sex.

[T] [F]   52. Condoms are generally ineffective against the human immunodeficiency virus.

[T] [F]   53. The eggs of pubic lice can survive for days on towels or sheets.

[T] [F]   54. A person who has no symptoms does not have to worry about having gonorrhea, chlamydia, or syphilis.

[T] [F]   55. Only females can contract trichomoniasis and monilial infections.

[T] [F]   56. Herpes can be cured with a drug called acyclovir.

[T] [F]   57. The human papillomaviruses that cause cervical cancer are the same as those that cause genital warts.

[T] [F]   58. Regular douching decreases the risk of pelvic inflammatory disease.

[T] [F]   59. The major symptom of the primary stage of syphilis is a rash.

[T] [F]   60. Recurrent herpes attacks are generally more painful, and last longer, than the first (primary) attack.

[T] [F]   61. Herpes is the leading infectious cause of blindness in the United States.

[T] [F]   62. Hepatitis A is most often spread by nonsexual means.

[T] [F]   63. Worldwide, most cases of HIV infection (the virus that causes AIDS) are contracted by sex between heterosexuals.

[T] [F]   64. Generally speaking, people who get AIDS this year are those who became infected with HIV 5 to 15+ years ago.

[T] [F]   65. Death by AIDS can generally be prevented by early treatment with the drug AZT.

[T] [F]   66. To minimize their chance of a vaginal infection, women should wear panties made of synthetic fabrics.

[T] [F]   67. Cystitis can sometimes be caused by vigorous intercourse.

[T] [F]   68. People who get HIV are extremely contagious in the first 60 days after exposure.

| T | | F | 69. Among young Americans aged 25 to 44, AIDS causes more deaths than accidents, cancer, or heart disease.

B.   MATCHING

Possible Symptoms

_____ 70. craterlike, painful sores

_____ 71. itchless, painless rash all over the body

_____ 72. puslike discharge and/or burning during urination

_____ 73. intense itching caused by grayish, six-legged parasites

_____ 74. thick, white, cheesy vaginal discharge and intense itching

_____ 75. loss of appetite, fatigue, slow recovery from colds and flus, continuous yeast infections, purple blotches on skin, pneumonia

_____ 76. cauliflower-like growths

_____ 77. severe abdominal pain and fever

_____ 78. scaling skin caused by pearly mites

_____ 79. large, ulcerlike, painless sore

_____ 80. fluid-filled blisters

_____ 81. copious, foamy, yellowish-green vaginal discharge and odor

_____ 82. wartlike growths that look like small pimples filled with a kernel of corn

_____ 83. thin, clear discharge and irritation of the urethra

_____ 84. jaundiced or yellow tinge of skin and eyes

_____ 85. large ulcers (gummas) appear on the skin and bones; damage to the heart and nervous system

_____ 86. inflammation of the bladder

Infection (or Infestation)

a. chancroid

b. chlamydia

c. gonorrhea

d. hepatitis

e. herpes

f. HIV infection (AIDS)

g. molluscum contagiosum

h. moniliasis (yeast infection)

i. PID

j. primary stage syphilis

k. cystitis

l. secondary stage syphilis

m. scabies

n. trichomoniasis

o. venereal warts (human papillomavirus infection)

p. late stage syphilis

q. pubic lice

C.   FILL IN THE BLANKS

87. Trichomoniasis, pubic lice, and scabies are all caused by _____.

88. Inflammation of the vagina is referred to as _____.

89. In women, untreated gonorrhea or chlamydia can lead to _____.

90. A woman who has had _____ is at high risk of getting cancer of the cervix.

91. The sexually transmitted disease that impairs the immune system is called _____.

92. Trichomoniasis, moniliasis, and bacterial vaginosis are all _____.

93. A viral liver infection that can be sexually transmitted is _____.

94. The most common viral sexually transmitted disease in the United States is _____.

95. The drug that is prescribed to relieve the symptoms of herpes is _____.

96. Two serious possible consequences of PID are _____ and _____.

97. Three sexually transmitted diseases that can be passed from an infected pregnant female to the fetus are _____, _____, and _____.

98. _____ is the most common thing that brings on recurrent herpes attacks.

99. The bacteria that cause gonorrhea and chlamydia live on _____.

100. Any inflammation of the urethra not caused by the gonococcus is called _____.

101. In tropical countries, chlamydia is responsible for an STD called _____.

102. _____ is a sexually transmitted disease for which many more women show symptoms than men.

103. Antibiotics commonly lead to _____ infections.

104. _____ live in the large intestine and can be transmitted during sex, but are generally acquired by children through nonsexual means.

105. Many people diagnosed with gonorrhea are also found to have _____.

106. HIV attacks immune system cells called _____.

107. People with HIV are most contagious (when) _____.

108. The most common "AIDS" test tests for _____.

109. Gonorrhea, chlamydia, syphilis, herpes, HPV infection, HIV infection, trichomoniasis: For which of these diseases do women usually not have visible symptoms in the initial stage? _____

110. Of the diseases listed in the previous question, for which do men usually not show symptoms in the initial stage? _____

111. The best ways to avoid sexually transmitted diseases are _____ and _____.

CHAPTER 6 INTERACTIVE REVIEW

There are well over one million births to unwed females in the United States every year. Nearly half of these are to teenagers. The teen pregnancy rate in the United States is (1)_____ as high as in most other developed countries. Unfortunately, the teens most likely to have babies are those least prepared to take care of them.

Worldwide, there is need for effective contraceptive technology. The world population is expected to double by the middle of the next century, yet already there are many parts of the world experiencing food shortages and mass starvation.

While all the methods of birth control discussed in this chapter are better than using nothing, some are more effective than others. Relatively ineffective methods include withdrawal, douching, and breast-feeding. Fertility awareness methods (the (2)_____ , (3)_____ , and (4)_____ methods) rely on calculating when (5)_____ will occur and abstaining from intercourse during that period. The failure rates for these methods are higher than for most others. (6)_____ work by killing sperm and are generally used in combination with a barrier method of contraception (condoms, (7)_____ , (8)_____ , and (9)_____). Barrier methods block sperm from getting into the (10)_____ . Spermicides and barrier methods often interfere with spontaneity, but for people who are not in a monogamous relationship, a major advantage of these methods (not offered by other methods) is that they (11)_____ .

Intrauterine devices (IUDs) have had a reputation for causing serious problems, but today's IUDs are safe as well as highly effective. However, they are recommended only for women in long-term monogamous relationships who have completed their families. The combination birth control pill contains synthetic (12)_____ and (13)_____ and works by preventing ovulation. The pills used today contain a low dosage of estrogen and are safer than the high-dosage pills used in the past. Nevertheless, there are certain groups of women who, for medical reasons, should not take the pill. (14)_____ (the shot good for 3 months) and (15)_____ (the implant good for 5 years) contain only progestin and are believed to be safer than the pill. All three hormonal methods of contraception have theoretical failure rates of less than 1 percent.

If you consider male and female sterilization techniques together, more Americans rely on sterilization for birth control than any other method. In a vasectomy, the (16)_____ is tied off and cut. Afterwards, the male still ejaculates during orgasm, but his ejaculation contains no sperm. For a (17)_____ or (18)_____ , a woman's Fallopian tubes are cut, cauterized, or blocked by clips. The failure rate is close to zero.

For women who have an unplanned or unwanted pregnancy, one option is abortion. Various techniques can be used to terminate pregnancy, including hormones or chemicals, scraping or suctioning away of the endometrium, and induced labor. The Supreme Court has recently made several decisions affecting the availability of abortion in the United States.

It is important that you choose an effective contraceptive technique *before* you have sexual intercourse. A questionnaire is provided at the end of the chapter that is designed to help you decide which method is best for you.

CHAPTER 6 SELF-TEST

A. TRUE OR FALSE

[T] [F] 19. The rates for births to unmarried teenage girls has decreased since 1970 because of increased use of contraceptives.

[T] [F] 20. The world population is expected to stabilize by the year 2000 because of increased use of birth control.

[T] [F] 21. The U.S. fertility rate is presently about 2.0 births per woman.

[T] [F] 22. If the theoretical failure rate for a contraceptive method is 20 percent, then for 100 couples who start using the method, about 20 of them will have conceived after 3 years.

[T] [F] 23. In order for a woman to get pregnant, she must have an orgasm.

[T] [F] 24. More couples rely on sterilization than on the birth control pill.

[T] [F] 25. It is possible for a girl to get pregnant as soon as she starts having menstrual periods.

[T] [F] 26. The combination birth control pill reduces the risk of cancer of the endometrium and ovaries.

CHAPTER SIX

[T]   [F]   27. A relatively effective method of birth control for women is to wash out the contents of the vagina immediately after sexual intercourse.

[T]   [F]   28. The birth control pill reduces the risk of getting a sexually transmitted disease.

[T]   [F]   29. Abortion was allowed by the Catholic church until the late 1800s.

[T]   [F]   30. A vasectomy works as birth control by preventing ejaculation.

[T]   [F]   31. If carefully washed and dried, condoms can be used safely on more than one occasion.

[T]   [F]   32. Taking antibiotics makes the birth control pill less effective.

[T]   [F]   33. Legal abortions do not increase a woman's later risk of infertility, miscarriage, or a low birth-weight baby.

[T]   [F]   34. A diaphragm works by being inserted into the uterus and blocking sperm.

[T]   [F]   35. Because IUDs are so effective, they are highly recommended for young, sexually active women.

[T]   [F]   36. The major difference between the cervical cap and the diaphragm is that the cervical cap does not need to be used with spermicide.

[T]   [F]   37. Most daughters of teenaged mothers become teenage mothers themselves.

[T]   [F]   38. Breast-feeding a baby inhibits the release of follicle-stimulating hormone from a woman's pituitary gland.

[T]   [F]   39. With perfect use, fertility awareness methods are as effective as the birth control pill.

[T]   [F]   40. Spermicides help to kill HIV, the virus that causes AIDS.

[T]   [F]   41. Pregnancy and childbirth result in more maternal deaths than the birth control pill.

[T]   [F]   42. In the future it will probably be possible to be vaccinated to prevent pregnancy (as is done for the flu).

[T]   [F]   43. The French abortion pill, RU 486, allows women to have abortions in the privacy of their own home.

[T]   [F]   44. Rubber condoms are more effective than "skin" condoms for prevention of STDs.

[T]   [F]   45. Nearly a third of all pregnancies to unwed teens in this country end in abortion.

[T]   [F]   46. The female condom is actually an intravaginal pouch.

[T]   [F]   47. Use of the contraceptive sponge substantially increases a woman's chance of toxic shock syndrome.

[T]   [F]   48. Most women over the age of 40 can continue to take the combination birth control pill.

[T]   [F]   49. Once inserted under the skin, Norplant must remain in place for 5 years.

[T]   [F]   50. The contraceptive sponge and diaphragm offer women some protection against gonorrhea and chlamydia.

B.   MATCHING (SOME ANSWERS CAN BE USED MORE THAN ONCE)

Contraceptive Method

_____ 51. breast-feeding

_____ 52. calendar method

_____ 53. basal body temperature method

_____ 54. Billings method

_____ 55. spermicides

_____ 56. male condom

_____ 57. female condom

_____ 58. diaphragm

_____ 59. cervical cap

Method of Operation

a. It was once thought that it worked by preventing implantation, but now known to work by preventing fertilization.

b. active ingredient kills sperm

c. prevents release of FSH

d. noticing changes in cervical mucus to determine when to abstain from intercourse

e. prevents sperm deposited in the vagina from getting into the uterus

f. Fallopian tubes are tied, cut, cauterized, or blocked by clips

g. contains enough spermicide to be effective for 24 hours

h. blocks sperm from getting into the vagina

i. uses simple mathematical formula to determine when to abstain from intercourse

j. progestins prevent ovulation

_____ 60. contraceptive
   sponge

_____ 61. IUD

_____ 62. combination pill

_____ 63. Depo-Provera

_____ 64. Norplant

_____ 65. vasectomy

_____ 66. tubal ligation

_____ 67. laparoscopy

k. noticing changes in resting temperature to determine when to abstain from intercourse

l. vas deferens is tied and cut off

m. synthetic estrogen helps to prevent ovulation

C. FILL IN THE BLANKS

68. The actual use failure rates of contraception are higher than the theoretical rates mainly because some people do not use the methods _____ or _____ .

69. Withdrawal is not a highly effective method of birth control because of secretions from _____ .

70. After a vasectomy, a male is not sterile until _____ .

71. Fertility awareness methods require that a couple abstain from sexual intercourse from near the end of _____ until several days after _____ .

72. For breast-feeding to be effective as a birth control method, a mother must allow her baby to nurse _____ .

73. A _____ resembles a large thimble and fits over the cervix by suction.

74. If a woman's shortest recorded menstrual cycle is 25 days, and her longest is 31 days, by the calendar method she should abstain from intercourse from day _____ to day _____ .

75. Women's basal body temperature _____ 24 to 72 hours after ovulation.

76. Women's cervical mucus becomes _____ at the time of ovulation.

77. The active ingredient in most spermicides is _____ .

78. Rubber condoms should not be used in combination with _____ lubricants.

79. The IUD is regarded as a safe contraceptive method for women _____ .

80. Name three nonprescription barrier types of contraception: _____ , _____ , and _____ .

81. The combination birth control pill is made less effective if a woman takes _____ .

82. The most common side effect of Depo-Provera and Norplant is _____ .

83. Name five birth control techniques that offer women some protection against STDs: _____ , _____ , _____ , _____ , and _____ .

84. One study that compared male and female sterilization techniques concluded that the _____ technique was preferable in every way.

85. In cases of rape, emergency birth control can be provided within the first few days by _____ .

86. If used properly and consistently, the most effective nonprescription, nonsurgical method of birth control is _____ .

87. The most effective reversible method(s) of birth control is(are) _____ .

CHAPTER 7 INTERACTIVE REVIEW

Sexual intercourse can result in conception on only about 4 days of the menstrual cycle (from about (1)_____ days before (2)_____ to about (3)_____ day afterwards). Fertilization usually occurs within a (4)_____ and implantation normally occurs in the (5)_____ of the uterus. Implantation of a fertilized egg at any other location is called an (6)_____ pregnancy and the most common cause is scarring of the Fallopian tubes due to (7)_____. Pregnancy tests are positive if a woman's urine or blood contains a hormone secreted by the developing placenta called (8)_____.

Pregnancy is divided into three 3-month intervals called (9)_____. After implantation, the conceptus is called an (10)_____ for the first (11)_____ months and then a (12)_____ for the last (13)_____ months of pregnancy. An expectant mother can first feel her unborn baby moving (an experience called (14)_____) during the (15)_____ month of pregnancy. Sexual intercourse during pregnancy is generally thought not to be harmful to the fetus, although some health professionals recommend that a pregnant woman not engage in intercourse during the ninth month of pregnancy.

There are many possible causes of complications of pregnancy. Substances that can cross the "placental barrier" and harm the unborn baby are called (16)_____. Examples include viruses, smoking, alcohol, cocaine and other drugs, and environmental hazards. Fetal abnormalities can often be detected by ultrasound or by a variety of invasive techniques such as chorionic sampling, (17)_____, celocentesis, and fetoscopy. Today, it is sometimes possible to perform surgery on a fetus while it is still in the uterus.

Prepared childbirth courses attempt to break the (18)_____ cycle through education and preparation. Lamaze and other techniques generally include a "coach" (usually the woman's partner) to help the expectant mother through labor and delivery. These methods hold to a philosophy that the mother-to-be and coach should be in control of the birthing process and that anesthetics should not be used unless absolutely necessary. Today, there is a growing movement back to having birth in the home (or a homelike environment), usually with the aid of a nurse- (19)_____ rather than a physician.

The actual birthing experience is known as labor. Before giving birth, many women experience "false labor." False labor is distinguished from true labor by the timing and length of (20)_____ and by the (21)_____ of the cervix. Labor proceeds in three stages. The initial or (22)_____ stage usually lasts from 6 to 13 hours, although each stage of labor varies a great deal from woman to woman and even from birth to birth in the same woman. The (23)_____ breaks (or is broken by the physician) just prior to or during this stage. The last part of the first stage of labor is called the (24)_____. It marks the beginning of the birth process. In the second stage of labor the cervix is (25)_____ and the fetus begins moving through the birth canal. The baby usually enters the world (26)_____ first, and after delivery the (27)_____ is cut. In the third stage of labor the (28)_____ detaches from the uterus and leaves the mother's body. If complications develop during childbirth, the baby can be delivered surgically through the mother's abdomen by a (29)_____. Today, in most cases it is considered safe for women who have previously had a C-section to deliver vaginally during subsequent deliveries.

An increasing number of U.S. women are breast-feeding their babies. Mothers' milk contains many infection-fighting (30)_____ and is easier to digest than cows' milk. After giving birth, many women experience a case of the blues, called (31)_____. Hormone changes, lack of sleep, and new demands can all contribute to this. Most physicians advise that women not resume sexual intercourse for (32)_____ weeks after delivery. Studies find that after the transition to parenthood, happiness within a relationship is related to (33)_____.

Infertility affects about one in (34)_____ couples in the United States. About (35)_____ percent are due to problems with the male, (36)_____ percent with the female, and about (37)_____ percent with problems to both partners. In men, infertility is usually caused either by blockage of the duct system or (38)_____. For the latter, a procedure called (39)_____ is often used. In women, infertility is usually the result of blocked (40)_____ or a failure to (41)_____.

Today, infertile couples may be helped by a variety of assisted reproductive procedures in which an egg is fertilized outside of a woman's body and then placed into her uterus (called (42)_____) or Fallopian tube (called (43)_____), or in which both eggs and sperm are placed into a Fallopian tube (called (44)_____). These techniques have allowed some postmenopausal women to have children as well. For many infertile couples, adoption has proven to be a rewarding alternative.

CHAPTER 7 SELF-TEST

A.   TRUE OR FALSE

[T] [F]   45. At conception the one-celled organism is called an embryo.

[T] [F]   46. A primary follicle first begins to mature under stimulation of luteinizing hormone.

[T] [F]   47. About 75 percent of all conceptions either fail to implant or are spontaneously aborted within the first 6 weeks.

[T] [F]   48. "Morning sickness" is most common during the last trimester of pregnancy.

[T] [F]   49. Men sometimes experience symptoms of pregnancy while their partners are pregnant.

[T] [F]   50. An expectant mother cannot feel her unborn baby moving inside her ("quickening") until the second trimester.

[T] [F]   51. Sexual intercourse during the seventh and eighth months of pregnancy is often harmful to the mother and/or fetus.

[T] [F]   52. Drugs can adversely affect the fetus, but smoking, while hazardous to the mother, has little effect.

[T] [F]   53. If a woman is Rh positive and her fetus is Rh negative, the condition is called Rh incompatibility.

[T] [F]   54. The only noninvasive technique for examining a fetus inside the uterus is ultrasound.

[T] [F]   55. One beer (or one glass of wine) a day is thought to be acceptable when a woman is pregnant.

[T] [F]   56. One of the most common causes of scarring of the Fallopian tubes is untreated gonorrhea and chlamydia.

[T] [F]   57. "Prepared childbirth" means having a baby without the use of anesthetics.

[T] [F]   58. A baby is born during the third stage of labor.

[T] [F]   59. If a woman has an ectopic pregnancy, she has an increased risk of future pregnancies also being ectopic.

[T] [F]   60. Women who have delivered babies by cesarean section usually can deliver vaginally in subsequent pregnancies.

[T] [F]   61. Natural filters protect the baby from alcohol, drugs, and pollutants during breast-feeding.

[T] [F]   62. "Test tube babies" refers to the process whereby conception and embryological development (i.e., first 2 months) occurs outside the mother's body.

[T] [F]   63. Secondary infertility (inability to conceive after having had one child) is more common than primary infertility.

[T] [F]   64. Some studies have found that the average sperm count in men today is less than half of what it was in men 50 years ago.

[T] [F]   65. Artificial insemination refers to when an egg is fertilized by synthetically manufactured sperm.

[T] [F]   66. Preembryos can be screened for genetic defects.

[T] [F]   67. With assisted reproductive techniques, women over 60 can have babies if they wish to.

[T] [F]   68. "Morning sickness" can be effectively treated with hormones.

[T] [F]   69. True labor is marked by the onset of Braxton-Hicks contractions.

[T] [F]   70. In Lamaze and some other prepared childbirth programs, pain is controlled by using focal points, effleurage, and breathing techniques.

B.   MATCHING (MATCH THE PROBLEM WITH THE TREATMENT OR SOLUTION)

_____ 71. artificial insemination

_____ 72. balloon tuboplasty

a. Susan has a tubal (ectopic) pregnancy.

b. Sherry and John cannot conceive because she is not having regular menstrual cycles.

c. Harriet's physician is worried that her perineum might tear during delivery.

——— 73. cesarean section

——— 74. chorionic
sampling (or
amniocentesis, or
fetoscopy)

——— 75. episiotomy

——— 76. fertility drugs

——— 77. fetal monitor

——— 78. fetal surgery

——— 79. gamete
intrafallopian
transfer

——— 80. in vitro
fertilization

——— 81. laparoscopic
surgery

——— 82. surrogate mother

——— 83. zygote
intrafallopian
transfer

d. Carol and David cannot conceive because he has a low sperm count.

e. Maria and John cannot conceive. Eggs taken from Maria are fertilized by sperm from John and the fertilized eggs are placed into one of Maria's Fallopian tubes.

f. Phyllis is not yet fully dilated and her baby is in distress.

g. Diane cannot carry a fetus during pregnancy but she and Frank want to have a baby that is biologically theirs.

h. Mary is in labor and her physician wishes to keep track of the unborn baby's vital signs.

i. Shelly and Mark cannot conceive. Eggs taken from Shelly are fertilized by sperm from Mark and then placed into Shelly's uterus.

j. Cindy and Bert cannot conceive because she has blocked Fallopian tubes, but they have ruled out assisted reproductive techniques.

k. Linda and Walter's unborn baby has a life-threatening urinary tract infection.

l. Joan and Tom are worried that their unborn baby may have an abnormality.

m. Betty and Sam cannot conceive. Eggs taken from Betty and sperm taken from Sam are placed directly into one of her Fallopian tubes.

C.   FILL IN THE BLANKS

84. Zygote, _____ , _____ , embryo, fetus.

85. The major link between the developing baby and the mother is the _____ .

86. A pregnant woman who has gained excessive weight and has high blood pressure and swollen joints may have _____ .

87. Before birth the fetus' head drops lower in the uterus. This is called _____ .

88. Three rules of thumb to determine if labor has begun are _____ , _____ , and _____ .

89. The _____ trimester is the time when a developing fetus is generally most susceptible to harmful substances.

90. The vast majority of ectopic pregnancies are _____ pregnancies.

91. In 1990, the Institute of Medicine recommended that normal-weight women gain _____ pounds during pregnancy.

92. By the time a fertilized egg has reached the uterus it is a fluid-filled sphere called a _____ .

93. A noninvasive technique for examining a fetus is _____ .

94. The part of a baby that normally comes into the birth canal first is _____ .

95. The cervix becomes fully dilated during the _____ stage of labor.

96. An egg remains ripe only for about _____ after ovulation.

97. The fetus is protected in a thick-skinned sac called the _____ .

98. _____ , _____ , and _____ are three procedures used by physicians during labor and childbirth that many experts feel are done far too routinely (and unnecessarily).

99. For a baby to have any chance of surviving, it must develop in the uterus for at least _____ weeks.

100. If a woman _____ during pregnancy, it increases the risk of low birthweight spontaneous abortions, and sudden infant death syndrome.

CHAPTER 8 INTERACTIVE REVIEW

(1)_____ is your subjective sense of being male or female. It is influenced by both biological and social factors. A person's genetic sex is determined at conception by the combination of an egg, which has an X chromosome for gender, and a sperm, which can have either an X or a Y chromosome. (2)_____ combinations usually result in girls, while (3)_____ combinations usually produce boys. There are over 70 known irregularities in chromosome combinations. These include males with one or more extra X chromosomes ((4)_____ Syndrome), females with only one X chromosome ((5)_____ Syndrome), and females with Triple-X Syndrome.

Hormones determine whether an embryo will develop anatomically as a male or female. Unless there are high levels of (6)_____ at this critical stage of prenatal development, nature has programmed the body to develop into a (7)_____ . Hormone abnormalities before birth can result in a mismatch between genetic and anatomical sex, or a baby whose external genitalia are ambiguous in appearance. Some individuals feel that they are trapped inside a body of the wrong gender, a feeling called (8)_____ . Persons whose gender identity does not match their biological gender are called (9)_____ . They often elect to undergo sex reassignment surgery.

Three psychological theories, although very different in their explanations, suggest that gender identity is learned. (10)_____ theory emphasizes unconscious identification with the same gender parent, while (11)_____ theory emphasizes the role of reinforcement and imitation. Cognitive-developmental theory states that children do not acquire the concept of (12)_____ until the age of (13)_____ .

(14)_____ are norms (what is considered appropriate) about the behaviors and attitudes of men and women. They vary from culture to culture and can change over time within the same culture. (15)_____ theory emphasizes how gender roles are integrated within the individual early in life as part of the individual's personality. The development of gender roles begins before a child develops gender identity or gender constancy. (16)_____ theory emphasizes the role of the environment or social context in influencing the way gender roles develop over the lifespan.

Masculinity and femininity were once viewed as opposite ends of a unidimensional continuum, but today they are generally viewed as (17)_____ constructs. This has led to the theory of (18)_____ , which says that a person can be both masculine and feminine and that this is the healthiest of all gender roles because of the flexibility it gives individuals in different situations.

Parents, teachers, the media, and peers are all powerful influences on the process of socialization and gender role development. Gender is possibly the first social category learned by children. When children cognitively organize the world according to gender, they create gender (19)_____ . Children raised in single-parent households tend to be more (20)_____ than children raised in two-parent households. As individuals become adults they generally acquire more complex sets of gender roles and for both genders there is an integration of gender roles. Continued belief in stereotypic gender roles can adversely affect one's personal and sexual relations with a partner.

Traditional gender roles in our culture evolved over time in response to social forces. Those forces have been changing (such as women in the work force) and as a result gender roles are in a state of transition. This may encourage individuals to base their behaviors, beliefs, and attitudes on human roles rather than being limited by rigid gender role expectations.

CHAPTER 8 SELF-TEST

A. TRUE OR FALSE

- ☐ T ☐ F   21. By the age of 3, children know their gender but do not understand that it cannot change.
- ☐ T ☐ F   22. In all cultures studied thus far, males are independent, aggressive, and make the important decisions, while females are emotional, nurturant, and considered too weak to do hard labor.
- ☐ T ☐ F   23. In the absence of testosterone during embryological development, we would all be born anatomically female.
- ☐ T ☐ F   24. Fathers tend to treat their children in more gender-stereotypic ways than do mothers.
- ☐ T ☐ F   25. According to microstructural theory, the way to change gender roles is not to retrain individuals but to restructure the social environment.
- ☐ T ☐ F   26. Transsexual is a term for a type of homosexual.
- ☐ T ☐ F   27. "Tomboy" behavior in girls is usually better tolerated by peers, parents, and teachers than is "effeminate" behavior in boys.

[T] [F] 28. Double standards often still exist in two-career families.

[T] [F] 29. According to social learning theory, imitation is a process by which children may learn gender identity and gender roles.

[T] [F] 30. Turner's syndrome results from an extra Y chromosome.

[T] [F] 31. Parents who assume "traditional" gender roles behave differently toward their male and female children.

[T] [F] 32. The rise of industrialization helped create the male gender role as independent and unemotional.

[T] [F] 33. Gender role is the way you express your gender identity.

[T] [F] 34. The most common cause of pseudohermaphroditism in males is androgen insensitivity syndrome.

[T] [F] 35. Males' and females' hypothalamus are different.

[T] [F] 36. A transsexual is someone who cross-dresses for sexual arousal.

[T] [F] 37. Children do not show gender-stereotyped behavior until they have developed gender constancy.

[T] [F] 38. A recent study found that young children view gender in dualistic terms, but as they grow older they come to view gender as a unidimensional construct.

[T] [F] 39. Some cultures have a practice called couvade in which males act out giving birth.

[T] [F] 40. There is little noticeable difference in the behavior of boys and girls before the age of 2.

[T] [F] 41. As people grow older, they are more able to rely on information about an individual to make judgments, even when the information is not consistent with stereotyped gender roles.

[T] [F] 42. Fewer than half of women with young children are in the labor force.

[T] [F] 43. As a result of converging gender roles, men and women no longer differ with regard to permissive attitudes about casual sex.

[T] [F] 44. Pleck's gender role strain perspective contends that the problem for the male gender role is that men are confronted by contradictory expectations in their early socialization and their adult life experience.

B. MATCHING (SOME QUESTIONS HAVE MORE THAN ONE ANSWER)

———— 45. Bob is low in instrumental orientation ("getting the job done") and has great affective concern for the welfare of others.

———— 46. Frank prefers men as sexual partners.

———— 47. Susan cannot reproduce, is short with a webbed neck, and has one X chromosome.

———— 48. Joe is neither instrumental nor expressive, assertive nor emotional.

———— 49. David's body did not respond to testosterone during prenatal development; he has female genitalia and undescended testes.

———— 50. Sam was born with a very small penis that looked like a clitoris, an incomplete scrotum, and a short closed vaginal cavity. At puberty his voice deepened, his testes descended, and his "clitoris" grew to become a penis.

———— 51. Wayne is both instrumental and expressive, assertive and emotional.

———— 52. Phillip believes he is a woman trapped in a male body.

———— 53. Sharon is slightly retarded and has an extra X chromosome.

———— 54. Carol has an enlarged clitoris and labia because of too much masculinizing hormone during fetal development.

a. adrenogenital syndrome
b .androgen insensitivity syndrome
c. androgynous individual
d. DHT-deficient individual
e. "feminine" on Bem Sex Role Inventory
f. gender dysphoric
g. hermaphrodite
h. homosexual
i. Klinefelter's Syndrome
j. pseudohermaphrodite
k. stereotyped individual
l. transsexual
m. Triple-X Syndrome
n. Turner's Syndrome
o. undifferentiated individual

_____ 55. Mike believes that men should be assertive, aggressive, success-oriented, unemotional, and play little role in house and children responsibilities.

_____ 56. Harold is tall with long arms and has a small penis, shrunken testes, low sexual desire, and an extra X chromosome.

_____ 57. Barbara is genetically a female, but has both male and female reproductive systems as a result of her primitive gonads failing to differentiate during the embryonic stage.

C.   FILL IN THE BLANKS

58. A child's knowledge that his or her sex does not change is called _____ in cognitive-developmental theory.

59. According to Cancian, gender roles for males and females did not start to differ until the _____.

60. According to _____ theory, an individual's gender role results from society's expectations of male and female behavior.

61. According to Freud, children acquire the gender identity of the same-sexed parent through the process of _____ .

62. The process of internalizing society's beliefs is called _____ .

63. Oversimplified, rigid beliefs that all members of a particular gender have distinct behavioral and emotional characteristics are called _____ .

64. On Bem's Sex Role Inventory, a person who scores low on both dimensions is called _____.

65. The duct system in embryos that can develop into the female reproductive system is called the _____ duct system.

66. According to Freud, children acquire their gender identity in the _____ stage of psychosexual development.

67. If an individual scores high on both the femininity dimension and the masculine dimension of the Bem Sex Role Inventory, he or she would be called _____ .

68. Money and Ehrhardt (1972) stated, "Nature's rule is, it would appear, that to masculinize, something must be added." The something is _____ .

69. According to Freud, gender identity is acquired when children resolve the _____ complex.

70. A _____ cross-dresses for sexual arousal and gratification, whereas a _____ cross-dresses because he or she truly believes they are a member of the opposite sex.

71. In social learning explanations of gender identity development, when children watch their mothers and fathers and copy them it is called _____ .

72. The _____ view of gender role development holds that biological influences establish predetermined limits to the effects of cultural influences.

73. According to Bem, masculine is to instrumental as feminine is to _____ .

74. According to Kagan, boy's and girl's behaviors do not differ at the age of _____ .

75. People who watch a lot of television generally believe in more _____ gender roles.

76. Some languages classify all nouns as either masculine or feminine. This is an example of _____ .

77. A recent study found that young people rely on _____ as judgment cues, but as they grow older they increasingly rely on more _____ information.

78. If research with single-parent households is correct, then a greater proportion of African-American children will grow up to be _____ than is true for Caucasian children.

79. The finding that cross-gender role characteristics often emerge among older men and women has been referred to as the _____ model of gender role development.

80. As a general rule, men have considerably more permissive attitudes about _____ than do women.

CHAPTER 9 INTERACTIVE REVIEW

....

In this chapter, sexual orientation is defined as (1)_____ consistently made after adolescence in the presence of clear alternatives. Isolated instances of sexual behavior may or may not reflect one's sexual orientation. Recent surveys indicate that (2)_____ percent of the adult male population and about (3)_____ of the adult female population have a homosexual orientation. About 20 percent of males (and a lower percentage of females) have had sex with a same-gender individual on at least one occasion, but fewer than 5 percent regard themselves as bisexual. A true bisexual would have a rating of (4)_____ on Kinsey's 7-point rating scale.

The (5)_____ of the vast majority of homosexuals and bisexuals is just as strong and consistent with their anatomical gender as is found among heterosexuals. One's conformity or nonconformity with gender (6)_____ does not predict one's sexual orientation. A great many homosexuals and bisexuals do not walk, talk, dress, or act any differently than anyone else.

There are three major explanations for the origins of sexual orientation. Psychoanalytic explanations state that heterosexuality is the "normal" outcome and that homosexuality results from problems in resolving the (7)_____ complex. Some of Freud's followers believed that homosexual males had (8)_____ mothers and (9)_____ fathers, while homosexual females had (10)_____ fathers and (11)_____ mothers. However, later research does not generally support these claims. Homosexuals, as well as heterosexuals, have all kinds of parents, both good and bad, caring and cold. (12)_____ regards homosexuality and heterosexuality as learned behaviors; good or rewarding experiences with individuals of one gender and/or bad experiences with individuals of the other gender (particularly during adolescence) would lead to a particular orientation. However, social and cultural studies show that environment alone cannot explain sexual orientation. In the (13)_____ society in Melanesia, all boys engage in homosexual acts for many years, yet the large majority grow up to have a heterosexual orientation.

Recent studies suggest that biology plays a major role in the origin of sexual orientation. Studies with twins indicate a (14)_____ factor while anatomical studies have found differences in the (15)_____ of heterosexuals and homosexuals. Many researchers believe that differences in (16)_____ before or shortly after we are born predispose us to a particular sexual orientation. Nearly all agree that biological and social/cultural influences (17)_____ to produce sexual orientation.

Anthropologists find that most societies are (18)_____ tolerant of homosexuality than prevailing attitudes in the United States. Attitudes about homosexuality have varied considerably in Western culture. The (19)_____ and (20)_____ accepted homosexuality, as did even the early Christians. It was not until St. (21)_____ that homosexuality came to be viewed as unnatural or "against the laws of nature," and not until the 1600s and 1700s that it was regarded as criminal. In the 1800s, the medical (psychiatric) model regarded it as an illness and homosexual individuals were regarded as pathological people in need of being "cured." It was not until 1973 that the American Psychiatric Association removed homosexuality as an official mental illness. Nevertheless, most people in the United States continue to have a harsh and negative attitude.

The process of (22)_____ or identifying oneself as homosexual involves several, often painful, stages. The first stage is (23)_____ . In the final stages, the individual attempts to gain the acceptance and understanding of friends, family, and co-workers. This is difficult in a society filled with (24)_____ , an irrational fear of homosexuality. Experts believe that antigay prejudice often reflects attempts to affirm one's own manhood (or womanhood).

Prior to the 1970s, opportunities for homosexuals to meet were limited to a few bars, bathhouses, and public bathrooms. Today, most metropolitan areas have well-established homosexual communities where individuals can openly associate. Women, whether straight or lesbian, tend to value (25)_____ in their relations. Prior to the 1980s, many gays engaged in impersonal sex with numerous partners, but today there is a greater emphasis in the gay community on establishing relationships.

At the time this book was written, homosexual marriages were illegal in all 50 states. Most Americans oppose the idea of openly homosexual individuals raising children (even their own), yet research shows that most parental sexual abuse is committed by heterosexuals and that children raised by homosexual parents grow up to have normal gender identities and gender roles, and almost always a heterosexual orientation. This last finding again suggests a greater role for biology than environment in the origin of sexual orientation, and it is the hope of those researchers conducting biological studies that their findings will promote greater understanding and tolerance.

CHAPTER 9 SELF-TEST

A. TRUE OR FALSE

T ☐ F ☐ 26. In some cultures, homosexual behavior is considered normal for males during adolescence.

T ☐ F ☐ 27. Homosexuals usually act and/or dress differently from heterosexuals.

T ☐ F ☐ 28. Freud said that homosexuality was not an illness.

T ☐ F ☐ 29. It is common for heterosexuals to have homosexual fantasies.

T ☐ F ☐ 30. Bisexuals are people who are afraid to admit (to themselves) their real homosexuality.

T ☐ F ☐ 31. Most homosexuals are unhappy with their sexual orientation and would like to become heterosexual.

T ☐ F ☐ 32. A homosexual orientation indicates a gender identity problem.

T ☐ F ☐ 33. A male homosexual can be made heterosexual by administering large doses of testosterone.

T ☐ F ☐ 34. People who have had homosexual experiences are by definition homosexual in orientation.

T ☐ F ☐ 35. "Coming out" is regarded as a form of exhibitionism and is generally unhealthy.

T ☐ F ☐ 36. Attitudes about homosexuality are learned and what is learned depends on the time and place in which a person is raised.

T ☐ F ☐ 37. Although being homosexual is no longer criminal, in many states it is against the law to engage in homosexual behaviors.

T ☐ F ☐ 38. Freud believed that all people were capable of becoming either heterosexual or homosexual, depending on their early childhood experiences.

T ☐ F ☐ 39. Researchers have found a higher rate of homosexuality among identical twins than among non-identical twins.

T ☐ F ☐ 40. Homosexual parents are more likely than heterosexual parents to molest their children.

T ☐ F ☐ 41. A bisexual is anyone who has had sex with both men and women.

T ☐ F ☐ 42. More recent studies support Kinsey's findings that 10 percent of American males are predominantly homosexual.

T ☐ F ☐ 43. Homosexual experiences before age 15 is a good predictor of adult sexual orientation.

T ☐ F ☐ 44. Bisexuals have fewer opposite-sex fantasies than heterosexuals and fewer same-sex fantasies than homosexuals.

T ☐ F ☐ 45. Many homosexuals and bisexuals have gender dysphoria.

T ☐ F ☐ 46. Most female homosexuals have not had pleasurable sexual relations with men.

T ☐ F ☐ 47. Sexual orientation is usually well established by adolescence.

T ☐ F ☐ 48. Extremely effeminate boys ("sissy boys") always develop a homosexual orientation.

T ☐ F ☐ 49. If one identical twin is homosexual, the other twin always is too.

T ☐ F ☐ 50. Studies have found that areas of the hypothalamus (in the brain) are different in heterosexuals and homosexuals.

T ☐ F ☐ 51. Male rats in which sex hormones have been manipulated shortly after birth often show female sexual behavior.

T ☐ F ☐ 52. Among major Western industrialized countries, only the United States and Britain bar known homosexuals from the military.

T ☐ F ☐ 53. Most homosexuals adopt a single role ("masculine" or "feminine") in sexual relationships.

T ☐ F ☐ 54. Children raised by openly homosexual parents are more likely to develop a homosexual orientation than children raised by heterosexual parents.

B.   MATCHING

_____ 55. George is a zero on Kinsey's rating scale.

_____ 56. Henry has had a few same-gender sexual experiences, but has had sex only with women since he turned 15 ten years ago.

_____ 57. Joyce has been married and enjoyed sexual relations with her husband, but now prefers sexual relations with women.

_____ 58. Frank has had sex with both men and women.

_____ 59. Michael believes he is a woman and has sex only with men.

_____ 60. Carl sometimes enjoys sex with women, but prefers sexual relations with men.

_____ 61. Tom is 12 years old and his few sexual experiences have been exclusively with boys his age.

_____ 62. Alice enjoys sex with men most of the time, but she often enjoys sex with women as well.

_____ 63. Robin has had sex only with men, but occasionally has homosexual fantasies.

_____ 64. Matthew occasionally goes to bathhouses and lets other men give him oral-genital sex.

_____ 65. Mary's gender identity is not consistent with her anatomical gender.

_____ 66. Steve is 19 years old and his only sexual experiences have been with women, but all his sexual fantasies are about men.

a. probably heterosexual
b. probably homosexual
c. probably bisexual
d. probably transsexual
e. not enough information to make a guess

C.   FILL IN THE BLANKS

67. In lesbian relationships, rubbing the genitals together is called _____.

68. In this book, sexual orientation is defined as distinct preferences consistently made after _____ in the presence of clear alternatives.

69. Humphreys (1970) called the practice of men giving oral sex to other men in public bathrooms _____ _____.

70. _____ and _____ believed (incorrectly) that homosexuality resulted from reversed gender roles.

71. Freud called individuals who kept their homosexual tendencies hidden from their conscious mind _____ _____.

72. Simon LeVay found that a part of the brain called the _____ was different in heterosexuals and homosexuals.

73. Researchers believe that hormones may affect sexual orientation during what time of life? _____

74. In this chapter, it is concluded that biological factors probably _____ individuals to a particular sexual orientation.

75. Many homosexuals refer to heterosexuals as _____.

76. The four stages of the coming out process are: (a) _____, (b) _____, (c) _____, and (d) _____.

77. Bell and Weinberg (1978) described homosexuals who were happy in their sexual orientation and in a monogamous relationship as _____ .

78. Many male homosexuals have changed their sexual lifestyles because of _____ .

79. Name four nonliving homosexuals who made significant contributions to humankind: (a) _____ , (b) _____ , (c) _____ , and (d) _____ .

CHAPTER 10 INTERACTIVE REVIEW

People are sexual beings from the moment of birth. In infancy, self-stimulation of the genitals is motivated by a general attempt to explore the body and seek pleasure. As children grow, their curiosity about their bodies continues and, during early childhood, reaches a peak in the (1)_____ -year age period. Early childhood games such as "house" or "doctor" allow exploration of same-sex and opposite-sex individuals. In the initial school-age years, children develop a sense of (2)_____ . Although overt sexual play may decrease, curiosity about the human body and sexuality does not.

(3)_____ is the time in life in which an individual becomes capable of reproduction. Many bodily changes occur, the result of changing (4)_____ levels, and these physical changes require many adjustments for young adolescents. Unfortunately, many young teens acquire a negative attitude about their bodies as a result of their parents' reactions to normal events such as menstruation and nocturnal emissions.

Interest in sex increases dramatically at puberty and earlier childhood games evolve into more erotic and consciously sexual games such as "spin the bottle." The most important issue in the lives of most adolescents is (5)_____ , and during these years there is a focus on body image and physical characteristics. Almost all teenaged boys and a majority of girls masturbate, usually accompanied by sexual fantasies. Sex therapists feel that masturbation is a safe and healthy sexual outlet for teenagers. Adolescents' interpersonal sexual experiences generally begin with holding hands, followed in order by embracing, (6)_____ , (7)_____ , and, for many, sexual intercourse. Surveys find that most boys and girls have engaged in sexual intercourse by age (8)_____ , and nearly three fourths have done so by the time they complete high school. For some teens, however, sexual relations is not a positive experience, yet many engage in it because of (9)_____ . The teenage pregnancy rate in the United States is one of the highest among industrialized countries.

The average age at marriage has steadily increased into the mid-twenties. Most young adults believe that premarital sex, especially in a "serious" relationship, is acceptable. Most have also had two or more sexual partners, often in a lifestyle pattern called (10)_____ .

By the time people are in their mid-twenties, most people's sexual lifestyle is characterized by (11)_____ , either in marriage or cohabitation. In all cultures the idealistic goal is a (12)_____ . Throughout the world, men value female promiscuity when pursuing short-term relationships, but when choosing a long-term mate, men in most cultures value (13)_____ . When choosing a long-term mate, women generally prefer men who can offer them (14)_____ . Despite the ideal, about a third of married men and about a quarter of married women eventually engage in extramarital relations. Some do so with the consent of their mate.

Most young adults underestimate the frequency of sex practiced by older adults. Sexual activity is highest for people in their (15)_____ , and only gradually declines up through the early 60's. Surveys indicate that married people have sex more often than singles and are happier with their sex lives than are singles. Still, over half of all marriages in the United States end in divorce. About three fourths of divorced people remarry, and for some marriage is just another form of serial monogamy.

As women grow older their menstrual cycles become irregular and eventually stop entirely, called (16)_____ . This usually occurs in the late forties or early fifties, and the change in hormones can result in hot flashes, a decrease in (17)_____ , and osteoporosis. These conditions can be reversed with (18)_____ replacement therapy. Experts feel that men normally do not experience menopause, but they do show a gradual decline in (19)_____ beginning in their late teens. This also results in some physical changes such as a decline in muscle mass and strength, less firm erections, less forceful ejaculations, and longer (20)_____ periods. However, most elderly people continue to enjoy sexual relations as long as they remain otherwise healthy and have a partner. For healthy couples, the best predictor of whether or not they will enjoy sex in old age is (21)_____ .

CHAPTER 10 SELF-TEST

A.   TRUE OR FALSE

T F   22. Ultrasound recordings have found male fetuses to have erections while still inside the uterus.

T F   23. Children cannot masturbate to orgasm until puberty.

T F   24. The growth of pubic hair on girls is the result of increased levels of testosterone.

T F   25. If a child is found engaging in sexual exploration games with another child of the same sex before age seven it means the child is probably gay.

T	F	26. Gagnon believes that teenage masturbation is the single most powerful predictor of adult sexuality.
T	F	27. Couples who lived together before marriage are less likely than other couples to get divorced.
T	F	28. In a study of 202 men and women aged 80 to 102, it was found that nearly half still engaged in sexual intercourse.
T	F	29. The lack of vaginal lubrication in women who have undergone menopause is an indicator that their sex life is coming to an end.
T	F	30. The average married couple in their twenties or thirties has sex more often than young singles.
T	F	31. Adults almost always quit masturbating after they are married.
T	F	32. The average age at which girls have their first menstrual cycle has been decreasing over the last two centuries.
T	F	33. "Hot flashes" are due, in part, to increasing levels of pituitary hormones.
T	F	34. Sexual fantasies are the same for males and females during adolescence.
T	F	35. The best predictor of sexual activity for older women is the amount of vaginal lubrication when they were younger.
T	F	36. A heart attack almost always causes older males to become impotent.
T	F	37. Boys often develop enlarged breasts during puberty.
T	F	38. Early studies found that babies could die from emotional neglect.
T	F	39. In early childhood it is normal for children to engage in sexual behaviors that imitate adults.
T	F	40. The way parents react to the sexuality of their children is generally an indication of the way they feel about their own sexuality.
T	F	41. Most U.S. children develop a sense of modesty about exposing their bodies in public beginning in kindergarten.
T	F	42. There is no physical reason why elderly couples cannot continue to have sexual intercourse.
T	F	43. In terms of hormone changes with aging, men's and women's hormone changes are very much alike.
T	F	44. In men, the production of sperm generally stops by the early fifties.
T	F	45. Most women show a decreased interest in sex after menopause.
T	F	46. In some cultures hot flashes are uncommon among postmenopausal women.
T	F	47. Pubertal development in boys lags about 2 years behind development in girls.
T	F	48. If an adult male is castrated, it substantially raises his voice.
T	F	49. Girls as young as 6 or 7 have given birth.
T	F	50. Most teenage girls experience severe pain during their first sexual intercourse.
T	F	51. The sexual activity of young adults is generally different from younger and older age groups.
T	F	52. Most young adults limit their premarital sexual activity to "serious" relationships.
T	F	53. Men and women are more likely to be upset at their partner having a sexual relationship with someone else than they are about them having an emotional attachment.
T	F	54. There is a good relationship between social background (religious and political views) and whether or not one engages in extramarital affairs.
T	F	55. The divorce rate for open-marriage couples is lower than that for sexually monogamous couples.

B.   MATCHING: WHICH HORMONE CHANGES ARE MOST LIKELY ASSOCIATED WITH THE FOLLOWING PHYSICAL OR BEHAVIORAL CHANGES?

_____ 56. breast development in girls

_____ 57. vaginal dryness at menopause

_____ 58. hot flashes in women

_____ 59. development of sweat glands (body odor, acne)

a. increase in estrogen
b. decrease in estrogen
c. increase in testosterone
d. decrease in testosterone
e. increase in FSH and LH

———— 60. gynecomastia

———— 61. pubic hair and body hair

———— 62. menarche

———— 63. less firm erection and longer refractory period

———— 64. reverses effects of menopause

———— 65. decreased sexual desire in women (review from Chapter 3)

———— 66. decreased sexual desire in men (review from Chapter 3)

C. FILL IN THE BLANKS

67. The decline in sexual activity among older, single women is most often due to _____.

68. When sexual development begins before age 9 it is called _____.

69. According to Jean Piaget, before the age of 2 children are _____.

70. The change that occurs in women in the few years that precede and follow menopause is called _____.

71. Before age 2, bodily exploration is usually confined to _____.

72. Freud referred to what in this chapter is called the initial school-age years as the _____ stage of psychosexual development.

73. Development of breasts and growth of facial hair are examples of _____.

74. The first experience many males have with ejaculation is a "wet dream" or _____.

75. For many teenage girls, the need for _____ is an important part of finding their self-identity.

76. Throughout the world men tend to engage in casual sex to _____.

77. About 80 percent of all societies allow men to _____.

78. Women are most concerned about _____ infidelity by their mates.

79. Whitehurst believes that the two things most likely to lead to extramarital sex are _____ and _____.

80. From the thirties to the early sixties the frequency of sexual intercourse _____.

CHAPTER 11 INTERACTIVE REVIEW

This chapter presents several normal, adult sexual behaviors. "Normal" is defined from a statistical point of view, and is best thought of as a (1)_____ of behaviors or values. Thus, you should not regard yourself as abnormal if you have not engaged in all the behaviors discussed here.

Historically, masturbation has been presented as unnatural, immoral, and bad for one's physical and mental health. In his landmark surveys of 1948 and 1953, (2)_____ found that (3)_____ percent of men and (4)_____ percent of women had masturbated, thus demonstrating that it was, in fact, a very normal human sexual behavior. Modern medicine has also shown that masturbation has no negative medical consequences. Most men and women masturbate even when they are in sexual relationships. Most men, and probably most women, have also experienced orgasms during sleep, called (5)_____. They occur during a stage of sleep called (6)_____ , during which all men in good health (7)_____ and women experience (8)_____.

Compared to men, sexual fantasies by women tend to be just as explicit but more (9)_____. Although at times very sexually explicit, a fantasy does not mean that a person would actually want to do what he or she has fantasized. Fantasies are usually not an indication of sexual unhappiness or personality/psychological disorders.

The most common position of sexual intercourse in the United States is (10)_____-on-top, also called the (11)_____ position. However, there is no "correct" way of having sexual intercourse, except that which is right for you and your partner. Making your sexual encounters spontaneous, exciting, fulfilling, and not ritualized may mean exploring a variety of times, places, and positions.

Oral-genital sexual relations (properly referred to as (12)_____ and (13)_____) as a form of sexual expression has increased tremendously in popularity since Kinsey's time. In addition, a considerable number of heterosexual couples have tried anal intercourse on at least one occasion. However, just because many people may be exploring a particular form of expression does not mean it fits into everyone's value system.

A healthy and satisfying sexual relationship can contribute to one's overall physical and emotional well-being. (14)_____ individuals consider sex to be a positive and good thing, and feel free to choose when, where, and with whom to engage in a particular sexual activity.

CHAPTER 11 SELF-TEST

A.   TRUE OR FALSE

[T] [F]   15. People who masturbate to excess run the risk of serious medical problems.

[T] [F]   16. Kellogg's corn flakes and Graham crackers were developed as foods to prevent youthful masturbation.

[T] [F]   17. Women do not have nocturnal orgasms.

[T] [F]   18. Substantially more men have sexual fantasies than women.

[T] [F]   19. A person can be sexually healthy and choose not to have oral-genital sex, or even sexual intercourse.

[T] [F]   20. Male-on-top is the preferred position of intercourse in all but a few cultures.

[T] [F]   21. Masturbation is normal for men, but not for women.

[T] [F]   22. Studies have found that males masturbate in more varieties of ways than do females.

[T] [F]   23. Assuming that neither person has a sexually transmitted disease, oral-genital sex is no less hygienic than kissing.

[T] [F]   24. Most married people who masturbate do so because they are unhappy in their sexual relationships.

[T] [F]   25. The content of sexual fantasies usually does not indicate sexual unhappiness or personality/psychological problems.

[T] [F]   26. Therapists sometimes instruct their clients how to masturbate in order to help overcome sexual problems.

[T] [F]   27. "Wet dreams" are dreams with a sexual theme.

[T] [F]   28. Fantasizing about another person while having sex with your partner is usually an indication of a serious relationship problem.

[T] [F]   29. Hunt's survey found that most couples have had sexual intercourse in more than one position.

[T] [F]   30. No other behavior has increased as much in popularity since Kinsey's time as oral-genital sex.

[T] [F]   31. Anal intercourse between men and women is often a sign of latent homosexuality.

[T] [F]   32. Men's sexual fantasies are more explicit than women's.

[T] [F]   33. Surveys have consistently found that over 90 percent of men have masturbated by age 20.

[T] [F]   34. Generally speaking, men have sexual fantasies more often than women.

[T] [F]   35. More people with sexual partners masturbate than people who do not have a sexual partner.

B.   MATCHING (THE QUESTIONS HAVE MULTIPLE ANSWERS)

_____ 36. probably a sexually healthy person

_____ 37. probably a sexually unhealthy person

_____ 38. not enough information to tell

a. a 24-year-old man who has never had sexual relations
b. a 20-year-old woman who has had 15 sexual partners
c. a 20-year-old woman who is abstaining from sex, but is looking forward to sexual relations in a long-term relationship
d. a 20-year-old man who has had 15 sexual partners
e. someone who has had oral-genital sex and sexual intercourse in many positions
f. a male who engages in sex with many partners to prove to his peers his sexuality
g. someone who refuses to try oral-genital sex
h. a man who has had many sexual partners and regards them as sluts
i. someone who doesn't like oral-genital sex but always agrees to it
j. someone who engages in sex because they have low self-esteem
k. someone who has had many partners and regards his or her experiences positively
l. someone who masturbates every day
m. someone who has always been faithful to his or her partner and who feels guilty about desires to have sex with him or her
n. someone who enjoys trying new sexual experiences with his or her partner, but chooses not to engage in anal sex

C.   FILL IN THE BLANKS

39. Oral stimulation of a woman's genitals is called _____.

40. Approximately every 90 minutes during sleep, females experience _____ and males experience _____.

41. Couples should not engage in anal and vaginal intercourse without washing in between because _____ _____.

42. Perhaps the most common type of fantasy during sexual intercourse is _____.

43. The main reason that many people continue to masturbate after forming a sexual relationship is _____ _____.

44. Couples who always have sex in the same place and in the same manner risk letting their sex lives become _____.

45. Laumann and colleagues (1994) found that the two sexual behaviors most preferred by Americans are _____ and _____.

46. Laumann and colleagues also found that masturbation is mostly a reflection of _____.

47. The preferred manner of sexual intercourse in all known cultures is _____ .

48. _____ is the position of intercourse usually preferred in cultures where a woman's sexual satisfaction is considered to be as important as the man's.

49. Victorian-era physicians incorrectly believed that nocturnal emissions were caused by the same thing that causes _____ .

50. A sexually healthy person is someone who (a) _____ , and (b) _____ .

CHAPTER 12 INTERACTIVE REVIEW

There have probably been as many definitions and descriptions of love as there have been poets, philosophers, and scientists (who study love). Recent work has shown that although friendship and romantic love share many characteristics, romantic lovers differ from friends in terms of their (1)_____, (2)_____, (3)_____, and willingness to give the utmost when the other is in need. The feeling of romantic love initially includes physiological arousal, but it requires a (4)_____ to interpret the responses as love. Feelings of passion almost always decrease with time, and long-term happy relationships are based more on togetherness, trust, sharing, and affection, or what is called (5)_____ love.

The ability to love another person requires (6)_____ and (7)_____. (8)_____ is an emotional state that is aroused by a perceived threat to a valued relationship. It is more common in people who have low (9)_____ and/or who are personally unhappy in their lives, or who put great value on things like (10)_____. Love and sex share many things in common, but it is possible to enjoy sex without emotional involvement, and also possible to love without having sexual relations. Love can be (11)_____ and depend on another person's ability to satisfy our needs and desires, or it can be (12)_____ and not depend on the loved one meeting certain expectations and desires.

Robert Sternberg has suggested that liking, loving, and all other positive emotions we feel for other individuals can be understood by the combination of three components: intimacy, passion, and decision/commitment. By this triangular theory, (13)_____ is intimacy alone without passion or commitment. (14)_____ is liking plus feelings of passion without commitment, while (15)_____ love is intimacy and commitment without passion. (16)_____ love, or what Sternberg believes to be true love, requires all three components together.

In contrast to Sternberg, John Lee does not believe that there is only one type of love that should be viewed as true love. He proposes that there are many styles of loving. (17)_____ is based on an ideal of physical perfection; (18)_____ grows from friendship; (19)_____ is rational and practical; (20)_____ involves an intense emotional dependency; (21)_____ is self-centered; and (22)_____ puts the interest of the loved person first. According to Lee, the degree of happiness an individual feels in a loving relationship depends greatly on how well his or her love-style (23)_____ that of the loved one.

Relationships that last are generally more realistic than idealistic and based on companionship and affection rather than on passion. In order to maintain a relationship, a couple must substitute new shared activities for old ones as their lives change, and they also must develop skills to achieve greater (24)_____, those feelings and experiences that promote closeness and bondedness.

CHAPTER 12 SELF-TEST

A.   TRUE OR FALSE

[T] [F]   25. People rate best friends and lovers similarly on characteristics such as acceptance, trust, respect, mutual assistance, and understanding.

[T] [F]   26. Romantic relationships are generally more rewarding than friendships, but they are also more volatile and frustrating.

[T] [F]   27. According to Lee, a good match generally results from two love-styles that are far apart on his color wheel chart.

[T] [F]   28. According to Lee, love-styles are fixed and repetitive.

[T] [F]   29. As a general rule, people are most attracted to opposites.

[T] [F]   30. The decision and commitment to love another person without intimacy or passion is experienced as empty love, according to Sternberg.

[T] [F]   31. In the initiation of a relationship, men attach greater importance to physical attractiveness than do women.

[T] [F]   32. Long periods of sexual deprivation (including masturbation) can result in death for an adult.

[T] [F]   33. Contrary to popular belief, men are no more likely than women to enjoy sex without emotional involvement.

T ☐   F ☐   34. One of the major predictors of marital success is the number of pleasurable activities the couple shares.

T ☐   F ☐   35. Within a monogamous relationship, sexual intercourse and affection are synonymous.

T ☐   F ☐   36. Jealousy is most common in cultures that allow polygyny.

T ☐   F ☐   37. Men and women respond to jealousy in much the same way.

T ☐   F ☐   38. Feelings of romantic love are associated with the release of amphetamine-like chemicals in the brain.

T ☐   F ☐   39. The manner in which one is raised is important for acquiring a positive self-concept.

T ☐   F ☐   40. Self-disclosure is always important in a relationship, and the timing or mutuality of it does not really matter.

T ☐   F ☐   41. Men and women are most likely to become jealous to the perception of a partner's sexual infidelity.

T ☐   F ☐   42. Romantic love tends to be unconditional.

T ☐   F ☐   43. Anthropologists have found that romantic love is an idealized notion that is found almost exclusively in industrialized cultures where emphasis is on the individual.

T ☐   F ☐   44. Babies who are deprived of physical contact may sicken or die.

T ☐   F ☐   45. In order for a couple to become more intimate, it is important to withhold their negative feelings about each other.

T ☐   F ☐   46. Theoretically, humans are probably not capable of true agape.

B. MATCHING

_____ 47. agapic love

_____ 48. attachment

_____ 49. companionate love

_____ 50. conditional love

_____ 51. consummate love

_____ 52. empty love

_____ 53. erotic love

_____ 54. fatuous love

_____ 55. infatuated love

_____ 56. ludic love

_____ 57. manic love

_____ 58. pragmatic love

_____ 59. romantic love

_____ 60. storgic love

_____ 61. unconditional love

a. a highly idealized love based on physical beauty; these type of lovers are inclined to feel "love at first sight," but it usually doesn't last long

b. based on partner satisfying certain needs and desires; Maslow called it deficiency love

c. an affectionate type of love that develops from friendship slowly over time

d. results when commitment is made on the basis of passion without the experience of intimacy; leads to whirlwind romances that usually end when the passion starts to fade

e. a selfless love-style that puts the interest of the loved person ahead of his or her own, even if it means great sacrifice

f. does not depend on the loved one meeting certain expectations and desires; Maslow called it (being love)

g. commitment without intimacy or passion; often the first stage in arranged marriages

h. one's partner gives few positive rewards, other than predictability, for remaining in the relationship

i. a self-centered love in which the lover avoids commitment and treats love like a game

j. occurs when there is passionate arousal and liking without commitment; results from two people being drawn together both physically and emotionally

k. results when passion is felt in the absence of intimacy and commitment, and thus the lover is obsessed with the other person as an ideal; similar to what Lee calls erotic love

l. characterized by an intense emotional dependency on the attention and affection of the partner; "head over heels" love in which one is obsessed with the loved one

m. found only in relationships that include intimacy, passion, and commitment

n. the combination of intimacy and commitment without passion; based on togetherness, trust, sharing, and affection

o. a rational or practical style of love; this type of lover consciously looks for a compatible mate (a "good match")

C.   FILL IN THE BLANKS

62.   Infatuated love in Sternberg's model most closely resembles _____ in Lee's theoretical model.

63.   Companionate love in Sternberg's model most closely resembles _____ in Lee's theoretical model.

64.   St. Augustine's idea of love ("I want you to be") is probably closest to _____ in Lee's theoretical model.

65.   In order to experience complete love in Sternberg's model, a relationship must have _____, _____ , and _____ .

66.   According to Freud, love is the result of _____ .

67.   Davis and others report that most romantic lovers find that their mood depends on _____ of their feelings more so than in friendships.

68.   Feelings of romantic love are associated with an increase in three brain chemicals called _____, _____ , and _____ .

69.   Companionate love is often referred to as _____ love because it is not based on the fantasies and ideals of romantic love.

70.   In Hazen and Shaver's attachment theory of love, adults who do not fear abandonment and find it easy to get close to others are called _____ lovers.

71.   People who put great value on things like popularity, wealth, fame, and physical attractiveness are more likely than others to _____ .

72.   As a general rule, women are much more likely than men to experience jealousy to a partner's _____ infidelity.

73.   Dorothy Tennov coined the term _____ to describe extreme "head over heels" love in which one is obsessed with the loved one. This would be experienced in the type of love Lee called _____ .

74.   In Lee's model, _____ lovers feel that the act of loving is more important than the partner for whom it is expressed, and thus feel fulfilled even if their love is not reciprocated.

75.   Elaine Hatfield has suggested that couples can achieve greater intimacy by (a) _____, (b) _____ , (c) _____ , and (d) _____ .

76.   A large component of passion is novelty and fantasy. The decline of passion in a relationship is almost inevitable because of _____ .

CHAPTER 13 INTERACTIVE REVIEW

Studies have found that (1)_____ of all couples in the United States will eventually experience sexual problems. While some couples may grow apart and experience a variety of relationship problems (sex being just one indicator that there are other problems), even couples with a good relationship can experience sexual problems. It is common for two people in a relationship to differ in their preference for frequency and type of sex. This often results from different expectations and assumptions about sex. When this happens, it is best to consider the problem as the (2)_____ problem. If the problem persists and is causing stress and anxiety, it is advisable to seek professional help.

Sex therapists are trained to (3)_____ . They consider it unethical to (4)_____ . Most sexual problems are treated with (5)_____ developed by Masters and Johnson, psychosexual therapy, or a combination of both. Sexual therapy programs generally have many things in common and follow the (6)_____ model, an acronym for permission, limited information, specific suggestions, and intensive therapy. Each represents a successively more in-depth level of therapy. Most therapists will probably take a (7)_____ and (8)_____ history first. Some clients will need self-awareness exercises, but for most couples the first set of general exercises will be nondemand mutual pleasuring techniques called (9)_____ . After completing these, the couple will then be assigned specific exercises.

Many therapists believe that the most common problem of couples going to therapy is (10)_____ . This refers to a persistent and pervasive inhibition of sexual desire. In its most extreme form the avoidance of sex becomes phobic in nature and is called (11)_____ . This generally requires psychosexual therapy. At the other extreme, hypersexual individuals are distinguished by the (12)_____ with which they engage in sex. A controversial term for these persons is (13)_____ . Painful intercourse, or (14)_____ , can occur in either men or women, and can have a variety of causes, both organic and psychological.

The most common sexual problem specific to males is probably (15)_____ , which is usually defined as a recurrent and persistent absence of (16)_____ . Probably the most psychologically devastating male problem is (17)_____ , which can have organic and/or psychological causes. The most common psychological cause is (18)_____ . Difficulty reaching orgasm and ejaculating in a woman's vagina is called (19)_____ and usually has a psychological cause. Some men suffer from benign coital cephalalgia, or (20)_____ , while others suffer from long-lasting (often painful) erections, a condition called (21)_____ .

Some women experience involuntary contractions of the muscles surrounding the vaginal opening when they attempt intercourse, which results in pain. (22)_____ , as it is called, usually has a psychological cause. The vast majority of women who go to sexual therapy do so because of problems (23)_____ . This can be due to a variety of causes, including poor techniques by the partner, sexual repression during upbringing, and general relationship problems. It is not unusual when one member of a couple has a sexual problem for the partner to develop a corresponding sexual difficulty.

Homosexuals can have many of the same sexual problems experienced by heterosexuals, but often experience additional problems that arise from dealing with (24)_____ and/or (25)_____ .

CHAPTER 13 SELF-TEST

A. TRUE OR FALSE

[T] [F]   26. Bob wants to have sex twice a week, but is in a relationship with Sue, who wants to have sex every day. In this example, it is clear that Sue is hypersexual.

[T] [F]   27. Psychoanalysis has proven to be the most effective technique for treating most sexual problems.

[T] [F]   28. The most frequent sexual problem for women is difficulty reaching orgasm.

[T] [F]   29. Stimulation of the clitoris during intercourse should not be necessary, and a woman should be able to be orgasmic through intercourse alone.

[T] [F]   30. Sex therapists generally treat sexual problems by having sexual relations with their clients.

[T] [F]   31. Vaginismus is usually caused by psychological factors.

[T] [F]   32. Performance anxiety can cause sexual problems in men, but not women.

[T] [F]   33. The American Psychiatric Association defines a premature ejaculator as any male who usually reaches orgasm within 2 minutes of beginning sexual intercourse.

[T]   [F]   34. Most women who have difficulty reaching orgasm do not enjoy sex.

[T]   [F]   35. In order to help their clients, most sex therapists require that the clients stop masturbation.

[T]   [F]   36. Dyspareunia is usually caused by a physical problem.

[T]   [F]   37. Many men with psychologically caused erectile problems get full erections during sensate focus exercises.

[T]   [F]   38. Sexual problems in one partner in a relationship often lead to sexual problems in the other partner.

[T]   [F]   39. Masters and Johnson found that the success rate for treating sexual problems in homosexuals was generally higher than that for heterosexuals.

[T]   [F]   40. Female orgasm problems are always the result of insufficient stimulation.

[T]   [F]   41. Men and women often have different ideas about sex and affection.

[T]   [F]   42. If it feels good to you, it must feel good to your partner.

[T]   [F]   43. Most sex therapists today are omitting the medical history because most sex problems are psychologically caused.

[T]   [F]   44. Sexual surrogates are mostly former prostitutes.

[T]   [F]   45. Therapists are in agreement that hypersexuality is a form of addiction similar to addiction to alcohol or drugs.

[T]   [F]   46. Erectile problems are inevitable as men grow older.

[T]   [F]   47. A majority of erectile problems have a physical basis.

[T]   [F]   48. Headaches during orgasm occur mainly in men.

[T]   [F]   49. The sex therapy model presented in this chapter is applicable to most peoples of the world.

B.   MATCHING: FOR EACH OF THE SEXUAL PROBLEMS BELOW, MATCH WHICH TECHNIQUES THERAPISTS WOULD BE LIKELY TO USE (IN ORDER) ACCORDING TO YOUR TEXT. ANSWERS MAY BE USED MORE THEN ONCE.

_____ 50. hypoactive sexual desire

_____ 51. hypersexuality

_____ 52. dyspareunia

_____ 53. psychological erectile problem

_____ 54. premature ejaculation

_____ 55. male orgasmic disorder

_____ 56. benign coital cephalalgia

_____ 57. vaginismus

_____ 58. female orgasmic disorder

a. sensate focus
b. psychosexual (or psycho-)therapy
c. Kegel exercises
d. bridge maneuver
e. use of dilators
f. resume female-on-top position of intercourse
g. self-exploration and masturbation
h. tease technique
i. treat the internal discomfort (antidepressants or stabilizing drugs)
j. usually organic cause; treat specific organic cause
k. squeeze technique or stop-start technique
l. relaxation techniques or medications for high blood pressure

C.   FILL IN THE BLANK

59. When a man with no previous history of sexual problems starts to experience difficulty getting and/or maintaining an erection, it is called _____ .

60. Most women need stimulation of the _____ in order to reach orgasm, even during intercourse.

61. Most therapists believe that the _____ position has the most erotic potential for both people during intercourse.

62. Sex therapists generally take a medical history of their clients because some sexual problems have a _____ cause.

63. When a person begins to observe and evaluate his or her own sexual responses during sex it is called _____ , and it can be a cause of sexual problems.

64. PLISSIT is an acronym for _____ , _____ , _____ , and _____ .

65. The therapy technique used to reduce anxiety by slowly introducing elements of the anxiety-producing stimulus is called _____ .

66. Sensate focus exercises are _____ techniques.

67. Many therapists classify a person as having hypoactive sexual desire if they initiate an average of _____ _____ sexual experiences a month.

68. In probably half or more of couples who go to therapy for sexual desire problems, one or the other partner has _____ .

69. People who engage in sex compulsively are called _____ .

70. In men, painful intercourse can be caused by the foreskin of the penis being too tight, a condition called _____ .

71. In men, a life stress such as unemployment could lead to _____ .

72. If a man is totally unable to ejaculate in a woman's vagina it is called _____ .

73. Vaginismus is usually caused by _____ .

74. Therapists do not use the term "frigid" to describe women with orgasm problems because _____ .

75. Tantrism emphasizes _____ during sex.

76. Probably the most difficult sexual problem to treat successfully is _____ .

CHAPTER 14 INTERACTIVE REVIEW

This chapter considers three different ways to define a behavior as unconventional or abnormal. The (1)_____ approach defines a behavior as normal if most people do it. Therefore, unconventional behaviors are those that are engaged in by relatively few people. The (2)_____ approach looks at various behaviors to determine if they are customary within a given society. The (3)_____ approach evaluates the behaviors with respect to whether or not they cause an individual to feel distressed or guilty, and/or cause problems functioning efficiently in ordinary social and occupational roles. What is considered to be unconventional depends on the time and (4)_____ in which the behavior is displayed.

Paraphiliacs are individuals whose sexual arousal and gratification (5)_____ on behaviors (or fantasizing about behaviors) that are outside the usual and accepted sexual patterns for adults. Unusual behaviors that are used to enhance sexual activity with a partner, not to compete with him or her, are called (6)_____. (7)_____ refers to achieving sexual arousal when using or fantasizing about an inanimate object or a particular part of the body. (8)_____ refers to achieving sexual arousal and gratification from dressing as a member of the opposite sex. (9)_____ expose their genitals compulsively in inappropriate settings, while (10)_____ repeatedly make obscene phone calls for sexual arousal. (11)_____ prefer to seek sexual gratification by watching people undress(ed) without their knowledge or consent. Zoophiliacs prefer (12)_____ as sexual partners; pedophiliacs prefer (13)_____. (14)_____ intentionally inflict pain and/or humiliation on others for sexual arousal and gratification, while (15)_____ obtain sexual pleasure from having pain and/or humiliation inflicted on them.

Other paraphilias include (16)_____ (sexual arousal by the act of urination), (17)_____ (arousal by feces), (18)_____ (arousal by filth), (19)_____ (arousal by being given an enema), (20)_____ (rubbing one's genitals against others in public places), and necrophilia (sex with (21)_____). Recent studies have found that people who practice paraphilias often engage in more than one type.

The large majority of paraphiliacs are (22)_____. Most describe themselves as heterosexual, but have difficulty maintaining intimate (particularly erotic) relations. The paraphiliacs' behavior(s) allows them to have control over the objects of their sexual arousal. Therapy is generally unsuccessful in eliminating the paraphilia, often because the individual does not want to give it up.

CHAPTER 14 SELF-TEST

A.   TRUE OR FALSE

- [T] [F] 23. Freud considered oral-genital sex to be a sign of impaired psychosexual development.
- [T] [F] 24. All abnormal behaviors are called paraphilias.
- [T] [F] 25. Some of the more common fetishes involve leather, rubber, shoes, feet, and women's undergarments.
- [T] [F] 26. Most men who buy scanty, frilly panties for their female partners have a panty fetish.
- [T] [F] 27. Young children who occasionally dress up in clothing of the opposite sex usually grow up to be transvestites.
- [T] [F] 28. Most transvestites are heterosexual men and married.
- [T] [F] 29. Exhibitionists often behave as if they wish to be caught.
- [T] [F] 30. Strippers and nudists are the most common examples of exhibitionists.
- [T] [F] 31. The best way to react to an exhibitionist is to show disgust.
- [T] [F] 32. Most exhibitionists and voyeurs are harmless.
- [T] [F] 33. Voyeurs often like to go to nudist colonies to observe naked bodies.
- [T] [F] 34. A person may commit bestiality and not have a paraphilia.
- [T] [F] 35. Many child molesters are not pedophiles.
- [T] [F] 36. Sadomasochists act out highly structured scenarios in which pain-inducing behaviors are more symbolic than real.
- [T] [F] 37. About half of sadomasochists are women.
- [T] [F] 38. Most men involved in S & M prefer the submissive role, and are well-educated and successful.

☐ T ☐ F   39. Most paraphiliacs have difficulties with intimacy.

☐ T ☐ F   40. Most paraphiliacs wish to be cured.

B.   MATCHING (MATCH THE BEHAVIOR WITH THE NAME OF THE PARAPHILIA THAT *BEST* FITS IT):

_____ 41. bestiality

_____ 42. coprophilia

_____ 43. exhibitionism

_____ 44. fetishism

_____ 45. frotteurism

_____ 46. klismaphilia

_____ 47. masochism

_____ 48. mysophilia

_____ 49. necrophilia

_____ 50. pedophilia

_____ 51. sadism

_____ 52. stigmatophilia

_____ 53. telephone scatologia

_____ 54. transvestism

_____ 55. urophilia

_____ 56. voyeurism

a. Billy must seek crowded places in order to get away with this paraphilia.

b. Henry is trying to find employment in a morgue in order to act out his paraphiliac fantasies.

c. Joe has volunteered to serve as counselor at the elementary school's summer camp to have access to the objects of his sexual arousal.

d. John is highly aroused by watching his partner have a bowel movement.

e. Jim has sneaked out to the barn to find a four-footed sexual partner.

f. Allen is peeking in windows in order to become aroused.

g. Bert is hanging around the laundromat hoping to steal the object of his sexual desire from an unwashed basket of clothing.

h. Carl is crawling on his hands and knees and being pulled by a leash in order to get sexually aroused.

i. Stan asks his partner to urinate on him whenever they have sex.

j. Greg is wearing pink, frilly panties and a bra underneath his suit and tie.

k. Walter is waiting in his car at the grocery parking lot to show his penis to the first woman who walks by.

l. Susan gets highly aroused whenever she ties her partner up and orders him to lick her feet.

m. Sam is getting highly aroused by putting a rod into his urethra.

n. David is describing his erect penis to a woman in his class he has called but does not know.

o. Lenny is becoming highly aroused by his partner's nasal mucus.

p. Paul has paid a prostitute to lay him cross her lap and give him an enema.

C.   FILL IN THE BLANK

57. The first classification of sexual deviations was made by _____.

58. Transvestism is most closely related to _____.

59. Among early North American Indian tribes, a _____ was a highly respected male who cross-dressed and assumed behaviors of women.

60. The most frequently caught paraphiliac offenders are _____.

61. Telephone scatologia is most closely related to _____.

62. You should consider a voyeur to be potentially dangerous if he _____ or _____.

63. A variation of voyeurism in which a person repeatedly seeks sexual arousal by secretly watching sexual acts is called _____.

64. The act of having sex with an animal is called _____.

65. For pedophilia, sex researchers generally define a child as someone who is younger than _____.

66. Weinberg and others have found that the distinctive features in nonclinical sadomasochism are _____ _____ and _____.

67. Coprophiliacs are aroused by _____ or the act of _____.

68. Urophilia, coprophilia, mysophilia, and klismaphilia involve sexual arousal by _____ and thus might be considered specific types of _____.

69. The objects of paraphiliacs' sexual arousal (e.g., pair of used panties, a dead body, an animal, a young child) have in common that they are _____ .

70. If a paraphiliac's inappropriate sexual urges can be controlled, then the most successful therapy is _____ combined with _____ .

71. The _____ explanation for paraphilia is that it arises from society's expectation that men should dominate women.

CHAPTER 15 INTERACTIVE REVIEW

Historically, rape has been viewed as a violation of (1)_____ and victims were treated like "damaged goods." Even today in the United States many states will not prosecute a husband for raping his wife unless there is extreme physical harm to the victim.

There are about 100,000 reported cases of rape in the United States every year, but the actual number of rapes committed is many times greater. Most rapes are committed by (2)_____. Most victims are women between (3)_____ years of age, but anyone can be a victim of rape, including men. Rapists generally plan their crimes and seek victims who appear to be (4)_____.

Studies of convicted rapists reveal that most have (5)_____ IQs, have no history of psychiatric illness, are not oversexed, and have normal social skills. However, many were physically or sexually abused as children, or come from families in which they witnessed abuse by the father of the mother. Most rapists are (6)_____ men who repeat the crime and who lack internal controls and (7)_____.

Rape by a date or an acquaintance is no less real than rape by a stranger. Rape is rape. About 25 percent of college women have been forced into sex when they did not want to. About 15–33 percent of college men admit to using force to have sex on a date, while two thirds admit to using (8)_____ to have sex. Women, too, often use coercion to have sex, but the coercion used by females is generally (9)_____ while that used by males is generally (10)_____. Many adolescents and young adults believe that a man has the right to force a date to have sexual intercourse under some circumstances. Poor communication skills regarding sexual intentions also contribute to unwanted sexual activities.

Many rapes involve more than one assailant and these (11)_____ rapes are usually more violent than rapes committed by individuals. Marital rape, too, is often accompanied by severe beatings and physical abuse. Most states have laws that make it illegal for an adult to have sex with anyone under the age of consent—this is generally called (12)_____. The mentally handicapped are often protected by these laws as well.

There are several explanations for rape. Psychodynamic theories explain rape as resulting from psychopathology. Studies of convicted rapists have found that rapists can be divided into three types according to their motivation: (13)_____, (14)_____, and (15)_____. For these men, rape is not a crime of passion; it is a crime of violence and aggression. Based on what we now know of date rapists, some researchers have proposed a fourth type of rapist, the (16)_____ rapist, for whom the primary motivation is sex. Recent studies have shown that cultural factors, social learning, and interpersonal factors (a lack of shared meaning between men and women) also help explain why rape occurs. Rape is almost nonexistent in some societies, but is common in countries like the United States that promote and glorify (17)_____, and where large numbers of people conform to conservative stereotypic gender roles and men view relationships between the two sexes as (18)_____.

Many mistaken beliefs about rape are so widespread that they are called myths. The chapter considered four rape myths: (19)_____, (20)_____, (21)_____, and women frequently make false accusations of rape. None of these are true, but people who believe them tend to blame the victim for being raped.

Rape victims experience short- and long-term reactions in what is called (22)_____. In the acute phase a victim's reactions may be either expressive or (23)_____. In the period of (24)_____ the victim attempts to regain control of her or his life. Long-term sexual problems are not uncommon. The reactions of a victim's partner and family are important to the recovery process and it is crucial that they do not attribute blame to the victim.

If you are ever raped, it is important to report the crime immediately and get a medical exam as soon as possible. Do not wash, douche, or change clothes until the exam is completed. Today, most police forces have specially trained units, including counselors, to work with rape victims, and the U.S. Supreme Court has approved broad (25)_____ laws to protect victims from feeling like they are on trial during court proceedings.

There are three basic approaches to rape prevention. One focuses on the rapists and advocates the creation of safer physical environments and tougher laws and punishments. Another focuses on potential victims and suggests educating women to be less vulnerable to assault. The third, a (26)_____ perspective, advocates changing societal values and attitudes as to how men and women interact with one another.

Unwelcome sexual advances, requests for sexual favors, and other unwanted verbal or physical conduct of a sexual nature in the workplace or classroom is called (27)_____. The Supreme Court has ruled that this also includes the creation of a hostile or offensive work environment, and that a victim does not have to prove that sexual favors were demanded in exchange for job benefits. Companies and schools can be held liable for not taking immediate and appropriate corrective action.

We now know that sexual abuse of children is more widespread than previously believed. Most victims are molested by (28)_____. We can divide child molesters into two classifications: the (29)_____ molester or pedophile whose primary sexual orientation is to children, and the (30)_____ molester whose primary sexual interests are toward adults. Pedophiles have been further classified according to their psychological characteristics as either (31)_____ , (32)_____ , or aggressive. Of pedophiles who have been caught, those who target girls average about 20 victims each, while those who target boys average nearly (33)_____ victims each. Heterosexual pedophiles outnumber homosexual pedophiles by 11 to 1. The effects on children are often long-lasting, but there is no single "post-sexual-abuse-syndrome."

Sexual relations between relatives (who are too closely related to marry) is called incest. (34)_____ incest is five times more common than parent-child incest, although father(stepfather)-daughter incest accounts for 80 percent of arrests. Incestuous fathers often appear to be shy and family-oriented publicly, but are dominating and authoritarian in their own homes. In these cases, the mothers are usually aware that the incest is going on. Because the abuse in father-child incest is usually frequent and long term, the victims generally have a variety of long-lasting problems. It is important for children who have been sexually abused to receive counseling and support from professionals and organizations familiar with sexual abuse.

CHAPTER 15 SELF-TEST

A. TRUE OR FALSE

T F   35. An adult woman cannot be raped if she *truly* does not want to be raped.

T F   36. Rapists are generally young men who have a consenting sexual partner.

T F   37. Groth et al. (1977) found that rape was the sexual expression of aggression, not the aggressive expression of sexuality.

T F   38. Rape was originally considered to be a crime against a man's property.

T F   39. In about half of the 50 states, a husband cannot be prosecuted for rape of his wife unless there is extraordinary violence.

T F   40. The percentage of reported rapes that are false is lower than for most other crimes.

T F   41. Anyone can be a victim of rape, including any man.

T F   42. The majority of acquaintance rapes are reported to police, but never prosecuted.

T F   43. If a woman willingly engages in necking or petting with a man, she cannot charge him with rape if he then forces her to have sexual intercourse.

T F   44. Rapists are more likely to initiate their crimes outdoors than indoors.

T F   45. Most rapists prefer victims who are feisty and who will try to physically resist.

T F   46. Most rapists believe that their victims want to have sex with them, or deserve to be raped.

T F   47. About 55 percent of rapists are found to be psychotic.

T F   48. Date rape is not as real as rape by a stranger.

T F   49. Muehlenhard and colleagues found that over one third of college women had said "no" to a date when they really meant "yes" (to having sex).

T F   50. Well over half of young, adolescent boys and girls believe that a husband has the right to force his wife to have sexual intercourse against her will.

T F   51. Males who participate in gang rape tend to be younger than rapists who act alone.

T F   52. A man cannot be convicted of rape if the female agreed to have sexual intercourse.

T F   53. A man cannot be raped by a woman.

T F   54. Women who are raped usually have done something to provoke it.

T F   55. Many victims of rape do not show any emotional reactions afterwards.

T F   56. A man who tells sexual jokes, makes sexual references, and/or stares obsessively at a female co-worker cannot be prosecuted for sexual harassment unless he demands sexual favors.

T F   57. About 80 percent of all child molesters are known by their victims.

T F   58. Most pedophiles were themselves sexually abused as children.

T F   59. Pedophile is the term used by the American Psychiatric Association for all child molesters.

T ☐ F ☐ 60. Men who molest children generally begin their deviate behavior as teenagers.

T ☐ F ☐ 61. The Supreme Court has ruled that people being prosecuted for child sexual abuse have a constitutional right to face their accuser in court.

T ☐ F ☐ 62. Fathers who commit incest appear to most people to be quite average.

T ☐ F ☐ 63. In families with father-child incest, the large majority of mothers do not try to protect their children.

T ☐ F ☐ 64. Incestuous inbreeding (first cousins or closer in relation) is a universal taboo.

T ☐ F ☐ 65. Victims of sexual abuse tend to blame themselves.

B. MATCHING

_____ 66. aggressive pedophile

_____ 67. anger rapist

_____ 68. opportunistic rapist

_____ 69. personally immature pedophile

_____ 70. power rapist

_____ 71. preference molester

_____ 72. regressive pedophile

_____ 73. sadistic rapist

_____ 74. sexual harasser

_____ 75. situational molester

a. Herbert feels insecure and inadequate. He commits rape to reassure himself of his sexual adequacy, strength, and potency.

b. Frank's sexual urges are primarily toward adults, but he has fondled a child and had the child touch his penis. He considers his behavior abnormal.

c. Jim tells crude sexual jokes and makes sexual references to his female employees.

d. Steve has sex with prepubescent boys and beats them before and afterwards.

e. Joe is sexually aroused and impulsively forces his date to have sex with him when they are alone.

f. Albert loves it when his rape victims try to resist and enjoys hurting them for a prolonged time.

g. David has never had a successful relationship with a woman and seeks out children, who he can control, for sexual gratification.

h. Mike has no interest in adults as sexual partners. His sexual orientation is to children only.

i. Robert rapes because he despises all women, who he blames for his lack of success.

j. Tom has always had sexual relations with adults, but work and marital problems have led him to drink, and while feeling sexually inadequate, he molests a child.

C. FILL IN THE BLANKS

76. Mentally handicapped people are often protected against sexual abuse by the same laws that protect _____ .

77. Russell and Howell (1983) estimated that a woman living in the United States has a one in _____ chance of being raped in her lifetime.

78. The majority of rapists were _____ prior to the attack.

79. Give four examples of sexually coercive behavior: _____ , _____ , _____ , and _____ .

80. Give two characteristics of cultures that are "rape-free": _____ and _____ .

81. In _____ rape, the individual responsibility for things a person does can be diffused or forgotten.

82. Statutory rape laws make it illegal to have sex with anyone _____ .

83. A recent study found that _____ distinguishes the victims of male rape from other men.

84. Psychodynamic theories of rape explain it as resulting from _____ .

85. The majority of date rapes are probably committed by _____ rapists.

86. Men who look at scenes of aggression toward women become _____.

87. Men who normally are not aroused by rape scenes are likely to become aroused by such scenes if _____ or _____ .

88. A person who believes in rape myths is likely to _____ the victims.

89. In the _____ of the rape trauma syndrome, victims attempt to regain control of their lives.

90. Most large cities now have rape victim advocate programs that provide rape victims with _____.

91. In cases of rape where there is semen, rapists can be positively identified by _____.

92. A problem with the approaches to preventing rape that focus on laws and punishment and teaching women how best to avoid rape is that these approaches _____.

93. Charges of sexual harassment are usually prosecuted as civil suits under Title VII of the _____ of 1964.

94. Sexual harassment usually occurs in a relationship where there is _____.

95. Research has shown that the more a male believes in _____, the more accepting he is of sexual harassment.

96. A man who repeatedly prefers children for achieving sexual excitement is called a _____.

97. For the previous question, "children" refers to persons under the age of _____.

98. The least common type of pedophile is the _____.

99. Your text suggests that the best way to minimize the chance of your child being a victim of sexual abuse is to educate _____ and educate _____ .

100. In _____ families there are both multiple abusers and multiple victims, both across generations and within the same generation.

101. _____ incest is probably the least common type of incest.

102. In cases of father-child incest, a _____ approach is often chosen as therapy.

CHAPTER 16 INTERACTIVE REVIEW

In addition to laws that protect children and nonconsenting adults from sexual abuse, many states also have laws that attempt to regulate the sexual behaviors of consenting adults. Prostitution is illegal in all parts of the United States except for a few counties in (1)_____ . In a recent survey, (2)_____ percent of the male respondents indicated that they had paid for sex on at least one occasion. Female prostitutes can be divided into three types according to status: (3)_____ who solicit in public, brothel prostitutes and (4)_____ , and (5)_____ who generally work out of their own apartment. Male prostitutes who cater to homosexuals are called (6)_____ . The primary reason most individuals engage in prostitution is (7)_____ . Most prostitutes were sexually or physically abused as children and were loners. Most customers are white, (8)_____ , and (9)_____ . Opponents of prostitution argue that it spreads sexually transmitted diseases and is often associated with other crimes. Proponents of legalization argue that licensing and required health checks would reduce both STDs (including HIV infection) and the influence of organized crime.

The sale of sexually explicit material is a multibillion dollar a year business. This could not have happened, of course, if there were not a large demand for such material. According to surveys, about (10)_____ of Americans have seen an X-rated movie or video in the last year. The President's Commission of 1970 and subsequent researchers have generally concluded that exposure to nonviolent sexually explicit material has (11)_____ effect on individuals. Subsequent research has shown that many men are aroused by sexually explicit material depicting violence toward women. Exposure to sexually explicit material with violent themes often results in men becoming (12)_____ toward rape victims, having greater belief in (13)_____ , displaying (14)_____ to women, and indicating a greater likelihood that they would (15)_____ . However, behavioral scientists have concluded that it is the (16)_____ in this material, not (17)_____ , that is potentially harmful.

Most people find some types of sexually explicit material to be offensive, but attempts to censor or ban this material raise questions about First Amendment rights. What is (18)_____ to one person is pornography to another, and who is to decide where to draw the line? The one exception is sexually explicit material involving (19)_____ , for which persons can be prosecuted on the basis of abuse.

Several states have sodomy laws that prohibit (20)_____ and/or (21)_____ sex between consenting adults. Many people believe that they should have the right to decide for themselves what to do in privacy, but the Supreme Court has upheld the constitutionality of these laws.

Additional topics on the legality of sexual behavior are included in Chapters 7 (Pregnancy and Childbirth, see the section on surrogate mothers), 9 (Sexual Orientation), and 15 (Sexual Abuse).

CHAPTER 16 SELF-TEST

A. TRUE OR FALSE

T F 22. Most people who become prostitutes do so because of abnormal sexual needs.

T F 23. Kinsey found that in the 1940s, a majority of white males had had sex with a prostitute.

T F 24. When exposed to sexually explicit material, most people show an increase in sexual behavior.

T F 25. The 1970 President's Commission concluded that there was no significant link between exposure of adults to sexually explicit materials and sex crimes.

T F 26. In many states, a married couple caught having oral sex in the privacy of their own home can be sent to prison.

T F 27. Prostitution is the only sexual offense for which more women than men are prosecuted.

T F 28. Erotica and pornography are synonyms, and are really the same thing.

T F 29. When Denmark legalized the sale of hard-core pornographic material to adults, there was a marked decrease in sex crimes afterward.

T F 30. People are most aroused by looking at sexually explicit material showing behaviors they regard as normal.

T F 31. Adultery is a crime in nearly half of the 50 states.

T F 32. Prostitution was uncommon during the Victorian era.

T F 33. Men who use male prostitutes usually pay to give oral sex to the prostitute.

[T]   [F]   34. Many prostitutes enjoy sex with their customers.

[T]   [F]   35. HIV infection is uncommon among prostitutes, probably because most have their customers use condoms.

[T]   [F]   36. Nearly all junior high school boys and girls have looked at a sexually explicit magazine.

[T]   [F]   37. Many people use sexually explicit material as a source of sexual information.

[T]   [F]   38. A majority of both men and women are aroused by sexually explicit material.

[T]   [F]   39. There is substantial evidence that sex offenders have had more exposure to sexually explicit material than have nonoffenders.

[T]   [F]   40. Exposure to violent sexually explicit material often results in women having attitudes that are more supportive of sexual violence against women.

[T]   [F]   41. There is more violence against women shown in X-rated movies than in R-rated movies.

[T]   [F]   42. It is a crime to possess sexually explicit material (e.g., magazines, videos, photos) showing children.

B.   MATCHING

_____ 43. B-girl

_____ 44. brothel prostitute

_____ 45. call girl

_____ 46. gigolo

_____ 47. hustler

_____ 48. john

_____ 49. not a prostitute

_____ 50. pimp

_____ 51. streetwalker

a. Susan has sex for money at a legalized house in Nevada.

b. Joan has sex with her boss in the hope it will get her a promotion.

c. Hank works out of an escort service and is paid by older women to have sex.

d. Stephanie works out of her own apartment and her clients must make an appointment to have sex with her.

e. David takes 75 percent of the money earned by six women who do tricks on the west side of town.

f. Joe pays women to give him oral-genital sex.

g. Sam accepts money from men on the street who want to have sex with him.

h. Sally solicits for sex in a downtown bar.

i. Bonnie solicits men in public.

C.   FILL IN THE BLANKS

52. The feature that distinguishes a prostitute from other women who engage in illicit sexual intercourse is the _____ with which she offers herself to men for hire.

53. Sexual intercourse between a man and a woman who are not married is called _____.

54. A hustler is on the same status level as a female _____.

55. Pornography is distinguished from erotica in that it is literature or art with a sexual theme that is considered to be _____.

56. Laws that prohibit oral or anal sex are called _____ laws.

57. Recent evidence suggests that it is exposure to _____ more than sexual explicitness that results in potentially harmful attitude and behavioral changes.

58. In *Miller* v. *California*, 1973, the Supreme Court ruled that material was obscene if (a) _____, (b) _____, and (c) _____.

59. Most teenaged prostitutes are _____ children who have turned their first trick by the time they are 14.

60. The _____, passed in 1873, made the mailing of material considered to be obscene a felony.

61. Probably the foremost reason many people use sexually explicit material is _____.

CHAPTER 17 INTERACTIVE REVIEW

Communication is the exchange of information. Because of our culture's negative attitudes about sex and the negativity taught by most parents, many people feel uncomfortable talking about sex, even with their sexual partner. (1)_____ and power differences in a relationship also contribute to this difficulty.

You and your partner can get used to talking about sex together by discussing sexuality related articles in newspapers, books, and magazines. One of the first things you must do is agree on a comfortable (2)_____ to use when talking about sex. When talking about sexual differences or problems, be sure to emphasize the (3)_____ rather than the (4)_____ things that your partner does. That doesn't mean that you can never complain, but when you do so, focus on your partner's behavior rather than on his or her character.

Take responsibility for your own pleasure by expressing your feelings and desires to your partner in a clear, specific manner. Whenever possible, begin sentences with "I" rather than (5)_____ , (6)_____ , or (7)_____ . It is often easier to find out about your partner's sexual desires and needs if you first (8)_____ . However, good communication is a two-way street; it requires that you also become a good (9)_____ . In addition to verbal communication, we also communicate nonverbally with (give four examples) (10)_____ , (11)_____ , (12)_____ , and (13)_____ . Even with good communication skills people will not always agree, but it is possible to agree that you disagree.

It is equally important that parents learn to communicate with their children about sexuality in a positive manner. Your children will learn about sex whether or not you ever talk to them about it. (14)_____ begins in infancy and is received from their peers, the media, and your own behaviors. Children who have had sex education are (15)_____ likely to have sexual relations than those who have not. Avoid that one, long "birds and bees talk" approach; communication between parents and their children about sexuality should begin (16)_____ and be ongoing. The chapter presents guidelines for age-appropriate discussions about sexuality-related topics.

Discussions with your children about sexuality should be frank and explicit. You should strive to create an atmosphere of love and caring, so avoid (17)_____ and do not lecture to them. You can emphasize your own sexual values, but do not preach. Your own behavior will affect your child's attitudes and moral values, so don't let them overhear you use "dirty" language or tell "dirty" jokes, and teach them, by example, that affection is something positive. The only way you will be able to know whether or not your attempts to educate your children about sexuality have been successful is by their (18)_____ .

CHAPTER 17 SELF-TEST

A. TRUE OR FALSE

[T] [F] 19. You can prevent your children from learning about sex by never talking to them about it.

[T] [F] 20. Most children can be adequately taught about sexuality with one long, serious talk.

[T] [F] 21. Parents should teach the words "penis" and "vagina" to their children at the same time they teach them the names for their other body parts.

[T] [F] 22. Young adolescent males should be taught about menstruation.

[T] [F] 23. When discussing sex with their children, parents should insist that the children reveal their sexual attitudes and behavior.

[T] [F] 24. In order to dissuade your child from engaging in sex, you should emphasize the possible negative consequences (e.g., AIDS).

[T] [F] 25. It is okay to teach your child your values while teaching factual information.

[T] [F] 26. You should avoid open displays of affection with your partner (e.g., hugging, kissing) when your children are present.

[T] [F] 27. Your own sexual behavior and attitudes will likely serve as a role model for your children, whether or not you discuss sexuality with them.

[T] [F] 28. Generally speaking, men are naturally more "expert" at sex than are women.

[T] [F] 29. When talking to your partner about sex, use of the term "making love" is always better than saying "having sex" or "sexual intercourse."

☐T ☐F 30. The best time to talk about a sexual problem or difference with your partner is immediately after sex.

☐T ☐F 31. The best place to discuss a sexual problem or difference with your partner is in bed.

☐T ☐F 32. When you have a sexual difference or problem with your partner, you should never complain or express your anger.

☐T ☐F 33. When talking to your partner about your sexual attitudes and preferences, it is good to begin sentences with "we" because it emphasizes the relationship.

☐T ☐F 34. Giving your partner a massage can strengthen communication by making you a better listener.

☐T ☐F 35. When approaching your partner about differences in sexual attitudes or preferences, it is best to present all your criticisms at once.

B.   MATCHING: AT WHAT AGE (GRADE LEVEL) SHOULD YOU BEGIN TO TALK TO YOUR CHILD ABOUT THE FOLLOWING TOPICS?

———— 36. the changes that occur in boys and girls at puberty

———— 37. correct names for genitals

———— 38. the idea that human sexuality is natural and that sexual feelings are normal

———— 39. peer pressure and the right to say "no"

———— 40. What is AIDS? Can I get AIDS?

———— 41. promotion of nonstereotyped gender roles

———— 42. basics of reproduction and that our genitals and reproductive organs enable this

———— 43. integration of sexuality into the individual's value system

———— 44. awareness of exploitive relations

———— 45. how to express sexual feelings in appropriate ways

———— 46. people have body parts that feel good when touched

a. preschool
b. early elementary
c. upper elementary
d. junior high
e. high school

C.   FILL IN THE BLANKS

47. When expressing your desires to your partner, you should try to begin sentences with _____.

48. Intercourse means _____.

49. When communicating with another, it is important that there be agreement between the _____ and _____ aspects of communication.

50. When answering your child's questions about sex, be sure to make your answers _____-appropriate.

51. If you must criticize your partner, make sure you criticize his or her _____, not his or her _____.

52. With regards to sexual relations, you must take responsibility for _____.

ANSWERS—CHAPTER 1

1. their friends
2. the media
3. 85–90
4. sexuality
5. the Biblical Hebrews
6. Christians
7. St. Paul
8. St. Augustine
9. Queen Victoria
10. penicillin
11. the birth control pill and IUD
12. Sigmund Freud
13. Havelock Ellis
14. Alfred Kinsey
15. Masters and Johnson
16. true
17. false
18. false
19. false
20. false
21. false
22. false
23. false
24. true
25. true
26. false
27. true
28. false
29. false
30. f
31. p
32. g
33. n
34. h
35. m
36. i
37. d
38. o
39. c
40. a
41. j
42. Inis Baeg
43. leisure time, mobility, birth control, antibiotics
44. each possible sample of that size
45. Plato
46. Puritans
47. 2,000
48. body, soul
49. libido
50. spermatorrhea

ANSWERS—CHAPTER 2

1. ambivalent
2. vulva
3. mons veneris
4. labia majora
5. labia minora
6. clitoris
7. vaginal opening
8. urethral opening
9. mons veneris
10. outer surfaces of the labia majora
11. clitoris
12. penis
13. labia minora
14. vestibular area
15. hymen
16. poor
17. eight
18. vagina
19. uterus
20. Fallopian tubes
21. ovaries
22. vagina
23. vagina
24. Grafenberg spot
25. ovary
26. Fallopian tube
27. uterus
28. endometrium
29. clitoris
30. vaginal opening
31. cancer of the cervix
32. scrotum
33. testicles
34. corpora cavernosa
35. corpus spongiosum
36. glans
37. foreskin
38. circumcision
39. testicles
40. testosterone
41. epididymis
42. vas deferens
43. ejaculatory ducts
44. urethra
45. prostate gland
46. seminal vesicles
47. semen
48. Cowper's glands
49. testicles
50. prostate gland
51. true
52. true
53. false
54. true
55. false
56. false
57. true
58. false
59. false
60. false
61. true
62. true
63. false
64. false
65. false
66. false
67. true
68. false
69. false
70. false
71. c
72. d
73. e
74. h
75. a
76. f
77. b
78. i
79. p
80. k
81. l
82. m
83. n
84. g
85. j
86. o
87. q
88. Pap smear; cervical
89. prostate gland
90. labia majora
91. endometrium
92. blood
93. Cowper's glands
94. mons veneris
95. amount of fatty tissue
96. just after menstruation
97. Fallopian tubes
98. scrotum
99. ejaculatory ducts
100. seminal vesicles
101. after a warm bath or shower
102. Bartholin's glands
103. seminiferous tubules
104. cells of Leydig
105. clitoris
106. pubococcygeus (PC) muscle
107. front
108. testicular torsion
109. crura

ANSWERS—CHAPTER 3

1. endocrine
2. testosterone
3. estrogen
4. progesterone
5. pituitary gland
6. 28
7. follicle-stimulating hormone
8. follicle
9. follicular (or proliferative)
10. endometrium
11. FSH
12. luteinizing hormone
13. LH
14. ovulation
15. abdominal cavity
16. Fallopian tube
17. luteal (or secretory)
18. corpus luteum
19. endometrium
20. endometrium
21. menstruation
22. at least 7 days
23. estrous
24. estrus (ovulation)
25. taboos
26. shredded endometrial tissue
27. cervical mucus
28. blood
29. sperm production
30. interstitial cell-stimulating hormone (ICSH)
31. male hormones (e.g., testosterone)
32. high blood pressure; liver, prostate, and breast tumors; impaired reproductive funciton; masculinization in women; emotional/psychological problems
33. amenorrhea
34. 3–14
35. premenstrual syndrome (PMS)
36. with the start of menstruation
37. dysmenorrhea
38. prostaglandins
39. endometrial tissue grows outside the uterus
40. toxic shock syndrome
41. testosterone
42. estrogen
43. progesterone
44. testosterone
45. false
46. false
47. false
48. false (28 days is an average)
49. true
50. false
51. true
52. true
53. false
54. false (there is no strong eivdence for this)
55. false
56. true
57. false
58. true
59. true
60. true
61. false
62. false
63. h
64. d
65. n
66. j
67. l
68. k
69. b
70. m
71. f
72. o
73. e
74. i
75. a
76. c
77. g
78. pituitary
79. pheromones
80. maturation of a follicle
81. the menstrual cycle
82. follicle
83. corpus luteum
84. progesterone
85. menarche
86. orchiectomy
87. brain
88. testosterone
89. toxins produced by a bacterium (*Staphylococcus aureus*)
90. human chorionic gonadotropin (HCG)

ANSWERS—CHAPTER 4

1. Masters and Johnson
2. more similar
3. excitement
4. plateau
5. orgasm
6. resolution
7. sexual response cycle
8. Helen Kaplan
9. desire
10. vasocongestive
11. penis erection
12. vaginal lubrication
13. plateau
14. orgasmic platform
15. pulls back against the pubic bone and disappears beneath the clitoral hood
16. 50–75
17. sex-tension flush
18. rhythmic muscular contractions
19. the brain
20. similar
21. emission
22. expulsion
23. ejaculation
24. refractory period
25. multiple orgasms
26. resolution
27. 30 to 50
28. clitoral
29. clitoral
30. vaginal
31. clitoris
32. front
33. Grafenberg spot
34. emission of fluid
35. prostate gland
36. not important
37. aphrodisiacs
38. clitoridectomy
39. infibulation
40. true
41. true
42. false
43. true
44. not necessarily
45. true
46. false
47. true
48. false
49. true
50. false
51. false
52. true
53. true
54. true
55. false
56. true
57. false
58. true
59. false
60. true

61. d
62. b, g, j, k, l, n, s
63. a, c, f, i, q, r, t
64. e, p, u
65. h, m, o
66. b, c, g, i, k, q, t

67. vasocongestion, myotonia
68. semen
69. Freud
70. urethra
71. sex-tension flush

72. anaphrodisiacs
73. myotonia
74. emission
75. retrograde ejaculation
76. orgasmic platform
77. Grafenberg spot

78. refractory period
79. labia minora
80. the tenting type

ANSWERS—CHAPTER 5

1. four
2. bacteria
3. viruses
4. parasites
5. gonorrhea
6. chlamydia
7. syphilis
8. gonorrhea
9. chlamydia
10. pelvic inflammatory disease
11. syphilis
12. antibiotics
13. skin, skin
14. recurrent
15. liver
16. feces
17. blood or body fluids
18. human papilloma
19. human immunodeficiency virus
20. CD4
21. immune
22. opportunistic
23. 10
24. intimate sexual activity
25. blood
26. casual contact
27. men and women
28. infestations of parasites
29. trichomoniasis
30. monilial
31. bacterial vaginosis

32. false
33. true
34. true
35. false
36. true
37. false
38. false
39. true
40. true
41. false
42. false
43. true
44. true
45. false
46. true
47. false
48. false
49. false
50. true
51. true
52. false
53. true
54. false
55. false
56. false
57. false
58. false
59. false
60. false
61. true
62. true
63. true
64. true
65. false
66. false
67. true

68. true
69. true
70. a
71. l
72. c
73. q
74. h
75. f
76. o
77. i
78. m
79. j
80. e
81. n
82. g
83. b
84. d
85. p
86. k
87. parasites
88. vaginitis
89. pelvic inflammatory disease
90. human papillomavirus infection
91. human immunodeficiency virus infection
92. types of vaginitis
93. hepatitis
94. human papillomavirus infection
95. acyclovir

96. ectopic pregnancy, infertility
97. syphilis, human immunodeficiency virus, hepatitis
98. stress
99. mucous membranes
100. nongonococcal (or nonspecific) urethritis
101. lymphogranuloma venereum
102. trichomoniasis
103. yeast (moniliasis)
104. pinworms
105. chlamydia
106. CD4 cells
107. during the first 60 days and late in the infection (AIDS)
108. HIV antibodies
109. gonorrhea, chlamydia, syphilis (the chancre is often internal), HPV infection, HIV infection
110. HPV infection, HIV infection, trichomoniasis
111. always use condoms, abstain from sex until you are in a long-term monogamous relationship

ANSWERS—CHAPTER 6

1. over twice
2. calendar
3. basal body temperature

4. Billings
5. ovulation
6. spermicides
7. the diaphragm

8. the cervical cap
9. the contraceptive sponge
10. uterus

11. offer some protection against sexually transmitted diseases
12. estrogen

13. progesterone
14. Depo-Provera
15. Norplant
16. vas deferens
17. tubal ligation
18. laparoscopy
19. false
20. false
21. true
22. false
23. false
24. true
25. true
26. true
27. false
28. false
29. true
30. false
31. false
32. true
33. true
34. false
35. false
36. false

37. false
38. true
39. false
40. true
41. true
42. true
43. false
44. true
45. true
46. true
47. false
48. true
49. false
50. true
51. c
52. i
53. k
54. d
55. b, e
56. h
57. h
58. e
59. e
60. b, e, g

61. a
62. c, j, m
63. j
64. j
65. l
66. f
67. f
68. consistently, properly
69. the Cowper's glands
70. he has 12 to 16 ejaculations
71. menstruation, ovulation
72. on demand
73. cervical cap
74. seven, twenty
75. rises slightly
76. clear and slippery
77. nonoxynol-9
78. oil-based
79. in a stable, monogamous relationship who have

completed their families
80. male condom, female condom, contraceptive sponge
81. many types of antibiotics, barbiturates, analgesics, and tranquilizers
82. menstrual irregularities
83. male condom, female condom, diaphragm with spermicide, contraceptive sponge, spermicides
84. male
85. Ovral 2+2 (morning after pill)
86. male condom with spermicide
87. the hormonal methods

ANSWERS—CHAPTER 7

1. three
2. ovulation
3. one
4. Fallopian tube
5. endometrium
6. ectopic
7. chlamydia and/or gonorrhea
8. human chorionic gonadotropin (HCG)
9. trimesters
10. embryo
11. two
12. fetus
13. seven
14. quickening
15. fourth or fifth
16. teratogens
17. amniocentesis
18. fear-tension-pain
19. midwife
20. contractions
21. dilation

22. start-up
23. amniotic sac
24. transition phase
25. fully dilated
26. head
27. umbilical cord
28. placenta
29. cesarean
30. proteins
31. postpartum depression
32. six
33. the sharing of child-care and housekeeping responsibilities
34. 12
35. 40
36. 40
37. 20
38. a low sperm count
39. artificial insemination
40. Fallopian tubes

41. ovulate
42. in vitro fertilization
43. zygote intrafallopian transfer
44. gamete intrafallopian transfer
45. false
46. false
47. true
48. false
49. true
50. true
51. false
52. false
53. false
54. true
55. false
56. true
57. false
58. false
59. true
60. true
61. false

62. false
63. true
64. true
65. false
66. true
67. true
68. false
69. false
70. true
71. d
72. j
73. f
74. l
75. c
76. b
77. h
78. k
79. m
80. i
81. a
82. g
83. e
84. morula, blastocyst
85. umbilical cord

86. preeclampsia
87. lightening
88. contractions are coming 10 minutes apart (or sooner) on a regular basis; contractions are at least 30 seconds

long on a regular basis; cervix is dilated to at least two to three centimeters; cervix is at least 70 percent effaced
89. first

90. tubal
91. 25 to 35
92. blastocyst
93. ultrasound
94. the head
95. end of the first (beginning of the second)

96. 24 hours
97. amnion
98. episiotomies, prepping, cesarean sections
99. 23 to 24 weeks
100. smokes

ANSWERS—CHAPTER 8

1. gender identity
2. XX
3. XY
4. Klinefelter's
5. Turner's
6. testosterone
7. female
8. gender dysphoria
9. transsexuals
10. Freudian
11. learning
12. gender constancy
13. six or seven
14. gender roles
15. individualist
16. microstructural
17. independent
18. androgyny
19. schema
20. androgynous
21. true
22. false

23. true
24. true
25. true
26. false
27. true
28. true
29. true
30. false
31. true
32. true
33. true
34. true
35. true
36. false
37. false
38. true
39. true
40. true
41. true
42. false
43. false

44. true
45. e
46. h
47. n
48. o
49. b, j
50. b, d, j
51. c
52. f, l
53. m
54. a, j
55. k
56. i
57. g
58. gender constancy
59. 1800s (when the United States became industrialized)
60. microstructural
61. identification
62. socialization

63. stereotypes
64. undifferentiated
65. Mullerian
66. phallic
67. androgynous
68. testosterone
69. Oedipus
70. transvestite; transsexual
71. imitation
72. biological essentialism
73. expressive
74. two
75. stereotyped
76. gender schema
77. gender labels (stereotypes); individuating
78. androgynous
79. transcendent
80. casual sex

ANSWERS—CHAPTER 9

1. distinct preferences
2. three to five
3. one
4. 2, 3, or 4
5. gender identities
6. roles
7. Oepidus
8. domineering, overprotective
9. weak, detached
10. absent
11. cold, rejecting
12. social learning theory
13. Sambian
14. genetic

15. brains
16. hormones
17. interact
18. more
19. ancient Greeks
20. Romans
21. Thomas Aquinas
22. coming out
23. admitting to onself of a homosexual orientation
24. homophobia
25. commitment and romantic love
26. true

27. false
28. true
29. true
30. false
31. false
32. false
33. false
34. false
35. false
36. true
37. true
38. true
39. true
40. false
41. false

42. false
43. false
44. false
45. false
46. false
47. true
48. false
49. false
50. true
51. true
52. true
53. false
54. false
55. a
56. a

57. b
58. e
59. d
60. a
61. e
62. c
63. a
64. e
65. d

66. b
67. tribadism
68. adolescence
69. tearoom trade
70. Freud, Havelock Ellis
71. latent homosexuals
72. hypothalamus
73. before or shortly after birth

74. predispose
75. straights
76. admitting to oneself of a homosexual orientation; getting to know other homosexuals; telling family and friends of one's sexual

orientation; complete openness about one's homosexuality
77. close-coupled
78. AIDS
79. Socrates, Leonardo da Vinci, Michaelangelo, Gertrude Stein, Walt Whitman

ANSWERS—CHAPTER 10

1. three through five
2. modesty (and inhibitions about exposing their bodies in public)
3. puberty
4. hormone
5. self-identity
6. necking
7. petting
8. 17
9. peer pressure
10. serial monogamy
11. monogamy
12. lasting relationship
13. chastity
14. economic and physical protection
15. mid-twenties to mid-thirties
16. menopause
17. vaginal lubrication
18. estrogen

19. testosterone
20. refractory
21. their sexual activity when they were younger
22. true
23. false
24. true
25. false
26. true
27. false
28. true
29. false
30. true
31. false
32. true
33. true
34. false
35. false
36. false
37. true
38. true
39. false

40. true
41. true
42. false
43. false
44. false
45. false
46. true
47. true
48. false
49. true
50. false
51. true
52. true
53. false (true for men only)
54. false
55. false
56. a
57. b
58. e (caused by b)
59. c
60. a
61. c

62. e
63. d
64. a
65. d
66. d
67. lack of a partner
68. precocious puberty
69. egocentric
70. the climacteric
71. self-exploration
72. phallic
73. secondary sex characteristics
74. nocturnal emission
75. emotional intimacy
76. test their virility
77. have multiple wives
78. emotional
79. opportunity, alienation
80. declines only slightly

ANSWERS—CHAPTER 11

1. range
2. Kinsey
3. 92
4. 62
5. nocturnal orgasms
6. REM
7. have erections
8. vaginal lubrication
9. romantic
10. male
11. missionary

12. fellatio
13. cunnilingus
14. sexually healthy
15. false
16. true
17. false
18. false
19. true
20. false
21. false
22. false

23. true
24. false
25. true
26. true
27. no (not necessarily)
28. false
29. true
30. true
31. false
32. false
33. true

34. true
35. true
36. c, k, n
37. f, h, i, j, m
38. a, b, d, e, g, l
39. cunnilingus
40. vaginal lubrication, penile erection
41. of rectal bacteria
42. the replacement fantasy

43. variety
44. ritualized
45. vaginal intercourse, watching one's partner undress

46. a sexually active lifestyle
47. face-to-face
48. female-on-top

49. gonorrhea
50. feels comfortable with his or her sexuality; feels free to choose

whether or not he or she wishes to try a variety of sexual behaviors

ANSWERS—CHAPTER 12

1. fascination (preoccupation with the other person)
2. exclusiveness
3. sexual desire
4. cognitive component
5. companionate love
6. a positive self-concept
7. self-disclosure
8. jealousy
9. self-esteem
10. popularity, wealth, fame, and physical attractiveness
11. conditional
12. unconditional
13. liking
14. romantic love
15. companionate love
16. consummate love
17. eros
18. storge
19. pragma
20. mania
21. ludus
22. agape

23. matches
24. intimacy
25. true
26. true
27. false
28. false
29. false
30. true
31. true
32. false
33. false
34. true
35. false
36. false
37. false
38. true
39. true
40. false
41. false (true for men)
42. false
43. false
44. true
45. false
46. true
47. e
48. h

49. n
50. b
51. m
52. g
53. a
54. d
55. k
56. i
57. l
58. o
59. j
60. c
61. f
62. eros
63. storge
64. agape
65. passion, intimacy, and commitment
66. repression of sexuality from infancy through childhood
67. reciprocation
68. dopamine, norepinephrine, and phenylethylamine

69. realistic
70. secure
71. experience jealousy
72. emotional
73. limerance; mania
74. storgic eros
75. (a) both individuals accepting themselves as they are,
    (b) each individual recognizing his or her partner for what they are,
    (c) each individual feeling comfortable to express himself or herself,
    (d) learning to deal with your partner's reactions.
76. habituation

ANSWERS—CHAPTER 13

1. at least half
2. couple's
3. help people with sexual problems
4. have sex with a client
5. cognitive-behavioral therapy
6. PLISSIT
7. medical
8. sexual
9. sensate focus exercises
10. hypoactive sexual desire

11. sexual aversion
12. compulsiveness
13. sexual addicts
14. dyspareunia
15. premature ejaculation
16. reasonable voluntary control
17. erectile disorder
18. performance anxiety
19. orgasmic disorder
20. headaches after orgasm
21. priapism

22. vaginismus
23. reaching orgasm
24. HIV/AIDS
25. homophobic attitudes within society
26. false
27. false
28. true
29. false (not necessarily)
30. false
31. true
32. false
33. false

34. false
35. false
36. true
37. true
38. true
39. true
40. false
41. true
42. false
43. false
44. false
45. false
46. false

47. true
48. true
49. false
50. a, b
51. i, b
52. j
53. a, h, f
54. a, k, f
55. g, d
56. l
57. a, e

58. g, a, f (possibly c as well)
59. secondary erectile disorder
60. clitoris
61. female-on-top
62. physical
63. spectatoring
64. permission, limited information, specific suggestions, intensive therapy

65. systematic desensitization
66. nondemand mutual pleasuring
67. two or fewer
68. coexisting sexual problem
69. hypersexual individuals (some refer to them as sexual addicts)
70. phimosis

71. erectile disorder
72. ejaculatory incompetence
73. psychological problems
74. it has negative connotations about a woman's emotional responsivity
75. spiritual union
76. hypoactive sexual desire

ANSWERS—CHAPTER 14

1. statistical
2. sociological
3. psychological
4. place
5. depend almost exclusively
6. sexual variants
7. fetishism
8. transvestism
9. exhibitionists
10. telephone scatologists
11. voyeurs
12. animals
13. prepubertal children
14. sadists
15. masochists
16. urophilia
17. coprophilia
18. mysophilia
19. klismaphilia
20. frotteurism

21. dead bodies
22. males
23. true
24. false
25. true
26. false
27. false
28. true
29. true
30. false
31. false
32. true
33. false
34. true
35. true
36. true
37. false
38. true
39. true
40. false
41. e

42. d
43. k
44. g
45. a
46. p
47. h
48. o
49. b
50. c
51. l
52. m
53. n
54. j
55. i
56. f
57. Richard von Krafft-Ebing
58. fetishism
59. two-spirit (berdache)
60. exhibitionists
61. exhibitionism

62. tries to draw attention to the fact that he is watching; attempts to approach you or enters your building
63. scoptophilia
64. bestiality
65. 13 years old
66. domination, submission
67. feces, defecation
68. bodily discharges, fetishes
69. quiet, passive, and nonrejecting
70. desensitization, social skills training
71. social systems perspective

ANSWERS—CHAPTER 15

1. property
2. someone the victim knows
3. 16 and 24
4. vulnerable
5. average
6. young
7. empathy
8. coercion
9. verbal

10. physical
11. gang
12. statutory rape
13. power
14. anger
15. sadism
16. opportunistic
17. violence by men
18. adversarial
19. women who are raped usually

provoke it by their dress and behavior
20. women subconsciously want to be raped
21. no woman can be raped if she truly does not want it
22. rape trauma syndrome
23. controlled

24. long-term reorganization
25. rape shield
26. social systems
27. sexual harassment
28. someone they know
29. preference
30. situational
31. personally immature
32. regressive
33. 200

34. brother-sister
35. false
36. true
37. true
38. true
39. true
40. true
41. true
42. false
43. false
44. false
45. false
46. true
47. false
48. false
49. true
50. true
51. true
52. false
53. false
54. false
55. true
56. false
57. true
58. true
59. false
60. true

61. false
62. true
63. true
64. false
65. true
66. d
67. i
68. e
69. g
70. a
71. h
72. j
73. f
74. c
75. b
76. juveniles (persons under the "legal age of consent")
77. four
78. drinking
79. getting a partner intoxicated to have sex, physical (relentless) pressure, verbal pressure (e.g., anger), emotional/psychological

pressure (e.g., threatening to end the relationship)
80. boys are raised to be nurturant, not aggressive; boys are raised to view women as equals who share power and responsibility
81. gang
82. under the "legal age of consent"
83. nothing
84. psychopathology (a character disorder)
85. opportunistic
86. less sensitive to the victims and more accepting of sexual violence
87. they had been drinking, if a woman had made them angry
88. blame

89. period of long-term reorganization
90. a specially trained counselor
91. DNA
92. place the responsibility for preventing rape in the hands of the victim, thus women who are raped may feel that it was somehow their fault
93. Civil Rights Act
94. unequal power
95. traditional stereotypical gender roles
96. pedophile (preference molester)
97. 13
98. aggressive
99. yourself, your child
100. polyincestuous
101. mother-child
102. family-systems

ANSWERS—CHAPTER 16

1. Nevada
2. 20
3. streetwalkers
4. B-girls
5. call girls
6. hustlers
7. economics (the need for money)
8. middle class
9. married
10. a third
11. no harmful
12. less sympathetic
13. rape myths
14. increased hostility
15. commit rape themselves if they were certain they would not get caught
16. depictions of violence toward women

17. sexual explicitness
18. erotica
19. children
20. oral
21. anal
22. false
23. true
24. false
25. true
26. true
27. true
28. false
29. true
30. true
31. true
32. false
33. true
34. true
35. false
36. true
37. true

38. true
39. false
40. true
41. false
42. true
43. h
44. a
45. d
46. c
47. g
48. f
49. b
50. e
51. i
52. indiscrimination
53. fornication
54. streetwalker
55. obscene
56. sodomy

57. material portraying violence toward women
58. (a) by contemporary community standards it depicts patently offensive sexual conduct;
    (b) it lacks serious literary, artistic, political, or scientific value; and
    (c) it appeals to prurient interests
59. runaway or throwaway
60. Comstock law
61. they enjoy the sexual arousal it produces

ANSWERS—CHAPTER 17

1. stereotypic gender roles
2. vocabulary
3. positive
4. negative
5. you
6. why
7. we
8. self-disclose
9. listener
10. eye contact
11. facial expressions
12. interpersonal distance
13. touch
14. sexual learning
15. no more
16. in early childhood (preschool years)
17. scare tactics
18. willingness to come to you when they have questions and problems
19. false
20. false
21. true
22. true
23. false
24. false
25. true
26. false
27. true
28. false
29. false (not true for all couples in all instances)
30. false
31. false
32. false
33. false
34. true
35. false
36. c
37. a
38. c
39. d
40. b
41. b
42. b
43. e
44. d
45. e
46. b
47. "I"
48. communication
49. verbal, nonverbal
50. age
51. behavior, character
52. your own pleasure